THE OXFORD HA

THE ARCHAEOLOGY OF THE LEVANT

This Handbook aims to serve as a research guide to the archaeology of the Levant, an area situated at the crossroads of the ancient world that linked the eastern Mediterranean, Anatolia, Mesopotamia, and Egypt. The Levant as used here is a historical geographical term referring to a large area which today comprises the modern states of Israel, Jordan, Lebanon, western Syria, and Cyprus, as well as the West Bank, Gaza Strip, and the Sinai Peninsula.

Unique in its treatment of the entire region, it offers a comprehensive overview and analysis of the current state of the archaeology of the Levant within its larger cultural, historical, and socio-economic contexts. The Handbook also attempts to bridge the modern scholarly and political divide between archaeologists working in this highly contested region. Written by leading international scholars in the field, it focuses chronologically on the Neolithic through Persian periods—a time span during which the Levant was often in close contact with the imperial powers of Egypt, Anatolia, Assyria, Babylon, and Persia. This volume will serve as an invaluable reference work for those interested in a contextualised archaeological account of this region, beginning with the 'agricultural revolution' until the conquest of Alexander the Great that marked the end of the Persian period.

Margreet L. Steiner is an independent scholar, living in Leiden, The Netherlands.

Ann E. Killebrew is an Associate Professor at the Pennsylvania State University.

THE OXFORD HANDBOOK OF

THE
ARCHAEOLOGY
OF THE LEVANT

C.8000–332 BCE

Edited by

MARGREET L. STEINER

and

ANN E. KILLEBREW

OXFORD
UNIVERSITY PRESS

Great Clarendon Street, Oxford, OX2 6DP,
United Kingdom

Oxford University Press is a department of the University of Oxford.
It furthers the University's objective of excellence in research, scholarship,
and education by publishing worldwide. Oxford is a registered trade mark of
Oxford University Press in the UK and in certain other countries

© Oxford University Press 2014

The moral rights of the authors have been asserted

First published 2014
First published in paperback 2018

Published in the United States of America by Oxford University Press
198 Madison Avenue, New York, NY 10016, United States of America

British Library Cataloguing in Publication Data
Data available

Library of Congress Cataloging in Publication Data
Data available

ISBN 978-0-19-921297-2 (Hbk.)
ISBN 978-0-19-882256-1 (Pbk.)

Contents

PART I ARCHAEOLOGY OF THE LEVANT: BACKGROUND AND DEFINITIONS

PART II THE LEVANT AS THE CROSSROADS BETWEEN EMPIRES: EGYPT, ANATOLIA, MESOPOTAMIA, AND PERSIA

PART III THE ARCHAEOLOGICAL RECORD

A. THE NEOLITHIC PERIOD

B. THE CHALCOLITHIC PERIOD

LIST OF FIGURES

List of Tables

LIST OF CONTRIBUTORS

Peter M. M. G. Akkermans Professor, Faculty of Archaeology, Leiden University, The Netherlands

Gassia Artin Associated Researcher, Maison de l'Orient et de la Méditerranée, Université Lyon II, France

María Eugenia Aubet Director of Cuadernos de Arqueologia Mediterránea, Universidad Pompeu Fabra, Spain

Anna Belfer-Cohen Professor, Institute of Archaeology, Hebrew University of Jerusalem, Israel

David Ben-Shlomo Institute of Archaeology, Hebrew University of Jerusalem, Israel

Alison Betts Professor, Department of Archaeology, University of Sydney, Australia

Piotr Bienkowski Cultural Consultant, Scotland

Stephen J. Bourke Research Associate, Department of Archaeology, University of Sydney, Australia

Aaron A. Burke Associate Professor, Department of Near Eastern Languages and Cultures and the Cotsen Institute of Archaeology, University of California, Los Angeles, USA

Hanan Charaf Assistant Professor, Lebanese University, Beirut, Lebanon

Joanne Clarke Senior Lecturer, School of World Art Studies, University of East Anglia, UK

Susan L. Cohen Associate Professor, Department of History and Philosophy, Montana State University, USA

Lisa Cooper Associate Professor, Department of Classical, Near Eastern and Religious Studies, University of British Columbia, Canada

Thomas Davis Professor, Tandy Institute for Archaeology, Southwestern Baptist Theological Seminary, USA

Josette Elayi Chercheur honoraire, Centre National de la Recherche Scientifique, France

Bill Finlayson Director, Council for British Research in the Levant, UK

Peter M. Fischer Professor, Department of Historical Studies, Gothenburg University, Sweden

David Frankel Professor, Archaeology Program, La Trobe University, Australia

Hermann Genz Associate Professor, Department of History and Archaeology, American University of Beirut, Lebanon

Ayelet Gilboa Senior Lecturer, Department of Archaeology, University of Haifa, Israel

A. Nigel Goring-Morris Professor, Institute of Archaeology, Hebrew University of Jerusalem, Israel

Raphael Greenberg Associate Professor, Department of Archaeology and Ancient Near East, Tel Aviv University, Israel

Holger Gzella Professor, Leiden University Centre for Linguistics, Leiden University, The Netherlands

James W. Hardin Associate Professor, Department of Anthropology and Middle Eastern Cultures, Mississippi State University, USA

Marlies Heinz Professor, Department of Near Eastern Archaeology, University of Freiburg, Germany

Larry G. Herr Professor, Department of Religious Studies, Canadian University College, Canada

Maria Iacovou Professor, Department of History and Archaeology, University of Cyprus, Cyprus

Zeidan A. Kafafi Professor, Faculty of Archaeology and Anthropology, Yarmouk University, Jordan

Ann E. Killebrew Associate Professor, Department of Classics and Ancient Mediterranean Studies, Jewish Studies, and Anthropology, The Pennsylvania State University, USA

Horst Klengel Altorientalischen Seminar, Freie Universität Berlin, Germany

Sabina Kulemann-Ossen Associate Researcher, Department of Near Eastern Archaeology, University of Bern, Switzerland

Gunnar Lehmann Associate Professor, Deptartment of Bible, Archaeology and Ancient Near Eastern Studies, Ben-Gurion University of the Negev, Israel

Thomas E. Levy Professor, Department of Anthropology and Qualcomm Institute of Tele-communications and Information Technology, University of California, San Diego, USA

Marta Luciani Assistant Professor, Oriental Institute, University of Vienna, Austria

Stefania Mazzoni Professor, Department of History, Archaeology, Geography, Fine & Performing Arts, University of Florence, Italy

Pierre de Miroschedji Directeur de recherche émérite, Centre National de la Recherche Scientifique, France

Daniele Morandi Bonacossi Associate Professor, Department of History and Preservation of Cultural Heritage, University of Udine, Italy

Gregory D. Mumford Assistant Professor, Department of Anthropology, University of Alabama at Birmingham, USA

Nava Panitz-Cohen Research Associate, Institute of Archaeology, The Hebrew University of Jerusalem, Israel

Edgar Peltenburg[†] Professor of Archaeology, University of Edinburgh, UK

Kay Prag Research Affiliate, Manchester Museum, University of Manchester, UK

Suzanne Richard Professor, Department of History and Archaeology, Gannon University, USA

Yorke M. Rowan Research Associate, Oriental Institute, University of Chicago, USA

Hélène Sader Professor, Department of History and Archaeology, American University of Beirut, Lebanon

Tammi J. Schneider Professor, School of Religion, Claremont Graduate University, USA

Ilan Sharon Professor, Institute of Archaeology, Hebrew University of Jerusalem, Israel

E. Susan Sherratt Lecturer, Department of Archaeology, University of Sheffield, UK

Louise Steel Senior Lecturer, School of Archaeology, History and Anthropology, University of Wales, UK

Margreet L. Steiner Independent Researcher, Leiden, The Netherlands

Matthew J. Suriano Assistant Professor, The Joseph and Rebecca Meyerhoff Center for Jewish Studies, University of Maryland, College Park, USA

Jennifer M. Webb Research Fellow, Archaeology Program, La Trobe University, Australia

Harvey Weiss Professor, Near Eastern Archaeology and Environmental Studies, Yale University, USA

Randall W. Younker Professor, Seventh-day Adventist Theological Seminary, Andrews University, USA

Jeffrey R. Zorn Adjunct Associate Professor, Department of Near Eastern Studies, Cornell University, USA

MAP OF THE LEVANT

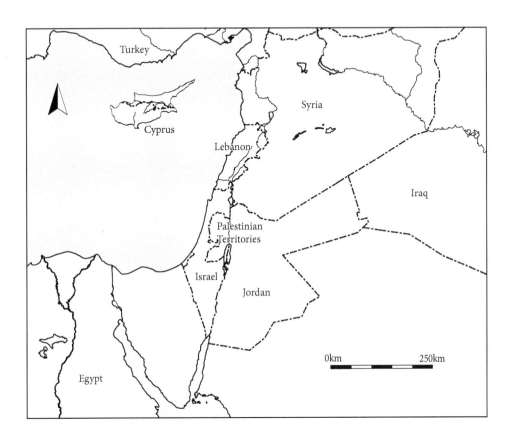

INTRODUCTION

ANN E. KILLEBREW AND MARGREET L. STEINER

When Oxford University Press approached us to edit a handbook on 'biblical archaeology', we were very honoured, but also apprehensive. Biblical archaeology has a multitude of definitions and traditions and, over the decades, this subfield of Old World archaeology had become increasingly controversial, contentious, and politicized. William F. Albright, often referred to as the 'father of biblical archaeology', defined biblical archaeology as encompassing 'all Biblical lands, from India to Spain, and from southern Russia to southern South Arabia and to the whole history of those lands, from about 10,000 BC or even earlier, to the present time' (Albright 1966: 13; for a recent overview of Albright's contribution, see Levy and Freedman 2009). This 'maximalist' view of the discipline was strongly rooted in American academic traditions, combined with a very positivist view of both the potential of archaeology and the biblical text's historicity. During much of the 20th century, biblical archaeology in the United States was too often hijacked by special interest groups. It became increasingly intertwined with sectarian, political, or other non-academic efforts to prove or disprove the Bible or employed to booster biblically based claims to land. Reflecting with the rise of a 'processual' and more science-based 'New Archaeology', in the 1980s William G. Dever was among the first to propose the term 'Syro-Palestinian' archaeology in an attempt to professionalize the discipline and encourage a more academic approach to 'biblical archaeology'.[1]

Outside the United States, the archaeology of the lands of the Bible tended to develop as a more academic and secular pursuit from its inception. For many professional Israeli archaeologists, the term 'biblical archaeology' signified a chronological designation, generally referring to the period from the Bronze Ages to the end of the Persian period of the southern Levant (Israel and Jordan). As a result, it lacked much of the religious overtones of American traditions, though at times was highly politicized (Bar-Yosef and Mazar 1982; Kletter 2006; for a Palestinian perspective, see Abu El-Haj 2001 and Yahya 2005). European scholars have generally avoided the designation 'biblical archaeology', preferring designations such as 'archaeology of Palestine', 'Syro-Palestinian archaeology', or 'archaeology of the Levant' (e.g.

---

[1] See e.g. Davis (2004) and Dever (2010) for critiques of the development of biblical archaeology in the US; regarding its political implications, see Silberman (1998); Scham (2008); see also Joffe (2010) for a critique. See most recently Levy (2010), who has proposed a return to a new biblical archaeology that he has designated 'historical biblical archaeology'.

Franken and Franken-Battershill 1963: 1; Kenyon 1971), although in the German-speaking academic world it is still a common term (e.g. Fritz 1985; Zwickel 2002). In recent decades, most archaeologists working in the Levant have distanced themselves from a biblical archaeology that far too often had been misused as a religious or political tool in a contested Middle East (see Davis, Ch. 3 below, for a history of archaeological research in the Levant).

An additional factor in our decision against editing a 'handbook of biblical archaeology' was the existence of numerous books already devoted to this topic (see e.g. Mazar 1990; Fritz 1985; Ben-Tor 1992; Levy 1998; Golden 2009). These treatments of the archaeology of the Holy Land are complemented by several publications that provide current overviews of the archaeology of Syria (Akkermans and Schwartz 2003) and Cyprus (Karageorghis 2002; Steel 2004; Knapp 2008). What was then and is still lacking today is a comprehensive volume on the archaeology of the whole of the Levant spanning the time from the Neolithic to the Persian period. This was the topic of the handbook that we ultimately proposed to Oxford University Press and is presented here.

The term 'Levant' is also notoriously ambiguous, with a variety of definitions, associations, and connotations, some derogatory in nature. It has been suggested that the first use of 'Levant' as a term for the eastern Mediterranean can be traced back to the 16th-century French *soleil levant*, probably in reference to the 'rising sun' in the east (Oppenheim 1996: 1099). In later times, 'Levantine' appears in numerous contexts to refer to European traders in the Levant but also to westernized local populations of the Levant that were usually involved in commerce, spoke numerous languages, and were cosmopolitan in character. Within its colonial context, the word developed a negative connotation, often employed as a denigrating term referring to a person engaged in unethical business transactions or indicating a state of cultural impurity (see e.g. Hochberg 2004: 220).

Also lacking is a consensus regarding the geographical borders of the Levant (see e.g. Hochberg 2004: 224 and n. 12). In this handbook, it includes the countries that border the eastern littoral of the Mediterranean, or, as it is referred to in Arabic, *bilād al-shām* ('the land of sham [Syria]', i.e. greater Syria). It encompasses the western region of the Fertile Crescent, an area south of the Taurus Mountains, bordered by the Mediterranean Sea on the west, and the north Arabian Desert and Mesopotamia to the east. It thus comprises the modern states of Syria southwest of the Euphrates, Lebanon, Israel, Jordan, and Cyprus, including the West Bank and Gaza (the Palestinian Territories), and Sinai (see Suriano, Ch. 1 below, for a detailed geographical description). In this volume, we use the term 'Cisjordan' to refer to the southern Levant west of the Jordan River encompassing the modern state of Israel and the Palestinian Territories and Transjordan to indicate the region east of the Jordan River, which includes the modern state of Jordan. This geographic definition of the Levant highlights its function throughout history as a land bridge, serving as the point of intersections for the criss-crossing of peoples and cultures from Europe, Asia, and Africa. As a consequence of location, this region has witnessed unique cultural interactions, hybridity, and confrontations that often fractured the population into local subcultures and multi-layered identities.[2]

---

[2] Recently, cultural hybridity and transculturalism have appeared with increasing frequency in archaeological literature relating to the Late Bronze and early Iron I periods (see e.g. Knapp 2008, Hitchcock 2011, and Stockhammer 2012a, 2012b for a detailed discussion of this concept; Killebrew, Ch. 39 below). These processes can emerge where two or more cultural entities overlap or come into close contact. Their manifestation can be both tangible and intangible, and is impacted by local geographic, cultural, and chronological contexts and region-specific factors. In this handbook, we suggest the use of the term 'Levantinism' to indicate hybridity in the specific context of the Levant.

Whether its original meaning was intended to be pejorative, contemporary definitions of Levantinism stress that the Levant is not exclusively eastern or western in its essence, but rather a 'hybrid of Middle Eastern and European values' (Halim 2010: 2). Recent fascination with the interaction between cultural fragmentation and hybridity or transculturalism, and coinciding with renewed interest in the Mediterranean defined as a place of cultural symbiosis (e.g. Braudel 1995; Horden and Purcell 2000), has led to the appropriation of the term 'Levantinism' to signify a richly stratified historical and cultural past, defined by its predilection for cultural fragmentation, creating multi-layered identities of its inhabitants (see e.g. Jacqueline Kahanoff's essays on Levantinism in Starr and Somekh 2011). It is in the spirit of these more recent contemplations on the nature of the Levant that we propose 'Levantinism' as the most appropriate designation for this region's cultural hybridity, with all its local peculiarities, as illustrated in the archaeological record presented in the chapters below.

The Oxford Handbook of the Archaeology of the Levant spans the Neolithic through to the end of the Persian period, ending with the era prior to the conquests of Alexander the Great. The Levant was often influenced by its more powerful neighbours, or even incorporated into the great empires of Egypt, Anatolia, Assyria, Babylonia, and Persia. As in the past, modern political boundaries that subdivide the Levant have created a diverse and fragmented political, cultural, and social landscape, a feature which is also reflected in the modern archaeological research of the region. Thus we aimed at including a broad range of diverse approaches to archaeological research in this area, including American, European, Cypriot, Australian, Israeli, and Arab researchers and scholarship. We invited both established and younger scholars to contribute to this volume, with the goal of presenting a variety of views and perspectives across the spectrum of well-established and innovative archaeological traditions.

The goal of this volume is to provide a comprehensive overview of the state of the art of the region in these periods, to describe the most important debates and discussions within the discipline, and to present a more integrated treatment of the archaeology of the region within its larger cultural and social context. Its fifty-five chapters explore the following major themes:

- *Archaeology of the Levant: Background and Definitions.* Chapters in this section include general topics and themes essential to the positioning of the discipline in its historical and geographical setting and in its relation to other fields of study.
- *The Levant as the Crossroads between Empires.* Here the interaction of the imperial powers of Egypt, the Hittites, Assyria, Babylonia, and Persia in the Levant is explored.
- *The Archaeological Record.* This section provides a general introduction to specific periods, followed by comprehensive treatments of each subregion in that period.

We are aware that the artificial subdivisions of the archaeology of the Levant are largely based on modern political borders rather than the geographical or cultural boundaries that had far greater influence on the region's archaeological development. Nevertheless we have chosen to describe the archaeological periods generally organized according to modern political boundaries, largely because we wanted to involve authors actually working in the region. And unfortunately, due to the modern political map of the region, it is seldom that archaeologists are able to conduct research in more than one country. Authors have been invited from the Arab countries, Israel, Europe, America, and Australia, based on their extended experience in and intimate knowledge of the periods and regions discussed.

We hope that *The Oxford Handbook of the Archaeology of the Levant* will serve as a timely and useful archaeological reference work and textbook for advanced students, at both undergraduate and graduate levels, professional archaeologists, and scholars in other disciplines including history, biblical studies, and the Ancient Near East, as well as a general resource for all who are interested in the archaeology of this region.

We take this opportunity to thank first and foremost our contributors to this volume. Their research, excavations in the area, and expertise made this volume possible. Our appreciation and thanks goes to Oxford University Press and especially to Hilary O'Shea, who invited us to edit this book, to its editors, Dorothy McCarthy and Taryn Cambell, and to Shereen Karmali who managed the production of the volume. We also would like to express our deepest appreciation and thanks to Heather Heidrich, who assisted with the copy editing and bibliographic checking of the references. Her professionalism and meticulous attention to detail during the first edit of the manuscripts improved the quality of the final book. Thanks are due to our graphic artist Willem Beex, who struggled with the (sometimes very) approximate maps that the contributors provided and succeeded in placing the hundreds of 'sites mentioned in the text' correctly on the fifty or so maps accompanying the chapters, to our great relief.

References

Abu El-Haj, N. (2001). *Facts on the Ground: Archaeological Practice and Territorial Self-Fashioning in Israeli Society*. Chicago: University of Chicago Press.

Akkermans, P. M. M. G., and G. M. Schwartz. (2003). *The Archaeology of Syria: From Complex Hunter-Gatherers to Early Urban Societies (c.16,000–300 BC)*. Cambridge: Cambridge University Press.

Albright, W. F. (1966). *Archaeology, Historical Analogy and Early Biblical Tradition*. Baton Rouge: Louisiana State University Press.

Bar-Yosef, O., and A. Mazar (1982). Israeli archaeology. *World Archaeology* 13: 310–25.

Ben-Tor, A. (ed.) (1992). *The Archaeology of Ancient Israel*, trans. R. Greenberg. New Haven, Conn.: Yale University Press.

Braudel, F. (1995). *The Mediterranean and the Mediterranean World in the Age of Philip II* (2 vols), trans. S. Reynolds. Berkeley: University of California Press.

Davis, T. W. (2004). *Shifting Sands: The Rise and Fall of Biblical Archaeology*. Oxford: Oxford University Press.

Dever, W. G. (2010). Does 'biblical archaeology' have a future? In Levy (2010: 349–60)

Franken, H. J., and C. A. Franken-Battershill (1963). *A Primer of Old Testament Archaeology*. Leiden: Brill.

Fritz, V. (1985). *Einführung in die Biblischen Archäologie*. Darmstadt: Wissenschaftliche Buchgesellschaft.

Golden, J. M. (2009). *Ancient Canaan and Israel: An Introduction*. Oxford: Oxford University Press.

Halim, H. (2010). Latter-day Levantinism, or 'Polypolis' in the Libretti of Bernard de Zogheb. *California Italian Studies* 1.1: 1–41. http://escholarship.org/uc/item/4t31n9vc. Accessed 15 Dec. 2011.

Hitchcock, L. A. (2011). 'Transculturalism' as a model for examining migration to Cyprus and Philistia at the end of the Bronze Age. *Ancient West and East* 10: 267–80.

Hochberg, G. Z. (2004). 'Permanent immigration': Jacqueline Kahanoff, Ronit Matalon and the impetus of Levantinism. *Boundary 2* 31.2: 219–43.

Horden, P., and N. Purcell (2000). *The Corrupting Sea: A Study of Mediterranean History.* Oxford: Blackwell.

Joffe, A. H. (2010). The changing place of biblical archaeology: exceptionalism or normal science? In Levy (2010: 328–48).

Karageorghis, V. (2002). *Early Cyprus: Crossroads of the Mediterranean.* Los Angeles, Calif.: J. Paul Getty Museum.

Kenyon, K. M. (1971). An essay on archaeological technique: the publication of results from the excavation of a tell. *Harvard Theological Review* 64: 271–9.

Kletter, R. (2006). *Just Past? The Making of Israeli Archaeology.* London: Equinox.

Knapp, A. B. (2008). *Prehistoric and Protohistoric Cyprus: Identity, Insularity, and Connectivity.* Oxford: Oxford University Press.

Levy, T. E. (ed.) (1998). *The Archaeology of Society in the Holy Land.* New York: Continuum.

——(ed.) (2010). *Historical Biblical Archaeology and the Future: The New Pragmatism.* London: Equinox.

——and D. N. Freedman. (2009). William Foxwell Albright: May 24, 1891–September 19, 1971. *Biographical Memoirs* 91: 2–29.

Mazar, A. (1990). *Archaeology of the Land of the Bible, vol. 1: 10,000–586 B.C.E.* New York: Doubleday.

Oppenheim, J.-M. R. (1996). Levantine. In R. S. Simon, P. Mattar, and R. W. Bulliet (eds), *Encyclopedia of the Modern Middle East*, vol. 3: *L–Sf.* New York: Macmillan, 1098–1100.

Scham, S. A. (2008). Disinheriting heritage: explorations in the contentious history of archaeology in the Middle East. In M. Liebmann and U. Z. Rizvi (eds), *Archaeology and the Postcolonial Critique.* Lanham, Md.: AltaMira, 165–76.

Silberman, N. A. (1998). Whose game is it anyway? The political and social transformations of American biblical archaeology. In L. Meskell (ed.), *Archaeology under Fire: Nationalism, Politics and Heritage in the Eastern Mediterranean and Middle East.* London: Routledge, 175–88.

Starr, D. A., and S. Somekh (eds) (2011). *Mongrels or Marvels: The Levantine Writings of Jacqueline Shohet Kahanoff.* Stanford, Calif.: Stanford University Press.

Steel, L. (2004). *Cyprus Before History: From the Earliest Settlers to the End of the Bronze Age.* London: Duckworth.

Stockhammer, P. W. (2012a). Conceptualizing cultural hybridization in archaeology. In Stockhammer (2012b: 43–58).

——(ed.) (2012b). *Conceptualizing Cultural Hybridization: A Transdisciplinary Approach.* Berlin: Springer.

Yahya, A. H. (2005). Archaeology and nationalism in the Holy Land. In S. Pollock and R. Bernbeck (eds), *Archaeologies of the Middle East: Critical Perspectives.* Oxford: Blackwell, 66–77.

Zwickel, W. (2002). *Einführung in die biblische Landes- und Altertumskunde.* Darmstadt: Wissenschaftliche Buchgesellschaft.

PART I

ARCHAEOLOGY OF THE LEVANT

Background and Definitions

CHAPTER 1

··

HISTORICAL GEOGRAPHY
OF THE ANCIENT LEVANT

··

MATTHEW J. SURIANO

The Levant consists of a stretch of southwestern Asia that forms a natural land bridge between Asia and Africa. Three prominent components define this general area from west-to-east: the Mediterranean, the great Syro-African Rift, and the vast desert expanse to the east. Today, several modern states occupy this area; yet in antiquity it saw the movements of innumerable peoples and political entities. These groups left behind historical sources that document much (though not all) of the Levant's topography. The place names of these sources are often preserved in the Arabic toponyms of the Levant, allowing a more accurate picture of the area from a historical perspective (Aharoni 1979: 105–30; Rainey and Notley 2006: 14–21). In addition, geological studies, together with the modern archaeological exploration of the Middle East, offer a more refined understanding of the ancient Levant both at site level and in a broader regional sense (Rainey and Notley 2006: 9–24). What follows is a broad, regional overview of the Levant that includes toponymic and topographical data drawn from both historical sources and modern archaeological work. Accordingly, the term 'historical geography' is an appropriate title for the descriptive survey presented in this chapter.

TERMINOLOGY

···

The term 'Levant', as used here, covers an area that is often referred to in archaeological works by other terms, most notably Syria-Palestine and North Syria (Dever 1997: 147; Silberman 1982: 123; Perkins 1949); therefore it is necessary to define the parameters of the following survey. The western coastline and the eastern deserts set the boundaries for the Levant, and these natural barriers will therefore serve as brackets for the area under discussion. The general limits of the Levant, as defined here, begin at the Plain of 'Amuq in the north and extend south until the Wâdī al-Arish, along the northern coast of Sinai. The 'Amuq is the northernmost of a series of faults and rifts, termed here the Syro-African Rift, that collectively form a great geographical trough comprising the Middle and Upper

Orontes, the Beqaʻ and Jordan Valleys, and the Arabah, and encompassing the Gulf of Aqaba and the Red Sea, before extending southward into the East African Rift. The Euphrates and the area around Jebel el-Bishrī mark the eastern boundary of the northern Levant, as does the Syrian Desert beyond the Anti-Lebanon range's eastern hinterland and Mount Hermon. This boundary continues south in the form of the highlands and eastern desert regions of Transjordan. Although the geographical boundaries described here are not absolute, the Litani River will mark the division of the northern Levant from the southern Levant. Cyprus is not part of the Levant geographically, but it is included on account of its proximity (and resulting cultural ties), as well as its geographical significance, size, and natural resources. Thus, the regional breakdown of this chapter consists of the northern Levant, Cyprus, and the southern Levant.

Northern Levant

The northern Levant (Fig. 1.1) can be subdivided in two halves, termed here 'lower' and 'upper', based on two factors. The first is the flow of the Orontes River and the second is the elevation of the upper half, which constitutes a large uplifted block with mountain ranges

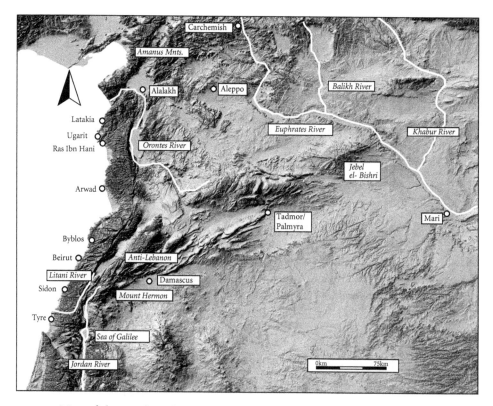

FIG. 1.1 Map of the northern Levant

(the Lebanon and Anti-Lebanon) that are higher in elevation than the ranges of the lower half. The division of the lower and upper regions of the northern Levant is Homs Gap.

Northern Levant: Lower

The northwestern mountains, collectively, are a chain of ranges that include the Amanus range (Nur Dağlari), Jabal al-Aqra', and the Jabal an-Nuṣayrīyah and Jabal az-Zawîyeh ranges. The Mediterranean Sea and the Orontes River determine the important gaps, depressions, and lowland regions that lie between these ranges. For instance, the Nuṣayrīyah range parallels the sea, distanced only by a coastal plain in the area of modern Latakia. The Nuṣayrīyah and the Zawîyeh ranges are separated by the flow of the Orontes, and both ranges form the eastern and western barriers of a fertile depression known today as the Al-Ghâb. The Orontes flows north and then sharply hooks westward and southwest to the sea at the Plain of 'Amuq. The Amanus range guards the northwestern side of the plain, standing opposite the Jabal al-Aqra' (Mount Ṣaphon) and the Jabal el-Ala in the south, and the Jabal Seman and the Kurt Dağ range in the east.

The Amanus range is a southwest-to-northeast trajectory that serves as a border between the Plains of Adana (classical Cilicia) and the 'Amuq to the south. The Amanus contains several important passes that control access between Anatolia and the eastern plateau of Syria, via the 'Amuq Plain. The Syrian Gates (Belen Pass) cross the southern half of the Amanus, connecting the 'Amuq with the Gulf of İskenderun and the Plain of Adana. Passage from Adana into the 'Amuq is also found in the northern extension of the Amanus at the Amanic Gates (Bahçe Pass). Ancient Sam'al (Zincirli, Turkey), whose name means 'north', stood at the eastern slopes of the Amanus, guarding entry into the Amanic Gates and the 'Amuq. At its southwestern tip, the Amanus forms a lateral promontory at the Mediterranean coast.

The Nuṣayrīyah range runs parallel along the coastland, north-to-south, offering some relief at the pass marked by the Nahr el-Kabîr, which separates the Nuṣayrīyah from Jabal al-Aqra' (Mount Ṣaphon). This pass continues east from here, between the Jabal el-Ala and the Jabal Zawîyeh, providing passage to the eastern plateau and Aleppo. Jabal el-Ala is positioned along the southern site of the 'Amuq (opposite the Amanus), to the northeast of the Nuṣayrīyah. Together with the Jabal al-Aqra' (to the west), el-Ala serves as the eastern flank of the Orontes as it passes north into the 'Amuq. The waters of the 'Afrin Su flow north of el-Ala, feeding into the Orontes to the southwest. The entrance to the 'Amuq follows the 'Afrin from the northeast, between the Kurt Dağ range and Jabal Seman.

The Plain of 'Amuq (the Plain of Antioch in classical sources) forms a northeast–southwest orientated trough that meets the sea at Samandağ, Turkey (Brice 1967: 210). This well-watered plain is actually a broad valley, the northernmost reach of the Syro-African Rift. The Amanus range guards the northwestern side of the plain, while Mount Ṣaphon and the Zawîyeh range flank the southern side, with the Orontes cutting between them (Akkermans and Schwartz 2003: 4–5). The Orontes makes its great western and southwestern hook as it passes Ṣaphon and plunges seaward through a gorge that drops 50m in a span of 16km. Tributaries from the northwest ('Afrin and Kara Su) once converged in a now-extinct lake (the Lake of Antioch), where their waters filtered into the Orontes.

The plain surrounding modern Latakia (classical 'Laodicea by the Sea') marks the coast-land, bounded on the north by Mount Ṣaphon, and corresponding to the Bronze Age king-dom of Ugarit. The eastern boundary follows the Jabal an-Nuṣayrīyah, probably referred to (in part if not as a whole) as the 'mountains of the Sun' in a Late Bronze Age cuneiform text that defines the local borders of Ugarit (van Soldt 2005: 55). Several tributaries that flow to the Mediterranean water this plain with two streams bordering the city of Ugarit (Ras-Shamra), the Nahr ed-Delbeh on the south and the Nahr Chbayyeb on the north (Yon 1992: 23). The Nahr el-Fidd debouches at the ancient harbor of Mahadu (Minet el-Beida). The ancient harbour probably extended much further inland, but the silting of the Fidd has created a greater distance today between Ugarit and the Mediterranean coast. The Bdamā Pass separates the Nuṣayrīyah range from Mount Ṣaphon. Several branches of the Nahr al-Kabir flow from the low-lying hills of this depression and converge to wind their way to the sea at a point near Latakia (Brice 1967). The Nahr es-Sinn, which preserves the ancient name Siyanu, reaches the sea at Arab al-Mulk and marks the southern boundary of the plain where the Nuṣayrīyah narrows the coastland towards the range's southern promontory. In antiquity, the southernmost harbour of this plain was at Tell Tueni (probably Gib'alā) in the vicinity of modern Jebleh (van Soldt 2005: 67).

The eastern plateau consists of the steppes surrounding Aleppo (ancient Ḥalab), watered by the Kuweik River, and the areas south until Jabal Abū Rujmayn and Jabal Bishrī (ancient Bashar: see Gelb 1938: 73). The Kuweik, which flows past Aleppo, is fed by sources north of the Kurt Dağ and is a western parallel to the Euphrates. In fact, Aleppo stands roughly midpoint for travel between the Euphrates and the Orontes (Brice 1967: 204–6). The rain-shadow effect of the northwestern mountains impedes precipitation in the eastern pla-teau, although enough rain occurs annually to enable the farming of crops as diverse as olive trees, grapes, and wheat (Akkermans and Schwartz 2003: 4). Due to the limestone marls and other sediments of the plain southwest of Aleppo, this part of the plateau has been an area of much cultivation and dense settlement patterns since antiquity (Mazzoni 2001: 108).

The Orontes River Valley, an extension of the Syro-African Rift, begins its winding course at the plain that lies between the modern city of Homs in the south and Ḥamā/ancient Ḥamath in the north (Bridgland et al. 2003: 1080). Often referred to as the Upper Orontes, this region drains the waters of the Beqa' Valley to the south. The northwestern flow of the river, with the Zawîyeh range along the east and Nuṣayrīyah at its southern and west-ern side, forms an alluvial depression referred to here as the Middle Orontes, the modern Al-Ghâb (Brice 1967: 209–10). The swift current of the Orontes (Al-Asi) is unmanageable for transportation purposes. Yet the river provides ample irrigation for the valley, support-ing dry-farming in the Upper Orontes and creating fertile wetlands in the Middle Orontes (Akkermans and Schwartz 2003: 4). Qarqar (Tell Qarqur, Syria), located at the northern end of the Ghâb, stood at the intersection of the Orontes and the east–west gap that connected Aleppo with the sea at Latakia (Brice 1967: 210). At this point, the Orontes flows northward between Jabal al-Aqra' and el-Ala, entering the 'Amuq.

Northern Levant: Upper

The Homs Gap, the natural division of the northern Levant, provides east–west access between the eastern plateau and the Mediterranean and connects with the north–south junction of the upper Orontes River Valley and the Beqaʿ. The uplifted block of the northern Levant's upper region is cut through by the Syro-African Rift Valley, here called the Beqaʿ, where it reaches its greatest elevation (915m). Although the Litani is the line of division between the northern and southern Levant, the coastlands of the northern Levant extend as far south as the Ras an-Naqoura/Rosh HaNiqra (the ladder of Tyre), approximately 15km south of Tyre.

Rising south of the Homs Gap, the Lebanon range forms a massive, unbroken phalanx that closely follows the Mediterranean coast along a northeast-to-southwest orientation. This high-elevation range is divided into districts according to altitude and geology (Brice 1967: 214–15). A chain of aquifers and springs emerge at the seam of a mid-elevation zone of sandstone outcropping and a high-elevation plateau. The waters that emerge from these sources are the result of winter runoff (snowmelt) and precipitation that seeps into the lime-stone of the high-elevation plateau (Brice 1967: 214). These sources water the western slopes and the lowlands below. The Lebanon range is cordoned off to the west by a narrow strip of coastland. Throughout history, this coastal region has benefited from the hinterland of the range's western slopes, and the Phoenician port cities of Gubla/Byblos (Jbail), Bêrût (Beirut), Tyre, and Sidon traded timber drawn from this region.

The Beqaʿ Valley (Al-Biqāʿ meaning 'the Valley') divides the Lebanon and the Anti-Lebanon ranges and forms a high plateau with its watershed in the vicinity of Baalbek (Brice 1967: 215). North of this point, the waters of the Beqaʿ feed into the Upper Orontes, while to the south the waters flow into the Litani River. The broad basin of the Beqaʿ (vary-ing between 12km and 20km in width east–west), with its abundant waters, forms large expanses of arable lands in the south. Travel, however, is impeded by the rising limestone ridges at the southern end of the Beqaʿ (beginning near modern Joub Jennine), which ulti-mately inhibit the flow of the Litani. At this point, the Litani cuts through several gorges before bending westward and terminating at the sea.

The Anti-Lebanon (ancient Sirion) stretches along a northeastern orientation (like the Lebanon range) with Mount Hermon (also known as Senir) at its southwest-ern head. In antiquity, the great divide between the Sirion and Lebanon Mountains (the Syro-African Rift) was explained in Tablet V of the *Standard Epic of Gilgamesh* as resulting from Gilgamesh's combat with the monster Humbaba (George 1990). Along the eastern slopes of the Anti-Lebanon is a hinterland (the Al-Ghutah oasis) that sur-rounds Damascus and is watered by the Nahr Barada, beginning in the Anti-Lebanon at the Az-Zabadāni depression. This area is known for its produce of apples, apricots, and walnuts (Brice 1967: 216); in the 9th century BCE, the Assyrian ruler Shalmaneser III boasted of his destruction of Damascus's orchards (*COS* 2.113D). To the south, the Nahr al-Awaj provides irrigation for a smaller sector of fertile lands. The general area, however, is semi-arid and precipitation is shielded by the Anti-Lebanon Mountains; further east is the arid expanse of the Syrian Desert. Yet the eastern periphery of the Anti-Lebanon and its hinterland has long afforded north–south travel, giving rise to the importance of Damascus and the emergence of the Kingdom of Aram-Damascus in the Iron Age (Pitard 1987). Passage from the north represents a convergence of two different points: from the northwest and the Homs Gap, and from the northeast (through Hauran) along a highway that passed Tadmor/Palmyra linking Mesopotamia with the Levant. From Damascus, the routes either continued south through Transjordan, or southwest through Bashan into the Syro-African Rift.

CYPRUS

The island of Cyprus is a geographical entity that is distinct from the Levant (Fig. 1.2). Nevertheless, the cultural connection between the two is significant due to the island's proximity to the eastern Mediterranean littoral, the advantages of its size (only Sicily and Sardinia are larger among Mediterranean islands), and its abundant resources. The geographical significance of the island is defined by factors that are both internal and external. The internal factors pertain to the local topography and physical setting of the island, while the external factors relate to the island's maritime landscape. This last factor involves Cyprus's important position within the eastern Mediterranean realm along with its accessibility owing to its coastline and harbours (see Blue 1997 and Knapp 1997; Gifford 1985). The Amarna letters mention Alashiya, which modern scholars have identified as Cyprus—an identification that has been strengthened by recent petrographic studies of the clay tablets mentioning Alashiya that seem to have originated in Cyprus (Goren et al. 2003).

Three principal features dominate the topography of Cyprus: the Kyrenia Mountains, the Mesaoria Plain, and the Troodos Mountains (Karageorghis 1982: 12–13). The Kyrenia, although in actuality a chain of mountains, forms a solid limestone massif that runs along the northern coast of the island. The northern slopes of the Kyrenia Mountains give way to a narrow strip of fertile coastlands due to rain shadow. Passage through this mountain range into the island's interior was possible through a pass southwest of modern Kyrenia as well as another that was southwest of modern Akanthou (Karageorghis 1982: 13–14). The dramatic Troodos Mountains cover most of western Cyprus, reaching as far as the Larnaca Lowlands to the southeast. The subsidiary ranges of the Troodos Mountains, with their steep valleys, are oriented in different directions due to various processes of geomorphology (uplifting

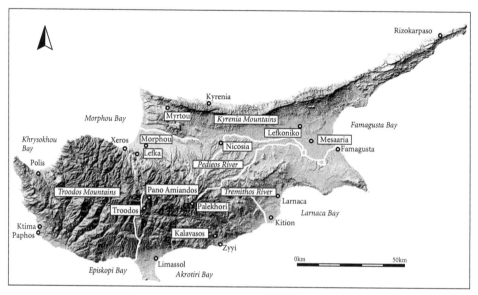

FIG. 1.2. Map of the island of Cyprus

and folding). This mountainous region, rich in copper, is the most prominent feature of Cyprus's geography. South of the Kyrenia and northeast of the Troodos Mountains is the Mesaoria Plain, hence the Greek name 'between the mountains'. The wide, flat area of the Mesaoria is bound by the Mediterranean to the east and south, and several seasonal rivers cut through the plain. The largest perennial river in Cyprus, the Pedieos, originates in the Troodos Mountains and winds its way northeast and east through the Mesaoria before terminating near Salamis in Famagusta Bay. The Tremithos River flows southeast through the area of the Mesaoria known as the Larnaca Lowlands, south of Kition (Gifford 1985: 45).

The maritime landscape of Cyprus is manifest in the ancient settlements of the lowland coastal regions (Knapp 1997), particularly in the south. The natural harbours of Cyprus are Famagusta Bay (on the east); Larnaca Bay, Akrotiri Bay, and Episkopi Bay (along the southern littoral, from east to west); and Khrysokhou Bay and Morphou Bay (along the northwestern coast). In antiquity, the principal maritime areas were located in the harbours of the southern littoral located near the Larnaca Lowlands (Kition and Hala Sultan Tekke), as well as the Akrotiri Penninsula (Blue 1997: 32–7). The southern littoral is near the coastlands of the eastern Mediterranean: this region of Cyprus is located roughly 100km from the northern Levant and 200km from the southern Levant.

SOUTHERN LEVANT

While the same geographical determinants as the northern Levant are at work here (i.e. the Mediterranean, the Syro-African Rift, and the eastern deserts), the southern Levant (Fig. 1.3) contains much more extensive coastal regions. Like the northern Levant, the southern Levant can be divided into two halves according to a river, in this case the Jordan; hence, Cisjordan and Transjordan. This conceptual division is imprecise, as the River Jordan, which begins as the Upper Jordan north of the Kinneret (Sea of Galilee/Lake Tiberias) terminates in the south at the Dead Sea. Yet the river follows the Syro-African Rift and lends its name to this great fault line for the area that spans the Kinneret in the north and the Red Sea (at the Gulf of 'Aqaba) in the south. The zones discussed here exclude the Sinai Peninsula, and out of necessity the regional survey will begin with a description of the Syro-African Rift, here called the Jordan Valley and the Arabah.

The great rift in the southern Levant is a lowland valley, distinct from its course in the northern Levant, where it is marked by its elevation. This distinction is evident in the contrast between the Marjoun Basin (500m), which is fed by the waters of the Litani, and the Huleh Basin (100m) to the south (Baly 1974: 191). From the north, entrance into the Huleh was made through passages at Dan (Tell el-Qâdī), in the northeast, or Abel-beth-maacah (Abil el-Qamḥ) in the northwest, with the site of Ḥazor (Tell el-Qadeḥ) standing watch over the valley. The Huleh is fed by springs and aquifers, most prominently those of Dan and Banias (Classical Paneas/Caesarea Philippi), which once met at a lake, now extinct. From here the waters form the Upper Jordan and flow southward. Eventually the river passes through a natural barrier of basalt that disgorges the waters into a low alluvial bank (the Plain of Bethsaida), where they meander to the Kinneret/Sea of Galilee. A lake (approximately 18×12km) that is slightly brackish due to mineral springs along its shores to the northwest, the Kinneret sits at roughly 200m below sea level (Baly 1974: 196). The periphery

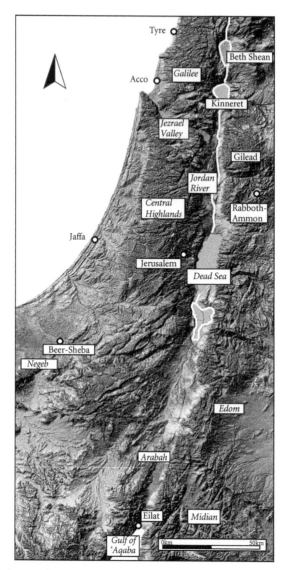

FIG. 1.3. Map of the southern Levant

of this lake is steeply guarded by hills on all sides, yet relief is found in small plains to the northwest (Gennesaret), the northeast (Bethsaida), and the south.

From the Kinneret, the Jordan River descends the Syro-African Rift southward, here called the Jordan Valley, eventually dropping several hundred metres in a span of roughly 100km. (For a brief description of the valley's geological history, see Raphael 1992: 969.) The valley begins to widen on the west side of the Jordan near the Beth Shean Valley, which guards the entrance to Jezreel through the smaller Harod Valley. The valley broadens further (the Ghor), on both the west and east, near the mouths of the Wâdī el-Far'ah (in the Cisjordan) and the Wâdī Zerqa (the Jabbok) in Transjordan, where it forms a relatively fertile eastern zone around Tell Deir 'Alla (possibly the location of Sukkoth). The span of this part of the plain is marked by the northern ford of the Jordan beside ed-Damieh (Adam; see Josh. 3: 16) and the southern ford near Jericho (Tell es-Sulṭân), with the Dead Sea as its southern boundary (Baly 1974: 199). The narrow banks of the Dead Sea are the lowest points of dry land on the earth (Orni and Efrat 1973: 98). This large saline lake (80×16km) is fed by several sources, in addition to the Jordan River, that include the waters of the Wâdī Zarqa Ma'in and the Wâdī Mujib (the Arnon) along its eastern bank as well as 'Ain Feshka and En-Gedi ('Ain-Jidi) along the west (MacDonald 2000: 29). The Jordan River stops at the Dead Sea, over 400m below sea level. To the south of this body of water is the Arabah, a broad, arid basin of saline soils and alluvial sands that extends to the Gulf of 'Aqaba and the ports of Elath and Ezion-Geber. The Arabah is bordered by the red granite hills of Edom (and Mount Seir) to the east and the limestone hills of the desert highlands to the west.

Cisjordan

This western portion of the southern Levant is bound by the Mediterranean Sea and includes extensive coastal regions. Often referred to as the Land of Canaan, the Cisjordan in the Iron Age was the cultural (and political) domain of the Canaanites and Philistines as well as the kingdoms of Israel and Judah with a Phoenician presence along the northern coast. The southern Levant, however, was both culturally and geographically diverse, and several zones can be discerned in the geomorphology of Cisjordan, excluding the Sinai Penninsula (cf. Raphael 1992: 968). The cultural and geographical importance of the Cisjordan is apparent in an ancient highway that passed through the region following the coastlands before penetrating the interior at the Jezreel Valley. This thoroughfare, known by scholars as the International Coastal Highway (or incorrectly as the Via Maris), ultimately connected Egypt and Mesopotamia (Rainey and Notley 2006: 165–6).

The mountains of the Galilee are divided by elevation between the upper Galilee to the north (which includes the south of Lebanon today) and the lower Galilee (Orni and Efrat 1973: 73–4). This division is known only from Roman period sources (Josephus, *War* 3.3.1) and Rabbinic literature, yet the geographical distinction between upper and lower is certainly implied in earlier sources (Josh. 19: 35–8; Rainey and Notley 2006: 38). The east–west valley of Beth-hakkerem, an eroded escarpment known as the Ash-Shagur Rift, separates the upper from the lower. The upper Galilee is primarily limestone and marked by faulting that created an up-warped region west of its watershed (Baly 1974: 153). The southern head of upper Galilee is Jabal Jarmaq (approximately 1,200m), called today Meron, although ancient Meron should be located further north in the vicinity of Jabal Marûn er-Râs (Rainey and Notley 2006: 38). The lower Galilee is composed of limestone slopes on the west, with considerable basalt exposures along its eastern bank (the plateau of Moreh; Baly 1974: 160). Along the western slopes, a series of valleys (escarpments created through faulting) allow access to the coast (Aharoni 1979: 28), the most important of which is the Beth-hakkerem, which connects with the coastal plain and Acco. The broad, arrowhead-shaped Jezreel Valley serves as the southern boundary of the Galilee. The wide alluvial plain contains some of the richest agricultural territory in the southern Levant, attested as early as the Amarna Letters. The Jezreel also offers access from the Syro-African Rift (via the Harod Valley and Beth Shean) westward to the coastal plain, and cities such as Megiddo grew in prominence commanding the valley's passages.

To the south are a series of Cenomanian hills that form the central highlands including the dome of Gilboa, which guards the Jezreel to the northwest and the Jordan Valley to the east. Valleys such as the Wâdī el-Farʿah and the Sahal Arrâbeh (Dothan Valley) divide the northern extension of the central highlands. The el-Farʿah is a northwest–southeast oriented corridor that cuts into the hills from the Syro-African Rift. To the west, the el-Farʿah connects with a trough-like valley that begins south of Shechem and stretches northeast to the Beth Shean Valley. In the Bronze Age (Middle Bronze–Late Bronze), Shechem commanded the northern hills, while during the Iron Age the focus of power shifted west of the watershed to Samaria, the capital of the northern kingdom of Israel.

The central highlands are divided between north and south by a saddle composed of two plateaus: a smaller northern plateau near Bethel and a second, larger plateau spanning a triangle between Mizpah (Tell en-Nasbeh), Gibeah (Tell el-Fûl), and Gibeon (el-Jib). This saddle provided access into the highlands from the east and west and allowed passage between the central ridges of the northern and southern highlands. Just south of these plateaus is Jerusalem, which sits slightly east of a central watershed ridge that distinguishes the southern highlands and runs just south of Hebron, comprising the heartland of the rural kingdom of Judah during the Iron Age. The slopes of the highlands east of the watershed drop sharply in elevation and experience low precipitation due to rain shadow, resulting in an arid steppe. This steppe, known as the wilderness (or *midbar*), spans the southern highlands (and the western shores of the Dead Sea) all the way to the north, just beyond the Wâdī el-Farʿah.

The coastal plains of the southern Levant begin south of the Ladder of Tyre at the Plain of Acco with its cities of Achzib and Acco. The promontory of the Carmel range marks the southern end of this plain, and here the coast extends westward and then south as it follows the lowland hills of the range in a small panhandle-shaped plain called Naphoth-Dor, after the important port (Dor) that was located here (1 Kgs. 4: 11; Rainey and Notley 2006: 175–6). The dominant culture of this region was Phoenician (ref. 1 Kgs. 9: 13), although this culture at times extended further south into the Plain of Sharon (*COS* 2.57 lines 18–19). The coastal area widens at the Sharon, and here the International Coastal Highway pierced the Jezreel Valley through a series of passes along the valley's southwestern slope (Aharoni et al. 2002: map 10), ultimately connecting the south (and Egypt) with the north (and Mesopotamia). A relatively broad expanse, the eastern zone of the Sharon is a fertile belt where alluvial soils deposited by the highlands are trapped by sandstone ridges. A spring at Aphek feeds the Nahr el-ʿAuja (modern Yarkon), and the river cuts westward to the small Philistine port of Tell el-Qasile and the sea, north of the ancient port of Jaffa. South of the river, the plain becomes Philistia, yet geologically it is similar to the Sharon, with sandstone ridges creating a fertile alluvial strip along its eastern periphery (Orni and Efrat 1973: 42–3; Karmon 1971: 222–3). In the Iron Age, this plain was dominated by five Philistine city-states, which effectively created a political map that was roughly trapezoidal in shape. Along the coast, these consisted of Ashdod (and its port Ashdod-Yam), Ashkelon, and further south, Gaza, while inland (and in the north) they were Ekron (Kh. el-Muqannaʾ) and Gath (Tell eṣ-Ṣafî). The plain gradually dies out in the south around Gaza, giving way to the sands and loess soils of the western Negeb.

To the west of the (southern) central highlands is a belt of lowland hills formed by Eocene outcroppings, and marked by a series of east–west valleys (Orni and Efrat 1973: 62–5). This region is called the Shephelah, a term derived from a Semitic root meaning 'low' (Rainey

1980). Although a similar geological formation occurs in a small patch along the Carmel range in the north (Finkelstein 1981: 84–94), it is most prominent in the south, where it parallels the Plain of Philistia. At the junction of the hard Cenomanian limestone of the central highlands and the soft Eocene hills of the Shephelah is a large north–south chalk trough that forms a natural boundary (Smith 1931: 147). The valleys that extend diagonally from this trough decrease in size as one travels southward; the large valleys of the Aijalon, Sorek, and Elah in the north are paralleled in the south with smaller systems that include two running past Mareshah (Tell Sandahanna)/Beit Guvrin and Lachish (Tell ed-Duweir) and another terminating at Tell el-Ḥesī in the coastal plain. The valleys collect runoff from the highlands to the east, resulting in wide beds of rendzina soils. The Shephelah was the agricultural belt of the kingdom of Judah during much of the Iron Age, and formed an effective screen separating the central highlands of Judah from the Plain of Philistia.

The dry eastern zone of the central highlands (the wilderness) converges south with the Arabah (Josh. 11: 16) and forms part of a large arid expanse that stretches westward to the Mediterranean and extends into the Sinai Peninsula. The modern term for this region (in Israel) is the Negev (Orni and Efrat 1973: 15–34), yet the ancient Negeb (as described in Egyptian and biblical sources) was much more circumscribed and was defined by two basins east and west of Beer-Sheba (Rainey 1984; Rainey and Notley 2006: 10; see Fig. 1.4). The western basin, which encompasses the Brook of Besor, is a larger area of mainly loess soils,

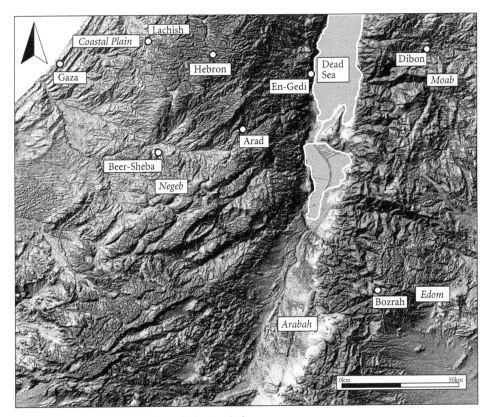

FIG. 1.4. Map of the Negeb and the Arabah

while the eastern Negeb wraps around the southern end of the central highlands (south of Hebron) in a basin around Arad. South of the Negeb is a series of ridges that are referred to in the Hebrew Bible as various 'wildernesses'. In this region are three circular depressions (or erosion cirques), known as the Makteshim, which are unmentioned in any ancient source but certainly played a decisive role in determining the routes of travel and trade. Important trade routes from the south, emanating from the Red Sea or the Arabian Peninsula, passed through the Arabah and the Negeb, terminating at Gaza and the Mediterranean Sea.

Transjordan

Composed of a series of highlands and plateaus, the boundary regions of Transjordan are the Syro-African Rift Valley (to the west) and the great eastern desert expanse (beginning in the north just below the Jebel Druze), along with the plateau of Bashan in the north and the southern mountains of Midian, near the Red Sea's Gulf of 'Aqaba. The eastern desert is actually a complex series of plateaus that are distinguished by geology and subtle changes in elevation most apparent in the expansive depression of the Wadi Sirhan, which is roughly 50–60km in width and 175km in length (Baly 1974: 243). North of the Wadi Sirhan is the basalt plateau of the Black Desert/Harrat ash-Shaba, which extends from the Jebel Druze plateau further north, and fades into a limestone plateau to the east (MacDonald 2000: 23–5), while to the south of the Sirhan lies the Flint Desert/Ardh as-Suwan (Baly 1974: 243). The difficult nature of the eastern desert made travel arduous, thus the main routes in Transjordan were north–south passages located along the highlands. The most important was a route, sometimes identified with the King's Highway (Num. 20: 1, 21: 22), which connected the Red Sea (through the ports of Elath and Ezion-Geber) and the Arabian Peninsula (via Midian) with the northern Levant and Mesopotamia, by way of Damascus (Aharoni et al. 2002: map 10).

In Transjordan's north, the massive basalt plateau of the Bashan (today's Golan Heights) emerges from the southern slopes of Hermon. The activities that produced this igneous rock are evident in the extinct volcanic cones that dot the landscape, resulting in a fertile soil that has supported agricultural production (both grain and wine) since antiquity. To the west, the Bashan breaks off sharply at the cliffs of the Kinneret, while to the south the Bashan stops at the deep Yarmûk Valley with its sizeable river. South of the Yarmûk is Gilead, an uplifted dome (approximately 900m) of Cenomanian limestone that represents an extension of an arch that once began in the southern highlands of Cisjordan, but is now cut by the Syro-African Rift/Jordan Valley (Baly 1974: 12). The az-Zarqa Ravine (Jabbok) wraps around Gilead as it travels north, where it separates the highlands from the arid eastern desert, before cutting west into the Jordan Valley, near Tell Deir 'Alla. In its northward flow, the Jabbok is fed by runoff from one of Gilead's two watersheds, while the other feeds into the Jordan to the west.

The waters of the Jabbok emerge from a source at Ammân (Rabbah/Rabboth Ammon). This basin is detached from the eastern desert by an upfold of Cenomanian limestone and is connected with the Syro-African Rift by a series of valleys to the west, separating Gilead from the plateau region of Moab (Baly 1974: 226). Moab, a tableland bisected by the Wâdī Mujib (Arnon Gorge), breaks off to the west with its embankments along the Dead Sea. The relatively level zones south of Gilead (Ammon and Moab) gradually ascend in elevation southward. The highlands of Edom (Fig. 1.4) begin their ascension south of the Wâdī al-Ḥasā (Zered) and form a geologically complex ridge-land (averaging 1,500m in height) that is divided by the Punon/Feinân Embayment (Baly 1974: 232–6). The rigid valleys of the Mountains of Midian fragment the southern highlands and form a zone of granite ridges that follow the Syro-African Rift south until the Red Sea and the important port of Ezion-Geber (Baly 1974: 244).

ACKNOWLEDGEMENTS

This chapter is dedicated to the memory of Anson F. Rainey, whose considerable contributions to the field have ensured the important place of historical geography in the study of the ancient Levant.

SUGGESTED READING

Aharoni, Y. (1979). *The Land of the Bible: A Historical Geography*, 2nd edn, trans. and ed. A. F. Rainey. Philadelphia: Westminster.

Bekker-Nielsen, T. (2004). *The Roads of Ancient Cyprus*. Copenhagen: Museum Tusculanum Press, University of Copenhagen.

Dorsey, D. A. (1991). *The Roads and Highways of Ancient Israel*. Baltimore, Md.: Johns Hopkins University Press.

Dussaud, R. (1927). *Topographie historique de la Syrie antique et médiévale*. Paris: Geuthner.

Knapp, A. B. (1990). Production, location and integration in Bronze Age Cyprus. *Current Anthropology* 31: 147–76.

—— (1994). Emergence, development and decline on Bronze Age Cyprus. In C. Mathers and S. Stoddart (eds), *Development and Decline in the Mediterranean Bronze Age*. Sheffield: Collis, 271–304.

Mittmann, S., and G. Schmitt (eds) (2001). *Tübinger Bibelatlas auf der Grundlage des Tübinger Atlas des Vorderen Orients (TAVO)/Tübingen Bible Atlas based on the Tübingen Atlas of the Near and Middle East*. Stuttgart: Deutsche Bibelgesellschaft.

Parpola, S., and M. Porter (eds) (2001). *The Helsinki Atlas of the Near East in the Neo-Assyrian Period*. Chebeague Island, Me.: Casco Bay Assyriological Institute/Helsinki: Neo-Assyrian Text Corpus Project.

Rainey, A. F., and R. S. Notley (2006). *The Sacred Bridge: Carta's Atlas of the Biblical World*. Jerusalem: Carta.

Scheffler, T. (2003). 'Fertile Crescent', 'Orient', 'Middle East': the changing mental maps of southwest Asia. *European Review of History* 10: 253–72.

REFERENCES

Aharoni, Y. (1979). *The Land of the Bible: A Historical Geography*, 2nd edn, trans. and ed. A. F. Rainey. Philadelphia: Westminster.

——M. Avi-Yonah, A. F. Rainey, and Z. Safrai (2002). *The Carta Bible Atlas*, 4th edn. Jerusalem: Carta.

Akkermans, P. M. M. G., and G. M. Schwartz (2003). *The Archaeology of Syria: From Complex Hunter-Gatherers to Early Urban Societies (c. 16000–300 BC)*. Cambridge: Cambridge University Press.

Baly, D. (1974). *The Geography of the Bible*, rev edn. New York: Harper & Row.

Blue, L. K. (1997). Cyprus and Cilicia: the typology and palaeogeography of second millennium harbors. In S. Swiny, R. L. Hohlfelder, and H. Wylde Swiny (eds), *Res Maritimae: Cyprus and the Eastern Mediterranean from Prehistory to Late Antiquity*. Atlanta, Ga.: Scholars, 31–44.

Brice, W. C. (1967). *South-West Asia*. London: University of London Press.

Bridgland, D. R., G. Philip, R . Westaway, and M. White (2003). A long Quaternary terrace sequence in the Orontes river valley, Syria: a record of uplift and of human occupation. *Current Science* 84: 1080–89.

COS = Hallo, W. W. (2003). *Context of Scripture* (3 vols). Leiden: Brill.

Dever, W. G. (1997). Syria-Palestine. In E. M. Meyers (ed.), *The Oxford Encyclopedia of Archaeology in the Near East*, vol. 5. New York: Oxford University Press, 147.

Finkelstein, I. (1981). The Shephelah of Israel. *Tel Aviv* 8: 84–94.

Gelb, I. J. (1938). Studies in the topography of western Asia. *American Journal of Semitic Languages and Literatures* 55: 66–85.

George, A. R. (1990). The day the Earth divided: a geological aetiology in the Babylonian Gilgamesh Epic. *Zeitschrift für Assyriologie* 80: 214–19.

Gifford, J. A. (1985). Paleogeography of ancient harbour sites of the Larnaca lowlands, southeastern Cyprus. In A. Raban (ed.), *Harbour Archaeology: Proceedings of the First International Workshop on Ancient Mediterranean Harbours, Caesarea Maritima, 24–28.6.83*. Oxford: British Archaeological Reports, 45–8.

Goren, Y., S. Bunimovitz, I. Finkelstein, and N. Na'aman (2003). The location of Alashiya: new evidence from petrographic investigation of Alashiyan tablets from El-Amarna and Ugarit. *American Journal of Archaeology* 107: 233–55.

Karageorghis, V. (1982). *Cyprus, from the Stone Age to the Romans*. London: Thames & Hudson.

Karmon, Y. (1971). *Israel: A Regional Geography*. New York: Wiley-Interscience.

Knapp, A. B. (1997). Mediterranean maritime landscapes: transport, trade, and society on Late Bronze Age Cyprus. In S. Swiny, R. L. Hohlfelder, and H. Wylde Swiny (eds), *Res Maritimae: Cyprus and the Eastern Mediterranean from Prehistory to Late Antiquity*. Atlanta, Ga.: Scholars, 153–62.

MacDonald, B. (2000). *East of the Jordan: Territories and Sites of the Hebrew Scriptures*. Boston, Mass.: American Schools of Oriental Research.

Mazzoni, S. (2001). Tell Afis and the Lu'ash in the Aramaean period. In P. M. M. Daviau, J. W. Wevers, and M. Weigl (eds), *The World of the Aramaeans*, vol. 2. Sheffield: Sheffield Academic, 99–114.

Orni, E., and E. Efrat (1973). *Geography of Israel*, 3rd edn. Philadelphia: Jewish Publication Society of America.

Perkins, A. L. (1949). *The Comparative Archeology of Early Mesopotamia*. Chicago: University of Chicago Press.

Pitard, W. T. (1987). *Ancient Damascus: A Historical Study of the Syrian City-State from Earliest Times until Its Fall to the Assyrians in 732 B.C.E.* Winona Lake, Ind.: Eisenbrauns.

Rainey, A. F. (1980). The administrative division of the Shephelah. *Tel Aviv* 7: 194–202.

——(1984). Early historical geography of the Negeb. In Z. Herzog (ed.), *Beer-Sheba II: The Early Iron Age Settlements*. Tel Aviv: Tel Aviv University, Institute of Archaeology, 88–104.

—— and R. S. Notley (2006). *The Sacred Bridge: Cartas Atlas of the Biblical World*. Jerusalem: Carta.

Raphael, C. N. (1992). Geography and the Bible (Palestine). In D. N. Freedman (ed.), *The Anchor Bible Dictionary*, vol. 2. New York: Doubleday, 964–77.

Silberman, N. A. (1982). *Digging for God and Country: Exploration, Archeology, and the Secret Struggle for the Holy Land, 1799–1917*. New York: Knopf.

Smith, G. A. (1931). *The Historical Geography of the Holy Land*, 25th edn. London: Hodder & Stoughton.

van Soldt, W. H. (2005). *The Topography of the City-State of Ugarit*. Münster: Ugarit.

Yon, M. (1992). Ugarit: the urban habitat. The present state of the archaeological picture. *Bulletin of the American Schools of Oriental Research* 286: 19–34.

CHAPTER 2

PEOPLES AND LANGUAGES OF THE LEVANT DURING THE BRONZE AND IRON AGES

HOLGER GZELLA

The study of peoples and languages of the Levant during the Bronze and Iron Ages offers fascinating insights into the long-term workings of successive politico-economic centres, contact-induced linguistic evolution, and far-reaching cultural paradigm shifts. As a conventional starting point, the time around 1550 BCE roughly coincides with the appearance of the first continuous attestations of some local languages used in Syria-Palestine instead of purely onomastic material scattered throughout earlier evidence. The fall of the Achaemenid Empire after Alexander's conquest in 332 BCE, by contrast, brought large parts of the region into enduring contact with Hellenistic culture and, later, with Roman administration, thereby serving as a *caesura*, albeit a weak one, often identified with the close of the 'Ancient Near East' proper in traditional historiography. Both ends of the time-frame constitute a compromise between the rational and the practical. During the intervening period, fortified cities under the competing authority of Egyptians and Hittites were transformed into or replaced by territorial states soon struggling again with the major empires of the day. This process triggered the emergence of new languages and forms of cultural self-awareness.

THE BRONZE AGE

While some distinct idioms, including Semitic ones, can already be identified in the Bronze Age, their origins and the erstwhile homelands of their speakers remain mysterious. Many linguists believe that the largest part of the population, Semitic-speaking peoples, had come in waves to Syria-Palestine from about 3000 BCE onwards (Sekine 1973), but there were no doubt sizeable amounts of other groups as well. After full urbanism in this region began early in the third millennium BCE, these peoples formed an area of interrelated cultures determined by a blend of mostly Mesopotamian and local traditions with many individual manifestations. Despite the fragmented physical geography, trade and migration, reinforced by the scarcity of natural resources, led to a high degree of mutual interaction and thus to intense language contact causing convergence of grammatical structures over the ages. This is when the tongues which are now for the most part classified as West Semitic or, depending on the underlying comparative framework, Northwest Semitic slowly emerged. Their oldest traces may be transcriptions of individual words and names in 20th–18th-century BCE Egyptian texts, leaving aside the problematic 'Proto-Sinaitic' inscriptions in a peculiar alphabetic script of which no universally accepted date and decipherment have yet been proposed. Eventually, the Syro-Palestinian dialects—to apply a concept from geographical rather than genealogical linguistics—clustered into Canaanite and Aramaic as polar ends of a once continuous, yet only partially attested, linguistic map by the beginning of the first millennium BCE, when several were promoted to written languages. Since literacy was largely restricted to professionals, chancellery idioms often conforming to supraregional standards make up most of the linguistic evidence. It is important to note that they do not represent contemporary vernaculars in any consistent way. Formal language can, in fact, lag behind developments in everyday usage even by centuries, whereas spelling conventions or simply the imperfections of the respective writing systems obscure subtle differences in pronunciation. Furthermore, a good proportion of the population lived in village societies outside the urban centres and the immediate hinterland, of which no written records survive.

Attempts to establish ethnic affinities along very general lines (e.g. West Semitic as opposed to Hurrian) are often based on onomastic data, but personal names were already subject to fashions at that time, and the mobility of people precludes too strict an association of a name with its bearer's place of origin and actual speech. The most important nomadic groups infiltrating the Levant in the Bronze Age, although no doubt not the only ones, belonged to the 'Amorites' (Streck 2000). Apparently, nomads and city-dwellers engaged throughout this period in 'dimorphic societies', fluctuating between sedentary life and pastoralism. The Amorite names appear mostly in cuneiform texts from the late third and early second millennia BCE. In light of certain grammatical phenomena, they reflect a separate (North-)West Semitic language, or set of dialects, which is unattested otherwise; but one does not know whether it was ever spoken during the period in question. Towards the end of the Late Bronze Age, another highly mobile and likewise heterogeneous though still enigmatic group of refugees and outlaws, the so-called 'apiru, appeared on the scene. Local rulers frequently referred to them as political enemies, but their identity cannot be established. Their name is often related to the first-millennium 'Hebrews'.

Akkadian and Hurrian

During the entire second millennium BCE, Akkadian, a cluster of distinct language varieties belonging to the East Semitic branch, and the syllabic cuneiform script dominated the textual record of the Levant. Both the language and its writing system are already attested in mid-third-millennium Mesopotamia, but especially the Middle Babylonian variety of Akkadian, widely used as a prestigious means of communication, spread far into the western periphery (George 2007). There, it formed intriguingly complex symbioses with admixtures of other Mesopotamian dialects and local West Semitic scribal cultures whose earlier history by and large defies reconstruction. A comprehensive study of Western Peripheral Akkadian would no doubt shed more light on this process. Linguistic contact with Egyptian and Hittite seems to have been much shallower, since their observable impact on the Syro-Palestinian languages is restricted to a few loanwords which nonetheless persist in the lexicon. In addition to that, some *Kulturwanderwörter* may have been borrowed from indigenous and foreign tongues which have otherwise disappeared completely.

By contrast, 15th- and 14th-century treaties, letters, and administrative documents from various city-states in Levantine Syria, such as Alalakh and Qatna, exhibit an extensive influence of Hurrian, a non-Semitic ergative-agglutinative language (Wegner 2007). Judging cumulatively from not only scores of personal names, but also from borrowings, grammatical convergence, and features of spelling practice (Márquez Rowe 1998), it seems to have acted as a 'pragmatically prominent' language among the scribal classes, even though its status as a vernacular spoken by a part of the wider population cannot be easily determined. The origin of the Hurrians in Syria and elsewhere is unknown, just like much of their culture and society. Many traces of Hurrian in the textual record supposedly result from the cultural radiance of the Mitanni Empire, and hence the prestige of its language, before the 13th century BCE. Several texts written in this yet little-known idiom and mostly pertaining to the local cult and school curriculum have also been unearthed in the coastal city of Ugarit—Ras Shamra in present-day Syria.

Ugarit

Thanks to more than 2000 published clay tablets in several languages underlining its thriving multicultural atmosphere (numerous discoveries of ongoing excavations during the past years still have to be published), society and daily life of Ugarit during the 13th and 12th centuries BCE are better documented than other places in Bronze Age Syria-Palestine. Semites, perhaps from different places of origin, constituted the main element of the population, enriched by a Hurrian component, as well as by expatriates not only from Phoenicia and Palestine but also from Cyprus, Egypt, and the Hittite kingdom (Vita 1999). The corpus of Akkadian material actually composed at Ugarit (rather than imported from Mesopotamia) comprises legal, economic, and epistolary texts in syllabic cuneiform, as well as multilingual word-lists for study purposes. Several peculiarities set their language apart from both normative Babylonian and other Western Peripheral varieties of Akkadian (Huehnergard 1989; van Soldt 1991). Some of those non-standard phenomena that occur more than sporadically, grammatical and lexical alike, conform to a common scribal tradition of 'Syro-Anatolian' Akkadian; many others, by contrast, reflect substrate influence of the local language. The latter, Ugaritic, is attested in 1000 published texts and fragments on clay tablets inscribed with an alphabetic cuneiform script (Bordreuil and Pardee 2009). This script thus displays an interesting fusion between the writing traditions of Mesopotamia and the Levant. Despite its otherwise strictly consonantal character and perhaps owing to Hurrian scribal education, it indicates the quality of a vowel following a glottal stop. According to the present majority opinion, Ugaritic belongs to the (North-) West Semitic language group and shares various features with Phoenician and Hebrew, although neither can count as its immediate successor, since it disappeared with the fall of Ugarit in 1175 BCE. Although its earlier history is shrouded in darkness, links with Amorite have been suggested. In addition to a few legal documents, many economic lists, and dozens of letters patterned after Akkadian models, an extensive body of mythological and ritual texts is the only direct evidence of Bronze Age Syro-Palestinian literary traditions and indigenous religious practice. The language of these poetic compositions diverges from prose in grammar (principally verbal syntax) and vocabulary, is in all likelihood more archaic, and appears to represent a more widespread, formulaic *Dichtersprache* whose reflexes can also be found in the earliest parts of the Hebrew Bible. Purportedly, alphabetic cuneiform had been introduced in order to commit such originally oral compositions to writing. Since a few letters sent to Ugarit from Phoenician cities and Asia Minor also employ Ugaritic cuneiform, this idiom and its script, possibly popularized by Ugaritic traders abroad, must have acquired some prestige in the course of time. As a consequence, its use gradually increased in Ugarit and the immediate vicinity, but variation in texts written abroad and the presence of different cuneiform alphabetic traditions in the same region point to a dialectal landscape which was far more complex than the surviving evidence makes one believe (Gzella 2010). For international affairs, however, scribes usually continued to resort to Akkadian, because it was more widely known.

Palestine

Further to the south, in Palestine, the linguistic situation bears witness to a similar distinction between Peripheral Akkadian for global purposes of communication and local vernaculars eclipsed by it. With the notable exception of seventeen 15th-century letters and administrative documents from Taanach near Megiddo, only a few, mostly small and fragmentary, Bronze Age cuneiform texts have been unearthed so far; the 91 objects from 28 sites are now conveniently assembled in Horowitz, Oshima, and Sanders (2006). They yield frustratingly little information on society and domestic affairs of the cosmopolitan city-states of this region, let alone on their literature and culture. This indicates that cuneiform writing was, if not less widespread, at any rate less deeply rooted than in Levantine Syria. Yet there is practically no evidence attesting the presence of flourishing scribal schools where masterpieces of Mesopotamian literature like the Gilgamesh Epic were studied.

More significantly, the Amarna letters—some 300 Akkadian cuneiform tablets dispatched from 14th-century vassal rulers of smaller cities along the Mediterranean coast and central Palestine (e.g. Byblos, Tyre, Akko, Jerusalem, Shechem, Gezer, and Ashkelon) to their overlord in Egypt and discovered at the capital of Amenhotep IV on the east bank of the Nile—represent an interesting case of language mixing. Many hybrid verbal forms and lexical items contain material akin to the Canaanite group of (North-)West Semitic (Rainey 1996), which is directly attested only from the Iron Age onwards. The presuppositions of the underlying linguistic code are controversial. Scholars often assume that the 'Canaanisms' mirror the respective scribe's native language in a pidginized form of Akkadian, if indeed the Akkadian 'layer' despite its complexities is not a purely graphic convention. Yet the restricted amount of variation in these texts does not necessarily imply geographical substrates. The hypothesis of an institutionalized contact idiom, on the other hand, is guided by the idea of a fossilized intermediary stage of learning Middle Babylonian by native speakers of Canaanite who originally, unlike their colleagues further to the north, were not exposed to a full training in Akkadian; this 'interlanguage' in turn became a supraregional standard.

THE IRON AGE

Following the population movements of the Early Iron Age and the resulting power vacuum, various local languages of the Syro-Palestinian city-states and tribal societies were promoted to chancellery idioms. This process coincided with the final breakthrough of alphabetic (or rather: *abjad*) writing in its various branches. The roots of the so-called linear alphabet may already lie in the first half of the second millennium, but it remained marginal for centuries (Sanders 2009: 76–155). A renewed self-assertion after a period of decline and the exhaustion of economic resources fostered radical changes in scribal culture, such as the use of a different script, the development of a fresh narrative prose style, and the rise of 'national languages' as a written means of expression. According to linguistic criteria, most of these can be assigned to either the 'Canaanite' or the 'Aramaic' branch of (North-) West Semitic. Others, by contrast, resist a straightforward classification. Since the transition period between 1200 and 1000 BCE is poorly documented (evidence mostly comes from some personal names on arrowheads: Hess 2007), their origin continues to cause debate. Owing to multilingualism, social prestige, or seemingly arbitrary decisions of a ruling dynasty, several forms of language contact, both natural and controlled, caused linguistic innovations to spread across the speech area from the centre to its periphery. Hence, the Iron Age languages of Syria-Palestine share a number of important features which clearly distinguish their grammatical structure from the one of their second-millennium ancestors: first, an older inflectional case system has been replaced by external marking of grammatical roles, chiefly the direct object; second, the semantics of tense, aspect, and modality were rearranged in different ways following the loss of some verbal forms and the rise of others; and third, a prepositive (Canaanite) or postpositive (Aramaic) definite article appeared in order to mark varying degrees of definiteness. These developments appear to be interconnected and were triggered by the loss of unstressed word-final vowels. Obviously, the limited amount of textual discoveries does not adequately represent the situation of colloquial speech at any moment.

Phoenician

Phoenician (Friedrich and Röllig 1999) was used in several small but ancient cities like Byblos, Tyre, and Sidon along the Mediterranean coast between Arwad and Mount Carmel; at times, their influence extended even further. From there colonists, merchants, and travellers brought the language and presumably also its alphabet to the Greek islands and as far west as Pyrgoi, Marseilles, and Spain from the 8th century BCE onwards. It was prestigious enough to be adopted as an official idiom in Anatolian Karatepe during the 8th and 7th centuries. These city-states were never formally united and the corpus of inscriptions, beginning in the 10th century BCE, exhibits a certain amount of historical and dialectal variation despite its largely formulaic character. This diversity was eclipsed by the growing influence of the dialect of Tyre and Sidon, often labelled 'Standard Phoenician'. The possible instances of substrate influence in second-millennium Ugaritic texts composed abroad, few though they are, may disclose forerunners of the languages of Iron Age Byblos and Tyre. A handful of 10th-century inscriptions from Byblos seem linguistically closer to that preceding stage than later Tyro-Sidonian. Consequently, the genesis of Phoenician is somewhat easier to trace than other Canaanite or Aramaic languages. Despite such differences, the inhabitants of the homeland and the colonies apparently shared a basically common culture and religion. Their pantheon at any rate resembles the one known from Ugarit. Phoenician continued to be used on the mainland into the Hellenistic and Roman periods for building, funerary, and dedicatory inscriptions. However, its status as a vernacular and the impact of Persian administration on the language situation in the Phoenician city-states are much more difficult to determine. In North Africa, Punic, an offshoot of Phoenician, remained in use until the 5th century CE. The Phoenician dialect group is closely related to the other first-millennium Canaanite languages, but has a number of common phonetic, morphological, and lexical peculiarities.

Canaanite

Conversely, in the hill country of Ephraim, Judah, and Transjordan, a remarkable growth in population led to the emergence of new settlements which eventually became monarchies, or, to be more cautious, 'extended chiefdoms' with unclear geographical boundaries. The underlying social conditions are subject to an ongoing discussion oscillating between the hypothesis of an influx from outside, based on the biblical exodus tradition with the subsequent conquest of Canaan (now often thought to be a later invention), and various models operating with the (multicausal?) consolidation of an internal, decentralized, population uprooted after a political or economic crisis. Linguistic evidence, generally neglected by theologians, historians, and archaeologists, points to a strong continuity of peoples and cultures since the Late Bronze Age, as second-millennium material already exhibits several phonological and morphological features of later Canaanite varieties. This fact, however, does not rule out the possibility of some newcomers being quickly integrated.

It is against such a background that Hebrew (Sáenz-Badillos 1993) emerged. The corpus of the Hebrew Bible has been unified over the course of many redactional processes, and the garb of later pronunciation traditions was arguably affected by Aramaic. Even so, traces of a once considerable internal diversity in historical, geographical, and social respects survive (Gianto 1996). Certain poetic compositions are widely considered to date from around the 11th century BCE. Their archaic, or archaizing, character results from the conventions of an earlier oral poetic tradition also reflected in Ugaritic epic. They exhibit peculiarities in the tense-aspect-mood system, the choice of words, and individual literary motives, such as the Divine Warrior. 'Classical' pre-exilic Hebrew, by contrast, shows several linguistic innovations, above all in the verbal syntax, which partly result from the development of a new narrative prose style taking the place of earlier epic. After the Babylonian Exile from 586 BCE onwards, Aramaic, later joined by Greek, gradually supplanted Hebrew for many everyday purposes in the heartland and exercised a growing impact on literary Hebrew which continued into Hellenistic and Roman times. A modest corpus of inscriptions dating from the 8th century BCE to the exile, which comprises chiefly letters and ostraca (Renz and Röllig 1995–2003), is essentially identical to pre-exilic biblical prose in morphology, syntax, and lexicon. However, they establish a clearer geographical distinction between a 'Northern' Hebrew variety which, being used during the independence of the 'Israelite' kingdom (until 722 BCE) in the Samarian hills and parts of central Transjordan and Galilee, was ostensibly closer to Phoenician, and a 'Southern' Judaean dialect with its centre at Jerusalem, later becoming the written prestige language of that area.

The few inscriptions from the Philistine pentapolis are difficult to distinguish from contemporary Hebrew. Some scholars nonetheless assign them to a discrete Canaanite dialect (Israel 1999); but since they date from centuries after the initial settlement of the Philistines, they say very little about the original Philistine language. The Philistines are often viewed as descendants of an Aegean or Cypriot contingent of the 'Sea Peoples' who arrived on the southwest coast of Canaan around 1185 BCE and acculturated soon thereafter.

Smaller epigraphic corpora from Transjordan to the east of the Dead Sea and the Jordan River, whose fragmented physical geography promoted regional diversity, also attest to a number of local chancellery languages with a more restricted sphere of influence (Parker 2002). They presuppose urbanization processes, perhaps even ethnogenesis, at some time during the Early Iron Age (the same region seems to have been inhabited by nomads in the Late Bronze Age) and employ either the Phoenician or the Aramaic branch of the alphabet.

Moabite is the one best known, thanks to a lengthy royal inscription of King Mesha/Mosha from c.835 BCE. Composed in a prose style very close to Southern Hebrew, by which it may have been inspired, this text refers to the king's delivery at the hands of the national god Kamosh and the erection of a mountain sanctuary. Some distinctive features warrant its classification as a separate Canaanite language, serving as the official idiom of the independent kingdom of Moab from the 9th (at the latest) to the 6th century BCE.

At that time, Ammon, which borders Moab in the north, also was a political entity with its own sovereign deity, Milkom, kings residing in Amman, and a standard language. The latter has been preserved in a few shorter royal inscriptions as well as in several ostraca and numerous seals. Its exact position within Canaanite is less clear.

Finally, the kingdom of Edom to the south of the Dead Sea existed from approximately the 8th to the 6th century BCE (it may have emerged even earlier). However, despite a specifically Edomite god, Qaws/Qos, and a capital, Bosra, its existing corpus of about thirty ostraca and seals can hardly be distinguished from Southern Hebrew on linguistic or paleographic grounds.

In addition, excavations in modern Deir 'Allā have unearthed a long but fragmentary plaster text written in red and black ink on a wall (Hoftijzer and van der Kooij 1991). It features the seer Bileam, son of Beor, who also appears in Numbers 22–24, but the context, supposedly a vision, is mysterious. Since Canaanite and Aramaic features occur side by side, its classification remains debated, as does the question whether this unique, literary witness reflects a historical language ('Gileadite') or artificial language mixing.

Some instances of variation in the Hebrew Bible, especially in the speech of foreigners (e.g. Judg. 12: 6 or some alleged irregularities in Job), may preserve traces of other languages or dialects, now long forgotten, of that ethnically heterogeneous area in which monarchies and tribal societies intersected.

Aramaic

While a continuous process of linguistic evolution thus correlates the Canaanite languages of the Iron Age with their Bronze Age ancestors, Aramaic (Beyer 1984: 23–71; 2004: 13–41) only becomes manifest at the beginning of the first millennium BCE. By that time, Aramean tribes had settled in various parts of Syria and Mesopotamia under unknown socioeconomic conditions (Younger 2007). The languages of these city-states appear at first in a number of royal inscriptions which exhibit certain local peculiarities, proving that the earliest known forms of Aramaic, recognizably distinct from Canaanite from the outset, were already diversified. Among them, Sam'alian, the official idiom of Sam'al in Asia Minor that supplanted Phoenician in the 8th century, occupies a special place. Because of its many peculiarities, Sam'alian has been categorized not to be Aramaic at all (for a recent discussion, see Pardee 2009: 66–9). Hence, the second-millennium ancestors of the Arameans were presumably nomads who spoke different dialects but did not write any of them.

Once Aramaic had become a written language, it rapidly conquered the Fertile Crescent from Egypt to Lake Urmia during the 8th–6th centuries BCE and thus promoted the alphabetic script in Syria, Mesopotamia, and elsewhere. Thanks to its grammatical flexibility and popularity among highly mobile speakers, (simplified?) varieties of Aramaic were employed for many legal, commercial, and communicative purposes during the Neo-Assyrian and Neo-Babylonian Empires, thus quickly restricting the use of Akkadian. When the Achaemenids adopted a Babylonian dialect of Aramaic as their lingua franca, it spread across the entire Near East to Central Asia and replaced many local idioms and scripts (Gzella 2008). This greatly standardized 'Official Aramaic' is best attested by dozens of letters and contracts on papyrus, as well as ostraca, discovered at Elephantine in Egypt, but also by epigraphic material from across the rest of the Achaemenid Empire, now including an official archive of letters and lists from Bactria. Moreover, it underlies the Aramaic parts of the Hebrew Bible. Under its surface, but influenced by its orthography and style, Aramaic vernaculars almost invisibly continued to develop and were themselves converted into written languages again in Hellenistic times. As a consequence, Aramaic maintained its position as the regnant language of the Ancient Near East for more than 1000 years until the advent of Islam. Having survived in various pockets, it is still spoken today.

Arabic

Long before the Islamic conquest, from the mid-9th century BCE onwards, groups subsumed under the generic term 'Arabs' were already attested (Versteegh 2001: 23–36; Krebernik 2008: 255–60). Any identification in ethnic, cultural, or social terms proves difficult. Yet personal names and perhaps also loanwords, which contain linguistic material evidently belonging to the heterogeneous 'Arabian' family of Semitic, controversial as to its subdivision and earlier history, occur throughout Syria-Palestine. Most of their bearers were supposedly nomads; the coexistence of Arabic and Aramaic names among them implies some kind of ethnic interference. During the Achaemenid period at the latest, certain North Arabian tribes also adopted Aramaic as a written language for international or representative purposes. Traces of the South Arabian sister branch of the alphabet throughout the Fertile Crescent illustrate long-distance connections extending even to the southwestern angle of the Arabian Peninsula, where various civilizations flourished early in the first millennium BCE and gained much wealth from the incense trade. Such connections may have promoted some form of contact with (North-)West Semitic languages and literary traditions, but this topic has not yet been thoroughly researched.

Given the extensive multilingualism of the Levant, with its continuous intertwining of official idioms and vernaculars in Bronze Age and Iron Age Syria-Palestine and the partial nature of the written evidence, it is difficult to establish ethnic and cultural boundaries on the basis of the surviving documents. This entails that the gap between 'peoples' and 'languages' often cannot be bridged. Until a theoretical framework has been developed which accounts for the linguistic status of the material in a more adequate manner, historical conclusions concerning population movements, sedentarization, and identity remain vulnerable. Even so, the Syro-Palestinian languages together with their oral and/or written traditions constitute perhaps the strongest bond between the Ancient Near Eastern civilizations and the modern Middle East.

SUGGESTED READING

Garr, W. R. (1985). *Dialect Geography of Syria-Palestine 1000–586 B.C.E.* Philadelphia: University of Pennsylvania Press.

Gianto, A. (2000). Amarna Akkadian as a contact language. In K. Van Lerberghe and G. Voet (eds), *Languages and Cultures in Contact: At the Crossroads of Civilizations in the Syro-Mesopotamian Realm*. Leuven: Peeters, 123–32.

—— (2008). Lost and found in the grammar of first-millennium Aramaic. In H. Gzella and M. L. Folmer (eds), *Aramaic in Its Historical and Linguistic Setting*. Wiesbaden: Harrassowitz, 11–26.

Ginsberg, H. L. (1970). The Northwest Semitic languages. In B. Mazar (ed.), *The World History of the Jewish People*, vol. 2: *Patriarchs*. Tel Aviv: Jewish History/New Brunswick, NJ: Rutgers University Press, 102–24.

Greenfield, J. C. (1969). Amurrite, Ugaritic and Canaanite. In *Proceedings of the International Conference on Semitic Studies Held in Jerusalem, 19–23 July 1965*. Jerusalem: Israel Academy of Sciences and Humanities, 92–101.

Gzella, H. (ed.) (2009). *Sprachen aus der Welt des Alten Testaments*. Darmstadt: Wissenschaftliche Buchgesellschaft.

—— (forthcoming). Northwest Semitic in general. In M. P. Streck and S. Weninger (eds), *Semitic Languages: An International Handbook*. Berlin: de Gruyter.

Harris, Z. S. (1939). *Development of the Canaanite Dialects: An Investigation in Linguistic History*. New Haven, Conn.: American Oriental Society.

Krebernik, M. (2007). Buchstabennamen, Lautwerte und Alphabetgeschichte. In R. Rollinger, A. Luther, and J. Wiesehöfer (eds), *Getrennte Wege? Kommunikation, Raum und Wahrnehmung in der Alten Welt*. Frankfurt am Main: Antike, 108–75.

Moran, W. L. (1961). The Hebrew language in its northwest Semitic background. In G. E. Wright (ed.), *The Bible and the Ancient Near East: Essays in Honor of William Foxwell Albright*, 53–72. Garden City, NJ: Doubleday. Reprinted in J. Huehnergard and S. Izreel (eds), *Amarna Studies: Collected Writings*. Winona Lake, Ind.: Eisenbrauns.

—— (ed. and trans.) (1992). *The Amarna Letters*. Baltimore, Md.: Johns Hopkins University Press.

REFERENCES

Beyer, K. (1984, 1994, 2004). *Die aramäischen Texte vom Toten Meer: samt den Inschriften aus Palästina, dem Testament Levis aus der Kairoer Genisa, der Fastenrolle und den alten talmudischen Zitaten: aramaistische Einleitung, Text, Übersetzung, Deutung, Grammatik/ Wörterbuch, deutsch-aramäische Wortliste, Register* (2 vols. and supplement). Göttingen: Vandenhoeck & Ruprecht.

Bordreuil, P., and D. G. Pardee (2009). *A Manual of Ugaritic* (English edn). Winona Lake, Ind.: Eisenbrauns.

Friedrich, J., and W. Röllig (1999). *Phönizisch-punische Grammatik*, 3rd edn, ed. M. G. Amadasi Guzzo with W. R. Mayer. Rome: Pontificio Istituto Biblico.

George, A. R. (2007). Babylonian and Assyrian: a history of Akkadian. In J. N. Postgate (ed.), *Languages of Iraq, Ancient and Modern*. London: British School of Archaeology in Iraq, 31–71.

Gianto, A. (1996). Variations in biblical Hebrew. *Biblica* 77: 493–508.

Gzella, H. (2008). The heritage of Imperial Aramaic in Eastern Aramaic. *Aramaic Studies* 6.1: 85–109.

——(2009). *Languages from the World of the Bible*. Berlin: de Gruyter.

——(2010). Linguistic variation in the Ugaritic letters and some implications thereof. In W. H. van Soldt (ed.), *Society and Administration in Ancient Ugarit*. Leiden: Nederlands Instituut voor het Nabije Oosten, 58–70.

——(2011). Northwest Semitic in general. In S. Weninger et al. (eds), *Semitic Languages: An International Handbook*. Berlin: de Gruyter, 425–51.

Hess, R. S. (2007). Arrowheads from Iron Age I. In K. L. Younger Jr. (ed.), *Ugarit at Seventy-Five*. Winona Lake, Ind.: Eisenbrauns, 113–29.

Hoftijzer, J., and G. van der Kooij (eds) (1991). *The Balaam Text from Deir Alla Re-Evaluated: Proceedings of the International Symposium Held at Leiden, 21–24 August 1989*. Leiden: Brill.

Horowitz, W., T. Oshima, and S. L. Sanders (2006). *Cuneiform in Canaan: Cuneiform Sources from the Land of Israel in Ancient Times*. Jerusalem: Israel Exploration Society, Hebrew University of Jerusalem.

Huehnergard, J. (1989). *The Akkadian of Ugarit*. Atlanta, Ga.: Scholars Press.

Israel, F. (1999). Un chiaramento di storia linguistica a Sir 50,26. In N. Calduch-Benages and J. Vermeylen (eds), *Treasures of Wisdom: Studies in Ben Sira and the Book of Wisdom*. Leuven: Peeters, 231–8.

Krebernik, M. (2008). Von Gindibu bis Muhammad: Stand, Probleme und Aufgaben altorientalistisch-arabistischer Philologie. In O. Jastrow, S. Talay, and H. Hafenrichter (eds), *Studien zur Semitistik und Arabistik: Festschrift für Hartmut Bobzin zum 60. Geburtstag*. Wiesbaden: Harrassowitz, 247–79.

Márquez Rowe, I. (1998). Notes on the Hurro-Akkadian of Alalaḫ in the mid-second millennium B.C.E. In S. Izreel, I. Singer, and R. Zadok (eds), *Past Links: Studies in the Languages and Cultures of the Ancient Near East*. Winona Lake, Ind.: Eisenbrauns, 63–78.

Pardee, D. G. (2009). A new Aramaic inscription from Zincirli. *Bulletin of the American Schools of Oriental Research* 356: 51–71.

Parker, S. B. (2002). Ammonite, Edomite, and Moabite. In J. Kaltner and S. L. McKenzie (eds), *Beyond Babel: A Handbook for Biblical Hebrew and Related Languages*. Leiden: Brill, 43–60.

Rainey, A. F. (1996). *Canaanite in the Amarna Tablets: A Linguistic Analysis of the Mixed Dialect Used by Scribes from Canaan* (4 vols). Leiden: Brill.

Renz, J., and W. Röllig (1995–2003). *Handbuch der althebräischen Epigraphik* (3 vols). Darmstadt: Wissenschaftliche Buchgesellschaft.

Sáenz-Badillos, A. (1993). *A History of the Hebrew Language*, trans. J. Elwolde. Cambridge: Cambridge University Press.

Sanders, S. L. (2009). *The Invention of Hebrew*. Urbana: University of Illinois Press.

Sekine, M. (1973). The subdivisions of the North-West Semitic language. *Journal of Semitic Studies* 18: 205–21.

Streck, M. P. (2000). *Das amurritische Onomastikon der altbabylonischen Zeit I*. Münster: Ugarit.

van Soldt, W. H. (1991). *Studies in the Akkadian of Ugarit: Dating and Grammar*. Kevelaer: Butzon & Bercker/Neukirchen-Vluyn: Neukirchener.

Versteegh, K. (2001). *The Arabic Language*. Edinburgh: Edinburgh University Press.

Vita, J.-P. (1999). The society of Ugarit. In W. G. E. Watson and N. Wyatt (eds), *Handbook of Ugaritic Studies*. Boston: Brill, 455–98.

Wegner, I. (2007). *Einführung in die hurritische Sprache*, 2nd rev edn. Wiesbaden: Harrassowitz.

Younger, K. L., Jr. (2007). The Late Bronze Age/Iron Age transition and the origins of the Arameans. In K. L. Younger Jr. (ed.), *Ugarit at Seventy-Five*. Winona Lake, Ind.: Eisenbrauns, 131–74.

CHAPTER 3

....

HISTORY OF RESEARCH

....

THOMAS DAVIS

Two centuries of archaeology in the Levant have resulted in an intensely examined archaeological record and provided a laboratory for theoretical models and methodologies. The Levant is a tapestry of cultures interwoven with strands of nationalism, colonialism, and politics. Archaeology in the Levant speaks directly to questions of identity, and as a consequence has often been appropriated by modern political ideologues.

OTTOMAN RULE

....

The weakness of the Ottoman Empire in the 19th century attracted the covetous gaze of the 'Great Powers'. The western European intelligentsia shared a generalized negative attitude toward Turkey and the Ottoman Empire, the reverse side of long-standing philhellenic attitudes (Frankel 2001). One of the byproducts of renewed European commercial and political interest in the region was increased antiquarian research and collecting. Many foreigners resident in the Levant began to collect and excavate for antiquities, motivated by religious beliefs, academic concerns, and basic acquisitiveness. Initial excavations carried out in this manner were essentially treasure hunts. One of the most colourful of these pillagers was the Russian and American consul on Cyprus, General Luigi Palma di Cesnola. He undertook large-scale plundering of tombs and other Cypriot sites and exported more than 10,000 items from the island; most of the collection ended up in the Metropolitan Museum in New York, where Cesnola was appointed as the first director.

In keeping with the prevailing social and academic milieu in western Europe, one expression of public interest in the region in the mid-19th century was the establishment of a plethora of academic and religious societies dedicated to Near Eastern archaeology. Great Britain in particular witnessed the establishment of the Palestine Exploration Fund, the Egypt Exploration Fund, the Cyprus Exploration Fund, and the Society of Biblical Archaeology. The United States entered the fray with the Palestine Exploration Society and, more successfully, in 1900 with the founding of the American Schools of Oriental Research (King 1983; Seger 2001).

The biblical connection was a primary factor behind much of the public and scholarly interest in archaeology in the Levant (Davis 2004). Edward Robinson, an American clergyman seeking to locate biblical sites based on his belief that ancient names were preserved in local Arabic usage, conducted the pioneering archaeological survey of Palestine. Conservative biblical scholars, inspired by the perceived success of Heinrich Schliemann in locating Homeric sites around the Aegean, sought to excavate the world of the Bible in the thousands of ancient 'tell' sites crowding the eastern Mediterranean. The discovery of important inscriptions such as the Siloam Inscription and the Moabite Stone added to the interest of biblical scholars in archaeological discoveries.

By the First World War, scholarly societies had spawned numerous foreign institutes in the Levant, principally in Jerusalem. Academic interest marched in step with political interests (Silberman 1982, 1989). British dominance in Egypt and Cyprus was balanced by a French focus on Syria and Lebanon, while German scholars worked in Anatolia. All of the 'Great Power' archaeological communities shared an interest in Palestine thanks to the biblical connection. The Palestine Exploration Fund followed up the pioneering survey work of Robinson with a monumental survey of Palestine, executed by serving British military officers demonstrating official support of research. Despite its geographical proximity to the Asian mainland, the interest in Cypriot archaeology was led by classical archaeologists. This resulted in the dominance of a Hellenocentric interpretive framework and a model of Cyprus as an intermediary between two cultural hemispheres of Asia and Europe (Frankel 2001).

The unique phenomenon of the tell site dominated the archeological agenda in the Levant (although not in Cyprus). Archaeologists active in this region employed a variety of different excavation methodologies to try and tell the 'tale of the *Tell*'. Sir Flinders Petrie, an English excavator working in Egypt, developed the principles of ceramic sequence dating while excavating Egyptian cemeteries, and came to Palestine to test this theory at Tell el-Hesi in 1890. He took advantage of an erosional cut in the mound there to gain a stratigraphic window to the site and provide an independent test for the idealized ceramic sequence. He established the importance of pottery for dating purposes, and coordinated ceramic typological changes with the stratigraphic changes in the tell. These two principles, ceramic typology and stratigraphy, are fundamental to archaeology. Unfortunately, Petrie diluted the importance of his work by only publishing 'types', i.e. a single specimen of each whole form, neglecting the sherd material completely.

Petrie also provided a fundamental framework for Late Bronze Age chronology in the Levant when he returned to Egypt and began excavations at the site of Tell el-Amarna in Egypt. This palace-city of the Egyptian New Kingdom ruler Amenhotep IV was only occupied for a short time, consequently yielding a closely dated assemblage of imported Mycenaean and Cypriot ceramics. Archaeologists working throughout the Near East would use this dated corpus as chronological markers to date local ceramic horizons.

Archaeologists focused on the excavation of tell sites because they were the remains of ancient cities, the home of the political and social elites of ancient civilizations. The primary aim of such excavations was chronology building to elucidate political history and the recovery of works of art and ancient texts. This reflected the desires of the western European and American intelligentsia and the membership of the funding societies, including societal elites linked to the burgeoning museum community. The relatively low level of expense involved in excavation in the Ottoman world also encouraged international archeology in the region. Indigenous involvement in the projects was, with rare exceptions, confined to providing the labour pool.

Archaeologists trained in the classical tradition brought trenching methods refined at classical sites such as Olympia in Greece to the Levant. The trench method was the most economical way to uncover elite structures at a tell. If a 'monumental building' was identified in a trench, the exposure would be widened to recover the floor plan and associated material of interest. German and Austrian excavators at the biblical sites of Megiddo and Jericho successfully employed the trench methodology. Meticulous architectural recordation was emphasized at the excavation of Tel Halaf in Syria by the German archaeologist Baron Max von Oppenheim. George Reisner, an American archaeologist at Samaria, was not interested in recovering building plans *per se*, and he used a more nuanced stratigraphic approach at Samaria. This reflected his understanding of a tell as a product of natural and human activity, not just building phases. At the time, however, the Palestinian ceramic chronology was not well understood, which prevented his innovative approach from being more successful.

Colonial domination

After the First World War, international archaeology expanded dramatically. The former Ottoman-controlled territories of Palestine, Jordan, Syria, Lebanon, and Cyprus, now under British and French oversight, were wide-open territory for archaeology. The British Mandatory government introduced new antiquities laws in October 1920. The archaeological permit process was much simpler than the old Turkish firman system, and the government retained the power to expropriate land for excavation. The new law used AD 1700 as a cut-off for archeological interest, reflecting the age of the village housing stock and betraying a subtle anti-Ottoman bias. The law made generous provision for sponsoring institutions to export recovered antiquities to Europe and America. This system was transferred to Cyprus and formed the basis of the modified antiquities laws of that British colony. It was at the instigation of a politically important local Cypriot that the antiquities laws were modified to allow the export of finds, to encourage foreign interest in archaeology on the island. The antiquities codes in the French Mandate of Syria adhered more closely to the stricter Ottoman model, but still allowed expeditions to have a division of finds. Sir Max Mallowan found the French regime in Syria more generous than the new tighter restrictions imposed in Iraq in the early 1930s, and began working in Syria (Mallowan 1977: 100). The British Museum excavations of Carchemish were undertaken to 'permit the recovery of numerous reliefs of the Neo-Hittite period' (Matthiae 1980: 19). William F. Albright, the director of the American School in Jerusalem, believed that tighter restrictions were scientifically preferable, but was concerned that tighter control 'greatly reduces the incentive to give money for excavation' (Albright 1921: 10).

Enlightened directors of antiquities, such as John Garstang in Palestine, Gerald Lankester Harding in Jordan, Henri Arnold Seyrig in Syria, and Peter Megaw in Cyprus, worked hard to promote archaeological research yet still protect archaeological resources as development in the region increased. New museums were constructed to encourage the display of artefacts in their home region, since before the First World War, the best finds (such as the

Alexander Sarcophagus from Sidon) from the Levant had been taken to Istanbul. Cyprus, under British administration since 1878, had had a museum since the late 19th century; a new structure built in the Edwardian period remains the home of the Cyprus Museum today. During the Depression, local antiquities authorities undertook large-scale clearance and stabilization of visible monuments such as the Venetian fortifications of Nicosia and Famagusta in Cyprus, and the huge crusader castle of Krac des Chevaliers in Syria. These projects provided much-needed local employment and raised awareness of the monuments.

The international community responded to the more open policies of colonial rule with enthusiasm. During the next two decades, American, Australian, Austrian, Belgian, British, Danish, Dutch, French, German, Italian, and Swedish excavators were active in the field. Active local archaeologists such as Eleazar Sukenik in Palestine and Porphyrios Dikaios in Cyprus, began to take field leadership roles in the colonial antiquities departments and in local academic settings. The political division of the Levant between British and French control accelerated a tendency amongst archaeologists to emphasize cultural divergences in their own studies of the ancient Near East. Albright, perhaps because he was an American, was able to retain a focus on the fundamental unities of the region and coined the term 'Syro-Palestinian archaeology' for the field, although most did not follow him in this (Albright 1938).

Archaeological methods reflected the exuberant self-confidence of the 'Roaring Twenties' (Davis 2003). Large-scale excavations were the order of the day in Syria and Palestine, many with museum sponsorship. The Oriental Institute from the University of Chicago planned a twenty-five-year campaign at the biblical site of Megiddo with the announced aim of total excavation of the 7.3ha mound. This was a huge undertaking, since the pre-excavation cultural deposits measured nearly 23m deep in places. The labour force was made up of local residents and specialist workmen trained by the antiquities departments. In more than forty seasons at the Lebanese site of Byblos, French teams under the direction of the Department of Antiquities attempted to excavate the entire site in 20cm levels, ignoring stratigraphic divisions. This method was ill suited to a tell site, and the publications make this failure clear. The excavations of Antioch, sponsored by a consortium of American museums, led to the discovery of more than 400 mosaics, many of which were exported from Syria to the sponsoring institutions. The excavations at Dura-Europos by Yale University recovered well-preserved frescos from a synagogue. These stayed in Syria and were placed in the new National Museum in Damascus.

Clarence S. Fisher, field director at both Megiddo and Beth Shean, advocated an area approach to excavation (as opposed to the trench method) since he saw a tell as a series of strata composed of architectural remains. Section drawings were used for the first time in the region at the Palestinian Antiquities Department excavations at Ashkelon. Aerial photography for archaeology was pioneered in the region by Antoine Poidebard in eastern Syria in the late 1920s. This was a by-product of the decision by France and Britain to police large areas of their mandated territories by air.

Rich individuals and companies continued to sponsor archaeology in the Levant. John D. Rockefeller provided US$1 million for the excavation by the Oriental Institute at Megiddo. Melvin Grove Kyle, a fundamentalist Presbyterian minister and seminary president, supported work at supposed biblical sites in Palestine. The Carlsberg Foundation funded the Danish work at Hama. George McFadden provided the major funding for the excavation of

Kourion on Cyprus in the 1930s. He was de facto director of the dig in the field, despite having no training in archaeology.

A major research emphasis throughout the region remained the chronological sequence. For the most part, Near Eastern archaeologists followed the traditional 'Three-Age' techno-evolutionary model pioneered in Scandinavia. Albright clarified the Palestinian ceramic chronology through his work at Tell Beit Mirsim. Harald Ingholt and his Danish colleagues at Hama provided the ceramic framework for northern Syria. Of crucial importance for ceramic chronology throughout the Levant was the Swedish Cyprus Expedition from 1927 to 1931. Einar Gjerstad and his Swedish colleagues refined and codified the Cypriot ceramic sequence. Since Cypriot pottery was widely exported in antiquity, it provided crucial cross-dating for sites in Palestine and Syria. Albright pioneered sherd-collecting archaeological surveys, and the newly solidified ceramic chronology made these forays viable. Thousands of new sites were recorded by various survey teams throughout the southern Levant during this period. Survey in Syria did not become widespread until after the Second World War (Matthiae 1980: 32).

Across the Levant, excavations explored sites from prehistory through the medieval period. The long-term excavations of the major Syrian coastal site of Ras Shamra (ancient Ugarit) starting in 1929 discovered texts in a new language that illuminated the Late Bronze Age world of the northern Levant and profoundly influenced biblical studies. The new texts discovered in these decades, such as the Ugaritic corpus, the Lachish Letters, and the Samaria Ostraca, were all directly relevant to the study of the Hebrew Bible, further encouraging biblical scholars' interest in archaeology. The Biblical Archaeology model dominated the interpretation of Bronze and Iron Age materials (Davis 2004). Biblically related textual discoveries culminated with the Dead Sea Scrolls immediately after the Second World War.

The Second World War brought a halt to most fieldwork in the region, although some small-scale work continued. Many archaeologists served in the armed forces of the various combatants, for example Claude Schaeffer and George McFadden. Nelson Glueck scouted for the Office of Strategic Services while continuing his archaeological survey work in southern Palestine (King 1983: 103).

National era

The end of the Second World War ushered in the postcolonial world in the Levant. Lebanon, Syria, Israel, Jordan, and Cyprus all achieved full independence by 1960. National archaeologists took over control of the various antiquities departments, directed significant excavations, and established departments of archaeology in the local universities. Regional museums were opened in urban centres throughout the region, widening the potential support base for archaeology among local residents. The new states imposed stricter controls over their archaeological heritage. For example, the Republic of Cyprus reversed the regulations of the colonial regime and eliminated the previous practice of artefact division between the excavation and the host government.

Understandably, nationalism became closely linked with archaeology in the new postcolonial states in the region after the Second World War. Since archaeology deals with questions of identity, the new states appropriated various cultures/peoples/eras of their past as part of the nation-building process. This encouraged the continued domination of a historical/cultural approach to archaeological explanation. In Israel, the archaeology of Eretz Israel intertwined with the ideology of the return and the search for roots by the thousands of new immigrants to the young state. Jordan and Syria both looked to the first flowering of Islamic culture in the region under the Umayyads. The archaeological record could be a source of national pride. The University of Rome excavations at Tell Mardikh recovered a massive cuneiform library that illuminated the vibrant urban culture of Syria in the third millennium BCE. The Jordanians also highlighted the achievements of the indigenous Arab Nabatean kingdom, particularly the site of Petra. The majority Greek Cypriot community on Cyprus heralded the Hellenic influence on the island, tracing their heritage back to Mycenaean immigrants at the end of the Bronze Age.

Levantine archaeology became truly worldwide, with teams from Japan, South America, and Eastern Europe joining Australian, North American, and Western European scholars in the field. The conflicts between the states in the region accelerated the scholarly tendency to cultural 'tunnel vision' by preventing direct archaeological cooperation across modern political boundaries. This was partially offset by the international scholars who continued to work in the newly independent states. International conferences held out-of-region usually provided the venue for cross-border archeological contacts.

The long hiatus in major research archaeology caused by the war allowed a new generation of scholars to reach positions of influence in Levantine archaeology. Yigael Yadin, after serving as chief of staff to the Israeli armed forces, joined the Hebrew University in 1954 and provided academic field training for the new generation of Israeli archaeologists through his large-scale, architecturally oriented excavations at Hazor (Mazar 1997: 48). These methods sought wide horizontal exposures, illuminating ancient city plans and major architectural units. The Hazor method became the signature Israeli excavation style. Yadin later excavated Masada, a site with deep emotional and historical ties for many Israelis. This excavation in the 1960s employed hundreds of volunteers from around the world, setting a pattern of student/volunteer archaeological labour that continues today. In Syria, the establishment of an archaeology programme by the University of Damascus encouraged more local students to become archaeologists than had been possible previously when they went to Europe for academic training.

A major methodological revolution occurred with Dame Kathleen Kenyon's excavation of Jericho in the area of Palestine under Jordanian control in the 1950s. Kenyon had trained at Verulamium, a Roman site in Britain directed by Sir Mortimer Wheeler. He used a stratigraphically oriented method, employing vertical sections. Kenyon applied the methods to the tell site of Jericho, excavating a series of relatively small square units separated by vertical sections between them (baulks) which provided a record of the vertical stratigraphy. This is driven by a stratigraphic understanding of a tell. The resulting methodology became known as 'Wheeler–Kenyon' in the Near Eastern archaeological literature. Kenyon's methodology in a variety of guises became the dominant field paradigm within the region, including Syria and Cyprus.

Recurring military conflict in the region profoundly affected archaeology. The new political realities after the Arab–Israeli War of 1967 created the need for new research centres in Amman to assist archaeologists active in Jordan. The Lebanese Civil War (1975–91) prevented most archaeological activity in that country; paradoxically, after the country stabilized, the destruction in Beirut provided the opportunity to study the previously inaccessible urban centre. The coup d'état against Cypriot President Makarios in July 1974 led to the invasion and occupation of northern Cyprus by the Turkish army. No internationally condoned archaeological excavations have been undertaken in the areas outside the direct control of the Republic of Cyprus. Turkish Republic archaeologists and Turkish Cypriot scholars have undertaken some excavation and survey work in the north of Cyprus, but these are not published internationally and have been condemned by the United Nations Educational, Scientific, and Cultural Organization (UNESCO) and the international community. This isolation is creating a 'significant bias in primary data' for Cypriot archaeology (Frankel 2001).

Since the Second World War, technological advances have accelerated the pace of theoretical and methodological change. The advent of radiocarbon dating in the 1950s revolutionized prehistoric archaeology. The multidisciplinary approach to archaeology, introduced into the Levant by Robert Braidwood and his fellow prehistorians, had become the norm for later period sites by the 1970s. Nautical archaeology has expanded rapidly in the region from the pioneering work in the 1960s of Michael and Susan Katzev on the Kyrenia ship off the coast of Cyprus, the first ancient hull raised in the Mediterranean. The advent of computers in the field created a data revolution. New questions could be asked, and Levantine archaeology is now much more in line with developments in the wider discipline of archaeology as processual and post-processual approaches have relegated traditional historical/biblical questions to a less dominant position (Dever 1981). This change has been reinforced by the impact of anthropologically oriented funding agencies in Europe and America. The use of new technologies in the field and the laboratory such as magnetometry, global positioning systems, digital photography, geographic information systems, and chemical provenience studies make significant contributions in the region.

Salvage archaeology became a dominant focus of the national antiquities departments after the 1967 war, when the resulting population displacement accelerated the already expanding pace of regional development (Akkermans and Schwartz 2003: 11). National infrastructure projects impacted vast tracts of landscape including countless archaeological sites. Examples include major water projects on the Euphrates and Khabur Rivers in Syria (cf. the Tabqa Dam project: Kelly-Buccellati 1997: 44) and the East Ghor Canal in Jordan. Archaeologists conducted extensive emergency site surveys and many rescue excavations. These regional studies encouraged a growing appreciation for the value of archaeological surveys, and provided raw data for new research questions including settlement pattern analyses, demographic studies, and landscape archaeology. The government of Jordan, in cooperation with the American Center of Oriental Research in Amman, developed an active and effective programem of Cultural Resource Management (CRM) in Jordan. A CRM conference held in 1992 acted as a catalyst to focus efforts on integrating cultural resources into the needs of development.

Public archaeology plays a key role in archaeological decision-making. All of the regional states have recognized the valuable economic contribution archaeology can make to the vital international tourist trade. Throughout the region, major sites have been designated as archaeological parks. Specialized tourist itineraries emphasizing religious and historical events have been created. Of necessity, the packaging of the past affects the way excavations were carried out and results presented. On occasion, excavation at a site or monument is halted to allow for the preservation and presentation of a particular historical moment in the history of the occupation of a site, despite unanswered questions. Individual projects are forced to consider the final status of the site and its conservation/public presentation as part of their research design.

In the 21st century, Levantine archaeology remains a vibrant, healthy discipline, a 'big tent' home to a wide variety of archaeological traditions. Its greatest strength lies in its wealth of accumulated primary data providing the basis for vibrant, foundational research into the story of the past.

Suggested Reading

Davis, T. W. (2004). *Shifting Sands: The Rise and Fall of Biblical Archaeology*. Oxford: Oxford University Press.

Kletter, R. (2006). *Just Past? The Making of Israeli Archaeology*. London: Equinox.

Silberman, N. A. (1989). *Between Past and Present: Archaeology, Ideology, and Nationalism in the Modern Middle East*. New York: Holt.

References

Akkermans, P. M. M. G., and G. M. Schwartz (2003). *The Archaeology of Syria: From Complex Hunter-Gatherers to Early Urban Societies (c. 16,000–300 BC)*. Cambridge: Cambridge University Press.

Albright, W. F. (1921). A tour on foot through Samaria and Galilee. *Bulletin of the American Schools of Oriental Research* 4: 7–13.

——(1938). The present state of Syro-Palestinian archaeology. In E. Grant (ed.), *The Haverford Symposium on Archaeology and the Bible*. New Haven, Conn.: American Schools of Oriental Research, 1–46.

Davis, T. W. (2003). Levantine archaeology. In S. Richard (ed.), *Near Eastern Archaeology: A Reader*. Winona Lake, Ind.: Eisenbrauns, 54–9.

——(2004). *Shifting Sands: The Rise and Fall of Biblical Archaeology*. Oxford: Oxford University Press.

Dever, W. G. (1981). The impact of the new archaeology on Syro-Palestinian archaeology. *Bulletin of the American Schools of Oriental Research* 242: 15–29.

Frankel, D. (2001). Cyprus. In T. Murray (ed.), *Encyclopedia of Archaeology: History and Discoveries*, vol. 1. Santa Barbara, Calif.: ABC-CLIO, 388–94.

Kelly-Buccellati, M. (1997). History of the field: archaeology in Syria. In E. M. Meyers (ed.), *The Oxford Encyclopedia of Archaeology in the Near East*, vol. 3. New York: Oxford University Press, 42–7.

King, P. J. (1983). *American Archaeology in the Mideast: A History of the American Schools of Oriental Research*. Philadelphia: American Schools of Oriental Research.

Mallowan, M. E. L. (1977). *Mallowan's Memoirs*. New York: Dodd, Mead.

Matthiae, P. (1980). *Ebla: An Empire Rediscovered*, trans. C. Holme. London: Hodder & Stoughton.

Mazar, A. (1997). History of the field: archaeology in Israel. In E. M. Meyers (ed.), *The Oxford Encyclopedia of Archaeology in the Near East*, vol. 3. New York: Oxford University Press, 47–51.

Seger, J. D. (ed.) (2001). *An ASOR Mosaic: A Centennial History of the American Schools of Oriental Research, 1900–2000.* Boston, Mass.: American Schools of Oriental Research.

Silberman, N. A. (1982). *Digging for God and Country: Exploration, Archeology and the Secret Struggle for the Holy Land, 1799–1917.* New York: Knopf.

—— (1989). *Between Past and Present: Archaeology, Ideology, and Nationalism in the Modern Middle East.* New York: Holt.

CHAPTER 4

··

LEVANTINE CHRONOLOGY

··

ILAN SHARON

In 1922 the directors of the schools of archaeology in Jerusalem met to decide on a common naming convention for archaeological periods in Palestine (Garstang et al. 1922). Up to that time, every researcher and excavation had used their own designations, including terms like 'Amorite' and 'Phoenician' periods (Petrie 1891: 14–17) or 'Pre-Semitic', and 'First Semitic' to 'Fourth Semitic' (Macalister 1912: xxi). The decision reached in this meeting was to use the European tripartite division for the naming of archaeological periods for the divisions dealt with by this handbook. The 'Stone Age', 'Bronze Age', and 'Iron Age' were each subdivided into 'Early', 'Middle', and 'Late' (with the exception of the Iron Age, which only had 'Early' and 'Late'—the latter now known as 'Persian'). Further subdivisions would be by Roman numerals and capital letters, e.g. MB IIA for the first subdivision within Middle Bronze Age II. Although ostensibly based on the level of technological knowhow, these names were 'translated' instantly to historical dates—e.g. the Late Bronze Age was taken as equivalent to the 18th and 19th Dynasties in Egypt, while the Iron I denoted the period from the entry of the Israelites into Canaan to the schism in the Israelite monarchy. This reflected the firm belief at the time that such events can be identified in the archaeological record easily enough to constitute viable benchmarks in archaeological time. Political happenstances such as dynastic changes were counted on both to provide the precise hinges between chronological periods and to link them to an absolute time-scale. Moreover, the three time-scales—archaeological, historical, and absolute—were seen as essentially fused, with the historical time-scale taking priority.[1]

William F. Albright was the first to use the new scheme in a systematic manner in his excavations at Tell Beit Mirsim (Albright 1932: xxi), a very influential and innovative project in its time, where there was an almost one-to-one correspondence between the proposed stratigraphic scheme and the newly devised chronological scheme. The influence of 'biblical

---

[1] E.g. when in 1937 a cartouche of Ramesses III was found with typically Late Bronze Age artefacts in Megiddo, the characteristic reaction was that Stratum VIIA (or at least its end) should be relegated to the Iron Age. Instead of extending the Late Bronze Age to include at least the beginning of the 20th Dynasty. Should, however, a historical event be re-dated (e.g. the end of the 19th Dynasty shifted from 1205 to 1186 BCE), then the date of the beginning of the Iron Age should change, and not the definition of what constitutes 'Iron Age'.

archaeology' and of Albright personally was such that the 'Jerusalem scheme' was quickly adopted for the archaeology of the entire Levant (with some significant exceptions, to be discussed below). For the most part, it still defines the terminology used today.

While the terms we use are often still the ones defined by Albright and his contemporaries, there has been over the years—and especially over the last score—an insidious shift in the meaning accorded to the named chronological entities. This has mainly been the result of continuing erosion of the confidence in historical dating. As the 20th century went by it became more obvious that the Levant was poor in primary epigraphic sources, including all manner of name-bearing artefacts, compared to its neighbours in the west, east, and north. This was coupled with growing theoretical discontent with the straightforward correlation of historical events and material culture change, and with growing doubts about the very historicity of some of the events being used as chronological criteria.

Thus the major periods are today broadly defined by macro-changes in social organization (Table 4.1); and artefact (usually ceramic) seriation provides the more precise articulation—for pinpointing both transitions between 'periods' and subdivisions within 'periods'. Absolute dates for the periods are increasingly supplied by radiometry, though dated epigraphic finds are used, of course, when found in context. Moreover, the different time-scales are usually conceived of as de-fused, with the seriational time-scale being primary.[2]

Table 4.1 The general framework for the chronology of the Levant. Note that not all the structural changes cited occur everywhere. Exceptions and reservations are listed in the text below

Neolithic	First farming villages
Chalcolithic	'Secondary products revolution' (?)
Early Bronze Age I (EB I)	'Urban revolution'—first cities
Early Bronze Age II–III (EB II–III)	Urban societies
Intermediate Bronze Age (IB)	(Partial) relapse to village-based societies
Middle Bronze Age (MB)	Resurgence of urban societies (city-states)
Late Bronze Age	City-states under vassalage to 'great kings'
Iron Age I	Partial collapse
Iron Age II	Urban societies (some city-states, some nation-states) to be incorporated within an imperial framework
Iron Age III/Persian	The entire Levant is a satrapy of the Persian Empire

[2] E.g. the current controversy relating to Iron Age I–IIA chronology (see below) involves debates about all of the following: (a) the historicity and dating of David and Solomon; (b) the beginning of [re-]urbanization of the highlands in Cis- and Transjordan; (c) the ceramic definition of assemblages as 'Iron Age I' or 'Iron Age IIA'; and (d) radiocarbon (or other absolute) dates of strata defined as 'Iron Age I' or 'Iron Age IIA'. There seems to be a consensus, though, that the criterion for defining *what is* 'Iron Age I' vs 'Iron Age IIA' should be Option C; i.e. should evidence come to light that there is urbanism and public architecture in highland sites with 'Iron Age I' assemblages, or should the name of Solomon appear in an 'Iron Age I' context, and whatever radiocarbon dates are assigned to these contexts, the definition of said contexts as either 'Iron Age I' or 'Iron Age IIA' (by ceramic seriation) would not change. It should perhaps be stressed that such 'consensus' is an agreement about a framework and not about contents, i.e. whether there is also an agreement on what ceramic attributes exactly denote 'Iron Age I' or 'Iron Age II' is a separate issue.

It should also be noted that this change in the conception of what an 'archaeological period' is has been implicit and gradual, and is not accepted unanimously or for all periods. For the beginning of the sequence herein discussed, the primacy (indeed the exclusivity) of material culture change as a chronological criterion has always been the case, for it had no history and its absolute dates were unknown (prior to the extension of the radiocarbon calibration curve). At the end of this sequence, the absolute, historical, and archaeological time-scales are still regarded as fused with historical events providing the articulation points within and between periods.

One exception to the consistent use of acronyms to name archaeological periods in this handbook concerns this late edge of the time-scale. This, of course, is still the case for periods later than those covered in this handbook (Hellenistic, Roman, etc.), as is indeed reflected in the names given to these periods. Two terms are used interchangeably or together to refer to the Persian period. In the northern Levant, it has been customary to refer to the archaeological period of the Babylonian and Achaemenid Empires by the name 'Iron Age III'. In the southern Levant, the terms 'Babylonian' and 'Persian' tend to be used for these periods.[3] In this chapter, the term 'Iron III/Persian period' is often employed to refer to this period of time (see Lehmann, Ch. 55 below). At any rate, when we use the term 'Period X' in this work, we imply a seriational unit, defined in terms of changes in material culture attributes. The absolute dates of this time-span and which historical events happened within it are regarded as secondary.

I noted above that the general scheme proposed for Palestine in the mid-1920s was not universally accepted. Some regions and sites in Syria are one exception. Whereas the Levant is almost completely circumscribed by sea, mountains, or deserts, it has no clear geographical and/or cultural border on its northeastern side. Thus investigators in these regions sometimes adopt Mesopotamian phasing schemes for their sites. The north and northeastern reaches of the Levant are also, in some periods, the notable exception to the dearth of datable epigraphic finds, and so direct historical dating of strata is sometimes feasible there.

The other exception is Cyprus. At about the same time of the aforementioned meeting in Jerusalem, the major archaeological enterprise—indeed, the first scientific excavation project to tackle the entire prehistory of the island—was the Swedish Cyprus Expedition.[4] The terminology adopted by them determines the chronological scheme in Cyprus to this day.[5] The Swedish Cyprus Expedition adopted the outlines of the Greek chronological scheme (as then current), substituting 'Cypriot' for 'Helladic'.[6] For the Iron Age, they added 'Cypro-' to the standard Greek nomenclature.[7] The subdivisions which were soon attached to the major periods do not, however, necessarily match the subdivisions in Greece.

Cyprus is a case unto itself in at least three other respects. For long periods, the island had little if any contacts with the mainland. Developments therefore tended to follow their own course, and correlations of Cypriot chronology with the rest of the Levant are in such periods difficult or impossible to make (except on absolute dates). Also, urbanization came late to Cyprus in the late Middle Cypriot/early Late Cypriot. Thus the broad changes in

[3] Note that the original scheme proposed by Albright also named this period 'Late Iron Age'.
[4] Though the Swedish Cyprus Expedition formally began its fieldwork in 1927, Einar Gjerstad had by that time already published his chronological model (Gjerstad 1926).
[5] The main addition to the Swedish Cyprus Expedition chronology for Cyprus is its extension to earlier cultures, not known to Gjerstad et al. (see below).
[6] As in 'Early Cypriot', 'Middle Cypriot', etc. instead of 'Early Bronze Age' or 'Middle Bronze Age'.
[7] As in 'Cypro-Geometric', 'Cypro-Archaic', etc.

social organization, which provide the *longue durée* structure to the chronology of the rest of the Levant, cannot do so in the case of early Cyprus. To this is tied yet a third factor: extreme conservativeness in ceramic traditions, evident both in the perseverance of certain wares and in persistent regionalism of wares and forms over long periods of time. All of the above make it extremely difficult, for instance, to define the transition from Early Cypriot to Middle Cypriot. By the Late Cypriot period, however, the island is fully integrated in the eastern Mediterranean economy, and chronological correlations, both within it and between it and the rest of the Levant, are numerous.

Unrelated to the conceptual change of what an 'archaeological period' is, which was gradual and rarely explicitly discussed, various changes in nomenclature were proposed and argued about over the years. These fall into several types.

First, there have been proposals to change the general naming framework without changing the definitions of the named units themselves or even their numbering. Several proposals called for changing the technological framework to one based on ethnonyms. The first edition of the *Encyclopedia of Archaeological Excavations in the Holy Land* (Avi-Yonah and Stern 1975) proposed to change 'Bronze' to 'Canaanite' and 'Iron' to 'Israelite'. Thus EB I would have become Early Canaanite I; and Iron II, Israelite II. Whether the term 'Canaanite' is in any way appropriate to the population of the EB I is of course moot. A similar scheme, avoiding the obvious pitfalls of ethnonyms by using regional designations instead, has been proposed by the ARCANE research programme for the third millennium (http://www. arcane.uni-tuebingen.de/index.html). Instead of Early Bronze, they propose the acronyms ENL (for the northern Levant), ESL (for the Southern Levant), and ECY (for Cyprus). Besides mere political correctness, such a regional scheme does provide extra flexibility inasmuch as it allows for different subdivisions within each region. At the other end of the spectrum were proposals to adopt an explicitly social-evolutionary chronological scheme. The first and perhaps most enduring was Kenyon's renaming of the EB I period as 'Proto-Urban'. She did not attempt, however, to extend this logic to the entire sequence. Such comprehensive suggestions were put forth by Finkelstein (1996) for the southern Levant and by Knapp (2008) for Cyprus. None of these attempts to 'reform' the entrenched names has enjoyed much support, and they are mentioned here mainly because students might occasionally encounter these alternative naming conventions.

A different type of naming debate concerns transitional periods which might, by their nature, be regarded as the end of the preceding epoch or the beginning of the succeeding one or be given an independent name which would accentuate the difference from both. The most salient of these is the one concerning the EB IV/Intermediate Bronze Age/MB I transition (see below). We have already mentioned the EB I/Proto-Urban. However, we shall see similar dithering at almost any transition, from Neolithic to Chalcolithic, Bronze to Iron Age, and even Iron Age to the Persian period.

An added difficulty in the case where an initial period 'XX I' is renamed is what to do with the vacated name. This dilemma is again most apparent in the case of MB I. If Albright's MB I is renamed EB IV or Intermediate Bronze, what do we do with the designation MB I? One option would be to rename MB II to MB I (or just Middle Bronze, as the original division was between MB I and MB II); this would create a second 'ripple effect' in that MB IIA, B, and C would now have to be renamed MB I, II, and III. In any case, a student reading the appellation 'MB I' would have to ask him/herself what chronological scheme the writer was using, for it would refer to one of two different entities. One way around this ambiguity would be *not* to rename the following period(s) and jump straight from EB IV to MB II. This, of course, also carries a seed of confusion.

Thus far we have dealt with cases where the same entities are differently named. In other cases, however, new periodization schemes have subdivided periods differently from hitherto. The result is that the named entities themselves are different. A case in point is the sub-periodization of the Iron Age. Albright's scheme, already mentioned, divided the 'Early Iron Age' of Israel into Early Iron I (up to the division of the Israelite monarchy) and Early Iron II (to the Babylonian exile); the division was a purely biblical one, so no material culture reference points were suggested. Based on the typo-stratigraphic sequence at Hazor, Aharoni and Amiran (1958) proposed a different subdivision—Iron Age I, II, and III.[8] Their Iron Age II comprised the last part of Albright's Early Iron I and the beginning of his Early Iron II.[9] Avi-Yonah and Stern (1975) took up this periodization, but renamed the entities so that Aharoni and Amiran's Iron Age II became Iron Age IIA and the Iron Age III became Iron Age IIB.[10] Aharoni and Aharoni later (1976) subdivided the Iron Age III, thus arriving at the convention used in this book—Iron I, IIA, IIB, and IIC.[11] For the northern Levant, Mazzoni (Ch. 45 below) uses a different tri-partite division wherein 'Iron Age III' denotes the period after the Assyrian conquest, i.e. parallel to the Iron IIC of the southern Levant. Similarly, the ceramically defined subdivision of the Iron Age I proposed by Gilboa and Sharon (2003) is incommensurate with the division used by Wright (1961), Avi-Yonah and Stern (1975), and Mazar (1990). The transition from Ir1a to Ir1b, delineated by ceramic seriation, probably falls somewhere in the middle of Wright's historically defined Iron Age IB.[12]

NEOLITHIC AND CHALCOLITHIC

Prehistorians in the Levant follow European traditions in defining cultures,[13] such as 'Khiamian', 'Sultanian', or 'Harifian'. Prior to the 'radiocarbon revolution' it has not always been possible, however, to isolate the spatial features from temporal ones, and hence to reliably judge which of these 'cultures' occupy coterminous spatial niches in the same chronological horizons—even today there is often no total agreement on that.

[8] Note that they dropped the 'Early' from the Iron Age altogether. By this time 'Persian period' was the common appellation for Albright's 'Late Iron Age' in the southern Levant.

[9] This scheme was also revolutionary in that it divorced archaeological periodization from historical dating. Aharoni and Amiran argued for a shift in ceramic traditions in the mid-9th century (the end of their Iron Age II), but had difficulty correlating this to any known historical event.

[10] Avi-Yonah and Stern (1975) also retreated onto 'safe' historical ground and ended the Iron Age IIA (Aharoni and Amiran's 'Iron Age II') with the schism of the Israelite monarchy. They did not, however, redefine the archaeological attributes of this division.

[11] The term 'Iron Age III' is particularly ambiguous. Aharoni, Amiran, and south Levantine archaeologists following their terminology use this term to denote both the period preceding the Assyrian destructions and the period succeeding it, up to the rise of the Achaemenid Empire (both Iron IIB and IIC as herein defined). In Syria it is sometimes limited to the period *after* the Assyrian destructions (as is the case in Mazzoni, Ch. 45 below), but at other times it denotes the Persian period (Elayi, Ch. 8).

[12] Note the use of different signs (Arab numerals and lower-case letters) to denote that the signified unit is different.

[13] In the limited sense of named spatio-temporally constrained complexes of self-similar assemblages.

The first enduring subdivision of the Neolithic was made by Kenyon, based on her excavations at Jericho. She divided the era into a 'pre-pottery' and a 'pottery' phase—each of which was further subdivided to make up Pre-Pottery Neolithic A, Pre-Pottery Neolithic B, Pottery Neolithic A, and Pottery Neolithic B. This scheme continued to be used in most subsequent works, the present one included. A slight change in naming convention is introduced in Goring-Morris and Belfer-Cohen (Ch. 11 below), whereby Late Neolithic (LN1 and LN2) is substituted for Pottery Neolithic A and B—the reasons being (a) that ceramics are (rarely) found already in PPNB and (b) that many Late Neolithic sites in the desert areas lack them altogether.

It soon became apparent, however, that not all *facies* of the Levantine Neolithic were present at Jericho. For one thing, in Jericho—and perhaps in the southern Levant as a whole—the formative stage of the Neolithic may be missing. Thus the Khiamian culture is regarded by some as preceding the PPNA. There is probably a gap between the Jericho PPNA and PPNB, within which falls a transitional culture (the so-called early PPNB), evident mainly in the northern Levant. A PPNC has been argued for 'Ain Ghazal, but it is not clear if it is a general chronological horizon or a localized culture of the Jordanian highlands, equivalent to late or terminal PPNB elsewhere.

Similar problems exist with the definition of Pottery Neolithic. The scheme put forward by Garfinkel (1999), where the Jericho PNA equals Yarmukian and PNB equals Wadi Rabah, is regarded by many as an oversimplification. The Yarmukian culture of Sha'ar Hagolan and Munhata doubtlessly reflects a very early phase of the Pottery Neolithic, while the Wadi Rabah culture presents a transition to the Chalcolithic. Jericho Stratum IX (=Kenyon's PNA) and Stratum VIII (PNB), as well as other cultures such as Lodian, Qatifian, and Besorian, fall in between, and are possibly partly contemporary with either or both.

A second debate (referred to above) is over the transition between the Neolithic and Chalcolithic. Maximizing views (e.g. Garfinkel 1999) define everything from Wadi Rabah onwards as Chalcolithic. A minimizing approach, such as the one followed here, includes only the classic sequence as found in Ghassul and chronologically comparable sites in the Chalcolithic. Note that in this case the transitional stage in debate may be longer than the core period itself. This reflects long-standing uncertainty as to what it is that should define a culture as Chalcolithic rather than Neolithic. The merit of a minimizing approach is that all Chalcolithic *facies* as herein defined share a cluster of common attributes which clearly divide them from the Neolithic, including new technologies (consistent appearance of copper and ivory working) and behavioural/mental attitudes (secondary burial in ossuaries). Absolute dates for the Neolithic sequence are perforce derived from radiocarbon.[14]

There is a possible gap in the early fifth millennium between the Wadi Rabah culture and the onset of classic Chalcolithic. Most of the radiocarbon dates that can be reliably assigned to the Wadi Rabah phase are in the late sixth millennium, though some do stretch into the early fifth. The problem is exacerbated by a sharp debate as to the relative sequence of supposedly transitional assemblages and the degree of 'Wadi Rabah-ness' which should be accorded to the earliest phases at Ghassul. Three solutions (or a combination thereof) have

---

[14] See http://www.exoriente.org/associated_projects/ppnd.php for an online database covering the late Epipaleolithic to PPNB, and Banning (2007) for a recent compilation of dates for the Late Neolithic, with Bayesian estimates for the beginning and end of (sub)phases. A general on-line database for Neolithic–Chalcolithic dates can be found at: http://context-database.uni-koeln.de/

been offered: (a) the Wadi Rabah culture lasts all the way to the middle of the fifth millennium; (b) the Ghassulian stretches all the way back to the early fifth, if not even into the sixth millennium (e.g. Blackham 2002; Banning 2002); or (c) some other culture (not Wadi Rabah and not Ghassulian) fills this gap, e.g. Garfinkel's (1999) Middle Chalcolithic, which at present is still mostly hypothetical. The apparent chronological difference in the present book for the end of the Neolithic in Syria (*c.*5300 BCE) versus the southern Levant (*c.*4500 BCE) stems from the fact that one chapter's authors (Goring-Morris and Belfer-Cohen, Ch. 11 below) chose Option A, while other chapters' authors (Akkermans and Betts, Chs 10 and 12 below) chose Option B or C.

Barring the occasional hunting party exploiting the island fauna, permanent human settlement on Cyprus probably occurred at some stage of the Levantine PPNA.[15] Throughout the eighth millennium, these populations seem to have stayed in touch with the northern Levant, and the development of Cypriot PPNB echoes that of the mainland. By *c.*7000 BCE, however, the Cypriot Neolithic was developing along a different course. One difference is the comparatively late introduction of pottery technology. Thus a separate era, termed 'Aceramic Neolithic' (or Khirokitia Culture), is defined for Cyprus. It lasts into the second half of the sixth millennium—i.e. by and large covering the Pottery Neolithic of the mainland. Similarly, the Cypriot Ceramic Neolithic (not to be confused with the Pottery Neolithic on the mainland) falls into the same time-slot as mainland Chalcolithic, as defined above. For the Cypriot Chalcolithic, see below.

EARLY BRONZE AGE

Both the chronology and very definition of the EB I[16] have changed rather drastically over recent decades. When Kenyon dubbed this period 'Proto-Urban' she really meant 'Pre-Urban'. As seen at the time, EB I was a period which had clear material culture affinities with the ensuing EB II–III, but the most distinctive attribute of the Early Bronze Age—urban lifestyle—has yet to appear. Excavation of EB I habitation sites has shown that EB IB (at least) is fully urban. On the other hand, it is now clear that what was initially seen as a rather short transitional period is a lengthy era in its own right.

Radiocarbon dates from both terminal Chalcolithic strata and early EB I confirm that the latter begins early in the fourth millennium.[17] This transition is marked more by changing

---

[15]   When Cypriot PPN was first discovered, it was considered to be coeval with an advanced phase of north Levantine PPNB. Carbon-14 dates in the ninth millennium cal. BCE from several PPN sites in Cyprus now move the colonization of the island to the PPNA (Manning et al. 2010).

[16]   Some publications may still refer to de Vaux's (1966) chronological scheme, in which the beginning of the conventional EB I is called Late Chalcolithic. Consequently, de Vaux's EB IB is the beginning of conventional EB II.

[17]   Just how early is the subject of some debate. A cluster of ^{14}C dates from the site of Afridar, which indicate a date at the very beginning of the fourth millennium, is belied by several later dates from Chalcolithic sites (Braun 2001). New dates from Teleilat Ghassul, however, show that occupation of the type site for the Ghassulian culture ended by *c.* 3900 BCE, which is in line with the earliest EB I dates (Bourke et al. 2004; Braun 2001).

ceramic styles (and perhaps some other features, such as burial customs) than by apparent social organization. The urban revolution which takes place during this period is not, however, accompanied by distinctive changes in the pottery repertoire or by other small finds. The end of the period can be correlated with the end of Dynasty 0 in Egypt by a number of serekhs of Narmer. Egyptologists variously date the beginning of Dynasty I to 3150–2950 BCE,[18] whereas the most recent radiocarbon-modelled Egyptian chronology would place it at the c.3025–2950 BCE range (Bronk-Ramsey et al. 2010).[19] Extant radiocarbon data from the Levant itself would seem to date the end of EB I somewhere in the 3250–3000 BCE range.[20]

As urbanization is no longer taken to be the benchmark for the onset of the EB II, it is again primarily ceramic factors that are used to differentiate between the two. Traditionally, it is the appearance of Abydos ware, found in 1st Dynasty tombs in Egypt and hence considered diagnostic or the historical correlation of 'Early Bronze Age' with the Old Kingdom, which defines the EB II. This distinction is not helped by the fact that different researchers refer by the same name to different attributes of different Levantine wares found in Old Kingdom Egypt, e.g. forms like the stump-based juglet, or decoration like dots painted in triangular fields. There are, however, additional ceramic phenomena which serve to mark the EB I/EB II transition—some prevalent pottery wares end, including grey burnished ware, while new ones appear, notably highly fired metallic ware with pattern combing.

The usual ceramic marker for the EB III is the appearance of the burnished red-and-black Khirbet Kerak ware. The use of this *fossile directeur* is limited by the fact that the distribution of this ware is confined to the inland valleys (from the 'Amuq to Jezreel). Moreover, similar wares are native to northeastern Anatolia (and further north and east) throughout the Early Bronze Age, and whether their southwards diffusion is sudden or gradual is moot. While secondary criteria for differentiating between early and late in the Early Bronze

---

[18] These estimates are mainly based on an Illahun Papyrus (dated to the Middle Kingdom on paleographical grounds) predicting a heliacal rising of Sothis on the sixteenth day of the eighth month in the seventh year of an unnamed pharaoh. Borchardt presumed this to be Sesortis III and Meyer calculated the date of this event to 1876–1872 BCE. To this is added the 950-year length of the Old Kingdom (according to the Turin Papyrus), 120 years from the beginning of the Middle Kingdom to the seventh year of Sesortis III, and the unknown length of the First Intermediate (see Shaw 2000 for a recent overview of Egyptian historical chronology).

[19] The Oxford Project modelled the entire 3rd–21st Dynasties sequence using ^{14}C dates on 188 regnal-year-dated organic objects (e.g. papyri) or organic objects from dated closed contexts (such as tombs), using the king-lists and regnal length data to estimate the minimal number of years between individual radiocarbon determinations wherever possible, but without resorting to either astronomical dating or 'dead reckoning' from a fixed datum. The earliest king dated in this manner is Djoser (first or second king of the 3rd Dynasty with a 95 per cent confidence range of 2691–2625 BCE). To this we must add c.325 regnal years between Djoser and Hor-Aha (Shaw 2000).

[20] The fullest current compilation and modeling of dates was done in the framework of the ARCANE project (Regev, de Miroschedji, and Boaretto 2012; Regev, de Miroschedji, Greenberg et al. 2012). However, a site-by-site analysis and sequencing of the radiocarbon dates show considerable deviations in the transition dates between phases labelled by their excavators EB I and EB II in different sites. This hints that the criteria conventionally used to differentiate between EB I and EB II are ill defined, or that different researchers use different definitions of these terms. The ARCANE group for the South Levant solves this apparent contradiction by positing a transitional period ('Early South Levant 3' in the ARCANE terminology) which encompasses both the end of the traditional EB IB and the beginning of EB II. A 3250/3150 BCE transition is also suggested by the data in Braun (2001), although he himself seems to prefer the conventional date, which is hardly supported by the data he cites, even after the

sequence do exist—both in ceramics and in other artefact groups, most notably glyptics—none is supraregional. Moreover, establishing that these regional changes occur more than approximately contemporaneously is difficult. Tying any of these to the traditional historical datum—the beginning of the 3rd Dynasty in Egypt (2700 BCE by the 'high' Egyptian chronology, 2600 BCE by the 'low', and 2690–2625 BCE (95%) by the ^{14}C-modelled Oxford chronology)—is well-nigh impossible. The existing radiocarbon record for the EB II/III in the Levant itself is still somewhat spotty, [21] but indicates a higher transition, perhaps c.2800 BCE or even earlier.

A note about Cyprus

Even when it was defined in pre-radiocarbon times, it was realized that the Cypriot Chalcolithic must have started later and lasted longer than its mainland counterparts. The justification for calling this particular temporal range Chalcolithic (apart from the very limited use of copper) is that it is clearly separated (by both a chronological and cultural gap) from the preceding Late Neolithic phase, and that the succeeding phase (the Philia culture) shows—apart from increased use of copper—cultural continuity with still later periods (Early Cypriot–Middle Cypriot) as well as some contact with the Anatolian mainland. The 'radiocarbon revolution' has had the effect of moving the Levantine Chalcolithic and Early Bronze back in time, and the Cypriot Chalcolithic forward. Thus the absolute dates of the Chalcolithic in Cyprus, as now defined (3900–2400 BCE)[22] nearly coincide with those of the mainland EB I–III.

INTERMEDIATE BRONZE AGE

Urban Early Bronze civilization collapsed in the southern Levant in the second half of the third millennium. There was widespread abandonment of large tell sites and a resurgence of village-based (and possibly semi-nomadic) lifestyle. Any explanation of this disintegration is inexorably tied to dating it. Early attempts to date this period historically were predicated on the assumption that this collapse can be equated with the First Intermediate in Egypt and/or the collapse of Ur III in Mesopotamia. The evidence for either of these is highly circumstantial and moreover puts the cart before the horse. One would like to use chronology as a yardstick to assess demographic processes, rather than vice versa.

Taking into account only radiocarbon dates from southern Levantine sites, the ARCANE team posits an EB III/Intermediate Bronze transition at 2500/2450 BCE for the Levant. The destruction of Palace G (Stratum IIB1) in Tell Mardikh gives us a chronological peg somewhere in the middle of the period, as both the palace itself and the succeeding phase

removal of archaeologically problematic dates and obvious outliers.

[21] The ARCANE dating for the beginning of the EB III stands, as these words are being written, at c.2900/2850 BCE (Regev, de Miroschedji, and Boaretto 2012; Regev, de Miroschedji, Greenberg, et al. forthcoming). This makes for an almost impossibly short EB II, unless the EB I is pushed back radically (see above). Anderson (2006) also provides a list of published dates, but hardly any argumentation.

[22] Peltenburg (1998: 4–21) still has the best compilation of dates.

display the typical caliciform pottery, which can be (loosely) correlated with the typical Intermediate Bronze pottery in the southern Levant. Inasmuch as this destruction can be attributed to either Sargon or Naram-Sin,[23] then it can be correlated with the rise of Akkad in Mesopotamia. Archi and Biga (2003) suggest an even earlier date for the demise of Palace G, based on synchronisms between the kings of Ebla and of Mari, which was destroyed by Sargon some years after the fall of Ebla, if these synchronisms hold. Recently, Lebeau (2012) combined the internal historical synchronisms and radiocarbon dates from Ebla, Mari, Tell Beydar, and Tell Brak to arrive at a date *c.*2340 BCE for the destruction of Ebla—independent of the conventional historical dating of Sargon. Note that accepting any of these dates pulls the chair from under the hypotheses that the collapse of Ur III is in any way connected to the collapse of urban society at the end of EB III in the Levant. In fact, by the zenith of the empire of Akkad in Mesopotamia, de-urbanization must have been well under way in the southern Levant.

It has to be borne in mind, moreover, that even in the Levant the collapse is far from total, but evident mainly in the south: not only is inland Syria unscathed, but Hama, Ebla, Selenkahiye, and Qatna reach their greatest extent in this period. If there was a demographic diminution or urban reduction in inland Syria, it was shorter and later then that of the coastal Levant. The situation on the Syrian coast is less clear. But even in Palestine, the concept of a non-urban intermediate between the Early and Middle Bronze Ages may have to be rethought. Some of the major tells (e.g. Megiddo, Hazor, Jericho, and possibly Lachish) were certainly occupied, and sites like Khirbet Iskander display almost all the attributes of full-fledged urbanism. Several other sites are quite extensive and have to be characterized as large villages if not actually cities.

As noted already, Albright's paradigm had named this period MB I. This was prompted by the view that there was a sharp break between this period and the preceding Early Bronze, and that the 'nomadic tribes' infiltrating the Levant at that time were Amorites (equated with the Amurru who reputedly destroyed Ur III), who settle and form the Canaanite culture of the Middle Bronze. This is no longer a common view. Nevertheless, the terminology of EB IV,[24] which is generally deemed more appropriate (especially in the Syrian sphere), implies a break between this period and the succeeding one. We chose to use the neutral Intermediate Bronze Age—a shortening of Intermediate Early Bronze/Middle Bronze Age.

MIDDLE BRONZE AGE

The problem of naming the subdivisions of the Middle Bronze Age once the Intermediate Bronze has been defined as a separate division has already been discussed. Traditionally, the Middle Bronze Age (MB II as defined if the Intermediate Bronze is called MB I) has a tripartite division (MB IIA, MB IIB, and MB IIC; or MB I, MB II, and MB III—if Albright's

---

[23] Both of them claimed to have captured Ebla, but that either of them was the destroyer of Phase G is of course a supposition. It goes without saying that they cannot *both* have destroyed it, and therefore one or both statements are empty boasts.

[24] Not to be confused with what Albright and Wright (and later Amiran) called EB IV, which is a largely hypothetical post-Khirbet Kerak phase of the EB III, later dubbed EB IIIB.

MB I is called EB IV or Intermediate Bronze). However, there seems to be no clear and generally agreed criteria for separating the two last subdivisions; indeed, in many parts of the Levant such a separation is impossible. Some of the writers in this handbook (Morandi Bonacossi, Charaf, and Cohen, Chs 28–30 below) therefore opt for a dual division (MB I and MB II), while Bourke (Ch. 31) uses the tripartite subdivision (MB I, MB II, and MB III). Thus Bourke's MB II (Albright's MB II B) should be equated with the early part of the MB II as defined by the others authors, while his MB III (Albright's MB II C) comprises the latter part.

From the beginning, the first part of the Middle Bronze Age (MB I as herein defined) has been equated with the Middle Kingdom in Egypt, and its second part (MB II) to the Hyksos period (Second Intermediate). Clues that point to a general correlation between these periods, known early on, included depictions of Canaanites bearing weapons of Middle Bronze Age type in Middle Kingdom tombs in Egypt, and metal versions of ubiquitous Middle Bronze pottery bowls found in the royal cemetery at Byblos together with cartouches of kings of the 12th and 13th Dynasties. Recent decades have added a wealth of information about the Egyptian–Levantine connection, not least due to the outstanding excavations at Tell Dab'a in the eastern Nile Delta.

As usual, the fine notation on the temporal scale is provided by pottery groups and, to some extent, metalwork. The hallmarks for the Middle Bronze are provided by the Levantine Painted ware of the (early) MB I and the Tell el-Yahudiyeh ware, which appears in the MB I and continues into MB II. Levantine Painted ware appears in Tell Dab'a in Phase H (late 12th–early 13th Dynasties) and perhaps slightly earlier in other Middle Kingdom contexts in Egypt (notably the Ezbet Rushdi temple, which was both built and destroyed during the 12th Dynasty). The earliest datable Egyptian exports to the Levant date to the reigns of Senusret II or III. This does not necessarily help pinpointing the *beginning* of the MB I, and dates anywhere between the beginning of the 12th Dynasty (*c.*2000 BCE) or even earlier and Senusret II (1900 BCE) have been proposed. The advanced stages of the MB I, in which red slipped ware with radial burnish gradually replaces the Levantine Painted ware group, are represented in Tell Dab'a in Phases G/1–3, which are datable to the latter part of the 13th Dynasty. Conversely, several 13th Dynasty scarabs appear in advanced MB I contexts in the Levant.

Several consistent suites of high-precision radiocarbon dates for *early* MB I horizons at Tel Ifshar and Tell el Hayyat indicate initial dates for the MB I in the 19th century BCE (Marcus 2003; see also updated list in Marcus 2010). Older measurements, with wider ranges, also extend into the 20th century BCE (and in some cases to the 21st), but, except for one or two anomalous dates, none is *necessarily* earlier than *c.*1900 BCE. This still leaves a wide gap between the earliest radiometric dates from Middle Bronze strata and those from reliable Intermediate Bronze contexts (e.g. the last stratum of Tell Abu en-Niaj), which are definitely before 2200 BCE. Clearly, much more radiocarbon work is needed in this area.

The few high-precision dates extant from late MB I contexts (e.g. at Tel Nami) generally agree with placing the MB I/II transition at *c.*1750 BCE, as traditionally maintained. A similar date is arrived at from a synchronism at Ebla. The name of Hotep-ib-ra Hornerjeryatef, a little-known ruler of the 12th Dynasty, gives a *terminus post quem* of *c.*1770 BCE to the royal tomb of King (?) Immeya buried under the floor of the late palace of Tell Mardikh. The funerary equipment (*inter alia* a metal bowl of the simple carinated type, a ceremonial eye axe, and a duckbill axe) date this tomb to an advanced phase of the MB I (Nigro 2009).

One chronological conundrum which must be mentioned concerning the Middle Bronze is the debate over the date of the first dynasty of Babylon. A general correspondence of this dynasty with the Middle Bronze has long been recognized due to the synchronisms afforded by Hammurabi's destruction of Mari and the conquest of Alalakh (most probably the destruction of Stratum VII) by Hattušili I. Pinpointing these events in terms of Levantine relative chronology (and/or in terms of the radiometric timescale) would establish— albeit indirectly—the long-sought 'early' synchronism between chronologies of Egypt and Mesopotamia, as well as peg the floating chronology of the Old Babylonian period. Recently the claim was made that dendrochronological dates from Anatolia support the 'middle' chronology (1792–1750 BCE for the reign of Hammurabi) (Manning et al. 2001).[25]

Cyprus up to the Late Bronze Age[26]

Radiometric chronology places the end of Cypriot Chalcolithic roughly in line with the end of the mainland Early Bronze. As the Late Cypriot period can be well correlated with the Late Bronze on the mainland, the Early Cypriot–Middle Cypriot sequence is by and large coeval with mainland Intermediate Bronze and Middle Bronze.

What was originally defined as two distinct periods (mainly in order to artificially fit them into the Minoan–Mycenaean scheme) actually forms a single cultural continuum. This is evident in terms both of prevalent lifestyle (villages practicing mixed agriculture, copper production) and of long-lasting, evolving ceramic traditions. Distinct development occurs only at the end of the period, which heralds the approaching urban revolution.

Traditional divisions within this period were established early, but were based almost exclusively on tomb material from the north. They also tended to underestimate non-temporal variability and the distinct regionalism on the island. Thus, these elaborate ceramic indices are often of little use for habitation site excavation—much less surface survey—on the south and west of the island.

This handbook adopts a less rigid framework, allowing for precision where possible but taking into account the essential continuity and fluidity of the sequence (Table 4.2). Note again the transition-period problems. The Philia culture, widespread at the beginning of the sequence, was defined only after a later *facies* had already been given the name EC I. Thus it stands outside the ordinary naming conventions. Chronologically, it partially overlaps the latest Late Chalcolithic. We classify it here as a distinct entity within the Early Cypriot to underscore its difference from Chalcolithic traditions and its standing at the head of the

[25] This is based on dates from constructional timber at Sarıkaya Palace at Acemhöyük and the Waršama Palace at Kültepe (Karum Kaneš Ib), and an indirect synchronism via Shamshi-Adad I of Assyria (whose name and those of his officials appear in both theses palaces) and Zimri-Lim of Mari with Hammurabi of Babylon. Note that whereas the 'high' chronology is ruled out if one accepts these synchronisms, the various 'low-middle' and 'low' options still exist, though they are less likely (e.g. if these structures were built well before the reign of Shamshi-Addad, or if the constructional timbers in them are reused from older structures).

[26] This section (as well as other references to Cypriot chronology) was adapted from a text given to me by David Frankel and Jenny Webb.

Table 4.2 Chronological scheme for Early Cypriot–Middle Cypriot Cyprus

Most general	General	Fine scale	Approximate years (±50)
Early Cypriot	Philia	Philia Bronze Age	2400–2200 BCE
	EC I–II	Early Cypriot I–II	2200–2100 BCE
	EC III–MC I	Early Cypriot III	2100–2000 BCE
Middle Cypriot		Middle Cypriot I	2000–1900 BCE
	MC II	Middle Cypriot II	1900–1800 BCE
	MC III–LC IA	Middle Cypriot III	1800–1700 BCE
Late Cypriot		Late Cypriot IA	1700–1650 BCE

Early Cypriot–Middle Cypriot tradition. Knapp's alternative Prehistoric Bronze Age I period conflates these distinct cultural and chronological entities.

At the end of the sequence is the transition into to Late Cypriot period, here labelled MC III–LC IA. Many of the manifestations of the Late Bronze high culture, including increased social elaboration, increased contacts with Egypt and the southern Levant, public architecture, and new ceramic traditions, gradually develop towards the end of the Middle Cypriot period. Meanwhile the distinguishing mark of the Late Cypriot culture—urbanization—is still lacking at the very beginning of the Late Cypriot. Hence the need for a distinct transitional phase, more or less equivalent to what Knapp refers to as the Protohistoric Bronze Age I period.

LATE BRONZE AGE

The Middle and Late Bronze Ages undoubtedly form a single cultural continuum. The structural difference between the two periods is that in the Late Bronze, the Canaanite city-states operate under an umbrella of 'great kings'. For most of the area considered in this volume, the overlord is Egyptian. While the northernmost parts are under Mitannian/Hittite control, the border between these powers shifted between the Euphrates and the headwaters of the Orontes, or even further south at times. What, if any, are the material culture correlates of this functional difference is moot.

A related and more readily visible development is the opening of the Mediterranean to commerce. However, this process is lengthy and gradual. Cypriot imports to the mainland Levant, and vice versa, had already begun in the later Middle Bronze Age. The occasional Middle Minoan sherd is to be found in Levantine Middle Bronze context also. Mycenaean imports, which *are* limited to the Late Bronze Age, are extremely rare at the beginning of the period. We are again constrained to use specific ceramic wares or 'families' to define the Late Bronze and sub-phases therein. These include Cypriot 'White Slip' and 'Base Ring' as well as the *dis*appearance of typical Middle Bronze wares such as the aforementioned Tell el-Yahudiyeh and Cypriot Red-on-Black. Several ceramic families are typical of the transitional Middle Bronze–Late Bronze phase (i.e. late MB II and LB I), including the Chocolate-on-Cream wares and Cypriot Bichrome.

The absolute date of the beginning of the Late Bronze is currently in debate. The annexation of the Levant to the Egyptian Empire is attributed to the first kings of the 18th Dynasty. Under Thutmose I the empire had already reached its furthest extent—the Euphrates River—although it is not considered to have stabilized till the campaigns of Thutmose III. The beginning of the 18th Dynasty is astronomically fixed to c.1550 BCE by a recorded observation.[27] A slightly earlier date is arrived at by 'dead reckoning' from the end of the Iron Age.[28] The Oxford Egyptian Chronology Project estimates a date of 1570–1545 BCE (95% range) for this event (Bronk-Ramsey et al. 2010: table 1). Since all the kings and the reign lengths for the New Kingdom (18th–20th Dynasties) are known, the New Kingdom is considered precisely dated by most Egyptologists.

Nevertheless, the date of the beginning of the Late Bronze is at present fiercely debated. Most researchers accept the broad contemporaneity of the beginning of the Levantine Late Bronze Age and the beginning of the Egyptian New Kingdom with the Aegean Late Minoan I. A significant peg for the latter is the volcanic eruption which buried the site of Thera in LM I. However, ice core dating on the Greenland icecap indicates that the tephra layer most likely associated with the Thera eruption dates to 1640–1620 BCE. Trees buried by that eruption on Santorini itself were radiocarbon dated (and wiggle-matched) to the last third of the 17th century. Besides the broad contemporaneity between LM I, LC I, LB I, and the New Kingdom (which would not preclude one of them starting earlier), the precise relative dating heavily depends on two Cypriot White Slip I bowls recovered from an indeterminate context in Thera. This is one of the wares usually considered to start in LC I, and it does not appear in the Levant prior to LB I, or in Egypt before the New Kingdom. Perhaps even more worrying is a sequence of radiocarbon measurements from Tell Dab'a, which also indicates that New Kingdom phases there begin as much as a century earlier than expected. As noted already, the Egyptian chronology itself seems to be soundly correlated with the radiocarbon time-scale. Thus the conundrum is whether one should stick to the conventional chronology for the beginning of the Levantine Late Bronze Age and explain away each of the above anomalies individually[29] or—once again—divorce the archaeological time-scale from political history and argue that the Levantine Late Bronze Age began *before* the region was incorporated into the Egyptian Empire.

Like the definition of the era itself, the subdivision of the Late Bronze Age is most easily achieved using imported wares and foreign correlations. Not only is the El Amarna period (c.1400–1330 BCE) the best historically illuminated phase of the Bronze Age as far as the southern Levant is concerned, but el-Amarna itself, the short-lived capital of Amenhotep IV, provides a neatly encapsulated reference point. Conveniently enough, this period nearly coincides with the span of Myc IIIA pottery, much of which was found at el-Amarna itself,

---

[27] A heliacal rise of Sothis is recorded on the ninth day of the third month of summer in the ninth year of Amenhotep I. Assuming this observation was made in Thebes (the capital of the 18th Dynasty) under ideal viewing conditions, this fixes this day to 1517 BCE, and the beginning of the 18th Dynasty to 1550 BCE. If the observation was made at some latitude further north (or a day or two too late), it might be up to a couple of decades earlier.

[28] This is complicated by unknown reign lengths and at least partial overlaps between rival dynasties in the Third Intermediate Period.

[29] For example, to argue that LC I/LM I/Late Helladic I do indeed start earlier but for some reason White Slip I is not imported to Egypt or the Levant prior to c.1550; and—independent of the above—the systematic shift evident in the Tell Dab'a radiometric dates is a problem specific to that site.

together with a few pieces which might be harbingers of the Myc IIIB style. The Uluburun shipwreck provides another closed assemblage that may be used as a benchmark. A gold ring with the name of Nefertiti proves the ship sunk within the reign of Amenhotep IV or (more likely) some short time after it (Pulak 2008). The Mycenaean pottery recovered is all Myc IIIA:2 (some *could* be Myc IIIB:1, but none is *necessarily* so). Dendrochronological analysis of wood from the ship and wiggle-matched radiocarbon dates indicate that the latest pieces of wood were cut a short time after 1320 BCE.

All of this data allows a tripartite division of the Late Bronze Age to pre-El Amarna, El Amarna, and post-El Amarna phases, more or less comparable to Late Helladic I–II, LH IIIA, and LH IIIB. Some textbooks (e.g. Amiran 1970) name these subdivision LB I, LB II, and LB III, while the more common designation is LB I, LB IIA, and LB IIB. In this volume, Heinz and Kulemann-Ossen (Ch. 35 below) and Panitz-Cohen (Ch. 36) use this last scheme.

Another possible scheme is to subdivide the Late Bronze using political history. In northern Syria, the watershed event is the takeover of Mittanian hegemony by the Hittite Empire at *c.*1350 BCE. This date is used by Luciani (Ch. 34) to divide the Late Bronze Age in Syria to LB I and LB II. Fischer (Ch. 37) correlates the Late Bronze in Jordan with Egyptian dynastic succession. He thus stretches his LB I to the end of the 18th Dynasty, at *c.* 1300 BCE.

Yet another LB III designation, not to be confused with the LB III in the Amiran scheme, is sometimes used to denote the transitional Late Bronze Age/Iron Age (see below, and Panitz-Cohen, Ch. 36).

IRON AGE

The transition from Bronze to Iron Age is again traumatic. It is ushered by the collapse or withdrawal of the 'great powers'; the virtual cessation of overseas trade in the highly visible fine-ware pottery that provided the benchmark for the classification of the Late Bronze Age; widespread destruction and abandonment of urban sites; and the foundation of alternative settlement patterns. All these indicate a deep socioeconomic and demographic rift, corroborated by the fact that the entities which coalesce after this crisis call themselves (when writing becomes widespread again) by different names, and variously delineate themselves vis-à-vis the Bronze Age inhabitants of the same spaces.

The fact that it is dramatic does not make this change any easier to define or to date. It is nowadays clear that the 'catastrophe' was not a singular event but was some time in the making, that it was not everywhere simultaneous, and that for a long while (perhaps the entire Iron I, i.e. some two centuries) some attributes and institutions of the *ancien régime* continue to function alongside the new.

We thus encounter the by-now familiar problem of transition periods: given that each of the polythetic attributes by which the shift is defined changes at its own pace, how does one define a beginning of a new era? First, it is important to note that two different stances are taken by the archaeologies of the mainland and that of Cyprus. For reasons which have to do mainly with the history of the discipline and former historical reconstruction, the archaeology of the Levant defines the beginning of the Iron Age more or less at the onset of the crisis (the point at which 'Israelites' and 'Sea Peoples' were presumed to have emerged in or entered Canaan); while that of Cyprus—following the practice of Greek archaeology—continue the Bronze Age until such time as the new order is firmly in place. Thus the LC III (A and B) are contemporaneous with the beginning of Iron I on the mainland, ending somewhere in the middle of it (the end of Iron IA, according to the terminology used here).

This is not the only problem, though. Destructions of Late Bronze sites vary in time, perhaps by as much as half a century or more. The fall of Hazor may have occurred as early as the mid-13th century. That of Ugarit was at least at the turn of the century and possibly a few decades later (during the reign of Merneptah, or, more likely, Seti II or Tausret). Sidon and Deir Alla were still functioning during the reign of Tausret, while Lachish was destroyed either during or after that of Ramesses III. Beth Shean and Megiddo were still flourishing in the latter king's reign, and the latest New Kingdom pharaoh to have left his cartouche in Canaan is Ramesses VI (in Megiddo, unfortunately out of context). Radiocarbon distributions from terminal Late Bronze destructions usually cover the same range—the last decades of the 13th to mid-12th centuries BCE.

In the southern Levant there are three other possible indices: the cessation of Late Bronze forms of pottery imports from Cyprus and Greece; the end of Egyptian influence in the Levant; and the appearance of the earliest Aegeanizing Philistine wares (the Monochrome, so-called Myc IIIC). Of these, the first most certainly precedes the latter two; but which of these takes precedence is debated. Finkelstein (1995) argues that Monochrome Philistine-bearing strata post-date those bearing Egyptian 20th-Dynasty finds, while others (e.g. Bunimovitz and Faust 2001) opt for contemporaneity. This leaves open the possibility that terminal Bronze Age strata with no imports (dubbed LB III by Ussishkin 1985), 20th-Dynasty Egyptian centres (Iron IA by the historical reckoning of Albright and his followers), and Monochrome Philistine sites are all more or less contemporary. In order to sidestep this issue, we name this phase 'Late Bronze/Iron Age transition'.

The Iron Age II is ushered in by re-urbanization and the re-establishment of higher culture (including writing and trading networks). Dating this transition, however, is not any easier. Lowland sites (in coastal Syria, Phoenicia, Philistia, and the rift valley systems), where good stratigraphic and typological sequences can be had, were never de-urbanized and to a certain extent at least retained small arts and trading connections. Highland sites are often quite poor and tend to have a thin stratigraphy. Moreover, it is in the nature of insular periods such as Iron I that pottery repertoires are quite localized (see above for a similar phenomenon in the IB). The lack of written or inscribed objects means that historical dates are virtually nonexistent. These problems are even worse on the Transjordanian Plateau. Being further away from the coast, overseas imports are rarer in the Late Bronze Age, and Cypriot, Phoenician, and Philistine ones nearly nonexistent in the Iron Age. Furthermore, re-urbanization cannot be used as a temporal reference point, since it may plausibly be argued that this process was widely staggered between the Mediterranean climate zone and the desert fringes.

Nevertheless, in the past this period was considered quite well dated in the southern Levant, based on an implicit trust in the biblical depiction of the crystallization of the Israelite tribal federation into the united monarchy of David and Solomon around 1000 BCE or just prior to it. This argument was bolstered by various secondary considerations such as the attribution of various terminal Iron I destruction layers (e.g. Qasile X, Megiddo VIB) to Davidic conquests; construction works such as six-chambered gates in Hazor, Megiddo, and Gezer to Solomon (Yadin 1958); and destructions at the *end* of Iron IIA to Shishak's campaign attributed by the book of Kings to the fifth year of Rehoboam (925 BCE). Critical views

of these biblical narratives, however, have led some to reject such attributions, and to propose radically different histories of the early monarchical period (e.g. Finkelstein 1996 and
many times since). This at a minimum points to the need to base archaeological chronology
on a less controversial foundation.

We thus fall back on pottery typology and radiometric dates. The usual criteria for the
beginning of Iron II are the end of the Philistine painted tradition in the southern Levant,
the spread of red slipped wares (hand-burnished in the southern Levant, Phoenician red
slip along the northern coasts, Black-on-Red in Cyprus), evolution within the Phoenician
bichrome tradition, and foreign imports, most importantly of the Cypro-Geometric III
horizon. Again, it must be stressed that all of the above are gradual and independent, and
none necessarily correlates with such criteria for state formation as urbanization and public
works. While mature Iron IIA strata such as Hazor X–IX or Megiddo VA–IVB display all of
these attributes, a horizon during which these are still vestigial can be delineated at some
sites, creating the usual transition period dilemma (see Killebrew, Ch. 39 below, regarding
the suggestion to divide Iron IIA into two sub-phases, early and late).

Several ambitious radiocarbon studies were launched in the late 1990s and 2000s to try to
give an absolute date to the Iron IIA, the results of which are still in debate. In general they
point out that the dates for the Iron IIA should be lowered somewhat. It encompasses all (or
at least most) of the 9th century BCE. There is less agreement about its beginning; Sharon et
al. (2007) opt for the end of the 10th century BCE, while Mazar prefers a date somewhere in
the first half of this century (Mazar and Bronk-Ramsey 2008). While the difference in years
is not large, the higher proposal can still support the biblical chronology of at least the end of
Solomon's kingdom within Iron IIA, while the lower does not.

Both low and amended high chronologies nowadays agree that the *beginning* of Iron IIB is
towards the end of the 9th century (note, however, that Hardin, Ch. 49 below, uses the conventional date of 930 BCE for this transition). The end of that sub-period is fixed by a series of
Assyrian destructions, which are historically dated to the end of the 8th century.[30] The most
significant among these is the destruction of Lachish by Sennacherib in 701 BCE, depicted
in the reliefs from his throne-room at Nineveh. Capitalizing on the typology of Olga Tufnell
(1953), Miriam and Yohanan Aharoni (1976) showed that later Iron Age destructions in
Judah can be typologically attributed to a late 8th-century horizon, comparable to Lachish
III, and a 7th/late 6th-century horizon comparable to Lachish II.[31] These articulate the distinction between Iron IIB and Iron IIC in the southern Levant. Such benchmarks are often
missing elsewhere in the Levant, either because the precise typological work was not done or
because of the lack of datable destructions. In the north, the wave of Assyrian destructions
started early (in the 9th century, rather than the end of the 8th), and there are no recorded
Assyrian campaigns into Jordan at all. Thus for these regions, most authors in this volume
use the designation 'Iron IIB–C'.

---

[30] Unfortunately, this cannot be verified by radiocarbon, as that period is already within the Hallstadt
Plateau in the calibration curve.

[31] Though nowadays this is considered to be a firm case of historical dating, it too was the subject of a
fierce debate. Tufnell's suggestion that Stratum III was the one destroyed by Sennacherib was rejected by
most of the authorities of the day. Only Ussishkin's re-excavation of the site in the 1970s and 1980s finally
settled the issue.

We noted already that in Cyprus the Late Cypriot period continues into what is already considered Iron I on the mainland (LC III). The so-called Cypro-Phoenician[32] Black-on-Red ware of CG III is one of the *fossiles directeurs* of the onset of the Iron II on the mainland. This establishes a correspondence of CG III with the mainland Iron IIA and leaves the CG I and the chronologically ill-defined CG II to correspond with the latter part of Iron I and the 'intermediate' Iron I/II—as is indeed testified by the numerous occurrences of these wares on the mainland and of (mainly Phoenician) imports on the island. At the other end of the Iron Age chronology, the beginning of Cypro-Archaic (*c.*750 BCE) fits fairly well with the transition from Iron IIB to Iron IIC.

IRON III/BABYLONIAN AND PERSIAN PERIODS

All the difficulties alluded to in the introduction are also present in the latest epoch covered by this volume. To begin with, naming conventions. Should these periods be referred to by demonyms (Babylonian/Persian periods), as is the convention in Israel, or by the more neutral Iron II used by others?[33] Using the names of the ruling polities to denote archaeological periods not only implies the historicity of that rule (which, at these late periods, is not really in doubt) but also that archaeological assemblages can be classified to such categories with sufficient accuracy in most, if not all, cases. Given that coins or other absolute date-bearing objects do not become common until the Hellenistic period, this is a serious issue.

That being said, the period is also beset by the usual transition phase problems at both ends. Should the Babylonian period be annexed to the Iron Age or to the Persian period? Given that assemblages roughly falling in the 7th century (Iron IIC; see above) can easily be discerned from those of the 5th century, would one expect Babylonian contexts to appear more Iron Age or more Persian? If one encounters artefacts typical of both in a not-quite-closed context (e.g. a fill, a multiple-inhumation tomb, or an old excavation report), is that a transitional assemblage, or merely a mixed one?

It is these problems which are at the nub of the debate about the Babylonian gap. Does the apparent scarcity of good 6th-century (and some would say even early 5th-century) contexts reflect a real demographic calamity, or only a gap in our knowledge? Do we simply not know how to recognize a Babylonian assemblage when we see one? Perhaps it is presumptuous to even assume we can date contexts to half-centuries without aid. Whatever the position one takes on the actual existence on a gap in the archaeological record in the 6th century (cf. Zorn, Ch. 54 below), the suggestion that a separate archaeological period should be devoted to the scant half-century of Neo-Babylonian rule of the Levant is premature.

Cyprus was under imperial hegemony—though in what form is not quite clear—from the end of the 8th century. Thus the Cypro-Archaic and Cypro-Classical periods more or less correspond to the period of Assyrian–Babylonian–Persian rule. The division between the two at 480/475 BCE finds no correspondence in mainland periodization, in which there are no agreed subdivisions of the Persian period 530–332 BCE. Although hinging the chronology of Cyprus—much less the entire Levant—on that of Athens is arguably even more

---

[32] Current provenience analysis indicates it is Cypriot and not Phoenician.
[33] See Mazzoni, Ch. 45 below, who uses Iron III to denote the 7th and 6th centuries BCE.

Table 4.3 Chronological table synthesizing the disparate names for the period divisions

Period	Alternate names		Absolute date	Cypriot chronology
PPNA			c.9750 BCE	PPNA
			c.8500 BCE	
PPNB				PPNB
			c.7750 BCE	
[PPNC]				
			c.6500 BCE	
Ln1	PNA, Early Pottery Neolithic			Aceramic Neolithic
			c.6000 BCE	
Ln2	PNB, Late PN, Early Chalcolithic			
			c.5500 BCE	
	[Middle Chalcolithic?]			
			c.4500 BCE	Ceramic Neolithic
Chalcolithic	Late Chalcolithic			
			3900/3700 BCE	
EB I	Proto-Urban			
			3200/3000 BCE	Chalcolithic
EB II				
			2850/2600 BCE	
EB III				
			2500/2300 BCE	
IB	MB I	EB IV		EC
			2200/1900 BCE	
MB I	MB IIA	MB I		MC I–II
			1750 BCE	
MB II(e)	MB IIB	MB II		
				MC III–LC IA
MB II(l)	MB IIC	MB III		
			1640/1540 BCE	
LB I	LB I	LB I		LC IB
			1400 BCE	
LB IIA	LB II			LC IIA
			1330/1300 BCE	
LB IIB	LB III	LB II		LC IIB–C
			1200/1150 BCE	
[LB/IR]	IA IA	LB III		LC IIIA
			1150/1100 BCE	
Iron I	IA IB			LC IIIB–CG IA
[Iron I/II]		Early IA IIA		CG IB–CG II
			1000/900 BCE	
Iron IIA	IA II			CG III
			925/800 BCE	
Iron IIB				
	IA III	IA II B–C	730/700 BCE	
Iron IIC				
			608/586 BCE	
	Babylonian	IA III		Cypro-Archaic
Iron III/Persian			530 BCE	
	Persian			
			475 BCE	
				Cypro-Classical
			330 BCE	

arbitrary than connecting it to political upheavals in Mesopotamia, Levantine archaeologists should take heed. Good assemblages of the end of the 6th century and the beginning of the 5th are as elusive as those of the Babylonian period. Whatever the explanation of the Babylonian gap, the early Persian period is phenomenologically similar. Moreover, 480 BCE forms a good heuristic cleavage point, inasmuch as Attic (and consequently Cypriot) pottery can easily be classified to Archaic versus Classical, and imports, especially of the former, become prevalent on mainland sites after the mid-5th century.

The end of the period should, in theory, be recognizable by the onset of Hellenization. Needless to say, Hellenization, however defined, did not happen overnight. Some regions annexed by Alexander had been—if not already settled by Greek speakers—holding close material culture conversations with them for centuries. In others, Hellenic traits would not influence the ingrained material culture until well into the Hellenistic period. Continuity rather than sudden changes being the case, there are grounds to disentwine in this case too the archaeological periodization from the historical one, and claim a Persian/Hellenistic transition period straddling the historical date of 332 BCE.

Whatever one's position on the name of this period, the apparently definite dates of its beginning and end are deceptive.

Based mainly on political history, Elayi suggests in Chapter 8 below a tripartite division of the Persian period: 539–486 BCE, 486–404 BCE, and 404–332 BCE. This scheme can perhaps be usefully adapted for archaeological dating as well, though of course the latter cannot be as precise. As noted already, 480/475 BCE can be a useful benchmark inasmuch as good classification criteria exist for Archaic–Classical Attic and Cypriot pottery, and both classes are to be found on many mainland sites. Fourth-century material culture assemblages can also be differentiated from 5th-century ones, both again using Attic typology, as well as changes in local wares. Coinage also begins to be a useful dating tool in many sites by the late Persian period.

Conclusion

Table 4.3 summarizes the prevalent subdivisions of the chronology of the Levant, as used in this volume and other contemporary publications.

References

Aharoni, M., and Y. Aharoni (1976). The stratification of Judean sites in the eighth and seventh centuries B.C.E. *Bulletin of the American Schools of Oriental Research* 224: 73–90.

Aharoni, Y., and R. Amiran (1958). A new scheme for the subdivision of the Iron Age in Palestine. *Israel Exploration Journal* 8: 171–84.

Albright, W. F. (1932). *The Excavation of Tell Beit Mirsim in Palestine: Joint Expedition of the Pittsburgh-Xenia Theological Seminary and the American School of Oriental Research in Jerusalem*, vol. 1: *The Pottery of the First Three Campaigns*. New Haven, Conn.: Yale University Press.

Amiran, R. (1970). *Ancient Pottery of the Holy Land: From Its Beginnings in the Neolithic Period to the End of the Iron Age*. New Brunswick, NJ: Rutgers University Press.

Anderson, R. W., Jr. (2006). Southern Palestinian chronology: two radiocarbon dates for the Early Bronze Age at Tell El-Hesi (Israel). *Radiocarbon* 48: 101–7.

Archi, A., and M. G. Biga (2003). A victory over Mari and the fall of Ebla. *Journal of Cuneiform Studies* 55: 1–44.

Avi-Yonah, M., and E. Stern (eds) (1975). *Encyclopedia of Archaeological Excavations in the Holy Land*. Jerusalem: Israel Exploration Society: Massada.

Banning, E. B. (2002). Consensus and debate on the Late Neolithic and Chalcolithic of the southern Levant. *Paléorient* 28: 143–56.

Banning, E. B.(2007). Wadi Rabah and related assemblages in the southern Levant: interpreting the radiocarbon evidence. *Paléorient* 33: 77–101.

Blackham, M. (2002). *Modeling Time and Transition in Prehistory: The Jordan Valley Chalcolithic (5500–3500 BC)*. Oxford: Archaeopress.

Bourke, S., U. Zoppi, J. Meadows, Q. Hua, and S. Gibbins (2004). The end of the Chalcolithic period in the South Jordan Valley: new 14C determinations from Teleilat Ghassul, Jordan. *Radiocarbon* 46: 315–23.

Borchardt, L. (1935). *Die Mittel zur seitlichen Festlegung von Punkten der ägyptischen Geschichte und ihre Anwendung*. Kairo.

Braun, E. (2001). Proto, Early Dynastic Egypt, and Early Bronze I–II of the southern Levant: some uneasy 14C correlations. *Radiocarbon* 43: 1279–95.

Bronk-Ramsey, C., M. W. Dee, J. M. Rowland, et al. (2010). Radiocarbon-based chronology for Dynastic Egypt. *Science* 328: 1554–7.

Bunimovitz, S., and A. Faust (2001). Chronological separation, geographical segregation, or ethnic demarcation? Ethnography and the Iron Age low chronology. *Bulletin of the American Schools of Oriental Research* 322: 1–10.

de Vaux, R. (1966). *Cambridge Ancient History*, vol. 1: *Palestine during the Neolithic and Chalcolithic Periods*, rev. edn. Cambridge: Cambridge University Press, 5–8.

Finkelstein, I. (1995). The date of the settlement of the Philistines in Canaan. *Tel Aviv* 22: 213–39.

Finkelstein, I. (1996). Toward a new periodization and nomenclature of the archeology of the southern Levant. In J. Cooper and G. Schwartz (eds), *The Study of the Ancient Near East in the Twenty-First Century*. Winona Lake, Ind.: Eisenbrauns, 103–24.

Garfinkel, Y. (1999). *Neolithic and Chalcolithic Pottery of the Southern Levant*. Jerusalem: Institute of Archaeology, Hebrew University of Jeruslaem.

Garstang, J., L. Vincent, W. F. Albright, and W. J. T. Phythian-Adams (1922). A new chronological classification of Palestinian archaeology. *Bulletin of the American Schools of Oriental Research* 7: 9.

Gilboa, A., and I. Sharon (2003). An archaeological contribution to the Early Iron Age chronological debate: alternative chronologies for Phoenicia and their effects on the Levant, Cyprus, and Greece. *Bulletin of American Schools of Oriental Research* 332: 7–80.

Gjerstad, E. (1926). Studies on prehistoric Cyprus. PhD dissertation, Uppsala University.

Knapp, A. B. (2008). *Prehistoric and Protohistoric Cyprus: Insularity, Connectivity, and Identity*. Oxford: Oxford University Press.

Lebeau, M. (2012). Dating the destructions of Ebla, Mari and Nagar from radiocarbon: with references to Egypt, combined with stratigraphy and historical data. In: H. Baker, K. Kaniuth, and A. Otto (eds.), *Stories of Long Ago: Festschrift für Michael D. Roaf*. Münster: Ugarit-Verlag, 301–22.

Macalister, R. A. S. (1912). *The Excavation of Gezer: 1902–1905 and 1907–1909* (3 vols). London: Published for the Committee of the Palestine Exploration Fund by J. Murray.

Manning, S. W., B. Kromer, P. I. Kuniholm, and M. W. Newton (2001). Anatolian tree-rings and a new chronology for the east Mediterranean Bronze–Iron Ages. *Science* 294: 2532–5.

Manning, S. W., C. McCartney, B. Kromer, and S. T. Stewart (2010). The Earlier Neolithic in Cyprus: recognition and dating of a Pre-pottery Neolithic A occupation. *Antiquity* 84: 693–706.

Marcus, E. S. (2003). Dating the Early Middle Bronze Age in the Southern Levant: a preliminary comparison of radiocarbon and archaeo-historical synchronizations. In M. Bietak (ed.), *The Synchronisation of Civilizations in the Eastern Mediterranean in the Second Millennium BC, II*. Vienna: Österreichischen Akademie der Wissenschaften, 95–110.

Marcus, E. S. (2010). Appendix B: Radiocarbon determinations from Middle Bronze Age Jordan Valley. In Aren M. Maeir (ed.), *In the Midst of the Jordan (Jos 4:10): The Jordan Valley during the Middle Bronze Age (circa 2000–1500 BCE); Archaeological and Historical Correlates*. Vienna: Österreichischen Akademie der Wissenschaften, 243–52.

Mazar, A. (1990). *Archaeology of the Land of the Bible*, vol. 1: *10,000–586 B.C.E*. New York: Anchor.

Mazar, A. and C. Bronk-Ramsey (2008). 14C Dates and the Iron Age chronology of Israel: a response. *Radiocarbon* 50: 159–80.

Meyer, E. (1904). *Aegyptische Chronologie*. Berlin.

Nigro, L. (2009). The eighteenth century BC princes of Byblos and Ebla and the chronology of the Middle Bronze Age. In *Interconnections in the Eastern Mediterranean: Lebanon in the Bronze and Iron Ages*. Beirut: Ministère de la Culture, Direction Générale des Antiquités, 159–75.

Peltenburg, E. J. (1998). *Lemba Archaeological Project (Cyprus)*, vol. 2, part 1A: *Excavations at Kissonerga-Mosphilia, 1979–1992*. Göteborg: Åströms.

Petrie, W. F. (1891). *Tell el Hesy (Lachish)*. London: Published for the Committee of the Palestine Exploration Fund by A. P. Watt.

Pulak, C. (2008). The Uluburun shipwreck and Late Bronze Age trade. In J. Aruz, K. Benzel, and J. M. Evans (eds), *Beyond Babylon: Art, Trade and Diplomacy in the Second Millennium B.C*. New York: Metropolitan Museum of Art/New Haven, Conn.: Yale University Press, 289–385.

Regev, J., P. de Miroschedji, and E. Boaretto (2012). Early Bronze Age chronology: radiocarbon dates and chronological models from Tel Yarmuth (Israel). *Radiocarbon* 54: 505–24.

Regev, J., P. de Miroschedji, R. Greenberg, E. Braun, Z. Greenhut, and E. Boaretto (2012). Radiocarbon chronology of the Early Bronze Age in the south Levant: new analyses for a high chronology. *Radiocarbon* 54: 525–66.

Sharon, I., A. Gilboa, A. J. T. Jull, and E. Boaretto (2007). Report on the first stage of the Iron Age Dating Project in Israel: supporting the low chronology. *Radiocarbon* 49: 1–46.

Shaw, I. (2000). Introduction: chronologies and cultural change in Egypt. In I. Shaw (ed.), *Oxford History of Ancient Egypt*. Oxford: Oxford University Press, 1–15.

Tufnell, O. (1953). *Lachish (Tell ed Duweir)*, vol. 3: *The Iron Age*. London: Published for the Trustees of the Late Sir Henry Wellcome by Oxford University Press.

Ussishkin, D. (1985). Levels VII and VI at Tel Lachish and the end of the Late Bronze Age in Canaan. In J. N. Tubb (ed.), *Palestine in the Bronze and Iron Ages: Papers in Honour of Olga Tufnell*. London: Institute of Archaeology, 213–30.

Wright, G. E. (1961). The Archaeology of Palestine. In G. E. Wright (ed.), *The Bible and the Ancient Near East: Essays in Honor of William Foxwell Albright*. Garden City, NY: Doubleday, 73–112.

Yadin, Y. (1958). Solomon's city wall and gate at Gezer. *Israel Exploration Journal* 8: 80–86.

PART II

THE LEVANT AS THE CROSSROADS BETWEEN EMPIRES

Egypt, Anatolia, Mesopotamia, and Persia

CHAPTER 5

EGYPT AND THE LEVANT

GREGORY D. MUMFORD

The intensity and nature of Egypto-Levantine relations have varied through time (see Table 5.1), encompassing overland and maritime commerce, diplomacy, alliances, emigration, imperialism, and deportations. Such cross-cultural relations incorporate varying importations and local adaptations by each host culture, including architecture, art, material culture, language, literature, and religion. In times of Egyptian strength and imperialism, such as the New Kingdom, early Saite period, and quite possibly the Protodynastic to Early Dynastic period, there is often a greater occurrence of Egyptian-style construction, monuments, diverse artefacts, transitory through permanent migrants, and other influence in the Levant. During such periods, trade still forms a major mechanism for transmitting Egyptian items and inspiring local-regional imitations, while Egyptian garrisons, transitory troops, emissaries, other personnel, and 'Egyptianized' Canaanites also play a substantial role in dispersing Egyptian materials and influence. During other periods of Egyptian prosperity, such as the Old and Middle Kingdoms, Egypt relaxes its interactions with Palestine, attacking it periodically and sometimes sharing greater maritime commerce with Syria. During low points in Egyptian political stability, such as the Intermediate periods, Egyptian exports and local-regional copies of Egyptian forms, motifs, and concepts generally decline with commerce often reflecting the main means of transferring Egyptian and Egyptian-style items and influence. On the other hand, the Hyksos domination of Egypt's eastern delta introduces more Levantine influences into Egypt; the Hyksos, however, also adopt aspects of Egyptian culture and relay Egyptian and Egyptian-style materials, products, and motifs abroad (e.g. 'Hyksos' scarabs). Other 'invaders', such as the Assyrian through Persian Empires, plunder Egypt of architectural elements (e.g. obelisks), statuary, artefacts, and people; most of these things are transported through the Levant and into the Mesopotamian heartland, while Phoenicia becomes an indirect imitator and exporter of Egyptian-style products throughout the Levant and Mediterranean.

PREDYNASTIC PERIOD

Chalcolithic to Early Bronze Age I

Egyptian imports first appear in Palestine during the Chalcolithic period, including a Naqada I-style calcite jar at Ghassul (Stager in Ehrich 1992: 26). North Sinai produced

Table 5.1. General correspondence between Egyptian dynasties and Levantine periods

Egyptian periods and dates (Shaw 2000)	Levantine periods and dates (Levy 1995)
Predynastic	
Badarian (South Egypt): c.4400–4000 BC	Chalcolithic 4500–3500 BC
Naqada I (Amratian): c.4000–3500 BC	
Naqada II (Gerzean): c.3500–3200 BC	Early Bronze Age IA–B 3500–3000 BC
Naqada III (Dynasty 0): c.3200–3000 BC	
Early Dynastic Period	
Dynasty 1: c.3000–2890 BC	Early Bronze Age II 3000–2700 BC
Dynasty 2: c.2890–2686 BC	(EB II sometimes terminated c.2900 BC)
Old Kingdom	
Dynasty 3: c.2686–2613 BC	Early Bronze Age III 2700–2200 BC
Dynasty 4: c.2613–2494 BC	(EB IV/MB I sometimes dated to c.2300 BC)
Dynasty 5: c.2494–2345 BC	
Dynasty 6: c.2345–2181 BC	
First Intermediate Period	Intermediate Bronze Age
Dyn. 7–mid-Dyn.11: c.2181–2055 BC	EB Age IV/MB Age I 2200–2000 BC
Middle Kingdom	Canaanites
Mid-Dyn.11–mid-Dyn.13: c.2055–1773 BC	Middle Bronze Age IIA 2000–1750 BC
Second Intermediate Period	Canaanites and 'Hyksos'
Dynasties 14 and 16: c.1773–1650 BC	Middle Bronze Age IIB 1750–1650 BC
Dynasties 15 and 17: c.1650–1550 BC	Middle Bronze Age IIC 1650–1550 BC
New Kingdom	Canaanite city-states
Early Dynasty 18: c.1550–1457 BC	Late Bronze Age IA 1550–1450 BC
Mid-Dynasty 18: c.1457–1390 BC	Late Bronze Age IB 1450–1400 BC
Late Dynasty 18: c.1390–1295 BC	Late Bronze Age IIA 1400–1300 BC
Dynasty 19: c.1295–1186 BC	Late Bronze Age IIB 1300–1200 BC
Early Dynasty 20: c.1186–1136 BC	Iron Age Sea Peoples, Israelites, Philistines:
Late Dynasty 20: c.1136–1069 BC	Iron Age IA 1200–1150 BC
	Iron Age IB 1150–1000 BC
Third Intermediate Period	Israel, Judah, Philistia, and other polities
Dynasty 21: c.1069–945 BC	Iron Age IB 1150–1000 BC
Dynasty 22: c.945–715 BC	Iron Age IIA 1000–925 BC
Dynasties 23–24: c.818–715 BC	Iron Age IIB 925–700 BC
Kushite-Saite period (early Late Period)	Assyrian–Babylonian Empires
King Piye (mainly Nubia) c.747–716 BC	Iron Age IIC 700–586 BC
Dynasty 25: c.716–664/656 BC	Babylonian period 586–539 BC
Dynasty 26: c.664–525 BC	
Late Period	
Dyn. 27 (Persian occupation): 525–404 BC	Persian period 539–332 BC
Dynasties 28–30: 404–343 BC	
Dyn. 31 (Persian occupation): 343–332 BC	

Ghassul-Beersheba pottery and Egyptian Red Polished pottery and palettes, attesting to overland traffic between Palestine and Egypt. Maadi, near the apex of Egypt's delta, exhibits Levantine-style subterranean dwellings, many donkey bones (i.e. pack animals), and copper ores, ingots, and artefacts from the Beer-Sheba region and Wadi Faynan (Levy 1995: 242). Maritime contact with Lebanon (and Afghanistan) is also demonstrated by the presence of cedar, pine, and cypress/juniper wood and lapis lazuli in Predynastic Egypt (Nicholson and Shaw 2000: 39, 349–52).

During EB I, Egypt's Naqada II–III cultures intensify trade with the emerging urban communities in Syria-Palestine: Egyptian artefacts appear throughout North Sinai and Palestine (see Braun 2009), reaching as far as Megiddo and Transjordan, and occur further north in Lebanon. Egyptian-style pottery is imported and locally made, perhaps being manufactured by Egyptian potters dwelling in Palestine. Egyptian-style vessels amount to 80 per cent of the ceramics in North Sinai and up to 20 per cent of the pottery at sites in southern Palestine (e.g. en-Besor). Some pots bear the serekh names of Kings Ka and 'Scorpion'; other Egyptian products include copper tools, flints, palettes, calcite and faience containers, clay sealings, mace-heads, jewellery, and Nile molluscs and catfish. Egyptian-style mud-brick buildings also appear (e.g. 'Ereini), while some human remains resemble 'African' (i.e. Egyptian) populations (Harrison 1993: 81–9). This may reflect Egyptian imperialism, peaceful colonization, or intense trade. Egyptian pottery, mace-heads, and palettes reach Byblos (Lebanon), with additional Egyptian pottery at Habuba Kabira (North Syria), and possible Egyptian-derived gold at Tepe Gawra (Mesopotamia) (Nigro 2007: 32–3). In conjunction with an intense Mesopotamian material presence and influence in late Predynastic–1st Dynasty Egypt, Syrian ports, such as Byblos, probably serve as conduits for maritime trade with Egypt (Mumford 2001a: 336).

EARLY DYNASTIC PERIOD

Early Bronze Age II

In the 1st Dynasty, Egyptian contact with southern Palestine intensifies and includes imported and locally made pottery, inscribed vessels (bearing the serekh names of kings Narmer, Hor-Aha, Den, and Anedjib?), clay sealings, stone vessels, a knife handle, and Egyptian-style architecture (e.g. Ai; 'Ereini). Narmer's name occurs on a potsherd (reassigned to Level III) from Arad, an important town along the copper trade routes from the southern Sinai and Wadi Faynan (Adams 2003: 18; Braun 2009: 36). The Palermo Stone, which lists pharaohs from the 1st–5th Dynasties, mentions Den attacking the *Iwnw*-peoples (known in southern Sinai during the Old Kingdom); commodity dockets from his reign also portray him smiting Asiatics. In the 2nd Dynasty, a dramatic drop occurred in Egypt's material/political (?) domination of southern Palestine: King Sekhemib-Perenmaat is identified on stone vessels that cite 'tribute of foreign lands', which might allude to residual political influence over Palestine (Wilkinson 1999: 155, 157). In general, however, Egypto-Levantine maritime commerce flourishes in the 2nd–6th Dynasties: the Palermo Stone notes ship-building by Khasekhemwy, whose name appears on a stone vessel at Byblos (Saghieh

1983: 104); a 2nd/3rd Dynasty calcite jar from Byblos names Neferseshemre (a scribe of the royal tree-cutters), while Egyptian-style pottery is found in the 'Amuq region of Syria (Akkermans and Schwartz 2003: 202).

OLD KINGDOM

Early Bronze Age III

Large Levantine urban centres prosper throughout EB III, but many sites are abandoned or destroyed toward the end of this period. EB III coincides with much of the 4th–6th Dynasties, when Egyptian artefacts diminish, but are still found in Palestine: e.g. Tel Yarmuth (de Miroschedji in van den Brink and Levy 2002: 47). Conversely, Old Kingdom Egypt produces a peak in Canaanite Combed Ware, possibly reflecting otherwise invisible Levantine trade or booty. For instance, the 5th Dynasty tombs of Inti and Khaemhesit illustrate Egyptian attacks against Asiatic strongholds (Kaplony in van den Brink and Levy 2002: 474).

The Palermo Stone alludes to maritime contact with Byblos to retrieve cedar, which is confirmed by cedar scaffolding in Sneferu's Dahshur pyramids. Sahure's mortuary temple portrays ships bringing bears, pottery, and male and female Asiatics to Egypt. A temple and cemetery at Byblos contain Egyptianizing architectural fragments (uraei friezes), statuary, stone vessels, and other items, some of which bear the names of most kings from the 4th–6th Dynasties (Saghieh 1983: 104–6). The intensity of Old Kingdom contact with Byblos may imply some Egyptian administrative control or alliance, securing this port for overland trade with Syria, Mesopotamia, and Afghanistan (e.g. lapis lazuli) (Akkermans and Schwartz 2003: 240). For example, Khafre and Pepy I's names are attested on items further inland at Ebla, while Menkaure is identified with artefacts from Cyprus (Matthiae in Oren 1997: 414).

FIRST INTERMEDIATE PERIOD

Intermediate Bronze Age

The Intermediate Bronze Age is marked by political decentralization in Egypt, dramatic de-urbanization in Palestine, a reappearance of seasonal settlements in North Sinai and the Negev, and somewhat impoverished settlements in Syria (Mumford 2006a: 57). Although few Egyptian artefacts appear in Palestine, Egyptian Medium Ware vessels and Palestinian 'caliciform' pottery occur at campsites across North Sinai (Oren in Stern 1993: 1388), which suggests some late Old Kingdom overland interactions with southern Palestine. Around this time, a mid-6th Dynasty official, Weni, claims to have led five military campaigns against Asiatic sand-dwellers somewhere in Sinai or Palestine (Simpson 2003: 402). Although Egypt maintained relations with Syria until the end of the 6th Dynasty, First Intermediate Period Egypt yields little evidence for trade, while later propagandistic texts (Ipuwer, Neferty, and

Merikare) harken back to Asiatic incursions, a cessation of trade with Byblos, and other problems.

MIDDLE KINGDOM

Middle Bronze Age IIA

MB IIA experiences the rebirth of urbanization in Palestine and a reunified Middle Kingdom state. Montuhotep II (11th Dynasty) claims he pacified hostile Asiatics and re-established trade; late 11th-Dynasty inscriptions reveal activity in Qedem (Syria), a siege of an Asiatic fort, a campaign against the Asiatics of Djaty, and a mission to obtain cedar from Lebanon (Callender in Shaw 2000: 152). In the 12th Dynasty, the Story of Sinuhe describes his flight to Syria-Palestine and encounters with Egyptian messengers, Egyptian fugitives(?), and people conversant in Egyptian, but omits mention of cities (Simpson 2003: 55); the Satire of Trades emphasizes the dangers of lions and Asiatics to Egyptian messengers travelling through Palestine. In another account, Amenemhat II sends troops in ten ships to Khentiu-she, on the Lebanese coast, to obtain raw materials, booty, and captives (Redford 1992: 78). In Senwosret III's reign, an Egyptian officer, Khusobek, claims to have killed an Asiatic warrior in an attack against Sekmem (Shechem?) (Bárta 2003: 127), while a commander of troops, under Amenemhet III, is described as 'opening the land of the Asiatic'.

The Egyptian execration texts list potential enemy towns, including Shechem, Ashkelon, Jerusalem, and Byblos, while inscriptions from Mit Rahina allude to treaties between Egypt and some Levantine city-states (Redford 1992: 87–93). In contrast, peaceful relations are evident with Byblos: the royal cemetery and temple have Egyptian-style architecture, statuary, stone vessels, and other artefacts with private and royal inscriptions (Amenemhet III–IV); nine royal tombs display Egyptian-style scenes, hieroglyphic texts, and titles ('count' and 'hereditary prince'), with evidence for the worship of Egyptian and Canaanite deities (Bárta 2003: 157). Ugarit has yielded probable Egyptian royal gifts: a statue of a daughter of Amenemhet II and two sphinxes of Amenemhet III (Yon 2006: 16).

Earlier theories for a Middle Kingdom empire in Palestine remain unfounded, especially since most 12th Dynasty statuary originates from later contexts. The otherwise abundant Middle Kingdom texts lack evidence for any imperial administration in Palestine, but recent investigations reveal more significant trade relations between Egypt and Palestine (Ilan in Levy 1995: 308); sites such as Tell Ifshar and Ashkelon are producing Egyptian-style pottery, calcite and faience vessels, scarabs, and jewellery (Cohen 2002: 83, 129; Marcus et al. 2008: 203). Some Cypro-Egyptian relations are also attested by pottery exchanged between both regions (Mumford 2001b: 360).

SECOND INTERMEDIATE PERIOD

Middle Bronze Age IIB

MB IIB experiences a continued growth in the number and size of settlements in Palestine, and prosperity in Syria; this coincides with the 13th Dynasty, and the 14th and 16th

Dynasties, which develop into the Hyksos and Theban kingdoms, respectively (Redford in Oren 1997). Although Egypt grows weaker politically, it maintains relations with Syria: Byblos contains items bearing the names of Amenemhet V, Sehetepib(en)re, and Neferhotep I. Neferhotep appears in a hieroglyphic text from a tomb stele of Prince Yantin, who also adopts an Egyptian-style sarcophagus. Jewellery from a palace at Ebla bears the name of Shetepibre (Matthiae in Oren 1997: 398), while Amenemhet V is cited on an artefact from Jericho. These strong links with Egypt are paralleled by a growing Levantine presence in the northeast delta: during the 13th Dynasty, Canaanite pottery increases from 20 per cent to 40 per cent at Avaris (Bietak 1996: 49). Further Asiatic influence occurs in copper-working, weaponry, contracted burials, associated donkey burials, and a seal of a deputy treasurer called Aamu ('the Asiatic'); Avaris has some Levantine-style temples, possibly dedicated to Baal-Zaphon; nearby Tell el-Yahudiyeh even adopts a Canaanite-style rampart fortification.

Middle Bronze Age IIC

MB IIC spans the Hyksos and Theban kingdoms of the 15th and 17th Dynasties, respectively, during which Hyksos Egypt exports jewellery, scarabs, and calcite vessels to the Levant. Some Canaanite officials apply Egyptian-style seals on amphorae: one Canaanite amphora sent to Avaris bore a hieroglyphic seal with an Egyptian title ('mayor') and Semitic name (*Shimw*). Residue analysis indicates the exportation of olive oil, probably wine, and possibly wheat to Egypt. Small perfume juglets ('Yahudiyeh' Ware) apparently originated in northern Palestine, but soon became manufactured throughout Syria-Palestine (e.g. Afula), Cyprus, and Egypt (Tell el-Dab'a), displaying local variants and trade between these regions (Bietak 1996: 55–63). The Kamose Stelae also describe the diversity of Levantine trade in a list of booty from Avaris' harbor: lapis lazuli, turquoise, silver, battle axes, oils, fats, honey, cedar, and precious woods (Redford in Oren 1997: 13–15). Cypriot contact with Avaris is attested by White Painted V–VI, Proto White Slip, White Slip I (?), and Bichrome pottery. Although scholars originally theorized that the Hyksos Empire encompassed the Levant, the evidence suggests only commercial and political alliances. King Ahmose ends this Asiatic domination, defeating the Hyksos at Avaris and pursuing them across North Sinai to Sharuhen (Tell el-'Ajjul?), which he captured after three years.

New Kingdom

Late Bronze Age IA

LB IA spans the early 18th Dynasty, during which Egypt began establishing its Levantine empire. Egypt applies periodic military force to pacify and extort annual tribute from city-states: various inscriptions allude to Ahmose fighting the Fenkhu in Syria, and capturing Asiatics and oxen. Redford (1992: 149) identifies a fragmentary text from Karnak Temple with Amenhotep I attacking Syria and retrieving unguents and other things from Qedem, Tunip, and elsewhere. A later text describes Thutmose I as having reached the Euphrates and erected a stele (Redford 2003: 74). Although official accounts assert that he faced no resistance, and collected cedar, copper, and gifts, several officers' biographies mention fighting, booty, and prisoners; Ahmose Pen-Nekhbet also describes fighting the Shasu-Bedouin for Thutmose II. During Hatshepsut's reign, the Speos Artemidos and other inscriptions allude to military activity in Syria-Palestine: this may represent an 'inspection tour' collecting tribute and cedar (Redford in Oren 1997: 16). Regarding selected Levantine sites and artefacts,[1] Egyptian and Egyptian-style items form 22 per cent, 10 per cent, and 7 per cent of non-pottery artefacts within mortuary, habitation, and cultic contexts, respectively (Mumford 2006b: 203): mainly ceramic, stone, and faience containers, clay sealings, jewellery (including scarab seals), toiletries, game pieces (Senet), and figurines. Aside from only two items bearing Thutmose I's name in Syria, the names of all other early 18th-Dynasty rulers appear on items throughout Palestine. Hence, in addition to trade, Egypt now begins extorting annual tribute and directly retrieving materials, products, livestock, and captives via intimidation and increasing raids.

Late Bronze Age IB

In Year 22, Thutmose III besieges Megiddo and captures many rulers from a coalition of 330 Levantine city-states led by the ruler of Kadesh. He accepts new oaths of allegiance, builds a fort in the Levant, and imposes more direct military control over Syria-Palestine. He consolidates the northern empire through sixteen further expeditions: inspection tours, tribute collection, and fighting in West Syria and Naharin (Mitanni) (Redford in Cline and O'Connor 2006: 332). Like Thutmose I, he reaches the Euphrates, where he places another stele, hunts elephants, and records exotic flora. His son, Amenhotep II, faces increasing rebellions in Syria (e.g. Takhsi, Ugarit, and Qatna) and Palestine (e.g. Shamash-Edom) (der Manuelian 1987). The next ruler, Thutmose IV, is notable for establishing peace and for a marriage alliance with Mitanni to counteract the expanding Hittite Empire (Anatolia). Despite this alliance, Thutmose IV needs to suppress rebellious Syrian vassals and establishes a fort nearby (Bryan 1991: 339–47); Egypt's Levantine empire is subdivided into provinces: Canaan (Palestine), Upe (Damscus to Beka Valley), and Amurru (West Syria), with headquarter cities at Gaza, Kumudi, and Ugarit (later Sumur); each regional headquarters receives a fort and storehouse with a commander and garrison (Redford 1992: 206–7).

During LB IB, Egyptian-style artefacts rise to 40 per cent in Levantine cemeteries, increase to 13 per cent in temples, and fall to 9 per cent in occupation contexts (Mumford 2006b: 203); a corresponding rise occurs in the quantities and dispersal of Egyptian royal name items (mostly scarabs). These Egyptian imports and local copies include ceramic, stone, faience, and glass containers, clay sealings, jewellery, toiletries, Senet pieces, figurines, utensils, axes, and a chariot fitting. Most of the items indicate luxury trade goods with a few products for domestic usage.

Late Bronze Age IIA

LB IIA begins with Amenhotep III, who publicizes his marriage to a Mitannian princess on commemorative scarabs sent to vassals and kingdoms in the eastern Mediterranean

---

[1] This writer conducted a study (Mumford 1998; 2006b; 2007) quantifying and assessing Egyptian and Egyptian-style artefacts from occupation, cultic, and mortuary contexts at a sample of twenty-four Late Bronze Age through early Persian-period Levantine sites.

(Weinstein 1998: 231–3). During this period, the Amarna letters, which span the reigns of Amenhotep III to Tutankhamun, provide a major source on relations between Egypt, its northern vassals, and Near Eastern kingdoms. The letters consist of clay tablets in Akkadian cuneiform and reveal conflict between Akhenaten's northernmost vassals. Despite frequent pleas to Akhenaten for aid, his western Syrian vassals of Sumur, Tunip, and Byblos are attacked and captured by another vassal: Amurru (Moran 1992: 139–223). Such neglect encourages Kadesh, a major vassal state straddling a strategic commercial route between Mesopotamia and the Mediterranean, to defect to the Hittite Empire, evading an apparent attempt to regain it in Year 15 (Schulman 1988: 56). Tutankhamun sends an army to resume control over Amurru (Davies 1995: 31–8), but its outcome is unclear and relations with Hatti deteriorate during his successor's reign: the Hittite Annals record that Šuppiluliumas attacked Egypt's northern frontier in retaliation for the alleged murder of a Hittite prince who had been sent to Egypt to marry a widowed Egyptian queen (Ankhesenamun?) (Goetze in Pritchard 1969: 319, 395).

At LB IIA sites, Egyptian artefacts fall sharply to 25 per cent and 7 per cent in mortuary and occupation contexts, but increase to 27 per cent in cultic settings (Mumford 2006b: 190, 203); royal name items also decline in quantity through this period. This trend argues for a reduction in Egyptian influence in everyday life in Canaan, while the rise in cultic contexts might imply the retention of increasingly valued votives (heirlooms?). On the other hand, the broad categories of Egyptianizing artefacts noted in LB IA–B continue, while some new types appear: a headrest, different figurines, and moulds for making Egyptian-type beads and amulets (Beth Shean and Tell el-'Ajjul) (Mumford 1997: 717). These sporadic moulds imply some efforts to supplement the decreasing (albeit still valued) imported Egyptian jewellery with cheaper local imitations.

Late Bronze Age IIB

LB IIB encompasses the 19th Dynasty and an intensification of Egyptian control and presence in the Levant. Inscriptions from Karnak Temple and elsewhere record Ramesses I and his co-regent, Sety I, repressing Shasu-Bedouin uprisings in Sinai-Palestine. Sety I also rescued Egyptian garrisons at Beth Shean and Rehab from attacks by Hamath, Pella, and the 'apiru (Kitchen 1993: 2, 93). The Hittite seizure of Cyprus and its copper mines probably encourages Sety I to expand copper mining in the Eastern Desert, Sinai, and southern Negev to maintain Egypt's war machine (see Hikade 1998). He briefly regained Kadesh in Years 5/6, erecting commemorative stelae at Kadesh, Tyre, Tell el-Shihab, and Beth Shean (Murnane 1990: 53). Hatti's reabsorption of Amurru and Kadesh prompted Ramesses II's Years 4–5 campaigns to retake them (Kitchen 1982: 51–62). Despite claims of victory, his failure to secure Kadesh generates rebellions throughout Palestine and emerging polities in 'Seir'/Edom and 'Moab' in Transjordan (Kitchen 1992: 26–9). He re-establishes control in Years 6/7, 8/9, and 10. By Year 21, a rising Assyrian threat encourages Hattusilis III to make peace with Ramesses II, who marries two Hittite princesses to cement relations with Hatti. Although peace and commerce continued between Hatti and Egypt, Merenptah needs to suppress rebellions in Palestine in Year 5, when 'Israel' is first listed amongst Egypt's enemies.

During LB IIB, but including the Late Bronze through to the end of Iron IA, a broad range of Egyptian gifts, payments, merchandise, possessions, livestock, personnel, and other influences reach Egyptian garrisons, merchants, and other residents in Canaan and Cyprus (see Jacobsson 1994); this includes the rulers, elite, and general populace amongst Egypt's Canaanite vassals and adjacent kingdoms. Texts from Amarna, Ugarit, Hattusas, and elsewhere cite Egyptian and Kushite residents, servants, traders, messengers, soldiers, and others serving and dwelling throughout Syria-Palestine (e.g. Ugarit) and sometimes mention marriages with Asiatics (Mumford 1998: 63–349). After being raised in pharaoh's household (*kap*) and adopting Egyptian language, dress, and customs, many Canaanite princes are returned to inherit and govern their city-states, thereby introducing a hybrid Egypto-Levantine influence into the local leadership and associated population.

At LB IIB sites, Egyptian and Egyptian-style artefacts remain high (25%) in mortuary assemblages, and rise to 13 per cent and 32 per cent in occupation and cultic contexts (Mumford 2006b: 190, 203). Egyptian-style items now display the greatest quantity and variety of types (Higginbotham 2000: 145–262). This continuity and increase probably reflect the intensification of Ramesside garrisons in Canaan, especially under Sety I and Ramesses II (Killebrew, Goldberg, and Rosen 2006: 51–83). Likewise royal name items increase in the early 19th Dynasty, but decline noticeably in the remainder of this period. Egyptian exports include raw materials ('ebony' logs, blue frit pigment), pottery jars and other containers for provisions (e.g. Nile molluscs (?), catfish, and grain), cultic items (e.g. female figurines and cobras), and luxury items (e.g. linen textiles, furniture, Senet boards, cosmetic kits, jewellery, and wine drinking sets). Such things were conveyed via state, temple, and private shipping, overland traffic, and cross-cultural correspondence (Mumford 2006b: 170). The presence of Egyptian and other types of weights emphasize the multicultural commerce between Canaan and its neighbours. The increasing local production of Egyptian domestic pottery and other items in LB IIB–Iron IA attests to both a greater influx of Egyptians and a Canaanite desire for cheaper Egyptian-style products.

Ramesside garrisons are particularly evident through Egyptian forts and housing at such sites as Beth Shean, Deir el-Balah (Fig. 5.1), Tel Mor (Barako 2007), Ashkelon (Stager 2008: 1580), Tel Aphek (Gadot and Yadin 2009), and Tell es-Saidiyeh (Tubb 1998: 90); these sites have yielded Egyptian-style chariot fittings, weaponry (mace-heads, *khepesh* swords, axe-heads), and other utensils. Some sites produced hieroglyphs on stone gateways, doorways, statuary, stelae, and various artefacts (e.g. jewellery); an Egyptian cursive script (hieratic) is also used by the imperial administration, for example on inscribed pottery vessels, jar sealings, a large stamp seal (of Ptah), and ostraca. Several pharaohs add commemorative monuments, especially Ramesses II, who is attested on stone blocks (Gaza), lintels (Jaffa, Byblos), and stelae from Beth Shean, Sheikh Said, Tyre, 'Adlun, Nahr el-Kelb, Byblos, and Keswé near Damascus (Mumford 2006b: 185). In Levels VIII–VI at Beth Shean (Fig. 5.2), Egyptian administrative and residential buildings are remodelled and contain Egyptian-style components: central columned halls, 'T-shaped' doorways, door jambs with hieroglyphic inscriptions, and stelae (James and McGovern 1993: 4). A reassessment of the fort at Deir el-Balah demonstrates that its adjacent 'reservoir' actually functioned as a quarry for mud bricks (Killebrew, Goldberg, and Rosen 2006: 97).

Egyptian influence also affects temples at garrison sites: the Level VII temple at Beth Shean has similarities to Egyptian shrines at el-Amarna and Deir el-Medineh, but is a hybrid Egypto-Levantine shrine. Alongside Levantine votives, it contains numerous Egyptian and Egyptian-style artefacts, including stelae reused in the Iron IA temple (James and McGovern 1993: 25); a similar hybrid temple and votives occur in Level VI at Lachish (Fig. 5.3), while

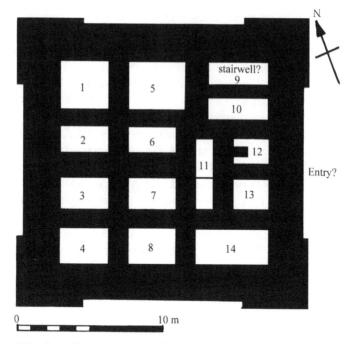

FIG. 5.1 New Kingdom fort at Deir el-Balah (adapted from Dothan 1982: 758)

elsewhere purely Levantine temples, such as Shrines F and H at Hazor, have produced fewer Egyptianizing items (Yadin 1975: 67, 95).

The garrison burials at Deir el-Balah, Tell el-Farah (S), and Beth Shean have produced locally made, Egyptian-derived terracotta anthropoid coffins (Fig. 5.4), local 'grotesque' variants, and sporadic funerary figurines (shawabtis). In addition, Deir el-Balah has yielded four mortuary stelae dedicated to Osiris (Fig. 5.5), while Tell es-Saidiyeh has evidence for mummification by Egyptian residents, or Canaanites emulating Egyptian elite burial practices: one adult's rib cage had been cut (possibly to remove internal organs); several bodies bore linen wrappings (preserved via impressions); a black resin ('bitumen') coating covered other bodies (Tubb 1998: 90).

Iron Age IA

Iron IA spans the early 20th Dynasty and the decline of Egypt's Levantine empire, during which Sea Peoples' coastal raids, and overland migrations by displaced populations, destroyed or transformed many eastern Mediterranean polities. Ramesses III claims victories in Palestine and the delta (Peden 1994a: 215), and later dispatches troops against hostile Bedouin in Seir and Edom. In a summation of his reign, the Great Harris Papyrus describes the temples of Amun (Thebes), Re (Heliopolis), and Ptah (Memphis) as owning estates in Syria-Palestine, including ships to retrieve annual revenues (Wilson in Pritchard 1969: 260). His successor, Ramesses IV, reportedly received tribute, cedar, and slaves from the Levant,

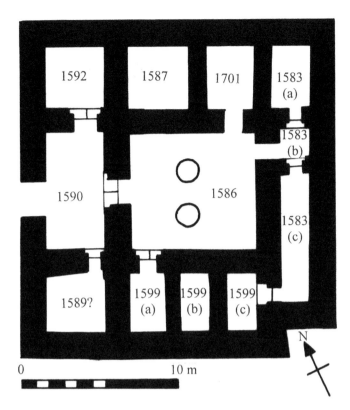

FIG. 5.2 LB IIB House 1500 at Beth Shean (adapted from James 1966: fig. 77)

and may have subjugated 'Asiatics' (Peden 1994b: 87, 93, 141). Egypt retains some control over Canaan as late as Ramesses VI, whose name occurs on a ring from Deir el-Balah, a bronze statue base at Megiddo, and possibly a scarab from Alalakh (Mumford 2006b: 185). Hence, this is a turbulent period in which Egypt exerts diminishing control and influence over its vassal states as far north as Beth Shean.

Egypt's presence and influence within the Levant apparently peaks during the Ramesside period, which is attested by both locally made Egyptian pottery and other artefacts and influences; non-pottery items from selected Iron IA sites reveal a similar rise in Egyptian-style influence in mortuary assemblages (35%) and occupation contexts (17%), with a drop to 26 per cent in cultic settings (Mumford 2006b: 203). These items contain a broad range of pottery, faience, stone, and metal containers, jar sealings, utensils, cosmetic kits, jewellery, Senet pieces, and cobra figurines. At Egypt's northern base at Beth Shean, Egypto-Levantine-style temples and adjacent houses are rebuilt in Stratum VI, but incorporate many earlier (i.e. Sety I and Ramesses II) Egyptian-style architectural pieces: column bases, papyrus capitals, cornice fragments, door jambs, lintels, and stelae. A statue of Ramesses III, a lintel of one of his officers, and other architectural fittings were reused in the Stratum V temple, but demonstrate the presence of an Iron IA Egyptian garrison here (Mazar in Stern 1993: 217). Likewise, Lachish yielded a bronze gate plaque of Ramesses III, confirming his control over another key Canaanite town (Ussishkin in Stern 1993: 904). The

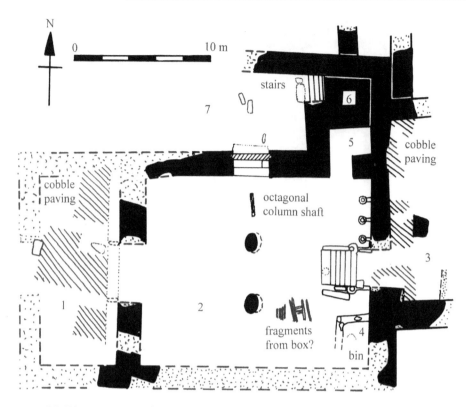

FIG. 5.3 LB IIB Egyptian-style acropolis temple at Lachish Level VI (adapted from Stern 1993: 901)

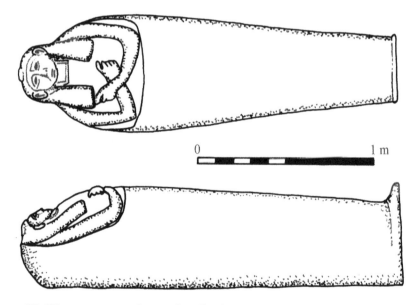

FIG. 5.4 LB IIB terracotta anthropoid coffin from Tomb 114 at Deir el-Balah (adapted from Dothan 1979: figs 8, 11)

FIG. 5.5 39cm-high kurkar stele of Amunemwia before Osiris (adapted from Ventura 1987: pl. 8A)

cemeteries at both Beth Shean and Lachish also contained Egyptian-style ceramic anthropoid coffins and some shawabtis. However, following Ramesses III, a definite decline affects the subsequent 20th-Dynasty royal name items and influence, which become restricted mostly within Egypt's shrinking northern empire (Mumford 2006b: 190).

Late New Kingdom to Third Intermediate period

Iron Age IB

The late New Kingdom through Third Intermediate period marks a virtual 'Dark Age' regarding textual sources on Egypto-Levantine relations. In early Iron IB, following the collapse of

Egypt's Levantine empire, Ramesses VIII–X are attested on royal name items from Gezer, Tell Farah (S), Beth Shemesh, and Tell Masos (Mumford 2007: 262), implying minimal Egyptian state-level contact with the eastern periphery of Philistia and southern Judea (Stager in Levy 1995: 336, fig. 2). Likewise, no evidence exists for any Egyptian campaigns into this region, despite Psusennes I's epithet: 'seizer of cities' (Redford 1992: 313). The fictitious Tale of Wenamun, composed in the late 20th Dynasty, describes Egyptian emissaries sailing to Byblos under Ramesses X(?)–XI to obtain cedar for the sacred barque of Amun (Wente in Simpson 2003: 116). This tale alludes to a Tjekker (Sikil) coastal settlement at Dor (northern Palestine), stressing Egypt's loss of prestige, economic decline, and reliance on foreign shipping. It indicates Egypt's diminished contact with Dor, Tyre, and Byblos, and describes Egypt sending royal gifts and payments of gold, silver, linen, papyrus rolls, ropes, cowhides, lentils, and fish to Byblos. It mentions an Egyptian butler and singer residing here; and a townsperson in Cyprus is described as knowing the Egyptian language. In addition, an Assyrian text notes that King Assurbelkala received an Egyptian gift of a crocodile and monkey (Kitchen 1986: 252, 267), demonstrating significant long-distance diplomacy by post-imperial Egypt.

The archaeological record also reveals quantitative shifts and continuity in Egypto-Levantine contact, albeit with a minimal presence in Philistia. Egyptian-style artefacts decrease noticeably in mortuary, occupation, and cultic contexts (Mumford 2007: 250, 273–7). However, these items now appear in broader social contexts than before, and include pottery, seal impressions, jewellery, luxury containers, figurines, weights, and game boards. The presence of imported Egyptian pottery at Dor and Tell Qasile demonstrate significant maritime commerce between Egypt and northern Palestine.

Iron Age IIA

Iron IIA spans the biblical period of Israel's emergence and domination over Philistia, Edom, Moab, Ammon, and Damascus. Various anachronistic biblical passages mention Egypt selling horses and chariots to Israel, Kushite and Egyptian retainers residing here, a campaign against Gezer, the marriage of an Egyptian princess to Solomon, and Egypt granting asylum to political refugees (e.g. Hadad of Edom and Jeroboam) (Mumford 2007: 239). Kitchen (1986: 280) argues that a scene of Siamun executing a captive holding a double axe may reflect an actual Egyptian campaign against Gezer (?); the best evidence for such activity, however, dates to Sheshonq I (biblical Shishak), who is attested as attacking this region (c.925 BC) in biblical accounts, the Karnak Temple List, Egyptian private texts (vague references), and a stele fragment from Megiddo (Kitchen 1986: 432–47). Although the scope and details of his campaign remain elusive, 1 Kgs. (14: 25–7) alleges that Shishak received temple and palace tribute from Jerusalem. Only these pharaohs appear on royal name items in Iron IIA Palestine: Siamun is cited on a scarab at Tell Farah (S), while Sheshonq I is mentioned on the Megiddo stele and via a statue from Byblos (Mumford 2007: 251). Egyptian exports and local/Phoenician copies also decrease markedly in Levantine occupation, cultic, and mortuary contexts: pottery, jewellery, luxury goods, weights, a game board, and Nile fish.

Iron Age IIB

In conjunction with Assyria's western expansion in Iron IIB, Egypt alters its attitude towards its Levantine neighbours: an oil jar of Osorkon II from the palace of Omri and

Ahab at Samaria suggests Egyptian diplomatic relations with Israel (Kitchen 1986: 324). The Assyrian Monolith Inscription shows that Egypt bolsters this relationship by contributing 1000 troops to a Levantine coalition that defeats Shalmaneser III's army at Qarqar *c*.853 BC. However, Shalmaneser III later receives exotic animals as tribute from Musri (Egypt) (Oppenheim in Pritchard 1969: 281, 610). In the following centuries, Assyria dominates Palestine (see Oppenheim in Pritchard 1969: 282–6) and Tiglath-pileser III invades the Levantine coast and establishes a 'warden' at Egypt's eastern frontier by 732 BC. Another Assyrian inscription describes Egypt granting asylum to Hanno, the ruler of Gaza. 2 Kgs. (17: 1–6) mentions King Hoshea of Israel requesting aid from 'So, King of Egypt' (Osorkon IV?), which galvanizes Shalmaneser V into besieging Samaria (725–720 BC); the Annals of Sargon II record him capturing Samaria (720 BC), deporting the population to Assyria, and defeating an Egyptian army. The Assur Prism lists Egypt as sending twelve large horses as a gift to Sargon II.

Egyptian-style artefacts decrease through this period, albeit with fluctuating quantities, in occupation and mortuary contexts (7–10%); an early Iron IIB shrine at Qasile yields few votive offerings, while a late Iron IIB Phoenician shrine at Sarepta held many Egyptian-style items (34%) (Mumford 2007: 262). All of these artefacts display the same broad categories as before, but contain greater diversity within each grouping. This overall decline in Egyptian exports and influence is also matched by relatively few Egyptian royal name items: a vase, scarab, and some statuary of Osorkon I–II at Samaria, Byblos, and in Cyprus.

KUSHITE–SAITE PERIOD

Iron Age IIC

Various inscriptions detail Assyria's expansion into Palestine and Egypt in Iron IIC (see Oppenheim in Pritchard 1969: 285–7). The Nimrud Prism ascribes to Sargon II the reopening of the 'sealed *karum*' (716 BC) and encouraging trade between Egypt, the Levant, and Assyria. The *karum* is best identified with a fortified settlement at Tell er-Ruqueish in southern Palestine (Oren in Stern 1993: 1293). The Annals of Sargon II and Prism A also relate that a Kushite ruler (Shabako?) initially cooperated with Sargon by extraditing a political fugitive: Yamani of Ashdod. In contrast, later biblical and Assyrian texts mention unnamed Kushite rulers (Shabitqu and Taharqa) allying themselves with Judah to fight Assyria in 701 BC (Eltekeh) and 681(?) BC (2 Kgs. 18: 13–37). From 616–605 BC, various Assyrian, Babylonian, and biblical texts describe Egypt assisting Assyria against the Babylonians, including defeating a Judean attempt to thwart Egypt at Megiddo and the eventual Babylonian defeat of the Assyrian and Egyptian armies at Carchemish and Hamath in 605 BC (Grayson 1975: 95–99; 2 Kgs. 23: 29–35).

This overall period and region witness a further decline in Egyptian-style artefacts and influence, albeit still retaining all the main categories seen in Iron IB–IIB (Mumford 2007: 277). Eight per cent of the tombs and graves from several sites yield Egyptian-style items amounting to 14 per cent of the mortuary assemblage. In contrast, Egyptianizing items composed only 3 per cent of selected occupation assemblages, while Egyptian-style votives form 5 per cent of the cultic offerings at three shrines. Other studies, however, reveal a notable presence in Egyptian-style pottery, artefacts, and influence in the 7th-century BC at sites such as Ashkelon and Ekron (Stern 2001: 233). For instance, Ekron yielded a cache of New Kingdom heirlooms in an Iron IIC context. The appearance of Egyptian hieratic script on scarabs, weights, and ostraca, including *hin*-grain measures at some Judean fortresses, parallel the close military and diplomatic relations between Egypt and Judah during this period (Stern 2001: 233–5). A slight increase also occurs in the quantity and dispersal of Egyptian royal name items throughout the Levant: Menkare, Shabako, Taharqa, Psamtek I, and Necho II (Mumford 2007: 262).

Babylonian period

Following his 605 BC victories, Nebuchadnezzar II consolidates Babylonia's control over Syria-Palestine. King Adon of Philistia sends a message to Egypt asking for aid (Porten 1981: 36), but his plea remained unanswered. Egypt defeats a Babylonian attack in 601 BC (Grayson 1975: 101); traces of this or another conflict may materialize in the early destruction debris at Tel Qedwa in northwest Sinai (Redford 1998: 52). Despite the 597 BC Babylonian capture of Jerusalem (Grayson 1975: 102), the Judeans continue sending ambassadors to Egypt to request military assistance (Ezek. 17: 11–17); an Egyptian response may be reflected via Papyrus Rylands IX, which records Psamtek II leading an undefined mission to Palestine in 591/590 BC. Lachish Ostracon III confirms the dispatch of a Judean military delegation to Egypt c.589 BC (Albright in Pritchard 1969: 321), which preceded Nebuchadnezzar II's siege and destruction of Jerusalem in 589–586 BC; Jer. 37: 5–11 notes an aborted Egyptian attempt (by Apries) to relieve the Babylonian siege. After the Babylonian sack of Jerusalem many Judeans flee to Egypt (Jer. 43: 5–13), which is supported by an influx of locally made Judean artefacts in the northeast delta (Holladay 2004: 405). At some point between 586 and 570 BC, Apries may have retaliated by sending an Egyptian army against Sidon, and a fleet against Tyre (Herodotus 2.160–6). Nebuchadnezzar II apparently fails to capture Egypt in 568/567 BC, while Herodotus (2.182) attributes Amasis with launching a subsequent successful naval attack against Cyprus. The Babylonian period also experiences a further decrease in Egyptian-style items, which still represent typical luxury products (Mumford 2007: 272). Ezek. 27: 2–15 describes other Egyptian exports as including fine linen for sail cloth (used especially by Tyre), ebony, and possibly ivory, while Jer. 38: 7 mentions a Kushite servant at the Judean court around this time. The discovery of a few royal name items of Amasis (at Sidon) and Psamtek III (at Beth Shemesh) imply continued Egyptian contact with parts of the Levant.

LATE PERIOD

Persian period

Persia supplants the Babylonian Empire in 539 BC and occupies and governs Egypt as a Persian province (satrapy) from 525–404 BC and 343–332 BC (see Ray 1988). Egypt regains its independence from 404 BC to 343 BC (Lloyd 1994), despite periodic Persian attacks (374/373 BC and 351 BC), and participates in or finances several counterattacks: in 381 BC,

Hakoris sends money, grain, and 50 fifty triremes to assist Evagoras of Cyprus against Persia. In 359 BC, Teos enters Palestine with Egyptian and Spartan troops, and 200 Athenian triremes, but is deposed en route by Nectanebo II, who aborts the campaign. In 346 BC, Nectanebo II dispatches 4000 mercenaries to Sidon. Despite such proactive Egyptian tactics, however, Persia manages to retake Egypt in 343 BC, holding it until Alexander the Great defeats Persia in 332 BC (Lloyd 1994).

Many Egyptian imports, and local/Phoenician imitations, appear throughout Syria-Palestine, including architecture (e.g. an Egyptian-style shrine at 'Amrit: Fig. 5.6), anthropoid sarcophagi (Gaza and mostly in Phoenicia), stelae with Egyptian deities and iconography (Byblos), pottery imitating stone alabastra (Palestine), Bes jars, figurines and amulets, containers of various materials, jewellery, seal impressions, toiletries (mirrors and kohl tubes), utensils (bronze dippers), Egyptian weight units, and some Egyptian coins (4th century BC) (Stern 1982: Index). Hybrid Egyptian and other architectural styles appear as far away as the Persian palace at Persepolis (Iran); the completion of Necho II's canal between the Nile and the Red Sea also enabled bulk shipping directly between Egypt and Persia. Hence, despite a visible decline in Egyptian-type items during the preceding Iron Age, the Persian Empire imposed peace and fostered widespread cross-cultural interactions throughout its empire via trade, migrant labour, art, architecture, language, literature, and codifying local laws.

0   5 m
(approximate scale)

FIG. 5.6 Phoenician/Egyptianizing Persian-period shrine at 'Amrit, Syria (adapted from Stern 1982: fig. 77)

SUGGESTED READING

Bietak, M. (2007). Egypt and the Levant. In T. A. H. Wilkinson (ed.), *The Egyptian World*. London: Routledge, 417–48.

Cohen, S. L. (2002). *Canaanites, Chronologies, and Connections: The Relationships of Middle Bronze IIA Canaan to Middle Kingdom Egypt*. Winona Lake, Ind.: Eisenbrauns.

Higginbotham, C. R. (2000). *Egyptianization and Elite Emulation in Ramesside Palestine: Governance and Accommodation on the Imperial Periphery*. Leiden: Brill.

Killebrew, A. E. (2005). *Biblical Peoples and Ethnicity: An Archaeological Study of Egyptians, Canaanites, Philistines, and Early Israel 1300–1100 B.C.E.* Atlanta, Ga.: Society of Biblical Literature.

Mark, S. (1997). *From Egypt to Mesopotamia: A Study of Predynastic Trade Routes*. College Station: Texas A&M University Press.

Morris, E. F. (2005). *The Architecture of Imperialism: Military Bases and the Evolution of Foreign Policy in Egypt's New Kingdom*. Brill: Leiden.

Redford, D. B. (2003). *The Wars in Syria and Palestine of Thutmose III*. Leiden: Brill.

Sowada, K. N. (2009). *Egypt in the Eastern Mediterranean during the Old Kingdom: An Archaeological Perspective*. Fribourg: Academic Press/Göttingen: Vandenhoeck & Ruprecht.

Spalinger, A. J. (2005). *War in Ancient Egypt: The New Kingdom*. Malden, Mass.: Blackwell.

Winnicki, J. K. (2009). *Late Egypt and Her Neighbours: Foreign Populations in Egypt in the First Millennium BC*, trans. Dorota Dzierzbicka. Warsaw: Warsaw University, Institute of Archaeology.

REFERENCES

Adams, R. B. (2003). External influences at Faynan during the Early Bronze Age: a re-analysis of Building I at Barqa el-Hetiye, Jordan. *Palestine Exploration Quarterly* 135: 6–21.

Akkermans, P. M. M. G., and G. M. Schwartz (2003). *The Archaeology of Syria: From Complex Hunter-Gatherers to Early Urban Societies (c.16,000–300 BC)*. Cambridge: Cambridge University Press.

Barako, T. J. (2007). *Tel Mor: The Moshe Dothan Excavations, 1959–1960*. Jerusalem: Israel Antiquities Authority.

Bárta, M. (2003). *Sinuhe, the Bible and the Patriarchs*, trans. R. Landgráfová. Prague: Set Out.

Bietak, M. (1996). *Avaris: The Capital of the Hyksos—Recent Excavations at Tell el-Daba*. London: British Museum Press.

Braun, E. (2009). South Levantine Early Bronze Age chronological correlations with Egypt in light of the Narmer Serekhs from Tel Erani and Arad: new interpretations. *British Museum Studies in Ancient Egypt and Sudan* 13: 25–48.

Bryan, B. M. (1991). *The Reign of Thutmose IV*. Baltimore, Md.: Johns Hopkins University Press.

Cline, E. H., and D. B. O'Connor (eds) (2006). *Thutmose III: A New Biography*. Ann Arbor: University of Michigan Press.

Cohen, S. L. (2002). *Canaanites, Chronologies, and Connections: The Relationships of Middle Bronze IIA Canaan to Middle Kingdom Egypt*. Winona Lake, Ind.: Eisenbrauns.

Davies, B. (trans.) (1995). *Egyptian Historical Records of the Later Eighteenth Dynasty, Fascicle VI*. Warminster: Aris & Phillips.

der Manuelian, P. (1987). *Studies in the Reign of Amenophis II*. Hildesheim: Gerstenberg.

Dothan, T. (1979). *Excavations at the Cemetery of Deir El-Balah*. Jerusalem: Institute of Archaeology, Hebrew University of Jerusalem.

—— (1982). Lost outpost of the Egyptian Empire. *National Geographic* 162: 739–69.

Ehrich, R. W. (ed.) (1992). *Chronologies in Old World Archaeology*, 3rd edn (2 vols). Chicago: University of Chicago Press.

Gadot, Y., and E. Yadin (2009). *Aphek-Antipatris II: The Remains on the Necropolis—The Moshe Kochavi and Pirhiya Beck Excavations*. Tel Aviv: Institute of Archaeology, Tel Aviv University.

Grayson, A. K. (1975). *Assyrian and Babylonian Chronicles*. Locust Valley, NY: Augustin.

Harrison, T. J. (1993). Economics with an entrepreneurial spirit: Early Bronze trade with Late Predynastic Egypt. *Biblical Archaeologist* 56: 81–93.

Higginbotham, C. R. (2000). *Egyptianization and Elite Emulation in Ramesside Palestine: Governance and Accommodation on the Imperial Periphery*. Leiden: Brill.

Hikade, T. (1998). Economic aspects of the New Kingdom: the expeditions to the copper mines of the Sinai. *Bulletin of the Australian Centre for Egyptology* 9: 43–52.

Holladay, J. S., Jr. (2004). Judaeans (and Phoenicians) in Egypt in the late seventh to sixth centuries B.C. In G. N. Knoppers and A. Hirsch (eds), *Egypt, Israel, and the Mediterranean World: Studies in Honor of Donald B. Redford*. Leiden: Brill, 404–38.

Jacobsson, I. (1994). *Aegyptiaca from Late Bronze Age Cyprus*. Jonsered: Åströms.

James, F. W. (1966). *The Iron Age at Beth Shan: A Study of Levels VI–IV*. Philadelphia: University Museum, University of Pennsylvania.

—— and P. E. McGovern (eds) (1993). *The Late Bronze Egyptian Garrison at Beth Shan: A Study of Levels VII and VIII* (2 vols). Philadelphia: University Museum, University of Pennsylvania.

Killebrew, A. E., P. Goldberg, and A. M. Rosen (2006). Deir el-Balah: a geological, archaeological, and historical reassessment of an Egyptianizing 13th and 12th century B.C.E. center. *Bulletin of the American Schools of Oriental Research* 343: 97–119.

Kitchen, K. A. (1982). *Pharaoh Triumphant: The Life and Times of Ramesses II King of Egypt*. Warminster: Aris & Phillips.

—— (1986). *The Third Intermediate Period, 1100–650* B.C. (2nd edn with supplement). Warminster: Aris & Phillips.

—— (1992). The Egyptian evidence on ancient Jordan. In P. Bienkowski (ed.), *Early Edom and Moab: The Beginning of the Iron Age in Southern Jordan*. Sheffield: Collis: National Museums and Galleries on Merseyside, 21–34.

—— (1993). *Ramesside Inscriptions: Translated and Annotated Translations*, vol. 2: *Ramesses II, Royal Inscriptions*. Oxford: Blackwell.

Levy, T. E. (ed.) (1995). *The Archaeology of Society in the Holy Land*. New York: Facts on File.

Lloyd, A. B. (1994). Egypt, 404–332 B.C. In D. M. Lewis, J. Boardman, S. Hornblower, and M. Ostwald (eds), *The Cambridge Ancient History*, vol. 6: *The Fourth Century* BC, 2nd edn. Cambridge: Cambridge University Press, 337–60.

Marcus, E. S., Y. Porath, R. Schiestl, A. Seiler, and S. M. Paley (2008). The Middle Kingdom Egyptian pottery from Middle Bronze Age IIa Tel Ifshar. *Ägypten und Levant* 18: 203–19.

Moran, W. L. (ed.) (1992). *The Amarna Letters*. Baltimore, Md.: Johns Hopkins University Press.

Mumford, G. D. (1997). Review of *The Late Bronze Egyptian Garrison at Beth Shan: A Study of Levels VII and VIII*, vols 1 and 2. *Journal of the American Oriental Society* 117: 715–19.

—— (1998). *International relations between Egypt, Sinai and Syria-Palestine in the Late Bronze Age to Early Persian period (Dynasties 18–26: c.1550–525 BC: a spatial and temporal analysis of the distribution and proportions of Egyptian(izing) artefacts and pottery in Sinai and selected sites in Syria-Palestine*. PhD dissertation, University of Toronto.

—— (2001a). Syria-Palestine. In D. B. Redford (ed.), *The Oxford Encyclopedia of Ancient Egypt*, vol. 3. Oxford: Oxford University Press, 335–43.

—— (2001b). Mediterranean area. In D. B. Redford (ed.), *The Oxford Encyclopedia of Ancient Egypt*, vol. 2. Oxford: Oxford University Press, 358–67.

—— (2006a). Tell Ras Budran (Site 345): defining Egypt's eastern frontier and mining operations in South Sinai during the Late Old Kingdom (Early EB IV/MB I). *Bulletin of the American Schools of Oriental Research* 342: 13–67.

—— (2006b). Egypt's New Kingdom Levantine Empire and Serabit el-Khadim, including a newly attested votive offering of Horemheb. *Journal of the Society for the Study of Egyptian Antiquities* 33: 159–203.

—— (2007). Egypto-Levantine relations during the Iron Age to Early Persian periods (Dynasties Late 20 to 26). In T. Schneider and K. M. Szpakowska (eds), *Egyptian Stories: A British Egyptological Tribute to Alan B. Lloyd on the Occasion of His Retirement*. Münster: Ugarit, 225–88.

Murnane, W. J. (1990). *The Road to Kadesh: A Historical Interpretation of the Battle Reliefs of King Sety I at Karnak*, 2nd edn. Chicago: Oriental Institute of the University of Chicago.

Nicholson, P. T., and I. Shaw (eds) (2000). *Ancient Egyptian Materials and Technology*. Cambridge: Cambridge University Press.

Nigro, L. (2007). Aside the spring: Byblos and Jericho from village to town in the second half of the 4th millennium BC. In L. Nigro (ed.), *Byblos and Jericho in the Early Bronze I: Social Dynamics and Cultural Interactions*. Rome: Università di Rome: La Sapienza, 1–45.

Oren, E. D. (ed.) (1997). *The Hyksos: New Historical and Archaeological Perspectives*. Philadelphia: University Museum, University of Pennsylvania.

Peden, A. J. (1994a). *Egyptian Historical Inscriptions of the Twentieth Dynasty*. Jonsered: Åströms.

—— (1994b). *The Reign of Ramesses IV*. Warminster: Aris & Phillips.

Porten, B. (1981). The identity of King Adon. *Biblical Archaeologist* 44: 36–52.

Pritchard, J. B. (ed.) (1969). *Ancient Near Eastern Texts: Relating to the Old Testament*, 3rd edn with supplement. Princeton, NJ: Princeton University Press.

Ray, J. D. (1988). Egypt 525–404 B.C. In J. Boardman, N. Hammond, D. M. Lewis, and M. Ostwald (eds), *The Cambridge Ancient History*, vol. 4: *Persia, Greece and the Western Mediterranean c. 525 to 479 B.C.*, 2nd edn. Cambridge: Cambridge University Press, 254–86.

Redford, D. B. (1992). *Egypt, Canaan, and Israel in Ancient Times*. Princeton, NJ: Princeton University Press.

—— (1998). Report on the 1993 and 1997 seasons at Tell Qedwa. *Journal of the American Research Center in Egypt* 35: 45–60.

—— (2003). *The Wars in Syria and Palestine of Thutmose III*. Leiden: Brill.

Saghieh, M. (1983). *Byblos in the Third Millennium B.C.: A Reconstruction of the Stratigraphy and a Study of the Cultural Connections*. Warminster: Aris & Phillips.

Schulman, A. R. (1988). Hittites, helmets and Amarna: Akhenaten's first Hittite war. In D. B. Redford (ed.), *The Akhenaten Temple Project*, vol. 2: *Rwd-Mnw, Foreigners and Inscriptions*. Toronto: Akhenaten Temple Project, 54–79.

Shaw, I. (ed.) (2000). *The Oxford History of Ancient Egypt*. Oxford: Oxford University Press.

Simpson, W. K. (ed.) (2003). *The Literature of Ancient Egypt: An Anthology of Stories, Instructions, Stelae, Autobiographies, and Poetry*, 3rd edn. New Haven, Conn.: Yale University Press.

Stager, L. E. (2008). Tel Ashkelon. In E. Stern (ed.), *The New Encyclopedia of Archaeological Excavations in the Holy Land*, vol. 5: *Supplementary Volume*. Jerusalem: Israel Exploration Society/Washington, DC: Biblical Archaeology Society, 1578–86.

Stern, E. (1982). *Material Culture of the Land of the Bible in the Persian Period 538–332* B.C. Warminster: Aris & Phillips/Jerusalem: Israel Exploration Society.

——(ed.) (1993). *The New Encyclopedia of Archaeological Excavations in the Holy Land* (4 vols). Jerusalem: Israel Exploration Society/New York: Simon & Schuster.

——(2001). *Archaeology of the Land of the Bible*, vol. 2: *The Assyrian, Babylonian, and Persian Periods, 732–332* B.C.E. New York: Doubleday.

Tubb, J. N. (1998). *Canaanites*. Norman: University of Oklahoma Press.

van den Brink, E. C. M., and T. E. Levy (eds) (2002). *Egypt and the Levant: Interrelations from the 4th through the Early 3rd Millennium B.C.E.* London: Leicester University Press.

Ventura, R. (1987). Four Egyptian funerary stelae from Deir el-Balah. *Israel Exploration Journal* 37: 105–15.

Weinstein, J. M. (1998). The world abroad: Egypt and the Levant in the reign of Amenhotep III. In D. B. O'Connor and E. H. Cline (eds), *Amenhotep III: Perspectives on His Reign*. Ann Arbor: University of Michigan Press, 223–36.

Wilkinson, T. A. H. (1999). *Early Dynastic Egypt*. New York: Routledge.

Yadin, Y. (1975). *Hazor: The Rediscovery of a Great Citadel of the Bible*. New York: Random House.

Yon, M. (2006). *The City of Ugarit at Tell Ras Shamra*. Winona Lake, Ind.: Eisenbrauns.

CHAPTER 6

....

ANATOLIA (HITTITES) AND THE LEVANT

....

HORST KLENGEL

During the late third and early second millennia, a new orientation of Near Eastern contact and trade is reflected by both archaeological and textual evidence (Klengel 2001: 349–55). Artefacts and settlement structures point to an increasing importance of the eastern Mediterranean areas of Syria/Palestine and Egypt, and Mesopotamian cuneiform texts refer to the lands of Magan (Oman) and Melukha (Indus Valley) as the origin of merchandise transported via the Persian Gulf to Mesopotamia, Syria, and the Nile Valley. A stone industry (including lapis lazuli and carnelian), which had developed in Badakhshan and in southern Iran—evidenced also by the carved stones from Jiroft—exported precious objects with inlays via Khusistan/Elam to Mesopotamia and from there to the Levant. As indicated by the cuneiform tablets from Ebla in northern Syria (late third millennium) and the material evidence from Gubla/Byblos in the central coastal area of the eastern Mediterranean, goods arrived there via the Euphrates, crossing northern Syria to the sea coast. Since the early second millennium, a desert route, leaving the valley of the Middle Euphrates for Tadmer (Palmyra) and Qatna (el-Mishrife), was used by the merchants travelling to the Levantine area (Klengel 2000: 239–40). Thus, progressive urbanization and the rising demand of the various local elites for prestigious foreign goods now became the essential incentive for the development of an interregional exchange in the eastern Mediterranean, i.e. between Egypt, the Syrian coastal centres, Cyprus with its rich copper deposits, and furthermore—by maritime trade following a sea route along the southern coast of Anatolia—the urban centres in the Aegean (Buchholz 1999).

This new orientation of trade, making the Levant a crossroad of land routes and maritime contacts, is clearly reflected by the archaeological material indicating both origin and routes of merchandise. Since the Middle Bronze Age, texts in Babylonian, Hittite, and Ugaritic, handed down on clay tablets, papyrus, and stone (Egyptian hieroglyphs), became the most important testimony for the development of an exchange of goods and ideas in the Near East. This multilingual textual tradition, in addition to increasing archaeological material from the various centres of the eastern Mediterranean, now considerably enlarges our knowledge of interregional contact and exchange. Economic development was closely connected with the regional palaces, their productive capacities, and commercial interests.

The palaces were able to finance the equipment of ships and crews and could also afford long-term enterprises, thus widening the horizon of trade. As a result, new elites developed in the centres of the Syrian Levant, acting as producers, customers, and mediators of goods.

HITTITE MILITARY INTERVENTION IN SYRIA

This increasing economic importance of the Levant became an incentive for foreign economic interest and military intervention. Texts from Mari on the Middle Euphrates, dating from the 18th century BC, point to the Syrian harbour city of Ugarit as an important centre of trade between the Euphrates region, Cyprus with its copper production, and Crete (Kaptaru/Caphtor). Also, King Hammurapi of Babylon (1792–1750 BC, according to the 'middle' chronology), had his own emissaries on the Levantine coast. The king of Babylon and merchants from contemporary Mari in the Euphrates Valley deposited tin—necessary for producing bronze—in Halab and Ugarit (Malamat 1998: 411–18). From Ugarit tin was sent to Crete, Qatna in central Syria, and Hazor—thus making Ugarit a hub of interregional trade in the Levant. At that time the land route to central Anatolia followed the Euphrates upstream, with Carchemish as an important station of departure, but this route was sometimes difficult to use because of climatic or security problems.

This economic and political development in the areas of the eastern Mediterranean made Syria a target of military campaigns led by the kings of neighbouring countries. Hittite troops, commanded by King Hattušili I (about 1650 BC) and then by his successor, Muršili I (about 1600 BC), crossed the eastern ranges of the Taurus to the fertile plains of northern Syria, finding there a rich booty and even including a prestigious raid as far as Babylon (Klengel 1992: 80–83). But these military activities did not result in any kind of provincial organization of the now subdued territories at the Levant, although Halab/Aleppo, the most important city of this region and prominent cult-place of the weather-god, was conquered. The Hittites made this central city, dominating the north Syrian plains and in control of important trade routes running through the area, a stronghold for their control of the region south of the Taurus Mountains. However there is no evidence that the Hittites tried to extend their rule to coastal Syria, including the harbour city of Ugarit, at this time.

This situation changed during the second half of the 14th century BC, when Hittite military campaigns beyond the Taurus Mountains started again under the rule of Šuppiluliuma I (about 1350 BC), this time resulting in well-organized Hittite political domination in Syria (Klengel 1992: 100–20). The great king of Hatti was now represented in Syria by a Hittite viceroy residing at Carchemish on the Euphrates, stemming directly from the family of the great king in Hattuša (Lackenbacher and Malbran-Labat 2005: 227–40). The local Syrian rulers were bound to the great king by a written treaty and a personal oath. Such treaties of subordination were discovered in the archives of Hattuša (Boghazköy) and also of Ugarit (Ras Shamra). These treaties included: Ugarit because of its important harbour and ability to act as mediator between the centres in the Levant; Halab/Aleppo because of its political and economic importance and its role as a prominent centre for the veneration of the weather-god; Amurru in the fertile plain of Homs, mediating access to the Mediterranean coast and to the Egyptian centres in Canaan; and Nukhashe, east of the upper Orontes.

These treaties were often renewed by each ruler's respective successors (Beckman 1999: 30–37, 50–64, 88–102).

Thus, from about the middle of the 14th century to the early 12th century, Syria between the eastern ranges of the Taurus and the plain of Homs, the coast of the Mediterranean Sea, and the Syrian Desert had become part of the Hittite Empire, including the important harbour city of Ugarit. The local rulers had to make a military alliance—both offensive and defensive—with the great king and his successors, and were obliged to extradite fugitives to them, to suppress uprisings against Hittite rule, and to pay annual tribute to Hattuša. This tribute consisted of gold and silver weighed out with the weights of the merchants of Hatti, special garments, dyed wool, or other special products produced by the countries that were subject to oath and treaty (Beckman 1999: 166–8, 175–7).

Ugarit under Hittite overlordship

As an important harbour city, with Ma'khadu as its main port and a fertile agrarian area between the close mountains and the seashore, Ugarit is mentioned in cuneiform texts as early as the early second millennium BC (Singer 1999: 603–733; cf. Klengel 1992: 130–51). During the 14th and 13th centuries BC, this city was the most important possession of the Hittite kings on the Levantine coast, a 'jewel in the crown of Hittite Syria' (Singer 1999: 648). The city was positioned favourably in a bay south of the Jabal al-Akra (*Casius mons*), a landmark of sea trade with Ugarit as a point of destination. A seal discovered at Tall Dab'a/Avaris from the time of the 13th Dynasty shows a god standing on two mountains, certainly the Jabal al-Akra, with an axe and a club in his hand—representing the fighting Ba'al (Klengel 2002: 30–31), the god protecting Ugarit. From inland Syria, Ugarit was accessible by mountain passes leading from the fertile plains of northern Syria to the coastal area. Ships approaching from the southern Levant could make use of a strong current running along the Syrian coast northward.

In southern Anatolia, the Taurus Mountains hampered access to the central Hittite territory, especially during the Anatolian winter, when, as it is noted in Hittite texts, 'the time had become too short' for further military or trading activities. During the favourable season travellers and merchants used a 'gap' in the mountain range by the Göksu River valley, allowing relatively easy access from the sea to central Anatolia and Hattuša. Thus, the harbour of Ura—located, as seems likely, not far from modern Silifke (Dinçol et al. 2000)—gained great importance in Hittite trade with the centres of the Levant and, especially, Ugarit (Klengel 2007: 383 7). As there is no evidence so far for an important commercial overland route connecting central Anatolia and the Aegean region (Seeher 2005: 33–44), thus the sea route along the southern coast of Anatolia was most probably used, as it was a rather short distance and its importance could be indicated by the shipwrecks of Cape Gelidonya and the farther westward Uluburun (Bass 2005: 303–30; Singer 2006: 242–62). The position of Ugarit and Troy, perhaps also Ura and centres close to eastern coast of Cyprus, could point to the preference of a certain distance from the sea in order to protect the harbour city from being attacked and plundered by foreigners coming across the sea.

Excavations undertaken in some prominent Late Bronze urban centres in the eastern Mediterranean between the Levant and the Aegean Sea have unearthed numerous monuments and literary testimonies pointing to an economic and cultural 'community' (*koiné*) mainly based upon the palace-households between the Levant and the Aegean. As an expression of this cultural identity, scenes of bull-leaping and certain 'western' vegetable motives were discovered at various sites of the eastern Mediterranean, such as Alalakh (Collon 1975: 60–1, fig.11.), Crete, and Avaris/Tall Dabʿa (Bietak 1999: 29) (cf. also the wall-paintings recently discovered at Qatna in middle Syria: Novák and Pfälzner 2002: 226–31). A frequent motif is also the weather-god Baʿal (-Saphon), lord of storm, thunder, and lightning, localized by the literary tradition of Ugarit on the Jabal al-Akra. Votive offerings to Baʿal excavated at his temple in Ugarit include the stone anchors of merchant ships, sometimes representing a considerable tonnage (Frost 1991: 335–408).

The presence of Hittites in Ugarit is clearly demonstrated by texts discovered in the cuneiform archives of the city (Neu 1995: 115–20). Treaties of subordination concluded by the Hittite king Šuppiluliuma I with Niqmadu II (Beckman 1999: 34–36), and by Muršili II with Niqmepa of Ugarit, deserve special attention (Beckman 1999: 64–69). In these, the Hittites established a political system in Syria as was already practised in Anatolia. It was based mainly on personal oaths sworn by relevant Syrian rulers and system of subordination, not on real political or even economic integration of controlled territories.

Texts from both Hattuša and Ugarit clearly point to a political subordination of Ugaritic rulers via overlordship to the Hittite kings. Hittite overlords were the highest authority and could intervene in Ugaritic dynastic affairs, as in the divorce of Ammistamru of Ugarit from a daughter of King Benteshina of Amurru (Beckman 1999: 180–81) and the Hittite viceroy Initeshub of Carchemish banishing the brothers of King Ammistamru II of Ugarit (Beckman 1999: 179–80). An edict of Muršili II was concerned with the boundaries of Ugarit and about the tribute of Ugarit to be paid to high Hittite officials (Beckman 1999:175–7).

URA AND THE HITTITE PARTICIPATION IN MEDITERRANEAN TRADE

Ugarit was certainly the most prominent harbour in Hittite Syria, and its rulers were bound by oath to Hattuša. It became the main foothold of Hittite power on the Levantine coast, both politically and economically. The Hittite vassal states in Syria were obliged to pay an annual tribute and to permanently house merchants of the Hittite king, who enjoyed a privileged status as his agents; they were also responsible for the transmission of yearly tribute from Ugarit to Hattuša. The local rulers granted anchorage capacities to Hittite ships, those of the Hittite royal house also among them (Beckman 1999: 178–9), including ships from Carchemish, which had the privilege of anchoring in Ugarit's inner harbour. The captains or crews of these ships were from other harbour cities of the Levant, such as Sidon or Akko, politically dominated by Egypt. Evidence that Syrian ships, sometimes also with a 'multinational' crew, could even arrive in Egypt was indicated by a now lost Egyptian painting in the Theban tomb of Kenamon, mayor of the southern city (Thebes) during the reign of Amenhotep III (1390–1352 BCE). It showed the arrival, unloading, and registration of a Syrian sailing ship (Davies and Faulkner 1947: 40–46).

It seems that Ura was directly subordinated to the Hittite great king. Lack of an administrative level between the local authorities of Ura and the overlord in Hattuša is evidenced in extant texts. Ura was connected with central Anatolia and Hattuša by a road running through the Göksu Valley to the plain of Mut, north of the Taurus Mountains and central Anatolia. A Hittite text (Košak 2003: 249–52) mentions merchants of Ura on the route to Zallara bringing with them a plenitude of workmen, cattle, sheep, horses, mules, donkeys, grain, and wine, in addition to precious items such as silver, gold, lapis lazuli, carnelian, 'Babylon-stone', mountain crystal, iron, copper, bronze, and tin. During the winter, when sea traffic was restricted by the weather, Uran merchants residing in Ugarit could then become a 'heavy burden' for the citizens of this prominent harbour by granting credit at a rather high interest rate—a business with negative social consequences.

Merchants from Ura acted as agents for the Hittite king and were responsible for the further transport of the tribute of Ugarit and other goods from the Hittite-dominated areas of the Levant to the king in Hattuša (Klengel 2007: 383–7). In the southern Levant, Ugarit had contacts with the other ports of the Levant north of Gubla/Byblos, the north-ernmost harbour under Egyptian rule. As evidenced by texts excavated at Ugarit, this port served at the same time as a naval base for ships acting on behalf of the Hittite crown, according to royal Hittite texts. From Ugarit ships could also take a route westward to the Aegean Sea following the southern coast of Asia Minor, i.e. mostly within view of the Anatolian mountains, though with the danger of shipwreck—as indicated by the ship-wrecks discovered near Uluburun and Cape Gelidonya—and of piracy. This maritime coastal traffic was all the more necessary as there was still no easy or secure overland route connecting Syria or central Anatolia with the Mycenaean centres (Seeher 2005: 33–44.; cf. also Singer 2006: 242–62).

These 'international' sea routes between the Syrian Levant and the Aegean centres were used by the Hittite government, and Ugarit was certainly the central place for participating in this trade. The relevant textual witness from Ugarit demonstrates that its harbour was one of the most important ports for 'international' sea trade in the Levant, although now under the political control of the Hittite government and its administrator. Here Egyptian or Syrian ships could take over further transport of goods to the Nile Delta, perhaps even upstream, as illustrated by the tomb-relief of Kenamun at Thebes (Davies and Faulkner 1947: 40–46). The Hittite king did not delegate this business to the local authorities of Ura or to ships belonging to the viceroy of Carchemish, entrusting it only to the king of Ugarit and his experts. Centres like Carchemish and Emar on the Euphrates probably profited from this trade, whereas Ashur on the Tigris, the growing military power of this period, did not participate directly. But the flourishing centres of northern Syria—among them Ugarit—could profit from Hittite protection. The treaty concluded by Šuppiluliuma I of Hatti with Niqmadu II of Ugarit mentions in its supplementary part a tribute to the Hittite king con-sisting of twelve minas and twenty shekels of gold, one cup equal to one mina in weight, four smaller linen garments, a large linen garment, 500 shekels of blue-purple wool, and 500 shekels of red-purple wool. The Hittite queen received from Ugarit a golden cup (thirty shekels in weight), one linen garment, and 100 shekels of blue-purple wool plus 100 shekels of red-purple wool (Beckman 1999: 167). Tribute to the highest officials of Hatti was added, consisting of golden cups, linen garments, and blue and red-purple wool. An inventory of the Ugaritic tribute paid to Hatti mentions gold, silver, wool dyed red or blue-purple, and linen garments (Beckman 1999: 168).

Other cuneiform texts handed down in Akkadian (Babylonian)—the 'international' language of diplomacy of the time—Hittite, or Ugaritic, point to a 'gift-exchange' between the Hittite kings and the pharaohs of Egypt, who controlled the southern Levant/Canaan (Edel 1994). Goods declared as gifts, with the expectation of reciprocity, are mentioned in letters exchanged between the kings of Hatti and the pharaoh; from Anatolia were sent trained horses (also for war chariots), herds of bulls, cattle, and sheep, from Egypt gold, silver, copper, fine garments, and other luxury items. Ugarit and the Cilician Ura served as mediators in this business, though Ura remained under direct Hittite control after the 'appanage kingdom' of Tarhuntassa had been created in the Taurus region as a province of its own east of the mouth of the Göksu River (Dinçol et al. 2000). The correspondence between Hatti and Egypt was sent through Hittite Syria and Egyptian Canaan, thus following a route that was similar to that taken by a Hittite princess, daughter of Hattušili III, and her escort when she travelled to Egypt for her marriage to Ramesses II (Klengel 2002: 130–39).

THE 'CRISIS YEARS': THE BREAKDOWN OF HATTI, UGARIT, AND THE ECONOMIC AND POLITICAL SYSTEMS OF THE LEVANT ABOUT 1200 BC

By the end of the Late Bronze Age, this system of trade and contact was threatened by both an economic crisis of the East Mediterranean world and the appearance of newcomers by ship. The so-called 'Sea Peoples', mentioned by their names in Egyptian texts dating about 1200 BC, left their native areas in the central and/or western parts of the Mediterranean— possibly forced to do so for survival. Traces of destruction in the Levant could be connected with raids by these peoples. However, this alone cannot explain the breakdown of political structures in various regions of the eastern Mediterranean at about the same time. Hittite (or Hieroglyphic Luwian) texts point to the arrival of new peoples who were, it seems, attracted by the wealth of the Levant. They contributed to the decay of the Levantine economy, which was exacerbated by a shortage of grain, as shown in texts from Hittite Anatolia mentioning 'years of hunger' (Klengel 1974: 165–74). Hatti called for help from Egypt—a country with an agriculture not dependent on rainfall at the right time and in sufficient quantity. This is reflected in the correspondence between the Hittite King Hattušili III and Pharaoh Ramesses II (Edel 1994). According to these letters, Egypt sent ships with grain to Hatti, perhaps via the harbour of Ura, but the Hittite king asked for further shipments because of the precarious situation in Anatolia, to which Ramesses replied: 'Look, I have now sent one ship, and another one I will send you next year. Your carpenters should draw a copy according to these ships, which I let bring you, and they [i.e. the Hittite ship-builders] should make for themselves a drawing...and they should build these ships accordingly and my brother [i.e. Hattušili III] shall make the ribs(?) in good quality' (Edel 1994: no. 79). In addition to a shortage of grain, there was also an epidemic in Anatolia and Syria, contributing to the decay of social relations and political stability. The Hittites had problems in their territories beyond the Taurus, and in Ugarit social unrest weakened royal authority. There are thus several factors, including economic and political, contributing to the decay of Hittite control that certainly encouraged western enemies to take advantage of the situation (Liverani 1995: 113–17).

The so-called Israel Stele, dating from the fifth year of the reign of Merenptah (1213–1203 BC), son of Ramesses II, refers to 'Israel' as an ethnic entity and gives an impression of the political situation in the Levant (Hornung 1983: 224–33). It mentions hostile 'Libyans', who were defeated by Merenptah, and the plunder of Canaan as it fell into social unrest. When the Egyptian Wenamun, living during the 22nd Dynasty in the 11th century BC, travelled to Gubla/Byblos in order to get timber for the holy boat of the god Amun, the political situation had changed considerably. Egypt no longer had its former strong position in the southern Levant; and Ugarit had lost its economic and political role in the Levant. It suffered from famine, an epidemic, and social unrest; the city was abandoned by its inhabitants and never resettled.

Suggested reading

Edel, E. (1994). *Die ägyptisch-hethitische Korrespondenz aus Boghazköi in babylonischer und hethitischer Sprache* (2 vols). Opladen: Westdeutscher.

Klengel, H. (1992). *Syria, 3000 to 300 BC: A Handbook of Political History*. Berlin: Akademie.

—— (1999). *Geschichte des hethitischen Reiches*. Leiden: Brill.

—— (2002). *Hattuschili und Ramses: Hethiter und Ägypter, ihr langer Weg zum Frieden*. Mainz: Philip von Zabern.

Seeher, J. (2005). Überlegungen zur Beziehung zwischen dem hethitischen Kernreich und der Westküste Anatoliens im 2. Jahrtausend v.Chr. In B. Horejs, R. Jung, E. Kaiser, and B. Terzan (eds), *Interpretationsraum Bronzezeit: Bernhard Hänsel von seinen Schülern gewidmet*. Bonn: Habelt, 33–44.

Singer, I. (1999). A political history of Ugarit. In W. G. E. Watson and N. Wyatt (eds), *Handbook of Ugaritic Studies*. Leiden: Brill, 603–733.

—— (2006). Ships bound for Lukka: a new interpretation of the companion letters RS 94.2530 and 94.2523. *Altorientalische Forschungen* 33: 242–62.

References

Bass, G. F. (2005). Die Schiffswracks der Bronzezeit im östlichen Mittelmeer. In U. Yalçin, C. Pulak, and R. Slotta (eds), *Das Schiff von Uluburun: Welthandel vor 3000 Jahren*. Bochum: Deutsches Bergbau-Museum, 303–8.

Beckman, G. M. (1999). *Hittite Diplomatic Texts*, 2nd edn, ed. H. A. Hoffner, Jr. Atlanta, Ga.: Scholars Press.

Bietak, M. (1999). L'archéologie de la Méditerranée orientale. In A. Caubet (ed.), *L'acrobate au taureau: les découvertes de Tell el-Dab'a (Égypte) et l'archéologie de la Méditerranée orientale (1800–1400 av. J.-C.)*. Paris: Documentation française, 29–81.

Buchholz, H.-G. (1999). *Ugarit, Zypern und Ägäis: Kulturbeziehungen im 2. Jahrtausend v.Chr.* Münster: Ugarit.

Collon, D. (1975). *The Seal Impressions from Tell Atchana/Alalakh*. Kevelaer: Butzon & Bercker.

Davies, N. de G., and R. O. Faulkner. (1947). A Syrian trading venture to Egypt. *Journal of Egyptian Archaeology* 33: 40–46.

Dinçol, A. M., J. Yakar, B. Dinçol, and A. Taffet (2000). The borders of the appanage kingdom of Tarhuntassa: a geographical and archaeological assessment. *Anatolica* 26: 1–29.

Edel, E. (1994). *Die ägyptisch-hethitische Korrespondenz aus Boghazköi in babylonischer und hethitischer Sprache* (2 vols). Opladen: Westdeutscher.

Frost, H. (1991). Anchors sacred and profane. In M. Yon (ed.), *Arts et industries de la pierre*. Paris: Éditions Recherche sur les civilisations, 355–410.

Hornung, E. (1983). Die Israelstele des Merenptah. In *Fontes atque pontes: eine Festgabe für Hellmut Brunner*. Wiesbaden: Harrassowitz, 224–33.

Klengel, H. (1974). Hungerjahre in Hatti. *Altorientalische Forschungen* 1: 165–74.

—— (1992). *Syria, 3000 to 300 BC: A Handbook of Political History*. Berlin: Akademie.

—— (2000). Qatna: ein historischer Überblick. *Mitteilungen der Deutschen Orient-Gesellschaft* 132: 239–52.

—— (2001). Zwischen Indus und Ägäis: zum überregionalen Austausch in der bronze- und frühen Eisenzeit. *Orientalistische Literaturzeitung* 96: 349–59.

—— (2002). *Hattuschili und Ramses: Hethiter und Ägypter, ihr langer Weg zum Frieden*. Mainz: Philip von Zabern.

—— (2007). Ura, Ugarit und der hethitische Mittelmeerhandel. In M. Alparslan, M. Doğan-Alparslan, and H. Peker (eds), *Belkıs Dinçol ve Ali Dinçol'a Armağan Vita*. Istanbul: Yayınları, 383–8.

Košak, S. (2003). A note on the 'Tale of the Merchants'. In G. M. Beckman, R. H. Beal, and J. G. McMahon (eds), *Hittite Studies in Honor of Harry A. Hoffner Jr. on the Occasion of His 65th Birthday*. Winona Lake, Ind.: Eisenbrauns, 249–52.

Lackenbacher, S., and F. Malbran-Labat (2005). Ugarit et les Hittites dans les archives de la 'Maison d'Urtenu'. *Studi micenei ed egeo-anatolici* 47: 227–40.

Liverani, M. (1995). La fin d'Ougarit: Quand? Pourquoi? Comment? In M. Yon, M. Sznycer, and P. Bordreuil (eds), *Le pays d'Ougarit autour de 1200 av. J.-C.: histoire et archéologie*. Paris: Éditions Recherche sur les civilisations, 113–17.

Malamat, A. (1998). Mari and its relations with the eastern Mediterranean. In M. Lubetski, C. Gottlieb, and S. R. Keller (eds), *Boundaries of the Ancient Near Eastern World: A Tribute to Cyrus H. Gordon*. Sheffield: Sheffield Academic, 411–18.

Neu, E. (1995). Hethiter und Hethitisch in Ugarit. In M. Dietrich and O. Loretz (eds), *Ugarit: Ein ostmediterranes Kulturzentrum im Alten Orient*, vol. 1: *Ugarit und seine altorientalische Umwelt*. Münster: Ugarit-Verlag, 115–29.

Novák, M., and P. Pfälzner (2002). Ausgrabungen in Tall Misrife-Qatna 2001: Vorbericht der deutschen Komponente der internationalen Kooperationprojektes. *Mitteilungen der Deutschen Orient-Gesellschaft* 134: 207–46.

Seeher, J. (2005). Überlegungen zur Beziehung zwischen dem hethitischen Kernreich und der Westküste Anatoliens im 2. Jahrtausend v.Chr. In B. Horejs, R. Jung, E. Kaiser, and B. Terzan (eds), *Interpretationsraum Bronzezeit: Bernhard Hänsel von seinen Schülern gewidmet*. Bonn: Habelt, 33–44.

Singer, I. (1999). A political history of Ugarit. In W. G. E. Watson and N. Wyatt (eds), *Handbook of Ugaritic Studies*. Leiden: Brill, 603–733.

—— (2006). Ships bound for Lukka: a new interpretation of the companion letters RS 94.2530 and 94.2523. *Altorientalische Forschungen* 33: 242–62.

CHAPTER 7

MESOPOTAMIA (ASSYRIANS AND BABYLONIANS) AND THE LEVANT

TAMMI J. SCHNEIDER

The Assyrians exploded from their traditional homeland in northern Mesopotamia to dominate the ancient Near East for several centuries during the first half of the first millennium BCE. The Babylonians, a southern Mesopotamian power that defeated the Assyrians in the late 7th century BCE, subsequently controlled most of the same territories that constituted the Assyrian Empire, until the conquest of the region by the Persians in 539 BCE (see Lehmann, Ch. 55 below). The Levant was but one of the areas that both the Assyrians and Babylonians sought to control, with varying degrees of success. The history and nature of the control exerted over the Levant by these two groups are documented by contemporary written documents left by the Assyrians and Babylonians, documentary evidence from non-Mesopotamian sources, biblical texts, and archaeological data (for recent treatments, see Melville et al. 2006; Strawn et al. 2006; Studevent-Hickman, Melville, and Noegel 2006; Kuhrt 1995: 473–546, 573–622; Stern 2001: 1–350). Together, these sources present a picture of repeated attempts to control the Levant through various means including military and diplomatic endeavours, and manipulation via control of local rulers.

Because the historical context orients the data and issues faced by both the dominating powers and the inhabitants of the Levant, this chapter will review the material chronologically, divided into three general trends: the period of initial Assyrian expansion (c.911–746 BCE) and its apogee in the Levant (c.745–632 BCE), followed shortly afterwards by Babylonian domination (c.626–539 BCE) of the region. Key issues facing Assyria and Babylonia, problems associated with imperial administration and control of the Levant, and an analysis of how the Levantine situation compares with other regions that formed part of the Assyrian and Babylonian Empires are addressed.

The Assyrian documentary evidence includes monumental reliefs that adorned the walls of their palaces, depicting their battles, tribute, and hunting expeditions; annals or yearly accounts that recorded their accomplishments; display texts (geographically organized accounts); and building inscriptions. Accomplishments of an Assyrian king entail conquering a city, country, or region; putting down a rebellion; lion hunting; receiving tribute; and expeditions to bring timber from Lebanon. These events were often depicted or inscribed on their palace walls, throne bases, royal stelae, cliff faces along the Tigris, Euphrates, and other smaller rivers, and on statues. Administrative documents have also been recovered including letters, tribute lists, astrologers' readings, treaties, and receipts from the various parties in Assyria and from Assyrian dignitaries to the subject nations (Grayson 1991; 1996).

Among the most important inscriptions are the Assyrian royal annals. These highly idealized accounts are written in the first person as though by the king. Characteristics of these texts include: praise is heaped upon the Assyrian king, no defeats are recounted, the text revels in detailed descriptions of war atrocities, and the numbers referring to victims and booty appear inflated. In the course of recounting the king's accomplishments, these annals include significant information regarding the empire's neighbours, but only in the context of problems created for the Assyrians (see e.g. Luckenbill 1926: 72–91, 109–18, 126–36, 138–77, 200–245, 253–62, 269–80 and Luckenbill 1927: 1–24, 69–71, 73–99, 115–53, 199–203, 216–23, 290–339).

An additional group of texts are the Mesopotamian Chronicles. Known for their brevity, they are written in third-person prose, with a date specified for every entry. The Chronicles list events in both Assyria and Babylonia, apparently in an effort to synchronize them and the relationship between the two regions over time, spanning the second half of the second millennium through to the first millennium BCE (Glassner 2004).

The focus of the Babylonian inscriptions differs from those of the Assyrian kings. They reflect a desire to relive the golden days of Babylonian independence during the second millennium BCE. This is expressed by an archaizing script and language, and in the boasts of resurrecting the religious and political agendas of their ancestors. As a result, when compared to the Assyrian texts, the Babylonian inscriptions lack information concerning contemporary historical events. The focus is not on campaigning but on renovation of temples, a traditional responsibility of the Babylonian kings. This provides useful information for understanding Babylonian culture but is less useful in determining the impact of their actions upon the Levant (Grayson 1975).

INITIAL ASSYRIAN EXPANSION

Assyria's expansion in the first millennium cannot be divorced from earlier territorial gains made by them during the reigns of Assur-uballit I (1363–1338 BCE) through Tukulti-Ninurta I (1243–1207 BCE) and Tiglath-pileser I (1114–1076 BCE). Both periods of Assyrian growth occurred at times of political turmoil in the region—in the first case by dynastic chaos in Mitanni resulting from Hittite invasions, especially during the reign of King Šuppiluliuma I, and in the second, by Aramean raids (van de Mieroop 2004: 130–31, 171–89). The second-millennium expansion of Assyria resulted in the establishment of administrative centres that survived into the first millennium BCE. In some cases, local rulers with an affinity for Assyria remained in power. The inscriptions of Assur-dan II (934–912 BCE) to Tukulti-Ninurta II (890–884 BCE) indicate that these kings continued to campaign in the territories west of the Habur and north of the Euphrates, previously conquered during the Middle Assyrian period, which they considered to belong to Assyria (van de Mieroop 2004: 227). Any local ruler who did not side with Assyria was considered to be in rebellion.

The 9th century BCE marks the beginning of 'Assyrianization', or the Neo-Assyrian period,[1] in the Levant. Assyrian interest in the Levant coincides with the emergence of new Iron Age polities following the crisis and resulting upheavals that characterized the end of the Late Bronze Age. In this initial period of expansion, Assyria's kings succeeded in extending its boundaries and bringing Assyria into contact with the Levant. Ambitious building projects in Assyria, accompanied by new forms of recording their achievements in writing and pictorially, set the stage for the more conscious growth that began much later, following the accession of Tiglath-pileser III (745–727 BCE; van de Mieroop 2004: 232).

Assurnasirpal II (883–859 BCE) was the first king to engage the post-second-millennium Iron Age Levant (Melville et al. 2006: 285–9). In Assyria he moved the political capital from Assur, which had been Assyria's political and religious capital from its beginnings, to Calah/Nimrud. At his new capital he began the tradition of adorning his palace with monumental reliefs that focused on territorial expansion and established the image of a powerful king. Following the successful 'pacification' of countries in northern Mesopotamia (Kutmuhu in the Upper Tigris Valley), the lower Khabur (Bit Halupe), and the Kashiari Mountains (Zauma), he moved westward. Assurnasirpal II then invaded the Aramean kingdom of Bit-Adini in the Jezirah, collecting tribute and hostages from its leader, Ahuni. The Assyrian army continued its march to the 'Great Sea of the land of Amurru', where Assurnasirpal II announced: 'I cleaned my weapons in the deep sea', and claimed to have received tribute from a number of rulers in the region including: Tyre, Sidon, Byblos, Mahallata, Maiza, Kaiza, Amurru, and Arvad (Luckenbill 1926: 166–7). Although Assurnasirpal II's engagement with the Levant was fleeting, it marked the beginning of an Assyrian presence in this region that was to continue until the fall of the Assyria.

The limited nature of control exercised over the region by the Assyrians becomes apparent during the reign of Assurnasirpal II's son and successor, Shalmaneser III (858–824 BCE; Yamada 2000; Melville et al. 2006: 289–93; see also Mazzoni, Ch. 45 below). The latter conducted campaigns in the region with the aim of receiving tribute and maintaining a physical presence. Each Assyrian king attempted, with varying degrees of success, to leave his mark in the Levant. Whereas Assurnasirpal II walked through the area easily, Shalmaneser III needed three campaigns to conquer the kingdom of Bit-Adini, transforming its capital, Til Barsib, into the provincial seat of Kar Shalmaneser (Quay of Shalmaneser). There he claimed to have built a palace that served as a base for future Assyrian operations. Evidence of this campaign to Bit-Adini appears in the display text with a relief of the king carved into the rock face along the upper Euphrates near the Kenk Gorge (Grayson 1996: 90–91). According to the Kurkh Monolith, in 853 BCE, Shalmaneser III met a group of 'twelve kings of the sea-coast' who formed a coalition to oppose him, including: Adad-idri (Hadadezer) the Damascene; Irhulenu the Hamathite; Ahab the Israelite; Matinu-Ba'al from the city of Arvad; Adunu-Ba'al from Sianu; Gindibu of Arabia; Ba'asa, son of Bit-Ruhubi the Ammonite; and the cities of Byblos, Musri, Irqanata, and Usanata (Grayson 1996: 11–24). Beaulieu

---

[1] The term 'Neo-Assyrian' has a variety of meanings. Its origins lie in art history where it marks the period beginning with the reign of Assurnasirpal II, the first Assyrian monarch to have monumental palace reliefs. Others prefer to define the beginning as coinciding with the rise of Assyria, beginning with the grandfather of Assurnasirpal II, Adad-nirari II (911–891 BCE). A third view attributes the beginning of the Neo-Assyrian period to the reign of Tiglath-pileser III due to his many administrative and organizational changes, and coinciding with the concept of an Assyrian empire.

suggests this is one of the first efforts to Assyrianize conquered lands and peoples (2007: 57). Noteworthy is the appearance of Ahab the Israelite, which represents the first documented evidence referring to a well-known ruler in the biblical text as a historical contemporary.

Despite Shalmaneser III's claims of success, he led three more expeditions against the area. Finally, because of internal issues, Adad-idri of Damascus was replaced by Hazael, 'the son of a nobody' (a usurper to the throne and therefore not royal); Shalmaneser III returned to the area, though without taking Damascus (Grayson 1996:118). On his way to the coast, he received tribute from Tyre, Sidon, and Jehu, king of Israel. Shalmaneser III's final set of annals are inscribed on the Black Obelisk, where five registers on the top record visually and list in writing the tribute from five different areas that constitute the farthest safe reaches of Assyria (Marcus 1987). Jehu is depicted kneeling before the Assyrian king, with his name and tribute appearing in the caption. However his name is not recorded within the body of this set of annals. There is no reference to this event in the Hebrew Bible.

Shalmaneser III's reign ends in revolt. His son and successor, Shamshi-Adad V (823–811 BCE), recorded how one of Shalmaneser III's other sons led the rebellion, listing the important cities that took part, which included the city of Assur (Grayson 1996: 180–83). By the time of Shamshi-Adad V's successor, Adad-nirari III (810–783 BCE), officials were recording their own inscriptions without referencing the king they served (Miller and Hayes 2006: 333). Also at issue is the status of the conquered areas, since the three inscriptions relating to Adad-nirari III's actions in the Levant provide slightly differing accounts (Grayson 1996: 203–18). In the Tell al-Rimah stele, the king claims to have subdued the lands of Amurru and Hatti, imposing upon them tax and tribute. Listed among these lands paying tax and tribute are Damascus and references to Joash (800–785 BCE) of Samaria and the people of Tyre and Sidon, suggesting that the Assyrians still exerted some control over this area (Grayson 1996: 209–12). The first Assyrian reference to 'palashtu' or 'Philistia' appears in Adad-nirari III's inscriptions where, in the Stone Slab, he claims to have subdued Amurru in its entirety, defining it as, 'Tyre, Sidon, Humri (Israel), Edom, Palashtu, as far as the great sea of the setting sun', and imposed tax and tribute upon them (Grayson 1996: 212–13).

ASSYRIA'S APOGEE

Assyria changes significantly when Tiglath-pileser III (745–727 BCE) accedes to the throne (Strawn et al. 2006: 331–3). In addition to campaigning annually, Tiglath-pileser III appears to have reorganized the army from one previously made up of Assyrians to a standing army composed of peoples from conquered areas. This changes the nature of the army and the concept of who is an Assyrian. The king also instituted administrative reforms that strengthened his position and reduced the independence and powers of others (such as Adad-nirari III's officials noted above). Finally, while previous Assyrian kings only periodically deported communities who had created problems for the Assyrians, under Tiglath-pileser III population deportations and resettlement in other regions became a regular policy. This cut the ties of the deported to their land, deities, and way of life, thus increasing their dependence upon Assyria, presumably in the hopes of securing their loyalty or, at least, subservience.

Tiglath-pileser III's policies transformed the Levant. On one of his earlier campaigns, which focused on the states in northwestern Syria (see Mazzoni, Ch. 45 below) and

Phoenicia, Tiglath-pileser III records tribute from Rezin, king of Damascus, Menachem from Bit-Omri (Israel), and Zabibe (the Arabs). Overall, the Assyrian impact on these regions differed. At Arslan Tash, a city fully incorporated into the empire as a provincial capital, a building filled with sculpture and ivory was excavated similar in layout to Assurnasirpal II's palace at Nimrud. Conversely, areas like the Golan, Gilead, and the kingdom of Geshur that revolted against the Assyrians were destroyed and their people deported (Stern 2001: 3).

As part of a repeating pattern, the western states formed anti-Assyrian coalitions, especially when Assyria's attention was focused elsewhere. The Levantine situation provides examples of differing Assyrian approaches to dealing with resistance from local communities. In Nimrud Letter 12 we learn that Assyrian troops were necessary to force 'the people to jump around' (apparently the troops were necessary to initiate some activity) in Tyre and Sidon because of restrictions on timber export to Philistia and Egypt (Saggs 1955: 128). This seems to contradict the royal inscriptions indicating that Tyre and Byblos were paying tribute (Tadmor 1994: 106, 171). Tiglath-pileser III's royal inscriptions (Summary Inscription 4:8: Tadmor 1994: 138–9) recount how Hanun of Gaza fled to Egypt before the Assyrians' weapons. As a result, the Assyrians conquered his city, confiscated his belongings, including his gods, and placed a royal image of Tiglath-pileser III in Gaza; yet later the king restored Hanun and turned Gaza into an Assyrian emporium (Tadmor 1994: 138–41). Israel is another example of how Assyria dealt with the Levantine states. According to a number of Tiglath-pileser III's royal inscriptions, Israel's King Pekah was assassinated, although it is unclear who was responsible (Tadmor 1994: 140–41). The biblical texts claim that Tiglath-pileser III then installed Hoshea on the throne of Bit-Omri; despite devastating the cities of Bit-Omri and carrying off its people, he did not destroy Samaria (2 Kgs. 15: 23–17: 2).

The situation in the west did not improve during the reign of subsequent kings. The only tidbit of information concerning the next king, Shalmaneser V (726–722 BCE), is a reference in the Babylonian Chronicle that 'he ravaged Samaria' (Glassner 2004: 194–5), an event confirmed by a biblical text (2 Kgs. 9–11). However, the biblical text does not record which Assyrian king captured Samaria and deported its people (2 Kgs. 17: 1–6). Sargon II appears to rise to power following the death of Shalmaneser V. His name 'true king' suggests he is a usurper of sorts, reinforced by the lack of a genealogy in his inscriptions (Luckenbill 1927: 25, 39, 45, 50–51, 55, 57–8, 60).

After Sargon II (721–705 BCE) had defeated the last resistance in the northern part of the Levant (see Mazzoni, Ch. 45 below), he was ready to turn to the southern areas again. A coalition in Syria revolted, led by Yaubidi, king of Hama, and Hanun of Gaza, the latter allied with Egypt. Qarqar was the place of battle and this time the Assyrians were successful. Hanun was captured and flayed (portrayed in detail on the walls of Sargon's palace), which probably strengthened Sargon II's position at home (Luckenbill 1926: 26–7). Eight years later the Egyptians instigated another revolt, which this time included Iamani of Ashdod, as well as the kingdoms of Judah, Edom, and Moab (Luckenbill 1926: 31–2).

During the reign of Sennacherib (704–681 BCE) Assyria's relationship with the Levant intensified, in part due to the many revolts against Assyrian interests. This king's reign has garnered a great deal of scholarly attention because of the amount of data, both textual and archaeological, some of it self-contradictory (Grabbe 2003). Despite this, some general trends are clear. This time Lule, king of Sidon, Sidka, king of Ashkelon, and Hezekiah, king of Judah, along with the inhabitants of Ekron, broke ties with Assyria (Luckenbill 1924: 29–34). Again, Assyrian reactions differ. Lule fled to Cyprus, Sidka was carried off to Assyria, Jerusalem was besieged but not captured (2 Kgs. 18: 13–19: 37 and Assyrian sources), and many of the cities in the area were captured or destroyed. Most famous of this second group is Lachish, which is not mentioned in the text of the campaign but is depicted in Assyrian reliefs. Excavations at the site confirm many elements including the siege ramp, the counter-defensive wall, and the devastation (Ussishkin 1982). Moab and Edom did not participate in this revolt. According to Assyrian inscriptions, Pedael, king of Ammon, Kamoshnadab of Moab, and Ayyaram of Edom sent tribute instead (Luckenbill 1924: 30).

Sennacherib eventually destroyed Babylon and was murdered in his palace, apparently by his own sons. Sennacherib's son Esarhaddon (680–669 BCE), after a dynastic crisis, finally acceded to the throne. As a result of Egyptian support of southern Levantine rebellions against Assyria, Esarhaddon focused his attention on conquering Egypt (Luckenbill 1927: 105). Inscriptions and archaeology suggest he developed military bases of operation and supplies in the Levantine region in anticipation of an attack on Egypt. For example, at Tell Jemmeh, an Assyrian vaulted building, similar in plan to those at Khorsabad, Nineveh, and Calah, appears to be a major staging ground for the Egyptian campaign. At Tel Sera', a large citadel with numerous storage rooms containing significant quantities of Assyrian 'Palace Ware' was constructed on top of the site of a violent conflagration, possibly attributed to Sennacherib (see e.g. Stern 2001: 21–6 for a summary of the evidence). In Esarhaddon's inscriptions the Moabite and Edomite kings continued as vassals listed as loyal along with the cities previously involved in revolts (Luckenbill 1927: 265).

Esarhaddon's initial attempt to conquer Egypt was successful but fleeting. After appointing new local kings, governors, officers, harbour overseers, officials, and administrative personnel, and imposing tribute, Esarhaddon returned to Assyria. Two years later, Taharqa, Egypt's ruler, was back, retook Memphis, and fermented rebellion against the Assyrians in the Nile Delta. On his return to Egypt to re-establish Assyrian control, Esarhaddon became ill in Harran and died before reaching Egypt (Glassner 2004: 208–9)

Prior to his death, in anticipation of an accession crisis, Esarhaddon forced his subjects to swear oaths of loyalty to his son, Assurbanipal (668–627 BCE), and appointed another son, Shamash-shum-ukin, to the throne of Babylon. Upon his death, the initial impact of this division was successful and the transition from Esarhaddon's reign to Assurbanipal's was smooth. The smooth transition from Esarhaddon's reign to Assurbanipal's accession allowed the new king to send his commander-in-chief immediately to the Levant to gather troops and supplies for the planned attack on Egypt. Following this successful campaign, the Assyrians uncovered plans of the next revolt early enough to capture the rebels and send them to Nineveh. Taharqa's son-in-law, Tandamane, occupied Memphis, causing Assurbanipal himself to lead his army to Egypt. When they entered Thebes, the Assyrian army ransacked and destroyed the city. When Egypt again rebelled later in Assurbanipal's reign, Assyria's troops were engaged elsewhere and could not return immediately. At the same time, trouble erupted in Babylonia, under the leadership of Assurbanipal's brother, Shamash-shum-ukin. In the end Shamash-shum-ukin set fire to his own palace and died in the flames. Ironically, Assurbanipal ruled Assyria at its zenith, but few records exist from the last twelve years of his reign (Luckenbill 1927: 291–409).

Following Assurbanipal's death, internal succession issues erupted and the political situation deteriorated rapidly. Assyria's weakened state led the Levantine states to sever ties and encouraged insurrection in Babylonia under the Neo-Babylonian king Nabopolassar (626–605 BCE). From 626 to 614 BCE wars ensued between Babylonia and Assyria, with details recorded in the Babylonian Chronicles (Glassner 2004: 219–25). Nabopolassar gained the upper hand and besieged Assur with a combined Babylonian–Median army, but did not succeed in conquering the city. Under Sin-shar-ishkun (622–612 BCE), Assyria gained the minimal and late support of Egypt, but it was not enough to withstand the Medes, who invaded Assyria and captured Assur in 612 BCE. However Assyrian resistance continued at Haran, where the Babylonians decisively defeated the Assyrians. Thus the Assyrian legacy ended, paving the way for Babylonia's rise to power.

BABYLONIAN DOMINATION

Babylonian hegemony in the Levant differed significantly from Assyrian practices. Under Assyria, the Levant was organized into semi-independent provinces, while Babylonian resources focused on the glorification of the city of Babylon (see e.g. Stern 2001: 303; regarding Assyrian and Babylonian administrative practices in the southern Levant, see Machinist 1992). Although the Babylonians conducted fewer military campaigns to the Levant, their conquests were more destructive. The nature of the Babylonian documentary evidence differs from the Assyrians, complicating the reconstruction of the historical situation of Babylonia's presence in the Levant (see e.g. Studevent-Hickman, Melville, and Noegel 2006). For a brief period of time, following the demise of Assyria and prior to the rise of Babylon, much of the Levant was under the influence of Egypt. Hints of this are recorded in Assyrian material and the Hebrew Bible (2 Kgs. 23: 28–30; 2 Chr. 35: 20–25). Due to the Egyptian presence in the Levant, the Babylonians may have been more focused on the Levant at the beginning of their control of it than the Assyrians. Though Nabopolassar was king, his son, Nebuchadnezzar II (604–562 BCE), conducted many of his military operations. His first task was ridding the Levant of the Egyptians. Beginning in the north, Nebuchadnezzar attacked the Egyptian garrison at Carchemesh in 606 BCE, successfully driving the Egyptians out of Syria. While continuing their campaign, the news of Nabopolassar's death reached the army on the border of Egypt, forcing Nebuchadnezzar to return to Babylon and take the throne. Shortly thereafter Nebuchadnezzar returned to the Levant to receive tribute from Damascus, Tyre, Sidon, and Jerusalem, destroying Ashkelon along the way because the city barred its gates against him. Nebuchadnezzar was forced to return to the region repeatedly due to local resistance to his control and Egypt's reluctance to surrender its influence over the area. Regarding Jerusalem, Nebuchadnezzar tried a few approaches, first besieging the city, taking its king, Jehoichin, hostage, placing Zedekiah on the throne, and deporting some inhabitants. When this failed, he finally besieged, captured, and destroyed the city, followed by the deportation of its citizens (2 Kgs. 24–5; Babylonian Chronicle in Glassner 2004: 231; see Lipschits 2005). Josephus claims that Moab also participated in the insurrection and was only brought back under Babylonian control five years after the fall of Jerusalem (*Ant.* 10.9.7).

Following the destructions in the Levant by Nebuchadnezzar, there are few records of campaigns. The end of Nebuchadnezzar's reign is obscure and the reign of his son, Awel-marduk (561–560 BCE), was short. He was replaced by Nergal-shar-usur, and his son, Labashi-Marduk, reigned for a very short time. They were succeeded by Nabonidus (555–539

BCE), who was not focused on campaigning and did not follow the important religious rituals of Babylon, especially those concerning their chief deity, Marduk (Glassner 2004: 235–9). Little is known of his reign or the motivation for some of his actions. For example, there is one reference in the Nabonidus Chronicle that he laid siege to the 'City of Edom' and may have captured it in the second half of the third year of his reign (Grayson 1975: 105). It is suggested that this city was Bozrah (modern Buseirah), though it is unclear why Nabonidus attacked. Another odd action by Nabonidus was his ten-year stay in Tema, an oasis town in the Arabian desert. In his absence Babylonia was ruled by his son, Bel-shar-usur, who did not have the support of the Babylonians. Thus, the Babylonian account of Nabonidus' stay in Tema emphasizes the consequences of his decision rather than the reasons for it, thereby providing modern scholars with little data to understand the relationship of the Babylonians with the Levant (Sack 2004: 17).

The Babylonians were far less interested campaigning and dominating the Levant than the Assyrians. The practical result of this for the Levant is that it was not until the Persian period that recovery would begin in the rest of the Levant.

SUGGESTED READING

Chavalas, M. W. (ed.) (2006). *The Ancient Near East: Historical Sources in Translation*. Malden, Mass.: Blackwell.

Grayson, A. K. (1975). *Assyrian and Babylonian Chronicles*. Locust Valley, NY: J. J. Augustin.

—— (1991). *Assyrian Rulers of the Early First Millennium BC I (1114–859 BC)*. Toronto: University of Toronto Press.

—— (1996). *Assyrian Rulers of the Early First Millennium BC II (858–745 BC)*. Toronto: University of Toronto Press.

Kuhrt, A. (1995). *The Ancient Near East, c. 3000–330 BC*, vol. 2: *From c. 1200 B.C. to c. 330 B.C.* London: Routledge.

Luckenbill, D. D. (1924). *The Annals of Sennacherib*. Chicago: University of Chicago Press.

—— (1926). *Ancient Records of Assyria and Babylonia*, vol. 1. Chicago: University of Chicago Press.

—— (1927) *Ancient Records of Assyria and Babylonia*, vol. 2. Chicago: University of Chicago Press.

Sasson, J. M. (ed.) (1995). *Civilizations of the Ancient Near East I–IV*. New York: Scribner.

Snell, D. C. (ed.) (2007). *A Companion to the Ancient Near East*. Malden, Mass.: Blackwell.

Tadmor, H. (1994). *The Inscriptions of Tiglath-Pileser III King of Assyria: Critical Edition, with Introductions, Translations, and Commentary*. Jerusalem: Israel Academy of Sciences and Humanities.

—— and S. Yamada (2011). *The Royal Inscriptions of Tiglath-Pileser III (744–727 BC) and Shalmaneser V (726–722 BC), Kings of Assyria*. Winona Lake, Ind.: Eisenbrauns, 2011.

REFERENCES

Beaulieu, P.-A. (2007). World hegemony, 900–300 BCE. In Snell (2007: 48–61).

Glassner, J.-J. (2004). *Mesopotamian Chronicles*, ed. B. R. Foster. Atlanta, Ga.: Society for Biblical Literature.

Grabbe, L. L. (ed.) (2003). 'Like a Bird in a Cage': The Invasion of Sennacherib in 701 BCE. London: Sheffield Academic.

Grayson, A. K. (1975). Assyrian and Babylonian Chronicles. Locust Valley, NY: J. J. Augustin.

—— (1991). Assyrian Rulers of the Early First Millennium BC I (1114–859 BC). Toronto: University of Toronto Press.

—— (1996). Assyrian Rulers of the Early First Millennium BC II (858–745 BC). Toronto: University of Toronto Press.

Kuhrt, A. (1995). The Ancient Near East, c. 3000–330 BC, vol. 2: From c. 1200 B.C. to c. 330 B.C. London: Routledge.

Lipschits, O. (2005). The Rise and Fall of Jerusalem: Judah under Babylonian Rule. Winona Lake, Ind.: Eisenbrauns.

Luckenbill, D. D. (1924). The Annals of Sennacherib. Chicago: University of Chicago Press.

—— (1926). Ancient Records of Assyria and Babylonia, vol. 1. Chicago: University of Chicago Press.

—— (1927) Ancient Records of Assyria and Babylonia, vol. 2. Chicago: University of Chicago Press.

Machinist, P. (1992). Palestine, administration of (Assyro-Babylonian). In D. N. Freedman (ed.), Anchor Bible Dictionary, vol. 5: O–Sh. New York: Doubleday, 69–81.

Marcus, M. I. (1987). Geography as an organizing principle in the imperial art of Shalmaneser III. Iraq 49: 77–90.

Melville, S. C., B. A. Strawn, B. B. Schmidt, and S. Noegel (2006). Neo-Assyrian and Syro-Palestinian texts I. In Chavalas (2006: 280–330).

Miller, J. M., and J. H. Hayes (2006). A History of Ancient Israel and Judah, 2nd edn. Louisville, Ky.: Westminster John Knox Press.

Sack, R. H. (2004). Images of Nebuchadnezzar: The Emergence of a Legend, 2nd edn. Selinsgrove, Penn.: Susquehanna University Press.

Saggs, H. W. F. (1955). Nimrud letters, 1952—Part II. Iraq 17: 126–60.

Stern, E. (2001). Archaeology of the Land of the Bible, vol. 2: The Assyrian, Babylonian, and Persian Periods, 732–332 BCE. New York: Doubleday.

Strawn, B. A., S. C. Melville, K. Greenwood, and S. Noegel (2006). Neo-Assyrian and Syro-Palestinian texts II. In Chavalas (2006: 331–81).

Studevent-Hickman, B., S. C. Melville, and S. Noegel (2006). Neo-Babylonian period texts from Babylonia and Syro-Palestine. In Chavalas (2006: 382–406).

Tadmor, H. (1994). The Inscriptions of Tiglath-Pileser III King of Assyria: Critical Edition, with Introductions, Translations, and Commentary. Jerusalem: Israel Academy of Sciences and Humanities.

Ussishkin, D. (1982). The Conquest of Lachish by Sennacherib. Tel Aviv: Institute of Archaeology, Tel Aviv University.

van de Mieroop, M. (2004). A History of the Ancient Near East ca. 3000–323 B.C. Malden, Mass.: Blackwell.

Yamada, S. (2000). The Construction of the Assyrian Empire: A Historical Study of the Inscriptions of Shalmaneser III (859–824 B.C.) Relating to His Campaigns to the West. Leiden: Brill.

CHAPTER 8

ACHAEMENID PERSIA AND THE LEVANT

JOSETTE ELAYI

In 539 BC Cyrus the Great overcame Nabonidus, the last Babylonian king, and the Levant fell into the Persian king's hands. Thus began the period of Persian rule, that was to last more than 200 years, until 332 BC. In order to take into account the double standpoint of archaeology (Iron III) and history (Persian period), the terminology chosen here for this period is the Iron III/Persian period (Elayi and Sayegh 1998: 8–9). History provides a useful chronological framework, recently completed by the annually dated Sidonian coinage from 401 to 333 BC (Elayi 2006: 11–43), that furnishes helpful markers for every scholar working in this field (Table 8.1).

However, the history of the Levant in the Iron III/Persian period is difficult to reconstruct, first because of the paucity of our sources, compared with the previous Neo-Assyrian and Neo-Babylonian periods and, even more, with the later Hellenistic period. The Persian, Elamite, and Babylonian inscriptions provide some information on the administration of the Levant. Under Achaemenid rule, Aramaic became the universal language for administration, appearing on monuments, ostraca, seals, and coins. However, legal deeds, long accounts, and archives were consigned to papyrus, and these documents have not been preserved due to the damp and salty soil of the Levantine coast. Inscriptions in other Northwest Semitic languages such as Hebrew are rare, except for Phoenician; Ammonite, Moabite, Edomite, and North and South Arabic inscriptions set up the difficult problem of their dating in the Iron III/Persian period. Greek and Cypriot syllabic inscriptions are also available, mainly for Cyprus. Some information on Persian contact with the Levant is provided by Greek and Latin sources, but mainly from a Greek point of view especially when they involved Greeks (e.g. Persian Wars). Finally, the relevant biblical material deals mainly with Judah, in the first generation of the so-called Restoration (c. 538–516 BC) and in the time of Ezra and Nehemiah (second half of the 5th century BC). Recent discussions about the relation between the Bible and Palestinian archaeology have focused on differences in methodology between these two fields, and on the fact that scholars in one or the other need to respect the methodological borders. A new and fruitful dialogue is needed between scholars involved in textual study and those recovering new data from fieldwork, including inscriptions (Elayi and Sapin 2000: 187–215).

Table 8.1. Concordance of the reigns of Persian and Phoenician kings during the Iron III/Persian period

Periods	Dates	Sidonian kings	Tyrian kings	Byblian kings	Aradian kings	Related events	Persian kings
550–526	549	Tabnit				Conquest of Phoenician cities by Cyrus II	Cyrus II (549–530)
	539						
	533	Amoashtart Eshmunazor II (14 years)	Hiram III (20 years: c.552–533)				
	532		Ittobaal IV (?) (from c.532)				
	530						Cambyses II (530–522)
525–501	525	Bodashtart (more than 7 years)				Campaign of Cambyses II in Egypt	
	522	Yatonmilk (?)					Smerdis (522) Darius I (522–486)
500–476	486	Anysos (?) Tetramnestos	Hiram IV (?) Mattan III	Shipitbaal III (?)	Ozbaal (?) Maharbaal		Xerxes I (486–465)
475–451	480			Urimilk II		Persian defeat of Salamis	
	479					Persian defeat of Mycalus	
	466			Yeharbaal		Persian defeat of Eurymedon	
	465						Artaxerxes I (465–424)
450–426	460/459					Persian defeat in Egypt	
	450	Baalshillem I		Yehawmilk		Persian defeat of Salamis (Cyprus)	

Period	Year			Events	Persian kings
425–401	424	Abdamon			Xerxes II (424–423)
	423	Baana			Darius II (423–404)
400–376	404	Baalshillem II (36 years: 401–366)	Elpaal		Artaxerxes II (404–359)
	401				
	394		Ozbaal	Victory of Cnidus	
	385–383			Capture of Tyre by Evagoras of Salamis	
	?			Failure of Persian campaign in Egypt	
	381			Persian victory of Kition and capture of Salamis (Cyprus)	
375–351	373			Failure of Persian campaign in Egypt	
				First revolt of satraps	
	369	Abdashtart I (14 years: 365–352)			
	365				
	c. 364			Athenian decree in honour of Abdashtart	
	359		Abdashtart	Tachos' expedition in Syria	Artaxerxes III (359–338)
				Flight to Sidon. Abdashtart I's revolt	
	355			End of Abdashtart I's revolt	
				Prisoners sent to Babylonia and Susa	
	353	Tennes (5 years: 351–347)	Addirmilk		Mazday's government on Transeuphratene (353–333)
	351			Failure of Persian campaign in Egypt	

(Continued)

Table 8.1. (Continued)

Periods	Dates	Sidonian kings	Tyrian kings	Byblian kings	Aradian kings	Related events	Persian kings
350–326	c. 350					Tennes' revolt	
	349		Ozmilk (17 years before 333)				
	347	Evagoras? (4 years: 346–343)					
	346					End of Tennes' revolt	
	343–342	Abcashtart II (10 years: 342–333)					
	342			Aynel	Abdashtart (?)	Persian reconquest of Egypt	
	339				Gerashtart (7 years before 333)		
	338						Arses (338–336)
	336						Darius III (336–330)
	333–332					Alexander's conquest of Phoenician cities	
	332	Abdalonym	Ozmilk (continuation)	Aynel (continuation?)	Gerashtart (continuation)		

Another difficulty related to the sources is that what little information we do have is unevenly distributed, with respect to both territorial extent and chronological span. The historical picture derived from the available data favours Phoenicia, Palestine, and Cyprus, whereas most of Syria, except for the coastal strip, and Transjordan to a lesser degree, are shrouded in almost complete darkness throughout the Iron III/Persian period (Sancisi-Weerdenburg and Kuhrt 1990: 207–62). In general for the Levant, the 4th century BC is better documented than the two previous centuries. Moreover, when interpreting the documentation, it is important to avoid some a priori approaches such as 'Biblocentrism', 'Hellenocentrism', and 'Iranocentrism' (Elayi and Sapin 1998: 29–33). Under these conditions, the meagre and varied information that can be gleaned from every region and type of sources illuminates the role played by the Persians in shaping the destinies of the peoples of the Levant. For convenience, this chapter will follow the historical chronology, considering at the same time the various fields of policy, administration, economy, and society, and focusing on the main questions still in debate. It is important to distinguish clearly what is secure from likely hypotheses and simple hypotheses of work, and to exclude resolutely hypotheses that are unlikely or obviously wrong.

THE CONQUEST AND ORGANIZATION
OF THE LEVANT (539–486 BC)

The exact date of the conquest of the different regions of the Levant still remains under discussion, especially for Judea and Cyprus: between 545 and 526/525 BC. However, the most likely date seems to be 539 BC, when Cyrus the Great captured Babylon, an event which meant the transition of the whole Neo-Babylonian Empire to under Persian domination (Briant 1996: 55–9). Cyrus replaced the last Babylonian king, Nabonidus, by the Iranian governor, Gobryas, and created a large government combining Babylonia and Transeuphratene. The exact definition of Transeuphratene is not simple because it encompasses several geographical entities based upon the period in question, sources cited, and its usage by the author. Generally speaking, it designates the region situated 'beyond the Euphrates', namely to the west of the river from the perspective of an observer situated to the east, in Mesopotamia or on the Iranian plateau (Elayi and Sapin 1998: 14–20). A number of problems come up in regard to its nature, unity, evolution, organization, and limits. Since we do not know by what term the Persians characterized the status of this area, modern authors use the term 'satrapy', corresponding to the fifth *nomos* of Herodotus. We still do not know to what extent Transeuphratene constituted a territorial, administrative, and fiscal unity, since its boundaries are elusive and underwent changes in the course of the two centuries of Achaemenid history. There is no agreement on the date and circumstances of the separation of Transeuphratene and Babylonia: in 503, 486, or between 486 and 420 BC, which seems to be the most cautious hypothesis. The boundaries of Transeuphratene roughly corresponded to the Levant, that is, all the area situated west of the Euphrates, up to the Amanus and the Habur northwards, and up to Cyprus on the west. The southern frontier is uncertain because we do not know whether the territory of the Arabs was included in Transeuphratene or formed a distinct area (Laperrousaz and Lemaire 1994: 24–30). Several hypotheses have been proposed for the capital of Transeuphratene: Tripolis and the springs of the Dardas, which are unlikely, and Damascus and Sidon, both good candidates.

What were the aims of the Persians in their conquest of the Levant? The Achaemenid policy followed that inaugurated by Tiglath-pileser III: the new territories were permanently integrated into the empire; political control was settled, based on the *adê* (oaths of loyalty), fiscal regulation, and military authority with stationed garrisons intended to prevent or suppress revolts and to prepare for further conquest. Territorial control was essential for the Persians; therefore they developed the existing network of roads, maintaining them with security (garrisons and guard stations) and using them for troop and logistical movements (supplies, reserves of water, and stocks of weapons). The defence of the Mediterranean front was important for the empire, which became more and more involved in westward maritime conquests, requiring a powerful navy. The administration of the Levant, probably unchanged during Cyrus' reign, was transformed by Cambyses and mainly by Darius I. The tribute paid by the different subjected peoples was at first irregular, then became yearly at the end of Darius' reign. They moreover had to pay different taxes, royal and satrapal, and they had various commitments to the Persians (Fig. 8.1).

Because the Levant lay at several crossroads, it was a very cosmopolitan region, which comprised at that time an extraordinary mosaic of governments of various kinds: provinces with local or Persian governors such as Judea, Samaria, and maybe Moab and Ammon; autonomous city-states such as Arwad, Byblos, Sidon, Tyre, Damascus, and the Cypriot cities; and client-states such as Arabia and Idumea. Persian population density in the occupied territories is debatable, with centralist and autonomist theses. The Iranist historians sometimes have a tendency to overvalue Persian power in the Levant, by arguing that it was an imperial-tributary state with a strong territorial hold and by using models of occupation compiled with data from well-documented provinces. Conversely, regionalist historians

FIG. 8.1 Silver Persian shekel, Group IVb of Stronach (private collection)

sometimes have the tendency to underestimate the indications of Persian territorial ascendancy. While the idea of centralization has merit, it is necessary to be aware of the great diversity in local governments and their socioeconomic and cultural intricacies, not only from one province to the other, but within the same province; and of the various expressions of Achaemenid power that cannot be isolated from their social and spatial-temporal dimensions (Elayi 1991: 77–89). As a general rule, the Persian kings used peaceful means for their domination, showing consideration for the religious beliefs of the subject populations (Elayi and Sapin 2001–2) (Fig. 8.2).

The Phoenician cities, fitting into the most privileged category of the autonomous tributary states, were allowed to retain their institutions and keep their autonomy. This preferential treatment was due to the Persian need for Phoenician war galleys; the use of these territories as strategic positions to control the coastal route and as bases of operation for the roads to Greek cities or Egypt; and the wealth generation for the Persians, including a *paradeisos* (royal forest reserve) in the Lebanese range belonging to Sidon. The relations between the Phoenician cities and the Persians in the 6th century BC are almost exclusively known through classical sources; they seem to have strengthened during the last stage of the Ionian revolt. Sidon was then an emerging city, which gained hegemony over other Phoenician cities. It was ruled by the so-called dynasty of Eshmunazor, now clearly dated to the second quarter till the end of the 6th or the beginning of the 5th century BC (Elayi and Elayi 2004: 593–611). Sidon was given Dor and Jaffa, as a reward for military deeds in the service of the Persians; this event seems to have inaugurated privileged relations with the Persian king.

FIG. 8.2 Marble bull protome of the Sidonian temple of Echmoun, influenced by Persian art (private collection)

According to Judean historiography, Cyrus II was not considered a conqueror but a liberator, since he allowed the exiled Judeans in Babylon to return to their country carrying their divine statues, rebuild the temple of Jerusalem, and restore the sacrificial cult. They came back and settled in Judea with a first governor, Sheshbassar, around 538 BC, then with Zerubbabel around 515 BC. According to Haggai's prophecy given in 521 BC, messianic hopes were centred on Zerubbabel, scion of the House of David. But his disappearance after 521 BC could have been due to his deposition by Persian authorities mistrusting a local dynasty. In fact, we lack a clear assessment of Persian imperial rule in Judea in order to know how it shaped and oriented the basic social constitution of the post-exilic community. Several questions are still in debate, such as the modalities of the return (myth of the mass return), the borders and size of Jerusalem (myth of the 'empty land'), the social and religious conflicts between the exiles and the 'people of the land', the imperial authorization, and the rebuilding of the temple (Watts 2001; Lipschits and Oeming 2006: 3–206). The measures taken by Cyrus in favour of Jerusalem seemed exceptional to the Judeans, but were probably usual from the Persian standpoint (Briant 1996: 56–8).

The Persian kings were no doubt interested in Arab cities such as Gaza, main outlet of the spice trade from Arabia controlled by the kingdom of Saba. The conquest of Egypt by Cambyses in 525 BC represented an important step in the history of the Sinai because the northern road had to be protected by military stations, especially close to the Pelusian Mouth, the 'door of Egypt' (Valbelle and Bonnet 1998: 61–87). Except for the Phoenician sites (Elayi 2000: 327–48), we have almost no information on northern and eastern Syria (Habur) and on the evolution of old Aramaic kingdoms (Lipiński 2000: 347–407). According to classical sources, Damascus was a great provincial capital. There was perhaps a Persian *paradeisos* at the source of the Dardas and lands belonging to Parysatis in Aleppo area. Cyprus was a crossroad between the Greek world and the Near East with several ethnic elements (Eteocypriot, Greek, and Phoenician): it was maybe not conquered in 539 BC, still remaining a tributary of Pharaoh Amasis for some years. Then it entered the category of autonomous tributary states, like the Phoenician cities (Colombier 1991: 21–43). Following the Greek cities, the Cypriot cities started minting their coins from the end of the 6th century BC. They took part in the Ionian revolt in 499/497 BC: the Persians landed on the island and besieged some cities such as Paphos and Soloi (over five months), suppressing the revolt.

THE LEVANT UNDER PERSIAN DOMINATION IN THE 5TH CENTURY (486–404 BC)

This period is also ill-known and mainly through Greek and Jewish sources. The thesis of the decadence of the Persian Empire starting in 479 BC is due to the deformation of Greek sources and to the idea of 'Asiatic despotism': it is now abandoned (Briant 1996: 531–4). In 486 BC the new Persian king, Xerxes I, had to face the revolts of Egypt and Babylonia. He also had to continue the policy of his father, Darius, in particular the project of campaign against Greece. The Persian Wars had nothing like the same importance for Athens as for the Persian king. However, all the Persian campaigns westwards (480–450 BC), involving Levantine populations, ended in defeats: Salamis of Greece (480 BC), Mycalus (479 BC), Eurymedon (466 BC), Egypt (460/59 BC), and Salamis of Cyprus (450 BC).

The Phoenician cities of Sidon, Tyre, and Arwad took part in these campaigns with their own navies requisitioned by the Persians and each of them commanded by their respective king (Elayi and Elayi 2004: 593–635). Following a period of naval victories, privileged relations were established between Xerxes and the king of Sidon during the Second Persian War. However, after the disaster of Salamis, Xerxes put to death the Phoenicians responsible. The relations afterwards between the Phoenician and Persian kings deteriorated, especially since it was quite costly for the Phoenicians to repair and build new war galleys. The following defeats were probably very damaging for them too.

At that time, some scattered pieces of evidence show a growth of Athenian imperialism in the Levant. The Athenian gravestone of individuals from the Erechtheid tribe who died in 459 or 458 BC, at the beginning of the Egyptian campaign, names Cyprus, Egypt, and Phoenicia. An inscription from Samos mentions the capture of Phoenician ships by the Samians, probably during the same campaign. In general, the satraps played an increasing role in the Persian Empire. During the second half of the 5th century BC, the Phoenician navies never fought but were used by the Persians either as a threat or as a promise of help with an element of manipulation, especially in the events of Samos in 441/439 and 412–409 BC. About that time, the city of Byblos built its own navy; it began to mint coinage shortly before 450 BC, followed by Tyre, Sidon, and Arwad (Elayi and Elayi 2009).

In the Persian Wars the Cypriot cities played a role similar to that of the Phoenician ones, providing the Persians with their navies. They numbered around ten but decreased during the Iron III/Persian period. This political evolution was more linked to internal conflicts than to interventions of Persians or Greeks (Collombier 1991). It is too simple to explain these political struggles by the existence of two parties, pro-Greek and pro-Persian. In fact, the pan-Hellenism and Athenian help (the naval expedition of Pausanias in 478 BC, Athenian struggles of 460/459 BC, and the campaign of Cimon in 450 BC) did not significantly change the political situation of Cyprus. Around 450 BC, King Ozbaal of Kition seized the city of Idalion. Shortly afterwards a Tyrian seized power at Salamis and another named Abdemon did the same around 415 BC.

The main sources for the history of Judea during this period are the books of Ezra and Nehemiah. They lack certainty on some crucial basic data such as their date, the authenticity of the Persian documents quoted, and the missions of Ezra and Nehemiah, both ostensibly acting as imperial functionaries (Lipschits and Oeming 2006: 531–70). The thesis of a revolt in Judea around 484 BC, reported in Ezra, seems to have no grounds. It is difficult to assess the authenticity of the accusation made against the inhabitants of Judea and Jerusalem by their neighbours, and of the anti-Persian activities that forced the authorities to take stern action. Nehemiah, the 'governor', was obviously given responsibility by Artaxerxes I for a specific mission: to rebuild and repopulate Jerusalem as a fortified city and capital of a 'province', to restore social order, and to ensure the proper functioning of the cult. He carried out a second mission of a more socio-religious character: to organize the administration of the temple, reasserting the value of the Sabbath and marriages between Judeans. Ezra, the 'scribe of the Law of the God of heaven', was sent on a juridical inspection, to enforce in Judea the 'Law of the King'. The Persian chancellery would probably choose its officials mandated in this way from the most loyal and easily controllable families, preferably in the diaspora close to the central power. They tolerated politico-administrative and socio-religious initiatives like those of Nehemiah and Ezra, insofar as they reinforced the internal cohesion and fidelity to them (Fried 2004). We note, however, that there is no indication of a dynasty of governors in this province, as was the case in Samaria, where this did not present the same risk of messianic temptations and therefore of revolts. Culturally speaking, Samaria and Judea had much in common. Thus attempts at self-definition may have been necessary for some of the elite in Jerusalem, precisely because of the similarities between the Yahwists living in the two territories. If some sort of sanctuary or temple already existed on Mount Gerizim during the Iron III/Persian period, this would have added further impetus for Jerusalem temple scribes to authenticate the distinctive positions of their city and shrine (Lipschits and Oeming 2006: 265–89). However, the so-called Samarian schism occurred probably later than the Persian period.

DISTURBANCES AND CHANGES IN THE LEVANT (404–332 BC)

The reign of Darius II (423–404 BC) had been marked, in the western part of the empire, by a relative peace that allowed the power of the satraps to be consolidated. The 4th century BC was a period of successive disturbances in the region, characterized by several rebel movements of local and satrapal authorities, under the reigns of Artaxerxes II, Artaxerxes III, Arses, and Darius III. Mazday brought together under his control the satrapies of Cilicia and Transeuphratene; he did not hold the title of satrap, however, but that of 'attendant to Transeuphratene and Cilicia' (Fig. 8.3). In contrast to the passive attitude of Darius II, Artaxerxes III actively sought to restore order to Asia Minor and Egypt. However, the so-called Great Revolt of Satraps, a joint operation against the weakened power of the Persian Empire in order to end it, was an invention by Greek writers, as was the theory of Persian decadence (Briant 1996: 675–94).

FIG. 8.3 Reverse of a silver double shekel minted in Sidon by the Persian satrap Mazday, Year 18 of his reign (= 336 BC) (Elayi and Elayi 2004: no. 1982)

After the Athenian defeats of 405 BC, Conon took refuge under Evagoras of Salamis and was given the responsibility of preparing the Cypriot navies against Sparta by the satrap Pharnabazus. The political situation had completely changed because of the increasing role of the satraps and of the new alliances between Greek cities and Persians. Evagoras (412/411–374/373 BC) progressively conquered most cities of Cyprus and even the Phoenician city of Kition in 392 or 387 BC (Collombier 1991: 35–7). After having been loyal to the Persians, he revolted during 391/390 BC, with the help of Athens and Egypt. He possibly landed in Cilicia and in Phoenicia, where he (symbolically) seized Tyre around 385–383 BC. The Persians won a naval victory at Kition while they besieged Salamis in 383/381: Cyprus went back under Persian control and had to pay tribute, but Evagoras kept the throne of Salamis. According to Diodorus, there were then nine cities, Tamassos having been sold to Pumyaton, king of Kition, between 362 and 351 BC. Nikokles of Salamis, being on friendly terms with Abdashtart I of Sidon, probably supported his revolt against Artaxerxes III, just as all Cypriot cities supported Tennes' revolt according to Diodorus.

The relations between the Persian kings and the Phoenician cities are relatively well documented for the 4th century BC, especially Sidon, with a precise chronology. In 394 BC, the Persians defeated the Spartans at the battle of Cnidus; they were mainly supported by the Phoenician navies, the first being the Sidonian one under the command of its king, Baalshillem II (401–366 BC), possibly named Saktôn ('shipowner') in a Greek papyrus (Elayi 2005: 49–52). The Phoenician navies probably took part in the Persian campaign against Egypt around 385/383 BC, which was a failure. They do not seem to have participated in the Persian reconquest of Cyprus around 383/381 BC, possibly due to damaged sustained in Egypt. However, they took part in the second campaign of Egypt that was mainly prepared in the territory of Tyre (Akko), since they had enough time to rebuild their war galleys: this campaign ended again in failure in 373 BC. From around 369 BC, several revolts of satraps broke out such as those of Datames and Ariobarzanes. There are two opposing theories: the first is maximalist, including all the revolts in a unique coalition, and the second is minimalist, considering each revolt as a local separate event of no consequence for the Persian Empire. The second theory is probably more realistic, but without excluding the existence of various alliances. We do not know whether the Phoenician navies took part in the expeditions sent by Artaxerxes III against the revolted satraps, but it is possible, since they were always loyal to him, in spite of difficulties.

When Abdashtart I succeeded his father, Baalshillem II, on the throne of Sidon, he was obliged to take emergency measures in order to face the difficulties, such as a devaluation of his coinage in 365 BC (Elayi 2005). After having established some alliances with Athens, Egypt, and Salamis on Cyprus, he decided to revolt against the Persians around 360 or 359 BC, taking advantage of an invasion of Phoenicia by Pharaoh Tachos. He probably defeated the army of Belesys and Mazday, sent by Artaxerxes III against him around 358/356. The revolt was finally suppressed in 355 BC, when Sidonian prisoners were sent to Babylon and Susa, but Abdashtart I was left on the throne. In 353 BC, Artaxerxes III put the satrap Mazday in charge of Transeuphratene and especially Sidon, where he minted his satrapian coinage, annually dated from 353 to 333 BC in parallel with Sidonian coinage (Elayi and Elayi 2004: 659–67). The revolt of Abdashtart I was a grave political error: his city met with more and more economic difficulties, exacerbated by a heavy Persian military presence, and lost several advantages, in particular territorial, much to the benefit of Tyre, its rival city. The situation of Sidon became worse after the failure of the Persian campaign in Egypt in 351 BC, when

Tennes decided to revolt anew against the Persians. It was severely suppressed by Artaxerxes III in 347 BC, the last year inscribed on Tennes' coinage. A foreign king (Evagoras?) was set on the throne (346–343 BC) until the Persian reconquest of Egypt, followed by a pro-Persian Sidonian king, Abdashtart II (342–333 BC).

As for Judea and Samaria, late sources mention a revolt linked with the Sidonian and Cypriot revolts, the destruction of Jericho, and the deportation of Judeans, but this information is questionable. However, there were a relatively large number of sites in Palestine that were destroyed during the second third of the 4th century BC, even if all these destructions are not necessarily linked with revolts. The documents of Wadi ed-Daliyeh reveal a Samarian revolt around 335–333 BC, the latest Tyrian coin found there being dated of 335 BC (Year 15). In northern Arabia, the kingdom of Qedar controlled, from the second half of the 5th century BC, south Palestine to Lachish, the Sinai, the south of Transjordan, and the Hijaz. Thus the Qedarite kings controlled most Arab tribes.

It seems that the whole region had undergone important changes relating to political control between the end of the 5th century BC and the beginning of the Hellenistic period. The Nabateans perhaps made their appearance, more or less taking the place of the Qedarites, and a new province was created: Idumaea. The most probable hypothesis would amount to linking these changes to a reorganization of the south of Palestine by the Persians in the 4th century BC. The successive revolts that shook the region could explain why the Persian authorities had felt the need for an administrative and military reorganization, perhaps during the energetic reign of Artaxerxes III. This reorganization seems to have been carried out at the expense of the Arab kingdom of Qedar, which would have taken part in the Cypriot revolt of Evagoras, who had the support of Pharaoh Achoris. The extent of the new province of Idumaea at the time of its creation is difficult to determine precisely; probably it included all the territory to the south of the province of Judea, from Lachish, Maresha, Hebron, and Ein Gedi as far as the Negev. It was probably also at this time that the city of Gaza was placed under the orders of a Persian military governor (Elayi and Sapin 1998: 154–6). Several hundred Aramaic ostraca, which began to appear in 1985 on the antiquities black market, probably dating between 362 and 312 BC, are connected with Achaemenid administration. Most of them seem to record taxes in kind (barley, wheat, oil, etc.) having entered the storerooms of Makkedah, identified with Khirbet el-Kom, and also taxes to be paid in silver (Lemaire 1996; 2002). The existence of a province of Ammon at that time can be deduced from the existence of a kingdom until 582 BC, and of a province in the Hellenistic period, and is confirmed by two seals and an inscription of Ma'in dated from the 5th century BC. The existence of a province of Moab can also be presumed from its existence before and after the Iron III/Persian period, but no discovery has confirmed this (Laperrousaz and Lemaire 1994: 46–51).

The short reign of Darius III (336–330 BC) was mainly occupied by military preparations against Alexander the Great, since he was aware of the Macedonian threat. According to classical sources, the Phoenician navies still had first place in the Persian navy, which was composed then of 400 war galleys (Fig. 8.4). When Alexander crossed the Hellespont with his army in 334 BC, he had only 160 war galleys and transport ships. It is impossible to understand why the Persian navy was absent, arriving only a few weeks later at Miletus, when the city was already in Alexander's hands. Several hypotheses were given to explain this absence: slow progress of the Persian forces, absence of strategy, the effect of surprise, or sending the navy against Pharaoh Khabbabash's revolt in Egypt; this last hypothesis would be more likely on condition that this revolt was simultaneous. However, Darius III remained master of the sea thanks to his powerful navy. The strategy of Alexander was then to conquer

FIG. 8.4 Obverse of a silver double shekel minted by Abdashtart I, king of Sidon, representing a war galley used by the Persians, Year 7 of his reign (=359 BC) (Elayi and Elayi 2004: no. 1292)

the Phoenician cities in order to get possession of their navies (Elayi and Elayi 2004: 682–7). The different reactions of the cities are known through classical sources which present Alexander as a liberator and the resistance of Tyre as a will for independence: however, it is understandable that Sidon was fed up with Persian oppression since 347 BC. But it must be kept in mind that Alexander's conquest was based on the territorial organization of Darius III's empire and on the collaboration with the state officials of the previous regime.

SUGGESTED READING

Briant, P. (1996). *Histoire de l'empire perse: de Cyrus à Alexandre*. Paris: Fayard.

—— (2002). *From Cyrus to Alexander: A History of the Persian Empire*. Winona Lake, Ind.: Eisenbrauns.

Collombier, A.-M. (1991). Organisation du territoire et pouvoirs locaux dans l'île de Chypre à l'époque perse. *Transeuphratène* 4: 21–43.

Elayi, J. (2000). Les sites phéniciens de Syrie au Fer III/Perse: bilan et perspectives de recherche. In G. Bunnens (ed.), *Essays on Syria in the Iron Age*. Leuven: Peeters, 327–48.

—— (2005). *'Abd'aštart Ier/Straton de Sidon: un roi phénicien entre Orient et Occident*. Paris: Gabalda.

——(2006). An updated chronology of the reigns of Phoenician kings during the Persian period (539–333 BCE). *Transeuphratène* 32: 11–43.

—— and J. Sapin (1998). *Beyond the River: New Perspectives on Transeuphratene*. Sheffield: Sheffield Academic.

—— (2000). *Quinze ans de recherche (1985–2000) sur la Transeuphratène à l'époque perse*. Paris: Gabalda.

—— (eds) (2001–2). *Actes du Ve Colloque international La Transeuphratène à l'époque perse: religions, croyances, rites et images*. Paris: Gabalda.

Laperrousaz, E.-M., and A. Lemaire (1994). *La Palestine à l'époque perse*. Paris: Cerf.

Lipschits, O., and M. Oeming (eds) (2006). *Judah and the Judeans in the Persian Period*. Winona Lake, Ind.: Eisenbrauns.

REFERENCES

Briant, P. (1996). *Histoire de l'empire perse: de Cyrus à Alexandre*. Paris: Fayard.

Collombier, A.-M. (1991). Organisation du territoire et pouvoirs locaux dans l'île de Chypre à l'époque perse. *Transeuphratène* 4: 21–43.

Elayi, J. (1991). La domination perse sur les cités phéniciennes. In *Atti del II Congresso Internazionale di Studi Fenici e Punici, Roma, 9–14 novembre 1987* (3 vols). Rome: Consiglio Nazionale delle Ricerche, 77–85.

——(2000). Les sites phéniciens de Syrie au Fer III/Perse: bilan et perspectives de recherche. In G. Bunnens (ed.), *Essays on Syria in the Iron Age*. Leuven: Peeters, 327–48.

——(2005). *'Abd'aštart Ier/Straton de Sidon: un roi phénicien entre Orient et Occident*. Paris: Gabalda.

——(2006). An updated chronology of the reigns of Phoenician kings during the Persian period (539–333 BCE). *Transeuphratène* 32: 11–43.

——and A. G. Elayi (2004). *Le monnayage de la cité phénicienne de Sidon à l'époque perse (Ve–IVe s. av. J.-C.)*. Paris: Gabalda.

——(2009). *The Coinage of the Phoenician City of Tyre in the Persian Period (5th–4th cent. BCE)*. Leuven: Peeters.

—— and J. Sapin (1998). *Beyond the River: New Perspectives on Transeuphratene*, trans. J. E. Crowley. Sheffield: Sheffield Academic.

—— (eds) (2000). *Actes du IVe Colloque international La Transeuphratène à l'époque perse: économie, commerce et monnaie*. Paris: Gabalda.

—— (eds) (2001–2). *Actes du Ve Colloque international La Transeuphratène à l'époque perse: religions, croyances, rites et images*. Paris: Gabalda.

—— and H. Sayegh (2000). *Un quartier du port phénicien de Beyrouth au Fer III/Perse*, vol. 2: *Archéologie et histoire*. Paris: Gabalda.

Fried, L. S. (2004). *The Priest and the Great King: Temple–Palace Relations in the Persian Empire*. Winona Lake, Ind.: Eisenbrauns.

Laperrousaz, E.-M., and A. Lemaire (1994). *La Palestine à l'époque perse*. Paris: Cerf.

Lemaire, A. (1996). *Nouvelles inscriptions araméennes d'Idumée*, vol. 1: *Au Musée d'Israël*. Paris: Gabalda

——(2002). *Nouvelles inscriptions araméennes d'Idumée*, vol. 2: *Collections Moussaïeff, Jeselsohn, Welch et divers*. Paris: Gabalda.

Lipiński, E. (2000). *The Aramaeans: Their Ancient History, Culture, Religion*. Leuven: Peeters.

Lipschits, O., and M. Ocming (cds) (2006). *Judah and the Judeans in the Persian Period*. Winona Lake, Ind.: Eisenbrauns.

Sancisi-Weerdenburg, H., and A. Kuhrt (eds) (1990). *Centre and Periphery: Proceedings of the Groningen 1986 Achaemenid History Workshop*. Leiden: Nederlands Instituut voor het Nabije Oosten.

Valbelle, D., and C. Bonnet (eds) (1998). *Le Sinaï durant l'antiquité et le Moyen Âge: 4000 ans d'histoire pour un désert*. Paris: Errance.

Watts, J. W. (ed.) (2001). *Persia and Torah: The Theory of Imperial Authorization of the Pentateuch*. Atlanta, Ga.: Society of Biblical Literature.

PART III

THE ARCHAEOLOGICAL
RECORD

Section A The Neolithic Period

CHAPTER 9

INTRODUCTION TO THE LEVANT DURING THE NEOLITHIC PERIOD

BILL FINLAYSON

The Neolithic in the Levant has been a major focus of archaeological research, and a number of the big themes of human development are associated with it. During this period (*c*.9750–5850 cal. BC), people in the Levant began to live in sedentary communities and farm for the first time in the world. This change was so important that it has been described as one of the major events of human history: the Neolithic revolution (Childe 1964). From an 'agricultural revolution' (Barker 2006), which brought all the major components of western Eurasian farming together, to a 'symbolic revolution', which has been argued as the start of religion and even the identification of gods (Cauvin 2000), and a 'cognitive revolution' that brought about the modern mind (Renfrew 2003; 2007; Watkins 2004a), the Neolithic is often seen as *the* critical period upon which all subsequent developments including population rise and urbanism depend.

The core idea of the Neolithic revolves around the appearance of the sedentary farmer, developing from hunter-gatherer societies. These terms appear intuitively simple and obvious, but they contain both a rich background of our own cultural understanding and a very wide range of possibilities. From our perspective, hunter-gatherers are primitive and different, farmers are familiar. Farmers live in villages, located in agricultural landscapes, while hunter-gatherers live in camps in the wild. These conceptual differences are at the heart of why so many people see the Neolithic as revolutionary. But they are based upon modern conceptions; our concept of what is wild, what farming is, and what villages are. Using our modern terminology in a simplistic way to describe the early Holocene is misleading. To start, the hunter-gatherer background was not one of highly mobile people living in a marginal environment, but one which already shared many of the traits of the earliest Neolithic populations, including developments towards a sedentary life and possibly greater management of food resources. Within the early Neolithic this process simply continued, albeit with an increasing pace of change. People did not suddenly become either fully sedentary or farmers. They began to do more to cultivate wild plants and manage wild animals at the same time as gradually making more elaborate settlements and developing new strategies to allow them to stay together in increasingly larger groups.

It is in the nature of the stadial sequences (Neolithic, Bronze Age, etc.) we use to divide prehistory to make it appear as if revolutions occur between each phase. The Neolithic of the Levant is no different in this regard, and conventionally starts with the Holocene and a bang. Although the Neolithic is typically characterized as a dramatic and rapid transformation in the subsistence, social, and symbolic systems used by humans, these so-called Neolithic developments are rooted deeper in time, in the late Pleistocene. Furthermore, the key changes we associate with the Neolithic, which include the appearance of large settled communities and farming, do not occur until very late in the Neolithic. From the early days of field research in the Levant the traditional European definition of the Neolithic (characterized by the appearance of polished stone tools, pottery, and agriculture) had to be modified, most notably with the introduction of a Pre-Pottery Neolithic (divided into a PPNA and a PPNB, with subsequent addition of a PPNC, and subdivision of the PPNB into an Early, Middle, and Late), indicating that the economic and social changes did not all happen at the same time. The reality revealed by research is much more messy, but probably much more interesting.

The four regional explorations that follow all employ slightly different chronological terminologies to discuss the Neolithic, but each explains their usage. For the most part none of the authors claims that their terminologies relate to regional cultures. The diversity of regionally based terminology becomes greater towards the end of the Neolithic. Akkermans' discussion of the Syrian Neolithic ends in c.5300 BC, while Goring-Morris and Belfer-Cohen include cultures up to 4500 BC as Late Neolithic 2, and Clarke takes the Neolithic in Cyprus to 3900 BC. Part of this discrepancy lies in variation in what is described as Chalcolithic, with the Late Neolithic 2 in the southern Levant being included by some scholars within that period, while the equivalent chronological period is more routinely classified thus in Syria. Some scholars see these differences as mainly semantic (e.g. Banning 2007a), while others (e.g. Bourke 2007; Gilead 2007) consider that their distinction between Neolithic and Chalcolithic reflects real differences in society and economy as discussed later in this volume. Such arguments on the early prehistory of the Levant continue to relate to a pre-radiocarbon dating use of 'cultural types' to develop regional chronologies. Neolithic archaeology is still affected by the debate on the reality of these 'cultures', which are generally defined in the earlier Neolithic mainly through flint tool typologies, with pottery taking over as the principal determining factor in the later Neolithic.

For the purpose of this review, I will discuss the following themes: history of research, regional geography, chronology, sedentary behaviour, society and belief, and subsistence economy. Far from being completely arbitrary divisions, each of these topics are interlinked, but first have to be unpacked a little to avoid the traps set by hindsight and the so-called Neolithic package.

History of research

Archaeological exploration of Neolithic cultures in the Near East has a long history, beginning with Kathleen Kenyon's investigations at Jericho during the 1950s. In large part, this deep research tradition makes the region so productive for study now. In theory we are beyond the phase of initial pioneering research, where every new site was a major discovery, and we now have a rich database to draw on and analyse. In practice, every new site still seems capable of generating surprising new information and Neolithic research is still pioneering in terms of the use of new analytical techniques. In the Upper Euphrates area, new evidence from sites such as Jerf el-Ahmar (Stordeur, Helmer, and Willcox 1997) (and just beyond the bounds of this volume in Turkey at Gobekli Tepe: Schmidt 2001) has dramatically changed our understanding of the northern late PPNA and early PPNB, in terms both of the sequence of events and of the presence of an elaborate communal and ritual architecture. Similarly, new work in the southern Levant beyond the Mediterranean Woodland Zone has changed our perception of the extent and nature of the PPNA in that area, no longer being understood as a marginal area, but the location of substantial settlements (e.g. Finlayson et al. 2003; Finlayson and Mithen 2007). In addition, new excavation results in the southern Levant have also radically changed our understanding of the transition from the PPNA to PPNB (e.g. Edwards et al. 2004) from a picture where it was assumed that the PPNB in the south commenced later than in the north, the 'centre of innovation', to a view that sees all regions as contributors to the overall processes of change.

REGIONAL GEOGRAPHY AND ENVIRONMENT

The Levant is characterized by an extremely varied landscape and climate. There are a number of major different environmental zones represented in the region, broadly divided into the Mediterranean Woodland Zone, encompassing the coastal region and some highland areas that catch sufficient rain to support similar woodland; the semi-arid steppes that run east of the highlands; and the arid desert areas. There are other significantly different environments, including the Euphrates River Valley and the Jordan Valley, as well as variations within the major zones, such as the high Anti-Lebanon Mountains, the coastal strip, major spring locations, and the oases in the East. These provide an enormous range of environments, creating different possibilities for subsistence strategies across the region for hunter-gatherers, cultivators, and early farmers alike.

Research investigating the relationship between environment and human approaches to subsistence has gone hand in hand with Neolithic research since the early days. The geographical diversity of the region, coupled with significant climate change events, undoubtedly had a significant impact on the people and the plant and animal resources they exploited. Major shifts in regional climatic conditions are an important feature of the Neolithic, from its beginning at the end of the Younger Dryas (the final cold and dry spell of the last glacial period) which may have been an important trigger for economic change, to the Holocene (with warmer and wetter conditions), to the so-called Year 8,200 Event, a short dry phase that may have contributed to the decline in PPNB population centres, especially in the more arid zone. Paleoenvironmental research is ongoing to understand how major global climate change events impacted the Levant and how such conditions may have affected each of the environmental zones within the Levant, including the availability of water, the seasonality of rainfall, sea level changes, and the distribution of the wild progenitors of the major plant species that were eventually to become domesticated.

The combination of new evidence and interpretation means that we constantly have to re-evaluate the relationship between human behaviour and environment (see Robinson et al. 2006 for a recent review).

The following chapters discuss the Neolithic as divided by modern state boundaries. To some extent, as can be seen in the different treatments offered, these boundaries reflect differing modern research interests, but it is important to emphasize that they do not exactly reflect Neolithic regional expressions, perhaps with the exception of Cyprus, although Clarke is at pains to emphasize that Cyprus is not isolated by the sea. The boundaries between Neolithic regions are generally related to geographic features, such as the Jordan Valley, or the 'hilly flanks' of the Fertile Crescent (e.g. Braidwood et al. 1983), or the Upper Euphrates. In other places there are no geographic boundaries, as in southern Syria, where the sites around Damascus (Tell Aswad and Tell Ramad) appear more as part of the southern Levant than the rest of the country; the Upper Euphrates region continues into modern Turkey, and to the east and south of Syria there are no sharp boundaries with Iraq and northern Mesopotamia, where early sites such as Qermez Dere and Nemrik are important and Mesopotamian relationships in the Later Neolithic are huge. The Levant is also part of a wider region, including at least the modern countries of Turkey, Iraq, and Iran, which are also part of the overall Neolithic process, but with different local expressions.

These large-scale divisions are now being broken down into smaller regions. All of the following chapters on the mainland subdivide the areas they examine in terms of environmental variation. The chapter on Cisjordan (Ch. 11) moves a step further to indicate that there are culturally based local differences. Recent papers have begun to explore some of these local provinces (e.g. Sayej 2001, examining PPN sites in southern Jordan). This awareness of diversity within the Levant is part of a developing debate (Gebel 2004; Rollefson and Gebel 2004; Warburton 2004; Watkins 2003) that centres on a mosaic of different 'Neolithics', with much of the dynamism of the period resulting from their interaction.

CHRONOLOGY

Many of the traits that we recognize as being 'Neolithic', perhaps especially an increase in sedentary behaviour, have their roots in earlier, Epipaleolithic periods as noted both by Akkermans and by Goring-Morris and Belfer-Cohen (Chs 10 and 11 below). (We can argue that the process of neolithization starts before the Neolithic, but the main concern here is with the construction of our Neolithic chronology.) The Neolithic of the Levant has continued to employ culture-chronological schemes based on material culture (especially on ceramics in the Late Neolithic)—schemes that were first developed from a very small numbers of sites (cf. Manning 2007). Campbell's analysis of periodization (2007) clearly illustrates the problems with this approach, where many of the divisions between the units result from gaps in the sequence at the original excavated sites. Such an approach inevitably leads to searches for the origins of these archaeologically defined units and an emphasis on transition with the assumption that each unit, whether it is the Late PPNB or the Yamourkian, is internally homogeneous and coherent. At times the argument seems to boil down to semantics, but some authors still place great weight on the meaning of the cultural periods.

Whether one accepts Goring-Morris and Belfer-Cohen's argument that there is a distinct Khiamian phase at the beginning of the PPNA (largely defined by flint tool typology) and that this appears more Natufian than Neolithic in character, the debate remains, at least partly, an exercise in definition. In southern Jordan the distinctions and boundaries between a Khiamian and a later PPNA do not seem at all clear (cf. Edwards et al. 2004), although there are changes in architecture and material culture during the course of the PPNA. Culture history terminology tends to rely on limited material culture elements, and this causes problems. For example, despite the appearance of pottery and the consequent identification of a Late Neolithic, Goring-Morris and Belfer-Cohen (Ch. 11) note that the Late Neolithic 1 is otherwise more like a Late PPNB than the Late Neolithic 2. Culture history emphasizes the significance of stadial periods, but then requires transitional periods, such as the Halaf–Ubaid Transition, to manage the change from one to another. Coupled with these problems, there remain the concerns alluded to above regarding the tendency to use labels with differing meanings—a problem most notable with the Late Neolithic. While many authors define the Qatifian as Late Neolithic (Late Neolithic 2 in this volume), there are others who regard it not only as Chalcolithic but as Middle Chalcolithic (Garfinkel 1999).

Our dating evidence has been poor, with a fairly thin dataset of radiocarbon determinations; many of them come from early in the process of radiocarbon dating, with large errors, often on poorly contextualized samples, on samples that are unidentified, or possibly on old wood (cf. Aurenche et al. 2001). Banning (2007b) provides a useful summary of the state of the art with regard to chronology and 'culture', at least with regard to the Late Neolithic. Even now, with notable exceptions (e.g. Campbell 2007, Banning 2007c, Edwards et al. 2004), radiocarbon interpretation remains basic, and techniques such as Bayesian analysis are rarely applied.

Campbell notes the rather counterintuitive point: the more dates we obtain, the more problems we will have with cultural-chronological approaches, as 'the poorly synchronized beginnings and endings of periods' will become more problematic (Campbell 2007: 107). Synthetic accounts have been able, using a very broad brush, to gloss over the problems and suggest that we understand the big picture. Campbell argues that this is a false premise, and that we need to work from the bottom up with detailed individual site and subregional chronologies. Increasing regionalization over time may simply appear more obvious with the greater plasticity of ceramic styles—as noted by Goring-Morris and Belfer-Cohen with regard to the differentiation between Yarmukian and Lodian/Jericho IX regions in the southern Levant. Even before the production of ceramics, subregions should be important as the basic building blocks for our study, rather than the regional or transregional approaches, which tended to dominate in the past, and might help us avoid some of the chronological problems we face.

SEDENTARY BEHAVIOUR

Sedentary behaviour is a separate issue from farming, although the two have often been conflated. There are examples of highly mobile 'swidden' farmers and shifting cultivation, and fairly static hunter-gatherer societies. The excavation of Jericho and its spectacular Early Neolithic architecture at the beginning of the discovery of the Neolithic period provided a bias towards associating substantial architecture with farming. We now see the massive PPNA architecture as belonging to a period before farming had developed, although people were cultivating wild cereals in the Jordan Valley.

Sedentary behaviour is a matter of degree, and it is difficult to demonstrate the level of sedentism in prehistoric communities. Certainly, permanence of architecture is not a sure indicator of permanence of people—as in the recent history of the area, solid buildings may indicate storage rather than permanent people. Sedentism in the preceding Early Natufian may well have been overstated (Olszewski 1991), and in any case, by the Younger Dryas and Later Natufian, it appears likely that the level of sedentism had declined before the start of the Neolithic. Early–Middle PPNB Shaqarat Msaiad had evidence of blocked doors, suggesting to that people were used to periodically leaving the settlement. From Qermez Dere in the north (just outside our study area in northern Iraq) to Wadi Faynan 16 in southern Jordan, there is mounting evidence that with the PPNA came a concern for sweeping out rubbish, generally perceived as an indication of an increased degree of sedentism (Watkins 1990; Hardy-Smith and Edwards 2004).

One of the most striking developments in sedentism was the large settlements of the LPPNB, mostly along the top of the mountains along the east side of the rift valley in Jordan. Here it appears that at some existing MPPNB settlements and some new foundations, populations grew substantially, with sites becoming both larger and more densely occupied. In the period of these LPPNB sites, some of the best examples of ritual architecture occur in the south, described variously as cultic shrines and temples, possibly reflecting new ways of organizing communities with larger populations. These large sites appear to collapse suddenly, possibly due to climate change, overexploitation of the environment around the site, population stress, or a combination of all three. Later large sites in the ceramic Neolithic do not show the same range of community structures, and it is possible (as noted both by Akkermans and by Goring-Morris and Belfer-Cohen) that ceramic Neolithic population densities within these sites are much lower than in the LPPNB. Whether the patchy nature indicates distinct wards within a community, as argued here for Sha'ar Hagolan, or chronologically distinct moves within a 'site', as argued for Tell Sabi Abyad, is moot.

In the Late PPNB and onwards, there are new developments in the nature of sedentism with the development of symbiotic communities able to live in more arid areas. Such behaviour may well have its roots in hunter-gatherer-style economies, where task groups leave the main base camp to procure resources from seasonal task camps. The arid-land camps located in the Jafr Basin may represent an example of this and pre-date nomadic pastoralism (Fujii 2007). If Fujii is right, these camps used seasonal water to grow crops, not rear animals. Nomadic pastoralism has been argued to develop with the appearance of domestic animals at Azraq, and by the Late Neolithic, a distinct *facies* of the population appears to have lived in the arid lands, although there is no direct evidence that the sophisticated practices we would regard as 'nomadic pastoralism' had developed. It appears probable that all of these communities in the arid regions had close relationships to, or perhaps were parts of, more settled communities in the better-watered lands.

SOCIETY AND BELIEF

Much has been written in recent years about the importance of changing beliefs and new ways of organizing the society that came with increased sedentism, increased population density, and a greater cultural materialization. The impression that a major ideological change took place is confirmed by the discovery of plastered skulls at Jericho and subsequent examples at other sites in the southern Levant, the later discovery of plaster statues from the MPPNB at 'Ain Ghazal in Jordan, the more recent discovery of communal and ritual buildings at EPPNB sites on the Upper Euphrates, and an increased repertoire of naturalistic figurative art. These have been interpreted as the birth of religion (cf. Cauvin 2000) or as a cognitive revolution (Watkins 2004b) and the development of a more stratified society, although others (e.g. Kuijt 2004) have argued that, for a long time, PPNB society was trying to maintain an egalitarian ideal.

Akkermans argues that in the Upper Euphrates from the PPNA through the PPNB, the sites that have been excavated are not solely 'domestic villages' but 'cult centres at the same time', possibly serving not only their own populations but also populations of mobile hunter-gatherer groups. Cult centres appear both in the Upper Euphrates, where Gobekli Tepe in particular has been seen as a major regional centre, and also at Kfar HaHoresh and Nahal Hemar in Israel, which appear to have served different functions within a rich ritual landscape.

Subsistence economy

Ancient hunting and gathering economies tend to be compared with modern hunter-gatherer societies, despite the chronological gulf between them. Much of the 'revolution' perceived in the Neolithic is between societies reconstructed using modern analogies and 'farming' societies, who probably also still relied substantially on wild resources. For much of the period concerned, practices such as tending wild plants (cultivation) and management of wild animals would have formed an important part of subsistence economics. In modern terms, some of these societies might well have been described as hunter-gatherer rather than farming. In practice, however, many of the societies of the Levantine Neolithic should not be described as either, but as economies that included a range of practices combining the exploitation of wild resources with elements of food production. While there was an increased reliance on managed plants and animals by the end of the PPNB, there is no simple unidirectional development sequence, and much regional variation depends in part on local environment and vegetation conditions.

In-depth studies of plant and animal remains have been a mainstay of Neolithic research. The identification of morphological characteristics as well as diagnostic markers indicating human manipulation of plants and animals have been key in determining what form of plant and animal management was in place and whether we can really describe it as 'farming'. Traditional paleobotanical and zooarchaeological analysis as well as new genetic approaches strongly suggest that domestication took place in a number of different locations, with some taxa probably being domesticated several times within the region (Fernández et al. 2006; Willcox, Fornite, and Herveux 2008; Zeder 2009). New approaches are steadily being added to the battery of techniques that can be employed. Phytolith analysis is being examined for its potential to overcome some of the taphonomic limitations associated with carbonized seeds as well as to investigate the introduction of irrigation (e.g. Rosen 1987), and isotope studies are increasingly being used to examine issues of sedentism and animal management practices (Makarewicz and Tuross 2009). Together these studies suggest a complex and varied process of domestication for both plants and animals.

The domesticated wheat, barley, sheep, and goats that are often described as part of the Neolithic farming package, and therefore understood as the core elements of what makes the Neolithic so important, only gradually emerge during the Pre-Pottery Neolithic. In economic terms, the Levantine Neolithic is what has been described in other parts of the world as 'diffuse' early farming (Vrydaghs and Denham 2007), where there is much variation between communities and no sharp divide between hunter-gatherer societies and those practising various levels of activities that we might describe as farming. Paleobotanical evidence suggests that PPNA plant exploitation included cultivation of morphologically wild cereals, legumes and possibly figs as well as a continued reliance on the gathering of wild plant resources, including small-seeded grasses and almonds. There is increasing evidence suggesting the intensification of plant management during the PPNB, indicated by the appearance of domesticated traits (e.g. tough rachis, larger grain size). While humans began manipulating plant resources during the PPNA, it is not until c.1,000 years later during the PPNB that clear evidence of animal management can be seen, and only by the LPPNB does it appear to dominate. Evidence suggests that there was no single domestication event, but different taxa were domesticated in different places several times and that domesticates were moved (e.g. sheep being introduced to the southern Levant and the entire package, most probably including wild animals) to Cyprus. Arguments that a form of nomadic pastoralism develops in the PPNC, specifically in the use of the arid eastern areas of Jordan, are based only on circumstantial evidence, such as suggestions that the corridor houses of the PPNC settlement at 'Ain Ghazal were only seasonally occupied and that the presence of sheep and goat remains found at sites around Azraq relate to seasonal movements.

The abandonment of the large LPPNB settlements has been explained in terms of local landscape destruction through overexploitation by humans of plant resources, either directly through deforestation for fuel, or indirectly though overgrazing by sheep and goats. While this has been the subject of considerable debate, a key point is that there is very little evidence for PPNB soil management—an important part of any stable sedentary agricultural system. This may change in the Late Neolithic, where early evidence for terracing and possibly fertilizing with manure may be visible in the region at Dhra' associated with Late Neolithic finds (Kuijt, Finlayson, and MacKay 2007). In general there seem to be striking changes in the landscape during the Late Neolithic, with populations apparently more diffusely spread in smaller settlements, a phenomenon best illustrated by research in the Wadi Ziqlab (Banning 1996). The relatively rare, large Late Neolithic sites, such as Sha'ar Hagolan and Tell Sabi Abyad, as noted above, may in fact be palimpsests of smaller occupations over time.

CONCLUSION

The Levant is often perceived as the region where we know the most about the Neolithic transition as a result of its long history of research. Although there is evidence for similar processes at work in the wider region and a need for more research beyond the Levant, it is also very clear that the quantity of data now available in the Levant enables a more in-depth style of research. However, despite the many years of work undertaken, we are still discovering how little we know. Having been rather dismissive of the cultural history created by comparative studies of material culture over large regions, I would re-emphasize that the basic building blocks for our research should be local histories, to allow us to escape from the oversimplified cultural evolutionary deterministic approaches that see every change as either a failure or the next step on a cultural ladder.

Architectural, material, cultural, and economic diversity is ubiquitous throughout the Neolithic. At the same time, strong common threads that gradually emerge at different times in different places suggest there was significant interaction between the various communities. Economic relationships gradually develop in a fairly uniform manner across the region, and by the end of the Neolithic a way of life, combining economic and social factors, had surfaced, providing a basis for subsequent developments eventually leading to urbanism. Through the application of new techniques and the development of new ways of understanding what is taking place, the coming years promise an ever-changing story of the Neolithic in the Levant.

SUGGESTED READING

Barker, G. (2006). *The Agricultural Revolution in Prehistory: Why Did Foragers Become Farmers?* Oxford: Oxford University Press

Cauvin, J. (2000). *The Birth of Gods and the Origins of Agriculture*, trans. T. Watkins. Cambridge: Cambridge University Press.

Manning, S. W. (2007). Beyond dates to chronology: rethinking the Neolithic–Chalcolithic Levant. *Paléorient* 33: 5–10.

Renfrew, C. (2007). *Prehistory: The Making of the Human Mind*. London: Weidenfeld & Nicolson.

REFERENCES

Aurenche, O., P. Galet, E. Régagnon-Caroline, and J. Évin (2001). Proto-Neolithic and Neolithic cultures in the Middle East: the birth of agriculture, livestock raising, and ceramics—a calibrated 14C chronology 12,500–5500 cal BC. *Radiocarbon* 43: 1191–1202.

Banning, E. B. (1996). Highlands and lowlands: problems and survey frameworks for rural archaeology in the Near East. *Bulletin of the American Schools of Oriental Research* 301: 25–46.

—— (2007a). Time and tradition in the transition from Late Neolithic to Chalcolithic: summary and conclusions. Paléorient 33: 137–42.

—— (2007b). Introduction. *Paléorient* 33: 11–14.

—— (2007c). Wadi Rabah and related assemblages in the southern Levant: interpreting the radiocarbon evidence. *Paléorient* 33: 77–101.

Barker, G. (2006). *The Agricultural Revolution in Prehistory: Why Did Foragers Become Farmers?* Oxford: Oxford University Press

Bourke, S. J. (2007). The Late Neolithic/Early Chalcolithic transition at Teleilat Ghassul: context, chronology and culture. *Paléorient* 33: 15–32.

Braidwood, L. S., R. J. Braidwood, B. Howe, C. Reed, and P. J. Watson (eds) (1983). *Prehistoric Archeology along the Zagros Flanks*. Chicago: Oriental Institute of the University of Chicago.

Campbell, S. (2007). Rethinking Halaf chronologies. *Paléorient* 33: 103–36.

Cauvin, J. (2000). *The Birth of Gods and the Origins of Agriculture*, trans. T. Watkins. Cambridge: Cambridge University Press.

Childe, V. G. (1964). *What Happened in History*, rev. edn. Harmondsworth: Penguin.

Edwards, P. C., J. Meadows, G. Sayej, and M. Westaway (2004). From the PPNA to the PPNB: new views from the southern Levant after excavations at Zahrat adh-Dhra 2 in Jordan. *Paléorient* 30: 21–60.

Fernández, H., S. Hughes, J.-D. Vigne, et al. (2006). Divergent mtDNA lineages of goats in an Early Neolithic site, far from the initial domestication areas. *Proceedings of the National Academy of the Sciences of the Unites States of America* 103: 15375–9.

Finlayson, B., I. Kuijt, T. Arpin, et al. (2003). Dhra Excavation Project: 2002 Interim Report. *Levant* 35: 1–38.

——— and S. J. Mithen (2007). *The Early Prehistory of Wadi Faynan, Southern Jordan: Archaeological Survey of Wadis Faynan, Ghuwayr and al-Bustan and Evaluation of the Pre-Pottery Neolithic A Site of WF16*. Oxford: Council for British Research in the Levant and Oxbow Books.

Fujii, S. (2007). PPNB barrage systems at Wadi Abu Tulayha and Wadi Ar-Ruwayshid ash-Sharqi: a preliminary report of the 2006 Spring Field Season of the Jafr Basin Prehistoric Project Phase 2. *Annual of the Department of Antiquities of Jordan* 51: 403–28.

Garfinkel, Y. (1999). *Neolithic and Chalcolithic Pottery of the Southern Levant*. Jerusalem: Institute of Archaeology, Hebrew University of Jerusalem.

Gebel, H.-G. (2004). There was no center: the polycentric evolution of the Near Eastern Neolithic. *Neo-Lithics* 1/04: 28–32.

Gilead, I. (2007). The Besorian: a pre-Ghassulian cultural entity. *Paléorient* 33: 33–49.

Hardy-Smith, T., and P. C. Edwards (2004). The garbage crisis in prehistory: artefact discard patterns at the early Natufian site of Wadi Hammeh 27 and the origins of household refuse disposal strategies. *Journal of Anthropological Archaeology* 23: 253–89.

Kuijt, I. (2004). When the walls came down: social organization, ideology and the 'collapse' of the Pre-Pottery Neolithic. In H.-D. Bienert, H.-G. K. Gebel, and R. Neef (eds), *Proceedings of the Symposium on Central Settlements in Neolithic Jordan, Held in Wadi Musa, Jordan, 21st–25th of July, 1997*. Berlin: Ex oriente.

——— B. Finlayson, and J. MacKay (2007). Pottery Neolithic landscape modification at Dhra. *Antiquity* 81: 106–18.

Makarewicz, C., and N. Tuross (2009). Variation in goat diet through the later Pre-Pottery Neolithic: diachronic shifts in human approaches to caprine management at Basta. In J. J. Shea and D. E. Lieberman (eds), *Transitions in Prehistory: Essays in Honor of Ofer Bar-Yosef*. Oxford: Oxbow, 285–302.

Manning, S. W. (2007). Beyond dates to chronology: rethinking the Neolithic–Chalcolithic Levant. *Paléorient* 33: 5–10.

Olszewski, D. (1991). Social complexity in the Natufian? Assessing the relationship of ideas and data. In G. A. Clark (ed.), *Perspectives on the Past: Theoretical Biases in Mediterranean Hunter-Gatherer Research*. Philadelphia: University of Pennsylvania Press, 322–40.

Renfrew, C. (2003). *Figuring It Out: What Are We? Where Do We Come From? The Parallel Vision of Artists and Archaeologists*. New York: Thames & Hudson.

——— (2007). *Prehistory: The Making of the Human Mind*. London: Weidenfeld & Nicolson.

Robinson, S., S. Black, B. Sellwood, and P. Valdes (2006). A review of palaeoclimates in the Levant and eastern Mediterranean from 25,000 to 5,000 years BP: setting the environmental background for the evolution of human civilisation. *Quaternary Science Review* 25: 1517–41.

Rollefson, G. O., and H.-G. K. Gebel (2004). Towards new frameworks: supra-regional concepts in Near Eastern Neolithization. *Neo-Lithics* 1/04: 21–2.

Rosen, A. M. (1987). Phytolith studies at Shiqmim. In T. D. Levy (ed.), *Shiqmim I: Studies Concerning Chalcolithic Societies in the Northern Negev Desert, Israel (1982–1984)*, vol. 1. Oxford: British Archaeological Reports, 243–9.

Sayej, G. J. (2001). A new Pre-Pottery Neolithic, a cultural region in Jordan: the Dead Sea Basin. In A. Walmsley (ed.), *Australians Uncovering Ancient Jordan: Fifty Years of Middle Eastern Archaeology*. Sydney: Research Institute for Humanities and Social Sciences, University of Sydney, 225–32.

Schmidt, K. (2001). Göbekli Tepe, southeastern Turkey: a preliminary report on the 1995–1999 excavations. *Paléorient* 26: 45–54.

Stordeur, D., D. Helmer, and G. Willcox (1997). Jerf el Ahmar: un nouveau site de l'horizon PPNA sur le moyen Euphrates syrien. *Bulletin de la Société Préhistorique Française* 94: 282–5.

Vrydaghs, L., and T. Denham (2007). Rethinking agriculture: introductory thoughts. In T. Denham, J. Iriarte, and L. Vrydaghs (eds), *Rethinking Agriculture: Archaeological and Ethnoarchaeological Perspectives*. Walnut Creek, Calif.: Left Coast Press, 1–15.

Warburton, D. (2004). Review of *Towards New Frameworks: Supra-Regional Concepts in Near Eastern Neolithization: A Report on the 4th Icaane Workshop (Berlin, 1–2 April 2004)*, organized by H. G. K. Gebel, M. Özdoğan, G. Rollefson, and K. Schmidt. *Paléorient* 30: 183–8.

Watkins, T. (1990). The origins of house and home? *World Archaeology* 21: 336–47.

——(2003). Developing socio-cultural networks. *Neo-Lithics* 2/03: 36–7.

——(2004a). Architecture and theatres of memory in the Neolithic of southwest Asia. In E. DeMarrais, C. Gosden, and C. Renfrew (eds), *Rethinking Materiality: The Engagement of Mind with the Material World*. Cambridge: McDonald Institute for Archaeological Research, 97–106.

——(2004b). Building houses, framing concepts, constructing worlds. *Paléorient* 30: 5–23.

Willcox, G., S. Fornite, and L. Herveux (2008). Early Holocene cultivation before domestication in northern Syria. *Vegetational History and Archaeobotany* 17: 313–25.

Zeder, M. A. (2009). The Neolithic macro-(r)evolution: macroevolutionary theory and the study of culture change. *Journal of Archaeological Research* 17: 1–63.

CHAPTER 10

THE NORTHERN LEVANT DURING THE NEOLITHIC PERIOD
Damascus and Beyond

PETER M. M. G. AKKERMANS

The purpose of this chapter is to briefly consider the nature and scale of settlement in Syria and Lebanon during the Neolithic (*c*.10,000–5300 cal. BC) and their implications for occupation in other parts of the Levant. In Syria, intensive fieldwork since the 1960s in the middle Euphrates area and in the Jezireh to the east of it has produced a formidable wealth of information. Dozens of Neolithic settlements have been located in surface surveys, and excavations have been initiated at many of them (Fig. 10.1).

The unravelling of their complex histories continuously amplifies and alters earlier propositions and conclusions on the evolution of Neolithic communities in this part of the Near East from the early tenth to the late sixth millennium BC. In contrast, the data from western Syria and Lebanon are not as plentiful as those of the middle Euphrates region and the expanse of steppe further east. The northern Levant has been conspicuously under-investigated for the Neolithic, with the greater part of the research efforts spent on surveys of different scale and intensity, less on excavations. The sites—their layout, architecture, material culture, economy, chronology, etc.—are still imperfectly understood, the more so because fieldwork was often done many years ago according to standards of recovery very different from today.

As to chronology, I shall rely on the conventional division of the Neolithic into two broad, successive phases, i.e. an early (aceramic) Neolithic phase (*c*.10,000–6900 cal. BC) and a late (ceramic) Neolithic phase (*c*.6900–5300 cal. BC). Primarily on the basis of its lithics, the early period is usually subdivided into the Pre-Pottery Neolithic A (PPNA, *c*.10,000–8700 cal. BC) and the Pre-Pottery Neolithic B (PPNB, *c*.8700–6900 cal. BC), the latter with its Early, Middle, Late, and Final stages. Late Neolithic relative chronology is usually based on developments in pottery typology and technology, which have led to a complex (and often very confusing) array of ceramic phases, with considerable local and regional variety (cf. Cauvin and Cauvin 1993; Cauvin 2000; Akkermans and Schwartz 2003).

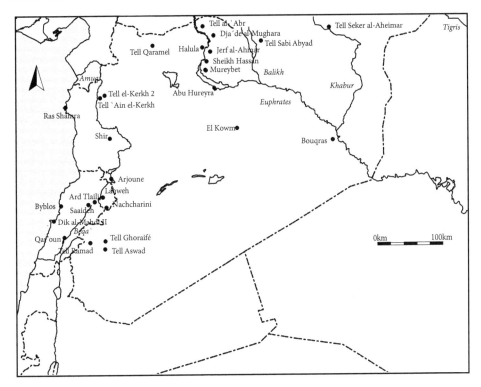

FIG. 10.1 Map of Neolithic sites in the northern Levant

NEOLITHIC BEGINNINGS ON
THE MIDDLE EUPHRATES

Sedentary village life and the inception of the farming economy are usually considered to characterize the beginning of the Neolithic in Syria and the Levant around the middle of the tenth millennium BC. It is, however, important to realize that the first steps towards sedentism were taken much earlier, at places such as Abu Hureyra I and Mureybet IA in the eleventh millennium BC, and that the full-scale adoption of agriculture and stock rearing took place thousands of years later, at the sites of the eighth millennium BC. Agriculture was not a necessary prerequisite of sedentary life, nor were sedentary settlers always farmers. Moreover, the sedentary lifestyle initially seems to have concerned only a relatively small number of people at a handful of small and dispersed sites, with evidence of sometimes long-lasting, albeit not necessarily year-round, occupation. Sites of the earliest Neolithic (PPNA, 10,000–8700 cal. BC) have been identified at a few places along the Euphrates: Mureybet, Sheikh Hassan, Jerf al-Ahmar, and Tell al-'Abr. No other site of this period is known in the interior of Syria. The number of occupations from the subsequent Early and Middle PPNB phases (c.8700–7500 cal. BC) is very small as well, with one or two of the earlier sites still in use for some time, the others abandoned, and a few newly founded (at different moments in time), such as Dja'de al-Mughara, Abu Hureyra, and Halula. Although later overburdens obscure the early deposits in most cases, leaving us uncertain about their size, it seems safe to assume that many if not all were small occupations less than 0.5–1ha in size, probably inhabited by a few dozen rather than hundreds of people (Akkermans and Schwartz 2003 and references therein).

Architecture at these sites consisted of round or oval, sometimes semi-subterranean dwellings 3–6m across, occasionally divided into smaller compartments for living, cooking, and storage. Wall paintings occurred in a few cases. PPNA Jerf al-Ahmar and Tell al-'Abr have also revealed a spectacular kind of architecture that was probably related to community-wide ritual and ceremony rather than to ordinary living: large, round, and wholly subterranean buildings embellished with benches and carved upright stone slabs, ornamented with friezes of triangles, undulating lines, human figures, and birds of prey (Fig. 10.2; cf. Stordeur et al. 2000). Another remarkable find, although of later date (*c.*8000 cal. BC), was the *Maison des Morts* at Dja'de al-Mughara, containing the skeletal remains of at least 38 individuals interred in a variety of ways (Coqueugniot 1998). These sites, it seems, were domestic villages and cult centres at the same time, serving perhaps not only the needs of their own occupants but also those of small, transitory hunter-gatherer groups in their vicinity (Akkermans 2004).

By 9000 cal. BC the round architecture was slowly replaced by rectangular structures, built of *pisé* on stone, sometimes strengthened with wooden poles. Dja'de al-Mughara, less than 1ha in size, revealed small, single-roomed houses which had been repeatedly renewed, suggestive of some permanence of settlement, although there were insubstantial, short-lived structures as well. Sites such as Abu Hureyra and Halula may have grown into sizeable villages from around 8000 cal. BC onwards, assumed to have covered as many as 7–8ha by the end of the eighth millennium, although it is not always clear how much later occupations contributed to the size of the mounds as we see them today.

In the domain of subsistence, the sites revealed an overwhelming predominance of wild resources over possible cultigens and domesticated animals. Early efforts at cultivation, such as at Abu Hureyra (cf. Moore, Hillman, and Legge 2000), seem to have had a highly restricted, local impact; it was not until the eighth millennium that the communities were firmly tied to the farming economy. Middle PPNB Abu Hureyra had a range of domestic

FIG. 10.2 Circular, subterranean architecture at Jerf al-Ahmar, *c.*9000 cal. BC (photograph D. Stordeur)

plants which occurred together with their wild counterparts. In contrast, nearby Halula contained no evidence for wild crop plants, suggesting that its settlers brought species such as wheat, barley, and flax in a fully domesticated form. The contribution of domestic animals (sheep and goats) to the diet was modest in the beginning but increased significantly in the late eighth millennium (up to 65–75% of the animal bone at Abu Hureyra; e.g. Moore, Hillman, and Legge 2000).

In the late PPNB (c.7500–7000 cal. BC), the number of sites increased substantially—dozens of sites have been identified for this period, usually in the form of settlement mounds with proof of sustained occupation over long spans of time. Early farming villages also began to appear in regions used rarely or not at all by settled communities so far, such as the Khabur and Balikh Basins. Most sites were small, one hectare or less, although there were a few larger settlements as well (Abu Hureyra, Halula, Bouqras, and Seker al-Aheimar). They were characterized by regularity and order in the pattern of house construction, indicative of the careful planning and organization of occupation. The houses were rectangular in plan, although in different variants, and often stood tightly together. They regularly had white-plastered floors, burnished to a shine and sometimes painted in red ochre, as at Tell Halula. Halula also yielded evidence of stone works of impressive scale, such as the huge retaining wall at least 28m long and 4m high, which undoubtedly required the effort of the local community in its entirety (Akkermans and Schwartz 2003 and references therein).

Not all sites grew into villages with long sequences of use. Although their precise date in the PPNB sequence is uncertain, several ephemeral, short-lived occupations covering a few hundred square metres at most have been located in the Euphrates Valley. Briefly used camps also occurred in caves and rock shelters in the Jebel ed-Douara and the Palmyrene, and at many of the open-air flint-working localities in their vicinity. Similar occupations have been found in western Syria and Lebanon, such as in caves high in the Anti-Lebanon and in the plains in its foothills. Small occupations, with a few, scattered lithics being the sole traces of use, were found at places such as Tell aux Scies and Dik al-Mahdi II on the Lebanese coast, and at Saaideh in the Beqa' Valley (Moore 1978; Cauvin 2000; Akkermans and Schwartz 2003). It is still unclear whether these sites should be interpreted as forager encampments in their own right, or whether they resulted from logistical forays from larger, more permanently used settlements located elsewhere.

EARLY NEOLITHIC WESTERN SYRIA AND LEBANON

The evidence for settlement in western Syria and Lebanon in the early stages of the Neolithic is extremely meagre. So far, research has produced only a few small sites lying far apart. Excavation at Tell Qaramel, north of Aleppo, has revealed wall fragments and other occupational debris ascribed to the PPNA period (c.9000 cal. BC) (Mazurowski 2003). Surface finds suggest the presence of another site of this period at Tell Chehab in the Palmyrene foothills east of Homs. PPNA-type lithics, including notched-based Al-Khiam points, have also been found in soundings at Nachcharini Cave high in the Anti-Lebanon, just inside the Lebanese border, and on the surface of the open-air stations of Borj Barajne and 'Tell aux

Haches' in the coastal dunes near Beirut. These were undoubtedly the temporary shelters of hunter-gatherer parties (Copeland 1991).

The overall scarcity of settlement continued up to the mid-eighth millennium BC. A small, short-lived occupation, dated to around 8500 cal. BC, has recently been identified at Tell 'Ain el-Kerkh near Idlib, in the form of a 1m-deep deposit excavated over an area of 5×5m and containing several shallow hearths (Tsuneki et al. 2006). More substantial evidence for settlement in this period comes from 5ha Tell Aswad near Damascus, where occupation started in the early PPNB, not in the PPNA as was assumed for a long time. Tell Aswad was first excavated in two very small soundings in the early 1970s, and at the time data were restricted to ash lenses, pits, fireplaces, and some wall fragments. Renewed excavations since 2001 have revealed single-roomed, elliptical or rectilinear mud-brick structures with rounded corners, up to 7m in diameter with a base for a roof pillar in the centre. Groups of storage bins were along the walls, whereas hearths stood in the open yards surrounding the buildings. Significantly, buildings at Tell Aswad were relatively short-lived, with little or no evidence for reconstruction. Settlement at the site seems to have shifted back and forth over the mound continuously; areas inhabited at one time were turned into open spaces at another time, and vice versa. Although its precise date is still uncertain, there was also an area specifically intended for burial and funeral ritual, with at least 25 individuals, in the form of either complete skeletal remains, skeletons without their skulls, or groups of skulls. An extraordinary find was the cache of four skulls remodelled with plaster to produce a life-like image of the human face (Fig. 10.3; cf. Stordeur 2003a; 2003b). Such plastering of skulls had earlier been attested a short distance west of Tell Aswad at Tell Ramad (de Contenson 2000), as well as at a series of sites in the southern Levant, such as Jericho, Beisamoun, and 'Ain Ghazal.

Less than a decade ago it was still believed that Neolithic habitation in coastal Syria and Lebanon did not occur until the mid-eighth millennium BC, with the beginning of the Late PPNB (Cauvin 2000). This view is unlikely to be correct. The supposed vacuum is being filled in with sites such as Tells Qaramel and 'Ain el-Kerkh, which by themselves imply the existence of other Neolithic sites in the northern Levant. The small communities cannot

FIG. 10.3 A group of four human skulls remodelled with plaster, found at PPNB Tell Aswad near Damascus (photograph D. Stordeur)

have operated entirely on their own, if only to ensure their biological survival. Sites may have been obliterated by the far-reaching effects of erosion, urbanization, and modern agriculture, or they may have become buried below later settlement mounds or underneath alluvial fans and wash from higher-situated areas (e.g. the site of Saaideh in the Beqaʿ was found by chance in an irrigation ditch over 3m below present-day field level). An intensified search will undoubtedly lead to the discovery of more sites. It is important to realize that the sparseness of settlement in the northern Levant in the earliest Neolithic is not unlike that of inland Syria; although researched much better, the interior, too, has yielded only a handful of small occupations at a considerable distance from each other along the Euphrates and its tributaries. But given the size of the area and the length of the period, many dozens or even hundreds of sites must have once existed in Syria and the Levant during the early Neolithic (c.10,000–7500 cal. BC). The majority of these as yet 'invisible' sites were, I believe, not settlement mounds but ephemeral, short-lived occupations with thin depositional strata and low archaeological visibility. Thus, small, temporary camps rather than large, permanent settlements may once have littered the landscape, and continual mobility rather than long-term stay may have been dominant in the earliest Neolithic (Akkermans 2004).

Research into the late PPNB has concentrated on a few settlement mounds of relatively large size and prominent visibility. Most sites, however, are known only from the finds on their surfaces. They often seem to have been isolated in the landscape, suggesting highly dispersed occupation of low regional intensity, although this may easily reflect the history and nature of archaeological investigation. In the Damascus area small villages were newly founded at Ghoraifé and Ramad. Ghoraifé failed to produce a coherent building plan, but nearby 2ha Tell Ramad had a series of widely spaced, semi-subterranean structures of roughly oval form, 3m or 4m in diameter, in its lowest Level I (de Contenson 2000). On the Mediterranean littoral, Ras Shamra VC and Byblos 'Néolithique ancien' have yielded aceramic layers of probably late eighth-millennium date, including rectangular houses on stone foundations with white-plastered floors. Similar architecture was found at Labweh in the Beqaʿ and, more recently, at Tell ʿAin el-Kerkh in the Rouj Basin.

LATE NEOLITHIC DEVELOPMENTS

Northeastern Syria

The first occurrence of ceramics in the seventh millennium BC has always been understood as a watershed in the prehistory of Syria and the Levant, distinguishing the early from the late Neolithic and assumed to be pivotal in the transformation of the local communities in the centuries that followed. However, recent excavation at Tell Sabi Abyad has shown that the introduction of pottery initially made little or no difference to the Neolithic way of life. There was much continuity in site distribution, community organization, material culture, subsistence, etc., indicating that the change at the transition from the early, aceramic to the later, ceramic Neolithic may have been much less profound than is often believed. In the beginning, pottery—generally relatively crude products in simple shapes (Fig. 10.4)—was probably little more than a useful type of container. It was not until seven or eight centuries after its first appearance, with the rise of the elaborate painted-pottery styles at the very end

FIG. 10.4 Early seventh-millennium pottery found at Tell Sabi Abyad in northeastern Syria (photograph P. Akkermans)

of the seventh millennium, that ceramics may have acquired a wider significance, serving in social networks as gifts or emblems of local identity and allegiance (Akkermans et al. 2006). Moreover, the manufacture and use of ceramics did not follow a simple, unilateral trajectory from one place to another. The earliest pottery was found in occupations radiocarbon-dated at c.7000–6800 cal. BC along the northern and northwestern fringes of the Fertile Crescent, at places such as Tell Sabi Abyad (Nieuwenhuyse 2006), Tell Seker al-Aheimar (Nishiaki and Le Mière 2005), and, more recently, Shir near Hama (Bartl, Hijazi, and Haidar 2006), whereas it was adopted much later in its advanced rather than incipient form in eastern Syria and the interior desert, such as in the El Kowm Oasis.

Seventh-millennium occupation along the Euphrates and in the plains of the Jezireh further east continued to be largely confined to settlement mounds with often lengthy sequences, but there were also shallow and short-lived sites, particularly towards the end of the period. The density of settlement fluctuated through time and varied from region to region. Settlements were, as before, of restricted size, in the range of 0.5–2ha, used by relatively small groups. There may have been a few more sizeable sites, such as Bouqras in eastern Syria, which probaly had as many as 180 houses over a 3ha area inhabited by 700–1000 people in the mid-seventh millennium BC. It remains to be seen, however, whether such high population estimates are always significant, considering the limited archaeological exposures (and hence limited insight into the overall organization of the settlement), as well as the growing evidence for continually shifting occupations and localized abandonments *within* the sites in the course of generations.

The architecture, made of *pisé* or mud bricks, ranged from small, single-roomed structures to large rectangular dwellings with many rooms of various sizes and elaborate tripartite buildings, each composed of three or four long rooms often divided into smaller compartments (Fig. 10.5). They either stood tightly together, as at Bouqras, or were widely spaced with extensive yards containing hearths, kilns, and silos between them, as at Tell Sabi Abyad. The settlement at Bouqras had a consistent and well-ordered pattern of house construction, suggestive of careful planning from the start. Elsewhere the communities came about in a much more 'organic' manner, allowing for individual preferences and swift adjustments to

FIG. 10.5 Tripartite architecture built upon a large mud-brick platform at Tell Sabi Abyad III, *c*.7000–6800 BC (photograph P. Akkermans)

changing needs through time. Tell Sabi Abyad and several other sites in its vicinity have provided evidence of large mud-brick platforms measuring around 10×7×0.7m, sometimes provided with low staircases. They stood prominently on the slope of the mound, where they served as foundations for the architecture built on top of them.

Tell Sabi Abyad has also provided evidence for important changes in the nature of settlement and the associated material culture at the end of the seventh millennium, *c*.6200 cal. BC (possibly in association with an abrupt climate change around this time; cf. Alley et al. 1997). This moment of renewal coincided with shifts in the location of habitation as well as the appearance of new types of architecture, including extensive multi-roomed storehouses and small circular dwellings (*tholoi*). There were changes in the lithic industry, including new types of projectile points, and in the manufacture of pottery, which occurred in many complex shapes, decorations, and wares different from the earlier products. It involved innovations such as the abundant use of spindle whorls and, very significantly, the introduction of stamp seals and sealings as indicators of property and the organization of controlled storage. The role of other artefact categories, such as vessels made of stone (*vaisselle blanche*), decreased substantially. Change also took place in the treatment of the dead, including the common occurrence of burial gifts and the development of graveyards. Last but not least, there were significant adjustments in the subsistence economy, involving an increase in pastoralism and mobility. Animals may have been exploited not only for their meat but for their 'secondary products', as can be deduced from milk residues on ceramics and the mass occurrence of spindle whorls, suggesting changes in textile production involving wool (Akkermans and Schwartz 2003; Akkermans et al. 2006).

The distinctive change at about 6200 cal. BC was not local but can be seen in various degrees at many sites in Syria and elsewhere. It ushered in considerable regional differentiation in the material culture and the organization of settlement. It is probably not a coincidence that many sites in the southern Levant underwent a metamorphosis with the onset of the Yarmukian period at about the same time, including, among other things, the introduction of circular architecture and pottery (many hundreds of years after its emergence in Syria).

Insight into community life in Syria at the close of the seventh millennium can be obtained from a number of recent excavations along the Euphrates and its tributaries. One example is the so-called Burnt Village at Tell Sabi Abyad, 1–2ha in size and consisting of extensive, closely spaced rectangular granaries and storehouses surrounded by many small round structures, which ended in a conflagration around 6000 cal. BC. Rich inventories have been recovered from the burnt buildings, including pottery, stone vessels, flint and obsidian implements, ground-stone tools, figurines, personal ornaments, and hundreds of clay sealings with stamp-seal impressions. Settlements like this, it has been argued, provided facilities of many kinds not only to their own sedentary populations but also to pastoralists roaming the surrounding steppe environments. The settlements were centres of production, storage, exchange, and distribution, and the scenes of all kinds of social engagements (Akkermans and Schwartz 2003). On the opposite side of the spectrum, there were small stations or camp sites with evidence of episodic settlement, as in the El Kowm area and other marginal areas in central and eastern Syria (Cauvin 1990).

Intricately painted ceramics occurred in ever-increasing quantities and developed into the famous painted-pottery styles of the end of the seventh and the beginning of the sixth millennia BC, such as the Samarra and Halaf, distributed over regions sometimes larger than modern states (although there was much internal diversity). The characteristic pottery is found at many sites, in association with circular buildings, with or without rectangular antechambers, containing hearths and other domestic installations. Rectangular buildings consisting of small cellular rooms occurred occasionally, and probably served as the communities' central storehouses. In many areas of sixth-millennium Syria there were considerably more sites than before, although they were usually very small and short-lived, reflecting a continually shifting pattern of settlement over the landscape. Occupations were easily established and easily deserted, often within one or two generations. Mobility and living in small, dispersed parties, it seems, were extremely important. At the very end of the sixth millennium, not only did rectangular architecture regain its predominance but there was also a renewed emphasis on permanent, long-term settlement in selected places, resulting in the build-up of substantial mounds.

Northern Levant

In western Syria, and probably in Lebanon as well, pottery appeared more or less at the same time as it did in the Syrian interior, around 7000–6800 BC, as shown by recent excavations at Shir in the vicinity of Hama (Bartl, Hijazi, and Haidar 2006). Other evidence in this direction has come from small soundings at Tell el-Kerkh 2 north of Shir and, to the south, at Tell Ramad near Damascus (Tsuneki and Miyake 1996; de Contenson 2000). The local pottery styles are commonly grouped together as 'Dark-Faced Burnished Ware' on the basis of the 1930s excavations at Tells Judaidah and Dhahab in the 'Amuq Plain (Braidwood and Braidwood 1960). The 'Amuq framework has often been transferred uncritically to other parts of Syria, but recent research has begun to refine and expand the 'Amuq data with attention shifting to internal diversity and regional differentiation. Long considered to have been the earliest pottery in the west, Dark-Faced Burnished Ware may now have a predecessor in the 'Kerkh Ware' of the lowest ceramic levels at Tell el-Kerkh 2 (Tsuneki and Miyake 1996). Southern Levantine Yarmukian-style pottery of the late seventh millennium occurred on the coast at Byblos—the northernmost site currently known with this kind of pottery (Garfinkel 1999).

During the course of the seventh millennium BC, settlements became well established in the varied landscapes of western Syria and Lebanon. Surface reconnaissance suggests an overall increase of sites in this period. For example, the Rouj area in the Early Neolithic (PPNB) contained only one or two sites, in contrast to the Late Neolithic represented by some fourteen occupations. A recent survey west of Homs has produced only one PPNB site, but twelve sites of Late Neolithic date (Haïdar-Boustani et al. 2007). Occupations also began to appear in regions that were apparently devoid of permanent settlement prior to the seventh millennium, such as the 'Amuq Plain in the northwest. However, we cannot assume that the sites are all contemporary. It is all too easy to conclude that more sites mean more sedentary occupation or an increase in population, but the number of sites in use at any given moment was probably (very) low.

The architecture at these sites was rectangular, ranging from relatively large storehouses made of many tiny cubicles hardly more than 1m² in size at Tell el-Kerkh 2 to small single-roomed structures of mud bricks on stone foundations at Tell Ramad. They tend to be free-standing, with lanes and yards containing hearths, ovens, and silos. Ramad in its final Level III has failed to produce a single building so far; instead, there were large pits sunk into the earlier phases, interpreted as temporary shelters used by pastoralists.

The history of settlement in the sixth millennium BC is among the poorest known in the northern Levant so far. There was a range of sites with varying amounts and degrees of materials of both southern Levantine and northeastern Syrian/Anatolian derivation. North Mesopotamian Halaf-style pottery, either locally produced or imported, extended as far west as Ras Shamra on the Mediterranean and as far south as Arjoune on the Orontes in Syria and Ard Tlaili in the Beqa' in the Lebanon. At these southern occupations the characteristic painted wares were found in (very) small quantities together with many burnished and unburnished ceramics that display a close resemblance to the southern Levantine Wadi Rabah pottery (Garfinkel 1999; Parr 2003). Such ceramics with a southern affinity also occurred to some extent at Byblos in its 'Néolithique moyen'—a short-lived phase following the Yarmukian-related layers. There is, however, evidence for local and regional trends in the pottery (and in the other material-culture categories, for that matter) from the northern Levant which requires first of all an evaluation in its own terms, rather than the rigid imposition of ceramic frameworks established in other, remote areas.

Excavations have been restricted to small samples at a few sites, and their chronologies often remain uncertain. Both Byblos and Ras Shamra on the Mediterranean had rectangular architecture, instead of the round buildings so typical of this period elsewhere in Syria. Free-standing single and multi-roomed, rectangular structures also occurred at Tell 'Ain el-Kerkh as well as at neighbouring Tell el-Kerkh 2 in association with circular buildings up to 2.5m in diameter. The round features had a restricted lifetime and were repeatedly renewed in the same spot (Iwasaki and Tsuneki 2003). At Arjoune there were shallow pits and what may have been the lower portions of roughly circular, subterranean structures, sunk to about a metre into the natural rock and filled with occupational debris—possibly the emplacements for small dwellings used only seasonally by a migrant population (Parr 2003).

The long-established mounds in the Damascus area seem to have been abandoned by about 6000 cal. BC at the latest, and any data on their sixth-millennium successors are highly inconclusive. Surveys in the foothills of the Anti-Lebanon and along the Barada River west of Damascus have located sites that might date from this period, but these seem to have been little more than small and ephemeral occupations (de Contenson 1985). Investigation in the Homs region and in the Lebanese Beqaʿ Gap have revealed both surface stations and settlement mounds with materials of often unspecified Neolithic/Chalcolithic date (Philip et al. 2005). The Lebanese sites are usually dated with reference to Byblos, although the sequence established there many years ago is not without (severe) difficulties. On the Lebanese coast and in the southern Beqaʿ Valley there were a series of localities (Qarʾoun, Nabi Zair, Mejdel Anjar, etc.) known only from their surface materials, which probably served as factory sites at which flint was obtained and worked. Some were small stations with little depth of deposit, others had very extensive artefact scatters, although these probably reflect successive occupations over long periods of time rather than a single large site. One cave (Bezez, southwest of Sidon) has been reported also to contain the typical lithic industry (sometimes described as 'Heavy Neolithic'), consisting of large scrapers, cores, flakes, blades, and roughed-out axes, chisels, and picks. The date of these sites is still problematic, although most are believed to fit in the sixth millennium BC and later (cf. Cauvin 1968; Moore 1978).

CONCLUDING REMARKS

Throughout the Neolithic, we see a number of sizeable settlement mounds scattered over the landscape, with often monumental visibility, long sequences, complex histories, and permanency of settlement, as well as many more small to very small occupations, inhabited by small groups for shorter or longer time spans. Settlements were not built to last forever; sites were abandoned everywhere, some for good, others for dozens or hundreds of years. There was a steady movement of communities, either wholesale or in part, inspired by subsistence strategies and changes in the availability of local resources, as well as by many opportunistic reasons, including diseases, vermin infestations, and everyday social tensions and disputes. This mobility must have contributed to the growth of a range of social networks of varying intensity, and to the establishment of often temporary and fluctuating groupings and alliances.

The evidence for any form of explicit social segmentation or institutionalized hierarchies in the Neolithic communities, to a degree that would leave firm traces in the archaeological record, is equivocal at best. Probably, authority was temporary and in the hands of individuals—elders, heads of family, etc.—who shifted routinely from the specific tasks of leaders to the ordinary domestic work of commoners as daily circumstances changed. The scale of the Neolithic communities was too small to permit a great deal of social distance between their members. Any relations of dominance were handled situationally and face to face, instead of in the form of clear-cut chiefly ranking or a centralized village authority.

It is tempting to attribute regional economic or political predominance to the handful of larger, long-lived sites in each region that may sometimes have grown as large as 10–15ha, probably housing many hundreds or perhaps even thousands of people. However, it is important to realize that site size is not necessarily the same as settlement size, let alone population size. Sites were not always inhabited in their entirety or continuously, but often reflected a small, shifting occupation from one part of the site to another. Large sites were not necessarily organized differently from small ones; in many respects they may simply have been extended, aggregated versions of the many small villages, rather than prehistoric 'urban centres' with all the usual connotations. In this perspective, the lack of consistent signs of social ranking even within the large sites, such as significant differences in house size or inventories, comes as no surprise (Hole 2000; Akkermans and Schwartz 2003; Akkermans et al. 2006).

SUGGESTED READING

Akkermans, P. M. M. G., and G. M. Schwartz (2003). *The Archaeology of Syria: From Complex Hunter-Gatherers to Early Urban Societies (c.16,000–300 BC)*. Cambridge: Cambridge University Press.

Cauvin, J. (2000). *The Birth of the Gods and the Origins of Agriculture*, trans. T. Watkins. Cambridge: Cambridge University Press.

Mellaart, J. (1975). *The Neolithic of the Near East*. London: Thames & Hudson.

REFERENCES

Akkermans, P. M. M. G. (2004). Hunter-gatherer continuity: the transition from the Epipalaeolithic to the Neolithic in Syria. In O. Aurenche, M. Le Mière, and P. Sanlaville (eds), *From the River to the Sea: The Palaeolithic and the Neolithic on the Euphrates and in the Northern Levant*. Oxford: Archaeopress, 281–93.

——R. Cappers, C. Cavallo, O. Nieuwenhuyse, B. Nilhamn, and I. N. Otte (2006). Investigating the Early Pottery Neolithic of northern Syria: new evidence from Tell Sabi Abyad. *American Journal of Archaeology* 110: 123–56.

—— and G. M. Schwartz (2003). *The Archaeology of Syria: From Complex Hunter-Gatherers to Early Urban Societies (ca. 16,000–300 BC)*. Cambridge: Cambridge University Press.

Alley, R. B., P. A. Mayewski, T. Sowers, M. Stuiver, K. C. Taylor, and P. U. Clark (1997). Holocene climatic instability: a prominent, widespread event 8200 yr ago. *Geology* 25: 483–6.

Bartl, K., M. Hijazi, and A. Haidar (2006). The Late Neolithic Site of Shir: preliminary report of the German–Syrian Cooperation Project 2006. *Neo-Lithics* 2/06: 15–18.

Braidwood, R. J., and L. S. Braidwood (1960). *Excavations in the Plain of Antioch*, vol. 1: *The Earlier Assemblages, Phases A–J*. Chicago: University of Chicago Press.

Cauvin, J. (1968). *Fouilles de Byblos IV: les outillages néolithiques de Byblos et du littoral libanais*. Paris: Maisonneuve.

—— (1990). Nomadisme néolithique en zone aride: l'oasis d'El Kowm (Syrie). In M. Paolo, M. N. van Loon, and H. Weiss (eds), *Resurrecting the Past: A Joint Tribute to Adnan Bounni*. Istanbul: Nederlands Historisch-Archaeologisch Instituut te Istanbul, 41–7.

—— (2000). *The Birth of the Gods and the Origins of Agriculture*, trans. T. Watkins. Cambridge: Cambridge University Press.

Cauvin, M.-C., and J. Cauvin (1993). La séquence néolithique PPNB au Levant nord. *Paléorient* 19: 23–8.

Copeland, L. (1991). Natufian sites in Lebanon. In O. Bar-Yosef and F. R. Valla (eds), *The Natufian Culture in the Levant*. Ann Arbor, Mich.: International Monographs in Prehistory, 27–42.

Coqueugniot, É. (1998). Djade el Mughara (Moyen-Euphrate), un village néolithique dans son environnement naturel à la veille de la domestication. In M. Fortin and O. Aurenche (eds), *Espace naturel, espace habité en Syrie du Nord (10e-2e millénaires av. J-C.): Actes du colloque tenu à l'Université Laval (Québec) du 5 au 7 mai 1997*. Quebec: Canadian Society for Mesopotamian Studies/Lyon: Maison de l'Orient méditerranéen, 109–14.

de Contenson, H. (1985). La région de Damas au Néolithique. *Annales archéologiques arabes syriennes* 35: 9–29.

—— (2000). *Ramad: site néolithique en Damascéne (Syrie) aux VIIIe et VIIe millénaires avant lére chrétienne*. Beirut: Institut français d'archéologie du Proche-Orient.

Garfinkel, Y. (1999). *Neolithic and Chalcolithic Pottery of the Southern Levant*. Jerusalem: Institute of Archaeology, Hebrew University of Jerusalem.

Haïdar-Boustani, M., J. J. Ibáñez, M. Al-Maqdissi, Á. Armendáriz, J. González Urquijo, and L. Teira (2007). New data on the Epipalaeolithic and Neolithic of the Homs Gap: three campaigns of archaeological survey (2004–2006). *Neo-Lithics* 1/07: 3–9.

Hole, F. (2000). Is size important? Function and hierarchy in Neolithic settlements. In I. Kuijt (ed.), *Life in Neolithic Farming Communities: Social Organization, Identity, and Differentiation*. New York: Kluwer Academic/Plenum, 191–209.

Iwasaki, T., and A. Tsuneki (eds) (2003). *Archaeology of the Rouj Basin: A Regional Study of the Transition from Village to City in Northwest Syria*. Tsukuba: Department of Archaeology, Institute of History and Anthropology, University of Tsukuba.

Mazurowski, R. F. (2003). Tell Qaramel Excavations 2003. *Polish Archaeology in the Mediterranean* 15: 355–70.

Moore, A. M. T. (1978). *The Neolithic of the Levant*. PhD dissertation, Oxford University.

—— G. C. Hillman, and A. J. Legge (2000). *Village on the Euphrates: From Foraging to Farming at Abu Hureyra*. Oxford: Oxford University Press.

Nieuwenhuyse, O. P. (2006). The earliest ceramics from Tell Sabi Abyad, Syria. *Leiden Journal of Pottery Studies* 22: 111–28.

Nishiaki, Y., and M. Le Mière (2005). The oldest Pottery Neolithic of Upper Mesopotamia: new evidence from Tell Seker al-Aheimar, the Khabur, northeast Syria. *Paléorient* 31: 55–68.

Parr, P. J. (ed.) (2003). *Excavations at Arjoune, Syria*. Oxford: Archaeopress.

Philip, G., M. Abdulkarim, P. Newson, et al. (2005). Settlement and landscape development in the Homs region, Syria: report on work undertaken during 2001–2003. *Levant* 37: 21–42.

Stordeur, D. (2003a). Tell Aswad: résultats préliminaires des campagnes 2001 et 2002. *Neo-Lithics* 1/03: 7–15.

—— (2003b). Des crânes surmodelés à Tell Aswad de Damascène (PPNB-Syrie). *Paléorient* 29: 109–15.

—— M. Brenet, G. Der Aprahamian, and J.-C. Roux (2000). Les bâtiments communautaires de Jerf el Ahmar et Mureybet horizon PPNA (Syrie). *Paléorient* 26: 29–44.

Tsuneki, A., and Y. Miyake (1996). The earliest pottery sequence of the Levant: new data from Tell el-Kerkh 2, northern Syria. *Paléorient* 22: 109–23.

—— M. Arimura, O. Maeda, K. Tanno, and T. Anezaki (2006). The Early PPNB in the north Levant: a new perspective from Tell Ain el-Kerkh, northwest Syria. *Paléorient* 32: 47–71.

CHAPTER 11

THE SOUTHERN LEVANT (CISJORDAN) DURING THE NEOLITHIC PERIOD

A. NIGEL GORING-MORRIS
AND ANNA BELFER-COHEN

INTRODUCTION

The Near Eastern Neolithic corresponds to revolutionary transformations in the human condition, setting the stage for later developments prior to the emergence of urban life. Theoretical constructs varying from climatic determinism through human vitalism to demographic and social triggers, co-evolutionary symbiotic human–plant relationships, and linguistic and multi-factor models have all been hypothesized to explain these processes (Kuijt 2000; Kuijt and Goring-Morris 2002; Simmons 2007 and references therein). Yet such models frequently preceded the hard data available. In recent decades the situation has improved markedly as numerous field projects have generated copious quantities of evidence (Fig. 11.1).

The period witnessed significant demographic growth when village communities were established, subsisting first on cultivation and foraging, then on agriculture, and finally on agropastoralism (Bar-Yosef 2001). Yet in order to begin to understand transformations associated with 'Neolithization' processes, it is crucial to note that many seminal developments were initiated during the preceding Epipaleolithic Natufian. Furthermore, 'Neolithization' involved not only plant and animal domestication but also the management of fire, water, and plastic materials as well as ritual and social interactions; these processes were neither linear nor directed (Goring-Morris and Belfer-Cohen 2010a). Wide-ranging cultural interaction spheres emerged throughout the Levant, of which the southern Levant (in and west of the Rift Valley), formed a small component of broader regional systems (Bar-Yosef and Belfer-Cohen 1989; Bar-Yosef and Bar-Yosef Mayer 2002). Subsistence shifted unevenly in time and space to domesticated plants and animals, with foraging still being important (Horwitz et al. 2000). The 'desert and the sown' dichotomy, present earlier, continued with the introduction of pastoralism midway through the

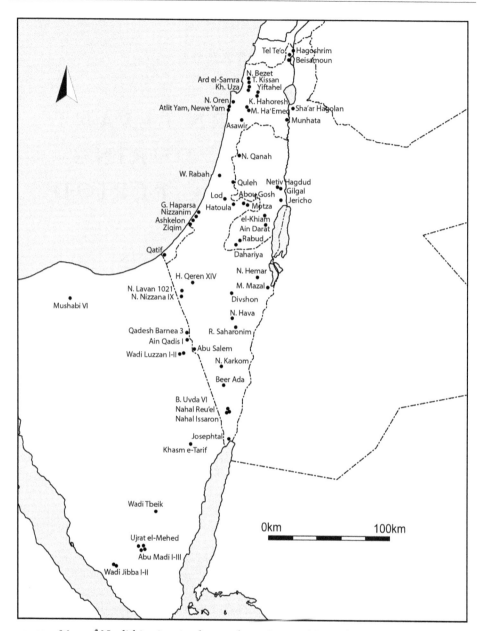

FIG. 11.1 Map of Neolithic sites in the southern Levant (Cisjordan)

Neolithic sequence (Goring-Morris 1993). Communal, cultic installations and paraphernalia, and their contextual associations, attest to intensive ritual practices within settlements in spatially discrete locales. A range of prestige and other items were exchanged, often over considerable distances. Innate social tensions were exacerbated by discrepancies in the accumulation of material, social, and ritual wealth within and between communities. Mechanisms for dissipating resulting 'scalar' stress (tensions arising from larger numbers of decision-makers within communities) involved the emergence of increasing social and ritual complexity and, possibly, ranking. The role of interpersonal and even intercommunity violence remains uncertain and merits detailed study. Furthermore, the effects of long-term sedentism and the introduction of domestic animals into villages raise issues of contagious—including zoonotic (i.e. animal-borne)—and other diseases (Goring-Morris and Belfer-Cohen 2010b).

THE CHRONO-CULTURAL FRAMEWORK

While evidence for Neolithic settlement in the Levant was reported much earlier, it was only with Kenyon's investigations in the 1950s at Tell es-Sultan (Jericho) that the four-phase terminological framework of Pre-Pottery Neolithic A (PPNA), Pre-Pottery Neolithic B (PPNB), Pottery Neolithic A (PNA), and Pottery Neolithic B (PNB) for the Neolithic was codified (see Table 11.1). While still widely used, with variations (e.g. Neolithic 1–4), numerous other appellations have also been used to describe specific industries, phases, and *facies* (see below).

The following presentation is arranged according to the traditional periodization, but with the PNA and PNB relabelled as Late Neolithic 1 and 2. Still, it should be noted that the PPNA probably shares greater commonalities with the Natufian than with the PPNB; while LN1 also could be more comfortably accommodated within the PPNB world; and LN2 has been argued to correspond more closely to the Chalcolithic. Adding to the confusion, ceramics first appear in small quantities during the PPNB, yet are virtually absent from the Pottery Neolithic desertic *facies*.

EARLY HOLOCENE ENVIRONMENTS

Independent sources for early Holocene environmental changes include: the Soreq cave speleothems (stalactites and stalagmites); the recently revised Hula pollen diagram chronology (rejecting the ^{14}C dates due to the 'reservoir effect'), based on correlations with other pollen sequences; deep sea cores; the eastern Mediterranean Sapropel 1 (a mud level consisting chiefly of decomposed organic matter formed at the bottom of a stagnant sea); and geomorphological evidence (e.g. Bar-Matthews, Ayalon, and Kaufman 1997; van Zeist, Baruch, and Bottema 2009). Climatic fluctuations generally correlate well with the archaeological evidence of changing settlement patterns.

In the southern Levant at least, the cumulative effects of the Younger Dryas cold climatic event on later Natufian developments were significant. PPNA conditions improved, becoming warmer and more humid, albeit with a tendency towards torrential rains. Perhaps most significantly, this enabled relative increases of cereal-type grasses. The PPNB is marked by increasingly humid conditions, reaching its highest values through the entire Holocene during the Late PPNB (the early Holocene climatic optimum). The '8,200 yr. event' (=6200 cal. BC) marks a rapid, short deterioration that likely played a major role in the demise of the PPNB (Weninger et al. 2009). Conditions thereupon improved somewhat, although the Late Neolithic is marked by environmental instability with climatic fluctuations.

Table 11.1 Chronology and paleoenvironments of Neolithic entities west of the Rift Valley, with principal sites by region

	cal. BC	Mediterranean zone	Arid zone	Environment
PPNA (Khiamian + Late Harifian)	~9750–9500	Salibiya IX, Hatoula, Poleg 18M, Huzuk Musa	Abu Salem, Shunera VI	Younger Dryas (~11,250–9,450 cal. bc) Cold & dry Low Dead Sea levels
Sultanian + Epi-Harifian	9500–8500	Nahal Oren, Gesher, Netiv Hagdud, Gilgal I, Jericho, Quleh, Hatoula, Neve Ilan, el-Khiam, Ein Darat	Abu Madi I, N. Lavan 108	Warmer, more humid & torrential Mediterranean ~50m bsl
Early PPNB	8500–8250	K. HaHoresh, Sefunim IV, el-Wad, Nahal Oren II, Mikhmoret, Motza VI	N. Lavan 1009, N. Boqer, Abu Salem II	Increasing humidity High Dead Sea Levels
Middle PPNB	8250–7500	N. Betzet I, Kh. Galil, Yiftahel, K. HaHoresh, Mishmar HaEmeq, N. Oren II, T. Ro'im V, T. Eli III, Munhata 4–6, Jericho, Abu Gosh, Motza V, Kh. Rabud, N. Hemar	Divshon, N. Nizzana IX, Ramat Matred V–VII, N. Lavan 1021, Mushabi VI, Ein Qadis I, N. Reu'el, W. Tbeik, Abu Madi III, Gebel Rubshah, N. Qetura	
Late PPNB	7500–7000	Beisamoun, Ard el-Samra C/4, Ein Miri, Yiftahel, K. HaHoresh, Mishmar HaEmeq, T. Eli, Munhata 3?, Atlit Yam?, Abu Gosh, Jericho?	N. Efe, Mushabi VI, N. Aqrav I, II, IV, V, Abu Madi I/8, Ujrat el-Mehed, W. Jibba I–II, N. Issaron, Ujrat Suleiman I–III	Mediterranean ~30m bsl
Final PPNB (+ Tuwailan)	7000–6400	Hagoshrim VI, T. Teo XI–XIII, T. Ro'im, Beisamoun, T. Eli?, Yiftahel, Kh. Uza 21, Atlit Yam, Ashkelon	Mezad Mazal, N. Issaron, Hamifgash III–V, Har Qeren XIV, Nahal Efe?, W. Jibba II	Mediterranean ~25m bsl

Late Neolithic 1 (*Yarmukian*)	~6,400–5,750	T. Teo IX–X, Hagoshrim V, K. Giladi, Beisamoun, T. Eli, Sha'ar Hagolan, Munhata 2B, N. Betzet I & II/2b Ard el-Samra, Yiftahel IV–V, Kh. Uza 20, T. Qishion, N. Zehora II, Mishmar HaEmeq, Atlit Yam, N. Qanah cave, Abu Gosh, Motza IVb, Rehov HaBashan	Qadesh Barnea 3, Beer Ada, N. Issaron	???8,200 yr event??? (cal. bp) Cooler & drier Mediterranean ~15 m bsl Rapid drop in Dead Sea level
Jericho IX/ Lodian	~5,800–5,500	Horvat Galil, T. Kabri, Kh. Abu Zureik, T. Yosef HaYeshana, Asawir VII, Jericho IX, Motza IVb, N. Timna, Lod (Neve Yarak), Nizzanim, Givat Haparsa, Ziqim	Qadesh Barnea 31, N. Issaron	Unstable conditions Low Dead Sea levels
Late Neolithic 2 (*Wadi Rabah, Qatifian, Besoran*)	~5,500–4,500	T. Teo VIII, Hagoshrim IV, Hayonim Terrace, Kh. Uza 19–16, N. Betzet I–II, T. Kabri, Ard el-Samra, Mishmar HaEmeq, Abu Zureiq, Ein el-Jarba, N. Zehora I, II, T. Hanan, Ein el-Jarba, Kfar Galim, Megadim, K. Samir, Neve Yam, Asawir VI, N. Qanah cave, Herzliya, W. Rabah, Lower Horvat Illin, T. Turmus, Beisamoun, T. Yosef HaYeshana, Jericho VIII, Motza IVa, Qumran cave	Ramat Nof, Qatif Y-3, Besor D, M, P, Shunera V, Ramat Saharonim, Wadi Luzan I–III, N. Zihor, Biqat Uvda 6, 9 lower, N. Issaron, Josephtal (Eilat), Khasm et-Tarif	Unstable conditions Mediterranean ~5 m bsl

Mediterranean Sea levels gradually rose during the Holocene from a low of *c.*70m below sea level during the early Natufian to *c.*15m during the Final PPNB and *c.*5m below sea level during LN2. The Dead Sea also witnessed major fluctuations, causing its contraction during the Late Neolithic to just the northern basin (Stein et al. 2010).

ARCHAIC SETTLEMENTS OF THE PPNA (C. 9750–8500 CAL. BC)

The local PPNA displays considerable elements of continuity from the preceding Natufian, with the 'Khiamian' representing a short-lived transition phenomenon after the cold spell of the Younger Dryas. Residual Mediterranean final Natufian/Khiamian communities probably combined with Negev and Sinai Harifian refugees and populations from else-where to aggregate into larger communities around more viable locales in ecotonal (inter-section of two or more ecological zones) settings, close to more dependable water sources in lowland settings (Kuijt and Goring-Morris 2002; Goring-Morris and Belfer-Cohen 2011).

From this catalytic situation, Sultanian (*c.*9500–8500 cal. BC) settlements emerged, in a linear arrangement, mostly along the western flanks of the Rift Valley at intervals of 15–20km (Gesher, Huzuk Musa, Netiv Hagdud, Gilgal I, Jericho, el-Khiam, and 'Ain Darat). Sites vary in size from *c.*0.1ha to 2.5ha (e.g. Bar-Yosef and Gopher 1994; Bar-Yosef, Goring-Morris, and Gopher 2010). Smaller settlements also occur on the western fringes of the central mountain ridge (Nahal Oren, Quleh, Modi'in, and Hatoula), but rarely within the coastal plain itself (e.g. Kuijt 1994; Kuijt and Goring-Morris 2002; Zbenovich 2006). Small, specific seasonal occupations were found within the central hills. The Negev and Sinai were virtually devoid of occupants at this time, with the small encampment at Abu Madi I, in the high mountains of the southern Sinai, probably representing an 'epi-Harifian' (end of the final Epipaleolithic) site (Bar-Yosef 1991).

At the nodal site of Jericho, the tower and wall represent a spectacular and unique com-munal PPNA endeavour (Kenyon and Holland 1982; 1983). The tower is widely accepted as representing a hallowed locale or shrine (perhaps even with topographic/celestial align-ments) and associated silos (Fig. 11.2). The wall has been interpreted either as a defence against flooding or as delineating a sacred precinct, perhaps a cemetery (Bar-Yosef 1986; Barkai and Liran 2008; Naveh 2003; Ronen and Adler 2001). Other burials are found in and under houses and sometimes in abandoned structures, at times including post-mortem skull removal, a Natufian innovation (Kuijt 1996).

PPNA domicile was based upon nuclear families in spaced, short-lived (and easily flam-mable) oval semi-subterranean structures (Fig. 11.3: 1–4). Construction was of wattle and daub or, somewhat later, of mud-brick on stone foundations with wooden posts and beams to support flat roofing and *pisé* floors, sometimes with interior partitions. Interior furniture includes stone-lined hearths and ovens, large cup-marked slabs, bins, and external storage silos.

PPNA subsistence integrated incipient farming (cultivation) and foraging, including hunting. Species cultivated comprised wild barley (*Hordeum spontaneum*) and wild oats (*Avena sterilis*), while foraging focused on nutlets of wild pistachio (*Pistacia atlantica*),

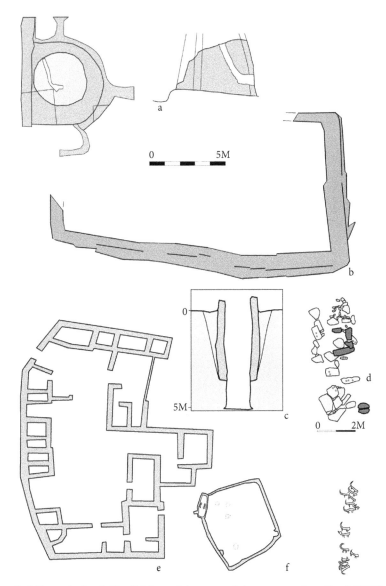

FIG. 11.2 Public and ritual Neolithic architecture: (a) tower and wall of PPNA Jericho; (b) massive podium at PPNB Kfar HaHoresh; (c) well at Final PPNB Atlit Yam; (d) monoliths and cup-marked slabs of ritual complex at Final PPNB Atlit Yam; (e) public complex at LN1 Sha'ar Hagolan; (f) sanctuary and pebble drawings at LN2 Biqat Uvda. Note different scales

acorns of wild oak (*Quercus ithaburensis*), and (possibly domesticated) fig (*Ficus carica*). Legumes and pulses include *Lens* sp. (lentil) and *Vicia* sp. (broad bean) (Kislev, Hartmann, and Noy 2010). Overhunting and the deterioration of conditions during the late Natufian had probably already brought about a decline in the medium-sized mammalian prey available (Horwitz et al. 2010); yet the emphasis on gazelle was still marked, together with

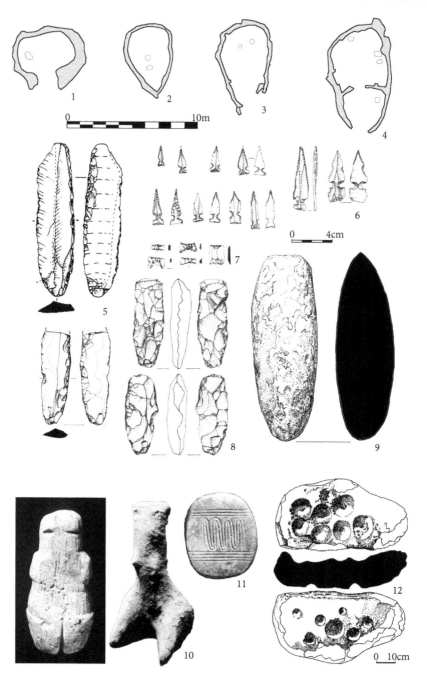

FIG. 11.3 Characteristic elements of PPNA material culture: (1–4) oval habitations; (5) sickle blades; (6) Khiam points; (7) Hagdud truncations; (8) tranchet axes; (9) limestone axe (celt); (10) anthropomorphic figurines (limestone and clay); (11) decorative motif; (12) cup-holed slab. Note different scales

aurochs, wild boar, and some wild goat. At the same time, one can observe an emphasis upon smaller species, including hare and avian species, especially waterfowl (the Rift Valley and the coastal plain are major thoroughfares for annual bird migrations). Fox (*Vulpes*) appear in some quantity, a factor that may be related to increased human sedentism, since it is a synanthropic (i.e. ecologically associated with humans) species, perhaps primarily for pelts. The only domesticated animal is the dog (already present during the Natufian).

Amongst the small finds, the chipped stone tool assemblages display innovations, including arrowheads, sickle-blades, bifacial tranchet axes and chisels, and pecked stone axes, reflecting developments in hunting, reaping, and carpentry activities (Fig. 11.3: 5–8) (Belfer-Cohen 1994). Groundstone tool assemblages shift from earlier narrow deep mortars characteristic of the late Natufian to shallow, v-shaped cup-marked slabs and platters (Fig. 11.3: 12), together with a variety of *manos* (handstones), pounders, and celts (Fig. 11.3: 9) (Rosenberg 2008; Wright 2005). When preserved, sophisticated basketry is also documented (Schick 2010).

Ritual objects include anthropomorphic and zoomorphic figurines in soft limestone and baked clay as well as incised geometric designs on slabs and pendants (Fig. 11.3: 10–11) (e.g. Goren and Biton 2010; Hershman and Belfer-Cohen 2010). Wide-ranging and complex exchange networks are documented, involving marine molluscs (from the Mediterranean and Red Seas) and exotic minerals (obsidian and greenstone), as well as asphalt (for hafting and lining baskets) and perhaps also salt (e.g. Bar-Yosef Mayer 2005; Bar-Yosef Mayer and Porat 2008). Certain localities (e.g. Jericho) appear to have served as hubs for redistribution networks.

Causes for the demise of the PPNA remain elusive, although lowered water tables and climatic considerations should be taken into consideration; few if any sites display evidence of direct continuity with the PPNB.

VILLAGES OF THE PRE-POTTERY
NEOLITHIC B (C.8500–6400 CAL. BC)

The PPNB coincides with significant and ongoing climatic amelioration throughout the Levant. Initially, during the Early PPNB, settlement density was sparse (e.g. Motza, Kfar HaHoresh, Michmoret, and Nahal Lavan 109), but then it steadily increased, reaching a peak during the Late PPNB–Final PPNB. These were indeed 'good' times as vegetation zones expanded and faunal populations rebounded. An eastward population shift is documented during the PPNB, as the major focus of settlement (and innovation) was now along the (later) 'King's Highway' in Transjordan, although 'megasites' are also found within the Jordan Valley (Goring-Morris, Hovers, and Belfer-Cohen 2009). Even when PPNA sites were reoccupied, it was only after a hiatus (Jericho, Nahal Oren), or by local realignment (Gesher–Munhata). Concurrently, seasonally mobile forager populations revisited or recolonized the arid periphery in the Negev and Sinai (Bar-Yosef 1984; Goring-Morris 1993).

Recent investigations have conclusively documented the presence of a previously debated and short-lived, local Early PPNB phase displaying considerable elements of continuity from the PPNA (Khalaily et al. 2007). This is followed by the more widespread and substantial settlements of the Middle, Late, and Final PPNB. While some view the Final PPNB (or

PPNC) as a distinct entity, it seems more pertinent to view it as the culmination of PPNB developments.

Mediterranean-zone PPNB settlements are located close to secure water sources and arable land. Some villages in the Rift Valley are substantial, often approximating the size of PPNB 'megasites' east of the Rift, but sites elsewhere in or at the edges of alluvial valleys tend to be more modest in scope, rarely exceeding 4ha. There is little evidence for sites along the Mediterranean littoral prior to the Final PPNB (e.g. Atlit Yam and Ashkelon); however, this may be biased by presently submerged offshore sites (Galili et al. 2004). Few if any settlements were occupied throughout the entire c.2000-year duration of the PPNB, perhaps reflecting a need to periodically relocate as agricultural yields declined in the absence of crop rotation or systematic fertilization of fields. Hunting probably focused on 'neutral' hilly areas.

Domestic Middle/Late PPNB architecture is locally represented by individual, large-roomed, rectangular structures, often divided into three sections (the 'megaron' or 'pier-house' concept), probably occupied by nuclear families (Fig. 11.4: 1) (Goring-Morris and Belfer-Cohen 2008; Kenyon and Holland 1983; Lechevallier 1978). Houses were usually built of mud-brick on stone foundations with large posts to support roofing; there is no clear evidence that structures west of the Rift Valley were more than one storey high. Copious quantities of lime plaster were manufactured on-site for flooring and walls (Garfinkel 1988; Goren and Goring-Morris 2008). Hearths and silos are found within houses, while in outer, open areas numerous hearths, ovens, kilns, fire pits, etc. indicate intensive pyrotechnical activities, whether for cooking, plaster production, or for baking clay and other items.

Unusual installations include massive, long walls traversing some sites (e.g. Middle/Late PPNB Abu Gosh and Final PPNB Atlit Yam), the functions of which remain uncertain, but they could reflect the delineation of wards within settlements. The >5m-deep wells at FPPNB Atlit Yam demonstrate sophisticated comprehension of hydrological principles (Galili and Nir 1993).

During the PPNB there was clear intensification of ritual activities, many deriving from Natufian practices. Ritual precincts, sometimes with anthropomorphic monoliths (*masseboth*), cup-marked slabs (Atlit Yam), and pavement-lined structures are found at the edges of sites (Mishmar Ha'Emeq) (Barzilai and Getzov 2008; Galili et al. 2005). The mortuary-cum-cult site of Kfar HaHoresh, with a massive walled podium/precinct, is located in the Nazareth hills; the secluded Judean desert cave of Nahal Hemar served as a storage locale for ritual paraphernalia marking the boundary between the 'sown and the desert' (Bar-Yosef and Alon 1988; Goring-Morris 2008). Other cave sites were also sporadically used (Belfer-Cohen and Goring-Morris 2007).

Burials are found within villages, often concentrated in special areas, as well as in separate sites. Within-settlement burial places are usually insufficient for the settlement size and intensity, so that off-site disposal of some deceased, as at secluded Kfar HaHoresh, is likely. Burial customs often continued previous traditions, such as post-mortem skull removal, applied to both sexes and even children, but this was by no means ubiquitous. Occasionally it involved impressive plaster modelling of facial features (Jericho, Beisamoun, Yiftahel, and Kfar HaHoresh) or of wigs (Nahal Hemar). In addition to primary interments with varied associations (plaster-capped pits, cists, walls, and numerous hearths), there is evidence for dismemberment and manipulation of corpses (Eshed, Hershkovitz, and Goring-Morris 2008; Goring-Morris 2005). There tend to be more carefully arranged multiple burials in

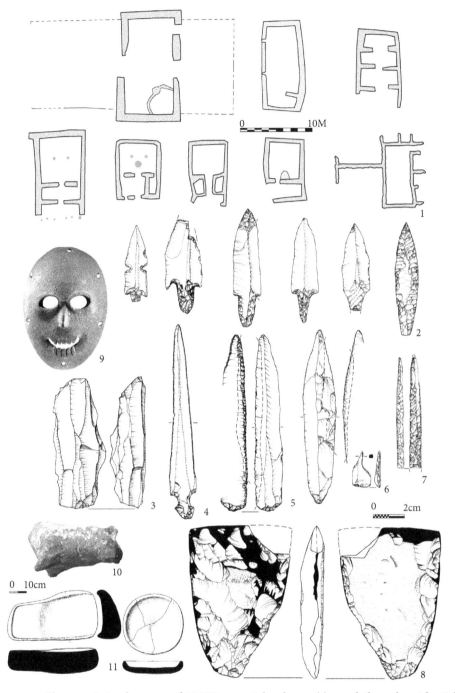

FIG. 11.4 Characteristic elements of PPNB material culture: (1) quadrilateral residential structures; (2) projectile points; (3) naviform core; (4) Nahal Hemar knife; (5) sickle blades; (6) awl; (7) borer; (8) polished axe; (9) mask; (10) zoomorphic clay figurine; (11) quern and platter. Note different scales

the Late PPNB, but it remains unclear whether these reflect diseases, violence, and/or other agents. Grave goods are located in and around burials, comprising lithics, groundstone, molluscs, polished pebbles, and animal motifs—whether the actual remains of foxes, gazelles, or aurochs or, in one case, an arrangement of human long bones, perhaps in the shape of an animal.

Other ritual elements include baked clay and stone anthropomorphic and zoomorphic figurines that are common in sites throughout the Mediterranean zone. Elaborate stone masks (er-Ram, Duma, and Nahal Hemar) and large lime-plaster sculptures (Jericho and Nahal Hemar) are characteristic cultic paraphernalia in Judea (Fig. 11.4: 9), as in neighbouring areas east of the Rift Valley.

Subsistence involved combinations of farming, foraging, hunting, herding, and fishing, depending on the specific location and phase (Horwitz et al. 2000). But, whereas primarily domesticated cereals (*Hordeum* sp. and *Triticum* sp.) were farmed in and east of the Rift, further west the emphasis was on pulses (*Lens culinaris* and *Vicia fabia*) (Garfinkel 1988); this may correlate with the presence of stepped 'saddle' or 'trough' querns, found only in the Rift Valley, while symmetrical basin querns are typical further west (Fig. 11.4: 11). For animals, a similar pattern emerges, with domestic goat (*Capra hircus*) present in the Jordan Valley, while further west gazelle continued to be the favoured prey, with goats only being introduced from the Late PPNB onwards. Other species include wild boar and aurochs, the latter especially in marshy areas, such as the coastal plain and Hula Valley. Fox, hare (*Lepus capensis*), and some bird remains indicate the smaller hunted elements. Contextual evidence indicates that aurochs (caches at Atlit Yam, Kfar HaHoresh, and Motza) and also foxes were imbued with symbolic attributes beyond that of diet (Galili 2004; Goring-Morris and Horwitz 2007; Sapir-Hen et al. 2009).

Much has been written concerning the hallmark PPNB 'naviform' chipped stone technology; but bidirectional blade technologies actually account for only a small proportion of PPNB lithic assemblages, especially in the Mediterranean zone (Barzilai 2009). Most production is actually ad hoc flake-based in nature. Bidirectional (naviform) technology was preferentially employed to provide elongated, symmetrical blade blanks for the more standardized tool classes (Fig. 11.4: 3)—sickle blades, large exquisitely fashioned arrowheads, borers, and burins/chanfreins (and the enigmatic Nahal Hemar knives, restricted to the eponymous site) (Fig. 11.4: 2, 5, 7) (Gopher 1994). There are diachronic and regional trends in the specifics of the technique; incipient craft specialization is represented by the exquisite blade stock at Early PPNB Motza. While good sources of raw material were available west of the Rift Valley (e.g. the Middle–Late PPNB beige 'Sollelim' flint near Yiftahel), Early–Middle PPNB purple/pink flint blanks were likely to have been procured by exchange from communities east of the Rift Valley (e.g. 'Ain Ghazal). Bifacials represent a separate *chaîne opératoire*, initially continuing PPNA tranchet sharpening techniques, but later shifting to polished ends to provide more durable cutting edges (Fig. 11.4: 8) (Barkai 2005).

Extensive, sophisticated basketry, matting, and weaving industries are indicated by the bone tool assemblages and impressions; and at Nahal Hemar by the preserved items themselves, indicating the range of organic items normally absent (Bar-Yosef and Alon 1988). Flax (*Linum usitatissimum*) was already domesticated for use through weaving.

Exchange of exotic prestige items involved intensification of previous PPNA patterns—Mediterranean, Red Sea, and freshwater molluscs, obsidian, cinnabar, asphalt, and various greenstones, deriving from Sinai, the Arava, Transjordan, Saudi Arabia, northern Syria/

Cyprus, Iraq, and central Anatolia (Bar-Yosef Mayer 2005; Bar-Yosef Mayer and Porat 2008). The exotics were used as cylinders, beads, pendants, votive axes, polished pebbles, incised tokens, etc. Such ornaments or talismans were individually rather than mass-produced. Bone, wood, fired clay and plaster beads and figurines (Fig. 11.4: 10) are also documented, some being coloured with powdered pigments. Poorly fired pottery and lime 'white ware' appear in small quantities. Clay tokens may indicate notational devices.

Beginning with the Early PPNB, but especially during the Middle–Late PPNB, the arid zones of the Negev and Sinai were reoccupied by foragers who continued to be seasonally mobile, albeit interacting with their neighbouring kinsmen (Bar-Yosef 1984; Goring-Morris 1993). A central Negev and north Sinai province probably interacted with communities to the north; another province in the southern Negev and southern Sinai interacted primarily with southern Edom across the southern Arava. Base camps rarely exceeded 150m², and featured small beehive-type clusters of rounded stone huts with organic superstructures (Fig. 11.5). Hunting focused on gazelle and ibex, depending on the specific topographic setting, together with some wild ass and hare. Marine molluscs (almost absent in the central Negev province) were systematically collected on the eastern (Red Sea) coast of Sinai for exchange northwards by way of Biqat Uvda to the southern Edom mega-sites and thence along the 'King's Highway'. Insofar as burials are documented in the south Sinai province, skull removal was not practised, perhaps paralleling Late PPNB cist/chamber burial practices in southern Edom (Hershkovitz, Bar-Yosef, and Arensburg 1994).

The Final PPNB 'Tuwailan' industry of the western Negev includes workshop sites for large cortical knives (e.g. Har Qeren XIV) that probably represent connections with the southern coastal plain (e.g. Ashkelon) and/or the Black Desert in Transjordan (Betts 1998; Garfinkel and Dag 2008; Goring-Morris, Gopher, and Rosen 1994).

The gradual demise of PPNB lifeways should perhaps be considered as resulting from combinations of the unforeseen and deleterious consequences of living in large, long-term sedentary settlements with ecological degradation in their vicinity, declining yields, contagious diseases, and perhaps even inter-community violence, exacerbated by the brief but rapid climatic deterioration c.6400 cal. BC (the so-called '8,200 yr. event') (Goring-Morris and Belfer-Cohen 2010b; and see papers in *Neo-Lithics* 1/10).

THE LATE NEOLITHIC 1 (C.6400–5500 CAL. BC)

In many respects the earlier part of the Late Neolithic represents what can best be termed as an 'epi-PPNB' village phenomenon. For historical reasons, the appearance of pottery in quantity at this time has often been interpreted as heralding a complete break with the Pre-Pottery Neolithic; yet there is actually considerable evidence for continuity (see below).

Two LN1 cultural entities have been defined within the Mediterranean zone: the 'Yarmukian' (c.6400–5750 cal. BC) and the 'Lodian/Jericho IX' (c.5800–5500 cal. BC) (Garfinkel 1993; Gopher 1995; Gopher and Gophna 1993). There has been considerable debate as to whether these represent regional differences (with the former located mostly north of the latter), a chronological succession, or, and most probably, combinations of both, not unlike the regionalization already apparent during the PPNB.

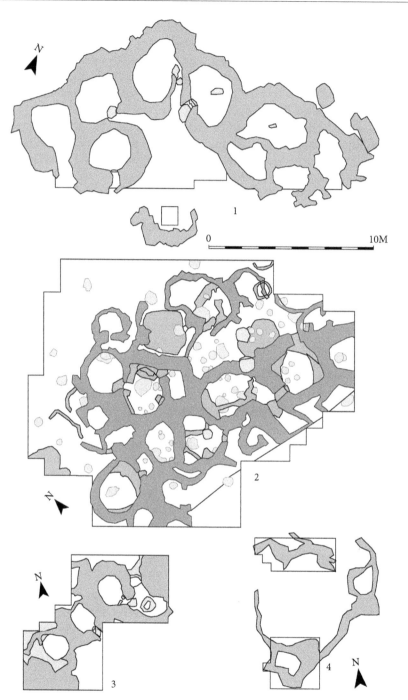

FIG. 11.5 Desert architecture: (1) beehive plan of Late PPNB Wadi Jibba I; (2) plan of Late PPNB Nahal Issaron; (3) plan of Early PPNB Abu Salem; (4) plan of animal enclosure and associated structures at LN2 Kvish Harif

Mediterranean zone sites are usually found at low elevations, whether along the Rift Valley or in the coastal plain, as well as at the edges of the major alluvial valleys, where fully agricultural subsistence based on domesticated plants (wheat, barley, and legumes) and animals (sheep, goat, cattle, and pigs) could be practised, as reliance on hunting and foraging declined.

The 'mega-site' of Sha'ar Hagolan, without doubt the largest known and probably focal Yarmukian site (15ha), is favourably located on the alluvial fan of the Yarmuk River in the central Jordan Valley (Garfinkel and Miller 2002). However, other sites are much more modest in scope. Whether Sha'ar Hagolan really displays 'early signs of urban concepts' (Ben-Shlomo and Garfinkel 2009) remains moot, as systematic surveys indicate patchy densities across the site (akin to those of the later Beersheva Chalcolithic sites). A more parsimonious interpretation is that the settlement comprised spatially discrete, perhaps clan-based clusters of wards. Still, there is a notable shift from previous PPNB domiciles to one of walled residential compounds, separated by alleys. These nuclear family compounds were walled with central courtyards, rectangular houses, and storage and cooking facilities. Such arrangements presumably reflect increasing concerns with privatization as well as providing penning for herded animals.

A possible communal structure, Building II in Area E, may be present; c.75 per cent of the clay and stone figurines in Area E derive from open areas within this complex, as did a concentration of three human skulls. Another probable communal endeavour is represented by the well.

The coil-made pottery of the LN1 includes storage and cooking vessels, as well as finer wares, often with distinctive herringbone incised and/or painted decorations; both the globular shapes and decorative motifs probably mimic (earlier PPN) basketry.

Amongst the lithic assemblages, projectile points (now including small pressure-flaked arrows) are found in relatively lower frequencies than previously, while deeply denticulated sickle blades, awls, burins, and bifacials are common (Matskevich 2005). Still, it is important to note some initial continuity of the (PPNB) bidirectional blade technology to produce blade blanks (Barzilai and Garfinkel 2006).

The relative quantities and sources of exotic prestige items shift, with smaller quantities of obsidian, marine molluscs, and greenstone items. Beads begin to be mass produced (Wright, Critchley, and Garrard 2008).

With regard to ritual, a special site is Nahal Qanah cave, the difficult access to and contents of which recall Nahal Hemar cave (Gopher and Tsuk 1991). The rich assemblage of large and small, more or less elaborate human figurines in clay and stone are a hallmark of the Yarmukian, albeit with differential concentrations from one site to the next (Garfinkel 1993). While very distinctive, certain iconographic elements again reflect origins in the PPNB, as do the zoomorphic figurines and geometric motifs. There are very few human burials within either Yarmukian or Lodian settlements, indicating that the deceased were disposed of either in such a manner as to leave no remains or, more probably, in currently undetected separate cemetery areas or sites.

The shift from foraging to pastoralism in the southern deserts remains poorly documented, although it was probably introduced from southern and eastern Transjordan (and/or the southern coastal plain) some time during the seventh millennium, and thence eventually to the Nile Delta (Bar-Yosef and Khazanov 1992). Qadesh Barnea 3 and Beer Ada, the latter with what appears to be an animal corral, probably represent early manifestations of this process (Gopher 2010). However, with the rapid shift away from foraging (and especially hunting) to pastoralism, site visibility declines, since the material culture remains rarely include diagnostic attributes amongst the lithic assemblages (except for specialized bead workshops) and pottery is absent.

THE LATE NEOLITHIC 2 (C.5500–4500 CAL. BC)

With the shift to the LN2, 'Wadi Rabah' settlements are found throughout the Mediterranean zone. The tendency for smaller, dispersed clan-based settlements continues, although a few larger regional central sites are still documented in favourable localities such as the Hula Valley (e.g. Hagoshrim IV), and northern (e.g. Kabri, Tel Kissan) and central coastal plain (e.g. Tel Asawir) (Gopher and Gophna 1993; Getzov 2008; Getzov et al. 2009; Yannai 2006; Zviely et al. 2006).

Wadi Rabah residential architecture presages the Chalcolithic in featuring rectangular broad-room (mud-brick?) houses on stone foundations with raised floors, together with associated circular storage and other features including pits and hearths within walled compounds. Indeed, the increasing quantities of elaborately incised stamps and tokens may reflect increasing concerns with privatization and marks of ownership (Eirikh-Rose 2004).

It is somewhat surprising that, in contrast to the desert, there is presently little if any obvious evidence of communal, public, or ritual architectural endeavours during LN2 within the Mediterranean zone. But this may simply indicate that insufficient exposures have been opened in large tells covered by later settlements.

Subsistence by now was almost entirely agropastoral, comprising the full suite of domestic plants (including olive exploitation if not actual domestication) and animals, with hunting rarely accounting for more than 10 per cent of faunal remains (Horwitz 1988; 2002; Marom and Bar-Oz 2009).

The ceramic repertoire, still handmade, has a limited range of shapes and sizes and includes bow rims; there are also distinctive burnished black and red wares (Garfinkel 1999; Gopher 1995; Gopher and Goren 1995). Among the lithics, projectile points virtually disappear, while short, rectangular sickle segments displaying invasive pressure flaking (sometimes with spaced denticulation), burins, and bifacials are common. Stone and clay sling shots are a distinctive addition to the small finds repertoire (Rosenberg 2009), as are spindle whorls and loom weights for weaving.

With regard to burial practices, only a few individual articulated remains have been recovered from within settlements with the exception of child jar burials (Gopher and Orrelle 1995). Still, the edge of the submerged site of Neve Yam displays a cemetery area with cist graves for individual burials (Galili et al. 2005).

Largely paralleling the Wadi Rabah in the northern Negev are the still poorly documented 'Qatifian' and later 'Besoran' settlements (Abadi-Reiss and Gilead 2010; Gilead 1990; Goren 1990). Further south in the Negev and Sinai, the mobile pastoralist adaptation continues, seemingly with greater intensification than before, albeit with few recognizable settlements as at Kvish Harif (Rosen 1984). But a notable innovation during LN2 here is the widespread appearance of open-air sanctuaries, heralding a long-lasting 'desert tradition'.

They are usually situated in remote, hyper-arid areas, adjacent to prominent topographic features. Clusters of such sanctuaries are documented in Ramat Saharonim, Biqat Uvda, the Eilat mountains, and Khasm et-Tarif (Avner 2002; Rosen et al. 2007; Yogev and Avner 1983). Sanctuaries are sometimes megalithic in nature and a few appear to have celestial alignments; others feature associated large-scale pebble drawings and clusters of large or small stele, *masseboth*, and hearths. Most are almost devoid of diagnostic material remains. The cemetery site of Josephtal near Eilat features cist burials, including a cache of skulls and numerous grave goods, wooden posts, and stone monoliths, as well as numerous hearths (Avner 1991). Carbon-14 dates commonly indicate continuity into the Chalcolithic.

DISCUSSION

While the Neolithic represents a period of major social and economic transformations, many material culture elements and practices can actually be traced to the late Epipaleolithic Natufian, when the first sedentary hamlets began to coalesce. So too, continuity can be traced from the PPNB through at least the earlier LN1. During the course of the Neolithic, wide-ranging cultural interaction spheres emerged throughout the Levant, of which the southern Levant, in and west of the Rift Valley, formed but a small component of broader regional systems. Following the Natufian, the centre of innovation shifted to the northern Levant. Nevertheless, there is considerable debate as to whether developments were polycentric, as opposed to central innovations in the north with secondary dispersion to the southern Levant. It seems likely there were elements of both; unquestionably, within the southern Levant the main PPNA axis was within the Rift Valley, while during the PPNB it shifted eastwards to higher elevations. During the LN, more pronounced regionalization is discerned, with primary developments in and west of the Rift Valley.

Recent evidence from both Cyprus and the northern Levant demonstrates that the processes of plant and animal domestication were much more complex than previously thought. The 'wild–domestic' spectrum was by no means binary, but involved prolonged manipulation of plant and animal species, some of which were either never or only very much later domesticated. Furthermore, it has even been proposed that milking, commonly associated with the later 'secondary products revolution', actually may have begun much earlier, during the Pre-Pottery Neolithic.

As global and community sizes increased, new social and ritual regulatory mechanisms were necessary to address the resulting stresses and inequalities within and between communities. Solutions involved realignments, together with embellishments and intensifications of previous traditions, many first apparent in the Natufian. Although Neolithic intra-community relationships were primarily kin-based, ritual behaviours were likely to have been both public and exclusionary in nature.

The 'agricultural revolution' is widely associated with the concept of the 'mother goddess'. Yet, inasmuch as gender can be identified amongst all Neolithic anthromorphic figurines, phallic depictions are a constant and significant element, indicating a more balanced perspective between the genders.

The issue of hierarchical ranking remains debatable. PPNA settlements already display considerable variability in size and contents, and PPNB mortuary data certainly indicate differential treatments of the deceased; but whether this also related to the living is currently uncertain. So, too, questions as to the nature of interpersonal and inter-community interactions (including violence) remain to be systematically addressed. Indeed, the emergence of incipient craft specialization during the Pre-Pottery Neolithic often focused around exchange networks of prestige items (e.g. flint blades and knives, minerals, and marine molluscs) and technologies (e.g. pyrotechnology and hydrology), presaging later developments (e.g. ceramics). Still, notwithstanding the scale and scope of accomplishments in the PPNB *koiné*, its lack of crucial social, organizational, and technological elements appears ultimately to have prevented it from developing into fully-fledged urban societies, and communities dispersed into generally smaller settlements. To summarize, the course of 'Neolithization' in the Near East was not a linear process leading to the establishment of urban centres and city-states, as thought in the past. Actually, it took another period, the whole of the Chalcolithic, to reach this stage in human history.

Acknowledgements

Part of the research on which this contribution is based was supported by grants to Nigel Goring-Morris from the Israel Science Foundation funded by the Israel Academy of Sciences (Grants 840/01, 558/04, and 755/07). We are grateful to Omry Barzilai, Yossi Garfinkel, Nimrod Getzov, Avi Gopher, Hamudi Khalaily, Ofer Marder, and Yanir Milevski for lively discussions; however, we naturally take full responsibility for the views expressed herein.

Suggested reading

Banning, E. B. (1998). The Neolithic period: triumphs of architecture, agriculture, and art. *Near Eastern Archaeology* 61: 188–237.

Bar-Yosef, O. (2001). New views on the origins of agriculture in southwestern Asia. *Review of Archaeology* 22: 5–15.

Gopher, A. (1995). Early pottery-bearing groups in Israel: the Pottery Neolithic period. In T. D. Levy (ed.), *The Archaeology of Society in the Holy Land*. New York: Facts on File, 205–25.

Goring-Morris, A. N., and A. Belfer-Cohen (2008). A roof over one's head: developments in Near Eastern residential architecture across the Epipalaeolithic–Neolithic transition. In J.-P. Bocquet-Appel and O. Bar-Yosef (eds), *The Neolithic Demographic Transition and Its Consequences*. Dordrecht: Springer, 239–86.

Horwitz, L. K., E. Tchernov, P. Ducos, et al. (2000). Animal domestication in the southern Levant. *Paléorient* 25: 63–80.

Kuijt, I. (ed.) (2000). *Life in Neolithic Farming Communities: Social Organization, Identity, and Differentiation*. New York: Kluwer Academic/Plenum.

—— and Goring-Morris, A. N. (2002). Foraging, farming and social complexity in the Pre-Pottery Neolithic of the south-central Levant: a review and synthesis. *Journal of World Prehistory* 16: 361–440.

Rosen, S. A. (2008). Desert pastoral nomadism in the *longue durée*: a case study from the Negev and the southern Levantine Deserts. In H. Barnard and W. Wendrich (eds), *The Archaeology of Mobility: Old and New World Nomadism.* Los Angeles: Cotsen Institute of Archaeology, University of California, 115–40.

Simmons, A. H. (2007). *The Neolithic Revolution in the Near East: Transforming the Human Landscape.* Tucson: University of Arizona Press.

REFERENCES

Abadi-Reiss, Y., and I. Gilead (2010). The transition of Neolithic–Chalcolithic in the southern Levant: recent research of cultural assemblages from the site of Qatif. In P. Matthiae, F. Pinnock, L. Nigro and N. Marchetti (eds), *Proceedings of the 6th International Congress of the Archaeology of the Ancient Near East,* Volume II, pp. 27-38. Wiesbaden: Harrassowitz.

Avner, U. (1991). Late Neolithic–Early Chalcolithic burial site in Eilat. *American Journal of Archaeology* 95: 496–7.

—— (2002). *Studies in the material and spiritual culture of the Negev populations, during the 6th–3rd millennia B.C.* PhD dissertation, Hebrew University of Jerusalem.

Barkai, R. (2005). *Flint and Stone Axes as Cultural Markers: Socio-Economic Changes as Reflected in Holocene Flint Tool Industries of the Southern Levant.* Berlin: Ex oriente.

—— and R. Liran (2008). Midsummer sunset at Neolithic Jericho. *Time and Mind* 1: 273–84.

Bar-Matthews, M., A. Ayalon, and A. Kaufman (1997). Late Quaternary paleoclimate in the eastern Mediterranean region from stable isotope analysis of speleothems at Soreq Cave, Israel. *Quaternary Research* 47: 155–68.

Bar-Yosef, O. (1984). Seasonality among Neolithic hunter-gatherers in southern Sinai. In J. Clutton-Brock and C. Grigson (eds), *Animals and Archaeology,* vol. 3: *Early Herders and Their Flocks.* Oxford: British Archaeological Reports, 145–60.

—— (1986). The walls of Jericho: an alternative explanation. *Current Anthropology* 27: 157–62.

—— (1991). The Early Neolithic of the Levant: recent advances. *Review of Archaeology* 12: 1–18.

—— (2001). From sedentary foragers to village hierarchies: the emergence of social institutions. In W. G. Runciman (ed.), *The Origin of Human Social Institutions.* Oxford: Oxford University Press for the British Academy, 1–38.

—— and D. Alon (1988). *Nahal Hemar Cave.* Jerusalem: Department of Antiquities and Museums.

—— and D. E. Bar-Yosef Mayer (2002). Early Neolithic tribes in the Levant. In W. A. Parkinson (ed.), *The Archaeology of Tribal Societies.* Ann Arbor, Mich.: International Monographs in Prehistory, 340–71.

—— and A. Belfer-Cohen (1989). The Levantine 'PPNB' interaction sphere. In I. Hershkovitz (ed.), *People and Culture in Change: Proceedings of the Second Symposium on Upper Palaeolithic, Mesolithic, and Neolithic Populations of Europe and the Mediterranean Basin.* Oxford: British Archaeological Reports, 59–72.

—— and A. Gopher (eds) (1994). *An Early Neolithic Village in the Jordan Valley, pt 1: The Archaeology of Netiv Hagdud.* Cambridge, Mass.: Peabody Museum of Archaeology and Ethnology, Harvard University.

—— A. N. Goring-Morris, and A. Gopher (eds) (2010). *Gilgal: Excavations at Early Neolithic Sites in the Lower Jordan Valley—The Excavations of Tamar Noy.* Oakville, Conn.: David Brown/Oxbow.

—— and A. M. Khazanov (eds) (1992). *Pastoralism in the Levant: Archaeological Materials in Anthropological Perspectives.* Madison, Wis.: Prehistory Press.

Bar-Yosef Mayer, D. E. (2005). The exploitation of shells as beads in the Palaeolithic and Neolithic of the Levant. *Paléorient* 31: 176–85.

—— and N. Porat (2008). Green stone beads at the dawn of agriculture. *Proceedings of the National Academy of Science* (USA) 105: 8548–51.

Barzilai, O. (2009). *Social complexity in the southern Levantine PPNB as reflected through lithic studies: the bidirectional blade industries*. PhD dissertation, Hebrew University of Jerusalem.

—— and Y. Garfinkel (2006). Bidirectional blade technology after the PPNB: new evidence from Sha'ar Hagolan, Israel. *Neo-Lithics* 1/06: 27–31.

—— and N. Getzov (2008). Mishmar Ha'emeq: a Neolithic site in the Jezreel Valley. *Neo-Lithics* 2/08: 12–17.

Belfer-Cohen, A. (1994). The Lithic continuity in the Jordan Valley: Natufian unto the PPNA. In H. G. Gebel and S. K. Kozlowski (eds), *Neolithic Chipped Stone Industries of the Fertile Crescent: Proceedings of the First Workshop on PPN Chipped Lithic Industries, Seminar für Vorderasiatische Altertumskunde, Free University of Berlin, 29th March–2nd April, 1993*. Berlin: Ex oriente, 91–100.

—— and A. N. Goring-Morris (2007). A new look at old assemblages: a cautionary tale. In L. Astruc, D. Binder, and F. Brioids (eds), *Systèmes techniques et communautés du Néolithique Précéramique au Proche-Orient: Actes du 5e Colloque international, Fréjus, du 29 février au 5 mars 2004*. Antibes: Éditions APDCA, 15–24.

Ben-Shlomo, D., and Y. Garfinkel (2009). Sha'ar Hagolan and new insights on Near Eastern proto-historic urban concepts. *Oxford Journal of Archaeology* 28: 189–209.

Betts, A. (ed.) (1998). *The Harra and the Hamad: Excavations and Surveys in Eastern Jordan*, Volume 1. Sheffield: Sheffield Academic.

Garfinkel (2009). Sha'ar Hagolan and new insights on Near Eastern proto-historic urban concepts. *Oxford Journal of Archaeology* 28: 189–209.

Eirikh-Rose, A. (2004). Geometric patterns on pebbles: early identity symbols? In E. J. Peltenburg and A. Wasse (eds), *Neolithic Revolution: New Perspectives on Southwest Asia in Light of Recent Discoveries on Cyprus*. Oxford: Oxbow, 145–62.

Eshed, V., I. Hershkovitz, and A. N. Goring-Morris (2008). A re-evaluation of burial customs in the Pre-Pottery Neolithic B in light of paleodemographic analysis of the human remains from Kfar HaHoresh, Israel. *Paléorient* 34: 91–103.

Galili, E. (2004). *Submerged settlements of the ninth to seventh millennia BP off the Carmel coast*. PhD dissertation, Tel Aviv University.

—— A. Gopher, V. Eshed, and I. Hershkovitz (2005). Burial practices at the submerged Pre-Pottery Neolithic site of Atlit-Yam, northern coast of Israel. *Bulletin of the American School of Oriental Research* 339: 1–19.

—— A. Gopher, B. Rosen, and L. K. Horwitz (2004). The emergence of the Mediterranean fishing village in the Levant and the anomaly of Neolithic Cyprus. In E. J. Peltenburg and A. Wasse (eds), *Neolithic Revolution: New Perspectives on Southwest Asia in Light of Recent Discoveries on Cyprus*. Oxford: Oxbow, 91–101.

—— and Y. Nir (1993). The submerged Pre-Pottery Neolithic water well of Atlit-Yam, northern Israel, and its palaeoenvironmental implications. *The Holocene* 3: 265–70.

Garfinkel, Y. (1988). Burnt lime products and social implications in the Pre-Pottery Neolithic B villages in the Near East. *Paléorient* 13: 69–76.

—— (1993). The Yarmukian Culture in Israel. *Paléorient* 19: 115–33.

—— (ed.) (1999). *The Yarmukians: Neolithic Art from Sha'ar Hagolan*. Jerusalem: Bible Lands Museum.

—— and D. Dag (eds) (2008). *Neolithic Ashkelon.* Jerusalem: Institute of Archaeology, Hebrew University of Jerusalem.

—— and M. A. Miller (eds) (2002). *Sha'ar Hagolan 1: Neolithic Art in Context.* Oxford: Oxbow Books/Jerusalem: Institute of Archaeology, Hebrew University of Jerusalem.

Getzov, N. (2008). Ha-Goshrim. In E. Stern (ed.), *The New Encyclopedia of Archaeological Excavations in the Holy Land*, vol. 5: *Supplementary Volume.* Jerusalem: Israel Exploration Society/Washington, DC: Biblical Archaeology Society, 1759–61.

——O. Barzilai, G. Le Dosseur, et al. (2009). Nahal Betzet II and Ard el Samra: two late prehistoric sites and settlement patterns in the Akko Plain. *Mitekufat Haeven* 39: 81–158.

Gilead, I. (1990). The transition Neolithic–Chalcolithic and the Qatifian of the northern Negev and Sinai. *Levant* 22: 47–63.

Gopher, A. (1994). *Arrowheads of the Neolithic Levant: A Seriation Analysis.* Winona Lake, Ind.: Eisenbrauns.

—— (1995). Early pottery-bearing groups in Israel: the Pottery Neolithic period. In T. D. Levy (ed.), *The Archaeology of Society in the Holy Land.* New York: Facts on File, 205–25.

—— (2010). Qadesh Barnea 3: a Neolithic site in the western Negev highlands. *Mitekufat Haeven* 40: 183–218.

—— and R. Gophna (1993). Cultures of the eighth and seventh millennium BP in the southern Levant: a review for the 1990s. *Journal of World Prehistory* 7: 297–353.

—— and Y. Goren (1995). The beginnings of pottery production in the southern Levant: a model. In P. Vincenzini (ed.), *The Ceramics Cultural Heritage.* Faenza: Techna, 21–8.

—— and E. Orrelle (1995). New data on burials from the Pottery Neolithic period (sixth–fifth millennium BC) in Israel. In S. Campbell and A. Green (eds), *The Archaeology of Death in the Ancient Near East.* Oxford: Oxbow, 24–8.

—— and T. Tsuk (1991). *Ancient Gold: Rare Finds from Nahal Qanah Cave.* Jerusalem: Israel Museum.

Goren, Y. (1990). The Qatifian culture in southern Israel and Transjordan: additional aspects for its definition. *Mitekufat Haeven* 23: 100–112.

—— and R. Biton (2010). Technology of the fired clay objects from Gilgal. In Bar-Yosef et al. (2010: 217–22).

—— and A. N. Goring-Morris (2008). Early pyrotechnology in the Near East: experimental lime plaster production at the PPNB site of Kfar HaHoresh, Israel. *Geoarchaeology* 23: 779–98.

Goring-Morris, A. N. (1993). From foraging to herding in the Negev and Sinai: the Early to Late Neolithic transition. *Paléorient*, 19: 63–89.

—— (2005). Life, death and the emergence of differential status in the Near Eastern Neolithic: evidence from Kfar HaHoresh, Lower Galilee, Israel. In J. Clark (ed.), *Archaeological Perspectives on the Transmission and Transformation of Culture in the Eastern Mediterranean.* Oxford: Oxbow, 89–105.

—— (2008). Kefar Ha-Horesh. In E. Stern (ed.), *The New Encyclopedia of Archaeological Excavations in the Holy Land*, vol. 5: *Supplementary Volume.* Jerusalem: Israel Exploration Society/Washington, DC: Biblical Archaeology Society, 1907–9.

—— (2010a). Different ways of being, different ways of seeing . . . changing worldviews in the Near East. In B. Finlayson and G. Warren (eds), *Landscapes in Transition.* Oxford: Oxbow, 9–22.

—— (2010b). 'Great expectations', or, the inevitable collapse of the Early Neolithic in the Near East. In M. S. Bandy and J. R. Fox (eds), *Becoming Villagers: Comparing Early Village Societies.* Tucson: University of Arizona Press, 62–77.

—— (2011). Neolithization processes in the Levant: the outer envelope. *Current Anthropology* 52(S4): S195– S208.

—— (forthcoming). Neolithisation processes in the Levant: the outer envelope. *Current Anthropology*.

—— and A. Belfer-Cohen (2008). A roof over one's head: developments in Near Eastern residential architecture across the Epipalaeolithic–Neolithic transition. In J.-P. Bocquet-Appel and O. Bar-Yosef (eds), *The Neolithic Demographic Transition and Its Consequences*. Dordrecht: Springer, 239–86.

—— and L. K. Horwitz (2007). Funerals and feasts in the Near Eastern Pre-Pottery Neolithic B. *Antiquity* 81: 902–19.

—— A. Gopher, and S. A. Rosen (1994). The Neolithic Tuwailan cortical knife industry of the Negev, Israel. In H. G. Gebel and S. K. Kozlowski (eds), *Neolithic Chipped Stone Industries of the Fertile Crescent: Proceedings of the First Workshop on PPN Chipped Lithic Industries, Seminar für Vorderasiatische Altertumskunde, Free University of Berlin, 29th March–2nd April, 1993*. Berlin: Ex oriente, 511–25.

—— E. Hovers, and A. Belfer-Cohen (2009).The dynamics of Pleistocene settlement patterns and human adaptations in the Levant—an overview. In J. J. Shea and D. Lieberman (eds), *Transitions in Prehistory: Papers in Honor of Ofer Bar-Yosef*. Oakville, CT: David Brown/Oxbow, 187–254.

Hershkovitz, I., O. Bar-Yosef, and B. Arensburg (1994). The Pre-Pottery Neolithic populations of south Sinai and their relations to other circum-Mediterranean groups: an anthropological study. *Paléorient* 20: 59–84.

Hershman, D., and A. Belfer-Cohen (2010). 'It's magic!' Artistic and symbolic material manifestations from the Gilgal sites. In Bar-Yosef et al. (2010: 185–216).

Horwitz, L. K. (1988). Bone remains from Tel Neve Yam. *Mitekufat Haeven* 21: 99–109.

—— (2002). Fauna from the Wadi Rabah site of Abu Zureiq. *Israel Exploration Journal* 52: 167–78.

—— T. Simmons, O. Lernau, and E. Tchernov (2010). Fauna from the sites of Gilgal I, II and III. In Bar-Yosef et al. (2010: 263–96).

—— E. Tchernov, P. Ducos, et al. (2000). Animal domestication in the southern Levant. *Paléorient*, 25: 63–80.

Kenyon, K. M., and T. A. Holland (eds) (1982). *Excavations at Jericho*, vol. 4: *The Pottery Type Series and Other Finds*. London: British School of Archaeology in Jerusalem.

—— (eds) (1983). *Excavations at Jericho*, vol. 5. London: British School of Archaeology in Jerusalem.

Khalaily, H., O. Bar-Yosef, O. Barzilai, et al. (2007). Excavations at Motza in the Judean Hills and the Early Pre-Pottery Neolithic B in the southern Levant. *Paléorient* 33: 5–37.

Kislev, M. E., A. Hartmann, and T. Noy (2010). The vegetal subsistence of Gilgal I as reflected in the assemblage of House 11. In Bar-Yosef et al. (2010: 251–8).

Kuijt, I. (1994). Pre-Pottery Neolithic A settlement variability: evidence for sociopolitical developments in the southern Levant. *Journal of Mediterranean Archaeology* 7: 165–92.

—— (1996). Negotiating equality through ritual: a consideration of Late Natufian and Pre-Pottery Neolithic A period mortuary practices. *Journal of Anthropological Archaeology* 15: 313–36.

—— (2000). *Life in Neolithic Farming Communities: Social Organization, Identity, and Differentiation*. New York: Kluwer Academic/Plenum.

—— and A. N. Goring-Morris (2002). Foraging, farming and social complexity in the Pre-Pottery Neolithic of the south-central Levant: a review and synthesis. *Journal of World Prehistory* 16: 361–440.

Lechevallier, M. (1978). *Abou Gosh et Beisamoun: deux gisements du VIIe millénaire avant l'ère chrétienne en Israël*. Paris: Association Paléorient.

Marom, N., and G. Bar-Oz (2009). 'Man made oases': Neolithic patterns of wild ungulate exploitation and their consequences for the domestication of pigs and cattle. *Before Farming* 2009: 1–12.

Matskevich, Z. (2005). *The lithic assemblage of Sha'ar Hagolan: typo-technological and chrono-cultural aspects.* MA thesis, Hebrew University of Jerusalem.

Naveh, D. (2003). PPNA Jericho: a socio-political perspective. *Cambridge Archaeological Journal* 13: 83–96.

Ronen, A., and D. Adler (2001). The walls of Jericho were magical. *Archaeology, Ethnology and Anthropology of Eurasia* 2: 97–103.

Rosen, S. A. (1984). Kvish Harif: preliminary investigation at a Late Neolithic site in the central Negev. *Paléorient* 10: 111–21.

—— F. Bocquentin, Y. Avni, and N. Porat (2007). Investigations at Ramat Saharonim: a desert Neolithic sacred precinct in the central Negev. *Bulletin of the American School of Oriental Research* 346: 1–27.

Rosenberg, D. (2008). Serving meals making a home: the PPNA limestone vessel industry of the southern Levant. *Paléorient* 34: 23–32.

—— (2009). Flying stones: the slingstones of the Wadi Rabah Culture. *Paléorient* 35: 99–112.

Sapir-Hen, L., G. Bar-Oz, H. Khalaily, and T. Dayan (2009). Gazelle exploitation in the Early Neolithic site of Motza, Israel: the last of the gazelle hunters in the southern Levant. *Journal of Archaeological Science* 36: 1538–46.

Schick, T. (2010). Basketry finds from Gilgal. In Bar-Yosef, O., A. N. Goring-Morris, and A. Gopher (eds), *Gilgal: Excavations at Early Neolithic Sites in the Lower Jordan Valley: The Excavations of Tamar Noy.* Oakville, Conn.: David Brown/Oxbow, 245–50.

Simmons, A. H. (2007). *The Neolithic Revolution in the Near East: Transforming the Human Landscape.* Tucson: University of Arizona Press.

Stein, M., A. Torfstein, I. Gavrieli, and Y. Yechieli (2010). Abrupt aridities and salt deposition in the post-glacial Dead Sea and their North Atlantic connection. *Quaternary Science Review* 29: 567–75.

van Zeist, W., U. Baruch, and S. Bottema (2009). Holocene palaeoecology of the Hula area, northeastern Israel. In E. Kaptijn and L. P. Petit (eds), *A Timeless Vale: Archaeological and Related Essays on the Jordan Valley in Honour of Gerrit van der Kooij on the Occasion of His Sixty-Fifth Birthday.* Leiden: Leiden University Press, 29–64.

Weninger, B., L. Clare, E. J. Rohling, et al. (2009). The impact of rapid climate change on prehistoric societies during the Holocene in the eastern Mediterranean. *Documenta Praehistorica* 36: 7–59.

Wright, K. I. (2005). The emergence of cooking in western Asia. *Archaeology International* 2004–5: 33–7.

—— P. Critchley, and A. Garrard (2008). Stone bead technologies and early craft specialization: insights from two Neolithic sites in eastern Jordan. *Levant* 40: 131–65.

Yannai, E. (2006). *'En Esur ('Ein Asawir) I: Excavations at a Protohistoric Site in the Coastal Plain of Israel.* Jerusalem: Israel Antiquities Authority.

Yogev, O., and U. Avner (1983). Excavation at the Neolithic sanctuary at Biq'at 'Uvda. *Excavations and Surveys in Israel* 2: 14–15.

Zbenovich, V. (2006). Salvage excavations at a Pre-Pottery Neolithic site at Modiin. *'Atiqot* 51: 1–15.

Zviely, D., D. Sivan, A. Ecker, et al. (2006). Holocene evolution of the Haifa Bay area, Israel, and its influence on ancient tell settlements. *Holocene* 16: 849–61.

CHAPTER 12

....

THE SOUTHERN LEVANT (TRANSJORDAN) DURING THE NEOLITHIC PERIOD

....

ALISON BETTS

Jordan is a region marked by a highly diverse landscape, a characteristic which had a significant impact on the nature and distribution of Neolithic sites. The low-lying floor of the Rift Valley with its mild winter climate was attractive for settlement, which was by necessity concentrated along the numerous streams running down to the Jordan River. The steep slopes of the valley were thickly forested, inhabited by predators, and unattractive to settlement, although in the middle reaches of the larger wadis some sites were established on small river terraces. The well-watered highlands above the valley offered sheltered rolling country with a variety of ecological zones and numerous small springs.

To the east the land flattens out and grows gradually drier. A band of good steppe provides seasonal grazing, but this grows sparser until the land becomes semi-desert. Much of the steppe is limestone, strewn with a thin bed of chert gravels, but across the middle lies a band of rough basalt country, cut by deep gorges and covered by fields of black boulders. The hunting and grazing opportunities offered by the steppe were only fully exploited in the later Neolithic. In the far south of Jordan the geology changes as the limestone gives way to heavily weathered sandstone. Above the Wadi Arabah, the rock forms dense blocks sliced by narrow clefts, while further east the land opens up into high isolated mesas interspersed with wide sandy canyons. Early Neolithic sites appeared in the sandstone foothills near the floor of Wadi Arabah while, a little later and higher up in the hills, springs among the sandstone clefts supported small settlements (Fig.12.1).

Pre-Pottery Neolithic A

....

The Pre-Pottery Neolithic A (PPNA) period represents the first fragile appearance of Neolithic village settlements in the southern Levant. These are largely concentrated in the lower part of the Rift Valley. While the massive tower at Jericho on the west bank of the

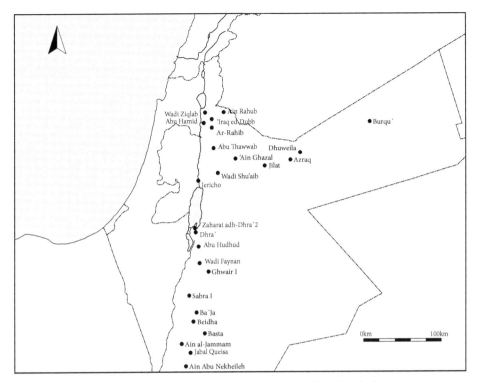

FIG. 12.1 Map of Neolithic sites in the southern Levant (Transjordan)

Jordan River gives an indication of the important cultural changes that were taking place at this time, only hints of these can be seen at other contemporary sites in the early Neolithic heartland. A small number of PPNA sites have been found in Jordan; one, the cave site of 'Iraq ed-Dubb (Kuijt 2002–2004), within the well-watered Mediterranean woodland zone in the mid-Jordan Valley; three open-air sites, Dhra' (Kuijt and Mahasneh 1998), Wadi Faynan 16 (Finlayson and Mithen 2007), and Zaharat adh-Dhra 2 (Edwards and Higham 2001) in the steppic landscape at the southern end of the Dead Sea; and two ephemeral campsites, Sabra 1 in the Petra region (Gebel 1988) and Jabal Queisa to the east in the Judayid Basin (Henry 1982; 1995).

'Iraq ed-Dubb is a small site within a rock shelter cut into a limestone escarpment overlooking Wadi al-Yabis. The shelter appears to have been used sporadically over several hundred years. Small, rounded stone structures were found inside the cave. The floors were covered with layers of mud plaster, which in some cases sealed sub-floor burials. Fittings included hearths, grinding stones, and low platforms. The site was visited and used by small groups of people with an economy that included hunting, gathering, and some plant cultivation. Given the location of the site within a steep river valley, it is likely that the cultivation took place elsewhere.

The sites at the southern end of the Dead Sea are quite different from the 'Iraq ed-Dubb rock shelter. They are open-air sites with clusters of rounded structures, some of which were domestic and others which may have been used for specialized activities. There are differences in their toolkits, which suggest that despite their relative proximity they were occupied by groups with similar economies but distinct cultural traditions (Mithen and Finlayson 2007: 485). The landscape today is arid, but pollen and charcoal recovered from the sites indicates a moister and more heavily vegetated environment in the PPNA period. The economy of the inhabitants of Wadi Faynan 16 and Dhraʿ was based on hunting and gathering, but Zaharat adh-Dhraʿ 2 had evidence for wheat, barley, and pulses that may have been in the early stages of cultivation (Edwards and Higham 2001: 144). At Zaharat adh-Dhraʿ 2 there was also evidence for long-distance exchange mechanisms in the form of saltwater dentalium shells and obsidian which must have been traded from a source in Anatolia. Chipped stone tool technology is characterized by the use of single-platform blade and bladelet cores. Typically diagnostic tools include projectile points with notched bases and tranchet axes (Fig. 12.2).

Following the evidence from Jericho, the PPNA has traditionally been seen as representing the earliest sedentary agricultural societies in the Near East. The Jordanian sites indicate that people on the east bank of the Jordan were moving in this direction, but remained only partially sedentary and were still just beginning to experiment with plant cultivation. Sites are concentrated within the Rift Valley. This contrasts with a much more widely dispersed pattern of land use in the preceding Late Natufian, where sites have been found from the Jordan Valley to far out in the eastern steppe (Olszewski 2001: 57).

PRE-POTTERY NEOLITHIC B

By contrast with the PPNA, the Pre-Pottery Neolithic B (PPNB) period represents the full flourishing of the Neolithic village phenomenon. This period is strongly represented in Jordan. A wide variety of sites are found in almost all kinds of ecological niches, and demonstrate an extraordinary wealth of cultural complexity in all aspects of life from architecture to spiritual beliefs. The economy developed linearly with increasing reliance on cultivated plants and goat herding, although hunting and gathering still formed an important part of the subsistence base.

The Early Pre-Pottery Neolithic B (EPPNB) is archaeologically ephemeral with few well-substantiated sites in Jordan (Edwards et al. 2004). Three possibly fall into this category: Ar-Rahib in Wadi al-Yabis (Kuijt and Goring-Morris 2002: 382), Abu Hudhud in Wadi al-Hasa (Rollefson 1994; 2001: 70), and Wadi Jilat 7 in the eastern steppe (Garrard, Baird, and Byrd 1994; Garrard, Baird, Colledge, et al. 1994). There is no clear evidence for a smooth transition from the PPNA to the PPNB, and this has encouraged deeper analysis of the EPPNB (Gopher 1994; Kuijt 1997; 2003; Edwards et al. 2004). One plausible line of inquiry is that the appearance of the southern EPPNB was the result of cultural stimulus and possibly migration from Syria to the south (Edwards et al. 2004).

By contrast with the ephemeral evidence for the EPPNB, the Middle Pre-Pottery Neolithic (MPPNB) is strongly represented. Sites range from substantial villages such as ʿAin Ghazal and Wadi Shuʿaib with complex rectangular buildings, probably indicating a largely sedentary population, to smaller sites still with rounded buildings, such as Beidha, Shaqarat Mazyad, and ʿAin Abu Nukheilah, perhaps with a lesser degree of fully sedentary occupation (Gebel 2004). The transition to the Late Pre-Pottery Neolithic B (LPPNB) saw the rise of new and sometimes much larger settlements along the eastern margins of the Rift Valley.

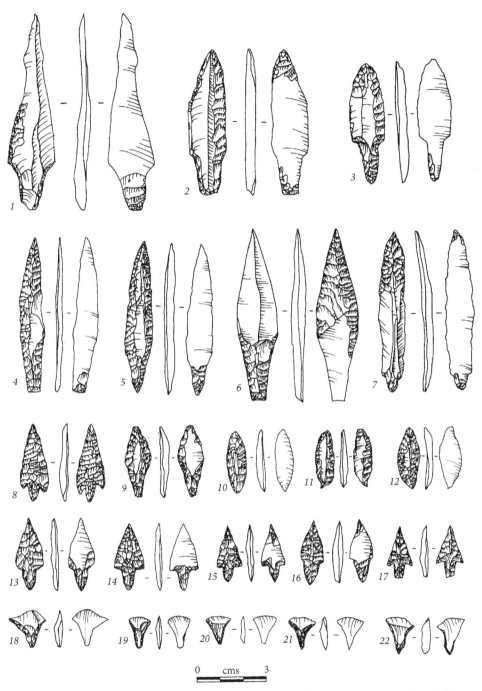

FIG. 12.2 Dhuweila PPNB and LN chipped stone projectile points. (Drawings by A. Betts)

'Ain Ghazal and Wadi Shu'aib saw continuity of settlement, while new villages appeared to the south, sites such as As-Safiya, Basta, and 'Ain Jammam. These LPPNB sites are remarkable for their large size, up to at least 15ha in some cases, and for their complex and densely packed architecture (Bienert 2004). Changes in settlement density may have influenced changes in cult practice, while pressure on resources may have provided the impetus for movements of population into the steppe. Starting in the MPPNB and reaching a floruit in the LPPNB, there was an expansion eastwards into the semi-arid steppic zones. Seasonally occupied sites in Wadi Jilat were established by at least the MPPNB (Garrard, Baird, and Byrd 1994; Garrard, Baird, Colledge, et al. 1994) and in the LPPNB there was extensive use of the basalt *harra* by mobile populations hunting gazelle east of al-Azraq (Betts 1998).

PPNB villages do not follow the settlement patterns of the preceding PPNA. They are newly established sites located in the upper reaches of valleys leading down to the Jordan Rift and on the highland plateau. A cluster of sites has been found in the sandstone massifs of the hills around Petra in the south of the country. The earliest of these is Shaqarat Mazyad, identified as early MPPNB in date (Hermansen et al. 2006), followed by Beidha (Byrd 2005) in the late MPPNB, and then Ba'ja in the Late PPNB (Bienert and Gebel 2004). The sites, in particular Beidha, show the remarkably sophisticated development of architecture during this period. Domestic buildings were constructed from the local sandstone. The earliest structures were curvilinear and semi-subterranean with timber roofing supports set into rough, cobblestone walls, an architectural form which finds parallels in the PPNA of northern Syria (Stordeur et al. 2000). This form was followed by the introduction of above-ground circular buildings as well as sub-rectangular and rectangular buildings with walls constructed of carefully cut and laid sandstone slabs. The rectangular structures became more complex with the introduction of the corridor building comprising two internally subdivided stories, one below ground and one above. The upper stories were open-plan with plastered floors, while the earthen-floored basements were divided into many small alcoves opening off the central corridor. At the later site of Ba'ja and further east at Basta, these developed further into close-packed, terraced, multi-storeyed buildings consisting of many small rectangular cells with some large, possibly open, courts (Bienert and Gebel 2004; Gebel et al. 2004) (Fig. 12.3).

In the central highlands the transition from MPPNB to LPPNB was marked by shifts in population that had a highly significant impact on existing settlements there. Sites such as 'Ain Ghazal witnessed a rapid increase in settlement size and consequent changes in type and density of structures (Banning 2004). There is increasing sophistication in architectural construction and variety in building forms, together with indications of specialized use of space within settlements. Specialized function, perhaps cult activity, may also be identifiable in whole buildings, specifically the LPPNB cult building and the PPNC 'special building' at 'Ain Ghazal (Rollefson 1998). The cult building was circular with a large central hole. Below the well-made plaster floor, four stone-lined channels led towards the outside walls (Fig. 12.4). Upright slabs, niches, and plastered benches mark out other buildings at 'Ain Ghazal, Ghwair 1, and 'Ain Jammam (Rollefson 1997; Simmons and Najjar 1996; Waheeb and Fino 1997).

Sites in the steppe were occupied only on a seasonal basis and have much more ephemeral architecture. The remains consist of circular and sub-circular units defined by parallel rings of stone slabs placed upright on their sides. In the basaltic region, low stone walls were also used. It is likely that these stone rings provided the substructure for tents made probably

FIG. 12.3 The LPPNB site of Ba'ja (photo courtesy of the Ba'ja Neolithic Project)

FIG. 12.4 'Ain Ghazal LPPNB cult building (photo courtesy of G. O. Rollefson)

from animal skins. Sites tend to cluster around seasonal water sources such as the gorge at Wadi Jilat and around the lake at al-Azraq (Garrard, Baird, Colledge, et al. 1994; Garrard, Baird, and Byrd 1994). East of al-Azraq in the basalt region, numerous hilltop knapping sites attest to the importance of this area for hunting. The LPPNB hunting camp of Dhuweila yielded a faunal assemblage consisting of over 90 per cent gazelle, and was associated with the use of large stone walled animal traps (desert kites) (Betts 1998).

The PPNB is characterized by a rich diversity of ritual practices, some related to death and burial. The period is marked by a paucity of burials, with the small number of skeletons recovered suggesting that in most cases either disposal of the dead took place away from the settlement or earlier burials were removed to make way for new ones (Bienert et al. 2004). Where bodies have been found, they were most commonly buried in a crouched position under the floors. At 'Ain Ghazal, bodies have also been found in areas of waste disposal (Rollefson 2001), while at Ba'ja excavations revealed a burial chamber containing the remains of at least three adults and nine infants (Bienert et al. 2004: 162). Human skull burials and headless skeletons have been documented at several sites including Basta, Beidha, and 'Ain Ghazal (Bienert 2004: 35). At 'Ain Ghazal, caches of three or four skulls were buried in tight clusters, some of them partially plastered, clearly in the same tradition as the well-known examples from Jericho, with carefully modelled human features (Rollefson 1983; 1986).

A second important parallel with Jericho is the discovery at 'Ain Ghazal of carefully buried groups of lime plaster anthropomorphic statues (Rollefson 1983; 1986). There are both full figures and busts, some with a wide body supporting two heads (Fig. 12.5). They vary in size up to a metre in height, and were constructed by modelling the clay on a reed base. The faces were simply shaped to show eyes, a nose, and mouth, with the eyes outlined using black mastic. Traces of paint are visible on the surface of the plaster. Before being buried, the figurines may have been displayed. The reed cores extended through the base and could have been used to anchor the statues into a floor surface. Numbers of small clay and, more rarely, stone animal figurines may have served a more personal role in the spiritual life of the community (Rollefson 2001: 76). Slivers of flint embedded in some of this site's examples suggest some form of 'hunting magic'. 'Ain Ghazal appears to illustrate changes in cult practice from the MPPNB into the LPPNB, possibly associated with social changes brought about by the rapidly increasing size of the settlement (Rollefson 2004: 150). Sub-floor decapitated burials were a common feature of the MPPNB settlement, and the plastered skulls appear to

FIG. 12.5 'Ain Ghazal plaster statues (image courtesy G. O. Rollefson)

be associated exclusively with the MPPNB, as do the plaster statues. The LPPNB sees the appearance of specialized buildings that imply changes in forms of cult practice towards rituals that involved a wider community of participants. A different form of cult practice may perhaps be seen in finely carved representations of gazelle from the hunters' camp at Dhuweila, which illustrate an expression of feeling towards their prey, whether spiritual or not (Betts 1998).

Personal ornaments have been found in burial and non-burial contexts at a number of sites. Stone rings for use as bracelets or clothing fasteners were manufactured at Ba'ja and found across the PPNB zone, even out into the steppe (Bienert and Gebel 2004; Betts 1998). Carved and pierced mother-of-pearl had a similarly wide distribution. Most examples were simple plaques with two holes but some, such as those from LPPNB Basta (Gebel et al. 2004: 97), were quite ornate. Stone and shell beads were also recovered from a number of sites.

The causes of the major changes and developments in this dynamic period are poorly understood. There is no doubt that there is a massive increase in site size and intra-settlement density in the LPPNB, as well as the establishment of new, often large settlements in the south of the country. It has been suggested that this occurred as a response to expansion by MPPNB populations from the Mediterranean highlands west of the Rift Valley, where many MPPNB sites seem to have been abandoned (Rollefson 2004: 147; Gebel 2004). To the east of the Rift Valley villages were established in new environmental zones which offered sheltered locations, plentiful water, rich resources, and access to the grasslands of the eastern steppes with their vast herds of game. It was also this period that saw the rise of highly organized hunting practices in the basalt zone as well as the first moves towards mobile pastoralism in the steppe. The diversity in settlement size and environmental locations among LPPNB sites has provoked discussion about the nature of their economic interdependence. There is evidence for trade, exchange, and shared technologies, yet there does not appear to be a hierarchical system in place, but rather a series of independent adaptations to varying regional opportunities supported by inter-site exchange mechanisms (Gebel 2004; Rollefson 2004).

The LPPNB was, however, an unsustainable socioeconomic system, and ultimately it collapsed, leaving most of the major sites abandoned. Initially the settled population adapted to more congested living and probably, as suggested by the evidence from 'Ain Ghazal, established coping mechanisms to manage social stress. Environmental stress has been suggested by Rollefson as a determining factor in the demise of these large LPPNB sites (Rollefson and Köhler-Rollefson 1993), but others have argued against it. There is no evidence from Basta, for example, to suggest environmental decline (Gebel 2004: 15). Movements out into the good steppe and the appearance of incipient pastoralism as an element in hunting and foraging subsistence strategies have been viewed as an additional response to pressures on the LPPNB economic structure (Rollefson 2004: 149). The nature of these movements, however, is the subject of some debate surrounding the precise stimuli and whether this resulted in seasonal or permanent use of the steppe (Martin 1999; Betts 2008). By the LPPNB evidence indicates that domestic goats constituted almost 70 per cent of the faunal remains at 'Ain Ghazal. Rollefson and Köhler-Rollefson have argued that to relieve pressure on resources in the immediate surroundings of the settlement, these were herded on a seasonal basis into the steppe (Rollefson and Köhler-Rollefson 1993; Rollefson 2004: 146). The first appearance of caprids on short-term occupation sites in the steppe has been documented in Wadi Jilat in the terminal PPNB/PPNC (Horwitz et al. 1999: 69).

PRE-POTTERY NEOLITHIC C

As the rich and dynamic culture of the Pre-Pottery Neolithic B came to an end, it was assumed for a long time that there was a break in occupation, the *hiatus palestinien*, before the reappearance of a now dispersed population living in small agricultural hamlets. Evidence from Jordan, most particularly 'Ain Ghazal, has shown that not all sites in prime locations were abandoned immediately at the end of the PPNB. At 'Ain Ghazal there is evidence for a transitional stage, the PPNC, underlying the Late Neolithic Yarmoukian occupation. PPNC levels have also been identified at Wadi Shu'aib (Rollefson 2001: 86ff.). The period is characterized by a great number of significant changes. The lithic technology shifts, with the abandonment of the naviform core and the appearance of smaller projectile points. Faunal remains, at least at 'Ain Ghazal, indicate a dominance of sheep over goats, while cattle and pigs may also have been domesticated. The size of the settled population declined as the dense two-storeyed housing of the LPPNB gave way to smaller and simpler single-room buildings. In the steppe there is evidence for continuity from the LPPNB into the Late Neolithic at Wadi Jilat, and also Burqu' much further to the east, where ovicaprids gradually rise in importance until they represent almost 50 per cent of the faunal remains (Horwitz et al. 1999; Betts 2008).

LATE (POTTERY) NEOLITHIC

With the appearance of ceramics as typological indicators, the Pottery Neolithic appears more complex and ill-defined. The Yarmoukian with its distinctive incised vessels is best represented. The two key Yarmoukian Late Neolithic sites in the verdant regions of Jordan are 'Ain Ghazal, with its important evidence for continuity from the earlier PPN, and Jebel Abu Thawwab in the hill country south of Jerash. Other known sites are all in the north of the country: 'Ain Rahub near Irbid (Muheisen et al. 1988) and Wadi Shu'aib (Simmons et al. 1989). Jebel Abu Thawwab was a new foundation, located close to a perennially flowing wadi. Domestic architecture included both round and rectilinear structures. Pottery was handmade, decorated with light-coloured slip, as well as red painted or incised herringbone designs (Kafafi 2001). At 'Ain Ghazal the buildings were mostly rectilinear, with the exception of some rings of stones, perhaps used as tent bases, and an unusual circular building with remarkably thick walls (Rollefson 2001). Settlement density was much reduced, with spaces of up to 15m between houses at 'Ain Ghazal (Rollefson 2001: 95). Chipped stone tools include high numbers of truncation burins. The faunal remains indicate a predominance of sheep and goat with some evidence for pigs and cattle. Gazelle, onager, and wild goat were still hunted. Botanical remains from 'Ain Rahub show that emmer, einkorn, and hulled barley were cultivated as well as flax (Muheisen et al. 1988).

Other ceramic traditions are less well represented. The Pottery Neolithic A (Jericho IX) appears dominant in the south, most notably at the site of Dhra' (Finlayson et al. 2003). In the north, the Wadi Rabah tradition has been identified in Wadi Ziqlab (Banning 1996) and at Abu Hamid on the east bank of the Jordan River (Kafafi 1998). For the later part of the period in the south the Qatifian, best known from the northern Negev and Sinai, has been identified at 'Ain Waida in Wadi Dhra' (Kuijt and Chesson 2002).

In the steppe, the Late Neolithic is a time of dynamic growth. There is a marked increase in the number of sites, generally associated with the appearance of domesticated animals on sites far out into the semi-arid regions (Betts 2008). This period sees the first sustained use of the deep steppe beyond the basalt region, probably associated with incipient nomadic pastoralism, but faunal remains on steppic sites show that wild game still provided up to half of the meat consumed by these early hunter-herders. Lithic assemblages indicate regional differences between the steppe and the verdant areas, with a strong dominance of truncation burins on many sites.

The end of the Neolithic is also somewhat ill-defined, as it merges into the succeeding Chalcolithic without a significant break. In the verdant regions the Jordanian Chalcolithic post-dates the Qatifian but may be contemporaneous with later Wadi Rabah (Rollefson 2001: 96; Bourke 2001: 111). In the steppe, evidence for the Neolithic to Chalcolithic transition is extremely sparse, but there are indications that it may have been a time of economic change as herding became increasingly dominant in the subsistence economy (Tarawneh 2007).

SUGGESTED READING

Betts, A. (1998). *The Harra and the Hamad: Excavations and Surveys in Eastern Jordan*, vol. 1. Sheffield: Sheffield Academic.

Byrd, B. (2005). *Early Village Life at Beidha, Jordan: Neolithic Spatial Organisation and Vernacular Architecture: The Excavations of Mrs Diana Kirkbride-Helbæk*. Oxford: Oxford University Press.

Kafafi, Z. A. (1998). The Late Neolithic in Jordan. In D. O. Henry (ed.), *The Prehistoric Archaeology of Jordan*. Oxford: Archaeopress, 127–39.

Kuijt, I., and A. N. Goring-Morris (2002). Foraging, farming, and social complexity in the Pre-Pottery Neolithic of the southern Levant: a review and synthesis. *Journal of World Prehistory* 16: 361–440.

Rollefson, G. O. (2001). The Neolithic period. In B. MacDonald, R. Adams, and P. Bienkowski (eds), *The Archaeology of Jordan*. Sheffield: Sheffield Academic, 67–105.

REFERENCES

Banning, E. B. (1996). Highlands and lowlands: problems and survey frameworks for rural archaeology in the Near East. *Bulletin of the American Schools of Oriental Research* 301: 25–45.

—— (2004). Changes in the spatial organization of Transjordanian settlements from Middle PPNB to Late Neolithic. In II.-D. Bienert, H.-G. K. Gebel, and R. Neef (eds), *Central Settlements in Neolithic Jordan: Proceedings of a Symposium Held in Wadi Musa, Jordan, 21st–25th of July, 1997*. Berlin: Ex oriente, 215–32.

Betts, A. (1998). *The Harra and the Hamad: Excavations and Surveys in Eastern Jordan*, vol. 1. Sheffield: Sheffield Academic.

—— (2008). Things to do with sheep and goats: Neolithic hunter-forager-herders in north Arabia. In H. Barnard and W. Wendrich (eds), *The Archaeology of Mobility: Old World and New World Nomadism*. Los Angeles: Cotsen Institute of Archaeology, University of California, 25–42.

Bienert, H.-D. (2004). The Pre-Pottery Neolithic B (PPNB) in Jordan: first steps towards proto-urban societies? In H.-D. Bienert, H.-G. K. Gebel, and R. Neef (eds), *Central Settlements in Neolithic Jordan: Proceedings of a Symposium Held in Wadi Musa, Jordan, 21st–25th of July, 1997*. Berlin: Ex oriente, 21–40.

—— and H.-G. K. Gebel (2004). Summary on Ba'ja 1997 and insights from the later seasons. In H.-D. Bienert, H.-G. K. Gebel, and R. Neef (eds), *Central Settlements in Neolithic Jordan: Proceedings of a Symposium Held in Wadi Musa, Jordan, 21st–25th of July, 1997*. Berlin: Ex oriente, 119–44.

—— M. Bonogofsky, H.-G. K. Gebel, I. Kuijt, and G. O. Rollefson (2004). Where are the dead? In H.-D. Bienert, H.-G. K. Gebel, and R. Neef (eds), *Central Settlements in Neolithic Jordan: Proceedings of a Symposium Held in Wadi Musa, Jordan, 21st–25th of July, 1997*. Berlin: Ex oriente, 157–76.

Bourke, S. J. (2001). The Chalcolithic period. In B. MacDonald, R. Adams, and P. Bienkowski (eds), *The Archaeology of Jordan*. Sheffield: Sheffield Academic, 107–62.

Byrd, B. F. (2005). *Early Village Life at Beidha, Jordan: Neolithic Spatial Organisation and Vernacular Architecture. The Excavations of Mrs Diana Kirkbride-Helbæk*. Oxford: Oxford University Press.

Edwards, P. C., and T. F. G. Higham (2001). Zaharat adh-Dhra' 2 and the Dead Sea Plain at the dawn of the Holocene. In A. Walmesley (ed.), *Australians Uncovering Ancient Jordan: Fifty Years of Middle Eastern Archaeology*. Sydney: Research Institute for Humanities and Social Sciences, University of Sydney/Jordan: Department of Antiquities of Jordan, 139–52.

—— J. Meadows, G. Sayej, and M. Westaway (2004). From the PPNA to the PPNB: new views from the southern Levant after excavations at Zaharat adh-Dhra' 2 in Jordan. *Paléorient* 30: 21–60.

Finlayson, B., I. Kuijt, T. Arpin, et al. (2003). Dhra', excavation project, 2002 interim report. *Levant* 35: 1–38.

—— and S. J. Mithen (eds) (2007). *The Early Prehistory of Wadi Faynan, Southern Jordan*. Oxford: Oxbow.

Garrard, A. N., D. Baird, and B. F. Byrd (1994). The chronological basis and significance of the Late Paleolithic and Neolithic sequence in the Azraq Basin, Jordan. In O. Bar-Yosef and R. S. Kra (eds), *Late Quaternary Chronology and Paleoclimates of the Eastern Mediterranean*. Tucson, Ariz.: Radiocarbon/Cambridge, Mass.: American School of Prehistoric Research, 177–99.

—— D. Baird, S. Colledge, L. Martin, and K. Wright (1994). Prehistoric environment and settlement in the Azraq Basin: an interim report on the 1987 and 1988 excavation seasons. *Levant* 26: 73–109.

Gebel, H.-G. K. (1988). Late Epipaleolithic–Aceramic Neolithic sites in the Petra area. In A. N. Garrard and H.-G. K. Gebel (eds), *The Prehistory of Jordan: The State of Research in 1986, pt 1*. Oxford: British Archaeological Reports, 67–100.

—— (2004). Central to what? The centrality issue of the LPPNB mega-site phenomenon in Jordan. In H.-D. Bienert, H.-G. K. Gebel, and R. Neef (eds), *Central Settlements in Neolithic Jordan: Proceedings of a Symposium Held in Wadi Musa, Jordan, 21st–25th of July, 1997*. Berlin: Ex oriente, 1–19.

—— M. Muheisen, H. J. Nissen, and N. Qadi (2004). Late PPNB Basta: results of 1992. In H.-D. Bienert, H.-G. K. Gebel, and R. Neef (eds), *Central Settlements in Neolithic Jordan:*

Proceedings of a Symposium Held in Wadi Musa, Jordan, 21st–25th of July, 1997. Berlin: Ex oriente, 71–104.

Gopher, A. (1994). *Arrowheads of the Neolithic Levant: A Seriation Analysis*. Winona Lake, Ind.: Eisenbrauns.

Henry, D. O. (1982). The prehistory of southern Jordan and relationships with the Levant. *Journal of Field Archaeology* 9: 417–44.

—— (1995). *Prehistoric Cultural Ecology and Evolution: Insights from Southern Jordan*. New York: Plenum.

Hermansen, B. D., I. Thuesen, C. Hoffmann Jensen, M. Kinzel, and M. Bille (2006). Shkârat Msaied: the 2005 season of excavations—a short preliminary report. *Neo-Lithics* 1/06: 3–7.

Horwitz, L. K., E. Tchernov, P. Ducos, et al. (1999). Animal domestication in the southern Levant. *Paléorient* 25: 63–80.

Kafafi, Z. A. (1998). The Late Neolithic in Jordan. In D. O. Henry (ed.), *The Prehistoric Archaeology of Jordan*. Oxford: Archaeopress, 127–39.

—— (2001). *Jebel Abu Thawwab (Er-Rumman), Central Jordan*. Berlin: Ex oriente.

Kuijt, I. (1997). Trying to fit round houses into square holes: re-examining the timing of the south-central Levantine Pre-Pottery Neolithic A and Pre-Pottery Neolithic B cultural transition. In H.-G. K. Gebel, Z. A. Kafafi, and G. O. Rollefson (eds), *The Prehistory of Jordan II: Perspectives from 1997*. Berlin: Ex oriente, 193–202.

—— (2002–2004). Pre-Pottery Neolithic A and Late Natufian at 'Iraq ed-Dubb, Jordan. *Journal of Field Archaeology* 29: 291–308.

—— (2003). Between foraging and farming: critically evaluating the archaeological evidence for the southern Levantine Early Pre-Pottery Neolithic B Period. *Turkish Academy of Sciences Journal of Archaeology* 6: 7–25.

—— and M. Chesson (2002). Excavations at 'Ain Waida', Jordan: new insights into Pottery Neolithic lifeways in the southern Levant. *Paléorient* 28: 109–22.

—— and A. N. Goring-Morris (2002). Foraging, farming, and social complexity in the Pre-Pottery Neolithic of the southern Levant: a review and synthesis. *Journal of World Prehistory* 16: 361–440.

—— and H. Mahasneh (1998). Dhra': an Early Neolithic village in the southern Jordan Valley. *Journal of Field Archaeology* 25: 153–61.

Martin, L. A. (1999). Mammal remains from the eastern Jordanian Neolithic, and the nature of caprine herding in the steppe. *Paléorient* 25: 87–104.

Mithen, S. J., and B. Finlayson (2007). WF16 and the Pre-Pottery Neolithic A of the southern Levant. In B. Finlayson and S. J. Mithen (eds), *The Early Prehistory of Wadi Faynan, Southern Jordan: Archaeological Survey of Wadis Faynan, Ghuwayr and al-Bustan and Evaluation of the Pre-Pottery Neolithic A Site of WF16*. Oxford: Oxbow, 470–86.

Muheisen, M., H.-G. K. Gebel, C. Hannss, and R. Neef (1988). 'Ain Rahub: a new Final Natufian and Yarmoukian site near Irbid. In A. N. Garrard and H.-G. K. Gebel (eds), *The Prehistory of Jordan: The State of Research in 1986, Part II*. Oxford: British Archaeological Reports, 472–502.

Olszewski, D. I. (2001). The Paleolithic period, including the Epipaleolithic. In B. MacDonald, R. Adams, and P. Bienkowski (eds), *The Archaeology of Jordan*. Sheffield: Sheffield Academic, 31–65.

Rollefson, G. O. (1983). Ritual and ceremony at Neolithic 'Ain Ghazal (Jordan). *Paléorient* 9: 29–38.

—— (1986). Neolithic 'Ain Ghazal (Jordan): ritual and ceremony II. *Paléorient* 12: 45–52.

—— (1994). Abu Hudhud (WHS 1008): an EPPNB settlement in the Wadi el-Hasa, southern Jordan. In S. K. Kozlowski and H.-G. K. Gebel (eds), *Neolithic Chipped Stone Industries of the Fertile Crescent: Proceedings of the First Workshop on PPN Chipped Lithic Industries, Seminar für Vorderasiatische Altertumskunde, Free University of Berlin, 29th March–2nd April, 1993*. Berlin: Ex oriente, 159–60.

—— (1997). Changes in architecture and social organization at 'Ain Ghazal. In H.-G. K. Gebel, Z. A. Kafafi, and G. O. Rollefson (eds), *The Prehistory of Jordan II: Perspectives from 1997*. Berlin: Ex oriente, 287–307.

—— (1998). Neolithic 'Ain Ghazal: ritual and ceremony III. *Paléorient* 24: 43–58.

—— (2001). The Neolithic period. In B. MacDonald, R. Adams, and P. Bienkowski (eds), *The Archaeology of Jordan*. Sheffield: Sheffield Academic, 67–105.

—— (2004). The character of LPPNB social organization. In H.-D. Bienert, H.-G. K. Gebel, and R. Neef (eds), *Central Settlements in Neolithic Jordan: Proceedings of a Symposium Held in Wadi Musa, Jordan, 21st–25th of July, 1997*. Berlin: Ex oriente, 145–55.

—— and I. Köhler-Rollefson (1993). PPNC adaptations in the first half of the 6th millennium B.C. *Paléorient* 19: 33–42.

Simmons, A. H., Z. A. Kafafi, G. O. Rollefson, and K. Moyer (1989). Test excavations at Wadi Shui'eib: a major Neolithic settlement in central Jordan. *Annual of the Department of Antiquities of Jordan* 33: 27–42.

—— and M. Najjar (1996). Current investigations at Ghwair I, a Neolithic settlement in southern Jordan. *Neo-Lithics* 2/96: 6–7.

Stordeur, D., M. Brent, G. der Aprahamian, and J.-C. Roux (2000). Les bâtiments communautaires de Jerf el Ahmar et Mureybet horizon PPNA (Syrie). *Paléorient* 26: 29–44.

Tarawneh, M. B. (2007). *Pastoral nomadism in the southern Levant during the Chalcolithic period: new evidence from eastern Bayir* (2 vols). PhD dissertation, University of Sydney.

Waheeb, M., and N. Fino (1997). 'Ayn el-Jammam: a Neolithic site near Ras en-Naqb, southern Jordan. In H.-G. K. Gebel, Z. A. Kafafi, and G. O. Rollefson (eds), *The Prehistory of Jordan II: Perspectives from 1997*. Berlin: Ex oriente, 215–20.

....

CHAPTER 13

CYPRUS DURING THE NEOLITHIC PERIOD

....

JOANNE CLARKE

INTRODUCTION

....

Until recently, Cyprus was rarely included in debates on the prehistory of the Levant, residing instead in scholarship on the Mediterranean, where it regularly formed part of discussions on island archaeology (Cherry 2004; Knapp and Blake 2005; Waldren and Ensenyat
2002). This was not wholly by choice; indeed, some scholars of Cypriot archaeology were
at pains to have it incorporated into Near Eastern discourse from an early date (Peltenburg
1978; 1985). The reasons were instead partly historical and partly the result of a complete
lack of evidence for external connections before excavations at Parekklisha-Shillourokambos
(hereafter Shillourokambos) and Kissonerga-Mylouthkia (hereafter Mylouthkia) a decade
ago.

During the 1950s and 1960s, interpretations of the Cypriot Neolithic were based almost
exclusively on excavations undertaken by Porphyrios Dikaios at the late eighth- and
seventh-millennia BC site Khirokitia and the fifth-millennium BC site Sotira (Dikaios
1953; 1961). By the 1970s many more excavations at Neolithic sites were under way,
including renewed work at Khirokitia (Le Brun 1984; 1989; 1994) and new excavations at
Kalavasos-Tenta (hereafter Tenta) (Todd 1987; 2005), Cape Andreas-Kastros (hereafter
Kastros) (Le Brun 1981), and two sites in the north of the island, Philia-Drakos A (hereafter Philia) and Ayios Epiktitos-Vrysi (hereafter Vrysi) (Peltenburg 1982; Watkins 1970).
These were supplemented by the work of the Cyprus Survey and by test excavations at
Klepini-Troulli (hereafter Troulli) (Dikaios and Stewart 1962), Petra tou Limniti (Gjerstad
1934), and Kalavasos-Site A (hereafter Kokkinoyia) (Dikaios and Stewart 1962) (Fig. 13.1).

Despite the intensification of Neolithic research, lack of evidence for mainland origins for
these early settled communities persisted, as did the view that Khirokitia and its contemporaries represented the earliest colonization of the island (Le Brun 1986, but see Stanley Price
1977 and Watkins 1973: 47–9 for alternative hypotheses).

Excavations in the 1990s at four sites pre-dating Khirokitia have led to significant revi-
sions in our understanding of the prehistory of Cyprus. In the first instance, it is now clear

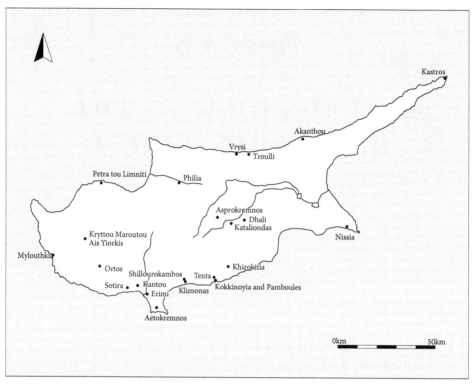

FIG. 13.1 Map of Neolithic sites in Cyprus

from the work undertaken at Akrotiri-Aetokremnos (hereafter Aetokremnos) that Cyprus
was visited by terminal epipaleolithic hunter-fisher groups from the Levant in the eleventh millennium BC (Simmons 1999; 2001; 2003; 2004a), and that these groups may have
continued to visit the island, or indeed may have settled on the island in the tenth millennium BC (see McCartney et al. 2006; Manning et al. 2010; and Vigne 2012 for the most
recent discussions on possible tenth-millennium BC sites on the island). In the second
instance, evidence from Mylouthkia, Shillourokambos, and Akanthou-Arkosyko (hereafter Akanthou) on the north coast indicates that farmer-herder groups, probably from
the northern Levantine coastal region (although perhaps not exclusively: see Simmons
2004a: 11 and Şevketoğlu 2002 for alternative locales), settled on the island in the ninth
millennium BC and went on to form the basis of the subsequent Khirokitian in the late
eighth and seventh millennia BC (Guilaine 2003a; 2003b; Guilaine et al. 2000; Peltenburg,
Colledge, et al. 2000; 2001; Peltenburg, Croft, et al. 2001; Peltenburg 2003). Other revi-
sions in our understanding of the Cypriot prehistoric record include acceptance of the
possibility of more than one colonizing event, from more than one region of the eastern
Mediterranean littoral (see Kuijt 2004; McCartney 2007; Simmons 2004b) and the likelihood of continued contact between Cyprus and the mainland Levant throughout the
whole of the Neolithic period, either in the form of exchange of knowledge, or personnel,
or the replenishment of depleted food stock (Clarke 2007a; McCartney 2007; Peltenburg
and Wasse 2004).

Not surprisingly, debates persist on why evidence for contact is equivocal in the archaeo-logical record after the eighth millennium BC. Archaeologists continue to search for expla-nations as to why, with so much circumstantial evidence in support of contact, the Cypriot prehistoric record bears so little resemblance to that of the mainland, either prior to coloni-zation of the island by Early PPNB settlers in the ninth millennium BC or indeed soon after. One recent theory considers the possibility that the inhabitants of Cyprus had a tendency toward insularity, effectively structuring and maintaining their own cultural boundaries (Clarke 2003; McCartney 2007; McCartney and Todd 2005). Another theory argues that low population density and low resource stress halted intensification, a process that continued largely unabated on the mainland and which ultimately resulted in the rise of complexity in the fourth millennium BC (Wasse 2007).

PERIODIZATION

The first relative chronology for Cyprus was constructed by Dikaios on the basis of his excavations at Khirokitia, Sotira, and Erimi. Khirokitia became the type site for the late eighth-and seventh-millennia BC (Dikaios' Neolithic 1a), Sotira became the type site for the fifth-millennium BC (Dikaios' Neolithic 1b), and Erimi became the type site for the fourth-millennium BC (Dikaios' Chalcolithic 1).

Very recently there has been considerable debate and a review of the chronologi-cal labelling for the Neolithic period. As new discoveries fill gaps in the archaeological record, existing periodizations are being expanded in ways that are unwieldy. Peltenburg, Colledge, et al. (2001) have argued for the use of a chrono-typological terminology that highlights links between Cyprus and the mainland in the earlier part of the Neolithic, in particular the use of the term 'Cypro-PPNB' to define the ninth and early eighth millennia BC and the sites that fall within this time-frame. This however, leads to inconsistency, as there are periods of time when Cyprus does not show links with the mainland and differ-ent terminology is used (e.g. the Khirokitian). Guilaine and counterparts use the terms Early, Middle, and Late Aceramic (Guilaine 2003a; 2003b; Guilaine et al. 2000), which approximate to Peltenburg's Cypro-Early PPNB, Cypro-Middle PPNB, and Cypro-Late PPNB; but Guilaine's terminology poses problems should there be the confirmation of a tenth-millennium BC presence on the island which would require another (even earlier) term to describe it.

Because of a lack of internal consistency in the Cypriot chrono-terminology and poor temporal synchronization with the mainland sequence, it is my view that it is better, when discussing prehistoric Cyprus in relation to the Near East, to refer to chronological periods of time, such as the eighth millennium BC, the seventh millennium BC, and so on. Comparing the 'Khirokitian' with the 'Yarmoukian' is unhelpful because they do not occupy exactly the same temporal space; the Khirokitian, for example, overlaps significantly with the PPNC. Instead, disregarding cultural labels opens the way for useful comparisons of a wide range of variables influencing and affecting both regions. Similarities between Cyprus and the main-land may be highlighted where they exist, while also continuing to acknowledge that there are significant differences. The simplest way to achieve this without significantly changing existing terminology is to use chronological periods as the primary descriptor. When it is

Chronological period	Chrono-typological timeframe	Cultural name	Dates cal. BC
11th mil.	Terminal Epipaleolithic?	Akrotiri phase	c. 10,900–9900 BC
10th mil.	Early Neolithic	no evidence	c. 9900–8800 BC
early-9th mil.	Early Neolithic	Late-PPNA	c. 8800–8500 BC
mid-9th mil.	Early Neolithic	Cypro-EPPNB	c. 8500–8200 BC
late-9th to 8th mil.	Early Neolithic	Cypro-MPPNB	c. 8200–7600 BC
mid- to late-8th mil.	Early Neolithic	Cypro-LPPNB	c. 7600–6900 BC
late-8th to 6th mil.	Early Neolithic	Khirokitian	c. 7000–5500/5000 BC
mid-6th to mid-5th mil.	Gap		c. 5500–4750/4500 BC
mid-5th to early-4th mil.	Late (ceramic) Neolithic	Sotiran	c. 4500–3900 BC

FIG. 13.2. Chronological chart showing concurrence of Cyprus and the Levant

necessary to differentiate, or when further clarification is necessary, then cultural terminology may be employed.

I adopt the periodization outlined in Clarke (2007a: 28) and reproduced in Fig. 13.2.

THE ELEVENTH MILLENNIUM BC

Aetokremnos is the only excavated site on the island attributable to the terminal Epipaleolithic period (but see Ammerman et al. 2006 for further sites attributable to this period). It is being included in this chapter because it is important for understanding the processes that eventually led to the colonization of Cyprus in the ninth millennium BC. Median radiocarbon determinations place it between the early eleventh and early tenth millennia BC (IntCal04.14c: Reimer et al. 2004). Robinson et al. (2006) have recently re-dated the Younger Dryas stadial in southwest Asia to 10,600–10,000 uncal. BP, which when calibrated using IntCal04 equates approximately to 10,785–9400 BC at one standard deviation. Thus, the Aetokremnos paleontological and cultural layers correspond in calendar years to the entire Younger Dryas cold, arid event.

Aetokremnos is a small rock-shelter located on the southern coast of the Akrotiri peninsula (Fig. 13.1 above). It has been the subject of controversy due to the excavator's assertion that the human inhabitants probably hunted the endemic fauna, possibly to extinction (Ammerman and Noller 2005; Simmons 2007: 231). The lowest stratum, Stratum 4, is dominated by over 200,000 disarticulated pygmy hippopotami and elephant bones, representing over 500 individuals. Stratum 2, a cultural layer above this but separated by a sterile layer (Stratum 3), contained chipped stone, casual hearths, beads, shells, bird bones, and a small number of pygmy hippopotami bones (Simmons 2004a: 3). Although the bones in Stratum 4 are disarticulated, there are no cut marks on any pieces. Having said this, 29 per cent of the bones show signs of burning, which the excavator argues supports his theory of human intervention in the extinction (Simmons 2004a: 8). Significantly, Strata 2 and 4 cannot be separated radiometrically, and therefore, whatever the nature of their contextual relationship, the extinction of the endemic fauna happened at approximately the same time that humans appeared at Aetokremnos. Of the extinction, Wasse contends: 'The highly ephemeral nature of the terminal Epipaleolithic archaeological horizon as currently understood makes it unlikely that humans were present on the island in sufficient numbers to be implicated in the extinction of the endemic Pleistocene fauna' (2007: 56). Wasse's view is supported by Bromage, who suggests that the extreme cold and arid climate typifying the Younger Dryas may have resulted in the drying up of standing pools of water and in the reduction of seasonally available woodland resources upon which pygmy hippopotami depended (Bromage et al. 2002: 423–5).

Wasse has recently summarized the importance of Aetokremnos for our understanding of wider Levantine late Epipaleolithic economic intensification. In his view, 'a growing preoccupation with the large-scale processing and storage of plant food resources from the early thirteenth millennium cal. BP (eleventh millennium BC) in the Levant has been linked to resource stress associated with the retreat of the woodland and its plant-food resources during the Younger Dryas. The intensive exploitation of increasingly crowded site catchments may have contributed to the expansion during the late Epipaleolithic period into the sub-desert steppe and southern desert zones of the Levant. It now seems increasingly likely that the emergence of the terminal Epipaleolithic of Cyprus might have been part of the same process' (Wasse 2007: 57).

If Aetokremnos does indeed represent part of the process of economic expansion during the eleventh millennium BC in the Levant, there is no evidence of where these people came from or indeed where they went. Although the chipped stone assemblage would not be out of place in the Levantine Epipaleolithic, the very high proportion of microliths and thumbnail scrapers is atypical of most Levantine terminal Epipaleolithic assemblages (Simmons 2004a: 8–10). Ultimately more evidence is required to solve the riddle of Aetokremnos.

THE TENTH MILLENNIUM BC

Recent archaeological work has identified sites on the island that appear to fall in the chronological gap between the utilization of the rock shelter at Aetokremnos and the colonization of the island in the ninth millennium BC. Research is in its infancy, but the most promising sites identified to-date are Ayia Vavara-Asprokremnos (hereafter Asprokremnos) and Ayios Tychonas Klimonas (hereafter Klimonas), which have been tentatively attributed to a Cypriot *facies* of the PPNA (McCartney et al. 2006; Manning et al. 2010; Vigne et al. 2012). Perhaps the most interesting feature of both sites at our present understanding is that the mammal component of the small faunal assemblages so far recovered is dominated by wild boar (Croft 2006; Vigne et al. 2012). The presence of small numbers of pig bones at Aetokremnos has led Wasse to surmise that pigs may have become feral, replacing the ecological niche left by pygmy hippopotami, and that 'a sizeable pig population might have become established on Cyprus by the second half of the 12th millennium cal. BP' (2007: 57). It is not unfeasible, then, that humans continued to predate a feral pig population in the tenth millennium BC and perhaps contributed to their domestication by the ninth millennium BC.

THE NINTH AND EIGHTH MILLENNIA BC

The significance of excavations at Mylouthkia and Shillourokambos was not simply the discovery on Cyprus of sites that filled the gap between Aetokremnos and Khirokitia; the whole paradigm within which Cypriot prehistorians had worked shifted. For the first time archaeologists recognized that Cyprus was not peripheral to cultural change in southwest Asia but integral to it. Also for the first time, experts in mainland southwest Asian prehistory were eager to enter the debate, a sign that Cyprus had finally penetrated mainstream discourse (Colledge 2004; Galili et al. 2004; Horwitz, Tchernov, and Hongo 2004). Within Cypriot research, archaeologists began to accept that the colonization of Cyprus was not a simple linear event, involving one or more migration episodes, stocking a previously uninhabited island with both food and people, but a complex web of different forms of contact, arising from different parts of the Mediterranean littoral at different times and ostensibly for different reasons.

At present, the most important data for understanding this crucial period comes from the rather unprepossessing site Shillourokambos, a small agricultural hamlet located in the low hills south of the Troodos Mountains (Fig. 13.1 above). The data from Shillourokambos are supplemented by results from excavations at four further sites, Tenta, Mylouthkia, Akanthou, and Kryttou Maroutou Ais Yiorkis.

Four occupation phases have been recorded at Shillourokambos, dating from the mid-ninth millennium BC (IntCal04; Reimer et al. 2004) to the late eighth millennium BC (Guilaine et al. 2000); these have been labelled the Early Phases A and B, the Middle Phase, and the Late Phase. In addition there is a Late Neolithic component documented by a number of subterranean features that bear considerable resemblance to features uncovered at Kokkinoyia, c.4000 BC (Clarke 2004; 2007b).

The initial occupation at Shillourokambos (known as the Early Phase A) is characterized by a large triangular feature, appearing as long channels and a series of post holes cut into the bedrock. Several archaeologists have suggested that it may have been used to pen animals (Guilaine 2003b: 7; Peltenburg, Colledge, et al. 2001: 39), which lends support to the theory that some of the earliest introduced faunal species, if not domesticated, were at least managed for food and breeding purposes. To the Early Phase A may also be assigned a deep well-like feature approximately 1m in diameter and nearly 4.5m deep (Guilaine 2003b: 5). Later, in the Early Phase B another well, 5.4m deep, contained a possible plaster figurine, stone wall fragments, lithics, and obsidian (Guilaine 2003b: 8). At Mylouthkia, a series of wells, broadly contemporary with the examples from Shillourokambos, were deliberately filled when they went out of use. One particular well (133) contained large numbers of ground stone vessel fragments and hammerstones. The deposition of these objects appears to have been purposeful, as the sample represented only a partial assemblage; other items, such as querns, rubbers, mortars, and pestles, were missing (Peltenburg, Colledge, et al.

2001: 48). In addition, Peltenburg sees the deposition of human crania in Well 133 as evidence of deliberate insertion in the tradition of PPNA–B skull detachment and reburial on the mainland (Peltenburg, Colledge, et al. 2001: 54). Although Well 114 at Shillourokambos resembles the Mylouthkia wells in many important features, there has been no suggestion of intentional deposition.

The first evidence of domestic architecture comes from the Early Phase B, where traces of walls were found which may have preceded what became fully-fledged circular structures in the Middle and Late Phases (Guilaine 2003b: 12). The presence of circular architecture in the Late Phase, dating to the end of the eighth millennium BC, offers strong evidence for continuity into the Khirokitian.

Akanthou, on the north coast, offers further insight into ninth-millennium BC settlement on the island. It is located close to the coast within sight of the Taurus Mountains on the Anatolian mainland. It has produced both curvilinear and rectangular architecture with well-made plaster floors, sometimes coloured red with ochre (Şevketoğlu 2002: 103). In addition to a number of small, cross-hatched incised bowls, and beads and tokens made of picrolite (a local stone found in only two river valleys in southern Cyprus), Akanthou has also produced over 1000 pieces of obsidian, originating from Gollü Dag in Cappadocia (Briois, Gratuze, and Guilaine 1997; Peltenburg 2003: 30–34) and which include both tools and debitage. This strongly suggests that obsidian was coming into the island in quantity, being worked at sites like Akanthou, and then possibly redistributed around the island (Şevketoğlu 2002: 103). The very high proportion of obsidian at Akanthou in comparison with other contemporary and later sites on the island suggests that Akanthou was possibly a landfall site. The presence of obsidian blades and incised picrolite beads and tokens at both Shillourokambos (Guilaine 2003a: 334) and Akanthou may indicate that these two materials were exchanged across long distances and were perhaps accorded special value.

A number of crucial indices of colonization have been recognized in the ninth-millennium BC deposits from sites around the island (Fig. 13.3). The first is a stone tool technology characterized by blade production from large bipolar cores made on high-quality translucent chert (Guilaine et al. 2000: 79; McCartney 1999: 7). This very specific *chaîne opératoire* is a type fossil of northern Syria in the Early PPNB. Significantly, Peltenburg, Colledge, et al. (2000: 848) have noted 'archaic epipaleolithic/PPNA traits' within the assemblages of Shillourokambos, Mylouthkia, and Tenta, which may have importance for the increasing evidence for human activity on the island in the tenth millennium BC. The second index is the introduction of a suite of founder species of plants and animals, some of which were successful and some of which (e.g. cattle) were not (Colledge 2004; Horwitz, Tchernov, and Hongo 2004; Peltenburg, Colledge, et al. 2000; 2001; Peltenburg, Croft, et al. 2001; Vigne 2001). Debate over the significance of these introductions has been ongoing for some years, and is discussed in detail below. It is, however, interesting to note that cattle disappear from the Cypriot archaeological record not long after their introduction to the island, suggesting that the expenditure of energy needed to maintain a cattle population was greater than the overall return (Wasse 2007: 61). The third index is the predominance of curvilinear architecture from the ninth millennium BC onwards, which harks back to curvilinear prototypes in the Levant. Although rectangular architecture has been recorded at both Akanthou (Şevketoğlu 2002) and Khirokitia (Le Brun, pers. comm.) a tradition of circular architecture survives virtually unchanged in Cyprus until the end of the fifth millennium BC (Clarke 2007a: 114). Peltenburg (2004: 74) has argued that the continued use of circular architecture

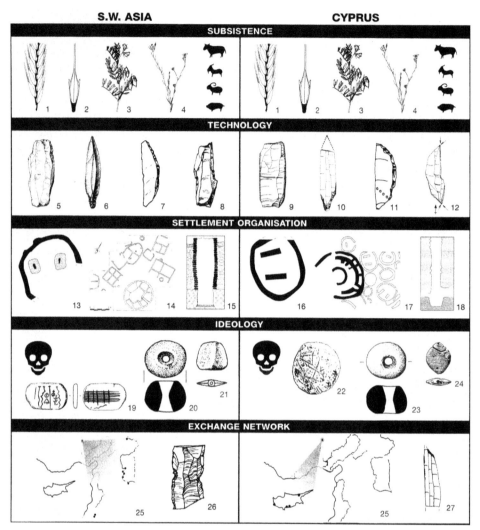

FIG. 13.3 Indices of colonization of Cyprus from the mainland during the PPNB (from Peltenburg, Colledge, et al. 2001: 35–64, esp. 38, fig. 2; courtesy E. J. Peltenburg)

on Cyprus, long after its virtual disappearance on the mainland, suggests that innovation in building traditions in Cyprus stopped sometime after colonization in the ninth millennium BC. The fourth index of colonization is a similarity between Cyprus and the mainland in aspects of art and representation. Comparisons have been drawn with PPNA and Early PPNB imagery from sites in the Euphrates Basin, including Dja'de al-Mughara, Jerf al-Ahmar, and Navali Çori. Schematic rendering of female and male imagery, animal imagery (in particular a stone cat's head from Shillourokambos, which bears a striking resemblance to a similar feline head from Jerf al-Ahmar in northern Syria), and geometric signs have broadly similar counterparts on the mainland (Guilaine 2003a: 329; Stordeur 2003: 363–8). Finally, a fifth index is the possibility of skull reburial at Mylouthkia, reminiscent of the PPNA and PPNB tradition of skull removal on the mainland. Taken together, these indices suggest that a wave of farmers and herders, originating from somewhere in the northern Levant, settled in Cyprus during the middle of the ninth millennium BC.

Perhaps the most important research on this period is related to the evidence it provides for how, where, and when domestication happened. At Shillourokambos in the earliest occupation levels, wild-type sheep, goats, cattle, pigs, and Mesopotamian fallow deer have been reported (Vigne 2001). By the latest phase (c.7500–7000 BC), the full suite of Cypriot Neolithic species was present on the island, including cat, dog, fox, and mouse. There is considerable debate as to whether herd species were introduced as domesticates or as wild animals. Guilaine et al. (2000) and Vigne (2001) report that domestic pigs were present in the earliest levels at Shillourokambos, cattle were probably wild, caprines were either domestic or managed animals, and fallow deer were hunted. This view is largely contested by Horwitz, Tchernov, and Hongo (2004: 43), who have argued that 'the earliest introduced animals comprise species for which there is no evidence for their domestication on the mainland, [secondly] the Cypriot fauna are morphometrically indistinguishable from wild animals and [thirdly], their age and sex ratios as well as body-part representation may as easily be interpreted as due to intentional selection during hunting and butchery as to domestication.' Again we can turn to Wasse for a counterargument: 'The fact that all four of the taxa that constitute the earliest farmyard domesticates, viz. goats, sheep, pigs and cattle, are represented alongside a range of domestic cereals and pulses in itself suggests that one is dealing with the introduction of agriculture to the island' (2007: 58).

THE SEVENTH AND SIXTH MILLENNIA BC

Although the seventh millennium BC is probably one of the better-known periods in Cypriot prehistory, very few sites have actually been excavated or published in detail. The most important and most extensively excavated is the type site Khirokitia. Although it gives its name to the period, it is widely viewed as unrepresentative of the seventh and sixth millennia BC due to its larger population aggregate (Peltenburg 2004: 84). More typical of the period are the smaller agricultural hamlets and ephemeral camps located in a wide range of environmental zones. Sites located on the coast include Petra tou Limniti, Troulli, and Kastros, and sites in the ecotone zone between the mountains and the sea include Khirokitia and Tenta. Inland sites that are yet to be fully defined include Kholetria-Ortos (hereafter Ortos), Dhali-Agridhi (hereafter Dhali), and Kataliondas-Kourvellos (hereafter Kataliondas) (Fig. 13.1 above). Although there is broad similarity across different types of sites, there are also significant differences in the material record, in daily activities and economic strategies, and in the organization and layout of space. The seventh millennium BC was a period of consolidation and population expansion, but it was an egalitarian society which, aside from limited evidence from Khirokitia, displays virtually no evidence of social hierarchy, storage surplus, specialized exchange networks, or ritual behaviour. Most settlement information comes from Khirokitia, Kastros (Le Brun 1981; 1984; 1989; 1994; Le Brun and Daune-Le Brun 2010), and to a lesser extent Troulli (Dikaios and Stewart 1962: 63–72). However, Ortos (Simmons 1994; 1996), Dhali (Lehavy 1974; 1989), and Kataliondas (Morrison and Watkins 1974) indicate that not all seventh-millennium BC sites were settlements; some appear to have been seasonally occupied.

Khirokitia is the largest of the seventh-millennium BC sites. It is located on the slopes and summit of a small promontory, which is skirted at the base by the Maroni River (Fig. 13.1 above). The site stretches 180m up the slope of the hill and is enclosed on its western side by a wall, built at the same time as the village. A second wall was constructed some time later, after the village had expanded beyond the original wall. Le Brun (2002: 25) has argued that the construction of the wall contemporaneously with the building of the village shows fore-thought, planning, and considerable mobilization of manpower, features not characteristic of any other site on the island at this time. There are at least two entrances into the village located along the length of the wall. The one surviving example indicates careful planning. Restriction or control of access into and out of the village appears to have been important as the entrance changes direction, doubling back on itself twice. Indeed, security appears to have been a primary consideration in the location and construction of settlements from the seventh millennium BC onwards.

Architecture displays both uniformity and variation across the island. Buildings were cir-cular in plan, with diameters of between 3m and 5m. At Khirokitia, three or four buildings were usually arranged in a circle around a small open courtyard containing grinding imple-ments and basins. Entrances usually faced inwards onto the central courtyard. Internal fixtures and fittings included central hearths, benches, and a range of domestic food prepa-ration installations. Some of the huts had internal partition walls or platforms, organizing internal space into clearly demarcated areas.

At Khirokitia and Tenta, the dead were buried beneath the floors of buildings in small, simple pits, often with one or more large stones placed on the body. There is no clear indica-tion of social status, expressed through differential degrees of elaboration of burial, types of grave offerings, or through spatial distribution and arrangement (Le Brun 2002: 27). The burial of the dead under house floors is a feature that is also characteristic of early farm-ing communities in southwest Asia. Some prehistorians have made the connection between increased sedentism, land ownership, and burial placement during the transition into the Neolithic period, and it may be that burials beneath domestic space represented some form of bridge between the living and their deceased ancestors (Goring-Morris 2000: 128), per-haps as a way of emphasizing permanency of place in the landscape and, with it, access or ownership of land.

At smaller settlements like Kastros, space is informally structured, buildings are less substantial, and construction methods differ from those at Khirokitia (Le Brun 1981: 21). Buildings are usually double-walled with radial partitions, a construction technique that was common in the northern Levant in the PPNB (Peltenburg 2004) but is not noted at Khirokitia until very late in the sequence. There are three burials recorded at Kastros, one containing an adult and an infant, and two further burials badly damaged by erosion. The one preserved example is extramural, which Le Brun notes does not accord with the pattern known from Khirokitia (1981: 28). Although it is dangerous to speculate on the basis of so little evidence, the combined differences between Khirokitia and Kastros, in settlement layout, organization, population aggregation, and burial data may suggest that intensifica-tion at Khirokitia led to changes in social strategies. Control of land and pressures on graz-ing may have been a problem for Khirokitia alone. Support for this argument comes from Wasse, who notes that 'the shift from a predominance of Mesopotamian fallow deer in the faunal record of Khirokitia to caprines at a time when the site was expanding beyond its boundaries, is unique evidence for economic intensification' (2007: 62).

THE FIFTH MILLENNIUM BC

The Early Neolithic period ended before 5500 BC, perhaps as a result of the collapse of Khirokitia, which was unable to match its need to intensify resource output with its ability to increase its degree of social complexity. Certainly, mainland comparisons show that both were necessary for social evolution.

After the collapse of Khirokitia there is a gap in the radiocarbon sequence of (conservatively) up to 1000 years. When the archaeological record resumes, it is characterized by continuity with, and change from, the Early Neolithic period. Small villages of approximately 100 persons were located along the north and east coasts of the island or inland in the southern ecotone zone between the Troodos Mountains and the sea. Some villages were positioned on sites vacated by seventh-millennium BC inhabitants, such as Troulli and a re-occupation of Khirokitia, whereas others were newly established in the fifth millennium BC, such as Philia, Sotira, Kantou-Koufovounos (hereafter Kantou), and Paralimni-Nissia (hereafter Nissia). All shared the innovation of pottery manufacture, which appeared on a wide scale around 4500 BC.

At present there is very little data for the intervening period between the demise of the Early Neolithic and the establishment of the Late Neolithic. Some evidence comes from the small ephemeral campsite Dhali, which appears to have been utilized in the late sixth millennium BC by people who had no pottery and then again in the early fifth millennium BC by people who did.

By the middle of the fifth millennium BC, small agricultural hamlets had sprung up across the island, most of which appear to have been occupied all year round. Within the confines of local geography and topography, settlement layouts are broadly similar across the island. Sites on coastal promontories share the same features with sites located on hill-tops in the foothills of the Troodos Mountains. Importantly, most aspects of the cultural record, apart from the way in which pottery was decorated, are virtually identical. Houses were free-standing mono-cellular constructions, 3–4m in diameter, sometimes with internal partitions, attached annexes, or subsidiary buildings. Fixtures and fittings included food-producing installations, benches, and bins. Hearths were located usually in one corner of the room or slightly off-centre, and comprised a raised platform with a central ash pit. In many instances groups of conjoined houses were arranged around open spaces (Dikaios 1961; Peltenburg 1982).

Very little burial evidence exists for the fifth millennium BC, but it is clear that at Sotira, the presence of an extramural cemetery containing twelve pit burials lends further support to the theory that fifth-millennium BC society was largely sedentary.

Probably the most important development in the fifth millennium BC was the widespread use of pottery. Very small quantities of low-fired ceramics were discovered at Khirokitia in the 1950s, including the head and upper torso of an anthropomorphic figurine (Dikaios and Stewart 1962: 48, fig. 25, 1063) and at least five vessels. Recently Peltenburg (pers. comm.) has discovered low-fired ceramics at Mylouthkia which pre-date the examples from Khirokitia, but by how long is not yet known. In any event, the presence of pottery at Mylouthkia indicates that Cypriot societies were aware of and used ceramics on a limited scale during the seventh millennium BC. Why pottery was not adopted more widely until the fifth millennium BC is not clear (but for a review, see Clarke 2007a: 97–9).

A Cypriot version of Dark-Faced Burnished Ware (Cypro-DFBW) is the first pottery to appear in the fifth millennium BC. It is found at Dhali and in the deepest layers at Philia. There is evidence to indicate technological connections with pockets of the mainland where DFBW was still occurring as late as the fifth millennium BC, for example Arjoune in the central Levant (Campbell, Mathias, and Phillips 2003: 37). Within a relatively short space of time Cypro-DFBW begins to be painted in a variety of positive designs in red paint directly onto the dark burnished surface of the pot (Fig. 13.4). At Philia this tradition appears to have developed quickly into fully fledged Red-on-White Ware that comes to characterize the northern, eastern, and possibly western parts of Cyprus throughout the fifth millennium BC. In the southern central part of the island the principal pottery decoration is combing, where the red paint is removed while still wet with a multiple tool. One interesting aspect of the Cypriot Neolithic pottery tradition is that there appears to be clearly defined regional variation. Not only do different decorative traditions dominate different parts of

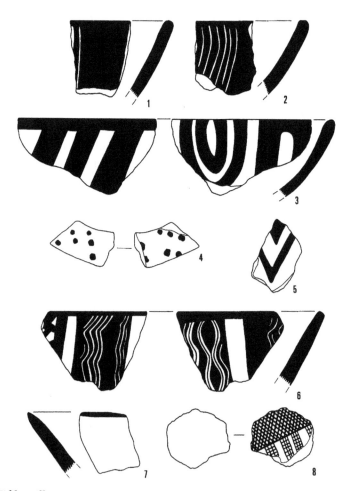

FIG. 13.4 Fifth-millennium painted pottery from Cyprus: (1, 2) Combed Ware; (3–5) Red-on-White Ware; (6) Painted and Combed Ware; (7, 8) pottery of the Neolithic/Early Chalcolithic transition

the island at the same time but there are very specific non-random patterns of variation between sites. This variation has been interpreted as structured identity, used by the small island populations to reduce risk as they negotiated there social and economic relationships (Clarke 2001; 2003).

Ultimately, the Neolithic period in Cyprus is perhaps one of the most intriguing periods in the prehistory of the Near East. The very peculiar material culture patterning that can be documented in much of the archaeological record offers insights into cultural change in the wider region. Themes such as cultural transmission and transformation in time and space, identity and the role of agency in the maintenance of social systems, bio-evolutionary theory and its relevance to long-term cultural change, human exploitation of marginal environments, and *refugia* in times of environmental pressure can be investigated through the archaeological record of Neolithic Cyprus, and may eventually have much wider significance for Near Eastern prehistory in general.

SUGGESTED READING

Clarke, J., with contributions by C. McCartney and A. Wasse (2007). *On the Margins of Southwest Asia: Cyprus during the 6th to 4th Millennia BC.* Oxford: Oxbow.

Guilaine, J. (2003). Parekklisha-Shillourokambos: périodisation et aménagements domestiques. In J. Guilaine and A. Le Brun (eds), *Le néolithique de Chypre: actes du colloque international organisé par le Département des antiquités de Chypre et l'École française d'Athènes, Nicosie, 17–19 mai 2001.* Athens: École Française d'Athènes, 3–14.

Peltenburg, E. J. (2004). Social space in early sedentary communities of southwest Asia and Cyprus. In E. J. Peltenburg and A. Wasse (eds), *Neolithic Revolution: New Perspectives on Southwest Asia in Light of Recent Discoveries on Cyprus.* Oxford: Oxbow, 71–90.

REFERENCES

Ammerman, A. J., and J. S. Noller (2005). New light on Aetokremnos. *World Archaeology* 37: 533–43.

—— P. Flourentzos, C. McCartney, J. S. Noller, and D. Sorabji (2006). Two new early sites on Cyprus. *Report of the Department of Antiquities of Cyprus* 2006: 1–21.

Briois, F., B. Gratuze, and J. Guilaine (1997). Obsidiennes du site néolithique précéramique de Shillourokambos (Chypre). *Paléorient* 23: 95–112.

Bromage, T., W. Dirks, H. Erdjument-Bromage, et al. (2002). A life history and climate change solution to the evolution and extinction of insular dwarves: a Cypriot experience. In Waldren and Ensenyat (2002: 420–27).

Campbell, S., V. T. Mathias, and C. S. Phillips (2003). The prehistoric pottery from Trenches V, VI and VII. In P. J. Parr (ed.), *Excavations at Arjoune, Syria.* Oxford: Archaeopress, 31–70.

Cherry, J. (2004). Mediterranean island prehistory: what's different, what's new? In S. M. Fitzpatrick (ed.), *Voyages of Discovery: The Archaeology of Islands.* Westport, Conn.: Praeger, 233–48.

Clarke, J. (2001). Style and society in Ceramic Neolithic Cyprus. *Levant* 33: 65–80.

—— (2003). Insularity and identity in prehistoric Cyprus. In J. Guilaine and A. Le Brun (eds), *Le néolithique de Chypre: actes du colloque international organisé par le Département des antiquités de Chypre et l'École française d'Athènes, Nicosie, 17–19 mai 2001*. Athens: École française d'Athènes, 203–18.

—— (2004). Excavations at Kalavasos-Kokkinoyia and Kalavasos-Pamboules 2002–3. *Report of the Department of Antiquities of Cyprus* 2004: 51–71.

—— with contributions by C. McCartney and A. Wasse (2007a). *On the Margins of Southwest Asia: Cyprus during the 6th to 4th Millennia BC*. Oxford: Oxbow.

—— (2007b). Site diversity in Cyprus in the late 5th millennium cal. BC: evidence from Kalavasos Kokkinoyia. *Levant* 39: 13–26.

Colledge, S. (2004). Reappraisal of the archaeobotanical evidence for the emergence and dispersal of 'founder crops'. In Peltenburg and Wasse (2004: 49–60).

Croft, P. (2006). *Animal Remains from Ayia Vavara Asprokremnos*. Unpublished manuscript.

Dikaios, P. (1953). *Khirokitia: Final Report on the Excavation of a Neolithic Settlement in Cyprus on Behalf of the Department of Antiquities, 1936–1946*. Oxford: Oxford University Press.

—— (1961). *Sotira*. Philadelphia: University Museum, University of Pennsylvania.

—— and J. R. Stewart (1962). *The Stone Age and the Early Bronze Age in Cyprus*. Lund: Swedish Cyprus Expedition.

Galili, E., A. Gopher, B. Rosen, and L. K. Horwitz (2004). The emergence of the Mediterranean fishing village in the Levant and the anomaly of Neolithic Cyprus. In Peltenburg and Wasse (2004: 91–102).

Gjerstad, E. (1934). *The Swedish Cyprus Expedition 1: Finds and Results of the Excavations in Cyprus, 1927–1931*. Stockholm: Swedish Cyprus Expedition.

Goring-Morris, A. N. (2000). The quick and the dead: the social context of Aceramic Neolithic mortuary practices as seen from Kfar HaHoresh. In I. Kuijt (ed.), *Life in Neolithic Farming Communities: Social Organization, Identity, and Differentiation*. New York: Kluwer Academic/Plenum, 103–36.

Guilaine, J. (2003a). Objets (symboliques) et parures de Parekklisha-Shillourokambos. In J. Guilaine and A. Le Brun (eds), *Le néolithique de Chypre: actes du colloque international organisé par le Département des antiquités de Chypre et l'École française d'Athènes, Nicosie, 17–19 mai 2001*. Athens: École française d'Athènes, 329–40.

—— (2003b). Parekklisha-Shillourokambos: périodisation et aménagements domestiques. In J. Guilaine and A. Le Brun (eds), *Le néolithique de Chypre: actes du colloque international organisé par le Département des antiquités de Chypre et l'École française d'Athènes, Nicosie, 17–19 mai 2001*. Athens: École française d'Athènes, 3–14.

—— F. Briois, J.-D. Vigne, and I. Carrère (2000). Découverte d'un Néolithique précéramique ancien chypriote (fin 9e, début 8e millénaires cal. BC), apparenté au PPNB ancien/moyen du Levant nord. *Comptes rendus de l'Académie des sciences, series 2: Sciences de la terre et des planètes* 300: 75–82.

Horwitz, L. K., E. Tchernov, and H. Hongo (2004). The domestic status of the early Neolithic fauna of Cyprus: a view from the mainland. In Peltenburg and Wasse (2004: 35–48).

Knapp, A. B., and E. Blake (2005). Prehistory in the Mediterranean: the connecting and corrupting sea. In E. Blake and A. B. Knapp (eds), *The Archaeology of Mediterranean Prehistory*. Malden, Mass.: Blackwell, 1–23.

Kuijt, I. (2004). Cyprus as a regional Neolithic entity: do researchers need to revisit the concept of the Levantine PPNB interaction sphere? *Neo-Lithics* 1/04: 8–9.

Le Brun, A. (1981). *Un site néolithique précéramique en Chypre: Cap Andreas-Kastros*. Paris: Éditions Recherche sur les civilisations.

——(1984). *Fouilles récentes à Khirokitia (Chypre), 1977–1981* (2 vols). Paris: Éditions Recherche sur les civilisations.

—— (1986). Khirokitia: une civilisation originale? In V. Karageorghis (ed.), *Acts of the International Archaeological Symposium 'Cyprus between the Orient and the Occident', Nicosia, 8–14 September 1985.* Nicosia: Department of Antiquities of Cyprus, 1–11.

—— (1989), *Fouilles récentes à Khirokitia (Chypre), 1983–1986.* Paris: Éditions Recherche sur les civilisations.

—— (1994), *Fouilles récentes à Khirokitia (Chypre), 1988–1991.* Paris: Éditions Recherche sur les civilisations.

—— (2002). Neolithic society in Cyprus: a tentative analysis. In D. Bolger and N. J. Serwint (eds), *Engendering Aphrodite: Women and Society in Ancient Cyprus.* Boston: American Schools of Oriental Research, 23–31.

—— and O. Daune-Le Brun (2010). Khirokitia (Chypre): la taille et les pulsations de l'établissement néolithique pré-céramique, nouvelles données. *Paléorient* 35: 67–76.

Lehavy, Y. (1974). Excavations at Neolithic Dhali-Agridhi, part 1: Excavation report. In L. E. Stager, A. M. Walker, and G. E. Wright (eds), *American Expedition to Idalion, Cyprus: First Preliminary Report, Seasons of 1971 and 1972.* Cambridge, Mass.: American Schools of Oriental Research, 95–102.

—— (1989). Excavations at Dhali-Agridhi: 1972, 1974, 1976. In L. E. Stager and A. M. Walker (eds), *American Expedition to Idalion, Cyprus, 1973–1980.* Chicago: Oriental Institute of the University of Chicago, 203–43.

Manning, S. W., C. McCartney, B. Kromer, S. T. Stewart (2010). The earlier Neolithic in Cyprus: recognition and dating of a Pre-Pottery Neolithic A occupation. *Antiquity* 84: 693–706.

McCartney, C. (1999). Opposed platform core technology and the Cypriot Aceramic Neolithic. *Neo-Lithics* 1/99: 7–10.

—— (2007). Lithics. In J. Clarke, *On the Margins of Southwest Asia: Cyprus during the 6th to 4th Millennia BC.* Oxford: Oxbow, 72–90.

—— S. W. Manning, D. Sewell, and S. Stewart. (2006). Elaborating Early Neolithic Cyprus: report on the 2005 field season. *Report of the Department of Antiquities of Cyprus* 2006: 39–62.

—— and I. A. Todd (2005). Chipped stone. In I. A. Todd (ed.), *Vasilikos Valley Project 7: Excavations at Kalavasos-Tenta II*, vol. 2. Sävedalen: Åströms, 177–264.

Morrison, I., and T. Watkins (1974). Kataliontas-Kourvellos: a survey of an Aceramic Neolithic site and its environs in Cyprus. *Palestine Exploration Quarterly* 106: 67–75.

Peltenburg, E. J. (1978). The Sotira Culture: regional diversity and cultural unity in Late Neolithic Cyprus. *Levant* 10: 55–74.

—— (1982). *Vrysi, a Subterranean Settlement in Cyprus: Excavations at Prehistoric Ayios Epiktitos-Vrysi 1969–73.* Warminster: Aris & Phillips.

—— (1985). Ras Shamra IVC and the prehistory of Cyprus. In T. Papadopoulos and S. Chatzistyllis (eds), *Actes du Deuxième Congrès International des Études Chypriotes.* Nicosia: Society of Cypriot Studies, 27–41.

—— (2004). Social space in early sedentary communities of southwest Asia and Cyprus. In Peltenburg and Wasse (2004: 71–90).

—— with D. Bolger, S. Colledge, et al. (2003). *The Colonisation and Settlement of Cyprus: Investigations at Kissonerga-Mylouthkia 1976–1996.* Sävedalen: Åströms.

—— S. Colledge, P. Croft, A. Jackson, C. McCartney, and M. A. Murray (2000). Agro-pastoralist colonization of Cyprus in the 10th millennium BP: initial assessments. *Antiquity* 74: 844–53.

—— S. Colledge, P. Croft, A. Jackson, C. McCartney, and M. A. Murray (2001). Neolithic dispersals from the Levantine corridor: a Mediterranean perspective. *Levant* 33: 35–64.

—— P. Croft, A. Jackson, C. McCartney, and M. A. Murray (2001). Well-established colonists: Mylouthkia 1 and the Cypro-Pre-Pottery Neolithic B. In S. Swiny (ed.), *The Earliest Prehistory of Cyprus: From Colonization to Exploitation*. Boston: American Schools of Oriental Research, 61–94.

—— and A. Wasse (eds) (2004). *Neolithic Revolution: New Perspectives on Southwest Asia in Light of Recent Discoveries on Cyprus*. Oxford: Oxbow.

Reimer, P. J., M. G. L. Baillie, E. Bard, et al. (2004). IntCal04 terrestrial radiocarbon age calibration, 0–26 cal kyr BP. *Radiocarbon* 46: 1029–58.

Robinson, S. A., S. Black, B. W. Sellwood, and P. J. Valdes (2006). A review of palaeoclimates and palaeoenvironments in the Levant and eastern Mediterranean from 25,000 to 5,000 years BP: setting the environmental background for the evolution of human civilisation. *Quaternary Science Review* 25: 1517–41.

Şevketoğlu, M. (2002). Akanthou-Arkosyko (Tatlısu-Çiftlikdüzü): the Anatolian connections in the 9th millennium BC. In Waldren and Ensenyat (2002: 98–106).

Simmons, A. H. (1994). Preliminary report on the 1993 test excavations at Kholetria-Ortos, Paphos District. *Report of the Department of Antiquities of Cyprus* 1994: 39–44.

—— (1996). Preliminary report on the multidisciplinary investigations at Neolithic Kholetria-Ortos, Paphos District. *Report of the Department of Antiquities of Cyprus* 1996: 29–44.

—— (1999). *Faunal Extinction in an Island Society: Pygmy Hippopotamus Hunters of Cyprus*. New York: Kluwer Academic/Plenum.

—— (2001). The first humans and last pygmy hippopotami of Cyprus. In S. Swiny (ed.), *The Earliest Prehistory of Cyprus: From Colonization to Exploitation*. Boston: American Schools of Oriental Research, 1–18.

—— (2003). Villages without walls, cows without corrals. In J. Guilaine and A. Le Brun (eds), *Le néolithique de Chypre: actes du colloque international organisé par le Département des antiquités de Chypre et l'École française d'Athènes, Nicosie, 17–19 mai 2001*. Athens: École française d'Athènes, 61–70.

—— (2004a). Bitter Hippos of Cyprus: the island's first occupants and last endemic animals— setting the stage for colonization. In Peltenburg and Wasse (2004: 1–14).

—— (2004b). The Mediterranean PPNB interaction sphere. *Neo-Lithics* 1/04: 16–18.

—— (2007). *The Neolithic Revolution in the Near East: Transforming the Human Landscape*. Tuscon: University of Arizona Press.

Stanley Price, N. (1977). Khirokitia and the initial settlement of Cyprus. *Levant* 9: 66–89.

Stordeur, D. (2003). De la vallée de l' Euphrate à Chypre? À la recherche d'indices de relations au Néolithique. In J. Guilaine and A. Le Brun (eds), *Le néolithique de Chypre: actes du colloque international organisé par le Département des antiquités de Chypre et l'École française d'Athènes, Nicosie, 17–19 mai 2001*. Athens: École française d'Athènes, 353–71.

Todd, I. A. (ed.) (1987). *Vasilikos Valley Project 6: Excavations at Kalavasos-Tenta*, vol. 1. Gothenburg: Åströms.

—— (ed.) (2005). *Vasilikos Valley Project 7: Excavations at Kalavasos-Tenta*, vol. 2. Sävedalen: Åströms.

Vigne, J.-D. (2001). The large mammals of Early Aceramic Neolithic Cyprus: preliminary results from Parekklisha *Shillourokambos*. In S. Swiny (ed.), *The Earliest Prehistory of Cyprus: From Colonization to Exploitation*. Boston: American Schools of Oriental Research, 55–60.

—— F. Briois, A. Zazzo, G. Willcox, T. Cucchi, S. Thiébault, I. Carrère, Y. Franel, R. Touquet, C. Martin, C. Moreau, C. Comby, and J. Guilaine (2012). First wave of cultivators spread to Cyprus at least 10,600 years ago. *Proceedings of the National Academy of Sciences*: 109: 8445–9.

Waldren, W. H., and J. A. Ensenyat (eds) (2002). *World Islands in Prehistory: International Insular Investigations.* Oxford: Archaeopress.

Wasse, A. (2007). Climate, economy and change: Cyprus and the Levant during the Late Pleistocene–Mid Holocene. In Clarke (2007a: 43–63).

Watkins, T. (1970). Philia-Drakos Site A: pottery, stratigraphy, chronology. *Report of the Department of Antiquities of Cyprus* 1970: 1–9.

—— (1973). Some problems of the Neolithic and Chalcolithic period in Cyprus. *Report of the Department of Antiquities of Cyprus* 1973: 34–61.

SECTION B

THE CHALCOLITHIC PERIOD

CHAPTER 14

....

INTRODUCTION TO THE LEVANT DURING THE CHALCOLITHIC PERIOD
Regional Perspectives

....

THOMAS E. LEVY

In terms of social, economic, ideological, and technological change, the Protohistoric period in the Levant is one of the most critical time periods, as it provides the background for the rise of the earliest urban centres in the region. The sociopolitical phenomenon of urbanism is closely linked to the rise of institutionalized social inequality and the formation of the earliest state-level societies—what Gary Feinman and Joyce Marcus refer to as 'Archaic States' (Feinman and Marcus 1998). Corresponding mostly with the late fifth–early fourth millennia BCE, Chalcolithic societies in the Levant witnessed remarkable achievements (and failures) in terms of social evolutionary processes that laid the foundation for the emergence of these archaic states in the following Early Bronze Age. Central to the Chalcolithic period in the Levant is the 'metallurgical revolution' (Levy 2007), when smelting technologies emerged which enabled people to develop unprecedented pyro-technologies that produced the first non-ferrous metals, some of which included alloying copper with other elements. The word 'Chalcolithic' is formed by χαλκός *khalkos* 'copper' + λίθος *lithos* 'stone' and reflects a technological/temporal framework that Old World and especially Near Eastern archaeologists have used since the 19th century CE to order the archaeological record. It recognizes the importance of the adoption of metal technology, and distinguishes this formative period from the preceding Neolithic and succeeding Bronze Age linked to early urbanism. If the Levant includes the eastern Mediterranean countries of Syria, Lebanon, Israel, the Palestinian Territories, Jordan, and the Sinai Peninsula, then the coverage of the Chalcolithic period represented in this volume is incomplete. The areas that lack systematic treatment include most of Syria (only the coastal zone is discussed here: see Artin, Ch. 15 below) and the Sinai. Geographically, these two areas are situated on the northernmost and southernmost extremities of the Levantine region near the major core areas of ancient Near Eastern civilization in Anatolia/Mesopotamia and Egypt. Both are important contact zones between the Levant and the traditional centres of early state formation in the 'Fertile Crescent'. Thus, the absence of data from these areas leaves some gaps in understanding the nature of pan-regional social interaction along the lines that have been studied in some other research projects (van den Brink and Levy 2002). However, it is rare to have overviews of Israel/Palestine, Jordan, Lebanon, coastal Syria, and the island of Cyprus together in one volume. When considered as a whole, it is possible to detect different socio-evolutionary trajectories and processes responsible for culture change during the Chalcolithic in the relatively small region of the Levant that extends for approximately 1000×400km along the eastern Mediterranean seaboard. The following is an overview of some of these trends based primarily on the chapters presented in this section for the different Levantine regions where Chalcolithic research has been summarized.

MODERN POLITICS AND CHALCOLITHIC RESEARCH

One of the questions implicit in the archaeological summaries of the different Levantine regions is: just how representative is the picture of the Chalcolithic period that we have? The archaeological landscapes of the Levant are determined first by research accessibility, depending on the degree of political stability in the region; second, by the research questions posed by principal investigators who can obtain the necessary funding for field work; and finally, in some cases, by cultural resource management directives by the modern nation-state governments that determine which geographic regions should be investigated having regard to the impact of development on the land.

Israel/Palestinian Territories and Jordan

The largest number of Chalcolithic research projects in the Levant have been conducted in Israel and Jordan. Since the first excavations at Teleilat Ghassul by the Pontifical Biblical Institute in the 1920s–30s and after the Chalcolithic period was first defined in the Levant by W. F. Albright in 1932 (Levy and Freedman 2008), there have been bursts of long-term Chalcolithic research projects in the southern Levant, in spite of the multitude of armed conflicts that have affected this region. In the 1950s and early 1960s the French National Scientific Research Centre (CNRS) sponsored extensive excavations in the northern Negev and Jordan Valley in the newly established state of Israel; and in the 1980s and early 1990s basic research with highly focused major Chalcolithic projects took place when the Hebrew Union College–University of California, San Diego and Ben-Gurion University of the Negev carried out major expeditions in the northern Negev; the University of Sydney conducted renewed large-scale excavation at Teleilat Ghassul, and the CNRS–Yarmouk University conducted excavations in the Jordan Valley.

While the initial excavations at Ghassul were aimed at solving biblical history questions (was this the site of Sodom or Gomorrah?), once it was established that the site reflected a previously undocumented phase in the ancient Near East between the earliest settled villages of the Neolithic period and the earliest urban centres of the Early Bronze Age, it became one of largest non-biblical archaeology excavation projects of the early 20th century. Since then, as Yorke Rowan points out in his chapter, a series of major long-term Chalcolithic regional research projects were carried out in the northern Negev Desert in the 1950s by Jean Perrot, and in the late 1970s to early 1990s by Thomas Levy and David Alon, and by Issac Gilead, that were 'pure research' focused on socioeconomic questions. Similar projects took place in the Golan Heights (Epstein 1998). However, in a reassessment of Chalcolithic research in the Golan Heights, Zeidan Kafafi questions the underlying role of modern political realities on Epstein's interpretation of the Golan Chalcolithic culture as a highly localized culture firmly rooted on this small plateau or a more regional phenomenon (Kafafi 2010). The peace treaties that emerged in the late 1970s and early 1990s between Israel and its neighbours in Egypt and Jordan, and the creation of Google Earth and other web-based information technologies, opened previously 'academically closed' borders to broader methods of investigation that even affect Chalcolithic research.

By the early 1990s, intensive development in Israel led to a marked increase in 'rescue' excavations that revealed remarkable Chalcolithic sites all over the country (Gal, Smithline, and Shalem 1997; Goren and Fabian 2002; Scheftelowitz and Oren 2004). The 'rescue' work was carried out by the Israel Antiquities Authority, universities, and newly formed small cultural resource management companies. In Jordan, as shown by Kafafi, long-term Chalcolithic research was continued at the Chalcolithic type-site Teleilat Ghassul by Australian archaeologists (Bourke 2002; Hennessy 1982; Seaton 2008), along with new large-scale investigations by French and Jordanian researchers at Abu Hamid, who followed in the secular tradition of prehistoric archaeology established by Perrot in the 1950s (Dollfus and Kafafi 1988).

However, since the mid-1990s, it has been the fortuitous discovery at open-air sites in the Hula Valley (Tel Teo) and spectacular burial cave sites such as Nahal Qanah in the West Bank (Gopher and Tsuk 1996), Shoham in the Lod Valley (van den Brink and Gophna 2005), Palmahim (Gorzalczany 2007), and in the Judean Desert (Schick 1998) that have created another surge in Chalcolithic research. While some basic Chalcolithic research has taken place outside the scope of rescue excavations in the southern Levant (Lovell et al. 2006; Lovell et al. 2005; Lovell et al. 2007), these projects have not made the spectacular material discoveries that lead to fundamental changes in conceptualizing culture change in the southern Levant during the fifth–fourth millennia BCE.

Based on the above, we can identify a number of 'bursts' in Chalcolithic research over the past 90 years that are distinguished by large-scale field projects aimed specifically at this period. These large-scale interdisciplinary projects have set a high benchmark and left rich data-sets for integrated views of the sociopolitical-religious nature of the Levantine Chalcolithic in Israel and Jordan that are still being researched and published (Commenge-Pellerin 1987; 1990; Gilead 1995; Levy 1987; 2006; Lovell 2001; Seaton 2008).

Syria/Lebanon

The literature review provided by Gassia Artin shows that very few 'new' large-scale long-term Chalcolithic research projects have been carried out in Lebanon since the major expeditions at sites such as Sidon and Byblos. The political upheavals that have plagued Lebanon since the civil war broke out have no doubt contributed to this problem. Coastal Syria has not been the locus of new Chalcolithic projects, although later periods continue to be investigated at Ras Shamra/Ugarit. Since the 1990s, political stability and governmental priorities have encouraged investigations in environmentally impacted regions such as the Tishrin Dam in the northern interior of Syria, providing important new Chalcolithic data. The University of Chicago's new excavation project at Tell Zeidan on the east bank of the Balikh River in northeast Syria (an effort to establish a joint American–Syrian project that focuses on questions of broad social evolutionary interest) is setting the stage for a major reassessment of the Chalcolithic period in northern Mesopotamia, with a focus on radiocarbon dating and the procurement of paleoenvironmental data (Stein 2009).

Chalcolithic research cycles for the Lebanese–Syrian coast vary significantly from those mentioned above, in that rescue excavations seem to have driven most Chalcolithic research in this region for many decades.

Cyprus

Despite the Turkish occupation of the northern part of Cyprus since 1974, long-term research projects concerning the Chalcolithic period have flourished, especially those carried out in Kalavasos by Ian Todd and those at Lemba, Kissonerga Mosphilia, and Souskiou-Vathyrkakas directed by Edgar Peltenberg who in Chapter 18 below provides an overview of the period in the Republic of Cyprus.

Similar Chalcolithic research cycles to those of Israel/Palestinian territories and Jordan are reflected on Cyprus (see above).

CHRONOLOGICAL CONSIDERATIONS

Chronological frameworks are essential for understanding socioeconomic trends through time. In the Levant, the two major methods used for chronology building are relative methods based on changes in indigenous pottery styles from well-stratified sites and absolute dating techniques that include cross-dating based on imported artefacts from regions with strong chronologies (usually Egypt) and radiocarbon dating methods. It is difficult to marshal the total number of radiocarbon dates currently available for the different regions of the Levant. According to Artin, the northern Levant is very much in need of concerted efforts at applying radiocarbon dating to stratified archaeology sites in Lebanon and Syria. The new excavations at Tell Zeidan have already produced twelve radiocarbon dates that help establish a new radiometric-based chronology for Chalcolithic Syria. As highlighted in Peltenberg's chapter, relative chronologies play a more important role in establishing a temporal framework for the Chalcolithic period on Cyprus. On the other hand, researchers in the southern Levant have relied on high-precision radiocarbon dating for over twenty years to construct their chronologies. For example, 44 ^{14}C dates have been published for Teleilat Ghassul and 42 for Shiqmim (Bourke et al. 2001; Bourke et al. 2004; Burton and Levy 2001; Joffe and Dessel 1995). At present, there are well over 200 radiocarbon dates for the southern Levant. A tentative pan-regional comparative chronology for the Levant is presented in Table 14.1. This chronological scheme is based primarily on radiocarbon dates from the southern Levant (Israel, Palestinian Territories, and Jordan) and the summary essays here,

Table 14.1 Pan-regional comparative chronology of the Levantine Chalcolithic period

	Southern Levant	Syria	Lebanon	Egypt	Cyprus
5300–4500 BCE	**Late Neolithic** Yarmukian, Qatifian, Jericho IX/Lodian Wadi Rabah, Besorian, and Qatif Y3; Tell Wadi Faynan [baulk, Square A, Locus 23]; Abu Hamid [Middle? Upper?]; Sukas [G11, Layer 58]; Ziqlab [200 Area A]; Ghassul [AXI 10.15, AXI 9.37, AXI 13.7, GII 66.55], Pella [32D 42.37, 32F 17.18, 32D 80.3, 28A 44.7]; Jabal Quaysa [J24]; Shiqmim [IV, Upper Village]; Golan [Site 21]	Ubaid ('Northern Ubaid')	Ras Shamra IIIC Turkman Period 4B	Merimda Early	Late Ceramic Neolithic
4500–4200 BCE	**Normative Chalcolithic** Pella [32F 17.18, 32.D 80.3, Area XIV]; Thawwab [Post-Neo']; Golan Faras Silo Abu Hamid [Middle, Upper, and Lower?]; Ghassul [AXI 11.14, GII 64.4, QI 13.1, NI 11.7, GII 55.11, GIII 10.10, AII]; Qalat Mudiq IV; Abu Snesleh Tell Wadi Faynan [Square A, Locus 8]; Nahal Qanah Gold Deposit Gilat [Phase III], Shiqmim [Phases IV, III, II]; Bir es-Safadi [lower]	Late Chalcolithic–1	Eneolithique ancien		Ceramic Neolithic
4200–3800 BCE?	Ghassul [G III 10.10, AII, E XXIII, AII baulk]; Abu Hamid [Upper?]; Tall Shuna N. [EII43, EI 12/13]; Golan Harbush	Late Chalcolithic–2		Hemamieh (Badarian) Merimda Late Naqada KH1 (Early)	

(continued)

Table 14.1 (Continued)

	Southern Levant	Syria	Lebanon	Egypt	Cyprus
	Shiqmim [Phases II–I]; Bir es-Safadi [Middle, Upper]; Horvat Beter [Early, Late]	Habuba Kabira		Naqada NT (Early)	Early Chalcolithic (3900–3400 BCE); Mylouthkia [Period 2]; Erimi [Layers 1–2]; Kissonerga
3800–3700/3600 BCE?	**Final Chalcolithic** Gilat [Phase II]; Nahal Mishmar [Mat hoard]; Golan Harbush	Late Chalcolithic–3	Eneolithique recent	Naqada KH3; Maadi Early; Maadi Early Hierkonpolis Site 29 Naqada II b	
3600–3300 BCE	**Early Bronze IA** Halif Terrace [IIIc], Tour Ikhbeineh	Late Chalcolithic–4		Buto Ib, Maadi	Middle Chalcolithic (3400–2900 BCE); Ayios Epiktitos-Mezarlik; Lapithos-Alonia ton Plakon; Lemba [Period 2]; Kissonerga [3A–B]; Souskiou complex
3300–3000 BCE	**Early Bronze IB** Halif Terrace IIIA–B Site H Tel Erani D En Besor III Halif Terrace II A–B	Late Chalcolithic–5 (Late Uruk expansion into the north) Amuq G		Naqada IIc–d2 Late Dynasty 0–Early Dynasty 1	Late Chalcolithic (2800–2400 BCE) Kissonerga 4a–b; Ambelikou-Ayios Georghious; Ovgos Valley

which provide at present the best chronological anchor for assessing some regional trends during the Chalcolithic.

SOCIAL EVOLUTIONARY TRENDS

Perhaps the underlying theme that makes the Chalcolithic period of critical scholarly interest is that it precedes the emergence of the first fortified settlements that are commonly linked to the beginnings of urbanism in the Levant. As such, the Chalcolithic period throughout the Levant holds many of the clues concerning fundamental changes in social organization, ideology, subsistence, technology, and trade and exchange that led to more complex urban societies. This has made the Chalcolithic period an important platform for debating the processes that led to the rise of social inequality, the nature of social organization at this time, and the period's relationship to transformations in the preceding Neolithic and succeeding Early Bronze Age. Due to the effects of 20th- and early 21st-century politics and economics on Levantine Chalcolithic research, our understanding of cultural evolution across the region during this formative period is varied. In discussing this problem, underlying all the contributions to this volume is an understanding that social evolution is not a unilinear process, but one made up of shifting peaks and troughs of social complexity. In some cases, the data is simply not sufficient to probe this aspect of ancient cultural systems. Artin takes a clear-eyed view of the situation in Lebanon and the Syrian coast by stating that there are problems with the physical anthropology data from the Byblos tombs (some of the best Chalcolithic data from Lebanon, but excavated more than 60 years ago), making it extremely difficult to link gender with grave goods in order to determine the presence of chiefdom organizations. The situation is different in Israel and the Palestinian Territories, where more recently discovered burial caves like those at Nahal Qanah and the Cave of the Warrior have been adequately studied by biological anthropologists, and a link between prestige goods (gold at Nahal Qanah and rich textiles at the Cave of the Warrior) and gender ranking has been established. Furthermore, the many studies of craft specialization linked to copper metallurgy at Chalcolithic sites, especially in the Beersheva Valley, demonstrate the key role that its control played in the coalition building of nascent chiefdoms in that region. When these data are coupled with the concomitant rise of pan-regional religious centres in Jordan at Teleilat Ghassul, the Judean Desert site of Ein Gedi, and Gilat in the northern Negev, one can see a package of social changes that are manifest with the emergence of chiefdoms in a number of geographic regions in the southern Levant. The data is succinctly summarized by Rowan and Kafafi in Chapers 16 and 17 below (see also Lovell and Rowan 2011).

The situation on Cyprus has a different tempo to that of the Levantine mainland. As highlighted in Table 14.1, the Chalcolithic period in Cyprus is just beginning when it is ending on the mainland. On the basis of both radiocarbon dating and comparative chronologies, Peltenberg is able to show that major sociopolitical changes occurred in Cyprus through three main phases. During the early phase (3900–3400 BCE), an ideology of egalitarianism prevailed when settlement was highly mobile and experienced fission. By the middle phase (3400–2900 BCE), signs of social inequality began to prevail which, as in the southern Levant, were linked to ritual intensification. In addition, it seems that copper metallurgy was beginning to be appropriated from the mainland and contributed to prestige enhancement, as evidenced in mortuary displays. By the late period (*c.*2880–2400 BCE), a similar 'package' of socioeconomic change was in place on Cyprus, demonstrating at least one emergent group at Kissonerga developed an institutionalized social ranking principle, manifest in what Peltenberg refers to as an 'ideology of economic control'.

Conclusion

While there are differences concerning the trajectories, tempo, and measures of complexity of Chalcolithic societies in the southern Levant, there is no question that social, economic, ideological, and technological developments during the fifth–fourth millennia BCE played a key role in setting the stage for the archaic states that evolved in the eastern Mediterranean during the third millennium. In terms of future research, more long-term, large-scale basic research projects are needed. The recent trend has been for rescue archaeology to dictate the direction and pace of Chalcolithic research, and the result has been fewer problem-oriented investigations. Higher-precision radiocarbon dating needs to be applied in order to more accurately test cultural models for this formative period. To make more Chalcolithic datasets available to the world scholarly community, cyber-archaeology methods need to be adopted by researchers (Levy et al. 2010). Finally, the local universities of the Levant will need to increasingly take charge of developing the large-scale research programmes needed to uncover new insights regarding this key period.

References

Bourke, S. J. (2002). Teleilat Ghassul: foreign relations in the Late Chalcolithic period. In van den Brink and Levy (2002: 154–64).

—— E. Lawson, J. L. Lovell, Q. Hua, U. Zoppi, and M. Barbetti (2001). The chronology of the Ghassulian Chalcolithic period in the southern Levant: new 14C determinations from Teleilat Ghassul, Jordan. *Radiocarbon* 43: 1217–22.

—— U. Zoppi, J. Meadows, Q. Hua, and S. Gibbins (2004). The end of the Chalcolithic period in the South Jordan Valley: new 14C determinations from Teleilat Ghassul, Jordan. *Radiocarbon* 46: 315–23.

Burton, M., and T. E. Levy (2001). The Chalcolithic radiocarbon record and its use in southern Levantine archaeology. *Radiocarbon* 43: 1223–46.

Commenge-Pellerin, C. (1987). *La poterie d'Abou Matar et de l'Ouadi Zoumeili (Beershéva) au IVe millénaire avant l'ère chrétienne*. Paris: Association Paléorient.

—— (1990). *La poterie de Safadi (Beershéva) au IVe millénaire avant l'ère chrétienne*. Paris: Association Paléorient.

Dollfus, G., and Z. A. Kafafi (1988). *Abu Hamid: village du 4e millénaire de la vallée du Jourdain*. Amman: Centre culturel français and Département des antiquités de Jourdanie.

Epstein, C. (1998). *The Chalcolithic Culture of the Golan*. Jerusalem: Israel Antiquities Authority.

Feinman, G. M., and J. Marcus (eds) (1998). *Archaic States*. Santa Fe, NM: School of American Research Press.

Gal, Z., H. Smithline, and D. Shalem (1997). A Chalcolithic burial cave in Peqi'in, Upper-Galilee. *Israel Exploration Journal* 47: 145–54.

Gilead, I. (ed.) (1995). *Grar: A Chalcolithic Site in the Northern Negev*. Beer-Sheva: Ben-Gurion University of the Negev Press.

Gopher, A., and T. Tsuk (eds) (1996). *The Nahal Qanah Cave: Earliest Gold in the Southern Levant*. Tel Aviv: Institute of Archaeology, Tel Aviv University.

Goren, Y., and P. Fabian (2002). *Kissufim Road: A Chalcolitihic Mortuary Site*. Jerusalem: Israel Antiquities Authority.

Gorzalczany, A. (2007). Centre and periphery in ancient Israel: new approximations to Chalcolithic funerary practices in the coastal plain. *Antiguo Oriente* 5: 205–30.

Hennessy, J. B. (1982). Teleilat Ghassul: its place in the archaeology of Jordan. *Studies in the History and Archaeology of Jordan* 1: 55–8.

Joffe, A. H., and J. P. Dessel (1995). Redefining chronology and terminology for the Chalcolithic of the southern Levant. *Current Anthropology* 36: 507–18.

Kafafi, Z. A. (2010). The Chalcolithic period in the Golan Heights: a regional or local culture. *Paléorient* 36: 141–57.

Levy, T. E. (ed.) (1987). *Shiqmim I: Studies concerning Chalcolithic Societies in the Northern Negev Desert, Israel (1982–1984)* (2 vols). Oxford: British Archaeological Reports.

—— (ed.) (2006). *Archaeology, Anthropology and Cult: The Sanctuary at Gilat, Israel*. London: Equinox.

—— (2007). *Journey to the Copper Age: Archaeology in the Holy Land*. San Diego, Calif.: San Diego Museum of Man.

—— and D. N. Freedman (2008). *William Foxwell Albright 1891–1971: A Biographical Memoir*. National Academy of Sciences. http://www.bibleinterp.com/articles/albright5.shtml

—— V. Petrovic, T. Wypych, et al. (2010). On-site digital archaeology 3.0 and cyber-archaeology: into the future of the past—new developments, delivery and the creation of a data avalanche. In M. Forte (ed.), *Cyber-Archaeology*. Oxford: Archaeopress, 135–53.

Lovell, J. L. (2001). *The Late Neolithic and Chalcolithic Periods in the Southern Levant: New Data from the Site of Teleilat Ghassul, Jordan*. Oxford: Archaeopress.

—— J. Meadows, T. J. Adams, et al. (2006). The second preliminary report of the Wadi Rayyan Archaeological Project: the first season of excavations at El-Khawarji. *Annual of the Department of Antiquities of Jordan* 50: 33–59.

—— T. Richter, P. B. McLaren, I. K. McRae, and A. I. Abu Shmeis (2005). The first preliminary report of the Wadi Rayyan Archaeological Project: the survey of el Khawarij. *Annual of the Department of Antiquities, Jordan* 49: 189–200.

—— and Y. M. Rowan (eds) (2011). *Culture, Chronology and the Chalcolithic: Theory and Transition*. Oxford: Oxbow.

—— D. Thomas, H. Miller, et al. (2007). The third preliminary report of the Wadi Rayyan Archaeological Project: the second season of excavations at el-Khawarij. *Annual of the Department of Antiquities of Jordan* 51: 103–40.

Scheftelowitz, N., and R. Oren (2004). *Giv'at ha-Oranim: A Chalcolithic Site*. Tel Aviv: Emery and Claire Yass Publications in Archaeology.

Schick, T. (ed.) (1998). *The Cave of the Warrior: A Fourth Millennium Burial in the Judean Desert*. Jerusalem: Israel Antiquities Authority.

Seaton, P. (2008). *Chalcolithic Cult and Risk Management at Teleilat Ghassul: The Area E Sanctuary*. Oxford: Archaeopress.

Stein, G. (2009). Tell Zeidan. *Annual Report of the Oriental Institute* 2008–9: 126–38.

van den Brink, E. C. M., and R. Gophna (2005). *Shoham (North): Late Chalcolithic Burial Caves in the Lod Valley, Israel*. Jerusalem: Israel Antiquities Authority.

—— and T. E. Levy (eds) (2002). *Egypt and the Levant: Interrelations from the 4th through the Early 3rd Millennium B.C.E.* London: Leicester University Press.

CHAPTER 15

THE NORTHERN LEVANT DURING THE CHALCOLITHIC PERIOD
The Lebanese–Syrian Coast

GASSIA ARTIN

The Chalcolithic period of the Levant was a transition between the end of the Neolithic period and the beginning of the Bronze Age, constituting an important and complex phase in the evolution of prehistoric societies. During this period, new technical advancements of great importance were developed in the arts of stone tool production and metallurgy. The debate amongst scholars as to whether the Chalcolithic period should be included in the Early Bronze Age or whether it should be considered a distinct transitional phase between the Neolithic period and the Bronze Age has made the study of the Chalcolithic complicated and controversial (for further discussion, see Genz, Ch. 21 below).

This chapter presents certain aspects of the Chalcolithic period on the Lebanese–Syrian coast, with an emphasis on spatial organization as well as the social and economic developments of its societies.

CHRONOLOGICAL AND ARCHAEOLOGICAL DATA

The archaeological data from the coastal regions of Lebanon and Syria are unfortunately rare for the Chalcolithic, as only a limited number of sites are known and have been investigated. In addition, the absence of precise dating for the majority of these sites, the varying quality of the different archaeological methods employed (much of the previous fieldwork was carried out using standards that differ from current methods of practice, and the findings were insufficiently described), the inadequate empirical information produced, and the poor conservation of the archaeological material recovered prevent a thorough investigation of these regions in this period. While the Chalcolithic continues certain 'prehistoric' traditions, such as the production and use of lithic tools, there were also innovations in the development of new types of arrowheads, blades, metal objects, and funerary practices.

The Chalcolithic in Lebanon is best illustrated by the sites of Byblos, Sidon-Dakerman, Khalde II (or Khan el-Asis), and Minet ed-Dalieh on the coast, and Mengez and Kfar Gerra (known as 'Djelal en Namous') located inland (Fig. 15.1). Other settlements dating from the Chalcolithic were discovered during surveys, and the materials gathered were the result of surface collections (Burkhalter 1946–8; Besançon and Hours 1970; 1971; Copeland and Wescombe 1965; 1966). Due to the absence of stratigraphical sequences, the archaeological material collected was never scientifically dated or studied in detail.

In Lebanon, Byblos is the only site to date that shows continuous human occupation and that has been almost entirely excavated (Dunand 1973). Excavations of Chalcolithic Byblos reveal jar burials (2,097 tombs) and an exceptionally rich and varied corpus of grave goods (3,652 objects) (Artin 2009). The chronology of human occupation on the Lebanese coast is essentially based on the Byblos excavations. Maurice Dunand (1950;

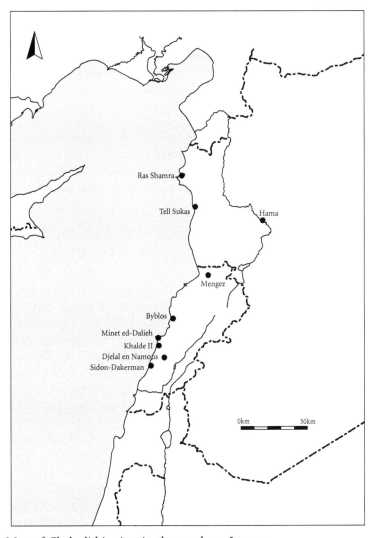

FIG. 15.1 Map of Chalcolithic sites in the northern Levant

1973) used the term 'énéolithique' to describe this archaeological period, which he further divided into two phases: the 'énéolithique ancien' (5700–5000 BP or 4500–3700 cal. BC), which corresponded to the 'levées' XXXIX–XXXVIII of Byblos, and the 'énéolithique récent' (5000–4200 BP or 3700–3000 cal. BC), which corresponded to the 'levées' XXXVIII–XXXIII of Byblos. (For data used in the calibrated chronology, see Hours et al. 1994.)

Our knowledge of the Chalcolithic in Lebanon is further enhanced by the excavations undertaken at the sites of Sidon-Dakerman, situated 70km south of Byblos (Saidah 1977; 1979), Khalde II or Khan el Asis, about 1km north of Khalde (Saidah 1969), and Minet ed-Dalieh, situated at the far end of the Ras Beyrouth promontory where a large number of triangular tools (later named after the site) were found (Cauvin 1962; 1968).

In Syria, the Chalcolithic is best illustrated by the excavations of Ras Shamra, Level IIIB (Schaeffer 1962; de Contenson 1992), the surveys of Tell Sukas IX, Levels M2 and M1 on the coast (Oldenburg 1991), and the site of Hama, Level K, further west (Fugmann 1958; Thuesen 1988). Due to the construction of the Tichrine Dam in the middle of the Euphrates in the 1990s, intensive fieldwork and rescue excavations were undertaken by international archaeological missions in northern Syria, revealing other sites and prompting rescue excavations at the sites of Tell Kosak Shamali (Nishiaki and Matsutani 2001) and Tell el Abr (Hammade and Yamazaki 2006). The information obtained from these represent an important reference point for this period in northern Syria.

Authors use various terms such as 'Ubaid' and 'Uruk' to designate the Chalcolithic in this region. Akkermans (1988) produced a chronology for the northern Levant (in particular, Syria and northern Mesopotamia) based on a detailed analysis of the ceramic assemblages dating from the Chalcolithic. However, a comparative study of the different chronological phases of the northern Levant with an analysis of the stratigraphic layers and radiocarbon dating is still needed.

SPATIAL ORGANIZATION OF SITES

During the Chalcolithic, the spatial occupation of settlements is characterized by both dwellings (houses, silos, and paved roads) and funerary structures (plain, cave, and jar burials) in close proximity to one another.

The traditional methods used in archaeological surveys and excavations of the coastal regions do not permit an in-depth study of the spatial organization of villages. Nor do they allow for the comparison of tombs and habitation structures at different points and over periods of time. It is therefore difficult both to obtain an overall picture of the spatial organization and to analyse the relationship that once existed between the world of the living and the world of the dead.

The excavations of different coastal sites in the Levant where jar burials have been found reveal a common factor: primary burial was either inside or in the immediate vicinity of dwellings. However, it is impossible to scientifically confirm that these burials date from the same period as the habitation structures. At Sidon-Dakerman, and in some rare cases at Byblos, Hama, and Ras Shamra, tombs were found directly underneath the dwellings; but the available data does not prove that a relationship existed between the two, nor does it indicate that the dwellings and burials were from the same period.

ARCHITECTURAL STRUCTURES

The architecture of the Chalcolithic at Byblos is characterized by single-room, stone-wall houses (termed 'logis' by Dunand to designate houses), that were sometimes fairly large in size (9×6m). These rectangular structures have right angle corners inside and rounded corners outside (Fig. 15.2). By the end of the Chalcolithic, the rectangular structure evolves into a circular one (with an approximate diameter of 5–6m). This development is unique to Byblos, as circular structures were replaced by rectangular ones at other sites.

Stone and pebble constructed houses were not aligned, nor did they stand tightly together like the dwellings of the Neolithic. Open spaces, devoid of any structure, could have served as roads, work areas, meeting places, or even as burial areas where construction was prohibited. On the basis of recorded data, we can assume that the spatial organization of Byblos during the second half of the Chalcolithic involved new forms of funerary practices.

At Sidon-Dakerman, well-preserved, isolated, single-room, stone-wall houses with an ellipsoidal plan were discovered in various sizes and orientations, measuring on average 8×4m (Figs 15.3 and 15.4). Several of the houses had been burnt and the plastered floors, which had been hardened by the fire, preserved the imprints of reeds.

At the site of Khalde II (Saidah 1969), the foundations of oval houses with and without their apses still intact (similar in size and form to those of Sidon-Dakerman) were found.

The architecture of Ras Shamra is represented by stone rectangular constructions with many rooms, some of which have paved stone floors, circular silos, and walls partly covered with plaster. At the site of Hama, rectangular houses with one to two rooms made of mud-brick (*pisé*) were found.

FIG. 15.2 Example of a rectangular habitation structure from Byblos, Lebanon (Archives Fonds Dunand © Ministère de la Culture/Direction Général des Antiquités)

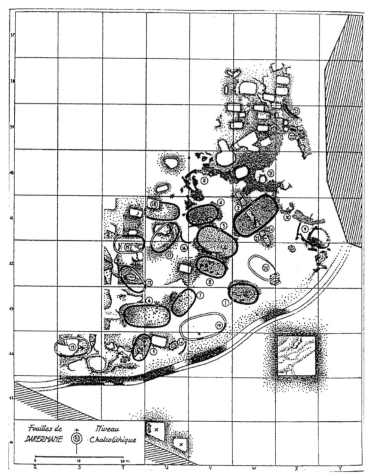

FIG. 15.3 Plan of the Chalcolithic settlement at Sidon-Dakerman, Lebanon (Saidah 1979)

No defensive installations were ever discovered on these sites. We can assume that in Byblos the promontory formed by two hills would have provided protection for the village from its neighbours. The excavations of the southern side of Sidon-Dakerman, however, revealed the existence of a fortification wall covering a distance of about 60m. We do not know if the village was entirely surrounded by such a fortification.

FUNERARY PRACTICES

In the fourth millennium BC, the tradition of jar burials, already in use during the Neolithic period, continued in the coastal sites of the northern Levant.

These sites revealed that immature individuals were generally placed under large fragments of ceramics or in large bowls or small jars, which were associated with the habitation structures.

A rich variety of funerary goods was found in Byblos. The site has 2,097 tombs, 2,059 of which are jar burials (Fig. 15.5) (Artin 2009). These large jars had domestic and funerary

FIG. 15.4 Example of an ellipsoidal habitation structure from Sidon-Dakerman, Lebanon (courtesy J. Cauvin)

FIG. 15.5 The funerary context in Byblos: jar burials (Archives Fonds Dunand © Ministère de la Culture/Direction Général des Antiquités)

usages. A total of 3,652 objects were found, including ceramics, ornaments, bone artefacts and objects made of gold and silver (Artin 2009). The grave goods are extremely diverse, and included ceramics, metal, and stone artefacts. The lithic industry included stone implements and weapons (either flaked or polished), the bone industry tools made of bone and/or ivory, and the art objects and ornaments (non-functional items) included human or animal figurines, as well as amulets, necklaces, bracelets, beads, and pendants made of different materials. In comparison to Byblos, the majority of the jar burials at the other sites contain only a small number of grave goods or ornaments. A flint flake found on the pelvis of a skeleton in Tomb 4 at Sidon-Dakerman is a notable exception (Hours 1979).

At the site of Ras Shamra, the tradition of jar burials was reserved for children, who were buried underneath houses or in their immediate vicinity. In Hama, jar burials were used for both children and adults, similar to the funerary practices observed at Byblos. These child jar inhumations, buried underneath the habitation structures, contained no grave goods. At Sidon-Dakerman, however, only adult jar burials were discovered in the Chalcolithic layers (Saidah 1977; 1979; de Contenson 1982).

Contrary to the coastal habitations, the stone structures of inland Lebanon, such as the 'megalithic necropolis' of Mengez (Tallon 1959; 1964), are not situated near the habitation structures. These stone constructions are attributed to nomad shepherds (Steimer 1996; Steimer-Herbert 2000). Funerary chambers built into soft stone were discovered without habitations in close proximity also at the site of Kfer Garra, 10km east of Sidon (Guigues 1937).

SOCIAL ORGANIZATION AND ECONOMIC DEVELOPMENT

Unfortunately, in the absence of stratigraphic and chronological data, it is impossible either to reconstruct the plans of the sequence of villages built at Byblos or to define their social and economic development. However, we can present an interpretation based on the study of the 'necropolis' and by the artefacts found on the site.

Social organization

The close proximity of habitation structures to the tombs seems to suggest the sedentary nature of these societies. In Byblos, the spatial analysis of the different zones revealed no difference between the burials of adults and children. Other areas in the Levant during the Chalcolithic reveal that adults and children were treated differently and were buried in separate zones.

It would be risky to formulate hypotheses about the social hierarchy that existed at the time. Current debates concern the degree of complexity in Chalcolithic societies, and in particular of their structures and social organization: were these egalitarian or chiefdom-type societies (Gilead 1993; Levy 1998)? Although funerary practices are frequently used to demonstrate the complexity of Chalcolithic societies in the southern Levant, the nature of the funerary goods does not indicate the social status of the individual, nor do they determine a hierarchy. Likewise, it cannot be confirmed that those buried were contemporary with one another (Masset 1990). The settlements lasted for over 1000 years, during which new techniques and materials were introduced and developed, making it impossible to establish social hierarchy based exclusively on the presence or absence of certain objects or types of material. Maurice Chéhab (1949–50) considered the tombs of Byblos to be those of chiefs, since they were rich in grave goods and included many metal objects. In a similar manner and without certainty, the weapons, daggers, and mace-heads that were deposited in the jars were always attributed to adult males, while ornaments were considered to have been for the females. These assumptions do not confirm the existence of 'chiefdoms', however. The tombs containing weapons were found to be not necessarily the richest in funerary goods, nor were they always connected with male subjects.

Furthermore, the funerary material found in the jars of Byblos include commonly used objects (fish-hooks and ornaments) as well as objects specifically made for inhumation, such as ceramics which were not resistant enough for functional use. The presence of objects made especially for inhumation implies that the deceased were not always buried with their personal belongings. Thus, the available data does not facilitate any attempt at establishing social differentiation.

ECONOMIC DEVELOPMENT

Economic life on the coastal sites was varied and based upon herding (enclosures and bone remains of domesticated animals), agriculture (barley, cereals, olive pits, and jars), fishing (fish-hooks), hunting (weapons and bone remains of wild animals), and crafts (ornaments, tools, and ceramics).

Due to the rise in specialized activities, crafts, and newly developed artisan production techniques, a large number of geological (flint) and environmental (quality timber) resources that were abundant at the coastal sites acquired a higher economic value.

The standardized ceramic objects at the coastal sites were probably the products of specialized artisans (Balfet 1962). The rarity of decoration demonstrates that the potter-artisans were mainly preoccupied with producing a large quantity of recipients for everyday use. It is interesting to note that most of the ceramic objects that were placed in funerary jars were the common household wares produced for the community in Byblos (Dunand 1973).

The stone industry of this period is characterized by a variety of blades, sickles, arrowheads, daggers, and triangles. The 'Canaanean blade' and 'Minet ed-Dalieh' techniques were used for blades and triangles respectively. The triangles, made of grey flint, which appear to be identical to the Cenomanien flint of Minet ed-Dalieh, were found on different sites, suggesting that they were imported from specialized workshops and not produced *in situ*. However, Minet ed-Dalieh was probably not the only workshop of this type, as similar triangles were also discovered at Ras Shamra and more inland, 5–20km east of Beyrouth, at Sin el-fil, Meyrouba, and Djelal en Namous. These discoveries reveal the intensification of exchange during the Chalcolithic.

Practical and ornamental artefacts made of bones were found in Ras Shamra and Byblos. The use of bone was not seen during the early phase of the Chalcholitic in Byblos. This site is an interesting example, demonstrating the development of this material. The quantitative study of the grave objects indicates that the stone grave goods (found in abundance) and bone funerary goods were present in the zones corresponding to the early phase. Their frequency diminished progressively as the site moved toward the south and east (middle phase), and then disappeared completely in the north area (final phase). This coincides with the addition and development of a new material, metal, including copper, gold, and, most notably, silver.

Bone objects were gradually replaced by metal ones, which were more resistant and flexible in the early phase of the Chalcolithic. Copper was mainly used for the fabrication of hunting weapons and arms (arrow heads, daggers, etc.), though its usage remained rare. The most frequently utilized metal was silver, largely used for the fabrication of ornaments. Despite the fact that fishing seems to have been an important activity for the coastal regions, as evidenced by the very large quantities of fish bones discovered during the excavations, only a small number of commonly used metal objects such as fish-hooks have been discovered. This may be because these objects were rare or perhaps reutilized (Artin 2009). Note that the first example of the use of metal was a fish-hook discovered in a funerary context at Byblos, and the oldest copper tool discovered in the excavations of Ras Shamra was also a fish-hook.

Despite the large number and exceptional quality of objects made of metal (silver, copper, and gold) discovered at Byblos and Ras Shamra, no trace of a metallurgical industry has ever been found on these sites. The presence of these objects is probably linked to commercial activities with Palestine, Egypt, and Anatolia, but this can only be proved through metal analysis (Epstein 2001; Prag 1986).

CONCLUSION

The well-known sites of the Lebanese–Syrian coast dating from the Chalcolithic period reveal some of the economic, cultural, and social characteristics of these prehistoric Levantine societies. The available data does not allow for a more precise definition of the social and economic organization of these Chalcolithic societies. However, the hypotheses presented here may help to set the priorities and objectives for future excavations in the region. Pre-existing archaeological data must be scientifically verified by means of control surveys at sites that were never explored, and samples of archaeological material must be re-examined and analysed in greater detail.

SUGGESTED READING

Artin, G. (2010). The necropolis and dwellings of Byblos during the Chalcolithic period: new interpretations. *Near Eastern Archaeology* 73: 74–84.
Dunand, M. (1973). *Fouilles de Byblos V: l'architecture, les tombes, le matériel domestique des origines néolithiques à l'avènement urbain* (2 vols). Paris: Maisonneuve.
Epstein, C. (2001). The significance of ceramic assemblages in Chalcolithic burial contexts in Israel and neighbouring regions in the southern Levant. *Levant* 33: 81–94.
Golden, J. M. (2010). *Dawn of the Metal Age: Technology and Society during the Levantine Chalcolithic*. London: Equinox.
Prag, K. (1986). Byblos and Egypt in the fourth millennium B.C. *Levant* 18: 59–74.

REFERENCES:

Akkermans, P. M. M. G. (1988). An updated chronology for the Northern Ubaid and Late Chalcolithic periods in Syria: new evidence from Tell Hammam et-Turkman. *Iraq* 50: 109–45.
Artin, G. (2009). *La nécropole énéolithique de Byblos: nouvelles interprétations*. Oxford: Archaeopress.

Balfet, H. (1962). *Céramique ancienne au Proche-Orient (Israël et Liban, VIIe–IIIe millénaires): étude technique*. PhD dissertation, Université de Paris.

Besançon, J., and F. Hours (1970). Préhistoire et géomorphologie: les formes du relief et les dépôts quaternaires dans la région de Joubb Jannine (Béqaa méridionale, Liban) (pt 1). *Hannon* 5: 64–95.

—— (1971). Préhistoire et géomorphologie: les formes du relief et les dépôts quaternaires dans la région de Joubb Jannine (Béqaa méridionale, Liban) (pt 2). *Hannon* 6: 29–135.

Burkhalter, L. 1946–8. Bibliographie préhistorique. *Bulletin du Musée de Beyrouth* 8: 10, 130–53.

Cauvin, J. (1962). Les industries lithiques du tell de Byblos. *L'Anthropologie* 66: 488–502.

—— (1968). *Fouilles de Byblos IV: les outillages néolithiques de Byblos et du littoral libanais*. Paris: Maisonneuve.

Chéhab, M. H. (1949–50). Date de tombes des chefs d'époque énéolithique trouvées à Byblos. *Bulletin du Musée de Beyrouth* 9: 75–85.

Copeland, L., and P. J. Wescombe (1965). Inventory of Stone Age sites in Lebanon, pt 1: West-central Lebanon. *Mélanges de l'Université Saint Joseph* 41: 29–175.

—— (1966). Inventory of Stone Age sites in Lebanon, pt 2: North–south–east central Lebanon. *Mélanges de l'Université Saint Joseph* 42: 1–174.

de Contenson, H. (1982). À propos du niveau chalcolithique de Dakerman. In *Archéologie au Levant: recueil à la mémoire de Roger Saidah*. Lyon: Maison de l'Orient/Paris: Boccard, 79–85.

—— (1992). *Préhistoire de Ras Shamra: les sondages stratigraphiques de 1955 à 1976* (2 vols). Paris: Recherche sur les civilisations.

Dunand, M. (1950). Chronologie des plus anciennes installations de Byblos. *Revue biblique* 57: 583–603.

—— (1973). *Fouilles de Byblos V: l'architecture, les tombes, le matériel domestique des origines néolithiques à l'avènement urbain* (2 vols). Paris: Maisonneuve.

Epstein, C. (2001). The significance of ceramic assemblages in Chalcolithic burial contexts in Israel and neighboring regions in the southern Levant. *Levant* 33: 81–94.

Fugmann, E. (1958). *Hama: fouilles et recherché, 1931–1938*, vol. 2, pt 1: *L'architecture des périodes préhellénistiques*. Copenhagen: Fondation Carlsberg.

Gilead, I. (1993). Sociopolitical organization in the northern Negev at the end of the Chalcolithic period. In A. Biran and J. Aviram (eds), *Biblical Archaeology Today 1990: Proceedings of the Second International Congress on Biblical Archaeology, Jerusalem, June–July 1990*. Jerusalem: Israel Exploration Society/Israel Academy of Sciences and Humanities, 82–97.

Guigues, P. E . (1937). Lébé'a, Kafer-Garra, Qrayé: nécropoles de la région sidonienne. *Bulletin du Musée de Beyrouth* 1: 35–76.

Hammade, H., and Y. Yamazaki (2006). *Tell al Abr (Syria): Ubaid and Uruk Periods*. Louvain: Peeters.

Hours, F. (1979). L'industrie lithique de Saïda-Dakerman. *Berytus* 27: 57–75.

—— O. Aurenche, J. Cauvin, M.-C. Cauvin, L. Copeland, and P. Sanlaville (1994). *Atlas des sites du Proche-Orient (14000–5700 BP)* (2 vols). Lyon: Maison de l'Orient/Paris: Boccard.

Levy, T. E. (ed.) (1998). *The Archaeology of Society in the Holy Land*. Leicester: Leicester University Press.

Masset, C. (1990). À la recherche des hiérarchies sociales. *Les nouvelles de l'archéologie* 40: 47–8.

Nishiaki, Y., and T. Matsutani (eds) (2001). *Tell Kosak Shamali: The Archaeological Investigations on the Upper Euphrates, Syria*, vol. 1: *Chalcolithic Architecture and Earlier Prehistoric Remains*. Tokyo: University Museum, University of Tokyo/Oxford: Oxbow.

Oldenburg, E. (1991). *Sukas IX: The Chalcolithic and the Early Bronze Periods*. Copenhagen: Royal Danish Academy of Sciences and Letters.

Prag, K. (1986). Byblos and Egypt in the fourth millennium B.C. *Levant* 18: 59–74.

Saidah, R. (1969). Archaeology in the Lebanon, 1968–1969. *Berytus* 18: 119–43.

——(1977). *Sidon et la Phénicie méridionale au XIVème siècle avant J.C. dans le contexte proche-oriental et egéen: à propos des tombes de Dakerman* (2 vols). PhD dissertation, Université de Paris I.

——(1979). Fouilles de Sidon-Dakerman: l'agglomération chalcolithique. *Berytus* 27: 29–55.

Schaeffer, C. F.-A. (1962). Les fondements préhistoriques d'Ugarit du Néolithique précéramique au début du Bronze Moyen: observations stratigraphiques, chronologiques et céramologiques. In C. F.-A. Schaeffer (ed.), *Ugaritica 4: découvertes des XVIIIe et XIXe campagnes, 1954–1955*. Paris: Geuthner, 151–251.

Steimer, T. (1996). *Les monuments mégalithiques de la région de Mengez (nord Liban)*. Diplôme d'Études Approfondies, Université de Paris I, Panthéon-Sorbonne.

Steimer-Herbet, T. (2000). Étude des monuments mégalithiques de Mengez (Liban) d'après les carnets de fouilles du R. P. Tallon (1959–1969). *Syria* 77: 11–21.

Tallon, M. E. (1959). Tumulus et mégalithes du Hermel et de la Beqã du nord. *Mélanges de l'Université Saint Joseph* 36: 93–100.

——(1964). Les monuments mégalithiques de Mengez. *Bulletin du Musée de Beyrouth* 16–17: 7–19.

Thuesen, I. (1988). *Hama: fouilles et recherches de la Fondation Carlsberg 1931–1938*, vol. 1: *The Pre- and Protohistoric Periods*. Copenhagen: Nationalmuseets.

CHAPTER 16

THE SOUTHERN LEVANT (CISJORDAN) DURING THE CHALCOLITHIC PERIOD

YORKE M. ROWAN

Fundamental changes in craft production, mortuary practices, settlement sizes and patterns, and subsistence economy occurred during the mid-fifth to early fourth millennia in the southern Levant. The impact these changes had on social organization and power relations are interpreted differently, although there is no doubt that greater complexity in socio-political organization was established in some areas (Fig. 16.1).

TERMINOLOGY AND CHRONOLOGY

First recognized at the site of Teleilat al-Ghassul, the Chalcolithic is sometimes referred to as the 'Ghassulian', a term coined by Neuville in 1930. Some use 'Ghassulian' in a narrower sense to describe particular assemblages, and therefore its definition is debated. W. F. Albright first introduced the term 'Chalcolithic' to describe ceramic styles preceding those of the Early Bronze Age. The Chalcolithic spans the period from approximately 4500 to 3700/3600 BC; for the early fifth millennium, a period of transition, terminological and chronological issues remain unresolved. Radiocarbon dates suggest some sites existed earlier (Gilat and Teleilat al-Ghassul) and overlap with sites having more recent radiocarbon sequences [e.g. Shiqmim (c. 4700–3700 BC): Burton and Levy 2001]. Terms for periods, phases, and 'cultures', including Jericho VIII/IX, Lodian, Coastal Neolithic, Besorian, Qatifian, Tsafian, and Wadi Rabah, mark the transition between the Late Neolithic and Chalcolithic. A few scholars regard the Wadi Rabah phase (or culture) as part of the Chalcolithic, but handmade pottery, absence of copper, less sophisticated technological crafting, and mortuary practices suggest Late Neolithic traditions, although there is no sharp break between the two. The paucity of radiocarbon dates associated with these entities means that distinguishing chronological

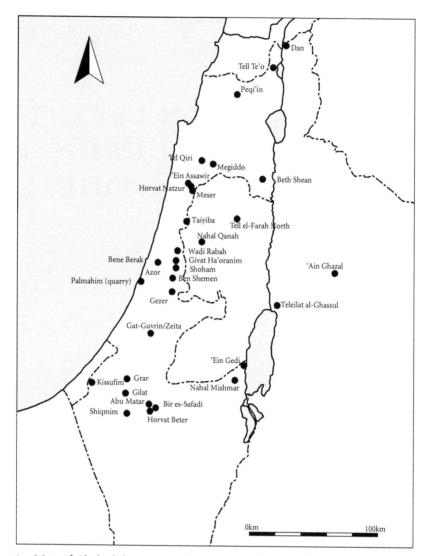

FIG. 16.1 Map of Chalcolithic sites in the southern Levant (Cisjordan)

phases from regional variation (or 'cultures') based on small ceramic assemblages is premature. Compounding this problem is the evident regionalism, with major distinctions of the Golan, Hula Valley, Jordan Valley, Nahal Grar/Patish, and Beersheva Valley based on mortuary practices, architecture, material culture, and faunal patterns. Our perspectives are formed in part by intensive research areas (Beersheva, Golan, and the Jordan Valley) where preservation is good and modern development less destructive. Early investigations carried out by Jean Perrot (1955) at the large settlements of Tell Abu Matar and Bir es-Safadi in the northern Negev revealed impressive material culture and subterranean complexes that led many scholars to believe that an influx of immigrants settled the region (Fig. 16.2). With increased excavations of Late Neolithic and Chalcolithic sites, continuity of pottery and flint assemblages led most to accept the indigenous inspiration for changes.

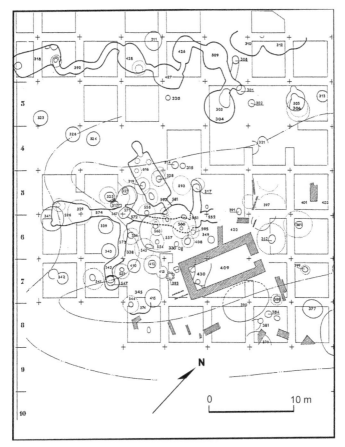

FIG. 16.2 Bir es-Safadi site plan, southern corner. Rectilinear wall foundations are rep-resented by dark shading. Curvilinear features represent subterranean cells and tunnels (adapted from Commenge-Pellerin 1990: fig. 2a; source: Daniel Ladiray, Archive CRFJ)

SUBSISTENCE ECONOMY

Neolithic patterns of mixed subsistence undergo a general intensification marked by increased storage capacity, suggesting amplification in agropastoral productivity. Most pop-ulations are sedentary, with foraging pastoralists in the southern and eastern arid regions of Jordan, southern Israel, and Sinai. Cereal and legume cultivation of einkorn and emmer wheat, six- and two-rowed barley, chickpeas, lentils, and peas established dietary compo-nents among the sedentary communities from the northern Negev to the Golan (and cer-tainly beyond), and from the Mediterranean coastal plain to the eastern highlands and plateau of Jordan. Farming employed simple basin irrigation techniques (Rosen 1987).

The submerged Wadi Rabah site of Kfar Samir indicates that olive, one of the earli-est cultivated fruit trees, was already exploited in the Late Neolithic. Although debated,

FIG. 16.3 Special vessels from Gilat. From left, the zoomorphic 'Ram with Cornets', 'Gilat Lady' with a churn balanced on her head, and a cornet (photograph Kenneth Garrett)

domestic olives (*Olea europea*) appear to be established by the Chalcolithic, on the basis of evidence from Teleilat al-Ghassul and Nahal Mishmar; the former included pits and wood. Charred olive wood from sites in the Jordan Valley support domestication, it is argued, because firewood would not have been carried far beyond the natural habitat. The prevalence of olive pits and wood at sites across the region seem to support the presence of domesticated trees. Other domesticates include date, fig, peach, pomegranate, almond, walnut, and pistachio.

Faunal assemblages are dominated by domesticated sheep, goat, and cattle with highly variable distribution of pigs reflecting environmental constraints. Grigson (1998) notes the absence of pig at Beersheva sites in contrast to sites slightly further north or toward the coast. Increasing frequencies of pig from south to north in the Jordan Valley may also reflect moister conditions to the north. Ovicaprine frequencies typically dominate faunal assemblages, but cattle contribute nearly 70 per cent of the meat (Grigson 1998: 251). Thorough field methods and optimal conditions for preservation produce faunal profiles that may include small amounts of fish, equids, dog, hare, gazelle, birds, ostrich, fox, and hyena. The hunting of hartebeest and gazelle may continue in a limited role. Low quantities of pulses, sickles, and pigs may indicate greater reliance on animal products at Beersheva sites.

Levy (1983; 1992) posits that nomadic or semi-nomadic specialized pastoralists grazed ovicaprine herds in the northern Negev and coastal zones, viewing smaller sites (e.g. Nahal Sekher) as pastoralist camps in a larger migration system. Gilead (1992) views these as short-term herder encampments from local habitation sites. Grigson (1998) argues that a sedentary model with limited transhumant pastoralism is more likely.

Changes in age-class patterns, skeletal morphology, and pathology of cattle, possibly reflecting their use for drafting, all support increased secondary products exploitation (Sherratt 1981). Pack animals are also indicated by the statuary examples such as the 'Ein Gedi bull carrying a churn and the ram with cornets from Gilat (Fig. 16.3). Evidence from Gilat, the largest published Chalcolithic faunal assemblage, suggests that herding strategies focused on wool production rather than milk (Grigson 2006); the extensive spindle whorl and bone tool collection indicates intensive spinning and weaving (Levy et al. 2006). With the possible exception of grape cultivation, much of the mixed agropastoral subsistence economy in the Mediterranean, based on crop agriculture, animal husbandry, and horticulture, was established by the Chalcolithic.

HOUSEHOLDS, VILLAGES, AND REGIONAL SETTLEMENT PATTERNS

Extensive exposure of Chalcolithic settlements is limited to a few regions (Golan, Jordan Valley, and northern Negev), skewing our view of intramural spatial arrangements. Domestic space generally includes rectangular broadroom structures of mud-brick or stone with an entrance through a longer wall. Varying in size from 15×6m to 5.5×2.5m, broadrooms often include an internal low bench along a wall, smaller internal partitioning walls, and post-holes in the centre for roof beam supports. Hearths, earthen pits, or silos are frequently found associated with these rooms or attached courtyards, with large ceramic vessels substituted in the rocky terrain of the Golan. Broadroom structures in the Golan adjoining one another end-to-end with shared short walls were termed 'chain houses'. Alleys between houses and courtyards, curvilinear structures, and small rectangular platforms constructed of flat stones are also found.

Dwelling sizes are variable, but without clear concentrations of elite structures or precincts. Large village sites in the Beersheva region such as Shiqmim, Bir es-Safadi, Abu Matar, and Horvat Beter are known for the subterranean complexes excavated into the hard-packed loess. These pits, tunnels, and underground chambers probably extended all along the wadi terrace at Shiqmim. Subterranean chambers, many with pits in the floors, ranged from small to large oval chambers (c.1.5×3.0–3.0×7.0m) linked by tunnels with a few smaller dividing walls and human burials in the chambers and pits. As at Bir es-Safadi, prestige items were found in the subterranean features at Shiqmim, including a unique vial, a handle, and other items of ivory. Contemporary with the surface village, subterranean complexes may have served as storage areas, defensive hiding areas (Levy et al. 1991), and burial zones (Rowan and Ilan 2013).

The earlier Late Neolithic patterns of dispersed small villages with little integration changes; although smaller villages are common, some sites are as large as ten hectares. In the northern Negev, a dramatic increase over the Neolithic heralds a major expansion of Chalcolithic settlements into a semi-arid zone, where a rank-size distribution of Beersheva Basin sites existed; Abu Matar, Bir es-Safadi, and Shiqmim are clearly larger than other smaller sites in the region (Levy 1987; Levy, Burton, and Rowan 2006).

Modern development and agriculture as well as ancient reoccupation have impacted many northern sites; in the Hula Valley, our knowledge is limited to a few sites such as

Tel Te'o and Tel Turmus. Areas such as the Galilee and central highlands were occupied, although settlements seem limited in size. In the Lower Galilee, larger sites (e.g. Beit Netofa, Beit Ha-Emeq, Horvat Usa, Marj Rabba, and Tel Qiri) are known and appear to be associated with an expansion in the number of settlement sites. Western highland and foothill sites are generally small without evidence of larger central sites. Surveys of the Mediterranean coastal plain indicate the presence of larger sites such as 'Ein Assawir, Natzur, Meser, and sites near Dor. Early excavation techniques of mixed deposits at deeply stratified tell sites such as Beth Shean, Gezer, Megiddo, and Tell el-Farah North prevent simple chronostratigraphic interpretations, but frequently include Chalcolithic material culture.

CRAFT PRODUCTION

Material culture production dramatically changes during the late fifth millennium, although general techniques and artefact forms of the preceding Late Neolithic endure. Chalcolithic ceramics are marked by a significant increase in forms, decoration, and quality over earlier traditions, with miniature forms, combinations of wheel- and handmade elements, and regional aspects of decoration and variation. As with other aspects of the material culture repertoire, however, regionalism complicates interpretation. Ceramic assemblages from the northern Negev, such as Grar, Gilat, Shiqmim, Bir es-Safadi, and Abu Matar, are well known (Commenge-Pellerin 1987; 1990). Excavation reports from Tel Te'o and the Golan underscore the regional nature of decoration and forms. Smaller, narrower soundings at sites in the Jordan Valley, many from decades ago, leave ceramic-based chronologies contentious (e.g. Banning 2002; Garfinkel 1999; Lovell 2001).

Pottery includes a diverse array of closed and open forms. Common open forms include 'V-shaped' bowls, pithoi, pedestalled fenestrated stands, basins, and large bowls; other forms include hole-mouths, globular pots, and necked jars. Less common but considered hallmarks of the period are 'churns' (spindle-shaped necked vessels) possibly used for butter and yoghurt production. Some vessels are restricted in distribution, such as the long, slender, pointed-base cornets (Fig. 16.3), rare at Beersheva and Golan sites, but common at Gilat, Grar, Ghassul, and 'Ein Gedi. Pedestaled fenestrated stands are also common, but found in significantly higher relative frequencies at mortuary and other ritual sites. Large thick-walled vessels known as 'torpedo jars' found at Gilat were manufactured from clays originating in a variety of southern petrographic zones; gas chromatography indicates these apparently served as olive oil containers (Burton and Levy 2006).

Pottery production techniques and distribution networks expanded. Manufacturing techniques included wheel use, slab, coil, and composite techniques. Wheel use was variable and more prevalent in Beersheva assemblages, for example, than at Gilat, where rather than maximizing efficiency, wheel use for more complicated forms required greater investment of time and attention. Most ceramic vessels were manufactured of locally available clays, but some, such as the 'Cream Ware' vessels found at northern Negev sites as well as Ghassul and Tel Gezer, were manufactured of finely sorted clays derived from Eocene chalk deposits.

Chipped stone assemblages exhibit broadly similar frequencies of flake production for expedient tools with much smaller quantities of specialized types, some manufactured at specialized sites or workshops. Continuity with Neolithic forms is apparent, although arrowheads essentially disappear except in the most arid zones. Celt (chisels, axes, and adzes) and blade workshops are known at Wadi Ghazzeh sites, and production sites for tabular scrapers are proposed in the western Negev, Jordan, and Sinai. Salvage excavations in Beersheva recently unearthed a massive blade-manufacturing workshop. Some variability in localized adaptations or traditions may be visible in lithics; for instance, sickle blade distribution indicates that the Beersheva sites have lower relative frequencies in contrast to sites such as Grar and Gilat. Microborers, microendscrapers, prismatic blades, and 'stars' (multi-perforators?) all occur in low frequencies and are geographically limited.

Ground stone artefacts include implements used for millennia such as grinding slabs, handstones, mortars, pestles, and assorted utilized cobbles and pebbles. Rare materials or intensive labour investment in artefacts such as mace-heads, violin-shaped figurines, palettes, and basalt bowls represent an increase of prestige stone objects over the Late Neolithic (Rowan and Golden 2009). Two general forms of the ubiquitous basalt bowls are found, open forms and pedestaled fenestrated bowls (Amiran and Porat 1984), but more elaborate subtypes are found in association with mortuary contexts such as Peqi'in, Nahal Qanah, Shoham, and, possibly, Givat Ha'oranim (van den Brink, Rowan, and Braun 1999; van den Brink and Gophna 2005; Gopher and Tsuk 1996). X-ray fluorescence provenience analyses eliminated some proposed sources for both types of bowls; many were made from basalts in the Golan (Philip and Williams-Thorpe 1993). Evidence for production sites is limited, although possible preforms are known from Golan sites and Natzur. Distance to basalt sources, difficulty of manufacture, and fine workmanship indicate that many elaborate bowls were created by skilled producers, although their rarity and non-standardized forms argue against full-time specialists.

Specialized production is evident in copper smelting, which first begins during the Chalcolithic. The absence of copper at many sites may reflect chronological or sociological factors. Copper objects are typically grouped into two broad categories, 'utilitarian' tools (adzes, axes, chisels, and awls), cast in open moulds with oxide-rich ores, and prestige/cultic items, manufactured using lost-wax casting techniques with 'arsenical' copper (mace-heads, standards, 'crowns', and vessels). This perception of a dual industry remains largely accurate, although more complex than originally conceived (Potazkin and Bar-Avi 1980; Key 1980; Shalev and Northover 1987). Some prestige or cultic items are manufactured of relatively pure copper and others include widely varying metal compositions (Tadmor et al. 1995)—'arsenical' copper is now known to include antimony or high nickel content ores rather than an alloy; Golden (2010) terms the latter 'complex metals'. These were preferred for lost wax casting because of their superior hardness, appearance, and casting qualities (lower melting point and fluidity). The division between utilitarian and prestige objects is misleading, because the wax casting technique would be more functional (harder) for the tools, which rarely indicate hard use and were probably also symbolically important prestigious objects (Rowan and Golden 2009).

Structure, texture, and chemical composition suggest that ores from the Wadi Feynan were smelted at northern Negev sites such as Shiqmim and Abu Matar (Timna and Sinai are other possible sources). The complex antimony or arsenical coppers derive from more distant areas such as Transcaucasia, Azerbaijan, Syria, and southern Sinai. Turquoise extraction in the Sinai suggests that Chalcolithic populations had contact with these distant southern areas for mineral resources. Local production of one mace-head (Shalev et al. 1992) and some ingots or lumps suggest complex ore was imported for local smelting.

The sophistication of copper production is highlighted by the spectacular discovery at the Nahal Mishmar cave, the 'Cave of the Treasure' (Fig. 16.4). Bundled in a reed mat and placed in a cave located in a sheer cliff face, the collection included 'crowns', over 100 standards, more than 200 mace-heads, jars, and tools of copper as well as a few ivory objects. Most scholars agree that the objects were associated with ritual (cultic) practices, although why they were secreted in this remote location remains the object of speculation. Copper objects found in other caves exhibit similar iconographic elements, such as the standard with ibex horns and crown with horns recovered from Givat Ha'oranim. These and complex metal items from Nahal Qanah and Peqi'in extend the range of copper implements well beyond the northern Negev area. The discovery of eight gold and electrum rings at the rich Nahal Qanah burial cave indicates the mastery of a new metal-to-smelting process, which may have necessitated new extraction techniques. The gold may have originated in Nubia, with similar rings depicted in later pharaonic tomb paintings.

Copper smelting offers evidence for a move beyond domestic production. Ores were non-local and difficult to obtain, and smelting skills would have been uncommon. Manufacturing, on the other hand, was apparently household-based, using local ores, with no evidence for centralized workshops or attachment to elite structures (Golden, Levy, and Hauptmann 2001). Indirect evidence suggests that complex metals were produced in the southern Levant, and this production may have been controlled (Levy and Shalev 1989). Most finished copper items are found in mortuary contexts or in structured deposits, hinting at elite, possibly ritual specialist, patronage.

FIG. 16.4 Copper and ivory artefacts from the 'Cave of the Treasure' wrapped in a reed mat and secreted in a cliff cave at Nahal Mishmar (photograph Kenneth Garrett)

INTERREGIONAL AND INTRAREGIONAL EXCHANGE

Long-distance exchange expands dramatically in contrast to the Neolithic, with gold, obsidian, turquoise, copper ores, and shells indicative of long-range contacts. Obsidian, derived from three different Anatolian sources, is very rare (Yellin, Levy, and Rowan 1996). Marine and freshwater shells were derived from the Mediterranean, Red Sea, and the Nile River. Most freshwater bivalves, such as *Chambardia rubens* (formerly *Aspatharia rubens*), are Nilotic and found at sites in the south, but these might have been more easily accessible because the Pelusiac branch of the Nile reached the northern Sinai during the fifth and fourth millennia. Likewise, rare ivory finds such as the perforated ivory tusks (e.g. Nahal Qanah and Nahal Mishmar), statuettes (e.g. Bir es-Safadi and Abu Matar), hairpin, vial, and handle (e.g. Shiqmim), and bowls (e.g. Bir es-Safadi and Shiqmim) are primarily limited to southern Palestine. Contact with Egypt is clear, even if indirect and limited in scale; recently recognized steatite beads may derive from Egypt. Pre-dynastic Egyptian vessels are extremely rare and limited to a few places, such as Gilat, 'Ein Gedi, Wadi Zeita, and sites in northeastern Sinai. Equally unusual are Levantine sherds in Predynastic Egyptian contexts, although examples were documented at a Badarian tomb. Forms typical of the southern Chalcolithic such as churns, V-shaped bowls, and pedestalled fenestrated vessels recovered at the Nile Delta site of Tell el-Fara'in/Buto were made of local clays.

Materials such as copper, hematite, and basalt indicate extensive intraregional exchange, with much more limited quantities of amazonite, calcite, carnelian, chlorite-schist, diorite, gabbro, granite, jasper, scoria, and turquoise (Rowan et al. 2006). Some flint, such as that used for the prismatic (wide, symmetrical) blades and tabular scrapers (made on wide cortical flakes), also formed an important facet of exchange. One of the most visible aspects of material movements is basalt, a valued material at sites distant from probable sources. Other materials, such as bitumen, salt, or oils, are difficult to trace but probably also formed essential exchange items.

MORTUARY PRACTICES

Intramural burial of the dead continues earlier traditions, but significant new burial practices indicate fundamental shifts in cultural attitudes to death. Most intramural primary burials are single, but multiple burials are also known. Extramural burials are diverse. Mortuary structures include caves, subterranean chambers, and grave circles mostly for secondary burial that includes a spectrum of associated material culture. Clay and stone ossuaries for secondary interments vary from simple to elaborately decorated and modelled (Fig. 16.5). Elaborate structural ossuaries ('house' ossuaries) frequently have painted faces as well as modelled features such as noses, breasts, tools, and beams. Other items include stone and ceramic tubs, large jars with a window on the side, and large vessels re-used for human remains (Perrot and Ladiray 1980). Peqi'in, the northern Galilee mortuary cave site, highlights the imaginative variety of elaborately modelled and painted ossuary features, introducing new features such as modelled heads with mouths, arms and hands, twin heads, and a diversity of painted decorations.

FIG. 16.5 Chalcolithic clay ossuaries for the secondary burial of human remains (photograph Kenneth Garrett)

Cave burials range from simple chambers hewn into bedrock such as Azor, Ben Shemen, Bene Berak, Palmahim, and Taiyiba to extensive karstic chambers and passages such as Nahal Qanah, Peqi'in, and Shoham. All include secondary remains and ossuaries, typically shattered through reuse, roof collapse, and modern destruction. Constructed shelves for placement of mortuary goods are common, as are stelae, pavements for ossuaries, and hewn roof-supporting pillars (in non-karstic caves).

More arid regions include clusters of grave circles such as those at Adeimah, Nahal Sekher, and Shiqmim. The most thoroughly documented example, Shiqmim, consists of clusters of stone cists and circles extending approximately 1km along the chalk hills above the village. The cists (found at only one cemetery) may have acted as excarination pits, but no human remains were found. Secondary burials in the circles may have come from other communities as well as Shiqmim.

Burials are also known from the Judean Desert region (e.g. Cave of the Horror, Wadi Makkukh, and Ketef Jericho), including the remarkable preservation of the Cave of the Warrior, a fully articulated burial with a 7m woven shroud, bow with arrows, prismatic blades, and wooden bowl, all treated with powdered ochre (Schick 1998).

Diverse grave goods include pottery and basalt vessels, copper, ivory, beads, and mace-heads, but some burials have no finds. Funerary artefacts are more commonly associated with secondary burials, although the Nahal Mishmar deposit is an exception (if one considers it mortuary). New variants of mortuary practices continue to be discovered, such as the semi-subterranean structures with large stone ossuary tubs near Palmahim near the Mediterranean coast. Kissufim, also on the southern coastal plain, includes ossuaries, stelae, pendants, and vessels deposited in and around a rectangular mud-brick subterranean structure with benches and wall niches (Goren and Fabian 2002). Mortuary contexts indicate differential access to distant exotic materials, sophisticated technology, and the ability to remove these goods from circulation through disposal in graves. Nevertheless, association of specific prestige goods with individuals is rarely possible, rendering identification of ascribed status and hierarchically ranked societies difficult. Likewise, mortuary structures rarely required extensive labour investments, although cave modifications and subterranean complexes certainly required some effort.

Religion, ritual, and expressive culture

Our evidence for insights into ritual practices derives from architectural forms, structured deposits, burial practices, and sophisticated artefact forms and motifs in diverse materials.

Extramural and intramural places existed for ritual practices. 'Ein Gedi, situated on a promontory near a spring on the western bank of the Dead Sea, is a widely accepted example. Four structures are joined by an enclosing wall: two gates, a lateral rectilinear chamber, and the main sanctuary broadroom. In the centre of the courtyard, a shallow stone feature may have been for libations, a tree, or some other function. A stone bench was built along the wall interior of the sanctuary, and a stone-built arc may have held the hard limestone pedestal recovered nearby. Small shallow pits containing fenestrated stands, cornet sherds, and horn cores were found here. A zoomorphic figurine with churns on its back and a Predynastic Egyptian alabaster vessel fragment were also recovered. The concentration of fenestrated stands, cornets, and animal horn cores underscore the ritual function of 'Ein Gedi (Ussishkin 1980).

In contrast, the regional ritual centre of Gilat includes domestic artefacts as well as a high concentration of exotica made of non-local materials (Levy 2006; Rowan et al. 2006). Architecture includes rectilinear and rounded structures, most of mud-brick, as well as large hearths, small platforms ($c.$1×1m), and an extraordinary number of pits that complicate the stratigraphy. The unparalleled artefact assemblage includes eccentric ceramics, large quantities of basalt vessels, ceramic anthropomorphic and zoomorphic statuettes, mace-heads, and a dog burial with a mortuary vessel. The 76 enigmatic violin-shaped figurine fragments (minimum number of individuals = 53) exceed the total number of all others found in the Levant. Most pottery is manufactured from local clays, yet high proportions of hole-mouths and churns were made of non-local clays. The torpedo jars, found almost exclusively at Gilat, exhibit different petrographic origins, suggesting that many were made elsewhere and imported; gas chromatography indicates vegetal lipids, probably olive oil residue (Burton and Levy 2006). The two figurative ceramic vessels, the Gilat Lady and the Ram with Cornets, are unique but include recognizable elements (Fig. 16.3). The seated female holds a churn on her head and an object under her arm, possibly a fenestrated stand or rolled mat. Similar in profile to the Nahal Mishmar copper 'crowns', her seat may represent a cult stand or a birthing stool.

Intramural ritual space is also known. At Shiqmim, several rebuilding phases of a long 'temenos' wall, a semi-circular altar, and caches of pottery vessels signify an area of repeated ritual practice situated next to the subterranean complex, possibly used for storage (Levy et al. 1991). Bourke (2001) observed similar functional continuity through time and spatial parallels between the Area E (Tulayl 5) sanctuary precinct and storage at Ghassul.

Violin-shaped figurines, ivory figurines, ossuaries, and other material culture share an iconographic vocabulary linking ritually significant artefacts. The upper torsos of violin-shaped figurines are sometimes paralleled by ossuary facades, where the Ghassulian characteristics of prominent nose and eyes are common; these facial characteristics are found on the basalt 'cult' stands of the Golan and northern Jordan plateau, the ivory figurines, and a few Nahal Mishmar copper items. A small bone figurine from Shiqmim combined these Ghassulian features and the violin-shaped profile.

Stone palettes, fenestrated stands, mace-heads, and stelae represent ritual equipment. These suggest a cohesive regional belief system inclusive of 'cultural units' as defined by ceramic patterns (Rowan and Golden 2009). This wealth stands in contrast to the Early Bronze (I) Age, when such iconography and exotica nearly disappear.

Some scholars argue that the absence of impressive burial monuments, rich individual burials, and limited hierarchical settlement patterns indicate informal and limited power (Gilead 1988). The role of ritual leader would be temporary and situational rather than permanent and inherited. Others argue for an elite presence, including full-time religious practitioners (priests) who controlled ritual practice (Levy 1998; 2006). Conflicting interpretations highlight the data's ambiguities, and suggest the possibility that a variety of religious practitioners operated within the region for different clienteles or purposes (Rowan and Ilan 2007). The diversity of intramural village spatial arrangements, regional settlement patterns, mortuary practices, and prestige goods suggest that some areas may have experienced hierarchically organized, territorial middle-range societies, while others did not.

SUGGESTED READING

Bar-Adon, P. (ed.) (1980). *The Cave of the Treasure: The Finds from the Caves in Naḥal Mishmar*, trans. I. Pommerantz. Jerusalem: Israel Exploration Society.

Epstein, C. (1998). *The Chalcolithic Culture of the Golan*. Jerusalem: Israel Antiquities Authority.

Golden, J. M. (2010). *Dawn of the Metal Age: Technology and Society during the Levantine Chalcolithic*. London: Equinox.

Levy, T. E. (1998). Cult, metallurgy and rank societies: Chalcolithic period (ca. 4500–3500 BCE). In T. E. Levy (ed.), *The Archaeology of Society in the Holy Land*. London: Leicester University Press, 226–44.

Rosen, S. A. (1997). *Lithics after the Stone Age: A Handbook of Stone Tools from the Levant*. Walnut Creek, Calif.: AltaMira.

REFERENCES

Amiran, R., and N. Porat (1984). The basalt vessels of the Chalcolithic and Early Bronze Age. *Tel Aviv* 11: 11–19.

Banning, E. B. (2002). Consensus and debate on the Late Neolithic and Chalcolithic of the southern Levant. *Paléorient* 28: 143–56.

Bourke, S. J. (2001). The Chalcolithic period. In B. Macdonald, R. Adams, and P. Bienkowski (eds), *The Archaeology of Jordan*. Sheffield: Sheffield Academic, 107–63

Burton, M., and T. E. Levy (2001). The Chalcolithic radiocarbon record and its use in southern Levantine archaeology. *Radiocarbon* 43: 1223–46.

—— (2006). Appendix I: Organic residue analysis of selected vessels from Gilat—Gilat torpedo jars. In Levy (2006: 849–62).

Commenge-Pellerin, C. (1987). *La poterie d'Abou Matar et de l'Ouadi Zoumeili (Beershéva) au IVe millénaire avant l'ère chrétienne.* Paris: Association Paléorient.

—— (1990). *La poterie de Safadi (Beershéva) au IVe millénaire avant l'ère chrétienne.* Paris: Association Paléorient.

Garfinkel, Y. (1999). *Neolithic and Chalcolithic Pottery of the Southern Levant.* Jerusalem: Institute of Archaeology, Hebrew University of Jerusalem.

Gilead, I. (1988). The Chalcolithic period in the Levant. *Journal of World Prehistory* 2: 397–443.

—— (1992). Farmers and herders in southern Israel during the Chalcolithic period. In O. Bar-Yosef and A. M. Khazanov (eds), *Pastoralism in the Levant: Archaeological Materials in Anthropological Perspectives.* Madison, Wis.: Prehistory, 29–42.

Golden, J. M. (2010). *Dawn of the Metal Age: Technology and Society during the Levantine Chalcolithic.* London: Equinox.

—— T. E. Levy, and A. Hauptmann (2001). Recent discoveries concerning ancient metallurgy at the Chalcolithic (ca. 4000 B.C.) village of Shiqmim, Israel. *Journal of Archaeological Science* 9: 951–63.

Gopher, A., and T. Tsuk (1996). *The Nahal Qanah Cave: Earliest Gold in the Southern Levant.* Tel Aviv: Institute of Archaeology, Tel Aviv University.

Goren, Y., and P. Fabian (2002). *Kissufim Road: A Chalcolithic Mortuary Site.* Jerusalem: Israel Antiquities Authority.

Grigson, C. (1998). Plough and pasture in the early economy of the southern Levant. In T. E. Levy (ed.), *The Archaeology of Society in the Holy Land.* London: Leicester University Press, 245–68.

—— (2006). Farming? Feasting? Herding? Large mammals from the Chalcolithic of Gilat. In Levy (2006: 215–319).

Key, C. A. (1980). Trace element composition of the copper and copper alloys of the Nahal Mishmar Hoard. In P. Bar-Adon (ed.), *The Cave of the Treasure: The Finds from the Caves in Naḥal Mishmar,* trans. I. Pommerantz. Jerusalem: Israel Exploration Society, 238–43.

Levy, T. E. (1983). The emergence of specialized pastoralism in the southern Levant. *World Archaeology* 15: 15–36.

—— (ed.) (1987). *Shiqmim I: Studies Concerning Chalcolithic Societies in the Northern Negev Desert, Israel (1982–1984)* (2 vols). Oxford: British Archaeological Reports.

—— (1992). Transhumance, subsistence, and social evolution. In O. Bar-Yosef and A. M. Khazanov (eds), *Pastoralism in the Levant: Archaeological Materials in Anthropological Perspectives.* Madison, Wis.: Prehistory, 65–82.

—— (1998). Cult, metallurgy and rank societies: Chalcolithic period (ca. 4500–3500 BCE). In T. E. Levy (ed.), *The Archaeology of Society in the Holy Land.* London: Leicester University Press, 226–44.

—— (ed.) (2006). *Archaeology, Anthropology and Cult: The Sanctuary at Gilat, Israel.* London: Equinox.

—— M. Burton, and Y. M. Rowan (2006). Chalcolithic hamlet excavations near Shiqmim, Negev Desert, Israel. *Journal of Field Archaeology* 31: 41–60.

—— W. Conner, Y. M. Rowan, and D. Alon (2006). The intensification of production at Gilat: textile production. In Levy (2006: 705–38).

——C. Grigson, A. Holl, P. Goldberg, Y. M. Rowan, and P. Smith (1991). Subterranean settlement and adaptation in the Negev Desert, ca. 4500–3700 BC. *National Geographic Research and Exploration* 7: 394–413.

——and S. Shalev (1989). Prehistoric metalworking in the southern Levant: archaeometallurgy and social perspectives. *World Archaeology* 20: 353–72.

Lovell, J. L. (2001). *The Late Neolithic and Chalcolithic Periods in the Southern Levant: New Data from the Site of Teleilat Ghassul, Jordan*. Oxford: Archaeopress.

Neuville, R. (1930). Notes de préhistoire palestinienne II. *Journal of the Palestine Oriental Society* 10: 193–221.

Perrot, J. (1955). The excavations at Tell Abu Matar, near Beersheba. *Israel Exploration Journal* 5: 17–41, 73–84, 167–89.

Perrot, J., and D. Ladiray (1980). *Tombes à ossuaires de la région côtière palestinienne au IVe millénaire avant l'ère chrétienne*. Paris: Association Paléorient/Jerusalem: Centre de recherches préhistoriques français de Jérusalem.

Philip, G., and O. Williams-Thorpe (1993). A provenance study of Jordanian basalt vessels of the Chalcolithic and Early Bronze Age I periods. *Paléorient* 19: 51–63.

Potazkin, R., and K. Bar-Avi (1980). A material investigation of metal objects from the Nahal Mishmar Hoard. In P. Bar-Adon (ed.), *The Cave of the Treasure: The Finds from the Caves in Nahal Mishmar*, trans. I. Pommerantz. Jerusalem: Israel Exploration Society, 235–7.

Rosen, A. M. (1987). Phytolith studies at Shiqmim. In Levy (1987: 243–9).

Rowan, Y. M., and J. M. Golden (2009). The Chalcolithic period of the southern Levant: a synthetic review. *Journal of World Prehistory* 22: 1–92.

—— and D. Ilan (2007). The meaning of ritual diversity in the Chalcolithic of the southern Levant. In D. A. Barrowclough and C. Malone (eds), *Cult in Context: Reconsidering Ritual in Archaeology*. Oxford: Oxbow, 249–56.

——T. E. Levy, D. Alon, and Y. Goren (2006). Gilat's ground stone assemblage: stone fenestrated stands, bowls, palettes and related artifacts. In Levy (2006: 575–684).

Schick, T. (ed.) (1998). *The Cave of the Warrior: A Fourth Millennium Burial in the Judean Desert*. Jerusalem: Israel Antiquities Authority.

Shalev, S., Y. Goren, T. E. Levy, and J. P. Northover (1992). A Chalcolithic mace head from the Negev, Israel: technological aspects and cultural implications. *Archaeometry* 34: 63–71.

—— and J. P. Northover (1987). The Chalcolithic metal and metalworking from Shiqmim. In Levy (1987: 357–71).

Sherratt, A. (1981). Plough and pastoralism: aspects of the secondary products revolution. In I. Hodder, G. L. Isaac, and N. Hammond (eds), *Patterns of the Past: Studies in Honour of David Clarke*. Cambridge: Cambridge University Press, 261–305.

Tadmor, M., D. Kedem, F. Begemann, A. Hauptmann, E. Pernicka, and S. Schmitt-Strecker (1995). The Nahal Mishmar Hoard from the Judean Desert: technology, composition, and provenance. *'Atiqot* 27: 95–148.

Ussishkin, D. (1980). The Ghassulian shrine at En Gedi. *Tel Aviv* 7: 1–44.

van den Brink, E. C. M., and R. Gophna (2005). *Shoham (North): Late Chalcolithic Burial Caves in the Lod Valley, Israel*. Israel Antiquities Authority Reports 27. Jerusalem: Israel Antiquities Authority.

van den Brink, E. C. M., Y. M. Rowan, and E. Braun (1999). Pedestalled Basalt Bowls of the Chalcolithic: new variations. *Israel Exploration Journal* 49: 161–83.

Yellin, J., T. E. Levy, and Y. M. Rowan (1996). New evidence on prehistoric trade routes: the Obsidian evidence from Gilat, Israel. *Journal of Field Archaeology* 23: 361–8.

CHAPTER 17

THE SOUTHERN LEVANT (TRANSJORDAN) DURING THE CHALCOLITHIC PERIOD

Jordan (c.4500–3500 BC)

ZEIDAN A. KAFAFI

INTRODUCTION

Chalcolithic archaeological remains in Jordan were first identified accidentally during a search for the 'five lost cities' of the Bible in the 1920s by researchers of the Pontifical Biblical Institute in Jerusalem. This search led them to a group of low mounds named Teleilat el-Ghassul about five kilometres to the northeast of the Dead Sea. Since excavations there, other sites of the same cultural sphere have been discovered.

Most scholars agree that during the second half of the fifth millennium BC the whole of the southern Levant witnessed both a continuation of Neolithic cultural elements and the appearance of new villages with a new archaeological culture, and changes in the type of settlement patterns and economy. Although some of the Late Neolithic sites continued to be occupied from the Late Neolithic to the Chalcolithic, the Chalcolithic's mixed farming communities reached the semi-arid environmental zones—unlike the Late Neolithic settlements, which are located primarily in areas very close to water resources (Levy 1995: 229).

Many earlier scholars (e.g. Kenyon 1960: 70; de Vaux 1966) considered these cultural changes to arise from newcomers originating in Jordan. Perrot (1978) suggested that parts of these cultural developments were local, and Hennessy, on the basis of his excavations at Teleilat el-Ghassul and Tabqat Fahil, agreed with the model of local development.

It is often difficult to distinguish the type of life practised by the farming communities assigned to the Late Neolithic from those of the Chalcolithic. In order to establish a more

precise understanding of the Chalcolithic culture in Jordan, more research should be conducted covering broader geographic regions, beyond the Jordan Valley sites. Archaeological
Surveys and excavations in the vicinity of 'Aqaba have shed new light on the archaeology
of south Jordan during the fourth millennium BC (Khalil and Eichmann 1999; 2001). On
the basis of the metallurgical studies conducted in the Wadi Feinan and 'Aqaba areas, it has
been deduced that the inhabitants mined and traded copper (Hauptmann 2000; Khalil and
Riederer 1998) although precise dating to the Chalcolithic remains problematic. However,
the dates of c.4500–3500 BC are the most acceptable for the Chalcolithic period in Jordan
(Levy 1995).

SITES AND SETTINGS

Chalcolithic settlements are found throughout Jordan (Fig. 17.1), but archaeological surveys indicate a concentration of Chalcolithic habitation in the Jordan Valley (Mellaart
1956; Kafafi 1982; Gustavson-Gaube 1986; Helms 1987; 1989; Kareem 1989; Leonard
1989; McNicoll, Edwards, and Hanbury-Tenison 1992; Bourke et al. 1994; 1995; Bourke,
McLaren, and Mairs 1998), possibly related to floodwater management strategies for agricultural purposes. It may, however, also reflect the small number of archaeological projects
outside the Jordan Valley. The settlement on the plateaus and uplands are concentrated primarily along wadis and close to permanent water resources (Mabry and Palumbo 1988;
1992; Kafafi and Vieweger 2000); smaller sites were found along the upper part of the wadi
system (Bourke 2001: 113). Chalcolithic inhabitants of the plateaus practised pastoralism
in addition to agriculture, perhaps reflecting environmental factors. A good example of this
is the site of Abu Snesleh, located in the steppe region (Lehmann et al. 1991; Kerner 1992;
Lamprichs 1998). Excavations and surveys in the regions bordering the Jordan Valley, east
of the Dead Sea and in the Wadi Araba, such as Wadi az-Zarqa, Wadi Feinan, Wadi Fidan,
and 'Aqaba, produced various settlement types (Najjar et al. 1990; 'Amr et al. 1993; 1996;
Caneva et al. 2001). In the Jordan Valley, Abu Hamid (c.10ha) (Dollfus and Kafafi 1986;
1988) and Teleilat el-Ghassul (c.20ha) represent the emergence of centres which coordinated social, economic, and religious activities. The site of Teleilat el-Ghassul is characterized as a planned village (Mallon, Koeppel, and Neuville 1934).

The Wadi el-Hasa Survey produced several fourth-millennium sites (MacDonald 1988:
131). Many were described as sherd and lithic scatters, while only a few showed architectural features. Several Chalcolithic sites, including Chalcolithic mining areas at various sites,
were uncovered in the Feinan region (Hauptmann 2000: 122). However, these sites may be
assigned to the latest phase of the Chalcolithic and predominantly the Early Bronze Age.

The Ras en-Naqab Survey (Henry 1992) produced many sites attributed to the
Chalcolithic culture; only two of them (Jebel el-Jill Site J14 and Jebel Queisa Site J24)
yielded (curvilinear) structures. The analysis of the faunal remains indicates a nomadic
pastoralist economy (Henry 1995: 353–74). The excavation of Tell Magass revealed rectangular stone structures (Khalil 1987; 1992; 1995), pottery vessels such as bowls, basins,
and jars, and flint tools. Metallurgical studies of copper found at Magass showed that the
copper ores originate in Timna, on the other side of Wadi 'Arabah (Khalil and Eichmann

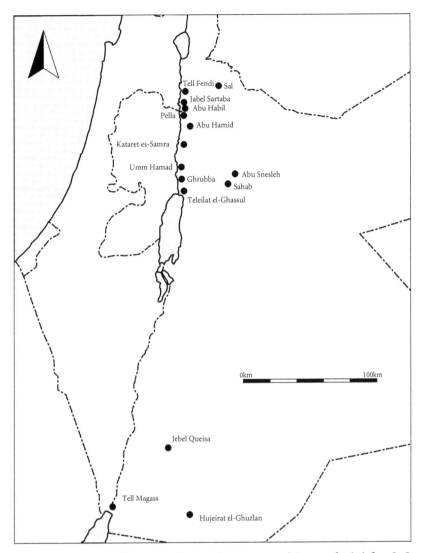

FIG. 17.1 Map of Chalcolithic sites in the southern Levant (Transjordan) (after S. Savage)

1999: 518). Unfortunately, we have little information about Chalcolithic settlements in the Badia area.

ARCHITECTURE

In Jordan during the Chalcolithic period, houses were built either of mud-bricks or stones. Some of these buildings are described as domestic houses and others as ritual structures. In addition, cave dwellings are registered, such as those at Sahab. A study of the architectural remains excavated in Jordan is presented below.

Residential constructions

Rectangular houses

Many rectangular buildings, some of which may have been used for residential purposes, were uncovered at the sites of Abu Hamid (Fig. 17.2), Teleilat el-Ghassul, and Jabel Sartaba, three kilometres east of Pella. The rectangular houses excavated at Teleilat el-Ghassul consisted of rooms surrounding a courtyard. These houses were built of mud-bricks laid directly over the land surface. In some cases foundation trenches were dug; in others, one or two rows of undressed stones served as foundations for the buildings. The roofs were made of a layer of reeds covered by another layer of mud (Hennessy 1969: 5). The floors of the rooms were made of either beaten earth or plaster. The courtyard was made to accommodate the activities of daily life. Several types of pits with different functions and *tabouns* (bread ovens) were excavated in the courtyard.

At Abu Hamid, different types of architecture and building techniques were identified (Dollfus et al. 1988). Generally, a house here consisted of a roofed broadroom with an attached open or partially roofed courtyard. The houses were assembled around larger open or public spaces (Bourke 2001: 120). Also, several types of pits for storage and firing were dug into areas adjacent to the houses.

Rounded architectural stone features (platforms) in connection with rectangular houses have been noticed at the sites of Abu Hamid and Teleilat el-Ghassul, measuring 1m–2m in diameter. Some have a pit dug into the centre. Hennessy argues that this kind of feature might have been used for dying purposes (1969: 7).

FIG. 17.2 Excavated structures at Abu Hamid

Apsidal houses

This type of building is usually rectangular in shape, with short, curved walls. In Jordan only one example, made of mud-brick, was excavated at Teleilat el-Ghassul (Hennessy 1969: 7), but it was found at Palestinian sites as well, such as Sheikh Meser. This kind of building started during the sixth millennium and became very common during the third millennium BC.

Cave dwellings

In the fourth millennium BC the inhabitants of the southern Levant lived part of the year in caves. Examples of this were recorded at Sahab and Wadi Hisma in Jordan. At Sahab, the caves were connected with built houses and had plastered floors with a wall built in front of the entrance (Ibrahim 1989).

Ritual buildings

In spite of the large number of fourth-millennium sites excavated in Jordan, only one example of a ritual building has been found, at Teleilat el-Ghassul. This building has a rectangular shape similar to the building excavated at 'Ein Gedi on the western shore of the Dead Sea. A single ^{14}C date of 3700 BC has been obtained from the Teleilat el-Ghassul temple building (Hennessy 1982: 56).

BURIAL CUSTOMS

Burial customs during the fourth millennium BC in the southern part of the Levant differed from one region to another. Infant burials excavated at Abu Hamid and Teleilat el-Ghassul show that the deceased child was put inside a jar and buried in one corner of the house (Mallon, Koeppel, and Neuville 1934: 48–50, pl. 25). Unfortunately, no adult burials were uncovered at the site of Abu Hamid, but a few were excavated at Teleilat el-Ghassul (Hennessy 1969: 7, pl. VIIa).

First, it has been argued—on the basis of archaeological excavations conducted in the south of the Levant—that adult burials may only be found outside residential areas (Levy and Alon 1982). Nevertheless, recent excavations conducted at Shiqmim, Gilat, Gerar, and other sites in the Neqab contradict this (Rowan, Ch. 16 above).

TOOLS AND OBJECTS OF DAILY USE

Clay vessels

The pottery assemblage of the Chalcolithic shows that new types of pottery vessels were manufactured during this period (Fig. 17.3). New decorative motifs were used such as painted decorations, which consisted of red bands, geometrical designs, and red lines. Incised decorations also occurred on fourth-millennium pottery sherds and consisted of

FIG. 17.3 Pottery vessels excavated at Abu Hamid (photograph Yousef Zubi)

diagonal, parallel, and wavy lines without much recognizable structure, applied to the pot while it was leather-hard and prior to firing. Applied decorations, such as rope-moulding decorated with thumb indentations, nail impressions, and reed impressions forming crescent shapes, were found (Amiran 1969).

Chalcolithic potters used pits to fire their pots, as evidenced at Abu Hamid. These pits mostly had round openings and were 0.5–1.0m deep. No kilns dated to the fourth millennium BC have been encountered in Jordan.

Manufacturing techniques for clay vessels included handmade 'coiling' and slow-wheel techniques or turning, as on the small V-shaped bowls excavated at Abu Hamid (Roux and Courty 1997). The most popular vessel types are cornets, cups, bowls, small jars, hole-mouth jars, large jars, fenestrated bowls, spoons, and churns (Amiran 1969). Although churns and cornets are common, they do not appear at all sites.

Archaeologists assume that during the fifth and fourth millennia BC craftsmanship evolved and specialization developed. Kerner (1997; 2001) defines specialization as 'a regularized and permanent production system in which consumers and producers are dependent on each other'.

Metal objects

Smelting and smithing of metals started in the Near East as early as the fifth millennium BC. The most notable example is the collection of copper objects found in a cave in Nahal Mishmar, to the west of the Dead Sea. Only a few everyday copper objects have been uncovered at sites in Jordan (e.g. Teleilat el-Ghassul and Abu Hamid). Good-quality copper ores are quite abundant on both sides of Wadi Araba (Hauptmann 2000), and miners' settlements were found in the region such as Fidan 4, dated to the Early Bronze Age. Although several

Late Chalcolithic/Early Bronze Age sites were excavated in the southern part of Jordan, such as Magass and Hujeirat el-Ghuzlan, no Chalcolithic mining camps were found inside the mining area. So it seems that during the Late Chalcolithic people used to mine copper from the surface or from shallow pits and then leave. It was only during the Early Bronze Age that people stayed in the mining area to practise smelting directly near the main source.

Bone tools

No ivory figurines like those found at sites near Beer es-Saba' (Perrot 1959) have been recovered in Jordan. But pointed bone objects as needles and piercers as well as bone jewellery were found (Mallon, Koeppel, and Neuville 1934: 77, 79, pls 30, 31; Dollfus and Kafafi 1993: 251; fig. 3).

Stone tools and vessels

Flint tools

The flint tool assemblages excavated in the Chalcolithic levels of Jordan include several types of tools such as picks, adzes, chisels, blades, sickle blades, piercers, scrapers, and, rarely, arrowheads. Most of these served an agricultural purpose and were used for wood cutting. Hunting did not play a large role in subsistence as in earlier periods. The presence of the sickle blades does not mean that they were only used for reaping domesticated crops; they may have also been used to cut wild plants (see Coqueugniot 1988).

Perforated discs were usually made of a tabular flint, and have different shapes: rounded, elliptical, crescent, and star-shaped. The function of this type of tool is still obscure; it has been proposed that it was used to treat sheep wool to prepare it for weaving.

Grinding stones

A large number of grinding stones was uncovered in Jordan. Most of these were made of basalt, but some were made of limestone, calcite, or sandstone. Several types have been recognized such as hand stones (*manos*) and grinding slabs (*metates*), and mortars and pestles (Wright and Qadi 1988).

Fenestrated bowls

This vessel type consists of two parts: the upper part is a bowl, while the lower part consists of a high fenestrated stand. Some archaeologists argue that this form of vessel may have been used for ritual purposes (Rowan, Ch. 16 above) as an incense-burner. These stone items are usually made of basalt, although analogous forms in limestone and clay are also known.

Mace-heads

Groups of mace-heads dated to the fourth millennium BC were found at Abu Hamid, Teleilat Ghassul, and Bab edh-Dhra'. They are rounded, elliptical, or pear-shaped and made of calcite, alabaster, or basalt. There is some doubt that these objects were used as weapons.

Basalt stands

These were encountered for the first time in the Golan Heights (Epstein 1977). These stands are pillar-shaped, reaching up to a height of half a metre, with the top shaped to form a bowl. Below the rim of the bowl, most pillars show stylized human or animal features such as a nose, beard, or eyes in high relief. Basalt stands (different in style) have also been found in the northern part of Jordan (e.g. the village of Sal).

Basketry and weaving

Although no baskets or cloth remains have been found in Jordan (due to the perishable nature of the material), evidence of this kind of manufacture has been noted. Mat impressions are visible on the bases of some pottery vessels, and spindle whorls are found in large quantities at fourth-millennium BC sites (Dollfus et al. 1988: 581; Vaillant 1988: 44–6).

ART

Small figurines of humans and animals made of clay were found at most of the Chalcolithic sites in Jordan. At Abu Hamid a large number of animal figurines dated to the fifth and fourth millennia BC were excavated in pits in the middle levels. Some were complete, others unfinished, and lumps of clay were found very close to them, showing that they had been made on site (Dollfus and Kafafi 1995). Limestone or green stones in the shape of a violin are thought to represent human figurines and are considered one of the Chalcolithic's typical items. These were found at Abu Hamid and Teleilat el-Ghassul.

At Abu Hamid a clay vessel in the shape of a laden animal was recovered, representing either a ram or a bull with a pot on its back (Fig. 17.4). The function of such a vessel is still unclear, but some scholars argue that it could have a ritual purpose (Alon 1976; Alon and Levy 1989).

In 1992, fragments of wall paintings were found at the site of Abu Hamid, dating to the late fifth millennium BC (Dollfus and Kafafi 1993). The design is linear with broad straight lines (yellow and red) intersected by a series of thinner red vertical and curved lines. Fresco paintings of the fourth millennium BC were first found at Teleilat el-Ghassul, showing stylized human and animal representations, stars, and geometrical designs (Fig. 17.5). The frescoes depict ceremonial processions, mythical figures, and strange animals (Mallon, Koeppel, and Neuville 1934: pls 66–71; Koeppel 1940: pls 5–8; Elliot 1977; Cameron 1981).

CHALCOLITHIC SHRINES
AND CULT OBJECTS IN JORDAN

The archaeology of religion is a difficult and challenging subject, since the material remains of ancient cults, especially from the prehistoric periods, are often very few. The paucity of Jordanian sanctuary sites with associated *in situ* artefacts means that little is known about the role of cult in the Chalcolithic societies of Jordan. However, through the study of site

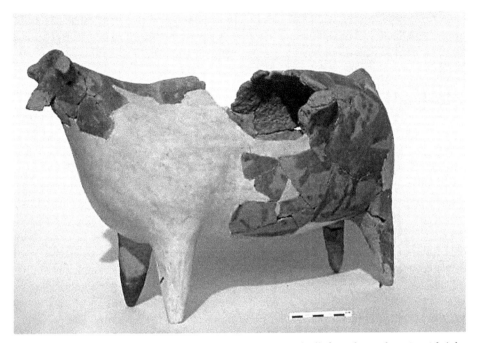

FIG. 17.4 A clay vessel representing either a ram or a bull found at Abu Hamid (photograph Yousef Zubi)

FIG. 17.5 Fresco painting from Teleilat el-Ghassul (after the catalogue of the exhibition 'Faces of the Orient: 10,000 Years of Art and Culture from Jordan', Altes Museum, Berlin, October 2004)

architecture, especially at Teleilat el-Ghassul, in conjunction with a wide range of portable objects from the key Chalcolithic sites in Jordan, such as Abu Hamid, it has been possible to answer some of the questions regarding cult during the Chalcolithic period in Jordan.

Cult/ritual buildings

In spite of the large number of excavated and surveyed Chalcolithic sites in Jordan and Palestine, only a few yielded structures identified as public sanctuaries (cf. Rowan, Ch. 16 above; Levy 1995: 235) or shrines (Gonen 1992: 63).

At Teleilat el-Ghassul, Hennessy uncovered two buildings in a mound (Area E) described as sanctuaries (Hennessy 1982: 56). The buildings were enclosed by stone and mud-brick walls at the northern and western sides, and are similar in layout to the one at 'Ein Gedi. Hennessy argues that both buildings appeared to have been in use for some time, as evidenced by resurfaced floors. The existence of cultic buildings in Teleilat el-Ghassul might also be reinforced by the results of the earlier excavations, where spectacular, prominent wall frescoes have been found. The walls of the two buildings mentioned above are one metre thick and are composed of an outer line of heavy boulders, lined with two rows of mud-brick, and an inner face of smaller stones. It seems that the floors and walls were plastered and painted (Hennessy 1982: 56). One of the two buildings also had a series of wall paintings. Benches lined the south wall of the so-called Sanctuary B, and a wide platform built outside the central doorway was noted. The doorways of both buildings opened onto a shallow stone step leading down to a sunken floor. Inside the buildings, cult vessels and clay figurines were found.

At the other excavated Chalcolithic sites in Jordan (e.g. Jebel Sartaba and Abu Hamid), no cultic buildings were discovered. However, many portable objects and art items such as human and animal figurines, laden animals, fresco painting, basalt pillars, and fenestrated bowls and cornets, although not excavated in a clearly sacred context, suggest cult significance in their form and motifs (cf. Rowan, Ch. 16 above).

Although the scant evidence excavated at Jordanian sites cannot help in providing a clear picture of the religious practices during the fourth millennium BC, it demonstrates the possibility of a common iconographic vocabulary or belief system in all regions in the south of the Levant. This is evidenced by the widespread distribution of the violin figurines and the common decorated motifs of the basalt pillars.

SUBSISTENCE ECONOMY

Archaeological excavations at Chalcolithic sites in Jordan produced considerable evidence for horticulture, especially during the last phase of the Chalcolithic period. Olive harvesting seems to have been practised in the Jordan Valley and the hilly regions of Jordan. Remains of olive trees and olive stones were excavated at Teleilat el-Ghassul, Tell Abu Hamid (Neef 1988), and in the Golan Heights (Epstein 1977). Those from Teleilat el-Ghassul may have been grown under irrigated conditions (Zohary and Spiegel-Roy 1975). Floodwater irrigation systems are well documented during the Chalcolithic in the Negev (Levy 1995: 230).

In addition, with the expansion of the Chalcolithic settlements into the arid lands of Jordan such as the Jordan Valley and to the south, new developments in agrotechnology might have been started. The well-known flint chisel, thought to have been made for cutting wood, might also have been used for ploughing or digging irrigation channels. By the latest phase of the Chalcolithic, deep ploughing appeared in the Jordanian hilly areas, as attested at Wadi Qattar to the east of Amman ('Amr et al. 1993). This was possible after the domestication of the donkey, as has been well documented by Late Chalcolithic clay models (Epstein 1985; Grigson 1995). In general, cereals, legumes, and fruits were produced as food.

Faunal remains, found at Abu Hamid, suggest that pigs constituted the largest portion of animals consumed during the Chalcolithic. But other sites such as Shuna, Pella, and Snesleh show a very different picture. The main food animals recognized at these sites were cattle, ovicaprines, and pigs. The study of Abu Hamid's animal bones indicated that pigs were slaughtered when very young, while ovicaprines and cattle were kept for a longer time. This has been explained as an implied emphasis on ovicaprine and cattle milk production (Dollfus and Kafafi 1986; Dollfus et al. 1988). The same age-class harvest pattern was also recognized at the Late Chalcolithic levels in Tabaqat Fahl and Teleilat el-Ghassul (Bourke 2001: 118).

Evidence of herding activities is available at most Chalcolithic sites. At Abu Hamid, winter pasturing at some distance from the main site suggests the existence of a well-established pastoral component during the beginning of the fourth millennium (Dollfus and Kafafi 1988: 28).

Recent publications of the archaeozoological remains from Teleilat el-Ghassul indicate that there is a marked change between the Late Neolithic and the beginning of the Chalcolithic. During the Late Neolithic, cattle were predominant; sheep and goats were secondary, never exceeding 40 per cent of the meat consumed (Mairs 1995). The same study shows that there is a dramatic increase in aged cattle from the beginning of the Chalcolithic, suggesting they were preserved for reasons of protein efficiency. Also, the percentage of sheep and goats declined from 40 per cent during the Late Neolithic to less than 20 per cent at the beginning of the Chalcolithic (Lovell 2001: 16).

More recently, excavations at Wadi Feinan, Wadi Fidan and Magass produced a new insight into the organization of the Chalcolithic inhabitants of Jordan. Despite the fact that the most notable example of copper metal objects from the south of the Levant was found at Nahal Mishmar on the western shore of the Dead Sea, copper-working was clearly significant at Wadi Feinan and Magass in Jordan.

Finally, craft specialization is the hallmark of the societies of the Chalcolithic period in southern Levant. Farmers, herders, copper metalworking specialists, potters, flint knappers, sculptors, painters, and jewellery makers were the handworkers who lived in the Levant during the fourth millennium BC (Kerner 2001).

SUGGESTED READING

Bourke, S. J. (1997). The 'pre-Ghassulian' sequence at Teleilat Ghassul: Sydney University excavations 1975–1995. In H.-G. K. Gebel, Z. A. Kafafi, and G. O. Rollefson (eds), *The Prehistory of Jordan II: Perspectives from 1997*. Berlin: Ex oriente, 395–417.

——(2001). The Chalcolithic period. In B. MacDonald, R. Adams, and P. Bienkowski (eds), *The Archaeology of Jordan*. Sheffield: Sheffield Academic, 107–62.

Dollfus, G., and Z. A. Kafafi (2001). Jordan in the fourth millennium. In *Studies in the History and Archaeology of Jordan VII*. Amman: Department of Antiquities of Jordan, 163–72.

Kerner, S. (2001). *Das Chalkolithikum in der südlichen Levante: die Entwicklung handwerklicher Spezialisierung und ihre Beziehung zu gesellschaftlicher Komplexität*. Rahden: Leidorf.

Lovell, J. L. (2001). *The Late Neolithic and Chalcolithic Periods in the Southern Levant: New Data from the Site of Teleilat Ghassul, Jordan*. Oxford: Archaeopress.

References

Alon, D. (1976). The cult vessels from Gilat. *'Atiqot* 11: 116–18.

—— and T. E. Levy (1989). The archaeology of cult and the Chalcolithic sanctuary at Gilat. *Journal of Mediterranean Archaeology* 2: 163–221.

Amiran, R. (1969). *Ancient Pottery of the Holy Land: From Its Beginnings in the Neolithic Period to the End of the Iron Age*. Jerusalem: Massada Press.

'Amr, K., M. Najjar, S. Kerner, K. Reilly, and D. W. McCreery (1993). Wadi al-Qattar salvage excavation 1989. *Annual of the Department of Antiquities of Jordan* 37: 263–78.

—— K. Hamdan, S. Helms, and L. Mohamadieh (1996). Archaeological survey of the east coast of the Dead Sea, phase I: Suwayma, az-Zara and Umm Sidra. *Annual of the Department of Antiquities of Jordan* 40: 429–49.

Bourke, S. J. (2001). The Chalcolithic period. In B. MacDonald, R. Adams, and P. Bienkowski (eds), *The Archaeology of Jordan*. Sheffield: Sheffield Academic, 107–62.

—— P. L. Seaton, R. T. Sparks, J. L. Lovell, and L. D. Mairs (1995). Preliminary report on a first season of renewal excavations at Teleilat Ghassul by the University of Sydney, 1994. *Annual of the Department of Antiquities of Jordan* 39: 31–64.

—— R. T. Sparks, K. N. Sowada, and L. D. Mairs (1994). Preliminary report on the fourteenth season of excavation by the University of Sydney at Pella in Jordan. *Annual of the Department of Antiquities of Jordan* 38: 81–126.

—— P. B. McLaren, and L. D. Mairs (1998). Preliminary report on the University of Sydney's sixteenth and seventeenth seasons of excavations at Pella (Tabaqat Fahl) in 1994/1995. *Annual of the Department of Antiquities of Jordan* 42: 179–213.

Cameron, D. O. (1981). *The Ghassulian Wall-Paintings*. London: Kenyon-Deane.

Caneva, I., M. Hatamleh, Z. A. Kafafi, et al. (2001). The Wadi az-Zarqa'/Wadi ad-Dulayl archaeological project: report on the 1997 and 1999 fieldwork seasons. *Annual of the Department of Antiquities of Jordan* 45: 83–119.

Coqueugniot, E. (1988). Preliminary study of the flint industry from Abu Hamid. In Dollfus and Kafafi (1988: 39–43).

de Vaux, R. (1966). Palestine during the Neolithic and Chalcolithic periods. In I. E. S. Edwards, C. J. Gadd, and N. G. L. Hammond (eds), *Cambridge Ancient History*, vol. 1, pt 2. Cambridge: Cambridge University Press, 498–520.

Dollfus, G., and Z. A. Kafafi (1986). Abu Hamid, Jordanie: premiers résultats. *Paléorient* 12: 91–100.

—— (eds) (1988). *Abu Hamid: Village du 4e millénaire de la Vallée du Jordanie*. Amman: French Cultural Centre/Department of Antiquities of Jordan.

—— (1993). Recent researches at Abu Hamid. *Annual of the Department of Antiquities of Jordan* 37: 241–63.

—— (1995). Représentations humaines et animales sur le site d'Abu Hamid (milieu du VIIème–début du VIème millénaire av. JC). In K. 'Amr, F. Zayadine, and M. Zaghlul (eds), *Studies in the History and Archaeology of Jordan V*. Amman: Department of Antiquities, 437–49.

—— J. Rewerski, A. N. Garrard, and H.-G. K. Gebel (1988). Abu Hamid, an early fourth millennium site in the Jordan Valley. In A. N. Garrard and H.-G. K. Gebel (eds), *The Prehistory of Jordan: The State of Research in 1986*, vol. 1. Oxford: British Archaeological Reports, 567–601.

Elliot, C. (1977). The religious beliefs of the Ghassulians, 4000–3100 BC. *Palestine Exploration Quarterly* 109: 3–25.

Epstein, C. (1977). The Chalcolithic culture of the Golan. *Biblical Archaeologist* 40/2: 57–62.

—— (1985). Laden animal figurines from the Chalcolithic Period in Palestine. *Bulletin of the American Schools of Oriental Research* 258: 53–62.

Gonen, R. (1992). The Chalcolithic period. In A. Ben-Tor (ed.), *The Archaeology of Ancient Israel*. New Haven, Conn.: Yale University Press/Tel Aviv: Open University of Israel, 40–80.

Grigson, C. (1995). Plough and pasture in the early economy of the southern Levant. In T. E. Levy (ed.), *Archaeology of Society in the Holy Land*. London: Leicester University Press, 245–68.

Gustavson-Gaube, C. (1986). Tall ash-Shuna North 1984–85. *Archiv für Orientforschung* 31: 283–6.

Hauptmann, A. (2000). *Zur frühen Metallurgie des Kupfers in Fenan/Jordanien*. Bochum: Deutsches Bergbau-Museum.

Helms, S. W. (1987). Jawa, Tell Umm Hammad and the EBI/Late Chalcolithic landscape. *Levant* 19: 49–81.

—— (1989). 'Um Hammad (Tell). In D. Homès-Fredricq and J. B. Hennessy (eds), *Archaeology of Jordan II, 2: Field Reports—Sites L–Z*. Leuven: Peeters, 581–9.

Hennessy, J. B. (1969). Preliminary report on a first season of excavation at Teleilat Ghassul. *Levant* 1: 1–24.

—— (1982). Teleilat Ghassul: its place in the archaeology of Jordan. In A. Hadidi (ed.), *Studies in the History and Archaeology of Jordan*. Amman: Department of Antiquities, 55–8.

Henry, D. O. (1992). Seasonal movements of fourth millennium pastoral nomads in Wadi Hisma. In M. Zaghloul, K. 'Amr, F. Zayadine, R. Nabeel, and N. R. Tawfiq (eds), *Studies in the History and Archaeology of Jordan IV*. Amman: Department of Antiquities of Jordan, 137–43.

—— (1995). *Prehistoric Cultural Ecology and Evolution: Insights from Southern Jordan*. New York: Plenum.

Ibrahim, M. (1989). Sahab. In D. Homès-Fredricq and J. B. Hennessy (eds), *Archaeology of Jordan II, 2: Field Reports—Sites L–Z*. Leuven: Peeters, 516–20.

Kafafi, Z. A. (1982). *The Neolithic of Jordan (East Bank)*. PhD dissertation, Freie Universität Berlin.

—— and D. Vieweger (2000). Geoelectric and archaeological work at Sal, Jordan: a preliminary report on the 1999 season at the Chalcolithic and Early Bronze Age site. *Annual of the Department of Antiquities of Jordan* 44: 173–92.

Kareem, J. (1989). Tell Fendi: Jisr Sheikh Hussein Project, 1986. *Annual of the Department of Antiquities of Jordan* 38: 97–109.

Kenyon, K. M. (1960). *Archaeology of the Holy Land*. New York: Praeger.

Kerner, S. (1992). Excavations in Abu Snesleh: Middle Bronze Age and Chalcolithic architecture in central Jordan. In S. Kerner (ed.), *The Near East in Antiquity: German Contributions to the Archaeology of Jordan, Palestine, Syria, Lebanon, and Egypt*. Amman: Goethe-Institut/Al Kutba Publishers, 43–54.

—— (1997). Specialization in the Chalcolithic in the southern Levant. In H.-G. K. Gebel, Z. A. Kafafi, and G. O. Rollefson (eds), *The Prehistory of Jordan II: Perspectives from 1997*. Berlin: Ex oriente, 419–29.

—— (2001). *Das Chalkolithikum in der südlichen Levante: die Entwicklung handwerklicher Spezialisierung und ihre Beziehung zu gesellschaftlicher Komplexität*. Rahden: Leidorf.

Khalil, L. A. (1987). Preliminary report on the 1985 excavation at el-Magass-Aqaba. *Annual of the Department of Antiquities of Jordan* 31: 481–5.

—— (1992). Some technological features from a Chalcolithic site at Magass-Aqaba. In *Studies in the History and Archaeology of Jordan IV*. Amman: Department of Antiquities of Jordan, 143–8.

—— (1995). A second season of excavations at Al-Magass-Aqaba, 1990. *Annual of the Department of Antiquities of Jordan* 39: 65–79.

—— and R. Eichmann (1999). Archaeological survey and excavation at Wadi al-Yutum and Tall Al-Magass area–'Aqaba (ASEYM): a preliminary report on the first season in 1998. *Annual of the Department of Antiquities of Jordan* 43: 501–20.

—— (2001). Archaeological survey and excavation at the Wadi Al-Yutum and Magass area–Al-'Aqaba (ASEYM): a preliminary report on the second season in 2000. *Annual of the Department of Antiquities of Jordan* 45: 195–204.

—— and J. Riederer (1998). Examination of copper metallurgical remains from a Chalcolithic site at Tall al-Magass, Jordan. *Damaszener Mitteilungen* 10: 1–9.

Koeppel, R. (1940). *Teleilat Ghassul II: compte rendu des fouilles de l'Institut biblique pontifical 1932–36*. Rome: Institut biblique pontifical.

Lamprichs, R. (1998). *Abu Snesleh: Ergebnisse der Ausgrabungen 1990 und 1992—Einfuehrung, Stratigraphie, Architektur*. Rahden: Leidorf.

Lehmann, G., R. Lamprichs, S. Kerner, and R. Bernbeck (1991). The 1990 excavations at Abu Snesleh: preliminary report. *Annual of the Department of Antiquities of Jordan* 35: 41–65.

Leonard, A., Jr (1989). A Chalcolithic Fine Ware from Kataret es-Samra in the Jordan Valley. *Bulletin of the American Schools of Oriental Research* 276: 3–14.

Levy, T. E. (1995). Cult, metallurgy and rank societies, Chalcolithic period (ca. 4500–3200 BC). In T. E. Levy (ed.), *The Archaeology of Society in the Holy Land*. New York: Facts on File, 226–44.

—— and D. Alon (1982). The Chalcolithic mortuary sites near Mezad Aluf, northern Negev Desert: a preliminary study. *Bulletin of the American Schools of Oriental Research* 248: 37–59.

Lovell, J. L. (2001). *The Late Neolithic and Chalcolithic Periods in the Southern Levant: New Data from the Site Teleilat Ghassul, Jordan*. Oxford: British Archaeological Reports.

Mabry, J., and G. Palumbo (1988). The 1987 Wadi el-Yabis survey. *Annual of the Department of Antiquities of Jordan* 32: 275–305.

—— (1992). Environmental, economic, and political constraints on ancient settlement patterns in the Wadi el-Yabis region. In *Studies in the History and Archaeology of Jordan, IV*. Amman: Department of Antiquities of Jordan, 67–72.

MacDonald, B. (1988). *The Wadi el Hasa Archaeological Survey 1979-1983, West-Central Jordan*. Waterloo: Wilfrid Laurier University Press.

Mairs, L. D. (1995). Report on the faunal remains from Al-Ghassul. *Annual of the Department of Antiquities of Jordan* 39: 58–60.

Mallon, A., R. Koeppel, and R. Neuville (1934). *Teleilat Ghassul I: compte rendu des fouilles de l'Institut biblique pontifical 1929–32.* Rome: Piazza della Pilotta.

McNicoll, A. W., P. C. Edwards, and J. Hanbury-Tenison (1992). *Pella in Jordan 2: The Second Interim Report of the Joint University of Sydney and the College of Wooster Excavations at Pella, 1982–1985.* Sydney: Meditarch.

Mellaart, J. (1956). The Neolithic site of Ghrubba. *Annual of the Department of Antiquities of Jordan* 3: 24–40.

Najjar, M., A. Abu Dayyeh, E. Suleiman, G. Weisgerber, and A. Hauptmann (1990). Tell Wadi Feinan: the first Pottery Neolithic tell in the south of Jordan. *Annual of the Department of Antiquities of Jordan* 34: 27–56.

Neef, R. (1988). Les activités agricoles et horticoles. In Dollfus and Kafafi (1988: 29–30).

Perrot, J. (1959). Statuettes en ivoire et autres objets en ivoire et en os provenant des gisements préhistoriques de la région des Beersheba. *Syria* 36: 8–19.

——(1978). *Syrien-Palaestina I: von den Ursprung bis zur Bronzzeit.* Genf: Nagel.

Roux, V., and M.-A. Courty (1997). Les bols élaborés au tour d'Abu Hamid: rupture technique au 4e millénaire avant J.-C. dans le Levant-sud. *Paléorient* 23: 25–43.

Vaillant, N. (1988). Les techniques de la céramique. In Dollfus and Kafafi (1988: 44–6).

Wright, K., and N. Qadi (1988). Transformation, préparation et consommation des aliments. In Dollfus and Kafafi (1988: 34–6).

Zohary, D., and P. Spiegel-Roy (1975). Beginnings of fruit growing in the Old World. *Science* 187: 319–27.

....

CHAPTER 18

CYPRUS DURING THE CHALCOLITHIC PERIOD

....

EDGAR PELTENBURG[†]

The Chalcolithic period of Cypriot prehistory, *c.*3900–2400 BCE, occupied a much shorter interlude between the better-known Late Neolithic and Early Bronze Age periods in the earlier standard works of Dikaios (1962) and Catling (1966). Calibrated radiocarbon dates dramatically altered this assessment, which was largely based on restricted, internal ceramic sequences in the virtual absence of cross-dates from imports or exports (Peltenburg 2003: 260; Todd and Croft 2004: 218–19). Their absence, moreover, indicates a lack of engagement with the outside world, a choice by the islanders to express their different identity from Levantine mainlanders. Chief amongst the contrasts are resolutely circular building traditions recalling PPNA and Khirokitian modes, prevalence of deer-focused subsistence economy, absence of urbanism, and a lack of tell-based occupations. Some of these features are typical of residential instability. A major issue of Cypriot prehistory, therefore, is an understanding of the ecological, political, and economic causes of this pattern. Islanders' exclusionary social behaviour started to break down towards the end of the period, but we must be mindful that current evidence is heavily biased to the southwest, so our understanding of developments could alter significantly when we obtain data from other parts of the island.

PERIODIZATION

....

On the basis largely of limited soundings at settlement sites, Dikaios (1962) divided the Chalcolithic into Periods I and II. More recently discovered radiocarbon-dated sites disclosed the existence of Chalcolithic sites that antedated the classic material of Chalcolithic I Erimi-*Pamboules* (henceforth Erimi) (Fig. 18.1). The settlements of Late Phase Ayios Epiktitos-*Vrysi*, Kalavasos-*Ayious*, and Kissonerga-*Mylouthkia* (henceforth *Vrysi*, *Ayious*, and *Mylouthkia*) rendered the I–II numerical phasing redundant. A revised terminology, Early–Middle–Late, was introduced to cope with the fuller record of some 1,500 years (e.g. Steel 2004: 13, 83–118). An alternative nomenclature privileges cultural stages by referring to the entire period as the 'Erimi culture' (Knapp 1990; 1994). Since significantly distinct

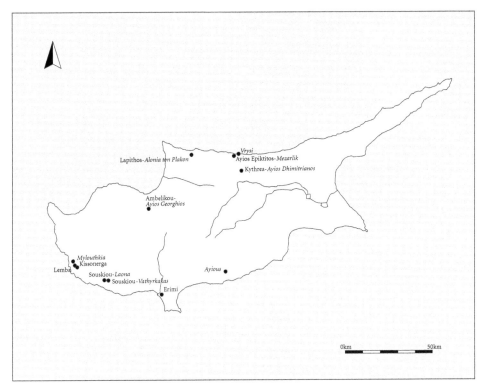

FIG. 18.1 Map of selected Chalcolithic sites in Cyprus

social and other developments characterize each of the Early, Middle, and Late periods, they are considered in turn here.

EARLY CHALCOLITHIC (C.3900–3400 BCE)

A major, island-wide restructuring of settlement occurred *c*.4000 BCE. After expanding beyond their walled enclosures, Late Neolithic communities such as those at Philia-*Drakos A* and Paralimni-*Nissia* abandoned their villages and sought other settings (Clarke 2007: 118, 122–5). This process involved a demographic shift to the west of the island, which has few signs of Neolithic occupation but which became the most densely populated region during the Chalcolithic. A key question that concerns scholars is the synchronicity of desertions. If strictly contemporary, then a general, sudden catastrophe, like Dikaios' suggestion of an earthquake, may have overwhelmed the system (cf. Clarke 2007: 118). On the other hand, if there was a more gradual transformation, then old and new traditions may have coexisted for some time. We need more dates, but whatever the outcome of the debate, scholars agree that this was a significant, indigenous transformation, and that the island was continuously occupied throughout the transition (Knapp 1994).

Timbered settlements

In addition to realigned settlement patterns, the most obvious innovation of the Early Chalcolithic is a switch from stone-based to timber-framed architecture accompanied by extensive subterranean activity, sometimes considered as evidence for squatter settlement and architectural retrenchment. Pit sites can include elaborate tunnel complexes (Todd and Croft 2004). Virtually all traces of flimsy above-ground structures at *Ayious*, *Mylouthkia* Period 2, and Erimi Layers I–II were removed by erosion, but the frequency of post-holes and, inside the pits, daub indicates the existence of timber-framed structures (Todd and Croft 2004; Peltenburg 2003; Dikaios 1962: 113–16). In contrast to these slight buildings is an extensive wall-and-ditch that enclosed all or part of Early Chalcolithic *Mylouthkia*. Traced intermittently for a length of 170m, the 2.7×4.4m ditch implies significant mobilization of communal labour and the existence there of a major centre (Peltenburg 2003: xxxii).

Dikaios interpreted the pits as pit houses, but it is important to note that they lack the floors and installations of subsequent above-ground buildings (Dikaios 1962: 106, 131–5). Many may have been dug to extract building material. Bell-shaped pits at Kissonerga-*Mosphilia* (henceforth Kissonerga) were used for grain storage (Peltenburg 1998: 242). Exceptional Pit 1 at *Mylouthkia*, however, has a sequence of four light internal timber structures interleaved with secondary burials (Peltenburg 2003: 261–3). Key sequences exist at Erimi, *Mylouthkia*, and Kissonerga, where stone structures succeed earlier hollows and timber buildings. These new stone buildings contain expanded numbers and varieties of artefacts indicating greater investment in sedentary behaviour.

While the Early Chalcolithic timber-framed houses manifest new cultural conventions in Cyprus, there are strong signs of continuity with groups that lived in the sub-rectangular stone houses of the preceding Late Neolithic. This is evident in the recurrence of the same types of installations, tunnels, wall-and-ditch enclosures, and in the gradual evolution of artefact types (Thomas 2005; Clarke 2007). Figurines, for example, gradually evolve from the cylindrical phallus-shaped objects of the Late Neolithic into cylinders with arm stubs in the Early Chalcolithic, and fully articulated head, arms, and legs subsequently.

Models of change

The persistence of so many earlier traditions raises the question of why community housing and location altered so radically. Two commonly proposed models provide insight into the nature of small-scale society and economy of Chalcolithic Cyprus as a whole.

In a social model, the main driver for the persistence of small egalitarian communities coupled with the frequent dislocation of settlement is a strategy of fission to resolve or mitigate intra-community tensions and to impede the development of elites (Peltenburg 1993). Mobility and fission belonged to an ideology of egalitarianism. They constituted structuring forces of Chalcolithic society. In this reconstruction, groups moved to other locations, or displacements occurred within long-lived, but episodically occupied, non-tell sites. Lacking coercive controls, groups only had weak mechanisms to deal with demographic stress. This may have occurred at the end of the Late Neolithic, when expanding communities dispersed in the face of clear signs of population growth. It is considered an inadequate explanation by some (e.g. Steel 2004: 82), and so accelerated processes of aridification may also have prompted social instability and a general movement to the wetter west (cf. Brooks 2006). Incomers had to clear woodland for the establishment of new settlements there and elsewhere, prompting a trend towards construction of post-frame houses (Peltenburg 2003: 272–3).

An economic model posits the long-term existence on the island of more mobile societies engaged in hunting Mesopotamian fallow deer, in sharp contrast to the mainland (Clarke 2007). Aridification at this time enhanced options for low-intensity occupations and hunting strategies. Such an emphasis would account for the exceptionally high proportion of deer bone on archaeological sites (Croft 1991). Mylouthkians, however, were also farmers, to judge from the occurrence of significant quantities of cereals and pulses, together with numerous rubbing stones and querns (Peltenburg 2003: 239–45, 264). A variant of this model refers to dual subsistence strategies of agropastoralism and deer hunting in which settlement relocation acted as a self-regulating response to depleted soil fertility, drought, disease, and other disasters, and the means to keep population and social hierarchies in check (Held 1993; Knapp 1994). Aspects of both models probably came into play at different times.

MIDDLE CHALCOLITHIC (C. 3400–2900 BCE)

Significant population growth, flourishing arts and crafts, an island-wide symbolic system, signs of social inequalities, and a decline in deer hunting characterize what is often regarded as the *floruit* of prehistoric Cyprus (Steel 2004: 108). Stone-based circular buildings occur together with a relatively homogenous material culture throughout the island except in the east.

Settlements with stone-based structures

Circular, monocellular structures occur in the north at Ayios Epiktitos-*Mezarlik* and Lapithos-*Alonia ton Plakon* (Dikaios 1936: 74; Gjerstad et al. 1934: 19–33). They were located in well-watered locales like the five circular structures up to 6m in diameter at Kythrea-*Ayios Dhimitrianos* on the edge of the central Mesaoria (Gjerstad et al. 1934: 277–301). In the south, Erimi yielded a sequence of increasingly robust structures up to 7m in diameter.

Some idea of the size and layout of these settlements is provided by the western sites of Lemba-*Lakkous* (henceforth, Lemba) Period 2 and Kissonerga 3A–B (Peltenburg 1985; 1998). In the former, buildings were set contiguously, with an isolated structure containing a unique statuette some 100m downslope beside earlier buildings and a graveyard. A two-tier arrangement existed at apparently undefended Kissonerga 3B (Fig. 18.2). At its core, separated from less substantial buildings by a wall, ditch, and paved track, lay a raised compound of three imposing circular structures and one rectilinear structure set around an open court, a manifestation of a newly ascendant group. Kissonerga may have extended over several hectares, but it is unlikely to have been crowded with buildings. Other sites consist of terraced dwelling on hillsides, as at Souskiou-*Laona*. Major issues concern the causes of this unprecedented florescence in some 80 sites of the period and the culture's socioeconomic

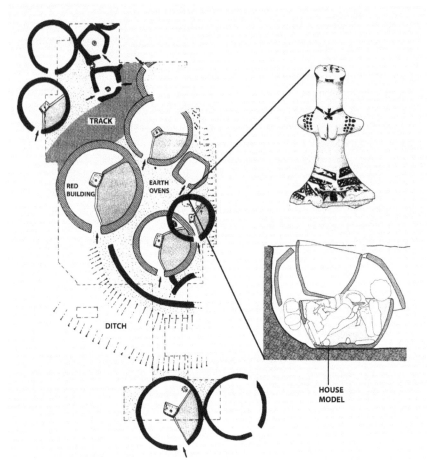

FIG. 18.2 Kissonerga Period 3B plan showing position of ritual deposit (bottom right) in elevated compound, together with one of the figurines from the house model (top right)

organization, especially in view of Flannery's (1972) general model that postulates an equation between circular houses and more temporary residence, a more sharing, communal lifestyle, and polygynous extended systems.

The Chalcolithic house

The pervasive free-standing circular house had four functional segments, without internal party walls (Fig. 18.3). Cooking, sleeping/reception, and storage of food and tools occupied fixed spaces in relation to entrances that tended to face southeast. We can infer these functions from recurrent material culture patterning, the result of leaving large quantities of perfectly usable artefacts *in situ* on floors. The buildings framed a unifying experience for the inhabitants, one that also incorporated the dead. They were interred beside the sleeping

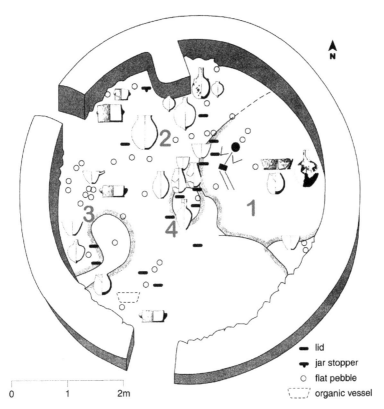

FIG. 18.3 *Mylouthkia* burnt Building 200, with juvenile *in situ*, as a template of standard Chalcolithic house arrangements: (1) reception/sleeping segment; (2) cooking and storage; (3) work and tool storage; and (4) hearth. Note that only a selection of objects is shown

segment of the house, on the side of the rising sun, or in the shell of abandoned structures. We can also infer ritual closure of some houses from burnt Building 200 at *Mylouthkia*, in which a juvenile lay prone beside the hearth. Experiments on replicate buildings have shown that destruction by fire must have been deliberate and could not happen as a result of accident.

Intensification of ritual activity

Ritual intensification and symbolic displays accompanied an increase of population. The most evocative instance of this comes from a unique non-mortuary deposit at Kissonerga (Peltenburg 1991). Contents and context are critical to an understanding of ritual in society. Cut into a pit filled with heat-cracked stones was a space filled with a painted pottery house model overflowing with some fifty objects including an anthropomorphic vessel, a model stool, eight pottery and ten stone human figurines, eighteen tools, a pristine triton shell, and a bone needle (Fig. 18.2). Abandonment customs here parallel ordinary house abandonments, except that the value or power of these special components needed to be broken. Participants intentionally smashed figurines, snapped off decorative relief above the entrance and doorpost loop of the house model, and concealed its elaborate painted decoration with a thick white coating. The model faithfully depicts recovered house features such as painted walls, hearth shape, and floor ridges. It was even placed so that its doorway was oriented like those of extant buildings. The most explicit of the associated figurines depict females seated on a stool and shown in the act of birth. Scholars have applied this evidence for an engendered study of society, taking account of the context of the ritual which suggests that feasting and public display played a significant role (Bolger 2003).

The remarkable deposition event took place in the courtyard of the elevated compound. In it were numerous earth ovens, otherwise rare on the island, and presumably used for special foods and food preparation. Beside the ovens and deposit stood the Red Building, the largest known structure of prehistoric Cyprus. On its floor were capacious bowls suitable for serving large numbers of people. Their exceptional painted decoration, including swirling patterns, must have made a memorable visual impact. Feasts and display seem to have been instrumental in sustaining the new social organization.

Birthing symbolism permeated society. The much-discussed iconic blue/green picrolite figurines are generally believed to represent cruciform-shaped females in schematic birth-giving postures, abbreviations of the birthing figurines in the Kissonerga 3B Period ritual deposit (Bolger 2003; Steel 2004: 99–103). Found throughout the island, but especially in the west, they are the culmination of a stylization trend that began in the Early Chalcolithic (Fig. 18.4). They hung as centrepieces on necklaces, and are found in habitation and burial contexts, particularly in the exceptionally rich cemeteries at Souskiou-*Laona* and *Vathyrkakas*.

Souskiou: a ritual centre

The Souskiou complex may have served as a regional integrative centre based on elaborate mortuary practices, ritual, technological innovation, and exchange (Peltenburg 2006). It consists of a small settlement on the Laona slopes and five Middle Chalcolithic cemeteries comprising deep bell-shaped pits cut into flat bedrock. In a radical departure from the usual single burial practice, up to fourteen individuals were interred in the tombs. Funerary specialists carefully lodged skulls in rows on top of bone stacks in secondary burial rites. We need to understand such a novel collective system in cemeteries in terms of local systems of meaning. The new emphasis on house-based communities and farming during the Middle Chalcolithic suggests some relationship between these novel tombs, houses, and intergenerational ties linked to hereditary claims on property and territory. To judge from the extraordinarily large Souskiou-*Vathyrkakas* Tomb 73, with unusual funerary goods and mortuary behaviour, overt display of status differences existed amongst social peers of this corporate society (Fig. 18.5). According to Manning (1993), the cemeteries represent the development of lineages with certain social rights and social status.

Increased grave offerings include an unprecedented variety of picrolite embellishments, figurines, imaginative pottery vessels such as centaurs and the introduction of new materials. Competition for valued symbolic items led to intensification of production *c.*3000 BCE. Faience and copper make their appearance in this context of ritual display. They may even have been produced at Souskiou, which was a centre of picrolite production. The raw material was mainly procured from the Kouris River which flowed past Erimi, and hence access to it necessitated interregional contacts. It is not yet possible to state if the copper

FIG. 18.4 Cruciform figurine of exceptional mottled picrolite, from Souskiou-*Vathyrkakas* Tomb 85 (photograph Edgar Peltenburg)

and faience involved the appropriation of new technologies from the mainland, where these materials have a longer history, but in the case of copper, we see that the impetus for its adoption came from prestige enhancement during mortuary display and not just utilitarian needs (cf. Steel 2004: 95).

The extraordinary status of Souskiou as a regional centre at the eastern border of the Ktima lowlands is also evident from the small size of the short-lived settlement, which is unlikely to have generated the hundreds of people who were buried in the adjacent cemeteries. Few children were found in the tombs, so it seems that mourners carried selected adults to Souskiou for burial.

The development of inequalities

In comparison to the Early Chalcolithic, later fourth-millennium BCE society exhibits social inequalities and status differences whereby ranking between sites, houses, and the Souskiou tombs is marked by size differences, access to key foods, provision of feasts,

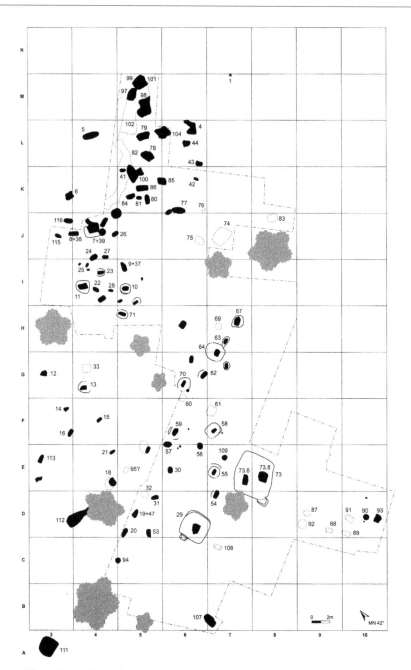

FIG. 18.5 Plan of Middle Chalcolithic Souskiou-*Vathyrkakas* cemetery. Black indicates numbered graves; grey indicates trees; broken line indicates recent excavation area, with earlier excavated and looted tombs to the west

and control of ritual. How did such inequalities come about? Kissonerga furnishes a key insight into one of the processes (Peltenburg 1998: 241–9). During Period 3A, inhabitants transferred what had hitherto been communal, public food preparation and storage indoors. In contrast to Flannery's model mentioned above, the development of circular structures now is associated with more sedentary behaviour and privatization that subverted the earlier corporate mode. The new social dynamic fostered more autonomous household behaviour, as is evident in the Period 3B elevated compound. Activities there are sometimes ascribed to consensual caretakers, indicating rudimentary rank amongst social elders, but the buildings conform to houses, so a higher-status household is more likely (cf. Held 1993). How much authority did this group possess? At 50m², the open space where the ritual took place could not hold many people and so it was probably a low-level integrative facility serving only to integrate a portion of the community, unlike the cemeteries of Souskiou.

The emergence of social inequalities occurred together with a greater investment in pig breeding and caprine herding, and with a gradual decline in deer hunting (Croft 1991). Increased population, intensification of subsistence resource acquisition, and ritual and intergenerational ties all played a part in social reordering: the task remains to differentiate correlations from causation. In addition, tensions may underlie the Middle Chalcolithic focus on the house/birth/female set and ideologies linked to subsistence. If, as in some ethnographic instances, hunting was important to concepts of masculinity, we should consider gender relations in negotiations for status within this increasingly sedentarized egalitarian society.

LATE CHALCOLITHIC (C. 2800–2400 BCE)

Consideration of this stage of the Chalcolithic is overshadowed by discussion of what it can tell us about one of the most profound transformations that occurred in Cypriot prehistory, namely, processes involving the start of the Early Bronze Age (see Webb, Ch. 24 below). It should, however, be understood in its own terms. Unfortunately, the evidence is extremely patchy.

Middle Chalcolithic society did not evolve institutionalized social hierarchies, but seems to have fissioned shortly after the ascendancy of the Kissonerga 3B elevated compound group, a dispersal facilitated by continuing low population density. At the end of the period, settlement at Erimi, for example, shifted after centuries of continuous development in the same location. There follows a gap of about two centuries in our records during which adverse reaction to the arrogation of powers seen at Kissonerga may possibly have taken place. This suggestion is supported by the virtual disappearance during the Late Chalcolithic of the highly visual cruciform birthing figures, the symbol of the ideological basis of so much of Middle Chalcolithic society.

The new Red-and-Black Stroke Burnished Ware, a thin-walled monochrome class of pottery that depends for decorative effect on the subtle interplay of red and black tones, marks the Late Chalcolithic in the west (Bolger 2007). Painted Red-on-White pottery, the hallmark of the Middle Chalcolithic, disappeared in some western centres. Other changes include the introduction of conical stones, possible tokens, rare stamp seals, annular shell rings, and chamber tombs. Continuity is nonetheless evident in the reoccupation of some Middle Chalcolithic sites and in the persistence of the circular house format, even though modifications are evident (Peltenburg 1998).

Shifting sociopolitical strategies

Whereas society empowered groups who seem to have laid claim to ritual authority in the Middle Chalcolithic, a newly emergent group at Kissonerga successfully instigated an ideology of economic control in the Late Chalcolithic. This is most evident from the Pithos House at Kissonerga 4a, belonging to the first of two Late Chalcolithic levels at that large settlement. Named after some 58 storage vessels that occupied over half the floor space, its contents provide an unrivalled insight into Cypriot society in the first half of the third millennium BC. Over 300 objects were trapped in a destructive fire here, together with the burnt remains of a baby. Inferred activities include bulk storage of comestibles (c.4,000 litres), tool storage (e.g. 30 axes and 17 adzes), food processing, metal and other specialized craft production, redistribution, and possibly olive oil processing. Regarded as a special building by some (Held 1993: 28), the installations and organization of space conform to standard house arrangements, and so it was probably an elite household. Its members were able to exercise economic management of people, labour, and resources on an unprecedented scale, whether for aggrandisement or benign management of social surplus (Steel 2004: 112–13).

A more egalitarian social structure reappears in the 4b settlement that follows what was probably a deliberate destruction of the Pithos House. Considered together, destruction and transformation point to a rejection of the concentration of economic resources in a single household. Such violent resistance to the concentration of power is plausible if we accept that equality was the default mode of Chalcolithic Cyprus. Autonomous 4b households consist of two to five structures arranged in adjacent unwalled compounds. As most buildings are small and with hearths, related individuals may have occupied separate quarters. The compound plan is clearest at Lemba, where there is an arc of subsidiary buildings appended onto a major structure that had access via 'libation holes' to five graves below its floor (Peltenburg 1985: 326–8). They were normal Chalcolithic grave pits, unlike the chamber tombs which appeared now at the larger site of Kissonerga. Chambers provided space for multiple burials and grave goods. They are the earliest examples of types that were to become standard during the subsequent Bronze and Iron Ages.

Economic intensification is evident in the Late Chalcolithic from the expanded repertoire of heavier food-processing tools, storage facilities, and increase of livestock. Several causes have been suggested for this change: increased population stress (Croft 1991), resource stress (Peltenburg 1998), and surplus production by emergent elites to sponsor the acquisition of exotics in prestige exchange (Manning 1993). There is some evidence in support of the first two propositions, but the last depends on what may have been happening in the north, and here we have only the most limited exposures. Ambelikou-*Ayios Georghios* with its circular Late Chalcolithic building and sites in the Ovgos Valley have no exotics, although it is probable that painted Cypriot pottery was exported from here to EB II Tarsus (Dikaios 1962: 141–55, 201–3). The more extensive record at Kissonerga rather suggests the appropriation of foreign ways expressed in an insular selection and adaptation of distant customs.

The nature of foreign and intra-island contacts

The inception of meaningful trans-maritime relations may have already begun in Middle Chalcolithic Cyprus (above), but it was in the Late Chalcolithic contact phase that this gradual process is discernible (Peltenburg 1998: 256–7). Links were multidirectional, although southwest Anatolia seems to have been a key zone within expanding interaction spheres. While faience beads may have been imported from the Levantine mainland, other changes imply emulation rather than prestige exchanges. Consumption patterns now emphasize pouring vessels and small bowl portions in Red-and-Black Stroke Burnished Ware that recall southwest Anatolian shapes, decorations, and finishes. These novel drinking and eating customs suggest new foodways in terms of food preparation, type of foods consumed, conventions of the meal, and how they reflect/create family life and status. Textile production also begins to follow northerly traditions, to judge from the appearance of fine, decorated spindle whorls. Locally produced stamp seals have Anatolian precursors. Some of these innovations occur early in Kissonerga 4, and so technology and social identity were in a state of flux amongst Late Chalcolithic islanders before Philia traits appear on the island (see Webb, Ch. 24 below). For example, copper tools and spurred shell pendants, sometimes regarded as Philia intrusions at Kissonerga, occur there in 4a, before diagnostic Philia material makes its first tentative appearance in 4b (cf. Frankel 2005).

Foreign interactions in the Late Chalcolithic mark a growing acceptance of external traditions with which the islanders may have been familiar but hitherto largely chose to reject. There may also have been some contacts with Philia-phase newcomers in the north of the island during Kissonerga 4b, but it is only in Period 5 of the site that new agricultural techniques (cattle) and diagnostic Philia Red Polished pottery are well established. Once that happened, the community soon abandoned Kissonerga. Lemba had already been destroyed, and most if not all Late Chalcolithic sites in the west were deserted. We are uncertain what happened to this once-thriving population. In the north of the island, where there may have been more interaction between Late Chalcolithic and Philia groups, the latter came to dominate, with few signs of acculturation between the groups (cf. Webb, Ch. 24 below). Contacts between them may well have prompted the disintegration of the Chalcolithic cultural system and marginalization of most of its people. A priority for future research is access to information about developments in the early third millennium and from the north of the island if we are to properly evaluate Late Chalcolithic Cyprus.

SUGGESTED READING

A Campo, A. (1994). *Anthropomorphic Representations in Prehistoric Cyprus: A Formal and Symbolic Analysis of Figurines, c. 3500–1800 B.C.* Jonsered: Åströms.

Karageorghis, V. (1982). *Cyprus: From the Stone Age to the Romans.* London: Thames & Hudson.

Keswani, P. (1994). The social context of animal husbandry in early agricultural societies: ethnographic insights and an archaeological example from Cyprus. *Journal of Anthropological Archaeology* 13: 255–77.

Peltenburg, E. J. (1990). Neolithic to Late Bronze Ages. In D. Hunt (ed.), *Footprints in Cyprus: An Illustrated History,* 2nd rev. edn. London: Trigraph, 1–21.

Stanley Price, N. (1979). *Early Prehistoric Settlement in Cyprus: A Review and Gazetteer of Sites, c.6500–3000 B.C.* Oxford: British Archaeological Reports.

Vagnetti, L. (1980). Figurines and minor objects from a Chalcolithic cemetery at Souskiou-Vathyrkakas (Cyprus). *Studi micenei ed egeo-anatolici* 21: 17–72.

Weiss, H., M.-A. Courty, W. Wetterstrom, R. Meadow, F. Guichard, L. Senior, and A. Curnow. (1993). The genesis and collapse of the Akkadian Empire. In M. Liverani (ed.), *Akkad, the First World Empire: Structure, Ideology, Traditions.* Padua: Sargon, 131–55.

References

Bolger, D. (2003). *Gender in Ancient Cyprus: Narratives of Change on a Mediterranean Island.* Walnut Creek, Calif.: AltaMira.

—— (2007). Cultural interaction in 3rd millennium B.C. Cyprus: evidence of ceramics. In S. Antoniadou and A. Pace (eds), *Mediterranean Crossroads.* Athens: Pierides Foundation, 162–86.

Brooks, N. (2006). Cultural responses to aridity in the Middle Holocene and increased social complexity. *Quarternary International* 151: 29–49.

Catling, H. W. (1966). Cyprus in the Neolithic and Chalcolithic periods. In I. E. S. Edwards, C. J. Gadd, and N. G. L. Hammond (eds), *Cambridge Ancient History*, vol. 1, pt 1: *Prolegomena and Prehistory.* Cambridge: Cambridge University Press, 539–56.

Clarke, J., with C. McCartney and A. Wasse (2007). *On the Margins of Southwest Asia: Cyprus during the 6th to 4th Millennia BC.* Oxford: Oxbow.

Croft, P. (1991). Man and beast in Chalcolithic Cyprus. *Bulletin of the American Schools of Oriental Research* 282–3: 63–79.

Dikaios, P. (1936). The excavations at Erimi, 1933–1935. *Report of the Department of Antiquities, Cyprus* 1936: 1–81.

—— (1962). The Stone Age. In P. Dikaios and J. Stewart, *The Stone Age and the Early Bronze Age in Cyprus.* Lund: Swedish Cyprus Expedition, 1–204.

Flannery, K. V. (1972). The origins of the village as a settlement type in Mesoamerica and the Near East: a comparative study. In P. J. Ucko, R. Tringham, and G. W. Dimbleby (eds), *Man, Settlement and Urbanism: Proceedings of a Meeting of the Research Seminar in Archaeology and Related Subjects Held at the Institute of Archaeology, London University.* London: Duckworth, 23–53.

Frankel, D. (2005). Becoming Bronze Age: acculturation and enculturation in 3rd millennium B.C.E. Cyprus. In J. Clarke (ed.), *Archaeological Perspectives on the Transmission and Transformation of Culture in the Eastern Mediterranean.* Oxford: Oxbow, 18–24.

Gjerstad, E., J. Lindros, E. Sjöqvist, and A. Westholm (1934). *The Swedish Cyprus Expedition: Finds and Results of the Excavations in Cyprus 1927–1931* (4 vols). Stockholm: Swedish Cyprus Expedition.

Held, S. O. (1993). Insularity as a modifier of culture change: the case of prehistoric Cyprus. *Bulletin of the American Schools of Oriental Research* 292: 25–34.

Knapp, A. B. (1990). Production, location and integration in Bronze Age Cyprus. *Current Anthropology* 31: 147–76.

—— with S. O. Held and S. W. Manning. (1994). The prehistory of Cyprus: problems and prospects. *Journal of World Prehistory* 8: 377–453.

Manning, S. W. (1993). Prestige, distinction, and competition: the anatomy of socioeconomic complexity in fourth to second millennium B.C.E. Cyprus. *Bulletin of the American Schools of Oriental Research* 292: 35–58.

Peltenburg, E. J. (1985). *Excavations at Lemba-Lakkous 1976–1983*. Gothenburg: Åströms.

—— (1991). *A Ceremonial Area at Kissonerga*. Gothernburg: Åströms.

—— (1993). Settlement discontinuity and resistance to complexity in Cyprus, ca. 4500–2500 B.C.E. *Bulletin of the American Schools of Oriental Research* 292: 9–23.

—— (1998). *Excavations at Kissonerga-Mosphilia, 1979–1992* (2 vols). Jonsered: Åströms.

—— (ed.) (2006). *The Chalcolithic Cemetery of Souskiou-Vathyrkakas, Cyprus: Results of the Investigations of Four Missions from 1950 to 1997*. Nicosia: Department of Antiquities.

—— with D. Bolger, S. Colledge, et al. (2003). *The Colonisation and Settlement of Cyprus: Investigations at Kissonerga-Mylouthkia 1976–1996*. Sävedalen: Åströms.

Steel, L. (2004). *Cyprus before History: From the Earliest Settlers to the End of the Bronze Age*. London: Duckworth.

Thomas, G. (2005). House form and cultural identity in Chalcolithic Cyprus. In J. Clarke (ed.), *Archaeological Perspectives on the Transmission and Transformation of Culture in the Eastern Mediterranean*. Oxford: Oxbow, 118–24.

Todd, I. A., and P. Croft (2004). *Vasilikos Valley Project 8: Excavations at Kalavasos-Ayious*. Sävedalen: Åströms.

SECTION C

THE EARLY AND INTERMEDIATE BRONZE AGES

CHAPTER 19

....

INTRODUCTION TO THE LEVANT DURING THE EARLY BRONZE AGE

....

RAPHAEL GREENBERG

Urbanism, and the route taken by different societies towards it, is the primary story of the Early Bronze Age Levant and of six of the seven chapters in the following section: Israel/Palestine and Jordan (de Miroschedji, Richard, and Prag) and Lebanon and western Syria (Genz, Cooper, and Weiss). Cyprus, the subject of the the seventh chapter, was never urbanized, although some of the characteristics of mainland Early Bronze society made their way to the island in the late third millennium. Bracketed between the emerging literate civilizations of Egypt and Mesopotamia, the regions composing the eastern Mediterranean littoral reveal a striking disparity in terms of their 'trajectory' toward urban life—a disparity expressed in the divergent periodization used in each region. Whereas the demise of the Ghassulian Chalcolithic within the first half of the fourth millennium BCE is perceived as the starting point of a new Early Bronze trajectory in the southern Levant, the northern coastal areas emerge from the Chalcolithic only at the tail end of the fourth millennium. And while the high point of urban development in the southern Levant occurs before—even well before—2500 BCE, north Levantine urbanism (often characterized as 'the second urban revolution') is a feature of the second half of the millennium. If this is not merely an artefact of different rates of excavation in the two regions, or of radically differing perceptions of urbanism among archaeologists, then a deeper significance must be sought: the relative position of the two regions at the interstices of Egyptian and Mesopotamian civilizations might be a good starting point for such a search. From a Mediterranean perspective, the southern Levant is the precocious urbanizer, passing the torch to the northern Levant in the mid-third millennium. The close chronological fit between sociopolitical developments in the Levant and the trajectory of Egyptian involvement in Asia can hardly be accidental; Egypt should always be kept in view as a keen observer of and player in Levantine affairs.

The following review attempts to bring together some of the central themes of the individual chapters, using a broad chronological and regional approach. It begins with the southern Levantine routes toward urbanism in the earlier part of the Early Bronze Age (*sensu lato*) and then expands its scope to the northern Levant in the middle part of the period. In late Early Bronze the focus moves northward, as the southern area takes on the character of a political and cultural margin.

Early Levantine Early Bronze: from village to town in the southern Levant (c.3600–2800 bce)

At about 3800 bce, on the cusp between the late Chalcolithic and the Early Bronze I, a person of standing was interred in a cave in the Judean Desert. Only a single imperishable object—a fine Canaanean flint knife—lay beside the skeleton, a male aged over 50 years, but the perishable goods preserved in the dry desert climate spoke of the man's elevated status: leather sandals, an exquisitely worked bow with arrows, a willow staff, a wooden bowl, and metre upon metre of linen textile (Schick 1998). Absent were the symbolic and ideological trappings that used to dominate Chalcolithic mortuary rites, metaphors of that culture's concern with the fecundity of the herd and with the prestige associated with rare metals, semi-precious stones, and exotic shells. Here, the materials accompanying the deceased reflected different preoccupations—hunting and agriculture—as well as raw power, the ability of this leader to command large resources of labour, both in life and death.

In many ways, the new order reflected in the Wadi Makkukh burial was that of the Early Bronze Age. Discarding the ideological superstructure of the Chalcolithic and the economic infrastructure that went along with it, Early Bronze people in the Levant focused on the fundamental building blocks of sedentary and semi-sedentary life: agriculture, horticulture, and herding. These were labour-intensive tasks at a time when labour may well have been scarce: the ability to command labour was to become a standard of power in the Early Bronze Age.

The earliest phase of the Levantine Bronze Age, EB IA, has only recently come into its own as an archaeological entity, both in chronological and cultural terms. Clearly, it is post-Chalcolithic in terms of social and economic organization. It is also quite distant from the agglomerated village society that appears to presage the advent of urbanism in the late EB I. Early EB I settlement, on either side of the Jordan River and well into Lebanon and southern Syria, may be characterized as extensive rather than intensive, dispersed rather than agglutinative. It was spread thin in the landscape, with a tendency to mobility. Social formations were small and segmented; craft specialization and long-distance contacts were limited. And yet strands of ideological cohesiveness can be traced, as well as receptiveness to interaction with outside world that was to have significant consequences in the following period.

EB IB represents the coming of age of Early Bronze village society. In what was clearly a checquered and uneven transition, dispersed populations began to come together in permanent villages. These villages became thick on the ground in some regions and a number of them grew to enormous size (30 hectares and upwards), taking on some functions of regional centres. Large cemeteries appeared, characterized by multiple-burial tomb caves. It has been suggested that some of the villages were fortified, in effect becoming towns. The evidence is, however, equivocal.

One of the most significant aspects of the late EB I southern Levant is the sizeable impact of late Predynastic/early Dynastic Egypt—whether as a colonial installation, a strong cultural influence, or an economic and political motivation for local self-organization. Wengrow (2006: 135–50) and Yekutieli (2006) have suggested that Egypt sought to acquire advanced agricultural technologies in the southern coastal plains. The recruitment of labour might have been another of the tasks taken on by Egyptians who, like their southern Levantine counterparts, were always strapped for working hands. There can be little doubt that the Egyptian presence motivated self-organization in the Levantine villages that interacted with them; by the same token, the sudden withdrawal of Egypt at the end of EB I would have had profound consequences.

Southern Levantine urbanization

The transition to EB II in the southern Levant is marked by significant changes in settlement distribution, site size and organization, household architecture, subsistence practices, and material culture. There are fewer sites in all regions, and they are usually large and densely built up, indicating a concentration of settlement. These sites are located at the edge of the arable soils, at locations that afford control of land, transportation routes, or both. At some continuously occupied sites in the valleys, the EB II settlements show a clear break with the earlier villages: they occupy only the highest part of the previous spread, moving away from alluvial soils and forming a dense walled cluster of houses.

Taking the disparate elements of EB II southern Levantine urbanism as a whole, there is a pervasive sense of what de Miroschedji terms 'deep change'. This does not represent a wholesale transition to rigid urban hierarchies, but there is a unified sense of purpose that betrays a shared ideology. The landscape becomes one of walled communities that share, as noted by Richard, a broad spectrum of material culture and of practices associated with that material culture—be it the daily time-space routines associated with agglomerated settlement and constraints on house size, or the manner in which food is prepared or staples stored. The agents of this change are EB I village people, who were evidently stimulated to action by some sort of crisis of faith in the prevailing system. What this crisis actually consisted of we do not know. Judging by the location of the core area of change—the inner plains, hills, and valleys of the southern Levant—the proximity of a massive Egyptian presence in EB I should be significant, although Joffe (1993: 58) has pointed out that EB II urbanism actually owes very little to Egyptian ideas of power or of administration (while having obvious homologies with Mesopotamian urbanism). It can therefore be suggested that the swift withdrawal of Egyptian agents from southwest Canaan during or soon after the reign of Narmer created a power vacuum in the southern Levant that was soon filled. This was a window of opportunity for local power brokers and social entrepreneurs to effect change while taking control of the overland trade with Egypt. The residual Egyptian interest legitimized the new order, but was of brief duration. Egyptian trade was soon to take the maritime route toward the northern Levantine coast, and was to have a significant impact on the northern Levantine littoral from the second quarter of the third millennium onward.

Within sites, the construction of town walls—some hardly exceeding 2m in width, others quite massive—appears to be one of the first acts of the new order. Other urban concepts, such as planning, zoning of private and public activities, or centralization of some economic activities, are more or less in evidence in accordance with geographical location or length and continuity of occupation. Thus, for example, Arad manifests a relatively low level of urban integration—slender fortifications with many gates that evade centralized surveillance, and an interior organization based on multi-purpose house compounds—whereas a site such as Tell el-Far'ah North exhibits massive fortification with a monumental gate, a street grid, and a tendency toward smaller, probably two-storeyed, houses in dense domestic insulae. Despite these differences, there is a noticeable uniformity between the various sites: the town walls show similarity of construction over great distances, houses are typically rectilinear, many of them incorporating a central pillared broadroom, and there are few examples of architectural display within towns: where temples and palaces have been identified, they seem hardly prominent within the townscape. In terms of landscape, the establishment of walled sites—large and small—created a series of prominent points of reference, many of which were to become tells, that is, long-standing nodes of human interaction over millennia.

A strong sense of uniformity pervades the material culture of the EB II as well. Large ceramic production centres catering to extensive regions have been posited (Greenberg 2003) for both north (North Canaanite Metallic Ware) and south (Arad ceramic industries). There is also a notable similarity between the products of these different centres, extending to some of the smallest details of production. These point to a significant change in the scale of organized ceramic production, probably correlating with other elements of social organization. Richard suggests a similar intensification in metal production and distribution from Feinan.

Trajectories to urbanism

Early Bronze Age society, from its inception, was to focus on the land and its bounty, on communal action, and on relatively egalitarian manifestations of material wealth and wellbeing. In this sense, early EB I could be seen as the beginning of a trajectory. In other senses, however, the relation between EB I society and settlement and later movement toward urbanism remains very tenuous. Many sites and even entire regions of EB I settlement constituted 'false starts', some being abandoned even before the onset of EB IB. In fact, one would be hard pressed to identify a single site that may be said to record a continuous, gradual progression toward urbanism. A punctuated progression should be imagined; an accumulation of short trajectories adding up—through a process of horizontal transmission—to the evolutionary whole. To what extent this 'whole' was truly urban remains a contentious issue. Richard appears to indicate that the southern Levantine system falls into no known typology, combining elements of heterarchy (the absence of hierarchal centres and primate polities) with a shared sense of purpose that would have integrated the many different communities. This is an appealing notion, and one that is best suited to the EB II, since the following period—as will be shown below—suggests considerable social flux and disintegration.

Northern Levant: the impact of Uruk

If the Egyptian intervention in southwest Canaan was the indirect cause of the southern Levantine brand of urbanization, might we not expect a similar impact to have been sustained by the northern Levant in the wake of the Uruk intervention in northern Syria and the Upper Euphrates? Why was the Mesopotamian urban ideology so slow in coming to western Syria? To phrase it differently, what prevented social agents from translating the ideas of Mesopotamian urbanism into a northern Levantine context? The answer seems to lie in the realm of motive. Information on urban configurations was surely present, but there was no powerful motivation for change. This absence of motivation must be linked to the weak interest that the Uruk culture had in the Mediterranean coast and the friction of distance in relation to Egypt. At the start of the third millennium, western Syria was not yet coveted for its resources, nor did it have any intermediary role in the relations between east and west, or between north and south.

It is therefore not, in all probability, an accident of discovery or of perception that the northeastern Mediterranean littoral was late in joining the move toward urbanism. Both Genz and Cooper indicate that if any move toward urbanism was made in the first quarter of the third millennium, it was not comparable in extent or impact to contemporary developments further south. This was to change with the increased role of Old Kingdom Egypt in Byblos and points north.

MIDDLE LEVANTINE EARLY BRONZE: SOUTHERN PEAK AND COLLAPSE, URBANISM MOVES NORTHWARD (C.2800–2400 BCE)

The EB II in the southern Levant may be seen as preparatory to the full-fledged urbanism—on a Levantine scale—of the EB III. This urbanism, however, is hedged by uncertainty. What may appear to be a continuous sequence of settlement augmentation and architectural escalation building up to a stunning collapse might actually be a series of punctuated and localized episodes of growth and decline. By late EB III, these episodes had created an attenuated landscape composed of a few heavily fortified centres and a large 'invisible' mobile component that would later acquire the form of dispersed, rural/pastoral Intermediate Bronze Age settlements.

There are several important walled sites—no more than a dozen in all—that show a long stratigraphic sequence. These centres are often excessively fortified with massive walls, towers, and bastions. They exhibit new features illustrative of elite aggrandisement and the creation of wealth and status disparities that had been suppressed in EB II: palaces (Yarmuth and Megiddo), monumental temples (Megiddo, Ai, and Khirbet ez-Zeraqun), and ostentatious elements of material culture (e.g. outsized platters, apparently used in competitive feasting). The sequence of palaces at Yarmuth exhibits not only meticulous planning but a careful choreography of ceremonial and economic time-space routines, suggestive of a developed ideology of social stratification.

Many other sites, however, have fewer strata and seem to cover only part of the sequence, particularly its earlier part. This is especially true of the highlands east of the Jordan, where urbanism never quite attained the peaks seen to the west (Philip 2001: 183). The mortuary evidence throughout the southern Levant does not provide much evidence for social stratification: in the few excavated cemeteries, burials are collective and kin-based (Chesson 1999). Moreover, if we are to presume a continuous build-up of interacting and competing urban sites, some source of energy must be supplied, whether external (increased trade or other kinds of interaction) or internal (intensification of agricultural production through expansion and/or technological innovation). In addition, we would expect a burgeoning elite stratum to bolster its legitimacy by building up a network of strategic connections with similar groups in neighboring regions.

As it appears, there is only a brief and geographically limited episode of external influx, represented by the immigration of people carrying a variant of Early Transcaucasian culture expressed in the introduction of Khirbet Kerak Ware. As time wears on, the external links of the southern Levantine towns appear very limited indeed; no new technologies are evidenced, and the countryside appears to be gradually abandoned, with fewer and fewer large sites accounting for an increasing proportion of the total settlement. Nor do we see an outstanding development of elite power or wealth, beyond the specific sites noted above where palatial structures and temple complexes were identified. Early Bronze social power had always been dependent on the ability to control labour and amass staple products. But by the end of Early Bronze III, at 2400 BCE or shortly thereafter, some of these towns may have been little more than a hollow shell, no longer able to control or distribute agricultural produce (Rosen 1995). As de Miroschedji indicates, collapse was systemic, rather than violent. The fortified centres simply failed.

Northern Levant

Even as the southern Levant reached the zenith of its urbanism and then entered a prolonged decline, the northern Levant was beginning to show elements of increased integration and centralization. Byblos, increasingly patronized by kings of the 3rd to 6th Dynasties of Egypt, grew in size and in political and cultic stature; and although it is still difficult to gauge its impact on the Lebanese coastal area as a whole, it may well have fuelled the nascence of the small-scale fortified polities noted by Genz. To the north, Cooper notes increased settlement at some of the major tell sites along the coast and inland, with possible evidence for the emergence of the ruling dynasty at Tell Mardikh/Ebla that was to have such a decisive influence on EB IV Syria. The production of a northern Levantine coastal version of North Canaanite Metallic Ware is particularly striking. It suggests that the same conditions that had earlier brought this ceramic to prominence in the southern Levant, i.e. its pre-eminent suitability to the transport of oils and resins over great distances, were implicated in its north Levantine coastal revival. With the establishment of the 'Byblos run' (the sea route between Asia and Egypt), the trademark jar was adapted to serve the new shipping route.

The establishment of long-distance interaction along the coast doubtless brought western Syria into the purview of the rapidly growing economies of the Upper and Middle Euphrates. Although the evidence for trade connections between Anatolia or Mari and western Syria does not seem to pre-date the mid-third millennium, the recognition that this area could be a hub of sea trade between western Asia, Cyprus, and Egypt must have its roots in this period. It is in this context that the influx of Early Transcaucasian migrants into western Syria, which may have begun some generations before their arrival in the Jordan Valley, should be seen. These migrants appear to have carried with them technological and possibly horticultural knowledge gained in the distant northern periphery. Travelling great distances and penetrating and adapting to a broad range of habitats, they seem to have played a role in the transmission of this knowledge to the various civilizations with which they came into (apparently peaceful) contact.

LATE LEVANTINE EARLY BRONZE: NORTHERN CORE, SOUTHERN PERIPHERY (C.2400–2000)

The latter part of the Early Bronze Age (EB IV in the north, EB IV or IBA in the south) was characterized by urban collapse and ruralization in the south and, by contrast, a 'second urban revolution' (S. Mazzoni, cited in Akkermans and Schwartz 2003) in the north, accompanied by what appears to be the temporary inclusion of Cyprus in the Anatolian interaction sphere. Tell Mardikh/Ebla is the epicentre of the new urban order in the northern Levant, but the spread of northern Levantine urbanization was rapid and thorough, creating a new landscape of towns and dependent villages.

There can be little doubt that a significant element in the 'explosion' of settlement in western Syria and the concomitant meteoric rise of the kingdom of Ebla is the increased interest of Mesopotamian polities in the region. The culture and language of the ruling dynasty had close Mesopotamian affinities, and the success of Ebla attracted competition and violent confrontations with Mari and with Akkadian kings. Nonetheless, the west Syrian polities were very much self-centred: that is, their main source of wealth was the organization of agricultural and pastoral production within the territories under their control or influence, and trade in textiles and other local products with north Syrian and Mesopotamian cities. There seems to be only a limited exploitation by the west Syrian polities of their strategic position in relation to high-value products such as Lebanese timber, Anatolian silver, Cypriot copper, or Egyptian gold and other preciosities. This is not to say that they did not acquire or trade in such products (occasionally in significant quantities), but fundamentally, theirs was very much a third-millennium staple finance economy based on corporate strategies of accruing power. This can be observed in the settlement pattern itself, oriented toward the interior and based on agropastoral intensification. Thus, Cooper notes intense settlement at both old and new sites in the Orontes Valley and the Ghab depression, the establishment of a grain-processing and storage centre at Mishrifeh-Qatna, or the construction, *de novo*, of an urban 'colony' at el-Rawda, on the desert margin, apparently intended to exploit agropastoral resources in previously uninhabited regions. Prestige items, especially tin, gold, and lapis lazuli of distant eastern origin no doubt obtained by virtue of long-distance gift exchanges or tribute collection, served to exhibit and legitimize the power of the ruling elite, in the same manner that precious oils and resins from the southern Levant (EB II) or northern Levant (EB III–IV) functioned in the Egyptian context.

Within such an economic and political regime, and given the high cost of overland transport of bulk commodities, sheer distance constrained the connectivity of the third-millennium polities, effectively preventing the emergence of global networks. Within the kingdom of Ebla, the texts suggest the existence of a powerful bureaucracy and highly centralized economic system. This produced relatively small core areas with a limited periphery, beyond which we would expect to find marginal areas, i.e. areas affected sporadically by the core, but contributing little to its economy and development. This was to change dramatically in the second millennium, when very broad networks utilized entrepreneurial trade along the major rivers and throughout the eastern Mediterranean basin to create systems of truly global extent.

Cyprus provides a case in point. Colonized, as it seems, by Anatolians around 2400 BCE, the island was briefly incorporated in a westward-looking trade network, before entering a centuries-long period of isolation. Although within striking distance of the northern Levantine polities, it did not enter into a significant relation with the Levantine littoral until well into the second millennium BCE.

The definition of what constituted the margin of urban Syria would best apply to the greater part of the Intermediate Bronze Age southern Levant. Despite regional differences— urban collapse was more decisive and regeneration of village life was slow and sporadic west of the Jordan River, whereas the transition to village life east of the Jordan was far less dramatic—there is very little evidence of independent cultural production or of the kind of reciprocal relationship that would characterize an urban periphery. Nonetheless, there are several elements of elite self-definition and of ritual that connect Intermediate Bronze Age societies of the southern Levant with those of the north. These include quantities of Syrian-style wheel-made ceramic drinking-sets (cups, beakers, and teapots) as well as tin-bronzes found in cultic and mortuary contexts in or near the northern valleys, and the silver goblet from 'Ein Samiya in the central hills. More broadly, the cup and teapot that crop up in all local wares can be understood as representing the emulation of elite drinking practices evident at many Syrian sites and most prominently in Ebla itself. Against a background of small-scale, segmented rural-pastoral settlement, the effort spent in mortuary rites and individual differentiation is striking. It seems to indicate the beginning of a fundamental shift in the collective value system that had informed much of the third millennium.

The final centuries of the third millennium set the stage for the transformations of the second millennium BCE. Widespread abandonments and population shifts, cogently argued by Weiss in his contribution on the Intermediate Bronze Age to be the result of abrupt climatic deterioration, affected large portions of the Near East. Almost uniquely in this expanse, the northern Levant shows little evidence of decline at the end of the millennium. Locally advantageous conditions in the Orontes Valley and at other locations along the Mediterranean littoral—as well as social and technological responses at sites such as Ebla— permitted communities to survive the deteriorating climatic conditions of the late third to early second millennia and even to thrive. Despite evidence for incursions and destructions, sites such as Byblos and Arqa on the coast maintain their standing, and urban Ebla quickly recovered after its mid-EB IV destruction. Egyptian contact was maintained until the end of the 6th Dynasty (c. 2191 BCE) and probably beyond, if only sporadically. These same towns were the springboard for an urban regeneration that was to quickly move across the entire Levant after 2000 BCE. But this new movement was sparked by a significant change in leadership and perspective that melded time-honoured strategies of collective action with the more exclusionary 'network' strategies associated with the burgeoning internationalism of the second millennium BCE. Eventually this would lead to the reinstatement of the southern Levant as the cultural and political centre of the eastern Mediterranean littoral, but this lies outside the scope of this chapter.

REFERENCES

Akkermans, P. M. M. G., and G. M. Schwartz (2003). *The Archaeology of Syria: From Complex Hunter-Gatherers to Early Urban Societies (c. 16,000–300 BC)*. Cambridge: Cambridge University Press.

Chesson, M. S. (1999). Libraries of the dead: Early Bronze Age charnel houses and social identity at urban Bab edh-Dhra', Jordan. *Journal of Anthropological Archaeology* 18: 137–64.

Greenberg, R. (2003). Early Bronze Age Megiddo and Beth Shean: discontinuous settlement in sociopolitical context. *Journal of Mediterranean Archaeology* 16: 17–32.

Joffe, A. H. (1993). *Settlement and Society in the Early Bronze Age I and II, Southern Levant: Complementarity and Contradiction in a Small-Scale Complex Society*. Sheffield: Sheffield Academic.

Philip, G. (2001). The Early Bronze I–III Ages. In B. MacDonald, R. B. Adams, and P. Bienkowski (eds), *The Archaeology of Jordan*. Sheffield: Sheffield Academic, 163–232.

Rosen, A. M. (1995). The social response to environmental change in Early Bronze Age Canaan. *Journal of Anthropological Archaeology* 14: 26–44.

Schick, T. (1998). *The Cave of the Warrior: A Fourth Millennium Burial in the Judean Desert*. Jerusalem: Israel Antiquities Authority.

Wengrow, D. (2006). *The Archaeology of Early Egypt: Social Transformations in North-East Africa, 10,000 to 2650 BC*. Cambridge: Cambridge University Press.

Yekutieli, Y. (2006). The ceramics of Tel 'Erani, layer C. *Glasnik* 22: 225–42.

CHAPTER 20

THE NORTHERN LEVANT (SYRIA) DURING THE EARLY BRONZE AGE

LISA COOPER

GEOGRAPHY OF WESTERN SYRIA

Presented here is an overview of the archaeology for the western part of Syria, this region forming part of the northern Levant (Fig. 20.1). Geographically, the region includes the Mediterranean coastal plain and the fertile valley of the Orontes River to the east, separated from the coast by the Jebel Ansariyeh Mountains. The Syrian steppe, a semi-arid region that was sparsely inhabited in antiquity, lies to the east of the Orontes Valley beyond the modern cities of Hama and Homs. The relatively fertile Idlib Plain to the north, which is separated from the Orontes Valley by the Zawiye Mountains, was home to several important ancient settlements, as was the region further to the north in the vicinity of Aleppo, watered by the Nahr el-Quweiq. In the south, below the dry steppe around Damascus, the Hawran basalt plateau covers much of southern Syria. Although the Hawran is relatively arid, the volcanic composition of its soil made possible agricultural activities and provided vegetation for pastoral pursuits.

CHRONOLOGY

Like other parts of the Levant, the terminology used to express the chronology of the third millennium BCE in western Syria is the Early Bronze Age, which has been divided up into four sub-periods: EB I and EB II (*c.*3100–2600 BCE; neither is yet well defined in western Syria), EB III (*c.*2600–2450 BCE), and EB IV (*c.*2450–2000 BCE). These sub-periods do not coincide perfectly with the Early Bronze phases of Palestine and Transjordan, which generally have earlier start dates and are longer in duration. Moreover, unlike the southern Levant, where the term 'Intermediate Bronze Age' has been popularly adopted to refer to the last three centuries of the third millennium BCE, the term does not apply well in western

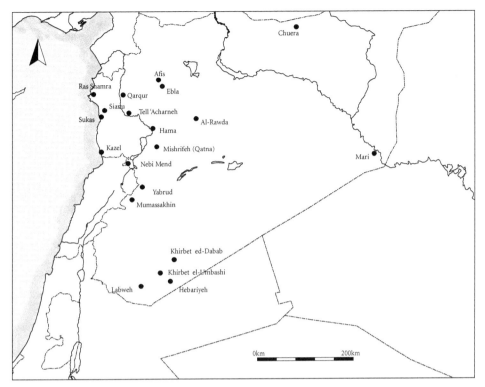

FIG. 20.1 Map of Early Bronze Age sites in the northern Levant (Syria)

Syria. Here, the designation 'EB IV' is widely used. This period, which begins around 2450 BCE and continues to 2000 BCE, represents the culmination of urban life in western Syria. The EB IV of Syria, therefore, contrasts significantly to the Intermediate Bronze Age in the southern Levant, which experienced a period of de-urbanization, and whose characteristics of tribalism and small-scale agropastoralism indicate a significant cultural break from the earlier phases of the Early Bronze Age (Dever 1995: 295).

The chronology of the Early Bronze Age is based largely on developments observed within the pottery assemblages of a few key sites whose occupations span much of the third millennium BCE. The large mounded site of Hama on the Orontes River is particularly informative. An enormous sounding dug in the centre of the tell by a Danish team in the 1930s penetrated into occupation layers dating back to prehistoric times (Neolithic, Halaf, and Ubaid periods). Settlement continued at the site through the Bronze and Iron Ages up to the medieval period. In the sounding, architectural remains, associated pottery, and other artefacts mark the progress of time. Periods K and J and their associated phases represent most of the Early Bronze Age, with Period K, Phases 9–1 covering EB I–III, while Period J, Phases 8–1 covers the EB IV (Fugmann 1958: 24–85; Thuesen 1988: 186).

The 'Amuq Plain has provided another important sequence with which many chronological synchronisms have been established for western Syria. Located today in the Hatay province of Turkey immediately to the north and west of Syria, this region is composed of a broad fertile plain watered by the lower reaches of the Orontes River before its final course into the Mediterranean Sea. On behalf of the Oriental Institute of the University of Chicago, Robert Braidwood carried out an archaeological survey of the 'Amuq Plain in the 1930s. Braidwood was able to identify 178 ancient sites, eight of which were subjected to further excavations. The pottery and other artefacts recovered from these excavations were pieced together to form a chronological sequence comprising Phases A–J, which span the Neolithic through to the end of the Early Bronze Age (Braidwood and Braidwood 1960). 'Amuq Phases G and H roughly correspond to the first phases of the Early Bronze Age (EB I–III), while 'Amuq Phases I and J fit within the EB IV period at the end of the third millennium BCE.

Early Bronze I–II

Chronological findings obtained from relative pottery sequences, and a few radiocarbon dates from stratified contexts both within and adjacent to western Syria, place the beginning of the Early Bronze Age in western Syria around 3100 BCE. This date corresponds roughly to the end of the period of the Uruk culture, which originated in southern Mesopotamia and whose presence and influence spread into many parts of the Near East, including Syria. Some sites in western Syria such as the settlement at Hama testify to the Uruk culture, as evidenced by the presence of the distinctive Uruk-related bevel-rimmed bowls in the early phases of Period K (Thuesen 1988: 181). But apart from this evidence, the overall picture in western Syria is that of the development of a local culture, with some traditions carrying over from the earlier Chalcolithic and only a low degree of contact and influence from urbanized societies existing elsewhere in the Near East at this time. Excavations have not penetrated extensively into levels of EB I and II in western Syria, with the exception of a few sites such as Hama, and so our understanding of the size and complexity of settlements during this time is far from complete (Mazzoni 2002: 71). It is suspected, however, that most settlements consisted of small, non-literate farming or pastoral communities with no political centralization and only a low degree of economic differentiation and social stratification (Akkermans and Schwartz 2003: 226).

One exception to this overall picture comes from the dry, basalt region of the Hawran in the south, where French investigations have brought to light several settlements with habitation spanning the third millennium BCE. Particularly noteworthy for the first quarter of the third millennium BCE is the site of Khirbet ed-Dabab, where a 1.6ha settlement, comprising 60–80 houses associated with a monumental tomb, was identified. Some of the houses are multi-roomed, and the quality of their construction, larger size, and their proximity to the monumental tomb indicate the presence of a social hierarchy at the settlement and the possible domination of the community by a chiefly lineage (Braemer, Échallier, and Taraqji 2004: 366–7). The architecture and pottery from this site have parallels with EB II sites further to the south in Palestine and Jordan, indicating a southern orientation to this site (Braemer, Échallier, and Taraqji 2004: 74).

Early Bronze III

With the onset of EB III, changes in western Syria become more apparent in terms of settlement development and material culture. More is known about this period thanks to larger exposures of EB III occupation at tell sites and several distinctive classes of pottery.

By EB III, there are signs of growing complexity in western Syria. At Ebla, excavations on the south slope of the acropolis have brought to light Building G2, a large structure with rooms that are presumed to have a storage function. Complementing this evidence is the presence of a large grain-storage silo that was found in another area of the acropolis, directly underneath part of the later Palace G of the EB IV period. Excavations in the area to the northeast of Palace G from EB IV have revealed an earlier building where a large quantity of chipped stone flakes and a core were found on the floor, signifying the storage and working of flint, and possibly indicating some kind of control over this material and its use for production of functional implements (Mazzoni 2003: 180). Overall, the picture at Ebla seems to be one of developing economic and craft specialization and the stockpiling of various goods and foodstuffs for the consumption of the settlement's elite. It may well be that by this time a royal dynasty has emerged at Ebla, and that the structures excavated on the acropolis from this period represent parts of the site's earliest palatial complex.

On the coast, EB III occupation has been noted at several sites (e.g. Ras Shamra, Tell Sukas, and Tell Sianu), while further inland in the Orontes Valley, sites such as Qarqur, Hama (Period K4–1), Mishrifeh/Qatna, and Tell Nebi Mend were all inhabited during this period. Domestic units and associated storage installations appear as the principal remains, although the architectural data are still too few to ascertain the true size and complexity of these sites. The EB III pottery recovered from these sites is marked by a dramatic improvement in the ceramic industry in terms of technology and production. Much of the pottery takes the form of a mineral-tempered Simple Ware, and overall, ceramic fabrics are more standardized and homogeneous throughout the territory (Mazzoni 2002: 73).

Apart from Simple Ware, a distinctive pottery, known variously as Early Transcaucasian Ware, Red-Black Burnished Ware, and Khirbet Kerak Ware, is strongly attested during the EB III, even though its first appearance in the region may go back as early as the Late Chalcolithic (Mazzoni 2002: 71). The designation Khirbet Kerak Ware, named after the site in northern Palestine where pottery of this type was found in copious quantities, is the term used here. The vessels are handmade, covered with slip, and are characterized by black and red colours produced in part by specific firing conditions in the kiln. The ware has also been burnished by hand to a high lustre, and can often be ribbed, fluted, or additionally decorated with plastic appliqué or incised and filled decorations (Fig. 20.2a,b) (Mazzoni 2002: 74). Khirbet Kerak Ware commonly appears as sinuous-sided bowls and cups, open-mouthed jars or kraters, and lids and andirons. Because of its similarities, in both form and production technology, to pottery found to the northeast into Anatolia and even as far away as the Transcaucasian regions of Georgia, Armenia, and eastern Turkey, Khirbet Kerak Ware is seen as an exotic element in the local repertoire, and may indicate the presence of a foreign group whose origins may be traced back to these regions to the northeast.

In the ʿAmuq Plain, Khirbet Kerak Ware is very abundant at some sites, constituting sometimes more than half of the total assemblage for the period (in Phase H) (Braidwood and Braidwood 1960: 352). This ware is also abundantly found in Palestine and Transjordan to the south, showing up in particular in the region around Lake Tiberias, the eastern Jezreel, and northern Jordan Valley (Philip 1999: 36). In western Syria, Khirbet Kerak Ware has been found at Ras Shamra (IIIA1 and 2) and in its neighbourhood (de Contenson 1989: 320–25), and elsewhere along the coast, such as the Jebeleh region to the south. It is rarer inland, although it is well attested at Tell Qarqur on the Orontes, and further inland to the north at Ebla. Khirbet Kerak Ware is found at the site of Hama, although it is very scarce if

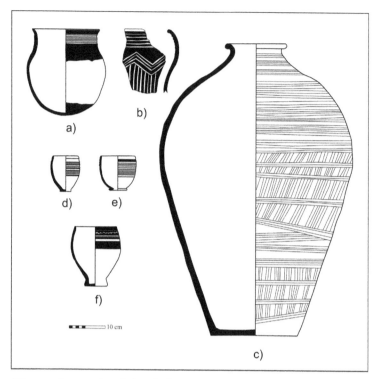

FIG. 20.2 Diagnostic vessels of the Early Bronze Age of western Syria (a, b, d–f: after Mazzoni 2002: pls. XXXIII: 34, 39; XXXVIII: 82–3; XLV: 142; c: after de Contenson 1989: fig. 4c)

not absent at sites further to the south, such as Tell Nebi Mend and Mishrifeh/Qatna (Philip 1999: 36). It may be significant to note that while Khirbet Kerak Ware was certainly present at many sites in the EB III period in Syria, it does not appear to have been found in the same quantities as attested in the ʿAmuq Plain and in the southern Levant, suggesting that a slightly different set of social and economic variables affected its production, distribution, and consumption in Syria.

If the presence of Khirbet Kerak Ware does signal a migrant population that had settled in the Levantine regions, as many scholars continue to believe, it remains to be concluded precisely why these peoples settled in these areas, while avoiding other parts of the Near East. Moreover, what accounts for the incredible longevity of this ware, which persisted for at least 300 years and continued to be manufactured according to very specific techniques and styles that made it a very visible and separate ceramic group from the local assemblages in which it was found? Our understanding of this enigmatic ware is still incomplete, and support has dwindled for interpretations that favour Khirbet Kerak Ware as representative of travelling craftsmen such as potters or bronze workers over a long distance who continued to produce vessels in the style of their homeland (Batiuk 2005: 226; Greenberg and Goren 2009: 130–31). A recent proposal argues that the Khirbet Kerak Ware producers were viniculturers, who specialized in wine-making and used the pottery for the storage and consumption of their specialized product, and whose production became fuelled by elite demand (Batiuk, pers. comm.). Certainly, Khirbet Kerak Ware's connection to social phenomena—its relation to elite consumption or its reflection of specific Near Eastern identities—figures in the discussions of several scholars (e.g. Philip 1999). Whatever the case, one must still take into account the ware's long presence in the Levant, and, while it is acknowledged that a variety of local factors affected its presence and symbolic significance from place to place, its technology and the style of several components of its assemblage remained essentially the same throughout the whole region.

Another distinctive pottery ware makes its first appearance in the EB III of western Syria, although it also continues into EB IV in significant quantities (Mazzoni 2002: 75). This pottery is known by a variety of names: Pattern Combed Ware or Cross-Combed Ware, according to its distinctive surface decoration; or Metallic Ware, referring to its dense metallic-like paste. The ware is invariably handmade, with a well-fired fabric. In Syria, it usually takes the form of restricted-necked jars (Bounni and al-Maqdissi 1994: 19). The walls of the jars are usually light and thin, and the bases are flat. The light combing on the surface of the jar is found on the body of the vessel from the neck downward, and although often appearing simply as horizontal bands, it can also run vertically and obliquely (Fig. 20.2c) (Bounni and al-Maqdissi 1994: 26).

Cross-Combed jars are well attested on the Syrian coast, having been found at Ras Shamra (de Contenson 1989: fig. 4), Tell Sianu, Tell Sukas, and at Tell Kazel near the Syrian–Lebanese border (Bounni and al-Maqdissi 1994: 20–25). As one travels inland in Syria, however, one observes a drop in the frequency of these vessels. Cross-Combed vessels are rare at Hama and Ebla (where they occur in EB IV contexts) and are virtually unknown further to the east. Nevertheless, in the Orontes Valley at Tell Nebi Mend and Tell 'Acharneh and its environs, several examples have been reported (Cooper 2006: 147–8), indicating that this is not an exclusively coastal phenomenon. Cross-Combed Ware is also attested in southern Syria, at sites such as Khirbet el-Umbashi and Labweh (Braemer, Échallier, and Taraqji 2004: 306).

Interestingly, vessels with the same distinctive pattern-comb decoration and metallic fabric have been found in the southern Levant, where they are usually referred to as Metallic Ware vessels. Their greatest popularity appears to have been in EB II in Palestine (c.3000–2700 BCE) before diminishing in number in the subsequent EB III period of Palestine (c.2700–2300 BCE) (Greenberg and Porat 1996: 12). Their appearance thus significantly pre-dates their presence and popularity in Syria. What accounts for this discrepancy in the date of the manufacture and production of Cross-Combed vessels in the Levant remains uncertain, but it may be linked to the varying demand by both local and foreign markets for these vessels and the goods they contained. It has been suggested that the jars are related to the production, transport, and consumption of olive oil, since they have been found in their greatest abundance in areas where olive trees would have been grown prolifically in antiquity (Bounni and al-Maqdissi 1994: 29; Mazzoni 2002: 75). Whatever their function, petrographic analysis of the wares shows that the jars often travelled well beyond their places of production, thus reflecting the presence of a regional trade network system within what was probably an increasingly favourable economic market.

EARLY BRONZE IV

It is with the EB IV of western Syria that the region enjoys the full flowering of urbanism and the prominence of elements associated with that phenomenon: the presence of a stratified society with elite groups and royal dynasties, long-distance trade in exotic and precious materials, and growing centralization with economic and political authority emanating from key centres which endeavoured to control the production and distribution of various agricultural and luxury products. The development of this urban society in western Syria does appear to have grown out of trends originating in the preceding EB III, as demonstrated principally by the evidence from Ebla, but it may also have received some momentum from Mesopotamia, which was experiencing a flourishing urban culture of its own at this time, and which was more accessible due to improved lines of trade and communication with Syria.

Nowhere in western Syria is urbanism more realized than at the site of Ebla. The site is distinguished by a 60ha tell that is divided into a central high mound ('acropolis'), surrounding 'lower city', and outer fortifications. It was on the slope of the central acropolis that Italian excavators found a vast mud-brick structure dubbed 'Palace G', which is dated principally to the 24th century BCE (Mardikh IIB1) and which corresponds to the first part of EB IV in western Syria. This was the residence of the king of Ebla, or the 'en' as he was called in the language of Ebla. Palace G comprised not only a large court and adjacent ceremonial wing where the king and his royal officials received audiences and carried out palatial administrative activities, but also private royal apartments, storage rooms, workshops, and kitchens (Matthiae 1981: 65–111).

The wealth of the king and his royal establishment is indicated not only by the sheer size and complexity of this vast palace at Ebla, but by the richness of some of the objects found within it. Several kilograms of unworked chunks of lapis lazuli, a valuable semi-precious stone imported from distant eastern Afghanistan, for example, were found in rooms of the palace. It seems plausible that the Ebla palace had a trade monopoly over this product, and oversaw its distribution to other Near Eastern regions and Egypt. The presence of the lid of an alabaster vase inscribed with the name of Pepi I, a pharaoh of the 6th Dynasty of the Old Kingdom, certainly confirms Ebla's relationship with Egypt and its royal court at this time.

The most important discovery made in Palace G was that of archive rooms filled with thousands of cuneiform tablets (17,000 or more) which document the business and political affairs of the Ebla kings and their palace officials over a period of about fifty years before the palace was violently destroyed by fire. The presence and use of cuneiform at Ebla indicates that the city had significant contacts with Sumer in southern Mesopotamia, from which the script emanated, although the language of the tablets was a local Semitic dialect (Eblaite). From the Ebla tablets, we know that the palace administration employed thousands of officials, artisans, and labourers, and paid them with food rations in return for their services (Akkermans and Schwartz 2003: 239). The tablets also reveal that the palace had a large sheep-rearing industry, owning several thousand sheep distributed over fields in territories far beyond the immediate vicinity of the city. It would appear the sheep were mainly raised for their wool, which was processed into textiles in the palace's cloth workshops and consequently redistributed through trade or given as gifts to local workers, officials, and foreign dignitaries.

Many cities, towns, and territories are mentioned in the Ebla texts, and the Ebla kings expended considerable energy in entering into relationships with the people of those places, through trade partnerships, political alliances, or outright conquests. From these tablets it appears that during the height of its wealth, Ebla's power extended over an extremely large part of western Syria. Moreover, Ebla had economic and political interests in the Euphrates

Valley to the east, as attested by the numerous tablets that refer to that region and repeated conflicts with Mari, another Syrian superpower which was vying for authority over this region and the resources which it contained or provided access to. Nevertheless, it has been difficult to understand precisely the mechanisms by which Ebla exerted its influence and supremacy over such a wide region and the extent to which it actually *controlled* various territories. Did other lesser Syrian kingdoms become dependants of Ebla, relinquishing their own economic and political autonomy to the Ebla king and his high officials? Or did such polities simply recognize the supremacy of Ebla while remaining essentially independent? Although this issue still needs to be fully explored using available textual and archaeological evidence, the overall picture seems to be that Ebla had a loose and somewhat transitory hold of other populations, perhaps dominating them without actually maintaining a constant military or administrative presence. Power and influence were exercised by having subject countries swear allegiance, pay tribute, and perform other services in the name of their Ebla overlord. In return, Ebla awarded gifts to loyal vassals.

To date, no other excavated site in western Syria matches the palatial character of Ebla. Nevertheless, there was quite an explosion of settlements at this time across all of Syria, judging by the number of sites with EB IV pottery and other artefacts that have been identified by surface prospection and excavations. Some of these settlements exhibit features that reflect an increasingly urban environment and well-established contacts with other sites that were probably facilitated by trade, political alliances, and various social relationships.

Early Bronze IV occupation has been found at sites along the Mediterranean coast (e.g. Ras Shamra and Tell Sianu). This period is also known from sites such as Mumassakhin and Yabrud in the Damascus region as well as a number of rock-cut shaft tombs in that area. In the Hawran region of southern Syria, several sites, such as Khirbet el-Umbashi, have extensive EB IV remains. The site, whose stone architecture is still visible on the surface, has evidence for massive deposits of butchered and burned animal bones. Pastoralism, particularly the keeping of sheep and goats, was clearly the main economy of this site. Moreover, elaborate water-harvesting systems, identified at Khirbet el-Umbashi, Khirbet ed-Dabab, and Hebariyeh, which entailed diverting water from the nearby wadis through a system of dams and channels into large reservoirs, ensured a plentiful water supply for humans and animals in this region of minimal rainfall (Akkermans and Schwartz 2003: 267–8; Braemer, Échallier, and Taraqji 2004: 248–58).

In the area of the Orontes Valley and to the north, sites with long sequences of Early Bronze occupation, namely Tell Nebi Mend, Hama, Qarqur, and Tell Afis, continued to be occupied in EB IV. Several EB IV tombs and cemeteries have also been found in this region, usually comprising rock-cut shaft graves that contained a wealth of metal and ceramic grave offerings.

Thanks to archaeological surveys, which have endeavoured to document and map ancient sites on the basis of their surface remains, principally pottery, many additional sites with EB IV occupation have been identified. Survey work has been particularly brisk in parts of the Orontes Valley, where the intensification of agricultural practices and a growing population have threatened to destroy or eradicate ancient sites altogether. Surveys in the area above and below Hama have successfully located several sites dating to the EB IV period. They have confirmed that urbanism and the attendant increase in settlement and population density did not occur until the late third millennium BCE (Bartl and al-Maqdissi 2007: 247–8). Moreover, while the majority of the sites in the area are small and probably do not represent more than farming villages, a few larger sites were also found, and indicate that urban centres such as Hama and Mishrifeh/Qatna were not the only large settlements in this part of the Middle Orontes Valley (Bartl and al-Maqdissi 2007: 250). The same observation has also been made in the Ghab depression of the Orontes Valley to the north and west of Hama, where sites with large EB IV occupations were found within only a few kilometres of one another (e.g. Tell 'Acharneh and Tell Ahmed are separated by just over 4km). It may be possible to interpret the density of settlement in the Orontes Valley as the result of the substantial fertility of the land and also the area's location along an important east–west route that linked points further inland with the Mediterranean coast (Cooper 2007). Last, it has been observed that settlements occupied during the EB IV continued to be occupied in the subsequent Middle Bronze Age, with little evidence of any settlement hiatus in between (Bartl and al-Maqdissi 2007: 248). The same pattern has been recognized in the marl landscape around Homs, to the south of the Hama region, where survey has reported settlement activity in both the EB IV and the consequent Middle Bronze (Philip 2007: 239). This observation significantly differs from the pattern observed elsewhere, especially the southern Levant, where the majority of Middle Bronze Age settlements were founded on sites having no previous Intermediate Bronze Age occupation.

Excavations at the site of Mishrifeh/Qatna, located to the east of the Orontes River and about 18km northeast of the Syrian city of Homs, have now revealed considerable evidence for EB IV occupation. Investigations by the joint Syrian–Italian–German archaeological mission have confirmed that the site was about 25ha in size at this time, and supported a sizeable and dense residential sector as well as numerous constructions for the storage and processing of surplus agricultural produce, especially grain (Morandi Bonacossi 2007: 67–71). It is suggested that such large-scale agricultural facilities, located on the central acropolis mound of this site, indicate the presence of a central institution at Mishrifeh which controlled the stockpiling, processing, and redistribution of this produce. Such evidence points to the urban character of Mishrifeh, as does the presence of an EB IVA shaft grave, known as Tomb IV. Discovered in the 1920s by the French archaeologist du Mesnil du Buisson, this burial contained 40 individuals together with a rich assemblage of funerary gifts including nearly 300 pottery vessels, metal weapons, metals pins, and various beads and other ornaments made out of faience and carnelian. The elite group or family that is represented by this grave clearly had abundant access to many expensive materials, some of which were obtained through trade over extremely long distances (Morandi Bonacossi 2007: 70–71).

Mishrifeh's position near the western edge of the central Syrian steppe made it a strategic stopping place for trading caravans and other transports making their way across the steppe from points along the Euphrates River to the east, whose waterway provided a crucial avenue of trade and communications between Mesopotamia and other parts of the Near East. Mishrifeh's success in the EB IV period might also be attributable to the large-scale exploitation of its hinterland, which, with proper management, could have supported a successful regime of both agriculture and pastoralism. The same might be true of the 'arid margins' of the Syrian steppe to the northeast of Hama and Homs, where the proliferation of EB IV settlements indicate successful attempts to harness the agricultural potential of the various micro-environments of this region and to maintain large flocks of sheep and goats. Interestingly, some of these sites have surprising urban-like features. Noteworthy among these is the site of al-Rawda, which has been the subject of archaeological investigations by a Franco-Syria mission since 2002. Located about 70km to the northeast of Mishrifeh/Qatna in the arid Syrian steppe, the 15ha settlement was founded around 2400 BCE at the start of the EB IV period and appears to have persisted until the end of the third millennium BCE. Geomagnetic investigations have revealed that al-Rawda was composed of a dense array of structures linked to one another by radial and concentric streets, and surrounded by a fortified enclosure (Castel and Peltenburg 2007: 604). This urban entity, which appears to have been constructed according to a preconceived design, is not unlike other circular cities in Syria to the north and east, especially the Early Bronze settlements at Mari and Tell Chuera (Castel and Peltenburg 2007: 612). At least two of the buildings functioned as temples within a large religious precinct, one of which has a temple *in antis* plan, known from elsewhere in Syria beginning in the Early Bronze Age. Altogether, many of the features of al-Rawda show associations with many other parts of Syria besides western Syria, reflecting the breadth of its far-reaching contacts. Al-Rawda not only prospered from trade between east and western Syria, but was also supported by a mixed agropastoral economy which featured carefully irrigated crops and the keeping of extensive flocks of sheep and goats. All of this is remarkable for a city that was founded *de novo* in the middle of an arid steppe, leading one to wonder if the site's creation was the result of a policy directed by state authorities elsewhere and their conscious attempts to colonize and exploit unsettled zones to maximize their economic and political value (Castel and Peltenburg 2007: 612–13).

The EB IV period of western Syria is easily recognized by its distinctive pottery assemblage, examples of which can be found throughout the western part of Syria from north to south, although admittedly, the proportions of diagnostic types vary considerably from region to region. One of the principal features of EB IV assemblages is the straight-sided drinking cup or goblet. It is fairly tall and cylindrical in shape, tapering to a base which is characterized by a flat foot or small ring base. It is also characterized by corrugations on the outer walls as well as slightly beaded or swollen rims (Fig. 20.2d,e). The fabric of the goblet is frequently of a metallic nature, having been well fired to a grey or deep red colour. The goblet's prolific and unique form, showing up in large quantities in western Syria and even into the southern Levant, has prompted the use of the term 'caliciform culture'—named after the distinctive chalice-shape of the cups—to describe these vessels and its related wares. The goblet is most numerous at the site of Hama in Level J—it is often referred in the literature as the 'Hama beaker'—as well as at Ebla, where it was found in great numbers at Royal Palace G. The standardized shape and size of the goblet and its large quantities indicate that pottery production had intensified in EB IV, and that potters had become highly proficient, efficient, and specialized in their ability to reproduce the same vessel forms many times over. This trend clearly seems to have evolved alongside the development of urbanization within western Syria and the attendant rise in the demand for craft goods.

The goblets functioned as drinking vessels, possibly being used frequently within the context of rituals and celebrations, where drinking among participants, particularly elites, was a way of solidifying social connections with one another and showcasing their special status within the increasingly complex, urban societies from which they came (Mazzoni 2003: 185–7). It is interesting to note in this context that such goblets and other associated caliciform wares such as teapots also made their way into the Intermediate Bronze Age assemblages of some Palestinian sites to the south. Rather than attributing their presence to the migrations of new peoples or, alternatively, seeing them as imported wares, these vessels are judged to constitute a kind of locally produced elite serving set that imitated the well-made caliciform assemblage of the urban centres of Syria to the north. It has been argued that elite members of Palestinian society, or would-be elites, were locally producing and con-suming these wares to highlight their special status. Unlike Syria, Palestinian society at the end of the third millennium BCE had become strongly de-urbanized, and all of the symbols of elite power and patronage that had operated in the earlier periods had disappeared. Thus people were looking now to Syria, still in the full flower of urbanism, to emulate elite behav-iour and the material symbols of that behaviour (Bunimovitz and Greenberg 2004: 27–8).

The caliciform pottery of the EB IV did not go unchanged for the duration of this period. The goblet was transformed into a painted ware, characterized by horizontal wavy bands of black and red paint (Fig. 20.2f) (Mazzoni 2002: 79). This major change marks the division between EB IVA, which coincides with the use of Ebla's Palace G and archives (2450–2300 BCE), and EB IVB, which marks the period coming after Palace G was destroyed, and then continues for the next three centuries to the end of the third millennium (2300–2000 BCE). It is interesting to note that at almost all of the excavated and surveyed sites in western Syria described above, both EB IVA and EB IVB types of 'caliciform' goblets have been encoun-tered. Moreover, other ceramic forms, which appeared in the earlier phase, continue to be produced and consumed at these sites. This would signify an overall continuity in settle-ment and cultural traditions throughout most of western Syria, despite the end of Ebla's Palace G and the demise of the presumed authority that it had wielded over a vast territory.

The destruction of Ebla's Palace G was the work of either Sargon or Naram-Sin of the Akkadian Dynasty of Mesopotamia, or a king belonging to the rival city-state of Mari. Nonetheless, even at Ebla, while the destruction of Palace G was a major event, it was not followed by a site-wide interruption in occupation. A building known as the Archaic Palace, located in the northern part of the city's lower town, appears to have replaced Palace G as the royal residence in EB IVB. The floors of other buildings found elsewhere in the lower town (Area T) and a section of a massive mud-brick town wall at the north end of the city are also dated to the last centuries of the third millennium BCE, indicating that Ebla was probably still a large settlement at this time (Pinnock 2009: 69–71).

The current evidence suggests that during EB IVB, western Syria did not experience any marked decline. On the contrary, this appears as a time of prosperity and relative stability which continued until around 2000 BCE. This picture, therefore, represents a somewhat dif-ferent history compared to other parts of Syria to the east, where settlement disruptions were considerable. The imperialistic efforts of Akkadian rulers to conquer existing and compet-ing centres of wealth and influence led to the destruction of several cities. If settlements were reoccupied, they show signs of major transformations in architecture and the appearance of administrative trappings which reflect a heavy Akkadian imperial presence (Akkermans and Schwartz 2003: 278–82). Fluctuations in the climate, especially increased aridity and atmospheric dust, are also thought to have caused considerable upheavals in the last centu-ries of the third millennium BCE (Weiss, Ch. 25 below). The result of these events led to the collapse of agricultural regimes and the abandonment and population displacement of many settlements, particularly in the Khabur region of northeastern Syria. The Euphrates Valley of Syria also experienced some type of upheaval, as evidenced by the abandonment of impor-tant centres such as Tell Banat. Nevertheless, this 'crisis' was not as marked in the Euphrates as in the Khabur, and one sees the survival of several urban settlements, such as Tell es-Sweyhat, which continued to thrive for several more centuries (Cooper 2006: 264–6). Last, mention has already been made of the last three centuries of the third millennium in the southern Levant, when urban society ceased to exist and intensified agriculture, industry, and trade gave way to a kind of 'ruralization', in which a diversified subsistence economy based on small-scale farming and pastoral nomadism prevailed (Dever 1995: 282). In contrast to these Near Eastern regions, much of western Syria appears to have weathered these unsettling forces remarkably well, not really experiencing any kind of disruption until after the end of the Early Bronze Age beginning around 2000 BC. At this time, a few sites appeared to have suffered destructions, abandonment, or settlement diminution (e.g. Umm al-Marra and surrounding areas of the Jabbul Plain; Nichols and Weber 2006: 46). But this period of demise did not last for long, and not all parts of the region, on present evidence, appear to have been so adversely affected.

So what accounts for the long duration of Early Bronze Age settlement and urban society in western Syria? The answer is still largely uncertain, although we might suggest that this region's distance from major parts of the Near East from which some of the most significant destabilizing effects emanated, namely Mesopotamia and Egypt, accounts for its longevity. Whatever the case, the relatively peaceful centuries of EB IV paved the way for the rapid urban renewal that took place in the succeeding Middle Bronze Age, and allowed for the continuation of occupation at most of the major western Syrian sites such as Ebla, Hama, and Mishrifeh (see Morandi Bonacossi, Ch. 28 below).

Suggested reading

Akkermans, P. M. M. G., and G. M. Schwartz (2003). *The Archaeology of Syria: From Complex Hunter-Gatherers to Early Urban Societies (c.16,000–300 BCE)*. Cambridge: Cambridge University Press.

Matthiae, P. (1981). *Ebla: An Empire Rediscovered*, trans. C. Holme. Garden City, NY: Doubleday.

Mazzoni, S. (2002). The ancient Bronze Age pottery tradition in northwestern central Syria. In M. al-Maqdissi, V. Matoïan, and C. Nicolle (eds), *Céramique de l'âge du Bronze en Syrie I: La Syrie du sud et la vallée de l'Oronte*. Beirut: Institut français d'archéologie du Proche-Orient, 69–96.

Morandi Bonacossi, D. (ed.) (2007). *Urban and Natural Landscapes of an Ancient Syrian Capital: Settlement and Environment at Tell Mishrifeh/Qatna and in Central-Western Syria. Proceedings of the International Conference Held in Udine, 9–11 December 2004*. Udine: Forum.

References

Akkermans, P. M. M. G., and G. M. Schwartz (2003). *The Archaeology of Syria: From Complex Hunter-Gatherers to Early Urban Societies (c.16,000–300 BCE)*. Cambridge: Cambridge University Press.

Bartl, K., and M. al-Maqdissi (2007). Ancient settlements in the middle Orontes region between ar-Rastan and Qal'at Shayzar: first results of archaeological surface investigations 2003–2004. In Morandi Bonacossi (2007: 243–52).

Batiuk, S. D. (2005). *Migration theory and the distribution of the Early Transcaucasian culture*. PhD dissertation, University of Toronto.

Bounni, A., and M. al-Maqdissi (1994). La céramique peignée à la lumière des fouilles syriennes à Tell Sianu. In P. Calmeyer, K. Hecker, L. Jakob-Rost, and C. Walker (eds), *Beiträge zur Altorientalischen Archäologie und Altertumskunde: Festschrift für Barthel Hrouda zum 65. Geburstag*. Wiesbaden: Harrassowitz, 19–29.

Braemer, F., J.-C. Échallier, and A. Taraqji (2004). *Khirbet al Umbashi: villages et campements de pasteurs dans la 'désert noir' à l'âge du Bronze—Travaux de la mission conjointe franco-syrienne 1991–1996*. Beirut: Institut français d'archéologie du Proche-Orient.

Braidwood, R. J., and L. S. Braidwood (1960). *Excavations in the Plain of Antioch I: The Earlier Asemblages, Phases A–J*. Chicago: University of Chicago Press.

Bunimovitz, S., and R. Greenberg (2004). Revealed in their cups: Syrian drinking customs in Intermediate Bronze Age Canaan. *Bulletin of the American Schools of Oriental Research* 334: 19–31.

Castel, C., and E. J. Peltenburg (2007). Urbanism on the margins: third millennium BC al-Rawda in the arid zone of Syria. *Antiquity* 81: 601–16.

Cooper, L. (2006). The pottery from Tell 'Acharneh, pt 1: Typological considerations and dating according to excavated areas in the upper and lower towns, 1998–2002. In M. Fortin (ed.), *Tell 'Acharneh, 1998–2004: rapports préliminaires sur les campagnes de fouilles et saison d'études*. Turnhout: Brepols, 140–90.

——(2007). Exploring the heartland of the Early Bronze Age 'caliciform' culture. *Journal of the Canadian Society for Mesopotamian Studies* 2: 43–50.

de Contenson, H. (1989). Rapports entre la Palestine et Ras Shamra-Ugarit au Bronze ancien. In P. de Miroschedji (ed.), *L'urbanisation de la Palestine à l'âge du Bronze ancien: bilan et perspectives des recherches actuelles*. Oxford: British Archaeological Reports, 317–29.

Dever, W. G. (1995). Social structure in the Early Bronze IV period in Palestine. In T. E. Levy (ed.), *The Archaeology of Society in the Holy Land*. London: Leicester University Press, 282–96.

Fugmann, E. (1958). *Hama: fouilles et recherches, 1931–1938*, vol. 2.1: *L'architecture des périodes pré-hellénistiques*. Copenhagen: Nationalmuseet.

Greenberg, R., and Y. Goren (2009). Migrating technologies at the cusp of the Early Bronze III. *Tel Aviv* 36: 129–34.

——and N. Porat (1996). A third millennium Levantine pottery production center: typology, petrography, and provenance of the Metallic Ware of northern Israel and adjacent regions. *Bulletin of the American Schools of Oriental Research* 301: 5–24.

Matthiae, P. (1981). *Ebla: An Empire Rediscovered*, trans. C. Holme. Garden City, NY: Doubleday.

Mazzoni, S. (2002). The ancient Bronze Age pottery tradition in northwestern central Syria. In M. al-Maqdissi, V. Matoïan, and C. Nicolle (eds), *Céramique de l'âge du Bronze en Syrie I: La Syrie du sud et la vallée de l'Oronte*. Beirut: Institut français d'archéologie du Proche-Orient, 69–96.

——(2003). Ebla: crafts and power in an emergent state of third millennium BC Syria. *Journal of Mediterranean Archaeology* 16: 173–91.

Morandi Bonacossi, D. (2007). Qatna and its hinterland during the Bronze and Iron Ages: a preliminary reconstruction of urbanism and settlement in the Mishrifeh region. In Morandi Bonacossi (2007: 65–90).

Nichols, J. J., and J. A. Weber (2006). Amorites, onagers, and social reorganization in Middle Bronze Age Syria. In G. M. Schwartz and J. J. Nichols (eds), *After Collapse: The Regeneration of Complex Societies*. Tucson: University of Arizona Press, 38–57.

Philip, G. (1999). Complexity and diversity in the southern Levant during the third millennium BC: the evidence of Khirbet Kerak Ware. *Journal of Mediterranean Archaeology* 12: 26–57.

—— (2007). Natural and cultural aspects of the development of the marl landscape east of Lake Qatina during the Bronze and Iron Ages. In Morandi Bonacossi (2007: 233–42).

Pinnock, F. (2009). EBIVB–MBI in northern Syria: crisis and change of a mature urban civilization. In P. J. Parr (ed.), *The Levant in Transition: Proceedings of a Conference Held at the British Museum on 20–21 April 2004*. Leeds: Maney, 69–79.

Thuesen, I. (1988). *Hama: fouilles et recherches, 1931–1938*, vol. 1: *The Pre- and Protohistoric Periods*. Copenhagen: Nationalmuseet.

CHAPTER 21

....

THE NORTHERN LEVANT (LEBANON) DURING THE EARLY BRONZE AGE

....

HERMANN GENZ

The Early Bronze Age is certainly one of the less well-known periods in Lebanon. Although about 140 sites are known (not including the so-called Shepherd Neolithic sites), few of them have been excavated and even fewer were adequately published (Fig. 21.1). The state of knowledge on the Early Bronze Age in Lebanon is very uneven. While the majority of excavations are situated along the coast, systematic surveys in the coastal plain—with the exception of the Akkar Plain (Bartl 2002; Thalmann 2006: 209–23)—are still lacking. The Beqaʻ Plain, on the contrary, has been extensively surveyed (Marfoe 1995), but no sites have been excavated down to the level of the Early Bronze. The exploration of the mountainous regions of Lebanon and the Anti-Lebanon ranges only began in recent years and is still in a very preliminary stage (Bonatz 2002; Garrard and Yazbeck 2004).

So far no generally accepted chronological terminology exists for the Early Bronze Age in Lebanon. Definitions for specific sub-periods are generally lacking, and terms such as 'Early Bronze III' are often used quite haphazardly.

For the lack of a better alternative, the chronological terminology that has been established for the southern Levant will be employed here (see Table 21.1).

A further subdivision of these periods, as suggested for the southern Levant, cannot be applied to Lebanon with the material evidence currently available. Even a differentiation between EB II and III remains somewhat hazy, and both periods will be treated together in the following. The absolute dates suggested here are based on radiocarbon measurements from the southern Levant. The few radiocarbon dates available from Lebanon up to now (Table 21.2) do not contradict these suggested datings; only EB IV seems to have begun somewhat earlier than in the southern Levant (Thalmann 2006: 15). (Two additional radiocarbon dates from EB III levels in Sidon have recently been discussed (Ramsey and Doumet-Serhal 2006), but as they are not yet fully published, they have not been incorporated into Table 21.2. Further, as yet unpublished radiocarbon dates are now available for Tell Arqa and Tell Fadous-Kfarabida.)

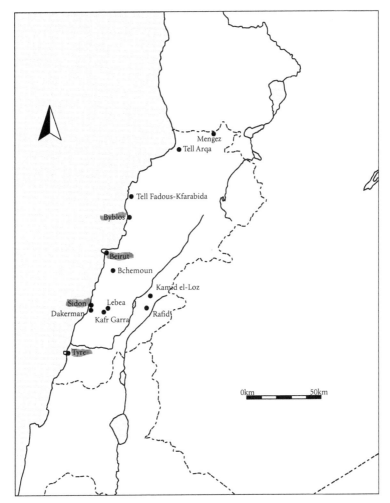

FIG. 21.1 Map of Early Bronze Age sites in the northern Levant (Lebanon)

THE EARLY BRONZE AGE I

The term 'Early Bronze Age I' so far has hardly been used for Lebanon. There is, however, a growing suspicion that the 'Énéolithique récent' of Byblos (Artin 2005) and the 'Chalcolithic' of Sidon-Dakerman at least partly represent this so far ill-defined period. Lauffray (2008: 25–65) uses the term 'proto-urbaine' for the later part of this period.

The settlements of Byblos and Sidon-Dakerman are characterized by oval houses, which are a typical feature of EB I in the southern Levant (Braun 1989). Other aspects of the material culture of these sites such as the widespread use of Canaanean blades (Cauvin 1968: 182–5; Hours 1979: 65–72), the pottery of the 'Énéolithique récent' at Byblos (Dunand 1973: 268–301; Ben-Tor 1989: 46–50), and the presence of a Grey Burnished bowl at Kamid el-Loz

Table 21.1 Chronological terminology of the Early Bronze Age in Lebanon

Period	Absolute dates	Byblos (Dunand)	Byblos (Saghieh)	Byblos (Lauffray)	Tell Fadous-Kfarabida	Tell Arqa	Sidon	Tyre	Other sites
Early Bronze Age IV	2000 – 2400	Epoque Amorite (Inst. VII)	J II	Periode de Style Piqueté III–IV	Phase V	Niveau 15	?	XIX	el-Hourriye
			J I			Niveau 16		XX	Rafid
Early Bronze Age III	2400 – 2800	Inst. VI	K IV	Periode de Style Piqueté I–II	Phase IV	Niveau 17	?	XXI	
			K III		Phase III		Stratum 6	–	
		Inst. V	K II	Periode de Grosses Fondations	Phase II	Niveau 18	Stratum 5	XXVII	
Early Bronze Age II	2800 – 3000	Inst. IV	K I	Periode de Style Sableux		Niveau 19	Stratum 4		
							Stratum 3		Lebea
Early Bronze Age I	3000 – 3600	Inst. III	L	Epoque Proto-Urbaine	Phase I	?	Stratum 1		Kafr Garra
		Enéolithique récent (Inst. II)							Sidon-Dakerman

Table 21.2 Available radiocarbon dates from Lebanon

Site	Sample No.	BP date	BC date (two sigma range)	Material	Source	Period
Tell Arqa, Level 15A	LY 5749	3600 ± 50	2112–1884	Seeds	Thalmann 2006: 230	EB IV
Tell Arqa, Level 16A–B	VERA 2278	3804 ± 29	2340–2130	Seeds	Thalmann 2006: 230	EB IV
Tell Arqa, Level 16A–B	VERA 2277	3842 ± 28	2410–2190	Seeds	Thalmann 2006: 230	EB IV
Tell Arqa, Level 16D	LY 2988	3609 ± 164	2448–1577	Charcoal	Thalmann 2006: 230	EB IV
Tell Arqa, Level 16D–E	LY 2987	3883 ± 169	2851–1919	Charcoal	Thalmann 2006: 230	EB IV
Tell Arqa, Level 16E	LY 2968	4205 ± 173	3305–2328	Charcoal	Thalmann 2006: 230	EB IV
Tell Fadous-Kfarabida Phase IV	KIA 40115	3955 ± 25	2567–2522; 2498–2436; 2421–2403; 2379–2349	Olive pit	Genz et al. 2009: 82	EB III
Tell Fadous-Kfarabida, Phase IV	KIA 40113	4065 ± 25	2839–2814; 2677–2557; 2555–2550; 2537–2491	Olive pit	Genz et al. 2009: 82	EB III
Tell Fadous-Kfarabida, Phase III	KIA 37205	4101 ± 23	2858–2810; 2750–2723; 2700–2576	Olive pit	Genz et al. 2009: 82	EB III
Tell Fadous-Kfarabida, Phase III	KIA 40114	4120 ± 25	2864–2806; 2760–2580	Olive pit	Genz et al. 2009: 82	EB III
Tell Fadous-Kfarabida, Phase III	KIA 26795	4120 ± 25	2864–2807; 2778–2771; 2760–2718; 2706–2616; 2614–2579	Olive pit	Badreshany et al. 2005: 82	EB III
Tell Fadous-Kfarabida, Phase III	KIA 26794	4140 ± 25	2872–2800; 2784–2621; 2608–2600	Olive pit	Badreshany et al. 2005: 81	EB III
Tell Fadous-Kfarabida, Phase III	KIA 37204	4154 ± 28	2876–2832; 2820–2632	Olive pit	Genz et al. 2009: 82	EB III
Tell Fadous-Kfarabida, Phase III	KIA 26796	4230 ± 25	2900–2861; 2809–2756; 2721–2702	Olive pit	Badreshany et al. 2005: 83	EB III
Sidon-Dakerman, Tomb 1	MC 559	4570 ± 90	3629–3016	300g of human bones	Saidah 1979: 47	EB I
Tell Fadous-Kfarabida, Phase I	KIA 37203	5039 ± 31	3951–3762; 3724–3715	Olive pit	Genz et al. 2009: 82	EB I/ Chalco- lithic

(Marfoe 1995: fig. 44.5) testify to strong connections to the EB I of the southern Levant. The only available radiocarbon date from this period in Lebanon (MC 559 from Sidon-Dakerman) unfortunately has a very wide margin, but again comfortably falls into the range of the EB I farther south. (For this problem, compare also Artin, Ch. 15 above, who chooses to retain the traditional terminology of Dunand until further clarification from new stratigraphic and radiocarbon evidence becomes available.)

So far only two settlements have provided sufficient evidence for architectural features. At Byblos, monocellular buildings are either oval or rectangular with rounded corners (Dunand 1973: 217–46). The rectangular buildings seem to represent a later stage, thus suggesting a possible subdivision of EB I. With the exception of a possible sanctuary in the vicinity of the 'Sacred Well' (Dunand 1973: 235–41), no special or outstanding buildings are attested, and the orientation of the individual buildings seems to follow the natural topography rather than a preconceived plan. Twenty-five oval buildings were uncovered at Sidon-Dakerman in an excavated area of 2,500m² (Saidah 1979). Again no unified orientation is recognizable. On its southern side, the settlement is enclosed by a wall made of compact clay soil with facades consisting of undressed stones, c.2m wide and approximately 3m high, exposed on a length of 60m. The sloping facades of this wall make it unlikely that it served as a fortification wall.

Individual burials in large jars are commonly encountered in Byblos (Dunand 1973: 246–5; Artin 2005) and Sidon-Dakerman (Saidah 1979: 42 and figs 14 and 15). The jars were either placed under the floors of houses or in the open spaces between the buildings. While some of these burials from Byblos contained quite rich inventories of gold and silver jewellery as well as copper weapons, other burials were poorly equipped (Artin 2005). This certainly indicates differences in social rank. At Tell Fadous-Kfarabida two child burials, one of them interred in a cooking pot (Fig. 21.2d), are the only features that can be attributed to this period so far (Badreshany, Genz and Sader 2005: 28–9). Besides the jar burials, multiple burials in caves are also attested at Byblos, and at Kafr Garra in the hinterland of Sidon an extramural burial cave has been discovered (Guigues 1937: 56–61).

The pottery of the EB I (Fig. 21.2) is entirely handmade. In Byblos, incised decoration as well as red or reddish-brown slip is frequently encountered (Dunand 1973: 268–301). Several of the large burial jars bear impressions of stamp seals on handles or shoulders (Dunand 1945: 25–58; Dunand 1973: 328–9). An identical stamp seal impression has recently been found at Tell Fadous-Kfarabida (Fig. 21.2e).

Although the use of metals such as copper for daggers and fishing hooks, as well as silver and gold for jewellery, is attested in several of the Byblos tombs (Dunand 1973: 311–13; Artin 2005: 234–6), the majority of tools representing a wide range of different types consist of flint (Cauvin 1968: 177–201; Dunand 1973: 301–4; Hours 1979). Typical are the so-called Canaanean sickle blades, tabular scrapers, and axes.

Due to the absence of systematic paleobotanical and paleozoological studies, little can be said about the economy of the EB I settlements. For Sidon-Dakerman at least the presence of shells and fish bones has been noted (Hours 1979: 57). Several of the tombs at Byblos contained remains of food offerings such as bones of cattle, sheep, goat, and fish as well as shells and snails. Plant remains are also attested, among them grains of wheat and barley, lentils, and olive pits (Artin 2005: 238–9).

The often-postulated close ties between Byblos and Egypt during this period are generally based on stylistic comparisons of such types as mace-heads and ivory figurines (Prag 1986) rather than on identifications of actual imports. The nature and extent of the relations

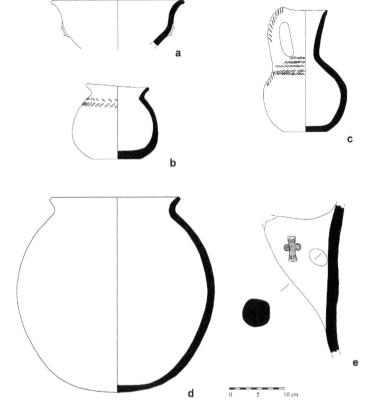

FIG. 21.2 Early Bronze Age I pottery from Lebanon: (a) Kamid el-Loz (after Marfoe 1995: fig. 44.5); (b, c) Byblos (after Dunand 1973: figs 156.24692 and 163.6682); (d–e) Tell Fadous-Kfarabida

between Byblos and Egypt thus remains a matter of debate. Yet the use of non-local materials such as metals or obsidian demonstrates that at least Byblos must have had far-reaching contacts.

The transition from the EB I to EB II remains entirely unclear for the time being. At Byblos this is largely due to the stratigraphic problems resulting from the inadequate excavation methodology. At Sidon the transition is obscured by a hiatus (Stratum 2) in the stratigraphic sequence (Doumet-Serhal 2006a: 13), whereas Sidon-Dakerman was completely abandoned towards the end of the EB I. At Tell Fadous-Kfarabida the limited exposure of the earliest levels does not allow us to draw any conclusions on the nature of the transition, while at Tell Arqa EB I levels have not been reached yet.

EARLY BRONZE AGE II–III

Sites and settlement systems

Byblos is certainly the most extensively excavated EB II–III site in Lebanon. Unfortunately an understanding of the development and layout of the settlement is greatly hampered by the inadequate excavation methodology and incomplete publication (Montet 1928; Dunand 1939; 1954; Lauffray 2008). Numerous reconstructions varying considerably in detail have been proposed. The analyses of Saghieh (1983) and Lauffray (2008) will be adopted here, as they represent the most detailed studies undertaken so far. In Saghieh's terminology, EB II–III is represented by Phases KI to KIV, which show a continuous development of the architectural as well as the ceramic traditions. Lauffray, on the other hand, uses architectural styles to subdivide the third millennium levels (Table 21.1).

Architectural remains have also been uncovered at Tell Arqa (Thalmann 2009: 16–19), Sidon (Doumet-Serhal 2006a–c), Tell Fadous-Kfarabida (Genz 2010: 104–8), and to very limited extents at Beirut (Badre 1997: 14) and Tyre (Bikai 1978: 5–6).

Due to these rather limited excavations, little can be said about site size and the layout of the settlements. The Early Bronze Age settlement of Byblos covers an area of 5ha and is divided into different quarters by a network of streets (Saghieh 1983; Lauffray 2008). At the end of EB III (Phase KIV) Byblos was destroyed by a severe conflagration, but the settlement was immediately rebuilt and continued to show urban characteristics in EB IV (Phases JI and JII). Despite its small size of only 1.5ha (Badreshany, Genz and Sader 2005: 104), Tell Fadous-Kfarabida (Fig. 21.3) clearly seems to show an urban layout with a densely built-up interior with public buildings in Phases III and IV (EB III) (Genz 2010). In Phase IV, the layout of the settlement changed dramatically, with a large columned hall (Building 3) being erected partly above earlier domestic dwellings (Fig. 21.3).

Tell Arqa may have covered up to 4.5ha in the Early Bronze Age (Thalmann 2006: 19). At this site a longer sequence of Early Bronze layers is present below the extensively excavated EB IV, but the exploration of these levels is currently in progress (Thalmann 2006: 17; 2009; 2010: 88–9). Nothing is known of the size of the other sites due to the limited extent of excavations.

Fortification systems, which are supposed to be characteristic of urban sites in the Levant, are so far only attested at Byblos (Saghieh 1983: 65–6; Lauffray 2008: 289–324) and Tell Fadous-Kfarabida (Genz 2010: 109). Whereas Saghieh (1983: 65–6) claims that the earliest fortification at Byblos was only erected at the beginning of EB III, according to Lauffray (2008: 289–324) the site was fortified from the beginning of EB II onwards. The earliest fortification consisted of a simple wall, whereas the later stages were reinforced by buttresses on the inside and an earthen rampart on the outside. At least three gates are attested. At Tell Fadous-Kfarabida, on the other hand, the fortification consists of a simple wall built against the slope of the natural hill. A stairway abutting the outer face presumably led to a yet unexcavated gate. Public buildings of a cultic nature are so far only attested at Byblos. The two main sanctuaries, the so-called Temple of Balaat Gebal and the Temple en L, are situated in the centre of the site. Smaller temples and sanctuaries are found in all quarters (Saghieh 1983: 119–28; Lauffray 2008). A possible palace or administrative building was excavated in the western part of Byblos (Lauffray 2008: 431–44). Due to its incomplete preservation, little can be said about its size and layout. According to their size, layout, and central position on the site, Buildings 3 and 4 at Tell Fadous-Kfarabida are interpreted as public buildings as well, probably of an administrative nature. Building 4, spanning both Phases III and IV, is unfortunately only incompletely preserved. It extended for at least 20m in a north–south direction. The discovery of a stairwell suggests the presence of at least one upper storey. Several rooms clearly were for food preparation on a larger scale. Even more revealing is Building 3 from Phase IV. It is a large, freestanding, one-roomed structure with interior dimensions of 6×8m and 15 pillar bases for massive wooden columns that probably supported an upper storey. As no evidence for domestic activities was found, the building most probably served an administrative purpose (Fig. 21.3).

FIG. 21.3 Architecture of the Early Bronze Age III (Phases III and IV) at Tell Fadous-Kfarabida (drawing Sidney Rempel)

Domestic dwellings generally seem to consist of several rooms, and the buildings are separated by narrow streets. Entire domestic quarters have been uncovered at Byblos (Saghieh 1983; Lauffray 2008), and the more limited evidence from Sidon (Doumet-Serhal 2006a–b), Tell Arqa (Thalmann 2009: 16–19; 2010: 88–9), and Tell Fadous-Kfarabida (Genz 2010: 104–8) seems to confirm the picture gained at Byblos. A typical feature of domestic dwellings in Lebanon from EB II–IV seems to be column bases placed in the corners or along the walls of the rooms. Such positions for columns are attested at Tell Fadous-Kfarabida (Genz 2010: 104), Tell Arqa (Thalmann 2009: 16–17), Byblos (Lauffray 2008: 69–71, 192–4, 283–4), and Sidon (Doumet-Serhal 2006c: 136).

Building materials vary from site to site. While at Byblos and Tell Fadous-Kfarabida limestone was used exclusively, at Sidon (Doumet-Serhal 2006b) mud-brick seems to have been preferred. The factors leading to the choice of building materials remain obscure for the time being, as both limestone and mud are widely available in the coastal plain.

Due to this rather limited evidence, little can be said about site sizes and settlement hierarchies during EB II–III. Survey work undertaken in the Beqa' Valley (Marfoe 1995; 1998: 115–28) and the Akkar Plain (Thalmann 2006: 209–18) seems to indicate a tripartite settlement hierarchy, with the largest sites measuring around 4ha or more and sites of secondary order measuring 2–4ha, whereas tertiary sites are always smaller than 1ha. The distribution of centres or first-order sites leads Marfoe (1998: 115–28) to reconstruct independent political units encompassing c.50km², which he terms 'city-states' or 'petty kingdoms'. Yet the existence of public buildings at the small site of Tell Fadous-Kfarabida suggests a more sophisticated sociopolitical organization encompassing administrative subcentres. Tell Fadous-Kfarabida most probably belonged to the political and economic sphere of Byblos.

In addition, a certain level of sociopolitical complexity in Early Bronze Age Lebanon is indicated by the presence of cylinder-seal impressions on pottery found at Byblos (Dunand 1945: 59–70), Bchemoun (Copeland and Wescombe 1965: 72), Sidon (Doumet-Serhal 2006a: 259–70), and Tell Fadous-Kfarabida (Fig. 21.4), which are best explained as a marking system developed and used by administrative elites. The presence of actual cylinder seals at Tell Fadous-Kfarabida, interestingly, is restricted to buildings of a public nature. A remarkable find from EB II levels at Tell Fadous-Kfarabida is a scale beam made of bone. The small size of the object (only 9.7cm long) suggests that only small quantities could be weighed, possibly precious metals, spices, or drugs. Similar objects from the third millennium BC are so far only attested in western Anatolia and the Aegean, making the object from Tell Fadous-Kfarabida the oldest scale beam in the Levant (Genz 2011). Its discovery demonstrates the existence of sophisticated economic transactions in the Levant around the time when more complex settlements emerge.

Burial customs

Burial customs seem to have changed considerably with the beginning of the EB II. The typical EB II–III tombs consist of rock-cut chambers outside the settlements, such as attested at Byblos (Baramki 1973) and Lebea (Guigues 1937: 42–56). Unfortunately, no anthropological studies have been undertaken, but the size of the chambers and the number of grave goods suggest multiple interments, possibly representing family tombs. Prestige items seem to be lacking, but it has to be admitted that the two EB II–III burials known so far from

FIG. 21.4 Cylinder seal impression on a sherd from Tell Fadous-Kfarabida (photograph Hermann Genz)

Lebanon were not found during regular excavations, so objects may have been removed during the accidental discoveries.

As evidenced by the excavations undertaken by Tallon at Mengez, dolmens were certainly used for burials during the Early Bronze Age (Steimer-Herbet 2000). However, the frequent looting and later reuse of these structures precludes a clear picture of Early Bronze burial customs here, and their relationship to the Early Bronze settlements also remains unclear. As dolmens are mainly restricted to less fertile regions in the northern and eastern parts of the country, an association with pastoralist communities is at least possible (Marfoe 1995: 82).

Society and economy

Typical for the pottery of the EB II and III are drinking vessels such as bowls and cups (Fig. 21.5a, c, d), juglets (Fig. 21.5e), jugs (Fig. 21.5f), jars (Fig. 21.5g), hole-mouth cooking pots (Fig. 21.5h), and four-spouted lamps (Fig. 21.5b). New modes of production can

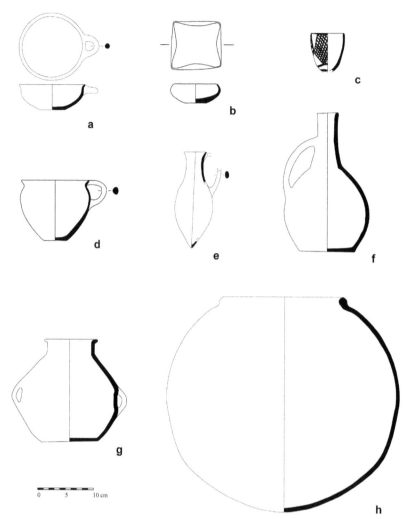

FIG. 21.5 Early Bronze Age II–III pottery from Lebanon: (a, b, d, e, h) Tell Fadous-Kfarabida; (c) Tell Arqa (after Thalmann 2006: pl. 47.4); (f, g) Lebea (after Guigues 1937: figs 10 and 11)

be observed, which involve the frequent use of rotary devices at least for smaller vessels as well as better firing techniques suggesting the use of real kilns. This tendency towards mass production also led to a greater standardization of pottery throughout the Levant. While regional variations in the pottery repertoire can still be observed, certain types such as one-handled red polished jugs (Fig. 21.5f) and two-handled storage jars with combed surfaces (Fig. 21.5g) are now found throughout the Levant, and testify to the existence of strong interregional and international commercial networks. Regional developments, on the other hand, are attested by dark painted pottery (Fig. 21.5c), which so far is restricted to Tell Arqa in northern Lebanon.

Flint continues to be used for a wide variety of tools (Yazbeck in Doumet-Serhal 2006a: 295–300; Thalmann 2010: 93–5). However, a growing importance of metal implements is indicated by the disappearance of several types of lithic tools such as axes and adzes. Undoubtedly these were replaced by metal tools.

As Tell Fadous-Kfarabida and Sidon so far are the only Early Bronze sites in Lebanon from which plant remains have been sampled and studied, little can be said about the agricultural economy of Early Bronze sites in Lebanon. A comparison with the better evidence from the southern Levant shows no surprises in the material from Tell Fadous-Kfarabida and Sidon: wheat and barley were the most important crops, but tree products, especially grapes and olives, also played a considerable role (Badreshany, Genz, and Sader 2005: 84–8; Genz et al. 2009: 110–16; De Moulins 2009).

The situation is only slightly better in regards to the archaeozoological record. Again, only for the two coastal sites of Tell Fadous-Kfarabida (Badreshany, Genz and Sader 2005: 89–92; Genz et al. 2009: 84–94) and Sidon (Vila in Doumet-Serhal 2006a: 301–38) are analyses of the animal bones available. An extensive use of marine resources is attested at both sites, which clearly shows that fishing and collecting shells contributed significantly to the diet of the inhabitants of Early Bronze coastal settlements. The mammalian remains from Tell Fadous-Kfarabida consist of the usual assemblage of domesticates, with sheep and goat predominating, followed by bovids. Hunting seems to have played a marginal role, possibly indicating a densely settled landscape from which wild animals had largely disappeared. Sidon, on the other hand, contains a surprisingly high proportion of game alongside the usual range of domesticated mammals.

Whereas the Early Bronze Age settlements mainly relied on a mixed strategy, with farming complemented by animal husbandry, there are indications that during this period, pastoral communities also existed. Evidence for such communities is provided by about 60 sites of the so-called Shepherd Neolithic, usually represented by small flint scatters without any evidence of pottery in marginal areas of the northern Beqaʿ Valley and Anti-Lebanon, which are less suited for agriculture (Marfoe 1995: 77–82). While a few surveyed sites might suggest an association between the Shepherd Neolithic and EB II–III, evidence for the precise dating of the Shepherd Neolithic is still lacking. In addition, dolmens have been associated with pastoralist elements of the society as well (Marfoe 1995: 82). While the frequent association of dolmen fields with Shepherd Neolithic sites seems to confirm this assumption, dolmens, in contrast to the typical Shepherd Neolithic sites, have produced Early Bronze Age pottery (Steimer-Herbet 2000).

Contacts with Egypt

From at least the end of the 2nd Dynasty throughout the Old Kingdom, a lively contact between Byblos and Egypt is attested. Numerous inscribed Egyptian objects dating from the end of the 2nd to the later 6th Dynasty have been found at Byblos (Saghieh 1983: 99, 104–6; Sowada 2009: 128–41), and in addition Byblos is mentioned in Egyptian sources from the Old Kingdom. Egypt's interest in the region was mainly sparked by the rich resources of timber available in the hinterland of Byblos, but other tree products, such as resin used for mummification, as well as agricultural products, such as wine and possibly olive oil, may have played a role. The precise mechanisms of connections between Byblos and Egypt are as yet unknown, but a direct political domination of Byblos by Egypt can certainly be ruled out. According to the textual evidence from Egypt as well as the vast number of Egyptian objects from Byblos, this city was certainly the main trading partner for the Egyptians. However, occasional finds of Egyptian objects from other sites, such as a cylinder seal from Tyre (Ward in Bikai 1978: 84) and a flint knife from Sidon (Yazbeck in Doumet-Serhal 2006a: 293), suggest that other sites along the coast of the central Levant also participated in this trade.

The end of the Early Bronze Age III

The end of EB III at Byblos is marked by a major destruction layer. Dunand (1952) and many scholars following him have attributed this destruction to the invading Amorites. However, in recent years this theory has gone out of favour. It should be noted that similar destruction layers marking the end of EB III are not yet attested at other sites in Lebanon. Clearly a major crisis of urban settlements can be noted in many parts of the Levant and even beyond around that time, but this is more likely due to a combination of various factors involving climatic changes (see Weiss, Ch. 25 below) and their consequences, such as increased competition for diminishing resources. It is remarkable, however, that this crisis in the central Levant did not lead to a complete breakdown of the urban systems, as was the case in most parts of the southern Levant (see Prag, Ch. 26 below). Urban settlements in Lebanon underwent a certain amount of change and restructuring, but continued into EB IV, as evidenced by Byblos and Tell Arqa.

SUGGESTED READING

Doumet-Serhal, C. (2006). *The Early Bronze Age in Sidon: 'College Site' Excavations (1998–2000–2001)*. Beirut: Institut français du Proche-Orient.

Genz, H. (2010). Recent excavations at Tell Fadous-Kfarabida. *Near Eastern Archaeology* 73: 102–13.

Marfoe, L. (1995). *Kamid el-Loz 13: The Prehistoric and Early Historic Context of the Site*. Bonn: Habelt.

Saghieh, M. (1983). *Byblos in the Third Millennium B.C.: A Reconstruction of the Stratigraphy and a Study of the Cultural Connections*. Warminster: Aris & Phillips.

Thalmann, J.-P. (2006). *Tell Arqa I: Les niveaux de l'âge du Bronze*. Beirut: Institut français du Proche-Orient.

REFERENCES

Artin, G. (2005). L'ensemble funéraire de Byblos: étude de la 'Nécropole Énéolithique'. *Bulletin d'archéologie et d'architecture libanaises* 9: 223–47.

Badre, L. (1997). Bey 003 preliminary report: excavations of the American University of Beirut Museum, 1993–1996. *Bulletin d'archéologie et d'architecture libanaises* 2: 6–94.

Badreshany, K., H. Genz, and H. S. Sader (2005). An Early Bronze Age site on the Lebanese coast: Tell Fadous-Kfarabida 2004 and 2005. Final report. *Bulletin d'archéologie et d'architecture libanaises* 9: 5–115.

Baramki, D. C. (1973). A tomb of the Early and Middle Bronze Age at Byblos. *Bulletin du Musée du Beyrouth* 26: 27–30.

Bartl, K. (2002). Archäologische Untersuchungen in der südlichen Akkar-Ebene, Nordlibanon: Vorläufige Ergebnisse einer Oberflächenprospektion. In R. Eichmann (ed.), *Ausgrabungen und Surveys im Vorderen Orient I*. Rahden: Leidorf, 23–48.

Ben-Tor, A. (1989). Byblos and Early Bronze I Palestine. In P. de Miroschedji (ed.), *L'urbanisation de la Palestine à l'âge du Bronze ancien: bilan et perspectives des recherches actuelles*. Oxford: British Archaeological Reports, 41–52.

Bikai, P. M. (1978). *The Pottery of Tyre*. Warminster: Aris & Phillips.

Bonatz, D., with N. Ali and C. Jauss (2002). Preliminary remarks on an archaeological survey in the Anti-Lebanon. *Bulletin d'archéologie et d'architecture libanaises* 6: 283–307.

Braun, E. (1989). The problem of the apsidal house: new aspects of Early Bronze domestic architecture in Israel, Jordan and Lebanon. *Palestine Exploration Quarterly* 121: 1–43.

Cauvin, J. (1968). *Fouilles de Byblos IV: les outillages néolithiques de Byblos et du littoral libanais*. Paris: Maisonneuve.

Copeland, L., and P. J. Wescombe (1965). Inventory of Stone-Age sites in Lebanon, pt 1: West-central Lebanon. *Mélanges de l'Université Saint-Joseph* 41: 29–175.

De Moulins, D. (2009). Sidon grain from the storerooms. *Archaeology and History in Lebanon* 29: 11–15.

Doumet-Serhal, C. (2006a). *The Early Bronze Age in Sidon: 'College Site' Excavations (1998–2000–2001)*. Beirut: Institut français du Proche-Orient.

——(2006b). Sidon: a mud brick building at the close of the third millennium BC. *Archaeology and History in Lebanon* 27: 4–17.

——(2006c). Eighth and ninth season of excavation (2006–2007) at Sidon: preliminary report. *Bulletin d'archéologie et d'architecture libanaises* 10: 131–65.

Dunand, M. (1939). *Fouilles de Byblos I, 1926–1932*. Paris: Geuthner.

——(1945). *Byblia grammata: documents et recherches sur le développement de l'écriture en Phénicie*. Beirut: Ministère de l'éducation nationale et des beaux-arts.

——(1952). Byblos au temps du Bronze ancien et de la conquête amorite. *Revue biblique* 59: 82–90.

——(1954). *Fouilles de Byblos II, 1933–1938*. Paris: Geuthner.

——(1973). *Fouilles de Byblos V: l'architecture, les tombes, le matériel domestique, des origines néolithiques a l'avènement urbain*. Paris: Maisonneuve.

Garrard, A. N., and C. Yazbeck (2004). Qadisha Valley Prehistoric Project (northern Lebanon): results of the 2003 survey season. *Bulletin d'archéologie et d'architecture libanaises* 8: 5–46.

Genz, H. (2010). Recent excavations at Tell Fadous-Kfarabida. *Near Eastern Archaeology* 73: 102–13.

——(2011). Restoring the balance: an Early Bronze Age scale beam from Tell Fadous-Kfarabida, Lebanon. *Antiquity* 85: 839–50.

—— C. Çakırlar, A. Damick, et al. (2009). Excavations at Tell Fadous-Kfarabida: preliminary report on the 2009 season of excavations. *Bulletin d'archéologie et d'architecture libanaises* 13: 71–123.

Guigues, P. É. (1937). Lébé'a, Kafer Garra, Qrayé: nécropoles de la région sidonienne. *Bulletin du Musée de Beyrouth* 1: 35–76.

Hours, F. (1979). Industrie lithique de Saida-Dakerman. *Berytus* 27: 57–76.

Lauffray, J. (2008). *Fouilles de Byblos VI: L'urbanisme et l'architecture—de l'époque proto-urbaine à l'occupation amorite (de l'Énéolithique à l'âge du Bronze II)*. Beirut: Institut français du Proche-Orient.

Marfoe, L. (1995). *Kamid el-Loz 13: The Prehistoric and Early Historic Context of the Site*. Bonn: Habelt.

—— (1998). *Kamid el-Loz 14: Settlement History of the Biqa' up to the Iron Age.* Bonn: Habelt.

Montet, P. (1928). *Byblos et l'Égypte: quatre campagnes de fouilles à Gebeil, 1921–1922–1923–1924.* Paris: Geuthner.

Prag, K. (1986). Byblos and Egypt in the fourth millennium B.C. *Levant* 18: 59–74.

Ramsey, C., and C. Doumet-Serhal (2006). Carbon 14 analysis from a new Early Bronze Age III building at Sidon. *Archaeology and History in Lebanon* 27: 18–22.

Saghieh, M. (1983). *Byblos in the Third Millennium B.C.: A Reconstruction of the Stratigraphy and a Study of the Cultural Connections.* Warminster: Aris & Phillips.

Saidah, R. (1979). Fouilles de Sidon-Dakerman: l'agglomération chalcolithique. *Berytus* 27: 29–55.

Sowada, K. N. (2009). *Egypt in the Eastern Mediterranean during the Old Kingdom: An Archaeological Perspective.* Fribourg: Academic/Göttingen: Vandenhoeck & Ruprecht.

Steimer-Herbet, T. (2000). Étude des monuments mégalithiques de Mengez (Liban) d'après les carnets de fouilles du R. P. M. Tallon (1959–1969). *Syria* 77: 11–21.

Thalmann, J.-P. (2006). *Tell Arqa I: les niveaux de l'âge du Bronze.* Beirut: Institut français du Proche-Orient.

—— (2009). The Early Bronze Age: foreign relations in the light of recent excavations at Tell Arqa. In A.-M. Maïla-Afeiche (ed.), *Interconnections in the Eastern Mediterranean: Lebanon in the Bronze and Iron Ages.* Beirut: Ministère de la culture, Direction générale des antiquités 15–28.

—— (2010). Tell Arqa: a prosperous city during the Bronze Age. *Near Eastern Archaeology* 73: 86–101.

....

CHAPTER 22

THE SOUTHERN LEVANT (CISJORDAN) DURING THE EARLY BRONZE AGE

....

PIERRE DE MIROSCHEDJI

INTRODUCTION

....

Towards the middle of the fourth millennium BC, a new world emerged in the Near East. While Mesopotamia and Egypt began a path toward state formation, at the southern tip of the Fertile Crescent, Palestine also underwent rapid and deep changes, albeit on a more modest scale. Their first manifestations, around 3700 BC, signal the end of the Late Chalcolithic period and the beginning of the Early Bronze Age.

The new civilization represents a radical transformation of the social and cultural landscape marked by the appearance of the first cities and the development of a complex and hierarchized society, culturally homogeneous, based on a Mediterranean agrarian economy. It heralds the emergence of the main traits of Canaanite civilization in the Bronze Age. Lasting for more than a millennium, it constitutes the first of three urban cycles before the Middle Bronze and the Iron Ages (Finkelstein 1995; de Miroschedji 2009).

The Early Bronze Age is traditionally divided into three sub-periods, each itself comprising several phases: Early Bronze (EB) I, which is a formative period, essentially pre-urban; and EB II and III, characterized by the development of urban fortified settlements (Ben-Tor 1992).

EARLY BRONZE I

....

Sequence and chronology

On the basis of radiocarbon calibrated dates, EB I lasted almost six centuries, between *c.*3700 and *c.*3100 BC. During this long time-span, important changes took place, leading to strong differences between the beginning and the end of the period. Archaeologists therefore differentiate between an early phase (EB IA), c.3700–3400 BC, a late phase (EB IB), c.3400–3200 BC, and a terminal phase (Final EB IB), c.3200–3100/3000 BC, which is transitional with the following EB II period (Regev, de Miroschedji, and Boaretto 2012; Regev et al. 2012).

The modalities of the transition between the Late Chalcolithic and EB I are still poorly understood. In the southern coastal plain, there are indications of a smooth transition (Braun 2011). Everywhere else, the beginning of a new period is felt rather abruptly in subsistence modes, pattern of settlement, material culture, foreign relations, funerary practices, and cult.

Subsistence modes

At the beginning of the new civilization, a new subsistence economy emerged during the fourth millennium, which characterized the Mediterranean zone from this time onward (de Miroschedji 1971: 87–91; Stager 1985; Grigson 1995). It is a mixed agropastoral economy based on agriculture (cereals and leguminous), horticulture (olive and vine), and animal husbandry (cattle, sheep and goats—pig whenever possible—and donkey domesticated in the EB I: Ovadia 1992; Hizmi 2004). The significant rise of a sedentary population in the Early Bronze Age suggests that both the surface of arable lands and productivity increased, a consequence of the development of floodwater farming (Rosen 2007: 128–49) and the introduction of the plough, possibly in the EB I. The development of horticulture represents the most important agricultural innovation since the Neolithic, which had a considerable impact on economic and social organization.

Pattern of settlement

The advent of a new subsistence economy was soon translated onto the settlement map (Fig. 22.1) (Getzov, Paz, and Gophna 2001). The first striking feature is the settlement hiatus: most of the Late Chalcolithic settlements were abandoned and a number of the EB I settlements are newly founded, a movement which implies a strong sedentarization process.

In addition the sharp increase in the number of sites is remarkable, suggesting a significant demographic rise, at least for the sedentary segment of the population.

Another conspicuous change concerns the spatial distribution of sites: previously almost empty, the hilly areas and the central highlands witnessed the foundation of numerous small settlements, some of which became major cities in the Bronze and Iron Ages (de Miroschedji 1971: 76–84; Getzov, Paz, and Gophna 2001). At the same time, scores of small settlements inhabited by transhumant pastoralists appeared in the semi-arid southern margins of the Negev (Rosen 2008: 123).

The process of sedentarization, however, was not uniform. In some areas, such as the central Shephelah region, two phases can be identified: the first marked by the founding of new settlements, the second by the abandonment of some and the grouping of their inhabitants into a few larger sites, one of which became a regional centre in the following period. Elsewhere the focal point of future settlement seems to have been a cemetery established initially at the centre of the territory inhabited by people still broadly semi-nomadic. Such a process may have triggered the founding of sites like Tell el-Fârʻah, Jericho, and especially

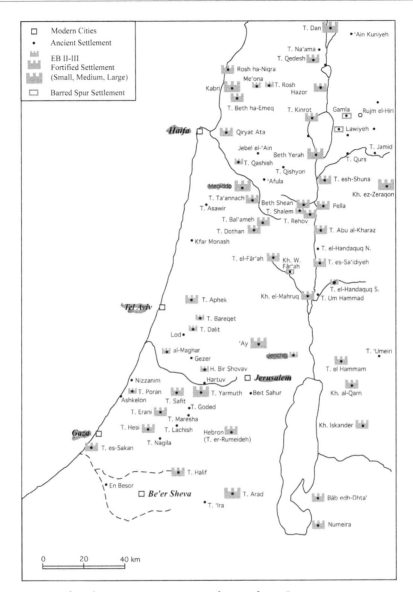

FIG. 22.1 Map of Early Bronze Age sites in the southern Levant

Bâb edh-Dhra', where there is evidence of the use of a large necropolis by several distinct groups of semi-nomadic pastoralists prior to the establishment of a sizeable permanent settlement (Rast 1992; Harrison 2001).

Character of settlements

These EB IA–B settlements were all villages. They rarely exceeded an area of 5ha, although some were very large, sometimes larger than the EB II–III cities that succeeded them: 16ha at

Yarmuth, 25ha at Beth Yerah and Megiddo. But excavations suggest that they were sparsely built, with dwellings disorderly distributed and separated by open spaces.

These dwellings were mostly of the courtyard type (a broadroom preceded by a courtyard), attested in the southern Levant since the Late Neolithic (Fig. 22.2 top right). Another kind of dwelling, considered a hallmark of the EB IA, is represented by oval or elongated houses with apses at both ends (Braun 1989). These are found on a dozen of settlements in the north of Israel and along its coast down to Ashkelon, as well as in Lebanon.

Some EB IB settlements also enclosed multi-roomed buildings used for storage, cultic activities, and various other purposes. At Hartuv, a public building, comprising several rooms and covering some 500m², was interpreted as a sanctuary due to the presence in its

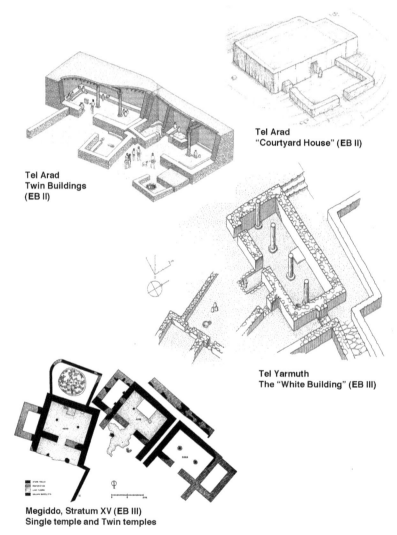

Tel Arad
"Courtyard House" (EB II)

Tel Arad
Twin Buildings
(EB II)

Tel Yarmuth
The "White Building" (EB III)

Megiddo, Stratum XV (EB III)
Single temple and Twin temples

FIG. 22.2 Examples of domestic and public buildings. Top right and centre left: R. Amiran et al., Site Sheet Arad (Israel Museum, n.d., in Hebrew, drawing by L. Ritmeyer). Centre right: © Tel Yarmuth Archaeological Expedition. Bottom left: Loud 1948: 80, fig. 180

main hall of a row of nine standing stones (*masseboth*) aligned along the long wall opposite the entrance (Mazar and de Miroschedji 1996). At Megiddo (Strata J-2 and J-3), two super-imposed EB IB temples each comprised a large hall, also of the broadroom type, with an axial row of pillar bases, preceded by a paved courtyard surrounded by an enclosure wall (Finkelstein and Ussishkin 2000: 38–55).

There is increasing evidence that the urbanization process began to accelerate at the very end of the EB IB. Although the presence of fortifications remains uncertain, except on some transitional EB I–EB II sites in the north and an Egyptian site in the south (Tell es-Sakan: see below), some sites (e.g. Qiryat Ata) show an increasing density of dwellings, suggesting a constriction of the settlement which took on a progressively urban character (Faust and Golani 2008). Megiddo testifies to the appearance of monumental architecture on a scale unmatched before the EB III: in the transitional EB IB–II Stratum J-4, the new temple measured 50×30m with walls up to 3.6m wide (Finkelstein, Ussishkin, and Peersmann 2006: 36–50). It was clearly a regional cultic centre, attracting the resources of a large part of the Plain of Israel.

Material culture

The EB I material culture represents a sharp break with the preceding Late Chalcolithic.

Local particularisms are conspicuous in the realm of pottery (Stager 1992: 29–30; Braun 2009; forthcoming; Bar 2010). EB I pottery shows a great diversity which goes well beyond the three categories (red, painted, and grey burnished) often invoked to describe it. Red and common wares present several regional varieties with few connections between them, while there are at least three kinds of painted wares. Burnished Grey Ware is an enduring EB I tradition mainly in the north of the country, although there is no clear relationship between the sinuous-sided grey burnished bowls, which typify the northern EB IA, and those found during the following phase. An important feature of the EB IB pottery in the north is the appearance of carefully finished red burnished vessels, forerunners of the EB II so-called Abydos Ware (see below). Although not common, the use of tournettes for wheel-shaping vessels is well attested in the north during the EB IB (Roux and de Miroschedji 2009).

Metallurgy underwent significant developments. In the area of Feinan, on the eastern border of the Aravah Valley, mining activities changed scale and nature during the Early Bronze Age (Hauptmann 2003). New copper veins were exploited, refining operations were conducted on site, and the ingots were probably exported to settlements located in the heart of Palestine. Metallurgical productions were less prestige-oriented than in the Late Chalcolithic and now more varied and widespread. Gold and silver were also imported for the manufacture of beads and small vessels (Philip and Rehren 1996).

The more widespread use of copper implements is suggested by the impoverishment of the flint tool kit (Rosen 1997). The latter comprises only the so-called Canaanean blades, whose appearance heralds the beginning of the Early Bronze Age in the entire Near East, alongside tabular scrapers, borers, and several ad hoc tools with no peculiar characteristics.

Ground stone objects and implements were mainly imported from peripheral areas (Golan and Negev) (Milevski 2008). Two types of basalt stone vessels are known during the EB I, different from but with the same provenience as those of the Late Chalcolithic (Braun 1990; Philip and Williams-Thorpe 2000).

A remarkable innovation in northern Israel is the adoption of the cylinder seal, an indi-rect result of an Urukian influence exerted on Syria and the Lebanese coast (Ben-Tor 1978; de Miroschedji 1997). EB I cylinder seals are decorated with naturalistic design represented in a flat relief suggesting that they were carved in wood. Following the Levantine practice, they were not rolled on jar or door sealings, but on the shoulders of pithoi before firing. It is, however, uncertain whether their introduction reveals the appearance of new administra-tive practices, although the transitional EB IB–EB II Megiddo temple of Stratum J-4 sug-gests that impressive economic development took place at this time.

Foreign contacts

The EB I is a period of increasing foreign contacts, direct or indirect, in a Near Eastern con-text of rapidly developing interconnections.

There is no clear evidence of direct contacts with Syria. Some EB IB red burnished jugs found in northern Palestine present morphological features vaguely reminiscent of contem-porary vessels from the Urukian colonies in northern Syria. More significant, a group of EB IB vessels found in graves at Tarsus suggests the possibility of occasional contacts, prob-ably maritime (Hennessy 1967: 38), a possibility borne out by the discovery of two imported southeast Anatolian vessels in a final EB IB funerary context at Tel Asawir (Yannai and Braun 2001: fig. 22.1:19–20).

On the other hand, the relations with Egypt were intensive and widespread (de Miroschedji 2002; Braun and van den Brink 2008). However, they illustrate a completely different situation since they took place in the framework of an Egyptian colonial enterprise affecting mainly the southwestern part of Palestine.

The interaction between the two countries was a dynamic process. Following an initial phase of sporadic exchanges in the Late Chalcolithic, the relations developed during the EB I at the rhythm of the emergence of the Egyptian state. The increase of the mining activi-ties at Feinan, the expansion of horticulture, the domestication of the donkey as a beast of burden, and the progress in navigation techniques created the *sine qua non* conditions for the establishment of regular exchange relations.

The EB IA saw the first evidence of Egyptian presence along the north coast of Sinai and in a small area at the south of the coastal plain in search of copper and other local products. The EB IB witnessed a considerable development of the Egyptian presence in many settle-ments of southwestern Palestine which became a *de facto* Egyptian colonial territory, from where local products, mainly oil and wine, were exported to Egypt. This interaction culmi-nated during the Final EB IB, contemporary in Egypt with Dynasty 0 and the beginning of the First Dynasty. The Egyptian colonial domain was then administered by Egyptian offi-cials probably residing in the Egyptian fortified settlement of Tell es-Sakan (de Miroschedji et al. 2001) and in *entrepôts* like En Besor (Gophna 1995) and trading outposts like Tel Erani (Brandl 1989). The Kfar Monash hoard of copper tools and weapons is another testimony of the Egyptian presence in the coastal plain (Tadmor 2002; Sebbane 2003).

Funerary practices

For a long time, burials were the major source of information on the EB I. Several scores of tombs, isolated or grouped in cemeteries near settlements, have been excavated. In the

Mediterranean zone, they consist of artificial caves accessed through a lateral shaft (de Miroschedji 2000a). Each tomb was used for collective burials during a long span of time, presumably by an extended family or clan, so that hundreds of skeletons were sometimes accumulated in disorder. In most cases, especially at Jericho at the end of the period, it seems that primary burials were practised.

In the semi-arid peripheries, secondary burials in tombs built above ground prevailed. They belong to several distinct traditions. Dolmenic burials exist in the Golan and its western periphery, on the Jordanian Plateau, and in the Jordan Valley (Zohar 1992). In some areas of the Negev and in southern Sinai are found built tombs in the shape of a circular (Sinai) or a square room (Negev) (Bar-Yosef et al. 1986; Haiman 1992); these *nawamis* and their variants are part of a funerary tradition typical of the southern deserts that can be traced to Oman through the Arabian Peninsula from the EB I onward.

Cult and religion

Indirect evidence attesting to the importance of funerary rituals is provided by the appearance during the EB I of cultic vessels, sometimes found in tombs (Amiran 1986; 1989; Greenberg 2001: 83–8). The same vessels might have been used in public rituals. There is evidence of temples within a settlement at Hartuv, and especially at Megiddo (see above). Presumably these temples were dedicated to a fertility goddess, as in the Chalcolithic and the EB II–III periods (see below).

Early Bronze II–III

Sequence and chronology

A synchronism between the final EB IB and Narmer, *c.*3100 BC, suggests that the EB I–II transition took place during the 31st century BC at the latest (Amiran 1965; 1969; Regev et al. 2012). Although stratigraphically gradual, it was culturally striking, marked by the appearance of fortified cities—a radically new factor which entailed deep social changes, immediately perceptible in the organization of the settlements and in the nature of the material culture.

Further synchronisms, albeit imprecise, imply that the EB II lasted for more than two centuries, until *c.*2900/2850 BC (Regev, de Miroschedji, and Boaretto 2012; Regev et al. 2012). The transition from EB II to EB III is indicated by clear changes in the material culture in the south and by the appearance of Khirbet Kerak Ware (see below) in the north. There are indications of local disturbances leading to the abandonment of several important sites in some areas (the Huleh Basin, the Jordan Valley, the central coastal plain, and the northern Negev), but elsewhere there are strong signs of an expansion of settlements, especially in the southern coastal plain, reoccupied after several centuries of virtual abandonment (Greenberg 2002: 95–100; de Miroschedji 2006: 70–73; Getzov, Paz, and Gophna 2001).

The EB III essentially paralleled the Egyptian Old Kingdom, until *c.*2500/2400 BC. It represents the zenith of the Early Bronze civilization in the southern Levant, when sites reached their maximum extension and monumental architecture developed.

Pattern of settlement

The EB II witnessed a sudden acceleration of the urbanization process marked by the abandonment of numerous EB I villages whose inhabitants moved to some settlements which were rapidly transformed into urban fortified sites (Fig. 22.1) (Getzov, Paz, and Gophna 2001).

As a result, a hierarchy emerged between large fortified sites, which could be regional centres; medium-sized or small fortified settlements, some of which may have been dependent on the former; villages of various sizes; permanent or semi-permanent hamlets; and camps. There was considerable regional variation in the density and nature of settlements: some areas (the northern part of the country and the Shephelah) were heavily populated and accommodated large urban settlements; whereas other areas, in particular the northern Negev, had only villages and a single fortified site in the EB II (Tel Arad). From the distribution of isolated tombs and megalithic burials, it is clear that a sizeable segment of the population was mobile.

Fortified cities

The construction of ramparts was a response to local situations of insecurity linked to the gradual development of a political system which, during six or seven centuries, fragmented the greater part of the Mediterranean area of the southern Levant into rival city-states, periodically engaged in local conflicts. Some settlements were surrounded by fortifications right from the beginning of the EB II, but most were fortified only in the course of the period, or even only at the beginning of the EB III. In some cases the city wall was erected on virgin soil; in others it was built over the ruins of dwellings and the settlement shrank accordingly.

About fifty fortified sites are known west of the Jordan River (Fig. 22.1) (Getzov, Paz, and Gophna 2001). The smallest cover about 2ha or 3ha (Jericho); the largest exceed 15ha (Yarmuth (18ha), Beth Yerah (25ha), the average being between 5ha and 12ha (Megiddo, Tell el-Fârʻah, Tel Arad, Ai, etc.). The strength of fortifications reveals a hierarchy between major cities, whose fortifications can reach, as in Tel Yarmuth, a thickness of up to 40m (de Miroschedji 1990), and those which, by comparison, evoke rather fortified towns, like Tel Arad (Amiran et al. 1978; Amiran and Ilan 1996).

In use for several centuries, these fortifications were subjected to successive modifications and restorations (Figs 22.3 and 22.4) (Ben-Tor 1992; Kempinski 1992a). The walls proper vary in thickness from 2.5m to 9m, and consist usually of a stone base, up to 7m high, and brick superstructures. They include defensive works such as semi-circular or quadrangular towers or bastions placed at regular intervals. At Tel Yarmuth (Fig. 22.3 top and centre right), there were possibly as many as 30 bastions, each 20m long, 8–10m wide and at least 6m high, with two or three inner rooms. Approach to these walls was often prevented by a glacis of earth and stone or bricks, the largest of which, up to 10m high, are forerunners of the Middle Bronze glacis (Fig. 22.3 bottom). City gates were either simple openings in the rampart or present complex arrangements with flanking towers and offset access (Fig. 22.3, centre left and right) (Herzog 1988).

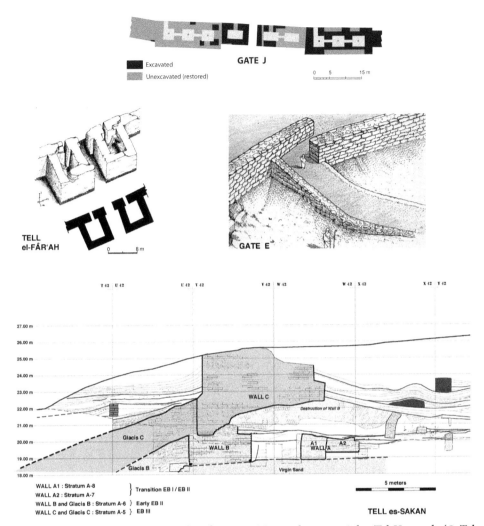

FIG. 22.3 Examples of EB II–III fortifications. Top and centre right: Tel Yarmuth (© Tel Yarmuth Archaeological Expedition). Centre left: Vaux 1962: 223, fig. 1. Bottom: Tell es-Sakan (Tell es-Sakan French–Palestinian Archaeological Expedition)

Urban organization

Excavations provide only a glimpse of the inner organization of some cities (Fig. 22.4). They appear densely built in their totality and may have sheltered between 1,000 and 3,000 inhabitants. In the few cases where the transition from EB I to EB II could be observed (Qiryat Ata and Beth Yerah), it shows the rapid transformation of the layout of dwellings and settlements (Faust and Golani 2008).

There are, however, marked regional differences in the character of the EB II–III settlements. Tel Arad in the northern Negev, a region where nomadic pastoralism was predominant, is an example at the lower end of the spectrum of urban complexity (Finkelstein 1995:

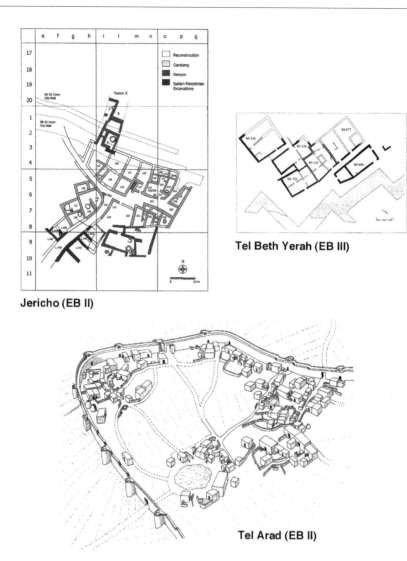

Jericho (EB II)

Tel Beth Yerah (EB III)

Tel Arad (EB II)

FIG. 22.4 Examples of urban layouts. Top left: Nigro 2010: fig. 4.45. Top right: Greenberg et al. 2006: fig. 5.43. Bottom: Amiran and Ilan 1992: 38, Abb. 23

67–86; Herzog 1997: 44–62). The town is formed by the juxtaposition of dwelling units separated from each other by open spaces used for circulation (Fig. 22.4 bottom). Each unit probably sheltered a family. Their inner organization evokes a camp of pastoral nomads surrounded by a fence: each area comprised a main broadroom instead of a tent, and of some annexes distributed along an enclosure wall. Their agglomeration gives to the settlement the appearance of a vast petrified encampment.

The difference is striking with the most urbanized centres found in the Mediterranean region, such as Tel Bareqet, Tell el-Fârʿah, and Qiryat Ata in EB II, or Tel Yarmuth, Beth Yerah (Fig. 22.4 top right), and Jericho (Fig. 22.4 top left) in EB III. The domestic dwellings usually comprised one or two rooms, a courtyard, and one or two storerooms (de Miroschedji

1999; Ilan 2001; Greenberg et al. 2006; Paz and Paz 2007; Faust and Golani 2008). They were closely imbricated and their grouping formed insulae bordered by streets, some paved; an insula presumably hosted an extended family. This kind of urban structure reveals a social organization and a degree of urban integration much more complex than in the northern Negev.

Public buildings

The cities enclosed some public buildings, identified by their size, their layout, and the unusual quality of their building techniques. The typical temples follow the tradition of the preceding period and consist of a large oblong hall with an axial row of pillar bases (Kempinski 1992b; Sala 2007); this hall was doubled in the case of the twin temples(?) of Tel Arad, possibly dedicated to a divine couple (Fig. 22.2 centre left) (Amiran et al. 1978; Sala 2007: 163–75). A courtyard in front of the hall may open onto one or several rooms and contain various installations (basins, hearths, and offering platform). Another kind of layout, which has Syrian connections, is the pseudo-megaron, attested by temples (including a twin temple) at EB III Megiddo (Strata XVII–XV/J-7) (Fig. 22.2 bottom left): it consists of an *in antis* portico with two pillars opening onto a slightly oblong main hall with an axial row of pillars (Loud 1948: 70–78; Finkelstein and Ussishkin 2000: 68–71; Sala 2007: 219–40). A large circular offering platform accessed by steps is attached to the single temple of Megiddo (Sala 2007: 214–19) and a comparable structure was found in connection with the temples of Khirbet ez-Zeraqun (Genz 2010).

Palaces (in the strictest sense) are not attested before the EB III. At Megiddo, a partially excavated palace (Building 3177), comprising about twenty rooms, corridors, and inner courtyards, was located close to the temple area (Loud 1948: 70–76; Nigro 1995: 16–23). At Tel Yarmuth, two superimposed palaces dating from the late EB III were brought to light (de Miroschedji 2003; 2008). Palace B2 was erected over the ruins of a violently destroyed dwelling quarter. It covered at least 1,750m² and included more than 26 rooms and courtyards. Completely razed after a short existence, it was replaced by Palace B1, of large and truly monumental proportions (Fig. 22.5). Bordered by domestic living quarters and erected on a partially artificial terrace after extensive ground levelling and terracing, Palace B1 is a quadrilateral measuring 84x72.5m (*c.*6000m²) enclosed by a thick peripheral wall with deep foundations and inner buttresses. Elaborate planning methods were applied, resulting in a regular orthogonal inner layout, with measurement based on a cubit of 52.5cm, similar to the Egyptian royal cubit (de Miroschedji 2001a). Although its inner space was partly destroyed, excavations have uncovered two large courtyards and more than forty rooms, corridors, and small inner courtyards, including a dozen storerooms filled with pithoi (de Miroschedji 2006). The entrance opened onto a hypostyle hall measuring 17×13.9m, leading to a forecourt and then to a large (70m²) reception hall. The building techniques are of exceptional quality: wall masonry, brickwork, preparation of thresholds, and pebbled floors, drainage channels converging toward a large, well-shaped water reservoir—all these elements bear witness to a remarkable architectural sophistication.

Other public buildings are few. The foundations of large monumental constructions have been identified at Tel Yarmuth, but their nature is uncertain. In an EB III stratum of the

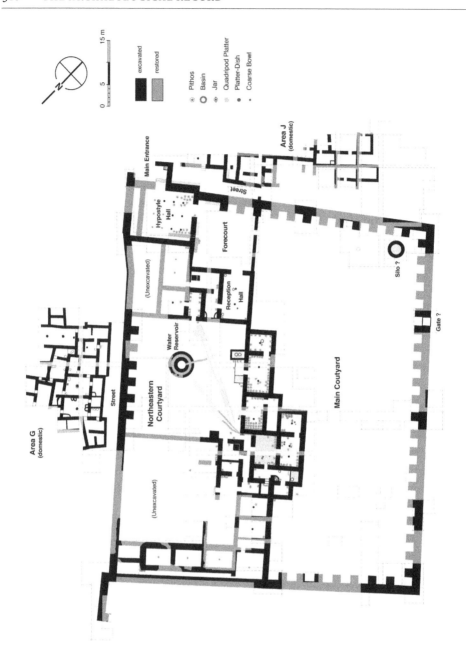

FIG. 22.5 Tel Yarmuth: plan of Palace B1 and adjacent domestic quarters. *In situ* vessels are shown in the excavated storerooms (© Tel Yarmuth Archaeological Expedition)

same site a building was uncovered (the 'White Building') (Fig. 22.2 centre right) which was initially identified as a temple (de Miroschedji 1988; 1999), but which was more probably a patrician house. An EB III monumental granary discovered at Beth Yerah gives an idea of the quantity of grain surpluses stored by a community under the authority of its leaders (Mazar 2001; Greenberg and Paz 2006).

City-states

The palaces of Yarmuth and Megiddo and the granary of Beth Yerah testify that the major cities of EB II–III Palestine were real city-states, characterized by a strong social hierarchy, a hereditary centralized power, and the functioning of a palatial economy. In smaller cities, however, the sociopolitical organization was presumably less complex and more comparable to that of chiefdoms. This diversity explains why the evaluations made by scholars of Early Bronze achievements on the scale of urban complexity are so diverse: seen from east of the Jordan river, the prevalent image is that of a heterarchical society whose members reside in corporate villages, some of which were fortified (Chesson and Philip 2003; Savage, Falconer, and Harrison 2007). But seen from west of the Jordan river, the landscape is much more contrasted, and shows many city-states with monumental architecture and evidence of political and economic centralization involving rather large territories (de Miroschedji 2006).

Economy

The economic basis of the Early Bronze city-states was essentially the same as in the preceding EB I period, but on a larger and more intensive scale. Horticulture, in particular, was widespread and had a decisive social impact, as suggested by the number of vessels (jugs and combed jars), used to contain oil and wine, and the frequency of their importation in Egypt (Hennessy 1967: 49–60, 71–3; Sowada 2009). Animal husbandry concentrated on cattle, sheep, and goats (Horwitz and Tchernov 1989; Hesse and Wapnish 2002). Three trends should be mentioned: the reluctance to consume pig, evident in the faunal spectrum of several sites; an emphasis on milk herds, indicated by the frequency of older female sheep and goats in faunal samples; and the preferential breeding of sheep, which implies a development of textile activities and a heavier reliance on the (semi-)nomadic pastoral component of the population as a provider of meat.

Material culture

Pottery

The changes in pottery from EB I to EB II are marked by the appearance of new shapes which characterize the EB II–III. Most prominent among them are the carinated platters, a hallmark of the period. Regional particularisms fade away, except between north and south (Greenberg forthcoming; de Miroschedji forthcoming).

There is no technological revolution, but trends perceptible earlier are now more manifest. The percentage of wheel-fashioned vessels increased and several basalt tournettes were identified (Roux and de Miroschedji 2009). Many vessels were fired at high temperature in closed kilns, one of which, quite elaborate, was discovered at Tell el-Fâr'ah (Vaux 1955).

These kilns imply the existence of resident professional potters. Pottery workshops, exporting their production over a wide area, are attested by the frequency of potters' marks and the standardization of pottery shapes and surface treatments within a site or a region, and especially by the widespread distribution of some specialized ceramics. The best example of the latter is the EB II–III Northern Metallic Ware, whose production centre may have been located in the Hulah Valley and whose distribution area covers the northern half of the southern Levant (Greenberg and Porat 1996).

Another example of high-quality production is the so-called Abydos Ware, named after the site in Egypt where it has been imported in abundance from the southern Levant during EB II. It consists mainly of red burnished or painted jugs (Amiran 1974). In EB III, several types of red simple or pattern-burnished vessels continue this tradition. Noteworthy among these display vessels are the late EB III 'giant' platters found in Yarmuth, with a diameter of up to 90cm.

The Khirbet Kerak Ware, named after a site (Hebrew Tel Beth Yerah) on the southern shore of the Sea of Galilee where it was first identified, represents a phenomenon of a different kind, since it was introduced by immigrants of northern origin (Philip 1999; de Miroschedji 2000b; Greenberg 2007). It is characterized by a specific manufacturing technique, typology, and decoration, with no local antecedents. The vessels are handmade and have a highly burnished red or red and black slip. The shapes are mostly bowls and craters with sharply sinuous profiles. The decoration is either incised or in relief. Found mainly in the plain of Israel and its vicinity, these remarkable vessels were distributed, albeit in small quantities, in the rest of the southern Levant. Considered prestigious, they have been imitated to produce hybrid vessels, combining the characteristics of the Khirbet Kerak Ware with local Canaanite shape. Frequently associated with this ware, the 'andirons' are horseshoe-shaped objects sometimes bearing an anthropomorphic incised decoration. They replicate large domestic hearths found in eastern Anatolia, and may have been used as portable hearths or pot stands with a symbolic connotation (de Miroschedji 2000b).

Metallurgy

The increase of mining activities during the EB II–III at Feinan, Timna, and in the southern Sinai brought about the expansion of the metallurgical production (Hauptmann 2003), indicated by the higher frequency and diversity of tools and weapons. This metallurgy concerned only copper: appearing in Mesopotamia around 2500 BC, bronze was still unknown in the southern Levant.

Art

Stamp and cylinder seals are frequent in EB II–III in northern and central Palestine, and were used to mark the shoulder or neck of jars as in the EB I. Decorations are geometric or naturalistic, showing animals and/or human beings (Ben-Tor 1978; de Miroschedji 1997).

Animal or human figurines are widespread. Bone or ivory bulls' heads should also be mentioned (de Miroschedji 1993), as well as bone handles decorated with geometric designs, a kind also attested in contemporary Syria (Genz 2003).

Foreign relations

In the EB II–III, there is more evidence of interregional and foreign contacts. To the south, Palestine maintained sustained relations with the Negev and Sinai during EB II (Amiran, Beit-Arieh, and Glass 1973; Finkelstein 1995: 67–86; Beit-Arieh 2003). The urban developments around the Mediterranean zone created a strong demand for raw material and manufactured objects produced by pastoral nomads of the southern deserts. Their products converged on Tel Arad, whose prosperity depended on the intensity of these exchange networks. Their cessation at the end of the EB II, possibly as a consequence of Egyptian control of the Sinaitic Peninsula at the beginning of the Old Kingdom, provoked the simultaneous abandonment of Tel Arad and of the seasonal sites of the Negev and Sinai. No EB III sites have been identified in the southern deserts. The network based on the copper of Feinan, however, continued to function but was diverted to the north of the Aravah, leading to the prosperity of sites like Numeira and Bab edh-Dhraʿ on the eastern shore of the Dead Sea.

The nature of the relations between Egypt and Palestine changed drastically at the beginning of EB II. There was no need for the Egyptians to maintain colonies in southwestern Palestine now that trading partners could be found locally among the leaders of the newly founded city-states. Consequently, the Egyptian colonies were abandoned and the Egyptians instead established direct contacts with the Palestinian city-states, exchanging presents for local products (de Miroschedji 2002). Their economic interests had also changed: rather than oil and wine, they were now looking for wood, resins, and perfumed oil—all products to be found further north (Sowada 2009: 245–8). Therefore they developed maritime instead of overland connections, mainly with northern Palestine. The frequency of these imports is shown by many scores of Canaanite jugs and bottles found in royal and noble tombs of the First Dynasty. In exchange, the Palestinians received objects of prestige, mainly stone vessels, of which a rich collection originate from the temple of Ai (Amiran 1970).

These relations faded away with the beginning of EB III, when Egypt developed privileged relations with Byblos, as a result of growing interest in cedar wood and of progress in navigation techniques (Marcus 2002; Sowada 2009: 248–55). Palestine was then essentially bypassed by Egyptian maritime trading expeditions. Contacts with southern Palestine existed nevertheless. Funerary bas-reliefs, wall paintings, and inscriptions testify to military expeditions, both maritime and overland, conducted by the Egyptians along the Palestinian coast at the end of the Old Kingdom (de Miroschedji 2012).

Relations between Palestine and the areas situated to the north (Lebanon, Syria, and Anatolia) are evidenced by only a few imported objects with northern affinities (Hennessy 1967: 79–83). The clearest instance of northern contacts is provided by the sudden influx of the Khirbet Kerak Ware, whose abundance and characteristics suggest that it was introduced, not as a result of trade connections, but rather with the arrival of immigrants (de Miroschedji 2000b; Greenberg 2007). Given the absence of way stations to illustrate their progression between Syria and Palestine, they may have come by sea (Philip 1999).

Funerary practices

In the Mediterranean zone, EB II–III funerary practices continued those of the preceding period. The sepulchral caves were often used for massive collective burials, up to several hundred individuals. In the steppic and semi-arid peripheries, the practice of above-ground megalithic burials expanded. In the Negev, EB II settlements are frequently associated with fields of tumuli, usually located on higher ground in order to be clearly visible and demarcate territories (Haiman 1992). In the north, especially in the Golan, many dolmens situated in predominantly pastoral areas may be dated to that period (Vinitzky 1992; Greenberg

2002: 79). It has been suggested that the megalithic complex of Rujm el-Hiri in the central Golan, the largest of its kind known in the Near East, should be ascribed to EB II–III (Mizrachi 1992; Aveni and Mizrachi 1998).

Cult and religion

The temples excavated as well as a few cultic objects and cylinder-seal imprints give a glimpse into cultic practices. Cultic objects consist of votive beds and votive shrines in terracotta, cultic stands, and cultic bowls on a pedestal foot (de Miroschedji 2001b). The cylinder-seal imprints suggest that the main deity was, as in the Late Chalcolithic period, a fertility goddess, while the twin temples hint at the existence of a divine couple, with a male deity perhaps associated with vegetation. Indeed, some imprints show either a man approaching a woman at the gate of a building, presumably the temple of the goddess, or their sexual intercourse; hence they evoke the ritual of the sacred marriage intended to ensure fertility on earth (de Miroschedji 2011).

The collapse of the Early Bronze Age civilization

The Early Bronze civilization just described collapsed in the course of the 25th century BC. All the EB III cities were deserted and many were never resettled. Palestine then plunged into a kind of 'Dark Age', presenting for several centuries a landscape of villages and encampments of pastoral nomads, before the reurbanization process which marks the beginning of the Middle Bronze I. The causes of this rather swift collapse of a civilization apparently so dynamic are yet uncertain. Once popular, the hypothesis of a massive Amorite invasion has long been discarded for lack of archaeological testimonies. Other hypotheses have been put forward which invoke climatic, social, and political crises, each on solid ground. A combination of these factors is most probable, triggering a domino effect all over the southern Levant.

The collapse of Early Bronze civilization appears as a large-scale systemic phenomenon (de Miroschedji 2009). It emphasizes the structural fragility of sedentary societies living at the fringe of the Fertile Crescent. Their history is marked by the succession of periods of expansion and contraction, urbanization and deurbanization. In the *longue durée* of the history of Palestine, the Early Bronze corresponds to the first efflorescence of an urban civilization, a kind of rehearsal before the golden age of Canaanite civilization in the Middle Bronze Age.

Suggested reading

Ben-Tor, A. (1992). The Early Bronze Age. In A. Ben-Tor (ed.), *The Archaeology of Ancient Israel*. New Haven, Conn.: Yale University Press/Tel Aviv: Open University of Israel, 81–125.

Esse, D. L. (1991). *Subsistence, Trade, and Social Change in Early Bronze Age Palestine*. Chicago: Oriental Institute of the University of Chicago.

Greenberg, R. (2002). *Early Urbanizations in the Levant: A Regional Narrative*. London: Leicester University Press.

Joffe, A. H. (1993). *Settlement and Society in the Early Bronze Age I and II, Southern Levant: Complementarity and Contradiction in a Small-Scale Complex Society*. Sheffield: Sheffield Academic.

Maeir, A. M., and P. de Miroschedji (eds) (2006). *'I Will Speak the Riddles of Ancient Times': Archaeological and Historical Studies in Honor of Amihai Mazar on the Occasion of His Sixtieth Birthday*, vol. 1. Winona Lake, Ind.: Eisenbrauns, 3–112.

Mazar, A. (1990). *Archaeology of the Land of the Bible, 10,000–586 B.C.E.* New York: Doubleday, 91–150.

Miroschedji, P. de (ed.) (1989). *L'urbanisation de la Palestine à l'âge du Bronze ancien: bilan et perspectives des recherches actuelles* (2 vols). Oxford: British Archaeological Reports.

Philip, G., and D. Baird (eds) (2000). *Ceramics and Change in the Early Bronze Age of the Southern Levant*. Sheffield: Sheffield Academic.

Stager, L. E. (1992). The periodization of Palestine from Neolithic through Early Bronze times. In R. W. Ehrich (ed.), *Chronologies in Old World Archaeology*, vol. 1, 3rd edn. Chicago: University of Chicago Press, 22–41.

van den Brink, E. C. M., and T. E. Levy (eds) (2002). *Egypt and the Levant: Interrelations from the 4th through the Early 3rd Millennium BCE*. London: Leicester University Press.

——and E. Yannai (eds) (2002). *In Quest of Ancient Settlements and Landscapes: Archaeological Studies in Honour of Ram Gophna*. Tel Aviv: Tel Aviv University.

Wolff, S. R. (ed.) (2001). *Studies in the Archaeology of Israel and Neighboring Lands in Memory of Douglas L. Esse*. Chicago: Oriental Institute, University of Chicago/Atlanta, Ga.: American Schools of Oriental Research.

References

Amiran, R. (1965). A preliminary note on the synchronism between the Early Bronze Age strata of Arad and the First Dynasty. *Bulletin of the American Schools of Oriental Research* 179: 30–33.

——(1969). A second note on the synchronism between Early Bronze Arad and the First Dynasty. *Bulletin of the American Schools of Oriental Research* 195: 50–53.

——(1970). The Egyptian alabaster vessels from Ai. *Israel Exploration Journal* 20: 170–79.

——(1974). The Painted Pottery Style of the Early Bronze II period in Palestine. *Levant* 6: 65–8.

——(1986). Some cult-and-art objects of the EB I Period. In M. Kelly-Buccellati, P. Matthiae, and M. N. van Loon (eds), *Insight Through Images: Studies in Honor of Edith Porada*. Malibu, Calif.: Undena, 7–13.

——(1989). An Early Bronze I basalt cult-bowl with ibex reliefs. *Israel Museum Journal* 8: 17–23.

——and O. Ilan (1992). *Arad: eine 5000 Jahre Stadt in der Wüste Negev, Israel*. Neumünster: K. Wachholtz.

——(eds) (1996). *Early Arad II, The Chalcolithic and Early Bronze IB Settlements and the Early Bronze II City, Architecture and Town Planning: Sixth to Eighteenth Seasons of Excavations, 1971–1978, 1980–1984.* Jerusalem: Israel Museum/Israel Exploration Society.

——I. Beit-Arieh, and J. Glass (1973). The interrelationship between Arad and sites in southern Sinai in the Early Bronze Age II (preliminary report). *Israel Exploration Journal* 23: 193–7.

——U. Paran, Y. Shiloh, R. Brown, Y. Tsafrir, and A. Ben-Tor (1978). *Early Arad, The Chalcolithic Settlement and the Early Bronze Age City: First–Fifth Seasons of Excavations, 1962–1966.* Jerusalem: Israel Museum/Israel Exploration Society.

Aveni, A. F., and Y. Mizrachi (1998). The geometry and astronomy of Rujm el-Hiri, a megalithic site in the southern Levant. *Journal of Field Archaeology* 25: 475–96.

Bar, S. (2010). Early Bronze Age I 'Umm Hamad Ware': a study in regionalism. *Palestine Exploration Quarterly* 142: 82–94.

Bar-Yosef, O., A. Belfer-Cohen, A. Goren, et al. (1986). Nawamis and habitation sites near Gebel Gunna, southern Sinaï. *Israel Exploration Journal* 36: 121–67.

Beit-Arieh, I. (2003). *Archaeology of Sinai: The Ophir Expedition.* Tel Aviv: Emery and Claire Yass Publications in Archaeology.

Ben-Tor, A. (1978). *Cylinder Seals of Third Millenium Palestine.* Cambridge: American Schools of Oriental Research.

——(1992). The Early Bronze Age. In A. Ben-Tor (ed.), *The Archaeology of Ancient Israel.* New Haven, Conn.: Yale University Press/Tel Aviv: Open University of Israel, 81–125.

Brandl, B. (1989). Observations on the Early Bronze Age strata of Tel Erani. In de Miroschedji (1989: ii.357–87).

Braun, E. (1989). The problem of the apsidal house: new aspects of Early Bronze I domestic architecture in Israel, Jordan, and Lebanon. *Palestine Exploration Quarterly* 121: 1–43.

——(1990). Basalt bowls of the EB I horizon in the southern Levant. *Paléorient* 16: 87–96.

——(2009). Social development in Early Bronze Age I of the southern Levant: reflections on evidence for different modes of ceramic productions. In S. A. Rosen and V. Roux (eds), *Techniques and People: Anthropological Perspectives on Technology in the Archaeology of the Proto-Historic and Early Historic Periods in the Southern Levant.* Paris: De Boccard, 233–52.

——(2011). The transition from Chalcolithic to Early Bronze I in the southern Levant: a 'lost horizon' slowly revealed. In J. L. Lovell and Y. M. Rowan (eds), *Culture, Chronology and the Chalcolithic: Theory in Transition.* Oxford: Oxbow, 160–77.

——(forthcoming). Early Bronze Age I (3700–3100/3050). In S. Gitin and E. Yannai (eds), *The Pottery of Ancient Israel and Its Neighbors,* vol. 1. Jerusalem: Israel Exploration Society/ W. F. Albright Institute of Archaeological Research/Israel Antiquities Authority.

——and E. C. M. van den Brink (2008). Appraising south Levantine–Egyptian interaction: recent discoveries from Israel and Egypt. In B. Midant-Reynes and Y. Tristant (eds), *Egypt at Its Origins 2: Proceedings of the International Conference 'Origin of the State, Predynastic and Early Dynastic Egypt', Toulouse (France), 5th–8th September 2005.* Leuven: Peeters, 643–75.

Chesson, M. S., and G. Philip (2003). Tales of the city? 'Urbanism' in the Early Bronze Age Levant from Mediterranean and Levantine perspectives. *Journal of Mediterranean Archaeology* 16: 3–16.

Milevski, I. (2008). The exchange of ground stone tools and vessels during the Early Bronze Age in the southern Levant. In Y. M. Rowan and J. R. Ebening (eds), *New Approaches to Old Stones: Recent Studies of Ground Stone Artifacts.* London: Equinox, 116–29.

Miroschedji, P. de (1971). *L'époque pré-urbaine en Palestine.* Paris: Gabalda.

—— (1988). *Yarmouth 1: Rapport sur les trois premières campagnes de fouilles à Tel Yarmouth (Israël), 1980–1982.* Paris: Recherche sur les civilisations.

—— (1990). The Early Bronze Age fortifications at Tel Yarmuth: an interim statement. *Eretz-Israel* 21: 48*–61*.

—— (1993). Note sur les têtes de taureau en os, en ivoire et en pierre du Bronze ancien de Palestine. In M. Heltzer, A. Segal, and D. Kaufman (eds), *Studies in the Archaeology and History of Ancient Israel in Honor of Moshe Dothan.* Haifa: Haifa University Press, 29*–40*.

—— (1997). La glyptique palestinienne du Bronze ancien. In A. Caubet (ed.), *De Chypre à la Bactriane: les sceaux du Proche-Orient ancien.* Paris: La Documentation française, Musée du Louvre, 189–227.

—— (1999). Yarmuth: the dawn of city-states in southern Canaan. *Near Eastern Archaeology* 62: 2–19.

—— (2000a). Les sépultures hypogées au Levant des IVe–IIe millénaires. In *L'ipogeismo nel Mediterraneo: origini, sviluppo, quadri culturali.* Sassari: Università degli Studi di Sassari, Facoltà di lettere e filosofia, 29–82.

—— (2000b). La céramique de Khirbet Kérak en Syro-Palestine: état de la question. In C. Marro and H. Hauptmann (eds), *Chronologies des pays du Caucase et de l'Euphrate aux IVe–IIIe millénaires.* Paris: Institut français d'études anatoliennes d'Istanbul, 255–78.

—— (2001a). Notes on Early Bronze Age metrology and the birth of architecture in Palestine. In S. R. Wolff (ed.), *Studies in the Archaeology of Israel and Neighboring Lands in Memory of Douglas L. Esse.* Chicago: Oriental Institute, University of Chicago/Atlanta, Ga.: American Schools of Oriental Research, 465–91.

—— (2001b). Les 'maquettes architecturales' palestiniennes. In B. Muller (ed.), *Maquettes architecturales de l'Antiquité, regards croisés: Proche-Orient, Egypte, Chypre, bassin égéen et Grèce, du néolithique à l'époque hellénistique.* Paris: De Boccard, 43–85.

—— (2002). The socio-political dynamics of Egyptian–Canaanite interaction in the Early Bronze Age. In van den Brink and Levy (2002: 39–57).

—— (2003). The Late Early Bronze Age III Palace B1 at Tel Yarmuth: a descriptive summary. *Eretz-Israel* 27: 153*–70*.

—— (2006). At the dawn of history: sociopolitical developments in southwestern Canaan in Early Bronze Age III. In A. M. Maeir and P. de Miroschedji (eds), *'I Will Speak the Riddles of Ancient Times': Archaeological and Historical Studies in Honor of Amihai Mazar on the Occasion of His Sixtieth Birthday,* vol. 1. Winona Lake, Ind.: Eisenbrauns, 55–78.

—— (2008). Jarmuth, Tel. In E. Stern (ed.), *The New Encyclopedia of Archaeological Excavations in the Holy Land,* vol. 5: *Supplementary Volume.* Jerusalem: Israel Exploration Society/Washington, DC: Biblical Archaeology Society, 1792–7.

—— (2009). Rise and collapse in the southern Levant in the Early Bronze Age. In A. Cardarelli, A. Cazzella, M. Frangipane, and R. Peroni (eds), *Reasons for Change: Birth, Decline and Collapse of Societies from the End of the Fourth to the Beginning of the First Millennium BC.* Rome: Università degli Studi di Roma 'La Sapienza', 101–29.

—— (2011). At the origin of Canaanite cult and religion: the Early Bronze Age fertility ritual in Palestine. *Eretz Israel* 74*–103*.

—— (2012). Egypt and southern Canaan in the third millennium BCE: Uni's Asiatic campaigns revisited. In S. Ahituv, M. Gruber, G. Lehmann, and Z. Talshir (eds), *All the Wisdom of the East: Studies in Near Eastern Archaeology and History in Honor of Eliezer D. Oren.* Fribourg: Academic Press/Göttingen: Vandenhoeck & Ruprecht, 265–92.

—— (forthcoming). Early Bronze Age III (2700–2200). In S. Gitin and E. Yannai (eds), *The Pottery of Ancient Israel and Its Neighbors*, vol. 1. Jerusalem: Israel Exploration Society/ W.F. Albright Institute of Archaeological Research/Israel Antiquities Authority.

—— M. Sadek, D. Faltings, et al. (2001). Les fouilles de Tell es-Sakan (Gaza): nouvelles données sur les contacts égypto-cananéens aux IVe–IIIe millénaires. *Paléorient* 27: 75–104.

Faust, A., and A. Golani (2008). A community in transition: the Early Bronze Age site of Qiryat Ata as a test case. *Tel Aviv* 35: 215–43.

Finkelstein, I. (1995). *Living on the Fringe: The Archaeology and History of the Negev, Sinai and Neighbouring Regions in the Bronze and Iron Ages*. Sheffield: Sheffield Academic.

—— and D. Ussishkin (2000). Area J. In I. Finkelstein, D. Ussishkin, and B. Halpern (eds), *Megiddo III: The 1992–1996 Seasons*. Tel Aviv: Tel Aviv University, 25–74.

—— and J. Peersmann (2006). Area J (the 1998–2000 seasons). In I. Finkelstein, D. Ussishkin, and B. Halpern (eds), *Megiddo IV: The 1998–2002 Seasons*. Tel Aviv: Tel Aviv University, 29–53.

Genz, H. (2003). *Ritzverzierte Knochenhülsen des dritten Jahrtausends im Ostmittelmeerraum: eine Studie zu den frühen Kulturverbindungen zwischen Levante und Ägäis*. Wiesbaden: Harrassowitz.

—— (2010). Thoughts on the function of public buildings in the Early Bronze Age southern Levant. In D. Bolger and L. C. Maguire (eds), *The Development of Pre-State Communities in the Ancient Near East: Studies in Honor of Edgar Peltenburg*. Oxford: Oxbow, 46–52.

Getzov, N., Y. Paz, and R. Gophna (2001). *Shifting Urban Landscapes during the Early Bronze Age in the Land of Israel*. Tel Aviv: Tel Aviv University.

Gophna, R. (1995). *Excavations at 'En Besor*. Tel Aviv: Ramot, Tel Aviv University.

Greenberg, R. (2001). An Early Bronze Age I and II tomb at Gadot, in the Hula Valley. *'Atiqot* 42: 79–94.

—— (2002). *Early Urbanizations in the Levant: A Regional Narrative*. London: Leicester University Press.

—— (2007). Transcaucasian colors: Khirbet Kerak Ware at Khirbet Kerak (Tel Beth Yerah). In B. Lyonnet (ed.), *Les cultures du Caucase, VIe–IIIe millénaires avant notre ère: leurs relations avec le Proche-Orient*. Paris: Éditions Recherche sur les civilisations, 257–68.

—— (forthcoming). Early Bronze Age II (3100/3050–2800/2750). In S. Gitin and E. Yannai (eds), *The Pottery of Ancient Israel and Its Neighbors*, vol. 1. Jerusalem: Israel Exploration Society/W. F. Albright Institute of Archaeological Research/Israel Antiquities Authority.

—— E. Eisenberg, S. Paz, and Y. Paz (2006). *Beth Yerah: The Early Bronze Age Mound*, vol. 1: *Excavation Reports, 1933–1986*. Jerusalem: Israel Antiquities Authority.

—— and S. Paz (2006). The granary at Tel Beth Yerah: new assessments. *Qadmoniot* 39.132: 98–103 [Hebrew].

—— and N. Porat (1996). A third millennium Levantine pottery production centre: typology, petrography, and provenience of the Metallic Ware of northern Israel and adjacent region. *Bulletin of the American Schools of Oriental Research* 301: 5–24.

Grigson, C. (1995). Plough and pasture in the early economy of the southern Levant. In T. E. Levy (ed.), *The Archaeology of Society in the Holy Land*. London: Leicester University Press, 245–68.

Haiman, M. (1992). Cairn burials and cairn fields in the Negev. *Bulletin of the American Schools of Oriental Research* 287: 25–45.

Harrison, T. J. (2001). Early Bronze social organization as reflected in burial patterns from the southern Levant. In S. R. Wolff (ed.), *Studies in the Archaeology of Israel and Neighboring Lands in Memory of Douglas L. Esse*. Chicago: Oriental Institute, University of Chicago/ Atlanta, Ga.: American Schools of Oriental Research, 215–36.

Hauptmann, A. (2003). Developments in copper metallurgy during the fourth and third millennia BC at Feinan, Jordan. In P. T. Craddock and J. Lang (eds), *Mining and Metal Production through the Ages*. London: British Museum Press, 90–100.

Hennessy, J. B. (1967). *The Foreign Relations of Palestine during the Early Bronze Age*. London: Quaritch.

Herzog, Z. (1988). *Der Stadttor in Israel und in den Nachbarländern*. Mainz: von Zabern.

—— (1997). *Archaeology of the City: Urban Planning in Ancient Israel and Its Social Implications*. Tel Aviv: Tel Aviv University.

Hesse, B., and P. Wapnish (2002). An archaeozoological perspective on the cultural use of mammals in the Levant. In B. J. Collins (ed.), *A History of the Animal World in the Ancient Near East*. Leiden: Brill, 457–91.

Hizmi, H. (2004). An Early Bronze Age saddle donkey figurine from Khirbet el-Makhruq and the emerging appearance of beast of burden figurines. In H. Hizmi and A. De-Groot (eds), *Burial Caves and Sites in Judea and Samaria from the Bronze and Iron Ages*. Jerusalem: Israel Antiquities Authority, 309–24.

Horwitz, L. K., and E. Tchernov (1989). Animal exploitation in the Early Bronze Age of the southern Levant: an overview. In de Miroschedji (1989: i.279–96).

Ilan, O. (2001). Household archaeology at Arad and Ai in the Early Bronze Age II. In S. R. Wolff (ed.), *Studies in the Archaeology of Israel and Neighboring Lands in Memory of Douglas L. Esse*. Chicago: Oriental Institute, University of Chicago/Atlanta, Ga.: American Schools of Oriental Research, 317–54.

Kempinski, A. (1992a). Fortifications, public buildings, and town planning in the Early Bronze Age. In A. Kempinski and R. Reich (eds), *The Architecture of Ancient Israel from the Prehistoric to the Persian Periods in Memory of Immanuel (Munya) Dunayevsky*. Jerusalem: Israel Exploration Society, 68–80.

—— (1992b). Chalcolithic and Early Bronze Age temples. In A. Kempinski and R. Reich (eds), *The Architecture of Ancient Israel from the Prehistoric to the Persian Periods in Memory of Immanuel (Munya) Dunayevsky*. Jerusalem: Israel Exploration Society, 53–9.

Loud, G. (1948). *Megiddo II: Seasons of 1935–39* (2 vols). Chicago: University of Chicago Press.

Marcus, E. (2002). Early seafaring and maritime activity in the southern Levant from prehistory through the third millennium BCE. In van den Brink and Levy (2002: 403–17).

Mazar, A. (2001). On the significance of the Early Bronze III granary building at Beit Yerah. In S. R. Wolff (ed.), *Studies in the Archaeology of Israel and Neighboring Lands in Memory of Douglas L. Esse*. Chicago: Oriental Institute, University of Chicago/Atlanta, Ga.: American Schools of Oriental Research, 447–63.

—— and P. de Miroschedji (1996). Hartuv: an aspect of the Early Bronze Age I culture of southern Israel. *Bulletin of the American Schools of Oriental Research* 302: 1–40.

Mizrachi, Y. (1992). Mystery circles. *Biblical Archaeology Review* 18: 47–57.

Nigro, L. (1995). *Ricerche sull'architettura palaziale della Palestina nelle età del Bronzo e del Ferro: contesto archeologico e sviluppo storico*. Rome: Università degli studi di Roma 'La Sapienza'.

—— with contributions by M. Sala (2010). *Tell es-Sultan/Jericho in the Early Bronze Age II (3000–2700 BC): The Rise of an Early Palestinian City*. Rome: Università degli studi di Roma 'La Sapienza'.

Ovadia, E. (1992). The domestication of the ass and pack transport by animals: a case of technological change. In O. Bar-Yosef and A. M. Khazanov (eds), *Pastoralism in the Levant: Archaeological Materials in Anthropological Perspective*. Madison, Wis.: Prehistory, 19–28.

Paz, Y., and S. Paz (2007). Tel Bareket: excavations in a fortified city of the Early Bronze Age II in the central coastal plain. *Qadmoniot* 40.134: 82–8 [Hebrew].

Philip, G. (1999). Complexity and diversity in the southern Levant during the third millennium BC: the evidence of Khirbet Kerak Ware. *Journal of Mediterranean Archaeology* 12: 26–57.

—— and T. Rehren (1996). Fourth millennium BC silver from Tell esh-Shuna, Jordan: archaeometallurgical investigation and some thoughts on ceramic skeuomorphs. *Oxford Journal of Archaeology* 15: 129–50.

—— and O. Williams-Thorpe (2000). The production and distribution of ground stone artefacts in the southern Levant during the 5th–4th millennia BC: some implications of geochemical and petrographic analysis. In P. Matthiae, A. Enea, L. Peyronel, and F. Pinnock (eds), *Proceedings of the First International Congress on the Archaeology of the Ancient Near East, Rome, May 18th–23rd 1998*, vol. 2. Rome: Università degli studi di Roma 'La Sapienza', Dipartimento di scienze storiche, archeologiche e antropologiche dell'antichità, 1379–96.

Rast, W. E. (1992). Tombs, kinship indicators, and the biblical ancestors. *Eretz-Israel* 23: 112*–19*.

Regev, J., P. de Miroschedji, and E. Boaretto (2012). Early Bronze Age chronology: radiocarbon chronological models from Tel Yarmuth (Israel). *Radiocarbon* 54: 505–24.

——, P. de Miroschedji, R. Greenberg, E. Braun, Z. Greenhut, and E. Boaretto (2012). Chronology of the Early Bronze Age in the South Levant: a new analysis. *Radiocarbon* 54: 525–66.

Rosen, A. M. (2007). *Civilizing Climate: Social Responses to Climate Change in the Ancient Near East*. Lanham, Md.: AltaMira.

Rosen, S. A. (1997). *Lithics after the Stone Age: A Handbook of Stone Tools from the Levant*. Walnut Creek, Calif.: AltaMira.

—— (2008). Desert pastoral nomadism in the *longue durée*: a case study from the Negev and the southern Levantine deserts. In H. Barnard and W. Wendrich (eds), *The Archaeology of Mobility: Old World and New World Nomadism*. Los Angeles: Cotsen Institute of Archaeology, University of California at Los Angeles, 115–40.

Roux, V., and P. de Miroschedji (2009). Revisiting the history of the potter's wheel in the southern Levant. *Levant* 41: 155–73.

Sala, M. (2007). *L'architettura sacra della Palestina nell'età del Bronzo Antico I–III: contesto archeologico, analisi architettonica et sviluppo storico*. Rome: Università degli Studi di Roma 'La Sapienza'.

Savage, S. H., S. E. Falconer, and T. J. Harrison (2007). The Early Bronze Age city-states of the southern Levant: neither cities nor states. In T. E. Levy, P. M. M. Daviau, R. W. Younker, and M. Shaer (eds), *Crossing Jordan: North American Contribution to the Archaeology of Jordan*. Winona Lake, Ind.: Eisenbrauns, 285–97.

Sebbane, M. (2003). The Kfar Monash Hoard: a reevaluation. *Eretz-Israel* 27: 169–84 [Hebrew].

Sowada, K. N. (2009). *Egypt in the Eastern Mediterranean during the Old Kingdom: An Archaeological Perspective*. Fribourg: Academic Press/Göttingen: Vandenhoeck & Ruprecht.

Stager, L. E. (1985). The first fruits of civilization. In J. N. Tubb (ed.), *Palestine in the Bronze and Iron Ages: Papers in Honor of Olga Tufnell*. London: Institute of Archaeology, 172–88.

—— (1992). The periodization of Palestine from Neolithic through Early Bronze times. In R. W. Ehrich (ed.), *Chronologies in Old World Archaeology*, vol. 1, 3rd edn. Chicago: University of Chicago Press, 22–41.

Tadmor, M. (2002). The Kfar Monash hoard again: a view from Egypt and Nubia. In van den Brink and Levy (2002: 239–51).

Vaux, R. de (1955). Les fouilles de Tell el-Fâr'ah, près Naplouse: cinquième campagne: rapport préliminaire. *Revue biblique* 62: 540–89.

——. (1962). Les fouilles de Tell el-Far'ah *Revue biblique* 69: 212–53.

Vinitzky, L. (1992). The date of the dolmens in the Golan and Galilee: a reassessment. *Tel Aviv* 19: 100–112.

Yannai, E., and E. Braun (2001). Anatolian and Egyptian imports from Late EB I at Ain Assawir, Israel. *Bulletin of the American Schools of Oriental Research* 321: 41–56.

Zohar, M. (1992). Megalithic cemeteries in the Levant. In O. Bar-Yosef and A. M. Khazanov (eds), *Pastoralism in the Levant: Archaeological Materials in Anthropological Perspective.* Madison, Wis.: Prehistory, 43–63.

CHAPTER 23

THE SOUTHERN LEVANT (TRANSJORDAN) DURING THE EARLY BRONZE AGE

SUZANNE RICHARD

INTRODUCTION

Previous reconstructions of the Early Bronze Age have drawn primarily from the more intensely excavated Mediterranean corridor, i.e. Cisjordan (western Palestine/Israel). Thus, surveys on the Early Bronze Age of Jordan are relatively recent and few (Philip 2001; 2008; Palumbo 2001; 2008—primarily EB IV; Prag 2001) but add immensely to earlier multi-period works (e.g. Dornemann 1983; Homès-Fredericq and Hennessy 1989), or to the still invaluable *Explorations in Eastern Palestine* series (Glueck 1934; 1935; 1939; 1951). Of the excavated Early Bronze sites, the final publication of Bab adh-Dhra' is of enormous importance, since it provides a rare (Jericho in Cisjordan is another) stratigraphic report on a continuously occupied EB I–IV site (Schaub and Rast 1989; Rast and Schaub 2003).

Intense survey over the past several decades has illuminated some 1000 EB I/II/III sites, as listed in the JADIS database (Savage, Falconer, and Harrison 2007: 288). But doubtless it is the discovery in the Faynan of the 'largest Early Bronze Age copper "manufactory" in the ancient Near East' (Levy et al. 2002: 425) that has quickened the pace of research in the period. The Faynan's importance for the period was recognized early on (Richard 1987: 30) and, in fact, the Faynan today is at the centre of research on the role that copper production and distribution played in the development of Early Bronze civilization in both Jordan and Cisjordan.

This chapter will attempt to: (1) highlight the compelling scholarly issues and theoretical approaches driving current research; (2) craft an updated précis of the relevant archaeological data; and (3) assess reconstructions of the period. It is hoped that such an overview will reveal insights about Early Bronze society in Jordan, and about the role played by exchange networks in the emergence of new sociopolitical institutions, as epitomized in the fortified sites. In this author's view, Jordan's Early Bronze era, though distinctive, emerges with greater clarity in the context of southern Levantine 'Canaanite' (or Proto-Canaanite) civilization as well as of the broader landscape of the ancient Near East or, recently, the Mediterranean world (Joffe 2004). Such a broader landscape reflects newer 'global' approaches in scholarship now being applied to Jordan (LaBianca 2007). Further, although this chapter focuses on the EB I–III periods, in this author's view the Early Bronze ends with EB IV, discussed elsewhere in this volume as the 'Intermediate Bronze Age'. A significant contribution of recent work in Jordan, in fact, is the discovery of EB IV sedentary sites that witness continuity (not a total break, as earlier believed) with the Early Bronze tradition, albeit its 'last gasp' (Dever 1973; Richard 1987; Richard et al. 2010; Rast and Schaub 2003; Nigro 2006).

The dates and subdivisions followed here are: EB I (3600–3100 BCE); EB II (3100–2750 BCE); EB III (2750–2300 BCE); and EB IV (2300–2000 BCE). The higher EB I chronology is in line with recent trends, affirmed by recalibrated radiometric (^{14}C) dates from Late Chalcolithic and EB I Jordanian sites, such as Tulayat-Ghassul, Abu al-Kharaz, and Tall ash-Shuna (Dessel and Joffe 2000). Given a growing corpus of higher EB III and EB IV ^{14}C determinations from southern Levantine sites, it is likely that the above dates will shift upwards. For example, ^{14}C determinations at Khirbat Iskandar suggest that the EB IV begins around 2500 (Regev et al. 2012).

COMPELLING SCHOLARLY ISSUES AND THEORETICAL APPROACHES

Two decades after writing a 'state of the art' piece on the Early Bronze and urbanism (Richard 1987, updated in 2003), arguably, the main issue upon which syntheses of the period still hinge is the question of whether the EB II–III was 'truly' urban. And if so, what was its genesis and why did it collapse? If not, what stage of political development do the walled sites of the southern Levant and, in particular, Jordan, epitomize? Although reflecting a scholarly preoccupation with processual and neo-evolutionary anthropological frameworks, i.e. the 'rise, fall, and regeneration of civilization' and cyclical models of sedentism/nomadism, these questions nonetheless remain, but are examined by newer, post-processual approaches.

Scholars now question unilinear political trajectories in the development of urbanism and chiefdoms, as formulated by Childe and Service. There is a general tendency to downplay outmoded cultural historical concepts such as diffusion and invasion to explain change, as popularized by Albright and Kenyon. Moreover, critiques of earlier surveys of the period cite bias ('urbanocentric') toward elites and hierarchical systems and/or too heavy a reliance on systems theory as a model of change. Today, scholars consider multilinear trajectories, variability, and diversity of lifeways (post-processual concerns) with a view to grasping the uniqueness of the particular society, region, site, the occupants as well as the individual.

Raising compelling questions about the nature of Early Bronze society/societies, a cadre of scholars working in Jordan has contributed newer innovative paradigms. These distinctive but complementary approaches deconstruct traditional views of urbanism in the Early Bronze by stressing ruralism (Falconer 1994) or heterarchical over against hierarchical systems (Philip 2001; Harrison 2001), or by writing a different narrative about past lifeways (Chesson 2003). A related approach, the model of 'interconnectivity', attempts to distinguish global influences (neighbouring higher civilizations, 'empires') from indigenous cultural development in Jordan (LaBianca 2007). The question is: how do these newer views resonate with the kindred culture of Cisjordan, where variations of urban models dominate (Joffe 1993; Greenberg 2002; de Miroschedji 2002)?

To reformulate the central question in light of newer trends, do the organizational strategies of the EB II–III reflect hierarchy (i.e. centralized, elite-driven urban society) or heterarchy (i.e. decentralized, kinship-based village (rural) society)? Or is there some middle ground between these seemingly polar viewpoints? Whether more 'urban' or more heterarchical, current scholarship stresses multiple and variable evolutionary trajectories at the regional level (Stein 1998). Moreover, is Jordan in the Early Bronze inherently different from contemporary Cisjordan? This chapter may not resolve these issues, but it will attempt to identify Jordan's distinctiveness and its interconnectedness in the Early Bronze, as well as to assess reconstructions of the period.

Traditional view of Early Bronze society: urbanism

Traditionally, the era has been seen as the first experiment in the southern Levant of urbanism (i.e. city and town life). Its attendant complex institutions are thought to parallel, more or less, the contemporary (late fourth/early third millennia BCE) rise of the 'city-states' or 'state' in neighbouring Mesopotamia and Egypt (and also the Indus Valley). An EB I proto-urban phase is followed by an urban EB II–III era that ends in a period of collapse, the post-urban EB IV period. If there has been scholarly consensus, it is that the *realia* of southern Levantine 'urbanism' fall short when compared with neighbouring states. In other words, the EB II–III walled sites of the southern Levant are not 'urban' in the classic sense as represented by the primary states. The latter include: a wealthy elite; four-tiered organizational hierarchies; vast cities of great populations; state-sponsored craft specialization; huge surpluses; international exchange and far-flung dispersion of identifying cultural markers; and, especially, writing.

Newer approaches, in fact, now question whether Early Bronze datasets (fortified sites; settlement hierarchies (hinting at sociopolitical hierarchies); public buildings like palaces and temples; large storage facilities; craft specialization; interregional and international exchange networks; moderate evidence for elites; moderate evidence for a system of notation (sealings and potmarks); cultural uniformity (suggestive of integrative mechanisms); floral, faunal, and climatic data; and, frankly, contrast with the EB I/EB IV periods) even reflect urbanism, particularly when judged against Mesopotamia (Falconer 1994; Philip 2001; Chesson and Philip 2003; Savage, Falconer, and Harrison 2007). Virtually no one debates the rise of state institutions in the Iron Age (first millennium BCE), or that urban institutions manifest themselves in the Middle Bronze/Late Bronze Ages (second millennium BCE) of the southern Levant.

For some time, scholars have wrestled with identifying the precise nature of Early Bronze society, usually citing a type of urbanism that is somewhere between secondary, derivative, small-scale, 'low-level', a peer polity, or unique (e.g. Richard 1987; 2003; Esse 1989; de Miroschedji 1989; Joffe 1993; Finkelstein 1995; Prag 2001). More recently, scholars have been seeking to illuminate variant regional processes, utilizing newer theoretical frameworks, such as diverse regional 'urbanizations', 'archaic states', 'world systems', or considering newer approaches to the chiefdom model (Stein 1998; Feinman and Marcus 1998; Greenberg 2002; see Levy and van den Brink 2002).

ALTERNATIVE (I.E. NON-URBAN) EXPLANATORY MODELS

'Ruralism'

On the basis of his excavations at Abu an-Ni'aj (EB IV) and Tall al-Hayyat (EB IV–Middle Bronze) in Jordan, and deep-time settlement patterns, Falconer believes that 'rural complexity and autonomy'—not classic (Mesopotamian) urbanism—were the fundamental characteristics of Canaanite (Early Bronze–Late Bronze) society (1994: 127). Classic urbanism involves a high level of political and economic control exerted by the centre over satellite and hinterland sites (e.g. Mesopotamian city-states). Utilizing a rank/size distribution of sites vis-à-vis exploitable agricultural areas, Falconer did not find a level of integration normally associated with patterns of urban dominance; rather, he found patterns of rural self-sufficiency.

In this model, EB II–III walled sites are 'epiphenomena' in a rural heartland; that is, they represent a rare experiment in increased complexity (central sites/cities) within a predominantly rural system. Even in such times, Falconer maintains, the rural sites are only loosely related to the cities and towns, preferring to remain autonomous. This model neatly explains the unique character of EB II–III 'urbanism'. It also provides an explanation for the continuation of the rural settlements in the post-collapse (EB IV) period: since the rural sites are independent and not totally integrated with central sites, they can adapt to turbulent periods and are less likely to collapse. In the latest conceptualization of the model, based on site cluster analysis, Falconer and others now question whether city-states or cities even existed in the Early Bronze in Jordan, and throughout the southern Levant (Savage, Falconer, and Harrison 2007).

'Heterarchy'

Similarly, on the basis of classic urban criteria as a barometer and a growing body of literature on heterarchy (Ehrenreich, Crumley, and Levy 1995), Philip argues that Jordan's Early Bronze Age (and the southern Levant, generally) is not urban, but rather exemplifies a corporate type of political organization (2001; 2008). In a tightly woven argument, he suggests a plausible alternative explanation to Early Bronze datasets (above). Rather than the hierarchically organized urban setting where elites dominate and control the city, its satellites, and the rural area politically and economically, the EB II–III walled sites are more like independent 'corporate villages'. The political structure is based on a type of shared (i.e. horizontal power) communal organization in which individual households bind together, probably along kinship lineages, the outgrowth of which being the corporate village ('supra-house community clusters'). Although kinship lineages are hierarchically ranked, parallel lineages would share power, perhaps the strongest clans asserting themselves.

Complementing the 'corporate village' view, several settlement studies find little evidence for integration of sites and also opt for heterarchy as an explanatory model (e.g. Harrison 1997; 2001; Savage, Falconer, and Harrison 2007). Harrison's work in the Madaba Plains is premissed on the view that, rather than scale (i.e. site size and settlement hierarchy), the more pertinent method to investigate political/economic organizational strategies is to focus on the level of regional integration of sites. Discerning internal kinship ranking within a clan or household in her study of the charnel house burials at Bab adh Dhra', Chesson (2003) goes further, to narrate how each community may have functioned autonomously in a separate polity (her 'house society').

'Great and little traditions' or 'interconnectivity'

This long-term study of cultural interactions in Jordan from the Early Bronze to the Ottoman period focuses on discerning not just the impact of elite or 'great' traditions (e.g. Egyptian and Mesopotamian 'empires') on local or indigenous cultures, but also the essential components of each tradition. LaBianca developed this framework to help explain the cyclical episodes of sedentarization/nomadization against the historically documented 'great traditions' that have swept over Jordan and/or influenced local polities and traditions (LaBianca 2007). His testing of the model in the Madaba Plains found diverse, heterarchical organizational strategies—as seen in kinship patterns, both tribal and at the household level—rather than centralized hierarchical patterns.

With these various theoretical constructs (urbanism/ruralism, hierarchy/heterarchy, house society, and interconnectivity) percolating in the background, the following is a précis of select EB I–III and post-collapse archaeological data. (For a somewhat different interpretation and detailed treatment of the data, see Philip 2001; 2008; for the post-collapse EB IV period, see Palumbo 2001; 2008).

THE ARCHAEOLOGICAL PICTURE IN EARLY BRONZE JORDAN: A PRÉCIS

The EB I period

Overview

Some fifteen site clusters (*c.* 300 sites) are dispersed throughout Jordan in EB I (Savage, Falconer, and Harrison 2007: 218), stretching from the Yarmuk River in the north to the Faynan in the south. Echoing broad organizational developments in Cisjordan, sites in Jordan show nucleated rounded residences in EB IA (Jawa and Jabal al-Mutawwaq), multiple-roomed, rectangular residences in EB IB (e.g. Bab edh-Dhra' and Tall ash-Shuna), and fortified settlements by the end of the period (Tall Abu al-Kharaz, Tall as-Sa'adiya, and Jawa). But the isolated EB IA cemetery at Bab edh-Dhra', the presence of rounded/rectangular structures at Tall ash-Shuna (EB IA) and Tall Abu al-Kharaz (EB IB), the ceremonial site of al-Murayghat, and the astonishing hydraulic system and fortifications of Jawa attest to considerable variability in the period (see Fig. 23.1).

Such diversity usually defines a regionalized society, much like the preceding Late Chalcolithic. Unlike the latter (probably a chiefdom in political terms), however, growth in social complexity and interregional exchange in the EB I eventuated in a dramatic settlement pattern shift and the virtual universal fortification of sites by EB II. Lowland/upland

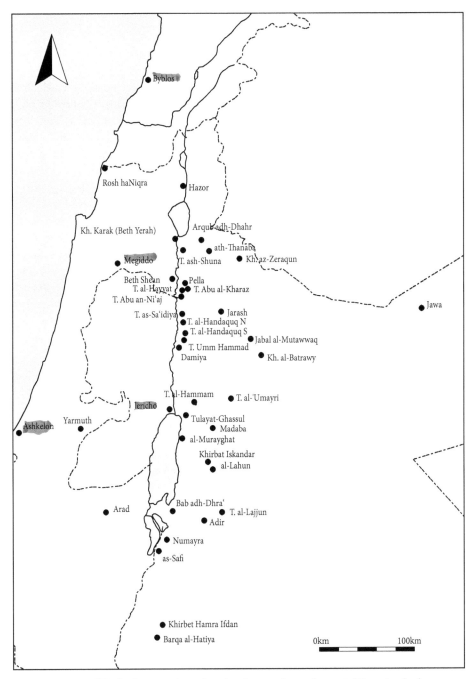

FIG. 23.1 Map of Early Bronze Age sites in the southern Levant (Transjordan)

settlement patterns suggest a developing interface between two economic strategies, presumably exploitative for surplus product: agriculture/horticulture (grape and olive especially) in the lowlands and pastoralism (wool/dairy) in the uplands. Still debated are the mechanisms driving developing complexity in this 500-year period, although international exchange networks, the growth of agricultural surpluses, and developing specialization in metallurgy are all pivotal.

Indigenous/foreign influences and exchange

Scholars increasingly highlight cultural continuities with the preceding Late Chalcolithic in, for example, architecture, metallurgy, and ceramics, rather than a complete break, as once thought. There are also northern (Byblos, Mesopotamia, and Anatolia) foreign influences evident in the drooped spout teapots, cylinder seals, and arsenic, copper, and silver, as well as south Syrian links with Jawa's unique fortifications, sophisticated hydraulic systems, and possible Uruk IV pottery traditions. Most agree, however, that the major spur to social complexity was the EB I–II exchange network with Egypt. Southern Cisjordan was the epicentre of trade with Egypt (Levy and van den Brink 2002), where quantities of metals and Canaanite vessels were found in Predynastic/Dynasty 0 tombs at Maadi and Naqada. But excavations at the village site of Wadi Fidan 4 show that the Faynan in southern Jordan supplied the copper. Egyptian imports found at Bab adh-Dhraʿ and Abu al-Kharaz (alabaster mace-heads and pottery) point to additional links in this international exchange network. The latter site's imports, early fortifications, and granary (Fischer 2008) add support to the east–west trade of agricultural surpluses to emporia like Arad and Ashkelon in southern Cisjordan, as outlined by Stager (2001).

Material culture

Generally, sites evince an earlier (EB IA) and later (EB IB) phase, but two cultural orbits emerge: northern Jordan/Cisjordan and the Jordan Valley—as far east as Jabal ad-Druze and southern Syria based on ceramics from Tall Umm Hammad and Jawa (Betts 1992)—and southern Jordan/Cisjordan. Amidst varying local ceramic traditions, grey burnished and 'band slip' wares in the north contrast with 'line-group' and red slipped wares in the south, the latter becoming the standard by EB II. Other craft specializations denote a growing standardization: 'Canaanean' flint knives, tabular scrapers, flat-sectioned copper awls, and basalt ground stone vessels. Metals specialization and developing complexity are evident in the exchange networks in the north (high arsenic content copper from Anatolia, imports of silver from Syria, and a workshop at Tall ash-Shuna) and in the south (Faynan-sourced copper in Egypt and Wadi Fidan 4 copper workshop).

Burial

Regionalization abounds: a unique charnel house and shaft tombs in the south (Fig. 23.2; Bab adh-Dhraʿ), dolmens in the north/north-central (Damiya, Jarash, Tall al-ʿUmayri, and Jabal al-Mutawwaq, and Wadi Yabis), cists/underground chambers (Khirbat Iskandar and as-Safi), and caves elsewhere (epecially Jericho and Cisjordan generally). The diversity of burial types appears to correspond to the dispersed settlement pattern of regionalized village

FIG. 23.2 Bab adh-Dhraʿ EB I and II tombs plus EB III charnel house (photographs courtesy R. Thomas Schaub)

cultures. The tombs contain remains interpreted as pastoral—Bab adh-Dhraʿ EB IA shaft tombs with bone pile and line of skulls—and as sedentary—the Bab adh-Dhraʿ EB IB tombs with primary burials and a new ceramic assemblage (Schaub and Rast 1989: 548–57). Even megalithic structures, once accepted as pastoral tombs/territorial markers, reveal sedentary practices, e.g. the dolmen at al-ʿUmayri (Herr and Clark 2009: 71–3).

The EB II period

Overview

In Jordan, as in Cisjordan, a major settlement shift occurred: twelve clusters (around 100 sites) indicate an agglomeration of population in fewer, but larger (and fortified) sites, particularly in optimal agricultural areas, but clusters in the south centred on Bab adh-Dhraʿ and on the Faynan continue. This shift also reveals distinctions among neighbouring sites, indicative of a developing intraregional complexity, for example, at Khirbet al-Batrawy (Douglas 2006: 49–62), Tall Madaba (Harrison 2001: 192), and Khirbet az-Zeraqun (Kamlah 2001), as well as in Cisjordan (see Greenberg 2002: 29–90 and Joffe 1993: 85). Yet the level of integration is debated (Savage, Falconer, and Harrison 2007: 293–4). The discontinuous occupational pattern at some sites, e.g. gap at Pella, Tall ash-Shuna (in Cisjordan: Megiddo and Beth Shean), and abandonment of sites at the end of EB II, e.g. Tall as-Saʿadiya (in Cisjordan: Arad), could reflect a lack of urban integration (Philip 2001; Harrison 2001) or simply a diverse (or non-linear) evolution as at Beth Shean (Greenberg 2002).

The uniformity of Canaanite material culture throughout the southern Levant is striking, especially the red slipped and burnished wares, in comparison with the preceding regionalized cultures. As evidence for growing social complexity and a developing stratified society, note the dramatic transformation of the landscape from dispersed villages to agglomerative fortified sites with square towers in Jordan, specialized crafts and industries, special purpose buildings, intensification of metals production in the Faynan, and what is evidently a notation system of cylinder seals, sealings, and potmarks, indicative of a level of administrative control or ownership.

Foreign influences and exchange

The late EB I/EB II is the *floruit* of agricultural and metals trade with Egypt via *entrepôts* in Cisjordan. Egyptian imports and/or storage facilities (Abu el-Kharaz, Tall as-Saʿadiya, Pella, and Bab adh-Dhraʿ) continue to evidence this international trade. In the Faynan, a shift takes place from village workshops to specialized smelting sites near the mines. Fifty-six of the latter affirm the intensification of metal production. Study of the sophisticated production process suggests a highly organized, labour-intensive industry hinting a fairly high level of centralization (Adams 2002: 23–4). This transformation is coeval with a reorganization of trade at the epicentre in southern Cisjordan, where Arad is the centre (see de Miroschedji 2002). The Faynan, as seen at Barqa al-Hatiya, now exhibits a typical 'Canaanite' culture found throughout the southern Levant beginning in EB II.

In northern Jordan, imports of fine Galilean metallic ware found at Abu al-Kharaz, Tall ash-Shuna, Khirbet al-Batrawy, and Pella indicate that interregional exchange networks continue to operate. Extensive evidence for the production of olive oil and wine are confirmed by the stone presses, vats, and storage vessels (combed ware coated with lime), as well as special rooms and buildings (al-Lahun, Abu al-Kharaz, and Tall as-Saʻadiya in particular) and transport vessels (the Abydos jug). These evidences, when combined with the greater frequency of seals, sealings, and potmarks, are suggestive of centres exhibiting either owner-ship or some form of centralized control. It is difficult not to posit elites controlling the spe-cialized areas devoted to olive oil, wine, or textiles in a building thought to be a palace at Tall as-Saʻadiya (Fig. 23.3; Tubb 1993).

Material culture

The Chalcolithic/Early Bronze broad room architectural tradition continues in the domestic and public spheres. Organizational changes normally interpreted as reflecting the presence of social elites include: fortifications (gates and towers), public sectors, including an upper site or acropolis, palatial/special-purpose buildings (Tall as-Saʻadiya and Khirbet az-Zaraqun (Figs. 24.4 and 24.5); Arad in Cisjordan); granaries/storage (Pella, Tall as-Saʻadiya, and Tell Abu e-Kharaz), and sophisticated water installations (Tell Handaquq N, Tall al-Lahun, Tall az-Zaraqun, and Tall Jalul). There are craft specializations of olive oil/wine industries, cop-per, and pottery. Other indications are the spindle whorls and associated weaving equip-ment found in workshops, the 'Canaanean' flint knives, and high-status dining ware found at Tall as-Saʻadiya.

Burial

Unlike the EB I, burial sites are not well attested in the period. Jericho is the best known in Cisjordan. In Jordan, there are caves at Arqub adh-Dhar and Tall al-ʻUmayri and a cem-etery at Bab adh-Dhraʻ (Fig. 23.2), where a shaft tomb and a charnel house date to EB II (the remaining charnel houses ranging from EB II-III, based on pottery). The scarcity of burial remains is a bit of a mystery. There are various theories (see Ilan 2002), includ-ing the proposition that the dolmens, which are in the orbit of the sedentary sites, may have been the graves of the people from the EB II fortified sites. There is, however, little if any evidence for this view. What is clear is that the remains of beads, metals, and pot-tery reflect a paucity of conspicuous wealth in graves, which is counterindicative of elites when compared with the northern Levant (Syria) and Mesopotamia. The suggestion that non-traditional symbols of wealth, such as agriculture or copper, could be a regional 'elite' alternative has merit and would be another indication of a variant strategy in the southern Levant for displaying unequal access to resources. The view that staples of the local econ-omy represent a type of 'staple wealth/finance' is gaining adherents (Joffe 1993: 59–60; Philip 2001; Genz 2003).

The EB III period

Overview

Larger clusters (18) of about 250 sites in Jordan coincide with a peak in level of sociopo-litical complexity in EB III, including greater integration (Savage, Falconer, and Harrison 2007: 208). The clusters show growth particularly in the Central and Southern Plateau

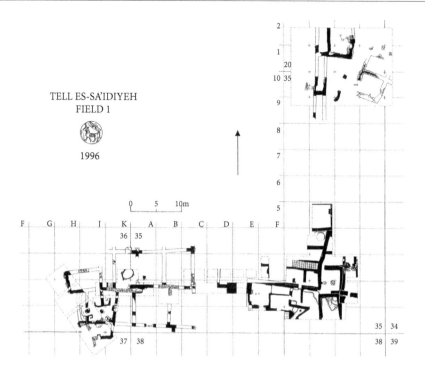

TELL ES-SAʾIDIYEH
FIELD 1

1996

FIG. 23.3 Tall as-Saʿadiya plan of the palace; below: the palace and olive oil production (drawing and photograph courtesy Jonathan N. Tubb)

areas. The expanded fortifications at sites (5–15m-wide strengthened defences) give the appearance of central regional sites, whether isolated like Khirbet al-Batrawy or with a network of sites, such as Bab adh-Dhraʿ and Numayra, the Madaba Plains sites (including Khirbat Iskandar), Tall al-Hammam, and Tall az-Zaraqun (Kamlah 2001; see Greenberg 2002 and Joffe 1993 for Cisjordan). The size of sites (less than 25ha) and convex rank-size settlement distribution do not meet the criteria for a 'classic' urban hierarchical pattern (Savage, Falconer, and Harrison 2007: 294). In this period, copper production reaches its peak in the Faynan.

Looking at more traditional data indicative of complex sociopolitical organization, centralization, and elites, there are massive defence systems and burgeoning public sectors, including cultic precincts, palaces, and storerooms. In Cisjordan, the palatial site of Yarmuth (40m-wide defences) and granary at Khirbet Kerak (Beth Yerah) are extraordinary. In Jordan, excavations at Khirbet al-Batrawy (Nigro 2006; 2008; 2010) are revealing domestic and public sectors (a temple and, recently, a palace). One may predict that excavations at the major centre of Tall al-Hammam with its satellite sites (Collins, Hamdan, and Byers 2009) will likewise reveal significant public sectors. Current work suggests that both upper and lower mounds (36ha) were fortified, making it the largest Early Bronze site in Jordan. But the best evidence comes from Khirbet az-Zaraqun (Fig. 23.4), with its upper and lower cities, size (8ha), fortifications, palace, and cultic compound paralleling Megiddo in a remarkable way. That these two sites were regional cult centres is self-evident. They illustrate continued close interaction in the northern sphere and, importantly, demonstrate the standardization of religious 'Canaanite' practices as echoed elsewhere (e.g. cultic precinct at Bab adh-Dhraʿ).There is a strong tradition of 'standing stones' in Jordan that are generally dated to EB III and EB IV at sites such as Adir, Bab adh-Dhraʿ, al-Lajjun, and Khirbat Iskandar. Whether ancestral, territorial, or burial markers, these monoliths represent another aspect of the symbolic world of the Early Bronze peoples.

Foreign influences and exchange

Egyptian trade is greatly diminished in EB III, but still evident, for example, gold jewellery and cosmetic palettes at Bab adh-Dhraʿ (see de Miroschedji 2002: 45–7 for Cisjordan). The Faynan metals industry, however, peaks in the EB III, estimated at 300–500 tonnes of copper produced (Adams 2002: 25). The intensity of mining, the moulds, finalized products, and ingots all support the industrialized nature of the 'manufactory' (Fig. 23.5) of Khirbet Hamra Ifdan (Adams 2002) and by inference Jordan's important metals exchange network in the EB III. The question is: who was controlling and organizing this phenomenal industry? The nearest EB III sites in the south were Bab adh-Dhraʿ and its sister site Numayra, and Yarmuth in Cisjordan.

In the north, the highly burnished red/black Anatolian Khirbet Kerak Ware is a benchmark for EB III. This ware and local imitations are found at a variety of northern sites in Jordan (and Cisjordan), but is attested as far south at Bab adh-Dhraʿ. Broad links with ceramics and metals assemblages in Syria point to continued interconnections. The presence of alloys at Bab adh-Dhraʿ and Tall az-Zaraqun attests to imports of tin and other metals from Anatolia. Evidence for notation, such as cylinder seals and potmarks, continue. Although such evidence is found at a number of sites, the largest collections are at Khirbet az-Zeraqun and Bab adh-Dhraʿ (Genz 2001).

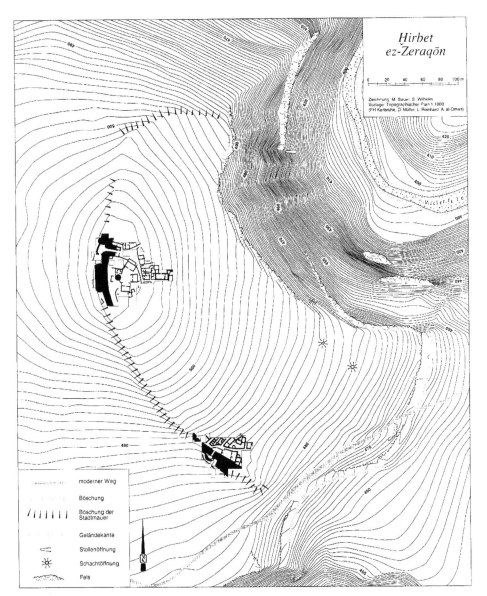

FIG. 23.4 Khirbet az-Zeraqun general plan of the site

Material culture

The period generally divides into EB IIIA and B. High-status objects appear at Bab adh-Dhra' (e.g. palettes, two of five known crescentic axe-heads; one of five known ceramic bull's heads; tin-bronze daggers, decorated bone tubes, and gold jewellery), Numayra and Tall Abu al-Kharaz (metal objects), Khirbet al-Betrawy (cache of copper axe-heads), and Tall az-Zaraqun (Egyptian palettes, gold leaf jewellery, gold beads, and decorated bone tubes). There is a range of fascinating finds at Yarmuth (de Miroschedji 1999). Other specialized industries include weaving, lithics, olive oil/wine industries, pottery, ground stone, and

FIG. 23.5 Khirbet Hamrat Ifdan, Jordan, where the main casting activities took place. Examples include casting moulds (1, 3, and 6), melted copper from crucible (2), and metal tools (4–5) (photo courtesy Thomas E. Levy)

cordage, especially clear from storerooms of pithoi as well as luxury items, such as Khirbet al-Batrawy and Khirbat Iskandar (Richard and Long 2006).

Burial

Jericho and Bab adh-Dhraʿ remain the best-known cemeteries. At the latter, ten charnel houses were excavated (Fig. 23.2). These 'houses of the dead', echoing domestic/temple broad room traditions, held from 46 to 200 individuals and included prestige items (see Chesson and Schaub 2007; Schaub and Rast 1989). Although 'conspicuous' wealth in burials remains elusive, given the exotic gifts (as well as those mentioned above) such as ostrich eggs, faience, lapis, and alabaster—unquestionably evidence of interregional and international exchange—one could make a case for elites in the larger charnel houses. The close connection between the assemblages of the living and the dead is an Early Bronze tradition that continues into EB IV, as clearly shown at Khirbat Iskandar (Richard et al. 2010).

Post-EB III collapse

Overview

The destruction and/or abandonment of every walled site by the end of EB III connects the southern Levant with widespread collapse in the Near East (Dalfes, Kukla, and Weiss 1997). Earlier suggestions of climate deterioration (Richard 1980: 25), among other factors, seem more cogent now, given a growing corpus of evidence suggesting dryer conditions (see Cordova 2007 and bibliography cited therein). Not to be discounted are other factors, such as warfare (Egyptian evidences) and the human exploitation of the landscape—the engine fuelling EB II–III societal growth. There are numerous theories about cultural change (Long 2003). (For a case study of one response to collapse, see Richard and Long 2009.) A regionalized settlement pattern of 250–300 sites witnesses to a period of significant social change in EB IV (from fortified to rural sites, in a shift to a lower median site size). Yet a high degree of site continuity (EB III–IV) is evidenced in the northern and central areas of Jordan, as shown by survey (Palumbo 2001). Tell occupation is more significant than previously thought; e.g. Bab adh-Dhra', Khirbat Iskandar, Tall az-Zeraqun, Khirbet al-Batrawy, Tall al-Hammam, and in Cisjordan, Jericho, Hazor, Megiddo (sacred complex), Khirbet Kerak (Beth Yerah), and Rosh haNiqra. Rural complexity and continuity is found in the EB III/IV cultic area at Bab adh-Dhra', six phases of occupation and mud-brick houses at Abu an Ni'aj, and two or three major phases at Khirbat Iskandar. The latter includes a 'gateway', a storeroom complex, numerous multi-roomed structures, and reuse of the earlier fortifications (Richard and Long 2009; Richard et al. 2010).

Thus, for Jordan at least, a sociopolitical devolution (from EB III), rather than a complete break and new population, still seems a cogent interpretation of the available data. As the excavators of the long, continuously occupied site of Bab adh-Dhra' conclude, the shifts noted in EB IV probably represent 'adaptations of an ongoing, perhaps remnant, population to new economic and social conditions...' (Rast and Schaub 2003: 448). In Jordan, the multiphase EB IV settlements evince a remarkable rural response of continuity, reorganization, and change in a post-collapse period. In Cisjordan, although there are numerous sedentary villages, a reversion to pastoralism and a severe sociocultural break are usually emphasized, based on the perspective of the hundreds of one-period sites in the marginal Negev Desert.

In Jordan, the Faynan's operations (mining, manufacturing, and distribution) at Khirbet Hamra Ifdan affirm continuity with the preceding period (Adams 2002). As Hauptmann notes about the EB II–IV in the Faynan, 'it is sensible to treat these periods as one' (2007: 275). Moreover, ceramic and metallurgical links with Negev/Sinai sites suggest a revitalized overland trade network with Egypt, perhaps hinted at in the slightly later Beni-Hasan tomb painting from Middle Egypt. Northern metal networks continue unabated (arsenic copper and tin bronze). Tin bronze daggers at Bab adh-Dhra' and a unique spearhead from Khirbat Iskandar hint at unequal access to this rare alloy prior to widespread bronze technology in the Middle Bronze (Richard 2006). As has been clear for some time now, there is a growing list of continuities with the succeeding era. Thus, the significance of the EB IV rural population's role in the re-emergence of town life in the Middle Bronze should not be underestimated.

RECONSTRUCTIONS OF THE EARLY BRONZE IN JORDAN

Jordan's distinctiveness and interconnectedness

Regardless of the theoretical approach, the above précis infers a 1,600-year cultural development, namely: (a) a regionalized political landscape with developing social complexity in EB I, spurred on by international exchange networks, northern contacts, agricultural surpluses, and metallurgy; (b) widespread complex organizational strategies (walled sites, public architecture, metals specialization, and sophisticated exchange networks) in EB II; (c) a higher degree of sociopolitical and economic organization (larger heavily fortified sites, regional cult sites, palaces, and metals manufacturing in EB III; and, finally, (d) a regionalized political landscape exhibiting rural complexity (multiphase sedentary sites/specialized pastoral nomadism) in the EB IV. This reconstruction resonates with Cisjordan generally, but there are important differences.

Whether it is fewer excavated sites, environmental marginality (Prag 2001), or peripheral geographical location (i.e. a 'fall-off' exchange curve vis-à-vis Egypt), Jordan's EB II–III sites generally do not exhibit the wealth, size, or population mass of sites in the Mediterranean corridor, yet they share common traditions and evince comparability in many instances. For example, there is no known palatial economy such as at Yarmuth, yet Tall az-Zaraqun's virtual mirror image of Megiddo's public/cultic acropolis suggests some equivalency of complexity and religious uniformity. Although not as numerous as in Cisjordan, Jordan's large walled sites are comparable in size: Tall Madaba (13ha), Handaquq S (16ha), Lajjun (20ha), ath-Thanaba (19ha), Tall al-Hammam (36ha), and Khirbet az-Zeraqun (8ha). Also, the cultural/economic integration pointed out between Jordan and Cisjordan in the north and south renders it difficult to posit vastly different organizational strategies. Thus if Cisjordan is 'urban' or 'urban-like', one would expect comparability of similar entities in Jordan, as posited in a peer-polity model of urbanism (Finkelstein 1995).

Current research is in the process of clarifying the impact of the Faynan copper industry on the Early Bronze in Jordan, as well as in Cisjordan (Hauptmann 2007). What are the sociopolitical links between the Faynan and the trading epicentre in EB I–II? An equally compelling question is: who controlled the mines and trade throughout the Early Bronze, including the EB IV? At the peak of copper production and distribution in the EB III, there is a palatial economy not far to the northwest, but Bab adh-Dhra' and Numayra are the closest centres. As for the EB IV, a strong sedentary base and documented flow of pottery and metals westward suggest control within Jordan. What we do know is that the Faynan played a pivotal role in Levantine metallurgy—one that connects Jordan's metals trade with Cisjordan and the Mediterranean coast, both southward to the Nile Delta and northward toward Galilee (Hauptmann 2007: 308). Metals and other trade goods in north and south Jordan, as described earlier, affirm the linkages with international exchange routes.

Jordan's distinctiveness in the Early Bronze, apart from localized traditions (e.g. unique burial traditions at Bab adh-Dhra'), is its continuous cultural development from EB I (or earlier) through EB IV (or later). The strong EB III/IV continuity contrasts with the picture in Cisjordan. These divergent paths following collapse find their parallels in Syria, the former paralleled by continuity in the Euphrates Valley sites, the latter by the pronounced break of the Khabur Plains sites (Cooper 2006: 34).

It may be said that the EB II–III was a highpoint in Jordan not to be surpassed until the Iron Age in the late second/early first millennia BCE. The real crux of the matter is how to interpret the level of sociopolitical complexity of the walled sites.

An assessment of reconstructions

'Classic' urbanism

One thing is now abundantly clear, if it was not before: 'classic' Mesopotamian urbanism (= state) is not a relevant concept for Jordan or for the southern Levant in the Early Bronze. This has been shown by comparative analysis and quantitative settlement pattern study.

'Ruralism'

Despite Falconer's questionable thesis that Canaanite (i.e. the Early Bronze–Late Bronze) civilization is essentially rural and the 'cities' epiphenomena, the model offers a provocative explanation for the distinctive nature of the EB II–III walled sites. Yet the thesis sidesteps the issue of the evolving social complexity from dispersed village to agglomerative forti-fied walled sites, and glosses over an increasingly complex landscape in the second millen-nium BCE (Middle Bronze–Late Bronze), which most would agree is urban. Nevertheless, rural complexity is indeed a significant concept, illuminated by Falconer's excavations at EB IV–Middle Bronze sites and clearly evidenced at Khirbat Iskandar and Tall al-Hayyat. When compared with the EB IV–early Middle Bronze rural sites, the EB II–III fortified sites surely reflect a difference in kind, not in degree of rural complexity.

'Heterarchy'

The wholesale shift from a hierarchical to a heterarchical paradigm for the Early Bronze requires some getting used to, yet the strengths of such a flexible approach are apparent. The perspective on 'corporate villages', intraregional diversity (rather than integration), and the coexistence of communal (shared power) along with kinship lineages (vertical or hier-archical power) all strike a chord. It offers tantalizing new perspectives on the society rep-resented by the walled sites, de-emphasizing normative culture and stressing variability at the regional, site, and house level. It is a post-processual theoretical construct that offers an explanation for Jordan's distinct trajectory in the period.

Although a plausible alternative interpretation of Early Bronze datasets, one senses, how-ever, the heuristic use of the conceptual model, which is fine, since it has inspired an innova-tive bottom-to-top analysis of Early Bronze society. However, its overemphasis on variability and diversity could be seen as one-sided, as was deemed the 'urbanocentric' perspective. At the risk of being labelled a neo-evolutionist, I have to say that the model obscures homolo-gous traits and developmental stages from EB I–IV, viz. the view that the walled sites ('cor-porate villages') are merely at one end of a continuum of villages. It understates the abundant evidence for cultural uniformity, as detailed above. Without texts, one remains to be con-vinced that the corporate body (not an elite) handles exchange, erects and maintains the fortifications, manages the temple and public (including palace) complexes, and controls the metals industry, especially in EB III. Nevertheless, as noted earlier, the archaeological datasets lend themselves to both urban and non-urban scenarios.

The quantitative evidence of the settlement (rank/size and cluster analysis) studies, dis-cussed above, is impressive and compelling, but heavily reliant on survey data. As others have noted, the comparison with Mesopotamia is an 'apples and oranges' argument: set-tlement pattern studies of the Mesopotamian heartland reveal vastly populated and huge cities, ruled by kings, in political control of a three-to-four-tiered hinterland. More difficult is the view that each community operated as a separate polity with independent governing structures, much like 'house societies' known from the ethnographic literature. The regional and international exchange networks discussed earlier, when combined with the cultural uniformity throughout the southern Levant, suggest more integrative, complex, overarching organizational strategies than the heterarchical model envisions for the EB II–III era.

Finally, the model of 'great and little traditions' is a new and thought-provoking way of capturing indigenous traditions and a local heritage from the overarching dominant culture of neighbouring states and empires. Its utility for the Madaba Plains area, especially the historical periods, seems more apparent than for the Early Bronze, although related core–periphery or interaction models have been applied to southern Cisjordan's relations with Egypt (Levy and van den Brink 2002). Although this perspective on Jordan stresses heterarchical relationships that are essentially tribal, the concept lends itself also to distinguishing the indigenous 'urban' response to the complex city-states in Mesopotamia.

Extrapolating from the various conceptual frameworks briefly discussed above, it is apparent that a view of Jordan as heterarchical in the Early Bronze is emerging. From the perspective of Cisjordan, generally, it appears that hierarchies, palace economies, and differing urbanizations are major scholarly approaches (de Miroschedji 2002; Greenberg 2002). Presumably the future (not this author) will decide if heterarchy has staying power for Jordan, or, further, if the suggestion that it is an overarching theoretical construct applicable to the entire southern Levant in the Early Bronze will be borne out. Nonetheless, heterarchical approaches have provided a 'bottom-up' perspective on 'local actors' in the households and communities, a narrative about the peoples of the Early Bronze not heretofore seen.

Future directions

Although mere suggestions in this short essay, newer approaches to studies of chiefdoms and states (mentioned earlier) offer alternative explanations for a higher degree of complexity and centralization in the southern Levant than envisioned by heterarchy. Could Jordan in the EB II–III era represent a chiefdom or chieftancy? There is mostly a difference in degree between a chiefdom and an urban level of political organization (see Renfrew and Bahn 2008: 207–20). The acceptance that the Late Chalcolithic cultures—Tulaylat Ghassul in Jordan and the Negev cultures in Cisjordan—represent (cultic elite) chiefdoms is growing. Several studies have theorized that the continuities with EB I could indicate that a chiefdom reappeared in EB II–III, possibly morphing into one of 'staple wealth/finance', with its emphasis on staples such as agriculture, horticulture, and metallurgy. Hints of chiefs—a text at Nahal Tillah in southern Cisjordan (Levy and van den Brink 2002: 28–9; de Miroschedji 2002), and the early second-millennium Egyptian Execration texts—add enticingly to this alternative.

Also, post-processual insights into diversity and variability offer new avenues for understanding the various exponents of urbanism, which is highly distinctive even among the pristine states. It is clear that for Jordan and the southern Levant generally, the starting point is the notion that, if urban, it is small-scale, incipient, scalar—in other words a unique trajectory, not paralleled elsewhere. Future research and theoretical modelling will hopefully determine more convincingly the order of complexity and degree of centralization as represented in the Early Bronze sites. Although in order to highlight differences, it may appear in this chapter that heterarchy and hierarchy are exclusive, heterarchical relationships are actually the building blocks of more complex hierarchical systems as well. This new research will help to differentiate both trends, which are diversity and the larger integrative currents in the Early Bronze. Ultimately, the question is whether the 'whole is greater than the sum of its parts'. It seems so to this author.

ACKNOWLEDGEMENTS

I would like to thank several colleagues who were kind enough to read earlier drafts of this chapter but who of course bear no responsibility for the content; they are Jesse C. Long, Jr, William G. Dever, Tim Harrison, and Sten LaBianca. Also, thanks go to the colleagues who provided material for illustration.

SUGGESTED READING

Fischer, P. (2008). Tell Abu al-Kharaz: a bead in the Jordan Valley. *Near Eastern Archaeology* 71: 196–213.

Ilan, D. (2002). Mortuary practices in Early Bronze Age Canaan. *Near Eastern Archaeology* 65: 92–104.

Levy, T. E., P. M. M. Daviau, R. W. Younker, and M. Shaer (2007). *Crossing Jordan: North American Contributions to the Archaeology of Jordan*. London: Equinox.

Miroschedji, P. de (1999). Yarmouth: the dawn of city-states in southern Canaan. *Near Eastern Archaeology* 62: 2–19.

Renfrew, C., and P. Bahn (2008). *Archaeology: Theories, Methods and Practice*, 5th edn. London: Thames & Hudson.

Richard, S. (1987). Early Bronze Age in Palestine: the rise and collapse of urbanism. *Biblical Archaeologist* 50.1: 22–43.

—— (2003). The Early Bronze Age in the southern Levant. In S. Richard (ed.), *Near Eastern Archaeology: A Reader*. Winona Lake, Ind.: Eisenbrauns, 286–302.

—— and J. C. Long, Jr. (2007). Khirbet Iskander: a city in collapse at the end of the Early Bronze Age. In Levy et al. (2007: 269–76).

Savage, S. H., S. E. Falconer, and T. J. Harrison. (2007). The Early Bronze Age city states of the outhern Levant: neither cities nor states. In Levy et al. (2007: 285–97).

REFERENCES

Adams, R. B. (2002). From farms to factories: the development of copper production at Faynan during the Early Bronze Age. In B. S. Ottaway and E. C. Wagner (eds), *Metals and Society: Papers from a Session Held at the European Association of Archaeologists Sixth Annual Meeting in Lisbon 2000*. Oxford: Archaeopress, 21–32.

Betts, A. V. G. (1992). *Excavations at Tell Um Hammad 1982–1984: The Early Assemblages (EB I–II)*. Edinburgh: Edinburgh University Press.

Chesson, M. S. (2003). Households, houses, neighborhoods and corporate villages: modeling the Early Bronze Age as a house society. *Journal of Mediterranean Archaeology* 16: 79–102.

—— and G. Philip (2003). Tales of the city? 'Urbanism' in the Early Bronze Age Levant from Mediterranean and Levantine perspectives. *Journal of Mediterranean Archaeology* 16: 3–16.

—— and R. T. Schaub (2007). Death and dying on the Dead Sea Plain: Fifa, al-Khanazir and Bab adh-Dhra' cemeteries. In T. E. Levy, P. M. M. Daviau, R. W. Younker, and M. Shaer (eds), *Crossing Jordan: North American Contributions to the Archaeology of Jordan*. London: Equinox, 253–60.

Collins, S., K. Hamdan, and G. A. Byers (2009). Tall al-Hammam: preliminary report on four seasons of excavation (2006–2009). *Annual of the Department of Antiquities of Jordan* 53: 385–414.

Cooper, L. (2006). The demise and regeneration of Bronze Age urban centers in the Euphrates Valley of Syria. In G. M. Schwartz and J. J. Nichols (eds), *After Collapse: The Regeneration of Complex Societies*. Tucson: University of Arizona Press, 18–37.

Cordova, C. E. (2007). *Millennial Landscape Change in Jordan: Geoarchaeology and Cultural Ecology*. Tucson: University of Arizona Press.

Dalfes, H. N., G. Kukla, and H. Weiss (eds) (1997). *Third Millennium BC Climate Change and Old World Collapse*. Berlin: Springer.

Dessel, J. P., and A. H. Joffe (2000). Alternative approaches to Early Bronze Age Pottery. In G. Philip and D. Baird (eds), *Ceramics and Change in the Early Bronze Age of the Southern Levant*. Sheffield: Sheffield Academic, 31–58.

Dever, W. G. (1973). The EB IV–MB I Horizon in Transjordan and southern Palestine. *Bulletin of the American Schools of Oriental Research* 210: 37–63.

Dornemann, R. H. (1983). *The Archaeology of the Transjordan in the Bronze and Iron Ages*. Milwaukee, Wis.: Milwaukee Public Museum.

Douglas, K. (2006). Occupational history of the Early Bronze Age in the upper Wadi az-Zarqa. In Nigro (2006: 49–62).

Ehrenreich, R. M., C. L. Crumley, and J. E. Levy (eds) (1995). *Heterarchy and the Analysis of Complex Societies*. Arlington, Va.: American Anthropological Association.

Esse, D. L. (1989). Secondary state formation and collapse in Early Bronze Age Palestine. In P. de Miroschedji (ed.), *L'urbanisation de la Palestine à l'âge du Bronze ancien: bilan et perspectives des recherches actuelles*. Oxford: British Archaeological Reports, 81–96.

Falconer, S. E. (1994). The development and decline of Bronze Age civilisation in the Levant: a reassessment of urbanism and ruralism. In C. Mathers and S. Stoddart (eds), *Development and Decline in the Mediterranean Bronze Age*. Sheffield: Collis, 305–33.

Feinman, G. M., and J. Marcus (eds) (1998). *Archaic States*. Santa Fe, NM: School of American Research Press.

Finkelstein, I. (1995). Two notes on Early Bronze Age urbanization and urbanism. *Tel Aviv* 22: 47–69.

Fischer, P. M. (2008). Tell Abu al-Kharaz: a bead in the Jordan Valley. *Near Eastern Archaeology* 71: 196–213.

Genz, H. (2001). Early Bronze Age potmarks from Khirbet az-Zayraqun: some aspects concerning their meaning. In *Studies in the History and Archaeology of Jordan VII*. Amman: Department of Antiquities, Jordan, 217–28.

——(2003). Cash crop production and storage in the Early Bronze Age southern Levant. *Journal of Mediterranean Archaeology* 16: 59–78.

Glueck, N. (1934). *Explorations in Eastern Palestine I* (2 vols). New Haven, Conn.: American Schools of Oriental Research.

—— (1935). *Explorations in Eastern Palestine II*. New Haven, Conn.: American Schools of Oriental Research.

—— (1939). *Exploration in Eastern Palestine III*. New Haven, Conn.: American Schools of Oriental Research.

—— (1951). *Exploration in Eastern Palestine IV* (2 vols). New Haven, Conn.: American Schools of Oriental Research.

Greenberg, R. (2002). *Early Urbanizations in the Levant: A Regional Narrative*. London: Leicester University Press

Harrison, T. J. (1997). Shifting patterns of settlement in the highlands of central Jordan during the Early Bronze Age. *Bulletin of the American Schools of Oriental Research* 306: 1–37.

—— (2001). Urban or rural? The development of regional communities in the highlands of Jordan during the third millennium. In *Studies in the History and Archaeology of Jordan VII*. Amman: Department of Antiquities, Jordan, 191–6.

Hauptmann, A. (2007). *The Archaeometallurgy of Copper: Evidence from Faynan, Jordan*. Berlin: Springer.

Herr, L. G., and D. R. Clark (2009). From the Stone Age to the Middle Ages in Jordan: digging up Tall al-'Umayri. *Near Eastern Archaeology* 72: 68–97.

Homès-Fredericq, D., and J. B. Hennessy (eds) (1989). *Archaeology of Jordan, vols 2.1 and 2.2: Field Reports: Surveys and Sites A–K and L–Z*. Leuven: Peeters.

Ilan, D. (2002). Mortuary practices in Early Bronze Age Canaan. *Near Eastern Archaeology* 65: 92–104.

Joffe, A. H. (1993). *Settlement and Society in the Early Bronze Age I and II, Southern Levant: Complementarity and Contradiction in a Small-Scale Complex Society*. Sheffield: Sheffield University Press.

—— (2004). Athens and Jerusalem in the third millennium: culture, comparison, and the evolution of social complexity. *Journal of Mediterranean Archaeology* 17: 247–67.

Kamlah, J. (2001). Patterns of regionalism: the plateau of northern Jordan during the Early Bronze Age in light of the Zayraqun survey. In G. Bisheh, M. Zaghloul, and I. Kehrberg (eds), *Studies in the History and Archaeology of Jordan VI*. Amman: Department of Antiquities, Jordan, 211–15.

LaBianca, Ø. S. (2007). Great and little traditions: a framework for studying cultural interaction through the ages in Jordan. In F. al-Khraysheh (ed.), *Studies in the History and Archaeology of Jordan IX*. Amman: Department of Antiquities, Jordan, 275–89.

Levy, T. E., R. B. Adams, A. Hauptmann, M. Prange, S. Schmitt-Strecker, and M. Najjar (2002). Early Bronze Age metallurgy: a newly discovered copper manufactory in southern Jordan. *Antiquity* 76: 425–37.

—— and E. C. M. van den Brink (2002). Interaction models, Egypt and the Levantine periphery. In E. C. M. van den Brink and T. E. Levy (eds), *Egypt and the Levant: Interrelations from the 4th through the Early 3rd millennium BCE*. London: Leicester University Press, 3–37.

Long, J. C., Jr (2003). Theory in archaeology: culture change at the end of the Early Bronze Age. In S. Richard (ed.), *Near Eastern Archaeology: A Reader*. Winona Lake, Ind.: Eisenbrauns, 308–18.

Miroschedji, P. de (1989). Le processus d'urbanisation en Palestine au Bronze Ancien: chronologie et rythmes. In P. de Miroschedji (ed.), *L'urbanisation de la Palestine à l'âge du*

Bronze ancien: bilan et perspectives des recherches actuelles. Oxford: British Archaeological Reports, 63–80.

—— (1999). Yarmouth: the dawn of city-states in southern Canaan. *Near Eastern Archaeology* 62: 2–19.

—— (2002). The socio-political dynamics of Egyptian–Canaanite interaction in the Early Bronze Age. In E. C. M. van den Brink and T. E. Levy (eds), *Egypt and the Levant: Interrelations from the 4th through the Early 3rd millennium BCE*. London: Leicester University Press, 39–57.

Nigro, L. (ed.) (2006). *Khirbet al-Batrawy: An Early Bronze Age Fortified Town in North-Central Jordan. Preliminary Report of the First Season of Excavations (2005)*. Rome: Università di Roma 'La Sapienza'.

—— (2008). *Khirbet al-Batrawy II: The EB II City-Gate, the EB II–III Fortifications, the EB II–III Temple. Preliminary Report of the Second (2006) and Third (2007) Seasons of Excavations*. Rome: Università di Roma 'La Sapienza'.

—— (2010). *In the Palace of the Copper Axes: Khirbet al-Batrawy—The Discovery of a Forgotten City of the III Millennium BC in Jordan*. Rome: Università di Roma 'La Sapienza'.

Palumbo, G. (2001). The Early Bronze Age IV. In B. MacDonald, R. B. Adams, and P. Bienkowski (eds), *The Archaeology of Jordan*. Sheffield: Sheffield Academic, 163–232.

—— (2008). The Early Bronze Age IV. In R. B. Adams (ed.), *Jordan: An Archaeological Reader*. London: Equinox, 227–62.

Philip, G. (2001). The Early Bronze I–III Age. In B. MacDonald, R. Adams, and P. Bienkowski (eds), *The Archaeology of Jordan*. Sheffield: Sheffield University Press, 163–232.

—— (2008). The Early Bronze I–III. In R. B. Adams (ed.), *Jordan: An Archaeological Reader*. London: Equinox, 161–226.

Prag, K. (2001). The third millennium in Jordan: a perspective, past and future. In *Studies in the History and Archaeology of Jordan VII*. Amman: Department of Antiquities, Jordan, 179–90.

Rast, W. E., and R. T. Schaub (2003). *Bab edh-Dhra': Excavations at the Town Site (1975–1981), pt 1: Test*. Winona Lake, Ind.: Eisenbrauns

Regev, J., P. de Miroschedji, R. Greenberg, E. Braun, Z. Greenhut, and E. Boaretto (2012). Chronology of the Early Bronze Age in the southern Levant: new analysis for a high chronology. *Radiocarbon* 54: 525–66.

Renfrew, C., and P. G. Bahn (2008). *Archaeology: Theories, Methods and Practice*, 5th edn. London: Thames & Hudson.

Richard, S. (1980). Toward a consensus of opinion on the end of the Early Bronze Age in Palestine-Transjordan. *Bulletin of the American Schools of Oriental Research* 237: 5–34.

—— (1987). Early Bronze Age in Palestine: the rise and collapse of urbanism. *Biblical Archaeologist* 50.1: 22–43.

—— (2003). The Early Bronze Age in the southern Levant. In S. Richard (ed.), *Near Eastern Archaeology: A Reader*. Winona Lake, Ind.: Eisenbrauns, 286–302.

—— (2006). Early Bronze IV transitions: an archaeometallurgical study. In S. Gitin, J. E. Wright, and J. P. Dessel (eds), *Confronting the Past: Archaeological and Historical Essays on Ancient Israel in Honor of William G. Dever*. Winona Lake, Ind.: Eisenbrauns, 119–32.

—— (2009). Khirbet Iskander, Jordan and Early Bronze IV Studies: a view from a tell. In P. J. Parr (ed.), *The Levant in Transition: Proceedings of a Conference Held at the British Museum on 20–21 April 2004*. London: Maney, 90–100.

—— and J. C. Long, Jr. (2006). Three seasons of excavations at Khirbet Iskander, Jordan: 1997, 2000, 2004. *Annual of the Department of Antiquities, Jordan* 49: 261–76.

—— P. S. Holdorf, and G. Peterman (eds) (2010). *Khirbet Iskandar: Final Report on the Early Bronze IV Area C Gateway and Cemeteries.* Boston: American Schools of Oriental Research.

Savage, S. H., S. E. Falconer, and T. J. Harrison (2007). The Early Bronze Age city states of the southern Levant: neither cities nor states. In T. E. Levy, P. M. M. Daviau, R. W. Younker, and M. Shaer (eds), *Crossing Jordan: North American Contributions to the Archaeology of Jordan.* London: Equinox, 285–97.

Schaub, R. T., and W. E. Rast (1989). *Bab edh-Dhraʿ: Excavations in the Cemetery Directed by Paul W. Lapp (1965–67).* Winona Lake, Ind.: Eisenbrauns.

Stager, L. E. (2001). Port power in the Early and the Middle Bronze Age: the organization of maritime trade and hinterland production. In S. R. Wolff (ed.), *Studies in the Archaeology of Israel and Neighbouring Lands in Memory of Douglas L. Esse.* Chicago: Oriental Institute of the University of Chicago/Atlanta, Ga.: American Schools of Oriental Research, 625–38.

Stein, G. J. (1998). Heterogeneity, power, and political economy: some current research issues in the archaeology of Old World complex societies. *Journal of Archaeological Research* 6: 1–44.

Tubb, J. N. (1993). Tell es-Saʿidiyeh: interim report on the sixth season of excavations. *Palestine Exploration Quarterly* 125: 50–74.

CHAPTER 24

CYPRUS DURING THE EARLY BRONZE AGE

JENNIFER M. WEBB

INTRODUCTION

The Early Bronze Age in Cyprus (*c.*2400–2000 BCE) is a substantially later phenomenon than the Early Bronze Age in the Levant (*c.*3500–2300 BCE). The developmental trajectory of the island in this period is also radically different from the surrounding mainland. While settlements elsewhere were progressing toward urbanization, those in Cyprus remained at the village level. Some hierarchical ordering of settlements existed, with smaller and more marginal villages linked with larger centres, but there do not appear to have been any pre-eminent population centres where inherent stimuli to changes in social and economic structure might have evolved. Villages were not fortified and there is no evidence for writing, sealing systems, centralized storage, communal buildings, cult centres, or major inequalities in wealth or status.

CHRONOLOGY AND TERMINOLOGY

The Cypriot Early Bronze Age is conventionally divided into three phases (Early Cypriot (hereafter EC) I, II, and III). There is now general agreement that the period began around 2500/2400 BCE, roughly coinciding with the end of EB II in Anatolia. In 1962 Stewart published a fine-scale ceramic chronology, based on material from north coast cemeteries, in which he added subdivisions to the basic structure (e.g. EC IIIA, IIIB). Recent work elsewhere on the island has led to the development of more complex regional sequences, and produced radiocarbon dates in keeping with the absolute chronology suggested in Table 24.1. A significant development has been the clarification of the chronological position of the so-called Philia culture. Dikaios identified this variety of Early Cypriot material culture in 1947, regarding it as antecedent to the better-known EC I, while Stewart believed it to be a contemporary regional variant (Webb 2002). The discovery of Philia deposits underlying and therefore pre-dating those of EC I at the stratified settlement of Marki has

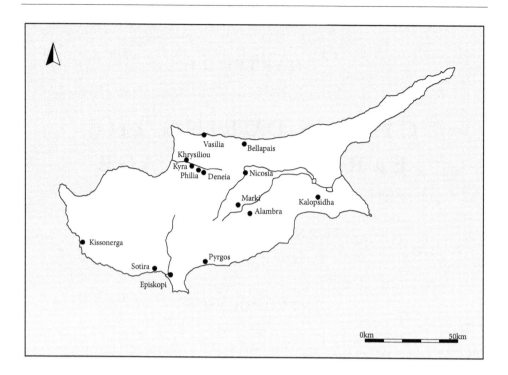

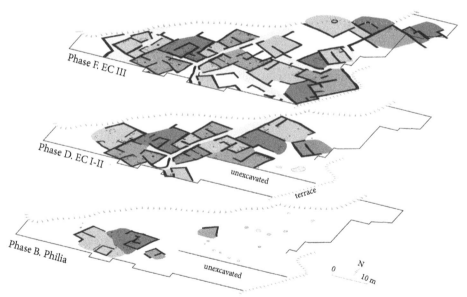

FIG. 24.1 (a) Map of Early Bronze Age sites in Cyprus. (b) Marki Alonia: plan of excavated area in Phases B, D, and F (excavations 1991–2000)

Table 24.1 Phasing of Cypriot Early Bronze Age

Early Cypriot Bronze Age	Philia *facies*	2400–2200 BCE
	Early Cypriot I–II	2200–2100 BCE
	Early Cypriot III	2100–2000 BCE

resolved the debate in favour of Dikaios (Frankel and Webb 2006). In order to preserve the entrenched three-stage nomenclature, this initial period of the Early Bronze Age is referred to as the Philia phase or *facies* (for an alternative chronological schema for the Cypriot Bronze Age, see Knapp 1994).

ORIGINS

The beginning of the Early Bronze Age is marked by major innovations in technology, economy, and society. These include the first systematic exploitation of the island's copper resources and the introduction of cattle, donkeys, and probably new breeds of goats and sheep, agricultural technologies (including the sole-ard plough), rectilinear architecture, extramural burial, chamber tombs and other aspects of mortuary behaviour, new ceramic wares, techniques, and forms, and a range of domestic technologies and practices. Evidence for these is associated with the Philia cultural system (Dikaios 1962: 152–76; Stewart 1962), which shows some chronological overlap with the Late Chalcolithic and, as already noted, stands at the beginning of the Early Bronze Age sequence (EC I–III).

Most scholars accept that southwestern Anatolia or/and Cilicia are the likely source of most, if not all, of these innovations. The process by which they reached Cyprus, however, has long been a source of controversy. Internal development (Stewart 1962: 270; Manning 1993; Knapp 2001) and population movement or migration have both been suggested (Dikaios 1962: 202–3; Catling 1971; Gjerstad 1980: 11–13; Webb and Frankel 1999; Frankel 2000). Recently, Peltenburg (2007) and Bolger (2007) have argued for a more complex, longer-term process, whereby contacts between Cyprus and Anatolia during the Late Chalcolithic were followed by intensive interaction culminating in the arrival of settlers at the beginning of the Philia period.

Recent evidence also suggests that the north coast of the island was active within a long-distance maritime interaction sphere, linking southeastern Anatolia to the east Aegean, the Cyclades, and mainland Greece as early as 2400 BCE (Webb et al. 2006). Direct or indirect participation in this 'Anatolian Trade Network' (Şahoğlu 2005) appears to have involved the importation of copper ingots and copper and bronze artefacts. This may have provided the initiative for an exploration of the island and subsequent development of a local industry.

This more nuanced picture of the island's interregional contacts provides a new context within which to understand the advent of the Early Bronze Age, and suggests that much of importance remains to be discovered about the island's external relations in the mid- and early late third millennium. Excavation on the north coast, halted since 1974, will be crucial in this regard, with sites in the vicinity of Vasilia of key significance.

The archaeological record

Bronze Age settlement in Cyprus was long thought to have been characterized by short-term, shifting occupation within favoured areas (Catling 1962: 131). It is now clear, however, that settlements with multiple chronological components were the norm. At Marki, occupation lasted for some 500 years, from the Philia *facies* to MC II. Similar indications of Philia to EC III or later habitation are indicated for settlements at Nicosia, Deneia, Sotira, and Pyrgos (Webb and Frankel 1999: 10–13; Fig. 24.1a,b).

Few Philia phase settlements have been excavated, and only Marki has produced a substantial exposure (Frankel and Webb 2006). Philia burials are better represented, with tomb groups documented at Vasilia on the north coast, Philia, Kyra, Khrysiliou, and Deneia in the Ovgos Valley, Marki and Nicosia in the central plain, and Episkopi, Sotira, and Kissonerga in the south and southwest (Webb and Frankel 1999: 7–12). A recent survey of Early and Middle Cypriot settlement by Georgiou (2007) identified 44 sites of EC I–II and 345 of EC III and MC I–II, suggesting very significant population growth toward the end of the third millennium. In EC I–II a chain of new sites was established along the south coast, while EC III saw a general expansion into coastal areas, copper-bearing zones, and the eastern and western regions. Only two Early Cypriot settlements have been excavated. Marki was occupied throughout the period. The remains at Sotira date primarily to EC III (Fig. 24.2). In this chapter these sites take on an importance beyond any they had in antiquity. New excavations will undoubtedly change the picture, possibly very significantly.

Regional demography

The Philia *facies* coincided with a restructuring of Chalcolithic communities and the establishment of new settlements and resource networks. Philia communities targeted the cupriferous zone of the northwestern Troodos, at the same time establishing villages in agriculturally productive terrain, along transportation routes, and at coastal outlets. While some

FIG. 24.2 View of excavations at Sotira *Kaminoudhia* (photograph courtesy Stuart Swiny)

foundations were short-lived, elsewhere the distinctive ceramic and other material traits of the Philia *facies* developed into those characteristic of the Early Cypriot period. This process, which is currently visible only at Marki but may be inferred for other settlements, represents an evolutionary development consistent with a history of unbroken occupation.

Population estimates for Marki range from a few dozen in the earliest phase to several hundred people in EC III (Frankel and Webb 2001; Webb and Frankel 2004). If such small founding populations were typical of the dispersed communities established during the Philia, few are likely to have been viable as biological populations or large enough to ensure that craft skills and more specialized technologies were transmitted from one generation to the next. These small founder communities must have been dependent on exchanges of people and goods and the maintenance of close relationships between villages and larger centres such as those at Ayia Paraskevi and Vasilia. This appears to have led to a marked similarity in material culture across the island and an emphasis on shared symbols of identity and alliance.

The success of these microcolonizations and their descendant populations resulted in the establishment of new cultural patterns which became increasingly distinctive at the regional level. These include an array of new pottery shapes and decorative motifs, an increase in the size of settlements, and changes in household size and structure. This seems to have been accomplished both through population growth and through processes of acculturation and integration, which transformed both Philia and indigenous communities into a more broadly based Early Cypriot system. The development of distinct cultural regionalism during EC I and II suggests the increasing importance of regional centres as the focus of alliance and exchange, with a concomitant decrease in multiple, smaller-scale interactions. While regional 'boundaries' are yet to be defined, at Marki ceramic links were strongest with the south in EC I–II. By EC III imports from the north coast, southwest, and perhaps also the east of the island testify to the establishment of broader, island-wide networks.

HOUSEHOLD AND COMMUNITY

Our knowledge of Early Cypriot domestic architecture has greatly advanced with the recent excavation and publication of 33 households at Marki (Frankel and Webb 2006). Here compounds with large courtyards and small interior rooms were the norm from first settlement. A single entrance provided access to an informally (in the earliest phases) and later formally enclosed courtyard. Toward the rear of the courtyard two or three inner rooms built of mud-bricks on stone foundations were located side by side or one behind the other. Additional privacy was provided by short screen walls placed to block views of hearths from exterior and interior passages and doorways.

At least one interior room in each compound was furnished with a hearth with a semicircular or rectangular plaster fender, set against a low wall bench. Rectangular wall bins were probably used for short-term food storage, perhaps in connection with mealing bins. Ovens were located in interior rooms from EC I and several units had substantial stone work benches. Courtyards were furnished with clusters of floor emplacements, animal pens, and informal work stations.

Most artefacts were found in hearth units. They suggest that the processing and small-scale storage of cereals and other commodities, spinning and weaving, chipped and ground stone tool production, and perhaps wood- and hide-working were routinely carried out in hearth rooms, along with the preparation, serving, and consumption of food. Other interior spaces were probably reserved for storage and sleeping.

There was a general continuity of compound size and structure through time, with most occupying around 100m². None is sufficiently larger or better built than others to suggest systemic differences in household function or in the wealth and status of the occupants. Similarly, while there is some variation in the number and size of facilities and rooms, there is nothing in the nature of the internal fittings or discard residues to suggest significant differences in economic capacity or acquisition or consumption behaviour.

At a finer scale of analysis, the evolution of domestic buildings at Marki reveals subtle changes with important implications for understanding the nature of social space. During the Philia phase, courtyards were defined by light fences or informally demarcated by animal pens, outhouses, or lean-tos. Evidence for a range of activities implies production and consumption beyond the scale of the individual 'family', seen also in the presence of large courtyard ovens and freestanding storerooms. This suggests a sharing of resources and cooperative relationships between kin-related households.

These relatively open relationships gave way to a more spatially segregated system in EC I, when substantial stone walls were built to enclose courtyards on three sides, leaving fairly wide entrances from surrounding open spaces. By EC III courtyards were fully enclosed with access via narrow entrances or internal passageways. Alongside these developments, there was a rise in the number and size of interior rooms and an increased reliance on formally defined access routes. These changes suggest an increasing desire for household privacy, perhaps linked with a greater emphasis on private property, intergenerational inheritance, and the control and manipulation of space.

This coincided with increases in the size of the community and of individual families, and with improved economic security at the household level. The social and economic cooperation visible during the Philia may have been a survival mechanism in a community numbering only a few dozen people, dispersed among a handful of households in relatively inhospitable terrain. Within a hundred years this was replaced by self-contained households, suggesting that residential units were now secure enough to meet the majority of their needs and survive as independent economic entities. This is likely to reflect the creation of reliable production and risk-management systems, and to have been accompanied by a desire to establish and maintain private ownership of buildings, land, livestock, and other resources.

The domestic architecture at Sotira has been characterized as 'agglutinative' (Wright 1992: 307; Swiny 2003: 64–71). The system, however, matches the complexity of the Marki architecture and may also represent the end-product of settlement growth and a series of minor and major renovations. Although courtyards were not specifically identified, the basic house form is again one in which linked rooms lead off from one another and are sometimes accessed through narrow passageways.

Villages like Marki and Sotira were probably autonomous communities in which both the land and its products were owned by extended family units, rather than collectively or by outsiders. This is suggested by the size and structure of house compounds, the presence of interior storage facilities, and the lack of evidence for communal enterprises. This village type and its implied mode of social organization appear to have been relatively rare in the ancient Near East (Faust 2005), but are likely to have been the norm in Early Bronze Age Cyprus. A key difference is the absence of urban sites on the island at this time. While a settlement hierarchy existed, it was not one which involved the dominance of rural villages by regional or urban centres with enforced payment by the latter of taxes, tribute, or agricultural surpluses.

This lack of urban pressure may go some way toward explaining the absence of fortifications on Cyprus. Apart from an enigmatic series of stone blocks on the edge of the Philia phase settlement at Marki, which may have been associated with an enclosure (Frankel and Webb 2006: 26, fig. 11.2), there is no evidence for boundary walls at any Early Cypriot settlement. This is likely to reflect well-integrated, interdependent, and permeable inter-site relationships rather than a lack of capacity to invest in such measures. This impression of open communities and relative stability is strengthened by the rarity of weaponry among metal artefacts until the latter years of EC III (Keswani 2004: 77, table 4.15), an absence of evidence for violent destruction or forced abandonment (except as a result of earthquake), and the location of settlements in open terrain.

Regional interaction

The Early Bronze Age in Cyprus was a period of autonomous development, with networks of small, largely self-sustaining villages loosely grouped into non-centralized regional communities and organized along household and kin-based lines. It seems likely that political, economic, and social networking was mediated through these kinship systems, operating primarily at the local level, rather than through structured alliances with economic and political elites based in regional centres. Such inter- and intraregional connections as are visible, largely through the ceramic record, suggest an economy shaped by local demand and dependent on small-scale interactions.

For the Philia period a more specific model can be suggested of larger centres at Vasilia, Nicosia, and elsewhere, and clusters of settlement, such as that in the Philia-Deneia region, with peripheral villages in appropriate resource zones. Movement of goods, people, and livestock no doubt served to cement mutual obligations and reinforce shared identities as well as to reduce competition. Given the small size of settlements like Marki, interaction at the regional level would also have been necessary for the demographic viability of both human and animal populations. While cereal and pulse crops were probably the dietary mainstay, livestock played an important role in supplementing the subsistence economy and providing transport and traction.

During the Philia period a common set of high quality, handmade eating and drinking vessels in Red Polished Philia and other minor wares was in use across the island (Fig. 24.3). Judging from their presence in all excavated tombs and all Philia deposits at Marki, use of these vessels was not restricted. Rather, members of these communities appear to have shared a common ideology and etiquette with respect to appropriate ceramic forms for the consumption of food and drink and, by extrapolation, a common cuisine, array of foodstuffs, and cooking and serving techniques. This must also reflect the existence of effective mechanisms for moving pottery and other commodities across the landscape and maintaining common symbolic behaviours at widely dispersed sites. This is seen not only in the similarity of pottery form and decoration but also in the widespread use of personal ornaments, such as spiral earrings and annular pendants, and may be evident also in the distribution of raw materials, such as picrolite and copper.

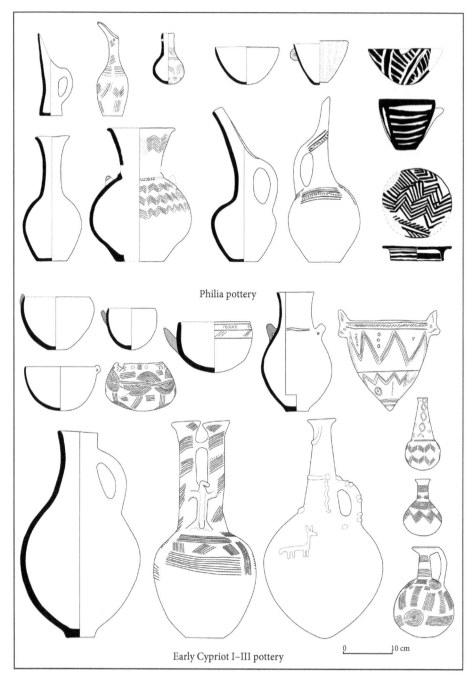

Philia pottery

Early Cypriot I–III pottery

0   10 cm

FIG. 24.3 Philia and EC I–III pottery (prepared by Jennifer M. Webb)

Sometime around 2250 BCE this cohesive system gave way to the more regionally distinctive material culture of EC I, reflecting localized patterns of interaction within and between settlements. Although drawing on Philia traditions and developing in broadly similar ways across the island, EC I–II ceramics display identifiable regional differences. Red Polished I

South Coast Ware, in use in the southwest, is both closest to its Philia antecedents and most clearly different from other ceramic style zones. Similarly, differences in vessel form and decoration separate Red Polished I–II Wares of the south and central parts of the island from those of the north coast.

A key element in this development of regionalism appears to have been an increase in population, which changed relationships within and between settlements. This is likely to have promoted the distribution of raw materials and manufactured goods, while the imperatives for exogamous marriage partners would have been significantly reduced. Kinship through intermarriage probably still served, however, as the primary mechanism linking different sites and facilitating the flow of goods and concepts.

By EC III regional ceramic styles were largely replaced by common forms of Red Polished Ware, predominantly of north coast origin. Toward the end of the period there is also an increased presence of metal goods in north coast cemeteries and some evidence, albeit limited, for imported objects and a renewed flow of tin to the island. This suggests that the north coast played a significant role in initiating extra-island contacts around 2000 BCE and establishing networks which enabled a flow of raw metal and/or finished goods from mining and production sites to the north.

In other aspects Early Cypriot society appears to have been essentially homogeneous, though few settlements have been excavated and future work may reveal significant regional diversity in architectural forms and domestic and industrial activities.

RESOURCE ACQUISITION, PRODUCTION, AND DISTRIBUTION

Most Early Bronze Age inhabitants of Cyprus were probably engaged in agricultural pursuits. At Marki a sustainable agricultural system was in place from the outset, with cattle, sheep, goats, pigs, and donkeys, in conjunction with wheat, barley, olives, pulses, and grapes, providing sufficient resources for an expanding population (Croft 2006; Adams and Simmons 1996). The high incidence of grain harvesting and processing equipment suggests a particularly heavy reliance on cereal cultivation. Cattle provided over half the meat supply and probably also served as a form of 'indirect storage' against the periodic failure of crops and as a means of establishing social ties through exchange (Keswani 1994).

Cypriot copper ores were exploited throughout the period. The organization of this industry, however, is still poorly understood. Several ingot moulds from Marki were probably used to cast ore from nearby sources by metalsmiths operating as autonomous individuals (Fig. 24.4). Unfortunately no metal-working locales have been excavated, and the scale and context of production remain unknown. The largest mould-produced casts estimated to have weighed 1.25kg (Frankel and Webb 2006: 216–17, pl. 57). This suggests production beyond local needs, but the mechanisms by which metal moved from production to manufacturing and redistribution locales are unclear.

There is also evidence for craft specialization in relation to local resources at Sotira. Here, worked picrolite, a coloured stone from the nearby Kouris riverbed used in the production of ornaments, was recovered throughout the excavated area, indicating widespread household production (Swiny 2003: 237). The excavators suggest that Sotira was a centre of transit and exchange related to a regional trade in this material (Herscher 2003: 194).

FIG. 24.4 Stone casting moulds from Marki *Alonia* (photograph courtesy Rudy Frank)

Earlier arguments for household production of ceramics (Frankel 1988) are difficult to sustain in view of estimated breakage and replacement rates at Marki (Frankel and Webb 2001; 2006: 149–53). The basic unit of pottery production is unlikely to be the individual household when replacement requirements fall below a level of economic efficiency. Other factors, including the age and gender structure of the household and the scheduling of other activities, are also likely to impose constraints. In the case of Marki, where replacement rates per household were probably below a dozen vessels per year, production requirements may have been more efficiently met by a small number of potting households engaged in part-time manufacture and exchange. This level of production, which may be characterized as 'elementary specialization', is likely to have been structurally linked to kin-related or other residence groups.

RELIGIOUS ORGANIZATION, RITUAL, AND BURIAL CUSTOMS

Evidence for ritual practice is surprisingly elusive. No cult buildings have been excavated, though a special purpose is argued for a complex at Sotira (S. Swiny, pers. comm.). While this may be due to the limited exposures available, it seems unlikely that Cypriot villages will ever produce the freestanding temples found in Early Bronze towns and villages in the Levant.

A terracotta model from Bellapais *Vounous* and three abbreviated versions from the Kalopsidha and Marki regions (Fig. 24.5), probably of EC III date, have been identified as depictions of open-air sanctuaries (Dikaios 1940: 118; Åström 1966: 14–15; Karageorghis 1970). The nature of the activities shown, however, has been vigorously debated, and alternative interpretations range from funerary (Frankel and Tamvaki 1973) to entirely secular (Morris 1985). Peltenburg (1994) has proposed that the *Vounous* model presents a symbolic representation of new authority structures in which males, bulls, and transcendent powers were dominant. Such a hierarchical ordering of social and gender relationships may well have developed toward the end of the Early Cypriot.

FIG. 24.5 Terracotta 'shrine model' from the Marki region (courtesy Cyprus Museum)

Small zoomorphic figurines appear at Marki from late EC II. The animals represented are oxen and most probably bulls. An association with patterned behaviour is suggested by the fact that most show exposure to fire and appear to have been deliberately damaged (Webb and Frankel 2001). Other iconographic data also link domestic animals, and in particular cattle, to communal ritual activity, most obviously in the case of horned uprights on the *Vounous* and other models. These highlight the socio-ideological importance of this species in prehistoric Bronze Age Cyprus.

Human figurines, primarily depicting females and infants, appear from EC III. It has often been assumed that they were manufactured for funerary use, leading to their identification as representations of a fertility goddess responsible for restoring life to the dead, effigies of mortal women, and symbols of the continuity of human existence (see Bolger 2003: 93–122 with references). The recovery of fragmentary examples in Early and Middle Cypriot deposits at Marki and Alambra (Frankel and Webb 2006: 155–7; Mogelonsky 1996), however, leaves no doubt that they were also in use in settlements. As with most prehistoric figurine assemblages, the function and identity of these objects remain uncertain. Their increasing numbers from EC III may, however, reflect a growing desire to control the reproductive potential of adult females in an intensive agricultural economy.

Burial in pit or rock-cut chamber tombs in extramural cemeteries was the norm through the Early Bronze, although there is evidence also for the occasional disposal of individuals within settlements (Frankel and Webb 2006: 283–5). Chamber tombs contained one or more burials accompanied by quantities of ceramic and, to a lesser extent, metal grave goods. In a major study of Cypriot Bronze Age mortuary behaviour, Keswani (2004: 37–83) argues that funerary celebrations became more protracted and elaborate during this period and sometimes involved rites of secondary treatment and reburial. This is interpreted as indicating the increasing centrality of mortuary ritual as an occasion for prestige competition and the negotiation of social identity rather than the emergence of hereditary elites, in keeping with the view that Early Cypriot communities were as yet weakly stratified (Keswani 2004: 38, 77–8, 83).

FOREIGN INFLUENCES

For some time following the inception of the Early Bronze Age, Cyprus must have remained in contact with the Anatolian mainland and a participant in the interregional metal trade. The lack of tin and the absence of imported copper in EC I–III suggest, however, that this interaction was not maintained and that Cyprus dropped out of the interregional commodity network around 2300 BC. The last quarter of the third millennium also witnessed a decline in authoritative structures and settlement contraction and dispersal in Upper Mesopotamia, Syria, and the Levant, perhaps as a result of changing environmental conditions (Peltenburg 2000). This impacted significantly on interregional trade and politics, and may have helped bring about the end of the 'Anatolian Trade Network' (Şahoğlu 2005: 354).

During the last centuries of the third millennium, Cyprus was largely, if not entirely, isolated from the outside world. No imports have been identified with the exception of a single jar from *Vounous*, which appears to have reached the island from Syria in EC II (Ross 1994). Tin-bronze reappears around 2000 BC, at much the same time as Assyrian trading colonies were established at Kültepe and elsewhere. These colonies changed the dynamics of tin production and distribution within Anatolia and established new regional interaction systems (Yener 2000: 15, 75), which may have been responsible for the island's re-entry into long-distance exchange networks. A gradual increase in external contacts, particularly with the Aegean, and the increasing wealth of north coast communities are among the few material markers of the transition to the Middle Bronze Age on the island.

SUGGESTED READING

Knapp, A. B. (2008). *Prehistoric and Protohistoric Cyprus: Identity, Insularity, and Connectivity*. Oxford: Oxford University Press.
Steel, L. (2004). *Cyprus Before History: From the Earliest Settlers to the End of the Bronze Age*. London: Duckworth.
Swiny, S. (1997). The Early Bronze Age. In T. Papadopoullos (ed.), *A History of Cyprus*, vol. 1. Nicosia: Makarios Foundation, 171–212.

REFERENCES

Adams, R., and D. Simmons (1996). Archaeobotanical remains. In Frankel and Webb (2006: 223–6).
Åström, P. (1966). *Excavations at Kalopsidha and Ayios Iakovos in Cyprus*. Lund: Åströms.

Bolger, D. R. (2003). *Gender in Ancient Cyprus: Narratives of Social Change on a Mediterranean Island*. Walnut Creek, Calif.: AltaMira.

—— (2007). Cultural interaction in 3rd millennium B.C. Cyprus: evidence of ceramics. In S. Antoniadou and A. Pace (eds), *Mediterranean Crossroads*. Athens: Pierides Foundation, 162–86.

Catling, H. W. (1962). Patterns of settlement in Bronze Age Cyprus. *Opuscula Atheniensia* 4: 129–69.

—— (1971). Cyprus in the Early Bronze Age. In I. E. S. Edwards, C. J. Gadd, and N. G. L. Hammond (eds), *The Cambridge Ancient History*, vol. 1, pt 2, 3rd edn. Cambridge: Cambridge University Press, 802–23.

Croft, P. W. (2006). Animal bones. In Frankel and Webb (2006: 263–81).

Dikaios, P. (1940). *The Excavations at Vounous-Bellapais in Cyprus 1931–2*. Oxford: Printed by John Johnson for the Society of Antiquaries of London.

—— (1962). The Stone Age. In P. Dikaios and J. R. Stewart, *The Stone Age and the Early Bronze Age in Cyprus*. Lund: Swedish Cyprus Expedition, 1–204.

Faust, A. (2005). The Canaanite village: social structure of Middle Bronze Age rural communities. *Levant* 37: 105–25.

Frankel, D. (1988). Pottery production in prehistoric Bronze Age Cyprus: assessing the problem. *Journal of Mediterranean Archaeology* 1: 27–55.

—— (2000). Migration and ethnicity in prehistoric Cyprus: technology as *habitus*. *European Journal of Archaeology* 3: 167–87.

—— and A. Tamvaki (1973). Cypriote shrine models and decorated tombs. *Australian Journal of Biblical Archaeology* 2: 39–44.

—— and J. M. Webb (2001). Population, households, and ceramic consumption in a prehistoric Cypriot village. *Journal of Field Archaeology* 28: 115–29.

———— (2006). *Marki Alonia: An Early and Middle Bronze Age Settlement in Cyprus, Excavations 1995–2000*. Sävedalen: Åströms.

Georgiou, G. (2007). *The topography of human settlement in Cyprus in the Early and Middle Bronze Ages* [Greek]. PhD dissertation, University of Cyprus.

Gjerstad, E. (1980). The origin and chronology of the Early Bronze Age in Cyprus. *Report of the Department of Antiquities, Cyprus* 1980: 1–16.

Herscher, E. (2003). The ceramics, with an appendix on pottery in the Chalcolithic tradition by Clark A. Waltz. In S. Swiny, G. R. Rapp, and E. Herscher, *Sotira Kaminoudhia: An Early Bronze Age Site in Cyprus*. Boston: American Schools of Oriental Research, 145–204.

Karageorghis, V. (1970). Two religious documents of the Early Cypriot Bronze Age. *Report of the Department of Antiquities, Cyprus* 1970: 10–13.

Keswani, P. (1994). The social context of animal husbandry in early agricultural societies: ethnographic insights and an archaeological example from Cyprus. *Journal of Anthropological Archaeology* 13: 255–77.

—— (2004). *Mortuary Ritual and Society in Bronze Age Cyprus*. London: Equinox.

Knapp, A. B. (1994). The prehistory of Cyprus: problems and prospects. *Journal of World Prehistory* 8: 377–453.

—— (2001). Archaeology and ethnicity: a dangerous liaison. *Archaeologia Cypria* 4: 29–46.

Manning, S. W. (1993). Prestige, distinction, and competition: the anatomy of socioeconomic complexity in fourth to second millennium B.C.E. Cyprus. *Bulletin of the American Schools of Oriental Research* 292: 35–58.

Mogelonsky, M. K. (1996). Figurines. In J. E. Coleman, J. A. Barlow, M. K. Mogelonsky, and K. W. Schaar, *Alambra: A Middle Bronze Age Settlement in Cyprus—Archaeological Investigations by Cornell University, 1974–1985*. Jonsered: Åströms, 199–217.

Morris, D. (1985). *The Art of Ancient Cyprus: with a Check-List of the Author's Collection*. Oxford: Phaidon.

Peltenburg, E. J. (1994). Constructing authority: the Vounous enclosure model. *Opuscula Atheniensia* 20: 157–62.

—— (2000). From nucleation to dispersal: late third millennium BC settlement pattern transformation in the Near East and Aegean. In O. Rouault and M. Waefler (eds), *La Djezire et L'Euphrate syriens de la protohistoire à la fin du II. Millénaire av. J.-C.: tendances dans l'interprétation historique des données nouvelles*. Brepols: Turnhout, 183–206.

—— (2007). East Mediterranean interaction in the 3rd millennium BC. In S. Antoniadou and A. Pace (eds), *Mediterranean Crossroads*. Athens: Pierides Foundation, 139–59.

Ross, J. F. (1994). The Vounous jars revisited. *Bulletin of the American Schools of Oriental Research* 296: 15–30.

Şahoğlu, V. (2005). The Anatolian trade network and the Izmir region during the Early Bronze Age. *Oxford Journal of Archaeology* 24: 339–61.

Stewart, J. R. (1962). The Early Cypriote Bronze Age. In P. Dikaios and J. R. Stewart, *The Stone Age and the Early Bronze Age in Cyprus*. Lund: Swedish Cyprus Expedition, 205–401.

Swiny, S. (2003). The settlement. In S. Swiny, G. R. Rapp, and E. Herscher, *Sotira Kaminoudhia: An Early Bronze Age Site in Cyprus*. Boston: American Schools of Oriental Research, 9–101.

Webb, J. M. (2002). *Exploring Bronze Age Cyprus: Australian Perspectives*. Armidale: University of New England.

—— and D. Frankel (1999). Characterizing the Philia *facies*: material culture, chronology, and the origin of the Bronze Age in Cyprus. *American Journal of Archaeology* 103: 3–43.

—— (2001). Clay cattle from Marki: iconography and ideology in Early and Middle Bronze Age Cyprus. *Archaeologia Cypria* 4: 71–82.

—— (2004). Intensive site survey: implications for estimating settlement size, population and duration in prehistoric Bronze Age Cyprus. In M. Iacovou (ed.), *Archaeological Field Survey in Cyprus: Past History, Future Potentials*. London: British School at Athens, 125–38.

——Z. A. Stos, and N. H. Gale (2006). Early Bronze Age metal trade in the eastern Mediterranean: new compositional and lead isotope evidence from Cyprus. *Oxford Journal of Archaeology* 25: 261–88.

Wright, G. R. H. (1992). *Ancient Building in Cyprus*. Leiden: Brill.

Yener, K. A. (2000). *The Domestication of Metals: The Rise of Complex Metal Industries in Anatolia*. Leiden: Brill.

....

CHAPTER 25

THE NORTHERN LEVANT DURING THE INTERMEDIATE BRONZE AGE

Altered Trajectories

....

HARVEY WEISS

Societies adapted quickly to altered dry-farming cereal production at the onset and terminus of the 4.2–3.9 ka BP (4200–3900 years ago, or 2200–1900 BCE) abrupt climate change. Relatively high-resolution and independent archaeological and paleoclimate records document that the period of abrupt climate change began with: (1) regional abandonments; (2) habitat-tracking to riparian, paludal, and karst spring-fed refugia; and (3) nomadization (subsistence transfer from agriculture to pastoral nomadism). Adaptive social responses at the termination of the abrupt climate change included: (1) sedentarization; (2) political state formation; (3) increased and enhanced surplus agroproduction; and (4) politico-territorial expansion. This 300-year period provides, therefore, an alluring Holocene example of societal responses to abrupt climate change across the eastern Mediterranean and west Asian landscapes, and in particular across steep gradient ecotones of modern Syria and Lebanon. Most of these societal processes have previously been categorized archaeologically and historically as components of the unexplained 'Intermediate Bronze Age', 'Early Bronze–Middle Bronze Transition', 'Akkadian collapse', and 'Amoritization'. The relatively highly resolved data currently available for the 4.2–3.9 ka BP abrupt climate change and the Intermediate Bronze Age of West Asia (2200–1900 BCE) have focused much paleoclimate and archaeological research on the period, even though century-scale Holocene climate changes different in their characteristics (abrupt, high-magnitude) also occurred at 8.2 (Weninger et al. 2009), 5.2 (Staubwasser and Weiss 2006), and 3.2 (Kaniewski et al. 2010) ka BP.

THE PALEOCLIMATE RECORD: 4.2–3.9 KA BP ABRUPT CLIMATE CHANGE

....

Moisture-laden North Atlantic cyclonic westerlies seasonally break into the Mediterranean trough and provide the winter precipitation needed for dry farming along the northern plains and mountain valleys of West Asia, as well as the spring melt that sustains Euphrates floodplain agriculture in Syria and Tigris–Euphrates irrigation agriculture in southern Iraq (Cullen et al. 2002; Lionello et al. 2006; Luterbacher et al. 2006). The annual variability in this seasonal precipitation during the modern instrumental period diverges from what is now known of the changes in the pre-instrumental period, which shows several century-scale disruptions with abrupt onsets and terminations. High-resolution paleoclimate proxy records, including lake, marine, speleothem, and glacial cores with annual resolution, document these century-scale excursions within the relative frequencies of stable isotopes, usually oxygen and carbon, as well as pollen and aeolian dust. The 4.2 ka BP–3.9 ka BP abrupt climate change is now well recorded globally and, within the limits of chronological resolution, synchronously (e.g. North America: Dean 1997; Zhang and Hebda 2005; Booth et al. 2005; Li, Yu, and Kodama 2007; Fisher et al. 2008; Menounos et al. 2008; South America: Thompson 2000; Baker et al. 2009; Licciardi et al. 2009; West Asia: Staubwasser and Weiss 2006; East Asia: Schettler et al. 2006; Wang et al. 2005; Liu et al. 2010). In the Mediterranean and western Asia, the 4.2 ka BP excursion was a sudden cooling and aridification, the product of a still unexplained weakening of North Atlantic cyclogenesis (Cullen et al. 2000; Cullen and deMenocal 2000; Weiss 2000; Bond et al. 2001) or deflection of the westerlies. Three hundred years later, westerlies-borne precipitation bounced abruptly back to its pre-aridification event levels.

THE MULTI-PROXY STACK

The distribution of the proxy climate change variables is illustrated in Fig. 25.1, a multi-proxy stack from the Mediterranean westerlies region and, as well, the glacial core at Kilimanjaro (Thompson et al. 2002), indicating the larger-scale regions similarly affected. The Gulf of Oman marine core (Cullen et al. 2000) displays a carbonate and dolomite dust spike of 300 years and provides both the radiocarbon and tephrochronological linkage with 2200 BCE Tell Leilan (Weiss et al. 1993). The Lake Van core (Lemcke and Sturm 1997) quartz is background dust, understood as a function of aridification beginning at 2190 BCE. The dust does not represent suddenly intensified Mesopotamian agriculture, which would have caused a relatively minor disturbance; more intensive agricultural activity in southern Mesopotamia, such as during the Sassanian dynasty, did not generate similar dust spikes. In fact, similar dust spikes occur at Italian lake cores synchronously with precipitous *natural* deforestation (di Rita and Magri 2009; Magri and Parra 2002). Noticeably, however, some of the other Van proxies do not show this spike. The Gölhisar lake core in southwest Turkey (Eastwood et al. 1999) provides the same dust spike, and the parallel increases and decreases in $\delta^{18}O$, a proxy for precipitation decreases and increases in these realms (Leng et al. 2010; Fairchild et al. 2006). Dead Sea levels fell *c*.45m during this same period, then returned to a higher than previous level for the following 600 years, until the Late Bronze Age collapse (Migowski et al. 2006; Frumkin 2009; Kaniewski et al. 2010). The highest density of data points within a proxy record for this region, *c*.15-year intervals, is the Red Sea core at Shaban Deep (Arz, Lamy, and Pätzold 2006), where the $\delta^{18}O$ spike is constrained to *c*.250 years. One attempt at a transfer of proxy values to precipitation values is from Soreq Cave, near Jerusalem, where the $\delta^{18}O$ speleothem spike has been estimated to reflect a 30 per cent precipitation reduction (Bar-Matthews, Ayalon, and Kaufman 1997; Enzel

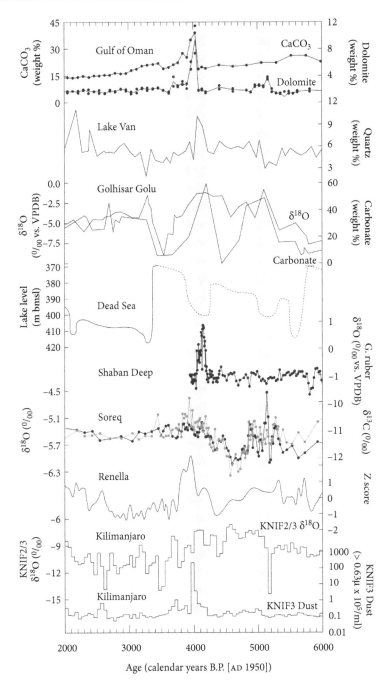

FIG. 25.1 Multi-proxy stack of Mediterranean westerlies and Kilimanjaro, displaying the 5.2 and 4.2 ka BP abrupt climate change events within marine, lake, speleothem, and glacial records (H. Weiss and M. Besonen; cf. Weiss et al. 2012: fig. 26)

et al. 2003; Jex et al. 2010). The synchronous Soreq $\delta^{13}C$ spike, also reported at Gölhisar (Leng et al. 2010), probably reflects a sharp increase in drought-advantage C4 vegetation although the Th/U dates around this event at Soreq Cave have large standard deviations (Bar-Matthews and Ayalon 2004: 381). In Italy, the Renella flowstone's Z score (Drysdale et al. 2006) records a precipitous aridification event that also appears in several Italian lake records (e.g. Magny et al. 2007; Magri and Parra 2002). Lastly, the 'Middle Holocene Dust Event' record from the Kilimanjaro glacial cores (Thompson et al. 2002; Davis and Thompson 2006), with annual ice lamination dating, is slightly divergent chronologically, but numerous well-dated East African lake level reductions, the product of synchronous deflection of the Indian Ocean monsoon and Somali jet sources for the Nile, independently conform to the Kilimanjaro and Mediterranean westerlies record (Gasse 2000; Gasse and van Campo 1994). The East African lake level records explain the synchronous diminution of Nile flow coincident with the First Intermediate Period in Egypt (Stanley et al. 2003).

The 4.2 ka BP event noted in Anatolian lake pollen cores (Weiss 2000) has been amplified considerably, but at low chrono-resolution (e.g., Kuzucuoğlu et al. 2011). At Gölhisar, the $\delta^{13}C$ spike (Leng et al. 2010; Eastwood et al. 2007) is synchronous with the carbonate and $\delta^{18}O$ spikes (Fig. 25.1). At Eski Acigöl, mesic trees declined with falling lake levels (Roberts et al. 2001). Pollen, charcoals, benthic foraminifera, and geochemistry confirm these observations at Aegean and Levantine seas (Schmiedl et al. 2010; Kotthoff et al. 2008), Lake Van, Turkey (Wick, Lemcke, and Sturm 2003), Maharlu, central Iran (Djamali et al. 2009), Malatya (Masi et al. 2012), and the Caspian Sea (Leroy et al. 2007, 2013).

Recent research has focused on the components of the aridification event. Tuscan and Albanian lake core pollen and geochemistry suggest brief initial and terminal humid phases (Magny et al. 2009), and the mini-spikes of $\delta^{18}O$ at Soreq Cave have been interpreted as short droughts between wetter stretches (Kuzucuoğlu 2007). The latter, however, are not congruent with higher-resolution samples, the Soreq $\delta^{13}C$ record, nor the numerous Mediterranean and western hemisphere paleoarchives. Similarly, a time-transgressive quality (Roberts et al. 2001) is supported by neither the available chronological resolution nor the regional and global chronologies.

The uniquely resolved multi-proxy analysis of a 10cm diameter subfossil *Tamarix* stem from a Mount Sedom (Dead Sea) diapir included three radiocarbon dates with 60–80-year standard deviations, 109 carbon and nitrogen stable isotope measurements from rings dated by interpolation of the calibrated radiocarbon dates' peak probabilities, and transfer of the $\delta^{13}C$ measurements to modern precipitation values. The *Tamarix* stem analyses document three or four successive multi-decadal droughts that reduced regional precipitation by 50 per cent between 2200 and 1900 BCE (Frumkin 2009).

THE ARCHAEOLOGICAL RECORD: REGIONAL SOCIAL RESPONSES (2200–1900 BCE)

Across Syria and Lebanon are five regions distinguished by their precipitation and hydrological resources: dry-farming plains, semi-arid steppe, rivers, swamps, and karstic springs. These were the stage for the adaptive social responses to the abrupt climate changes: political collapse and regional abandonment, nomadization, and habitat-tracking (Coope 1979; Eldredge 1985: 10; Grosjean, Núñez, and Cartajena 2005), followed by resettlement, political consolidation, and state expansion.

The Khabur Plains and the Akkadian Empire

The Akkadian extraction and deployment of cereal revenues from the rain-fed agricultural regions of Mesopotamia extended from Susa through Kirkuk/Nuzi, Erbil/Arbilu, Mosul/Nineveh to the Khabur Plains of northeast Syria dominated by Leilan/Shekhna, Mozan/Urkesh, and Brak/Nagar. At those cities the depth and extent of the Akkadian control is manifest in the monumental public buildings, Akkadian administrative texts, school texts (de Lillis-Forrest, Milano and Mori 2007), and standardized flat-based sila ration bowls (Senior and Weiss 1992). Impressive epigraphic representations also include the name-stamped foundation bricks at Brak's Naram-Sin fortress (Mallowan 1947: 66, pl. lxiv), the sealing of the daughter of Naram-Sin, wife of the ruler, at Mozan/Urkesh (Buccellati and Kelly-Buccellati 2002), and the seal impression of Haya-abum, the Akkadian *šabra*, at Tell Leilan (de Lillis-Forrest et al. 2004). As in other Akkadian imperialized domains, the target was cereal production revenues to augment the irrigation-agriculture imperial economy in southern Mesopotamia. One imperial Akkadian document, purchased in Baghdad by the British Museum shortly after Rassam's excavations at nearby Sippar, records receipt of 29 metric tonnes of barley, or 20,000 man-days of rations, from a city named Nagar (Sommerfeld, Archi, and Weiss 2004). These were probably the transported harvest of Akkadian-controlled lands in the high cereal-yield areas around Leilan and Mozan, where a cultivated hectare or two, at 1,200 kg/ha (Weiss 1986), produced c.400 man-days of barley rations for Akkadian workers. This combination of high yields and extensive cultivable land could have sustained multiples of the regional Akkadian-period population and imperialized cereal revenues, and did so only 300 years later (Fig. 25.2) (Ristvet and Weiss 2013).

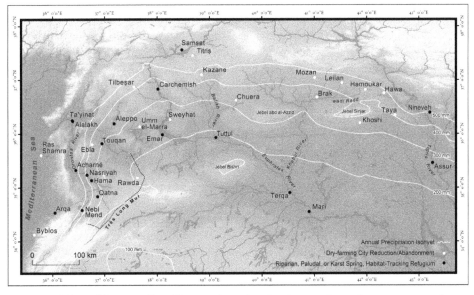

FIG. 25.2 Map of Intermediate Bronze Age sites in the northern Levant, 4.2–3.9 ka BP. Dry-farming settlement diminished while riparian, paludal, and karstic refugia settlement expanded. The Très Long Mur was constructed and the Jebel Bishri became the pastoralists' regional cemetery (Weiss 2012: Fig. 5)

When precipitation dropped *c*.30–50% during the 4.2 ka BP abrupt climate change, the Khabur Plains' cultivable land areas narrowed (Staubwasser and Weiss 2006: figs 4 and 5) and regional cereal yields plummeted. Previously marginal production areas, such as the area around Brak, dropped below limits of cereal dry farming. The Akkadians departed suddenly, and with them so did the indigenous regional population. The Tell Leilan Region Survey, a 30km-wide north–south 1,650km² transect through the heart of the eastern Khabur Plains, documents an 87% reduction in settled area for the period immediately after the Leilan Akkadian Administrative Building abandonment (Fig. 25.2) (Ristvet and Weiss 2013; Weiss 2012).

The elimination of imperial revenues from the Khabur and the other imperialized dry-farming plains truncated imperialized grain flow to the Akkadian capital. Evocative epi-grams for the subsequent Akkadian collapse in southern Mesopotamia include 'On its canal-bank tow-paths the grass grew long' (*The Curse of Akkade*: Black et al. 2004: 124), 'Who was king, who was not king' (Sumerian King List: Glassner 1993: 140), and, in north-ern Mesopotamia, 'seven generations since the Fall of Akkad' (Shamshi-Adad: Grayson 1987: 53; Glassner 1993: 22), and of Shamshi-Adad's predecessors, 'the seventeen [Amorite] kings who lived in tents' (Assyrian King List: Glassner 1993: 147). The contemporary epi-graphic record for the Akkadian collapse (Glassner 1986) is now amplified and quantified through recent archaeological measurement of regional site abandonments, site-size reduc-tions, and their rates of change on the Khabur Plains, as well as by the new paleoclimate records for abrupt climate change.

The Akkadians built several public structures at the north and south edges of the *c*.40ha Tell Brak/Nagar acropolis. At the southern edge, the massive Naram-Sin fortress was prob-ably intended for regional grain harvest storage, but this building was probably still unfin-ished at the site's desertion: its walls were still under construction, a prepared floor was laid upon only one of four courtyards (Mallowan 1947), and re-excavation shows the walls' foundation trench, but no working/living exterior floor (Oates, Oates, and McDonald 2001: fig. 15). The unprovenienced sealing of Talpuš-atili of Nagar may date from shortly after the desertion, but the lack of evidence for a 'Hurrian period' rebuilding of the fortress sug-gests a fantasy as evanescent as its Ur III tablets and seal impressions (Sallaberger 2007: 432). Elsewhere on the acropolis, two elaborate Akkadian administrative buildings (FS and SS) and ceramic assemblages (McMahon 2012) were abandoned after ritual filling and seal-ing (Oates, Oates, and McDonald 2001). Synchronously, the Akkadian-period lower town at the southern edge of the acropolis was also evacuated (Ur, Karsgaard, and Oates 2011). Succeeding the Akkadian collapse and abandonments were a few short-lived houses of the ill-defined Period N in Area CH (Oates, Oates, and McDonald 2001). Similarly, the ram-shackle, post-Akkadian *pisé* construction on top of the formal mud-brick Akkadian build-ing in Area TC was abandoned at *c*.2200 BCE and never reoccupied (Emberling et al. 2012). The Brak occupational hiatus extended thereafter until the 19th-century Khabur Ware peri-od's precipitation bounce-back, when some domestic construction appeared at the western (HH) and northwestern (HN) edges of the acropolis (McDonald and Jackson 2003).

Akkadian-controlled, 90ha Tell Leilan/Shekhna was similarly abandoned at *c*.2200 BCE. 'The Unfinished Building' on the southern side of the Leilan acropolis's Akkadian street was without a finished interior floor, with its walls built to only three or four mud-brick courses above dressed basalt block bases (like those used at the Mozan Akkadian palace), when the city was deserted (Ristvet and Weiss 2000; de Lillis-Forrest et al. 2004; Weiss et al. 2012).

Fragments of similar unfinished walls have been retrieved at nearby Mohammed Diyab (Nicolle 2012). At the glacis-protected Akkadian palace across the street, where grain harvests were collected and processed, clay balls for tablet manufacture and blank clay tablets were left on a palace room floor when the Akkadians walked away from the acropolis (Weiss et al. 2012). Lastly, the walled residential lower town of c.75ha was abandoned (Weiss 1990). On top of the abandoned Akkadian palace, a four-room house was built around a courtyard (Fig. 25.4; Leilan Period IIc), and is the only post-Akkadian construction yet detected within the site. Numerous radiocarbon dates from the Akkadian palace and its post-Akkadian house indicate that the remnant reoccupation here and at the other, infrequent, post-Akkadian Khabur Plains occupations survived 30–50 years after the Tell Leilan Akkadian palace abandonment (Weiss et al. 2012; Fig. 25.3).

At 120ha Tell Mozan/Urkesh, close to the Tur Abdin Mountains, the Akkadian-period palace of large dressed basalt blocks and mud-brick construction (Buccellati and Kelly-Buccellati 2000) lacks high-resolution radiocarbon dates but was abandoned at the same time as the Akkadian collapse at Brak and Leilan. Here, the indigenous population also abandoned the lower town, and the city was reduced to a less than 20ha town at a remnant Tur Abdin stream refugium (Pfälzner, Wissing, and Hübner 2004; Weiss 2012). This was the period of Atal-shen and Tish-atal of 'Urkesh and Nawar', the latter settlement possibly located 30km northeast at Gir Nawaz (Sallaberger 2007).

Recent studies based on excavation-retrieved archaeobotanical samples and an early paleoclimate model (Bryson 1997) conclude that Mozan environs did not experience an arid climate excursion during this period (e.g., Deckers et al. 2010). However, archaeobotanical records, whether at Mozan, Brak (Charles and Bogard 2001), or elsewhere, are not *paleoclimate* proxies; rather, they are the social products of a cultural filter. Meanwhile, the paleoclimate model used in the Mozan study had been rejected because the frequency and intensity of the Mediterranean westerlies was unknown (Bryson and Bryson 2000: 80–81).

Elsewhere across the Khabur Plains, the hastened search for and excavation of post-Akkadian settlement has so far produced three occupations, two certainly very small, and all abandoned quickly. At Tell Arbid, 45km south of Tell Mozan, the estimated 4ha Akkadian occupation, yet unexcavated, was reduced c.20%, and comprised a Main Building, its renovations, and abandonment. Radiocarbon dates indicate that this remnant settlement, like the other 'post-Akkadian' settlements, lasted only 30–50 years (Koliński 2012).

At 12ha Chagar Bazar, 22km south of Mozan, alongside the Wadi Khanzir and the 'old road' from Hasseke to Qamishli, post-Akkadian occupation comprised but 1ha at the c.5ha southern mound: the terminal 'Bâtiment 1', a four-room house, possibly two-storey and 'communal'. No radiocarbon dates are available, but the ceramic assemblage is similar to that of Leilan IIc. The earlier Akkadian occupation, as yet untested, may have extended across 10ha (Tunca, McMahon, and Baghdo 2007).

'Late third millennium' occupations, only preliminarily divided into Akkadian and post-Akkadian periods and without radiocarbon dates, have been surveyed and excavated at 100ha Hamoukar, still further east. After its Akkadian or post-Akkadian building abandonment, and a number of early post-Akkadian pits (Gibson 2001; Gibson et al. 2002; Ur 2002), Hamoukar was not reoccupied. Along the Jaghjagh River, at Tell Barri, the Akkadian settlement was abandoned, a kiln area briefly reoccupied about 75 years later, and then abandoned again until Khabur Ware times (Pecorella and Pierobon 2004: 21, 29; Orsi 2008, 2012). West of the Jaghjagh River, a Tell Beydar temple was still used during the early Akkadian period but was abandoned subsequently (Van der Stede 2005). In general, Khabur Plain post-Akkadian sedentary settlement was reduced greatly, a short-lived step to almost three centuries of desertion similar to the synchronous settlement history of dry-farming Palestine (Gophna 1992). The Akkadian collapse on the Khabur Plains was, therefore, a two-phase regional process manifest within the synchronous public building and lower town abandonments at Leilan, Mozan, and Brak, accompanied by the widespread rural settlement abandonment that is visible in the Leilan Regional Survey (Arrivabeni 2012; Ristvet 2012; Weiss 2012; Weiss et al. 2012).

The Euphrates River

Away and apart from the Akkadian imperialized realms, state polities and region-wide settlements were similarly affected by precipitation reduction and agricultural dislocation. Euphrates flow was probably diminished, but did not cease during this period. Hence habitat-tracking from dry-farming areas to Euphrates River settlements in Syria and southern Mesopotamia was one response of dry-farming sedentary agriculturalists and seasonal transhumant pastoralists as well (Weiss et al. 1993; de Boucheman 1934). Urban settlement flourished and expanded along the middle Euphrates during this *shakkanaku* period at Mari and its environs (Geyer and Monchambert 2003; Butterlin 2007: 242), as at Tuttul (Miglus, Strommenger, and Achwan 2007) and Emar, greater than 40ha (Faist and Finkbeiner 2002: 191). Settlement along the Balikh River was always limited, as Balikh spring flow from karstic 'Ain al-Arus was less than 6m^3 per second, within a channel that rarely exceeded 6m across (Wirth 1971). Here the small town at Hammam et-Turkman shows evidence of abandonment during this period (Curvers 1991; Wilkinson 1998). Just south of the Taurus, settlement system collapse and abandonment occurred within the rain-fed agriculture Karababa Basin at and around 43ha Titriş Höyük, which was then reduced to 3ha (Algaze et al. 1996). The same pattern is obtained with abandonments at 56ha Tilbeşar west of Carchemish within the Sajour River drainage (Kepinski 2007) and 100ha Kazane Höyük near Urfa (Creekmore 2010). Further south, along the Euphrates, however, settlement expanded greatly during this period in the Carchemish region, where a definitive study of that 40ha site is now in progress (Marchetti 2012). Tell es-Sweyhat, a 45ha settlement located, curiously, 4km east of the Euphrates, at the 200–300mm limit of dry farming, was occupied extensively to *c.*2150 BCE in Period 4, and then abandoned thereafter in Period 5, with Period 6 poorly preserved building levels extending only to the early transition to the Middle Bronze Age (Danti and Zettler 2007: 176). The Euphrates drainage region, therefore, indicates continued and thriving occupation during this period along the river, the target of habitat-tracking, and pronounced abandonment in the drainage's dry-farming zones. Similar habitat-tracking should have targeted the adjacent Anatolian plateau, within the Tur Abdin/Diyarbakr region of higher precipitation (Weiss and Courty 1993: 144), as has been suggested for the Upper Tigris/Batman region (Laneri et al. 2008).

Dry-farming western Syria and the steppe

The wealth and power of Ebla on the Idlib Plain made it the famous target of the Mari coalition that destroyed its palace in *c.*2300 BC (Archi and Biga 2003). Following a short occupational hiatus, the succeeding EB IVB city of this time period was reduced in size while ruled from the Archaic Palace with its unique water cisterns. The palace construction, however, remained unfinished, probably like the buildings at Leilan, Mohammed Diyab, and Brak, and the city was destroyed again in *c*.2000 BCE (Matthiae 1995a; 1995b; Fiorentino et al. 2008). Around this time, habitat-tracking to the Madekh Swamp, terminus of the Qoueiq River, resulted in the settlement at Tell Touqan (Baffi and Peyronel 2013).

Further east, at the limits of dry-farming cultivation prior to 2200 BC, the eastern Jabbul Plain, with the 20ha town at Umm el-Marra, was abandoned during the aridification period (Nichols 2004). To the south, Rawda, in the semi-arid marginal zone, was also abandoned after *c*.400 years of occupation. There the radial planned town (Castel and Peltenburg 2007), a major unexplained phenomenon from the Khabur Plains to the Orontes River, was the settlement outpost facing, or replaced by, the Très Long Mur during the aridification excursion.

The Très Long Mur (Fig. 25.3) was constructed of rough, calcareous, and basalt boulders along a 220km distance following precisely the precipitation isohyets of the western steppe (Geyer et al. 2010). This western analogue to the contemporary 'Repeller of the Amorites' wall in southern Mesopotamia delimited and protected urban agricultural territory from expanding Amorite, steppe nomad populations—described famously as the people 'who know not agriculture' in *The Curse of Akkade*. The extended pastoralist cemeteries of this

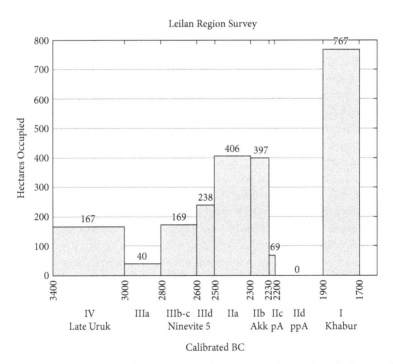

FIG. 25.3 Leilan Region Survey histogram, preliminary analysis of settled areas showing sedentary population reductions during 5.2 and 4.2 ka BP abrupt climate change events. Minor 'post-Akkadian settlement' persisted for a few decades after initiation of the 4.2 ka BP abrupt climate change (Weiss 2012: Fig. 3)

period at the Jebel Bishri, probably mirroring tribal units in the spatial distribution of stone-lined and cairn-marked inhumations, is now under intensive survey and excavation (Ohnuma 2010).

The regional expansion of pastoralism is visible at the edge of the steppe, 'The Black Desert', at Khirbet al-Umbashi (Braemer, Échallier, and Taraqji 2004), some 70km southeast of Damascus, where settlement grew from 6ha to 60ha during this period and comprised *c.*250 large stone houses. Subsistence here was non-agricultural, exclusively dependent upon sheep/goat herding and dairy production, with no evidence for hierarchical organization. This settlement type extended across the Syro-Palestinian marginal steppe, but was mostly abandoned at *c.*3.9 ka BP with the sudden return of pre-abrupt climate change precipitation levels.

Orontes River

The Orontes River provides a unique environmental contrast with the Jabbul and Idlib Plains. The karstic 'Ain ez-Zarka, its source, drains a slow infiltration system with 10 billion m^3 of phreatic zone storage and a mean residence currently around 40 years (Bakalowicz, El Hakim, and El-Hajj 2008) that is extended downstream by other springs.

Hence, during this 300-year period of reduced precipitation, the Orontes River attracted and sustained large, habitat-tracking, sedentary agricultural populations (al-Maqdissi 2010). The karstic springs of the Jebel Ansariyeh, Lebanon/Anti-Lebanon, Orontes system include three at 100ha Mishrifé/Qatna that were dammed to create a >70ha lake during the city's late third-millennium growth (Fig. 25.5) (Cremaschi 2007; Morandi Bonacossi 2009). Survey and excavation along the Orontes River have also documented the sudden synchronous growth of square-walled, Qatna-like, 76ha Nasriyah, the smaller, but similarly square-walled, Tell She'irat (al-Maqdissi 2010), and the first occupations at 70ha Acharné (Fortin 2007), probably ancient Tunip, where 175 karst springs debouch into the paludal Ghab depression (Voûte 1961).

The 'Amuq Plain, at the terminus of Orontes River karst aquifer flow, provided the cultivable landscape for urban settlement at Ta'yinat and Atchana probably beginning at this period (Yener 2005: 173). On the western side of the Jebel Ansariyeh, along the fertile littoral, karstic springs provided for the villages of the Akkar Plain and the town at Tell Arqa, where settlement and paleobotanical remains indicating bountiful agriculture are robustly radiocarbon-dated to this period (Thalmann 2006). Coastal Syria and Lebanon lack karstic springs apart from Jeita Cave, along the Nahr el-Kalb Valley near Beirut (Verheyden et al. 2008). Hence population reductions and site abandonments were experienced at 23ha Ras Shamra/Ugarit between Levels III and II (Yon 1997: 16), at similarly sized Byblos (Saghieh 1983) down the coast, and at Sianu (al-Maqdissi 2006), while occupation continued in some areas of 12ha Tweini at the seaside conjunction of two rivers (Bretschneider and Van Lerberghe 2008).

3.9 KA BP

The abrupt return of pre-4.2 ka BP annual precipitation returned dry farming to the Khabur Plains on the east and to the fertile *terra rossa* plains of Aleppo and Idlib on the

FIG. 25.4 Stratigraphic profile of abandonment and reoccupation. Tell Leilan, 1989, Operation 8, one of the Lower Town soundings recording the abandonment at 2200 BCE (stratum 3, terminal Akkadian period) and the reoccupation at c.1900 BCE (stratum 1, Khabur Ware period). Excavation in 2006 and 2008 revealed a four-room post-Akkadian occupation of the Acropolis northwest Akkadian palace, the only post-Akkadian occupation recovered at the 90ha site (Weiss et al. 1993: Fig. 5)

west. The resettlement of formerly arid and abandoned territories was the second stage of Amoritization, the sedentarization of the Amorite pastoral nomads, dramatically recorded in their archaeologically retrieved settlements within the Leilan Region Survey (Fig. 25.3), well-recorded epigraphically, and thereafter famously engaged in military struggles for control of newly opened lands and agricultural wealth during the 19th and 18th centuries BCE, which initiate the succeeding Middle Bronze Age. While the physical return of dry-farming lands is now clear, the social forces behind this resettlement remain to be explored.

CONCLUSIONS

Some archaeological perspectives on late third-millennium Syria and Lebanon view them as featureless isotropic planes, separate from the available and rich environmental and paleoclimatic data, and thereby provide a settlement and abandonment profile that is at once reductionist and stochastic (e.g. Marro and Kuzucuoğlu 2007; Schwartz 2007). The

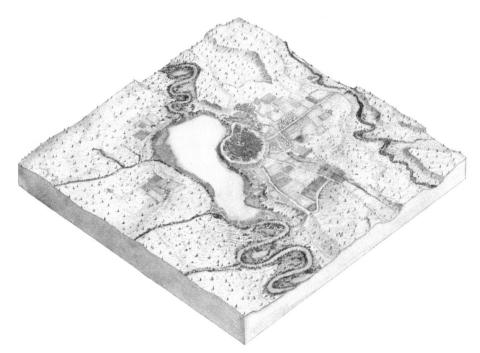

FIG. 25.5 A reconstruction of the settlement at Qatna where Mauro Cremaschi's cores and analyses identified dammed karst spring flow that produced a reservoir of more than 70ha for the settlement's expanding population at *c*.2200 BC (courtesy Daniele Morandi Bonacossi)

patterning of social responses to the late third-millennium abrupt climate excursion across hydrologically varied plains stands in marked contrast, however, to the apparent randomness within only two-dimensional views. Interpretations that champion the conscious self-determinism of these ancient societies evaporate alongside the illusory randomness. The non-imperialized settlements in dry-farming terrains collapsed unless situated, like Iktanu (Prag 2007), adjacent to karst springs. Likewise, the Akkadian Empire, barely a generation old, was expanding when it collapsed suddenly: (1) The 'Seventeen Kings against Naram-Sin' had been defeated (Westenholz 1997); (2) monumental imperial Akkadian architecture was in the course of construction at Leilan, Mohammed Diyab, and Brak; and (3) the marriage of Naram-Sin's daughter had successfully sealed the Akkadian alliance at Mozan.

The steppic, riparian, paludal, and karstic resources of Syria and Lebanon were the adaptively utilized theatre for the dramatic social and environmental interactions, and the altered trajectories at the 4.2–3.9 ka BP abrupt climate change. Societies responded to the abrupt climate change with political collapse, regional abandonment, nomadization, and habitat tracking to sustainable agricultural regions. These adaptations provided demographic and social resilience across the West Asian landscape at 2200 BCE, as did sedentarization and dry-farming resettlement at 1900 BCE, although the latter processes await explanation.

The accessibility of testable, reproducible, paleoclimate proxies extends, therefore, collapse research horizons beyond the concatenation of imagined events to the quantification of transfer functions and rates of climate change that are now well documented globally.

Similarly, quantification of the dynamics and variability within adaptive regional habitat tracking, nomadization, and sedentarization are new archaeological challenges for this and other prehistoric and early historic abrupt climate change research.

ACKNOWLEDGEMENTS

Figure 25.1 was created with the assistance of Mark Besonen (University of Massachusetts, Amherst); Figure 25.2 with Justin Kosslyn (Yale University), Lauren Ristvet (University of Pennsylvania), and M. Arrivabeni (FU Berlin); and Figure 25.3 with Stacey Maples (Yale University). I also thank Paolo Matthiae and Frances Pinnock (Ebla); Geoff Emberling and Augusta McMahon (Brak); Michel al-Maqdissi and Dominique Parayre (Orontes Survey and Nasriyah); Ł. Rutkowski (Arbid); Uwe Finkbeiner (Emar); Salam al-Kuntar for our expedition to the ʿAin ez-Zarqa sources of the Orontes; Kazuyo Ohnuma, Yoshihiro Nishiaki, Sumio Fujii, Minna Lönnqvist, and Jan-Waalke Meyer (Jebel Bishri); and Frank Braemer (Khirbet al Umbashi) for graciously sharing detailed knowledge of their research.

SUGGESTED READING

Geyer, B., N. Awad, M. Al-Dbiyat, Y. Calvet, and M.-O. Rousset (2010). Un 'très long mur' dans la steppe syrienne. *Paléorient 36.2: 57–72.*

Luterbacher, J., E. Xoplaki, C. Casty, et al. (2013). Mediterranean climate variability over the last centuries: a review. In P. Lionello, P. Malanotte-Rizzoli, and R. Boscolo (eds), *Mediterranean Climate Variability.* Amsterdam: Elsevier, 27–148.

Morandi Bonacossi, D. (ed.) (2007). *Urban and Natural Landscape of an Ancient Syrian Capital: Settlement and Environment at Tell Mishrifeh/Qatna and in Central-Western Syria.* Udine: Forum.

Ohnuma, K. (ed.) (2010). *Formation of Tribal Communities: Integrated Research in the Middle Euphrates, Syria.* Tokyo: Kokushikan University.

Parr, P. J. (ed.) (2009). *The Levant in Transition: Proceedings of a Conference Held at the British Museum on 20–21 April 2004.* Leeds: Maney.

Ristvet, L., and H. Weiss (2013). The Hābūr region in Old Babylonian Period. In W. Orthmann (ed.), *The History and Archaeology of Syria,* vol. 1. Saarbrücken: Saarbrücker Verlag.

Sallaberger, W. (2007). From urban culture to nomadism: a history of upper Mesopotamia in the late third millennium. In C. Kuzucuoğlu and C. Marro (eds), *Sociétés humaines et changement climatique à la fin du troisième millénaire: une crise a-t-elle eu lieu en haute Mésopotamie?* Istanbul: Institut français d'études anatoliennes Georges-Dumézil, 417–56.

Staubwasser, M., and H. Weiss (2006). Holocene climate and cultural evolution in Late Prehistoric–Early Historic West Asia. *Quaternary Research* 66: 372–87.

Weiss, H. (ed.) (2012) *Seven Generations Since the Fall of Akkad.* Wiesbaden: Harrassowitz

Weiss, H., M.-A. Courty, W. Wetterstrom, et al. (1993). The genesis and collapse of third millennium North Mesopotamian civilization. *Science* 261: 995–1004.

Wirth, E. (1971). *Syrien: eine geographische Landeskunde.* Darmstadt: Wissenschaftliche Buchgesellschaft.

References

Algaze, G., J. Kelly, T. Matney, and D. Schlee (1996). Late EBA urban structure at Titris Höyük, southeastern Turkey: the 1995 season. *Anatolica* 22: 129–43.

al-Maqdissi, M. (2006). Notes d'archéologie levantine VIII: stratigraphie du chantier B de Tell Sianu (plaine de Jablé). *Syria* 83: 229–46.

——(2010). Matériel pour l'étude de la ville en Syrie (deuxième partie)/Urban planning in Syria during the SUR (Second Urban Revolution) (mid-third millennium BC). In Ohnuma (2010: 131–46).

Archi, A., and M. G. Biga (2003). A victory over Mari and the fall of Ebla. *Journal of Cuneiform Studies* 55: 1–44.

Arz, H., F. Lamy, and J. Pätzold (2006). A pronounced dry event recorded around 4.2 kya in brine sediments from the northern Red Sea. *Quaternary Research* 66: 432–41.

Baffi, F. and L. Peyronel (2013). Early Bronze Age Tell Tuqan. In P. Matthiae and N. Marchetti (eds), *Ebla and Its Landscape*. Walnut Creek, Calif.: Left Coast, 195–214.

Bakalowicz, M., M. El Hakim, and A. El-Hajj (2008). Karst groundwater resources in the countries of the eastern Mediterranean: the example of Lebanon. *Environmental Geology* 54: 597–604.

Baker, P. A., S. C. Fritz, S. J. Burns, E. Ekdahl, and C. A. Rigsby (2009). The nature and origin of decadal to millennial scale climate variability in the southern tropics of South America: the Holocene record of Lago Umayo, Peru. In F. Vimeux, F. Sylvestre, and M. Khodri (eds), *Past Climate Variability in South America and Surrounding Regions: From the Last Glacial Maximum to the Holocene*. Dordrecht: Springer, 301–22.

Bar-Matthews, M., and A. Ayalon (2004). Speleothems as climate indicators: a case study from Soreq Cave located in the eastern Mediterranean region, Israel. In R. W. Battarbee, F. Gasse, and C. E. Stickley (eds), *Past Climate Variability through Europe and Africa*. Dordrecht: Springer, 363–91.

——and A. Kaufman (1997). Late Quaternary paleoclimate in the eastern Mediterranean region from stable isotope analysis of speleothems at Soreq Cave, Israel. *Quaternary Research* 47: 155–68.

Black, J. A., G. Cunningham, E. Robson, and G. Zólyomi (2004). *The Literature of Ancient Sumer*. Oxford: Oxford University Press.

Bond, G., B. Kromer, J. Beer, et al. (2001). Persistent solar influence on North Atlantic climate during the Holocene. *Science* 294: 2130–36.

Booth, R. K., S. T. Jackson, S. L. Forman, et al. (2005). A severe centennial-scale drought in mid-continental North America 4200 years ago and apparent global linkages. *The Holocene* 15: 321–8.

Braemer, F., J.-C. Échallier, and A. Taraqji (2004). *Khirbet al Umbashi: villages et campements de pasteurs dans le 'désert noir' (Syrie) à l'âge du Bronze*. Beirut: Institute français du Proche-Orient.

Bryson, R. R. (1997) Proxy indications of Holocene winter rains in southwest Asia compared with simulated rainfall. In H. Nuzhet Dalfes, G. Kukla, and H. Weiss (eds), *Third Millennium BC Climate Change and Old World Collapse*. Berlin: Springer, 465–73.

—— and R. U. Bryson (2000). Site-specific high-resolution models of the monsoon for Africa and Asia. *Global and Planetary Change* 26: 77–84.

Buccellati, G., and M. Kelly-Buccellati (2000). The royal palace of Urkesh: report on the 12th season at Tell Mozan/Urkesh—excavations in Area AA, June–October 1999. *Mitteilungen der Deutschen Orient-Gesellschaft zu Berlin* 132: 133–83.

—— (2002). Tar'am-Agade, daughter of Naram-Sin, at Urkesh. In L. al-Gailani Werr, J. Curtis, H. Martin, A. McMahon, J. Oates, and J. Reade (eds), *Of Pots and Plans: Papers on the Archaeology and History of Mesopotamia and Syria Presented to David Oates in Honour of His 75th Birthday*. London: NABU, 11–31.

Butterlin, P. (2007). Mari, les šakkanakku et la crise de la fin du troisième millénaire. In C. Kuzucuoğlu and C. Marro (eds), *Sociétés humaines et changement climatique à la fin du troisième millénaire: une crise a-t-elle eu lieu en haute Mésopotamie?* Istanbul: Institut français d'études anatoliennes Georges-Dumézil, 227–45.

Castel, C., and E. J. Peltenburg (2007). Urbanism on the margins: third millennium BC Al-Rawda in the Arid Zone of Syria. *Antiquity* 81: 601–16.

Charles, M., and A. Bogaard (2001) Third millennium BC charred plant remains from Tell Brak. In D. Oates, J. Oates, and H. McDonald (eds), *Excavations at Tell Brak*, vol. 2: *Nagar in the Third Millennium BC*. London: British School of Archaeology in Iraq/Cambridge: McDonald Institute for Archaeological Research, 301–26.

Coope, G. R. (1979). Late Cenozoic fossil coleoptera: evolution, biogeography, and ecology. *Annual Review of Ecology and Systematics* 10: 247–67.

Creekmore, A. (2010). The structure of upper Mesopotamian cities: insight from Fluxgate Gradiometer Survey at Kazane Höyük, southeastern Turkey. *Archaeological Prospection* 17/2: 73–88.

Cremaschi, M. (2007). Qatna's lake: a geoarchaeological study of the Bronze Age capital. In Morandi Bonacossi (2007: 93–104).

Cullen, H. M., and P. deMenocal (2000). North Atlantic influence on Tigris–Euphrates streamflow. *International Journal of Climatology* 20: 853–63.

—— S. Hemming, et al. (2000). Climate change and the collapse of the Akkadian Empire: evidence from the deep sea. *Geology* 28: 379–82.

—— A. Kaplan, P. A. Arkin, and P. deMenocal (2002). Impact of the North Atlantic oscillation on Middle Eastern climate and streamflow. *Climatic Change* 55: 315–38.

Curvers, H. H. (1991). *Bronze Age society in the Balikh drainage (Syria)*. PhD dissertation, University of Amsterdam.

Danti, M. D., and R. L. Zettler (2007). The Early Bronze Age in the Syrian north-west Jezireh: the Tell es-Sweyhat region. In E. J. Peltenburg (ed.), *Euphrates River Valley Settlement: The Carchemish Sector in the Third Millennium BC*. Oxford: Oxbow, 164–83.

Davis, M. E., and L. G. Thompson (2006). An Andean ice-core record of a Middle Holocene mega-drought in North Africa and Asia. *Annals of Glaciology* 43: 34–41.

Dean, W. E. (1997). Rates, timing, and cyclicity of Holocene Eolian activity in north-central United States: evidence from varved lake sediments. *Geology* 25: 331–4.

de Boucheman, A. (1934). La sédentarisation des nomades du désert de Syrie. *L'Asie française* 320: 140–43.

Deckers, K., M. Doll, P. Pfälzner, and S. Riehl (2010). *Development of the Environment, Subsistence and Settlement of the City of Urkeš and Its Region*. Wiesbaden: Harrassowitz.

de Lillis-Forrest, L. M., L. Milano, and L. Mori (2007). The Akkadian occupation in the northwest area of the Tell Leilan acropolis. *KASKAL* 4: 43–64.

—— T. Guilderson, and H. Weiss (2004). The Akkadian administration on the Tell Leilan acropolis: imperialism and cooptation on the Habur Plains. Online at: http://leilan.yale.edu/pubs/files/poster1/poster1.jpg

di Rita, F., and D. Magri (2009). Holocene drought, deforestation and evergreen vegetation development in the central Mediterranean: a 5500 year record from Lago Alimini Piccolo, Apulia, southeast Italy. *The Holocene* 19: 295–306.

Djamali, M., J.-L. De Beaulieu, N. F. Miller, et al. (2009). Vegetation history of the SE section of the Zagros Mountains during the last five millennia: a pollen record from the Maharlou Lake, Fars Province, Iran. *Vegetation History and Archaeobotany* 18: 123–36.

Drysdale, R., G. Zanchetta, J. Hellstrom, et al. (2006). Late Holocene drought responsible for the collapse of Old World civilizations is recorded in an Italian cave flowstone. *Geology* 34: 101–4.

Eastwood, W. J., M. J. Leng, N. Roberts, and B. Davis (2007). Holocene climate change in the eastern Mediterranean region: a comparison of stable isotope and pollen data from Lake Gölhissar, southwest Turkey. *Journal of Quaternary Science* 22: 327–41.

——N. Roberts, H. F. Lamb, and J. C. Tibby (1999). Holocene environmental change in southwest Turkey: a palaeoecological record of lake and catchment-related records. *Quaternary Science Reviews* 18: 671–95.

Eldredge, N. (1985). *Time Frames: The Evolution of Punctuated Equilibria.* Princeton, NJ: Princeton University Press.

Emberling, G., and H. McDonald (2003) Excavations at Tell Brak 2001–2002: preliminary report. *Iraq* 65: 1–75.

—— H. McDonald, J. Weber, and H. Wright (2012). After collapse: the post-Akkadian occupation in the Pisé Building, Tell Brak, in H. Weiss (ed.), *Seven Generations Since the Fall of Akkad.* Wiesbaden: Harrassowitz, pp. 65–87.

Fairchild, I. J., C. L. Smith, A. Baker, et al. (2006). Modification and preservation of environmental signals in speleothems. *Earth Science Reviews* 75: 105–53.

Faist, B., and U. Finkbeiner (2002). Emar: eine syrische Stadt unter hethitischer Herrschaft. In Kunst- und Ausstellungshalle der Bundesrepublik Deutschland GmbH (ed.), *Die Hethiter und ihr Reich: das Volk der 1000 Götter.* Stuttgart: Theiss, 190–95.

Fiorentino, G., V. Caracuta, L. Calcagnile, et al. (2008). Third millennium B.C. climate change in Syria highlighted by carbon stable isotopes analysis of 14C-AMS dated plant remains from Ebla. *Palaeogeography, Palaeoclimatology, Palaeoecology* 266: 51–8.

Fisher, D., E. Osterberg, A. Dyke, et al. (2008). The Mt Logan Holocene–Late Wisconsinan isotope record: tropical Pacific–Yukon connections. *The Holocene* 18: 667–77.

Fortin, M. (2007). La vallée du Ghab: nouvelle prospection archéologique. In Morandi Bonacossi (2007: 253–68).

Frumkin, A. (2009). Stable isotopes of a subfossil tamarix tree from the Dead Sea region, Israel, and their implications for the Intermediate Bronze Age environmental crisis. *Quaternary Research* 71: 319–28.

Gasse, F. (2000). Hydrological changes in the African tropics since the Last Glacial Maximum. *Quaternary Science Reviews* 20: 189–211.

—— and E. van Campo (1994). Abrupt post-glacial climate events in West Asia and North Africa monsoon domains. *Earth and Planetary Science Letters* 126: 435–56.

Geyer, B., N. Awad, M. Al-Dbiyat, Y. Calvet, and M.-O. Rousset (2010). Un 'très long mur' dans la steppe syrienne. *Paléorient* 36.2: 57–72.

—— and J.-Y. Monchambert (2003). *La basse vallée de l'Euphrate syrien: du Néolithique à l'avènement de l'islam—Géographie, archéologie et histoire* (2 vols). Beirut: Institut français d'archéologie du Proche-Orient.

Gibson, McG. (2001). Hamoukar: 2000–2001 annual report. *Oriental Institute Annual Reports.* Online at: http://oi.uchicago.edu/research/pubs/ar/00–01/hamoukar.html

——A. al-Azm, C. Reichel, et al. (2002). Hamoukar: a summary of three seasons of excavation. *Akkadica* 123: 11–34.

Glassner, J.-J. (1986). *La chute d'Akkadé: l'événement et sa mémoire.* Berlin: Reimer.

—— (1993). *Chroniques mésopotamiennes*. Paris: Belles Lettres.

Gophna, R. (1992). The Intermediate Bronze Age. In A. Ben-Tor (ed.), *The Archaeology of Ancient Israel*. New Haven, Conn.: Yale University Press/Tel Aviv: Open University of Israel, 126–58.

Göyünç, N., and W.-D. Hütteroth (1997). *Land an der Grenze: Osmanische Verwaltung im heutigen turkisch-syrisch-irakischen Grenzgebiet in 16. Jahrhundert*. Istanbul: EREN.

Grayson, A. K. (1987). *Assyrian Rulers of the Third and Second Millennia B.C.* Toronto: University of Toronto Press.

Grosjean, M., L. Núñez, and I. Cartajena (2005). Cultural response to climate change in the Atacama Desert. In M. A. Smith and P. P. Hesse (eds), *23 °S: Archaeology and Environmental History of the Southern Deserts*. Canberra: National Museum of Australia Press, 156–71.

Jex, N. C., A. Baker, I. J. Fairchild, et al. (2010). Calibration of speleothem $\delta^{18}O$ with instrumental climate records from Turkey. *Global and Planetary Change* 7: 207–17.

Kaniewski, D., É. Paulissen, E. van Campo, et al. (2010). Late second–early first millennium BC abrupt climate changes in coastal Syria and their possible significance for the history of the eastern Mediterranean. *Quaternary Research* 74: 207–15.

Kepinski, C. (2007). Continuity and break at the end of the third millennium B.C.: the data from Tilbeşar, Sajour Valley (southeastern Turkey). In C. Kuzucuoğlu and C. Marro (eds), *Sociétés humaines et changement climatique à la fin du troisième millénaire: une crise a-t-elle eu lieu en haute Mésopotamie?* Istanbul: Institut français d études anatoliennes Georges-Dumézil, 329–40.

Koliński, R. (2012). Generation count at Tell Arbid, Sector P, in H. Weiss (ed.), *Seven Generations Since the Fall of Akkad*. Wiesbaden: Harrassowitz, 109–28.

Kotthoff, U., U. C. Müller, J. Pross, et al. (2008). Late Glacial and Holocene vegetation dynamics in the Aegean region: an integrated view based on pollen data from marine and terrestrial archives. *The Holocene* 18: 1019–32.

Kuzucuoğlu, C. (2007). Climatic and environmental trends during the third millennium B.C. in Upper Mesopotamia. In C. Kuzucuoğlu and C. Marro (eds), *Sociétés humaines et changements climatiques à la fin du troisième millénaire: une crise a-t-elle eu lieu en Haute Mésopotamie?* Istanbul: Institut français d'études anatoliennes Georges-Dumézil, 459–80.

Laneri, N., M. Schwartz, J. Ur, et al. (2008). The Hirbemerdon Tepe archaeological project 2006–2007: a preliminary report on the Middle Bronze Age 'architectural complex' and the survey of the site catchment area. *Anatolica* 34: 177–240.

Lebeau, M., and J. Bretschneider (1997). Urbanisme et architecture. In P. Talon and K. Van Lerberghe (eds), *En Syrie: aux origines de l'écriture*. Turnhout: Brepols, 151–60.

Lemcke, G., and M. Sturm (1997). $\delta^{18}O$ and trace element measurements as proxy for the reconstruction of climate changes at Lake Van (Turkey): preliminary results. In H. Nüzhet Dalfes, G. Kukla, and H. Weiss (eds), *Third Millennium BC Climate Change and Old World Collapse*. Berlin: Springer, 653–78.

Leng, M. J., M. D. Jones, M. R. Frogley, W. J. Eastwood, C. P. Kendrick, and C. N. Roberts (2010). Detrital carbonate influences on bulk oxygen and carbon isotope composition of lacustrine sediments from the Mediterranean. *Global and Planetary Change* 71: 175–82.

Leroy, S. A. G., F. Marret, E. Gibert, F. Chalié, J.-L. Reyss, and K. Arpe (2007). River inflow and salinity changes in the Caspian Sea during the last 5500 years. *Quaternary Science Reviews* 26: 3359–83.

—— A. Kakroodi, S. Kroonenberg, H. Lahijani, H. Alimohammadian, A. Nigarov (2013). Holocene vegetation history and sea level changes in the SE corner of the Caspian Sea: relevance to SW Asia climate. *Quaternary Science Reviews* 70: 28–47.

Li, Y.-X., Z. Yu, and K. P. Kodama (2007). Sensitive moisture response to Holocene millennial-scale climate variations in the mid-Atlantic region, USA. *The Holocene* 17: 3–8.

Licciardi, J. M., J. M. Schaefer, J. R. Taggart, and D. C. Lund. (2009). Holocene glacier fluctuations in the Peruvian Andes indicate northern climate linkages. *Science 325*: 1677–9.

Lionello, P., P. Malanotte-Rizzoli, R. Boscolo, et al. (2006). The Mediterranean climate: an overview of the main characteristics and issues. In P. Lionello, P. Malanotte-Rizzoli, and R. Boscolo (eds), *Mediterranean Climate Variability*. Amsterdam: Elsevier, 1–26.

Liu, H., Z. Lin, X. Qi, M. Zhang, Z. Zhang, and J. Du (2010). Multiple analysis of variation of the East Asian monsoon during the Holocene. *Quaternary International* 213: 74–8.

Luterbacher, J., E. Xoplaki, C. Casty, et al. (2006). Mediterranean climate variability over the last centuries: a review. In P. Lionello, P. Malanotte-Rizzoli, and R. Boscolo (eds), *Mediterranean Climate Variability*. Amsterdam: Elsevier, 27–148.

Magny, M., J.-L. de Beaulieu, R. Drescher-Schneider, et al. (2007). Holocene climate changes in the central Mediterranean as recorded by lake-level fluctuations at Lake Accesa (Tuscany, Italy). *Quaternary Science Reviews* 26: 1736–58.

—— B. Vannièrre, G. Zanchetta, et al. (2009). Possible complexity of the climatic event around 4300–3800 cal. BP in the central and western Mediterranean. *The Holocene* 19: 823–33.

Magri, D., and I. Parra (2002). Late Quaternary western Mediterranean pollen records and African winds. *Earth and Planetary Sciences Letters* 200: 401–8.

Mallowan, N. (2012). Excavations at Brak and Chagar Bazar. *Iraq* 9: 1–259.

Marchetti, N. (1947). Karkemish on the Euphrates. *Near Eastern Archaeology* 75.3: 132–147.

Marro, C., and C. Kuzucuoğlu (2007). Northern Syria and upper Mesopotamia at the end of the third millennium B.C.: did a crisis take place? In C. Kuzucuoğlu and C. Marro (eds), *Sociétés humaines et changement climatique à la fin du troisième millénaire: une crise a-t-elle eu lieu en haute Mésopotamie?* Istanbul: Institut français d'études anatoliennes , 583–90.

Masi, A., L Sadori, G. Zanchetta, I. Baneschi, and M. Giardini (2013). Climatic interpretation of carbon isotope content of mid-Holocene archaeological charcoals from eastern Anatolia. *Quaternary International* 303: 64–72.

Matthiae, P. (1995a). The archaic palace at Ebla: a royal building between Early Bronze IVB and Middle Bronze Age I. In S. Gitin, J. E. Wright, and J. P. Dessel (eds), *Confronting the Past: Archaeological and Historical Essays on Ancient Israel in Honor of William G. Dever*. Winona Lake, Ind.: Eisenbrauns, 85–104.

—— (1995b). Fouilles à Ebla en 1993–1994: les palais de la ville basse nord. In *Comptes rendus des séances de l'année 1995, Académie des inscriptions et belles-lettres*, 651–81.

McDonald, H., and N. Jackson (2003). A house on the hill: second millennium investigations—the Middle Bronze Age. In R. Matthews (ed.), *Excavations at Tell Brak*, vol. 4: *Exploring an Upper Mesopotamian Regional Centre, 1994–1996*. Cambridge: McDonald Institute Research, 271–320.

McMahon, A. (2012). Post-Akkadian ceramic assemblages of the central Upper Khabur, in H. Weiss (ed.), *Seven Generations Since the Fall of Akkad*. Wiesbaden: Harrassowitz, 25–43.

Menounos, B., J. J. Clague, G. Osborn, B. H. Luckman, T. R. Lakeman, and R. Minkus (2008). Western Canadian glaciers advance in concert with climate change circa 4.2 ka. *Geophysical Research Letters* 35: L07501.

Miglus, P. A., E. Strommenger, and S. Achwan (2007). *Ausgrabungen in Tall Biʾa/Tuttul*, vol. 7: *Der Palast A*. Wiesbaden: Harrassowitz.

Migowski, C., M. Stein, S. Prasad, J. F. W. Negendank, and A. Agnon (2006). Holocene climate variability and cultural evolution in the Near East from the Dead Sea sedimentary record. *Quaternary Research* 66: 421–31.

Morandi Bonacossi, D. (2009). Tell Mishrife and its region during the EB IV and the EBA–MBA transition: a first assessment. In P. J. Parr (ed.), *The Levant in Transition: Proceedings of a Conference Held at the British Museum on 20–21 April 2004.* Leeds: Maney, 56–68.

Nicolle, C. (2012). Pre-Khabur occupations at Tell Mohammed Diyab (Syrian Jezirah). In H. Weiss (ed.), *Seven Generations Since the Fall of Akkad.* Wiesbaden: Harrassowitz, 129–44.

Nichols, J. (2004). *Amorite agro-pastoralism and the Early to Middle Bronze Age transition in Syria.* PhD dissertation, Johns Hopkins University.

Oates, D., J. Oates, and H. McDonald (2001). *Excavations at Tell Brak,* vol. 2: *Nagar in the Third Millennium BC.* London: British School of Archaeology in Iraq.

Ohnuma, K. (ed.) (2010). *Formation of Tribal Communities: Integrated Research in the Middle Euphrates, Syria.* Tokyo: Kokushikan University.

Orsi, V. (2008). La produzione ceramica a Tell Barri tra la fine del III e l'inizio del II millennio A.C. *La parola del passato* 63: 220–33.

Pecorella, P. E., and R. Pierobon (2004). *Tell Barri/Kahat: la campagna del 200—Relazione preliminare.* Florence: Firenze University Press.

Peltenburg, E. J. (2007). New perspectives on the Carchemish sector of the Middle Euphrates River Valley in the 3rd millennium BC. In E. J. Peltenburg (ed.), *Euphrates River Valley Settlement: The Carchemish Sector in the Third Millennium BC*—Levant Supplementary Series 5, 1–27.

Pfälzner, P., A. Wissing, and C. Hübner (2004). Urbanismus in der Unterstadt von Urkeš: Ergebnisse einer geomagnetischen Prospektion und eines archäologischen Surveys in der südöstlichen Unterstadt von Tall Mozan im Sommer 2002. *Mitteilungen der Deutschen Orient-Gesellschaft zu Berlin* 136: 41–86.

Prag, K. (2007). Water strategies in the Iktanu region of Jordan. *Studies in the History and Archaeology of Jordan* 9: 405–12.

Ristvet, L., and H. Weiss (2000). Imperial responses to environmental dynamics at late third millennium Tell Leilan. *Orient-Express* 2000/4: 94–9.

——(2013). The Hābūr region in the Old Babylonian Period. In W. Orthmann (ed.), *The History and Archaeology of Syria,* vol. 1. Saarbrücken: Saarbrücker Verlag.

Roberts, N., J. M. Reed, M. J. Leng, et al. (2001). The tempo of Holocene climatic change in the eastern Mediterranean region: new high-resolution crater-lake sediment data from central Turkey. *The Holocene* 11: 721–36.

Saghieh, M. (1983). *Byblos in the Third Millennium B.C.: A Reconstruction of the Stratigraphy and a Study of the Cultural Connections.* Warminster: Aris & Phillips.

Sallaberger, W. (2007). From urban culture to nomadism: a history of upper Mesopotamia in the late third millennium. In C. Kuzucuoğlu and C. Marro (eds), *Sociétés humaines et changement climatique à la fin du troisième millénaire: une crise a-t-elle eu lieu en haute Mésopotamie?* Istanbul: Institut français d'études anatoliennes Georges-Dumézil, 417–56.

Schettler, G., Q. Liu, J. Mingram, M. Stebich, and P. Dulski (2006). East-Asian monsoon variability between 15000 and 2000 cal. yr BP recorded in varved sediments of Lake Sihailongwan (northeastern China, Long Gang volcanic field). *The Holocene* 16: 1043–57.

Schmiedl, G., T. Kuhnt, W. Ehrmann, et al. (2010). Climatic forcing of eastern Mediterranean deep-water formation and benthic ecosystems during the past 22000 years. *Quaternary Science Reviews* 29: 3006–20.

Schwartz, G. M. (2007). Taking the long view on collapse: a Syrian perspective. In C. Kuzucuoğlu and C. Marro (eds), *Sociétés humaines et changement climatique à la fin du troisième millénaire: une crise a-t-elle eu lieu en haute Mésopotamie?* Istanbul: Institut français d'études anatoliennes Georges-Dumézil, 45–67.

Senior, L., and H. Weiss (1992). Tell Leilan 'sila bowls' and the Akkadian reorganization of Subarian agricultural production. *Orient-Express* 1992/2: 16–23.

Sommerfeld, W., A. Archi, and H. Weiss. (2004). Why 'Dada measured 40,000 liters of barley from Nagar for Sippar'. 4ICAANE Berlin 29 March–3 April 2004: http://leilan.yale.edu/pubs/files/poster2/poster2.jpg

Stanley, J.-D., M. D. Krom, R. A. Cliff, and J. C. Woodward (2003). Nile flow failure at the end of the Old Kingdom, Egypt: strontium isotopic and petrologic evidence. *Geoarchaeology* 18: 395–402.

Staubwasser, M., and H. Weiss (2006). Holocene climate and cultural evolution in Late Prehistoric–Early Historic West Asia. *Quaternary Research* 66: 372–87.

Thalmann, J.-P. (2006). *Tell Arqa I. Les niveaux de l'âge du Bronze* (3 vols). Beirut: Institut français du Proche-Orient.

Thompson, L. G. (2000). Ice core evidence for climate change in the tropics: implication for our future. *Quaternary Science Reviews* 19: 19–35.

—— E. Mosley-Thompson, M. E. Davis, et al. (2002). Kilimanjaro ice core records: evidence of Holocene climate change in tropical Africa. *Science* 298: 589–93.

Triantaphyllou, M. V., P. Ziveri, A. Gogou, et al. (2009). Late Glacial–Holocene climate variability at the south-eastern margin of the Aegean Sea. *Marine Geology* 266: 182–97.

Tunca, Ö., A. McMahon, and A. el-Massih Baghdo (2007). *Chagar Bazar (Syrie) II: Les vestiges 'post-akkadiennes' et études diverses.* Louvain: Peeters.

Ur, J. A. (2002). Settlement and landscape in northern Mesopotamia: the Tell Hamoukar survey 2000–2001. *Akkadica* 123: 57–88.

—— P. Karsgaard, and J. Oates (2011). The spatial dimensions of early Mesopotamian urbanism: the Tell Brak suburban survey, 2003–2006. *Iraq* 73: 1–19.

Van der Stede, V. (2005). The Akkadian occupation, in M. Lebeau and A.Suleiman (eds), Tell Beydar Nabada, an Early Bronze Age City in the Syrian Jezirah: 10 Years of Research (1992–2002). Damascus: Archaeological InstituteVerheyden, S., F. Nader, H. Cheng, L. Edwards, and R. Swennen (2008). Paleoclimate reconstruction in the Levant region from the geochemistry of a Holocene stalagmite from the Jeita Cave, Lebanon. *Quaternary Research* 70: 368–81.

Voûte, C. (1961). A comparison between some hydrological observations made in the Jurassic and Cenomian limestone mountains situated to the west and to the east of the Ghab Graben (U.A.R., Syria). In *Eaux souterraines dans les zones arides: colloque d'Athènes, 10–9–18–9, 1961.* Gentbrugge: Association international d'hydrologie scientifique, 160–66.

Wang, P., S. Clemens, L. Beaufort, et al. (2005). Evolution and variability of the Asian monsoon system: state of the art and outstanding issues. *Quaternary Science Reviews* 24: 595–629.

Weiss, H. (1986). The origins of Tell Leilan and the conquest of space. In H. Weiss (ed.), *The Origins of Cities in Dry Farming Syria and Mesopotamia in the Third Millennium B.C.* Guilford, Conn.: Four Quarters, 71–108.

—— (1990). Tell Leilan 1989: new data for mid-third millennium urbanization and state formation. *Mitteilungen der Deutschen Orient-Gesellschaft zu Berlin* 122: 193–218.

—— (2000). Beyond the Younger Dryas: collapse as adaptation to abrupt climate change in ancient west Asia and the eastern Mediterranean. In G. Bawden and R. M. Reycraft (eds), *Environmental Disaster and the Archaeology of Human Response.* Albuquerque, NM: Maxwell Museum of Anthropology, University of New Mexico, 75–98.

—— (2003). Ninevite 5 periods and processes. In E. Rova and H. Weiss (eds), *The Origins of North Mesopotamian Civilization: Ninevite 5 Chronology, Economy, Society*. Turnhout: Brepols, 593–624.

—— (2012). Quantifying collapse: the Late Third Millennium Khabur Plains, in H. Weiss (ed.), Seven Generations Since the Fall of Akkad. Wiesbaden: Harrassowitz, 102–14.

—— M.-A. Courty, W. Wetterstrom, et al. (1993). The genesis and collapse of the Akkadian Empire. In M. Liverani (ed.), *Akkad, The First World Empire: Structure, Ideology, Traditions*. Padua: Sargon, 131–55.

—— W. Wetterstrom, et al. (1993). The genesis and collapse of third millennium North Mesopotamian civilization. *Science* 261: 995–1004.

—— S.W. Manning, L. Ristvet, et al. (2012). Tell Leilan Akkadian imperialization, collapse and short-lived re-occupation defined by high-resolution radiocarbon dating, in H. Weiss (ed.), Seven Generations Since the Fall of Akkad. Wiesbaden: Harrassowitz, 193–217.

Weninger, B., L. Clare, E. Rohling, et al. (2009). The impact of rapid climate change on prehistoric societies during the Holocene in the eastern Mediterranean. *Documenta Praehistorica* 36: 7–59.

Westenholz, J. G. (1997). *Legends of the Kings of Akkade: The Texts*. Winona Lake, Ind.: Eisenbrauns.

Wick, L., G. Lemcke, and M. Sturm (2003). Evidence of Late Glacial and Holocene climatic change and human impact in eastern Anatolia: high-resolution pollen, charcoal, isotopic and geochemical records from the laminated sediments of Lake Van, Turkey. *The Holocene* 13: 665–75.

Wilkinson, T. J. (1998). Water and human settlement in the Balikh Valley, Syria: investigations from 1992–1995. *Journal of Field Archaeology* 25: 63–87.

Wirth, E. (1971). *Syrien: Eine geographische Landeskunde*. Darmstadt: Wissenschaftliche Buchgesellschaft.

Yener, K. A. (2005). Conclusions. In K. A. Yener (ed.), *The Amuq Valley Regional Projects*, vol. 1: *Surveys in the Plain of Antioch and Orontes Delta, Turkey, 1995–2002*. Chicago: Oriental Institute Press of the University of Chicago, 193–202.

Yon, M. (1997). Ugarit. In E. Meyers (ed.), *The Oxford Encyclopedia of Archaeology in the Near East*, vol. 5. New York: Oxford University Press, 255–62.

Zhjang, Q.-B., and R. J. Hebda (2005). Abrupt climate change and variability in the past four millennia of the southern Vancouver Island, Canada. *Geophysical Research Letters* 32: L16708.

....

CHAPTER 26

THE SOUTHERN LEVANT DURING THE INTERMEDIATE BRONZE AGE

....

KAY PRAG

A PERIOD OF CHANGE

....

The definition and chronology of the Intermediate Bronze Age in the southern Levant is based on a distinctive material assemblage, semi-historical links to Egypt, Syria, and Mesopotamia, and on relatively few ^{14}C dates (from Jericho, Niʻaj, Umm Hamad, and Bab edh-Dhraʻ: for the latter, see Weinstein 2003). It was long seen as a 'dark age' (e.g. Dever 1970: 132; Palumbo 1990), a 'non-urban' period, and a semi-nomadic or even nomadic interlude. Albright (1932; 1938), in his excavations at Tell Beit Mirsim between 1926 and 1932, defined the assemblage as belonging to the last phase of the Early Bronze and the earliest of the Middle Bronze, hence the terms 'EB IV' and 'MB I'. Versions of this terminology were used by Glueck, Tufnell, Amiran, Dever, Richard, and Palumbo among others. Later some applied just the EB IV terminology (e.g. Dever 1980: 35). The use of the term 'intermediate' is that of Iliffe (1937), followed by Kenyon, R. H. Smith, Lapp, Prag, Gophna, and Greenberg. Both terminologies have been applied to hypotheses relevant to processes of indigenous or externally induced change in the archaeological record.

Albright (1938: 16), Kenyon (1957: 186–209), and Amiran (1969: 79) had sparse stratified material of the early Intermediate Bronze with which to bridge the gap between EB III and the characteristic later Intermediate Bronze pottery which dominated many of the early excavations. They and others thus saw, not just the social, but also the ceramic change as a major break in the archaeological record, which was explained at that time as the result of external invasion by desert nomads or Amorite incomers.

Demonstrating continuity between the early and late phases of the Intermediate Bronze period is therefore important when considering its nature and its terminology, for it is a single, culturally distinctive and identifiable period, not to be terminologically divided between the more urban Early and Middle Bronze Ages. There is a stratigraphic break between EB III and Intermediate Bronze, marked by the destruction and/or abandonment of most EB III walled settlements, a process of uncertain duration, which was followed by marked social changes. There was an equally marked stratigraphic and cultural break at the end of the Intermediate Bronze Age. That there was a direct ancestral link between the EB III and the Intermediate Bronze populations is, however, quite clear and it is equally likely that there was demographic continuity into the second millennium. Many scholars have assumed a considerable degree of population continuity from Intermediate Bronze to Middle Bronze. In a similar but unquestioned fashion, demographic continuity with the Early and Middle dynastic periods is assumed for the First Intermediate Period in Egypt, despite a record of 'Asiatics' invading the Egyptian Delta.

The site of Tell Iktanu in the southeast end of the Jordan Valley, a village newly founded early in the Intermediate Bronze and first excavated in 1966, reinforced both a cultural derivation from EB III and the stratified sequence prolifically demonstrated continuity within two phases of the Intermediate Bronze period, with clear continuity from early to late Intermediate Bronze ceramics (Prag 1971; 1974). Phase 2 houses were rebuilt on the same alignments and often the same foundations as in Phase 1. Excavations at a number of sites, Umm Hamad Gharbi, Ni'aj, and Iskander among others, have since uncovered multiple phases of occupation within the Intermediate Bronze.

REGIONALISM

The pattern of society in the Intermediate Bronze reveals intense regionalism with very poorly defined boundaries in the central Levant (Fig. 26.1). A number of geographic subregions are definable: (1) the central coastal region; (2) the Beqa' of Lebanon on the headwaters of the Orontes and Litani Rivers; (3) south inland Syria, the Damascus region north to the Kalamun Ridges; (4) north Jordan (Yarmuk River); (5) central Jordan (Zarqa River); (6) south Jordan (Mujib River); (7) the Jordan Valley; (8) north Palestine (Jezreel Valley); (9) the central hill country of Palestine; (10) the south coast region; and (11) the Negev and Sinai.

Byblos and Arqa on the central coast reveal aspects of urbanism and little direct contact with the south. Sites in the Beqa' of Lebanon on the whole show links with the Homs region. At the heart of the Intermediate Bronze are some large settlements in the Jordan Valley and many smaller and sparser villages and farming communities around the tributary valleys. The regions occupied by the people of the Intermediate Bronze included land of rich agricultural and horticultural potential with c.400–800mm of annual rainfall (Prag 1974: 73). In areas of low rainfall—the Negev and southeast Syria, for example—there is evidence of communities virtually dependent on pastoralism and probably importing grain. There are around 1000 known campsites of Intermediate Bronze pastoralists found in the drier Negev (c.100mm annual rainfall). Gophna (in Parr 2009) has suggested that the south coastal area was abandoned during the early Intermediate Bronze, and recently Faust and Ashkenazy (2007) have suggested that the coastal area had already been virtually abandoned during the EB II/III periods, due to a spread of marshy conditions caused by increased precipitation, and that this situation probably continued during the Intermediate Bronze. The whole question of climate impact at this period has been debated for decades. It has been concluded that humidity was declining during the Early Bronze, but there is also clear evidence for incidents of heavy rainfall during the Intermediate Bronze (Prag 1986: 63), and perhaps therefore for short-term fluctuations in rainfall and drought which may have made conditions for farming difficult.

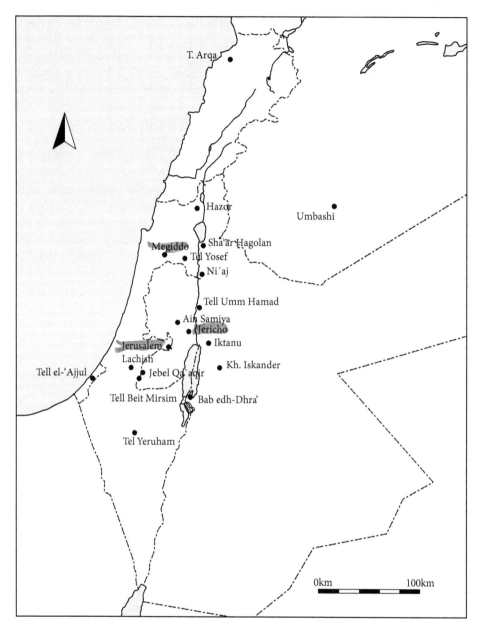

FIG. 26.1 Map of Intermediate Bronze Age sites in the southern Levant

THE ARCHAEOLOGY

Pottery

Virtually the entire ceramic repertoire of the Early Bronze was reprised during the Intermediate Bronze, including medium-sized bowls, deep basins, amphoriskoi, twin-vessels, jugs, holemouth jars (including those used as cooking pots), ledge handles (usually of the envelope ledge type), and flat-based storage jars with everted rims. The continued use of ledge handles confirms that these traditions are an indigenous heritage in the southern Levant, not involving external influences, for they are characteristic of pottery production in the south for over a millennium, but not of the north. The pottery is usually coil-built and finished on a turntable. The fabric is, however, quite distinct from that of the Early Bronze, generally thinner-walled and lighter in colour. Both these features compare with the contemporary pottery production of Syria; and other features, including the popularity of cups, four-spouted lamps, and the corrugation or grooving below the rims of vessels, also suggest strong influences from the north.

Although rare examples of cups are found during the Early Bronze, the popularity of cups during the Intermediate Bronze gave rise to the use of the word 'caliciform' to describe the period (Albright 1932: 8; Tufnell 1958: 41). In the early Intermediate Bronze Phase 1 at Iktanu, cups are found in red slipped, red burnished, and reserved slip varieties with narrowed or corrugated rims and either flat or 'waisted' bases (Fig. 26.2). The latter form is closely paralleled by the silver cup from an Intermediate Bronze tomb at Ain Samiya in Palestine (Stern 1993: 378; Prag in Parr 2009: 87–8). The use of red slip and burnish is inherited from the Early Bronze, but Phase 2 is characterized by the absence of red slip and burnish, and the cups, in light cream or buff fabric, are very plain. In post-Iktanu contexts, such as Jericho's tell, and in the northwest settlement and most of Cemetery 2000 at Lachish, they often have incised, band-combed decoration, a rather carinated wall, and are usually light coloured and described as wheel-made.

The results of chemical analyses (Falconer 1987) suggested a local distribution of the products of kilns, but the presence of kilns in Phase 1 at Iktanu (Prag 1988) and other Intermediate Bronze kilns at Beth Yerah, Jebel Qaʿaqir, Tel Yeruham, and Tel Yosef (Stern 1993: 255–9,

FIG. 26.2 Red slipped and burnished cup, Phase 1, Iktanu (photograph Kay Prag)

665–7, 1506–9; Gophna 1992: 145), along with the regional nature of the ceramics, suggests there were many local workshops, not just domestic production. Petrographic studies have confirmed this (Goren 1996). Pottery at Nahal Refaim was also locally produced, but much of the pottery from the Negev showed connections with central and southwest Jordan.

For illustration of the characteristic earlier Intermediate Bronze shapes, see e.g. Prag (1974: figs 3–8); for later Intermediate Bronze shapes, see e.g. Amiran (1969: 79–89), Kenyon and Holland (1982: 249–67), and Tufnell (1958: pls 6 and 7).

Stone and metal artefacts

The specialized Canaanean technique of blade production common throughout the Early Bronze continued in the Intermediate Bronze. The use of mortars and saddle querns (Fig. 26.3) also continues Early Bronze practices. These tools confirm the importance of grain and vegetable harvesting and processing in the economy. At Iktanu this equipment is found both in houses and in open areas, which may have been used for food processing.

In metal working, the Intermediate Bronze is characterized by a rich local copper industry, but analyses have revealed rare bronze weapons. High-status goods included long daggers, more rarely spears, fenestrated axes, and javelins. These weapons have usually been found buried with their owners, suggesting a warrior status and a relatively conspicuous consumption of material wealth. Ornaments including dress pins, some with curled heads, rings, and bracelets were found. Rare tools (axes, adzes, and chisels) are known, and many copper/bronze rivets, studs, and bands once attached to wooden objects were discovered in the Jericho tombs. Gold and silver objects are very rare.

Architecture

On many sites the strata containing Intermediate Bronze houses are thin, due to the relatively impermanent, short-lived nature of the occupation. The structures on the south hill at Iktanu were laid out on virgin ground, and were therefore not constrained by any pre-existing walls (Fig. 26.4).

FIG. 26.3 Typical Intermediate Bronze Age saddle quern from food processing Area E, Iktanu (photograph Kay Prag)

FIG. 26.4 Room, Phase 2, Iktanu, Area A14; from the southeast. Note the central column supports and the large saddle quern against the west wall (photograph Kay Prag)

The layout was pre-planned and new, comparable with those of towns along the central Euphrates (Prag 2011). The village was large and unwalled, with orthogonally laid out blocks of domestic structures separated by narrow earth roads. Intermediate Bronze structures vary regionally. Houses in agricultural areas are rectangular, thin-walled, usually of mudbrick on light stone foundations, but were considerably more solid at Arqa in the central coast region to the north. At Lachish, Jebel Qaʾaqir, and other sites, cave dwellings have been found. In the Negev, the dwellings tend to be agglomerations of simpler, rounded structures, interpreted as the dwellings of seasonal pastoralists. Very similar constructions were found at Umbashi in south inland Syria, also associated with a pastoralist population. Villages intermediate between rectangular and rounded agglutinative houses and animal pens have been found at Batrawy on the central Jordan plateau. The existence of campsites is likely. No monumental, clearly public buildings constructed during the Intermediate Bronze have yet been uncovered. Glueck proposed that many Intermediate Bronze sites in Jordan were fortified, but the construction date of these fortifications has not been verified, although Palumbo (1990: 132 and fig. 25) suggested competition for land in some marginal areas may have resulted in a few fortified settlements. At Iskander, located in southern Jordan where Early Bronze ceramic traditions appear to have lingered later in the Intermediate Bronze (Prag 1974: 78–9), the nature of continuity and reuse of Early Bronze fortifications is still under investigation.

Burial

Extensive cemeteries have been described as 'cities of the dead', and may have been central places for mobile communities in use over long periods with greater permanency of use. The presence of large cemeteries also appears to highlight social change between the Early Bronze and the Intermediate Bronze in the southern Levant, but they compare with the huge cemeteries of the third millennium unearthed in northern Syria. Intermediate Bronze tombs were diverse, including shaft graves, pits, cists, dolmens, cairns, tumuli, and caves.

The burial type may be linked as much to local geology as to burial tradition. Articulated and disarticulated burial practices are recorded, with normally one, perhaps up to three and rarely seven burials in each grave.

Economy

Generally the same products of an agropastoral regime were produced during Early Bronze, Intermediate Bronze, and Middle Bronze with cereals, fruits, legumes, sheep, goats, cattle, and pigs providing the basis of a subsistence economy. There is much greater emphasis on family-based production, and processing and storage (storage jars and ground silos) in the Intermediate Bronze (Fig. 26.5), with no evidence of communal facilities even in the larger settlements such as Iktanu, which could be a basis for large-scale trade. Horwitz (1989), in noting the importance of caprovine herding at Intermediate Bronze sites (up to 90% of the total fauna in the Negev and 80% at Refaim in the central hill country) and its suitability for seasonal pastoralism in arid regions, also discussed the environmental and proportional significance of pigs and cattle. Domesticated pigs (15% in the settlement at Refaim) indicated a sedentary community in an area with adequate water, and cattle (just 3% at Refaim) also limited the grazing/migration options. Cattle and pigs were also kept at Ni'aj in the Jordan Valley. Despite the relatively small proportion, the slaughter rate for cattle is generally lower than that for caprovines, and whether cattle were kept for ploughing, meat, milk, or leather products may indicate a disproportionate importance in the economy. There is no evidence for pigs at Iktanu, but cattle were kept. The extraordinary numbers of cattle bones and evidence for cattle rearing at Umbashi in southeast Syria confirms that they were a significant element in the contemporary economy (Braemer, Échallier, and Taraqji 2004). It must be concluded that a rural subsistence economy existed in the Intermediate Bronze, with little central political or community support against crop failure and natural or social disasters. Under such circumstances, small kin or tribal communities would have to move on with their animals in search of grazing elsewhere. Brawer (1988) calculated that a very

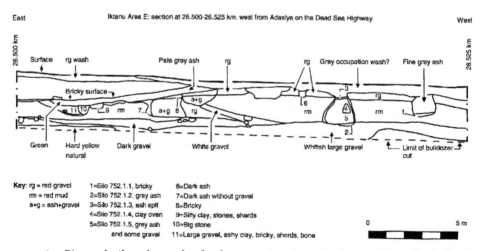

FIG. 26.5 Pits and silos above the food processing Area E, Iktanu. Note the bell silo IK.752.1.5 (courtesy Kay Prag)

large percentage of land in the southern Levant today is non-productive or suitable only for grazing. In the southern Levant, pastoralism may well have been the real backbone of the economy and in difficult times, such as the Intermediate Bronze, the necessary reversion strategy for the population.

TRADE

The primary evidence for long-distance trade during the Intermediate Bronze is in metal. Intermediate Bronze society used considerable quantities of copper, probably from the mines at Faynan, perhaps augmented from the north, via Syrian intermediaries, which may also be the source of the occasional appearance of tin, silver, and magnetite in the south. The presence of dress pins with curled heads, rare fenestrated axes, and the silver and the iconography of the cup found at Ain Samiya in the Palestinian hill country all indicate northern influences (Prag in Parr 2009). The copper ingots found at sites in the Negev suggest that metal was being traded across to Egypt, perhaps by pastoralists in exchange for grain, beads, and textiles (I owe the suggestion that textiles may have played a part in such trade to Caroline Grigson, pers. comm.). The emphasis on riverine settlement along the Jordan Valley and up the tributary streams also suggests pastoralism, and it is possible that cattle played a role in population movement and trade. The site of Umbashi in southern inland Syria during the last third of the third millennium had evidence for connections with both central Syria and the southern Levant, and for cattle breeding as well as sheep and goat pastoralism (Braemer, Échallier, and Taraqji 2004: 364).

Egypt had a long recorded history of taking slaves and cattle from the Levant, and during the weakness of the First Intermediate Period in Egypt (*c.* 2136–2023 BC), perhaps the Intermediate Bronze pastoralists took the opportunity to supply some of this need. Carnelian beads were found in Intermediate Bronze tombs at Ajjul (Petrie 1931: 3–4) and Tell Ashir in the Sharon region; some shell and gold beads in Intermediate Bronze tombs at Jericho were also imported goods (Prag 1986: 71–2); and in the tombs on the Mount of Olives, outside Jerusalem, beads of carnelian and blue paste/glaze were found (Prag 1995a: 239). Whether these items are residual, originating with the Early Bronze trade to Egypt, or indicate an ongoing contact with Egypt is not known.

Falconer (1987) has shown there was distribution in ceramics within regions. The varied pottery fabrics at Iktanu during Phase 1 suggest a variety of sources as well as a local production. Some northern white-painted grey wares filtered into the south, where rare fragments are found in the Madaba region and at Iskander.

SOCIETY

It seems most likely that Intermediate Bronze society was based on small-scale kinship, clan, or tribal networks, for there is virtually no evidence for elites or a hierarchical society, although Palumbo (1990: 120) suggested some evidence for social complexity. The intense regionalism exhibited reveals for the most part localized social networks. In this agropastoral society, there is considerable emphasis on herding, agriculture, horticulture, and food processing and storage. The large quantity of pottery, especially storage jars, deposited in shaft graves and found in settlements emphasizes the importance of grain storage and other commodities in a subsistence society without reliance on external support mechanisms. The number of querns and mortars in the houses at Iktanu suggests the hard daily routine of food processing. Villages may even have been used mostly as storage centres and seasonal quarters for mobile communities. Perhaps the cemeteries were also centres for burial of scattered, semi-nomadic communities, with above-ground tombs such as cairns and dolmens used as territorial markers (Prag 1995b).

Religion

No Intermediate Bronze temples have yet been identified (small shrines at Megiddo (Stern 1993: 1008) and Bab edh-Dhraʿ (Stern 1993: 135) are currently exceptions), but a number of cult places, mostly outside settlements, are known. The unique occurrence of a silver cup might suggest feasting, even elite banqueting, but the iconography indicates it had a cult aspect also. The bull-man on the Ain Samiya goblet (Stern 1993: 378) and the cattle horns in the Bab edh-Dhraʿ shrine place a ritual emphasis on cattle. The numbers of cups and jugs suggest communal drinking/feasting rituals either in these gathering places, in funerary rites, or even in more domestic settings, which may have replaced the temple rituals of the more urban societies of the Early Bronze. Standing stones in particular, though difficult to date, have frequently been attributed to the Intermediate Bronze and a useful summary of the lines of monoliths found in southern Jordan has been compiled by Ben-Ami (2008). Like dolmens, standing stones may also have been more permanent territorial markers and places of gathering for scattered communities than were more ephemeral settlements.

TRANSFORMATIONS

The models of explanation for social transformation vary greatly. Radical change, in the form of a new age, a 'Copper Age', was first distinguished by Petrie (1931: 3–4) at Ajjul, where he dated carnelian beads in square-shaft tombs to the early 6th Egyptian Dynasty (c.2362–2250 BC). Kenyon (1960: 136, 159–60) thought radical change was due to a great Amorite invasion which 'blotted out the preceding urban civilization of the Early Bronze Age'.

In her use of the Albright 'MB I' terminology, Amiran (1969: 79) wrote (of what we now know is the later Intermediate Bronze pottery): 'In examining the general character of the MB I assemblage, stress must be placed first and foremost on the break between this pottery and that of the Early Bronze Age. There is hardly a doubt that the new MB I civilization was instrumental in destroying the old. Although some reminiscences survive and remain embedded in the MB I repertoire, the new is much stronger than the traditional element.'

Albright (1932: 9, 11) saw analogies between Intermediate Bronze pottery (including 'caliciform' cups with grooved rims) and pottery from Syria, but decided that the early part of the Intermediate Bronze was 'essentially a supplementary phase of the preceding' Early Bronze (Albright 1960: 77), and just the later Intermediate Bronze band-incised pottery derived from Syrian prototypes; at first he assumed Palestine was overrun by nomadic tribes from the desert (Albright 1938: 16), but later thought this evidence was due to cultural 'diffusion', not movement of peoples (Albright 1960: 80). As he thought the migration of Abram 'may' have occurred during the latest stage of the Intermediate Bronze, one must presume that he did not entirely dismiss the movement of people.

External pressures from Egypt as factors of change have also been suggested, either as Egyptian military interventions under the 5th and early 6th Dynasties (Prag 1974: 103) or as due to the failure of the Egyptian 6th Dynasty, which led to the collapse of an important trade in wine and olive oil on which much of the urban prosperity of the southern Levant depended.

Others chose a more intermediate hypothesis, involving a complex explanation for social collapse due to both environmental and political events, followed by relatively peaceful infiltrations from central Syria (especially from the Euphrates zone) at the beginning of the period, succeeded by further cultural influences from Syria later in the Intermediate Bronze, with evidence for a degree of sedentism, agropastoralism, horticulture, and extensive cemeteries from the very beginning of the period (Prag 1971; 1974).

Dever (1970: 140) initially accepted the Amorite invasion hypothesis for the early Intermediate Bronze, followed by first nomadization and then sedentarization, but also noted the strength of the Early Bronze tradition in the seasonal settlement at Jebel Qa'aqir. By 1980 he had moved to a new terminology (EB IVA–C) embracing three phases of the Intermediate Bronze, abandoned the Amorite hypothesis in favor of Early Bronze collapse followed by an interlude of pastoral nomadism and gradual sedentarization (Dever 1980: 35, 58). While acknowledging Syrian influences, he argued against any invasion or large-scale migration (Dever 1980: 52). He still maintained a clear break with the following Middle Bronze.

An indigenous process of change has been widely accepted in more recent years. Change has been interpreted as a segment of a regular process of economic and administrative boom and bust, the rise and fall of urban societies reflected in 'repeated cycles of intensification and abatement' and the 'varying rates at which sedentarization and nomadization have occurred' (Geraty et al. 1986: 117–19; LaBianca 1990); of cycles of specialization and despecialization as factors in the rise and collapse of urbanism with the Intermediate Bronze seen as a period of declining urbanism (Richard and Long 1995: 82). Joffe (1993) also understood such a cycle from village agropastoralism to urbanism and back. Both Richard and Palumbo have argued for a high degree of residual urbanism, but the existence of city walls, particularly new-build city walls, has yet to be fully demonstrated.

The understanding of Intermediate Bronze society does have to account for significant change in the archaeological record. While Dever emphasizes the differences between the northern and southern Levant, I emphasize the new elements of change in the south, and their likely source in Syria; how one interprets the material evidence depends on whether one sees movement of people or just of cultural diffusion in the shape and decoration of a pot, the layout of a house or a town, the importance of large extramural cemeteries amongst a wider Levantine population which probably then, even more than today, had a shared West Semitic ethnicity and language.

Models of Early Bronze society have tended towards a process of urbanization through the third millennium. It seems likely that the collapse of this structure resulted in the removal of a developed urban support system with its centralized agricultural surpluses, territorial control, and trade-based wealth.

Demographic collapse followed the destruction and abandonment of town sites in Palestine, as suggested by estimates of total population in the Intermediate Bronze period (based on survey data, excluding the Negev) that the population shrank from a high of 150,000 during the EB II/III, to just 10–15,000 during the Intermediate Bronze (Gophna 1992: 156). Although these figures may be too drastic, they agree well with the statistics of a 'post-collapse society' (Tainter 1999) in the Intermediate Bronze as suggested by Faust (2007: 43, 48), and the fragmentation of the bulk of the surviving population to family, tribal, or kin-based subsistence agropastoralism. Dever, from a Palestinian perspective, wrote of this as a dispersal to the fringes, the margins (of Palestine or of the fertile land?). Shallow settlements such as that at Iktanu were more visible to archaeological surveys in regions not subject to subsequent building or modern agriculture. It is only in recent years that more evidence for sedentism has been emerging in Palestine itself, at sites such as Nahal Refaim and Hazor. In this process of change, of political weakness and instability, grazing and land rights were lost, leading to weaker, less stable communities, rather than urban protected territorial or 'state' ownership, and to a much lower level of more localized exchange systems. There are many ethnographic parallels for such periods of political weakness, of social fluidity, which leave the way open for the infiltration of territories by pastoralists and refugees.

The agency of destruction in EB III towns has not been resolved, whether due to inter-urban strife, competition for land, or destabilization and infiltration of already stretched resources, such as territorial rights and grazing rights, by refugees. The destruction was not the work of a successful invading army, for there was no subsequent urban re-consolidation. Directly after the collapse, the presence of so many new influences bearing on the impoverished inhabitants of the southern Levant still requires explanation. Archaeologists in the southern Levant tend to forget there were contemporary crises affecting even the towns and cities of Syria.

The importance of the Jordan Valley in this process of change should not be underestimated. It had been the location of many major defended Early Bronze towns—Pella, Kharaz, Hammam, Jericho, amongst others; and then was also the location of some of the largest known Intermediate Bronze unwalled sites, Sha'ar Hagolan (15ha, Stern 1993: 1340–43), Tel Yosef (100ha, Gophna 1992: 130), Umm Hamad (c.50ha, Prag 1971: 104–8), Meshra al-Abiad (c.30ha, Prag 1971: 108–9), and Iktanu (c.18ha); here there was not just fertile land and water, but also a major entry route for people, animals, goods, and ideas. It seems likely that radical changes in the southern Levant in the late third millennium were based on more substantial causes than just diffusion of ideas. Whether this can be attributed, at least in part, to peaceful infiltration following the collapse of urbanism, or whether the infiltration was part of the cause of collapse rather than a result, remains uncertain.

SUGGESTED READING

Gophna, R. (1992). The Intermediate Bronze Age. In A. Ben-Tor (ed.) The Archaeology of Ancient Israel, trans. R. Greenberg. New Haven, Conn.: Yale University Press/Tel Aviv: Open University of Israel, 126–58.

Goren, Y. (1996). The southern Levant during the Early Bronze Age IV: the petrographic perspective. Bulletin of the American Schools of Oriental Research 303: 33–72.

Horwitz, L. K. (1989). Sedentism in Early Bronze IV: a faunal perspective. Bulletin of the American Schools of Oriental Research 275: 16–25.

Palumbo, G. (1990). *The Early Bronze Age IV in the Southern Levant: Settlement Patterns, Economy, and Material Culture of a 'Dark Age'.* Rome: Università di Roma 'La Sapienza'.

Parr, P. J. (ed.) (2009). *The Levant in Transition: Proceedings of a Conference Held at the British Museum on 20–21 April 2004.* London: Maney.

Prag, K. (1974). The Intermediate Early Bronze–Middle Bronze Age: an interpretation of the evidence from Transjordan, Syria and Lebanon. *Levant* 6: 69–116.

REFERENCES

Albright, W. F. (1932). *The Excavation of Tell Beit Mirsim I: Pottery of the First Three Campaigns.* New Haven, Conn.: American Schools of Oriental Research.

——(1938). *The Excavation of Tell Beit Mirsim II: The Bronze Age.* New Haven, Conn.: American Schools of Oriental Research.

——(1960). *The Archaeology of Palestine*, rev. edn. Harmondsworth: Pelican.

Amiran, R. (1969). *Ancient Pottery of the Holy Land: From Its Beginnings in the Neolithic Period to the End of the Iron Age.* Jerusalem: Massada.

Ben-Ami, D. (2008). Monolithic pillars in Canaan: reconsidering the date of the High Place at Gezer. *Levant* 40: 17–28.

Braemer, F., J.-C. Échallier, and A. Taraqji (2004). *Khirbet Al Umbashi: villages et campements de pasteurs dans le 'désert noir' à l'âge du Bronze.* Beirut: Institut français d'archéologie du Proche-Orient.

Brawer, M. (1988). *Atlas of the Middle East.* New York: Macmillan/London: Collier Macmillan.

Dever, W. G. (1970). The 'Middle Bronze I Period' in Syria-Palestine. In J. A. Sanders (ed.), *Near Eastern Archaeology in the Twentieth Century: Essays in Honor of Nelson Glueck.* Garden City, NY: Doubleday, 132–63.

——(1980). New vistas on the EB IV ('MB I') horizon in Syria-Palestine. *Bulletin of the American Schools of Oriental Research* 237: 35–64.

Falconer, S. E. (1987). Village pottery production and exchange: a Jordan Valley perspective. In A. Hadidi (ed.), *Studies in the History and Archaeology of Jordan III.* Amman: Department of Antiquities/London: Routledge & Kegan Paul, 251–9.

Faust, A. (2007). Settlement dynamics and demographic fluctuations in Judah from the Late Iron Age to the Hellenistic period and the archaeology of Persian period Yehud. In Y. Levin (ed.), *A Time of Change: Judah and Its Neighbours during the Persian and Early Hellenistic Periods.* London: Continuum, 23–51.

——and Y. Ashkenazy (2007). Excess in precipitation as a cause for settlement decline along the Israeli coastal plain during the third millennium BC. *Quaternary Research* 68: 37–44.

Geraty, L. T., L. G. Herr, Ø. S. LaBianca, et al. (1986). Madaba Plains Project: a preliminary report of the 1984 season at Tell el-'Umeiri and vicinity. In W. E. Rast (ed.) *Preliminary Reports of ASOR-Sponsored Excavations 1980–84.* Winona Lake, Ind.: Eisenbrauns, 117–44.

Gophna, R. (1992). The Intermediate Bronze Age. In A. Ben-Tor (ed.) *The Archaeology of Ancient Israel.* New Haven, Conn.: Yale University Press/Tel Aviv: Open University of Israel, 126–58.

Goren, Y. (1996). The southern Levant during the Early Bronze Age IV: the petrographic perspective. *Bulletin of the American Schools of Oriental Research* 303: 33–72.

Horwitz, L. K. (1989). Sedentism in Early Bronze IV: a faunal perspective. *Bulletin of the American Schools of Oriental Research* 275: 16–25.

Iliffe, J. H. (1937). *A Short Guide to the Exhibition Illustrating the Stone and Bronze Ages in Palestine*. Jerusalem: Department of Antiquities.

Joffe, A. H. (1993). *Settlement and Society in the Early Bronze Age I and II, Southern Levant: Complementarity and Contradiction in a Small-Scale Complex Society*. Sheffield: Sheffield Academic.

Kenyon, K. M. (1957). *Digging Up Jericho*. London: Benn.

—— (1960). *Archaeology in the Holy Land*. London: Benn.

—— and T. A. Holland (1982). *Excavations at Jericho IV: The Pottery Type Series and Other Finds*. London: British School of Archaeology in Jerusalem.

LaBianca, Ø. S. (1990). *Sedentarization and Nomadization: Food System Cycles at Hesban and Vicinity in Transjordan*. Berrien Springs, Mich.: Andrews University Press.

Palumbo, G. (1990). *The Early Bronze Age IV in the Southern Levant: Settlement Patterns, Economy, and Material Culture of a 'Dark Age'*. Rome: Università di Roma 'La Sapienza'.

Parr, P. J. (ed.) (2009). *The Levant in Transition: Proceedings of a Conference Held at the British Museum on 20–21 April 2004*. London: Maney.

Petrie, W. M. F. (1931). *Ancient Gaza I: Tell el 'Ajjul*. London: British School of Archaeology in Egypt.

Prag, K. (1971). *A study of the Intermediate Early Bronze–Middle Bronze Age in Transjordan, Syria and Lebanon*. DPhil. dissertation, Oxford University.

—— (1974). The Intermediate Early Bronze–Middle Bronze Age: an interpretation of the evidence from Transjordan, Syria and Lebanon. *Levant* 6: 69–116.

—— (1986). The Intermediate Early Bronze–Middle Bronze Age sequences at Jericho and Tell Iktanu reviewed. *Bulletin of the American Schools of Oriental Research* 264: 61–72.

—— (1988). Kilns of the Intermediate Early Bronze–Middle Bronze Age at Tell Iktanu: a preliminary report, 1987 season. *Annual of the Department of Antiquities of Jordan* 32: 59–73.

—— (1995a). The Intermediate Early Bronze–Middle Bronze Age cemetery on the Mount of Olives. In I. Eshel and K. Prag (eds), *Excavations by K. M. Kenyon in Jerusalem 1961–1967 IV: The Iron Age Cave Deposits on the South-east Hill and Isolated Burials and Cemeteries Elsewhere*. Oxford: Oxford University Press for the British School of Archaeology in Jerusalem, 221–41.

—— (1995b). The Dead Sea dolmens: death and the landscape. In S. Campbell and A. Green (eds), *The Archaeology of Death in the Ancient Near East*. Oxford: Oxbow, 75–84.

—— (2011) The domestic unit at Tall Iktanu, its derivations and functions. In M. Chesson (ed.), *Daily Life, Materiality, and Complexity in Early Urban Communities of the Southern Levant. Papers in Honor of Walter E. Rast and R. Thomas Schaub*. Winona Lake, Ind.: Eisenbrauns, 55–76.

Richard, S., and J. C. Long, Jr. (1995). Archaeological expedition to Khirbat Iskandar and its vicinity, 1994. *Annual of the Department of the Antiquities of Jordan* 39: 81–92.

Stern, E. (ed.) (1993). *The New Encyclopedia of Archaeological Excavations in the Holy Land* (4 vols). Jerusalem: Israel Exploration Society & Carta/New York: Simon & Schuster.

Tainter, J. A. (1999). Post-collapse societies. In G. Barker (ed.) *Companion Encyclopedia of Archaeology*, vol. 2. London: Routledge, 988–1039.

Tufnell, O. (1958). *Lachish (Tell ed-Duweir) IV: The Bronze Age* (2 vols). London: Oxford University Press.

Weinstein, J. M. (2003). A new set of radiocarbon dates from the town site. In W. E. Rast and R. T. Schaub (eds), *Bab edh-Dhra': Excavations at the Town Site (1975–81)*, vol. 1. Winona Lake, Ind.: Eisenbrauns, 638–48.

SECTION D

THE MIDDLE BRONZE AGE

CHAPTER 27

INTRODUCTION TO THE LEVANT DURING THE MIDDLE BRONZE AGE

AARON A. BURKE

The original chronological divisions of the Middle Bronze Age in the Levant centred on historical synchronisms between the southern Levant and Egypt, and this framework was extended to the northern Levant. In recent years, however, distinct though related chronologies for these two regions have emerged. This is largely due to the different sets of relationships that both regions of the Levant had with neighbouring cultures, which is best exemplified by the regional coverage provided by two of the primary historical sources for these regions: the Execration Texts (for the south) and the Mari Letters (for the north). Limited contact between the northern Levant and Egypt has meant that inferences made about the history and archaeology of the Levant that are, for example, attributed to 'Hyksos' dominance during the MB III are mostly of relevance to the southern Levant (if not to only the southern part of this region). Indeed, the northern Levant was predominantly influenced by historical events in Anatolia and Mesopotamia, which included cultural and military incursions during the first half of the second millennium. Differences in the archaeological assemblages of the north and south are also cited as a basis for the adoption of different chronologies, although it can be argued that in many respects a cultural *koiné* was evident across the Levant by the start of the MB II.[1] Cyprus, however, did not share in this cultural *koiné*, and Middle Cypriot material culture was largely the product of endogenous developments, despite maritime contact with the Levant.

While challenges are faced in the adoption of a single chronological schema that adequately represents the historical and archaeological development of the Levant as a whole, to a large extent during the Middle Bronze Age the archaeology of the Levant, not including Cyprus, can now be discussed within an historical framework. This is due to the fact that sources, such as the Mari Letters, provide sufficient insights into Levantine culture to aid

---

[1] The terminology adopted in this treatment follows that used in recent treatments (e.g. Ilan 1995), abandoning the terms MB IIA–IIC to refer to the Middle Bronze Age since the old MB I is now regularly referred to as the EB IV.

our interpretation of the archaeological record, and vice versa. In fact, the Middle Bronze Age is the first archaeological period for which sources illuminate the history of both the northern and southern Levant (Klengel 1992: 39–83). It is also the first period for which the ethnicity of the Levant's inhabitants is revealed through personal names. The majority of individuals can be identified as ethnically Amorite (Akkadian *Amurru*/Sumerian MAR. TU 'Westerners'), a west Semitic group who are first identified in Mesopotamian sources at the end of the third millennium BC (see Gzella, Ch. 2 above). This cultural ascription is facilitated by references to kings, tribes, and historical figures that are identified by their Amorite names and customs in both the Execration Texts and Mari Letters. Correspondence both temporally and regionally between references in these texts, most evidently with the Execration Texts, permits the suggestion that Middle Bronze Age material culture should be predominantly identified as Amorite. While the process associated with the emergence of Amorite material culture, as wholly distinct from the urban EB IV culture that preceded it, is more difficult to identify in the northern Levant, the stark contrast that accompanies the shift between EB IV and MB I material culture in the south, for example with the reintroduction of fortified urban centres, serves as the clearest basis for identifying Middle Bronze Age material culture as that of the Amorites, as suggested by the names of Amorite rulers in the Execration Texts during the MB I. During the second half of the Middle Bronze Age, however, Hurrians constituted an increasing proportion of the Levantine population, particularly in the north. Unfortunately, it is impossible to identify the Cypriot population with a historically attested ethnic group owing to the absence of references to it in textual sources, but there is no basis for asserting the emergence of a new population during this period. In light of historical sources, archaeological studies focus primarily on three issues for the Middle Bronze Age: ethnicity, political organization, and the historical events that marked the transitions between each phase of the Middle Bronze Age. These are treated here within the historical-archaeological framework of Middle Bronze Age Levantine chronology.

MB I: THE RISE OF AMORITE KINGDOMS (C.1900–1700 BC)

The central question regarding the onset of the MB I (*c.*1900 BC) on the Levantine mainland concerns the relationship between the emergence of the Amorites and the ethnic associations of MB I material culture.[2] While settlement in the southern Levant during the preceding EB IV consisted predominantly of dispersed rural communities, the archaeological record of the northern Levant reveals that the transition between the EB IV and MB I was not dramatic. In nearly all respects the material culture of the northern Levant during the MB I appears to have evolved directly out of the preceding EB IV culture, which is most evident at Ebla (Tell Mardikh). Thus the emergence of the Amorites during the early second millennium was probably the result of a gradual process that had already begun in

---

[2] This work adopts the very low chronology as described by Manfred Bietak (2002) for Egypt and the Levant. Recent evidence from Mesopotamia suggests a similar downward shift of the chronology (Gasche et al. 1998). Indeed, whatever schema is chosen, it is necessary to emphasize that the same chronology must be adopted for both Egypt and Mesopotamia, as these chronologies are linked via the Middle Bronze Age stratigraphy of Hazor, which is identified in the Mari Letters (Ben-Tor 2004).

the northern Levant during the late third millennium. The identification of the material culture of the Levant as Amorite during the MB I is based, therefore, on textual sources. Nevertheless, a number of elements of the cultural assemblage of the Middle Bronze Age reveals the crystallization of Amorite identity, the consolidation of their political power, and the gradual spread of their culture southwards over the course of the MB I. Indeed, the rapid pace of cultural developments in the south during the MB I has obscured thus far distinct traces of an indigenous non-Amorite population during this period, and this has resulted in the widely held notion that the indigenous population emulated Amorite elite practices to the point of effectively becoming archaeologically indistinguishable. Nevertheless, the complicated nature of this process, which was undoubtedly protracted, will require closer study in the future.

Most explanations of the diffusion of Amorite culture have adhered to one of two models: military invasion or economic colonization. The so-called Amorite Hypothesis associated with the work of Kathleen Kenyon suggested that two waves of nomadic warriors, at the beginning and end of the EB IV, swept in from the steppes of Syria across the northern Levant and destroyed major settlements such as Ugarit, Byblos, and Ebla as they moved southwards (Kenyon 1966). More recent models, however, draw upon economic data associated with the arrival of Amorite culture in different parts of the Levant during the Middle Bronze Age (Gerstenblith 1983; Cohen 2002). Although these economic models seek to address the nuances of the archaeological data, it is much more likely that the spread of Amorite culture throughout the Levant from c.1900 to 1700 BC resulted from different social and economic circumstances, which were nevertheless associated with the establishment of Amorite cultural and political centres. Despite their differences, each of these models recognizes that the origins of MB I material culture associated with the Amorites are traced back to the northern Levant.

The spread of Amorite culture represents, therefore, a protracted process that resulted in the foundation of Amorite dynasties in the Levant, Mesopotamia, and Egypt from the end of the Ur III period in Mesopotamia (c.1900 BC) until the Amorite takeover of Avaris (c.1640 BC), the capital of the 'Hyksos' during the 15th Dynasty. The identity of Amorite rule at the start of the Middle Bronze Age may be owed to military campaigns by Mesopotamian kings into the northern Levant which began as early as Lugalzagesi (c.2250 BC) but continued through the Akkadian and Ur III periods (Burke 2008). Proponents of the Amorite Hypothesis mistakenly attributed the destruction of settlements connected with these campaigns to Amorite conquests. However, not only do the Amorites seem to have endured these military raids, but the raids may have ultimately contributed to the formation and consolidation of Amorite social and political identity from the EB IV to the MB I. Recent work in the late third-millennium levels of Umm el-Marra in the Jabbul may shed light on the details and chronology associated with the crystallization of Amorite ethnicity.

Dated to the 12th Dynasty, the Berlin group of Egyptian Execration Texts reveals that Amorite dynasties ruled a number of southern Levantine towns, such as Ashkelon, Byblos, Ullaza, and 'Irqatum (ancient 'Arqa). However, these texts do not permit the reconstruction of the duration of their rule, kinship affiliations, or territorial control. It is only by virtue of the Mari texts from the 17th century BC (early MB II) that Amorite polities, especially those in the north, are identified as kingdoms. Yamḥad (with Aleppo as its capital), Ugarit, Qatna, and Hazor are among the leading kingdoms of the Levant identified in the Mari Letters at the start of the MB II. Together, textual sources indicate that by the end of the MB I, Amorite kingdoms (the largest located in the north) dominated the entirety of the Levant from Aleppo to Ashkelon.

Archaeological evidence also supports the identification of these kingdoms. The leading indicator of political organization is the defences employed by these kingdoms (Burke 2008). Historical sources from Mesopotamia from the late third millennium through the first half of the second millennium indicate that long-distance military campaigns into the northern Levant occurred with regularity. In response to these campaigns Amorite rulers adopted a type of defence common to settlements in the Middle Euphrates during the third millennium. Massive earthen ramparts were crowned by thick mud-brick walls, which were supplemented by deep fosses. Together these devices were employed to repel siege machinery, specifically the battering ram (Akkadian *yašibum*) and the siege tower (Akkadian *dimtu*), as attested in the Mari archives. The capitals of Amorite kingdoms were always the largest settlements within their territories, and thus featured the most impressive examples of these features. During the MB I the layouts of large and medium-sized settlements were predominantly elliptical, as at Byblos, Ashkelon, Akko, and Burga. By the start of the MB II an almost entirely orthogonal layout was adopted, as seen at Ugarit, Qatna, Hazor, Dan, and Timnah (Tel Batash). The change in overall layout between these periods reflects the realization that defensibility could be improved by employing straight lengths of wall that were more easily defended from towers and bastions.

This explanation of the military concerns of Amorite kingdoms during the Middle Bronze Age supersedes earlier suggestions which asserted that conflicts between city-states were the primary motivation for the construction of fortifications or, more recently, that this process was predominantly one of conspicuous consumption and peer polity emulation. Although there is only limited evidence for the destruction of Levantine settlements as a result of conflict before the expansion of the Egyptian and Hittite Empires in the 16th century BC, the sustained threat posed by Mesopotamian powers such as Assyria and Mari up to the end of the MB II against northern Levantine states like Yamhad and Qatna required the construction and maintenance of these defences. Since Amorite kingdoms in the south could not rely on northern states as buffers against these threats, similar fortifications were constructed throughout the kingdoms of Byblos, Apum (ancient Damascus), Hazor, and Ashkelon from the MB I to MB II–III. It is also likely, as revealed by Sesostris III's campaign against *Skmm* (i.e. Shechem) mentioned in the Khu-Sebek stele (*c*.1850 BC), that Egypt posed an occasional threat. Functional reasons dictated, therefore, the investment of large quantities of human resources in the construction of defences throughout the Levant during the Middle Bronze Age. Nevertheless, royal inscriptions from Mesopotamia indicate that the construction process related to the defences of even the largest settlements probably did not last more than a couple of years.

Like the evidence for defensive architecture, the settlement pattern of the MB I reveals a north-to-south trend for the foundation of new settlements bearing Amorite material culture. The evidence can be divided into two major zones, which correspond to the main trade routes through the Levant: the Levantine coast from Ugarit to Ashkelon, and inland from Aleppo to Hazor. The evidence from the southern Levantine coast consists of the foundation of commercial ports such as Akko and Ashkelon, and the gradual establishment of enclaves east of them along wadi systems leading inland (Cohen 2002). This pattern is remarkably clear due to the resolution afforded by the MB I ceramic sequence from Tel Aphek (Kochavi, Beck, and Yadin 2000).

These settlement patterns appear to have developed as the result of long-distance trade networks. The new ports along the coast of Israel reveal what was probably initially a need for freshwater and foodstuffs for ships from Byblos making their way to Egypt. However, eventually these ports were identified as kingdoms in their own right, probably as demand grew in Egypt for olive oil and wine that could be abundantly produced in the southern Levant (Stager 2001). The items and ceramics found at Avaris and at sites along the Levantine coast suggest that in the MB I Canaanite ships began to transport copper from Cyprus, timber and resins from Lebanon, and wine and oil from Canaan, along with trinkets, to Egypt. The Mari texts provide unequivocal evidence that Alashiya (Cyprus) provided most of the copper needed in the Levant and Mesopotamia in this period, although archaeology on Cyprus has provided little to substantiate this picture. The earliest evidence for the Cypriot goods that accompanied the large quantities of copper to the Levant included Red-on-Black bowls and jugs, White Painted IV–VI jugs and juglets, and, with less frequency, amphorae, zoomorphic vessels, and bowls. Jewellery, scarabs, gold, carnelian, and faience and alabaster vessels were shipped from Egypt. Such Cypriot and Egyptian artefacts were thus deposited in tombs in the southern Levant during the MB I, while Tell el-Yehudiyeh Ware juglets are common to tombs throughout the southern Levant, Egypt, and Cyprus. Tin was also distributed through this network, and accounts for the proliferation of bronze weaponry and tools during the MB I. Foodstuffs such as Nile perch were also sent from Egypt.

The pattern of Amorite settlements along the inland route from Aleppo to Hazor reveals the economic impact of long-distance donkey caravans of the type depicted in the Beni Hasan tombs in Egypt dated to the 19th century BC, and similar caravans mentioned in the Mari texts at the start of the MB II. Tin was undoubtedly one of the major commodities moving southwards, while copper, wool, olive oil, and wine were shipped to Mesopotamia from the northern Levant. In this respect it appears that by the end of the MB I regional specializations are evident in the increasing shipment of surplus of goods to Egypt, Mesopotamia, and Anatolia. The most prominent of these goods included copper from Alashiya, timber and finished metal goods from the northern and central Levantine coast, olive oil and wine from the southern Levant, and wool and textiles from the inland northern Levant.

A major component of the archaeological record of the MB I consists of burials and their assemblages. MB I Amorite royal burials are attested at Byblos and Ebla, which should be identified as a district capital of Yamḥad at this time. Tombs I to III at Byblos, which were located on the western side of the mound (probably beneath the royal palace), date to the late 19th and early 18th centuries BC. In addition to gold and silver ceremonial weapons like the duckbill axe, mace, and dagger, they included exquisite examples of Middle Kingdom pectoral jewellery demonstrating the interest in traded goods from Egypt. So-called warrior burials of the MB I found throughout the Levant and the middle Euphrates region reveal a shared Amorite identity across the region. These burials consist of the interment of a single adult male and his weapons, often a duckbill axe and/or a dagger (Garfinkel 2001). These weapons were markers of social rank, perhaps indicating the role of these individuals as tribal warlords, as suggested in the Egyptian *Tale of Sinuhe*. Conspicuous for their rarity during this period are communal burial chambers, which become common only during the MB II–III. The itinerant nature of the Amorites, who were involved in long-distance trade during the MB I, may be suggested by this mortuary pattern. However, the interaction between Amorite groups arriving in the southern Levant during the early stages of the MB I with local EB IV communities remains to be studied further.

MB II: AMORITE RULE AND AMORITE KOINÉ (C.1700–1600 BC)

As demonstrated foremost by the occurrence of Amorite names, by the start of the MB II Amorite dynasties were established throughout the Levant and Mesopotamia. While it is impossible to determine to what extent dynasties in these two regions may have been consanguine, a shared Amorite identity resulted in the emergence of the first *koiné* culture of the Near East. Rulers throughout these regions appear to have spoken Amorite, although they corresponded with each other in Old Babylonian; they worshipped gods belonging to related pantheons; and they traced their identity to a common ancestry (i.e. the Tidnum), thus satisfying the criteria necessary for identifying them as an ethnic group (Kamp and Yoffee 1980: esp. 98). Despite this shared identity, the Mari texts reveal that Amorite dynasties in the northern Levant and Mesopotamia vied intensely for military supremacy.

During the MB II, fortifications were improved as rectilinear layouts, six-pier gates, and bastions were adopted at newly fortified centres (Burke 2008). These are evident at Ugarit, Qatna, Hazor, Tel Dan, and in the secondary settlements arrayed around these centres. Ashkelon's satellites, which included Yavneh-Yam, Ekron, Timnah, Lachish, Haror, and Tell el-'Ajjul, were fortified for the first time in this period, although many were already settled during the MB I (Cohen 2002). To one extent or another, urban planning must have followed in major settlements such as Qatna and Hazor after the massive efforts required in the construction of their fortifications (Kempinski 1992). An identifiable pattern of fortified settlements around Ashkelon during the MB II, for example, suggests a process of growth related to Ashkelon's consolidation of control over its hinterland following nearly two centuries of economic interaction with its neighbours (Burke 2008). While there is a lack of data for the settlement patterns associated with other Amorite centres which hampers comparisons across the region, it may be surmised that the process witnessed around Ashkelon was simply one of the last examples of Amorite territorial consolidation that occurred during the Middle Bronze Age. Far less evidence, including almost no evidence of fortifications, is available in Cyprus to permit a reconstruction of its political organization during this period.

Contemporaneous with political consolidation, during the MB II a process of settlement infilling began and continued through the MB III. While this process probably took place during the MB I in the northern Levant, it established a dense settlement pattern in the coastal plain of Israel by the end of the MB III. A seven-tier settlement hierarchy can be reconstructed for the Levant in this period (Burke 2008). From largest to smallest these include fortified political centres (e.g. Hazor and Qatna), secondary fortified provincial centres oriented to major political centres (e.g. Lachish), smaller fortified towns (e.g. Timnah), unfortified villages, fortresses (e.g. Burak and Mevorakh), watchtowers (Burke 2007), and farmsteads. While these settlements can be assigned individual size attributes, size is a relative criteria since, for example, Byblos, which was at the top of its settlement hierarchy, was less than 6ha in size while Ekron, which was a satellite of Ashkelon, was 22ha in size during the MB II. A site's role was more significant, therefore, than its size.

The nature of the political organization of the Levantine landscape, which is suggested by the fortifications employed and the settlement hierarchy, is also supported by several additional features. Political centres at the top of the rank-size hierarchy possessed large palaces with elaborate architecture and masonry, royal burial complexes, and royal statuary. Both royal capitals and their secondary fortified settlements preserve evidence of the palaces (of kings and provincial governors, respectively), cuneiform tablets (evidence of their administrative role), and impressively constructed *migdôl*-style temples (attesting the existence of a priestly class). The best excavated example of an MB II–III royal palace is found at Qatna. Although royal palaces in the Levant were built on a much smaller scale, they bear architectural similarities to Old Babylonian palaces at Mari and Šubat-Enlil in Mesopotamia. Located within large, well-fortified settlements, these palaces were adorned with grand central courtyards, throne rooms, carefully dressed orthostats and column bases, tiled floors, drainage systems, cedar beams, and plastered walls and floors—all of which suggest the employment of specialized labour. Evidence also exists for the presence of fresco-producing artisans from the Minoan Aegean, who were commissioned to paint elaborate scenes for certain rooms in the palaces of Qatna, Alalakh (modern Tell Atchana), and Avaris, as well as in residences at Kabri and Tell el-Burak. The palace at Qatna, as was no doubt the case at other Amorite capitals, functioned until it was destroyed in the Late Bronze Age (Novák 2004). Although the limited quantity of Old Babylonian texts from Levantine palaces is often compared with the numbers of texts from Mesopotamian sites, the difference is probably due to the limited number originally produced (and is thus relative to the size of the populations of these kingdoms) but is also largely the accident of preservation, since few Levantine sites appear to have been destroyed in conflagrations during the course of the MB II (cf. Alalakh VII).

The royal palace at Qatna, as was probably typical of other royal palaces, featured a subterranean royal burial complex. The conceptual layout of these complexes is effectively that of MB II–III cave burials, which are especially well attested in the southern Levant. The plan consisted of a shaft or entrance from the surface that led down to a central chamber from which doorways led into adjoining chambers. Individuals were laid out on benches, beds, or in niches within these chambers. DNA analysis of approximately 300 individuals interred in the Middle and Late Bronze Age cemetery at Ashkelon confirms the widely held belief that these tombs are those of the extended patriarchal households or, as in the case of Qatna's tombs, the royal household. Many of these tombs, as at Qatna, also continued to function during the Late Bronze Age, suggesting a high degree of cultural continuity between these periods. Faunal remains associated with both the royal and elite burials of patriarchal households reveal the remains of ritual feasting associated with burials customs or celebrations of the dead, if not both.

Palatial complexes at Alalakh (Level VII) and Ebla probably functioned as the residences of provincial governors, since these two sites were known vassals of Yamḥad, the capital of which was Halab (Aleppo). Thus, attempts should be made to distinguish between royal palaces and the residences of governors during the Middle Bronze Age. Palaces at Lachish and Megiddo, for example, should probably also be identified as those of provincial governors rather than those belonging to the rulers of city-states. This interpretation is supported by the collection of texts from Alalakh VII (Wiseman 1953), which reveal the administrative workings of the province of Mukish within the Amorite kingdom of Yamḥad. It is also supported by the discovery of individual collections of Old Babylonian tablets from sites such as Shechem, Gezer, and Hebron, which also possess characteristics of provincial centres. The characteristics shared by royal and provincial capitals have been conflated in the process of identifying city-states in the southern Levant, as opposed to kingdoms as identified for the northern Levant. Nevertheless, evidence, notably the size of Ashkelon and Hazor, both of which reveal traits of royal capitals, demonstrates the artificial nature of this characterization (Burke 2008). The theoretical framework described by the patrimonial household model provides a clear understanding of the social, economic, and political relationships embedded within this framework of domination (Schloen 2001).

Shared Amorite religious customs are revealed by a common temple type and a shared religious iconography. The so-called *migdôl*-style temple (Mazar 1992: 162–9), which is attested throughout the Levant by the MB II, is directly descended from the third-millennium temple type, as demonstrated at Ebla. This temple type featured a symmetrical plan with a direct-axis entry way, usually through a portico, that aligned with the dais at the rear of the building. The temple was rectangular in layout, and was longer than it was wide. A few examples featured a wall dividing the interior space, thus creating a tripartite structure, but most examples lack this feature. This temple type established a long tradition of temple construction in the Levant that continued into the Iron Age. Many of the MB II–III structures were renovated during the Late Bronze Age. While their exact function remains unknown, stelae or *masseboth* have been identified at Ebla, Hazor, Gezer, and Shechem, as at Mari. Almost no such evidence exists for cult places in Cyprus during this period.

The Amorite *koiné* that pervaded the Levant is evident among burial customs, temple and house architecture, religious and royal iconography, palatial architecture, and fortification strategies during the MB II. The architecture of large upper-class homes was typified by the Mesopotamian courtyard-style house (Kaplan 1971: 295–6). Many houses also featured vaulted burial chambers built below the house as found at Megiddo, and burial customs were frequently intramural. Common among these were infant jar burials below the floors of houses in the southern Levant, while in the north cooking pots were used to achieve the same end. Where vaulted family tombs could not be built below a house for one or another reason, individuals were often interred extramurally in caves or rock-cut tombs in nearby hillsides. In this respect, these burials were not entirely different from contemporary rock-cut tombs in Cyprus, which were employed for multiple interments presumably of extended family members over many decades.

MB III: *PAX AMORITICA* (C.1600–1530 BC)

Some scholars identify the final stage of the Middle Bronze Age in the southern Levant, the MB III (*c.*1600–1530 BC), as a distinct phase contemporaneous with the rule of the Hyksos in Egypt because of shared material culture assemblages with Avaris in Egypt, which include among other things Hyksos scarabs. While direct political relationships between the 15th Dynasty and the Amorites of the southern Levant cannot be inferred from this evidence alone, the socioeconomic and political environment in the Levant and the Egyptian Delta, which permitted the rise of an Amorite dynasty at Avaris, was clearly one of considerable peace, prosperity, and flourishing international trade towards the end of the Middle Bronze Age. This is evident in the abundance of traded Cypriot and Mycenaean wares that continued to be deposited in Amorite tombs in this period, and a continuation of the settlement process throughout the Levant that had begun during the MB II. In the highlands of the southern Levant, settlement proliferated during the MB III and a number of sites were fortified for the first time, including Shechem, Shiloh, and Hebron, seemingly after Jerusalem was fortified, suggesting the consolidation of power throughout this region during this period (Burke 2008).

While it is difficult to reconstruct developments in the settlement pattern in the northern Levant during this period, its wealth is represented in the archaeology of Alalakh and Ebla, both of which were provincial capitals in the kingdom of Yamḫad. These sites reflect the peak of the development of the Amorite *koiné* as reflected in palace and temple architecture, and burial customs. Alalakh also reveals the extent to which Hurrians were becoming a larger portion of the Levant's population. At Alalakh their presence is suggested by the occurrence of Hurrian names in the Alalakh tablets and a unique style of ceramics known as Nuzi Ware.

Although the MB III culture of the southern Levant is often identified as 'Hyksos' because of the role played by Levantine Asiatics in the rise of the 15th Dynasty (Bietak 1997), there is no basis for the identification of a territorial Hyksos state, ruled from Avaris and encompassing the southern Levant or Canaan. Rather, the retreat of the Hyksos to the southern Levant, insofar as it can be identified, simply reveals the socioeconomic relationships of the Amorite refugees. Sharuhen (Tell el-ʿAjjul?), besieged by Ahmose, was not the seat of an independent Hyksos kingdom but the first large and well-fortified settlement along the overland route into Canaan that may have sheltered a large part of this displaced population.

The end of the relatively short-lived *pax Amoritica* was brought about by the campaigns of the Hittite and Egyptian Empires which began *c*.1540 BC and lasted for two or three generations. Archaeological evidence of these events in both regions include destruction levels at nearly thirty major settlements in the southern Levant and settlements such as Alalakh, Ebla,[3] Afis, Tuqan, and Kadesh in the northern Levant (Burke 2008). While the relatively limited investment made in fortification construction during the MB III and a reliance on the maintenance of existing systems may have facilitated the collapse of Amorite rule, the dissolution of Amorite kingdoms is more likely to be reflective of the political fragmentation of and growing competition between states that characterized the Late Bronze Age.

SUGGESTED READING

Akkermans, P. M. M. G., and G. M. Schwartz (2003). *The Archaeology of Syria: From Complex Hunter-Gatherers to Early Urban Societies (c. 16,000–300 BC)*. Cambridge: Cambridge University Press.

Ilan, D. (1995). The dawn of internationalism: the Middle Bronze Age. In T. E. Levy (ed.), *The Archaeology of Society in the Holy Land*. New York: Facts on File, 297–319.

Kempinski, A. (1992). The Middle Bronze Age. In A. Ben-Tor (ed.), *The Archaeology of Ancient Israel*. New Haven, Conn.: Yale University Press/Tel Aviv: Open University of Israel, 159–210.

Klengel, H. (1992). *Syria, 3000 to 300 BC: A Handbook of Political History*. Berlin: Akademie.

Mazar, A. (1990). *Archaeology of the Land of the Bible*, vol. 1: *10,000–586 B.C.E.* New York: Doubleday.

Rainey, A. F., and R. S. Notley. (2006). *The Sacred Bridge: Carta's Atlas of the Biblical World*. Jerusalem: Carta.

---

[3] P. Matthiae suggests that this destruction should be attributed to Pizikarra of Nineveh, after *c.* 1524 BC (Matthiae 2006).

Redford, D. B. (1992). *Egypt, Canaan, and Israel in Ancient Times*. Princeton, NJ: Princeton University Press.

REFERENCES

Ben-Tor, A. (2004). Hazor and chronology. *Ägypten und Levante* 14: 45–67.

Bietak, M. (1997). The center of Hyksos rule: Avaris (Tell el-Dab'a). In E. D. Oren (ed.), *The Hyksos: New Historical and Archaeological Perspectives*. Philadelphia: University Museum, University of Pennsylvania, 87–139.

—— (2002). Relative and absolute chronology of the Middle Bronze Age: comments on the present state of research. In M. Bietak (ed.), *The Middle Bronze Age in the Levant: Proceedings of an International Conference on MB IIA Ceramic Material, Vienna, 24th–26th of January 2001*. Vienna: Österreichische Akademie der Wissenschaften, 29–42.

Burke, A. A. (2007). Magdalūma, Migdālîm, Magdoloi, and Majādīl: the historical geography and archaeology of the Magdalu (Migdāl). *Bulletin of the American Schools of Oriental Research* 346: 29–57.

—— (2008). *'Walled Up to Heaven': The Evolution of Middle Bronze Age Fortification Strategies in the Levant*. Winona Lake, Ind.: Eisenbrauns.

Cohen, S. L. (2002). *Canaanites, Chronology, and Connections: The Relationship of Middle Bronze IIA Canaan to Middle Kingdom Egypt*. Winona Lake, Ind.: Eisenbrauns.

Garfinkel, Y. (2001). Warrior burial customs in the Levant during the early second millennium B.C. In S. R. Wolff (ed.), *Studies in the Archaeology of Israel and Neighbouring Lands in Memory of Douglas L. Esse*. Winona Lake, Ind.: Eisenbrauns, 143–61.

Gasche, H., J. A. Armstrong, S. W. Cole, and V. G. Gurzadyan (1998). *Dating the Fall of Babylon: A Reappraisal of Second-Millennium Chronology*. Ghent: University of Ghent and the Oriental Institute of the University of Chicago.

Gerstenblith, P. (1983). *The Levant at the Beginning of the Middle Bronze Age*. New Haven, Conn.: American Schools of Oriental Research.

Ilan, D. (1995). The dawn of internationalism: the Middle Bronze Age. In T. E. Levy (ed.), *The Archaeology of Society in the Holy Land*. New York: Facts on File, 297–319.

Kamp, K. A., and N. Yoffee (1980). Ethnicity in ancient western Asia during the early second millennium BC: archaeological assessments and ethnoarchaeological prospective. *Bulletin of the American Schools of Oriental Research* 237: 85–104.

Kaplan, J. (1971). Mesopotamian elements in the Middle Bronze II culture of Palestine. *Journal of Near Eastern Studies* 30: 293–307.

Kempinski, A. (1992). Urbanization and town plans in the Middle Bronze Age II. In A. Kempinski and R. Reich (eds), *The Architecture of Ancient Israel: From the Prehistoric to the Persian Periods in Memory of Immanuel (Munya) Dunayevsky*. Jerusalem: Israel Exploration Society, 121–6.

Kenyon, K. M. (1966). *Amorites and Canaanites*. London: Oxford University Press for the British Academy.

Klengel, H. (1992). *Syria, 3000 to 300 BC: A Handbook of Political History*. Berlin: Akademie.

Kochavi, M., P. Beck, and E. Yadin (eds) (2000). *Aphek-Antipatris I: Excavation of Areas A and B, The 1972–1976 Seasons*. Tel Aviv: Tel Aviv University, Emery and Claire Yass Publications in Archaeology.

Matthiae, P. (2006). Archaeology of a destruction: the end of MB II Ebla in the light of myth and history. In E. Czerny, I. Hein, H. Hunger, D. Melman, and A. Schwab (eds), *Timelines: Studies in Honour of Manfred Bietak*, vol. 3. Leuven: Peeters, 39–51.

Mazar, A. (1992). Temples of the Middle and Late Bronze Ages and the Iron Age. In A. Kempinski and R. Reich (eds), *The Architecture of Ancient Israel: From the Prehistoric to the Persian Periods in Memory of Immanuel (Munya) Dunayevsky*. Jerusalem: Israel Exploration Society, 161–87.

Novák, M. (2004). The chronology of the Royal Palace of Qatna. *Ägypten und Levante* 14: 299–317.

Schloen, J. D. (2001). *The House of the Father as Fact and Symbol: Patrimonialism in Ugarit and the Ancient Near East*. Winona Lake, Ind.: Eisenbrauns.

Stager, L. E. (2001). Port power in the Early and Middle Bronze Age: the organization of maritime trade and hinterland production. In S. R. Wolff (ed.), *Studies in the Archaeology of Israel and Neighbouring Lands in Memory of Douglas L. Esse*. Winona Lake, Ind.: Eisenbrauns, 625–38.

Wiseman, D. J. (1953). *The Alalakh Tablets*. London: British Institute of Archaeology at Ankara.

CHAPTER 28

THE NORTHERN LEVANT (SYRIA) DURING THE MIDDLE BRONZE AGE

DANIELE MORANDI BONACOSSI

INTRODUCTION

After about a century of systematic research, the relative and absolute chronologies of the Middle Bronze Age in Syria west of the Euphrates have not yet been fully agreed upon by scholars. The current system of chronological reference is rooted in the stratigraphic and material culture sequences found at Tell Mardikh (Ebla), the principal 'type' site of western Syria (Matthiae 1997).[1] On this basis, the west Syrian Middle Bronze Age is divided into two segments, Middle Bronze Age I and II (c.2000–1600 BC), which correspond to Phases IIIA and IIIB in the Ebla stratigraphic sequence.

There are as yet no ^{14}C dates associated with the Ebla sequence, although important information has recently emerged from Italo-Syrian excavations under way in Mishrifeh (ancient Qatna). Two AMS radiocarbon determinations from Qatna's Phases 18 and 11–10, Area J suggest dates of around 2000 BC (interval 2040–1930 BC) for the transition between the EB IVB and MB I, and c.1600 BC or a little later (interval 1640–1510 BC) for the end of the MB II. A similar measurement for the beginning of the MB I comes from Tell Arqa in the Lebanese Akkar Plain (Thalmann 2006: 86). There has, however, been more debate concerning the end of the MB II, for which several archaeologists propose the 'ultra-low chronology' of about 1500 BC (Thalmann 2006: 135–6).

Although a general consensus reigns concerning the division of the Middle Bronze Age into two main phases, with a transition from one to the other at around 1800–1770 BC,[2] the division of the period into four subphases—which correspond to the internal subdivisions

---

[1] Stratigraphic sequences which encompass the entire Middle Bronze Age, or most of it, have also been found in Alalakh, Ugarit, and Hama, but problems with the stratigraphy or, as in the case of Qatna, of insufficient exposure, limit their usefulness. For recent revaluations of the Alalakh and Hama sequences, see Heinz (1992) and Nigro (2002).

[2] Radiocarbon dates for the MB I–II transition in this region are not available. There is a ^{14}C date of 1850/1800 BC for the MB I–II transition at Tell Arqa (Thalmann 2006: 135).

Table 28.1 Archaeological phasing and chronology in western Syria

Period	Mardikh	Alalakh	Hama	Synchronisms	Absolute Chronology
MB IA	IIIA1	XVI–XI	Hiatus H5–H3, Graves III, VI, I	Kültepe *karum* II	c.2000–1850 BC
MB IB	IIIA2	XI–IX	H3–H2, Graves X, II/1	End of M. IIIA2– beginning of III B1–Hotepibra 13th Dyn.	c.1850–1770 BC
MB IIA	IIIB1	VIII	H1, Grave II/1		c.1770–1700 BC
MB IIB	IIIB2	VII	Graves II/2, XIII, G	Destruction of M. IIIB2 under Mursili I	c.1700–1600 BC

of Mardikh (Ebla) IIIA and IIIB, established with regard to changes in material culture—is still under discussion. The Mardikh IIIA and IIIB subphases have been dated by means of a series of reliable synchronisms which anchor the sequence to an absolute chronology. At present, contemporaneity has been established between Mardikh IIIA1 and Kültepe *karum* II (1930–1836 BC), demonstrated by the presence of Eblaite seal imprints on tablets from Kanesh (Pinnock 2000), and between the end of Mardikh IIIA2 and the beginning of Mardikh IIIB1 on one hand and the Egyptian 13th Dynasty on the other, based on the discovery of a mace of Pharaoh Hotepibra (who reigned from 1770 to 1760 BC) in the tomb of the 'Lord of the Goats' (Scandone Matthiae 1979). The last synchronism is between the destruction of Mardikh IIIB2 and the end of the MB II at Ebla and the reign of Mursili I (Matthiae 2004: 343ff.). On this basis, the chronology summarized in Table 28.1 has recently been proposed for Mardikh (Pinnock 2005: 133–9) and Middle Bronze western Syria. It should be noted, however, that in the stratigraphic sequences of Mardikh and other sites in Levantine Syria and in the evolution of material culture in the region, there are no clear breaks or discontinuities such as would demonstrate unambiguously the existence and duration of the individual subphases within the Middle Bronze Age.[3] Furthermore, the Ebla pottery assemblages, which form the basis of these subdivisions, especially those regarding the Middle Bronze I (Mardikh IIIA1–2), have as yet only been published partially and selectively, giving priority to functionally remarkable contexts, while the important ceramic material from the Area P Archaic Palace (Phases II and III) and successive Intermediate Palace and the Area FF South Palace (Phase I) has not been published thus far.

For the moment, then, considering the strong continuity exhibited by the development of material culture during the Syrian Middle Bronze, it seems safer to regard as established only the division of the Middle Bronze Age into two main phases, MB I–II, beginning in about 2000 BC, with a transition at around 1800–1770 BC and finishing in about 1600 BC or slightly later.

---

[3] For a different definition of the Middle Bronze Age subphases at Mardikh, see Nigro (2002).

URBAN AND RURAL LANDSCAPES OF MIDDLE BRONZE WESTERN SYRIA: WHAT SETTLEMENT PATTERNS REVEAL

In the aftermath of the economic, political, social, and demographic crisis which gripped the Syrian city-states system in the last centuries of the third millennium BC (though in ways, and with consequences, which differed throughout the region), the beginning of the Middle Bronze Age marked a new development in the territorial structure and organization of Syrian urban civilization.

The onset of the Middle Bronze Age was characterized by the survival of a limited number of urban centres and a fabric of rural villages scattered throughout the territory, structured into weakly hierarchically organized settlement systems (Akkermans and Schwartz 2003: 288–332) and in some areas, for instance in the Upper and Middle Euphrates, not under the control of dominant towns and political entities (Cooper 2006). The time-scale, modalities, and causes of the regeneration of the urbanization process in Syria after the collapse or, at least, the regression of urban society towards the end of the third millennium BC constitute a complex problem, which has not yet been resolved due to the paucity of the available archaeological data (Schwartz 2006; Morandi Bonacossi 2009; see also Cooper, Ch. 20 above).

The accepted interpretation of the archaeological record has long emphasized the clear break between the third and second millennia BC with respect both to patterns of urban and rural settlement in Syria (particularly in eastern Syria) and the development of material culture. This seemed particularly evident with regard to new Middle Bronze town plans, innovative fortifications, and temple architecture as well as the production of pottery, weapons, and other metal objects, terracotta figurines, and seals.

Archaeological discoveries made during recent decades, however, necessitate a revision of the traditional representation of the regional settlement landscape (Fig. 28.1). The existence of a substantial continuity of settlement between the Early and Middle Bronze Age in numerous urban centres, particularly in the north and centre of Levantine Syria, has gradually emerged.

Continuity of occupation, although against a background of generalized decrease and regression of urbanization, has been found in numerous sites on the Upper and Middle Euphrates, such as Amarna, Shiukh Tahtani, Tell Ahmar, Tell Kabir, Hadidi, Munbaqa, Halawa A, Habuba Kabira North, Qannas, Emar, and Tell Bi'a (Cooper 2006: 26) and at Abu Danne and Umm el-Marra in the Jabbul area (Schwartz et al. 2003). Brief gaps in the occupation of several of these sites (Shiukh Tahtani, Qara Quzak, and Umm el-Marra) may be indicated by their pottery sequences, which suggest occasional short-lived periods of abandonment of the settlements at the end of the Early Bronze or at the beginning of the Middle Bronze (Cooper 2006: 37, Schwartz 2007: 47–55; Schwartz et al. 2003).

The evidence from Middle Bronze Age I Ebla is in marked contrast with this picture of urban decentralization which, however, took place against a general background of settlement continuity. Here, excavation has brought to light a vigorous urban centre covering 55ha, which grew up over the destruction layer of the preceding EB IVB city, surrounded by massive earthworks and equipped with at least two palace buildings and a temple: the Archaic Palace (Area P), the South Palace (Area FF), and the HH3 Temple (Matthiae 1997; 2002; 2004; 2006). In a not dissimilar fashion, the Tell Afis excavations have revealed the existence

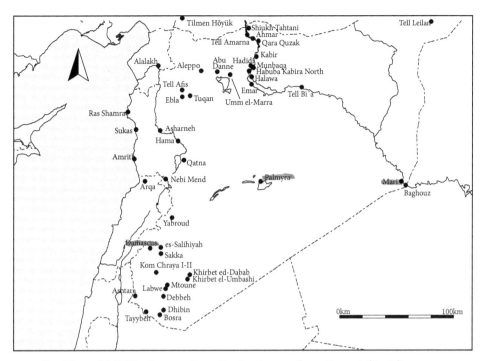

FIG. 28.1 Map of Middle Bronze Age sites in the northern Levant (Syria)

of a city with a walled acropolis and fortified lower city (Mazzoni 2005: 9). Continuity of occupation between EB IV and MB I is also found at Sukas, Tell Tuqan, Asharneh, Hama (if with a brief hiatus), Mishrifeh, Tell Arqa, and the majority of sites on the Akkar Plain, perhaps also at Nebi Mend.

The picture of settlement distribution in the region in the late third and early second millennia BC furnished by field walking surveys is, unfortunately, ambiguous due to the difficulty of distinguishing between MB I and II surface pottery assemblages. In the Jabbul region, survey results indicate a marked reduction in settlement at the onset of the MB I, while settlement data from surveys in the 'Amuq and the Sajur, Quweiq and Middle Orontes Valleys, the Tell Mastuma area, and around the Maath Basin make it possible to reconstruct only indistinct pictures of Middle Bronze occupation. Work in the Jazr region (Idlib), however, has yielded evidence of a marked continuity compared to the EB IVB, with uninterrupted occupation on most sites (Mazzoni 2005). Similar results were obtained from a recent survey of the Homs Plain. On the Akkar Plain during the MB I, the number of sites in fact increased with respect to the EB IV and the three-tiered settlement system which had emerged since the mid-third millennium was maintained (Thalmann 2007), while a slight reduction, though within a general framework of substantial settlement continuity, is to be seen in the region of Qatna, where a hierarchical settlement system had first appeared in the EB IV.

Survey evidence indicates that no shift in the settlement pattern occurs in these regions at the end of the third millennium. Middle Bronze I occupation is, on the other hand, virtually absent in the arid Badiyah region northeast of Salamiyeh where, with respect to EB IV, a drastic fall in levels of permanent settlement has been recorded (Geyer et al. 2007).

The settlement landscape in the Damascus region, and in southern Syria, is generally less clear. Around Damascus and in the Leja, occupation during the first half of the second millennium is concentrated in the MB II (Nicolle 2002). Further south in the Hawran, third to second-millennia BC settlement continuity is well documented only at Bosra and, especially, at Khirbet el-Umbashi in the Safa, where this specialized herdsmen's settlement reached its maximum size of 40ha during this very period and was surrounded by a network of villages associated with hydraulic installations (tanks and canals) for the collection and storage of rainwater (Braemer, Échallier, and Taraqji 2004).

The evidence outlined above shows that the overall picture of EB IVB–MB I settlement in Levantine Syria is characterized by an actual and substantial continuity of development which is in evident contrast with the marked break between 2200 and 1900 BC recorded by excavations and surveys in the Syrian Jezirah.

In a similar fashion, archaeological research in recent years and the concomitant accumulation of data regarding Syria's material culture at the start of the Middle Bronze have partly modified our ideas concerning the material culture development between the late third and early second millennia BC, emphasizing in particular its strong continuity with the EB IV. It is now clear, for example, that Syrian Middle Bronze earthwork fortifications developed from those of the second half of the third millennium (at Beydar, Leilan IIb, and Mari, Arbid), and that the *in antis* temples are directly descended from those of the earlier period. This may be seen at the *in antis* temples of Chuera, Bi'a, Halawa, Munbaqa (Steinbau 1), perhaps Habuba Kabira North, Tell Kabir, Qara Quzak, ar-Rawda and, recently, Ebla itself, where the largest EBA IVA 'Temple of the Rock' is overlain in the MB I–II by a second, smaller *in antis* temple (Matthiae 2006: fig. 16; see Fig. 28.5 below) and the Middle Bronze Age Ishtar Temple D on the acropolis developed from EB IVA and B temples of the same *in antis* type (Matthiae 2009: 762–77).

Cultural continuity is also evident in the evolution of pottery sequences, for example in the case of the Euphrates sites (Cooper 2006: 27) and also in the production of larger centres such as Ebla (Nigro 2002: 102), Tell Afis (Mazzoni 2005: 9), and Tell Mishrifeh (Morandi Bonacossi 2008), and smaller ones (e.g. Tell Arqa: Thalmann 2006: 101–6). Productions with transitional features have recently been identified from these sites, evident especially in some ceramic forms and fabrics, which nonetheless fit into a broader context that originated at the start of the Middle Bronze and is distinguished by the disappearance of the 'caliciform' tradition and changes in vessel shape, fabrics, decoration, surface treatments, and manufacturing techniques.

The available archaeological evidence has therefore revealed the existence in Syria of clear regional differences in settlement development between 2200 and 1900 BC, and a wide range of processes may be traced, ranging from the crisis of urbanism and the drastic interruption of occupation in the Syrian Jezirah to urban decentralization within a general trend towards settlement continuity in the Euphrates region, to the persistence and flourishing of urban life in various parts of north-central Levantine Syria, where third-millennium urbanization was a success and persisted, albeit in new forms, in the Middle Bronze. To the east and south of this strip, in ecologically less favourable areas such as those of the Badiyah and the south Syrian arid fringes, the MB I marks the disintegration or drastic regression of all forms of urban settlement.

It is no easy matter to explain such a diversified collection of settlement and urbanization development trends as found in Syria in the early Middle Bronze Age. In the debate on the collapse of urbanism at the end of the Early Bronze and the following regeneration of complex societies during the early Middle Bronze, several factors have been suggested which might have provided the driving force for the revitalization of statehood and urban life (Schwartz 2006: 9–12). In the case of the Syrian Euphrates, the reconstruction of social and economic complexity at the onset of the Middle Bronze was probably assisted by the interaction of several factors: a diversified agropastoral economy which gave the region economic and productive resilience and flexibility, independence from larger political entities and therefore non-involvement in the collapse of these, and its tribal character, which may have facilitated the implementation of more resilient kin-based inclusionary and corporate strategies, rather than exclusionary and rigidly organized approaches centred on state, elites, and the monopolistic control of sources of power (Cooper 2006).

Probably also a crucial factor at Umm el-Marra, in the Jabbul region, was the emergence of the new Amorite ethnic group, which seems to have gained legitimacy in the early second millennium through the restoration of symbols peculiar to the local authority of the previous period by means of the (certainly programmatic) construction of a ceremonial platform on the acropolis, immediately above the EB III–IV elite burial complex (Schwartz et al. 2003: 345). In the case of Umm el-Marra, emphasis has recently been placed on the role played in urban renewal by an increase in important productive activities, such as intensive hunting of the onager and its significance for an economy specialized in leatherworking and associated trade (Nichols and Weber 2006).

In the case of Levantine Syria, distinguished on one hand by highly favourable ecological conditions for a Mediterranean economy based on cereal dry-farming, the cultivation of olives and grapes, and pastoralism, and on basic continuity in the development of both settlement and urban life in comparison with the Syrian Jezirah and Euphrates Valley, the complex interaction of different factors which gave birth to the Middle Bronze 'Amorite' civilization must also have included some important additional element. This could well have been the survival—though with diminished vigour—of the institutions and symbols of the preceding third-millennium state and urban civilization, as may be seen above all from the extraordinary case of Ebla,[4] as well as from the uninterrupted urban life clearly recorded in sites such as Qatna and Tell Afis between the late EB IV and early MB I.

At least with regard to Levantine Syria, therefore, the time is ripe for a thoroughgoing revision of the 'dark age' theory and the model of collapse and subsequent regeneration in the early second millennium BC of statehood and urban civilization, which was imposed on the archaeological evidence of this region as a reflection of the 'crises' which characterized the urbanization of northeastern Syria on one hand and the southern Levant on the other.

The changes from which Syrian civilization emerged at the start of the MB I would seem rather to have been the result of longer-term economic, cultural, and social transformations certainly under way already during the EB IV and perhaps also due, as would be suggested by the instance of Tell Arqa (Thalmann 2007), to the development of a new system of interrelations between Syria's internal and coastal regions and the rise to power of the new Amorite cultural element. In fact at Arqa, after the destruction of the Level 15 settlement (c.2000 BC cal.), the area at the western end of the settlement was occupied by burials (including a 'warrior

---

[4] Here the Intermediate Palace was built over the EB IVB and MB I phases of the Archaic Palace, and the Middle Bronze Ishtar Temple of Area D and the 'Temple of the Rock' of Area HH were erected on top of sequences of EB IVA and B sacred buildings (Matthiae 2009).

tomb') at the onset of the MB I and by stone-built, corbelled silos, which mark a radical change in agricultural practices at the site in comparison with the preceding EB IV (Thalmann 2006: 32–50). The Level 14D burials show strong similarities with the material culture of early MB I internal Syria and probably indicate the arrival of newcomers from this area, who settled at the margins of the existing settlement without altering the composition and economic strategies of the local population, as may be deduced from the undisturbed continuity of the regional settlement pattern during the passage from the third to the second millennium BC.

An even greater growth in settlement number and population occurred in urban and rural Levantine Syria during the late MB I and especially the following MB II.

Throughout the region, surveys and excavations indicate a notable increase in settled sites and in the vitality of both urban and rural life. The phenomenon is evident in the Amuq Plain (Alalakh) and to the north, in the Islahiyeh Valley (Tilmen Höyük), the Sajur and the Quweiq Valleys, in Aleppo (citadel temple and Ansari), in the Jabbul (Umm el-Marra and Abu Danne) and Jazr (Afis), in the regions of Mastuma, Ebla, and the Maath Basin (Tuqan), in the entire Middle Orontes Valley, and even in the Badiyah, where, after the collapse of MB I settlement, a new network of sites protected by a system of fortresses, watchtowers, and advance forts emerged. The same situation is found in the coastal strip, at the foot of the Qalamoun Range (Yabrud), in the Damascus region (Tell es-Salihiyah, Sakka), in the Leja (Kom Chraya, Mtoune, Labwe), the Hawran (Ashtara, Tayybeh, Bosra, Dhibin, Debbeh), and the Safa (Khirbet ed-Dabab).

This strong growth in urban settlement and in the occupation of the west Syrian countryside from the end of the 19th century BC onwards is the result—besides of the presence of very productive dry-farming hinterlands with a Mediterranean economy—of the rise on the Syrian political scene of new regional states which derived part of their political and economic power from their strategic position at the intersection of trading routes that crossed the Levant. To the north, the kingdom of Yamḥad, with its capital at Aleppo, controlled the fertile region and commercial exchange between the Mediterranean coast and the Middle Euphrates. To the east, the kingdom of Mari functioned as 'gateway' or emporium to and from Babylon, Iran, and the Persian Gulf, while to the south, the kingdom of Qatna controlled central Syria between the Mediterranean and Palmyra and the trading routes leading to the Beqa' Valley, the Damascus region, southern Syria, and northern Palestine, where other similar states flourished, such as Tel Hazor and Laish (Tel Dan).

The political and economic relations—which are well documented in the Mari archive—among these territorial Amorite states located between the Mediterranean, Syria, Palestine, and Mesopotamia and within the wider context of a peer–polity interaction system characterized by political rivalries, military and interdynastic alliances, emulation, and competition, would certainly have provided a fertile soil for the intensification of agricultural and craft production, population and settlement growth, and the revitalization of the long-distance commercial networks which were the basis of the extraordinary development of urbanism in MB II Levantine Syria.

LANDSCAPES OF POWER: URBAN PLANNING AND PUBLIC ARCHITECTURE

Though exposure is in general insufficient to reveal much of the organization of MB II cities, excavations at Ebla have been extensive enough to give a picture of the essential plan of this capital city of one of the kingdoms under the domination of Yamḥad, while Woolley's digs at Tell Atchana (1955) have furnished an unfortunately much more partial picture of the capital of another vassal kingdom, that of Alalakh.

Ebla in the MB II was a large city (Fig. 28.2), girded by huge earthworks protected by forts (Matthiae 1997; 2002); the ramparts were passed by means of 'double-chambered' city gates. The circular fortified upper town was located almost at the city centre, its profile dominated by the Royal Palace E, residence of Elba's sovereigns, and Temple D, a palatine *in antis* temple dedicated to the cult of Ishtar. The base of the acropolis was surrounded by a ring of impressive public and religious buildings with at least three palace complexes and three main religious areas. The northern part included an *in antis* temple (Temple N) dedicated to Shamash; further west, over the Archaic Palace (the residence of Ebla's EB IVB rulers, which remained in use until the MB IA), the Intermediate Palace was built as well as the Northern Palace in the MB IIA, which was probably used for ceremonies related to kingship. To the south, there was a large sacred area dedicated to the goddess Ishtar, made up of the large *in antis* Temple P2 and the monumental cult Terrace P3. Continuing southwards, one would have encountered the great Western Palace, residence of the crown prince, below the flooring of which was situated the entrance to the tombs of the royal cemetery, Temple B, dedicated to Rashap, god of the underworld, and Sanctuary B2, probably reserved for the cult of defunct sovereigns. Beyond the sacred Area B, at the foot of the southern acropolis

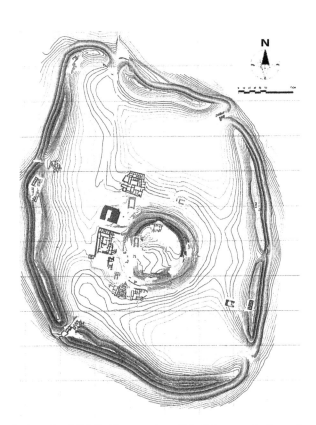

FIG. 28.2 Ebla during the Middle Bronze Age (Matthiae 2006: fig. 27)

slope, there was a residential quarter and the Southern Palace, interpreted as the residence of the 'Grand Vizier' of Ebla. The southeastern lower city contained a third religious area, centred on Temple HH2, perhaps dedicated to the god Hadad. Lastly, at the base of the western rampart, recent excavations have brought to light a residential quarter, dominated by the Western Residence, an imposing elite dwelling.

The walls surrounding the city of Umm el-Marra stood upon fortifications with a glacis; the central acropolis was fortified in the MB I with a defensive wall (Nichols and Weber 2006: 47–9). The site of Tuqan in the Maath Basin, an urban centre dependent on Ebla, was divided into acropolis and lower city; these were fortified by a wall reinforced by a glacis and a rampart which held up a wall equipped with circular towers, respectively (Baffi 2006).

Much less is known of the organization of the MB II cities of coastal Syria, such as Ras Shamra (Ugarit). Here, the presence of a defensive city wall is recorded, together with numerous single and multiple tombs, among which elaborate stone-corbelled collective burials contained imported Cypriot and Minoan pottery—clear evidence that Ugarit already formed part of a network of commercial ties in the Aegean in this period.

In the interior, in the Middle Orontes Valley, excavations at Tell Acharneh and Tell Mishrifeh (al-Maqdissi 2007; al-Maqdissi et al. 2002; Morandi Bonacossi 2007; Pfälzner 2007) have brought to light two urban centres fortified with enormous ramparts and, in the case of Qatna, 'twin-chambered' city gates. The city of Qatna, divided in the Middle Bronze Age into an upper and a lower town, covered an area of more than 100ha and had an extremely regular planned square layout and a roughly circular, probably walled, upper town.

Fortifications with walls or earthworks are also known from Sakka, on the Damascus Oasis, where the excavation is in progress of a probable summer residence of the Damascene rulers. This building is decorated with painted murals showing evident Egyptian influence (Taraqji 1999).

It was a characteristic of Middle Bronze Syrian cities (and of Levantine urban landscapes generally) that they were divided into a lower city and an acropolis, both of which were fortified with huge defensive earthen ramparts (Fig. 28.3) capped by fortresses and towers or walls. One may realistically imagine that such defensive architecture constituted an effective defence against archers armed with long-range composite bows, or siege machines and strategies (e.g. towers, sapping). However, it would seem also clear that these massive earthworks, fruit of an enormous effort of logistics, must also have fulfilled a powerful politico-ideological function, as symbols of power which expressed the relations of emulation and competition between the great Syrian peer-polities and their ambitions regarding regional power.

The scarcity of the residential quarters so far brought to light in Middle Bronze urban centres—in comparison with the plentiful evidence of monumental defensive, public, and religious architecture—has not as yet attracted careful reflection. As a matter of fact, housing quarters have been discovered only in Ebla, where the area occupied by private houses is extraordinarily limited. Similar situations have also been observed in other north Mesopotamian and Syrian Middle Bronze sites, such as Tell ar-Rimakh, Tell al-Hawa, Tell Leilan, and perhaps Mari (Morandi Bonacossi 2007: 80–82). The dearth of ordinary residential quarters might suggest that these urban centres were what might be called 'hollow cities', i.e. administrative shells characterized by numerous (often imposing) public buildings and

FIG. 28.3 Aerial view of Qatna's ramparts (Italian–Syrian Mission to Mishrifeh/Qatna)

low densities of inhabitants, who consisted basically of institutional personnel, but largely lacking extensive populations of ordinary residents.

According to the available archaeological evidence, the 'hollow cities' phenomenon seems to have arisen in Syria and northern Iraq at the beginning of the second millennium BC, and is in contrast with the impression conveyed by many mid- and late third-millennium urban centres, which were distinguished by close-packed urban neighbourhoods. This suggests that, with respect to the Early Bronze, a new 'idea' of 'city' is developed in Middle Bronze Syria, which dominates the countryside as a 'disembedded' capital essentially devoid of common residents and enclosing enormous fortified areas. These considerably exceeded the needs of the individual centres, and could also be viewed as an expression of the emulation and competition processes characteristic of peer–polity interaction.

Whether, and in what measure, the new urban ideology shared by Syrian regional states was one of the effects of the process of the 'Amoritization' of Syria and reflected the markedly tribal nature of Middle Bronze society, strongly permeated by the spirit of agrarian and pastoral nomadic kin groups who lived in villages and towns dispersed in the capitals' hinterlands, transcending the boundaries of closed urban environments, remains to be ascertained.

The urban landscapes and hierarchical settlement systems of Syrian territorial states in the Middle Bronze had as focal points the imposing palaces situated in the capital cities (Aleppo, Qatna, and Mari) and urban centres of second (Tilmen Höyük, Alalakh, and Ebla) or third rank (Sakka).

The palace architecture of western Syria shows the reciprocal influence of two different cultural traditions, one authentically Syro-Levantine and the other Syro-Mesopotamian. The first tradition may be seen in the palaces of Ebla, Alalakh, Tilmen Höyük, Qatna, and Sakka, and is distinguished by plans which are often asymmetrical, the absence of large courtyards surrounded by rooms (which are, on the contrary, typical of Mesopotamian and east Syrian palaces), the frequent occurrence of columns, hypostyle halls (occasionally also galleries), and the widespread use of basalt orthostats lining the lower walls and of wood-in-wall construction. The presence of royal hypogea (Ebla, Alalakh, Qatna, and Bi'a) and the arrangement of the reception suite with the throne room were also distinctive. The latter consisted of a tripartite structure, where a central hall with columns was flanked by wings with side rooms.

At Qatna, a typical palace of 'Syrian' type (the Eastern Palace) was built at the end of the MB IIA and abandoned at the end of the MB IIB (Morandi Bonacossi et al. 2009). At the same time (the end of the MB II) a new monumental palace building was erected above a MB I–II cemetery, exhibiting a combination of elements characteristic of the western Syrian tradition (absence of large courtyards, widespread use of basalt orthostats, wood, and columns, and the presence of a royal hypogeum) and typically Syro-Mesopotamian features (Fig. 28.4). The latter are evident in the articulation of the central reception suite of the palace: the large colonnaded audience chamber (Hall C) with access to the probable throne room (Hall B) and a second, even more monumental ceremonial chamber (Hall A), perhaps dedicated to the royal ancestor cult from which an underground corridor led to the royal burial chambers, well known for its final period of use in the Late Bronze Age. This arrangement can clearly be compared with that of Courtyard 106 and Rooms 64 and 65 of the 'Palace of Zimri-Lim' in Mari.

Several rooms of the Qatna palace were decorated with wall paintings of Aegean-type motifs, approximately contemporaneous with those found at Thera, Alalakh VII, Kabri, and Tell el-Dab'a. The painted scenes of miniature landscapes, which decorated the walls of Room N, probably had a religious function. The presence of wall paintings that were Aegean in technique, style, and iconography in Levantine palaces demonstrates that the courts of the Syro-Palestinian states participated in the network of far-flung interpalatial exchanges which connected the eastern Mediterranean and the Levant as far as the Nile Delta. However, the exact direction of cultural influence and its implications still need chronological confirmation.

In the same context, distinguished by long-distance trade and prestige relations, emulation and competition are to be understood by the Egyptian Middle Kingdom materials (statues, scarabs, ritual vases, and ceremonial weapons) found in the Qatna palace, together with finds from Ugarit and the 'Tomb of the Lord of the Goats' in the Ebla royal cemetery, and of course the Egyptianizing imagery abundantly documented in the glyptics from Yamḫad and Qatna, the wall paintings from Mari (around the investiture scene of Zimri-Lim) and Sakka (and recently from Tell Burak in the Lebanon), the ivories from the Ebla Northern Palace, as well as in the Egyptianizing precious metalwork (or imitations of Egyptian craftsmanship) from Byblos on the Lebanese coast. In this vast spectrum of artistic expression of Egyptian (as well as Aegean) provenance, inspiration, or imitation, the ideological effort on the part of the reigning Syrian dynasties to emulate the elite symbols of prestigious foreign state entities, thus legitimizing their own authority, stands out clearly.[5]

---

[5] The 'Tod treasure' found in the temple of Mont, Upper Egypt, and dated to the reign of Amenemhet II (1929–1895 BC) is also significant in this context. The objects which composed it (including seals and 153 silver vases of Syro-Anatolian origin) were probably individual gifts sent to the Egyptian pharaoh by a north Syrian ruler.

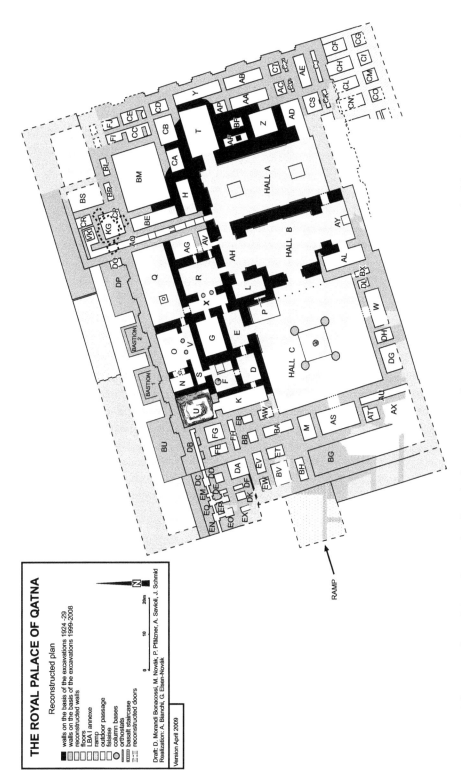

FIG. 28.4 Schematic plan of Qatna's Royal Palace (Italian–Syrian and German–Syrian Missions to Mishrifeh/Qatna)

Religious and Funerary Landscapes: Temples and Burials, Governance Strategies, and Society

The same aspiration on the part of royal Syrian dynasties to legitimize their status also permeates religion and funerary practice in western Syria.

In the major urban centres there were sacred areas centred on *in antis* temples, each of which had a cult chamber (with long axis aligned with that of the temple and a niche in the end wall for a statue of the god) preceded by a vestibule closed off by screening walls (Fig. 28.5). A tripartite variation on this plan, associated with royal palaces and found in Temple D in Ebla and the Alalakh VII temple, seems to have been employed for palace temples dedicated to the dynastic cult.

Middle Bronze Age *in antis* temples are found throughout the region, along the Euphrates (Mari, Bi'a, Munbaqa, and Qara Quzak) and in northwestern Syria (Tilmen Höyük, Alalakh, Aleppo, and Ebla), but not—to date, at least—in southern central Syria.

The widespread occurrence of a temple type derived, as outlined above, from Early Bronze Syrian prototypes emphasizes the marked uniformity and originality of the Syrian religious architectural tradition, which may be presumed to reflect a similar unity with respect to liturgical and ritual aspects. This is also indicated in epigraphic sources, which reveal the popularity of the cult of the goddess Ishtar, especially at Ebla, where the figure of Ishtar Eblaitu is dominant, together with Hadad (and his wife Khebat), whose great temple in Aleppo is currently being excavated and whose cult extended throughout the territory of Yamhad (including Alalakh and Ebla). Dagan was worshipped in the Euphrates Valley, from Mari to Tuttul and Emar. Hadad was probaly also venerated in Qatna, as suggested by the discovery there of a royal sealing in which the god is mentioned as the god of King Ishkhi-Hadad.

Particularly widespread in Amorite Syria were the cult of stones, known archaeologically and textually (through the Mari archives), and the cult of ancestors, based on the *kispum*-ritual in honour of royal forefathers, which is well documented along the Euphrates Valley and evidenced by the royal hypogea of Alalakh, Ebla, and Qatna. The extraordinary royal tomb of Qatna, the last (Late Bronze) phase of which has been recently brought to light (al-Maqdissi et al. 2003), was certainly built together with the palace at the end of the MB II, as is shown also by the recent discovery of a hypogeum (Tomb VII) containing over

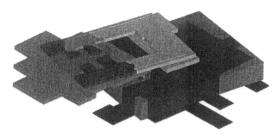

FIG. 28.5 Isometric view of the superimposed MB II and EB IVA 'Temples of the Rock', Ebla (Matthiae 2006: fig. 16)

50 secondary depositions under Room DA in the northwestern wing of the Royal Palace (Fig. 28.4), which was probably the secondary burial of individuals originally interred in the Royal Grave at the end of the MB II, whose skeletons, personal ornaments, and grave goods were later removed from their original location to make room for new burials.

The royal hypogea are the architecturally most striking manifestation of a phenomenon which is typical of Syrian Middle Bronze funerary practices: the disappearance of public above-ground sepulchres for the elite community's ancestors which had distinguished the regional funerary landscape during the latter half of the third millennium, particularly in the Euphrates Valley (Akkermans and Schwartz 2003: 322).[6] In the Middle Bronze these monumental mortuary complexes were replaced by underground tombs sited beneath royal palaces, by means of which royal power controlled the participation at funerary rituals and access to the deceased, which was limited to a restricted royal and (probably) elite circle. These changes in funerary practices on the part of Syrian royal courts and urban elites reflect the substitution in the governance strategies of the 'corporate' polity, which during the EB IV had permeated the practice of power, by 'exclusionary' approaches, by means of which 'leaders entrenched divisions within communities by taking absolute control of community ancestors' (Peltenburg 2009).

This development is archaeologically visible in Qatna (for example), where the royal palace was built over the necropolis of the Middle Bronze community for the purpose of taking symbolic possession of its ancestors, segregating them underneath the palace (which was, in turn, equipped with a royal hypogeum). This was manifestly an operation of appropriation and control of the community's past, a procedure which may also be seen at Tell Bi'a in the construction of Palace B and later Palace A (the latter with a hypogeum) on top of Mortuary Complex E of the mid-third millennium BC.

The process of appropriation of the community's ancestors (progressively substituted by those of the royal family), which appears to have been fully accomplished during the Middle Bronze, began earlier in EB IV, as may be seen from the case of Bi'a and the presence in Ebla of a royal hypogeum under Palace G that was never used (G4) and of two violated royal tombs under the throne room and Room 1 of the later Eastern Palace in Mari (Margueron 2004: 356–61). Yet again, profound changes that appear to distinguish Syrian Middle Bronze culture are deeply rooted in sociocultural processes which began earlier, in the second half of the third millennium BC.

The abandonment, on one hand, of visible and public ancestor monuments, which functioned as landmarks that structured the physical and mental map of a community and the corresponding segregation, on the other, of the royal ancestors within palace buildings are accompanied by a significant and certainly correlated change in the funerary record from extramural burials in cemeteries near settlements (which are especially widespread in the Euphrates Valley) to intramural mortuary facilities, which have been abundantly recorded at numerous sites, such as Shiukh Tahtani, Ebla, Ras Shamra, Sukas, Qatna, Arqa, and Sakka. Frequent infant and occasional adult burials are found beneath the floors of houses and courtyards. The denial by royalty and urban elites of community access to and participation in corporate mortuary rituals would seem to have determined the development

---

[6] See the monumental funerary complexes and tumuli of Gre Virike, Jerablus, Ahmar, Banat, and Umm el-Marra (Peltenburg 2009).

within Middle Bronze Syrian society of stronger ties of individualistic type with ancestors (Peltenburg 2009). This process of strengthening kinship affiliation is reflected in the adoption of private intramural burial customs, in which burial is associated with the domestic sphere, whereas the habit of multiple successive burial points to a strengthening also of familial affiliation.

Middle Bronze Age Syria's funerary record reveals the existence of considerable social stratification, evident both in tomb architecture, extending from simple burials in grave-cuts and jars, to multi-chambered underground shaft graves with multiple burials and stone-lined dolmen tombs, and in grave goods and personal ornaments. The simple grave cut and jar burials at Shiukh Tahtani, Ebla, and Qatna generally contain only a few vases which would have originally held the foodstuffs and drink that accompanied the deceased, and occasionally bronze weapons or personal ornaments. Richer grave goods are associated with members of the elite,[7] from the numerous shaft graves found in western Syria, the Sukas collective pit grave, the burials in disused grain stores in Amrith, and the dolmen tombs at Baghouz, Ras Shamra, Yabroud, Tayyibeh, Khirbet el-Umbashi as well as the tombs of the Ebla royal cemetery.

There seem also to be significant differences in tomb type and grave goods which are related to the age, rather than the social status, of the deceased. At Qatna, for example, infant burials up to about one year old had no grave goods, whereas children above one year were buried in grave cuts with pottery vases.

Western Syria within the wider context of the Levant: trends, problems, and future approaches

Excavations and surveys in recent years have shown that western Syria did not suffer greatly from the phenomenon of the collapse of statehood and urban civilization which hit much harder the complex societies in other parts of the Levant (especially the south) and Mesopotamia in the late third and early second millennia BC. As a result, the beginning of the Middle Bronze seems ever less an impenetrable 'dark age', and comes into clearer focus as a period distinguished by a fundamental continuity of urban and rural settlement and of the state political and administrative institutions under the control of kin-based Amorite groups, which took over political power and founded new ruling dynasties in the entire Syro-Mesopotamian region.

With the exception of the ecologically less favourable areas of the 'arid margins', where in the long run the EB IV urban experiment proved a failure, no major shift is recorded in the multi-tier settlement patterns that arose in many regions of Levantine Syria (Orontes Valley and coastal region) during the EB IV. Cities such as Ebla and Qatna were re-founded in accordance with new urban models on top of the remains of previous towns. New cities with

---

[7] They include notable quantities of pottery, amongst which Syro-Cilician Painted and Common Painted Ware jugs and other classes of high-quality pottery, such as Black, Red, and Orange Burnished Wares and Yahudiyeh Ware (Nigro 2003), personal ornaments (toggle pins, torques, rings, bracelets, and beads), and metal weapons (daggers, socketed spearheads, fenestrated axe-heads, and arrowheads).

monumental elite architecture, dominated by gigantic earthwork-based fortifications and walled acropolises, created a new urban landscape, strongly penetrated by symbolic features which profoundly structured the territory and landscapes of power of the new competing regional states. The amount of human labour needed for the construction of the enormous ramparts indicates that large urban centres must have exercised powerful control over their hinterlands.

This new Amorite 'heartland of cities' was sustained by a flourishing interregional exchange system and a strongly developed agropastoral economy, based on the dry culti-vation of cereals, in particular two-row barley, on the Mediterranean vine and olive crops, and on sheep/goat pastoralism that was strongly specialized compared to the third millen-nium, as indicated by the marked and widespread increase in ovicaprines and correspond-ing reduction in cattle and pigs registered at many sites.

Population growth and the intensification of agricultural and craft production in the region during the Middle Bronze were accompanied by signs of stress in the paleoenvi-ronmental record of many sites (Umm el-Marra and Qatna) most probably also related to increased deforestation in the area for reasons of agriculture, animal rearing, and produc-tion (massive use of wood as fuel for metallurgy and pottery mass production).[8]

In western Syria, as in Palestine, the considerable diffusion of tin-bronze in the place of copper has left clear evidence in the archaeological record, above all in the form of grave goods. Cuneiform sources, in particular the Kültepe and Mari archives, provide informa-tion about the metal supply networks, especially those relating to copper and tin. Syrian copper continued to arrive from the Anatolian Upper Euphrates, but Middle Bronze Cyprus came to play an important role in its supply. Mari functioned as a 'gateway' from which tin originating in Elam was distributed throughout western Syria and Palestine. Written sources indicate the existence of a *karum*, a foreign commercial supply centre, at Qatna, and similar arrangements may have also been present in the capitals of the territorial states fur-ther south, such as Damascus and Hazor. The Mari documents, in fact, speak of Babylonian emissaries living in the latter city.

In this cultural climate, open to trade, international contacts, and experimentation, tech-nological innovations also developed. True glass in the form of beads and small vessels seems to have appeared for the first time in Syria at Alalakh VII, probably as an offshoot of the pyrotechnology utilized for metallurgy and frit.

Pottery production acquired the characteristics of mass manufacture by specialized arti-sans, who worked in genuine pottery 'factories' probably managed by centralized institutions, such as that excavated at Qatna (Morandi Bonacossi 2008). The discovery of areas of pottery manufacture also in lower-ranking urban settlements such as Afis suggests that the capitals' hinterlands were more complex and economically independent than had been imagined. In any case, as is shown by many funerary objects from shaft graves, prestige items (e.g. weap-ons and luxury ware pottery) were also consumed in middle-sized and small towns.

The regional capitals' long-distance trading relations allowed them to acquire not only tin and copper for metal production but also a wide range of raw materials, such as timber for building, perfumed woods to be burnt in the temples, wine, cloth, fine white horses from Qatna, and luxury craft items, such as carts and litters (according to texts from Mari).

---

[8] For the anthropogenic impact on Qatna's environment, see Cremaschi et al. (2007).

The wide-ranging commercial ties of the larger western Syrian cities were also a crucial source of power for the local rulers, whose power base received legitimacy and increased strength from exchanges with the prestigious elites of Crete and the eastern Mediterranean, Mesopotamia, and Egypt. The circulation of itinerant specialized craftsmen, who decorated the walls of Levantine palaces with paintings of Minoan or Egyptian subjects and the markedly international styles shown by items of artistic production found in elite contexts (e.g. ivory inlays, glyptics, and precious metalwork) demonstrate that the Syrian territorial states' competitive participation in the vast system of interregional commercial networks was a main source of legitimacy.

Competition between territorial states and processes of emulation between communities in the manner of Renfrew's Peer Polity Interaction model would explain quite convincingly the rapid diffusion in Middle Bronze western Syria of a material culture both homogeneous and structurally receptive towards international interactions and cross-cultural contaminations.

Within this culturally composite but fundamentally unified milieu and strongly stratified social context where the Amorite elites had a monopoly on power, there existed a society which was only apparently culturally and ethnically monolithic. The Syrian texts, as well as the few tablets found in Palestine, reveal—alongside the prevalently Amorite onomastics— the persistence of Akkadian and the significant presence of Hurrian personal names, or at least Hurrian naming practices (Akkermans and Schwartz 2003).

The end of the Middle Bronze in northwest Syria is marked by the devastating destructions of Alalakh, Aleppo, and Ebla by the Hittite rulers Hattusili I and Mursili I and Pizikarra of Nineveh at the end of the 17th or the beginning of the 16th century BC. Archaeological sequences from south-central Syria, with the exception of the destruction level brought to light during the excavations at Sakka, do not show signs of violent interruption in settlement continuity. In general, from a cultural point of view, there is a gradual transition between the Middle Bronze and Late Bronze, distinguished by a complete continuity of occupation and material culture, especially with regard to pottery production.

In fact, we do not know precisely what happened between the end of the Middle Bronze and the onset of the Late Bronze, and what led to the crumbling of Middle Bronze political structures and the emergence throughout the Levant of a new geopolitical set-up. This occurred over a lengthy span of time, from the second half of 17th to the late 16th century BC. By analogy with what seems to have taken place in the southern Levant, where the archaeological record is rather more abundant, one could hypothesize that in the long term, the economic pressure exerted by the Syrian regional kingdoms on their hinterlands proved to be excessive. The depletion of economic and human resources for the benefit of the Amorite monarchies' gargantuan programmes of urban construction and defence, the expansion of non-productive elites, the growth of an intensified dry-farming agricultural regime, population increase, and environmental deterioration are all factors which could have undermined the economic base and also the foundation of consensus and legitimacy which guaranteed the social solidity and sense of ideological identity of Syria Middle Bronze political entities, triggering a process of disaggregation. This was subsequently accelerated, at least in northern Syria, by the destructive incursions of Hittite sovereigns and other northern Mesopotamian rulers.

Although many problems remain unsolved (the 'Amoritization' of Syria, the evolution of the material culture, and the collapse of the Middle Bronze territorial states), it should be borne in mind that their solution is rendered difficult above all by the present lack of accurate intraregional and interregional correlations between chronologies. Only the construction of a firm, absolute time-scale, based on a wide-ranging set of AMS radiocarbon determinations relating to continuous stratigraphic sequences from sites distributed over the various regions of western Syria, will allow us to tackle these problems effectively in the future.

ADDENDUM

After the submission of the chapter a new tripartite subdivision of the Middle Bronze Age (MBA I–III) has been proposed on the basis of selected archaeological contexts and ceramics from Qatna. The new evidence suggests that the Middle Bronze Age should be extended to include the entire 16th century BC, through addition of a third phase, the MB III (Iamoni and Morandi Bonacossi 2010–2011; Iamoni 2012).

SUGGESTED READING

Charpin, D., and N. Ziegler (2003). *Florilegium marianum V: Mari et le Proche-Orient à l'époque amorrite*. Paris: Société pour l'étude du Proche-Orient ancien.

Fleming, D. E. (2004). *Democracy's Ancient Ancestors: Mari and Early Collective Governance*. Cambridge: Cambridge University Press.

Gerstenblith, P. (1985). *The Levant and the Beginning of the Middle Bronze Age*. Philadelphia: American Schools of Oriental Research.

Klengel, H. (1992). *Syria 3000 to 300 B.C.: A Handbook of Political History*. Berlin: Akademie.

Matthiae, P. (1997). Ebla and Syria in the Middle Bronze Age. In E. D. Oren (ed.), *The Hyksos: New Historical and Archaeological Perspectives*. Philadelphia: University Museum, University of Pennsylvania, 379–414.

——(2010). *Ebla, la città del trono: archeologia e storia*. Turin: Einaudi.

REFERENCES

Akkermans, P. M. M. G., and G. M. Schwartz (2003). *The Archaeology of Syria: From Complex Hunter-Gatherers to Early Urban Societies (c. 16,000–300 BC)*. Cambridge: Cambridge University Press.

al-Maqdissi, M. (2007). Notes d'archéologie Levantine X: introduction aux travaux archéologiques syriens à Mishirfeh/Qatna au nord-est de Homs (Émèse). In D. Morandi Bonacossi (ed.), *Urban and Natural Landscapes of an Ancient Syrian Capital: Settlement and Environment at Tell Mishrifeh/Qatna and in Central-Western Syria*. Udine: Forum, 19–27.

—— H. Dohmann-Pfälzner, P. Pfälzner, and A. Suleiman (2003). Das königliche Hypogäum von Qatna: Bericht über die syrisch-deutsche Ausgrabung im November–Dezember 2002. *Mitteilungen der Deutschen Orient-Gesellschaft* 135: 189–218.

—— M. Luciani, D. Morandi Bonacossi, M. Novák, and P. Pfälzner (eds) (2002). *Excavating Qatna I: Preliminary Report on the 1999 and 2000 Campaigns of the Joint Syrian-Italian-German Archaeological Research Project at Tell Mishrifeh*. Damascus: Direction Général des Antiquités et des Musées de Syrie/Udine: University of Udine/Tübingen: University of Tübingen.

Baffi, F. (2006). *Tell Tuqan: ricerche archeologiche italiane nella regione del Maath (Siria)*. Galatina: Congedo.

Braemer, F., J.-C. Échallier, and A. Taraqji (2004). *Khirbet Al Umbashi: villages et campements de pasteurs dans le 'désert noir' à l'âge du Bronze*. Beirut: Institut français d'archéologie du Proche-Orient.

Cooper, L. (2006). The demise and regeneration of Bronze Age urban centers in the Euphrates Valley of Syria. In G. M. Schwartz and J. J. Nichols (eds), *After Collapse: The Regeneration of Complex Societies*. Tucson: University of Arizona Press, 18–37.

Cremaschi, M., A. Canci, L. Gourichon, et al. (2007).The environment of ancient Qatna: contributions from natural sciences and landscape archaeology. In D. Morandi Bonacossi (ed.), *Urban and Natural Landscapes of an Ancient Syrian Capital: Settlement and Environment at Tell Mishrifeh/Qatna and in Central-Western Syria*. Udine: Forum, 331–6.

Geyer, B., M. al-Dbiyat, N. Awad, et al. (2007). The arid margins of northern Syria: occupation of the land and modes of exploitation in the Bronze Age. In D. Morandi Bonacossi (ed.), *Urban and Natural Landscapes of an Ancient Syrian Capital: Settlement and Environment at Tell Mishrifeh/Qatna and in Central-Western Syria*. Udine: Forum, 269–81.

Heinz, M. (1992). *Tell Atchana/Alalakh: Die Schichten VII–XVII*. Kevelaer: Butzon & Bercker/ Neukirchen-Vluyn: Neukirchener.

Iamoni, M. (2012). *The MBA II and the LBA Pottery Horizons at Qatna: Innovation and Conservation in the Ceramic Tradition of a Regional Capital and Its Implications for the Second Millennium Syrian Chronology*. Udine: Forum Editrice.

—— and D. Morandi Bonacossi (2010–11). The Middle Bronze Age I–III pottery sequence from the Italian excavations at Mishrifeh/Qatna, Syria: archaeological contexts and ceramic evidence. *Berytus* 53–4.

Margueron, J.-C. (2004). *Mari: métropole de l'Euphrate au IIIe et au début du IIe millénaire av. J.-C*. Paris: Picard.

Matthiae, P. (1997). Tell Mardikh 1977–1996: vingt ans de fouilles et de découvertes—La renaissance d'Ebla amorrhéenne. *Akkadica* 101: 1–29.

—— (2002). A preliminary note on the MB I–II fortifications system at Ebla. *Damaszener Mitteilungen* 13: 29–51.

—— (2004). Le palais méridional dans la ville basse d'Ebla paléosyrienne: fouilles à Tell Mardikh (2002–2003). *Comptes rendus de l'Académie des inscriptions et belles-lettres* 2004: 301–46.

—— (2006). Un grand temple de l'époque des archives dans l'Ebla protosyrienne: fouilles à Tell Mardikh 2004–2005. *Comptes rendus de l'Académie des inscriptions et belles-lettres* 2006: 447–93.

—— (2009). Temples et reines de l'Ébla protosyrienne: résultats des fouilles à Tell Mardikh en 2007 et 2008. *Comptes rendus de l'Académie des inscriptions et belles-lettres* 2009: 747–92.

Mazzoni, S. (2005). Tell Afis (Siria), 2002–2004. *Egitto e Vicino Oriente* 28: 1–138.

Morandi Bonacossi, D. (2007). Qatna and its hinterland during the Bronze and Iron Ages: a preliminary reconstruction of urbanism and settlement in the Mishrifeh region. In D. Morandi Bonacossi (ed.), *Urban and Natural Landscapes of an Ancient Syrian Capital: Settlement and Environment at Tell Mishrifeh/Qatna and in Central-Western Syria*. Udine: Forum, 65–90.

—— (2008). The EB/MB transition at Tell Mishrifeh: stratigraphy, ceramics and absolute chronology: a preliminary review. In M. Bietak and E. Czerny (eds), *The Bronze Age in the Lebanon: Studies on the Archaeology and Chronology of Lebanon, Syria, and Egypt*. Vienna: Österreichische Akademie der Wissenschaften, 127–52.

—— (2009). Tell Mishrifeh and its region during the EBA IV and the EBA–MBA transition: a first assessment. In P. J. Parr (ed.), *The Levant in Transition: Proceedings of a Conference Held at the British Museum on 20–21 April 2004*. Leeds: Maney, 56–68.

—— M. Da Ros, G. Garna, M. Iamoni, and M. Merlino (2009). The 'Eastern Palace' and the residential architecture of Area T at Mishrifeh/Qatna: preliminary report on the 2006–2008 excavation campaigns of the Italian component of the Syro-Italian Archaeological Project. *Mesopotamia* 44: 61–112.

Nichols, J. J., and J. A. Weber (2006). Amorites, onagers, and social reorganization in Middle Bronze Age Syria. In G. M. Schwartz and J. J. Nichols (eds), *After Collapse: The Regeneration of Complex Societies*. Tucson: University of Arizona Press, 38–57.

Nicolle, C. (2002). Le céramique de l'âge du Bronze en Damascène. In M. Al-Maqdissi, V. Matoïan, and C. Nicolle (eds), *Céramique de l'Âge du Bronze en Syrie I: La Syrie du sud et la vallée de l'Oronte*. Beirut: Institut français d'archéologie du Proche-Orient, 51–64.

Nigro, L. (2002). The Middle Bronze Age pottery horizon of northern inner Syria on the basis of the stratified assemblages of Tell Mardikh and Hama. In M. Al-Maqdissi, V. Matoïan, and C. Nicolle (eds), *Céramique de l'Âge du Bronze en Syrie I: La Syrie du sud et la vallée de l'Oronte*. Beirut: Institut français d'archéologie du Proche-Orient, 97–128.

—— (2003). The smith and the king of Ebla: Tell el-Yahudiyeh Ware, metallic wares and the ceramic chronology of Middle Bronze Syria. In M. Bietak (ed.), *The Synchronisation of Civilisations in the Eastern Mediterranean in the Second Millennium B.C.: Proceedings of an International Symposium at Schloss Haindorf, 15th–17th of November 1996 and at the Austrian Academy, Vienna, 11th–12th of May 1998*, vol. 2. Vienna: Österreichische Akademie der Wissenschaften, 345–63.

Peltenburg, E. J. (2009). Enclosing the ancestors and the growth of socio-political complexity in Early Bronze Age Syria. In G. Bartoloni and M. Gilda Benedettini (eds), *Sepolti tra i vivi: evidenza ed interpretazione di contesti funerari in abitato*. Rome: Quasar, 214–48.

Pfälzner, P. (2007). Archaeological investigations in the Royal Palace of Qatna. In D. Morandi Bonacossi (ed.), *Urban and Natural Landscapes of an Ancient Syrian Capital: Settlement and Environment at Tell Mishrifeh/Qatna and in Central-Western Syria*. Udine: Forum, 29–64.

Pinnock, F. (2000). Some thoughts about the transmission of iconographies between north Syria and Cappadocia, end of the third–beginning of the second millennium BC. In P. Matthiae, A. Enea, L. Peyronel, and F. Pinnock (eds), *Proceedings of the First International Congress on the Archaeology of the Ancient Near East, Rome, May 18th–23rd 1998*. Rome: Università degli studi di Roma 'La Sapienza', Dipartimento di scienze storiche, archeologiche e antropologiche dell'antichità, 1397–1416.

—— (2005). *La ceramica del Palazzo Settentrionale del Bronzo Medio II*. Rome: Università degli Studi di Roma 'La Sapienza'.

Scandone Matthiae, G. (1979). Un oggetto faraonico della XIII dinastia dalla 'Tomba del Signore dei Capridi'. *Studi eblaiti* 1: 119–28.

Schwartz, G. M. (2006). From collapse to regeneration. In G. M. Schwartz and J. J. Nichols (eds), *After Collapse: The Regeneration of Complex Societies*. Tucson: University of Arizona Press, 3–18.

—— (2007). Taking the long view on collapse: a Syrian perspective. In C. Kuzucuoğlu and C. Marro (eds), *Sociétés humaines et changement climatique à la fin du troisième millénaire: une crise a-t-elle eu lieu en Haute Mésopotamie?* Istanbul: Institut français d'études anatoliennes Georges-Dumézil, 45–68.

—— H. H. Curvers, S. Dunham, and B. Stuart (2003). A third-millennium BC elite tomb and other new evidence from Tell Umm el-Marra, Syria. *American Journal of Archaeology* 107: 325–61.

Taraqji, A. (1999). Nouvelles découvertes sur les relations avec l'Égypte à Tell Sakka et à Keswé, dans la région de Damas. *Bulletin de la Société française d'égyptologie* 144 : 27–43.

Thalmann, J.-P. (2006). *Tell Arqa I: Les niveaux de l'âge du Bronze* (3 vols). Beirut: Institut français du Proche-Orient.

—— (2007). Settlement patterns and agriculture in the Akkar Plain during the late Early and Early Middle Bronze Ages. In D. Morandi Bonacossi (ed.), *Urban and Natural Landscapes of an Ancient Syrian Capital: Settlement and Environment at Tell Mishrifeh/Qatna and in Central-Western Syria*. Udine: Forum, 219–31.

Woolley, L. (1955). *Alalakh: An Account of the Excavations at Tell Atchana in the Hatay, 1937–1949*. Oxford: Oxford University Press.

CHAPTER 29

THE NORTHERN LEVANT (LEBANON) DURING THE MIDDLE BRONZE AGE

HANAN CHARAF

The Middle Bronze Age in Lebanon is a period of continuous development that started in the Early Bronze Age IV (EB IV). While the Beqaʿ Valley witnessed a sharp demographic recession at the end of the third millennium BC (Fig. 29.1), a phenomenon comparable to the collapse of urban culture in Palestine, the coast of Lebanon was largely unfazed by the turmoil in Syria and Palestine.

Even if some disruptive events affected Lebanese cities, such as the destruction of Byblos and Arqa, there was no dramatic lasting effect such as abandonment. Although new types of weapons, architecture, and burials were introduced in the MB I, the pottery reflects a gradual development from the EB IV. For this reason, it is somewhat difficult of speak of a new culture emerging in Lebanon at the dawn of the second millennium, as many 'older' cultural traits continued through to the Middle Bronze Age. The peaceful conditions that prevailed at this time allowed many sites, notably Arqa, Byblos, and Sidon, to flourish and develop political and economic ties with both neighbouring and remote regions. Byblos renewed ties with Egypt, which had been severed during the First Intermediate Period. As a result of these exchanges, there is a general trend of homogeneity in the Levantine Middle Bronze Age culture. Unfortunately, there is still much that we do not know about the Middle Bronze Age culture in Lebanon. This is primarily due to the paucity of excavated sites and a lack of synthesis of available data.

PERIODIZATION AND ABSOLUTE CHRONOLOGY

Based on the present state of research, the tripartite division of the Middle Bronze Age, whether the older Palestinian terminology (MB IIA, MB IIB, MB IIC) or the newly proposed one (MB I, MB II, MB III), does not fully apply to Lebanon. For this reason, some scholars working in Lebanon prefer to use their local site stratigraphy to define regional cultural periods. For example, Phase N at Tell Arqa corresponds *grosso modo* to the MB I and

FIG. 29.1 Map of Middle Bronze Age sites in the northern Levant (Lebanon)

Phase M to the MB II (Table 29.1). The Arqa system is valid for the entire plain of Akkar in northern Lebanon. Such periodizations are more accurate because they take into account local variations in the material culture. However, since the traditional tripartite system is still the only available chronological tool to identify and relate to unfamiliar periodizations, it is still encountered in the literature. Generally, a twofold division into MB I and MB II is preferred, but subdivisions are also employed. This is less so in MB I, where subdivisions are rarely used due to a lack of well-stratified MB I sequences. In MB II, the adoption of MB

Table 29.1 Comparative stratigraphy of Middle Bronze Age sites in Lebanon

Sites	Suggested relative chronology				
	MB I 2000 1800/1750				MB II 1550/1500
Tell Arqa	Level 14/Phase N				Level 13/Phase M
Mgharet al-Hourriyé	Cave tomb				
Ardé					Tombs
Tell Fadous		Tomb			
Byblos	Royal tombs/private rock-cut tombs/Temple of the Obelisks/*champs des offrandes*				Private rock-cut tombs
Sin el-Fil					Rock-cut tombs
Beirut	Fortification and Glacis Complex I/infant jar burial of Complex III/ Kharji shaft tombs 1 and 2				Monumental Gate Complex II / 'Treasure' and silo of Complex III
Sidon: College Site	Level 1	Level 2	Level 3	Level 4	Level 5
Lebe'a					Shaft tombs
Kafr Garra					Shaft tomb
Majdalouna					Shaft tomb
Ruweise	Pit child burial 14				Tombs
Tell el-Burak	Public building 'palace'				2 tombs
Sarepta					Stratum L
Tyre	Unattested in excavations				Unattested in excavations / Grave 3/ Stratum XVIII
Baalbek					3 tombs
Tell Hizzin					Tombs
Tell el-Ghassil	Level XI 1775		Level X 1650/1640	Level IX 1540	Level IX 1500
Kamed el-Loz	Building Period 8/Building Levels 22–21			Building Period 7/ Building Levels 20–17	Building Period 6/ Building Levels 16–14/ Temple 4/Palace P6

IIB and IIC is more frequent. Carbon-14 (^{14}C) dates supporting the absolute dating of the Middle Bronze Age are scarce, except for Tell Arqa, where charred wheat from the destruction of the latest EB IV settlement has helped establish the beginning of the MB I at around 2000 cal. BC. Since there was no stratigraphic break between the EB IV and the MB I, this date was also used as the *terminus post quem* for the MB I. Recent ^{14}C dates from Tell el-Burak confirm the latter date for the beginning of the MB I. The transition from the MB I to the MB II is more problematic. Carbon-14 dates from Tell Arqa place the transition from Level 14 to 13 at around 1850/1800 cal. BC, a date obtained from analysing bones from these two levels. An even lower date for the end of the MB I at around 1750 BC is also acceptable if we take into account regional correlations with Byblos.

For the time being, given the lack of archaeological evidence, we see no compelling reason to create an independent phase for the end of the Middle Bronze Age in Lebanon, as has been the case in Palestine, even though a few scholars support this idea, e.g. MB IIC (Doumet-Serhal 1995–6 for Tell el-Ghassil) or MB III (Marfoe 1995 for Kamed el-Loz). Arguments favouring such a subdivision are largely based on ceramic parallels with Palestine, possibly misrepresenting the end of the Middle Bronze Age in Lebanon. The dates assigned to the terminal Middle Bronze Age phase vary from 1560 to 1500 BC. None are supported by ^{14}C determinations, but are based instead on Egyptian chronology. Nevertheless, the dates do agree with the idea of a smooth transition into the Late Bronze Age, given the wide margin assigned to the end of the Middle Bronze Age.

SETTLEMENT PATTERNS AND POLITICAL ORGANIZATION

The few surveys carried out in the Akkar and the Beqaʿ indicate the Middle Bronze Age as one of the main periods of occupation in Lebanon, but an accurate modelling of settlement patterns is difficult to achieve for the whole country. The nature of occupation at some sites, except for Byblos, which retained its urban character, differed from the previous Early Bronze IV period. Large areas of Arqa, Sidon, and Tell el-Ghassil were converted into cemeteries during the early part of the Middle Bronze I, before transitioning into a period of uninterrupted urban development. Demographic pressures created new centres, preferably in arable zones near water sources such as springs and rivers. Surveys in the plain of Akkar show an increase in both the number and size of sites (Thalmann 2006: 215). Marshy areas in the centre of this plain, previously vacant, were now inhabited. These settlements, primarily tells, do not exceed 5ha in area for the largest ones (Bartl 1998–9: 175). This was the standard size of most Middle Bronze sites in Lebanon, and is modest in comparison to the large Syrian centres. The Akkar Plain was controlled by three small political entities, independent of one other with each probably functioning like a mini city-state (Thalmann 2002: 365; 2006: 214–15). Each of these (Arqa, Kazel, and Jamous) was fortified and controlled a network of smaller sites within a 10km radius. Following the same basic political characteristics encountered elsewhere in the Levant, the rulers must have been local notables or military men able to forge mini-states and extend their clout over a network of subservient sites. Smaller sites must have provided agricultural goods and a workforce to large centres in exchange for protection or some sort of financial reward. This type of hierarchical organization is typical of an urbanized culture and was probably the model adopted in other Lebanese areas as well. Three surveys of the Beqaʿ Valley show an increase of rural sites strategically located along the international trade route linking the Jordan Valley to inland Syria and Mesopotamia (Kuschke 1978; Marfoe 1995; Bonatz 2002). Two major sites, Kamed el-Loz and Tell Hizzin, profited from this lucrative thoroughfare. The marginal zones must have been occupied by nomads or pastoralists raising livestock. During the MB II, Byblos showed an increase in agriculture and displayed a dense habitation that spilled beyond the city ramparts, while Kamed el-Loz extended its occupational surface. Main coastal sites are recorded every 15–20km, indicating the radius of their influence. Many are established near natural bays where trading ships anchored, thus allowing them to prosper considerably. Others, situated more inland (Tell Humaira and Tell Ardé: see Salamé-Sarkis, 1972; 1973), might have used nearby rivers as additional means of circulation. All relied on the narrow plains sur-rounding them for subsistence agriculture and animal husbandry. Archaeobotanical studies around Sidon found a high percentage of olive pollen, indicating the extensive cultivation of this tree. A few sites (like Yanouh and Tadmor in the Byblos Mountains) were identified in high mountain terrain (Gatier et al. 2004: 141–9); however, their distribution does not yet permit any convincing explanation as to the type and spread of occupation in the regions where they were found. The high number of tombs found in the inland hills, especially in the south of Lebanon (Qrayé, Majdalouna, and Lebe'a: see Guigues 1937; 1938; 1939 and Chéhab 1940), hints at a dense occupation of nearby areas yet to be investigated. For reasons that are not yet fully understood, the intense settlement of Lebanon ended around the mid-dle of the second millennium. However, ripple effects from the turmoil that stirred Palestine and other regions at this time, and the decline of international trade, were probably among the major factors. Though many sites were abandoned, destroyed, or reduced in size, others like Arqa and Sidon continued to display a smooth transition from Middle Bronze to Late Bronze with minimal change in material culture.

Urban architectural traditions

The small number of excavated Middle Bronze sites severely restricts our knowledge about the various types of architecture. Urban architecture is mainly known from Byblos, where large parts of the city were uncovered in large-scale excavations conducted by M. Dunand. However, his controversial method of horizontal excavation in arbitrary 20cm increments has obscured our understanding of the city's development. Certainly, one of the most important building achievements of the Middle Bronze is the defensive system. The forti-fications at Byblos consisted of massive ramparts made of stone foundations, mud-brick superstructures, and watchtowers (Dunand 1954: pl. 212; 1963: 25). The MB II rampart at Beirut is particularly well preserved, with its limestone foundations preserved to a height of 12m and reinforced at regular intervals with engaged pillars (Badre 1997: 28–30). MB II ramparts at Kamed el-Loz and Arqa share the same layout, with a series of connecting rectangular rooms displaying a saw-edge profile and intermittent watchtowers (respectively, Marfoe 1995: 104; Thalmann 2006: 56). The glacis, introduced during the MB I in Beirut (Badre 1997: 23; 2001–2: 3) and Byblos, is also employed during the MB II (Byblos and pos-sibly Beirut with Glacis I). City gates were also fortified. The gate at Beirut, probably dating to the MB II, had a bent axis *en chicane* to help prevent direct attacks. Two corridor sea gates at Byblos from the MB I had stepped ramps to assist charioteers. Monumental defensive constructions required both tremendous effort and vast means to be built: only a strong central power had the financial means to carry them out. On the other hand, the increase in wealth and power of the Middle Bronze cities made them lucrative prey and pushed them into protecting their assets.

Few Lebanese sites offer examples of domestic architecture, making it impossible to draw any comprehensive conclusions that can be applied to the entire country. Byblos has large domestic rectangular buildings from the MB I. These lacked interior partition walls and were dispersed inside the city without any detectable urban pattern. With the flourish-ing of the MB II civilization came better-built houses with stone channels running under houses and courtyards laid with flagstone pavements. Basalt grinders and ovens indicate household activities such as wheat crushing and cooking. Bottle-shaped silos such as at Arqa (Thalmann 2007) were used for cereal storage. It is not clear if these chores were executed by the female members of the household. To the end of the MB II belongs a building at Sidon of which one room is excavated and constructed with carefully hewn stones and olive trees (*Olea europaea*) wood. Olive, oak (*Quercus sp. deciduous*), and strawberry trees were largely used as structural timber in the regions of Sidon (Marriner, de Beaulieu, and Morhange 2004; Asouti and Griffiths 2003) and Tyre due to a shortage of expensive cedar tree which does not grow at this latitude. The Tell el-Burak excavations recently uncovered a large, well-preserved mud-brick building established on an artificial mound (15m high and 100×120m wide). The mound was built from piles of stones retained by mud-brick walls. This structure, identified as a palace or an administrative building by the excavators (Kamlah and Sader 2003: 166) and dated to the MB I, has a rectangular shape with each of the four corners occupied by a square tower (Fig. 29.2). The floor plan displays a central courtyard, a kitchen, and several rooms. Room 10 contained frescoed wall paintings, the first to appear in a Middle Bronze Age site in Lebanon (Sader and Kamlah 2010: 137). The excavators believe that this free-standing structure, unlinked to any surrounding settlement, was commissioned by the

FIG. 29.2 Monumental building/'Palace' at Tell el-Burak (map courtesy of the German-Lebanese Excavation Project)

king of Sidon, who controlled the region. Excavations of an area overlooking the ancient harbour on the tell of Beirut yielded a large courtyard covered with plaster that must have belonged to a public building (perhaps a palace or a temple, as advocated by the excavator: Badre 2000: 35–9; 2001–2: 5–9; 2009: 253–8). Unfortunately, the dig was stopped before the rest of the building was investigated.

CULT

Temple and shrines

Cultic constructions are rare with the exception of Byblos, which houses the largest concentration of Middle Bronze Age temples in Lebanon. The best-preserved MB I sanctuary is the Temple of the Obelisks built over the remains of an older temple destroyed by fire at the end of the third millennium BC (Fig. 29.3). It is built on a podium and is surrounded by a courtyard.

The temple had a roof supported by pillars made from cedar, although pine was also used according to an inscription found on a stele. The Temple of the Obelisks has a tripartite plan that originated in Syria with a *cella* and a *pro-cella*. The *cella* contains a large hewn stone symbolizing the deity. The *pro-cella* has two antechambers equipped with several niches for offerings. Several cultic deposits were found buried under the floors. The courtyard contained a sacrificial area as well as dozens of standing stones or obelisks, including one bearing a hieroglyphic inscription dedicated by the seal-bearer of King Abishemou, beloved of Herishef-Rê (Dunand 1937–9: pl. 22). This Middle Kingdom-era Egyptian god could be the

FIG. 29.3 Temple of the Obelisks at Byblos (photo courtesy of Robert Mullins)

deity to whom this temple was dedicated. A workshop, identified by Dunand as a jewellery workshop, sat adjacent to the temple and probably specialized in crafts sold as votive offerings to pilgrims. Eight deposits totalling 1,306 *ex voto* offerings were recovered from the temple. These included faience figurines, metal weapons, and dozens of gilded bronze male figurines that have become the 'poster child' of the Ministry of Tourism of Lebanon. Inscriptions and several offering deposits indicate that the Temple of Baalat-Gebal built during the Early Bronze Age was still in use in the Middle Bronze Age. Besides Byblos, Kamed el-Loz is the only other site that has yielded MB II temple remains, but we lack a clear floor plan, since it was only partially uncovered.

Burial customs

Dozens of Middle Bronze Age tombs have been unearthed throughout Lebanon, most only summarily published or not at all. Moreover, the focus was primarily on the grave goods, leading to a general neglect of vital anthropological, faunal, and floral information. While Early Bronze Age tomb types (rock-cut chambers or jar burials) continue in use, the Middle Bronze Age saw an emergence of four new types: the shaft tomb, the earthen pit, the cist burial, and the built tomb (Genz and Sader 2007–8: 263–73). Their distribution shows that shaft and rock-cut tombs are absent from the Beqa' Valley, probably due to the lack of rock outcrops in this alluvial plain. Usually, rock-cut and shaft tombs are predominant outside the settlement while pit, cist, and jar burials are more common inside. Most of the latter were located under courtyards or open spaces (e.g. at Sidon and Sarepta (see Anderson 1988: 59–62), at Kamed el-Loz (see Hachmann 1969), and at Tyre (see Bikai 1978: 6)), but a few were found under room floors (Kamed el-Loz and Arqa). Adults were generally placed in rock-cut, shaft and built tombs, and earthen pits. Infants and children were usually laid in household storage jars intentionally broken and recycled as coffins. Some exceptions do occur. At Kamed el-Loz, the majority of children and infants were not buried in jars, and at Tell Arqa and Sidon (Doumet-Serhal 2010: 120), large storage jars were used as receptacles for adult burials. Body positions inside a grave vary, but infants and children are usually buried in a foetal position. There appears to be no preferred orientation for the tombs. The exception to inhumation as a burial practice during the Middle Bronze Age is Mgharet al-Hourriyé, where there is some evidence of cremation (Beayno, Mattar, and Abdul-Nour 2002: 144). The published forensic data does not point to any attempt at body preservation such as embalming or mummification, but the presence of pins and needles, generally in adult tombs, indicate that the dead were shrouded in a cloth. Burials are overwhelmingly primary, with one possible secondary internment at Tell el-Ghassil (Tomb 1) (Badre 1982). While more accurate investigations of anthropological remains are needed to assess the practice of secondary burial, both single and multiple successive burials are attested in all types of tomb. Generally, jar burials are single while rock-cut and shaft tombs are multiple. Tombs with multiple burials (as at Sidon, Doumet-Serhal 2001: 170) are thought to be familial or communal, though it is impossible to prove this theory. Generally, the burials contained funerary goods (pottery, jewellery, weapons, scarabs, and cosmetic boxes) that were locally made or imported from Egypt, Crete, or Cyprus. For the Middle Bronze tombs at Kamed el-Loz, Miron (1982) used the presence (or absence) of offerings, their number, and their quality to speculate on the social status of the deceased. At Arqa, except for one burial, all the other tombs contained a standardized funeral kit composed of globular pots, juglets, and platters. This led the excavator, J.-P. Thalmann (2006: 67), to regard these vessels as utilitarian *par excellence*, used as food containers rather than expressions of social differences. If so, then this might hint at belief in an afterlife. Indeed, animal bones (sheep, goat, cow, pig, and fish) found in some burials at Byblos, Sidon, Ruweise, Kamed el-Loz, and Arqa indicate food offerings. Portions and heads of sacrificed animals were found in at least eight tombs at Sidon (Doumet-Serhal 2004d: 19) and in four tombs at Arqa (Thalmann 2006: 65–7). A stele from Byblos lists the different foods (bread, beer, beef, and fowl) offered during the funerary repast. Animal bones mixed with human remains in Royal Tomb I at Byblos could suggest animal offerings or maybe ritual sacrifices in connection with the funeral. Ovens (*tannours*) and a mud-brick channel associated with burials at Sidon suggest funerary banquets for the dead (Doumet-Serhal 2002: 187; 2006b: 143–4; 2009: 241; 2010). Unfortunately, few published excavations (with the exception of Sidon) include studies of faunal remains; any general thesis concerning animal sacrifices or associated rituals is therefore speculative at best. Indeed, a study based on one site cannot be generalized to a region or to all of Lebanon.

Byblos is the only site where royal tombs were found (Dunand 1963: 66–9; Montet 1928; Virolleaud 1922). Eight shaft tombs dug into the rock contained the remains of local princes who lived during the reigns of the Egyptian pharaohs, Amenemhat III and IV, of the 12th Dynasty (Tombs I–IV) and the Hyksos period (Tombs VI–IX). The square or rectangular vertical shafts led to the funerary chambers, some of which had stone walls and floor paving. The bodies were buried in wood or stone coffins surrounded by opulent offerings, many of which were gifts from Egyptian royalty (Montet 1928: 155–238; Tufnell 1969). While the so-called Warrior Tomb at Arqa contained remains of a wood coffin (Thalmann 2006: 34), Byblos is the only site that has yielded evidence of stone coffins (Tombs I and IV, and possibly Tomb II). A number of Lebanese sites (Arqa, Sin el-Fil, Beirut, Lebe'a, and Sidon) contained tombs designated as warrior tombs because of the types of metal weapons they contained: duckbill axes, spears and arrowheads, and daggers and knives (Thalmann 2000: 50–54; Doumet-Serhal 2003a; 2004a; 2004b; 2008a: 10–11; 2008b: 19–41; Saidah 1993–4: 186–205). These types of tombs were widespread in the Levant during the MB I, with other examples found in Syria, Palestine, and Egypt.

MATERIAL CULTURE

Pottery is one of the few tools available to trace the evolution of the Middle Bronze material culture and to discern differences in regional developments. Piriform, cylindrical, and dipper juglets, so-called Canaanite jars, flaring carinated bowls, and radially burnished plates with in-turned rims are some of the popular productions found all over the Levant (Thalmann 2000: 55, 62). There are, however, clear technological traits, some unparalleled in Palestine, continuing from the previous EB IV period, like the use of the fast wheel. In most cases the Middle Bronze pottery is fine; it is frequently slipped and vertically burnished. But there are also regional variations: while Arqa's pottery is very fine and exceptionally well made, that of Byblos is rather crude. Paint is rarely used except on MB I jugs or jars imitating Cilician or Khabur wares. The corpus of MB I pottery comes essentially from Byblos, Arqa, Sidon, and Mgharet al-Hourriyé. It includes elongated jars with flat bases and tall necks, ovoid jugs with trefoil or cutaway mouths, dipper juglets with stepped rims, platters with flat bases and in-turned rims, and carinated small bowls (Thalmann 2002). Shoulders of large open kraters and jars are frequently incised with horizontal and wavy lines, a decoration influenced by Syrian designs. MB II ceramics contain globular or carinated bowls, large kraters with ledge rims and three incised lines on the shoulder, dipper juglets with button bases and double handles, ovoid jars, and red slipped jugs and bowls (Doumet-Serhal 2004d: 138–44; 2008a: 13; Thalmann 1998: 65–6). Cooking pots have a rounded body and a series of incised lines on the shoulder, a technique that appeared timidly at the end of the MB I. Flat-based cooking pots, very popular on Palestinian sites but relatively rare in Lebanon, appear at Tell Fadous (Genz 2010: 111) on the coast and Tell el-Ghassil in the Beqa'.

Tell Arqa has yielded an entire MB I potters' quarter with a decantation pit, firing structures, and kilns (Fig. 29.4). The firing pits were circular in shape and built of mud-brick (Thalmann 2000: 48–9). Jars were piled in an upright position, while smaller pots like carinated bowls or jugs were inserted in the empty spaces between the jars. Horseshoe-shaped kilns were used for firing medium-size pottery. There is no hint as to the gender of the potters.

Metalworking flourished during the Middle Bronze Age and was largely influenced by Egyptian and Syrian art. The tombs of Byblos offer a rich repertoire of metal objects (pectorals, teapots, and weapons) fabricated by local artisans who took liberties when adopting the Egyptian style. Tombs at Sidon which might have been involved in silver trade brought from the Taurus Mountains (Doumet-Serhal 2008a: 12) revealed an extensive use of silver (headbands, bracelets, and anklets) and bronze (rings and belts) adorning the deceased (Fig. 29.5). Weaponry underwent a radical change during the Middle Bronze Age with the introduction of new arms such as duckbill axes and socketed spearheads, copied from Mesopotamian and Syrian prototypes and mostly crafted in bronze and found in tombs or in temples (Gernez 2007; 2009). The duckbill or fenestrated axehead, introduced in the MB I, appears in tombs at Arqa (Thalmann 2010: 98), Byblos, Sidon (Doumet-Serhal 2003b: 180), and Baalbek and in deposits from the Temple of the Obelisks. During the MB II, Anatolian-style spearheads and socketed javelins appeared.

Other art productions such as metal figurines, toggle pins, cylinder seals, and ivory inlays were very popular in the Middle Bronze Age. Craft activities such as dyeing and weaving are yet to be documented archaeologically in this period. But a house uncovered at Arqa and dated to the MB II had three rectangular mud-brick plastered basins associated with a yet-unidentified craft activity (Thalmann 2006: 57).

TRADE AND INTERNATIONAL RELATIONS

Thanks to the stable political conditions, trade flourished during the Middle Bronze Age. All the coastal cities established reliable and active trade networks, as evidenced by findings at sites. They specialized in exporting sought-after goods such as olive oil, wine, and wood (a recent tablet from Sidon lists an inventory of wood) and importing foreign commodities (copper from Cyprus; fish, wheat, and gems from Egypt) for local consumption or resale. Contacts with northern Syria and eastern Turkey affected many aspects of material culture, especially architecture, ceramics, and metallurgy, and contributed to a relatively homogenized culture throughout the Levant. The abundance of silver objects in Sidon's

FIG. 29.4 Firing pit from Tell Arqa, Level 14 (photo and reconstruction of the structure courtesy of Jean-Paul Thalmann)

burials indicates intense trade with Anatolia and especially the Taurus Mountains where the ores originated (Véron and Le Roux 2004: Doumet-Serhal 2004c: 24, 28). Some of the bronze artefacts found in those burials were made with alloys imported from Cyprus and the Aegean (Véron, Poirier, and Le Roux 2009: 72). Many of the tombs found contained imported grave goods from Egypt, Crete, and Cyprus. Tomb I of the royal necropolis of

FIG. 29.5   Sidon, British Museum excavations. A grave of a young individual with pottery vessels and two silver rings in the left hand (photo courtesy Claude Doumet-Serhal)

Byblos contained an obsidian and gold vase inscribed with the throne name of the Egyptian pharaoh, Amenemhat III. Tomb II yielded another obsidian vase inscribed with the name of Amenemhat IV. Other tombs at Byblos (Baramki 1973: pl. IV:1), Beirut (Saidah 1993–4: 164–5), and Sidon (MacGillivray 2003) contained ceramic pots of Minoan Kamarès Ware. Sidon enjoyed active relationships with Egypt, as signified by more than 79 Egyptian jars and numerous scarabs (Doumet-Serhal 2008a: 20–23) found in tombs, while Byblos entertained exclusive relations with the superpower, as evidenced by the hundreds of objects (Montet 1928) and inscriptions found on the site. Egyptian scarabs were found also in numerous other tombs across Lebanon (e.g. at Ruweise (Tufnell 1975–6: 19) and Sin el-Fil (Chéhab 1939)). Petrographic analysis determined that pottery from Arqa was sent to Tell el-Dabʿa in Egypt (Forstner-Müller and Kopetzky 2009: 149). The pottery imported from Cyprus appears during the MB II, but its distribution shows it frequent in coastal sites but absent from sites in the Beqaʿ. Sidon and Arqa have yielded hundreds of Middle Cypriot imports (Charaf 2009). By contrast, Chocolate-on-White Ware produced in the Jordan Valley is present at Tell el-Ghassil (Doumet-Serhal 1996: 296) and Kamed el-Loz but is completely absent from coastal sites. Another hallmark import of the MB II is Tell el-Yehudiyeh Ware, found in small quantities at practically all Middle Bronze Age sites in Lebanon, but with Arqa (Charaf 2009), Byblos, and Sidon yielding the largest quantities. Evidence of local Levantine trade is found especially during the MB I with the occurrence of Palestinian Red, White, and Blue Ware (Doumet-Serhal 2006a: 43) and Syrian Levantine Painted Ware at Sidon (Bagh 2004) and Arqa.

TEXTUAL SOURCES

In contrast to Egypt, Mesopotamia, and eastern Syria, textual sources from Lebanon are rare, and this has hindered our understanding of many socioeconomic aspects of Middle

Bronze Age culture. What little we do know about customs is usually drawn from nearby regions such as Syria. The local population must have spoken a West Semitic language, but the diplomatic correspondence would have been conducted in Akkadian, the *lingua franca* of the Levant during the Middle Bronze Age. During the MB II, a new script was invented in Byblos which followed a graphic syllabic system of about 100 signs, some inspired by hieroglyphics. The Byblos syllabary, engraved on bronze plates and spatulas, was published by Dunand (1945), but remains undeciphered.

The few other inscriptions found in Lebanon are all written in hieroglyphics (Dunand 1937–9; Montet 1964). An inscription on a scarab found in MB II levels at Sidon mentions the city of *'Iay*, thought to be located in the Beqa' Valley (Loffet 2006). Even though the Byblos kings had Semitic names, they used the title *Haty-a* ('count') which was only conferred by the pharaoh. This clearly demonstrates the close ties between Byblos and Egypt during the 12th Dynasty. Two hieroglyphic inscriptions mentioning Byblian 'counts' were found at the site itself: one which refers to Count *Abishemou-Abi*, son of Count *Abishemou*, and the other to Count *Inten*, son of Count *Reyen* (Pritchard 1969: 229). A ruler of Byblos by the name of *Yantin-Hamu* is mentioned in a text found in the palace of Zimri-Lim, king of Mari. Assuming that *Inten* and *Yantin-Hamu* are the same person (Albright 1965), Lebanon has one of the earliest synchronisms between Egypt, Mesopotamia, and the Levant.

Ancient Lebanese cities are also mentioned in ancient texts. In the *Story of Sinuhe*, an Egyptian exile settles in an unidentified land called Yaa located east of Byblos, possibly the Beqa' Valley. He describes the daily rural life of this city rich in figs, grapes, olives, wine, milk, and honey. Several other cities (Arqa, Byblos, Ullaza, and Tyre) are mentioned in the Execration Texts of the 19th and 18th centuries BC.

SUGGESTED READING

Badre, L. (2000). Recently discovered Bronze Age temples: Middle Bronze Beirut and Late Bronze Tell Kazel. In P. Matthiae, A. Enea, L. Peyronel, and F. Pinnock (eds), *Proceedings of the First International Congress on the Archaeology of Ancient Near East, Rome, May 18th–23rd 1998*, vol. 1. Rome: Università degli Studi di Roma 'La Sapienza', Dipartimento di scienze storiche, archeologiche e antropologiche dell'antichità, 35–54.

Bagh, T. (2004). Levantine Painted Ware from the Middle Bronze Age tombs at Sidon: new material from the Lebanese coast. *Archaeology and History in Lebanon* 20: 40–57.

Doumet-Serhal, C. (2003). Weapons from the Middle Bronze Age burials at Sidon. *Archaeology and History in Lebanon* 18: 38–57.

Dunand, M. (1963). *Byblos, son histoire, ses ruines, ses légendes*. Beirut: Imprimerie Catholique.

Genz, H., and H. Sader (2007–8). Bronze Age funerary practices in Lebanon. *Archaeology and History in Lebanon* 26–27: 258–83.

Pritchard, J. B. (1969). *Ancient Near Eastern Texts Relating to the Old Testament*, 3rd edn. Princeton, NJ: Princeton University Press.

Thalmann, J.-P. (1998). Le Liban à l'âge du Bronze, du village à la cité-état. In *Liban, l'autre rive: exposition présentée à l'Institut du monde arabe du 27 octobre au 2 mai 1999*. Paris: Flammarion, 50–9.

References

Albright, W. F. (1965). Further light on the history of Middle-Bronze Byblos. *Bulletin of the American Schools of Oriental Research* 179: 38–43.

Anderson, W. P. (1988). *Sarepta I: The Late Bronze and Iron Age Strata of Area II, Y.* Beirut: Publications de l'Université Libanaise.

Asouti, E., and D. R. Griffiths. (2003). Identification of the wood used in the construction of the 'sunken room' at Sidon. *Archaeology and History in Lebanon* 18: 62–9.

Badre, L. (1982). Tell el-Ghassil: Tomb I. In *Archéologie au Levant: recueil à la mémoire de Roger Saidah*. Lyon: Maison de l'Orient Méditerranéen, 123–32.

—— (1997). Bey 003 preliminary report: excavations of the American University of Beirut Museum 1993–1996. *Bulletin d'archéologie et d'architecture libanaises* 2: 6–94.

—— (2000). Recently discovered Bronze Age temples: Middle Bronze Beirut and Late Bronze Tell Kazel. In P. Matthiae, A. Enea, L. Peyronel, and F. Pinnock (eds), *Proceedings of the First International Congress on the Archaeology of Ancient Near East, Rome, May 18th–23rd 1998*, vol. 1. Rome: Università degli Studi di Roma 'La Sapienza', Dipartimento di scienze storiche, archeologiche e antropologiche dell'antichità, 34–54.

—— (2001–2). The Bronze Age at Beirut: major results. *Aram* 13: 1–26.

—— (2009). The religious architecture in the Bronze Age: Middle Bronze Beirut and Late Bronze Tell Kazel. *Bulletin d'archéologie et d'architecture libanaises*, hors-série 6: 253–70.

Bagh, T. (2004). Levantine Painted Ware from the Middle Bronze Age tombs at Sidon: new material from the Lebanese coast. *Archaeology and History in Lebanon* 20: 40–57.

Baramki, D. C. (1973). A tomb of the Early and Middle Bronze Age at Byblos. *Bulletin du Musée de Beyrouth* 26: 27–30.

Bartl, K. (1998–9). Akkar Survey 1997: archaeological surface investigations in the Plain of Akkar/northern Lebanon. Preliminary results. *Bulletin d'archéologie et d'architecture libanaises* 3: 169–79.

Beayno, F., C. Mattar, and H. Abdul-Nour (2002). Mgharet al-Hourriyé (Karm Saddé, Caza de Zgharta): rapport préliminaire de la fouille de 2001. *Bulletin d'archéologie et d'architecture libanaises* 6: 135–78.

Bikai, P. M. (1978). *The Pottery of Tyre*. Warminster: Aris & Phillips.

Bonatz, D. (2002). Preliminary remarks on an archaeological survey in the Anti-Lebanon. *Bulletin d'archéologie et d'architecture libanaises* 6: 283–307.

Charaf, H. (2009). Arqa and its regional connections redux. *Bulletin d'archéologie et d'architecture libanaises*, hors-série 6: 295–310.

Chéhab, M. H. (1939). Tombe phénicienne de Sin el-Fil. In *Mélanges offerts à Monsieur René Dussaud*, vol. 2. Paris: Geuthner, 803–10.

—— (1940). Les tombes phéniciennes: Majdalouna. *Bulletin du Musée de Beyrouth* 4: 37–53.

Doumet-Serhal, C. (1995–6). Le Bronze Moyen IIB/C et le Bronze Récent I au Liban: l'évidence de Tell el-Ghassil. *Berytus* 42: 37–70.

—— (1996). *Les fouilles de Tell el-Ghassil de 1972 à 1974: étude du matériel*. Beirut: Institut français d'archéologie du Proche-Orient.

—— (2001). Third season of excavation at Sidon: preliminary report. *Bulletin d'archéologie et d'architecture libanaises* 5: 153–72.

—— (2002). Fourth season of excavation at Sidon: preliminary report. *Bulletin d'archéologie et d'architecture libanaises* 6: 179–210.

—— (2003a). Weapons from the Middle Bronze Age burials at Sidon. *Archaeology and History in Lebanon* 18: 38–57.

—— (2003b). Fifth season of excavation at Sidon: preliminary report. *Bulletin d'archéologie et d'architecture libanaises* 7: 175–207.

—— (2004a). Sidon (Lebanon): twenty Middle Bronze Age burials from the 2001 season of excavation. *Levant* 36: 89–154.

—— (2004b). Sixth and seventh seasons of excavation at Sidon: preliminary report. *Bulletin d'archéologie et d'architecture libanaises* 8: 47–82.

—— (2004c). Warrior Burial 27 at Sidon. *Archaeology and History in Lebanon* 20: 21–9.

—— (ed.) (2004d), in collaboration with A. Rabate and A. Resek. *Decade: A Decade of Archaeology and History in the Lebanon*. Beirut: Lebanese British Friends of the National Museum.

—— (2006a). Sidon: Mediterranean contacts in the Early and Middle Bronze Age: preliminary report. *Archaeology and History in Lebanon* 24: 34–47.

—— (2006b). Eighth and ninth season of excavation (2006–2007) at Sidon: preliminary report. *Bulletin d'archéologie et d'architecture libanaises*, 10: 131–68.

—— (2008a). The Kingdom of Sidon and its Mediterranean connections. In C. Doumet-Serhal (ed.), in collaboration with Anne Rebate and Andrea Resek, *Networking Patterns of the Bronze and Iron Age Levant: The Lebanon and Its Mediterranean Connections*. London: Lebanese British Friends of the National Museum, 1–70.

—— (2008b). The British Museum excavation at Sidon: markers for the chronology of the Early and Middle Bronze Age in Lebanon. In M. Bietak and E. Czerny (eds), *The Bronze Age in the Lebanon: Studies on the Archaeology and Chronology of Lebanon, Syria, and Egypt*. Vienna: Österreichische Akademie der Wissenschaften, 11–44.

—— (2009). Second millennium BC Levantine ceremonial feasts: Sidon, a case study. *Bulletin d'archéologie et d'architecture libanaises*, hors-série 6: 229–44.

—— (2010). Sidon during the Bronze Age: burials, rituals and feasting grounds at the College Site. *Near Eastern Archaeology* 73: 114–29.

Dunand, M. (1937–9). *Fouilles de Byblos*, vol. 1: *1926–1932* (2 vols). Paris: Geuthner.

—— (1945). *Byblia Grammata: documents et recherches sur le développement de l'écriture en Phénicie*. Beirut: République Libanaise, Ministère de l'Éducation National des Beaux-Arts.

—— (1954). *Fouilles de Byblos*, vol. 2: *1933–1938*. Paris: Maisonneuve.

—— (1963). *Byblos, son histoire, ses ruines, ses légendes*. Beirut: Imprimerie Catholique.

Forstner-Müller, I., and K. Kopetzky (2009). Egypt and Lebanon: new evidence for cultural exchanges in the first half of the 2nd millennium B.C. *Bulletin d'archéologie et d'architecture libanaises*, hors-série 6: 143–57.

Gatier, P.-L., C. Atallah, J.-S. Caillou, et al. (2004). Mission de Yanouh et de la haute vallée du Nahr Ibrahim: rapport préliminaire 2003–2004. *Bulletin d'archéologie et d'architecture libanaises* 8: 119–210.

Genz, H. (2010). Recent excavations at Tell Fadous-Kfarabida. *Near Eastern Archaeology* 73: 102–13.

—— and H. Sader (2007–8). Bronze Age funerary practices in Lebanon. *Archaeology and History in Lebanon* 26–27: 258–83.

Gernez, G. (2007). *L'armement en métal au Proche-Orient et Moyen-Orient: des origines à 1750 av. J.-C.* PhD dissertation, University of Paris I.

—— (2009). La place de l'armement levantin en Méditerranée orientale : influences, dynamiques et échanges au Bronze Ancien et Moyen (3300–1600 av. J.-C.). *Bulletin d'archéologie et d'architecture libanaises*, hors-série 6: 271–84.

Guigues, P.-É. (1937). Lébé'a, Kafer Garra, Qrayé: nécropoles de la région sidonienne. *Bulletin du Musée de Beyrouth* 1: 35–76.

—— (1938). Lébé'a, Kafer Garra, Qrayé: nécropoles de la région sidonienne (suite). *Bulletin du Musée de Beyrouth* 2: 27–72.

—— (1939). Lébé'a, Kafer Garra, Qrayé: nécropoles de la région sidonienne (fin). *Bulletin du Musée de Beyrouth* 3: 53–63.

Hachmann, R. (1969). Le cimetière de l'âge du Bronze Moyen sur la pente nord du Tell. *Bulletin du Musée de Beyrouth* 22: 77–84.

Kamlah, J., and H. Sader (2003). The Tell el-Burak Archaeological Project: preliminary report on the 2002 and 2003 seasons. *Bulletin d'archéologie et d'architecture libanaises* 7: 145–73.

Kuschke, A. (1978). Preliminary remarks on an archaeological survey in the northern Biqa. *Bulletin du Musée de Beyrouth* 30: 43–5.

Loffet, H. C. (2006). The Sidon Scaraboid S/3487. *Archaeology and History in Lebanon* 24: 78–85.

MacGillivray, J. A. (2003). A Middle Minoan Cup from Sidon. *Archaeology and History in Lebanon* 18: 20–4.

Marfoe, L. (1995). *Kamid el-Loz 13: The Prehistoric and Early Historic Context of the Site*, rev. and enlarged by R. Hachmann and C. Misamer. Bonn: Habelt.

Marriner, N., J.-L. de Beaulieu, and C. Morhange (2004). Note on the vegetation landscapes of Sidon and Tyre during antiquity. *Archaeology and History in Lebanon* 19: 86–91.

Miron, R. (1982). Die mittelbronzezeitlichen Gräber am Nordhang des Tells. In R. Hachmann (ed.), *Bericht über die Ergebnisse der Ausgrabungen in Kamid el-Loz in den Jahren 1971 bis 1974*. Bonn: Habelt, 101–21.

Montet, P. (1928). *Byblos et l'Égypte: quatre campagnes de fouilles à Gebeil, 1921–1922–1923–1924*. Paris: Geuthner.

—— (1964). Quatre nouvelles inscriptions hiéroglyphiques retrouvées à Byblos. *Kêmi* 17: 61–8.

Pritchard, J. B. (1969). *Ancient Near Eastern Texts Relating to the Old Testament*, 3rd edn. Princeton, NJ: Princeton University Press.

Sader, H., and J. Kamlah (2010). Tell el-Burak: a New Middle Bronze Age site from Lebanon. *Near Eastern Archaeology* 73: 130–41.

Saidah, R. (1993–4). Beirut in the Bronze Age: the Kharji tombs. *Berytus* 41: 137–210.

Salamé-Sarkis, H. (1972). Ardata-Ardé dans le Liban-Nord: une nouvelle cité cananéenne identifiée. *Mélanges de l'Université Saint-Joseph* 47: 123–45.

—— (1973). Chronique archéologique du Liban-Nord, II: 1973–1974. *Bulletin du Musée de Beyrouth* 26: 91–102.

Thalmann, J.-P. (1998). Le Liban à l'âge du Bronze: du village à la cité-état. In *Liban, l'autre rive: exposition présentée à l'Institut du monde arabe du 27 octobre au 2 mai 1999*. Paris: Flammarion, 50–9.

—— (2000). Tell Arqa. *Bulletin d'archéologie et d'architecture libanaises* 4: 5–74.

—— (2002). Pottery of the Early Middle Bronze Age at Tell Arqa and in the northern Levant. In M. Bietak (ed.), *The Middle Bronze Age in the Levant: Proceedings of an International Conference on MB IIA Ceramic Material, Vienna, 24th–26th of January 2001*. Vienna: Österreichische Akademie der Wissenschaften, 363–77.

—— (2006). *Tell Arqa-I: les niveaux de l'âge du Bronze* (2 vols). Beirut: Institut français d'archéologie du Proche-Orient.

—— (2007). Settlement patterns and agriculture in the Akkar Plain during the Late Early and Early Middle Bronze Ages. In D. Morandi Bonacossi (ed.), *Urban and Natural Landscapes of an Ancient Syrian Capital: Settlement and Environment at Tell Mishrifeh/Qatna and in Central-Western Syria.* Udine: Forum, 219–32.

—— (2010). Tell Arqa: a prosperous city during the Bronze Age. *Near Eastern Archaeology* 73: 86–101.

Tufnell, O. (1969). The pottery from royal tombs I–III at Byblos. *Berytus* 18: 5–33.

—— (1975–6). Tomb 66 at Ruweise, near Sidon. *Berytus* 24: 5–25.

Véron, A., and G. Le Roux (2004). Provenance of silver artefacts from Burial 27 at Sidon. *Archaeology and History in Lebanon* 20: 34–8.

—— G. A. Poirier and G. LeRoux (2009). Lead isotopes reveal the origin of Middle Bronze Age artefacts found in Sidon (Burial 42). *Archaeology and History in Lebanon* 29: 68–74.

Virolleaud, C. (1922). Découverte à Byblos d'une hypogée de la XIIe dynastie égyptienne. *Syria* 3: 273–90.

....

CHAPTER 30

THE SOUTHERN LEVANT (CISJORDAN) DURING THE MIDDLE BRONZE AGE

....

SUSAN L. COHEN

INTRODUCTION

....

The Middle Bronze Age in Canaan (*c.*1950/25–1550 BCE) stands as one of the formative eras in the history of the southern Levant. In particular, the Middle Bronze Age is traditionally hailed as a period of re-urbanization, during which, after a hiatus of almost three centuries, large urban sites, situated predominately along the coastal plans and on significant trade and communication routes, once more developed in the region. An intensification of settlement accompanied this urbanization throughout the region, as well as increased participation in international trade, technological progression, and innovation, marked by changes in metal and ceramic production and technologies and the development of more complex mortuary rites, all of which become notable as the hallmark of urban expression in the southern Levant.

Through the examination of the settlement patterns, site development, architecture, and material culture of the Middle Bronze Age of Israel/Palestine (hereafter referred to as Canaan), this chapter will attempt to integrate these forces for the development and progression of Canaanite Middle Bronze Age culture, with attention to the political, social, and economic systems that help define it. These developments within Canaanite society, together with those outside influences that act upon it, define the society and ultimately influence the production of the material remains; the material remains do not create the culture itself. To elucidate the development of the Middle Bronze Age in Canaan, therefore, this chapter will consider processes of urbanization, standardization, continuation, innovation, and progression as they are represented by different elements in the archaeological record.

THEORETICAL APPROACHES

....

Past approaches to the examination of Canaanite Middle Bronze Age society, influenced by the view of the Middle Bronze Age as one of rapid urbanization marked by new expressions of material culture with little or no connection to the preceding Intermediate Bronze Age, focused almost entirely on positing the exogenous origins of the era and its reliance on cultural and societal direction from regions outside Canaan, in particular the Bronze Age cultures in the northern Levant. These earliest models also tended towards the mono-causal, in which evidence for cultural change and societal development were subsumed under sweeping theories of population change. Known as the 'Amorite Hypothesis' (e.g. Kenyon 1966; Dever 1976), the model posited vast influxes of new ethnic groups into Canaan, bringing with them all the elements of the new culture identified in the region. Thus, the rise of cities, new ceramic typologies, metal technologies, and all other attributes of societal and cultural development progression and change could be subsumed under the simplistic correlation that pots equal people and, by extension, that cultural development equals population movements.

An important corollary to this view was the emphasis on the primacy of exogenous factors in the cultural development of the Middle Bronze Age. While scholars eventually recognized the sweeping assumption of vast population changes as too all-encompassing, newer models also concentrated on the means by which ideas, products, technologies, and other aspects of cultural change could be transmitted through external agencies to the region. As such, interpretations of the Middle Bronze Age that emphasized the importance of international trade (e.g. Gerstenblith 1983) received considerable attention in outlining social, cultural, and political developments. The ensuing progression of Middle Bronze Age culture was thus firmly grounded in explanations highlighting external factors that resulted in the implementation of an urban landscape, complete with all the trappings of urbanized society, in Canaan early in the second millennium BCE. This focus on external stimuli, however, while illuminating in regard to cultural connections within the greater region of the eastern Mediterranean world, also reduced the entire Middle Bronze Age culture of Canaan to a smaller and lesser version of societies elsewhere in the Levant, and obscured or diminished its own developments, trajectories, and unique formative paths, which ultimately gave rise to a powerful and independent urbanized specific Canaanite cultural entity.

Continued excavation and analysis, however, provided evidence to offset this predominately exogenous focus, and revealed an integrated pattern of site formation, interaction, innovation, and progression that combine to illustrate the existence of a complex culture that may clearly be identified as uniquely Canaanite, and not simply a shadow of larger and more advanced neighbours. Evidence regarding rural organization, continuity between the Middle Bronze Age and the preceding Intermediate Bronze Age, and above all, theoretical and methodological concerns regarding the validity of approaches and models that neglected internal developments served to spark the development of several competing and compelling models regarding the development of the Middle Bronze Age in Canaan. Included within these newer models are those that highlight the significance of rural complexity (e.g. Falconer 1994), Peer Polity interaction theory (e.g. Ilan 1998), world systems or core-periphery models (e.g. Cohen 2002), approaches positing urban-rural symbiosis (e.g. Cohen 2009), and others (e.g. Greenberg 2002; Maeir 2002).

Although differing in elements of detail and approach, these newer models are all characterized by attempts to incorporate local developments as well as external influences into integrated understandings of Middle Bronze Age Canaanite society. Below, therefore, the archaeological remains of the Middle Bronze Age will be examined in light of these ideas. Settlement patterns, urban growth, and the material culture of the Middle Bronze Age will be set forth with attention to the interactions and interconnections that influenced their development and dissemination in Canaan, and how they reflect on the indigenous and exogenous forces that gave rise to Middle Bronze Age Canaanite culture, and its connections with other contemporary societies in the Levant.

Terminology

The Middle Bronze Age in Canaan is conventionally divided into three basic periods, referred to in this volume as MB I, II, and III. It should be noted, however, that some aspects of the formative MB I period differ in significant ways from the ensuing mature period of the MB II and III, and that it is often difficult to differentiate finer distinctions between the latter two sub-periods. Where possible in this discussion, the distinction of subdivisions will be noted; in general, however, MB II and III will be treated together as the later portion of the Middle Bronze Age as a whole. It is also significant to note that many trends within the overall era developed at different rates between these sub-periods, which are fundamentally artificial divisions; it should not be inferred that there are significant cultural or developmental breaks as marked by these sub-eras. Rather, cultural development throughout the Middle Bronze Age proceeded smoothly while also progressing at different rates in different regions throughout Canaan.

Middle Bronze Age I

Settlement

A significant increase in settlement characterizes the initial phase of the Middle Bronze Age in Canaan, which is most evident in the coastal regions and along communication and transport routes, although surveys in all regions note an increase in settlement, including locations previously uninhabited in the Intermediate Bronze Age (Broshi and Gophna 1986; Gophna and Portugali 1988). Overall, settlement in MB I Canaan developed in a manner conducive to the rise of urban culture and the strengthening of trade and communication networks throughout the region (Fig. 30.1). In particular, settlement growth on the coastal plains provided support for the urban centres in these areas (Gophna and Beck 1981), whereas settlement in other parts of Canaan appears to have begun first along the east–west wadi systems, and then spread out into the rest of the region, thus providing a systemic network of support and growth focused on the larger urban sites at the end of each system (Cohen 2002).

In general most survey data reveal a slower pace in settlement and system development in the inland and southern regions in Canaan (Cohen 2002), thereby matching the basic pattern of urbanization noted throughout the region. Significantly, however, occupation dating to the earliest phases of MB I exists in marginal areas of Canaan as well, especially in the Jordan Valley region. In particular, Phases 5 and 4 at Tell el-Hayyat (Falconer 1994; Falconer and Fall 2006) and the cemetery at Gesher date to the early phases of MB I (Garfinkel and Cohen 2007); the occupational and mortuary traditions at both sites evince continuity with the preceding Intermediate Bronze Age (Cohen 2009). This evidence for continuity in local systems in regions well removed from the large urban centres highlights rural growth within

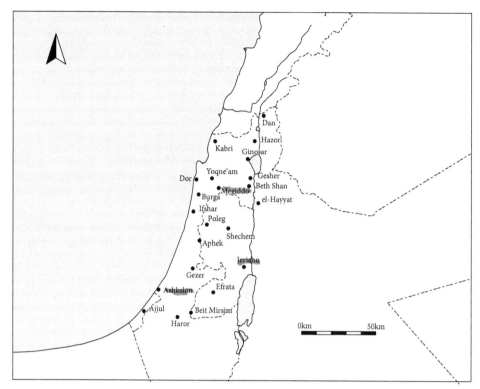

FIG. 30.1 Map of Middle Bronze Age sites in the southern Levant (Cisjordan)

Canaan that developed concurrently with external forces on the region, spurring the urbanizing character of the period.

Architecture

Significant architectural developments, in particular massive fortification systems, 'palace' architecture, and other public structures, all with clear antecedents in the northern Levant, also characterize the urbanizing nature of MB I. The massive mud-brick fortifications found at major urban sites clearly indicate northern influences. Their appearance in the early MB I strata of urban sites in Canaan, e.g. Ashkelon and Tel Dan, also highlights the rapid development of urban culture in Canaan. In addition to the fortifications at the larger cities, many smaller fortified sites founded in MB I in key strategic locations between the larger cities, such as Tel Poleg and Tel Burga, are situated in positions to support the growing urban culture. These sites contribute to a settlement hierarchy, whereby the smaller unfortified sites would have been controlled by the fortresses, which in turn helped to support the continued growth of large urban sites.

The growth of public architecture also reveals the centralized nature of the cities. Palaces, or, more appropriately, large public buildings, at sites such as Aphek, Megiddo, Tel Kabri, and Tel Ifshar, for example, point to the political organization of the urbanizing culture of MB I. The nature of the public architecture suggests the beginnings of 'palace economies' in which the political and economic systems in Canaan were dominated by a series of urban polities controlling settlement and resources in their hinterlands, and yet also relying on the resources and materials from those regions for their own continued maintenance, power, and growth.

Burial customs

MB I mortuary remains provide considerable information regarding Canaanite social structure. Burial type in MB I is considerably varied, and includes pit and cist burials and constructed tombs as well as rock-cut cave tombs (Hallote 1995; Ilan 1995); it has been suggested that these different methods are contingent on social ranking and stratifaction (Ilan 1998), although the different physical locations of the cemeteries should also be taken into account. It is important to note, however, that the age of the individual affects the burial type, as children were almost always interred in jars, often found in sub-mural contexts, whereas the cemeteries, either consisting of pit graves or rock-cut tombs, only yield adult remains.

During the course of MB I, as a general pattern, burial customs reflect a change from secondary to primary interments and, especially in the more urbanized areas, from single to multiple burials. MB I burials have been excavated at settlements and isolated cemeteries throughout all regions in Canaan, including Tell el-ʿAjjul, Efrata, Gesher, Ginosar, Jericho, and Megiddo (Fig. 30.2). While differing regionally, in general MB I burials do not have large quantities of associated grave goods; these tend to consist primarily of ceramics linked with basic subsistence and often metal weapons, such as daggers, javelin points, or duckbill axes. Significantly, cemeteries and tombs located in regions removed from urban centres also show strong continuity of mortuary traditions with those identified for the Intermediate Bronze Age culture (Cohen 2009).

Ceramics

The ceramic material excavated from the major urban centres provides the standard typology of the period, derived primarily from the excavations at Aphek (Beck 2000), and supplemented by the ceramic corpora from such sites as Megiddo, Jericho, Tel Ifshar, Kabri, and Tel Dan, among others. In the standard corpus, Middle Bronze Age I ceramic remains are characterized by cooking pots, both hand- and wheel-made, handleless jars with triangular rims, larger two-handled storage jars, often with an elongated folded rim, and a variety of open bowls, both hemispherical and with rounded carination (Fig. 30.3). Juglets are rare early in the period, and become more common throughout MB I; the cylindrical juglet appears only in the latest phases of MB I. In the earliest phases of MB I, surface treatment is characterized by horizontal combed decoration on store-jars; painted wares, particularly those with antecedents in the inland regions of Syria, are also characteristic of the early phases of the period. By the middle phases of MB I, red slip and burnishing becomes common. This finishing technique becomes one of the most characteristic features of the era; the ultra-thin, highly polished red slipped ware, found predominately at the large urban centres, exhibits a technological calibre not achieved again in this region for another millennium.

Ceramic remains from sites located outside the primary urban areas, however, provide evidence for local trends in ceramic development throughout MB I as well and, notably, also indicate a certain continuity with the preceding Intermediate Bronze Age ceramic repertoire.

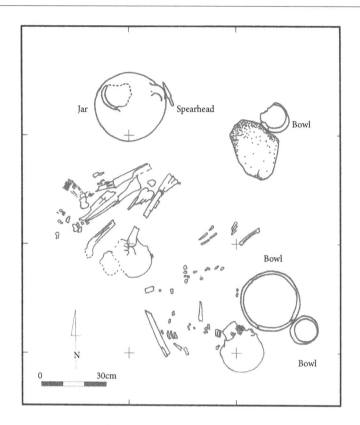

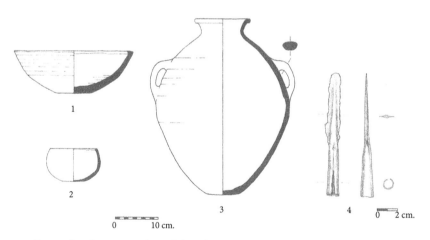

FIG. 30.2 Example of an MB I burial (Gesher cemetery burial) and the associated grave goods found (Garfinkel and Cohen 2007)

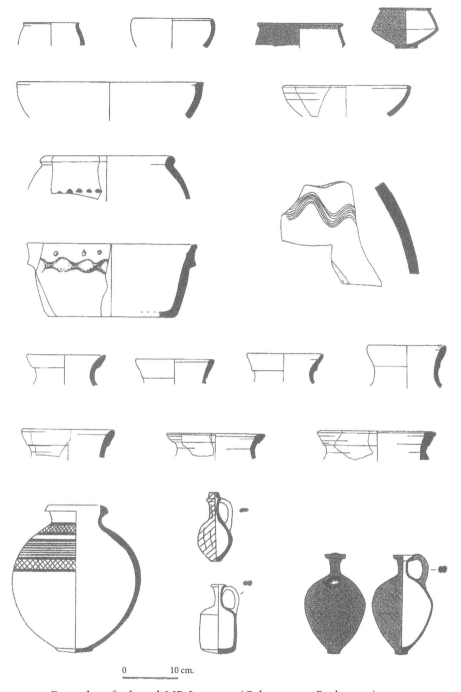

0   10 cm.

FIG. 30.3 Examples of selected MB I pottery (Cohen 2002; Beck 2000)

Sherd evidence from the earliest levels at Tell el-Hayyat (Phases 5–4) (Falconer 1994) and the whole vessels from Gesher (e.g. Graves 1, 16, and 18) (Garfinkel and Cohen 2007; Cohen and Bonfil 2007) show distinct continuity with the earlier era in both ware and form, and suggest the existence of regional ceramic traditions in regions such as the Jordan Valley that develop concurrently with the more standard repertoire present at the urban sites (Cohen 2009; Maeir 1997; 2002). Evidence found at Tell el-Hayyat for local pottery production and distribution in the Jordan Valley region also supports this supposition. Regional differences between northern and southern Canaan may also exist early in the period, although these need to be examined in further detail.

The regionalism of the early phases of MB I was short-lived; the trend toward ceramic standardization ceramics becomes increasingly apparent toward the end of the sub-period. Also notable is the evolution of utilitarian forms relevant to transportation and increased demand for production, most probably arising from evolving forces of urbanization and centralization; this is evident in the change from wide, flatter bottoms on the store-jars to increasingly pointed bases, which allow for stronger containers more suited for long-distance trade. The introduction of the fast wheel early in the sub-period, a technology with clear northern antecedents, also allows for the increased progression and standardization of the corpus as MB I progresses.

By the end of MB I, most of the regional characteristics present in the repertoire disappear from the corpus. In addition, many of the characteristic and highly distinctive surfaces treatments, such as red slip and burnish and the painted wares, become less common. External pressures may be responsible for this development, as standardization of material culture is an indicator of increase in production to meet external demands for goods and products; concurrently, the decline of regionalism also may reflect an increasing consolidation of power and control of the urban sites over the economic support systems derived from local networks.

Trade and foreign contact

Despite the importance placed on external influences in the formation of MB I Canaan, foreign imports found in stratigraphic contexts in MB I strata are relatively rare. The majority of imports, as to be expected, are from northern Levantine contexts, such as painted wares, weapons, and other small objects, such as cylinder seals. Like the ceramics, the typology of weapons in MB I has clear antecedents in the northern Levant; the characteristic weapons of MB I include the duckbill axe, the socketed spearhead, and the dagger with a pronounced midrib (Philip 1989). A change in metal technology, from arsenical bronze to tin-bronze, which allows for greater strength of the weapons, is significant as one of the characteristics of the age, although it should be noted that the use of both technologies, often at the same site, remains in use throughout MB I and may be noted as another example of gradual change in this formative first period of the Middle Bronze Age (Cohen 2009). In addition to northern materials, small, but significant amounts of imported materials from other regions have been excavated in Canaanite MB I stratified contexts. In particular, Cypriot wares have been excavated at Tel Dor, Ashkelon, and Kabri.

Although Egyptian imported materials are extremely scarce, a jar of Egyptian Marl C clay and sherds of other Egyptian vessels were excavated at Tel Ifshar (Stratum C) (Paley and Porath 1997; Marcus et al. 2008), and small quantities of Lisht Ware sherds have been found in MB I layers (Stratum XIV) in the gate complex at Ashkelon (Stager and Voss 2011). Scarabs, generally found in mortuary contexts such as the tombs at Tel Dan, while rare early in the era, become more common in the later phases of MB I. Although the amount of Egyptian material found in reliable contexts throughout Canaan is quite small, and while most of the influence on material cultural seems to have been from the north, the economic and political influence of Middle Kingdom Egypt on the development of MB I Canaan cannot be discounted. Egyptian evidence points to increasing interest in Canaan on the part of the 12th Dynasty pharaohs, as indicated by both the Berlin and Brussels sets of Execration Texts and the Khu-Sobek inscription. Thus, increased stimuli for production, trade, and subsequent settlement arising from Middle Kingdom Egypt's activities in the eastern Mediterranean no doubt also contributed to the growth of the social, economic, and political systems in MB I (Cohen 2002).

While the presence of imports, together with the northern-inspired nature of much of the ceramic corpus in general, supports the focus on trade and exogenous influences on Canaanite development, their relative scarcity would also indicate that external contacts alone are not sufficient to explain the development of the social, economic, and political systems in MB I Canaan. The very fact that most imports are concentrated at sites along the coast or at the urban sites situated along communication routes highlights the relatively limited extent of foreign influence into the interior regions of Canaan. While foreign contact may have helped stimulate urban growth, the local and rural systems in the hinterlands would have yielded whatever materials MB I Canaan provided in return for these items, such as olive oil, timber, bitumen, and other materials, thereby furthering the interactive nature of internal and external forces for continued urban growth in Canaan, and leading to the development of the mature Middle Bronze Age Canaanite culture in MB II and III.

Middle Bronze Age II and III

Settlement

The later phases of the Middle Bronze Age in Canaan are marked by a continuation of the developments begun in MB I, with increasing trends toward centralization of social, economic, and political systems, and further standardization of material culture. New settlements continued to be founded throughout the period, and MB II settlement expanded further into areas sparsely settled in MB I; overall, the pattern of growth changes. Settlement patterns in MB II and III reveal an agglomeration of population in the large urban centres, which themselves increase in size. For example, the sites of Gezer, Megiddo, and Jericho grew significantly, while Hazor reached the unprecedented size of 80ha. Correspondingly, settlement in the surrounding regions decreased in diversity and number (Ilan 1998). By MB III, survey data indicate an abandonment of smaller rural settlements and decrease in the rural population while concurrently showing an increasing centralization and concentration of population in the urban sites (Broshi and Gophna 1986). In particular, survey data in around the Kabri clearly indicate a shrinking of smaller regional settlement that occurred concomitantly with the continued growth of Kabri as a large, urban site with international connections in the eastern Mediterranean (Yasur-Landau, Cline, and Pierce 2008).

Architecture

The architecture of the mature Middle Bronze Age also indicates continued standardization: well-planned public buildings or 'elite' structures, as well as the massive fortification structures that exist at most of the larger cities throughout Canaan. The size and quality of these architectural features suggest the continued existence of a 'palace economy' system in which a centralized political power controlled the surrounding economies. Significantly, public architecture similar in style, although on a smaller scale, is attested at the smaller rural sites as well, such as the *migdol* temple at Tell el-Hayyat, which is almost identical in form (although far smaller in size) to those *migdol* temples at Haror and Shechem. The similarities of these structures speak towards the continued standardization of cultural elements throughout the later phases of the Middle Bronze Age, as well as the strength of the rural elements of the society.

Burial customs

The mortuary remains reveal the increasing wealth of Canaanite society in MB II and III. It is also notable that the quality and number of associated mortuary goods change, in general, from basic subsistence vessels and a high percentage of weapons identified in MB I contexts, to an increased number of 'luxury' ceramics, as well as scarabs, jewellery, and other items, together with a decrease in weapons in the later MB II and MB III phases (Hallote 1995). The larger amounts of grave goods, as well as the non-utilitarian nature of many of the offerings, point to a growing level of material wealth in MB II and III. These changes may be reflective of developments in social and political systems; as the urbanizing polities consolidated their power, emphasis on basic subsistence was replaced by increasing amounts of expendable wealth that could be deposited with the dead, as indicated by the large cemeteries found throughout the regions, such as the cave burials at Ashkelon, Jericho, and Megiddo, the tombs at Tel Dan, and the Courtyard Cemetery at Tell el-'Ajjul. The basic similarity of the artefacts found in mortuary contexts, however, also indicates that Canaanite cult and belief, like the rest of the society, became increasingly homogenized throughout the later phases of the Middle Bronze Age.

Ceramics

In MB II and III the ceramic repertoire loses the last elements of regionalism, at least as identified to date in the current corpus, derived from sites such as Aphek, Gezer, Hazor, Jericho, Megiddo, and Yoqne'am, among numerous others. Many of the aesthetic elements that typified MB I, such as the ultra-thin, red slipped and highly burnished forms, and painted wares disappear from the repertoire in MB II and III. Typologically, while many of the basic forms of MB I continue into the later phases, including rounded and carinated bowls and two-handled store-jars with pointed bases, these forms all show significant changes in form. The ring and/or disc base evolves to a higher 'trumpet' base on the bowls, juglets become more elongated and increasingly pointed at the base, while carination on bowls rises and becomes sharper throughout the period (Fig. 30.4).

The handmade cooking pot disappears from the corpus at the very beginning of MB II, to be replaced entirely by the wheel-made form with an everted triangular rim, which becomes more pronounced as the period progresses from MB II to MB III. The store-jars develop into the typical 'Canaanite' store-jar, with a high sharply carinated shoulder and straight-sided body tapering to a pointed base; the continued evolution of this form is most

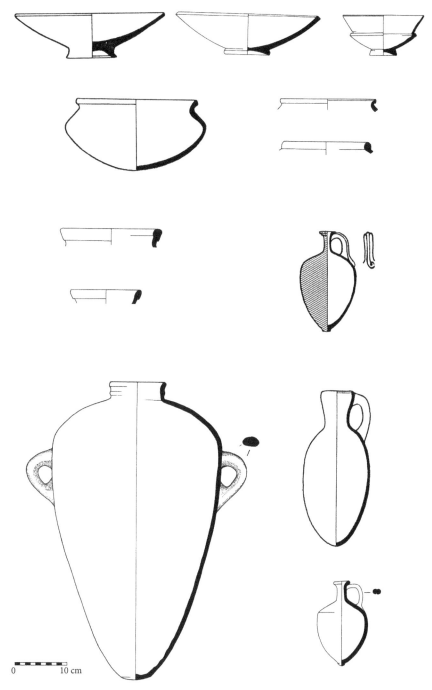

FIG. 30.4 Examples of selected MB II/III pottery (Amiran 1969; Ben-Tor, Ben-Ami, and Livneh 2005)

probably to be related to increasing Canaanite participation in international trade and transport, as evidenced by the millions of sherds of these jars found at Tell el-Dab'a (Avaris) in the Egyptian Delta (Bietak 1997). Overall, the general standardization of most forms by the end of MB III is such that, without additional specific chronological indicators, it is often very difficult to discern the difference between the late MB III and early LB I on the basis of ceramic type alone.

Trade and foreign contact

During MB II and III, foreign imports, such as metals, scarabs, and cylinder seals, while still relatively scarce, appear more regularly, particularly in tomb groups. It is still a matter of some debate whether Chocolate-on-White Ware may be considered a typological and chronological marker for the end of the MB III, but it may be noted that this ware does make its first appearance in Canaan in MB III, as do increased amounts of imported Cypriot material, such as Black-on-Red wares. Fresco fragments uncovered at Kabri (Area D, Stratum 3, Room 661) also attest to connections with regions in the Aegean world (Kempinski 2002). Recent excavations in the palace area at Kabri under the direction of E. Cline and A. Yasur-Landau have continued to uncover a complex large public building that clearly served at the administrative centre of a large and important urban site with far-flung international connections.

What is notable, however, are the large quantities of Canaanite exports found in other regions, such as the vast number of store jars excavated at Tell el-Dab'a in Egypt. These jars, most probably associated with the circulation of olive oil and wine, point to an increased network of contact, trade, and expansion on the part of the powerful Canaanite urban entities southward, leading to the development of the Hyksos occupation in Egypt, and are indicative of a Canaanite cultural continuum based on the urban society now firmly established as the hallmark of Middle Bronze Age in the southern Levant.

SUGGESTED READING

Gerstenblith, P. (1983). *The Levant at the Beginning of the Middle Bronze Age*. Philadelphia: American Schools of Oriental Research.
Ilan, D. (1998). The dawn of internationalism: the Middle Bronze Age. In T. E. Levy (ed.), *The Archaeology of Society on the Holy Land*. London: Leicester University Press.
Kempinski, A. (1992). The Middle Bronze Age. In A. Ben-Tor (ed.), *The Archaeology of Ancient Israel*. New Haven, Conn.: Yale University Press/Tel Aviv: Open University of Israel.
Mazar, A. (1990). *The Archaeology of the Land of the Bible*, vol. 1: *10,000–586 B.C.E.* New York: Doubleday.

REFERENCES

Amiran, R. (1969). *Ancient Pottery of the Holy Land: From Its Beginnings in the Neolithic Period to the End of the Iron Age*. Jerusalem: Masada.

Beck, P. (2000). The Middle Bronze Age IIA pottery repertoire: a comparative study. In M. Kochavi, P. Beck, and E. Yadin (eds), *Aphek-Antipatris I: Excavation of Areas A and B—The 1972–1976 Seasons*. Tel Aviv: Tel Aviv University, Sonia and Marco Nadler Institute of Archaeology, 239–54.

Ben-Tor, A. , D. Ben-Ami, and A. Livneh (2005). *Yoqne'am III: The Middle and Late Bronze Ages—Final Report of the Archaeological Excavations (1977–1988)*. Jerusalem: Institute of Archaeology, Hebrew University of Jerusalem in cooperation with Israel Exploration Society.

Bietak, M. (1997). The center of Hyksos rule: Avaris (Tell el-Dab'a). In E. D. Oren (ed.), *The Hyksos: New Historical and Archaeological Perspectives*. Philadelphia: University Museum, University of Pennsylvania, 87–139.

Broshi, M., and R. Gophna (1986). Middle Bronze Age II Palestine: its settlements and population. *Bulletin of the American Schools of Oriental Research* 261: 73–90.

Cohen, S. L. (2002). *Canaanites, Chronology, and Connections: The Relationship of Middle Bronze Age IIA Canaan to Middle Kingdom Egypt*. Winona Lake, Ind.: Eisenbrauns.

—— (2009). Continuities and discontinuities: a re-examination of the Intermediate Bronze Age–Middle Bronze Age transition in Canaan. *Bulletin of the American Schools of Oriental Research* 354: 1–13.

—— and R. Bonfil (2007). The pottery. In Y. Garfinkel and S. L. Cohen (eds), *The Middle Bronze Age Cemetery at Gesher: Final Report*. Boston, Mass.: American Schools of Oriental Research, 77–99.

Dever, W. G. (1976). The beginning of the Middle Bronze Age in Syria-Palestine. In F. Moore Cross, W. Lemke, and P. Miller (eds), *Magnalia Dei: The Mighty Acts of God*. Garden City, NJ: Doubleday, 3–38.

Falconer, S. E. (1994). Village economy and society in the Jordan Valley: a study of Bronze Age rural complexity. In G. M. Schwartz and S. E. Falconer (eds), *Archaeological Views from the Countryside*. Washington, DC: Smithsonian Institute Press, 121–42.

—— and P. L. Fall (2006). *Bronze Age Rural Ecology and Village Life at Tell el-Hayyat, Jordan*. Oxford: Archaeopress.

Garfinkel, Y., and S. L. Cohen (eds) (2007). *The Excavations at the Middle Bronze Age IIA Cemetery at Gesher: Final Report*. Boston, Mass.: American Schools of Oriental Research.

Gerstenblith, P. (1983). *The Levant at the Beginning of the Middle Bronze Age*. Philadelphia: American Schools of Oriental Research.

Gophna, R., and P. Beck (1981). The rural aspect of the settlement pattern of the coastal plain in the Middle Bronze Age II. *Tel Aviv* 8: 45–80.

—— and J. Portugali (1988). Settlement and demographic processes in Israel's coastal plain from the Chalcolithic to the Middle Bronze Age. *Bulletin of the American Schools of Oriental Research* 269: 11–28.

Greenberg, R. (2002). *Early Urbanizations in the Levant: A Regional Narrative*. London: Leicester University Press.

Hallote, R. S. (1995). Mortuary archaeology and the Middle Bronze Age southern Levant. *Journal of Mediterranean Archaeology* 8: 93–122.

Ilan, D. (1995). Mortuary practices at Tel Dan in the Middle Bronze Age: a reflection of Canaanite society and ideology. In S. Campbell and A. Green (eds), *The Archaeology of Death in the Ancient Near East*. Oxford: Oxbow, 117–39.

—— (1998). The dawn of internationalism: the Middle Bronze Age. In T. E. Levy (ed.), *The Archaeology of Society in the Holy Land*. London: Leicester University Press, 297–319.

Kempinski, A. (2002). *Tel Kabri: The 1986–1993 Excavation Seasons*. Tel Aviv: Emery and Claire Yass Publications in Archaeology, Institute of Archaeology, Tel Aviv University.

Kenyon, K. M. (1966). *Amorites and Canaanites*. London: Oxford University Press.

Maeir, A. M. (1997). *The material culture of the Central Jordan Valley during the Middle Bronze II period: pottery and settlement pattern* (2 vols). PhD dissertation, Hebrew University of Jerusalem.

—— (2002). Perspectives on the Early MB II Period in the Jordan Valley. In M. Bietak (ed.), *The Middle Bronze Age in the Levant: Proceedings of an International Conference on MB IIA Ceramic Material, Vienna, 24th–26th of January 2001*. Vienna: Österreichische Akademie der Wissenschaften, 261–7.

Marcus, E., Y. Porath, R. Schiestl, et al. (2008). The Middle Kingdom Egyptian pottery from Middle Bronze Age IIa Tel Ifshar. *Ägypten und Levante* 18: 203–19.

Paley, S. M., and Y. Porath (1997). Early Middle Bronze Age IIa remains at Tel el-Ifshar, Israel: a preliminary report. In E. D. Oren (ed.), *The Hyksos: New Historical and Archaeological Perspectives*. Philadelphia: University Museum, University of Pennsylvania, 369–78.

Philip, G. (1989). *Metal Weapons of the Early and Middle Bronze Ages in Syria-Palestine*, pts 1–2. Oxford: BAR International Series 526.

Yasur-Landau, A., E. H. Cline, and G. A. Pierce. (2008). Middle Bronze Age settlement patterns in the western Galilee, Israel. *Journal of Field Archaeology* 33: 59–83.

CHAPTER 31

THE SOUTHERN LEVANT (TRANSJORDAN) DURING THE MIDDLE BRONZE AGE

STEPHEN J. BOURKE

INTRODUCTION

The Middle Bronze was the first age of regular interregional contact and trade, and large-scale international conflict. The development of Jordanian culture throughout the Middle Bronze Age is a story of insularity and experimentation, of independence and empire. By the end of the Period, late Middle Bronze Age Jordan was a mature actor on an international stage.

RELATIVE AND ABSOLUTE CHRONOLOGY OF THE JORDANIAN MIDDLE BRONZE AGE

In recent times it has become customary to separate the Middle Bronze Age into three phases (MB I–III) with divisions linked to key phases in the Egyptian Middle Kingdom/Second Intermediate period relationship with Canaan (Falconer 2008); this tripartite relative chronology will be employed below.

The absolute chronology of the Jordanian Middle Bronze Age is more problematic. While an independent chronology based on radiometric data is desirable, there is currently insufficient data for such an endeavour. The beginning of the Middle Bronze resettlement wave occurred around 2000/1900 BC (Fischer (ed.) 2006: 243–4) with an end-point for Jordan around 1500 BC. There is no clear-cut evidence for a single late Middle Bronze horizon of destruction, but some of the Jordan Valley bottom settlements, such as Deir Alla and Abu Kharaz, were destroyed, although agency remains unclear (Fischer (ed.) 2006). However, cultural continuity with the succeeding Late Bronze Age is indicated throughout.

SETTLEMENT PATTERNS

The first MB I settlements cluster in the north/central Jordan Valley (Fig. 31.1). They were small and dispersed (Falconer 1987), but concentrated on the alluvial fans of lateral wadis.

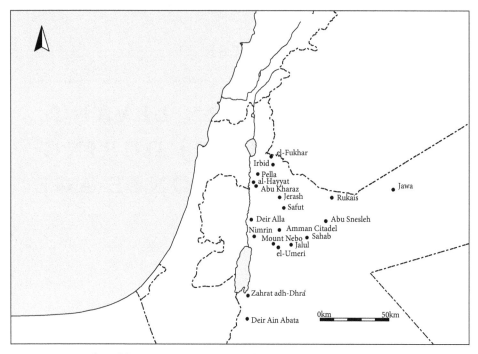

FIG. 31.1 Map of Middle Bronze Age sites in the southern Levant (Transjordan)

Whether due to intensified economic interaction, or increased population mobility, MB I culture displays links with Syria (Cohen 2005). Expansion into headwater regions of the adjacent uplands occurred by MB II, as competing demands for arable land forced flocks further away from valley's bottom pasturage. Resettlement of the south Jordan Valley occurred towards the end of the MB I (Prag 1992: 155; Flannigan, McCreery, and Yassine 1996: 289), grew in the MB II (Yassine 1988), and spread into the adjacent foothill zones during the MB III. The Jordan Plateau began to be resettled late in the MB I and, by the MB III, much of north/central Jordan was again densely settled.[1]

JORDAN VALLEY SETTLEMENTS

Pella

Pella was occupied throughout the Middle Bronze Age. The early Middle Bronze Age settlement was around 2ha in extent, located on the south-central region of the later tell site, and founded in the 20th century BC. Perhaps the eastern two-thirds (6ha) of the central mound of Khirbet Fahl was defended by a 3m-thick mud-brick wall by the end of the MB I (McLaren 2003: 13–15). There are three major exposures of Middle Bronze materials on the tell of

---

[1] For architecture of sites mentioned in this chapter, see Fig. 31.2; for non-ceramic artefacts, see Fig. 31.3; for Common Ware ceramic artefacts, see Fig. 31.4; and for non-standard ceramic artefacts, see Fig. 31.5.

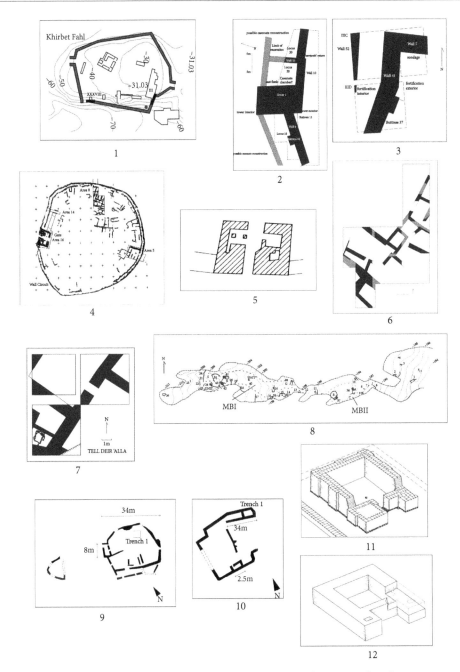

FIG. 31.2 Middle Bronze Age Jordan architecture: (1) Pella, MB I fortification circuit. (2) Pella, MB I Area XXVIII west fortification complex. (3) Pella, MB I Area III east fortification complex. (4) Rukais, MB III fortification circuit. (5) Rukais, MB III gateway. (6) Tell Abu Kharaz, MB III fortifications and domestic dwellings. (7) Deir Alla, Lower Town, MB III major structure. (8) Zad edh-Dhra 1, MB I settlement plan. (9) Wadi al-Ajib, MB I Site 42 farmstead. (10) Wadi al-Ajib, MB I Site 38 farmstead. (11) Tell al-Hayyat, MB II Phase 3 temple reconstruction. (12) Pella, MB III Phase 4 *migdol* temple reconstruction.

Khirbet Fahl and one on the eastern summit of the nearby fortified hilltop of Tell Husn. On Khirbet Fahl, the East Cut (Area III) unearthed a four-phase (Phases X–VI) sequence of defensive walls and associated domestic architecture, while excavations in the West Field (Area XXVIII) uncovered six phases (Phases A–F) of architecture associated with another section of the mud-brick fortifications, the latter featuring a 12×8 meter solid mud-brick tower (McLaren 2003: 17).

The South Field (Area XXXII) is the site of the massive *migdol* temple and associated structures under excavation since 1994 (Bourke 2004). There are four main phases (1–4) of Middle Bronze architecture and a number of intramural burials. Off-site, a series of extramural cemeteries surround the main tell. Of these, Area II (East Cemetery) and Area XI (Husn North) are the most significant, although robbed Middle Bronze cemeteries have been detected throughout the surrounding hinterland. Finally, on the eastern end of the Husn summit (Area XXXIV), fragments of an MB III fortified strongpoint have been explored below the extensive Byzantine fortress complex.

Tell al-Hayyat, Tell Abu Kharaz, Deir Alla, and Tell Nimrin

Located 6km southwest of Pella, the small (0.5ha) village site of Tell al-Hayyat was occupied throughout the Middle Bronze Age. Occupation is dominated by a long-lived, increasingly elaborate mud-brick shrine (Magness-Gardiner and Falconer 1994: 137), which has led to the suggestion that al-Hayyat was founded as a temple estate (Faust 2005). Two kilometres further southeast, a MB III settlement, some 1.5ha in extent, was located at Tell Abu Kharaz (Fischer (ed.) 2006). Initially unwalled, the later MB III settlement was heavily fortified by a 3m casemate wall to control access up the Wadi Rayyan.

Further to the south, 5km east of the Jordan at the mouth of the Wadi Zarqa, the 2ha site of Deir Alla was apparently first settled in the MB III period (van der Kooij in Fischer 2006). Mud-brick buildings have been detected on the southern and eastern peripheries, one containing elaborate metal weaponry (Fischer (ed.) 2006: 204–15). It may be that Deir Alla was fortified to control the valley bottom settlements and secure the trade route up the Wadi Zarqa.

The south Jordan Valley between the Wadis Zarqa and Shueib is largely devoid of Middle Bronze settlement. The 2ha site of Tell Nimrin is located on the eastern edge of the alluvial fan of the Wadi Shueib, 6km east of the Jordan River. Nimrin was occupied throughout the Middle Bronze Age. It was first settled in the MB I and heavily fortified in the MB III (Flannigan, McCreery, and Yassine 1996: 219) to control access up Wadi Shueib.

MAIN SETTLEMENTS OF THE NORTH JORDAN UPLANDS

Tell Irbid and Tell el-Fukhar, Quweilbeh/Abila, Tell Zira'a, el-Husn, and Jerash

Tell Irbid was probably the central polity on the north Jordan Plateau. Occupation began in the late MB I, with the basalt circuit wall, probably MB III in date (Lenzen and McQuitty

1989: 299). There is some slight evidence that the site was destroyed at the end of the Middle Bronze.

Most of the small lateral wadis that ran down off the northern plateau had some form of Middle Bronze settlement exploiting the rich agricultural soils at their heart. Eleven kilometres northeast of Irbid, the 1ha village of Tell el-Fukhar dominated Wadi Shellale. Probably founded in the late MB I (McGovern 1997: 421), it was heavily fortified in the MB III to control access up Wadi Shellale. Further to the west and some 16km north of Irbid, the 4ha Bronze Age mound of Tell Abila, located beside the verdant Wadi Quweilbeh, was certainly occupied during the Middle Bronze Age (Mare 1989: 483). Although little beyond sherds and tombs has been recovered to date, tell contours would suggest that this eminently defensible site was fortified by the MB III.

Around 28km west of Irbid, and dominating the east/west Wadi al-Arab, the finest natural accessway onto the plateau, the 3ha settlement of Tell Zira'a has at least two distinct Middle Bronze occupational phases, although their exact nature is still to be revealed (Vieweger and Häser 2007). The presence of Hyksos royal name scarabs suggests occupation in the MB III (Vieweger and Häser 2007: 8–9), and it seems probable that Zira'a controlled access onto the plateau from the west in this period.

Ten kilometres to the south of Irbid, the impressive high tell of el-Husn certainly has Middle Bronze occupation (Leonard 1987), with high contours implying (probable) Middle Bronze walling, suggesting that el-Husn was fortified to regulate movement along the main upland trunk road linking Irbid and Amman. Also on this upland trunk route, but 25km further south, classical Jerash was built over an approximately 4ha Bronze Age tell (Braemer 1989), first settled in the MB III.

Settlements of the Central Jordan Uplands

Amman, Tell Safut, Sahab, Tell el-Umeri, Madaba, Mount Nebo, and Tell Jalul

Amman was the longest-lived and most important Middle Bronze polity on the central Jordan Plateau. Occupation began late in MB I, and evidence from deep soundings (Greene and 'Amr 1992: 117) and rich tombs (Najjar 1991) suggest intensifying occupation through MB II–III. The 10ha Upper Qalaat was heavily fortified early in MB III (Zayadine, Najjar, and Greene 1987: 308).

Twelve kilometres to the north of Amman, 2ha Tell Safut was well positioned to regulate access down the Amman/Jerash road, and heavily fortified in MB III (Wimmer 1989: 514). A similar distance to the southeast of Amman, the 3ha settlement at Sahab controlled the eastern aspect of the Amman polity. Sahab was occupied from MB II and heavily fortified in MB III (Ibrahim 1989). Tell el-Umeri, the sole excavated Middle Bronze settlement south of Amman, lies approximately 10km to the southwest on the northern edge of the Madaba Plains. The 1.5ha settlement was heavily fortified late in MB III (Herr et al. 2002: 15–16), guarding access to Amman from the south.

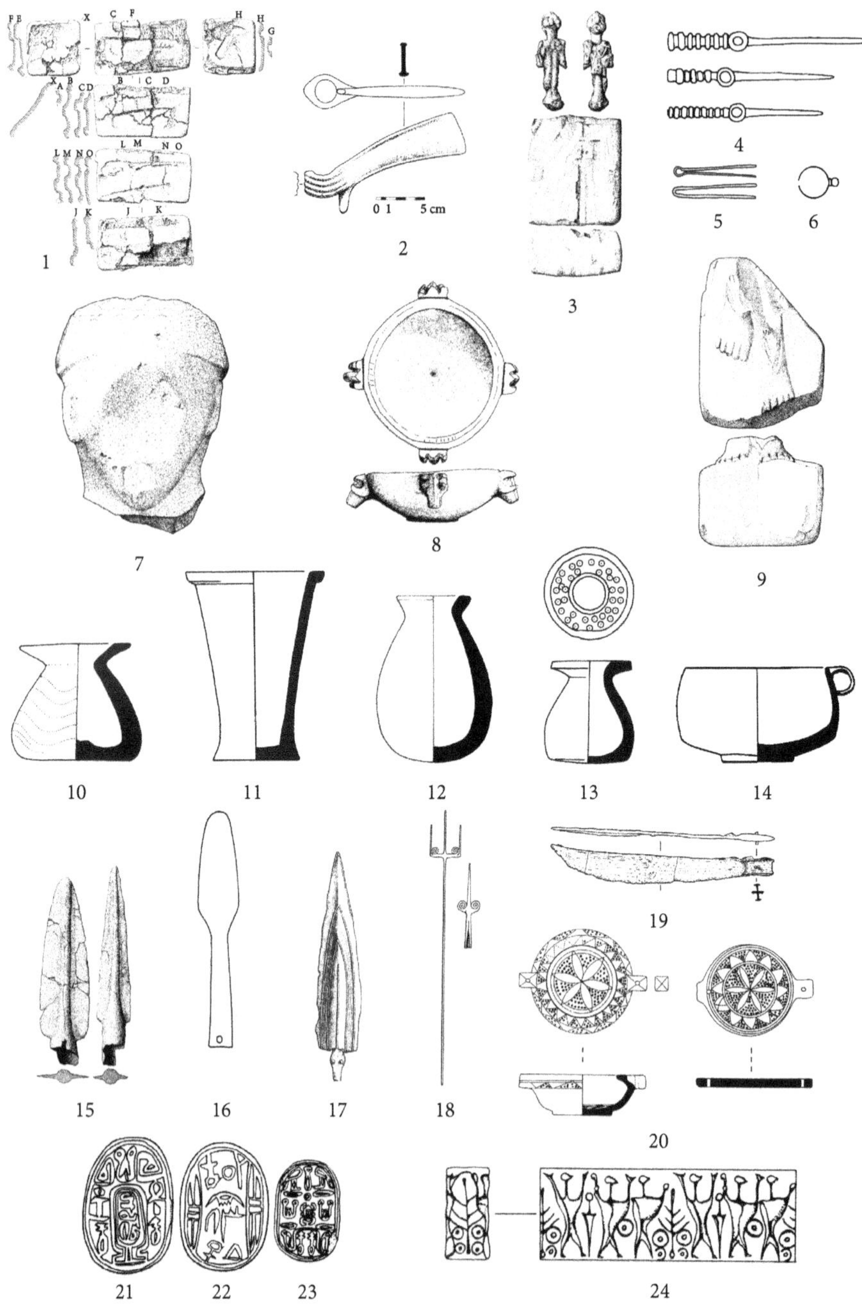

FIG. 31.3 Middle Bronze Age Jordan non-ceramic artefacts: (1) Rukais settlement, MB III baked clay tool block-mould; (2) Deir Alla settlement, MB III bronze shaft-hole axe; (3) Tell al-Hayyat Temple precinct, MB II baked clay figurine mould; (4) Pella Tomb 62, MB III bronze toggle pins; (5) Pella Tomb 62, MB III bronze tweezers; (6) Pella Tomb 62, MB III silver earring; (7) Pella Temple precinct, MB II basalt life-sized head; (8) Pella Temple precinct, MB III gypsum ram's-head-handled bowl; (9) Pella Temple precinct, MB I Fine Basalt Statuette fragment; (10) Pella Tomb 62, MB III alabaster squat alabastron; (11)

A second major polity may have been centred on Madaba, although there is little evidence to date to support such an attribution (Harrison 1997). If such a polity did exist, satellite settlements may have been located 8km northwest at Nebo and 10km east at Tell Jalul.

By MB III small settlements occupied most of the well-watered agricultural land north of Madaba, but settlement drops off sharply south of the Wadi Walla. No excavated settlements from the Kerak Plateau date from the Middle Bronze, but a tomb group from Umm Dimis suggests that at least some late Middle Bronze activity occurred around Balua'(Worschech 2003).

East Dead Sea settlements

Zahrat adh-Dhra 1, and Cairn Tomb fields at Bab edh-Dhra' and Deir Ain Abata

Recent work in the foothill zones of the Wadi Kerak at the 6ha MB I site of Zahrat adh-Dhra 1 has revealed a seasonally occupied settlement (Berelov 2006a). That a significant seasonally mobile population existed south of the Wadi Mujib is suggested by recent work on cairn cemeteries at Deir Ain Abata (Berelov 2001: 168) and Bab edh-Dhra' (Edwards et al. 2004: 194–5). It may be that the seasonally fertile region around Wadi Kerak was utilized by semi-nomadic groups throughout the Middle Bronze.

Eastern desert region

Tell Rukais, the Wadi al-Ajib, and Jawa

The Jordanian desert landscape south of the Jebel Druze was dominated by the 1ha settlement of Tell Rukais, located 2km from the Syrian border at the southern limit of cultivation. Rukais was occupied from late MB I and fortified in MB III (McLaren 2003: 20–21). It features a basalt circuit wall, stone tower, and six-chambered gate. A network of small farmsteads spread up Wadi al-Ajib from late MB I (Eames 2001: 242). Some 50km east of Rukais, a MB I settlement at Jawa consisted of an isolated caravanserai (Helms 1989).

FIG. 31.3 (continued) Pella Temple precinct, MB III alabaster flask; (12) Pella Tomb 62, MB III alabaster rounded aryballos; (13) Pella Tomb 62, MB III circle-incised alabaster squat alabastron; (14) Pella Temple precinct, MB III gypsum lug-handled bowl; (15) Tell al-Hayyat Temple precinct, MB II bronze spearhead; (16) Pella Tomb 62, MB III bronze socketed spearhead; (17) Pella settlement Burial F.98, MB II bronze dagger; (18) Deir Alla settlement, MB III bronze trident and harpoon head; (19) Pella Tomb 62, MB III bronze knife; (20) Pella Tomb 20, MB II incised alabaster dish and lid; (21) Pella Tomb 62, MB III steatite royal name scarab Apophis; (22) Pella Tomb 62, MB III steatite royal name scarab Nebuserre; (23) Pella Tomb 62, MB III Steatite royal name scarab Khamose; (24) Pella Tomb 62, MB III serpentine Cypriot Common-Style cylinder seal

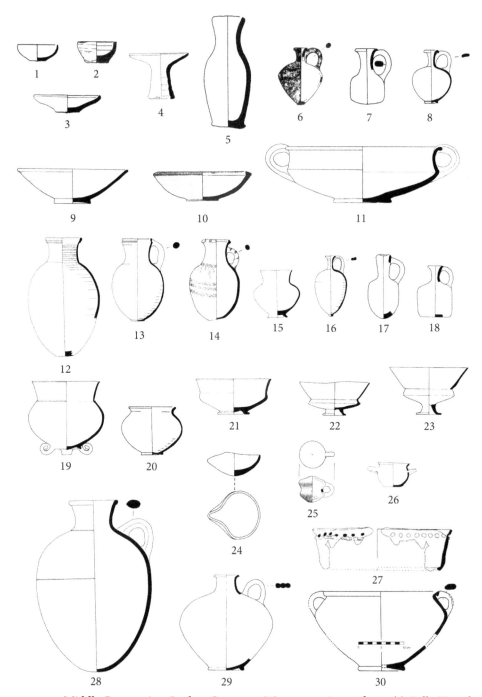

FIG. 31.4 Middle Bronze Age Jordan Common Ware ceramic artefacts: (1) Pella Temple precinct, MB III miniature rounded bowl; (2) Pella Temple precinct, MB III miniature bowl; (3) Pella Temple precinct, MB III miniature platter bowl; (4) Pella Temple precinct, MB III miniature funnel; (5) Pella Temple precinct, MB III miniature bottle; (6) Pella Tomb 22, MB II black slip burnished piriform juglet; (7) Pella Tomb 62, MB III miniature cylindrical juglet; (8) Pella settlement Burial F.98, MB II buff slip burnished

MATERIAL CULTURE

Introduction

The Middle Bronze material culture of Jordan passes through successive stages of import, imitation, and innovation (Sparks 2001b: 263). Early Middle Bronze architectural forms and luxury stone, metal, ceramic, and ivory artefacts all bear the hallmark of Syrian or Egyptian originals. However, as the Middle Bronze unfolds, increasingly skilled local workshops develop vibrant stone and ceramic industries. Imported luxury goods feature in MB II assemblages, but by MB III, skilfully executed local products compete with and often supplant imported goods. The gypsum industry (Sparks 2001b) and Chocolate-on-White ceramics (Donnelly 2004) are only two of the more obvious local industries that flourished in the MB III period.

Architecture

The MB I fortification system at Pella was constructed simply, consisting of a single-trace circuit featuring stone foundations and a mud-brick superstructure. None of the refinements that feature in later circuits (earthern ramparts, stone-faced glacis, or forward ditches) are present at Pella. MB III fortifications at Tell Nimrin, Amman, Sahab, and Tell el-Umeri display some of these elaborations. The sharp rise in fortification across the country during the MB III suggests heightened insecurity and growing militarization (Finkelstein 1992).

No palatial residences have been recovered from Middle Bronze Jordan. Substantial multi-room buildings are known from MB III Deir Alla and Pella. Modest domestic architecture is documented at Pella, Tell al-Hayyat, Abu Kharaz, Sahab, and Rukais, with rural farmsteads in Wadi al-Ajib and at Abu Snesleh and the stone caravanserai at Jawa. The little we know of Jordanian domestic and rural architecture suggests that it does not depart significantly from earlier Canaanite norms (Foucault-Forest 1997: 151–7).

Formal temples are known from Pella (Bourke 2004) and Tell al-Hayyat (Falconer and Fall 2006). The structures at these sites are of the Syrian anten-temple form. The modest (7×10m) but carefully constructed mud-brick structures at al-Hayyat span much of

FIG. 31.4 (*continued*) globular juglet; (9) Pella settlement, MB II platter bowl; (10) Pella settlement, MB I rounded bowl; (11) Pella settlement, MB III carinated krater; (12) Pella settlement, MB II tall narrow-necked jar; (13) Pella settlement Burial F.98, MB II ridge-neck jug; (14) Pella settlement, MB I red painted jug; (15) Pella Tomb 19, MB II fine globular bowl; (16) Pella Tomb 19, MB II fine piriform juglet; (17) Pella Tomb 62, MB III rounded dipper juglet; (18) Pella Tomb 62, MB III cylindrical juglet; (19) Pella Tomb 22, MB II hoop-footed White Slip globular bowl; (20) Pella settlement Burial F.98, MB II fine globular jar; (21) Pella Tomb 19, MB I Fine White Slip carinated bowl; (22) Pella Tomb 19, MB II Fine White Slip carinated bowl; (23) Pella Tomb 19, MB III Fine White Slip pedestalled carinated bowl; (24) Pella Tomb 62, MB III saucer lamp; (25) Pella Tomb 62, MB III ceramic rattle; (26) Pella Tomb 62, MB III ceramic spouted feeder bowl; (27) Zad edh-Dhra 1 settlement, MB I flat base upright piecrust cooking pot; (28) Pella Tomb 62, MB III rounded storage jar; (29) Pella Tomb 22, MB II large globular jug; and (30) Tell Abu Kharaz settlement, MB III round based everted-rim cooking pot

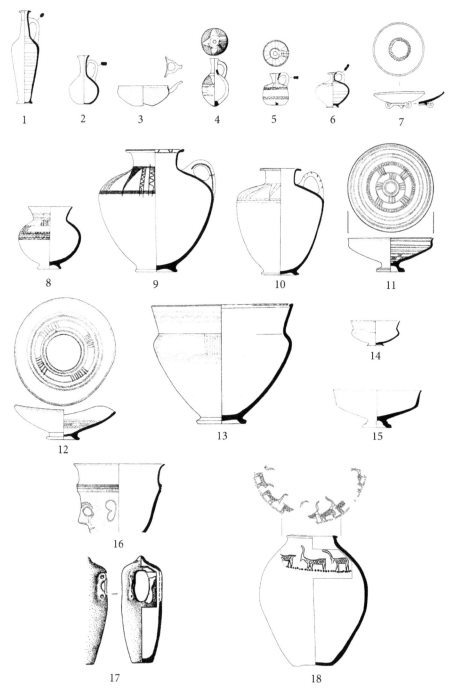

FIG. 31.5 Middle Bronze Age Jordan non-standard ceramic artefacts: (1) Pella Tomb 62, MB III Cypriot Red Lustrous Wheel-Made Ware jug; (2) Pella Tomb 62, MB III Cypriot Black Lustrous Wheel-Made Ware juglet; (3) Pella Tomb 62, MB III Cypriot Proto-Base Ring Ware wishbone-handled bowl; (4) Pella settlement, MB II Tell el-Yahudiyeh Ware piriform juglet; (5) Pella settlement, MB II Tell el-Yahudiyeh Ware globular juglet; (6) Pella settlement Burial F.106, MB II Tell el-Yahudiyeh Ware carinated juglet; (7) Pella

the Middle Bronze, whereas the Pella Fortress Temple is a huge stone-based *migdol* form (32×24m). There are at least two phases of smaller mud-brick temples below the stone *migdol* at Pella, but these earlier MB I–II structures are so badly disturbed by later foundation cuts that no coherent plans can be recovered.

Ceramic assemblages

Middle Bronze Jordanian ceramic assemblages do not depart markedly from Canaanite norms (Kempinski 1992), although distinctive features emerge as the Middle Bronze unfolds. Early Middle Bronze assemblages feature large, flat-based, straight-sided, piecrust-decorated cooking vessels at Zad edh-Dhra 1 and Pella, as well as small/medium chalky white slipped jug and jar forms, decorated with simple red-brown and black painted horizontal bands. Red slipped carinated bowls, stepped-rim jugs, juglets, and platter bowls are known from tomb and tell assemblages at Pella. A unique jar from early Middle Bronze Age Zad edh-Dhra 1 features an incised frieze of caprines, probably ibex (Berelov 2006b: 8–9). All forms are relatively 'heavy', as the fast wheel is sparingly employed. Painted decoration is dominated by simple linear bands and burnishing is rare.

Later Middle Bronze assemblages include smaller and more robust round-based everted-rim cooking vessels. Fragile early cooking vessels were fixed in cooking areas, while later Middle Bronze forms were more transportable, promoting better nutritional regimes. Later Middle Bronze jugs, bowls, and juglets were more commonly white-slipped, although both red and black slips occur. The fast wheel is ever more common with forms correspondingly finer and lighter. Carinated bowls feature high ring bases, sharply carinated bodies, and outflaring rims. While ovoid and piriform juglet forms continue, squat cylindrical juglets become more numerous, and wheel burnishing more common on large and small vessels. Painted decoration (mainly on jugs, jars, and bowls) in pseudo-bichrome (two browns) is common, although true bichrome (red/black) remains rare. Medium/large one- and two-handled storage jars become common, as do large multi-handled kraters.

Towards the end of the Middle Bronze, the locally produced Chocolate-on-White Ware is perhaps the most accomplished Jordanian Bronze Age ceramic. It was made on a fast wheel, slipped in brilliant burnished white slip, and carefully decorated in red-brown paint, featuring linear bands, solid pendant triangles, and framed wavy line motifs. The rare krater and the more popular jug and platter bowl forms show the ceramic ware at its best advantage, although amphoroid jars, carinated bowls, tankards, and cylindrical juglets are all known at Pella, which has the widest repertoire of forms (Donnelly 2004).

FIG. 31.5 (*continued*) settlement Burial F.106, MB II Tell el-Yahudiyeh Ware hoop-footed platter; (8) Pella Tomb 19, MB II White Slip Painted globular jar; (9) Pella Tomb 20, MB III Chocolate-on-White Ware large jug; (10) Pella Tomb 62, MB III Chocolate-on-White Ware large jug; (11) Pella Tomb 62, MB III Chocolate-on-White Ware carinated bowl; (12) Pella Tomb 62, MB III Chocolate-on-White Ware platter bowl; (13) Pella Tomb 62, MB III Chocolate-on-White Ware krater; (14) Pella Settlement, MB II White Slip Painted carinated bowl; (15) Pella Tomb 62, MB III White Slip carinated bowl; (16) Pella Tomb 18, MB III White Slip Painted face vase; (17) Wadi al-Ajib Site 42, MB II ceramic granary model shrine; and (18) Zad edh-Dhra 1, MB I zoomorphic antelope frieze-incised storage jar

Metallurgy

The main tool and weapon forms closely resemble the extensive tomb assemblage from Jericho, where metallographic analysis suggested manufacture from recycled metal scrap (Philip 1995: 529). Chemical analysis of a wide range of metal objects from Pella also favoured the use of recycled metal (Philip, Clogg, and Dungworth 2003: 89). It seems that all Jordanian bronze objects were made from exotic copper, probably sourced from Anatolia and Cyprus, with tin from southwest Afghanistan. The Faynan copper ores were not exploited during the Middle Bronze (Philip, Clogg, and Dungworth 2003: 93).

Metal tools and weapons were a feature of both occupation and burial contexts. A full range of weaponry (axes and short swords), tools (chisels and adzes), cultic exotica (figurines, a trident, and an ornate spearhead) and jewellery (toggle pins, hair-rings, and earrings) are known from Jordan Valley sites (see Fischer (ed.) 2006), more occasionally in upland Jordan (Najjar 1991). The typological range is small, and weapons and tools look much the same wherever they are found.

There is evidence for small-scale metalworking at Pella, Tell al-Hayyat, Tell Abu Kharaz, and more surprisingly in the eastern desert at Rukais, where an elaborate block mould was recovered (Betts and Braune 2001). These metal workers were capable of fashioning most of the main tool and weapon categories found in Middle Bronze deposits, suggesting that itinerant smiths could well have played a considerable role in maintaining and reworking tools and weaponry.

Stone vessels

The majority of Jordanian stone vessels were manufactured from locally available stone, fine basalts from the north Jordan uplands, and gypsums from the main lateral wadis emptying into the Jordan Valley Rift. Highly polished ring-based or more roughly executed tripod-footed basalt platters were common at Pella (Sparks 2001b), Tell Abu Kharaz (Fischer (ed.) 2006: 356), and Amman (Najjar 1991), perhaps employed as serving vessels and braziers respectively.

In the early Middle Bronze Egyptian calcite imports (mostly squat alabastra) dominated the fine vessel market, but in the later Middle Bronze Jordanian gypsum copies outnumbered Egyptian imports by three to one (Sparks 2001b: 260). As well, unique vessels in gypsum from MB III Pella suggest on-site manufacture, while imitation of ceramic forms in gypsum, and white-painted wooden imitations of gypsum ram's-head handled bowls (Sparks 2001b: 260–62), suggest a lively interplay between local craft media. Fine calcite vessels were still imported from Egypt, mainly squat alabastra, tear-drop vessels, and fine jars.

BURIAL CUSTOMS

In the MB I, intramural primary burial was the norm, with many examples at Pella (Fischer (ed.) 2006: 21–3), featuring built mud-brick chambers or simple ovoid pits. Departures from this rule include a rare multiple simultaneous burial from MB II Pella and a stone-lined cist containing several burials from MB III Pella.

From early in MB II most burials were in extramural chamber tombs, normally cut into the rock faces of nearby hillsides. The majority were single-chambered family tombs, containing 10–30 burials, interred successively. These small chamber tombs were in use for approximately 100 years, perhaps five to six generations. Chamber tombs from MB II–III are well documented at Pella, Quweilbeh, el-Husn, Amman, Mount Nebo, and Balu'.

Very large multiple-chambered tombs are rare, and only one Jordanian example is known, from Middle Bronze/Late Bronze Pella (Tomb 62). It contained approximately 150 individuals and over 2,000 objects (McNicoll et al. 1992: 69–81). Single examples of these large 'cache burials' are known from Shechem, Dothan, Gezer, and Jerusalem, and date between the MB III and LB II periods. Whether these mass burials are the result of single catastrophic events (pestilence, earthquake, or warfare) remains unclear, although the meagre evidence we do have argues against it. As all contain costly exotica, they may be the burial vaults of extended-family ruling lineages.

Trade and foreign relations

Textual evidence

Only a single Middle Kingdom Execration Text reference (Brussels E8) is confidently attributed to a Jordanian Middle Bronze centre, namely Pella, ruled by Apiru-Anu (Kitchen 1992: 23). Kitchen suggests *Rmt* (Brussels F3) for the later Ramoth Gilead (Tell er-Rumeith). However, as there is no evidence for Middle Bronze occupation at or near the site, Abila is a more probable candidate. Haram (Brussels E4) is generally located at the later Beth Haram, northeast of the Dead Sea. Haram cannot be located at Tell Iktanu, as there are no Middle Bronze remains on site, but as there is extensive Middle Bronze occupation at nearby Tell Hammam (Prag 1992: 155), it is a better candidate. The Execration Texts reflect a sketchy but nonetheless wide-ranging knowledge of Jordanian toponyms (Kitchen 1992: 21–3).

Trade in ceramics

Foreign ceramics are present at MB II Pella (Fischer (ed.) 2006: 49), including a Tell el-Yahudiyeh platter bowl and piriform and globular juglets. Yahudiyeh juglets are known on the plateau at Nebo (Mortensen and Thuesen 1998) and the Amman Citadel (Najjar 1991:120–21). These forms date from early in the 17th century BC, and suggest limited contact between Jordan and late Middle Kingdom Egypt.

In Middle Bronze/Late Bronze Pella, Cypriot ceramics occur in both burial and occupation assemblages. They include Proto-White Slip, White Slip I, Proto-Base Ring, and Black Lustrous Wheel-Made Wares. Most (but not all) are closed vessel forms and suggest small-scale trade in luxury oils and unguents. This limited trade with Cyprus is consistent with the upsurge in maritime activity throughout the eastern Mediterranean during the late Hyksos period.

By way of contrast with the import of foreign ceramics, the movement of the locally produced Chocolate-on-White Ware is revealing. While most Chocolate-on-White is found close to its major production centres in the central Jordan Valley, a small amount was exported north to Hazor and Tell es-Salihiyeh in the Damascene, west to Beth Shean,

Shechem, Megiddo, and Kabri, and south to Tell el-'Ajjul and Tell ed-Daba. While this indicates a far-flung trading network, it also underscores the very small scale of the endeavour.

Scarabs, seals, and beads

'Hyksos' design scarabs are very common in MB III (and later) contexts throughout Jordan (Eggler and Keel 2006). At Pella, over 80 examples have been recovered to date (Fischer (ed.) 2006: 52–3). They are recorded in smaller numbers from Tell el-Fukhar, Quweilbeh, Tell Zira'a, and Sahem in the north, and at Nebo, Amman, and Balu' in the south. 'Hyksos' design scarabs are very probably the property of local inhabitants, although their function and significance remains at issue. The ubiquity of design scarabs in burial contexts probably reflects a growing cultural intimacy (probably shared religious beliefs) between Jordanian and Egyptian elites, but this need not imply political association.

However, the presence of Hyksos 'royal name' scarabs in Pella Tomb 62 may suggest something more significant than acculturation (Smith 1973). Three scarabs have been identified as royal name scarabs, and a single jar seal-impression from the same tomb records a fourth royal name. The presence of royal name scarabs in Tomb 62 probably indicates closer, perhaps personal, relationships between local elites and Egyptian contemporaries at the very end of the MB III.

Evidence for interregional trade includes Baltic amber beads at MB III Abu Kharaz and lapis lazuli at MB III Pella. Further exotica from Middle Bronze Pella include an Old Babylonian hematite cylinder seal, late Middle Bronze Cypriot (or North Syrian) serpentine cylinder seals, and a recently discovered MB III Syrian (?) green jasper scarab, along with ivory, faience, gold, and silver.

SETTLEMENT AND SOCIETY

Late Middle Bronze settlement pattern analysis (Savage and Falconer 2003: 42) suggests that a series of independent polities coalesced out of the scattered agricultural villages of the early Middle Bronze, typically with a large, heavily fortified central site (Pella, Irbid, and Amman), surrounded by a constellation of border fortresses. These exist both in the intensively studied Jordan Valley (Pella and Deir Alla) and in the lesser-known Jordan uplands (Irbid and Amman, perhaps Madaba, Jerash, and Salt). The wealth (and unequal spread) of later Middle Bronze material culture provides strong evidence for the existence of an economically sophisticated, culturally diverse, and sharply stratified society, exactly the picture evoked from the written records at Mari, Ugarit, and Amarna.

Early Middle Bronze ruling elites may have viewed themselves as guardians of their peoples, but this 'warrior ethos' was more notional than real, with weaponry more symbolic of social status than employment. The sharp decline in weaponry in later Middle Bronze burials reflects changing elite culture emphasizing refined (Egyptian influenced) elegance (tweezers, shaving knives, and jewellery) over martial display. While this probably reflects a genuine change in social mores, it also indicates a change in military technology.

The scale of later Middle Bronze offensive warfare (massed chariots and professional archers) put the smaller city-states of the southern Levant at a decided disadvantage, prompting the massive fortifications that characterize later Middle Bronze Jordan. For a time this sufficed to insulate Jordan from the renascent Egyptians, but as the offensive power of the New Kingdom grew under Thutmosis III (c.1475 BC), Jordan fell under the sway of the expanding empire, bringing the brilliant culture of the Middle Bronze Age to a close.

Suggested reading

Falconer, S. E. (1987). *Heartland of villages: reconsidering early urbanism in the southern Levant.* PhD dissertation, University of Arizona.

Fischer, P. M. (ed.) (2006). *The Chronology of the Jordan Valley during the Middle and Late Bronze Ages: Pella, Tell Abu Al-Kharaz, and Tell Deir 'Alla.* Vienna: Österreichische Akademie der Wissenschaften.

Savage, S. H., and S. E. Falconer (2003). Spatial and statistical inference of Late Bronze Age polities in the southern Levant. *Bulletin of the American Schools of Oriental Research* 330: 31–45.

References

Berelov, I. (2001). ZAD 1: Stranded on the Dead Sea in the Middle Bronze Age. In A. G. Walmsley (ed.), *Australians Uncovering Ancient Jordan: Fifty Years of Middle Eastern Archaeology.* Sydney: Research Institute for Humanities and Social Sciences, University of Sydney, 165–72.

—— (2006a). *Occupation and Abandonment of Middle Bronze Age Zahrat adh-Dhra I, Jordan: The Behavioural Implications of Quantitative Ceramic Analyses.* Oxford: Archaeopress.

—— (2006b). The antelope jar from Zahrat adh-Dhra' 1 in Jordan: cultural and chronological implications of a rare zoomorphic incised decoration from the MB II period. *Palestine Exploration Quarterly* 138: 5–12.

Betts, A., and T. Braune (2001). A Middle Bronze Age block mould from Tell Rukais, Jordan. In A. G. Walmsley (ed.), *Australians Uncovering Ancient Jordan: Fifty Years of Middle Eastern Archaeology.* Sydney: Research Institute for Humanities and Social Sciences, University of Sydney, 233–8.

Bourke, S. J. (2004). Cult and archaeology at Pella in Jordan: excavating the Bronze and Iron Age temple precinct (1994–2001). *Journal and Proceedings of the Royal Society of New South Wales* 137: 1–31.

Braemer, F. (1989). Jerash. In D. Homès-Fredericq and J. Hennessy (eds), *Archaeology of Jordan II,1: Field Reports—Surveys and Sites A–K.* Leuven: Peeters, 316–19.

Cohen, S. (2005). The spearheads from the 2002–2004 excavations at Gesher. *Israel Exploration Journal* 55: 129–42.

Donnelly, P. F. (2004). Chocolate on White Ware: tomb and tell vessel typology at Pella. *Studies in the History and Archaeology of Jordan* 8: 97–108.

Eames, S. (2001). A gateway community in northern Jordan: the University of Sydney Hawran Project. *Studies in the History and Archaeology of Jordan* 7: 239–45.

Edwards, P. C., S. E. Falconer, P. L. Fall, A. Ariotti, and T. Swoveland (2004). Archaeology and environment of the Dead Sea Plain: preliminary results of the third season of investigations by the Joint La Trobe University/Arizona State University Project. *Annual of the Department of Antiquities of Jordan* 48: 181–202.

Eggler, J., and O. Keel (2006). *Corpus der Siegel-Amulette aus Jordanien: vom Neolithikum bis zur Perserzeit*. Fribourg: Academic Press/Göttingen: Vandenhoeck & Ruprecht.

Falconer, S. E. (1987). *Heartland of villages: reconsidering early urbanism in the southern Levant*. PhD dissertation, University of Arizona.

—— (2008). The Middle Bronze Age. In R. Adams (ed.), *Jordan: An Archaeological Reader*. London: Equinox, 263–80.

—— and P. L. Fall (2006). *Bronze Age Rural Ecology and Village Life at Tell el-Hayyat, Jordan*. Oxford: Archaeopress.

Faust, A. (2005). The Canaanite village: social structure of Middle Bronze Age rural communities. *Levant* 37: 105–25.

Finkelstein, I. (1992). Middle Bronze Age 'fortifications': a reflection of social organization and political formations. *Tel Aviv* 19: 201–20.

Fischer, P. M. (ed.) (2006). *The Chronology of the Jordan Valley during the Middle and Late Bronze Ages: Pella, Tell Abu Al-Kharaz, and Tell Deir 'Alla*. Vienna: Österreichische Akademie der Wissenschaften.

Flannigan, J. W., D. W. McCreery, and K. N. Yassine (1996). Tall Nimrim: preliminary report on the 1995 excavation and geological survey. *Annual of the Department of Antiquities of Jordan* 40: 271–92.

Foucault-Forest, C. (1997). Modèles d'organisation de l'espace dans l'habitat du Bronze Moyen et du Bronze Récent en Palestine. In C. Castel, M. al-Maqdissi, and F. Villeneuve (eds), *Les maisons dans la Syrie Antique de IIIe millénaire aux débuts de l'Islam:pratique et représentations de l'espace domestique*. Beirut: Institut français d'archéologie du Proche-Orient, 151–60.

Greene, J. A., and K. 'Amr (1992). Deep soundings on the lower terrace of the Amman citadel: final report. *Annual of the Department of Antiquities of Jordan* 36: 113–44.

Harrison, T. J. (1997). Shifting patterns of settlement in the highlands of central Jordan during the Early Bronze Age. *Bulletin of the American Schools of Oriental Research* 306: 1–37.

Helms, S. (1989). Jawa at the beginning of the Middle Bronze Age. *Levant* 21: 141–68.

Herr, L. G., D. R. Clark, L. T. Geraty, R. W. Younker, and Ø. S. La Bianca (eds) (2002). *Madaba Plains Project: The 1994 Season at Tall al-Umayri and Subsequent Studies*. Berrien Springs, Mich.: Andrews University Press in cooperation with the Institute of Archaeology.

Ibrahim, M. (1989). Sahab. In D. Homès-Fredericq and J. B. Hennessy (eds), *Archaeology of Jordan II,2: Field Reports: Sites L-Z*. Leuven: Peeters, 516–20.

Kempinski, A. (1992). The Middle Bronze Age. In A. Ben-Tor (ed.), *The Archaeology of Ancient Israel*. New Haven, Conn.: Yale University Press/Tel Aviv: Open University of Israel, 159–210.

Kitchen, K. A. (1992). The Egyptian evidence on ancient Jordan. In P. Bienkowski (ed.), *Early Edom and Moab: The Beginnings of the Iron Age in Southern Jordan*. Sheffield: National Museums and Galleries on Merseyside, 21–34.

Lenzen, C. J., and A. M. McQuitty (1989). Irbid (Tell). In D. Homès-Fredericq and J. B. Hennessy (eds), *Archaeology of Jordan II,1: Field Reports: Surveys and Sites A-K*. Leuven: Peeters, 298–300.

Leonard, A., Jr (1987). The Jarash–Tell el-Ḥuṣn Highway Survey. *Annual of the Department of Antiquities of Jordan* 31: 343–90.

Magness-Gardiner, B., and S. E. Falconer (1994). Community, polity and temple in a Middle Bronze Age Levantine village. *Journal of Mediterranean Archaeology* 7: 127–64.

Mare, W. H. (1989). Quweilbeh (Abila). In D. Homès-Fredericq and J. B. Hennessy (eds), *Archaeology of Jordan II,2: Field Reports: Sites L-Z*. Leuven: Peeters, 472–86.

McGovern, P. E. (1997). A ceramic sequence for northern Jordan: an archaeological and chemical perspective. *Studies in the History and Archaeology of Jordan* 6: 421–5.

McLaren, P. B. (2003). *The Military Architecture of Jordan during the Middle Bronze Age: New Evidence from Pella and Rukeis*. Oxford: Archaeopress.

McNicoll, A. W., P. C. Edwards, J. W. Hanbury-Tenison, et al. (1992). *Pella in Jordan 2: The Second Interim Report of the Joint University of Sydney and the College of Wooster Excavations at Pella, 1982–1985*. Sydney: Meditrach.

Mortensen, P., and I. Thuesen (1998). The prehistoric periods. In M. Piccirillo and E. Alliata (eds), *Mount Nebo: New Archaeological Excavations, 1967–1997*, vol. 1. Jerusalem: Stadium Biblicum Franciscanum, 85–99.

Najjar, M. (1991). A Middle Bronze Age tomb at the citadel of Amman. *Annual of the Department of Antiquities of Jordan* 35: 105–31.

Philip, G. (1995). The same but different: a comparison of Middle Bronze Age metalwork from Jericho and Tell ed-Dab'a. *Studies in the History and Archaeology of Jordan* 5: 523–30.

—— P. W. Clogg, and D. Dungworth (2003). Copper metallurgy in the Jordan Valley from the third to the first millennia BC: chemical, metallographic and lead isotope analyses of artefacts from Pella. *Levant* 35: 71–100.

Prag, K. (1992). Bronze Age settlement patterns in the South Jordan Valley: archaeology, environment and ethnology. *Studies in the History and Archaeology of Jordan* 4: 155–60.

Savage, S. H., and S. E. Falconer (2003). Spatial and statistical inference of Late Bronze Age polities in the southern Levant. *Bulletin of the American Schools of Oriental Research* 330: 31–45.

Smith, R. H. (1973). *Pella of the Decapolis 1: The 1967 Season of the College of Wooster Expedition to Pella*. Wooster, OH: College of Wooster.

Sparks, R. T. (2001a). Stone vessel workshops in the Levant: luxury products of a cosmopolitan age. In A. J. Shortland (ed.), *The Social Context of Technological Change: Egypt and the Near East, 1650–1550 BC*. Oxford: Oxbow, 93–112.

—— (2001b). Palestinian stone vessels: the evidence from Pella. *Studies in the History and Archaeology of Jordan* 7: 259–63.

Vieweger, D., and J. Häser (2007). Das Gadara Region Project: der Tell Zerā'a in den Jahren 2005 und 2006. *Zeitschrift des Deutschen Palästina-Vereins* 123: 1–27.

Wimmer, D. H. (1989). Safut. In D. Homès-Fredericq and J. B. Hennessy (eds), *Archaeology of Jordan II,2: Field Reports: Sites L–Z*. Leuven: Peeters, 512–15.

Worschech, U. (2003). *A Burial Cave at Umm Dimis, North of el-Balu'*. Frankfurt am Main: Lang.

Yassine, K. N. (1988). The East Jordan Valley Survey, 1976, pt 2. In K. N. Yassine (ed.), *Archaeology of Jordan: Essays and Reports*. Amman: Department of Archaeology, University of Jordan, 189–207.

Zayadine, F. S., M. Najjar, and J. A. Greene (1987). Recent excavations on the citadel of Amman (lower terrace): a preliminary report. *Annual of the Department of Antiquities of Jordan* 31: 299–311.

....

CHAPTER 32

CYPRUS DURING THE MIDDLE BRONZE AGE

....

DAVID FRANKEL

INTRODUCTION

....

During the three centuries of the Middle Bronze Age (about 2000/1950–1700/1650 BCE), Cyprus was transformed from a relatively isolated island with numerous small independent villages to one with increasing foreign connections and the initial development of larger centres. Even so, it is not until the very end of the period that there is any suggestion of centralized organization or a formal social, political, or economic hierarchy of sites. Nor was there any formal symbolic system used to signify ownership or status. In these and other respects Middle Cypriot society differed significantly from Middle Bronze Age societies elsewhere in the Levant: the equivalence of terminology reflects only archaeological labelling developed in the early history of research. Similarly, although archaeological distinctions can be made within continuously evolving ceramic and other traditions, the formally designated conventional periods within the Cypriot Bronze Age should not be taken to mark sharp points of change. No clear distinction can be made in the seamless development from Early Cypriot (EC) III to Middle Cypriot (MC) I early in the second millennium BCE, while the latest MC III elides into Late Cypriot (LC) IA during the 17th century BCE.

THE ARCHAEOLOGICAL RECORD

....

Three complementary datasets are available: extramural cemeteries of chamber tombs, settlement excavations, and evidence from surface surveys. Until the 1980s, the often-repeated comment that the Early and Middle Cypriot was known almost entirely from tombs was largely true, although the quality if not the quantity of funerary evidence was and is less than often thought (Fig. 32.1). Detailed ceramic typologies based on grave goods (Stewart 1962; Åström 1972) formed the basis of most discussion.

   Apart from Alambra *Mouttes* (Coleman et al. 1996), Marki *Alonia* (Frankel and Webb 1996; 2006), and Pyrgos *Mavroraki* (Belgiorno 2004), there is still very little settlement evidence available to provide stratigraphic confirmation of the ceramic chronology or for studies of most aspects of life and society. There is an uneven distribution of information from

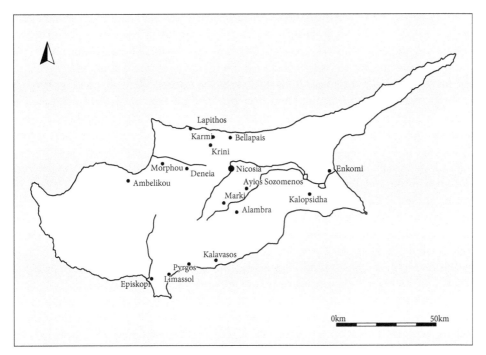

FIG. 32.1 Map of Middle Bronze Age sites in Cyprus

different areas of the island. An earlier bias toward cemeteries on the north coast and some central sites structured much of the formative analysis and classification. However, since 1974 no research has been carried out in the northern half of the island in the areas under Turkish Cypriot control, leading to a different bias in the data. Knowledge of site distribution is also patchy, although the pioneering work of the Cyprus Survey initiated by Catling in the 1950s is now supplemented by a few more focused regional studies and data from rescue excavations (Iacovou 2004; Georghiou 2006).

SETTLEMENTS, HOUSEHOLDS, AND COMMUNITY

Middle Cypriot settlements were, for the most part, open villages with no clear boundaries or evidence of fortifications. Only toward the very end of the period is there evidence of fortified sites, and these are generally poorly documented and understood. The extent of settlements can seldom be estimated from surface indications, especially as villages varied considerably in size and structure through time (Webb and Frankel 2004). At Marki, for example, it has been argued that a small Early Cypriot foundation by a handful of people grew to a maximum population on the order of 400 people spread over 4–6ha of settlement area in Middle Cypriot I (Frankel and Webb 2001; 2006).

Middle Cypriot I–II architecture is best known from excavations at Marki (Frankel and Webb 1996; 2006) and Alambra (Coleman et al. 1996). Although they are only 8km apart, there are significant differences between these two sites due to their specific geographical setting and the history of occupation revealed by limited excavations.

At Alambra, a row of rectangular houses sharing party walls was built into a shallow gully on the side of a hill. They were constructed, used, and abandoned over a short period of time with little evidence of renovation and modification, and are therefore relatively uniform in layout. A major transverse wall divided each house into a front and rear section, with the rear further divided to produce a total of three to five rooms. The front sections, through which the houses were entered, may have been partly or fully enclosed (their front walls may have been lost through erosion). The bedrock provided an uneven floor and the rear rooms and walls were partly set into and against the hillside. Walls were built primarily of the local chalk.

The larger area of Middle Cypriot domestic architecture at Marki, by contrast, was an end-product of a centuries-long history of building, renovation, and rebuilding in more open terrain (see Webb, Ch. 24 above) (Fig. 32.2). The layout of individual households varied. The majority, particularly when not constrained by existing structures, retained the traditional form of rectilinear multi-roomed compounds seen in the Early Cypriot period, with two or three small rooms at the back of walled courtyards. Some new household types developed: specifically single room units and compounds with no courtyards. In contrast to Alambra, the buildings at Marki were constructed of mould-made mud-bricks, laid on several courses of dry-stone walling. As in the earlier phases at the site, substantial emplacements, perhaps supports for storage vessels, were placed beside the courtyard walls; other built features, such as small rectangular bins, long, low plastered benches, and semicircular hearths, were set against interior walls (Fig. 32.3). The associated artefacts suggest a wide array of domestic activities and small-scale storage within each household.

Similar compounds with courtyards can be identified in the older excavations at EC III or MC I Alambra and MC III to LC I Kalopsidha (Åström 1972). They may have been in evidence, too, in the LC I village at Episkopi *Phaneromeni*, and represent a common pattern of household organization.

FIG. 32.2 Looking northeast across the main excavated area at Marki, 1999

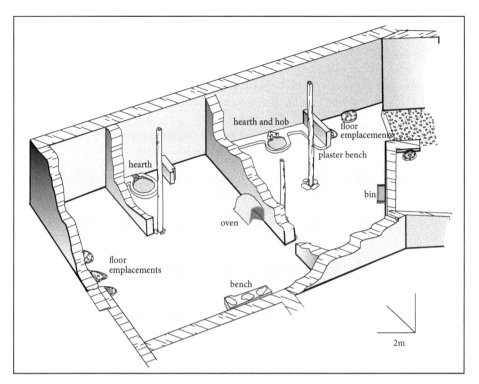

FIG. 32.3 Isometric reconstruction of a house at Marki, showing the location of hearths and other built-in features

While changing population and settlement size must have impacted the nature of social interaction and decision-making within communities, there is no suggestion in the domestic areas excavated at Marki and Alambra of any significant differences in house form, size, or function indicative of social or economic hierarchies or centralized control. As discussed in the chapter on the Early Cypriot period (Webb, Ch. 24 above), cooperation between households is visible in the earliest phases at Marki. However, the later, Middle Cypriot system at that site and at Alambra appears to favour more isolation between house compounds, regulating social interaction by restricting visual penetration and access. These changes may have been the result of the growth in settlement size, leading to lower levels of cooperation and regularity of contact between all members of the community. This in turn can be seen as associated with more formal social structures, and the ownership, inheritance, and control of resources. Increased size and attendant transformations in social organization may have been matched by changes in the physical structure of villages, which may have become fragmented once populations grew beyond about 400 people (Bintliff 1999: 527). While there is no direct evidence, this could account for the separation of the extensive cemetery areas observed at Deneia (Frankel and Webb 2007).

A different aspect of Middle Cypriot architecture is seen at Pyrgos, although the extent, structure, and dating of the large buildings currently being excavated are still uncertain (Belgiorno 2004). While the settlement undoubtedly had a longer history, the main excavated building, which was catastrophically destroyed, is probably MC III in date. It appears to have been used for substantial industrial and storage purposes. A large room or courtyard contained a series of *pithoi* containing olive oil. Adjacent spaces with small furnaces and associated equipment were used for working metals. It is also possible that other items—notably textiles—were produced in nearby areas.

There is less detail available for other MC III settlements, either because of poor preservation (Dali *Kafkallia* at Ayios Sozomenos (Overbeck and Swiny 1972) or because problems of access preclude further study (Krini *Merra*). These two settlements are among several fortified sites which appear to have been built late in the Middle Cypriot period or in LC I, especially in the centre of the island (Catling 1973; Peltenburg 1996).

Cemeteries, funerary customs, and ritual

Extensive burial grounds of chamber tombs are characteristic of the Middle Cypriot period, continuing the Early Cypriot tradition (Keswani 2004; 2005). These were sited at appropriate localities some distance from the parent settlements (at Marki the cemetery areas are over 500m from the settlement). The number of tombs is, however, hard to estimate. About 700 Early and Middle Cypriot tombs have been documented in the looted cemeteries at Marki (Frankel and Webb 1996), and some 1,300 (mainly Middle Cypriot) tombs survive at Deneia, where there were probably originally at least two or three times that number (Frankel and Webb 2007). The most extensive series of formally excavated Middle Cypriot tombs is at Lapithos *Vrysi tou Barba* (Gjerstad et al. 1934), with substantial numbers also published from Bellapais *Vounous* (Dikaios 1940; Stewart and Stewart 1950; Dunn-Vaturi 2003). Smaller numbers of tombs are documented from cemeteries elsewhere in the island but, apart from a few cases, such as Kalavasos and Limassol, are not well published.

As with settlements, variation in tomb form is partly related to local topography and geology and partly to cultural and historical factors (Fig. 32.4). The basic form consists of a dromos or entry shaft leading through a small stomion (doorway) into a larger underground chamber. These doorways were normally blocked by large stone slabs. In some cases two or more separate chambers shared a single entrance. At the north coast sites of Lapithos, Karmi, and Bellapais, the typical dromos sloped down to a horizontal entry to the chamber. On the limestone plateau areas at Deneia, where the ground surface consists of a hard capping above looser conglomerates, there were neatly cut square or circular vertical shafts about 1–1.5m in depth, with secondary narrower, tunnel-like shafts leading down into the chambers hollowed out of the lower unconsolidated soil. On hillslopes, however, short horizontal shafts led directly to the entrance of the chamber. Most tomb chambers are roughly circular or oval, but they vary considerably in size and shape. Where natural cavities under limestone capping were utilized, chambers can be exceptionally large.

The effort invested in tomb construction and the quantity of grave goods indicates that burial rites formed a significant aspect of social behaviour and identity. Most Middle Cypriot tombs were used for a series of successive burials, each accompanied by an array of grave goods providing an opportunity for conspicuous display related to the wealth or status of individuals or kin-groups.

Often previous burials and accompanying artefacts were unceremoniously moved aside to make space for new ones, although Keswani perceives occasional careful rearrangement

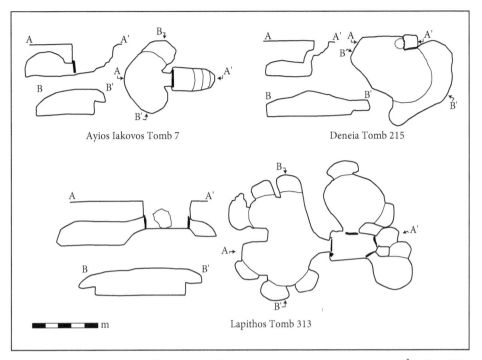

Ayios Iakovos Tomb 7

Deneia Tomb 215

Lapithos Tomb 313

FIG. 32.4 Examples of Middle Cypriot Bronze Age chamber tombs (after Åström 1972: figs 4 and 5; Frankel and Webb 2007)

of skulls of earlier interments (2005). Pots were the most common items deposited in tombs. While the more unusual shapes are likely to have been made specifically for funerary use, most were everyday types. Some show patterns of use-damage which indicates that they were in normal use before being deposited in the tombs (Dugay 1996). The lack of formal excavation of cemeteries and associated settlements precludes some aspects of comparison, but it is likely that finer, decorated vessels were preferentially selected (if not specifically made) for funerary use. There is insufficient evidence to demonstrate any systematic differential treatment of male, female, young, and old. The absence at many sites of remains of children remains problematic, and is certainly contradicted by the large number identified at Deneia (Frankel and Webb 2006). Identification of status on the basis of the quantity and nature of grave goods is confused by poor preservation and/or excavation, and the difficulty of estimating either the total number of burials or the association between sets of items and individuals. There does not, however, appear to be any neat separation of classes, suggesting a well-established hierarchy of wealth or status (Keswani 2005). The continuous use and reuse of tombs argues, however, for long-lasting family ownership, matching that suggested for household compounds at Marki.

Apart from funerary customs, there is no evidence at all of Middle Cypriot ritual distinct from an inherent ritualization in everyday life (cf. Bradley 2003), and no cult places have been identified (Webb 1999: 17). This has not inhibited speculation on the meaning or significance of an array of terracotta figures and models (discussed in Webb, Ch. 24 above).

Site distribution and settlement networks

Significant changes in settlement pattern took place during the Middle Cypriot period. Although settlement in the region followed at all times a primarily rural system, there was a trend toward a concentration of population in larger centres, and the foundation of new settlements late in the period.

Many, if not all, MC I sites were originally founded earlier in the Bronze Age, perhaps the result of an increase in population during EC III. Allowing for the difficulties arising from the varied intensity of survey coverage, a general spread of sites can be seen across most of the island, with the exception of the Troodos Range (where little archaeological research has been carried out). On the south coast there was a string of settlements a few kilometres apart on the rising ground 2–4km from the shore. A similar pattern was in evidence on the narrower coastal plain between the Kyrenia Range and the north coast. In the centre of the island, substantial sites were located in the vicinity of major rivers, such as the east-flowing Pedeios and Yialias and the west-flowing Ovgos, or in well-watered localities along the southern base of the Kyrenia Range. Other, perhaps smaller settlements were positioned at the interface between the sedimentary formations of the centre, close to the rich copper-bearing deposits in the foothills of the Troodos Range. There was, however, little or no settlement at this time along the low-lying, perhaps swampy eastern or western coasts of the central plain.

During MC II and into MC III some sites, such as Marki and Alambra, were abandoned. At these two sites this may have been due in part to changed climatic conditions and soil degradation through over-use, reducing the productivity of these less well-favoured areas of the northern foothills of the Troodos. It may also be attributed to a development of a different pattern of inter-site relationships. A more or less contemporary increase in the scale of the cemeteries at Deneia, Lapithos, and Nicosia *Ayia Paraskevi*, together with increased evidence of settlement at Kalopsida and Pyrgos, suggests a process of redistribution and consolidation of populations into fewer, larger settlements. Some of these centres may, in turn, have begun to decline in significance toward the end of MC III and beginning of LC I. At this time new sites on the coastal fringe of the central plain were established, notably at Morphou *Toumba tou Skourou* and Enkomi, which were to become the kernel of Late Cypriot urbanism. While a reduction of unhealthy or unproductive wetlands may account for the specific siting of these settlements, their coastal location can be regarded as part of the opening up of the overseas connections which led to their later pre-eminence.

Resource acquisition, production, and distribution

For MC I to II there is no significant change in patterns of resource use from the well-established practices of EC III. With few exceptions—most obviously metallurgy—there is little indication of any economic system beyond the household, village, or local regional level. It is possible to argue that evolving patterns of household structure seen at Marki (such as the presence of some households without courtyards) signify a divergence in household activities and possibly land ownership. If so, it would fit with a model of increasing specialization in manufactures such as pottery. Nevertheless, pottery production is best seen as carried out by part-time, individual elementary specialists, even during the later phases when the similarity of some types, such as White Painted Fine Line Style, suggest distinct workshops (Maguire 1991) or when other wares began to be exported to the Levant. During MC III, the reorganization of internal settlement patterns, coupled with an increasing export of goods, suggests some more complex and perhaps formal organization of storage and production. This certainly appears to be the case in the area excavated at Pyrgos, with its array of large pithoi and evidence of metallurgical workshops.

At both Marki and Alambra subsistence was, as earlier in the Bronze Age, based on a mixed agropastoral economy, with wheat and barley supplemented by an array of fruits and legumes. Apart from donkeys, presumably kept as beasts of burden, sheep, goats, and cattle were the main animals herded, with very small proportions of pigs, and some hunting of feral deer. At Marki goats became slightly more common in the Middle Cypriot than sheep, perhaps associated with changes to the local environment rather than with a more broad development. Age profiles of caprines suggest a slight increase in herding for milk, but at all times culling regimes indicate a greater concern for meat (and possibly wool) production (Croft in Frankel and Webb 2006).

The main metal used in the Middle Cypriot was copper from sources in the Troodos foothills. The presence of moulds and other processing equipment at Ambelikou *Aletri* (Merrillees 1984; Webb and Frankel 2013), Marki (Frankel and Webb 2006), and Alambra (see Gale, Stos-Gale, and Fasnacht in Coleman et al. 1996) indicates that copper was brought to these settlements from mines a few kilometres away for final processing and casting into small ingots for distribution across the island. This may have been a relatively small-scale industry operating as part of a mixed economy at these strategically placed sites. The MC III furnaces and anvils at Pyrgos suggest larger-scale production (Belgiorno 2004). It remains unclear whether there was any significant export of metal from the island at this time. However, as tin was imported throughout the Middle Cypriot, some reciprocal exchange of metals may have taken place.

INTERACTION AND SOCIAL NETWORKS

The earlier phases of the Middle Bronze Age can be characterized as a period of slow growth and general economic and social equilibrium, with the development of a relatively uniform and integrated system of smaller and larger villages in an egalitarian, horizontally integrated, and essentially rural system. Connections between neighbouring regions were most probably based on kinship and associated with a low level of exchange of goods for internal consumption within the island. That is, networks were largely built on social relationships which facilitated economic exchanges. In this way the distribution of some primary products (the most obvious of which is copper, but perhaps including shells, salt, flax, and possibly drugs) and some manufactured goods both stimulated and was facilitated by connections between villages based on intermarriage. During the Middle Cypriot this is most evident in the general distribution of major pottery wares and finer-scale stylistic variation within them (Fig. 32.5).

Although Red Polished pottery typical of the Early Cypriot continued as the dominant fabric, it is most common at northern, central, and southeastern sites and rare or absent in the southwest. Although the pottery is technologically similar, regional differences in shape

White Painted Ware

0 ___ 10cm   Red Polished Ware

Black Polished Ware

Drab Polished Ware   Red-on-Black Ware   Cooking pot   Black Slip Ware

FIG. 32.5 A selection of the Middle Cypriot Bronze Age pottery illustrating the main wares

and decoration show stylistic—and hence social—interaction zones. The Red Polished pottery from Marki and Alambra, in the centre of the island, is, for example, more similar to that from the southeast than the north coast, while a relatively close association can be seen in northern types and those from Deneia in the eastern part of the central plain. There is a generally similar distribution of the White Painted wares which are often regarded as the hallmark of the Middle Cypriot. Regional preferences for particular motifs and organizational structures demonstrate that most of this pottery was locally made, with patterns of similarity showing social connections between sites, best explained by the occasional movement of individual potters (Frankel 1974a; 1974b). The underlying correlation of geographical and social distance is cut across by other patterns of association suggesting links to the distribution of copper.

Drab Polished Ware was the predominant monochrome pottery in the southwest. Some examples of this pottery are found in central sites: many of these were perhaps containers for precious liquids. The distribution of some other wares was even more geographically restricted. Black Polished Ware, for example, was made and used primarily at Deneia, while the Karpas Peninsula was home to Red-on-Red and Red-on-Black Wares. The occasional example of these wares outside their area of manufacture shows that at least small quantities of pottery were carried from one site to another, although this is unlikely for the bulk of material—at least until the later phases of MC III, when Cypriot pottery began to be exported to the Levant and Egypt.

The later Middle Cypriot settlement pattern involved the development of larger centres and provided a platform for a new order of relationships, as kin-based networks gave way to commercial and more industrial-scale production. This facilitated the spread of foreign goods across the island. These developments were part of a transformed economic, if not political, landscape which foreshadowed that of the initial phase of the Late Cypriot period (LC IA), when centres such as Enkomi began to dominate broader territories. It is only at that time that more formal relationships can be suggested, with both commercial exchanges and an associated political dimension to establishing and controlling vertically integrated and asymmetrical networks.

External relations

In the early years of the Middle Bronze Age, some time after 2000 BCE, Cyprus began to be involved in broader eastern Mediterranean networks. It is unlikely, however, that Cypriots either initiated these connections or were anything other than minor players on the fringe of major developments of new trading systems. A handful of imports (several daggers and two pottery vessels) from Crete (Kehrberg 1995; cf. Keswani 2005: table 13) show occasional connections with expanding Middle Minoan activity made possible by the development of deep-hulled sailing ships. Cyprus may, however, have been no more than an occasional port of call outside the normal route of Minoan trading vessels.

The reappearance of tin-bronze from the beginning of Middle Cypriot is also part of this gradual opening up to the outside world. It may be no coincidence that it was about this time that new forms of commercial interaction were developing in Anatolia with the establishment of Assyrian trading colonies such as that at Kültepe, providing a context for the long-distance movement of tin and other primary products.

The extent to which Cypriot copper was systematically incorporated into the Anatolian and Aegean interaction sphere at this time is unclear.

There was, however, a rapid expansion of external interaction during MC III. Yehudiyeh juglets and other exotic items are found in many Cypriot sites. A reciprocal export of MC III–LC I pottery, especially later forms of White Painted Ware typical of the eastern part of the island (notably Pendant Line and Cross Line Style vessels), is also well documented at many sites in the Levant and Egypt. While smaller closed vessels might have been used to ship precious liquids, others must have been distributed in their own right. These exports argue for a large scale of pottery production, but the nature of both the internal system and the mechanisms involved in the exchange networks remain unknown.

Several examples of imported shaft-hole axes and associated elite goods (listed in Keswani 2005: table 13) also demonstrate the increasing scale and nature of contacts with the Levant during MC III. In addition, Cyprus (i.e. Alashiya) receives its first mention in 18th- and 17th-century tablets from Mari, Alalakh, and Babylon—a clear signal of involvement with the island and its resources by the more developed and complex societies on the mainland (Knapp 1996: 5, texts 2–11, 32). Although Cyprus remained an essentially rural and loosely integrated society on the fringes of the state-controlled market economies of the eastern Mediterranean, it is clear that the foundations for the fundamental shifts in social organization and economy that characterize Late Cypriot society were well in place by the end of the Middle Bronze Age.

Suggested reading

Barlow, J. A., D. R. Bolger, and B. Kling (eds) (1991). *Cypriot Ceramics: Reading the Prehistoric Record*. Philadelphia: University Museum of Archaeology and Anthropology, University of Pennsylvania.

Bolger, D. R. (2003). *Gender in Ancient Cyprus: Narratives of Social Change on a Mediterranean Island*. Walnut Creek, Calif.: AltaMira.

Karageorghis, V. (1991). *The Coroplastic Art of Ancient Cyprus 1: Chalcolithic–Late Cypriote I*. Nicosia: A. G. Leventis Foundation.

Knapp, A. B. (2008). *Prehistoric and Protohistoric Cyprus*. Oxford: Oxford University Press.

Rupp, D. (ed.) (1993). Perspectives on Cypriot social complexity. *Bulletin of the American Schools of Oriental Research* 292.

Steel, L. (2004). *Cyprus Before History: From the Earliest Settlers to the End of the Bronze Age*. London: Duckworth.

References

Åström, P. (1972). *The Middle Cypriote Bronze Age*. Lund: Swedish Cyprus Expedition.

Belgiorno, M. R. (2004). *Pyrgos Mavroraki: Advanced Technology in Bronze Age Cyprus*. Nicosia: Nicosia Archaeological Museum.

Bintliff, J. L. (1999). Settlement and territory. In G. Barker (ed.) *Companion Encyclopedia of Archaeology*, vol. 1. London: Routledge, 505–45.

Bradley, R. (2003). A life less ordinary: the ritualization of the domestic sphere in later prehistoric Europe. *Cambridge Archaeology Journal* 13: 5–23.

Catling, H. W. (1973). Cyprus in the Middle Bronze Age. In I. E. S. Edwards, C. J. Gadd, N. G. L. Hammond, and E. Sollberger (eds), *The Cambridge Ancient History*, vol. 2/1, 3rd edn. Cambridge: Cambridge University Press, 165–75.

Coleman, J. E., J. A. Barlow, M. K. Mogelonsky, and K. W. Schaar (1996). *Alambra: A Middle Bronze Age Settlement in Cyprus—Archaeological Investigations by Cornell University 1974–1985*. Jonsered: Åström.

Dikaios, P. (1940). The excavations at Vounous–Bellapais in Cyprus, 1931–1932. *Archaeologia* 88: 1–174.

Dugay, L. (1996). Specialised pottery production on Bronze Age Cyprus and pottery use-wear analysis. *Journal of Mediterranean Archaeology* 9: 167–92.

Dunn-Vaturi, A.-E. (2003), *Vounous: C.F.A. Schaeffer's Excavations in 1933—Tombs 49–79*. Jonsered: Åström.

Frankel, D. (1974a). *Middle Cypriot White Painted Pottery: An Analytical Study of the Decoration*. Gothenburg: Åström.

—— (1974b). Inter-site relationships in the Middle Bronze Age of Cyprus. *World Archaeology* 6: 190–208.

—— and J. M. Webb (1996). *Marki Alonia: An Early and Middle Bronze Age Town in Cyprus*, vol. 1: *Excavations 1990–1994*. Jonsered: Åström.

—— (2001). Population, households, and ceramic consumption in a prehistoric Cypriot village. *Journal of Field Archaeology* 28: 115–29.

—— (2006). *Marki Alonia: An Early and Middle Bronze Age Settlement in Cyprus*, vol. 2: *Excavations 1995–2000*. Jonsered: Åström.

—— (2007). *The Bronze Age Cemeteries at Deneia in Cyprus*. Sävedalen: Åström [with associated digital archive http://library.latrobe.edu.au/record=b2234894]

Georghiou, G. (2006). *The topography of human settlement in Cyprus in the Early and Middle Bronze Age* [Greek]. PhD dissertation, University of Cyprus.

Gjerstad, E., J. Lindros, E. Sjöqvist, and A. Westholm (1934). *The Swedish Cyprus Expedition: Finds and Results of the Excavations in Cyprus 1927–1931* (3 vols). Stockholm: Swedish Cyprus Expedition.

Iacovou, M. (ed.) (2004). *Archaeological Field Survey in Cyprus: Past History, Future Potentials*. London: British School at Athens.

Kehrberg, I. C. (1995). *Northern Cyprus in the Transition from the Early to the Middle Cypriot Period: Typology, Relative and Absolute Chronology of Some Early Cypriot III to Middle Cypriot I Tombs*. Jonsered: Åström.

Keswani, P. (2004). *Mortuary Ritual and Society in Bronze Age Cyprus*. London: Equinox.

—— (2005). Death, prestige, and copper in Bronze Age Cyprus. *American Journal of Archaeology* 109: 341–401.

Knapp, A. B. (ed.) (1996). *Near Eastern and Aegean Texts from the Third to the First Millennia BC*. Altamont, NY: Greece and Cyprus Research Centre.

Maguire, L. C. (1991). The classification of Middle Bronze Age painted pottery: wares, styles…workshops? In J. A. Barlow, D. R. Bolger, and B. Kling (eds), *Cypriot Ceramics: Reading the Prehistoric Record*. Philadelphia: University Museum of Archaeology and Anthropology, University of Pennsylvania, 59–66.

Merrillees, R. S. (1984). Ambelikou–*Aletri*: a preliminary report. *Report of the Department of Antiquities, Cyprus* 1984: 1–13.

Overbeck, J. C., and S. Swiny (1972). *Two Cypriot Bronze Age Sites at Kafkallia (Dhali)*. Gothenburg: Åström.

Peltenburg, E. J. (1996). From isolation to state formation in Cyprus, c. 3500–1500 BC. In V. Karageorghis and D. Michaelides (eds) *The Development of the Cypriot Economy from the Prehistoric Period to the Present Day*. Nicosia: University of Cyprus and the Bank of Cyprus, 17–44.

Stewart, E. M., and J. R. Stewart. (1950). *Vounous 1937–38: Field Report of the Excavations Sponsored by the British School at Athens*. Lund: Gleerup.

Stewart, J. R. (1962). The Early Cypriote Bronze Age. In P. Dikaios and J. R. Stewart, *The Stone Age and the Early Bronze Age in Cyprus*. Lund: Swedish Cyprus Expedition, 205–401.

Webb, J. M. (1999). *Ritual Architecture, Iconography and Practice in the Late Cypriot Bronze Age*. Jonsered: Åström.

—— and D. Frankel (2004). Intensive site survey: implications for estimating settlement size, population and duration in prehistoric Bronze Age Cyprus. In M. Iacovou (ed.), *Archaeological Field Survey in Cyprus: Past History, Future Potentials*. London: British School at Athens, 125–37.

—— and D. Frankel (2013). *Ambelikou Aletri. Metallurgy and Pottery Production in Middle Bronze Age Cyprus*. Uppsala Åström.

SECTION E

THE LATE BRONZE AGE

CHAPTER 33

INTRODUCTION TO THE LEVANT DURING THE LATE BRONZE AGE

E. SUSAN SHERRATT

CHRONOLOGY AND PERIODIZATION: TERMINOLOGY, ARCHAEOLOGY, AND TEXTS

The first thing that strikes one when contemplating the Late Bronze archaeology of the Levant (rather loosely and only partly logically defined for the purposes of this volume as comprising the modern states of Israel with Palestine, Jordan, Lebanon, Syria, and Cyprus) are the obstacles it presents to viewing it contextually as a coherent geographical area. This is partly because of modern geopolitical boundaries, which have ensured that the archaeologies of different national entities have tended to try to preserve their own distinctive integrity and to develop, maintain, or elaborate their own traditions and frameworks; even within those traditions and frameworks, archaeologists in many cases find it difficult to reach consensus. The Levant, as defined here, seems to suffer from the traditional European archaeological practice of proliferating new chronologies and associated terminologies, presumably in the hope of refining generalized frameworks which will allow one to slot 'events' at individual sites accurately into these, but probably also for other more obscure and archaeologically specific reasons. In any case, the effect may just be to cause confusion. Figure 33.1, a highly simplified summary of the particular chronological schemes for the Late Bronze Age used for the various regions by the authors of the following chapters, appears to illustrate this, with its cumbersome alternatives for the beginning of the Late Bronze Age in the case of Israel/Palestine and its hesitancy about the distinction between LB I and II in the case of Jordan. It underlines the difficulties faced by anyone hoping to hop across modern geopolitical boundaries and untangle the archaeological record of the Late Bronze Levant (or east Mediterranean) as a whole. If LB IIB starts half a century earlier in Lebanon than in neighbouring Israel/Palestine or Jordan, then what hope is there that outsiders faced with dealing with detailed site reports or even syntheses compiled within modern national boundaries can easily make sense of the terminology employed?

It is perhaps unfair to single out these difficulties, which in fact are only the tips of highly disputed icebergs when it comes to chronologies within any one of the individual regions. What they are symptoms of, however, are much deeper uncertainties about the role and purpose of archaeology in general in this part of the world, and about the roles, purposes, and natures of archaeological chronologies in particular. It all depends on the lenses through which the various archaeological records are viewed and interpreted. On the one hand, as most overtly in the case of Jordan (Fischer, Ch. 37 below), the archaeology and its interpretation are seen through the lens of Egyptian history, and not only is its Late Bronze chronology calibrated by the reigns of Egyptian pharaohs and their activities, but the fortunes of archaeological sites are actively tied into this history—to the extent that, in the case of Tell Abu al-Kharaz Phase V, the 'find a Pharaoh' system as described by Leonard (1988) comes into play, and the main question is one of whether it was destroyed by Thutmosis III during the Palestinian campaign in Year 22 of his reign or by his son Amenophis II some thirty years later. By contrast, at Kamid el-Loz in the Beqa' Valley, where Egyptian interests at times during the Late Bronze appear to have been no less active than in the central Jordan Valley, both temple and palace (or sections of it) were destroyed on several occasions without any seeming need to invoke particular pharaonic campaigns or other textually recorded conflicts as causes or date-calibrating mechanisms (Heinz and Kulemann-Ossen, Ch. 35 below; cf. Luciani, Ch. 34 below).

Parts of the Levant as archaeological (and chronological) peripheries of New Kingdom Egypt is one thing, but at the other extreme we have Cyprus, whose Late Bronze chronological framework owes nothing directly to Egypt, but rather has traditionally sought to align itself with the Aegean. This is why, in general, the Cypriot Late Bronze Age (Late Cypriot) currently appears to start earlier and, particularly, end later than the Late Bronze Age in its mainland neighbours just across the water (Fig. 33.1 and Steel, Ch. 38 below, Table 38.1, based on Merrillees 1992).[1] Here, well out of the reach of Egyptian history and with no readable historical documents of its own, the chronological framework since the 1930s has been built primarily around stylistic analysis of changes in pottery, originally elaborated somewhat precariously on the basis of pots found in tombs, many of these in use for long periods and in most of which it is impossible to distinguish the goods associated with successive burials.

Pottery, too, has affected aspects of the chronological frameworks of other regions, even where these are based primarily on text-generated historical punctuation marks such as the expulsion of the Hyksos or the destructions attributed to the invasions of the 'Sea Peoples' (Sharon, Ch. 4 above). Pottery along with other aspects of material culture, for example, have played some part in proposals to rename what was originally called LB IA in Israel/ Palestine to transitional Middle-to-Late Bronze or MB IIC–LB I (Panitz-Cohen, Ch. 36 below) and in the divisions of the Late Bronze Age and their terminology (in particular,

---

[1] This has not always been the case. Once upon a time, before attempts to date the volcanic eruption of Thera by various scientific means, the beginning of the Late Bronze Age in both the Aegean and Cyprus was aligned with the start of the Egyptian New Kingdom at *c.* 1550 BCE (Sjöqvist 1940: 197; cf. Manning 1995: 198–9); and C. F.-A. Schaeffer (1948: 392) made a brief but short-lived attempt to align the end of the Late Bronze Age in Cyprus with that at Ugarit (*c.*1200 BCE), before the scheme originally devised by the Swedish Cyprus Expedition, which brought it into line with the end of the Submycenaean ceramic phase in Greece (*c.*1050 BCE), reasserted itself. From current viewpoints at least, neither of these latter dates has very much to do directly with the switch to iron as a base metal.

Table 33.1 Chronologies of the Late Bronze Age Levant, from Chapters 34–38

	ISRAEL/PALESTINE	JORDAN	LEBANON	SYRIA	CYPRUS
1650					LC IA
					- - - - - -
1600				- - - - -	
1550	- - - - - - - - - -	- - - - - -	- - - - - - -		- - - - - -
	transitional MB-LB				
1500	or MB IIC-LB I or LB IA	LB IA	LB I	LBA I	LC IB
	- - - - - - - - - -				
1450		- - - - - -			- - - - - -
	LB IB	LB IB			LC IIA
1400		- - - - - -	- - - - - -		
	- - - - - - - - - -	LB IC	LB IIA		- - - - - -
		or LB IIA			
1350	LB IIA		- - - - - - -	- - - - -	LC IIB
1300	- - - - - - - - - -	- - - - - -	LB IIB	LBA II	- - - - - -
1250	LB IIB	LB II			LC IIC
		or LB IIB			
1200	- - - - - - - - - -		- - - - - - -	- - - - -	- - - - - -
	LB III				
1150	or Iron Age IA	- - - - - - -			LC IIIA
	- - - - - - - - - -				
1100					- - - - - -
					LC IIIB
1050					- - - - -

the decision to substitute LB IC for LB IIA) employed in the chapter on Jordan (Fischer, Ch. 37 below). To those immersed in a traditional culture-history approach to the archaeological record, in which pottery, architecture, burial customs, and the like were seen as reliable indicators of the advent of new groups of people, new regimes, or simply a new 'age', it has sometimes come as something of a surprise to find that pottery shows distinct continuities across such major 'historical' divisions as are supposedly denoted by the beginning or end of the Late Bronze Age.[2] Now that archaeologists have long got over such surprise, one might wonder why it is felt necessary to try to combine a ceramic-based chronology within the same framework as a historical chronology. By all means have them both, but they are quite separate things, not easily merged into a single integrated and readily comprehensible whole. For that matter, the idea that pottery can provide a universal chronological framework even within modern political boundaries is somewhat problematic; and in any case, the Levant has a long archaeological tradition of studying pottery with other questions in mind rather than simply the demands of broad chronological schemes (e.g. Kelso and Thorley 1943; Magrill and Middleton 2001; cf. Frankel 1991). A series of parallel

---

[2] Hence e.g. the once prevalent belief that collared-rim jars were a type associated exclusively with early Israelite settlers and therefore found only in the Early Iron Age—to the extent that the presence of a collared-rim jar was enough to proclaim the context in which it was found to be of unequivocal Early Iron Age date (Albright 1954: 118; Esse 1991).

but cross-cutting chronologies operating at different levels—from the highly localized phasing (including ceramic phasing) of individual sites based on stratigraphy (e.g. as at Kamid el-Loz (Heinz and Kulemann-Ossen, Ch. 35 below) or Tell Abu al-Kharaz (Fischer, Ch. 37 below)) to traditional broad period divisions based on the three-age system and supposedly major historical and societal changes, with ceramic linkages providing geographically ad hoc and specific links between individual aspects of the two—seems a more satisfactory way of approaching archaeological chronology than trying to squeeze everything in Procrustean fashion into a single overarching and universalized scheme.

A series of calibrated radiocarbon determinations from Phases V and VI at Tell Abu al-Kharaz (Fischer, Ch. 37: Table 37.2) reminds us that the Levant as a whole has only relatively recently embraced dating techniques such as calibrated radiocarbon (^{14}C) and (still at an extremely embryonic stage) dendrochronology (Lorentzen et al. 2010). Long dismissed on the grounds that the chronologies provided by tie-ins with historical texts were both more precise and accurate, even the most sophisticatedly calibrated short-life radiocarbon determinations still have difficulties in providing answers to the kinds of chronological questions typically asked of Late Bronze sites, such as which pharaonic campaign was responsible for the destruction of Tell Abu al-Kharaz Phase V.[3] What they do, however, like the series of radiocarbon determinations from LC IIC–early LC IIIA contexts on Cyprus (Manning et al. 2001; Steel, Ch. 38), is provide a check on approximate absolute datings achieved by another, more traditional means of ad hoc cross-linking—which seem, in this case, to be vindicated within perfectly tolerable degrees of approximation. Our frameworks, so far, seem robust enough as long as we do not press them to a level of precision which archaeology is incapable of delivering, and as long as we do not expect archaeology to provide precise chronological confirmation of the events recorded in historical documents.

POLITICAL STRUCTURES

The Late Bronze Age in the Levant is characterized by what Liverani (1987: 66–7) has called 'great kings' and 'small kings'—i.e. the major imperial powers of Egypt, Mitanni, and Hatti on the one hand and a multiplicity of city-states and kingdoms of varying size and extent on the other, some of which at various times became vassals of, or otherwise nominally subject to, the rulers of one or other of the 'great powers'. To the extent that we know about these, this is again because of contemporary documents recovered archaeologically, such as the archives at Ugarit and Alalakh (Luciani, Ch. 34) as well as Egyptian (Panitz-Cohen, Ch. 36) and Hittite correspondence, and other texts.[4] Because of

---

[3] Not helped by the fact that there are uncertainties within the Egyptian chronology itself, as between the 'high' and 'low' chronologies, which probably, however, amount to a difference of little more than a decade or so during the New Kingdom. For the most recent attempt to sort out the chronology of Dynastic Egypt using a relatively large series of radiocarbon determinations on short-lived samples from reasonably secure contexts, see Bronk Ramsey et al. (2010).

[4] It may be counted as a great blessing that so many royal and other administrative centres in the Levant maintained the Mesopotamian habit of recording and storing documents written on clay which they had initially adopted in the third millennium BC—a habit which, arguably, proceeded from and strengthened the ideal of inter-regional elite cohesion reflected in other aspects of Late Bronze material culture in the east Mediterranean. Outside Egypt, whatever was written on perishable materials, such as papyrus, wood, or leather, is now lost to us.

the historical imperative which drove much earlier archaeology in the region,[5] excavation has traditionally tended to focus on sites thought to be important, named or potentially named in the textual record, and above all likely to provide further archives. As a result, we know more about the material remains, official personnel, and political interrelationships of top-level centres in hierarchical structures than we do about more humble settlements, which are generally textless and anonymous. In recent decades, however, programmes of multi-period archaeological survey, both extensive and intensive, in many parts of the Levant have begun to fill in some of the gaps in our knowledge of human occupation in the Late Bronze Age as in other periods (see e.g. Panitz-Cohen, Ch. 36; Yener 2005). While these may not necessarily tell us everything we might like to know about the political relationships between major centres and their 'hinterlands' (or, indeed, about political boundaries (Panitz-Cohen, Ch. 36)), they do help to add a necessary degree of complexity to the picture and remove some of our earlier more simplistic assumptions and text-derived generalizations. In particular, they have, with the help of insights imported from such disciplines as political sociology or human geography, increased our appreciation of the probable diversity of political organization, which characterized the Late Bronze Levant as a whole (see Panitz-Cohen, Ch. 36).

On Cyprus, where we lack the assistance of readable indigenous texts and where external references to Alashiya—likely to refer to Cyprus or somewhere on Cyprus (Knapp 1996)—have the effect of raising rather than answering questions, the problem of political organization in the Late Bronze is still very much disputed (Steel, Ch. 38). On the face of it, given the naturally centrifugal geography of the island with its series of river valleys running down from the copper-bearing Troodos Massif and looking outwards towards the sea on the south, west, and east, and its narrow coastal strip backed by the Kyrenia Range in the north, it seems unlikely that the whole of Cyprus was ever politically controlled by any one centre, any more than it was in the later Archaic and Classical periods, when we can read the Cypriot syllabic inscriptions. That is not to say, however, that, especially perhaps in the early Late Bronze Age, a centre like Enkomi did not have a particularly dominant role in the island's political and economic relationships with the Levant (Peltenburg 1996; 2008) before, perhaps, other centres in the south of the island got in on the act, forming external relationships on their own account. Here, surveys combined with excavations in various parts of the southern section of the island have indicated the existence of different types of apparently specialized sites, ranging from farming villages, copper-mining and smelting communities, and probably seasonal pottery-production locations to what appear to be administrative centres dedicated to the processing of agricultural products and coastal cities engaged in trading and manufacture, with (by LC IIC at least) urban sanctuaries, city walls, and (in some cases) a regular grid layout (Steel, Ch. 38). It has every appearance of being a complex and highly dynamic pattern of political and economic structures, all the more visible, perhaps, because it is not channelled or distracted by textual information.

Despite the differences in the lenses through which we are able to see them, in both the Levantine mainland and Cyprus one receives the impression, at least in the case of centres involved in maritime trade, that political and mercantile power were very closely intertwined. At Ugarit, for instance, merchants were counted among the most elite stratum of society, and individuals such as Sinaranu doubled as 'royal' agents and mercantile operators

---

[5] What Bunimovitz has called 'the tyranny of the historical context' (1995: 328).

in their own right (Heltzer 1988). On Cyprus, it is hard to avoid the suggestion that the wealth, architectural elaboration, and religious appropriation characteristic of what Negbi (1986) has termed 'the climax of urban development' in the 13th–12th centuries also owed its existence to the manufacturing and trading activities of increasingly powerful guilds of merchants based in the coastal cities.

ECONOMIES

It is probably fair to say that the economic bases of the Levant in the Late Bronze Age were as diverse and complex as its political structures, and affected in similar measure by the needs and demands of imperial intervenors such as the Egyptians and Hittites. It could offer these not only desirable 'lifestyle' products, such as wine, olive oil, woollen textiles, timber, and hippopotamus ivory, but access via the overland and maritime routes which it straddled to distant sources of more 'exotic' materials, such as semi-precious and precious stones (especially lapis lazuli), amber, pigments, metals, incense, and techniques such as glass-making. The Levant (including Cyprus) was particularly attractive to both Hittites and Egyptians, neither of whom were naturally comfortable operating habitually or sufficiently flexibly on the open sea, because of the long-practised facility of its coastal centres in maritime expertise and trading. Egypt maintained its traditionally advantageous close links with Byblos, for instance, down to the Ramesside period (Heinz and Kulemann-Ossen, Ch. 35), while Ugarit with its ports of Minet el-Beida and Ras Ibn Hani would appear to have been of far more useful to the Hittite kings as a going concern, operating relatively freely under their vassalage from the 14th century onwards, than stultified by over-control or obliterated (Knapp and Cherry 1994: 136). Away from the sea, it is also notable that many of the main centres or kingdoms, or those in which surrounding powers were particularly interested, lie at crucial points or junctions along long-distance routes, either those running north and south along the Levantine Corridor or the Shephelah (e.g. Alalakh, Qatna, Kamid el-Loz, Hazor, Beth Shan, Shechem, and Lachish) or east and west, linking the coast with the inland valleys or with the Euphrates and beyond (e.g. Tell el-Far'ah South, Megiddo, Damascus, and Aleppo). On Cyprus, the steady—or in some cases rapid—growth of urban centres, such as Enkomi, Kition, and Hala Sultan Tekke on the southern and eastern coasts of the island during the course of the Late Bronze Age, along with the appearance of short-lived coastal trading settlements, such as Pyla-Kokkinokremos or Maa-Palaeokastro, also emphasize its importance in maritime route networks in this period (Steel, Ch. 38).

Some of our information about the role of agriculture and animal husbandry in the Late Bronze economies of the Levant comes from texts as well as from analyses of settlement pattern distributions, faunal and botanical remains, and (most recently) strontium isotopes (e.g. Hopkins 1997; Hesse and Wapnish 1997; Meiggs 2010). Archaeologically speaking, much of our evidence for interregional and long-distance contacts and exchange rests on pottery, the most ubiquitous and indestructible class of artefact in the archaeological record in this part of the world but one which is seldom, if ever, of interest to those responsible for creating our textual sources. Developments in methods of interrogating pottery over the last thirty to forty years, including such techniques as optical emission spectrography, neutron activation analysis, and petrographic analysis for helping to give clues as to composition and provenance, and organic residue analysis (still somewhat controversially—see e.g. Merrillees 1989; Bisset et al. 1994) for helping to indicate contents, have had the effect of answering some questions, but at the same time raising numerous others and in general of suggesting a picture full of hitherto undreamed-of complexities. While clay vessels can be used both as containers (e.g. the Canaanite jars which travelled widely within the Levant as transport vessels for such substances as olive oil, wine, and incense resins (Serpico et al. 2003; Smith et al. 2004; Pedrazzi 2007; Panitz-Cohen, Ch. 36)) and as goods traded in their own right, perhaps their greatest value—especially when it comes to this latter function—lies in their capacity to indicate routes and route or trading networks. Certain regions, such as Cyprus, building on the back of its copper exports (Steel, Ch. 38), made an additional living not only from producing pottery for trade elsewhere in the Levant but also from trading in the pottery produced by others. Much of the Aegean (or apparently Aegean) pottery often interpreted in the past as a symptom of direct and intimate relations between Aegean centres and the Levant in the Late Bronze, if not of Aegean 'colonies', is likely to have formed part of relatively low-level, opportunistic trade, channelled through Cypriot traders, or—during the 13th century in successive processes of import substitution—made on Cyprus or even at various places in the Levant itself (Panitz-Cohen, Ch. 36; Luciani, Ch. 34; Amiran 1961; Baramki 1973; Hankey 1981; Koehl 1985; Artzy 2006; Panitz-Cohen 2009: 256–8). Recent excavation of quayside discard deposits at Tell Abu Hawam has told us much about the range of places that ships which anchored there might have come from or recently visited, and have revealed a wealth of varied ceramic types, some of which, like pithoi and a staggering variety of cooking wares, rarely made it further inland and presumably represent vessels mainly for use on the ships themselves (Artzy 2006: 52–5). The most surprising discovery as a result of this excavation—that an apparently characteristically Cypriot ware as utilitarian and as visually unexciting as Plain White Wheelmade may actually also have been produced in the district around Tell Abu Hawam—raises all sorts of questions about the confidence with which we assign geographical and cultural labels to potsherds and readily use them to produce simplistic models of trade.

Material culture

It is probably true to say that, when it comes to Late Bronze architecture in the Levant, we still know more about the palaces, temples, and fortifications of the elite and their urban centres than we do about the more lowly villages, farms, or nomadic encampments of the rest of Levantine society, despite new insights in this latter regard mainly provided by survey work in various regions. Some of the palaces often excavated in the search for archives are impressively monumental and, in some cases, surprisingly standardized in their traditional layout and use of materials (cf. e.g. Alalakh Level IV, the Lower City Palace at Qatna, Hazor XIV–XIII: Luciani, Ch. 34; Heinz and Kulemann-Ossen, Ch. 35; Bonfil and Zarzecki-Peleg 2007). On Cyprus, we have nothing in the Late Bronze Age that anyone is yet willing to call a 'palace', with its connotations of royal absolutism and centralized politico-economic and ceremonial power, but we have several buildings of monumental size and design which compare not unfavourably in the scale and elaboration of their architecture to grand buildings further east. These include the 'administrative' Building X at Kalavasos-Ahios Dhimitrios (South 1984) and the enigmatically vast and imposing ashlar construction of Building 2 at

Alassa-Palaeotaverna (Hadjisavvas 1994). Cypriot temples, like those at Late Bronze Kition, also have a 'Levantine' look with their rectangular plans, pillared courtyards, and inner sanctuaries (cf. Karageorghis 1976: 55–7).

When it comes to other aspects of material culture, once one has put pottery into its proper perspective as a ubiquitous and everyday material of little immediate concern to the highest echelons of society, it becomes clear how much elite material symbols were dependent on a kind of jet-set 'logo' mentality which operated at a certain social level throughout the eastern Mediterranean and reflected its vision of itself as 'cosmopolitan' and well-connected. The elite *koiné* or 'international style' (Panitz-Cohen, Ch. 36; Feldman 2006), which was given a particular boost by the outward-looking artistic experimentation of Egyptian rulers during the Amarna period, manifested itself on elaborate objects of precious metal (vessels and jewellery) ivory, precious or semi-precious stone, vitreous materials, and doubtless also elaborately woven or painted textiles.[6] It also extended to particular materials and techniques, the latter sometimes facilitated by the exchange or loan of skilled craftsmen such as architects or sculptors (Caubet 1998; Zaccagnini 1983). Court life was further 'internationalized' by the gift and exchange of personnel, such as physicians and entertainers, and even of deities—thus contributing to the geographical spread of ideas concerning healing practices and divine abilities. All this had a 'trickle-down' effect (Panitz-Cohen, Ch. 36), whereby symbols and motifs gained currency within less exalted circles and were reproduced—whether as symbols with a perfectly understood meaning or merely as commonly recognized 'elite' symbols—in less exalted contexts and on less exalted media such as earthenware, while Levantine gods and goddesses, who always had an ability to run together and morph fairly effortlessly into one another, also increasingly came to belong to a fluid international pantheon whose members were easily accommodated in the most local of religious cultures and their languages. All this was facilitated—and indeed symbolized—by, on the one hand, the use of Akkadian as a lingua franca and, on the other, by the existence of polyglot and multiliterate communities at centres like Ugarit where Ugaritic, Akkadian, Egyptian, Hittite, Hurrian, and Cypriot are all found written in a variety of scripts (Luciani, Ch. 34). Even Cyprus (or some centre(s) on it), which, apart from a few imported inscribed items, has so far produced only documents written in its own Bronze Age syllabic script or scripts, seems to have managed to write (or arrange to have written for it) letters written in Akkadian in syllabic cuneiform, as the Alashiya letters from Amarna and Ugarit appear to testify.

SUMMARY

It is perhaps something of a cliché that the ancient Levant, throughout much of its history, lay at the centre of the world. It formed a corridor and junction between north and south, east and west; and the regions (based on modern political boundaries) which are treated individually in the following chapters have to be understood within the context of one another as well as in the wider context provided by Egypt, Anatolia, Mesopotamia, and the Mediterranean. In the Late Bronze Age it also acted as an active crucible in which

[6] In other words, the kinds of objects which rulers can be seen giving as gifts to one another in the Amarna letters and other correspondence.

ideas, technologies, materials, goods, and ideologies, some of them deriving originally from surrounding areas, were melted together to produce an eclectic cultural and ideological alloy with its own distinctive character, in which the Levant's central position in a wider 'civilized' world and its kaleidoscope of local or regional social, economic, or cultural identities were an explicit part of the mix. This was partly a function of its geography (as encompassing a series of articulation points on networks of long-distance land and sea routes stretching in all directions) and of its geophysical and ecological diversity with deserts, sea, plains, river valleys, and hill regions all within close proximity to one another; but it was also, ultimately, a function of its position as a mediating bridge between two of the world's first urban civilizations. In the Late Bronze Age, when Mitanni and particularly Egypt, followed by Hatti, sought to gain or maintain control and influence over large parts of the Levant for the sake of what it could offer them directly or indirectly, its position as the highly desired focus of outside attention heightened and accelerated this process. The Levant as a whole became an active participant in the creation of a more closely integrated economic and cultural world, and individual elements within it used this to their political and economic advantage, even if it meant that, at times, their territories became destructive battlegrounds. At the same time, the more commercial activities of the Levant's maritime mercantile centres had the effect of extending elements of Levantine economy and culture westward into the Mediterranean, not only to Cyprus but also (possibly largely through Cyprus) to the Aegean and beyond.

Cyprus, being an island, perhaps had particular advantages in being insulated from direct external military or political interference. Although Hittite documents seem to suggest that Alashiya was at various times under the control of the Hittite kings, this may have been little more than wishful thinking, even if the Hittites did have some dealings with Cyprus or an individual Cypriot centre or centres, and sometimes came into armed conflict with Cypriot ships (Hellbing 1979: 58). Like Ugarit, with which Enkomi at least seems to have close ties, the main advantage of the island's coastal urban centres was their extensive and increasingly diversified manufacture and entrepreneurial maritime trade, which they built up during the course of the Late Bronze Age. Unlike Ugarit, but like the mercantile city-states on the coast of modern Lebanon[7] (which found themselves in a largely interference-free zone between Egyptian and Hittite spheres after the battle at Kadesh in the early 13th century), these Cypriot coastal cities and their mercantile elites were in a good position to capitalize on this once empires started to disintegrate or recede and certain important Levantine polities were decapitated in the accompanying turmoil and competitive readjustments in the decades around 1200 BC (cf. Liverani 1987). One result was that they turned their attention further west, extending the direct east–west maritime trading routes as far as the Adriatic and Tyrrhenian Seas (Borgna 2000; Lo Schiavo 2003), paving the way for the complete linking of the Mediterranean finally accomplished by Phoenician maritime traders, based in a coastal city such as Tyre, no more than two or three centuries later.

---

[7] We now know a little more about the Late Bronze Age in some of these coastal cities thanks to urban excavations in recent years (see e.g. Doumet-Serhal 2004). However, the remains of this period are still poorly known as a result of the overburden and destruction caused by their continued and increasingly successful existence in the Early Iron Age and later. It is perhaps above all in this very important stretch of the Levantine coast that our current knowledge of the Late Bronze Age most frustratingly remains 'an incompletely assembled puzzle' (Heinz and Kulemann-Ossen, Ch. 35).

Suggested reading

Kuhrt, A. (1995). *The Ancient Near East, c. 3000–330 BC*, vol. 1. London: Routledge

Van de Mieroop, M. (2004). *A History of the Ancient Near East, ca. 3000–323 B.C.* Malden, Mass.: Blackwell.

References

Albright, W. F. (1954). *The Archaeology of Palestine*, rev. edn. Harmondsworth: Penguin.

Amiran, R. (1961). A Late Bronze Age II pottery group from a tomb in Jerusalem. *Eretz-Israel* 6: 25–37 [Hebrew with English summary].

Artzy, M. (2006). The Carmel coast during the second part of the Late Bronze Age: a center for eastern Mediterranean transshipping. *Bulletin of the American Schools of Oriental Research* 343: 45–64.

Baramki, D. C. (1973). The impact of the Mycenaeans on ancient Phoenicia. In P. Dikaios (ed.), *Acts of the International Archaeological Symposium, 'The Mycenaeans in the Eastern Mediterranean', Nicosia 27th March–2nd April 1972.* Cyprus: Ministry of Communications and Works, Department of Antiquities, 193–7.

Bisset, N. G., J. G. Bruhn, S. Curto, B. Holmstedt, U. Nyman, and M. H. Zenk (1994). Was opium known in the 18th Dynasty in Egypt? An examination of materials from the tomb of the chief royal architect Kha. *Ethnopharmacology* 41: 99–104.

Bonfil, R., and A. Zarzecki-Peleg (2007). The palace in the upper city of Hazor as an expression of a Syrian architectural paradigm. *Bulletin of the American Schools of Oriental Research* 348: 25–47.

Borgna, E. (2000). Osservazioni sulla presenza egeo-cipriota nella metallurgia della regioni comprese tra l'alto Adriatico e l'Europa centrale. In A. R. Giumlia-Mair (ed.), *Ancient Metallurgy between Oriental Alps and Pannonian Plain: Workshop, Trieste, 29–30 October 1998.* Aquileia: Associazione nazionale per Aquileia, 41–51.

Bronk Ramsey, C., M. W. Dee, J. M. Rowland, et al. (2010). Radiocarbon-based chronology for Dynastic Egypt. *Science* 328: 1554–7.

Bunimovitz, S. (1995). On the edge of empires: Late Bronze Age (1500–1200 BCE). In T. E. Levy (ed.), *The Archaeology of Society in the Holy Land.* London: Leicester University Press, 320–31.

Caubet, A. (1998). The international style: a point of view from the Levant and Syria. In E. H. Cline and D. Harris-Cline (eds), *The Aegean and the Orient in the Second Millennium: Proceedings of the 50th Anniversary Symposium, Cincinnati, 18–20 April 1997.* Liège: Histoire de l'art et archéologie de la Grèce antique, Université de Liège/Austin: Program in Aegean Scripts and Prehistory, University of Texas at Austin, 105–11.

Doumet-Serhal, C. (ed.) (2004). *Decade: A Decade of Archaeology and History in the Lebanon.* Beirut: Lebanese British Friends of the National Museum.

Esse, D. L. (1991). The collared rim pithos at Megiddo: ceramic distribution and ethnicity. *Journal of Near Eastern Studies* 51: 81–103.

Feldman, M. H. (2006). *Diplomacy by Design: Luxury Arts and an 'International Style' in the Ancient Near East, 1400–1200 BCE.* Chicago: University of Chicago Press.

Frankel, D. (1991). Ceramic variability: measurement and meaning. In J. A. Barlow, D. R. Bolger, and B. Kling (eds), *Cypriot Ceramics: Reading the Prehistoric Record.* Philadelphia: University Museum of Archaeology and Anthropology, University of Pennsylvania, 241–52.

Hadjisavvas, S. (1994). Alassa Archaeological Project 1991–1993. *Report of the Department of Antiquities, Cyprus* 1994: 107–14.

Hankey, V. (1981). Imported vessels of the Late Bronze Age at high places. In A. Biran (ed.), *Temples and High Places in Biblical Times: Proceedings of the Colloquium in Honor of the Centennial of Hebrew Union College-Jewish Institute of Religion, Jerusalem, 14–16 March 1977.* Jerusalem: Nelson Glueck School of Biblical Archaeology of Hebrew Union College/ Jewish Institute of Religion, 108–17.

Hellbing, L. (1979). *Alasia Problems.* Gothenburg: Åströms.

Heltzer, M. L. (1988). Sinaranu, son of Siginu, and the trade relations between Ugarit and Crete. *Minos*, n.s. 23: 7–13.

Hesse, B., and P. Wapnish (1997). Paleozoology. In E. M. Meyers (ed.) *The Oxford Encyclopedia of Archaeology in the Near East*, vol. 4. New York: Oxford University Press, 206–7.

Hopkins, D. (1997). Agriculture. In E. M. Meyers (ed.) *The Oxford Encyclopedia of Archaeology in the Near East*, vol. 1. New York: Oxford University Press, 22–30.

Karageorghis, V. (1976). *Kition: Mycenaean and Phoenician Discoveries in Cyprus*. London: Thames & Hudson.

Kelso, J. L., and J. P. Thorley (1943). The potter's technique at Tell Beit Mirsim, particularly in Stratum A. In W. F. Albright, *The Excavation of Tell Beit Mirsim*, vol. 3: *The Iron Age*. New Haven, Conn.: American Schools of Oriental Research, 86–142

Knapp, A. B. (ed.) (1996). *Sources for the History of Cyprus*, vol. 2: *Near Eastern and Aegean Texts from the Third to the First Millennia B.C.* Altamont, NY: Greece and Cyprus Research Center.

—— and J. F. Cherry (1994). *Provenience Studies and Bronze Age Cyprus: Production, Exchange and Politico-Economic Change.* Madison, Wis.: Prehistory.

Koehl, R. B. (1985). *Sarepta III: The Imported Bronze and Iron Age Wares from Area II, X—The University Museum of the University of Pennsylvania Excavations at Sarafand, Lebanon.* Beirut: Libraire orientale.

Leonard, A., Jr (1988). Some problems inherent in Mycenaean/Syro-Palestinian synchronisms. In E. B. French and K. A. Wardle (eds), *Problems in Greek Prehistory: Papers Presented at the Centenary Conference of the British School of Archaeology at Athens, Manchester, April 1986.* Bristol: Bristol Classical Press, 319–30.

Liverani, M. (1987). The collapse of the Near Eastern regional system at the end of the Bronze Age: the case of Syria. In M. J. Rowlands, M. T. Larsen, and K. Kristiansen (eds), *Centre and Periphery in the Ancient World.* Cambridge: Cambridge University Press, 66–73.

Lorentzen, B., C. B. Griggs, T. Wazny, J. M. Herlich, W. Guerra, and S. W. Manning (2010). Dendrochronology in Israel: a preliminary reconstruction of tree-ring response to climate and environment in the southern Levant. Abstract of paper delivered to the Annual Meeting of the Association of American Geographers, Washington, DC, April 2010. http:// communicate.aag.org/eseries/aag_org/program/AbstractDetail.cfm?AbstractID=29327 (accessed 20 June 2010).

Lo Schiavo, F. (2003). Sardinia between East and West: interconnections in the Mediterranean. In N. Stampolidis and V. Karageorghis (eds), ΠΛΟΕΣ—*Sea Routes: Interconnections in the Mediterranean 16th–6th c. BC.* Athens: University of Crete/A. G. Leventis Foundation, 15–34.

Magrill, P., and A. P. Middleton (2001). Did the potter's wheel go out of use in Late Bronze Age Palestine? *Antiquity* 75: 137–44.

Manning, S. W. (1995). *The Absolute Chronology of the Aegean Early Bronze Age: Archaeology, Radiocarbon, and History.* Sheffield: Sheffield Academic.

—— B. Weninger, A. K. South, et al. (2001). Absolute age range of the Late Cypriot IIC period on Cyprus. *Antiquity* 75: 328–40.

Meiggs, D. (2011). Herding practices, urban provisioning, and human mobility at Tell Atchana (Alalakh), Hatay: 2009 strontium isotope (^{87}Sr/^{86}Sr) results. In A. N. Toy, H. Dönmez, and Ö. Ötgün (eds), *Arkeometri Toplantısı Sonuçları (İstanbul—24-28 Mayıs 2010)*. Ankara: T. C. Kültür ve Turizm Bakanlığı Yayın, 51–68.

Merrillees, R. S. (1989). Highs and lows in the Holy Land: opium in biblical lands. *Eretz-Israel* 20: 148*–54*.

—— (1992). The absolute chronology of the Bronze Age in Cyprus: a revision. *Bulletin of the American Schools of Oriental Research* 288: 47–52.

Negbi, O. (1986). The climax of urban development in Bronze Age Cyprus. *Report of the Department of Antiquities, Cyprus* 1986: 97–121.

Panitz-Cohen, N. (2009). The local Canaanite pottery. In N. Panitz-Cohen and A. Mazar (eds), *Excavations at Tel Beth-Shean 1989–1996*, vol. 3: *The 13th–11th Century BCE Strata in Areas N and S*. Jerusalem: Israel Exploration Society/Institute of Archaeology, Hebrew University of Jerusalem, 195–285.

Pedrazzi, T. (2007). *Le giare da conservazione e trasporto del Levante: uno studio archeologico dell'economia fra Bronzo Tardo II e Ferro I (ca. 1400–900 a.C.)*. Pisa: ETS.

Peltenburg, E. J. (1996). From isolation to state formation in Cyprus, c. 3500–1500 B.C. In V. Karageorghis and D. Michaelides (eds), *The Development of the Cypriot Economy from the Prehistoric Period to the Present Day*. Nicosia: University of Cyprus, 17–43.

—— (2008). Nitovikla and Tell el-Burak: Cypriot mid-second millennium B.C. forts in a Levantine context. *Report of the Department of Antiquities, Cyprus* 2008: 145–59.

Schaeffer, C. F.-A. (1948). *Stratigraphie comparée et chronologie de l'Asie occidentale: IIIe et IIe millénaires*, vol. 1: *Syrie, Palestine, Asie mineure, Chypre, Perse et Caucase*. Oxford: Oxford University Press.

Serpico, M., J. Bourriau, L. Smith, Y. Goren, B. Stern, and C. Heron (2003). Commodities and containers: a project to study Canaanite amphorae imported into Egypt during the New Kingdom. In M. Bietak (ed.), *The Synchronisation of Civilisations in the Eastern Mediterranean in the Second Millennium B.C. II: Proceedings of the SCIEM 2000–EuroConference, Haindorf, 2nd of May-7th of May 2001*. Vienna: Österreichische Akademie der Wissenschaften, 365–75.

Sjöqvist, E. (1940). *Problems of the Late Cypriote Bronze Age*. Stockholm: Swedish Cyprus Expedition.

Smith, L., J. Bourriau, Y. Goren, M. Hughes, and M. Serpico (2004). The provenance of Canaanite amphorae found at Memphis and Amarna in the New Kingdom: results 2000–2002. In J. Bourriau and J. S. Phillips (eds), *Invention and Innovation: The Social Context of Technological Change*, vol. 2: *Egypt, the Aegean and the Near East, 1650–1150 BC*. Oxford: Oxbow, 55–77.

South, A. K. (1984). Kalavasos-*Ayios Dhimitrios* and the Late Bronze Age of Cyprus. In V. Karageorghs and J. D. Muhly (eds), *Cyprus at the Close of the Late Bronze Age*. Nicosia: A. G. Leventis Foundation, 11–17.

Yener, K. A. (ed.) (2005). *The Amuq Valley Regional Projects*, vol. 1: *Surveys in the Plain of Antioch and Orontes Delta, Turkey, 1995-2002*. Chicago: Oriental Institute of the University of Chicago.

Zaccagnini, C. (1983). Patterns of mobility among Ancient Near Eastern craftsmen. *Journal of Near Eastern Studies* 42: 245–64.

CHAPTER 34

....

THE NORTHERN LEVANT (SYRIA) DURING THE LATE BRONZE AGE
Small Kingdoms between the Supraregional Empires of the International Age

....

MARTA LUCIANI

THE HISTORICAL NARRATIVE

....

Geography, chronology, political structure, and population

Syria in the Late Bronze Age had become geographically central in a world which encompassed supraregional powers such as Egypt, Mittani, and the Hittites. This centrality, and its ability to absorb and reinterpret diverse stimuli in its material culture, make Syria unique in this phase.

The country, however, was divided into a number of different polities: the small kingdoms Mukish and Halab (Aleppo) in the north; Ugarit, Niya, and Nukhashe south of the first two; Amurru and Qatna in the centre; and Qadesh and Ube in the south. Their territories were bordered by the Levantine coast on the west and the Euphrates to the east.

Archaeological chronology of the Late Bronze in Syria (1600–1200 BC) is dependent on historical chronology. Because the period is located between two eras whose beginnings or ends are difficult to pinpoint, the above dates must be understood as conventional.[1]

Late Bronze I lasts to c.1350, i.e. to the end of the Mittani kingdom and the conquests of the New Kingdom Hittite ruler, Šuppiluliuma I. This phase is less well known than the

---

[1] The *end* of the Middle Bronze is a 'dark age' in the traditional sense of the word, because we do not have dated/datable written texts from this phase. And since our dating of the Late Bronze is based on the historical chronology, 'dark age' is, in historical terms, a pertinent description of the situation at the end of the Middle Bronze/beginning of the Late Bronze.

following one, LB II (1350–1200 BC), also called the International Age (or Amarna Age), for which data is more abundant.

A number of sites feature a continuous development between the Late Bronze and Iron Ages. Coastal and some inner Syrian sites (e.g. Ras Shamra/Ugarit and Meskene/Emar on the Euphrates) display widespread destruction levels at the end of the Late Bronze, not followed by consistent reoccupations. These destruction horizons have been traditionally attributed to the arrival of the 'Sea Peoples' or, in the case of the inland sites, to raiding Aramaic tribes.

While the culprits responsible for the ruin may not always coincide with those named in the written records, and destruction dates are still difficult to establish with precision (Ugarit and Tell Kazel have more than one conflagration horizon: Margueron 2004: 146; Badre 2006), it is a fact that significant change in settlement type and strategies, and a new sociocultural order emerge after this time, so that the turn of the 13th century may indeed be taken as a closing point for the Late Bronze Age in Syria and the surrounding regions (Sader 1992).

As both our archaeological and textual sources suggest, the northern Levant (Syria and southeastern Turkey: Fig. 34.1) shared to a great extent the same political structure as the southern Levant, whereas inner Syria featured a different one.

On the Euphrates a range of medium- to small-sized settlements are attested, where temples were the communal buildings and decision-making was shared by roughly egalitarian bodies (Akkermans and Schwartz 2003: 342). Not so in the coastal and Orontes regions, where the palatial structure and a more stratified society seem to prevail. The role of the temple was more discrete, and it does not seem to have been involved in economic or commercial activities (Liverani 2005).

Written sources from Alalah, Level IV, and Ugarit indicate that the population comprised the 'king's men', who at various levels were dependants of the royal administration (and therefore legally not free), and the free 'sons/children' of the country:[2] farmers and shepherds with family-owned land and flocks of sheep and goats. The highest rank of the 'king's men' was the military charioteer nobility—the *maryanni* class (Liverani 2005: 17–19).

In the Alalah IV palace there seems to be no functional distinction between a 'private' and an 'official' sphere in the activities of high-status members of society (von Dassow 2005: 50). In Ugarit and Qatna, differentiated findings in the royal palaces and the closeness to these buildings of elite residences (House of Yabninu and the Monumental Residence in Ugarit) support the observations made for Alalah.

Women are attested in all positions of the hierarchical echelon, and high-status women seem to have enjoyed significant power in middle Syrian society. Sealed tablets from Meskene/Emar indicate that women were involved in a noteworthy part of the bulk of the transactions, enjoying a discrete social and economic autonomy (Beyer 2001).

A rough estimation based on texts from Alalah/Mukish and Ugarit points to *c.*80 per cent of the population as residing in the countryside (Liverani 2005), with the majority of their produce and livestock sent into the city. The economy was mainly agricultural, including bovine herding. Northern Levantine urban contexts (Ugarit, Qatna, and Kamid el-Loz) ceased pig breeding in the Late Bronze, apparently in favour of arable land and intensive

[2] For a more detailed description and a different interpretation of the evidence in Alalah IV, see von Dassow 2008.

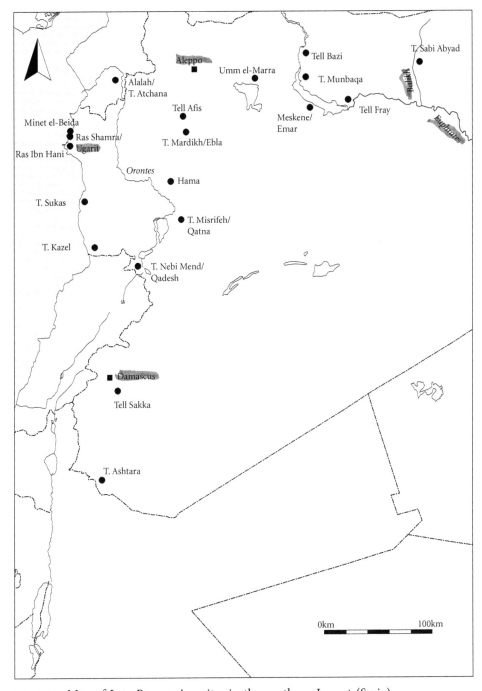

FIG. 34.1 Map of Late Bronze Age sites in the northern Levant (Syria)

sheep/goat rearing for meat, milk, and other secondary products. Wild boar, however, was hunted and part of the diet (Vila 2006).

The archaeological record

Settlement patterns and settlement topography

Surface surveys indicate a decrease in the number and size of settlements on the Levantine coast and inland Syria with respect to the preceding Middle Bronze Age. As the pottery record during the initial Late Bronze phase is quite conservative, it is difficult to identify the precise date of this change in settlement pattern. The surviving sites are concentrated close to favourable water sources, such as the Euphrates, Orontes, Qoweiq, and Afrin Rivers (Mazzoni 2002). However, continuity is definitely present in urban sites such as Hama and Tell Mishrifeh/Qatna, and partially also in Tell Mardikh/Ebla, as well as in Tell Sukas, Ugarit, and Alalah on the coast.

The previous structure of large urban settlements, featuring a division of the citadel from the lower town by means of fortifications, is not maintained in the Late Bronze, and a localization of the main city temple as separated from the palaces seems an innovation of this period (Matthiae 1997). City fortifications and ramparts are either maintained from the previous phase (Qatna) or founded anew or transformed (Alalah and Ugarit). However, precise topographic information is still lacking for most sites, with the exception of Ugarit, where large portions of the 13th-century city have been excavated and Tell Munbaqa or Tell Bazi (Otto 2008). Alalah and Qatna are known to a smaller extent, and various areas dating to the Late Bronze are now being investigated.

A specific type of agricultural/military small settlement is archaeologically attested east of the Euphrates, the *dimtu* or *dunnu* (e.g. Tell Sabi Abyad on the Balikh: Akkermans and Schwartz 2003: 350), which according to written documents must have also been present in the region of Ugarit.

Architecture

The centrality of the palace system in the northern Levant is well attested archaeologically in Alalah, capital of the kingdom of Mukish in the 'Amuq Plain (now Turkey); in Ugarit, capital of the coastal reign by the same name, and Ras Ibn Hani/Biruti(?), which also belong to it; and in Qatna, capital of the kingdom of the same name east of the Orontes Valley in central Syria, on the fringes of the steppe.

At Alalah the palace of Level IV (15th century BC) was founded southeast of the Levels V–IV fortress (Woolley 1955; von Dassow 2005: 33; Fig. 34.1). It is likely, but unproven, that this event is attributable to King Idrimi, whose inscribed statue has survived. To his successor, Niqmepa, belong most of the texts found in the two royal buildings (von Dassow 2005). The additions to the east may be attributed to his son, Ilimilimma. The extensive use of basalt orthostats for the wall bases as well as mud-brick and wood for the elevations is typical of contemporaneous Syrian palaces. The double-columned porch as an entrance and the side wing access to the longitudinal throne-room are features that become characteristic of later so-called *bit hilani* buildings. Also typical is the royal reception suite: a square room divided by columns from an adjoining broadroom. Its bent-axis approach is the norm, to which the Alalah Level IV palace eastern wing constitutes an exception. The Levels III–II fortress-palace built on top of Level IV testifies to its continued role as the administrative centre of the city throughout the Late Bronze.

Ugarit's Royal Palace, measuring c.6,500m^2 and with over 100 rooms, was part of a larger complex comprising a monumental gate to the west, a plaza, a guard post, and a small temple (formerly called the Hurrian Temple) as well as a monumental pillared building (Margueron 2004). The main underground sewer served the entire area.

The building was built between the 15th and the 13th centuries BC with embossed ashlars carefully fitted together, reinforced vertically with wooden beams (Yon 2006: 36), quarry stone, and mud-brick. At ground level were rooms, halls, and open courtyards (I–IV) with double-columned porches, including one with a garden and pavilion, and a (covered?) hall with a large shallow pool. Water was provided through underground canals from a well. One storage room was filled with jars. While the throne-room was accessed by visitors through a courtyard, the king entered it through a staircase from the upper floor. In its vicinity was a banquet hall (formerly called Courtyard VI). Under the floor of two rooms in the northern sector, stone burial vaults were located, similar to what is documented in private houses. At least one upper storey must have been present in the palace, probably where the residential quarters were located as well as some of the scribal offices and archives.

The palace was not only home to the royal family and their ancestors' cult but also the administrative centre of the kingdom, as the written records found in six different parts of the palace indicate. Akkadian and Ugaritic were the main written languages, but Egyptian hieroglyphic, Hittite, Hurrian, and Cypro-Minoan testify to intense international relations.

At Ras Ibn Hani, a small-scale centre less than 5km south of Ugarit, the Northern Palace featured a two-column porch opening onto the central courtyard serving as a throne-room. Epigraphic evidence seems to point to Ahatmilku, queen mother of Ammishtamru II, king of Ugarit (1260–1230 BC), as the person residing in this palace (Bounni and Lagarce 2004). Part of the inventory indicates the existence of workshops active during the final phase of use. Among others, metallurgy played a significant role, as indicated by a mould for oxhide-shaped ingots, a type known to be made of Cypriot copper (for a specimen from Ugarit, see Dardaillon 2004: 123).

The Royal Palace at Qatna, over one hectare in extent and located at the centre of the site on the artificial mound resulting from previous deposits, was one of the most impressive build-ings of its time. Its structure was organized around an expanded reception area comprising a square hall with four column bases, giving access to a throne-room-*cum*-ceremonial room. The layout is unique in the exaggerated proportions of the reception area, an original re-elaboration of themes only superficially reminiscent of earlier palaces (Matthiae 1997: 115). Service rooms occupied a smaller part of the surface. Cuneiform inventories of the goddess Ninegal's treasure and the archive of one the last kings of Qatna, Idanda, were also found (Pfälzner 2006). North of the site was the Lower City Palace (Fig. 34.2), built at a lesser alti-tude and smaller, but with distinct traditional palatial architectural features and containing written administrative records. Evidence of workshops for ivory within it (Luciani 2006a) may suggest a functional differentiation with the Royal Palace. Both palaces feature poly-chrome wall paintings with strong Aegean parallels (Luciani 2004; Pfälzner 2006).

A monumental residence was found immediately to the south of the Royal Palace on the central mound (al-Maqdissi 2003: 235–8). All palatial buildings in Qatna were in use

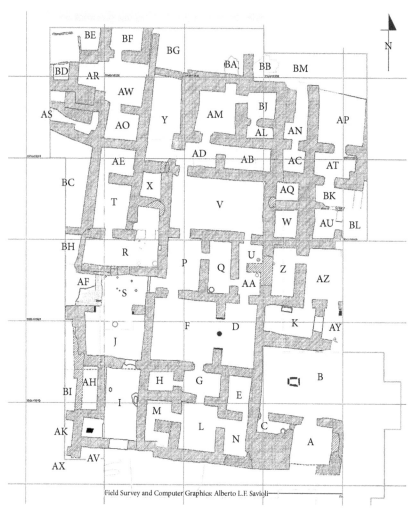

FIG. 34.2 Plan of the Lower City Palace in Tell Mishrifeh/Qatna (from Luciani 2006a: fig. 7; courtesy Peeters Publishers)

between the end of the Middle Bronze and the LB IIA periods, and are contemporaneous with Alalah IV but not with the last phase of use in Ugarit and Ras Ibn Hani.

The plans of various temples are known in this period: tower-like (Alalah and Ugarit) or with a short vestibule, sometime *in antis*, and a long room as *cella* (Emar: Temple South, Temple North, Temple 2; Tell Munbaqa, *Steinbaus* 1–4; Tell Fray Temple South and Tell Kazel Area IV) as well as with a broadroom as *cella* (Euphrates sites and further to the east). Whatever the differences in size and layout, it seems that the principle of an axial access/ entrance was a common feature, and one which descended from the Middle Bronze tradition. In comparison both with south Mesopotamian and with earlier Syrian examples, Late Bronze temples were usually rather small.

On the Euphrates sites, a lack of palatial structures has pointed to the hypothesis that temples may also have housed communal meetings of citizens (i.e. decision-making bodies) (Sallaberger, Einwag, and Otto 2006: 94). Nonetheless, private cultic activities were performed elsewhere too, as may be indicated by finds such as terracotta figurines in households.

Proper cemeteries dating to the Late Bronze are not known in Syria. Burials are attested in Alalah within the city, as single child or adult inhumation or cremations (already in the 15th century BC). They are beneath or close to houses, and rather poor in accompanying goods. The small numbers of graves may not account for the entire population (Woolley 1955: 201–23).

In Ugarit itself, in Ugarit's harbour, Minet el-Beida/Mahadu, and in Ras Ibn Hani, built-in stone vaulted chambers with access through a *dromos* were located beneath the floors of rooms. Most were plundered in antiquity, but those that were not contained jewellery and imported goods, such as Aegean and Cypriot pottery.

Of the *hypogea* uncovered under the Royal Palace of Qatna, at least two date to the Late Bronze, the main one featuring a multi-chamber, multiple burial, probably used by the royal family. Its access was guarded by two basalt statues. Expensive goods such as gold jewellery, amber, ivory, and semi-precious stones were preserved inside (Pfälzner 2006). An infant jar burial characterizes the last phase of use in the Lower City Palace (Luciani 2003: 153).

In the *dunnu* at Tell Sabi Abyad, several inhumation and cremation burials were discovered in abandoned rooms of the fortress, among them an important sealed double cremation (Akkermans and Smits 2008).

Residential architecture in Late Bronze Syria displays different types of units (McClellan 1997). Large and articulated houses with corridor rooms along one side were found in Alalah, while in Ugarit the whole spectrum, from small five-room houses to extended residences, was present. Light and access were provided by a central court. Ground level was used for storage, food preparation, and craft activities, while the upper storey was the residence. Some of the buildings had built-in drainage and bathroom facilities.

Different-size houses seem to be distributed throughout the site of Ugarit, mixing households of distinct functions and economic/social status in the same quarters of the city. This low degree of specialization in the urban setting is visible also in the Euphrates settlements in the diffusion of craft activity installations in different locations within one site. The variation of house types attested in the east (central-room and front-room houses) and urban centres on the coast seems to mirror the substantial diversity in productive, economic/social rank, and organization of these settlements.

In the Damascus oasis at Tell Sakka, Late Bronze pillared houses were uncovered above the Middle Bronze monumental building, with Egyptianizing wall paintings (Taraqji 1999).

Less is known about single-specialization Late Bronze productive areas. A pottery workshop is documented at Qatna (al-Maqdissi 2003: 223–5; for ivory, see Luciani 2006a), a kiln in Tell Sabi Abyad (Akkermans and Duistermaat 2001), and a metallurgical workshop in the south of Syria at the western Hawran site of Tell Ashtara (Akkermans and Schwartz 2003: 351).

Everyday artefacts and pottery

The presence in urban households in Ugarit of lithic industries for sickles indicates the wide participation of city-dwellers in agricultural activities (Cocqueugniot 2006). This confirms a picture of the city as including parts of the 'residual village' (Liverani 2005: 17).[3] Alloyed

---

[3] For a different interpretation of this data, see Schloen 2001.

copper was in use for a variety of everyday tools and weapons, but some of the first uses of iron are attested in Ugarit for ceremonial weapons with gold-inlayed hilts (Dardaillon 2004: 166).

In the production of terracotta figurines, the most common type attested is moulded, and features a woman holding her breasts. Elaborate terracotta house models are also present.

As for pottery, Alalah, Hama, Tell Nebi Mend/Qadesh (Bourke 1993), and Qatna (Luciani 2008) provide a sequence starting with the end of the Middle Bronze and extending into the initial Late Bronze Age. The LB II sequence is better documented at sites like Tell Kazel (Badre 2006) and Tell Afis (Mazzoni 2002).

The bulk of pottery was made of undecorated, wheelmade, drab specimens. Shapes such as the carinated goblet, with long, flaring neck, bowls with high carination, and hemispherical cups and shallow bowls with plain or slightly swollen rims, are shapes continued from the preceding period (McClellan 2007). 'Shoulder goblets', brown burnished shallow bowls with in-turned rims, are very characteristic, as are large kraters (Akkermans and Schwartz 2003: 332, Fig. 10.3). In the following LB II phase, a further trend towards a simplification of shapes and reduction in variants indicates processes of standardization in production. Disc and ring bases become less common, plates and bowls feature simple rims, and shapes find more parallels in Anatolian types (Mazzoni 2002: 129–32, pls lxi–lxiv).

Decorated classes (e.g. Fig. 34.3) such as the 'Nuzi Ware', featuring light geometric or floral motifs painted on a dark field of drinking-set shapes, are statistically unimportant but may have to be interpreted as a marker of the Mittani elite.

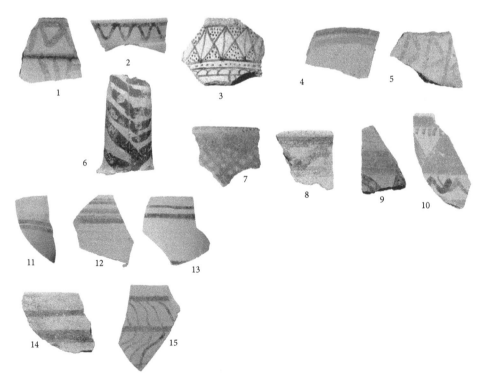

FIG. 34.3 Painted pottery from Area K in Tell Mishrifeh/Qatna (Luciani 2008: fig. 2; courtesy Österreichische Akademie der Wissenschaften)

Imported pottery represents an insignificant percentage (less than 1%; Monchambert 2004: 11) of the Syrian assemblages, even in coastal sites such as Ugarit. Late Cypriot pottery (Fig. 34.4) is introduced at the beginning of the Late Bronze period and is found, though in small quantities, as far east as the Euphrates. In the course of the transition to the LB II it is gradually replaced by Aegean, mostly Mycenaean, vessels and subsequently Levantine imitations. Imported non-container shapes, such as the rhyton, and the amphorid krater (most often with a chariot depiction), were made as a hybridizing production in Greece (Argolid) for export to the northern Levant. While in function they are associated with rituals and feasting, they played no role in high-level transactions and are not mentioned in the texts relating to palatial gift exchange. They should instead be interpreted as mass-produced goods for consumption by sub-elite and substitute-elite circuits (Sherratt 1999). A similar situation should be envisaged for Cypriot pottery.

Glass and faience (Caubet 2007), new materials widely used during this period, imitating precious stones in colour and precious metals in texture (e.g. granulation), should possibly also be interpreted as technological improvements fulfilling the growing demands of the local (sub- or substitute) elites.

Administrative practices: seals and sealings

Sealing practices of the Mittani period are attested on the Alalah IV tablets (Collon 1975) and in Nuzi, Iraq (besides fewer examples from Umm el-Marra, Tell Munbaqa, and Tell

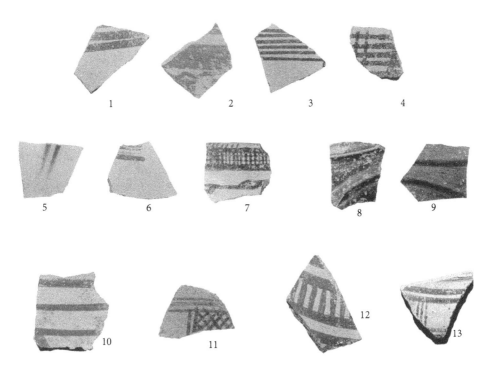

FIG. 34.4 Imported pottery from Area K in Tell Mishrifeh/Qatna (Luciani 2008: fig. 3; courtesy Österreichische Akademie der Wissenschaften)

Bazi). The succeeding Hittite rule of northern Syria is mirrored both in the Ugaritic and in the Emar sealings.

In the Mittani Elaborate Style, Babylonian and Syrian traditions are still recognizable in the main theme. An addition is the division of the subsidiary scene in two registers. However, Saushtatar's dynastic seal—used also by his successors as a legitimization tool—is innovative in the abandonment of clearly defined registers. Filling motives and fantastic creatures are plentiful. Egyptianizing elements, already in use in the Middle Bronze, are still present, but so are Aegean and Cappadocian motifs.

The Mittani Common Style is normally found in seals obtained using a new material—sintered quarz—which allowed increased production. However, the great number of seals of this type not attested as seal impressions point to use also as jewels or amulets. The scenes feature simple motifs carried out in a linear style (Salje 1990).

In Ugaritic production (a workshop is documented on the site) the representation of chariots in war and hunt scenes is frequent. Royal Hittite stamp seals are attested in Ugarit on the high-level documents that involved the Anatolian ruler, while the Hittite influence is also strongly recognizable in Emar throughout the corpus and also on commoners' cylinder seals. The acculturation produced by the Hittite milieu was so relevant that even people with Semitic names made use of Hittite or Syro-Hitttite seals (Beyer 2001).

Art, luxury, and prestige goods

Sculpture is not well known in this period, yet the few finds (e.g. Alalah, Idrimi statue: Matthiae 1997: 110; Ugarit, limestone figurine of a seated, bearded figure) exhibit features strongly reminiscent of Middle Bronze sculpture in themes (deified kings and gods) if not always in quality. Elements such as a cloak with padded rounded borders and oval tiara for kings (horned tiara for gods) are still in use.

Both on stone and even more in the small bronze figurines with gold and silver coating (Ugarit, sitting god El, smiting god Ba'al; Qatna, sitting deified ancestor king: Matthiae 1997: 111) the influence of Egyptian iconography is quite clear. It is visible in the smiting posture as well as in the short kilt and the pointed tiara similar to the Egyptian 'white crown'.

Beyond metal figurines, these elements appear most eloquently on the Ba'al stele (Yon 2004) and to a certain extent also in the ivory, lapis lazuli, and gold head (Gachet-Bizollon 2007: 304, fig. 55, pls 112 and 113) of a god (?), both from Ugarit. True Egyptian imports include statues and stelae (Ugarit, Qadesh, stele of Sethi I; Kiswé, near Damascus, stele of Ramesses II). Inscribed alabaster/calcite vessels were both imported (Ugarit and Qatna) and locally produced.

Elephant ivory is one of the precious materials used for the production of large and sophisticated artefacts pertaining to the royal circuits attested at Ugarit (carved table top, 'oliphant', head of a lion, female figurine: Gachet-Bizollon 2007: 304, fig. 55, pls 112 and 113) and now also at Qatna (Luciani 2006b) (Fig. 34.5). The Ugarit bed panel is the best example of a high-quality Syrian production reinterpreting Egyptian and Hittite iconographic elements in six scenes with a long hunt frieze at the top (Gachet-Bizollon 2007: 135ff., pls 25, 26, 79–84). On an ivory pyxis lid (Gachet-Bizollon 2007: 87ff., 235, pls. 13, 71), on the contrary, it is Aegean elements which are re-elaborated for the local market.

Hunting scenes were a favourite theme, as visible on both gold bowls found southwest of the Ba'al Temple in Ugarit. In one, the fantastic creatures and animals, and their syntax

FIG. 34.5 Elephant ivory face from the Lower City Palace in Tell Mishrifeh/Qatna (Luciani 2006a: fig. 10; courtesy Peeters Publishers)

mirror Mesopotamian, Egyptian, and Aegean influences. In the other, the charioteer driving the light, two-wheeled horse-drawn chariot (Calvet 2004), a Near Eastern technological innovation in Late Bronze warfare, is one of the most cherished royal motifs, also found in glyptic.

Gold is used for pendants representing the naked goddess with Hathoric headdress or for rings with inscribed personal names in hieroglyphic Hittite.

In the highly developed and ceremonial life of Late Bronze urban sites in Syria, luxury and prestige goods played an essential role. As documented in the rich international correspondence, gift exchange was practised at the highest echelons of politics and society not only as a means of acquiring staple wealth but even more as a means of participation in the international court system of the Amarna Age.

A SYNTHESIS

Notwithstanding the centrality of the palace and the urban context outlined above, the majority of the population lived in rural villages and the countryside. Therefore, our reconstruction concerns only a minority of the populace and our perspective is characterized by an urban bias.

While an overall continuity in art and architecture with the previous Middle Bronze period is apparent, especially in the first centuries of the Late Bronze Age and in specific aspects (religious architecture), two further opposing trends seem to be active during the Late Bronze in Syria.

On one hand, the introduction of innovative elements brought regionalization to the material culture (profane architecture, pottery, and glyptics). This tendency continues into the beginning of the Iron Age and will only be inverted later in the first millennium BC. On the other, we witness a shared language in the production of luxury and prestige goods stemming from and destined to the palatial circuit. For however spectacular these may have been, they were enjoyed by only a few. Nonetheless, the skills required in their production constitutes the basis of future high-quality craft production in the Iron Age.

Egyptian elements, already well attested in the Levant in the Middle Bronze, are still present and enjoy renewed popularity during the Late Bronze—not in architecture, but on high-level, moveable/transferable artefacts and monumental art. This does not, however, indicate tighter control or a higher degree of integration of the local Syrian communities with the Egyptian Empire as opposed to the control/integration obtained first by the Mittani and subsequently by the Hittites.

As the use of Mittanian dynastic sealings so far is not attested further south of the Alalah–Tell Brak line, notwithstanding the presence of the Mitanni inland (tablets from Tell Ashara/Terqa), we may imagine that Mittanian administrative grip on the central Syrian territory it claimed was not all-encompassing. However, the important role played by the Mittani culture should be traceable in the motives and syntax of their glyptics and in the presence of the Hurrian language and personal names as far south as Qatna and Tell Taannech.

Hittite culture and prestige, beyond the aspects observable through the iconography and style of rings or seals and sealings used in administration, do not appear as visible as the corresponding Egyptian and Mittani elements in the material culture record of Late Bronze Syria.

Whether in these small kingdoms internal power and social conflicts were so prevalent as to eventually cause the demise of the entire system (Liverani 2005) or whether a more unified, basically agrarian patrimonial society is the better explanatory model (Schloen 2001), the urban centres of western Syria participated in trade and contributed fully to the exchange of ideas and products, thus shaping for the first time the Levant's specific role—one which was to last until the Middle Ages—as a bridge between Egypt and Anatolia, the Aegean, and Mesopotamia.

Suggested reading

Bergoffen, C. J. (2005). *The Cypriot Bronze Age Pottery from Sir Leonard Woolley's Excavations at Alalakh (Tell Atchana).* Vienna: Österreichische Akademie der Wissenschaften.

Beuger, C., A. Hausleiter, and M. Luciani (eds) (forthcoming). *Recent Trends in the Study of the Late Bronze Age Ceramics in Syro-Mesopotamia and Neighbouring Regions—Proceedings of the International Workshop Held in Berlin, 2–5 November 2006.*

Cochavi-Rainey, Z., and C. Lilyquist (1999). *Royal Gifts in the Late Bronze Age Fourteenth to Thirteenth Centuries B.C.E.: Selected Texts Recording Gifts to Royal Personages.* Beer-Sheva: Ben-Gurion University of the Negev Press.

Duistermaat, K. (2008). *The Pots and Potters of Assyria: Technology and Organisation of Production, Ceramic Sequence and Vessel Function at Late Bronze Age Tell Sabi Abyad, Syria.* Turnhout: Brepols.

Feldman, M. H. (2006). *Diplomacy by Design: Luxury Arts and 'International Style' in the Ancient Near East, 1400–1200 BCE.* Chicago: University of Chicago Press.

Genz, H. (2006). Hethitische Präsenz im spätbronzezeitlichen Syrien: die archäologische Evidenz. *Baghdader Mitteilungen* 37: 499–509.

Landesmuseum Württember/Stuttgart (ed.) in collaboration with M. al-Maqdissi, D. Morandi Bonacossi, and P. Pfälzner (2009). *Schätze des Alten Syrien: Die Entdeckung des Königreichs Qatna.* Stuttgart: Landesmuseum Württember/Theiss.

Liverani, M. (1990). *Prestige and Interest: International Relations in the Near East, ca. 1600–1100 B.C.* Padua: Sargon.

—— (2011). Review of E. von Dassow (2008). *State and Society in the Late Bronze Age: Alalah under the Mittani Empire*. Bethesda, Md.: CDL, ff. 52, 244–7.

Manning, S. W., and L. Hulin (2005). Maritime commerce and geographies of mobility in the Late Bronze Age of the eastern Mediterranean: problematizations. In A. B. Knapp and E. Blake (eds), *The Archaeology of Mediterranean Prehistory*. Malden, Mass.: Blackwell, 270–302.

Moran, W. L. (ed.) (1992). *The Amarna Letters*. Baltimore, Md.: Johns Hopkins University Press.

Otto, A. (2006). *Alltag und Gesellschaft zur Spätbronzezeit: eine Fallstudie aus Tall Bazi (Syrien)*. Turnhout: Brepols.

—— (2008). Organization of Late Bronze Age cities in the Upper Syrian Euphrates Valley. In J. M. Córdoba Zolio, M. Molist Montaña, M. del Carmen Pérez Aparicio, I. Rubio, and S. Martínez (eds), *Proceedings of the 5th International Congress on the Archaeology of the Ancient Near East, Madrid, 3–8 April 2006*, vol. 2. Madrid: Ediciones Universidad Autónoma de Madrid, Centro Superior de Estudios sobre el Oriente Próximo y Egipto, 715–32.

Pfälzner, P., in collaboration with C. von Rüden (2008). Between the Aegean and Syria: the wall paintings from the royal palace of Qatna. In D. Bonatz, R. M. Czichon, and F. Janoscha Kreppner (eds), *Fundstellen: Gesammelte Schriften zur Archäologie und Geschichte Altvorderasiens ad Honorem Hartmut Kühne*. Wiesbaden: Harrassowitz, 95–118.

References

Akkermans, P. M. M. G., and K. Duistermaat (2001). A Middle Assyrian pottery kiln at Tell Sabi Abyad. In J.-W. Meyer, M. Novák, and A. Pruss (eds), *Beiträge zur vorderasiatischen Archäologie: Winfried Orthmann gewidmet*. Frankfurt: Johann Wolfgang Goethe-Universität, Archäologisches Institut, 12–19.

—— and G. M. Schwartz. (2003). *The Archaeology of Syria: From Complex Hunter-Gatherers to Early Urban Societies (c. 16,000–300 BC)*. Cambridge: Cambridge University Press.

—— and E. Smits (2008). A sealed double cremation at Middle Assyrian Tell Sabi Abyad, Syria. In D. Bonatz, R. M. Czichon, and F. Janoscha Kreppner (eds), *Fundstellen: Gesammelte Schriften zur Archäologie und Geschichte Altvorderasiens ad Honorem Hartmut Kühne*. Wiesbaden: Harrassowitz, 251–61.

al-Maqdissi, M. (2003). Ergebnisse der siebten und achten syrischen Grabungskampagne 2001 und 2002 in Mišrife-Qatna. *Mitteilungen der Deutschen Orient-Gesellschaft* 135: 219–45.

Badre, L. (2006). Tell Kazel-Simyra: a contribution to a relative chronological history in the eastern Mediterranean during the Late Bronze Age. *Bulletin of the American Schools of Oriental Research* 343: 65–95.

Beyer, D. (2001). *Emar IV, Les sceaux: Mission archéologique de Meskéné-Emar—recherches au pays d'Astata*. Fribourg: Éditions universitaires/Göttingen: Vandenhoeck & Ruprecht.

Bounni, A., and J. Lagarce (2004). Ras Ibn Hani. In Y. Calvet and G. Galliano (eds), *Le royaume d'Ougarit: aux origines de l'alphabet*. Paris: Somogy/Lyon: Musée des beaux-arts, 57.

Bourke, S. J. (1993). The transition from the Middle to the Late Bronze Age in Syria: the evidence from Tell Nebi Mend. *Levant* 25: 155–95.

Calvet, Y. (2004). Patère ornée d'une scène de chasse. In Y. Calvet and G. Galliano (eds), *Le royaume d'Ougarit: aux origines de l'alphabet*. Paris: Somogy/Lyon: Musée des beaux-arts, 30–31.

Caubet, A. (ed.) (2007). *Faïences et matières vitreuses de l'Orient ancien: études physico-chimique et catalogue des œuvres du Département des antiquités orientales.* Gand: Snoeck/ Paris: Musée du Louvre.

Cocqueugniot, É. (2006). Mari, Larsa, Ugarit et les outillages en silex à l'Âge du Bronze: réflexions sur le rôle et le statut du travail du silex au IIIe et IIe millénaires. In P. Butterlin, M. Lebeau, J.-Y. Monchambert, J. L. Montero Fenollós, and B. Muller (eds), *Les espaces syro-mésopotamiens: dimensions de l'expérience humaine au Proche-Orient ancien.* Turnhout: Brepols, 323–38.

Collon, D. (1975). *The Seal Impressions from Tell Atchana/Alalakh.* Kevelaer: Butzon & Bercker.

Dardaillon, E. (2004). L'importation du métal à Ougarit and Hache d'apparat. In Y. Calvet and G. Galliano (eds), *Le royaume d'Ougarit: aux origines de l'alphabet.* Paris: Somogy/Lyon: Musée des beaux-arts, 123, 166.

Gachet-Bizollon, J. (2007). *Les ivoires d'Ougarit et l'art des ivoiriers du Levant au Bronze récent.* Paris: Recherche sur les civilisations.

Liverani, M. (2005). *Israel's History and the History of Israel*, trans. C. Peri and P. Davies. London: Equinox.

Luciani, M. (2003). The lower city of Qatna in the Late Bronze and Iron Ages: Operation K. *Akkadica* 124: 144–63.

—— (2004). Palazzi, abitazioni e botteghe tra prima Età del Bronzo Tardo e Ferro nell'antica Qatna: il Cantiere K a Tell Mishrifeh. In A. Guidi and S. Ponchia (eds), *Ricerche archeologiche in Italia e in Siria: atti delle giornate di studio, Verona, 6–7 maggio 2002.* Padua: Sargon, 133–46.

—— (2006a). Palatial workshops at Qatna? *Baghdader Mitteilungen* 37: 403–29.

—— (2006b). Ivory at Qatna. In E. Czerny, I. Hein, H. Hunger, D. Melman, and A. Schwab (eds), *Timelines: Studies in Honour of Manfred Bietak.* Dudley, Mass.: Peeters, 17–38.

—— (2008). The Late Middle Bronze to early Late Bronze Age in Qatna, with special emphasis on decorated and imported pottery. In M. Bietak and E. Czerny (eds), *The Bronze Age in the Lebanon: Studies on the Archaeology and Chronology of Lebanon, Syria, and Egypt.* Vienna: Österreichische Akademie der Wissenschaften, 115–26.

Margueron, J.-C. (2004). Le palais royal d'Ougarit. In Y. Calvet and G. Galliano (eds), *Le royaume d'Ougarit: aux origines de l'alphabet.* Paris: Somogy/Lyon: Musée des beaux-arts, 143–9.

Matthiae, P. (1997). *La storia dell'arte dell'Oriente antico, 1600–700 a.C.: i primi imperi e i principati del ferro.* Milan: Electa.

Mazzoni, S. (2002). Late Bronze Age pottery production in northwestern central Syria. In M. al-Madqissi, V. Matoïan, and C. Nicolle (eds), *Céramique de l'Âge du bronze en Syrie, I: La Syrie du sud et la Vallée de l'Oronte.* Beirut: Institut français d'archéologie du Proche-Orient, 129–34.

McClellan, T. L. (1997). Houses and households in north Syria during the Late Bronze Age. In C. Castel, M. al-Maqdissi, and F. Villeneuve (eds), *Les maisons dans la Syrie antique du IIIe millénaire aux débuts de l'Islam: pratique et représentations de l'espace domestique.* Beirut: Institut français d'archéologie du Proche-Orient, 29–59.

—— (2007). Late Bronze Age pottery from the Upper Euphrates. In M. al-Madqissi, V. Matoïan, and C. Nicolle (eds), *Céramique de l'Âge du bronze en Syrie, II: L'Euphrate et la région de Jézireh.* Beirut: Institut français d'archéologie du Proche-Orient, 53–75.

Monchambert, J.-Y. (2004). *La céramique d'Ougarit: campagnes de fouilles 1975 et 1976.* Paris: Recherche sur les civilisations.

Pfälzner, P. (2006). Qatna B. Archäologisch. *Reallexikon der Assyriologie* 11: 161–70.

Sader, H. (1992). The 12th century B.C. in Syria: the problem of the rise of the Aramaeans. In W. A. Ward and M. S. Joukowsky (eds), *The Crisis Years: The 12th Century B.C. from Beyond the Danube to the Tigris*. Dubuque, Ia.: Kendall/Hunt, 157–63.

Salje, B. (1990). *Der 'Common Style' der Mitanni-Glyptik und die Glyptik der Levante und Zyperns in der späten Bronzezeit*. Mainz: von Zabern.

Sallaberger, W., B. Einwag, and A. Otto (2006). Schenkungen von Mittani-Königen an die Einwohner von Basīru: die zwei Urkunden aus Tall Bazi am Mittleren Euphrat. *Zeitschrift für Assyriologie* 96: 69–104.

Schloen, D. J. (2001). *The House of the Father as Fact and Symbol: Patrimonialism in Ugarit and the Ancient Near East*. Winona Lake, Ind.: Eisenbrauns.

Sherratt, E. S. (1999). *E pur si muove*: pots, markets and values in the second millennium Mediterranean. In J. P. Crielaard, V. Stissi, and G. J. van Wijngaarden (eds), *The Complex Past of Pottery: Production, Circulation and Consumption of Mycenaean and Greek Pottery (Sixteenth to Early Fifth Centuries BC)*. Amsterdam: Gieben, 163–211.

Taraqji, A. F. (1999). Nouvelles découvertes sur les relations avec l'Égypte à Tel Sakka et à Keswé, dans la région de Damas. *Bulletin de la Société française d'égyptologie* 144: 27–43.

Vila, E. (2006). Les restes de suidés: un marqueur archéologique au Levant? In B. Lion and C. Michel (eds), *De la domestication au tabou: le cas des suidés au Proche-Orient ancien*. Paris: De Boccard, 215–26.

von Dassow, E. (2005). Archives of Alalah IV in archaeological context. *Bulletin of the American Schools of Oriental Research* 338: 1–69.

——(2008). *State and Society in the Late Bronze Age: Alalah under the Mittani Empire*. Bethesda, Md.: CDL.

Woolley, L. (1955). *Alalakh: An Account of the Excavations at Tell Atchana in the Hatay, 1937–1949*. Oxford: Oxford University Press.

Yon, M. (2004). Stèle 'du Baal au foudre'. In Y. Calvet and G. Galliano (eds), *Le royaume d'Ougarit: aux origines de l'alphabet*. Paris: Somogy/Lyon: Musée des beaux-arts, 170.

——(2006). *The City of Ugarit at Tell Ras Shamra*. Winona Lake, Ind.: Eisenbrauns.

CHAPTER 35

....

THE NORTHERN LEVANT (LEBANON) DURING THE LATE BRONZE AGE

....

MARLIES HEINZ AND SABINA

KULEMANN-OSSEN

INTRODUCTION

....

The developments of the Late Bronze Age in Lebanon (*c.* 1550–1200 BC) can be examined from three different points of view: (1) from the inside to the inside; (2) from the inside to the outside; and (3) from the outside to the inside.

View from the inside to the inside

This view bases itself on the analysis of results and finds of the time period from each site, seeing these as evidence for and an expression of human action, and in their totality as a mirror of the cultural, economic, political, and societal developments of the Late Bronze Age in Lebanon.

View from the inside to the outside

This view is also based on the study of material remains. The approach from the inside to the outside forms the basis of a supposition where the world of things is seen to have the potential to provide information about 'us' and 'them'. The attribution of this potential is in turn based on the assumption that it is possible to distinguish between the existence of different social communities by looking at, among other things, the material remains (it is self-evident that pots are not people, but it is also a fact that different social communities have so far created different cultural expressions which, among other aspects, find their expression in different ensembles of material culture). The task for archaeological research in this view is to point out those characteristics in the remains that can be seen as indicators of 'us' and 'them' and which can be indicators of contact between the social entities.

(This is, however, not the task of this contribution; here the authors draw on the evidence of earlier archaeological research on the provenance of goods, which are elaborated upon below.)

In certain circumstances the view from the inside to the outside may make it possible to determine with greater precision the nature and background of the contact that took place between the Late Bronze sites in the territory of Lebanon and their near or distant neighbours, aside from statements based on the aforementioned evidence. This is the case where written records of the local elite on local, regional, and supraregional politics and on current affairs have been found in the sites' assemblages.

View from the outside to the inside

The history of the Late Bronze Age in the area of the Levant is characterized by a multitude of attempts by different political forces to establish themselves as hegemonic powers or foreign rulers over the locally established political and social formations. Clues to the political development of the time and region, and thus the progress of events, can be gleaned from the records of the foreign rulers, which were preserved in the archives of their political centres 'at home' as well as in the archives of the political dependencies in the occupied territories.

THE ARCHAEOLOGICAL EVIDENCE

View from the inside to the inside

Three settlement areas in the region of modern-day Lebanon were populated during the Late Bronze, not least because of their economic potential: the Akkar Plain in the north of the country, the entire coastal area from the north to the far south towards Tyre, and the Beqaʿ Valley, located between the Lebanon and Anti-Lebanon Mountains (Fig. 35.1). Our knowledge of the type and extent of settlement in these areas varies considerably from region to region and from site to site. The state of knowledge of the Late Bronze at the present time resembles an incompletely assembled puzzle. Nevertheless, the comparative analysis of the results and finds from selected settlements provides an initial clue to regional similarities in the cultural characteristics of Late Bronze Age Lebanon.

Settlement types and settlement system

The Late Bronze Age culture of Lebanon was an urban one, as some of the known urban settlements have shown (Arqa, Beirut, Kamid el-Loz, Tyre, Sidon, and Byblos[1]). Urban centres provided the surrounding villages with administrative services, while the villages provided the towns with the necessary means of subsistence. In these hierarchically constructed settlement systems, urban and village life were connected in a mutually conditional symbiosis, according to the results of studies in the region surrounding Arqa and

---

[1.] Sarepta and Tell el-Ghassil were not yet urban at the time, being still villages.

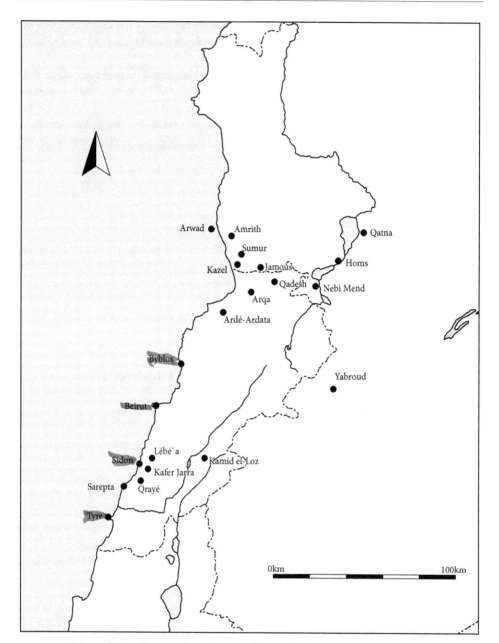

FIG. 35.1 Map of Late Bronze Age sites in the northern Levant (Lebanon)

Kamid el-Loz (Thalmann 2006: 190: Niveau 12, Phase L, LB I, about 1500–1400 BC; Marfoe 1995; 1998).

Urban space and fortified space

The towns were heavily fortified. In Arqa, in addition to the stone town wall, a tower supported the defensive nature of the fortification (Thalmann 2006: 69ff., fig. 93). Beirut, too, was surrounded by a city wall. There is evidence for this wall for the period from the 14th to the 13th century BC, but it is assumed that the Late Bronze fortifications were built on an older structure (Sader 1997: 401). In Kamid el-Loz the solid city wall ran immediately next to the area of the Late Bronze palace of Phase P4 (LB I–IIA, c. 1500/1450–1350 BC). Protection from external attack thus appears to have been vital, even though, as the history of events shows (see below), the most solid of fortifications could not prevent the takeover of the city by outsiders in all cases. In terms of town planning, the fortifications clearly and visibly marked the spatial inside and outside of the city, which in social contexts can be translated into 'us' and 'them', namely the sphere of those that belonged to the town's population and those who were not included in this group.

Living, ruling, and crafting

The activities of living and crafting took place within the city walls in close proximity to one another. Neither in Sarepta, located on the coast 16km south of Sidon, nor in Kamid el-Loz in the Beqa' Valley did the inhabitants fear the dangers and potential noise and smell pollution produced by crafts that used fire. In Sarepta the pottery kilns were located in the middle of the living areas (Khalifeh 1988: 11ff., 73ff. and pls 4–7; 81, 88: Period II, about 1450–1350 BC; Anderson 1988: 2ff., 386ff., pl. 6). In Kamid-el Loz the political conditions in the Late Bronze Age made an obvious demonstration of the political-social order necessary. At the highest topographical point of the settlement a palace was built, visible as a landmark from a distance and not to be overlooked in its significance for the town. As the oldest Late Bronze Phase 5 through Phase 4 building so far known, this palace was not just located adjacent to a metal workshop but could even be reached through the workshop (Adler and Penner 2001: 348). What characterized the spatial order of Late Bronze sites was not segregation of functions, but rather their immediate proximity to each other. (That Byblos should be included into the considerations here is obvious—the Amarna letters give accounts of the existence of a ruling elite of Byblos at the time; however, the archaeological evidence for the Late Bronze city of Byblos is lacking.)

Lives of the living and the dead

This observation of the location of the different functions in the settlement space recurred in the burial customs where—as attested in Arqa, Sarepta, and Kamid el-Loz—the life of the living was spatially indivisible from the 'life' of the dead. In Arqa the inhabitants buried their deceased in the middle of the settlement under floors and in courtyards (Thalmann 2006: 76ff. and fig. 93, Niveau 12, Phase L, LB I, about 1500–1400 BC). Adults and children, buried both individually and in groups, found their last resting place here. In Sarepta three graves were found in the settlement context. Although it cannot be determined for certain whether these were placed there at the time of the settlement or before the construction of the houses, it is still possible to establish that even in Sarepta the location of living space and burial place in one and the same place meant that one did not preclude the other (Anderson 1988: 59–67; 367–75 and pl. 3; 371: Grave 3, Stratum L, LB I; Stratum L, see 422; 17th–16th centuries BC).

   In the findings from Kamid el-Loz the connection of the living and the deceased to their previous surroundings becomes particularly clear. In the so-called Treasure House, a building that also functionally belonged to the Late Bronze palace, members of the elite, including two children, had been buried at great expense and accompanied by many grave goods (see below).

The Late Bronze Age burial customs in the above described contexts made sure that the dead all found their final resting places in the immediate vicinity of the bereaved—a rule that held good for all, independent of their age, gender, or status.

The deceased were provided with the objects of daily use, such as dishes, weapons, jewellery, and countless other artefacts. Whether these burial good customs can be seen as evidence that ownership of these goods was considered to be useful even in the afterlife, whether the burial goods illustrate the status ascribed to the dead, or whether the spectrum of grave goods was meant to illustrate what mourners could afford in terms of burial expense are questions that remain unanswered as long as there are no written records available on the subject.

The excavations in Beirut (Saidah 1993–4: 137ff.) and Tyre (Bikai 1978: 6) and the grave fields of Sidon (Saidah 2004; Jidejian 1968) also provided numerous clues to the burial customs in Lebanon during the Late Bronze Age. Unlike Arqa, Sarepta, and Kamid el-Loz, the connection between settlement context, burials, and cemeteries—that is to say the spatial connection between the living and the dead—has not yet been extensively investigated. (For the existence of Late Bronze Age grave goods in Iron Age graves in Byblos, see below.)

A great deal of attention was devoted to the burial of both children and adults and there were no partial burials or cremation burials; thus 'preserving' the 'entire' body must have been a necessary condition for a proper burial. Even though the background of the efforts expended on the burials has not been determined in detail, the visible care and effort of the living for the dead point to the significance the life of the dead had in that of the living.

A closer look at Kamid el-Loz: an example of a Late Bronze town in Lebanon

The networking of villages and towns in a hierarchically structured settlement system, the urban character and appearance of Late Bronze Age settlements, and the principle of spatial order within the towns (based not on functional segregation, but on the spatial integration of heterogeneous functions) can currently best be revealed by the results from Kamid el-Loz in the Beqa' Valley.

Kamid el-Loz and its neighbours

With a surface area of 240×300m, Kamid el-Loz was one of the larger settlements in the Beqa' Valley during the Late Bronze Age. The town was surrounded by a range of smaller settlements. Together, these formed a hierarchically structured settlement system with Kamid el-Loz at its head (Marfoe 1995; 1998; Bonatz 2002).

One of Kamid el-Loz's neighbouring settlements, which may have been integrated in this hierarchical settlement system, is Tell el-Ghassil, c.40km to the north of Kamid el-Loz in the central Beqa'. During the Late Bronze, Tell el-Ghassil had a size of 2.2ha. Marfoe characterizes this settlement as a large village 'of rather little importance within the settlement network of the Late Bronze Age Beqa'' (1998: 164). He based this characterization not just on the size of the settlement but also on the fact that the settlement during that time did not exhibit any functionally specialized architecture (such as temples, palaces, or administrative buildings)—that is to say, the functions associated with these buildings at that time in Tell el-Ghassil were probably not present and had not emerged in such a form that their representation in the constructed order was seen as necessary. That even villages were integrated in the global trade of the time is proved by the occurrence of Mycenaean and Cypriot pottery in Tell el-Ghasssil.

The townscape

The fortified Late Bronze town of *Kumidi* was constructed side by side with buildings in which the so-called 'ruling upper class' resided and conducted their administrative duties, as well as the living areas and handicraft quarters of the population. A palace, Treasure House, and workshop were located at the highest elevation of the settlement. Adjoining this zone to the north was an area with other official functions: the temple area, surrounded by residential houses.

The palace

The palace of Kamid el-Loz, so far only partially recorded, was repeatedly rebuilt during the course of the Late Bronze Age (Fig. 35.2). It was first widened (P5–P4), then made smaller (P3–P1) (Phase P5 to P1/LB I–IIB; mid-16th to late 12th century BC), and during the same building phase the number of storeys was reduced from two to one (Adler and Penner 2001: 348). From its establishment to the end of Phase P4, the palace was connected to the metal workshop mentioned previously. On several occasions fire destroyed sections of the palace, but the site and the building as a whole were not abandoned. The palace probably provided a place for both the political representation and the administration of the local community of *Kumidi*. This is suggested, among other things, by the cuneiform texts from Kamid el-Loz, which identified the settlement as the city of *Kumidi* known from the Amarna letters (see below) (Hachmann 1989: 89ff.).

The Treasure House

The so-called Treasure House, located to the north of the palace, was originally given its name because of the numerous objects that were found therein, which were due to its use as a funerary place (Fig. 35.3). The basic construction of the treasure house consisted of three rooms, a hallway, and beneath that a cellar. The rooms in the cellar, known as S and T, served as burial chambers for two children and one adult. The first to be buried was a child aged about seven years, followed by an adult male with the bodies placed in a row in Room T. The graves were destroyed at the same time. Despite this fact, a large number of objects, pottery, imported stone containers, and items made of glass, metal, ivory, and gold remained intact. Room S also served as a burial chamber, in this case for a female child aged about 8 years. This grave had also been destroyed, but here too numerous objects were found intact, many of them imported or made locally from imported raw materials, including gold ornaments and containers. The close proximity of the Treasure House to the palace, as well as the type of wealth indicated by the objects placed in the burial chambers (see below for a detailed discussion), lead us to believe that those buried here belonged to the circle of the so-called upper class in that community. This explains the wealth indicated in the graves of the children, who would probably not have been able to accumulate these riches in such a short time.

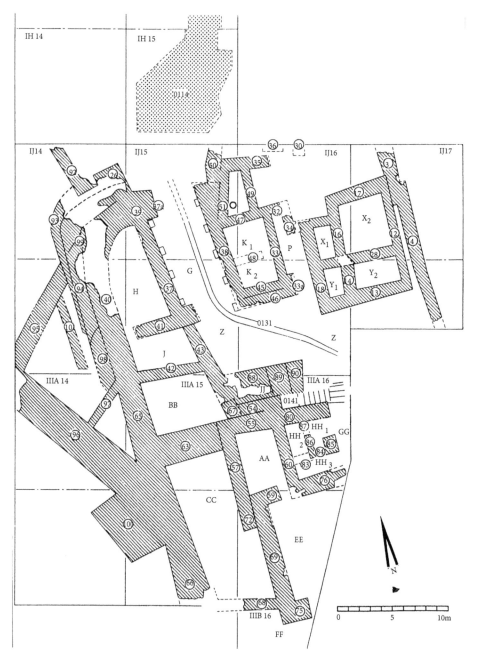

FIG. 35.2 Kamid el-Loz, palace of Building Stage 4a (Adler and Penner 2001: Abb. 128)

The temple

To the north of the town, not far from the palace and its associated buildings, lay the temple area (Fig. 35.4). The temple too was rebuilt several times during the Late Bronze

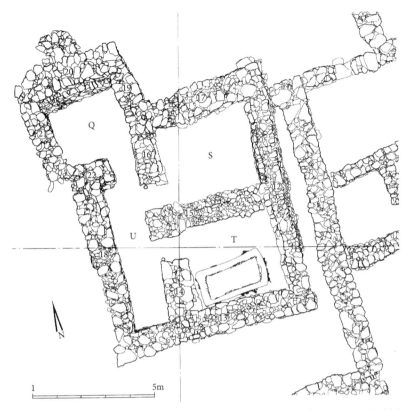

FIG. 35.3 Kamid el-Loz, Treasure House of Building Stage 4c (Miron 1990: Abb. 4)

(Hachmann 1996: 21; T3–T1, mid-16th to the end of 12th century BC), but unlike the palace, it gained in rooms and surface area as time went on, so that by the end of its use the original three-room construction had become a veritable double temple. This constant enlargement may be seen in connection with a continuous increase in importance of the institution, and a corresponding increase in the power of the priesthood of Kamid el-Loz. There too, the temple apparently served as both cult building and economic facility. In all the building phases the temple had economic sections, an alleyway to the north of it, and was surrounded by residential areas—that is to say it was embedded in the daily happenings of the settlement (Heinz et al. 2004: 106; Metzger 1991: 218ff.). The temple was destroyed on several occasions by fire, but its location was not abandoned and the building was resurrected.

The construction effort and configuration of the rooms, the finds in the buildings of Kamid el-Loz, the grave goods, and not least the information that can be gleaned from the texts found in Kamid el-Loz document the functional differentiation and the growing social hierarchy of the population. This differentiation was, however, countered by the built order of the public space and the principle of direct proximity of all functions and status groups, insofar as that they did not emphasize the segregation but rather the spatial proximity of the representatives of these functions and groups.

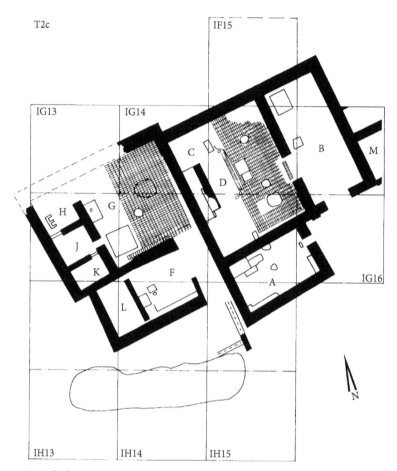

FIG. 35.4 Kamid el-Loz, temple of Building Stage T2c (Marfoe 1995: fig. 74)

View from the inside to the outside

The view from the inside to the outside is meant to help point out the regional and supraregional connections to which the inhabitants had access, established primarily on the material remains which, on the basis of stylistic characteristics and raw materials employed, could be identified as imports or copies in different settlements.

Pars pro toto? *The situation in Kamid el-Loz*

In Kamid el-Loz numerous goods found in the Treasure House, the temple, and the palace were identified as imports or locally manufactured imitations of 'foreign' originals.

The stone containers, the ornaments, and the ivory objects from the Treasure House in Kamid el-Loz suggest an Egyptian origin, mostly based on stylistic criteria. These suspicions are substantiated by the presence of a number of objects with name inscriptions that make an Egyptian origin more likely (Miron 1990).

An Egyptian-style stone vessel inscribed with the name of an Egyptian prince 'Rawoser' was found in Burial Room S (Fig. 35.5), while a ring with a scarab of Pharaoh Thutmosis III

FIG. 35.5 Kamid el-Loz, stone vessel with inscription ('Prince Rawoser') (Miron 1990: Abb. 16)

(1479–1425 BC) was found in Room T. In addition, numerous ceramic vessels appear to be Cretan and Cypriot in origin (Adler 1994: 140).

Besides a number of painted ceramics, the temple revealed cylinder seals, bronze statu-ettes, and other imported items made of ivory, silver, and gold (Metzger 1991). Numerous finds, in particular the ceramics, were Mycenaean in origin, while the bronze statuettes mainly came from the Syrian-Anatolian region. The Egyptian influence is clearly reflected in the silver sheets featuring a depiction of Hathor's head, while imports from the Mitanni are documented by the seal pictures (Kühne and Salje 1996).

Among the finds from the palace, the texts proved to be particularly informative, not just for the reconstruction of the regions with which the inhabitants and elite of Kamid el-Loz had connections, but also for the investigation of the background of these connections and a more precise date for this contact. The official correspondence of the administration was kept in the palace. Among the letters preserved there was one, written in Akkadian, and found in the debris from a fire in the palace during P4a, containing instructions from an Egyptian pharaoh to 'the man from Damascus': 'Send me the 'Apiru of the pastureland (?) concerning whom I send you as follows', 'I will settle them in the cities of the land of Kush insomuch as I have plundered them' (Morris 2005: 239).

A letter with almost identical wording was found in the Egyptian Amarna letters, which contained the correspondence of the pharaoh with the eastern world. The Amarna letter in question (EA 197), according to Morris, dates to the time of Akhenaten (Amenohotep IV 1350–1330 BC) and can be considered—because of the identical wording—to be contem-poraneous with the letter from Kamid. Who sent this letter to *Kumidi* and why it remained there is not known (Morris 2005: 239).

Based on the identification of the material remains in Kamid el-Loz, Egypt, Crete/ Mycenae, Cyprus, and the Syrian-Anatolian region are without doubt the regions that pro-vided goods, either directly or through intermediaries, which ended up in the hands of the local elite. The wide range of the contact area that can be determined from the finds at

Kamid el-Loz formed the rule rather than the exception in the Late Bronze in the region of Lebanon.

Trade, contacts, and exchange between the towns in Lebanon and the 'western' world

The finds from Byblos, Beirut, and Tyre also point to contacts with Egypt. In Byblos, stone blocks that originally belonged to a monumental building were inscribed with the name of Thutmosis III (Dunand 1939: pl. 27, nos. 1317 and 1318; Morris 2005: 120 and n. 23). When the local ruler, Ahiram, died in Byblos around 1000 BC (Heinz 2002: 167; Jidejian 1968: 30), one of the items placed in his grave was an alabaster vessel that had been inscribed with the name and title of the Egyptian Pharaoh Ramesses II (1290–1224 BC). That Beirut, too, had contact with Egypt is shown by a calcite vessel with the name Ramesses III (1184–1152 BC) from the so-called Kharji tombs (Saidah 1993–4: 170ff.).

The settlement of Tyre during the Late Bronze is primarily documented by residential houses and three graves that Bikai excavated and published in the 1970s (1978). The contacts of the town of Tyre with Egypt are authoritatively documented by the Amarna letters from the 14th century BC (Markoe 2003: 16).

Mycenaean and Cypriot pottery also appeared in the contexts mentioned. In Arqa the pottery attests to contact between the settlers and Cyprus at the beginning of the Late Bronze Age in the 16 to 15th centuries BC, as well as the importation of Mycenaean pottery from the 14th century BC (Thalmann 2006: 174ff.). Ahiram's grave in Byblos contained, besides the Egyptian vessel, ceramic finds from Cyprus, among them a decorated ivory fragment that points to contact with Mycenae, and an ivory box which, based on its craftsmanship and style, may come from Megiddo (c.1200 BC) (Jidejian 1968: 32 and fig. 100). The settlers in Beirut, Sarepta, Sidon, and Tyre also had direct or indirect contact with Crete/Mycenae and Cyprus, as shown by the pottery in burial and settlement contexts (Saidah 1993–4: 170ff.; 2004: 141–2; Koehl 1985; Bikai 1978).

In a letter (EA 89) from the king of Byblos to the Pharaoh Akhenaten (Markoe 2003: 16) the vast riches of the city of Tyre were described (with envy). Egypt, Palestine, and Cyprus were the trade and contact regions with which Tyre demonstrably had connections, even though the settlement picture cannot be reconstructed because of the lack of extended excavation (Bikai 1978).

Globalization in the Late Bronze Age: 'free trade' or Egyptian imports limited to the elite?

The spread and occurrence of imported items of Egyptian provenance and the ceramic finds from Mycenae and Cyprus give the impression that in Late Bronze settlements of the Levant, access to ceramics from Mycenae/Crete and Cyprus was open to a wider circle than access to goods from Egypt. This assumption is on the one hand based on the kind of imported Egyptian objects found in the towns of the Levant and, on the other, on the local context of the findings as in Kamid el-Loz. Objects of Egyptian origin appeared there in the above-mentioned grave at the 'treasure house', and its proximity to the palace, the extravagance of the mausoleum, and the numerous grave items given to the dead for the after-life allowed it to be identified as the burial of the elite. This identification is supported by those objects which, on the basis of the inscribed names (Prince 'Rawoser', Thutmosis III), could clearly be assigned to the sovereigns and region of Egypt. Further finds of Egyptian origin came from the inventory of the temple and the palace—in other words from the context of the cultic and political elite. Finds of Egyptian provenance from Beirut and Byblos were also characterized by the signature of Egyptian pharaohs.

Our assumption here is that vessels carrying the name of an Egyptian pharaoh must have originated from the possessions of the pharaoh in question, or at least from the sphere surrounding the pharaoh—in other words, out of the most powerful circles of the Egyptian elite. The context in Kamid el-Loz supports the proposition that only the political elite were in a position to acquire goods from the Egyptian elite. The exchange of goods between the elite, we further argue, was presumably part of the context of diplomacy in Late Bronze Lebanon, and the ritual exchange of goods was part of political communication on the highest level. Mycenaean and Cypriot ceramics also appeared in the contexts mentioned, and thus definitely belonged to the prestige goods of the times. But other than the Egyptian goods, they were never found exclusively in elite contexts, i.e. not reserved for the elite but, as suggested above, available for a wider circle of townspeople.

Conclusion: view from the inside towards the outside

The societies in the region of present-day Lebanon during the Late Bronze Age had far-reaching contacts that made it possible to access goods from far and wide in the known world of the time. In the second millennium BC 'globalization' was part of the already well-known phenomenon of trade in the Levant. The view from the inside to the outside documents both the range and directions of global relationships of the time, and in isolated cases even the background that led to these contacts.

Cyprus, Crete/Mycenae, Egypt, the Syrian-Anatolian area (Mitanni), and Palestine/Meggido, based on the evidence of material remains, made up the regions with which the inhabitants of the region of Lebanon were in direct or indirect contact and from which they acquired goods. Access to goods from Egypt, on current evidence, was limited to the elite of the towns. Cypriot and Mycenaean ceramics were probably also considered luxury or prestige items, but they were available to wider circles. Trade and exchange in the Lebanese towns in the Late Bronze were apparently concentrated on the west in its broadest sense. The Mesopotamian east as an economic partner for the Levant cannot be substantiated by the material remains.

View from the outside to the inside

The numerous imported goods and the range of regions with which the settlers in the Lebanon region maintained contact provide evidence of the interest of 'Lebanese societies' in the potentials, and the goods and products, of their most immediate and more distant neighbours. At the same time, the region of present-day Lebanon was of interest to the empires that came into being, or that already existed, during the Late Bronze in the surrounding area. In the mountains of Lebanon cedar trees grew, a raw material that all its neighbours coveted, and which in particular the rulers of wood-poor areas such as Egypt could not do without. The control of the area of Lebanon proved desirable, if not indispensable, for the rulers of these empires, as it was crossed by important overland routes that connected the north with the south and the east with the west (Heinz 2000). When globalization was an economic factor that could not be ignored and the world from Persia to Mycenae was united in a giant trade network (Sommer 2005), the control of the roads on which the exchange of goods depended was an important power factor in international events. The towns and villages of Late Bronze Lebanon together had access to an excellent infrastructure, as the view from the inside to the inside and from the inside to the outside have already shown, despite the gaps in the sources. Local, regional, and supraregional elites commanded complex administrations. There was a well-developed craft industry and the branches of economy that secured subsistence apparently also flourished. In other words, control of this region for foreign rulers would ideally mean not just that they would gain access to and power over economically vital goods and raw materials, but also that by using the local infrastructure they could take control of the human resources, labour, and skills in the region, thus expanding their net of imperial leadership over an increasingly large geographical horizon at relatively little expense.

What happened

In the Late Bronze Age the empires of Egypt, the Mitanni, the Hittites, and later also Assyria endeavoured to establish themselves politically in the economically important area of the Levant. The political activities of the rulers of the 18th Dynasty in Egypt saw the start of an important change in Egypt's relationship with its neighbours, including the Beqa' Valley. Thutmosis III (1479–1425 BC), the sixth pharaoh of the 18th Dynasty, was in the twenty-second year of his reign faced with a coalition of rulers from Palestine, Lebanon, and Syria who opposed the Egyptian claims to power in their territories. In a battle near Megiddo he defeated these rulers, conquered Meggido, an important city for supraregional trade, and thus established a foreign policy that allowed Egypt to act as an empire in the Near East. After sixteen additional campaigns, the Egyptian sphere of power included southern Lebanon, the Lebanese coast, and southern Syria as far as the line from Byblos to Damascus, including the Beqa' Valley. Through Thutmosis's strategy, the most important route through the Beqa' and one of the most important connections to the east via Damascus to the Euphrates and on to Mesopotamia fell under Egyptian control. Byblos, the most important harbour on the Mediterranean, also fell and stayed under the influence of Egypt. However, starting in Syria, the political circumstances turned unfavourable for Egypt in the time that followed. Alliances of local rulers repeatedly formed against Thutmosis III. In the second half of the 15th century BC the state of Hurri-Mitanni arose in northern Syria, and its claim to power soon spread to southern Syria. Thus the two empires battled over Syrian territory, which had an impact as far away as Lebanon. It was resolved when the two came to an agreement on the expansion of their spheres of authority. The Mitanni ruled northern Syria, while the other regions stayed under Egyptian administration. The sphere of Egyptian influence thus stretched along the coast to Ugarit, inland northwards as far as Qadesh, and to the Syrian trade town of Qatna. The two most important trade hubs of southern Syria, Qatna, and Damascus, remained initially under Egyptian sovereignty.

With a strengthening of the Hittite Empire a new curtailment of the foreign political supremacy of Egypt developed. The Hittite king Šuppiluliuma I (1380–1346 BC), a contemporary of Akhenaten among others, ousted the Mittani from northern Syria, took over the rule of this region, and thus threatened Egyptian interests in Syria. After military altercations between Egypt and the Hittites, a new division in the regional authority of Syria/

Lebanon took place. Ugarit, along with other smaller coastal towns and the town of Qatna, was added to the Hittite sphere of influence. Byblos and the Beqaʿ, including Damascus, on the other hand, remained under Egyptian sovereignty until the 19th Dynasty. The expansion of economic and military interests, along with the expansion of Egyptian political rule, thus had a significant impact on events in the area of Lebanon in the Late Bronze Age.

Kamid el-Loz: junction of supraregional long-distance roads and seat of Egyptian governors in the Beqaʿ Valley

In Kamid el-Loz, as far as we currently know, resource availability and demand came together in a classical way, and the town had many advantages. In the immediate hinterland Kamid el-Loz had access to fertile agricultural land and pastures. The settlement was strategically placed at the junction of large overland routes, thus enabling control of all movements through the plains (Hachmann and Kuschke 1966: 30; Heinz 2000; 2002). With this position and at a time in which supraregional trade and the control over territories were important factors within economic, foreign, and power politics, a town like Kamid el-Loz played a key role in the Beqaʿ Valley (Heinz 2000). Congruent settlement conditions as a general rule do not leave the political, economic, and cultural developments of an area unaffected. The rulers of the 18th Dynasty had already judged the location as favourable for the implementation of Egyptian imperial policy. The town's natural resources, its good infrastructure, and its integration into long-range trade relations fulfilled in an almost ideal way Egypt's demand for exactly those 'resources' on which they relied. The Beqaʿ Valley, in its function as the 'garden of Lebanon', provided precisely those resources that allowed the Egyptians to remain in the area for a longer period of time, and its excellent internal and external infrastructure served their economic and military needs optimally.

Kamid el-Loz: the Egyptian foreign, military, and economic politics, and the Beqaʿ Valley as a meeting point of cultures

Thutmosis's III (1479–1425 BC) campaigns reached as far as Lebanon (Morris 2005: 153). In his campaign lists *Kumidi* (*kmt*) is explicitly mentioned (Adler 1994: 142; Hachmann 1982: 156), but what is not known is what happened to *Kumidi* in the aftermath of the Egyptian foray. It is not until the reign of Pharaohs Amenhotep III (1388–1352 BC) and Akhenaten/Amenhotep IV (1350–1330 BC) that the historical events in and around *Kumidi* are known more clearly. It can be assumed that Egyptian troops already occupied *Kumidi*, among other towns, during the reign of Amenhotep III (Morris 2005: 254 and n. 155). At the time *Kumidi* was under the control of the local ruler Arahattu, known as such from an Amarna letter (EA 198). Arahattu had written to Amarna (the name of the addressee in Egypt has not been preserved) to assert his loyalty to the Egyptian power and to complain that he did not have a horse or cart in *Kumidi*, a concern that implicitly expressed the wish that this grievance be remedied so that Arahattu could personally come to Egypt to dispel the rumours of his lack of loyalty to the Egyptian court. As a character witness who could vouch for him, Arahattu named a diplomat, Hamashshi, who acted as ambassador for both Amenhotep III and later for Akhenaten in the Levant and Syria as well as Babylon (Hachmann 1982: 137ff.). The ambassador to the Egyptian pharaoh, so we assume, knew Arahattu because presumably Hamashshi stopped off in *Kumidi* on his journeys to the north. *Kumidi*'s location, as already described, made it an almost ideal stopping and meeting point for travellers. This assumption that *Kumidi* was a rest-stop on the way from Egypt to the north and east can be supported by two other letters which were found in the Palace at Kamid el-Loz (KL 69:277, 69:279). The letters in question were meant to be sent from Egypt to Syria but were apparently retained in *Kumidi*—Hachmann's suggestion that the messengers were attacked on their way past *Kumidi* is not without merit—and sheds new light on Arahattu's avowal of loyalty and the apparent mistrust of the Egyptian pharaoh concerning the reliability and faithfulness of the ruler of *Kumidi* (Hachmann 1982: 144–5). During Arahattu's reign, the Beqaʿ Valley was already under Egyptian control and Arahattu ruled under the supervision of the Egyptians. That is to say, the Egyptian policy was initially to rely on the local elite to further their political interests, thus keeping the representatives of the local government in office. But apparently the Egyptians' confidence in Arahattu had been weakened (Hachmann 1982).

The exact circumstances behind the apparent quarrel between the Egyptian occupational power and the local elite of Kamid el-Loz, and the reasons that eventually led to the removal of the local rulers from power, have not survived (Morris 2005: 240).

According to the written sources, *Kumidi* was turned into a gubernatorial seat under the control of an Egyptian administrator named Puhuru in the reign of Echnaton (1350–1330 BC). In other words, the political organization of *Kumidi* was adjusted (Morris 2005: 238). No further mention was made of a local king; instead the representation of Egyptian power was now in the hands of the *rabisu*, the aforementioned administrator. In order to control the Levant more effectively, the Egyptians divided the region into three provinces (Morris 2005: 239): Canaan, with its administrative seat in Gaza, Phoenicia and Amurra, which were ruled from Sumur, and the province of Upe, which was ruled from *Kumidi*. The functions and activities of the governors in *Kumidi* are relatively well known because of the Amarna letters. The administrator was responsible for maintaining law and order. He was in control of troops which in an emergency would be used against enemies of Egypt. When one of the administrators lost power in Byblos, Puhurru sent his troops from *Kumidi* to the coast to re-establish order. Puhurru was apparently a successful representative of Egyptian interests. Aside from Byblos, his political power stretched as far as Kadesh and Qatna, two towns that were ports of call for the caravans and thus important stopping-off places for international trade (Morris 2005: 238). Puhurru's tasks in *Kumidi* were related to the factors that created *Kumidi*'s economic and political potential, which probably led to the occupation of Kamid el-Loz/*Kumidi*: the control of the roads in order to secure the economic, military, and political interests of the Egyptians in the periphery of their empire. (According to Morris (2005: 252), at the end of the rule of Akhenaten *Kumidi* may also have lost its function as gubernatorial seat for the Egyptians and fallen under the control of Aziru of Amurra, king of Qatna. Not until the reign of Seti (1291–1278 BC) did *Kumidi* apparently once again fall under the rule of the Egyptian power (Morris 2005: 354).)

CONCLUSION: LEBANON IN THE LATE BRONZE AGE

The view from the inside to the inside showed the complex development of an urban culture in Lebanon during the Late Bronze Age. The view from the inside to the outside reveals a wider spectrum of regions that stood in direct and/or indirect contact with the towns in

Lebanon. Finally, the view from the outside to the inside documents how the spatial, political, economic, and cultural advantages of the Lebanon region, shown here *pars pro toto* for one site, could not just lead to an economic boom for a town or region, but could also have the opposite effect for the political autonomy of an advantaged region when it becomes useful for the expansion politics of a militarily superior empire.

Then as now, because of its natural advantages and its cultural and economic state of development, the region of Lebanon was a prosperous land; so prosperous and so well situated that the dominant powers could not (and up to date do not) resist to use the area for their own interest.

SUGGESTED READING

Doumet-Serhal, C. (ed.) (2008). *Networking Patterns of the Bronze and Iron Age Levant: The Lebanon and Its Mediterranean Connections*. Beirut: Lebanese British Friends of the National Museum.
—— A. Rabate, and A. Resek (eds) (2004). *Decade: A Decade of Archaeology and History in the Lebanon*. Beirut: Lebanese British Friends of the National Museum.
Eriksen, T. H. (2001). *Small Places, Large Issues: An Introduction to Social and Cultural Anthropology*, 2nd edn. London: Pluto Press.

REFERENCES

Adler, W. (1994). *Kamid el-Loz 11: Das 'Schatzhaus' im Palastbereich*. Bonn: Habelt.
—— and S. Penner (2001). *Kamid el-Loz 18: Die spätbronzezeitlichen Palastanlagen* (3 vols). Bonn: Habelt.
Anderson, W. P. (1988). *Sarepta I: The Late Bronze and Iron Age Strata of Area II, Y*. Beirut: Département des publications de l'Université libanaise.
Bikai, P. M. (1978). *The Pottery of Tyre*. Warminster: Aris & Phillips.
Bonatz, D. (2002). Preliminary remarks on an archaeological survey in the Anti-Lebanon. *Bulletin d'archéologie et d'architecture libanaises* 6: 283–307.
Dunand, M. (1939). *Fouilles de Byblos I, 1926–1932*. Paris: Geuthner.
Hachmann, R. (1982). 'Arahattu–Biriawaza–Puhuru. In R. Hachmann (ed.), *Ausgrabungen in Kamid el-Loz: Bericht über die Ergebnisse der Ausgrabungen in Kamid el-Loz in den Jahren 1971 bis 1974*. Bonn: Habelt, 137–61.
——(1989) *Kamid el-Loz 1963–1981: German Excavations in Lebanon, Part I*. Beirut: Faculty of Arts and Sciences, American University Beirut.
——(1996). *Kamid el-Loz 16: 'Schatzhaus'-Studien*. Bonn: Habelt.
—— and A. Kuschke (1966). *Bericht über die Ergebnisse der Ausgrabungen Kamid el-Loz (Libanon) in den Jahren 1963 und 1964*. Bonn: Habelt.
Heinz, M. (2000). Kamid el-Loz: Knotenpunkt überregionaler Fernstrassen und Sitz des ägyptischen Statthalters in der Beqa'a-Ebene: Archäologie im Libanon. *Antike Welt* 31: 359–68.
—— (2002). *Altsyrien und Libanon: Geschichte, Wirtschaft und Kultur vom Neolithikum bis Nebukadnezar*. Darmstadt: Wissenschaftliche Buchgesellschaft.
——S. Kulemann-Ossen, E. Wagner, C. Leschke, and J. Nieling (2004). Kamid el-Loz in the Beqa'a Plain/Lebanon: excavations in 2001, 2002 and 2004. *Bulletin d'archéologie et d'architecture libanaises* 8: 83–117.
Jidejian, N. (1968). *Byblos through the Ages*. Beirut: Dar el-Machreqe.

Khalifeh, I. (1988). *Sarepta II: The Late Bronze and Iron Age Periods of Area II, X.* Beirut: Département des publications de l'Université libanaise.

Koehl, R. B. (1985). *Sarepta III: The Imported Bronze and Iron Age Wares from Area II, X.* Beirut: Département des publications de l'Université libanaise.

Kühne, H., and B. Salje (1996). *Kamid el-Loz 15: Die Glyptik.* Bonn: Habelt.

Marfoe, L. (1995). *Kamid el-Loz 13: The Prehistoric and Early Historic Context of the Site.* Bonn: Habelt.

——(1998). *Kamid el-Loz 14: Settlement History of the Biqa' up to the Iron Age.* Bonn: Habelt.

Markoe, G. E. (2003). *Die Phönizier,* trans. T. Ohlsen. Stuttgart: Theiss.

Metzger, M. (1991). *Kamid el-Loz 7: Die spätbronzezeitlichen Tempelanlagen—Stratigraphie, Architektur und Installationen.* Habelt.

Miron, R. (1990). *Kamid el-Loz 10: Das Schatzhaus im Palastbereich—Die Funde.* Bonn: Habelt.

Morris, E. F. (2005). *The Architecture of Imperialism: Military Bases and the Evolution of Foreign Policy in Egypt's New Kingdom.* Leiden: Brill.

Sader, H. (1997). Den Ruinen entsteigt die Vergangenheit: Archäologie in Beirut. *Antike Welt* 28: 397–406.

Saidah, R. (1993–4). Beirut in the Bronze Age: the Khariji tombs. *Berytus* 41: 137–210.

——(2004). *Sidon et la Phénicie méridionale au Bronze récent: à propos des tombes de Dakerman.* Beirut: Institut français du Proche-Orient.

Sommer, M. (2005). *Die Phönizier: Handelsherren zwischen Orient und Okzident.* Stuttgart: Kröner.

Thalmann, J.-P. (2006). *Tell Arqa I: les niveaux de l'Âge du bronze* (3 vols). Beirut: Institut français du Proche-Orient.

CHAPTER 36

......

THE SOUTHERN LEVANT (CISJORDAN) DURING THE LATE BRONZE AGE

......

NAVA PANITZ-COHEN

The Late Bronze Age in the area of the Israel/Palestinian territories (termed here 'Canaan') was a period of prosperity and privation, submission and rebellion. It marked a high point of various technological, mercantile, and artistic endeavours while, at the same time, other aspects of ancient life experienced a decline.

Two seminal features characterized this period: the domination of the Egyptian Empire, which provides the chrono-historical as well as the political-cultural framework for the entire duration of this period, and the economic and cultural involvement of Canaan in the 'world system' network of the eastern Mediterranean and the ancient Near East.

It is this dialectic nature, along with the multitude of textual evidence and rich archaeological finds, that make the Late Bronze Age a pivotal period in the development of history, society, and culture in Canaan.

THE CHRONO-HISTORICAL FRAMEWORK

......

The subdivision of the Late Bronze Age in Canaan is intricately tied to the activities and policies of the Egyptian New Kingdom, the 18th–20th Dynasties, although also affected by local conditions and processes (Table 36.1). The absolute dates used here are those of the low chronology proposed by Kitchen (1987; 2007).

While its inner development is basically uncontentious, there is debate concerning the beginning and the end of this period, a feature that is, of course, typical of transitional periods in general. The initial phase of the Late Bronze (LB IA) was thought to have been 'officially' ushered in with the conquest of Avaris and the reunification of Egypt by Ahmose, the first pharaoh of the 18th Dynasty; his conquest of Saruhen (Tell el-'Ajjul) marks the expulsion of the Hyksos from Canaan and the beginning of Egyptian imperial control (1550 BCE). However, while the series of destructions of various MB IIB sites has been linked to this event, the picture was much more complex and the process of change in sociopolitical organization, settlement patterns, and material culture was gradual and intermittent. Other

Table 36.1 Periodization of the Late Bronze Age

Period	Date	Egyptian New Kingdom
LB III/Iron IA	1190–1140	20th Dynasty Ramesses III–Ramesses VI
LB IIB	1300–1190	19th Dynasty Tauseret
LB IIA	1375–1300	Late 18th Dynasty Amarna period
LB IB	1479–1375	Mid-18th Dynasty Thutmosis III–Amenophis III
LB IA	1550–1479	Early 18th Dynasty Ahmose-Hapshetsut

factors most probably also played a role in the transformation, such as natural disasters, internecine strife, nomadic incursions, previous and subsequent military campaigns, and migration of peoples such as the Hurrians (Weinstein 1981: 1; 1991; Hoffmeier 1989; Dever 1990: 76; 1992a: 48; 1997; Bietak 1991: 58–61; 2002: 37–8; Redford 1992: 139, n. 49, 148–9; Na'aman 1994; Bunimovitz 1995: 320–22, 330; Ilan 1995: 314–15; Hasel 1998: 4–5, n. 6). It has been suggested that the second half of the 16th century should be designated as 'transitional MB–LB' or 'MB IIC–LB I' (Bietak 1991; Dever 1992b: 16) in an attempt to accommodate both the short-term events and long-term processes that shaped the inception of the Late Bronze in Canaan.

It is with the ascension of Thutmosis III (1479 BCE) that the full-blown Late Bronze material culture patterns appear unequivocally in the archaeological record (Leonard 1989: 12–16; Mazar 1990: 232; Bietak 1991: 58–62; Ilan 1995: 315; Oren 2001). The reigns of Thutmosis III, Amenophis II, and most of Amenophis III are designated LB IB. Some scholars deny the validity of a subdivision into LB IA and LB IB for the latter 16th and the 15th centuries BCE, and use just LB I (Weinstein 1981: 12). However, it is justifiable to separate the two sub-periods in light of the different nature of the processes and events of each.

The following phase (LB IIA) covers the latter three-quarters of the 14th century BCE, including the end of the reign of Amenophis III and the so-called Amarna Age (Redford 1992: 169–88). The end of the Amarna interlude was followed by a much tightened control of Canaan by the rulers of the 19th Dynasty, covering all of the 13th century BCE. This phase (LB IIB) began with the military campaigns of Seti I (1295 BCE) and was dominated by the long-lived Ramesses II (1279–1212 BCE). The 19th Dynasty ended with brief reigns of Ramesses II's successors, the most prominent being Merenptah (1212–1204 BCE) and the last being Queen Tauseret, whose reign ended c.1190 BCE.

The 20th Dynasty constituted the 'swan song' of Egyptian domination of Canaan. The reign of Ramesses III terminated in c.1155 BCE and marked the virtual demise of the Egyptian Empire, though sparse Egyptian presence is attested until the reign of Ramesses VI down to c.1140 BCE (Weinstein 1992). The definition of this sub-period is the most debated, as it is characterized by almost equal shares of continuity and change. Continuity is represented by the aforesaid Egyptian presence, as well as many aspects of Canaanite material culture and settlements, particularly along the coast and in the northern valleys (Gonen 1992b). Change is underscored by destructions of key Canaanite sites, against the background of the breakdown of the geopolitical framework of the ancient Near East and the Mediterranean basin during the second half of the 13th until the early 12th centuries BCE (Ward and Joukowsky 1992; Drews 1993; Killebrew 2005: 33–49). This turmoil terminated the extensive international trade and triggered migratory movements throughout the region, particularly of the so-called Sea Peoples (Sandars 1985; Bietak 1993; Oren 2000; Killebrew 2005: 33–42). The long-lived Canaanite city-state system ultimately dissipated and an unprecedented regionalism took its place. This complex transitional period is designated LB III by some scholars (Ussishkin 2004: 74–5; Oren 2006), but is deemed Iron Age IA by others (Mazar 1990: 290, 296; Stern 1993: 1529), depending on how the material culture of the first half of the 12th century BCE is contextualized and whether the initial settlement of the Philistines is considered contemporary with or post-dating the 20th Dynasty (Finkelstein 2000; Barako 2007; Mazar 2007: 575–9; Yasur-Landau 2007). This final part of the Late Bronze is charac- terized by the reshuffling of sociopolitical boundaries between various groups—Egyptians, Canaanites, 'apiru, Shasu, Israelites, and Sea Peoples, some of whom disappeared and some who took centre stage in the subsequent Iron Age (Killebrew 2005).

SETTLEMENT PATTERNS, URBANIZATION, AND POPULATION

The nature and dynamics of Late Bronze settlement patterns, urbanization, and popula- tion are a prime window into the dialectics of Canaanite society, economy, and culture as a two-tier process which oscillated between autonomy and dependence.

The rash of destructions of MB IIB cities eventually culminated in a new settlement pat- tern (Fig. 36.1). Alongside a decrease in the amount of sites, the majority were now con- centrated along the coast and major inland valleys, with a decline in the erstwhile densely populated central hill country and Beersheba Valley. The net size of Late Bronze settlements also decreased, with a concomitant population reduction. These population shifts were also expressed in the refiguration of sedentary versus nomadic elements, with the latter gaining ground, particularly in the less populated peripheral regions (Gonen 1984; 1987; 1992b: 215; Mazar 1990: 239–40; Ahlström 1993: 220; Bunimovitz 1994; Savage and Falconer 2003). Late Bronze II saw a gradual increase in settlements (Bunimovitz 1995: 320–24; Killebrew 2005: 97), although Gonen (1984: 63; 1992b: 217) claimed that the increase in LB IIB is more of an optical illusion, since it took place mainly in centres of Egyptian admin- istration such as Tel Sher'a, Beth Shean, Jaffa, and Aphek, while other settlements were abandoned.

Although traditional scholarship has tended to homogenize the political organization of the Middle and Late Bronze city-states (i.e. Albright 1956: 91–2; Baumgarten 1992), recent evaluations using analytic methods taken from the fields of political sociology and human geography (Bunimovitz 1989; 1992; 1994; 1995; Finkelstein 1996; Savage and Falconer 2003; Jasmin 2006), survey data (Dagan 2000; 2004; Shavit 2000), and provenience stud- ies of the Amarna archive tablets (Goren, Finkelstein, and Na'aman 2004) have demon- strated that the Late Bronze political-territorial organization represented a more diverse and less integrated system than in the Middle Bronze. In place of a relatively small number of large MB IIB cities controlling broad hinterlands (Ilan 1995; Dever 1997), the Late Bronze comprised a cluster of rather small, semi-autonomous city-states of differential hierarchy,

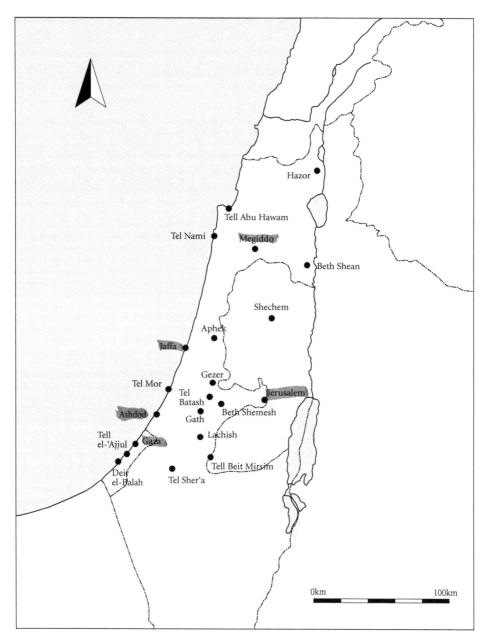

FIG. 36.1 Map of major Late Bronze Age sites of the southern Levant (Cisjordan)

both intra- and interregional (Strange 2000). Although there was a high degree of cultural continuity between the two periods, differences stemming from demographic depletion, Egyptian domination, and international commercial and cultural involvement are considerable (Killebrew 2005: 100).

The Late Bronze political system of small city-states most probably coalesced during the 15th century BCE, but the main source for its reconstruction and interpretation remains the Amarna letters (Na'aman 1975; 1997; 2000; Marfoe 1979; Liverani 1983; Bunimovitz 1989: 131–61; Moran 1992; Giles 1997; Goren, Finkelstein, and Na'aman 2004). Attempts to reconstruct the number of city-states and particularly to define the nature of their borders, have resulted in conflicting views, ranging from a number of 13–14 (Finkelstein 1996), or 17–18 (Bunimovitz 1989: 131–62), to 22–27 (Helck 1971; Gonen 1992b: 214; Na'aman 1997; Falconer and Savage 2003) (see Fig. 36.2).

A proposed *modus vivendi* is the round number of *c.*20 suggested in wake of the recent petrographic study of the Amarna tablets (Goren, Finkelstein, and Na'aman 2004: 320). The different evaluations are based on variable definitions of what constitutes a city-state (Hansen 2000), as well as on the question whether there was a 'no man's land' or fuzzy border between them (Na'aman 1997: 606–7) or whether it was a tightly organized system with no sparsely inhabited or poorly controlled border zones (Finkelstein 1996: 225–6; Goren, Finkelstein, and Na'aman 2004: 322). Another consequential issue is whether some kingdoms were more dominant than others. It seems probable that Hazor, Shechem, and possibly Gezer were of higher rank (Bienkowski 1987; Na'aman 1997; Zuckerman 2007: 12); Jerusalem (Finkelstein 1996: 243) and Gath (Uziel and Maeir 2005; Jasmin 2006: 174) are recent candidates for this list of 'territorial kingdoms'. This hierarchal inequality was most likely the result of assorted factors, such as differential access to resources (natural and human), geographic location (proximity to trade and military routes, or to peripheral nomadic areas), as well as the effects of direct Egyptian intervention (garrisons, governors' residencies, and temples).

Scholars have tried to understand the reasons for the overall smaller size of Late Bronze city-states as opposed to their MB II predecessors, as well as for the causes behind the constant strife between them. One model proposes that population depletion resulted in small urban elites competing for natural resources and sedentary manpower. The smaller size of the Late Bronze city-states was also impacted by the factor of 'economic feasibility', i.e. the distance that the relatively impoverished rural population would be willing to go to take advantage of the central place's services (Bunimovitz 1989: 71–100; 1994; 1995: 324–6). Explanations of Canaanite political fragmentation include disputes between the lowlands and the highlands, as the latter tried to regain power lost at the end of MB II (Finkelstein 1996; Savage and Falconer 2003: 40), as well as control of major trade routes and seizure of neighbouring agricultural land, which was at a premium due to Egyptian land confiscation and exploitation. A deliberate Egyptian policy of 'divide and rule' is apparently behind at least some of the internecine bickering, as well as of the relatively small size and unfortified state of most of these petty kingdoms (Gonen 1992b).

Analysis of the degree of urbanization by way of the material correlates of monumental public secular and religious architecture, as well as fortifications, has shown that these parameters decline in the Late Bronze (Gonen 1984; 1992b; London 1989). This is not to say that this period was non-urban, but rather that the scale and nature of urbanism was quantitatively and qualitatively different than before (Bunimovitz 1995: 324). While Bunimovitz postulated that the main players were the small urban centres and the non-sedentary elements, Falconer (1994: 329) suggested that the rural sector in the population became steadily more influential as the urban entities deteriorated (also Gonen 1992b: 218; Finkelstein 1996: 232). When evaluating the Late Bronze population, the dissident *'apiru* and the pastoralist Shasu must be considered alongside the sedentary rural and urban Canaanites (Greenberg 1955; Finkelstein 1992; Redford 1992: 179, 195; Rainey 1995; Goren, Finkelstein, and Na'aman 2004: 321). Immigration from Anatolia, Syria, and

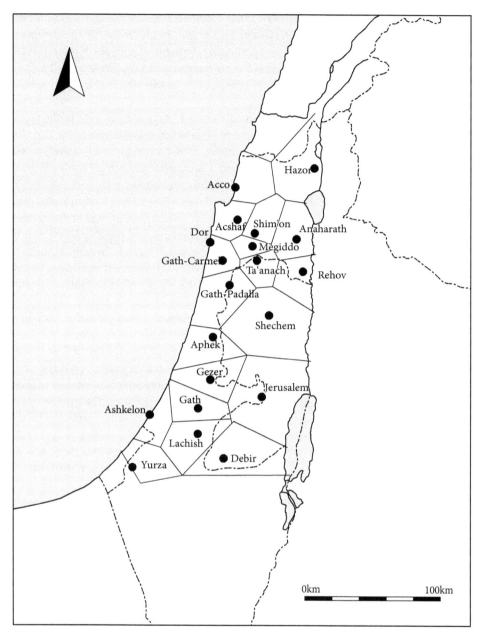

FIG. 36.2 Different proposals for the division of Canaanite city-states (based on Falconer and Savage 2003)

the Aegean world influenced the local population by the latter part of LB IIB (Mazar 1988a). The spatial and temporal diversity of burial types reflects regional and socioeconomic differences of the indigenous Canaanite population and their differential exposure to Egyptian influence, alongside a minority of burials that are an expression of foreign and nomadic groups (Gonen 1992a; Bunimovitz 1995: 331). Thus, while the urban and village Canaanites constituted the main bulk of the population, other socioeconomic and ethnic elements must be reckoned with when analysing Late Bronze society (Dever 1992c; Killebrew 2005).

THE IMPACT OF THE EGYPTIAN EMPIRE ON CANAAN

The 'shadow of Egyptian domination' (Mazar 1990) is the primary formative factor of the Canaanite Late Bronze Age, for better and (for the most part) for worse. The vassal status of the Canaanite city-states exposed the local population to ongoing economic stress of land confiscation, population deportation, and military raids, although also offering a preferred status and economic advantages for some (Knapp 1993: 85–6). The Egyptian domination was far from monolithic, having undergone alterations and adjustments that deeply impacted Canaanite culture, economy, and society during the 400-odd years of its duration.

The first seventy years of the 18th Dynasty (LB IA) were a moratorium for Canaan, when a new, more decentralized social equilibrium was being established which entailed shifts in political loyalties, with local elites turning from the Hyksos to the Egyptian 18th Dynasty in a process termed 'dynastic substitution', or having been replaced with new elements who would prove loyal to the latter (Bunimovitz 1989; 1995: 323–6; Ilan 1995: 315; Dever 1998: 112). On the basis of somewhat later sources such as Ugaritic texts and the Amarna letters, this new elite included civilian and military functionaries, such as the *maryannu*, as well as scribes, administrators, landowners, middlemen, and merchants (Heltzer 1976; Mazar 1990: 247; Ahlström 1993: 211). Egyptian administrative apparatus in Canaan was cursory, and it seems that the first potentates of the 18th Dynasty were content with oaths of loyalty and regular tribute by local princes (Redford 1992: 148–55, 200).

Egyptian involvement in Canaan expanded in proportion to their engagement with the Mitannian kingdom in northern Syria over the course of the 15th century BCE, with growing acknowledgement of the potential of Canaan as a launching place and buffer zone, as well as a valuable economic resource (Leonard 1989: 13; Ahlström 1993: 218; Hasel 1998: 117; Killebrew 2005: 51–92; Morris 2005). Following the peace treaty with Mitanni, the last part of LB IB was one of relative tranquility, with the *pax aegyptiaca* being especially lucrative for Egypt, although detrimental for Canaan, as an Egypt now free of international altercations increasingly set its sights on exploiting its northern province with labour and land confiscation, as well as taxes and tribute (Knapp 1987: 25; Redford 1992: 169). Egyptian administration of Canaan became more proactive at this time, though the details of its subdivision are debated (Na'aman 1999: 34).

It is difficult to assess the impact of the Amarna interlude in LB IIA on the Canaanite vassals, and scholarly opinion is divided as to whether this was an era of prosperity or weakness (Weinstein 1981: 15–16; Redford 1992: 175). Bienkowski (1989: 60); Giles (1997: 352), Knapp (1989: 65; 1993: 86), and Ahlström (1993: 241–2) view the minor squabbling of the petty kings of Canaan and their constant expressions of loyalty to Egypt as the very proof of viable Egyptian rule rather than as a breakdown; it was 'business as usual' that was simply frozen for modern eyes by dint of the discovery of the archive. On the other hand, the greatly intensified Egyptian involvement in Canaan during the subsequent 19th Dynasty is thought to be clinching evidence of a significant weakening of Egyptian control during the Amarna period (Weinstein 1981: 17; Leonard 1989: 16).

Not only is the political situation difficult to evaluate, but economic and social conditions are ambivalent as well. Scholars have deliberated as to the apparent disparity between certain aspects of material culture which demonstrate great wealth and artistic prowess (such as elabourate burial deposits, elegant ceramic imports, and high-quality luxury items), as opposed to others (such as local pottery technology and dearth of monumental architecture) which show decline (Gonen 1987; Knapp 1987: 26; 1989; Leibowitz 1987; 1989; Bienkowski 1989; Bunimovitz 1994: 9–10; Hasel 1998: 115–17). Was Canaan too poor to constitute a target for Egyptian exploitation (Ahituv 1978; Bienkowski 1989; Dever 1998: 111), or are the texts mentioning ample tribute, taxation, goods, manpower, and services commandeered by the Egyptians evidence of an economically sound province (Na'aman 1981; Weinstein 1981; Knapp 1989; 1992; Hasel 1998: 117)? Various reasons have been suggested for this incongruity, such as disparate socioeconomic conditions, ethnic entities, and settlement venues. One scenario points to a highly stratified society, whose ruling elite was preoccupied with maintaining their status at all costs through conspicuous consumption within the framework of Egyptian supremacy and status symbols, at the expense of the rural hinterland and ultimately, themselves (Bunimovitz 1994: 10–11; Bryan 1996; Higginbotham 2000). Others postulate that prosperity was enjoyed only in those regions where Egyptians were present or had clear vested interests, while poverty was the lot of those 'off the Egyptian track' (Bienkowski 1989). This 'complex pattern of economic decline and survival' (Bunimovitz 1995: 326) is to be understood against the background of the duality of life in Late Bronze Canaan, caught between local autonomy and imperial dependence.

The reign of the 19th Dynasty marked an unprecedented intensification of Egyptian presence in Canaan, well-attested in Egyptian sources by a step-up in punitive military campaigns, and in the archaeological record by the governors' residencies and garrison stations established at strategic locations (i.e. Deir el-Balah, Beth Shean, Jaffa, Gaza, Tel Mor, Lachish, Aphek, Tel Sher'a, and possibly Gezer and Megiddo), temples dedicated to Egyptian deities, and an increase in Egyptian and Egyptianized objects, inscriptions, and burial customs in the form of anthropoid coffins (Weinstein 1981: 17–22; Oren 1984; 2006; Gonen 1992a; Ahlström 1993: 251–3; Singer 1994: 284; Higginbotham 2000; Killebrew 2004: 342; 2005: 51–92; Killebrew, Goldberg, and Rosen 2006). Egyptian involvement in local craft production is evident, particularly in pottery manufacture (Cohen-Weinberger 1998; Killebrew 2004; 2005: 79–80; Oren 2006: 271; Martin 2011). An alternative explanation for this intensification entails the concept of 'elite emulation', wherein the surge of Egyptianization reflects local elites who acculturated the trappings of Egyptian culture as status symbols (Bryan 1996; Higginbotham 2000). However, it seems that while such a process might have occurred on some level, it does not sufficiently account for the intensified Egyptian involvement in Canaan, which was in fact the core of its Asiatic empire following the battle of Kadesh and the peace treaty with the Hittites. The nature of Egyptian presence in the 20th Dynasty, considered a continuation of the intense 19th Dynasty policy, has been questioned by Mazar (2007: 578), who postulates a weakening of imperial rule in face of the incursions of Sea Peoples and the general disturbances that shook the entire ancient Near East at this time.

THE PLACE OF CANAAN IN THE LATE BRONZE AGE 'WORLD SYSTEM'

The Late Bronze has been termed the 'age of internationalism' due to the extensive economic, cultural, political, and ideological interaction between Egypt, Mesopotamia, Anatolia, the Mycenaean world, Cyprus, and the Levant. The concept of a 'world system', taken from Wallerstein's analysis of the emergence of modern capitalism, is a convenient analytic framework in which to understand these processes (Kohl 1987; Knapp 1998; Killebrew 2005: 23–4). Globalization is still another heuristic framework currently being utilized in the analysis of the interconnected relations of the ancient Near East and the Mediterranean basin in the latter half of the second millennium BCE (Randsborg 2001; La Bianca and Scham 2006). These analyses emphasize the interaction between regions and political entities, wherein both major (core regions, palace systems) and minor (periphery and semi-periphery regions, small city-states) players impacted different and dynamically developing levels of the system. This fundamentally economic interaction was concomitant with a shared artistic *koiné* or 'international style' (Caubet 1998), whose material correlates reflected an ideology that served the great kings and high elites in the construction and consolidation of their status and power (Feldman 2006). This materiality and its associated social and ideological 'added value' trickled down to local elites of secondary city-states and even to lower social echelons ('sub-elite consumers': Sherratt and Sherratt 1991), so that virtually all social classes were able to partake in some way and on some level of the commercial contacts and absorb the ideological baggage that accompanied them (Zaccagnini 1987; Sherratt and Sherratt 1991; Caubet 1998: 112; Knapp 1998: 202–4; van Wijngaarden 2002).

Late Bronze Canaan was a secondary but significant participant in this system, as a 'semi-periphery' component (Killebrew 2005: 23) that served as a geographic, economic, cultural, and political interface and buffer zone between the larger powers of Egypt and the Hittite Empire (Leonard 1989). Despite its vassal state, Canaan enjoyed some degree of autonomy in the international trade network. Canaanites were involved in both shipbuilding and maintenance, although most of the known references and archaeological remains pertain to Ugarit (Wachsmann 1998). The active role of Canaanites as seamen is evidenced by the Syro-Palestinian finds in the Uluburun and Cape Gelidoniya shipwrecks that may be considered personal effects (Bass 1986: 296; Pulak 1997). The Canaanite storage jar was both widely traded and copied throughout the Mediterranean basin (Gunneweg, Perlman, and Asaro 1987; Mazar 1988b), so that not only did the contents of these jars figure in the trade interaction, but the jars themselves fulfilled an emblematic role of transmitting 'Canaanitism' throughout the world system.

Canaanite trade was not only an officially attached or palace-dependent commerce as were most of the mercantile endeavours of Greece, Cyprus, and Egypt, but rather the Canaanite merchants and seafarers apparently often operated as middlemen, mercenaries, or free agents in a kind of 'opportunistic sailor's trade' or 'entrepreneurial trade' (Artzy 1994; 1998). Such traders filled the niche of informal exchange of 'added-value products', such as pottery, less expensive substitutes for elite luxury items, and possibly scrap metal as well (Sherratt 1998). Certainly the ubiquity of Cypriot ceramic imports in virtually every Canaanite town is due, at least in part, to this informal but critical role of Canaanite seamen and sub-elite merchants. Gateway ports such as Tell Abu Hawam and Tel Nami were coastal emporia that served as the foci of this distribution to inland Canaan (Artzy 1994; 2007), most likely by way of regional hubs along the inland trade routes, such as Megiddo and Beth Shean in the northern valleys (Knapp 1993: 87).

MATERIAL CULTURE AND CANAANITE SOCIETY: DIVERSITY AND HOMOGENEITY

The material culture of the Late Bronze continued many features of the previous period, while developing unique patterns of its own. The various factors discussed above—the nature of the settlement pattern and degree of urbanization, the scope and makeup of the population, the Egyptian imperial presence, and the involvement of Canaan in the world system—are all crucial factors in the contextual interpretation of Late Bronze material culture, which demonstrated both rags and riches, autonomy and interdependence, and creativity and stagnation.

Canaanite temples were either a reuse of monumental MB II temples or newly built of rather heterogeneous plans, such as at Hazor, while some temples demonstrate Egyptian influence, especially in LB IIB, such as in Beth Shean Stratum Lower VI and Lachish Area P, Stratum VII (Mazar 1992). Few buildings that can be defined as administrative and/or royal palaces have been found; the most prominent examples include Hazor (Zuckerman 2007), Megiddo, and Tell el-'Ajjul (Oren 1992). Somewhat more frequent are the so-called patrician houses, found mostly at southern sites such as Ashdod, Tel Batash, Tell Beit Mirsim, and Beth Shemesh (Ben-Dov 1992; Oren 1992; Daviau 1993; Panitz-Cohen 2006b). These well-appointed dwellings attest to the comfortable status of certain sectors of the urban population. The diversity of burials, ranging from multiple interments in caves with thousands of pottery vessels to single-burial cist tombs accompanied by a well-defined funeral kit, reflects the socioeconomic multiplicity of the Canaanites, as well as other ethnic entities in the land (Gonen 1992a; Baker 2003). Specialized crafts such as glyptics, faience, metallurgy, pendants, and ivory and alabaster carving obtained a high level of achievement that was the outcome of long-lived local traditions, Egyptian auspices, and the exposure of Canaanite artisans to the styles and technologies of the world system cultural *koiné* (Kohl 1987; Leibowitz 1987; Gonen 1992b; Caubet 1998; Moorey 2001; Feldman 2006).

Although typologically there was continuity in the ceramics from MB IIB, pottery production experienced a certain technological decline, evident in the less plastic clays, a reduction in fast-wheel formation, warping and cracks due to unsuitable drying or firing conditions, and a narrower typological range (Amiran 1969: 125; Bienkowski 1986; Wood 1990: 18; Franken and London 1995; Killebrew 2005). Various reasons for these changes may be suggested, such as denied access to clay sources due to political strife, disruption of consumer and marketing patterns which dictated changes in production modes, and increased competition from affordable high quality imports (Panitz-Cohen 2006a: 276–83). Late Bronze pottery includes some of the most elaborately painted ware to be found in Canaan, indicating that alongside this technological decline, there often was no reduction in the quantity and the quality of certain production steps (Feinman, Upham, and Lightfoot 1981). The widespread imitation of ceramic imports (Prag 1985) was an integral facet of

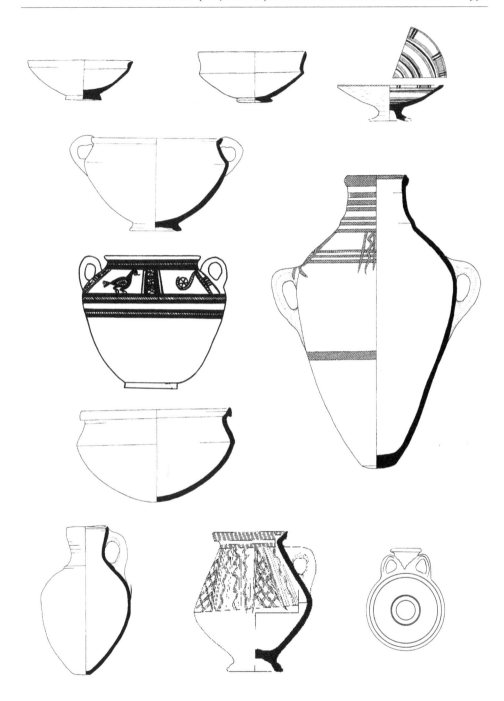

FIG. 36.3 Representative Canaanite pottery types

Late Bronze pottery production, as a conscious effort on the part of Canaanite potters to stimulate market competition with import substitution (Bergoffen 2006). Fig. 36.3 presents a sample of Late Bronze Canaanite pottery.

The typological and technological ceramic changes during LB I–LB IIA suggest that some of the plain pottery production was conducted in small–medium scale household workshops that involved elementary specialization and were geared to local distribution catchments (Killebrew 1998: 255). This marked a departure from the mostly centralized, specialized production and controlled distribution of the previous MB IIB. This change is assumed to be based on various factors, such as the above-mentioned technological decline, petrographic studies that show localized production for the same shapes throughout the country, a high degree of formal variation, and the use of different formation techniques to manufacture the same shapes (Panitz-Cohen 2006a: 275–83). Ethnographic analogies demonstrate how the reduction of sustenance from agriculture often prompts villagers to turn for subsistence to pottery making in household or nucleated household workshops (i.e. Arnold 1985: 171–96); extensive Egyptian land confiscation could have induced such a process in Late Bronze Canaan (Na'aman 1988; Panitz-Cohen 2009; 2010). The lack of a central authority (Egyptian or Canaanite elite) interested in controlling pottery production at this time was also one of the mechanisms that encouraged such a dispersed production mode (Rice 1987: 460). In LB IIB–LB III, a shift in the organization of production to a more centralized mode took place with the heightened intervention of the 19th and 20th Dynasties, at least in those towns and regions where Egyptian presence was most active (Panitz-Cohen 2009; 2010). Egyptian potters were brought to the garrison towns and Egyptian centres, and made Egyptian shapes locally using Egyptian technology, working alongside Canaanite potters, thus impacting local technology and distribution patterns (Knapp 1993; Cohen-Weinberger 1998; Killebrew 2005: 79–80), although there was virtually no typological cross-fertilization between the Canaanite and Egyptian traditions (Martin 2011; Oren 2006: 271).

An interesting issue is the homogeneity of Canaanite material culture during the Late Bronze Age, particularly the pottery, in a land that was politically fragmented and socio-economically disparate. A major factor that prompted this homogeneity was the pressure of Egyptian imperialistic policy, which solidified a well-defined group identity of 'us' and 'them' (Killebrew 2005: 11; see also Na'aman 1999). This external force joined the habitus of the long-lived Canaanite ceramic tradition that had its roots in the MB II and, as such, became emblematic of a shared identity, language, and cult. Both the technological style and the pervasive decorative motifs of Canaanite pottery served to form and reinforce the group identity of people who, despite the geopolitical borders between them, shared a common heritage with recognizable material correlates that was able to overcome the political fragmentation of the city-state confines. Social interaction of relocation, visits, labour exchange, and marriage connections that crossed the political borders were part of the adhesive that bound Canaanite self-identity. The intense Egyptian political and economic control of the 13th and early 12th centuries BCE, along with the influx of foreign immigrants and the rash of destructions of key Canaanite sites, resulted in a gradual breakdown of this cultural distinctiveness, aside from isolated pockets such as in the northern valleys, ultimately culminating in the new cultural segmentation of the Iron Age and ending the long-lived Canaanite culture that reached its zenith in the Late Bronze Age.

Suggested reading

Baumgarten, J. J. (1992). Urbanization in the Late Bronze Age. In A. Kempinski and R. Reich (eds), *The Architecture of Ancient Israel: From the Prehistoric to the Persian Periods.* Jerusalem: Israel Exploration Society, 143–50.

Bunimovitz, S. (1995). On the edge of empires: Late Bronze Age (1500–1200 BCE). In T. E. Levy (ed.), *The Archaeology of Society in the Holy Land.* New York: Facts on File, 320–31.

Finkelstein, I. (1996). The territorial-political system of Canaan in the Late Bronze Age. *Ugarit-Forschungen* 28: 221–55.

Gonen, R. (1984). Urban Canaan in the Late Bronze period. *Bulletin of the American Schools of Oriental Research* 253: 61–73.

—— (1992). The Late Bronze Age. In A. Ben-Tor (ed.), *The Archaeology of Ancient Israel.* New Haven, Conn.: Yale University Press/Tel Aviv: Open University of Israel, 211–57.

Hasel, M. G. (1998). *Domination and Resistance: Egyptian Military Activity in the Southern Levant, ca. 1300–1185 B.C.* Leiden: Brill.

Higginbotham, C. R. (2000). *Egyptianization and Elite Emulation in Ramesside Palestine: Governance and Accommodation on the Imperial Periphery.* Leiden: Brill.

Leonard, A., Jr (1989). The Late Bronze Age. *Biblical Archaeologist* 52: 4–39.

Mazar, A. (1990). In the shadow of Egyptian domination: the Late Bronze Age (ca. 1550–1200 B.C.E.). In *Archaeology of the Land of the Bible*, vol. 1: *10,000–586 B.C.E.* New York: Doubleday, 232–94.

Redford, D. B. (1990). *Egypt and Canaan in the New Kingdom*, ed. S. Ahituv. Beer-Sheva: Ben-Gurion University of the Negev Press.

References

Ahituv, S. (1978). Economic factors in the Egyptian conquest of Canaan. *Israel Exploration Journal* 28: 93–105.

Ahlström, G. W. (1993). *The History of Ancient Palestine from the Paleolithic Period to Alexander's Conquest*, ed. D. Edelman. Sheffield: JSOT Press.

Albright, W. F. (1956). *The Archaeology of Palestine*, rev. edn. Harmondsworth: Penguin.

Amiran, R. (1969). *Ancient Pottery of the Holy Land.* Jerusalem: Masada.

Arnold, D. E. (1985). *Ceramic Theory and Cultural Process.* Cambridge: Cambridge University Press.

Artzy, M. (1994). Incense, camels and collared rim jars: desert trade routes and maritime outlets in the second millennium. *Oxford Journal of Archaeology* 13.2: 121–47.

—— (1998). Routes, trade, boats and 'nomads of the sea'. In S. Gitin, A. Mazar, and E. Stern (eds), *Mediterranean Peoples in Transition: Thirteenth to Early Tenth Centuries BCE.* Jerusalem: Israel Exploration Society, 439–48.

—— (2007). Tell Abu Hawam: news from the Late Bronze Age. In M. Bietak and E. Czerny (eds), *The Synchronisation of Civilisations in the Eastern Mediterranean in the Second Millennium B.C.: Proceedings of the SCIEM 2000–2nd EuroConference, Vienna, 28th of May–1st of June 2003.* Vienna: Österreichische Akademie der Wissenschaften, 357–66.

Baker, J. L. (2003). *The Middle and Late Bronze Age tomb complex at Ashkelon, Israel: the architecture and the funeral kit.* PhD dissertation, Brown University.

Barako, T. J. (2007). Coexistence and impermeability: Egyptians and Philistines in southern Canaan during the twelfth century BCE. In M. Bietak and E. Czerny (eds), *The Synchronisation of Civilisations in the Eastern Mediterranean in the Second Millennium B.C.: Proceedings of the SCIEM 2000-2nd EuroConference, Vienna, 28th of May–1st of June 2003*. Vienna: Österreichische Akademie der Wissenschaften, 509–16.

Bass, G. F. (1986). A Bronze Age shipwreck at Ulu Burun (Kas): 1984 campaign. *American Journal of Archaeology* 90: 269–96

Baumgarten, J. J. (1992). Urbanization in the Late Bronze Age. In A. Kempinski and R. Reich (eds), *The Architecture of Ancient Israel: From the Prehistoric to the Persian Periods*. Jerusalem: Israel Exploration Society, 143–50.

Ben-Dov, M. (1992). Middle and Late Bronze Age dwellings. In A. Kempinski and R. Reich (eds), *The Architecture of Ancient Israel: From the Prehistoric to the Persian Periods*. Jerusalem: Israel Exploration Society, 99–104.

Bergoffen, C. J. (2006). Canaanite wheelmade imitations of Late Cypriot Base Ring II jugs. In E. Czerny, I. Hein, H. Hunger, D. Melman, and A. Schwab (eds), *Timelines: Studies in Honor of Manfred Bietak*. Leuven: Peeters, 331–8.

Bienkowski, P. (1986). *Jericho in the Late Bronze Age*. Warminster: Aris & Philips.

—— (1987). The role of Hazor in the Late Bronze Age. *Palestine Exploration Quarterly* 119: 50–61.

—— (1989). Prosperity and decline in LBA Canaan: a reply to Leibowitz and Knapp. *Bulletin of the American Schools of Oriental Research* 275: 59–61.

Bietak, M. (1991). Egypt and Canaan in the Middle Bronze Age. *Bulletin of the American Schools of Oriental Research* 281: 27–72.

—— (1993). The Sea Peoples and the end of the Egyptian administration in Canaan. In A. Biran and Y. Aviram (eds), *Biblical Archaeology Today: Proceedings of the Second International Congress on Biblical Archaeology, Jerusalem, June–July 1990*. Jerusalem: Israel Exploration Society/Israel Academy of Sciences and Humanities, 292–306.

—— (2002). Relative and absolute chronology of the Middle Bronze Age: comments on the present state of research. In M. Bietak (ed.), *The Middle Bronze Age in the Levant: Proceedings of an International Conference on MB IIA Ceramic Material, Vienna, 24th–26th of January 2001*. Vienna: Österreichische Akademie der Wissenschaften, 29–42.

Bryan, B. M. (1996). Art, empire and the end of the Late Bronze Age. In J. S. Cooper and G. M. Schwartz (eds), *The Study of the Ancient Near East in the Twenty-First Century*. Winona Lake, Ind.: Eisenbrauns, 33–79.

Bunimovitz, S. (1989). *The Land of Israel in the Late Bronze Age: a case study of socio-cultural change in a complex society* [Hebrew]. PhD dissertation, Tel Aviv University.

—— (1992). The beginning of the Late Bronze Age. *Eretz Israel* 23: 21–5 [Hebrew].

—— (1994). The problem of human resources in Late Bronze Age Palestine and its socioeconomic implications. *Ugarit-Forschungen* 26: 1–20.

—— (1995). On the edge of empires: Late Bronze Age (1500–1200 BCE). In T. E. Levy (ed.), *The Archaeology of Society in the Holy Land*. New York: Facts on File, 320–31.

Caubet, A. (1998). The international style: a point of view from the Levant and Syria. In E. H. Cline and D. Harris-Cline (eds), *The Aegean and the Orient in the Second Millennium: Proceedings of the 50th Anniversary Symposium, Cincinnati, 18–20 April 1997*. Liège: Université de Liège, Histoire de l'art et archéologie de la Grèce antique/Austin: University of Texas at Austin, Program in Aegean Scripts and Prehistory, 105–13.

Cohen-Weinberger, A. (1998). Petrographic analysis of the Egyptian forms from Stratum VI at Tel Beth-Shean. In S. Gitin, A. Mazar, and E. Stern (eds), *Mediterranean Peoples in Transition: Thirteenth to Tenth Centuries BCE*. Jerusalem: Israel Exploration Society, 406–12.

Dagan, Y. (2000). *The settlement in the Judean Shephelah in the second and first millennnia B.C.E.* [Hebrew]. PhD dissertation, Tel Aviv University.

—— (2004). Results of the survey: settlement patterns in the Lachish region. In D. Ussishkin (ed.), *Renewed Archaeological Excavations at Lachish (1973–1994)*, vol. 5. Tel Aviv: Emery and Claire Yass Publications in Archaeology, 2672–90.

Daviau, P. M. M. (1993). *Houses and Their Furnishings in Bronze Age Palestine: Domestic Activity Areas and Artefact Distribution in the Middle and Late Bronze Ages.* Sheffield: JSOT Press.

Dever, W. G. (1990). Hyksos, Egyptian destructions and the end of the Palestinian Middle Bronze Age. *Levant* 22: 75–82.

—— (1992a). The chronology of Syria-Palestine in the second millennium B.C. In M. Bietak (ed.), *High, Middle or Low? Acts of the Second International Colloquium on Absolute Chronology (The Bronze Age in the Eastern Mediterranean), Schloss Haindorf/Langenlois, Austria 12.–15. VIII 1990.* Vienna: Österreichische Akademie der Wissenschaften, 39–51.

—— (1992b). The chronology of Syria-Palestine in the second millennium B.C.E.: a review of current issues. *Bulletin of the American Schools of Oriental Research* 288: 1–25.

—— (1992c). The Late Bronze–Early Iron I horizon in Syria-Palestine: Egyptians, Canaanites, Sea Peoples, and Proto-Israelites. In Ward and Joukowsky (1992: 99–110).

—— (1997). Settlement patterns and chronology of Palestine in the Middle Bronze Age. In E. D. Oren (ed.), *The Hyksos: New Historical and Archaeological Perspectives.* Philadelphia: University Museum, University of Pennsylvania, 285–301.

—— (1998). Gezer, *A Crossroad in Ancient Israel* [Hebrew]. Tel Aviv: Kibbutz Meuchad/Israel Exploration Society/Israel Antiquities Authority.

Drews, R. (1993). *The End of the Bronze Age: Changes in Warfare and the Catastrophe ca. 1200 B.C.* Princeton, NJ: Princeton University Press.

Falconer, S. E. (1994). The development and decline of Bronze Age civilization in the southern Levant: a reassessment of urbanism and ruralism. In C. Mathers and S. Stoddart (eds), *Development and Decline in the Mediterranean Bronze Age.* Sheffield: J. R. Collins, 305–34

Feinman, G. M., S. Upham, and K. G. Lightfoot (1981). The production step measure: an ordinal index of labor input in ceramic manufacture. *American Antiquity* 46: 871–84.

Feldman, M. H. (2006). *Diplomacy by Design: Luxury Arts and an 'International Style' in the Ancient Near East, 1400–1200 BCE.* Chicago: University of Chicago Press.

Finkelstein, I. (1992). Pastoralism in the highlands of Canaan in the third and second millennia B.C.E. In O. Bar-Yosef and A. M. Khazaonv (eds), *Pastoralism in the Levant: Archaeological Materials in Anthropological Perspectives.* Madison, Wis.: Prehistory, 133–42.

—— (1996). The territorial-political system of Canaan in the Late Bronze Age. *Ugarit-Forschungen* 28: 221–55.

—— (2000). The Philistine settlements: when, where and how many? In E. D. Oren (ed.), *The Sea Peoples and Their World: A Reassessment.* Philadelphia: University Museum, 159–80.

Franken, H. J., and G. A. London (1995). Why painted pottery disappeared at the end of the second millennium BCE. *Biblical Archaeologist* 58.4: 214–22.

Giles, F. J. (1997). *The Amarna Age: Western Asia.* Warminster: Aris & Philips.

Gonen, R. (1984). Urban Canaan in the Late Bronze period. *Bulletin of the American Schools of Oriental Research* 253: 61–73.

—— (1987). Megiddo in the Late Bronze Age: another reassessment. *Levant* 19: 83–100.

—— (1992a). *Burial Patterns and Cultural Diversity in Late Bronze Age Canaan.* Winona Lake, Ind.: Eisenbrauns.

—— (1992b). The Late Bronze Age. In A. Ben-Tor (ed.), *The Archaeology of Ancient Israel.* New Haven, Conn.: Yale University Press/Tel Aviv: Open University of Israel, 211–57.

Goren, Y., I. Finkelstein, and N. Na'aman (2004). *Inscribed in Clay: Provenance Study of the Amarna Tablets and Other Ancient Near Eastern Texts.* Tel Aviv: Emery and Claire Yass Publications in Archaeology.

Greenberg, M. (1955). *The Hab/piru.* New Haven, Conn.: American Oriental Society.

Gunneweg, J., I. Perlman, and F. Asaro (1987). A Canaanite jar from Enkomi. *Israel Exploration Journal* 37: 168–72.

Hansen, M. H. (2000). Concepts of city-state and city-state culture. In M. H. Hansen (ed.), *A Comparative Study of Thirty City-State Cultures: An Investigation.* Copenhagen: Kongelige Danske Videnskabernes Selskab, 11–34.

Hasel, M. G. (1998). *Domination and Resistance: Egyptian Military Activity in the Southern Levant, ca. 1300–1185 B.C.* Leiden: Brill.

Helck, W. (1971). *Die Beziehungen Ägyptens zu Vorderasien im 3. und 2. Jahrtausend v. Chr.* Wiesbaden: Harrassowitz.

Heltzer, M. (1976). *The Rural Community in Ancient Ugarit.* Wiesbaden: Reichert.

Higginbotham, C. R. (2000). *Egyptianization and Elite Emulation in Ramesside Palestine: Governance and Accommodation on the Imperial Periphery.* Leiden: Brill.

Hoffmeier, J. K. (1989). Reconsidering Egypt's part in the termination of the Middle Bronze Age in Palestine. *Levant* 21: 181–93.

Ilan, D. (1995). The dawn of internationalism: the Middle Bronze Age. In T. E. Levy (ed.), *The Archaeology of Society in the Holy Land.* New York: Facts on File, 297–319.

Jasmin, M. (2006). Political organization of the city-states in southwestern Palestine in the Late Bronze Age IIB (13th century BC). In A. M. Maier and P. de Miroschedji (eds), *'I Will Speak the Riddles of Ancient Times': Archaeological and Historical Studies in Honor of Amihai Mazar on the Occasion of His Sixtieth Birthday,* vol. 1. Winona Lake, Ind.: Eisenbrauns, 161–91.

Killebrew, A. E. (1998). *Ceramic craft and technology during the Late Bronze and Early Iron Ages: the relationship between pottery technology, style and cultural diversity.* PhD dissertation, Hebrew University of Jerusalem.

—— (2004). New Kingdom Egyptian-style and Egyptian pottery in Canaan: implications for Egyptian rule in Canaan during the 19th and early 20th Dynasties. In G. N. Knoppers and A. Hirsch (eds), *Egypt, Israel and the Ancient Mediterranean World: Studies in Honor of Donald B. Redford.* Leiden: Brill, 309–44.

—— (2005). *Biblical Peoples and Ethnicity: An Archaeological Study of Egyptians, Canaanites, Philistines, and Early Israel, 1300–1100 B.C.E.* Atlanta, Ga.: Society of Biblical Literature.

—— P. Goldberg, and A. M. Rosen (2006). Deir el-Balah: a geological, archaeological, and historical reassessment of an Egyptianizing 13th and 12th century B.C.E. center. *Bulletin of the American Schools of Oriental Research* 343: 97–119.

Kitchen, K. A. (1987). The basics of Egyptian chronology in relation to the Bronze Age. In P. Åström (ed.), *High, Middle or Low? Acts of an International Colloquium on Absolute Chronology Held at the University of Gothenburg, 20th–22nd August 1987,* vol. 1. Gothenburg: Åströms, 37–55.

—— (2007). Egyptian and related chronologies: look sciences, no pots! In M. Bietak and E. Czerny (eds), *The Synchronisation of Civilisations in the Eastern Mediterranean in the Second Millennium B.C.: Proceedings of the SCIEM 2000–2nd EuroConference, Vienna, 28th of May–1st of June 2003.* Vienna: Österreichische Akademie der Wissenschaften, 163–72.

Knapp, A. B. (1987). Pots, PIXE and data processing at Pella in Jordan. *Bulletin of the American Schools of Oriental Research* 266: 1–30.

—— (1989). Response: independence, imperialism, and the Egyptian factor. *Bulletin of the American Schools of Oriental Research* 275: 64–8.

—— (1992). Independence and imperialism: politico-economic structures in the Bronze Age Levant. In A. B. Knapp (ed.), *Archaeology, Annales and Ethnohistory*. Cambridge: Cambridge University Press, 83–98.

—— (1993). *Society and Polity at Bronze Age Pella: An Annales Perspective*. Sheffield: Sheffield Academic.

—— (1998). Mediterranean Bronze Age trade: distance, power and place. In E. H. Cline and D. Harris-Cline (eds), *The Aegean and the Orient in the Second Millennium: Proceedings of the 50th Anniversary Symposium, Cincinnati, 18–20 April 1997*. Liège: Université de Liège, Histoire de l'art et archéologie de la Grèce antique/Austin: University of Texas at Austin, Program in Aegean Scripts and Prehistory, 193–207.

Kohl, P. (1987). The ancient economy, transferable technologies and the Bronze Age world-system: a view from the northeastern frontier of the ancient Near East. In M. J. Rowlands, M. T. Larsen, and K. Kristiansen (eds), *Centre and Periphery in the Ancient World*. Cambridge: Cambridge University Press, 143–64.

La Bianca, Ø. S., and S. A. Scham (eds) (2006). *Connectivity in Antiquity: Globalization as Long Term Historical Process*. London: Equinox.

Leonard, A., Jr (1989). The Late Bronze Age. *Biblical Archaeologist* 52.1: 4–39.

Leibowitz, H. (1987). Late Bronze II ivory work in Palestine: evidence of a cultural highpoint. *Bulletin of the American Schools of Oriental Research* 265: 3–24.

—— (1989). Response: LBIIB ivories and material culture of the Late Bronze Age. *Bulletin of the American Schools of Oriental Research* 275: 63–4.

Liverani, M. (1983). Political lexicon and political ideologies in the Amarna letters. *Berytus* 31: 41–56.

London, G. A. (1989). A comparison of two contemporaneous lifestyles of the late second millennium B.C. *Bulletin of the American Schools of Oriental Research* 273: 37–55.

Marfoe, L. (1979). The integrative transformation: patterns of socio-political organization in southern Syria. *Bulletin of the American Schools of Oriental Research* 234: 1–42.

Martin, M. A. S. (2007). A collection of Egyptian and Egyptian-style pottery at Beth Shean. In M. Bietak and E. Czerny (eds), *The Synchronisation of Civilisations in the Eastern Mediterranean in the Second Millennium B.C.: Proceedings of the SCIEM 2000–2nd EuroConference, Vienna, 28th of May–1st of June 2003*. Vienna: Österreichische Akademie der Wissenschaften, 375–88.

—— (2011). *Egyptian-Type Pottery in the Late Bronze Age Southern Levant*. Vienna: Österreichische Akademie der Wissenschaften.

Mazar, A. (1988a). Some aspects of the Sea Peoples settlement. In M. Heltzer and E. Lipiński (eds), *Society and Economy in the Eastern Mediterranean (c. 1500–1000 B.C.): Proceedings of the International Symposium Held at the University of Haifa from the 28th of April to the 2nd of May, 1985*. Leuven: Peeters, 251–60.

—— (1988b). A note on Canaanite jars from Enkomi. *Israel Exploration Journal* 38: 224–6.

—— (1990). *Archaeology of the Land of the Bible*, vol. 1: *10,000–586 B.C.E.* New York: Doubleday.

—— (1992). Temples of the Middle and Late Bronze Ages and the Iron Age. In A. Kempinski and R. Reich (eds), *The Architecture of Ancient Israel: From the Prehistoric to the Persian Periods*. Jerusalem: Israel Exploration Society, 161–89.

—— (2007). Myc IIIC in the Land of Israel: its distribution, date and significance. In M. Bietak and E. Czerny (eds), *The Synchronisation of Civilisations in the Eastern Mediterranean in the Second Millennium B.C.: Proceedings of the SCIEM 2000–2nd EuroConference, Vienna, 28th of May–1st of June 2003*. Vienna: Österreichische Akademie der Wissenschaften, 571–82.

Moorey, P. (2001). The mobility of artisans and opportunities for technology transfer between western Asia and Egypt in the Late Bronze Age. In A. J. Shortland (ed.), *The Social Context of Technological Change: Egypt and the Near East, 1650–1550 BC.* Oxford: Oxbow, 1–14.

Moran, W. L. (ed.) (1992). *The Amarna Letters.* Baltimore, Md.: Johns Hopkins University Press.

Morris, E. F. (2005). *The Architecture of Imperialism: Military Bases and the Evidence of Foreign Policy in Egypt's New Kingdom.* Leiden: Brill.

Na'aman, N. (1975). *The political disposition and historical development of Eretz-Israel according to the Amarna letters* [Hebrew]. PhD dissertation, Tel Aviv University.

—— (1981). Economic aspects of the Egyptian occupation of Canaan. *Israel Exploration Journal* 31: 172–85.

—— (1988). Pharaonic lands in the Jezreel Valley in the Late Bronze Age. In M. Heltzer and E. Lipiński (eds), *Society and Economy in the Eastern Mediterranean (c. 1500–1000 B.C.): Proceedings of the International Symposium Held at the University of Haifa from the 28th of April to the 2nd of May, 1985.* Leuven: Peeters, 177–85.

—— (1994). The Hurrians and the end of the Middle Bronze Age in Palestine. *Levant* 26: 175–87.

—— (1997). The network of Canaanite kingdoms and the city of Ashdod. *Ugarit-Forschungen* 29: 599–612.

—— (1999). Four notes on the size of Late Bronze Age Canaan. *Bulletin of the American Schools of Oriental Research* 313: 31–7.

—— (2000). The Egyptian–Canaanite correspondence. In R. Cohen and R. Westbrook (eds), *Amarna Diplomacy: The Beginning of International Relations.* Baltimore, Md.: Johns Hopkins University Press, 125–38.

Oren, E. D. (1984). 'Governors' residencies' in Canaan under the New Kingdom: a case study of Egyptian administration. *Journal for the Society of the Study of Egyptian Antiquities* 14: 37–56.

—— (1992). Palaces and patrician houses in the Middle and Late Bronze Ages. In A. Kempinski and R. Reich (eds), *The Architecture of Ancient Israel: From the Prehistoric to the Persian Periods.* Jerusalem: Israel Exploration Society, 105–20.

—— (ed.) (2000). *The Sea Peoples and Their World: A Reassessment.* Philadelphia: University Museum.

—— (2001). Early White Slip pottery in Canaan: spatial and chronological perspectives. In V. Karageorghis (ed.), *The White Slip Ware of Late Bronze Age Cyprus: Proceedings of an International Conference Organized by the Anastasios G. Leventis Foundation, Nicosia.* Vienna: Österreichische Akademie der Wissenschaften, 127–44.

—— (2006). An Egyptian marsh scene on pottery from Tel Ser'a: a case of Egyptianization in Late Bronze Age III Canaan. In A. M. Maier and P. de Miroschedji (eds), *'I Will Speak the Riddle of Ancient Times': Archaeological and Historical Studies in Honor of Amihai Mazar on the Occasion of His Sixtieth Birthday,* vol. 1. Winona Lake, Ind.: Eisenbrauns, 263–75.

Panitz-Cohen, N. (2006a). *Processes of ceramic change and continuity: Tel Batash in the second millennium BCE as a test case.* PhD dissertation, Hebrew University of Jerusalem.

—— (2006b). Distribution of finds, activity areas and population estimates. In N. Panitz-Cohen and A. Mazar (eds), *Timnah (Tel Batash) III: The Finds from the Second Millennium BCE.* Jerusalem: Institute of Archaeology, Hebrew University of Jerusalem, 173–94.

—— (2009). The organization of ceramic production during the transition from the Late Bronze Age to Iron Age I: Tel Batash as a test case. In C. Bachhuber and R. G. Roberts (eds), *Forces of Transformation: The End of the Bronze Age in the Mediterranean.* Oxford: Oxbow, 186–92.

—— (2010). Technological change in the organization of ceramic production at Tel Batash in the second millennium BCE. In S. A. Rosen and V. Roux (eds), *Techniques and People: Anthropological Perspectives on Technology in the Archaeology of the Proto-Historic and Early Historic Periods in the Southern Levant*. Paris: De Boccard.

Prag, K. (1985). The imitation of Cypriot wares in Late Bronze Age Palestine. In J. N. Tubb (ed.), *Palestine in the Bronze and Iron Ages: Papers in Honour of Olga Tufnell*. London: Institute of Archaeology, 154–66.

Pulak, C. (1997). The Uluburun shipwreck. In S. Swiny, R. L. Hohlfelder, and H. Wilde Swiny (eds), *Res Maritimae: Cyprus and the Eastern Mediterranean from Prehistory to Late Antiquity*. Atlanta, Ga.: Scholars Press, 233–62.

Rainey, A. F. (1995). Unruly elements in Late Bronze Canaanite society. In D. P. Wright, D. N. Freedman, and A. Hurvitz (eds), *Pomegranates and Golden Bells: Studies in Biblical, Jewish, and Near Eastern Ritual, Law, and Literature in Honor of Jacob Milgrom*. Winona Lake, Ind.: Eisenbrauns, 481–96.

Randsborg, K. (2001). Archaeological globalization: the first practitioners. *Acta Archaeologia* 72.2: 1–53.

Redford, D. B. (1992). *Egypt, Canaan and Israel in Ancient Times*. Princeton, NJ: Princeton University Press.

Rice, P. M. (1987). *Pottery Analysis: A Sourcebook*. Chicago: University of Chicago Press.

Sandars, N. K. (1985). *The Sea Peoples: Warriors of the Ancient Mediterranean*, rev. edn. London: Thames & Hudson.

Savage, S. H., and S. E. Falconer (2003). Spatial and statistical inference of Late Bronze Age polities in the southern Levant. *Bulletin of the American Schools of Oriental Research* 330: 31–45.

Shavit, A. (2000). Settlement patterns in the Ayalon Valley in the Bronze and Iron Ages. *Tel Aviv* 27: 189–230.

Sherratt, A. G., and E. S. Sherratt (1991). From luxuries to commodities: the nature of Mediterranean Bronze Age trading systems. In N. H. Gale (ed.), *Bronze Age Trade in the Mediterranean: Papers Presented at the Conference Held at Rewley House, Oxford in December 1989*. Jonsered: Åström, 351–86.

Sherratt, E. S. (1998). 'Sea Peoples' and the economic structure of the late second millennium in the eastern Mediterranean. In S. Gitin, A. Mazar, and E. Stern (eds), *Mediterranean Peoples in Transition: Thirteenth to Early Tenth Centuries BCE*. Jerusalem: Israel Exploration Society, 292–313.

Singer, I. (1994). Egyptians, Canaanites and Philistines in the period of the emergence of Israel. In I. Finkelstein and N. Na'aman (eds), *From Nomadism to Monarchy: Archaeological and Historical Aspects of Early Israel*. Jerusalem: Israel Exploration Society, 282–338.

Stern, E. (ed.) (1993). *The New Encyclopedia of Archaeological Excavations in the Holy Land* (4 vols). Jerusalem: Israel Exploration Society & Carta/London: Simon & Schuster.

Strange, J. (2000). The Palestinian city-states of the Bronze Age. In M. H. Hansen (ed.), *A Comparative Study of Thirty City-State Cultures: An Investigation*. Copenhagen: Kongelige Danske Videnskabernes Selskab, 67–76.

Ussishkin, D. J. (2004). A synopsis of stratigraphical, chronological and historical issues. In D. Usisshkin (ed.), *The Renewed Archaeological Excavations at Lachish (1973–1994)*. Tel Aviv: Emery and Claire Yass Publications in Archaeology, 50–119.

Uziel, J., and A. M. Maeir (2005). Scratching the surface at Gath: implications of the Tell es-Safi/ Gath surface survey. *Tel Aviv* 32: 50–75.

van Wijngaarden, G. J. (2002). *Use and Appreciation of Mycenaean Pottery in the Levant, Cyprus and Italy (1600–1200 BC)*. Amsterdam: Amsterdam University Press.

Wachsmann, S. (1998). *Seagoing Ships and Seamanship in the Bronze Age Levant*. College Station: Texas A&M University Press/London: Chatham.

Ward, W. A., and M. S. Joukowsky (eds) (1992). *The Crisis Years: The 12th Century B.C. from Beyond the Danube to the Tigris*. Dubuque, Ia.: Kendall/Hunt.

Weinstein, J. M. (1981). The Egyptian Empire in Palestine: a reassessment. *Bulletin of the American Schools of Oriental Research* 241: 1–28.

—— (1991). Egypt and the Middle Bronze IIC/Late Bronze IA transition in Palestine. *Levant* 23: 105–15.

—— (1992). The collapse of the Egyptian Empire in the southern Levant. In Ward and Joukowsky (1992: 142–50).

Wood, B. G. (1990). *The Sociology of Pottery in Ancient Palestine: The Ceramic Industry and the Diffusion of Ceramic Style in the Bronze and Iron Ages*. Sheffield: JSOT Press for the American Schools of Oriental Research.

Yasur-Landau, A. (2007). Let's do the time warp again: migration processes and the absolute chronology of the Philistine settlement. In M. Bietak and E. Czerny (eds), *The Synchronisation of Civilisations in the Eastern Mediterranean in the Second Millennium B.C.: Proceedings of the SCIEM 2000-2nd EuroConference, Vienna, 28th of May–1st of June 2003*. Vienna: Österreichische Akademie der Wissenschaften, 609–20.

Zaccagnini, C. (1987). Aspects of ceremonial exchange in the Near East during the late second millennium BC. In M. J. Rowlands, M. T. Larsen, and K. Kristiansen (eds), *Centre and Periphery in the Ancient World*. Cambridge: Cambridge University Press, 57–65.

Zuckerman, S. (2007). Anatomy of a destruction: crisis architecture, termination rituals, and the fall of Canaanite Hazor. *Journal of Mediterranean Archaeology* 20: 3–32.

CHAPTER 37

··

THE SOUTHERN LEVANT (TRANSJORDAN) DURING THE LATE BRONZE AGE

··

PETER M. FISCHER

INTRODUCTION

··

Following his surface surveys in Transjordan, Glueck (1951) advanced the theory that there was an occupational lacuna during most of the Middle and Late Bronze Ages in much of Transjordan—a conclusion which finds no support in the material evidence known today. Stratified remains have been ascertained from a number of sites in the Jordan Valley, the North Jordanian Plain, and the central portions of Jordan (Fig. 37.1).

This chapter concentrates mainly on the evidence from a few sites where regular excavations have taken place over a longer period and resulted in comprehensive reports. Chief amongst them are the Jordan Valley sites of Pella (Smith and Potts 1992; Bourke, Sparks, and Schroeder 2006), Tell Abu al-Kharaz (Fischer 2006a; 2006b), and Tell Deir ʿAlla (Franken 1992; van der Kooij 2006). The Beqaʿ Valley project has been published, but it deals mainly with burials from the Late Bronze to the early Iron Age (McGovern 1986). Another final publication, concerning a rich tomb from Sahem, close to the Yarmouk in north Jordan, is from approximately the same period (Fischer 1997).

In general, the archaeological evidence from Late Bronze Age Jordan is restricted mainly to north and central Jordan. Very little is known from the south of Jordan during this period. However, we know from Egyptian texts that the Shasu, who are best described as a social class of nomads, lived there.

THE TRANSITION FROM THE MIDDLE TO THE LATE BRONZE AGE

··

The reasoning for making a division between the two societies which dominated most of the second millennium BC, namely those of the Middle and Late Bronze Ages, should be briefly

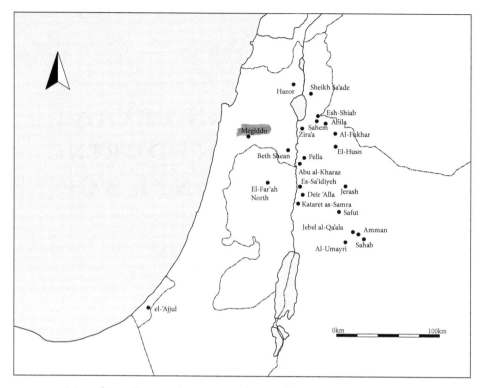

FIG. 37.1 Map of Late Bronze Age sites in the southern Levant (Transjordan)

discussed. Nobody would dispute that the cultural differences between the Middle and the Late Bronze Age of the southern Levant are much less accentuated than those between the Early and Middle Bronze Age, which are divided by quite a long transitional period of several hundreds of years (EB IV). There are, however, two markers that justify a division between the Middle and Late Bronze Age.

The first marker comprises the events which ended the Second Intermediate Period and the regime of the Hyksos of the 15th Dynasty. The Hyksos had their capital at Tell el-Dab'a/ Avaris in the Nile Delta, where they had ruled since the 17th century BC (or from around 1640 BC according to Bietak 2003). Ahmose from the Theban royal house, the founder of the 18th Dynasty, started his reign in 1550 BC according to High Egyptian chronology or in 1539 BC according to the Low Egyptian chronology (Kitchen 2002: 10). His warfare against the Hyksos and their final defeat and expulsion from the Nile Delta—and/or their possible assimilation according to new evidence from Tell el-Dab'a /Avaris (M. Bietak, pers. comm.)— are supposed to have happened about ten years after his accession. Other scholars still defend the hypothesis that the Hyksos were actually expelled and that they retreated to Palestine, a process which might have taken a number of years. According to this theory, Ahmose pursued the Hyksos into Palestine and conquered their stronghold of Sharhan/Sharuhen (very likely Tell el- 'Ajjul in Gaza), which fell after a siege of three years (e.g. Rainey 1993: 179). The events in the southwest of Palestine might then have lead to a general movement of people and a weakening and—in many cases—disintegration of the urban system of the Middle Bronze Age. The retreating Hyksos might have settled down in southern Palestine and expelled local people, who were forced to leave their homes and to settle somewhere further north and east. This migration could have resulted in the further movement of other people and affected Transjordan (cf. Fischer 2006a: 330).

It is highly likely that Palestine was affected in some way almost immediately by the start of Ahmose's warfare against the Hyksos. Therefore, the 'historical start' of the Late Bronze Age in the southern Levant, LB IA, is in the proposed chronological scheme (see Table 37.1) contemporary with the start of the reign of Ahmose at 1550/1539 BC. It has been said that their final defeat is supposed to have come ten years later, at 1540/1529 BC. Still lower absolute dates have recently been suggested by Krauss and Warburton (2009), who date the final defeat of the Hyksos as low as 1504 BC (not included in Table 37.1).

The second marker is the occurrence of certain changes in the nature of cultural remains, which took place over quite a long period in the southern Levant (see Middle–Late Bronze in Table 37.1). These changes were definitely not abrupt but rather slow, and can be observed in particular in the shapes and production techniques of locally produced pottery. Therefore the material culture suggests a transitional period between the outgoing Middle Bronze and the established Late Bronze (Table 37.1). The region's participation in intercultural trade is reflected by the gradual upsurge of imports from, especially, Cyprus and—later on—the Mycenaean sphere of culture. The gradual changes in the pottery repertoire are especially apparent in the steady artistic and qualitative decline of various types of Chocolate-on-White Ware, which flourished roughly during the MB III and LB IA (Fischer 1999).

Pottery production techniques are used by numerous archaeologists to distinguish between the Middle and Late Bronze Age. It is, for example, argued that much of the pottery from the second half of the Middle Bronze Age was well levigated, thrown on a fast wheel, thin-walled, relatively hard-fired, and usually of a high finish. Late Bronze Age pottery, in contrast, is said to be the product of a ceramic industry which again uses a slower wheel (Franken 1992: 149). This gave vessels with thicker walls which were also usually softer-fired than in the previous period. Nevertheless, this change was gradual, as is well reflected at Tell Abu al-Kharaz in the Jordan Valley: the end of Phase IV/2, the last MB III phase at Tell Abu al-Kharaz, which is marked by a destruction layer, is followed by the LB IA Phase V, which demonstrates only slightly changed pottery types and production techniques

Table 37.1 The revised terminology of the southern Levant and synchronization with Egypt

Revised	Earlier terms	Egyptian Dynasty (no. of pharaohs)	Pharaohs
MB	*MB*		
MB III	MB IIC	15 (6)	Hyksos
LB	*LB*		
LB IA	LB IA	18 (6)	Ahmose–Thutmosis III (22 yrs)
LB IB	LB IB	18 (3)	Thutmosis III (23 yrs)–IV
LB IC	LB IIA	18 (6)	Amenophis III–Haremhab
LB II	LB IIB	19 (4)	Ramesses I–Tewosret
LB II	LB IIB	20 (2)	Setnakht–Ramesses III

(Fischer 2006a: 215–80). Tell Deir 'Alla, some 30km to the south, also shows a destruction layer between the Middle and Late Bronze Age and pottery which is termed 'transitional MB/LB' (van der Kooij 2006: 216, fig. 13a; 223–4).

In summary, it should be stated that dates for the division between the Middle and Late Bronze Age and the subdivision of the Late Bronze Age based on the Egyptian genealogy provide us with supportive and easily assimilated absolute chronological information. Nevertheless, the application of excessively rigid chronological criteria to the material culture and, in particular, pottery shapes and production techniques in defining either period, or in sub-dividing the Late Bronze Age, is best avoided.

POLITICS, CHRONOLOGY, AND THE MATERIAL EVIDENCE

LB IA

The military campaigns in Palestine of several pharaohs of the 18th Dynasty, namely Ahmose (1550/1539–1525/1514 BC), Thutmosis I (1504/1493–1492/1481 BC), and Hatshepsut (1479–1457 BC), were few in number and limited in scale, and did not establish Egyptian supremacy there. Egyptian domination in Cisjordan was not established before the Palestinian campaign of Thutmosis III (1479–1425 BC), which marks the end of LB IA. It is, however, highly questionable whether Transjordan was of any major interest to Thutmosis III except for its easily plundered natural and man-produced resources (cf. Warburton 2001; Redford 1992).

The synchronization of destruction layers with historical events is tentative in the extreme. There is, for example, a destruction layer marking the end of the Phase V town of Tell Abu al-Kharaz. This phase, which is dated in the LB IA, is the most substantial and most productive of all Late Bronze Age phases at the site (V–VIII). There are four radiocarbon dates from Phase V, one from the fill above the Phase V floor, and two from the succeeding Phase VI (see Table 37.2). The historical date of the siege of Megiddo by Thutmosis III at 1457 BC and probable raids into Transjordan around that time are included in all seven calibrated radiocarbon dates in the 2σ range with a higher probability than 79.1 per cent, but six of them would also allow for the time of the Palestinian campaign of his son, Amenophis II (1427–1400 BC), around 1421 BC. The seventh radiocarbon date (OxA-5089), which is based on seeds from a burned down silo, however, would not permit a destruction date as late as during the reign of Amenophis II. Natural causes such as an earthquake, or local warfare, might also explain this destruction layer, but the possibility of an Egyptian attack should not be dismissed.

Interpreted settlement structures from this period are rare. Tell Abu al-Kharaz, the centre of a city-state, is a walled town with an administrative complex. The casemate system was taken over from the previous Phase IV/2 (MB III) and modified. A compound which is connected to the casemate system represents a centrally administered bakery, and includes stone-paved and plastered rooms with grain silos, a water cistern, several ovens, and working and storage spaces. Close to the bakery are installations which were used for the final crop processing and storage, and for the production of pottery (Fischer 2006a: e.g. 342–5). A temple complex is reported from Tell Deir 'Alla (Franken 1992; van der Kooij 2006: 218).

Table 37.2 Calibrated radiocarbon dates from Tell Abu al-Kharaz

Lab. no.	Material spot	δ¹³C (‰)	¹⁴C age (years BP)	Calibrated date (BC) 1σ range	2σ range	Phase
OxA-5089	seeds silo	$-23.2 \pm$ 0.5–1.0	3260 ± 50	1620(62.7%)1509 1476(05.5%)1463	1672(95.4%)1441	V
OxA-5090	seeds silo	$-23.4 \pm$ 0.5–1.0	3210 ± 60	1588(06.8%)1571 1527(61.4%)1424	1639(95.4%)1394	V
VERA-1411	wood oven	-27.0 ± 0.9	3120 ± 50	1490(01.5%)1480 1450(66.7%)1310	1520(95.4%)1260	V
VERA-1414	wood floor	-28.0 ± 0.8	3190 ± 30	1500(68.2%)1425	1520(95.4%)1410	V
VERA-1413	wood fill above floor	-24.4 ± 0.9	3145 ± 25	1440(65.3%)1390 1330(02.9%)1320	1500(08.3%)1470 1460(79.1%)1370 1340(08.0%)1310	V–VI
VERA-1408	wood/ seeds courtyard	-26.9 ± 0.9	3195 ± 30	1500(68.2%)1430	1520(95.4%)1410	VI
VERA-1415	wood fill	-25.6 ± 0.9	3195 ± 30	1500(68.2%)1430	1520(95.4%)1410	VI

Carinated Eggshell bowls, already existing in the MB III, were found in secure contexts at Tell Abu al-Kharaz together with Chocolate-on-White II, a further development of Chocolate-on-White I from Phase IV/2 (Fig. 37.2; concerning the classification of Chocolate-on-White Ware, see Fischer 1999). The decoration of common ware is often colourful, with shades from yellow to red to black, both bichrome and monochrome. Rounded bowls show a trend from raised ring bases to lower ring bases and concave disc bases. There is also a gradual development of the shape and position of the carination of carinated bowls from very much developed and low to less pronounced and higher. Gradual development can also be demonstrated in the cooking pot repertoire: triangular rims, slightly changed, were taken over from the previous phase. Lamps show a gradual change from slightly pinched to more distinctively pinched mouths, and deeper profiles. Pottery imports are rare and mainly restricted to those from Cyprus. Pella's examples of Cypriot Proto-White Slip and White Slip I are associated with Phase VB horizons, of which Phase VB2 approximately corresponds to Tell Abu al-Kharaz Phase V (cf. Fischer 2006b: 241, table 1). Much of the material from the rich Tomb 62 at Pella should be dated to LB IA. Tell Abu al-Kharaz Phase V produced sherds of two thin-walled bowls of Cypriot Base-Ring I Ware for which a synchronism to Late Cypriot IB is proposed.

LB IB

This period starts by convention after the battle of Megiddo in 1457 BC. The campaigns of Thutmosis III, Amenophis II, and Thutmosis IV (1400–1390 BC) might have had consequences for Transjordan. Finds of Egyptian origin are limited and there is, again, no firm evidence that Transjordan came under Egyptian rule if we exclude limited raids across the

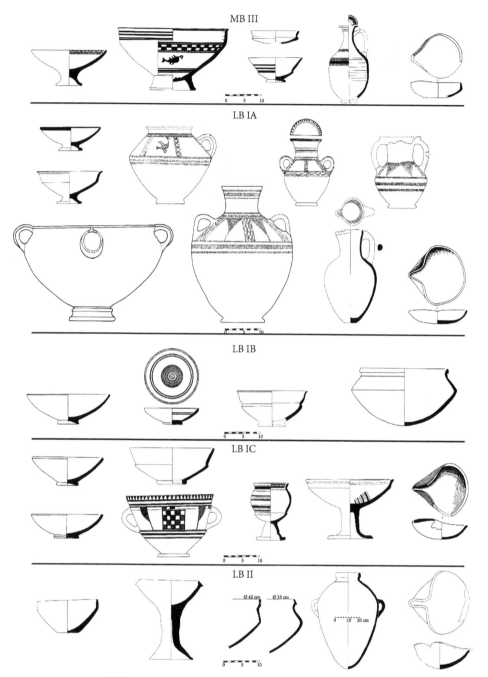

FIG. 37.2 Late Middle Bronze and Late Bronze ceramics from Tell Abu al-Kharaz (MB III–LB IC) and Tell Deir ʿAlla (LB II) (courtesy G. van der Kooij)

River Jordan and measures to secure routes through the area. It is here suggested that the city-states lying closest to the Egyptian-dominated Cisjordan, viz. Pella, Tell Abu al-Kharaz and Tell Deir 'Alla, were dependent on the benevolence of Egypt but kept a certain sovereignty and were left alone if they did not interfere with Egyptian interests, and as long as they provided the Egyptian forces with tributes in the form of products from farming, livestock holding, and natural resources such as timber.

The construction of the 'governor's residence' in the city-state of Pella (Phase VB), seems to be associated with this period or possibly earlier, i.e. LB IA/B (Bourke 1994; Bourke, Sparks, and Schroeder 2006). The Lion Box of wood with inlaid ivory was possibly in use in this period (Fig. 37.3). The style combines Egyptian, Syrian, and Mesopotamian features, but the box could be an heirloom from MB III. The material remains from Tell Abu al-Kharaz Phase VI and the temple from Phase VII are placed in this period. There are two radiocarbon dates from Tell Abu al-Kharaz Phase VI which seem to be in the upper range of what is feasible according to the stratigraphy. The degenerated Chocolate-on-White III from Phase VI defines the end of this ware. Phase VI and VII pottery, which also displays monochrome and, more rarely, bichrome decoration, mainly on carinated bowls, goblets, chalices, and biconical jugs, is characterized, inter alia, by rounded and carinated bowls where the low ring bases and the concave disc bases dominate. The stems of chalices become higher, and the mouths of lamps become more pinched. Cooking pots with dominating triangular and square rims are now more uniform in shape. Imports from Cyprus, for instance White Slip II and Base-Ring I, are more common now and were part of the find repertoire of the Phase VII temple at Tell Abu al-Kharaz.

FIG. 37.3 The Lion Box of wood with inlaid ivory from Pella (courtesy S. Bourke; photograph Ben Churcher, Pella Project)

LB IC

The next traditional subdivision of the Late Bronze Age in the southern Levant would be LB IIA, which by convention starts with the beginning of the reign of Amenophis III (1390–1352 BC). The reason for the traditional subdivision of the Late Bronze Age into LB I and LB II at the beginning of Amenophis III's reign seems, though, to be more the convenience of a mathematical split into two periods of approximately equal length than a distinct change in the material culture. I therefore suggest, on the strength of the material evidence, maintaining the LB I terminology and using the term LB IC for the period until the end of the 18th Dynasty. This subdivision also has support in the pottery repertoire (see below). The period of the reign of Amenophis III seems to have been peaceful in the area, because of the absence of major warfare and peaceful relations with the Mitanni Empire in the north. We eventually see a weakened Egyptian control of the northern provinces as Hittite influence increases, especially during the Amarna period. This apparently quite calm period includes, in addition to the pre-Amarna ruler Amenophis III, the rulers at Amarna, namely Amenophis IV/Echnaton (1352–1336 BC), Smenkhkare (1338–1336 BC), and, at Amarna and Thebes, Tutankhamun (1336–1327 BC), and the post-Amarna rulers Ay (1327–1323 BC) and Haremhab (1323–1295 BC). During the rule of Amenophis IV, the power of Mitanni was vanishing due to the increasing military supremacy of the Hittites.

The common ware pottery does not change very much. There is a tendency for imports from the Mycenaean sphere, especially from Late Helladic (LH) IIIA2 and onwards, to sur-pass the formerly predominant imports from Cyprus. The recently excavated temple-for-tress at Pella, which dates back to the MB III (around 1650 BC according to the excavator, S. Bourke), shows a major horizon of refurbishment in this period, around 1350 BC (S. Bourke, pers. comm.), and an alteration of the earlier square 'standard *migdol*' into a more rectan-gular shape which is close in proportion to the Phase VII temple at Tell Abu al-Kharaz. The temple at Tell Abu al-Kharaz was destroyed in the middle or possibly late 14th century; it contains, in addition to jewellery, many complete locally produced vessels and Cypriot imports. The site also demonstrates a casemate system close to the summit of the tell. Two finds from Tell Abu al-Kharaz should be highlighted: one is a stamp-seal of calcite with two heraldic antelopes standing against the tree of life (Fig. 37.4), and the other is a well-pre-served bronze figurine representing a male armed god, standing upright upon a plinth (Fig. 37.5). The lion-faced god is dressed in a skirt with a waistband. Above his forehead is the uraeus. He has trefoil headgear. The raised right hand holds a weapon behind the head. The left arm is extended forwards and the hand holds an oblong object. The left leg is human and set forward, but the right is a lion's leg with a lion's paw. The figurine, which might have been produced at Tell Abu al-Kharaz itself, probably for a local sanctuary, is an image of a male deity. It represents a cult or votive idol. Egyptian elements dominate our figurine, but it definitely cannot be described as an Egyptian work of art when all aspects of its iconography are considered.

LB II

This was again a period of fighting, mainly intended to restrict the increasing power of the Hittites in Syria, who had decisively defeated the Mitanni. Sethos I (1294–1279 BC),

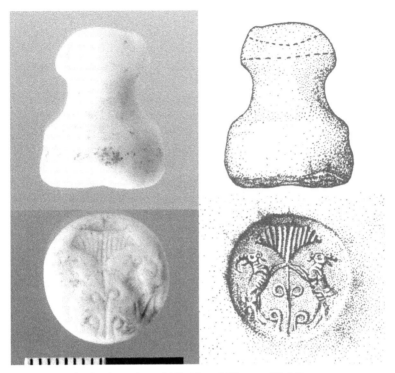

FIG. 37.4 Stamp-seal of calcite from Tell Abu al-Kharaz LB IC

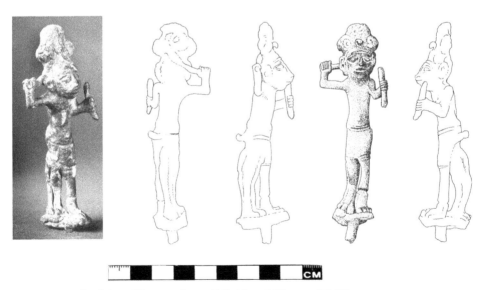

FIG. 37.5 Male deity of bronze from Tell Abu al-Kharaz LB IC

the son of Ramesses I, who ruled for only one year, made military excursions into the area (cf. Murnane 1990). Raids into Transjordan, for instance, were certainly carried out by Seti I and possibly Ramesses II (1279–1213 BC) or Egyptian vassals in Cisjordan. A short period of peace was followed by other wars under Ramesses II, which culminated in the battle against the Hittites at Kadesh during his second campaign. Ramesses II also quelled a revolt in Palestine. The treaty with the Hittites during the twenty-first year of his reign was followed by a peaceful period. The reign of Merenptah (1213–1203 BC) is the period when Egypt suffered from the most serious threat of invasion since the Hyksos period. Merenptah temporarily defeated the Libyans and the 'Sea Peoples' during the fifth year of his reign, and secured at least Cisjordan once again (Yurco 1978). Not much of relevance to Palestine can be reported from the end of the 19th Dynasty and the early 20th Dynasty except for the names and reigns of their rulers. After that we are well into the next major period, the Iron Age. The influence of Egypt in Palestine seems to have vanished at the end of the Late Bronze Age.

Several Jordanian sites bear witness to the renewed Egyptian interest in securing access to commodities from Transjordan during LB II. Pella's cultural decline during the 13th century is reflected by the lack of imports, luxury goods, and new architecture. Major cemeteries were abandoned, tombs became smaller and less elaborate, settlements in the hinterland almost vanished, and by the end of the Late Bronze Age (Phase IA) Pella, for instance, was nothing more than a deprived village. The temple at Pella from around 1350 BC, which succeeded the mighty original *migdol* temple from the MB III, was destroyed at the end of the Late Bronze Age, around 1150 BC, most likely by an earthquake. There is a possible destruction of Phase VIII at Tell Abu al-Kharaz which decisively terminated the Late Bronze Age culture of the town. This event is tentatively dated within the 13th century, when Sethos I and his son, Ramesses II, ruled. Tell Deir 'Alla Late Bronze Phases E–H are a good chronological indicator of the end of the Late Bronze Age (Franken 1992; van der Kooij 2006). Phase E (= Phase 12), to which the last phase of the above-mentioned temple belongs, suffered from severe destruction, possibly caused by an earthquake according to Franken (1992). Finds from this phase include LH IIIA2–B pottery and a faience vase with the cartouche of Queen Tawosret (1188–1186 BC). There is an obvious discrepancy of some decades between the date of (the later part of) LH IIIA2, i.e. the last quarter of the 13th century BC, and the reign of Tawosret, but this can be explained by the fact that Mycenaean pottery was certainly considered as luxury goods and kept for a considerable time. Stratum XII at Tell es-Sa'idiyeh in the Jordan Valley represents a transitional Late Bronze/Iron Age settlement, which was destroyed around 1150 BC according to Tubb and Chapman (1991: 100). Stratum XII contains a public building which is described as an outpost of the 20th Dynasty and an 'Egyptian governor's residence' on the strength of specific architectural traits found elsewhere in Cisjordan, for instance, at Beth Shean and Tell el-Far'ah South. At Tell al-Fukhar in the north of Jordan, a partly excavated structure, called a 'palace' by the excavators, is reported to have been abandoned at the end of the Late Bronze Age, reoccupied by squatters and finally destroyed by a conflagration (Strange 2001: 292). In summary, the Egyptian influence on Transjordan at the end of the Late Bronze Age seems to have been limited to the Jordan Valley on the meagre evidence of Egyptian finds in Transjordan. 'Egyptianizing architecture', for instance at Tell es-Sa'idiyeh (Tubb and Chapman 1991: 99, fig. 48), seems only to reflect a general trend or merely emulation.

Additional selected Late Bronze Age sites and cemeteries in Transjordan

The cemetery at Kataret as-Samra in the southern Jordan Valley produced pottery from major parts of the LB I and II, including Cypriot imports from the latter period (Leonard 1981). The northern part of Jordan reveals a number of Late Bronze Age settlements and cemeteries. A walled settlement with a temple, public structures, and tombs is reported from Irbid during the LB II. Abila demonstrates sparse Late Bronze Age remains, including tombs (Kafafi 1984). The fortified settlement of Tell al-Fukhar yielded a public building and imported items (Strange 1997). The rich tomb at Sahem, which produced numerous fine objects of gold, silver, bronze, and stone (see below), dates to the second part of the Late Bronze Age and the beginning of the Iron Age (Fischer 1997). Tell el-Husn, near Irbid, yielded finds from the Late Bronze Age. Jerash seems to include material from major parts of the Late Bronze Age (Braemer 1992). Recent excavations in the northwest of Jordan at Tell Zira'a exposed remains from the second part of the Late Bronze Age, from 'somewhere between 1450 and 1300 BC' according to the excavators (Vieweger and Häser 2007), which would correspond to our LB IB–C period according to radiocarbon dating. There are a number of adjoining rooms along the edge of the tell which are regarded as 'casemate chambers' with domestic structures on their inside. Cypriot and Mycenaean pottery, cylinder seals, and a few Egyptian/Egyptianizing finds are reported (Vieweger and Häser 2007).

The Amman area also shows a number of sites with Late Bronze Age remains. From Amman itself (Jebel al-Qaʻala) are finds that may be as early as from the beginning of the Late Bronze Age. There is a roughly 15m² square temple from approximately the 13th century BC at Amman Airport: it yielded numerous imports from the Cypriot, Mycenaean, and Egyptian sphere of culture (e.g. Hankey 1995). The fortified Tell Safut, which overlooks the Beqa' Valley to the northwest of Amman, produced Late Bronze Age remains including a seated bronze figurine deity. There are a number of tombs in the Beqa' Valley which are dated to LB I, II, and the early Iron Age: they contain, in addition to locally produced wares, imports in the shape of Cypriot Base-Ring II and White Slip II, and Mycenaean IIIA2–B (McGovern 1986). From the walled town of Sahab, southeast of Amman, a sequence from the beginning of the Late Bronze Age to the 13th century is reported. At Tell al-Umayri, to the south of Amman, a large structure standing on a rampart of MB III date has been excavated. It was probably built in the 14th century BC and burnt down in the late 14th or early 13th century BC: it is interpreted as a temple or a public building with significant cultic function (Bramlett 2004). Lehun, east of the Dead Sea, demonstrates a transitional Late Bronze/early Iron Age settlement (Homès-Fredericq 1997).

Burials

From what is published, it seems that the most common burial form during the Late Bronze Age in Transjordan was cave or rock-cut burials. These caves were reused during a longer period, as is demonstrated, for instance, by the three-chambered Tomb 62 at Pella: this tomb, which contained around 2,000 objects including 1,200 earthenware vessels, some from Cyprus, was in continuous use from the end of the Middle Bronze Age well into the Late Bronze Age (Smith and Potts 1992: 69–81). There is another rock-cut burial from Sahem near the Yarmouk from the second part of the Late Bronze Age and the beginning of the Iron Age (Fischer 1997). The tomb contained several hundred objects, including some of bronze, silver, and gold, figurines of fired clay and painted stone, and Egyptian/Egyptianizing objects, including the rare representation of a pharaoh's coronation ceremony on a gold-mounted Egyptian blue scarab attached with silver wire to a bronze ring: this is from the time of Ramesses II. There are also numerous locally made imitations of Mycenaean pottery from Sahem. Other cave burials are from the Beqa' Valley (McGovern 1986). These span the Late Bronze Age and the beginning of the Iron Age. The tombs included Cypriot and Mycenaean pottery, scarabs, and cylinder seals.

Pit and jar burials are reported from the vast cemetery at the lower mound of Tell es-Sa'idiyeh (Pritchard 1980; Tubb and Chapman 1991). The cemetery also contains tombs built of mud-brick. Most of the tombs are from the outgoing Late Bronze Age and include, in addition to numerous locally produced wares, imports from Cyprus, Mycenae, and Egypt, and fine objects of bronze, such as a 'wine set'. Some of the tombs (in addition to the architecture in the settlement) show Egyptianizing features. There is the rare report of cremation practices in the Amman Airport temple area (for discussion, see Hankey 1995).

Textual evidence related to Transjordan

The textual evidence is limited and the most important is presented here in chronological order. Pella is mentioned several times in New Kingdom texts and inscriptions, which are best associated with Phases V to II at Pella, of which parts of Phase V might correspond to the reign of Thutmosis III and Phase II roughly to the 12th century BC (Bourke, Sparks, and Schroeder 2006: 9, 30; Fischer 2006b: 241, table 1). There are a number of place names whose identification remains obscure in the great topographical list of Thutmosis III. Some are likely to have been located in Transjordan (cf. Kitchen 1992: 23–5) and they may include Tell Abu al-Kharaz (possibly Nos. 91 or 92: cf. Fischer 2006a: 337). Regardless of the exact location of these place names, the evidence for an Egyptian route through parts of Transjordan towards the north is fairly convincing. There is a possible mention of places in Transjordan in the Soleb list of Amenophis III, and there are Amarna letters which imply kinship links between Shechem and a number of 'brother polities', which mention King Mut-Balu of the city-state of Pella (EA 256; Knapp 1993). A stele with the name of Sethos I is reported from Tell ash-Shiab close to the Yarmouk River in north Jordan, and seems to be connected with his campaign against the nomadic tribes of the Shasu. Stelae from Beth Shean from the reigns of Sethos I and Ramesses II mention warfare in the area including Transjordan (Aharoni 1979: 166–70). A statue of Ramesses II from the temple of Luxor depicts a list of Asiatic places and names which include 'Moab' east of the Dead Sea. A stele with the cartouche of Ramesses II is reported from Sheik Sa'ade on the route to Damascus, which indicates Egyptian interests (Weinstein 1982: 20). Neither the material evidence nor the textual evidence provides indisputable proof that major parts of Transjordan were under Egyptian control during most of the Late Bronze Age. It is not unlikely that the eastern side of the Jordan Valley was under the strong influence of the Egyptian Empire from the time of Thutmosis III onwards, and this might include the city-states of Pella, Tell Abu al-Kharaz, and Tell Deir 'Alla. Nevertheless, as the military campaigns of Amenhotep II might imply, relations were certainly not unproblematic. The correspondence in the Amarna letters seems to leave little doubt that Egypt claimed loyalty from Mut-Balu of Pella. It is not clear, however, to what degree his allegiance met the Egyptian demands in practice. The campaigns of Sethos I and the stelae of Ramesses II in North Jordan and the Bashan would seem to demonstrate a growing Egyptian interest in Transjordan during the 19th Dynasty. The function of the Egyptian garrison at Beth Shean was to guarantee that the Jordan Valley area was under control, which was most probably non-intrusive as long as the Transjordanian city-states did not interfere with Egyptian interests, maintained an unthreatening attitude, and functioned as safeguards against nomadic tribes.

CONCLUDING REMARKS

There is no proof that Transjordan—with the possible exception of parts of the Jordan Valley during certain periods—was under Egyptian rule. The number of 'Egyptian' finds in Transjordan is limited, and would be further reduced if we scrutinized the production technique and inscriptions of scarabs from Transjordan: certainly many were not made in Egypt but are Palestinian products, maybe from Tell el-'Ajjul, from where approximately 1,300—the largest number of scarabs/scaraboids in the southern Levant—derive (Fischer and Sadeq 2000; 2002). Egypt was mainly interested in a stable Jordan Valley and secure routes through northern Jordan. A certain dependence on Egypt must be admitted; however, as long the Jordan Valley city-states did not come into conflict with Egyptian interests and as long as they provided tributes, they were left alone. After being the dominating system during most of the Middle and Late Bronzes, the city-state system collapsed by the end of the Late Bronze Age and was replaced by smaller but much more numerous rural villages which epitomize the start of the Iron Age. Population estimates from the fortified Middle and Late Bronze Age town of Tell Abu al-Kharaz are as follows (inhabitants in the surrounding plain and hinterland are not counted): Phase IV/1 and 2, the late Middle Bronze Age phases, might have had a population of 100–200 individuals. Phase V, which had the highest density, might have been inhabited by approximately up to 500 people. The figures for Phases VI–VIII are very probably as low as those from the late Middle Bronze Age, maybe even lower, viz. 100–200 individuals. These figures should be raised during times of conflict, when the surrounding dwellers retreated into the fortified town.

The main source of the relative prosperity of many settlements in the northern part of Jordan was almost certainly agriculture, the production of oil and wine, cattle breeding, and access to timber. These commodities were used for intraregional trading for coveted goods, mainly copper, and for imports such as tin/bronze, silver, gold, 'exotic' ceramics, and other luxurious merchandise, for instance, cosmetic oils and pigments from other regions. An additional source of income may have been tribute from trading caravans on their way through Jordan carrying incense and spices, for instance, from the south Arabian coast.

We know very little about the religious organization. Non-standardized sanctuaries were found at most major Late Bronze Age sites. They usually contain luxury goods, many of them imported. Mould-made images of fired-clay deities, usually of the upright Astarte type with the Egyptian-influenced Hathor coiffure, are not uncommon in sanctuaries or in tombs. There are the rare figurines of bronze deities, one in the shape of an upright, smiting, half-human, half-leonine god from Tell Abu al-Kharaz and another from Safut, showing a seated and smiling god. Both were originally attached to furniture, possibly a throne. The original *migdol* temple at Pella (MB III) demonstrates the characteristics of other Canaanite temples in the region, for instance, at Shechem and Hazor, which might point to a uniform religious faith in the region. The reconstructed temple from 1350 BC seems to have its closest architectural parallels in temples that have been excavated in the Nile Delta of Egypt (S. Bourke, pers. comm.).

The political supremacy of Egypt in the southern Levant was at its height from the time of Thutmosis III and well into the 14th century BC. It seems, in the case of Pella, that by 1350 BC the city was—at least nominally—under the control of Egypt despite the fact that there is no clear evidence of direct Egyptian occupation at Pella. The same could possibly be said about the city of Tell Abu al-Kharaz, just a few kilometres south of Pella: the long-term excavation project did not produce any indisputably Egyptian objects during the considerable Late Bronze Age occupation (Fischer 2006a; 2006b). It is of course possible that the Egyptians were more interested in the region of Pella because of convenient communication roads, and that they did not care about Tell Abu al-Kharaz, despite its supreme strategic position, as long as the city did not present any threat to them. It might also be the case that the 'Egyptian' design of the Pella temple merely mirrors the then dominating cultural and religious tendencies. The Iron Age temple, which replaced the temple from 1350 BC, shows a different orientation and deprived construction. One might conclude that these changes in the Iron Age reflect a breakdown of a common religious organization in the southern Levant as a result of the disintegration of the power of the Egyptian New Kingdom, which also led to the political and economic crumbling of the Levant into small, and often fairly poor, city-states.

SUGGESTED READING

Adams, R. B. (ed.) (2008). *Jordan: An Archaeological Reader*. London: Equinox.
James, F. W., and P. E. McGovern (1993). *The Late Bronze Age Egyptian Garrison at Beth Shan: A Study of Levels VII and VIII* (2 vols). Philadelphia: University Museum, University of Pennsylvania.
Mazar, A. (1990). *Archaeology of the Land of the Bible*, vol. 1: *10,000–586 B.C.E.* New York: Doubleday.
Weippert, H. (1988). *Palästina in vorhellenistischer Zeit*. Munich: Beck.

REFERENCES

Aharoni, Y. (1979). *The Land of the Bible*, ed. A. F. Rainey. London: Burns & Oates.
Bietak, M. (2003). Science versus archaeology: problems and consequences of high Aegean chronology. In M. Bietak (ed.), *The Synchronisation of Civilisations in the Eastern Mediterranean in the Second Millennium B.C. II: Proceedings of the SCIEM 2000-EuroConference, Haindorf, 2nd of May–7th of May 2001*. Vienna: Österreichische Akademie der Wissenschaften, 23–33.
Bourke, S. J. (1994). Excavations in Area IIIN/S: the Late Bronze Age palatial residence. *Annual of the Department of Antiquities of Jordan* 38: 81–109.
——R. T. Sparks, and M. Schroeder (2006). Pella in the Middle Bronze Age. In Fischer (2006b: 9–58).
Braemer, F. (1992). Occupation de sol dans la région de Jérash aux périodes du Bronze récent et du Fer. *Studies in the History and Archaeology of Jordan* 4: 191–98.

Bramlett, K. (2004). A Late Bronze Age cultic installation at Tall al-ʿUmayri, Jordan. *Near Eastern Archaeology* 67: 50–1.

Fischer, P. M. (1997). *A Late Bronze to Early Iron Age Tomb at Sahem, Jordan.* Wiesbaden: Harrassowitz.

——(1999). Chocolate-on-White Ware: typology, chronology, and provenance—The evidence from Tell Abu al-Kharaz, Jordan Valley. *Bulletin of the American Schools of Oriental Research* 313: 1–29.

——(2006a). *Tell Abu al-Kharaz in the Jordan Valley*, vol. 2: *The Middle and Late Bronze Ages.* Vienna: Österreichische Akademie der Wissenschaften.

——(ed.) (2006b). *The Chronology of the Jordan Valley during the Middle and Late Bronze Ages: Pella, Tell Abu al-Kharaz, and Tell Deir ʿAlla.* Vienna: Österreichische Akademie der Wissenschaften

——and M. Sadeq (2000). Tell el-ʿAjjul 1999: a joint Palestinian–Swedish field project—First season preliminary report. *Ägypten und Levante* 10: 211–26.

——(2002). Tell el-ʿAjjul 2000: second season preliminary report. *Ägypten und Levante* 12: 109–53.

Franken, H. J. (1992). *Excavations at Tell Deir ʿAlla*, vol. 2: *The Late Bronze Age Sanctuary.* Louvain: Peeters.

Glueck, N. (1951). Explorations in eastern Palestine IV. *Annual of the American Schools of Oriental Research* 25–8: 261–75.

Hankey, V. (1995). A Late Bronze Age temple at Amman airport: small finds and pottery discovered in 1955. In S. J. Bourke and J.-P. Descoeudres (eds), *Trade, Contact, and the Movement of Peoples in the Eastern Mediterranean: Studies in Honour of J. Basil Hennessy.* Sydney University: Meditarch, 169–85.

Homès-Fredericq, D. (1997). *Lehun.* Brussels: Cultura Wetteren.

Kafafi, Z. A. (1984). Late Bronze Age pottery from Qwelbe (Jordan). *Zeitschrift des Deutschen Palästina-Vereins* 100: 12–29.

Kitchen, K. A. (1992). The Egyptian evidence on ancient Jordan. In P. Bienkowski (ed.), *Early Edom and Moab: The Beginning of the Iron Age in Southern Jordan.* Sheffield: Collis, 21–34.

——(2002). Ancient Egyptian chronology for Aegeanists. *Mediterranean Archaeology and Archaeometry* 2/2: 5–12.

Knapp, A. B. (1993). *Society and Polity at Bronze Age Pella: An Annales Perspective.* Sheffield: Sheffield Academic.

Krauss, R., and D. A. Warburton (2009). The basis for the Egyptian dates. In D. A. Warburton (ed.), *Time's Up! Dating the Minoan Eruption of Santorini.* Athens: Danish Institute at Athens, 125–44.

Leonard, A., Jr. (1981). Kataret es-Samra: a Late Bronze Age cemetery in Transjordan? *Annual of the Department of Antiquities of Jordan* 25: 179–95.

McGovern, P. E. (1986). *The Late Bronze and Early Iron Ages of Central Transjordan: The Baqʿah Valley Project, 1977–1981.* Philadelphia: University Museum, University of Pennsylvania.

Murnane, W. J. (1990). *The Road to Kadesh: A Historical Interpretation of the Battle Reliefs of King Sety I at Karnak*, 2nd rev. edn. Chicago: Oriental Institute of the University of Chicago.

Pritchard, J. B. (1980). *The Cemetery at Tell es-Saʾidiyeh, Jordan.* Philadelphia: University Museum, University of Pennsylvania.

Rainey, A. F. (1993). Sharhan/Sharuhen: the problem of identification. *Eretz-Israel* 24: 178–87.

Redford, D. B. (1992). *Egypt, Canaan, and Israel in Ancient Times.* Princeton, NJ: Princeton University Press.

Smith, R. H., and T. F. Potts (1992). The Middle and Late Bronze Ages. In A. W. Nicoll, P. C. Edwards, J. Hanbury-Tenison, et al., *Pella in Jordan 2: The Second Interim Report of the Joint University of Sydney and the College of Wooster Excavations at Pella, 1982-1985*, Sydney: Meditarch, 35–81.

Strange, J. (1997). Tell el-Fukhar 1990–1993. *Studies in the History and Archaeology of Jordan* 6: 399–406.

——(2001). The Late Bronze Age. In B. MacDonald, R. B. Adams, and P. Bienkowski (eds), *The Archaeology of Jordan*. Sheffield: Sheffield Academic, 291–321.

Tubb, J. N., and R. L. Chapman. (1991). *Archaeology and the Bible*. London: British Museum Press.

van der Kooij, G. (2006). Tell Deir ʿAlla: the Middle and Late Bronze Age chronology. In Fischer (2006b: 199–226).

Vieweger, D., and J. Häser (2007). Tall Ziraʿa: five thousand years of Palestinian history on a single-settlement mound. *Near Eastern Archaeology* 70: 147–67.

Warburton, D. A. (2001). Egyptian campaigns in Jordan revisited. *Studies in the History and Archaeology of Jordan* 7: 233–7.

Weinstein, J. M. (1982). The Egyptian Empire in Palestine: a reassessment. *Bulletin of the American Schools of Oriental Research* 241: 1–28.

Yurco, F. J. (1978). Merneptah's Palestinian Campaign. *Society for the Study of Egyptian Antiquities* 8: 70.

CHAPTER 38

···

CYPRUS DURING THE LATE
BRONZE AGE

···

LOUISE STEEL

INTRODUCTION

···

The Late Bronze Age on Cyprus (*c.* 1650–1050 BC) (Fig. 38.1) was marked by a number of significant social and economic changes. There was a massive increase in settlement, which expanded into new, previously unoccupied areas; alongside this there is evidence for an

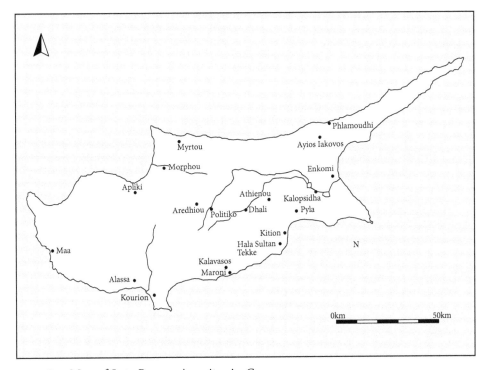

FIG. 38.1 Map of Late Bronze Age sites in Cyprus

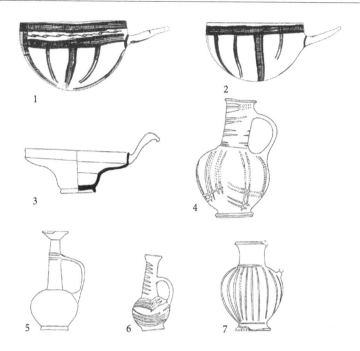

FIG. 38.2 White Slip and Base Ring pottery: (1) White Slip I hemispherical bowl (after Mee and Steel 1998: no. 205, pl. 39); (2) White Slip II hemispherical bowl (after Mee and Steel 1998: no. 75, pl. 14); (3) Base Ring II carinated cup (after Mee and Steel 1998: no. 66, pl. 11); (4) Base Ring II jug with painted decoration (after Mee and Steel 1998: no. 203, pl. 38); (5) Base Ring I juglet (bilbil) (after Mee and Steel 1998: no. 52, pl. 9; (6) Base Ring II juglet with painted decoration (after Mee and Steel 1998: no. 202, pl. 38); and (7) Bucchero jug (after Mee and Steel 1998: no. 67, pl. 11)

increasingly complex hierarchical settlement pattern, culminating in the rise of a number of urban centres along the southern coast by the 13th century BCE. The Late Bronze Age was also characterized by increased Cypriot involvement in maritime trade around the eastern basin of the Mediterranean, reaching a peak in the 14th and 13th centuries BCE. Cypriot participation in this trade was dependent on exploitation of the rich copper resources located in the foothills of the Troodos Mountains. The development of the copper trade allowed the emergence of an economic and possibly political elite, who controlled access to luxury imports and prestige goods. Although it is possible to categorize Late Bronze Age Cyprus as an urban civilization, particularly one that was in contact (trading and diplomatic) with the state systems of Egypt, the Aegean, and the Levant, the nature of the social, political, and economic organization on the island is still a matter of conjecture. Various models have been proposed, largely dependent on elite control of copper production and trade (Keswani 1993; 1996; Peltenburg 1996; Knapp 1997).

The Late Bronze Age on Cyprus is commonly termed the Late Cypriot period. This archaeological phase is defined by changes in the ceramic sequence and the appearance of new tableware: White Slip, Base Ring, and Monochrome (Fig. 38.2). The period has been further subdivided into a tripartite scheme of LC IA–B, LC IIA–C, and LC IIIA–B. These

Table 38.1 Absolute chronology of the Late Cypriot
(after Merrillees 1992: 51, table 2)

Terminology	Chronology
LC IA	1650–1550 BCE
LC IB	1550–1450 BCE
LC IIA	1450–1375 BCE
LC IIB	1375–1300 BCE
LC IIC	1300–1200 BCE
LC IIIA	1200–1100 BCE
LC IIIB	1100–1050 BCE

phases are likewise defined by the ceramic repertoire. LC II is characterized by a standardization of the White Slip and Base Ring Wares and the appearance of imported Mycenaean pottery. LC IIIA is defined by the gradual disappearance of Late Cypriot tableware and increasing local production of Mycenaean-style pottery (White Painted Wheelmade III). A complete transformation in the island's ceramic industry in LC IIIB is illustrated by the introduction of the Proto-White Painted Ware, ancestral to the pottery of Iron Age Cyprus. An alternative scheme has been proposed by Knapp (1994); the preceding Early and Middle Cypriot periods are termed the Prehistoric Bronze Age and the Late Cypriot period the Protohistoric Bronze Age (ProBA). Knapp proposes a tripartite division of the Protohistoric Bronze Age material. The MC III–LC I interface is lumped into a single transitional phase (ProBA I), the entire LC II period is designated ProBA II, and LC III is termed ProBA III. Absolute dates for the Late Cypriot period are largely derived from correlations with the chronologies of Egypt and the Near East (Merrillees 1992). Nonetheless, radiocarbon determinations from a number of sites have dated the LC IIC period to *c*.1340–1315 to 1200 ± 20/–10 BC, very close to the traditional dates derived from the Egyptian chronology (Manning et al. 2001) (Table 38.1).

THE ARCHAEOLOGICAL RECORD

The Late Cypriot period has been extensively explored. As for the Middle Bronze, three datasets are available: tomb groups, excavated settlements, and survey material. Initially knowledge of the Late Cypriot was almost entirely dependent on tombs; between 1893 and 1899 the British Museum excavated various Late Bronze tombs groups, most notably at Enkomi, and also at Kourion, Hala Sultan Tekke, and Maroni (Murray, Smith, and Walters 1900; Bailey 1976; Manning and Monks 1998). The finds from these excavations and other tomb groups excavated during the early years of the 20th century form the basis for the definition of the Cypriot Late Bronze Age.

Numerous Late Bronze settlements have been excavated since the pioneering work of the Swedish Cyprus Expedition (Gjerstad et al. 1934). For the most part excavation has concentrated on the towns around the coastal strip—Alassa, Hala Sultan Tekke, Kalavasos *Ayios Dhimitrios*, Maroni, and Morphou *Toumba tou Skourou*. The most extensively explored is Enkomi (Gjerstad et al. 1934; Schaeffer 1952; Dikaios 1969–71; Crewe 2007), located on the southeast coast. In contrast, knowledge of island's hinterland is largely dependent on survey data, in particular that collected by the Cyprus Survey in the 1950s (Catling 1962), supplemented more recently by a number of regional surveys (Iacovou 2004; 2007; 2008).

MC III–LC I TRANSITION

The transition between the Middle and Late Bronze Age on Cyprus was a period of seemingly violent social upheaval, characterized by a horizon of destruction and the wholesale abandonment of the Middle Cypriot settlements. Mass burials at Pendayia *Mandres*, Myrtou *Stephania*, and Ayios Iakovos *Melia*, identified by an unusually large number of skeletons with a disproportionately small number of grave goods, might be evidence for social instability and have been interpreted in terms of some catastrophic event, such as an epidemic or warfare (Åström 1972: 764). This, however, is not supported by the paleo-osteological evidence (Fischer 1986). The construction of fortresses along the Karpass Peninsula, the southern slopes of the Kyrenia Range, and the northeastern slopes of the Troodos Massif have also been seen as evidence for insecurity and population stress (Catling 1962: 141). Peltenburg (1996: 29–34), however, contends that the forts demonstrate the power of an emergent elite and are indicative of an initial stage of state formation on the island. For the most part MC III–LC I burials were not richly furnished and metal artefacts were rare. However, a small number of warrior burials have been identified in the copper-producing region of the northeast foothills of the Troodos Mountains. Military equipment included hook-tanged weapons, socketed axe-heads, and bronze belts, for example in Dhali *Kafkallia* Tomb G (Overbeck and Swiny 1972), stone mace-heads, and horse burials. In the newly established centres at Enkomi and Morphou *Toumba tou Skourou* there is some evidence for the emergence of a social and economic elite which had the ability to acquire imported luxuries. The range of imported valuables from Morphou includes Late Minoan IB pottery, silver trinkets, beads of faience, glass, carnelian and amethyst, hematite weights, cylinder seals, and ostrich eggs (Vermeule and Wolsky 1990). A similar range of goods was recovered from Enkomi French Tomb 32 (Courtois 1981).

SETTLEMENT

The Late Cypriot period witnessed a massive expansion in settlement and diversified use of the Cypriot landscape. A number of towns grew up around the coastal plains, the earliest being Morphou *Toumba tou Skourou* and Enkomi *Ayios Iakovos*. By the 13th century BCE the towns were organized on a grid system, suggesting a certain degree of central planning. Ashlar masonry was used in the construction of imposing public buildings. While the houses at Kourion *Bamboula* (Weinburg 1983) were large agglomerative structures, similar to the dwellings of the preceding Early and Middle Cypriot periods, the freestanding house built around an open court was more typical. Houses were equipped with cisterns, benches, pits, bins, and grinding installations for a variety of household activities. The inhabitants of the towns were primarily involved in diverse specialized activities and participated in international maritime trade. In addition to craft specialists, in particular those involved in metallurgical production, there is some evidence for religious elites and possibly for economic, bureaucratic elites. Central redistribution centres have been identified at Kalavasos *Ayios Dhimitrios* and Alassa *Paliotaverna* (South 1992; Hadjisavvas 2001; Knapp 2009). Both sites

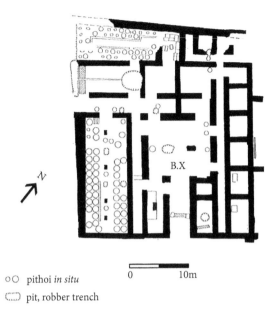

oO pithoi *in situ*

⊂⊃ pit, robber trench

0   10m

FIG. 38.3 Plan of Building X, Kalavasos *Ayios Dhimitrios* (after South 2000: fig. 1)

were dominated by a large ashlar building, which housed sizeable storage facilities. The two pithoi halls in Building X (Fig. 38.3), Kalavasos, contained more than 50 large pithoi and had an estimated storage capacity of around 50,000 litres (Keswani 1992). Even so, there is only limited evidence for the development of a literate bureaucracy to facilitate control over these economic activities. A small number of possible economic documents, written in the Cypro-Minoan script, have been found at Kalavasos and Enkomi, but their use is inconclusive (Smith 2002a).

The nature of occupation in the Cypriot hinterland is still a matter of conjecture. A three-tiered settlement hierarchy was posited by Catling (1962), based on survey data. This comprised the coastal urban centres, small mining communities, as represented by Apliki *Karamallos* (Taylor 1952; Kling and Muhly 2007), and farming villages. Recent excavations at Politiko *Phorades* have thrown light on the processes of copper extraction and primary smelting (Knapp and Kassianidou 2008). The site is characterized by unusually large quantities of archaeometallurgical finds, including 2.5 tonnes of copper slag, and numerous furnace and tuyère fragments. There is, however, no evidence for an associated settlement; this might indicate that copper working at this stage (LC I) was a seasonal activity. The very different nature of this site from Apliki *Karamallos*, which Keswani (1993) has posited as a local redistribution centre, might illustrate increasing centralized control over copper production by the urban communities as the Late Bronze Age progressed. The Late Cypriot rural hinterland has received little attention by archaeologists, and only a small number of possible farming villages or farmsteads have been identified, such as Analiondas *Palioklichia* (Webb and Frankel 1994) and Aredhiou *Vouppes* (Steel 2009). It has been suggested that these sites functioned as specialist agricultural production centres, which supported the mining communities in the Troodos foothills and the inhabitants of the coastal towns (Knapp 2003; Keswani and Knapp

2003). Specialist pottery production sites have also been documented at Sanidha *Moutti tou Ayiou Serkou* (Todd and Pilides 1993) and Morphou *Toumba tou Skourou* (Vermeule and Wolsky 1990).

COPPER WORKING

Copper formed the basis of the island's wealth during the Late Bronze Age, and copper production is frequently cited as a key factor in models of state formation. The LC I primary smelting site at Politiko *Phorades* (Knapp and Kassianidou 2008) demonstrates small-scale, seasonal operations at the beginning of the Late Bronze Age; however, metallurgical production increasingly came under control of the urban elites. Already in LC I there was central control over secondary copper production at Enkomi, within the imposing structure of the fortress (Dikaios 1969–71). The height of the Cypriot copper industry, however, dates to the 13th and 12th centuries BCE. Small mining villages, such as Apliki *Karamallos*, were involved in the procurement of the raw material and the initial smelt of the sulphide ores; the resultant furnace conglomerate was then transported to the coastal towns. The secondary smelt and the subsequent production of bronze goods (tools, weapons, and high-status, prestige goods such as tripod and four-sided stands) took place within the towns, under the close supervision of the urban elite. The frequent occurrence of metallurgical installations within the confines of the urban sanctuaries might indicate religious, state control over copper production in the latter stages of the Late Bronze (Knapp 1986).

FOREIGN CONTACTS AND THE ALASHIYA QUESTION

From beginning of the second millennium BCE Cyprus played an increasingly important role in maritime trade in the East Mediterranean. The earliest textual referrals to the island, dating to the 18th and 17th centuries BCE, are cuneiform references to Alashiya from Mari, Alalakh, and Babylon (Knapp 1996: 5, texts 2–11, 32). These texts document trade in copper. The evidence from the earliest levels at Enkomi indicates copper production at the site from LC I and moreover a close association between this activity and the acquisition of luxury imports. There is physical evidence for maritime trade in Cypriot copper, in the form of copper ingots, found as far west as Sardinia and Sicily, as well as a number of shipwreck sites in the Aegean and off the south coast of Turkey, dating between the 14th and 12th centuries. These ingots were standardized, weighing between 25kg and 28kg, implying close centralized control of the metals trade.

Cypriot pottery was widely exported throughout the East Mediterranean. Base Ring, White Slip, and Monochrome Wares were commonly exported to the Levant and Egypt (Gittlen 1981), but only in small quantities to the Aegean, most notably to Kommos (Watrous 1992). Although Hittite texts suggest close political links between Cyprus and the Hittite Empire, this is difficult to document archaeologically. Nonetheless, the large quantities of Red Lustrous arm-shaped vessels from Hittite sites might illustrate trade between the two civilizations. Moreover, rare high-status Hittite objects, including a silver figurine from a tomb at Kalavasos *Ayios Dhimitrios*, are attested. Despite the limited amount of Cypriot

FIG. 38.4 Imported Mycenaean stirrup jar from Aredhiou *Vouppes*

pottery in the Aegean, large quantities of Mycenaean ceramics were traded to Cyprus during the 14th and 13th centuries (Steel 1998); indeed, the island appears to have played a pivotal role in the procurement and dissemination of Mycenaean pottery throughout the region. The stirrup jar, a container for perfumed oils, was the most frequent import (Fig. 38.4), but a wide variety of forms are attested, most notably the pictorial kraters.

Raw materials, such as gold, ivory, and possibly glass, were imported and fashioned into luxury goods; in addition, high-status prestige imports, such as faience vases from Egypt and trinkets such as cylinder seals from Syria, were traded. New Kingdom Egyptian texts, namely the Annals of Thutmosis III and the Amarna archives, illustrate Cypriot participation in gift exchange and diplomatic envoys at the highest level. These texts document the payment of 'tribute'—horses, wood, lapis lazuli, and above all copper—from the king of Alashiya to the Egyptian pharaoh. Moreover, the Amarna letters clearly indicate the power of the ruler of Alashiya, who addressed the pharaoh as 'my brother'. Although the location of Alahsiya has been long disputed (Merrillees 1987), recent petrographic analyses of the Alashiya tablets from Amarna place their manufacture in the southern coast of Cyprus, in the vicinity of Alassa *Paliotaverna* and Kalavasos *Ayios Dhimitrios* (Goren et al. 2003)

BURIAL CUSTOMS

In contrast to the preceding Middle Cypriot, during the Late Bronze Age burial largely occurred within the boundary of the settlement, below streets, and in the courtyards of houses (Keswani 2004: 86–8). The typical burial facility was the rock-cut chamber tomb entered via a vertical shaft (the *dromos*). The tomb chambers tend to be smaller and less elaborate than their Early Cypriot–Middle Cypriot predecessors and variable in shape—circular, ovoid, and rectangular. Particularly elaborate tombs were constructed at Morphou

Toumba tou Skourou: between one and four chambers opened off from the central *dromos* (Vermeule and Wolsky 1990). Elaborate, large tombs were also constructed at Ayios Iakovos *Melia*. These had large niched chambers and were approached by long tapering *dromoi* (Gjerstad et al. 1934). Some tombs were furnished with rock-cut benches and niches cut into the walls of the chamber or *dromos*. The most common form of chamber tomb at Enkomi was a rounded chamber entered through the roof by a shaft-like *dromos*. Various other tomb types have been identified at Enkomi: the built tomb lined with ashlar blocks (Courtois, Lagarce, and Lagarce 1986), the *tholos* tomb (Johnstone 1971), and infant burials in Canaanite jars (Keswani 1989: 52). Typical burial ritual comprised multiple inhumations over several generations. There is some evidence for secondary burial practices (Keswani 2004: 88–104), in some cases comprising post-mortem manipulation of the skeletal remains and the deliberate, preferential recovery of long bones and skulls as an element of secondary burial (Goring 1989). In LC IIIA (12th century BCE) the shaft grave was introduced, comprising a rectangular cut in the bedrock, which might be lined with loose stones (Niklasson-Sönnerby 1987). Shaft graves housed between one and three individuals and the practice of secondary burial was abandoned. These shaft graves seem to reflect disruption to the social order on Cyprus in the 12th century; even so, some traditional rock-cut chamber tombs continued to be used, indicative of some social continuity during this period.

Burials were accompanied by a wide range of grave goods. Ceramic vessels were a prerequisite, largely comprising local fine ware pottery, such as White Slip hemispherical bowls and Base Ring juglets, and in the wealthier tombs imported Mycenaean vases. Chief amongst these was the pictorial krater; other Mycenaean imports include a range of small perfumed oil containers (stirrup jars and alabastra) (Steel 1998). Specialized forms, such as Mycenaean rhyta and Red Lustrous spindle bottles and arm-shaped vessels, are only rarely attested; these may have been used in libation ceremonies but their exact function is unclear. High-status grave goods included items of personal adornment fashioned from gold and silver, vases of glass, alabaster, faience, and ivories, used to enhance the social and economic position of the newly emergent urban elites (Keswani 2005: 393). Bronzes were rare until LC IIC–IIIA, when hemispherical bowls and weapons were deposited with the wealthier burials (Keswani 1989: 65). Although burials of the LC IIIA tended to be less richly furnished than in the preceding periods, there were occasional very wealthy assemblages, such as Tomb 23 at Hala Sultan Tekke and Evreti Tomb 8 (Keswani 2004: 129, 133).

RELIGION

A major change from the preceding Early and Middle Bronze Age was the development of special places for the formalized practice of cult. There is no certain evidence for the construction of religious buildings during LC I, although a stone podium associated with a concentration of Red-on-Black drinking vessels at Phlamoudhi *Vounari* has been interpreted as a location for the practice of public cult (al-Radi 1983).

In LC IIA the first religious buildings were constructed at Myrtou *Pigadhes* (Taylor 1957) (Fig. 38.5) and Athienou (Dothan and Ben-Tor 1983), and in LC IIC–IIIA there was an apparent explosion in religious activity throughout the island, with the construction of a

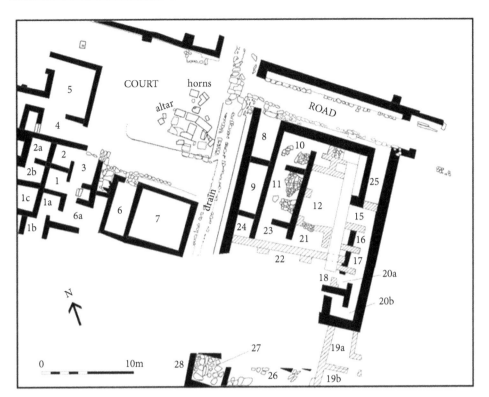

FIG. 38.5 Plan of Myrtou *Pigadhes* (after Taylor 1957: fig. 7)

number of sanctuaries in the coastal towns, most notably at Kition (Karageorghis and Demas 1985), Enkomi (Courtois 1971; Dikaios 1969–71), and Palaepaphos (Maier 1979). Although there was no canonical ground plan for Late Cypriot religious buildings, a number of common characteristics can be identified (Webb 1999; Knapp 2009). For the most part these were freestanding rectangular buildings, constructed on an east–west axis. They comprised a series of rooms, including a pillared hall, the *cella* (cult room), and an enclosed courtyard. The sanctuaries might be furnished with benches for the display of cult equipment, hearths, and stone platforms topped with horns of consecration (Webb 1999). The urban temples were constructed using ashlar masonry, and stepped column capitals were a typical feature.

All the sanctuaries were characterized by the accumulation of specialized objects and ritual paraphernalia. Large numbers of miniature vessels were recovered at Athienou and Kalopsidha *Koufos*; these might have been votive deposits, but otherwise there is limited evidence for votive offerings, such as figurines, until the final phase of the Late Bronze. The sanctuaries served as repositories for luxury prestige objects including bronze tripod stands, faience, glass and alabaster vessels, ivories, and seal-stones. Cult images were rare, with the exception of the Horned God and Ingot God, both from Enkomi. A large stone baetyl from Palaepaphos might have served as an aniconic cult image. Cult practices might be inferred from the physical remains in the sanctuaries. Incised ox scapulae, astragali, and worked shells were possibly used in divination practices. Accumulations of faunal remains (sheep, goat, cattle, and deer) were probably the remains of sacrifice and dining practices. Detailed analyses of the ceramic deposits suggest feasting and libation ceremonies. Religious control of copper production has also been suggested, given the proximity of the metal workshops and religious structures at Enkomi, Kition, Myrtou *Pigadhes*, and Athienou (Knapp 1986). More recently it has been proposed that the temples at Kition also controlled textile production (Smith 2002b).

THE END OF THE LATE BRONZE AGE

The end of the Late Bronze Age on Cyprus was marked by dramatic events which entailed significant changes in the island's social, political, and economic organization. There was a wave of destructions throughout the island at the beginning of the 12th century BCE (LC IIIA) (Karageorghis 1990), the sudden, violent nature of which is illustrated by the skeletons of children trapped and killed by falling mud-brick within the settlement at Enkomi and the occasional occurrence of slingshot. Many sites, such as Kalavasos *Ayios Dhimitrios*, Maroni *Vournes*, and Morphou *Toumba tou Skourou*, were abandoned. Other sites, destroyed at the beginning of the 12th century, were rebuilt. However, for the most part LC IIIA settlements were occupied only briefly before being finally abandoned (Myrtou *Pigadhes*, Apliki, Alassa, and Sinda) (see Iacovou 1989). The only urban centres with clear evidence for occupation throughout LC IIIA are Enkomi, Kition, Kourion, and Palaepaphos. A key feature was the construction of cyclopean-style fortifications at Kition and Enkomi. Possible defensive outposts were established at sites such as Pyla-*Kokkinokremos* and Maa-*Palaeokastro* (Karageorghis and Demas 1984; 1988) prior to the LC IIC/IIIA destructions. These disruptions on Cyprus were contemporary with a horizon of violent destructions throughout the eastern Mediterranean—events which appear to be described on the mortuary temple of Ramesses III at Medinet Habu and in contemporary texts from Ugarit. The possible role played by the Peleset/Philistines in the events in Cyprus is reiterated by apparent representations of Philistine warriors in characteristic feathered headdress on a seal-stone and an ivory box, both from Enkomi.

The cultural changes that characterize LC IIIA are usually attributed to an influx of Mycenaean settlers on Cyprus. Central to the argument is the transformation of the Cypriot pottery repertoire; namely large-scale, local production of Mycenaean-style pottery (variously termed Mycenaean IIIC:1b, Decorated LC III, Late Mycenaean IIIB, and White Painted Wheelmade (WPWM) III: Kling 1989; Sherratt 1991). Alongside this, the ancient Base Ring and White Slip Wares gradually fell from use and new forms of cooking pots were introduced, belonging to the Aegean tradition. Certainly, the pottery record reflects changing modes of preparation and consumption within the household and might be interpreted as an ethnic marker. Nonetheless, the issue is more complex. The initial manufacture of Aegean-style pottery in fact dates to LC IIC, prior to the destructions believed to herald the arrival of Aegean settlers. Instead, Sherratt (1991) has contended that the development of the WPWM III style was a byproduct of increasing centralization and standardization of craft production within the urban centres, rather than an ethnic marker, and that the shifts in ceramic production might indicate economic changes. Another change in the LC IIIA ceramic repertoire was the introduction of a class of coarse, handmade pottery used to make a variety of jars, bowls, and cups—the Handmade Burnished Ware or Barbarian Ware (Pilides 1994). Similar pottery has been identified in LH IIIB and IIIC deposits in the

Aegean, where it was intrusive to the indigenous wheelmade pottery. The appearance of the Handmade Burnished Ware on Cyprus has been attributed to elements of a displaced Aegean population; given its limited occurrence, however, the economic and social significance of the ware in Cyprus remains elusive. Other changes to the material culture of Cyprus include the introduction of various metal types, which further illustrate close cultural contact with the Aegean. These comprise a new dress accessory, the violin bow fibula, and a complex of warrior equipment—socketed spears, cut-and-thrust swords, and bronze greaves (Catling 1964). An architectural innovation of LC IIIA, also ascribed to Aegean colonists, was the large communal hall with central hearth. Similar structures have been identified in the southern Levant, at Ashdod, Tel Miqne, Ashkelon, and Tell Qasile. The Mycenaean megaron is thought to be the precursor to these halls (Karageorghis 1998).

LC IIIB (c.1100–1050 BCE) effectively marks the transition to the Iron Age. This phase is characterized by the introduction of a new ceramic tradition, the Proto-White Painted Ware (Iacovou 1988), ancestral to the ceramic industries of the Iron Age. The initial development of iron technology is attested in the form of small, curved knives with ivory handles (Sherratt 1994). Although there was a major breakdown in maritime trade within the Mediterranean, contacts persisted between Cyprus and the Levant, as indicated by the earliest imports of Phoenician pottery (Bikai 1987). There was a major shift in settlement pattern: the final abandonment of the ancient Late Bronze sites at the end of the 12th century BCE and the gradual establishment of new centres, which developed into the Iron Age city kingdoms (Iacovou 1994). Continuity into the 11th century has only been demonstrated for Enkomi and Kition (Courtois 1971; Karageorghis and Demas 1985), but this was confined to sanctuaries and, moreover, was short-lived. For the most part, the LC IIIB settlements are not archaeologically visible, covered by centuries of Iron Age, Hellenistic, and Roman occupation deposits; instead the main source of evidence are the newly established extramural cemeteries.

New burial practices indicate major social transformations in this period (Steel 1995). One of the key characteristics was the introduction of a new type of burial facility—the chamber tomb approached by a long, narrow *dromos*, similar to the tombs used on the Greek mainland throughout the Late Bronze. These tombs housed between one and three individuals with a modest array of grave goods. There were also significant changes in the practice of cult, indicated by the deposition of large numbers of female terracotta figurines, probably votives (Webb 1999: 213–15). Occasional larger, wheelmade figures were possibly representations of deities, such as the goddess with upraised arms (Webb 1999: 215). Many of these cultural changes appear to derive ultimately from the Aegean and are commonly viewed as evidence for a population movement from this area. All the changes documented in LC IIIB in effect laid the foundations for the development of a very different social order in the Iron Age, centred around the city-kingdoms.

SUGGESTED READING

Barlow, J. A., D. R. Bolger, and B. Kling (eds) (1991). *Cypriot Ceramics: Reading the Prehistoric Record*. Philadelphia: University Museum of Archaeology and Anthropology, University of Pennsylvania.

Bolger, D. R. (2003). *Gender in Ancient Cyprus: Narratives of Social Change on a Mediterranean Island*. Walnut Creek, Calif.: AltaMira.

Karageorghis, V. (1991). *The Coroplastic Art of Ancient Cyprus I: Chalcolithic–Late Cypriote I.* Nicosia: A. G. Leventis Foundation.

Knapp, A. B. (2009). *The Archaeology of Cyprus from the Earliest Prehistory through the Late Bronze Age.* Cambridge: Cambridge University Press.

Muhly, J. D., R. Maddin, and V. Karageorghis (eds) (1982). *Early Metallurgy in Cyprus, 4000–500 BC.* Nicosia: Pierides Foundation.

Peltenburg, E. J. (1989). *Early Society in Cyprus.* Edinburgh: Edinburgh University Press.

Smith, J. S. (ed.) (2002). *Script and Seal Use on Cyprus in the Bronze and Iron Ages.* Boston: Archaeological Institute of America.

Steel, L. (2004). *Cyprus Before History: From the Earliest Settlers to the End of the Bronze Age.* London: Duckworth.

REFERENCES

al-Radi, S. M. S. (1983). *Phlamoudhi Vounari: A Sanctuary Site in Cyprus.* Gothenburg: Åströms.

Åström, P. (1972). *The Late Cypriote Bronze Age: Architecture and Pottery.* Lund: Swedish Cyprus Expedition.

Bailey, D. M. (1976). The British Museum excavations at Hala Sultan Tekke in 1897 and 1898: the material in the British Museum. In P. Åström, D. M. Bailey, and V. Karageorghis (eds) *Hala Sultan Tekke 1: Excavations 1897–1971.* Gothenburg: Åströms, 1–32.

Bikai, P. M. (1987). *The Phoenician Pottery of Cyprus.* Nicosia: A. G. Leventis Foundation.

Catling, H. W. (1962). Patterns of settlement in Bronze Age Cyprus. *Opuscula Atheniensia* 4: 129–69.

——(1964). *Cypriot Bronzework in the Mycenaean World.* Oxford: Clarendon Press.

Courtois, J.-C. (1971). Le sanctuaire du Dieu au Lingot d'Enkomi-Alasia. In C. F.-A.Schaeffer (ed.), *Alasia I.* Paris: Klincksieck, 151–362.

——(1981). *Alasia II; Les tombes d'Enkomi—le mobilier funéraire.* Paris: Mission archéologique d'Alasia.

——J. Lagarce, and E. Lagarce. (1986). *Enkomi et le Bronze récent à Chypre.* Nicosia: Zavallis.

Crewe, L. (2007). *Early Enkomi: Regionalism, Trade and Society at the Beginning of the Late Bronze Age on Cyprus.* Oxford: Archaeopress.

Dikaios, P. (1969–71). *Enkomi: Excavations 1948–1958* (3 vols). Mainz am Rhein: von Zabern.

Dothan, T., and A. Ben-Tor (1983). *Excavations at Athienou, Cyprus, 1971–1972.* Jerusalem: Institute of Archaeology, Hebrew University of Jerusalem.

Fischer, P. M. (1986). *Prehistoric Cypriot Skulls: A Medico-Anthropological, Archaeological, and Micro-Analytical Investigation.* Gothenburg: Åströms.

Gittlen, B. M. (1981). The cultural and chronological implications of the Cypro-Palestinian trade during the Late Bronze Age. *Bulletin of the American Schools of Oriental Research* 241: 49–59.

Gjerstad, E., J. Lindros, E. Sjöqvist, and A. Westholm (1934). *The Swedish Cyprus Expedition: Finds and Results of the Excavations in Cyprus 1927–1931* (4 vols). Stockholm: Swedish Cyprus Expedition.

Goren, Y., S. Bunimovitz, I. Finkelstein, and N. Na'aman (2003). The location of Alashiya: new evidence from petrographic investigation of Alashiyan tablets from el-Amarna and Ugarit. *American Journal of Archaeology* 107: 233–55.

Goring, E. (1989). Death in everyday life: aspects of burial practices in the Late Bronze Age. In E. J. Peltenburg (ed.), *Early Society in Cyprus.* Edinburgh: Edinburgh University Press, 95–105.

Hadjisavvas, S. (2001). Crete and Cyprus: religion and script—The case of Alassa. In *Kreta und Zypern: Religion und Schrift*. Weilheim: Verein zur Förderung der Aufarbeitung der Hellenischen Geschichte, 205–31.

Iacovou, M. (1988). *The Pictorial Pottery of Eleventh Century B.C. Cyprus*. Gothenburg: Åströms.

—— (1989). Society and settlements in Late Cypriot III. In E. Peltenburg (ed.), *Early Society in Cyprus*. Edinburgh: Edinburgh University Press, 52–9.

—— (1994). The topography of eleventh century B.C. Cyprus. In V. Karageorghis (ed.), *Cyprus in the 11th Century B.C.: Proceedings of the International Symposium*. Nicosia: A. G. Leventis Foundation/University of Cyprus, 149–65.

—— (ed.) (2004). *Archaeological Field Survey in Cyprus: Past History, Future Potentials*. London: British School at Athens.

Johnstone, W. (1971). A Late Bronze Age Tholos tomb at Enkomi. In C. F.-A. Schaeffer (ed.) *Alasia I*. Paris: Klincksieck, 51–122.

Karageorghis, V. (1990). *The End of the Late Bronze Age in Cyprus*. Nicosia: Pierides Foundation

—— (1998). Hearths and bathtubs in Cyprus: a 'Sea Peoples' innovation? In S. Gitin, A. Mazar, and E. Stein (eds), *Mediterranean Peoples in Transition: Thirteenth to Early Tenth Century BCE*. Jerusalem: Israel Exploration Society, 276–82.

—— and M. V. Demas (1984). *Pyla-Kokkinokremos: A Late 13th-Century BC Fortified Settlement in Cyprus*. Nicosia: Department of Antiquities.

—— (1985). *Excavations at Kition 5/1: The Pre-Phoenician Levels, Areas I and II*. Nicosia: Department of Antiquities.

—— (1988). *Excavations at Maa-Palaeokastro 1979–1986* (2 vols). Nicosia: Department of Antiquities.

Keswani, P. S. (1989). Dimensions of social hierarchy in Late Bronze Age Cyprus: an analysis of the mortuary data from Enkomi. *Journal of Mediterranean Archaeology* 2: 49–86

—— (1992). Gas chromatography analyses of pithoi from Kalavasos-*Ayios Dhimitrios*: a preliminary report. *Reports of the Department of Antiquities, Cyprus*: 141–6.

—— (1993). Models of local exchange in Late Bronze Age Cyprus. *Bulletin of the American Schools of Oriental Research* 292: 73–83.

—— (1996). Hierarchies, heterarchies, and urbanization processes: the view from Bronze Age Cyprus. *Journal of Mediterranean Archaeology* 9: 211–49.

—— (2004). *Mortuary Ritual and Society in Bronze Age Cyprus*. London: Equinox.

—— (2005). Death, prestige, and copper in Bronze Age Cyprus. *American Journal of Archaeology* 109: 341–401.

—— and A. B. Knapp (2003). Bronze Age boundaries and social exchange in north-west Cyprus. *Oxford Journal of Archaeology* 22: 213–23.

Kling, B. (1989). *Mycenaean IIIC:1b and Related Pottery in Cyprus*. Gothenburg: Åströms.

—— and J. D. Muhly (eds) (2007). *Joan du Plat Taylor's Excavations at the Late Bronze Age Mining Settlement at Apliki Karamallos, Cyprus*. Sävedalen: Åströms.

Knapp, A. B. (1986). *Copper Production and Divine Protection: Archaeology, Ideology and Social Complexity on Bronze Age Cyprus*. Gothenburg: Åströms.

—— (1994). Emergence, development and decline on Bronze Age Cyprus. In C. Mathers and S. Stoddart (eds), *Development and Decline in the Mediterranean Bronze Age*. Sheffield: Collis, 221–304.

—— (ed.) (1996). *Near Eastern and Aegean Texts from the Third to the First Millennia BC*. Altamont, NY: Greece and Cyprus Research Centre.

—— (1997). *The Archaeology of Late Bronze Age Cypriot Society: The Study of Settlement, Survey and Landscape*. Glasgow: University of Glasgow, Department of Archaeology.

—— (2003). The archaeology of community on Bronze Age Cyprus: Politiko *Phorades* in context. *American Journal of Archaeology* 107: 559–80.

—— (2009). Monumental architecture, identity and memory. In *Bronze Age Architectural Traditions in the East Mediterranean: Diffusion and Diversity*. Weilheim: Verein zur Förderung der Aufarbeitung der Hellenischen Geschichte, 47–59.

—— and V. Kassianidou (2008). The archaeology of Late Bronze Age copper production: Politiko *Phorades* on Cyprus. *Anatolian Metal* 4: 135–47.

Maier, F. G. (1979). The Paphian shrine of Aphrodite and Crete. In *Acts of the International Archaeological Symposium The Relations Between Cyprus and Crete, ca. 2000–500 B.C.* Nicosia: Department of Antiquities, 228–35.

Manning, S. W., and S. Monks, with contributions by L. Steel, E. Ribeiro, and J. M. Weinstein. (1998). Late Cypriot Tombs at Maroni-*Tsaroukkas*, Cyprus. *Annual of the British School at Athens* 93: 297–351

—— B. Weninger, A. K. South, et al. (2001). Absolute age range of the Late Cypriot IIC period on Cyprus. *Antiquity* 75: 328–40.

Mee, C. B., and L. Steel (1998). *The Cypriote Collections in the University of Liverpool and the Williamson Art Gallery and Museum*. Jonsered: Åströms.

Merrillees, R. S. (1987). *Alashiya Revisted*. Paris: Gabalda.

—— (1992). The absolute chronology of the Bronze Age in Cyprus: a revision. *Bulletin of the American Schools of Oriental Research* 288: 47–52.

Murray, A. S., A. H. Smith, and H. B. Walters (1900). *Excavations in Cyprus (Bequest of Miss E. Turner to the British Museum)*. London: British Museum.

Niklasson-Sönnerby, K. (1987). Late Cypriote III shaft graves: burial customs of the last phase of the Bronze Age. In R. Laffineur (ed.), *Thanatos: les coutumes funéraires en Egée à l'Âge du bronze*. Liège: Université de l'État, Histoire d'art archéologie de la Grèce antique, 219–25.

Overbeck, J. C., and S. Swiny (1972). *Two Cypriot Bronze Age Sites at Kafkallia (Dhali)*. Gothenburg: Åströms.

Peltenburg, E. J. (1996). From isolation to state formation in Cyprus, c. 3500–1500 BC. In V. Karageorghis and D. Michaelides (eds), *The Development of the Cypriot Economy from the Prehistoric Period to the Present Day*. Nicosia: University of Cyprus and the Bank of Cyprus, 17–44.

Pilides, D. (1994). *Handmade Burnished Wares of the Late Bronze Age in Cyprus*. Jonsered: Åströms.

Schaeffer, C. F.-A. (1952). *Enkomi-Alasia: nouvelles missions en Chypre, 1946–1950*. Paris: Klincksieck.

Sherratt, E. S. (1991). Cypriot pottery of Aegean type in LC IIC–III: problems of classification, chronology and interpretation. In J. A. Barlow, D. R. Bolger, and B. Kling (eds), *Cypriot Ceramics: Reading the Prehistoric Record*. Philadelphia: University Museum of Archaeology and Anthropology, University of Pennsylvania, 185–98.

—— (1994). Commerce, iron and ideology: metallurgical innovation in 12th–11th century Cyprus. In V. Karageorghis (ed.), *Cyprus in the 11th Century B.C.: Proceedings of the International Symposium*. Nicosia: A. G. Leventis Foundation/University of Cyprus, 59–106.

Smith, J. (2002a). Problems and prospects in the study of script and seal use on Cyprus in the Bronze and Iron Ages. In J. S. Smith (ed.), *Script and Seal Use on Cyprus in the Bronze and Iron Ages*. Boston, Mass.: Archaeological Institute of America, 1–47

—— (2002b). Changes in the workplace: women and textile production on Late Bronze Age Cyprus. In D. R. Bolger and N. J. Serwint (eds), *Engendering Aphrodite: Women and Society in Ancient Cyprus*. Boston, Mass.: American Schools of Oriental Research, 281–312.

South, A. (1992). Kalavasos-*Ayios Dhimitrios* 1991. *Reports of the Department of Antiquities, Cyprus*: 133–40.

—— (2000). Late Bronze Age burials at Kalavasos-*Ayios Dhimitrios*. In G. Ioannides and S. A. Hadjistylli (eds), *Praktika tou Tritou Diethnous Kyprologikou Synedriou 1: Archaion Tmema*. Lefkosia: Society of Cypriot Studies, 345–64.

Steel, L. (1995). Differential burial practices in Cyprus at the transition from the Bronze Age to the Iron Age. In S. Campbell and A. Green (eds), *The Archaeology of Death in the Ancient Near East*. Oxford: Oxbow, 199–205.

—— (1998). The social impact of Mycenaean imported pottery in Cyprus. *Annual of the British School at Athens* 93: 285–96.

—— (2009). Exploring regional settlement on Cyprus in the Late Bronze Age: the rural hinterland. In I. Hein (ed.), *The Formation of Cyprus in the 2nd Millennium B.C.: Studies in Regionalism during the Middle and Late Bronze Ages*. Vienna: Österreichische Akademie der Wissenschaften, 134–45.

Taylor, J. du P. (1952). A Late Bronze Age settlement at Apliki, Cyprus. *Antiquaries Journal* 32: 133–67.

—— (1957). *Myrtou-Pigadhes: A Late Bronze Age Sanctuary in Cyprus*. London: Headley.

Todd, I. A., and D. Pilides (1993). Excavations at Sanidha 1992. *Reports of the Department of Antiquities, Cyprus*: 97–146.

Vermeule, E., and F. Z. Wolsky (1990). *Toumba tou Skourou: A Bronze Age Potter's Quarter on Morphou Bay in Cyprus*. Boston, Mass.: Harvard University/Museum of Fine Arts/Boston Cyprus Expedition.

Watrous, L. V. (1992). *Kommos III: The Late Bronze Age Pottery*. Princeton, NJ: Princeton University Press

Webb, J. M. (1999). *Ritual Architecture, Iconography and Practice in the Late Cypriot Bronze Age*. Jonsered: Åströms.

—— and D. Frankel (1994). Making an impression: storage and surplus finance in Late Bronze Age Cyprus. *Journal of Mediterranean Archaeology* 7: 5–26.

Weinburg, S. S. (1983). *Bamboula at Kourion: The Architecture*. Philadelphia: University Museum, University of Pennsylvania.

THE IRON
AGE I PERIOD

CHAPTER 39

···

INTRODUCTION TO THE LEVANT DURING THE TRANSITIONAL LATE BRONZE AGE/IRON AGE I AND IRON AGE I PERIODS

···

ANN E. KILLEBREW

The end of the Bronze Age (*c.*1200–1130 BCE) witnessed the demise of the Mycenaean palace system and the decline of the Late Bronze Age Hittite and Egyptian Empires, culminating in the collapse of the first 'Age of Internationalism' in the eastern Mediterranean. This Late Bronze 'golden age of heroes', romantically immortalized in the *Iliad*, is defined by economic, political, and cultural interconnectivity that was under the control of imperial networks and local royal palaces. Early scholarly treatments attributed the end of this era to a catastrophe or series of disasters—natural or man-made—that destroyed major Late Bronze Age centres. In this scenario, these destructions triggered migrations of displaced peoples, especially populations in the western Aegean. These groups, often referred to by the modern term 'Sea Peoples', were held responsible for the devastation of Late Bronze Age settlements further to the east that resulted in a 'dark age' lasting centuries (see e.g. Sandars 1978 and Wood 1996: 210–59 for overviews and bibliography)— a view that still prevails among some Aegeanists, particularly when dealing with the Levant. Recent studies reveal a far more complex network characterized by multidirectional cultural and socioeconomic interconnections that preceded and coincided with a more protracted demise of the Bronze Age that continued into the 12th century BCE (see e.g. Sherratt 2003; Maran 2004; Killebrew 2005a: 21–49; 2006–7; Artzy 2006a; Knapp 2008; Ben-Shlomo 2011; Hitchcock 2011, Sherratt, Ch. 33 above). Continuity, discontinuity, change, appropriation, diffusion, creolization, hybridity, transculturalism, interculturality, catastrophe, collapse, crisis, dislocation, migration, colonization, ethnogenesis, nucleation, reoccupation, abandonment, and a new term I have proposed, Levantinism (see Killebrew and Steiner, Introduction, above) are all descriptive terms that have been employed to characterize the instability and fluidity of the late 13th–11th centuries as evidenced in the archaeological record and reflected in the economic, political, and social structures of this period of time (see e.g. Ward and Joukowsky 1992; Drews 1993; Bachhuber and Roberts 2009).

To a large degree these multifaceted factors and influences still have not been adequately addressed in the academic literature (Killebrew 2010). The simplest hyper-diffusionist models that attempt to explain the transmission of cultural traits and practices via linear migration narratives continue to appear in recent publications on the topic (see e.g. Karageorghis 2002: 71–113; Dothan and Zukerman 2004; Mazar 2007; Yasur-Landau 2010). These west-to-east unidirectional notions of cultural purity and transmission are due in part to Eurocentric or Hellenocentric biases and western perceptions regarding the Levant that dominated scholarship in the 19th and 20th centuries (see e.g. Silberman 1998; Leriou 2002). This tendency has been abetted by the scant archaeological record for these periods in the underexplored regions of the eastern Mediterranean where large swathes of territory (e.g. the western coast of Asia Minor, Cilicia, and much of the northern Levant) remain *terra incognita* (see e.g. Lehmann 2008; Heinz and Kulemann-Ossen, Ch. 35 above, and Sader, Ch. 40 below). In the more extensively excavated and surveyed regions of Cyprus and the southern Levant, the complexity of the transitional Late Bronze/Iron I and the cultural regionalism of the Iron I Levant that demonstrate both continuity and change are incontrovertible. The archaeological evidence, as presented in the chapters below, illustrates the complexity of the 12th and 11th centuries BCE during which individual sites or regions and their populations experienced very different fates. Although research traditions and agendas vary, often based on a scholar's nationality or on modern political borders, the chapters below do share many common themes. In this introduction to the Iron I Levant, I highlight several interconnected topics addressed in the chapters below that are key to our understanding of this transformative period and are promising venues for future research.[1] Broadly speaking, these include settlement patterns, cultural regionalism, mechanisms of cultural transmission and contact, and the restructuring of social, political, and economic life on the local, regional, and supraregional levels (regarding key issues relating to chronology, see Sharon, Ch. 4 above).

SETTLEMENT PATTERNS, REGIONALISM, AND CULTURAL TRANSMISSION

Among the most distinguishing features of the 12th and 11th centuries BCE are the changes experienced in the demographic and material culture landscape. In contrast to the largely homogeneous material culture of the Levantine Late Bronze Age, the Iron I is characterized by cultural fragmentation and a variety of regionally defined settlement patterns and social, economic, and cultural boundaries (see e.g. Killebrew 2005b). Iron I cultural fragmentation tends to split along the Levant's diverse and well-defined geographical boundaries, a feature that doubtlessly played a major role in the region's history and cultural development. The natural tendency towards political, economic, and cultural regionalism was tempered by Mediterranean connectivity. Fragmentation was overridden only during periods when external empires and foreign imperialism succeeded in superimposing an

---

[1] Due to intense scholarly scrutiny and interest in the transitional Late Bronze/Iron I and Iron I periods, I am including an especially extensive and inclusive bibliography at the end of this introduction, which represents the wide range of approaches and interpretations of this transformative period of time as well as the most recent relevant archaeological discoveries in the Levant.

artificial political, economic, and cultural unity that temporarily conquered these natural boundaries. A case in point is the Late Bronze II period, during which the Levant experienced a *c*.200-year period of integration into 'global' economic and imperial political structures. However, this incorporation into larger world systems quickly splintered once again along the Levant's geographically defined fault lines during the subsequent early Iron Age following the collapse of the great Late Bronze Age empires and their networks.

The Levantine mainland and Cypriot coastal regions

Decentralized polities, or independent city-states that often were a continuation of settlement on sites previously occupied during the Late Bronze Age, characterized settlements along the coast and fertile valleys of the Iron I mainland Levant and Cyprus. These regions and their materialized hubs, which had played a key role in international maritime trade during the Late Bronze Age, were now freed from imperial control and exploitation to develop locally controlled and entrepreneurially driven networks. Those sites that survived the upheaval or were newly established in the Iron I generally experienced a period of relative prosperity (see Sader, Gilboa, and Iacovou, Chs 40, 41, and 43 below). Settlement patterns and the archaeological record along the northern Levantine coast remain less explored and documented than coastal regions to the south (see Sader, Ch. 40 below). What is emerging illustrates the complexity of this period, and the inadvisability of monolithic, meganarratives that mask the diversity of these local sequences. In the northernmost regions of the Levant, devastation (e.g. Ugarit), continuity (e.g. Ras el-Bassit), and the introduction of new material culture traits (e.g. Tell Kazel and Ras Ibn Hani) appear in the scant archaeological record. [2] A similar mixture of destruction, continuity, and change is beginning to emerge in Cilicia, including the Bay of İskenderun, and 'Amuq regions in present-day Turkey (see e.g. Gates 2010; Harrison 2010; Janeway 2011).

Farther south, along the Iron Age Phoenician coast, many Late Bronze Age centres survived without experiencing destruction (see Sader and Gilboa, Chs 40 and 41 below). The Iron I material culture of sites such as Tyre, Akko, and Tel Dor continue local Late Bronze Age ('Canaanite') traditions, with the appearance in relatively small quantities of Aegean- and Cypriot-style wares. Although the majority of settlements in the northern (north Syria) and central (Phoenicia) coastal regions continue indigenous Late Bronze Age traditions, excavations at several sites have uncovered Aegean-style material culture, either locally produced (e.g. Mycenaean IIIC wares at Sarepta) or smaller quantities of vessels that were

---

[2] The distinct regionalism and individuality of each site's development during this period of time is evident by the variety of Iron I assemblages. For example Aegean-style pottery and other artefacts similar to Late Cypriot IIIA styles appear at Ras Ibn Hani, a coastal site that served as the major port during the Iron I, replacing the destroyed city of Ugarit (du Piêd 2006–7). At nearby Tell Kazel, located along the northern coast of Syria, provenience studies show that Late Bronze II Mycenaean pottery was imported from the Greek mainland. These Greek imports cease near the end of the Bronze Age, to be replaced with locally produced Aegean-style wares (Badre et al. 2005). It is also noteworthy that locally produced Aegean-style pottery from Tell Kazel differs significantly from Cypriot and other Levantine Aegean-style assemblages (Jung 2011). In addition to the Aegean-style wares, other new pottery groups appear in the archaeological record at this time. These include Handmade Burnished Ware, uncovered at Tell Kazel and other Levantine and Cypriot sites, and/or talc ('steatite') fabric cooking pots from Ras Ibn Hani, Tell Tweini, and other north Syrian sites (see most recently Vansteenhuyse 2010 and du Piêd 2011).

imported from Cyprus or other areas of the eastern Aegean (Killebrew 1998; Koehl and Yellin 2007 for provenience studies on 'Simple Style' and other late Mycenaean III wares; Mazar 2007; Mountjoy 2011; Sader and Gilboa, Chs 40 and 41 below).

In the southern coastal plain of Israel and its neighbouring areas, the transitional Late Bronze/Iron I and early Iron I sites experience a variety of fates. Some sites are destroyed and resettled, either immediately or only after several decades by urban centres that are defined by their Aegean-style features (e.g. Ashdod and Ekron). A number of sites continued to serve as Egyptian administrative centres well into the 12th century BCE (e.g. Deir el-Balah, Tell el-Far'ah South, and Aphek; Killebrew 2005a: 51–92). Simultaneously, Late Bronze Age ceramic traditions continue at other 12th-century sites in the southern coastal region and neighbouring Shephelah (e.g. Tel Yarmouth (Jasmin 2006) and Beth Shemesh (Bunimovitz and Lederman 2011)).

With the decline and gradual retreat of 20th Dynasty Egypt from the southern Levant, the resulting power vacuum in the southern coastal plain witnessed the appearance of several fully developed large urban centres. Excavations at these revitalized cities constructed on Late Bronze Age settlements reveal a different settlement plan and a new Aegean-style material culture that dominates the cultural repertoire. The scholarly consensus today is that the sheer volume and suddenness of the appearance of significant quantities of Aegean-style pottery herald the arrival of new populations, known from New Kingdom Egyptian and biblical sources as the Peleset/Philistines (Killebrew 2005a: 197–245 for an overview; Gilboa, Ch. 41 below).

The earliest settlements are identified by the appearance of large quantities of Aegean-style material culture, especially Mycenaean IIIC middle/Monochrome Ware/Philistine 1 pottery, at Ekron, Gath, Ashdod, Ashkelon, and (most likely) Gaza—all sites that are named in the biblical account as key Philistines cities (Joshua 13:2–3). The early Philistine pottery and other aspects of their material culture demonstrate close stylistic parallels to Aegean-style assemblages on Cyprus (White Painted Wheelmade III pottery, bathtubs, hearths, incised scapulae, etc.) and at several sites in Cilicia, hinting at close ties between these three regions during the early 12th century (see e.g. Killebrew 2000; 2006–7; Gilboa, Ch. 41 below; Mountjoy 2013). More detailed studies that include the discoveries from recent excavations in Iron I levels at Ashkelon and Gath (Tel Zafit) are beginning to reveal variations even within the Philistine 1 material culture assemblages in the southern coastal plain, hinting at the diversity and mixed origins of the Philistine population groups at the different sites in Philistia (see e.g. Mountjoy 2010). Philistine influence spread during the 11th century, as testified by the expansion of Philistine material culture, most notably bichrome Philistine pottery, to surrounding sites in the southern coastal plain (see e.g. Dothan 1982; Ben-Shlomo 2010 for a stylistic analysis of Iron I and II Philistine iconography).

The archaeological evidence for Cyprus demonstrates both continuity and change, a situation indicated by the chronological terminology Late Cypriot IIIA and IIIB, approximately corresponding to the Iron I period on the mainland Levant. Some settlements are destroyed, others continue, and new settlements are established. The major 12th-century sites at Enkomi, Hala Sultan Tekke, Kition, and Paphos weathered the disintegration of the great empires, with urbanism, state functions, and copper production remaining intact (see Steel, Ch. 38 above, and Iacovou, Ch. 43 below). Aegean influence was already evident in the 14th and 13th centuries with the appearance of Mycenaean pottery, which was initially imported, and was later gradually replaced with locally produced Mycenaean-style pottery.

This process of Aegeanization continued during the 12th century, with the appearance of White Painted Wheelmade III pottery (also referred to as Mycenaean IIIC) and other Aegean-inspired wares (see Steel, Ch. 38 above). The resulting Aegean-style material culture incorporates Cypriot, Levantine, and both east and west Aegean components, a blending of cultural features which has been termed 'creolization' or 'hybridization' (Webster 2001; van Dommelen 2006; Stockhammer 2012). Interpretations differ regarding the significance of the prevalence of Aegean-style material on 12th-century Cyprus. These include large-scale migration and colonization to more nuanced processes of interaction that take into consideration external and internal stimuli such as long-term economic migration, creolization, hybridization and transculturalism, which would typify diverse urban populations (see e.g. Iacovou 2008; Iacovou, Chs 43 and 53 below; Knapp 2008: 249–97; Voskos and Knapp 2008 for recent discussions of the various views).

Inland regions

In contrast to coastal areas, where urban settlements often survived the transitional Late Bronze/Iron I, the archaeological evidence from inland regions points to a subsistence-level rural economy, especially during the 12th century. In the northern Levant, where only limited excavations have been conducted, many settlements in interior regions are modest agricultural villages or the remains of squatters who reoccupied Late Bronze Age sites. Iron I material culture is for the most part a continuation of Late Bronze Age traditions (see Sader, Ch. 40 below). Tell Afis, identified as Aramean Hazrek, represents the most complete Late Bronze–Iron I stratigraphic sequence in the northern Levant. As one of the most impressive mounds in the district of Idlib, it serves as a key type-site for the region. At Afis, the early Iron I occupation is characterized by domestic structures and a large degree of continuity with the earlier Late Bronze Age; however, several new cultural features appear in the Iron I. These include modest quantities of Iron I Aegean-style pottery and cylindrical loom weights (Venturi 2010; Cecchini 2011). By the 11th century, evidence exists for the beginnings of reurbanization, especially at Tell Afis, Aleppo, and 'Ain Dara, where monumental architecture makes an appearance. Further to the east, major Hittite sites such as Karkemish continue to play a major, albeit diminished, role (see Sader 2010; Ch. 40 below).

The interior regions of the southern Levant are more extensively documented. Small agricultural villages populate the hill country of Cisjordan. These rural settlements, often single-period sites, increase in number over time (see Gilboa, Ch. 41 below). This Iron I cultural landscape displays both continuity (e.g. aspects of the material culture) and discontinuity (e.g. demographic and settlement patterns). The evidence suggests that Iron I hill-country peoples are for the most part indigenous, but include the small numbers of newcomers and possibly the introduction of new ideologies. Considered together with the Merneptah Stela and the biblical account, this demographic shift and subsistence-level settlements have led many scholars to associate these highland villages and their inhabitants with the emergence and ethnogenesis of ancient Israel (see e.g. Dever 2003; Killebrew 2006; Faust 2006 and bibliography therein).

To the east of the Jordan River, settlement types and patterns vary according to geographic region. In the fertile Jordan Valley, sites situated on the valley floor on both sides of the river tend to be larger and more prosperous, and often continue Late Bronze Age occupation. In the highland regions, settlement patterns were uneven, with fewer Iron I sites in the more arid southern sections (for a recent overview, see van der Steen 2004). The transitional Late Bronze/Iron I period is especially well represented in the northern and central plateau regions. Although the archaeological evidence for Transjordan differs somewhat from Cisjordan, there are aspects of the material culture, such as pottery assemblages, that do demonstrate close ties between the two regions (see Herr, Ch. 42 below; regarding the ceramic assemblages, see Routledge 2008 and Steiner forthcoming). The two best-documented regions are Ammon and Moab, where recent excavations have revealed that Iron I highland sites in Jordan are often fortified, in contrast to the more modest and unwalled hamlets on the western side of the Jordan River. These large Transjordanian Iron I villages are typically protected by a casemate wall with a ring of pillared buildings. Most of these settlements were short-lived, either destroyed during the Iron I (e.g. Tall al-'Umayri) or abandoned (e.g. Khirbat al-Mudayna al-'Aliya). The majority of these sites lacked clear stratigraphic continuity between the transitional LB/Iron I and Iron I periods. One key exception is 'Umayri, which was occupied during the Late Bronze and transition to the early Iron I Age (see Herr, Ch. 42 below). As was the case in Cisjordan, the number of settlements and sedentary population in the Transjordanian highlands gradually increased over the course of the Iron I and into the Iron II period (see e.g. Routledge 2004; 2008; van der Steen 2004; Levy 2009).

ECONOMIC, POLITICAL, AND SOCIAL STRUCTURES

The disintegration of the great Late Bronze Age empires profoundly transformed the Iron I economic, political, and social landscapes of the Levant, as described in the following chapters. The restructuring of political systems and commercial activities from centralized palace- or elite-controlled networks to a period of increased political and economic autonomy represents a key factor in the transition from the Late Bronze to Iron Age.[3] The more archaeologically visible exchange of high-value gifts, prestige items, and tribute together with the exchange of peoples including slaves, craft specialists, and women that defined and cemented Late Bronze networks, shifted to mercantile activities dominated by entrepreneurial private agents and economic mercenaries or hirelings who also engaged in itinerant peddling (see e.g. Liverani 1987; Artzy 1997; Klengel 2000). These latter activities that define Iron I commercial interactions are less easily identified in the archaeological record, giving rise to the erroneous conclusion that regional systems of trade and communications ceased with the demise of the great imperial networks—a misconception now belied by evidence from recent excavations. A closer examination of the material culture suggests the creation of more circumscribed regional markets for new types of goods. These include the exchange of commodities in utilitarian Canaanite and

---

[3] However, one needs to acknowledge additional factors and agents involved in Late Bronze Age trade networks and the dissemination of goods, technology, and transmission of style or ideologies. See e.g. Manning and Hulin (2005) and Gates (2011) for a discussion of these less explored features of Late Bronze economic systems.

Phoenician commercial containers produced in various locations, Cypro-Geometric I wares, and Egyptian pottery found at Iron I sites along the Levantine coast. Limited exchange networks linked the coast, valleys, and highlands in the southern Levant, as revealed by interregional transport of massive collar-rim pithoi. These objects testify to modest interregional contacts and commercial ties. By the end of the Iron I period, evidence exists for expanded trade contacts that included Greece and Anatolia (see Gilboa, Ch. 41 below).

The circulation of copper and tin, the constituents of bronze, played a key role in Late Bronze Age high-level exchange systems (see e.g. Sherratt 2000). Coinciding with the end of the Late Bronze Age and Iron I periods, numerous bronze hoards have been recovered from Cyprus and the Levantine mainland (see Artzy 2006b for a detailed discussion of these hoards). These discoveries testify to the continuation of trade in metal and economic ties between the island, Phoenicia, and the copper-producing sites in the Arabah Valley, south of the Dead Sea (see Ben-Yosef et al. 2010 regarding Iron I copper production at Faynan, the largest copper ore deposit in the southern Levant). A typical feature of the Iron I is the increase in scrap metal and evidence of recycling, which probably signifies less formal modes of commercial exchange during this period. Coinciding with these changes, new metallurgical technologies resulted in the gradual increase in production of objects fashioned out of iron (see e.g. Sherratt 1994; 2003; Iacovou, Ch. 43 below regarding the evidence on Cyprus).

Decentralization is also reflected in the political restructuring that transpired during the Iron I period. Major coastal settlements and their associated hinterland were now freed of imperial exploitation and no longer a component of a cosmopolitan Late Bronze Age world system. These more independent city-states continued to dominate the coastal political landscape well into the later Iron Age (see e.g. Gilboa and Iacovou, Chs 41 and 43 below). In interior regions, rural agropastoral settlements of varying size characterize the highlands. The agrarian features and 'four-room houses' that typify the architecture of these villages have often been interpreted as representing decentralized egalitarian patrilineal households organized along kinship lines (see e.g. Stager 1985; Schloen 2001) and reflect a highly 'egalitarian ethos' (Faust 2006: 92–107). Others have challenged this reconstruction, proposing that a correlation exists between the size/prominence of a domestic complex and household wealth (Routledge 2008: 170–3; see also London 1989). Diversity is also reflected in the faunal record and Iron I animal economies. These differences reflect the variety of ecological and social strategies used by communities to adapt to their environments (Lev-Tov, Porter, and Routledge 2011). As noted above, variations and evidence for inequalities appear to be more pronounced in Transjordan, suggesting that early Iron Age rural settlements were not as egalitarian, stable, or autochthonous as presented in earlier studies (see e.g. Routledge 2009; Herr, Ch. 42 below).

The 12th and 11th centuries BCE, often depicted both by the ancients and modern scholars as a 'dark age', represent the transition from an interconnected 'globalized' world-systems network to more 'localized' and fragmented political, economic, and social landscapes. In the material culture record, continuity and change coexist alongside the winners and losers of this 'Age of Transformations'. Out of the ruins of the Bronze Age, the survivors developed their own local Iron I traditions that formed the foundations of the classical and biblical worlds of the later Iron Age and beyond. Archaeology continues to play a critical role in our understanding of this pivotal period of human history.

Suggested reading

Bunnens, G. (ed.) (2000). *Essays on Syria in the Iron Age*. Leuven: Peeters.

Dever, W. G. (2003). *Who Were the Israelites and Where Did They Come From?* Grand Rapids, Mich.: Eerdmans.

Gitin, S., A. Mazar, and E. Stern (eds) (1998). *Mediterranean Peoples in Transition: Thirteenth to Early Tenth Centuries BCE*. Jerusalem: Israel Exploration Society.

Grabbe, L. L. (ed.) (2008). *Israel in Transition: From Late Bronze II to Iron IIA (c. 1250–850 B.C.E.)*, vol. 1: *The Archaeology*. London: T. & T. Clark.

Killebrew, A. E. (2005a). *Biblical Peoples and Ethnicity: An Archaeological Study of Egyptians, Canaanites, Philistines, and Early Israel, 1300–1100 B.C.E.* Atlanta, Ga.: Society of Biblical Literature.

—— and G. Lehmann (eds) (2013). *The Philistines and Other "Sea Peoples" in Text and Archaeology*. Atlanta, Ga.: Society of Biblical Literature.

Knapp, A. B. (2008). *Prehistoric and Protohistoric Cyprus: Identity, Insularity, and Connectivity*. Oxford: Oxford University Press.

Liverani, M. (1987). The collapse of the Near Eastern regional system at the end of the Late Bronze Age: the case of Syria. In M. J. Rowlands, M. T. Larsen, and K. Kristiansen (eds), *Centre and Periphery in the Ancient World*. Cambridge: Cambridge University Press, 66–73.

Venturi, F. (ed.) (2010). *Societies in Transition: Evolutionary Processes in the Northern Levant between Late Bronze Age II and Early Iron Age*. Bologna: CLUEB.

Ward, W. A., and M. S. Joukowsky (eds) (1992). *The Crisis Years: The 12th Century B.C. from Beyond the Danube to the Tigris*. Dubuque, Ia.: Kendall/Hunt.

References

Artzy, M. (1997). Nomads of the sea. In S. Swiny, R. L. Hohlfelder, and H. W. Swiny (eds), *Res Maritimae: Cyprus and the Eastern Mediterranean from Prehistory to Late Antiquity*. Atlanta, Ga.: Scholars, 1–15.

—— (2006a). The Carmel coast during the second part of the Late Bronze Age: a center for eastern Mediterranean transshipping. *Bulletin of the American Schools of Oriental Research* 343: 45–64.

—— (2006b). *The Jatt Metal Hoard in Northern Canaanite/Phoenician and Cypriote Context*. Barcelona: Laboratorio de arqueología, Universidad Pompeu Fabra.

Bachhuber, C., and R. G. Roberts (eds) (2009). *Forces of Transformation: The End of the Bronze Age in the Mediterranean*. Oxford: Oxbow.

Badre, L., M.-C. Boileau, R. Jung, and H. Mommsen (2005). The provenance of Aegean- and Syrian-type pottery found at Tell Kazel (Syria). *Ägypten und Levante* 15: 15–47.

Ben-Shlomo, D. (2010). *Philistine Iconography: A Wealth of Style and Symbolism*. Fribourg: Academic/Göttingen: Vandenhoeck & Ruprecht.

——(2011). Early Iron Age domestic material culture in Philistia and an eastern Mediterranean *koiné*. In A. Yasur-Landau, J. R. Ebeling, and L. B. Mazow (eds), *Household Archaeology in Ancient Israel and Beyond*. Leiden: Brill, 183–206.

Ben-Yosef, E., T. E. Levy, T. Higham, M. Najjar, and L. Tauxe (2010). The beginning of Iron Age copper production in the southern Levant: new evidence from Khirbat al-Jariya, Faynan, Jordan. *Antiquity* 84: 724–46.

Bunimovitz, S., and Z. Lederman (2011). Canaanite resistance: the Philistines and Beth-Shemesh—A case study from Iron Age I. *Bulletin of the American Schools of Oriental Research* 364: 37–51.

Cecchini, S. M. (2011). Loomweights and the textile industry in north Syria in the Early Iron Age. In V. Karageorghis and O. Kouka (eds), *On Cooking Pots, Drinking Cups, Loomweights and Ethnicity in Bronze Age Cyprus and Neighbouring Regions: An International Archaeological Symposium Held in Nicosia, November 6th–7th 2010*. Nicosia: A. G. Leventis Foundation, 195–202.

Dever, W. G. (2003). *Who Were the Israelites and Where Did They Come From?* Grand Rapids, Mich.: Eerdmans.

Dothan, T. (1982). *The Philistines and Their Material Culture*, rev. and trans. New Haven, Conn.: Yale University Press.

——and A. Zukerman (2004). A preliminary study of the Mycenaean IIIC:1 pottery assemblages from Tel Miqne-Ekron and Ashdod. *Bulletin of the American Schools of Oriental Research* 333: 1–54.

Drews, R. (1993). *The End of the Bronze Age: Changes in Warfare and the Catastrophe ca. 1200 B.C.* Princeton, NJ: Princeton University Press.

du Piêd, L. (2006–7). The Early Iron Age in the northern Levant: continuity and change in the pottery assemblages from Ras el-Bassit and Ras Ibn Hani. *Scripta Mediterranea* 27–8: 161–85.

——(2011). Early Iron Age society in the northern Levant: architecture, pottery and finds. In V. Karageorghis and O. Kouka (eds), *On Cooking Pots, Drinking Cups, Loomweights and Ethnicity in Bronze Age Cyprus and Neighbouring Regions: An International Archaeological Symposium Held in Nicosia, November 6th–7th 2010*. Nicosia: A. G. Leventis Foundation, 219–36.

Faust, A. (2006). *Israel's Ethnogenesis: Settlement, Interaction, Expansion and Resistance*. London: Equinox.

Gates, M.-H. (2010). Potters and consumers in Cilicia and the Amuq during the 'Age of Transformations' (13th–10th centuries BC). In F. Venturi (ed.), *Societies in Transition: Evolutionary Processes in the Northern Levant between Late Bronze II and Early Iron Age*. Bologna: CLUEB, 65–81.

——(2011). Maritime business in the Bronze Age eastern Mediterranean: the view from its ports. In K. Duistermaat and I. Regulski (eds), *Intercultural Contacts in the Ancient Mediterranean: Proceedings of the International Conference at the Netherlands–Flemish Institute in Cairo, 25th to 29th October 2008*. Leuven: Peeters, 381–93.

Harrison, T. P. (2010). The Late Bronze/Early Iron Age Transition in the North Orontes Valley. In F. Venturi (ed.), *Societies in Transition: Evolutionary Processes in the Northern Levant between Late Bronze Age II and Early Iron Age*. Bologna: CLUEB, 83–102.

Hitchcock, L. A. (2011). 'Transculturalism' as a model for examining migration to Cyprus and Philistia at the end of the Bronze Age. *Ancient West and East* 10: 267–80.

Iacovou, M. (2008). Cultural and political configurations in Iron Age Cyprus: the sequel to a protohistoric episode. *American Journal of Archaeology* 112: 625–57.

Janeway, B. (2011). Mycenaean bowls at 12th/11th century BC Tell Tayinat (Amuq Valley). In V. Karageorghis and O. Kouka (eds), *On Cooking Pots, Drinking Cups, Loomweights and Ethnicity in Bronze Age Cyprus and Neighbouring Regions: An International Archaeological Symposium Held in Nicosia, November 6th–7th 2010*. Nicosia: A. G. Leventis Foundation, 167–85.

Jasmin, M. (2006). *L'Étude de la transition du Bronze récent II au Fer I en Palestine méridionale*. Oxford: Archaeopress.

Jung, R. (2011). Mycenaean vending cups in Syria? Thoughts about the unpainted Mycenaean pottery from Tell Kazel. In W. Gauss, M. Lindblom, R. A. K. Smith, and J. C. Wright (eds),

Our Cups Are Full: Pottery and Society in the Aegean Bronze Age. Oxford: Archaeopress, 121–32.

Karageorghis, V. (2002). *Early Cyprus: Crossroads of the Mediterranean*. Los Angeles, Calif.: J. Paul Getty Museum.

Killebrew, A. E. (1998). Aegean and Aegean-style material culture: diffusion or migration? In E. H. Cline and D. Harris-Cline (eds), *The Aegean and the Orient in the Second Millennium: Proceedings of the 50th Anniversary Symposium, Cincinnati, 18–20 April 1997*. Liège: Histoire de l'art et archéologie de la Grèce antique, Université de Liège/Austin: Program in Aegean Scripts and Prehistory, University of Texas at Austin, 159–70.

—— (2000). Aegean-style early Philistine pottery in Canaan during the Iron I Age: a stylistic analysis of Mycenaean IIIC:1b pottery and its associated wares. In E. D. Oren (ed.), *The Sea Peoples and Their World: A Reassessment*. Philadelphia: University Museum, University of Pennsylvania, 233–53.

—— (2005a). *Biblical Peoples and Ethnicity: An Archaeological Study of Egyptians, Canaanites, Philistines, and Early Israel 1300–1100 B.C.E.* Atlanta, Ga.: Society of Biblical Literature.

—— (2005b). Cultural homogenisation and diversity in Canaan during the 13th and 12th centuries BC. In J. Clarke (ed.), *Archaeological Perspectives on the Transmission and Transformation of Culture in the Eastern Mediterranean*. Oxford: Oxbow, 170–5.

—— (2006). The emergence of ancient Israel: the social boundaries of a 'mixed multitude' in Canaan. In A. M. Maeir and P. de Miroschedji, '*I Will Speak the Riddles of Ancient Times*': *Archaeological and Historical Studies in Honor of Amihai Mazar on the Occasion of His Sixtieth Birthday*, vol. 2. Winona Lake, Ind.: Eisenbrauns, 555–72.

—— (2006–7). The Philistines in context: the transmission and appropriation of Mycenaean-style culture in the east Aegean, southeastern coastal Anatolia and the Levant. *Scripta Mediterranea* 27–8: 245–66.

—— (2010). The Philistines and their material culture in context: future directions of historical biblical archaeology for the study of cultural transmission. In T. E. Levy (ed.), *Historical Biblical Archaeology and the Future: The New Pragmatism*. London: Equinox, 156–67.

Klengel, H. (2000). The 'crisis years' and the new political system in Early Iron Age Syria: some introductory remarks. In G. Bunnens (ed.), *Essays on Syria in the Iron Age*. Leuven: Peeters, 21–30.

Knapp, A. B. (2008). *Prehistoric and Protohistoric Cyprus: Identity, Insularity, and Connectivity*. Oxford: Oxford University Press.

Koehl, R. B., and J. Yellin (2007). What Aegean 'simple style' pottery reveals about interconnections in the 13th-century eastern Mediterranean. In P. Betancourt, M. C. Nelson, and H. Williams (eds), *Krinoi kai Limenes: Studies in Honor of Joseph and Maria Shaw*. Philadelphia: INSTAP Academic, 199–207.

Lehmann, G. (2008). North Syria and Cilicia, c. 1200–330 BCE. In C. Sagona (ed.), *Beyond the Homeland: Markers in Phoenician Chronology*. Leuven: Peeters, 205–46.

Leriou, N. (Anastasia) (2002). Constructing an archaeological narrative: the Hellenization of Cyprus. *Stanford Journal of Archaeology* 1, Internet Edition. http://www.stanford.edu/dept/archaeology/journal/newdraft/leriou/paper.pdf (accessed 15 Dec. 2011).

Lev-Tov, J. S. E., B. W. Porter, and B. E. Routledge (2011). Measuring local diversity in Early Iron Age animal economies: a view from Khirbat al-Mudayna al-'Aliya (Jordan). *Bulletin of the American Schools of Oriental Research* 361: 67–93.

Levy, T. E. (2009). Pastoral nomads and Iron Age metal production in ancient Edom. In J. Szuchman (ed.), *Nomads, Tribes and the State in the Ancient Near East: Cross-Disciplinary Perspectives*. Chicago: Oriental Institute of the University of Chicago, 147–77.

Liverani, M. (1987). The collapse of the Near Eastern regional system at the end of the Late Bronze Age: the case of Syria. In M. J. Rowlands, M. T. Larsen, and K. Kristiansen (eds), *Centre and Periphery in the Ancient World*. Cambridge: Cambridge University Press, 66–73.

London, G. (1989). A comparison of two contemporaneous lifestyles of the late second millennium B.C. *Bulletin of the American Schools of Oriental Research* 273: 37–55.

Manning, S. W., and L. Hulin (2005). Maritime commerce and geographies of mobility in the Late Bronze Age of the eastern Mediterranean: problematizations. In E. Blake and A. B. Knapp (eds), *The Archaeology of Mediterranean Prehistory*. Malden, Mass.: Blackwell, 270–302.

Maran, J. (2004). The spreading of objects and ideas in the Late Bronze Age eastern Mediterranean: two case examples from the Argolid of the 13th and 12th Centuries B.C. *Bulletin of the American Schools of Oriental Research* 336: 11–30.

Mazar, A. (2007). Myc IIIC in the Land of Israel: its distribution, date and significance. In M. Bietak and E. Czerny (eds), *The Synchronisation of Civilisations in the Eastern Mediterranean in the Second Millennium B.C. III: Proceedings of the SCIEM 2000—2nd EuroConference, Vienna, 28th of May–1st of June 2003*. Vienna: Österreichische Akademie der Wissenschaften, 571–82.

Mountjoy, P. (2010). A note on the mixed origins of some Philistine pottery. *Bulletin of the American Schools of Oriental Research* 359: 1–12.

—— (2011). An update on the provenance by neutron activation analysis of Near Eastern Mycenaean IIIC pottery groups with particular reference to Cyprus. In W. Gauss, M. Lindblom, R. A. K. Smith, and J. C. Wright (eds), *Our Cups Are Full: Pottery and Society in the Aegean Bronze Age*. Archaeopress: Oxford, 179–86.

—— (2013). The Mycenaean IIIC pottery of Tel Miqne-Ekron. In A. E. Killebrew and G. Lehmann (eds), *The Philistines and Other "Sea Peoples" in Text and Archaeology*. Atlanta, Ga.: Society of Biblical Literature, 53–75.

Routledge, B. E. (2004). *Moab in the Iron Age: Hegemony, Polity, Archaeology*. Philadelphia: University of Pennsylvania Press.

—— (2008). Thinking 'globally' and analysing 'locally': south-central Jordan in transition. In L. L. Grabbe (ed.), *Israel in Transition: From Late Bronze II to Iron IIA (c. 1250–850 BCE)*, vol. 1: *The Archaeology*. London: T. & T. Clark, 144–76.

—— (2009). Average families? House size variability in the southern Levantine Iron Age. In P. Dutcher-Walls (ed.), *The Family in Life and in Death: The Family in Ancient Israel— Sociological and Archaeological Perspectives*. New York: T&T Clark, 42–60.

Sader, H. (2010). The Aramaeans of Syria: some considerations on their origin and material culture. In A. Lemarie and B. Halpern (eds), *The Books of Kings: Sources, Composition, Historiography and Reception*. Leiden: Brill, 273–300.

Sandars, N. K. (1978). *The Sea Peoples: Warriors of the Ancient Mediterranean, 1250–1150 B.C.* London: Thames & Hudson.

Schloen, J. D. (2001). *The House of the Father as Fact and Symbol: Patrimonialism in Ugarit and the Ancient Near East*. Winona Lake, Ind.: Eisenbrauns.

Sherratt, E. S. (1994). Commerce, iron and ideology: metallurgical innovation in 12th–11th century Cyprus. In V. Karageorghis (ed.), *Cyprus in the 11th Century B.C.: Proceedings of the International Symposium*. Nicosia: A. G. Leventis Foundation, 59–108.

—— (2000). Circulation of metals and the end of the Bronze Age in the eastern Mediterranean. In C. F. E. Pare (ed.), *Metals Make the World Go Round: Supply and Circulation of Metals in Bronze Age Europe*. Oxford: Oxbow, 82–98.

—— (2003). The Mediterranean economy: 'globalization' at the end of the second millennium B.C.E. In W. G. Dever and S. Gitin (eds), *Symbiosis, Symbolism, and the Power of the Past:*

Canaan, Ancient Israel, and Their Neighbors from the Late Bronze Age through Roman Palaestina. Winona Lake, Ind.: Eisenbrauns, 37–62.

Silberman, N. A. (1998). The Sea Peoples, the Victorians, and us: modern social ideology and changing archaeological interpretation of the Late Bronze Age collapse. In S. Gitin, A. Mazar, and E. Stern (eds), *Mediterranean Peoples in Transition: Thirteenth to Early Tenth Centuries BCE in Honor of Professor Trude Dothan.* Jerusalem: Israel Exploration Society, 268–75.

Stager, L. E. (1985). The archaeology of the family in ancient Israel. *Bulletin of the American Schools of Oriental Research* 260: 1–35.

Steiner, M. (forthcoming). The Iron I pottery of Khirbat al-Lehun. *Bulletin of the American Schools of Oriental Research.*

Stockhammer, P. W. (2012). Conceptualizing cultural hybridization in archaeology. In P. W. Stockhammer (ed.), *Conceptualizing Cultural Hybridization: A Transdisciplinary Approach.* Berlin: Springer, 43–58.

van der Steen, E. J. (2004). *Tribes and Territories in Transition: The Central East Jordan Valley in the Late Bronze Age and Early Iron Age—A Study of the Sources.* Dudley, Mass.: Peeters.

van Dommelen, P. (2006). The orientalizing phenomenon: hybridity and material culture in the western Mediterranean. In C. Riva and N. C. Vella (eds), *Debating Orientalization: Multidisciplinary Approaches to Change in the Ancient Mediterranean.* London: Equinox, 135–52.

Vansteenhuyse, K. (2010). The Bronze to Iron Age transition at Tell Tweini (Syria). In F. Venturi (ed.), *Societies in Transition: Evolutionary Processes in the Northern Levant between Late Bronze Age II and Early Iron Age.* Bologna: CLUEB, 39–52.

Venturi, F. (2010). Cultural breakdown or evolution? The impact of changes in 12th century BC Tell Afis. In F. Venturi (ed.), *Societies in Transition: Evolutionary Processes in the Northern Levant between Late Bronze Age II and Early Iron Age.* Bologna: CLUEB, 1–28.

Voskos, I., and A. B. Knapp (2008). Cyprus at the end of the Late Bronze Age: crisis and colonization or continuity and hybridization? *American Journal of Archaeology* 112: 659–84.

Ward, W. A., and M. S. Joukowsky (eds) (1992). *The Crisis Years: The 12th Century B.C. from Beyond the Danube to the Tigris.* Dubuque, Ia.: Kendall/Hunt.

Webster, J. (2001). Creolizing the Roman provinces. *American Journal of Archaeology* 105: 209–25.

Wood, M. (1996). *In Search of the Trojan War,* updated edn. Berkeley: University of California Press.

Yasur-Landau, A. (2010). *The Philistines and Aegean Migration at the End of the Late Bronze Age.* Cambridge: Cambridge University Press.

CHAPTER 40

THE NORTHERN LEVANT DURING THE IRON AGE I PERIOD

HÉLÈNE SADER

Iron Age I was and still is largely considered to be one of the most puzzling 'dark ages' in the history of the central and northern Levant for two main reasons: the extreme rarity of the textual record and the ambiguity of the available archaeological data.

THE IRON AGE I IN LEBANON

Iron Age I is poorly documented in the archaeological record of Lebanon (Fig. 40.1). There is no established chronology and no accepted—or even suggested—periodization. All authors use the Palestinian and/or Cypriot terminology (Bikai 1978: 66; Anderson 1988: 390; Badre 1997: 60; Baramki 1961: 93; 1966: 33–4; Marfoe 1995: 159; Echt 1984: 60).

Surveys and excavations

Marfoe, who systematically surveyed the Lebanese Beqaʿ Valley, was able to identify 53 sites with Iron Age I strata (1995: 160, n. 137). The Lebanese Akkar Valley was surveyed in 1968 by an Italian team for the University of Rome, who visited fifteen tells, only two of which had Iron Age remains (Saidah 1969: 142). This survey was never published. Bartl recently undertook a new survey of the Lebanese Akkar Valley and spotted six sites with Iron Age remains, with the dating of only three certain (Bartl and Chaaya 2002: 29, table 1; see also Thalmann 2006: 210–11). Since the results of the Akkar survey are preliminary, there is no indication whether any of these sites was occupied in Iron Age I. The rest of the country was never surveyed and remains largely *terra incognita*.

In terms of excavations (Fig. 40.2), only a few sites have been regularly excavated and their results published. In the Beqaʿ Valley, Iron Age I levels are represented in Kamid el-Loz Building Periods 1–3 (Echt 1984: 60, Abb. 3, with no further subdivisions of the period and no suggested dates for the various building periods; see also Marfoe 1995: 159–61) and

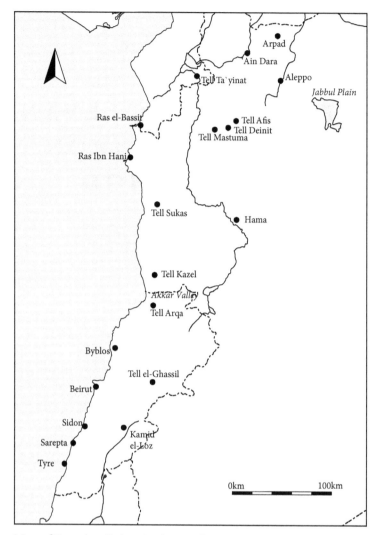

FIG. 40.1 Map of Iron Age I sites in the northern Levant

in Tell el-Ghassil (Baramki 1961; 1964; 1966; Joukowsky 1972: 206–7, 210–12) Area I, Levels 4–5 and Area III, Levels 3–6 (Baramki 1961: 93; Joukowsky 1972: 220). The Iron I period in the latter site begins in the 12th century BC after a period of abandonment and ends in the 9th century BC (Baramki 1961: 93; 1966: 38).

On the coast, excavations that have yielded Iron Age I layers are very few. In Tell Arqa Iron Age I was ascribed to Phase J (Thalmann 2000: fig. 15; 2006: 15, fig. 3). However, no remains dating to that period were found. The Byblos excavations were never properly published and no information is available for the period in question.

The evidence for Iron Age I in Beirut is highly controversial: in Area BEY 003, Badre identified a Late Bronze/Iron Age transitional phase characterized by the erection of a new fortification wall and glacis, which she calls 'Glacis II' and which dates to the end of LB

Figure 40.2 Summary of the archaeological evidence related to Iron Age I in Lebanon and Syria

Site	Transitional LBA/Iron Age I	Iron Age I strata	Iron Age I occupation	Proposed Dates
Tell el-Ghassil	Abandonment	Area I, Levels 4 & 5; Area III, Levels 3–6	Domestic occupation	c.1150–900 BC
Kamid el-Loz	Abandonment	Building Periods 1–3	Domestic occupation	No proposed dates
Tell Arqa	Abandonment	Period J	No settlement	c.14th–c.9th BC
Beirut	Destruction?	Phase IV?	Fortification? No settlement	End of 13th–c.9th BC?
Sidon	Destruction		No settlement	End of c.13th BC
Sarepta	No stratigraphic break	Area II, Y Str.F Area II, Y Str.E	Domestic occupation with industrial activity	c.1200/1190–1150/1125 c.1050–1025 BC
Sarepta	No stratigraphic break	Area II, X Per.V Area II, X Per. VI	Domestic occupation with industrial activity	c.1275–1150 BC c.1150–1025 BC
Tyre	No stratigraphic break	XIV	Domestic occupation with industrial activity	c.1200–1070/50 BC
Hama	Destruction	Stratum F2= cemetery Period I Stratum F1=cemetery Period II	Domestic settlement	c.1200–1075 BC c.1075–925 BC
Tell Afis	Destruction	Stratum VII= LB-IA Transition= Level 9b Iron Age I A= Levels 9c+8 Iron Age IB= Levels 7 + 6 Iron Age IC= Levels 5–3	Fortification, temple and Domestic occupation with industrial activity	c.1200–900 BC c.1200–1125 BC c.1125–1050 BC c.1050–950 BC c.950–900 BC
Tell Mastuma	No evidence	Level I-3	Domestic occupation	c.1200–1000 BC
Ras Ibn Hani	Destruction	Phases 1–3	Domestic occupation	c.1200–c.1150 1150–1050 c.1050–950 BC
Tell Sukas	Destruction	Period H2 early phase Period H2 later phase	Domestic occupation	c.1170–1050 BC c.1050–850 BC
Tell Sukas	Destruction	Iron I cremation cemeteries		c.1200–1000 BC
Tell Kazel	Destruction	Level 5 in Area II and 4–3 in Area IV	Temple	No proposed dates
Ain Dara	No evidence	Periods I and II	Temple	c.1300–1000 1000–900 BC
Tell Tayinat	No occupation	Levels 3–6	Domestic occupation	c.1200–1100 BC
Ras el-Bassit	Destruction	2 levels	Domestic occupation	No proposed dates
Aleppo	Destruction	Level?	Temple	c.1100–1000 BC

II (1997: 54, 64). The excavators of neighbouring areas, where the same structure (Glacis II) was attested, suggest a much lower date for its building: Finkbeiner dates it to Iron II (2001–2: 27–8) and Curvers to Iron II–III (2001–2: 57). On the other hand, in his reconstruction of the Beirut stratigraphy Curvers does not recognize any Iron I levels (2001–2: 59). This conclusion seems to fit the ceramic evidence retrieved on site, since no Iron I pottery is described or illustrated in any of the excavation reports. (All preliminary reports on the excavations of the upper city of Beirut have appeared in the second volume of *Bulletin d'archéologie et d'architecture libanaises*, 1997.)

The best-preserved evidence for Iron I on the coast comes from Sarepta Area II, Sounding X, Periods V–VI, and Sounding Y, Strata F–E (Khalifeh 1988: 102–24; Anderson 1988: 386–96) and from Tyre Level XIV (Bikai 1978: 65–6). Stratum F in Sounding Y was tentatively ascribed to the period between *c.*1200/1190–1150/1125 BC on the basis of Late Cypriot III and Mycenaean IIIC pottery (Anderson 1988: 390); Stratum E in the same sounding is dated to the period ranging between 1150/1125–1050/1025 BC; and Period V in Sounding X is dated *c.*1275–1150 BC (Khalifeh 1988: 113) and Period VI to *c.*1150–1025 BC (Khalifeh 1988: 124).

According to the Sarepta excavators (Anderson 1988: 386; Khalifeh 1988: 102, 113–14) there are no distinctive breaks in the occupational sequence and pottery traditions from G to F and from IV to V. Between Strata F–E and Periods V–VI there is also a gradual transition, with no distinct break in either the stratigraphy or the characteristic pottery types. On the basis of this evidence, Anderson concludes that 'Sarepta—and possibly most of the Phoenician coast—was not directly affected by the massive disturbances, attributed to the 'Sea Peoples' which occurred at the end of the Late Bronze Age in Syria, Palestine and elsewhere' (1988: 424). This conclusion is confirmed by the evidence of Periods V and VI of Sounding X.

In Tyre Stratum XIV 'extends from about 1200 BC to about 1070/50 BC and covers a period roughly equivalent to Palestinian Iron Age I and Late Cypriot III' (Bikai 1978: 66). The date of the end of the stratum was determined by the absence of Cypriot White Painted sherds, which indicates that this stratum must have ended before 1070/50 BC.

Society and economy

Iron Age I sites in the Beqa' Valley were clearly small rural settlements, as evidenced by the architecture, while the coastal sites such as Sarepta and Tyre provided evidence for industrial activity. Faunal analyses are available only from Kamid el-Loz for the whole Iron Age (Bökönyi 1990), while paleobotanical information is totally absent. There was a wide range of animal species in Kamid el-Loz in the Iron Age, enough to cover all the population needs. Noteworthy is the scarcity of pig bones and the overwhelming majority of ovids (Bökönyi 1990: 97, fig. 57).

The best-preserved and published domestic architecture during Iron I came from Kamid el-Loz. In Stratum 3, Level 8, domestic dwellings built on—and sometimes reusing—the ruins of the Late Bronze palace as well as others scattered on the tell surface were excavated (Echt 1984: 47; Marfoe 1995: 159–61). Sunken storage jars, silos, and *tannurs* determine the domestic character of the buildings. Complete house plans were retrieved from Stratum 2, Level 6. These houses (i.e. huts) stood on wooden pillars and their walls were made of reed and plastered with mud (Echt 1984: 43–4); they averaged 35–40m². Three house plans were identified: a one-room house, a trapeze-shaped house with a row of pillars inside, and a rect-angular house with a row of pillars placed along the width and not along the length of the room. The same type of hut was most probably used in Tell el-Ghassil, as suggested by the evidence from Areas I and III, where hardly any architectural remains besides *tannurs*, silos, and pithoi were found (Baramki 1966). The excavator concluded that the people were 'semi-nomadic squatters' (Baramki 1966: 32) and must have lived 'either in tents or some such flimsy structures' (Baramki 1966: 36).

The only sacred building of this period was found in Area I in Tell el-Ghassil. The build-ing was interpreted as a temple because of the presence of a large number of terracotta cult objects (Baramki 1961: 95, plan, figs. 1–3; 1964: 49, 52ff.). The temple is a one-room rectan-gular shrine with stone foundations and a stone-paved floor (Baramki 1964: 51). No other specific features are mentioned.

On the coast, the evidence suggests an economy based on industrial activity. In Sarepta part of a bilobate pottery kiln and refuse pits were discovered in Stratum F, suggesting that 'the architecture of this stratum was associated with the manufacture of pottery' (Anderson 1988: 88–9). The kiln continued to be in use in Stratum E2–1 (Anderson 1988: 90, 93) and the presence of a large number of bread ovens, mainly in E1, attest to the domestic character of the buildings. No complete house plan was, however, found. In Sounding X, both Periods V and VI are also characterized by a pottery workshop area and the presence of bilobate kilns (Khalifeh 1988: 102, 113). In Period VI a new building technique known as 'headers and stretchers' appears for the first time.

Tyre Stratum XIV has yielded fragments of domestic architecture with a *tannur* and stor-age bins cut into the floors as well as evidence for a bead industry (Bikai 1978: 8). A fire pit, probably used for the firing of the beads, was also found.

Pottery

The pottery repertoire of the Beqa' Valley in Iron I is uniform (Fig. 40.3). The Iron I pot-tery of Kamid el-Loz displays no notable change in any building period (Marfoe 1995: 160). Charateristic types are the cooking pots with vertical, inturned, or everted rims and hanging or horizontal flange, pithoi with thumb indentations around the collar, painted and unpainted jugs with loop handle to rim or below the rim, incense burners on tripod stands, and strainer jugs (Marfoe 1995: figs 103–6). No periodization based on pottery types can be made at this stage. The pottery of Tell el-Ghassil is very similar to that of Kamid el-Loz (Joukowsky 1972: pls 8–14, 24–9), and includes cooking pots, strainer jugs, incense burners on tripod bases, thumb-impressed pithoi, dipper juglets, and jars. No imports are mentioned.

On the coast, the ceramic repertoire is different. At Sarepta, the pottery of Stratum F (Anderson 1988: pls 29, 30) is in the tradition of the Late Bronze pottery with the emergence of six new types (Anderson 1988: 387). The pottery repertoire remains the same in both Stratum E (Anderson 1988: pls 31, 32) and Period VI (Khalifeh 1988: 124); however, changes are evi-dent in the surface treatment, with burnishing and painted decoration becoming more prev-alent (Khalifeh 1988: 121–2). There is a clear increase in pithoi and storage jars (Khalifeh 1988: 106), which according to Anderson (1988: 424) may hint at trade activitiy. In Tyre, the pottery (Bikai 1978: pls 38–41) is characterized by the rarity of imports, by the emergence of

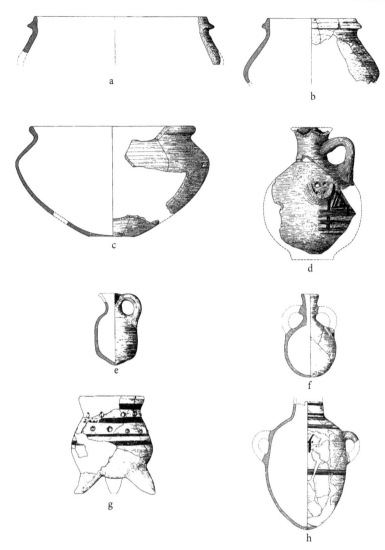

FIG. 40.3 Iron Age I pottery from Kamid el-Loz (scale 1:3) (from Marfoe 1995)

Cooking Pot Type 8 (Bikai 1978: 52) and of Plate Types 11–13 (Bikai 1978: 24–5), and by a noteworthy increase in Storage Jar Types SJ-11, SJ-12, and SJ-9 (Bikai 1978: 45–6).

Small finds

The Iron I strata were very poor in terms of small finds. Noteworthy are a potter's wheel (see Fig. 40.5i below), an iron dagger, and a sickle blade as well as a bronze anklet and tweezers (Fig. 40.5j) from Tell el-Ghassil (Baramki 1966: 35, 37, fig. 9).

Funerary practices

No tombs dated to Iron I were found in Lebanon. The recent excavations on the site of the Phoenician cemetery of al-Bass in Tyre have not yielded tombs from Iron I. Al-Bass Period I of the necropolis, which is dated by the excavators between the 11th and the mid-9th century BC (Aubet 2004: 458, 465), has provided only isolated finds which were discovered out of context.

THE IRON AGE I IN SYRIA

Iron I in Syria remains a rather dark age in spite of the fact that much of northern Syria has been systematically surveyed. The period's obscurity is partly due to the lack of a clear pottery sequence for that period from well-stratified contexts. (See Fig. 40.1.)

Surveys and excavations

The first systematic surveys in the 'Amuq Plain were conducted by Braidwood (1937). More recently, this region was re-investigated by the Oriental Institute of the University of Chicago (Yener 2005). The survey data (Harrison 2009a: 175–6; Janeway 2006–7: 126–7) indicated that the number of settlements doubled in the Early Iron Age ('Amuq Phase N) as compared to the previous Late Bronze Age and a large majority of them were new foundations of a small size indicating 'a "dispersal" of the population into small, rural settlements during the Iron Age' (Harrison 2009a: 176). Continuity with both the previous Late Bronze Age and the later Iron Age II is indicated by the fact that some early Iron sites reoccupied Late Bronze settlements and an even larger number continued to be settled in Iron II. In the latter period this settlement network 'developed into an integrated, urbanized regional entity' as Tell Ta'yinat reached a size of 35ha, thus becoming the dominant settlement and centre of the area with a cluster of small settlements in its vicinity. Sapin surveyed the Syrian Akkar from 1976 to 1979, but the survey results were only summarily published (Thalmann and al-Maqdissi 1989). In his brief statement, Sapin says that the beginning of the Iron Age is marked everywhere by a hiatus in the occupation, a gap attested at Tell Arqa in the Lebanese part of the Akkar Valley. Courtois (1973) visited some thirty sites in the Middle Orontes Valley but did not identify Iron I occupation on any of them. Matthers surveyed the area around Tell Rifaat and identified only one Iron I site (1978: fig. 2). Shaath (1985) visited sixteen sites around Tell Deinit in the Idlib region, but his survey was never published. In the same region, the Tell Afis Archaeological Project undertook a survey around Tell Afis in the Jazr Plain (Melis 2005; see also Ciafardoni 1992: 37–72). They identified several sites with Iron I occupation (Melis 2005: fig. 1), but the final survey results are still awaiting publication. The area around Tell Mastuma was also visited, but no specific Iron I occupation is mentioned (Wakita et al. 1993: 31–2; Tsuneki 2009: 50). The surface survey of Tell 'Ain Dara in the Afrin Valley has yielded Iron I material (Stone and Zimansky 1999: 11, fig. 12). Maxwell Hyslop et al. (1942) and more recently the Umm el-Marra Archaeological Project (Schwartz et al. 2000: 447ff.) surveyed the Jabbul Plain. The latter counted thirty-four Iron Age sites (Schwartz et al. 2000: 452, fig. 22), but they unfortunately do not refer to any Iron Age I settlement. In south Syria Iron I remains a mystery: in his survey, Braemer visited sixty sites but was not able to identify Iron I settlements. He uses the general terminology 'Fer' which covers all the Iron Age (Braemer 1984: figs 33–4).

In terms of excavations a few sites have yielded clear and stratified Iron I remains (see Fig. 40.2 above). On the coast, at Tell Ta'yinat, recent excavations have uncovered a clear sequence of four levels, Field Phases 6–3 in Field I dating to the 12th century BC (Harrison 2009a: 178; 2009b: 180; Janeway 2006–7: 128). The study of the pottery is still preliminary, but will certainly contribute to refining the periodization of Iron I in Syria. Other sites are: Ras Ibn Hani (Bounni et al. 1979; Bounni and Lagarce 1989: 94), where three phases of occupation dating respectively to 1200–1150, 1150–1050, and 1050–950 BC were identified (Bounni et al. 1981: 258, 269–70); Ras el-Bassit (Courbin 1986: 186–8), where two Iron Age I levels of occupation were found, although their clear separation was often difficult (du Piêd 2006–7: 162–3, n. 7); Tell Sukas (Riis 1961–2: 140; 1979: 51), where Iron I levels were excavated in Stratum H and in a cremation cemetery dated to the 12th–10th centuries BC near the southern harbour; and Tell Kazel (Badre 2006: 69), where the last occupational phase of Level 6 in Area II and Level 5 in Area IV represent the transitional Late Bronze–Iron occupation and Level 5 in Area II and Levels 4–3 in Area IV represent Iron Age I.

In central north Syria, Iron I levels are represented in Tell Mastuma (Wakita et al. 1995: 2) Level I-3 dated 12th–10th centuries BC;[1] in 'Ain Dara, where a clear occupation sequence in Iron I based on iconography was identified: Period I from 1300 to 1000 BC and Period 2 from 1000 to 900 BC (Abū 'Assāf 1990: 39); in Aleppo (Gonella, Khayyata, and Kohlmeyer 2005: 92–3; see also Kohlmeyer 2009: 197), where an Iron I temple dating to the 11th century was recently found indicating an occupation of the site at that period; and finally, at Hama (Riis 1948: 191–3; Fugmann 1958: 149), where Periods I–II of the cremation cemeteries as well as Stratum F on the tell were dated to Iron I. The pottery and small finds in the latter site allowed a clear subdivision of Iron I: Period I of the cemeteries and Substratum F2 are dated between 1200 and 1075 BC, and Period II and F1 between 1075 and 925 BC (see Fig. 40.2 above). In Tell Mishrifeh-Qatna the excavations have shown a hiatus in the occupation sequence in Iron I (al-Maqdissi and Souleiman 2008: 32, 35).

A clear periodization of the Iron I layers was achieved in Tell Afis, where Stratum VII was ascribed to Iron I and dated 1250–875 BC (Mazzoni 2005: 11–12). Soundings in several areas (see mainly Venturi 1998; 2000; 2005; Mazzoni 2000a; Cecchini 2005; Cecchini and Mazzoni 1998; Chitti 2005) have yielded a clear sequence of levels which could be accurately distinguished and dated on the basis of the ceramic repertoire. In Area E, where the sequence is clearest, the end of the Late Bronze is marked by the destruction of an important residential building ascribed to Level 10. This destruction was followed by a short period of abandonment and scattered occupation, Level 9c, which represents the intermediate Late Bronze Age/Iron Age I dated from the end of the 13th century to the first half of the 12th century BC. In Level 9b the site was resettled and the reoccupation consisted of pits and silos dated to c.1125 BC. Monochrome painted pottery influenced by Late Mycenaean and Cypriot culture makes its first appearance in this level. The following Levels, 9a–8, dated between 1125 and 1050 BC, Iron IA, are characterized by a drastic increase in monochrome painted pottery which is the main indicator of Iron I levels in Syria. In Levels 7–6, Iron IB, new urban planning and regular occupation of a domestic character are attested and dated between the second half of the 11th and the first half of the 10th centuries BC; Levels 5–3, Iron

---

[1] It is to be noted that in the final publication (Iwasaki et al. 2009: Fig. 3.2) the Iron I period is represented in the stratigraphic chart by a hiatus and the earliest part of Stratum I-2 Level D. [14]C dates indicate 'that the early phase of the Iron Age settlement at Tell Mastuma can be dated to the Iron Age I period, rather than the Iron Age II period (9th to 8th centuries BC), which we have considered in the previous preliminary reports' (Iwasaki et al. 2009: 523).

IC, are ascribed to the second half of the 10th century BC (see Mazzoni 2000b: table 1, which also clearly correlates Hama Stratum F and Periods I–II of the cemeteries with Levels 9b–3). The Tell Afis evidence clearly shows that in spite of the violent destruction of the LB II buildings and a short abandonment period, there is a clear continuity in the material culture, more specifically in the local ceramic assemblage (Venturi 1998: 128).

This continuity is not restricted to Tell Afis but is attested at all other excavated sites (Bounni et al. 1979: 243, 245; Lund 1986: 40–42; Fugmann 1958: 135, 266; Venturi 1998: 128).

Society and economy

The overwhelming majority of excavated Iron I sites have an economy predominantly based on agriculture with strong evidence for production, storage, and processing of food represented by silos, pithoi, and bread ovens. Paleobotanical and paleozoological analyses for Iron I are available only from Tell Afis (Wachter-Sarkady 1998: 465; Wilkens 1998; 2005). Preliminary results of the former indicate that cereals, principally barley, were the main crop during that period. Olive trees and grapes are also attested. The archaeozoological results have demonstrated the predominance of ovids (Wilkens 2005: 107–8), which explains the development of textile industry in that site. The large number of loomweights found in Tell Afis in Iron I levels (Cecchini 2000: 217) confirms the existence of this industry. The results also indicate a varied fauna ranging from sweet-water to steppe animals.

The rural character of the sites is clearly indicated by the architecture. Most Iron I sites had no public buildings and contained only dwellings characterized by domestic installations such as *tannurs*, silos, and pithoi indicating food processing and storage.

The Iron I settlement at Tell Mastuma showed some evidence for town planning: it had a horseshoe shape with a monumental entrance to the south and a series of well-outlined streets (Wakita et al. 1995: 12–14, figs. 3, 6–2), which continued through the Iron Age. The best examples for domestic architecture also come from this site, where three different types of Iron I house plans were excavated. They had stone foundations and mud-brick walls, and consisted of either two or three rooms differently arranged (Wakita et al. 1995: 41–3). They are similar to but smaller in size than the later Iron II houses (Wakita et al. 1995: 12). Hama Level F had at least three buildings, none of them however with a complete plan. They contained storage jars and ovens, and in one of them, several sling stones made of clay were found (Fugmann 1958: 141–2). In Tell Afis Area E, the residential area consists of one- to two-room houses surrounded by an open space with silos, the size of which was progressively reduced as new dwellings were built (Venturi 2000: 510ff.; 2005: 72; Chitti 2005: 66). From the coast no complete house plans were found.

Recent evidence has, however, demonstrated the existence of monumental religious architecture dating to Iron I, which was built in the Syrian Bronze Age tradition. At ʿAin Dara (Abū ʿAssāf 1990), Aleppo (Kohlmeyer 2000; 2009; Gonella, Khayyata, and Kohlmeyer 2005), and Tell Afis (Mazzoni 2011), monumental temples with sculptures were discovered. In Tell Kazel (Badre 2006: 77) the Late Bronze temple was rebuilt in Iron I: it has monumental features but no sculptures. The first phase of the ʿAin Dara temple is dated by the excavator on the basis of the iconography of the *cella* sculptures (Reliefs E1–E7) to the 13th–12th centuries BC, while the second is dated on the basis of the lions and the sphinxes of the façade and sides to the 10th century BC (Abū 'Assāf 1990: 39). Mazzoni dates the 'Ain Dara temple between 1150 and 1050 BC (2000b: 1048, table 1), while Kohlmeyer (2008: 123–4) opts for a foundation date of the temple *cella* in the late Hittite period and a second building phase of the temple in the 11th century BC. The Hieroglyphic Hittite inscriptions in the weather god temple in Aleppo, which were dated by Hawkins (2008; 2009; 2011) to the 11th century BC, ascribe the temple to this period, a date adopted by the excavator for the rebuilding of the temple in Iron I (Gonella, Khayyata and Kohlmeyer 2005: 92–3; Kohlmeyer 2009: 197). In August 2008 Mazzoni announced the discovery of an Iron I temple at Tell Afis. This temple was built on top of an earlier one, and two phases of occupation were identified (AIII.1–2). The earliest phase is dated by the pottery to the 11th century, while the second is dated to the 11th–10th centuries BC by a painted *kernos* with a bull head and a painted Cypro-Geometric I sherd with a bird. A cylinder seal representing the weather god might suggest an attribution of the building to the cult of this divinity (Mazzoni 2010: 365). All the sculptures in these temples indicate a clear Hittite influence and a cultural homogeneity. They attest to a rapid re-urbanization process, which started in the course of the 11th century BC.

The Iron I pottery (Fig. 40.4) indicates clear cultural contacts with neighbouring regions. On the coast, the main types of pottery attested at Ras Ibn Hani are Mycenaean IIIC:1 locally made painted kraters (Fig. 40.4g), storage jars, bichrome pottery, strainer jugs, and a new type of talc-tempered cooking pot called 'à la stéatite' (Fig. 40.4f), which continued to be produced until the end of Iron I (Bounni et al. 1979: figs. 25–8; see also du Piêd 2006–7: 169–77). The same type of cooking pot also appears at Ras el-Bassit (du Piêd 2006–7: 163–7, fig. 40.4c–e). In Tell Ta'yinat, Mycenaean IIIC:1 pottery is also the dominant type in Iron I with a wide range of forms. The pottery assemblage of Tell Ta'yinat also includes the so-called Philistine Cooking Jug, a 'distinctive cooking ware tradition [which] is commonly found in the Aegean and on Cyprus' (Harrison 2009b: 181).

In central north Syria, the pottery repertoire of Iron I consists of common and painted wares both locally made and in clear continuity with the ceramic vessels of the Late Bronze Age. It displays 'both a coastal Eastern Mediterranean and an Anatolian orientation' (Mazzoni 2000a: 36) and consists of jars, kraters, bowls, pilgrim flasks, cooking pots, and jugs (Riis 1948: 77–8 table; Fugmann 1958: fig. 165; Venturi 1998: figs 7–13; 2000: figs 6–9). The emergence and increasing numbers of locally made monochrome painted vessels with strong Late Mycenaean and Cypriot influence are characteristic of the Syrian Iron I (Venturi 1998: 128–9; 2000: 513ff.; Riis 1948: 80; Stone and Zimansky 1999: 30, 39; Wakita et al. 1995: 19, figs 7–9). The painted motifs are varied: horizontal circles, geometrical and animal motifs (Riis 1948: fig. 130A, B; Venturi 1998: 129). Finally, imported pottery is sometimes attested (Bonatz 1998; Riis 1948: 114; Venturi 2000: 522ff.) and confirms the trade contacts (Mazzoni 2000a: 36) suggested by the Anatolian and eastern Mediterranean influences on the locally produced vessels. The emergence of the red slipped burnished ware ushers the next Iron II phase (Harrison 2009b: 183; Venturi 2007: 297–300).

Small finds

The end of the second millennium BC witnesses the emergence of iron, which implies economic and technological developments. Iron objects appear for the first time but bronze objects continue to be used (Fig. 40.5). Bronze and iron weapons, socketed and riveted swords, spearheads, and arrowheads—leaf-shaped, with and without mid-ribs—as well as

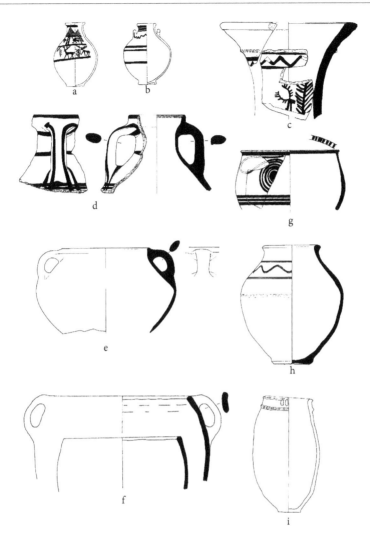

FIG. 40.4 Iron Age I common and painted pottery from Syria: Hama (a, b: scale 1:10); Tell Afis (c–e, h: scale 1:4); Ras Ibn Hani (g, f: scale 3/10); and Tell Mastuma (i: scale 1:16)

knives, sickle blades, and axe-heads, are attested at Hama (Riis 1948: 119–25; Fugmann 1958: fig. 165), Tell Mastuma (Wakita et al. 1995: 28, fig. 11, pl. 23), and Tell Afis (Venturi 1998: 131). Bronze and iron pins, needles, bracelets, anklets, and rings are also found. Stone vessels including mainly basalt bowls and grinders as well as weights and pestles were found at all the above-mentioned sites, and attest food processing activities. Loomweights, mainly of Aegean type, were found in almost every excavated site such as Tell Afis (Cecchini 2000) and Tell Ta'yinat (Harrison 2009b: 183), and a few fragments of clay figurines and moulds were also retrieved. Special mention should be made of the cylinder and stamp seals, examples of which were found in Hama (Riis 1948: 150ff.) and Tell Afis (Cecchini and Mazzoni 1998: 202, fig. 3). Beads, bone needles, and spatulae were also part of the small finds repertoire.

Funerary practices

Only two sites have yielded cemeteries dating to Iron I: Hama and Tell Sukas. They both attest the introduction of a new funerary practice in Syria, that of cremation (Riis 1948: 27ff.; 1961–2: 140; 1979: 51). The cremated remains of adults, children, and infants, sometimes mixed with burnt animal bones, were placed in cinerary urns covered with chalk and deposited in pits. Newborn and stillborn children were usually inhumated in kraters. The urn was often covered with a large bowl and both were wrapped in a cloth and accompanied by small vessels and a lamp. A commemorative stone stele indicated the location of the tomb. Among the most common funerary offerings are weapons, jewellery, beads, needles, and loomweights.

CONCLUSION

The transition from the Late Bronze to the Iron Age was traditionally believed to have been ushered in by the invasion of the 'Sea People' who, according to the inscriptions of the Egyptian pharaoh Ramesses III, burnt and destroyed all the Late Bronze cities of the Levant. The ensuing political vacuum allowed nomadic 'newcomers', bursting out of the desert, to settle the territory of inland Syria and Palestine, and waves of invaders to occupy the coast, creating new kingdoms a century or two later.

Recent epigraphic discoveries (Hawkins 1988; 1995; 2008; 2009) and the above archaeological evidence have largely discredited this view. The newly discovered Hittite-Luwian inscriptions seem to suggest that in north Syria, 'In key centres of Hittite power, such as Karkemish, Hittite imperial control appears to have survived in the form of diminished "rump" states ruled by dynastic lines with direct ancestral links to the royal family in Hattusa' (Harrison 2009b: 187), which explains the continuity in material culture and the progressive change that followed.

The transition from Late Bronze to Iron Age differed from site to site. The archaeological record showed that the transition took place either directly, with no stratigraphic break, as at Sarepta and Tyre, after a short period of abandonment, as in Kamid el-Loz and Tell el-Ghassil, or after a violent destruction, as in Ras Ibn Hani, Tell Sukas, and Tell Afis. With the exception of sites such as Tell Arqa, Sidon, and Qatna, which experienced an occupation vacuum in Iron I (Thalmann 1983: 217; 2006: 70; Doumet-Serhal 2002: 196, 201; al-Maqdissi and Souleiman 2008: 32, 35), most sites were almost immediately reoccupied and resumed agricultural, industrial, and trade activity. The above-mentioned disruptions were in most cases very short, and did not lead to regression in land occupation. On the contrary, survey results noted a substantial increase of settlements in Iron Age I, with a vast majority of small village sites (e.g. Schwartz et al. 2000: 452, fig. 22).

There is ample evidence for a population continuum in Iron I attested by Late Bronze surviving political institutions, architectural traditions, industries, and material culture. However, the emergence of painted pottery and of cremation as a new funerary practice may hint either at the arrival of some foreign groups or at the adoption of foreign traditions by the local population in Syria and Lebanon through trade contact. The transition from Late Bronze to Iron Age is understood today as the result of both internal and external fac-

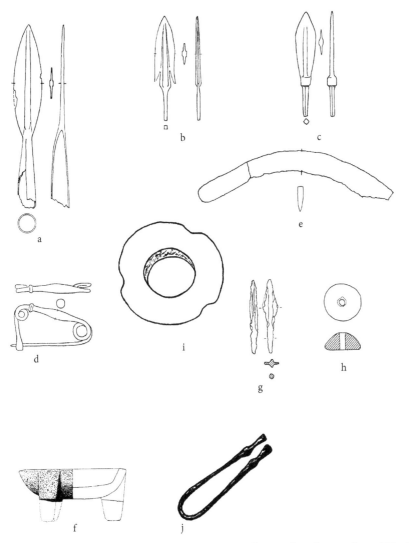

FIG 40.5 Iron Age I small finds from Hama (a–e: scale 1:2; f: scale 1:5, from Riis 1948); Tell Mastuma (g, h, scale 1:2, from Wakita et al. 1995), and Tell el-Ghassil (i: Scale 1:5; j: Scale 1:1, from Baramki 1961: no. 16; 1966: no. 19)

tors, and the direct causes of cultural change are sought in new socioeconomic conditions (Liverani 1987; Venturi 1998: 135–6; 2000: 531ff.).

SUGGESTED READING

Akkermans, P. M. M. G., and G. M. Schwartz (2003). *The Archaeology of Syria: From Complex Hunters-Gatherers to Early Urban Societies (ca. 16,000–300 BC)*. Cambridge: Cambridge University Press.

Harrison, T. P. (2009). Lifting the veil on a 'dark age': Ta'yinat and the North Orontes Valley during the Early Iron Age. In J. D. Schloen (ed.), *Exploring the Longue Durée: Essays in Honor of Lawrence E. Stager*. Winona Lake, Ind.: Eisenbrauns, 171–84.

—— (2009). Neo-Hittites in the 'Land of Palistin': renewed investigations at Tell Ta'yinat on the Plain of Antioch. *Near Eastern Archaeology* 72: 174–89.

Mazzoni, S. (2000). Syria and the periodization of the Iron Age: a cross-cultural perspective. In G. Bunnens (ed.), *Essays on Syria in the Iron Age*. Louvain: Peeters, 31–59.

Venturi, F. (2000). Le premier Âge du fer à Tell Afis et en Syrie septentrionale. In G. Bunnens (ed.), *Essays on Syria in the Iron Age*. Louvain: Peeters, 505–36.

REFERENCES

Abū Assāf, A. (1990). *Der Temple von 'Ain Dara*. Mainz am Rhein: von Zabern.

al-Maqdissi, M., and A. Souleiman (2008). Notes d'archéologie levantine, 13: Fouilles archéologiques syriennes à Mishrifeh/Qatna au nord-est de Homs (Émèse). In D. Bonatz, R. M. Czichon, and F. J. Kreppner (eds), *Fundstellen: Gesammelte Schriften zur Archäologie und Geschichte Vorderasiens ad honorem Hartmut Kühne*. Wiesbaden: Harrassowitz, 31–9.

Anderson, W. P. (1988). *Sarepta I: The Late Bronze and Iron Age Strata of Area II, Y*. Beirut: Lebanese University Publications.

Aubet, M. E. (2004). *The Phoenician Cemetery of Tyre-Al Bass: Excavations, 1997–1999*. Beirut: Ministère de la Culture, Direction Générale des Antiquités.

Badre, L. (1997). Bey 003 preliminary report. *Bulletin d'archéologie et d'architecture libanaises* 2: 6–94.

—— (2006). Tell Kazel-Simyra: a contribution to a relative chronological history in the eastern Mediterranean in the Late Bronze Age. *Bulletin of the American Schools of Oriental Research* 343: 65–95.

Baramki, D. C. (1961). Preliminary report on the excavations at Tell el Ghassil. *Bulletin du Musée de Beyrouth* 16: 87–97.

—— (1964). Second preliminary report on the excavations at Tell el Ghassil. *Bulletin du Musée de Beyrouth* 17: 47–103.

—— (1966). Third preliminary report on the excavations at Tell el Ghassil. *Bulletin du Musée de Beyrouth* 19: 29–49.

Bartl, K., and A. Chaaya (2002). Archäologische Untersuchungen der südlichen Akkar-Ebene, Nordlibanon: Vorläufige Ergebnisse einer Oberflächenprospektion. In R. Eichmann (ed.), *Ausgrabungen und Surveys im Vorderen Orient*, vol. 1. Rahden: Marie Leidorf, 23–48.

Bikai, P. M. (1978). *The Pottery of Tyre*. Warminster: Aris & Phillips.

Bökönyi, S. (1990). *Kamid el-Loz 12: Tierhaltung und Jagd—Tierknochenfunde der Ausgrabungen 1964 bis 1981*. Bonn: Habelt.

Bonatz, D. (1998). Imported pottery. In Cecchini and Mazzoni (1998 : 211–29).

Bounni, A., E. Lagarce, J. Lagarce, N. Saliby, and L. Badre (1979). Rapport préliminaire sur la troisième campagne de fouilles (1977) à Ras Ibn Hani (Syrie). *Syria* 56: 217–91.

—— and J. Lagarce (1989). Ras Ibn-Hani (mission franco-syrienne). In *Contribution française à l'archéologie syrienne (1969–1989)*. Damascus: Institut français d'archéologie du Proche Orient, 91–7.

—— E. Lagarce, et al. (1981). Rapport préliminaire sur la quatrième campagne de fouilles (1978) à Ibn Hani (Syrie). *Syria* 58: 215–97.

Braemer, F. (1984). Prospections archéologiques dans le Hawran (Syrie). *Syria* 61: 219–50.

Braidwood, R. J. (1937). *Mounds in the Plain of Antioch: An Archaeological Survey*. Chicago: University of Chicago Press.

Cecchini, S. (2000). The textile industry in northern Syria during the Iron Age according to the evidence of the Tell Afis excavations. In G. Bunnens (ed.), *Essays on Syria in the Iron Age*. Louvain: Peeters, 211–33.

—— (2005). Area N: presentazione e cronologia—Gli oggetti. In *Tell Afis, Siria 2002–2004: missioni archeologiche dell'Università di Pisa*. Pisa: PLUS, 77–82.

—— and S. Mazzoni (eds) (1998). *Tell Afis (Siria): scavi sull'acropoli 1988–1992*. Pisa: ETS.

Chitti, B. (2005). Area E4b nord: Bronzo Tardo II–Ferro I. In *Tell Afis, Siria 2002–2004: missioni archeologiche dell'Università di Pisa*. Pisa: PLUS, 62–9.

Ciafardoni, P. (1992). Insediamenti aramaici e pre-aramaici nella regione di Idlib. In S. Mazzoni (ed.), *Tell Afis e l'età del ferro*. Pisa: Giardini, 37–74.

Courbin, P. (1986). Bassit. *Syria* 63: 175–220

Courtois, J.-C. (1973). Prospection archeologique dans la moyenne vallée de l'Oronte. *Syria* 50: 53–99.

Curvers, H. (2001). The lower town of pre-classical Beirut. *Aram* 13: 51–72.

Doumet-Serhal, C. (2002). Fourth season of excavation at Sidon: preliminary report. *Bulletin d'archéologie et d'architecture libanaises* 6: 179–210.

du Piêd, L. (2006–7). The Early Iron Age in the northern Levant: continuity and change in the pottery assemblages from Ras el-Bassit and Ras Ibn Hani. *Scripta Mediterranea* 27–8: 161–85.

Echt, R. (1984). *Kamid el-Loz 5: Die Stratigraphie*. Habelt: Bonn.

Finkbeiner, U. (2001–2). BEY 020: the Iron Age fortification. *Aram* 13–14: 27–36.

Fugmann, E. (1958). *Hama: fouilles et recherches 1931–1938—L'architecture des périodes pré-hellénistiques*. Copenhagen: Fondation Carlsberg.

Gonella, J., W. Khayyata, and K. Kohlmeyer (2005). *Die Zitadelle von Aleppo und der Tempel des Wettergottes: Neue Forschungen und Entdeckungen*. Münster: Rhema.

Harrison, T. P. (2009a). Lifting the veil on a 'dark age': Ta'yinat and the North Orontes Valley during the Early Iron Age. In J. D. Schloen (ed.), *Exploring the Longue Durée: Essays in Honor of Lawrence E. Stager*. Winona Lake, Ind.: Eisenbrauns, 171–84.

—— (2009b). Neo-Hittites in the 'Land of Palistin': renewed investigations at Tell Ta'yinat on the Plain of Antioch. *Near Eastern Archaeology* 72: 174–89.

Hawkins, J. D. (1988). Kuzi-Teshub and the great kings of Karkamish. *Anatolian Studies* 38: 99–108.

—— (1995). 'Great kings' and 'country lords' at Malatya and Karkamiš. In T. P. J. van den Hout and J. de Roos (eds), *Studio Historiae Ardens: Ancient Near Eastern Studies Presented to Ph. H. J. Houwink ten Cate on the Occasion of His 65th Birthday*. Istanbul: Nederlands Historisch-Archaeologisch Instituut, 73–85.

—— (2008). *Cilicia, Aleppo and the Amuq: New Evidence on the Late Bronze–Iron Age Transition*. Paper presented at the Sixth International Congress on the Archaeology of the Ancient Near East (ICAANE), Rome.

—— (2009). Cilicia, the Amuq, and Aleppo: new light in a dark age. *Near Eastern Archaeology* 72: 164–73.

—— (2011). The inscriptions of the Aleppo Temple. *Anatolian Studies* 61: 35–54.

Iwasaki, T., S. Wakita, K. Ishida, and H. Wada (eds) (2009). *Tell Mastuma: An Iron Age Settlement in Northwest Syria*. Tokyo: Ancient Orient Museum.

Janeway, B. (2006–7). The nature and extent of Aegean contact at Tell Ta'yinat and vicinity in the Early Iron Age: evidence of the Sea Peoples? *Scripta Mediterranea* 27–8: 123–46.

Joukowsky, M. S. (1972). *The pottery of Tell el Ghassil in the Beqaʾa: a comparative study and analysis of the Iron Age and Bronze Age wares.* MA thesis, American University of Beirut.

Khalifeh, I. (1988). *Sarepta II: The Late Bronze and Iron Age Periods of Area II, X.* Beirut: Lebanese University Publications.

Kohlmeyer, K. (2000). *Der Tempel des Wettergottes von Aleppo,* ed. Gemeinsamen Kommission der Nordrhein-Westfälischen Akademie der Wissenschaften und der Gerda Henkel Stiftung. Münster: Rhema.

—— (2008). Zur Datierung der Skulpturen von ʿAin Dārā. In D. Bonatz, R. M. Czichon, and F. J. Kreppner (eds), *Fundstellen: Gesammelte Schriften zur Archäologie und Geschichte Vorderasiens ad honorem Hartmut Kühne.* Wiesbaden: Harrassowitz, 119–30.

—— (2009). The temple of the storm god in Aleppo during the Late Bronze and Early Iron Ages. *Near Eastern Archaeology* 72: 190–202.

Liverani, M. (1987). The collapse of the Near Eastern regional system at the end of the Bronze Age: the case of Syria. In M. J. Rowlands, M. T. Larsen, and K. Kristiansen (eds), *Center and Periphery in the Ancient World.* Cambridge: Cambridge University Press, 66–73.

Lund, J. (1986). *Sukas VIII: The Habitation Quarters.* Copenhagen: Kongelige Danske Videnskabernes Solskab/Munksgaard.

Marfoe, L. (1995). *Kamid el-Loz 13: The Prehistoric and Early Historic Context of the Site.* Habelt: Bonn.

Matthers, J. (1978). Tell Rifaʾat, 1977: preliminary report of an archaeological survey, I—Overall results of the survey. *Iraq* 40: 119–37.

Maxwell Hyslop, R., J. du Plat Taylor, M. V. Seton-Williams, and J. dʾA. Waechter (1942). An archaeological survey of the Plain of Jabbul, 1939. *Palestine Exploration Quarterly* 74: 8–40.

Mazzoni, S. (2000a). Syria and the periodization of the Iron Age: a cross-cultural perspective. In G. Bunnens (ed.), *Essays on Syria in the Iron Age.* Louvain: Peeters, 31–59.

—— (2000b). Crisis and change: the beginning of the Iron Age in Syria. In P. Matthiae, A. Enea, L. Peyronel, and F. Pinnock (eds), *Proceedings of the First International Conference on the Archaeology of the Ancient Near East, Rome, May 18th–23rd 1998,* vol. 2. Rome: Università degli studi di Roma ʿLa Sapienzaʾ, Dipartimento di scienze storiche, archeologiche e antropologiche dellʾantichità, 1043–55.

—— (2005). Tell Afis, the survey and the regional sequence. In *Tell Afis, Siria 2002–2004: missioni archeologiche dellʾUniversità di Pisa.* Pisa: PLUS, 5–14.

—— (2010). Syro-Hittite temples and the traditional *in antis* plan. In *Kulturlandschaft Syrien— Zentrum und Peripherie: Festschrift Jan-Waalke Meyer.* Münster: Ugarit-Verlag, 359–76.

—— (2011). Templi e corredi del culto a Tell Afis nellʾEtà del ferro e le tradizioni del Levante. *Byrsa* 15–16/2009: 27–54.

Melis, S. (2005). Note geomorfologiche e ipotesi geoarcheologiche sulla piana del Jazr. In *Tell Afis, Syria 2002–2004: missioni archeologiche dellʾUniversità di Pisa.* Pisa: ETS, 14–17.

Riis, P. J. (1948). *Hama: fouilles et recherches 1931–1938—Les cimetières à cremation.* Copenhagen: Gyldendalske Boghandel.

—— (1961–2). Lʾactivité de la Mission archéologique danoise sur la côte phénicienne en 1960. *Annales archéologiques arabes syriennes* 11–12: 133–44.

—— (1979). *Sūkās 6: The Graeco-Phoenician Cemetery and Sanctuary at the Southern Harbour.* Copenhagen: Munksgaard.

Saidah, R. (1969). Archaeology in the Lebanon 1968–1969. *Berytus* 18: 119–42.

Schwartz, G. M., H. H. Curvers, F. A. Gerritsen, J. A. MacCormack, N. F. Miller, and J. A. Weber (2000). Excavation and survey in the Jabbul Plain, western Syria: the Umm el-Marra Project 1996–1997. *American Journal of Archaeology* 104: 419–62.

Shaath, S. (1985). Fouilles archéologiques de Tell Deinit (District d'Idlib). *Syria* 62: 134.

Stone, E. C., and P. E. Zimansky (1999). *The Iron Age Settlement at 'Ain Dara, Syria: Survey and Soundings*. Oxford: Archaeopress.

Thalmann, J.-P. (1983). Les niveaux de l'Âge du bronze et de l'Âge du fer à Tell Arqa (Liban). In *Atti del I Congresso internazionale di studi fenici e punici*. Rome: Consiglio nazionale delle ricerche, 217–21.

—— (2000). Tell Arqa. *Bulletin d'archéologie et d'architecture libanaises* 4: 5–74.

—— (2006). *Tell Arqa 1: les niveaux de l'Âge du bronze*. Beirut: Institut français d'archéologie du Proche Orient.

—— and M. al-Maqdissi (1989). Prospection de la Trouée de Homs: les sites de la plaine du 'Akkar Syrien. In *Contribution française à l'archéologie syrienne (1969–1989)*. Damascus: Institut français d'archéologie du Proche Orient, 98–101.

Tsuneki, A. (2009). General overview of tell-type settlements around Tell Mastuma. In Iwasaki et al. (2009: 13–52).

Venturi, F. (1998). The Late Bronze II and Early Iron I Levels. In Cecchini and Mazzoni (1998: 123–62).

—— (2000). Le premier Âge du fer à Tell Afis et en Syrie septentrionale. In G. Bunnens (ed.), *Essays on Syria in the Iron Age*. Louvain: Peeters, 505–36.

—— (2005). Area E4b sud: Bronzo Tardo II–Ferro I. In *Tell Afis, Syria 2002–2004: missioni archeologiche dell'Università di Pisa*. Pisa: PLUS, 69–75.

—— (2007). *La Siria nell'età delle trasformazioni (XIII–X sec.a.C.): nuovi contribute dallo scavo di Tell Afis*. Bologna: CLUEB.

Wachter-Sarkady, C. (1998). Archaeobotanical investigations. In Cecchini and Mazzoni (1998: 451–80).

Wakita, S., I. Asano, H. Wada, A. Tsuneki, and T. Nakamura (1993). Tell Mastuma: a preliminary report of the excavations in Idlib, Syria, 1993. *Bulletin of the Ancient Orient Museum* 15: 23–49.

—— et al. (1995). Tell Mastuma: a preliminary report of the excavations at Idlib, Syria, in 1994 and 1995. *Bulletin of the Ancient Orient Museum* 16: 1–73.

Wilkens, B. (1998). The faunal remains. In Cecchini and Mazzoni (1998: 433–50).

—— (2005). Relazione preliminare sui resti faunistici provenienti dalle campagne di scavo 2002–2003–2004. In *Tell Afis, Syria 2002–2004: missioni archeologiche dell'Università di Pisa*. Pisa: PLUS, 104–11.

Yener, K. A. (ed.) (2005). *The Amuq Valley Regional Projects*, vol. 1: *Surveys in the Plain of Antioch and Orontes Delta, Turkey, 1995–2002*. Chicago: Oriental Institute Press of the University of Chicago.

CHAPTER 41

THE SOUTHERN LEVANT (CISJORDAN) DURING THE IRON AGE I PERIOD

AYELET GILBOA

INTRODUCTION

The world of Iron Age I in Canaan was a new one. It followed the near-total collapse of Late Bronze political, economic, and social patterns and witnessed a gradual crystallization of a new world order, culminating in Iron II with the formation of small territorial kingdoms. Concomitantly, new group identities were consolidated, and therefore Iron I should also be considered a period of ethnogenesis.

Indeed, traditionally this period has been interpreted mainly in terms of population influxes: 'Sea Peoples' to the coastal regions, 'Israelites' to the highlands, and Arameans to the north. No doubt, at least in parts of Canaan, new populations are definitely in evidence, but they are only part of many factors to be considered. Conversely, attempts to implement a *long durée* perspective have defined Iron I demographic and economic phenomena as just one further wave in the oscillating balance between urban/rural and/or sedentary/pastoral modes of existence, but this approach has a very limited explanatory potential. It is the juxtaposition of specific processes and events that must be considered. Most fundamental are the following:

1. The disappearance of the two imperial powers that dominated the region in the Late Bronze Age—Hatti and mainly Egypt, which to various extents controlled Canaan from the 16th century BCE. Though occasional Assyrian excursions reached the Mediterranean in the late 12th/early 11th centuries BCE, for the first time in centuries Canaan was free of external domination.
2. The collapse of the international commercial and symbolic networks of the Late Bronze Age, a substantial component of the economies of all participating societies. Canaan's direct contacts with the Aegean and beyond had nearly ceased altogether, and those with Cyprus were significantly lessened. The tail end of the Cypriot Bronze Age export is evidenced by very few 'Myc IIIC' containers, e.g. at Tel Keisan

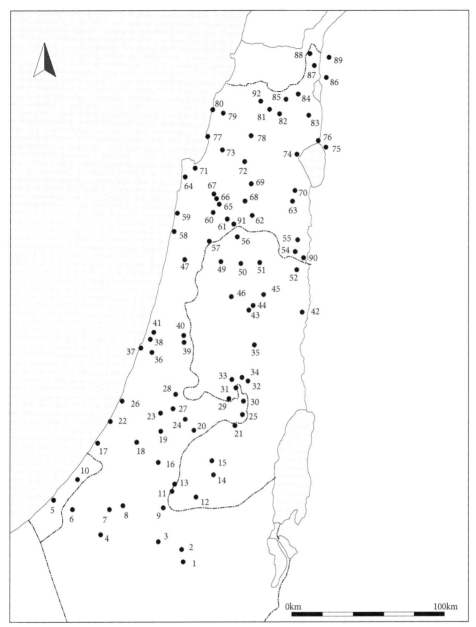

FIG. 41.1 Map of Iron Age I sites in the southern Levant (Cisjordan). (1) Tell Esdar; (2) Tel Masos; (3) Beersheba (Tel); (4) Tell el-Far'ah (South); (5) Deir el-Balah; (6) Tell Jemmeh; (7) Tel Haror; (8) Tel Sera; (9) Tell Halif; (10) Gaza; (11) Tell Beit Mirsim; (12) Kh. Rabud; (13) Tell Eitun; (14) Hebron; (15) Beth Zur; (16) Lachish; (17) Ashkelon; (18) Tel Zippor; (19) Tell es-Safi (Gath); (20) Tel Yarmuth; (21) Giloh; (22) Ashdod; (23) Tel Miqne (Ekron); (24) Beth Shemesh; (25) Jerusalem; (26) Tel Mor; (27) Tel Batash; (28) Gezer; (29) Gibeon; (30) Tell el-Ful; (31) Tell en-Nasbeh; (32) Ai; (33) Kh. Raddana; (34) Bethel; (35) Shiloh; (36) Azor; (37) Jaffa; (38) Tel Gerisa; (39) Aphek; (40) 'Izbet Sartah; (41) Tell Qasile; (42) Bedhat ash-Sha'ab; (43) Shechem; (44) Mount Ebal; (45) Tell el-Far'ah (North);

and Beth Shean (D'Agata et al. 2005). Even exchanges with neighbouring Egypt are only minimally attested for large tracts of Canaan. The disappearance of the 'state-administered' interregional exchanges also means that exchanges now assumed new, less centralized modes.

3. As part of these processes, the supply of Cypriot copper may have been severely disrupted and Egyptian mining activities in Timna in the 'Aravah Valley weakened. Concomitantly, the Feinan copper mines, in the eastern 'Aravah Valley, started to gain importance. This had crucial effects, since in Iron I bronze was still the principal metal used for tools and weapons. There was, however, no shortage of copper and bronze. Bronze artefacts are plentiful, but their production and recycling was fragmented, executed throughout Canaan's subregions, such as at Tel Dan, Tell el-Wawiyat, Dor, Yoqne'am, Megiddo, Khirbet Raddana, Beth Shemesh, Tell Qasile, and Tel Masos (Fig. 41.1; Artzy 2006).

4. The collapse of the Bronze Age *mappa mundi* also culminated in significant population dislocations. Some of these, of various scopes and compositions and originating in the west and north (the Aegean, Cyprus, Anatolia, and Syria), eventually settled in various parts of Canaan. Particularly, the final collapse of the Cypriot Bronze Age world, which occurred somewhat later than in other regions (i.e. the Late Cypriot IIIA/IIIB transition), had fundamental effects on Canaan.

5. The annihilation of the urban and commercial matrix of coastal Syria, especially the disappearance of Ugarit (*c.*1185 BCE) had profound effects, especially on coastal regions to the south.

6. Textual data and environmental studies hint that the termination of the Bronze Age world system coincided with or was even caused by a prolonged period of draught, affecting at least the Levant, Anatolia, and the Aegean. This, however, still needs further corroboration.

SUB-PERIODIZATION, NOMENCLATURE, CHRONOLOGY

Traditionally, Iron I in Canaan/Israel is dated between roughly 1200/1150–1000/980 BCE and correlated with the period of Israelite settlement and Judges narrated in the Bible.

Due to the fragmentation of material manifestations in the different Canaanite subregions, it is difficult to determine an all-encompassing chronological/terminological framework. Furthermore, the disappearance of Bronze Age administrations also means that inscribed artefacts enabling direct historical dating, for most of this period, are scarce.

FIG. 41.1 (*continued*) (46) Samaria; (47) Tel Zeror; (48) not used; (49) Kh. El-Hammam; (50) Dothan; (51) Daharat et-Tawileh ('Bull' site); (52) Tell el-Hammah; (53) not used; (54) Tel Rehov; (55) Beth Shean; (56) Ta'anach; (57) El-Ahwat; (58) Tel Mevorakh; (59) Dor; (60) 'En Haggit; (61) Megiddo; (62) 'Afula; (63) Tel Rekhesh; (64) Shiqmona; (65) Tel Qiri; (66) Yoqne'am; (67) Tel Qashish; (68) Migdal Ha-'Emeq; (69) Tel 'en-Zippori; (70) Tel Yin'am; (71) Tell Abu Hawam; (72) Tell el-Wawiyat; (73) Tell Keisan; (74) Tel Kinrot; (75) Tel Hadar; (76) Bethsaida; (77) 'Akko; (78) Carmiel; (79) Kabri; (80) Achziv; (81) Gush Halav; (82) Sasa; (83) Hazor; (84) Tel Kedesh; (85) Horvat 'Avot; (86) Tel Anafa; (87) Qiryat Shemona; (88) Tel Abel Beth Ma'acha; (89) Dan; (90) Tel Menorah; (91) Tel Qedesh; and (92) Har Adir

Sub-periodization is easier for the lowlands, where detailed stratigraphic sequences pro-duced variegated material culture media. For other regions, particularly the highlands, where sites typically offer very shallow stratigraphies and poor assortments of finds, and where research relies heavily on surveys, this is extremely difficult.

Chronologically, a fourfold division is employed here (based on Gilboa and Sharon 2003): Late Bronze/Iron transition; Iron 1a; Iron 1b; and Iron 1/2 transition. The Late Bronze/Iron Age transition is defined as the period immediately following the collapse of the Late Bronze Mediterranean network. Archaeologically it is definable by the final, near-total disappear-ance of Cypriot and Mycenaean ceramic imports in the Levant. Based on Egyptian finds in Canaan, the chronology of Mycenaean and Cypriot pottery in datable contexts such as Ugarit and Emar on the Euphrates, 'Myc IIIC' pottery at Beth Shean, and ^{14}C determina-tions, especially in Cyprus, this phase starts around 1190 BCE, coinciding with the ascen-sion of the Egyptian 20th Dynasty. Its end is defined here as the end of the Egyptian hold on Canaan, occurring somewhere between the latter part of Ramesses III's reign (end of reign c.1157 BCE) and that of Ramesses VI (ending c.1139 BCE), i.e. about 1140 BCE. This phase correlates mainly with LC IIIA in Cyprus and LH IIIC in the Aegean. In Philistia, it is then that Philistine Monochrome pottery ('local Mycenaean IIIC') starts to appear.

Iron 1a is easily defined in the lowlands. In the south ('Philistia') it is typified by the tran-sition from the 'Philistine Monochrome phase' to the 'Philistine Bichrome' one, and corre-lates with LC IIIB in Cyprus. Occurrences of Philistine Bichrome on the northern coast and northern valleys, and some ceramics in these regions that are also associated with LC IIIB, allow the integration of the northern coast and valleys into this framework. In the Aegean, this period parallels at least some portion of the sub-Mycenaean–early Proto-Geometric range, but evidence is still scarce. Traditionally, the end of this period is placed about 1050 BCE, which is the date employed here, but this is totally conjectured and currently cannot be assessed by radiometric determinations. Iron 1b as employed here is again discernible chiefly in the lowlands, recognizable mainly by the first occurrences of Phoenician Bichrome containers and Cypro-Geometric ceramics. Through these, this horizon can be specifically correlated with CG IA–mid CG I in Cyprus and more roughly with an unknown stretch of the early–mid-Proto-Geometric range of Euboea in Greece. Dating the end of this period is at present one of the most debated issues in Levantine archaeology (Finkelstein 2005; Mazar 2005; Sharon et al. 2007). Major occupations of this horizon, such as Tell Qasile on the Yarkon River (Stratum X), Megiddo in the Jezreel Valley (Stratum VIA), Tell Keisan in the 'Akko Plain (Stratum 9a–b), and Tel Kinrot near the Sea of Galilee (Stratum VI/V), end in destruction or abandonment, which have been attributed to Davidic conquests. Using biblical chronology, these have been dated around 1000/980 BCE. However, radiocarbon determinations allow for the possibility that this period also encompasses most of or even all the 10th century BCE. This, of course, would completely change our understand-ing of the way Iron I archaeological phenomena correlate with social, demographic, and political phenomena portrayed in the Bible, meaning that Iron I encompasses not only the 'Period of the Judges' but also the beginning of the monarchy (10th century BCE by biblical reckoning).

Lastly, in various regions of Canaan/Israel it has been realized recently that a fourth, tran-sitional Iron 1/2 period needs to be defined. This apparently short period has been segre-gated in a few sites only and some scholars define it as Early Iron IIA (e.g. Herzog and Singer Avitz 2006). This period correlates with CG IB/II in Cyprus and with Late Proto-Geometric Euboea, possibly starting parallel to Middle Proto-Geometric. Archaeologically, the *end* of this period is most easily recognized by the appearance in Canaan of Cypriot Black-on-Red Ware, which coincides with the main cultural phenomena defining Iron IIA in the Levant. Employing biblically derived chronology, this horizon could be dubbed 'Davidic' and date around the turn of the 11th century BCE. But new ^{14}C dating from Israel may point to a much later date, placing it around 925–900 BCE.

The end of Egyptian domination

During the 20th Dynasty (Late Bronze/Iron transition), Egypt gradually but terminally lost her imperial grip over Nubia and Canaan (Weinstein 1992; some Egyptian holdings in Canaan had already been relinquished by the 19th Dynasty). Egyptian control in this period is traceable mainly in southern Canaan and the Jordan Valley, where some Egyptian administrative centres are unequivocally attested until at least Ramesses III's reign. These are chiefly Beth Shean in the Jordan Valley (Stratum Lower VI), Tel Sera' (Tell esh-Shari'a; Stratum IX) in the western Negev, and Lachish in the Shephelah (Stratum VI). In Canaan, Egyptian artefacts bearing royal names (chiefly scarabs) fall off sharply after Ramesses III, even more so after Ramesses IV. Considering the social and political unrest in Egypt under Ramesses III, it is hardly conceivable that Egypt held any serious control over Canaan after him, but a bronze pedestal with the name of Ramesses VI at Megiddo, for example, may indicate some Egyptian activity somewhat later. Egyptian copper and turquoise mining and accompanying cultic activities at Timna in the 'Aravah and at Serabit el-Khadem in the southwestern Sinai continued until about the reign of Ramesses V or VI. In contrast, many sites in the Egyptian chain of forts, granaries, etc. along the 'Ways of Horus' (known in the Old Testament as the 'Way of the Philistines'), connecting Egypt and Canaan through northern Sinai, had fallen into disuse. Only rarely, such as at Haruba (Haruvit), is Egyptian activity clearly attested after the 19th Dynasty. Ramesses III's eighth-year battles (c. 1180 BCE), as recorded mainly on his mortuary temple at Medinet Habu, were the last time Egypt had fought against any foreign force for a very long while.

The clearest evidence for Egyptian presence is at Beth Shean, Stratum Lower VI (Mazar 2003), continuing from Strata IX through VII (of the 18th and 19th Dynasties) (Fig. 41.2). Two superimposed Egyptian administrative buildings were uncovered. The upper one, a 22×22m square building ('1500'), comprised small rooms around a central two-columned hall (probably provided with a clerestory) and exhibits Egyptian plan and Egyptian building techniques, such as T-shaped thresholds. As evident from accompanying hieroglyphic inscriptions, it was the seat of an Egyptian governor, Ramesses Weser-Khepesh, 'Overseer of the army of the Lord of the two lands'. He operated under Ramesses III, whose statue was erected somewhere in Beth Shean (but found in Stratum V). A well-planned domestic quarter east of this so-called residency, built according to a grid system, incorporated a temple (renovated from Stratum VII). It is of Canaanite tradition, but with some Egyptian-inspired elements, such as lotus-shaped column capitals, Egyptian-style friezes, and floors tinted with 'Egyptian Blue'. It is unclear which deity was worshipped here, and nothing clearly indicates Egyptian cult.

Substantial Egyptian presence at the site is also provided by other finds, such as Egyptian inscriptions, glyptics, and *bullae*, and by its Egyptianized ceramics (Martin 2006). Numerous Egyptian-looking vessels, mainly domestic, were manufactured locally, but

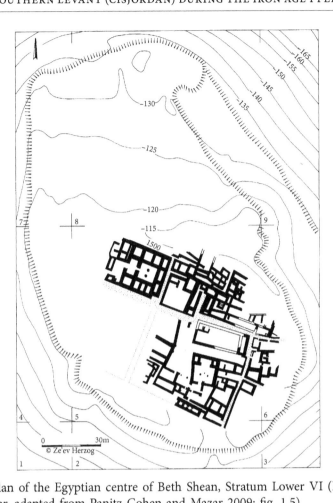

FIG. 41.2 Plan of the Egyptian centre of Beth Shean, Stratum Lower VI (LB/Ir) (courtesy A. Mazar, adapted from Panitz-Cohen and Mazar 2009: fig. 1.5)

employing Egyptian techniques. These quite crude vessels hardly had any clientele among the Canaanite population.

In the northern cemetery of Beth Shean, dozens of tubular clay anthropoid coffins were found, their lids shaped like human faces, some naturalistic and some schematic. They exemplify Egyptian burial customs and must have belonged to Egypt's functionaries at the site. It is difficult, however, to determine which of them parallel Stratum Lower VI.

At other sites, Egyptian control is best attested through Egyptian inscriptions. At Lachish VI and Tel Sera' IX, short Egyptian hieratic inscriptions on clay vessels/fragments, some of them recording the collection of grains, provide evidence for the collection of taxes in kind. At Lachish, a bronze plaque with cartouches of Ramesses III probably adorned some building. Otherwise, however, Egyptian impact on local material culture was marginal. Beyond Beth Shean, a few so-called residencies with central halls (Oren 1984) incorporate some Egyptian elements in layout and construction, but are a far cry from their 'prototypes'. But a few can be demonstrated to have functioned during the 20th Dynasty. At Lachish, similarly to Beth Shean, the so-called Acropolis Temple of Stratum VI (Ussishkin 2004) is essentially a

Canaanite temple, but with some unmistakable Egyptian-type furnishing, such as octagonal column bases and grooved columns that probably supported lotus capitals (found nearby). In addition to Beth Shean, clay anthropoid coffins in Cisjordan where uncovered at Tell el-Far'ah South and Lachish, the latter bearing an Egyptian hieroglyphic inscription.

Weighing this and other evidence (Higginbotham 2000), especially when contrasting the evidence with that regarding imperial presence in Nubia, it seems that Egyptian control over Canaan in this period was implemented by a limited number of Egyptian administrators and small garrisons, mostly through the Egyptian-acculturated Canaanite elites. These managed Egyptian interests and were personally dependent on Egypt's goodwill and backing.

The end of all these sites is marked by wholesale destructions, whose agents are difficult to identify. Postulated candidates are the 'Sea Peoples', 'Israelites', the Canaanite population, or the withdrawing Egyptians themselves.

The disappearance of Egypt from the Canaanite scene, especially in the south, was of paramount impact. On one hand, the country found itself free of the Egyptian taxation yoke and, more importantly, free of the need to feed pillaging armies on the move. On the other hand, however, social structure, particularly in the south, must have been deeply shaken. Old regime elites lost their support and perhaps legitimacy, and traditional landownership (including crown properties) was probably contested. Considering the fact that a mere 50 years earlier the cessation of Mediterranean trade had also deprived some of the elites of considerable revenues, this was a serious blow and rendered southern Canaan, more than any other region, amenable to social change and vulnerable to newcomers from west and north.

FRAGMENTATION: SUBREGIONS AND SUBCULTURES

The northern valleys and northern coast

Very few Canaanite towns in these regions survived into the Late Bronze/Iron horizon, notably Ta'anach, Period IA, and Megiddo, Stratum VIIA (Mazar 2002). The latter, rebuilt after the destruction of Stratum VIIB, exemplifies the same urban layout as its predecessor, comprising a ceremonial gate, a courtyard-type palace in the north, a renewed monumental *migdol* temple and adjoining quarter on the east, and residential quarters on the south. Continuity is also exemplified by the marked persistence of Canaanite ceramic practice and metalwork. The treasury of the northern palace produced a hoard comprising mainly hundreds of ivories. Stylistically, many of them are older than their 12th-century BCE find-context and the hoard seems to have been accumulated over a long period of time. In turn, the VIIA town too, alongside nearby Ta'anach, and the as yet poorly known settlement at Tell Keisan (in the 'Akko Plain; Stratum 13) was violently destroyed around the mid-12th century. Other than these sites, evidence for any substantial administrative centres in the northern lowlands in this horizon is scarce. Even such coastal *entrepôts* as Tell Abu Hawam and Dor did not yet reveal any attestations of Late Bronze/Iron settlement. More continuity, however, is traceable in the villages, especially in the Jezreel Valley.

It is only during Iron 1a, culminating in Iron 1b, that a new 'urban' system emerges, which bears little resemblance to the Late Bronze one. Megiddo, again, is the only site where continuity is discernible (Fig. 41.3; Halpern 2000). Stratum VIB, constructed above the ruins

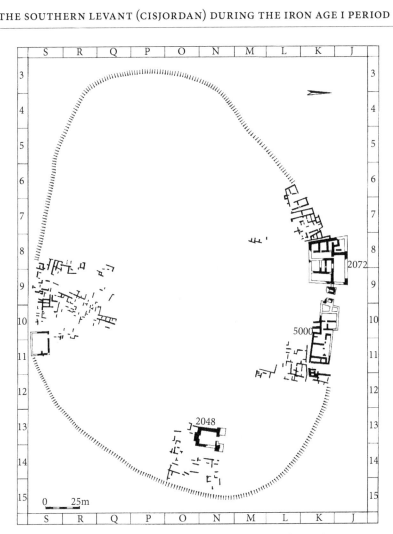

FIG. 41.3 Plan of Megiddo VIA (Ir1b) (from Herzog 1997: fig. 5.8)

of VIIA, starts as a modest affair and develops into a well-planned town (VIA), surprisingly similar to that of VIIA, and extending over the high tell and a lower terrace. Large administrative buildings of the courtyard building type (2072 and 5000) and a gate are again situated in the north and even the *migdol* temple (of Syrian architectural pedigree) is renewed—the latest attestation of this type of temple in Canaan. At Beth Shean, on the other hand, after a short-lived, partial reconstruction of the ex-Egyptian centre, there springs up a totally new town, in which the main edifices were two monumental buildings surrounded by auxiliary rooms (Strata Upper VI/Lower V). The northern edifice was a temple with an indirect approach and clear Canaanite Late Bronze antecedents, and the southern one was a large hall divided into 3×2 rows of pillars, which may have been a temple as well. In tandem, extensive urban centres were established where Late Bronze Age occupation was modest or nonexistent, but they differ from each other greatly. At Tel Kinrot on the northwestern shore of the Sea of Galilee (mainly Stratum VI/V), a 9ha fortified town was constructed, comprising a well-planned grid of mainly courtyard buildings, alleys and streets, some with stone-covered drainage channels (Fig. 41.4; Fritz and Münger 2002). Opposite Tel Kinrot, at Tel Hadar on the eastern shore of the Sea of Galilee (Stratum IV; Iron 1b or Iron 1/2), a unique architectural complex—a fortified enclosure with a tripartite building and adjacent six-chambered granary—served as a redistribution centre (Beck, Kochavi, and Yadin forthcoming).

At Tel Keisan (Strata 12–9) it is mainly the end of this sequence (Stratum 9a–b; Iron 1b) that is known. The town was unfortified, but characterized by meticulous planning, comprising buildings of identical size and complex inner partitioning (Humbert 1988). At Tell Abu Hawam in the southwestern 'Akko Plain (Levels Vc late–IV-2), the only continuity from the Late Bronze Age is the erection of an oblong temple (30) on the same spot and in a similar orientation where the Late Bronze temple (50) once stood. This seems to have been the only monumental building on the mound. The Late Bronze fort on the west has been abandoned, and other buildings were very modest. Subsequently, in the course of Iron 1b and Iron 1/2, new structures were built, having no Canaanite antecedents, but some corollaries in Syria. They are small (*c.*8×8m) square structures usually subdivided into three spaces. Towards the end of Iron I there is a complete change in the town's layout: a large structure of some administrative function ('Building 32-3') is erected on the southeast and adjacent to it, an annex comprising three long and narrow halls, separated by walls of alternating segments of fieldstones and large dressed stones. In Iron II, this 'tripartite' layout is to become typical for various public structures, serving various purposes. At Tell Abu Hawam, by its contents, it seems to have served as a storehouse, perhaps also as a commercial nexus.

At Dor, in Iron 1a, the modest Late Bronze town was supplanted by a 7ha town, which from its inception was fortified and densely built, characterized by 'Canaanite' courtyard buildings and a monumental inner citadel/acropolis overlooking its southern bay. Towards the end of this sequence (Iron 1b), a complex of huge buildings overlooking the southern bay was erected, that is one of the most monumental buildings known around the Mediterranean in this period. It comprises a massive stone structure with ashlar corners—one of the earliest attestations of this type of construction in the Iron Age. This building was surrounded by an

FIG. 41.4 View of Tel Kinrot VI/V (Ir1b) (courtesy S. Müenger)

FIG. 41.5 View of storage building overlooking the southern lagoon at Dor (Ir1b) (courtesy Tel Dor Excavation Project)

extensive mud-brick complex, part of which, as at Tel Keisan and Tel Hadar, comprised long and narrow halls (Fig. 41.5), but here the spaces were entered from their ceilings. This, and their contents, indicate that they were used for storage (Sharon and Gilboa 2013).

Ceramic traditions in all these regions (and likewise at Yoqne'am in the Jezreel Valley, Strata XVIII–XVII, and at Tel Rehov in the Jordan Valley, Levels D-5–D-4) reveal a basic continuity versus the Late Bronze Age. However, the habit of painting on pottery has been gradually abandoned and decorations are executed mostly on small commercial containers to promote their trade.

Supraregional contacts are attested mainly along the Carmel and Galilee coasts and to a lesser extent in the northern valleys. Especially, a continuous and extensive exchange with Cyprus is in evidence, which, however, is totally different from Late Bronze patterns. To Cyprus were shipped mainly some commodities packed in storage jars and small lentoid flasks, adorned with Late Bronze Age-derived painted decorations. In Iron 1b, part of the small containers start to be adorned in the so-called Phoenician Bichrome style—derived from an amalgamation of Canaanite and Cypriot decorative concepts (Fig. 41.6; Gilboa, Sharon, and Boaretto 2008). Cypriot presence, at least on the coast, is also indicated by some imports from Cyprus and local production of 'Myc IIIC' containers and drinking vessels (mainly at Akko); by an extensive local production of wavy-band pithoi in Cypriot style; by some previously unattested local production of skyphoi; and in Iron 1b, especially at Dor, by the import of significant amounts of Cypro-Geometric I tablewares (Gilboa 1999). Extensive, probably maritime, contacts with Egypt are attested mainly at Dor and probably at Akko, by numerous Egyptian jars and the import of Nile perch. Other exchanges, of more limited geographical scope, are exemplified by Philistine ('Bichrome') containers (mainly at Tel Keisan and Dor) and possibly by a multidirectional exchange between the coast, the valleys, and the Manasseh hills of some commodities packed in collared-rim pithoi. 'En Hagit, situated in Wadi Milh connecting the coast and the Jezreel Valley, may have been a way station or redistribution centre serving this network

Towards the end of Iron I, contacts with regions further north and west are attested by the presence at Tel Keisan (Iron 1b) and Dor (Iron 1/2) of silver originating in Anatolia, and

FIG. 41.6 Phoenician Bichrome containers from Yoqne'am and Tel Kinrot (Ir1b; courtesy A. Ben-Tor, Yoqne'am Excavations and S. Müenger, Kinneret Excavations)

possibly also the Aegean and even Sardinia, but the mechanisms by which this metal circulated are poorly known. Concurrently, very rare examples of Greek (Euboean) ceramics are known from Tel Hadar (Iron 1b) and Dor (Iron 1/2).

Thus, like their northerly neighbours on the Lebanese coast, the coastal centres of the Carmel Coast and 'Akko Plain benefited from the collapse of Bronze Age coastal Syria. They were probably also active, through sites in the northern valleys like Tel Kinrot, in the shipment of copper mined at Feinan. Entrepreneurial initiatives in these activities seem to have been much more prominent now than in the Late Bronze.

But even in these thriving towns, in some material culture respects, there is a decline from the Late Bronze Age. For example, prestige items (elaborate ivories, glass vessels, etc.) are hardly known, though technologies were probably retained through the production of simpler artefacts such as beads. Also, in this and other Canaanite regions, there was no significant literacy. Still, Proto-Canaanite inscriptions, known in Late Bronze contexts and in Iron IIA (subsequently developing into the various alphabetic scripts of the first millennium BCE), indicate that this knowledge must have been preserved. Some so-called Proto-Canaanite inscriptions have indeed been assigned to Iron I (chiefly an abecedarium at 'Izbet Sartah on the western fringes of the Samaria Hills, and short dedicatory inscriptions on bronze arrowheads), but none can be unequivocally assigned to Iron I.

Throughout the period, there is evidence of some Cypriots presence in the region, especially along the Carmel Coast, which had a central role in interregional commercial exchanges. Some of this population probably arrived in northern Canaan following the LC IIIA/IIIB disruptions on the island. Some newcomers from Syria are attested by designs on ceramics and by the introduction of lioness-headed cups of Syrian origin (at Dor and Megiddo). It is probably some of this new blend of Canaanite, Cypriot, and Syrian populations that is referred to by the Egyptians as *tj-k-r/SKL* (Gilboa 2005). In Medinet Habu, their clash with Ramesses III's armies in his fifth and eighth regnal years is described, among others people from the north and from the sea (dubbed by modern scholarship 'Sea Peoples'). The Egyptian Onomasticon of Amenope (mid-11th century or somewhat later) associates them with the Canaanite coast, and in the Tale of Wenamun (11th or 10th century BCE) they are described as residing at Dor. Some scholars identify them with a people named *Šikalayu*, mentioned in a 13th-century Ugaritic document as 'living on boats'.

The end of Iron I witnessed the gradual disintegration of this 'northern alliance'. At some sites (Megiddo, Yoqneʿam, Tel Keisan, Tel Hadar, and possibly also Tel Kinrot), this end is marked by violent destructions. At Megiddo and Yoqneʿam these are followed by the gradual development of totally different Iron II towns, while other sites where abandoned, at least for a while. Continuity into Iron IIA is attested mainly at Tel Keisan and Dor. The latter is the only town that passed into the Ir1/2 transitional period unscathed.

THE SOUTHERN COASTAL PLAIN, SHEPHELAH, AND NORTHERN NEGEV

Though surveys in these regions were intensive, it is very difficult to differentiate between late Late Bronze and early Iron Age pottery, and concomitantly to assess demographic processes in the Late Bronze/Iron transition. It seems, however, that during this transition the region underwent a significant demographic change. Similarly to the Late Bronze Age, settlement was mainly in larger-scale villages or towns, mainly on tell sites, with scant evidence of an integrated settlement hierarchy. However, the number of settlements had dwindled, a process especially evident in the southern part of this region, including the short-term abandonment of major sites, such as Lachish. Settlement is mostly attested in the north—in the environs of Tel Miqne-Ekron, Tell es-Safi-Gath, and to their west (the Ashdod area) (Finkelstein 2000). It is unclear, however, if the decline in the number of settlements also implies a decrease in population, or whether a process of nucleization may be postulated. Extensive resettlement of all these regions is only attested in Iron II. It is therefore the sequences in the major tell sites through which this period is best known, where the quite variegated picture attests to the growth of new urban centres during the Late Bronze/Iron Age transition, i.e. earlier than most of the northern towns. The clearest sequence is at Tel Miqne-Ekron on the eastern margins of the Shephelah (Strata VII–IV; the Late Bronze/ Iron transition till Ir1/2; Dothan 1998). There, a small Late Bronze town (Stratum VIII) was superimposed by a well-planned 20ha city, fortified by a solid wall, which exemplifies gradual urban growth, until it ended in destruction. At other sites (chiefly coastal Ashkelon, Levels 20–17 and Ashdod, Strata XIII–XI) no such significant growth and no obvious fortifications are attested, at least in the beginning, and at Ashdod it is obvious that some of the Late Bronze structures were re-used.

The most conspicuous phenomenon in these sites (and others, e.g. Tell es-Safi-Gath) is the sudden appearance in the Late Bronze/Iron horizon of significant amounts of locally produced table wares of 'western' derivation, alongside the local Canaanite repertoire. These, the so-called Myc IIIC or Philistine Monochrome (Dothan and Zukerman 2004), comprise mainly drinking and serving vessels (mostly bell-shaped skyphoi (Fig. 41.7) and kraters, and spouted jugs) whose shapes, decorations, and technology are foreign. Their exact stylistic associations in the west are still contested—the Aegean, Cyprus, Anatolia, or different combinations thereof—but they are especially close to contemporary 'Myc IIIC' wares in Cyprus. At all these sites during Iron Ia, this ware was gradually replaced by the so-called Philistine Bichrome vessels, also produced locally, which are geographically more widespread throughout the southern coast and Shephelah, including towns like Beth Shemesh, Tel Batash-Timnah, Tell Qasile on the Yarkon River, and many others, surviving until the end of Iron I (e.g. Bunimovitz 1990). This ware too forms only a small part of the ceramic assemblages, but it comprises a larger assortment of shapes than the preceding 'Philistine Monochrome'. In shapes and decorations 'Philistine Bichrome' owes much to the 'west', but Cypriot traditions on it are conspicuous, attesting to some new Cypriot impact. Local, Canaanite, and Egyptian traits are new features.

Throughout Iron I, foreign habits, mainly at Tel Miqne-Ekron, Ashkelon, and Ashdod, are attested by many other new phenomena (Stager 1995; Dothan 2003). Cooking jugs of Aegean and/or Cypriot types, alongside clay basins modelled after Cypriot types (*kalathoi*) and clay cylindrical 'spool-shaped' loomweights of Aegean or Cypriot derivation, attest to domestic routines of foreign ancestry. New dietary habits, chiefly a dramatic increase in the consumption of pigs (Killebrew and Lev-Tov 2008), reflect Aegean custom. Artefacts of foreign ceremonial associations are figurines—zoomorphic, male, and first and foremost the female 'Ashdoda' figurines (Ben-Shlomo and Press 2009).

A complete example from Ashdod (Fig. 41.8; Stratum XII) constitutes a schematic female figurine, painted in 'Philistine Bichrome', whose torso merges with the body of the chair. Her pinched bird-like face and *polos* headdress reveals Aegean or Cypriot style. Other

FIG. 41.7 'Philistine Monochrome' skyphos from Tel Miqne-Ekron, Stratum VII (courtesy Trude Dothan and Seymour Gitin, the Tel Miqne-Ekron Excavations)

0   2 cm

FIG. 41.8 'Ashdoda' figurine adorned in 'Philistine Bichrome' from Ashdod, Stratum XII
(courtesy Israel Antiquities Authority)

ceremonial objects betraying a Cypriot association are incised bovine scapulae and bimetallic knives. The latter are composed of iron blades attached by bronze rivets to ivory or bone
handles with a ring-shaped pommel. At Ashdod, two seals bear undeciphered signs, somewhat resembling Cypro-Minoan characters, and similarly at Ashkelon (Level 17, late Iron I)
an ostracon was inscribed in characters reminiscent of the Cypro-Minoan script.

From their inception, all these towns were densely built and reveal preplanned layouts
with architectural complexes, some of them domestic, aligned alongside streets intersecting
at right angles (especially at Ashkelon and Ashdod), with very little continuity with late Late
Bronze constructions. No clear foreign impact, however, can be detected in this architecture, and at Ashdod some of these buildings are possibly reminiscent of 'Canaanite' courtyard buildings. At Tell Qasile, by the end of this sequence (Stratum X, Iron Ib), buildings of
the 'four-room house' type and other pillared buildings are introduced, a rare occurrence in
Iron I outside the mountainous regions.

Tel Miqne-Ekron also produced structures of cultic nature. Initially these are very small
and simple, consisting of one space only (Stratum VII). Their inner furnishing includes
different combinations of benches alongside walls, especially oval or oblong mud-brick
hearths, sometimes supporting a column or flanked by two columns (a configuration also
known at Ashdod), and deep stone or clay oval basins ('bathtubs'). Such hearths, usually
coated with pebbles or potsherds, are also known from Ashkelon, Tell Qasile (keyhole-
shaped), and Ashdod. They were probably used for cooking during cultic or other social
activities. They have no local antecedents but are amply attested both in Cyprus, and, less so,
in the Aegean. A Cypriot or possibly Aegean origin is also evident for the 'bathtubs' (either
of stone or clay), known also from Ashkelon, Ashdod, and Tell Qasile, but their function

is yet unclear (industrial? cultic purification?). At Tel Miqne, Field IV, these modest cultic structures gradually grow into a densely built complex, which in Strata V–IV comprises a large building, probably of cultic nature ('Temple 350'; Fig. 41.9). It was entered through a square hall, whose entrance is flanked by two columns, which led into the main oblong hall, divided longitudinally by a row of columns and possibly containing a rounded pebble-surfaced hearth. One of the long sides of this hall opened into three small chambers with small altars or platforms. The building was dubbed a megaron on account of its *in antis* entrance. Though its plan is a far cry from the megara in Greece, some features (i.e. small cultic chambers) do have corollaries in Greece.

A unique sequence of small temples was uncovered at Tell Qasile (Strata XII–X, Iron Ia–b) and identified as 'Philistine' because of its abundance of 'Philistine Bichrome' asemblages. Here too, a small structure of one space gradually develops into two temples within a densely built quarter. Architecturally they belong to a Canaanite type of temple typified by modest dimensions, lack of symmetry, indirect access, inner benches, and platforms (Mazar 2000). Though similar temples are known in Cyprus and the Mycenaean world, it is difficult to pinpoint the exact origin of their plans. Likewise, the rich cultic paraphernalia in them is of a mixed heritage: Canaanite–Egyptian tradition (e.g. cylindrical cult stands, bird bowls, a mask, and *naoi*); Cypriot (*kernoi*, 'trick vases'); Syro-Anatolian (lioness-headed cups—also known from other sites in Philistia and outside it); and some unique objects.

It is unknown which deities were worshipped in all these 'temples'. The 'Ashdoda' figurines indicate a feminine deity and the double temples at Tell Qasile may point to the worship of a couple. Customarily the female deities are taken to represent the great Aegean 'Mother Goddess', though an association with Syro-Anatolian deities has also been suggested (Yasur-Landau 2001; Singer 1992).

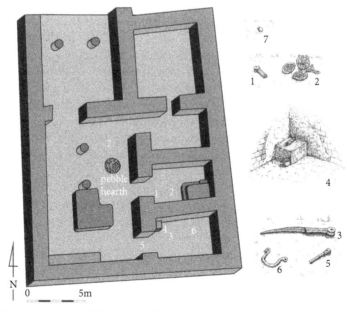

FIG. 41.9 Temple 350 at Tel Miqne-Ekron, Stratum V (courtesy Trude Dothan and Seymour Gitin, the Tel Miqne-Ekron Excavations)

The burial grounds of these Philistine sites are yet to be discovered. At other sites in this geographical sphere (mainly Tell el-Far'ah South, Azor, Gezer, and Tel 'Eton ('Eitun)), burial practices vary, but most continue from the Late Bronze. Most burials are simple, single and primary burials in oblong pits or in 'cist' tombs (lined by brick or stones). In some instances (e.g. Azor) burial was conducted in single or double clay vessels, mostly jars, and cremations are known mainly at Azor and Tell el-Far'ah South. Occasionally, multiple burials were conducted in large rock-hewn chamber tombs. In Cemetery 500 at Tell el-Far'ah South, five conspicuous rock-cut tombs, hewn in a row, exhibited a meticulously executed trapezoidal shape, a long, stepped-entrance *dromos* (corridor), some Philistine Bichrome pottery, and a few lids of clay anthropoid coffins. They were thus dubbed 'Philistine'. A Cypriot origin for this layout is likely, and the long *dromoi* are paralleled mainly in the Aegean (and in Cyprus during LC IIIB). However, it cannot be ruled out that the shape of these tombs developed at Tell el-Far'ah South locally, from similar tombs dating to the Middle Bronze Age.

Clearly, then, as early as the Late Bronze/Iron horizon, parallel to the end of Egyptian domination, new populations arrived in these regions from Cyprus, and possibly the Aegean and coastal Asia Minor, but their numbers cannot be assessed. The social and economic havoc caused by Egypt's withdrawal, to which these populations contributed, left a chaotic environment in which they rapidly became a significant component of society. There is no doubt that these people—or rather, the mixture of locals and newcomers—are who the Bible and Egyptian records refer to as *plst*/Philistines. In Egypt, these *palastu* are mainly described alongside the *tj-k-r/Skl* and other groups in Ramesses III's inscriptions and reliefs at Medinet Habu, in Papyrus Harris I, and, like these, Amenope's Onomasticon associates them with the Canaanite coast. In the Bible, the Philistines are considered Israel's major foe during the 'Period of the Judges'. They are associated with the southern coast and Shephelah, and are recognized to have originated overseas (oftentimes specifically at *Kaftor,* to be identified with Crete or Cyprus). Politically, each city and hinterland was an independent entity, and the region never united to form a 'state', a situation that remained practically unchanged until the end of the Iron Age.

It was suggested that the rise of Philistine towns should be linked to a realignment of interregional commercial networks, and that, among other things, they functioned as shipping centres for copper, now produced mainly in Feinan. At present, however, this has not been confirmed by archaeological data. The emergence of Tel Masos in the eastern Negev, the only substantial site in this sparsely populated desert on the route from the 'Aravah to the Philistine coast, has been postulated as owing its existence to this new network (another site here is Tel Esdar). However, Masos starts to be important only in Ir1/2 (Stratum II).

Some exchange with the northern coastal areas is attested in Philistia by Phoenician commercial containers, but collared-rim jars, for example, are absent and elaborate metal artefacts typifying other regions in Canaan (and Cyprus) are few. Commercial contacts with Egypt involved mainly the extensive import of Egyptian fish. Evidence for overseas commercial contact is very scarce (Barako 2000), significantly less so than on the northern coast, though at Ashkelon some silver apparently originates in Sardinia.

During the transition to Iron II, some of the Philistine sites were destroyed and diminished in importance (Tell Qasile, Tel Miqne-Ekron; partly also Ashdod XI). Continuity is attested mainly at Ashkelon, Ashdod, and Tell es-Safi-Gath, which will hold centre stage in the next period.

THE MOUNTAINOUS REGIONS

Galilee and its eastern margins

In the Late Bronze Age the mountainous regions of the Galilee were sparsely settled, and larger-scale towns are known mainly around the Hula Valley (Hazor and Dan) and in Lower Galilee (e.g. Tel Hannathon and Tel Rekhesh). Hazor (XIII) and Dan (VII) are gradually destroyed and abandoned. Throughout Iron I, no urban sites are known in these regions, and lower and Upper Galilee, including to a certain extent their eastern margins (especially the Hula Valley), undergo a drastic demographic change. Following the destructions, either directly (at Dan) or after a gap (Hazor), new villages and hamlets gradually grow on these tells (Hazor XII/XI, Ben-Ami 2001; and especially Dan VI–IVB, Biran 1994: 125–46). Initially, they are characterized mainly by abundant stone-lined silos, pits, and other installations, utilizing a very modest architecture. Gradually, architecture evolves, silos become less frequent, and the storage of grain is conducted mainly in pithoi.

Concurrently, dozens of apparently similar small villages, some partially excavated (mainly in Upper Galilee and its vicinity, such as Sasa III–I, Tel Harashim, Horvat 'Avot, and Tel Anafa, but also in Lower Galilee, such as Carmiel) and some known only from surveys were established, chiefly on new terrain or over long deserted sites.

More continuity is attested in the rural sphere, where some Late Bronze small towns, villages, and hamlets continued to exist, such as Tel Yin'am, Tel 'En Zippori, and Tell el-Wawiyat in Lower Galilee (Dessel 1999; but they largely do not continue to Iron II). No intra- or inter-site hierarchy can be detected in those settlements, though towards late Iron I, larger sites like Dan, and possibly Tel Kedesh and Tel Abel Beth Ma'acah, may have functioned as regional centres.

Horvat 'Avot and Carmiel seem to have been composed of an oval chain of rooms enclosing a large open space. At Carmiel the use of pillars is a rare occurrence of construction methods known mainly in the central hill country.

This seems to have been a very loosely integrated system, most probably comprising kin-based settlements, practising a combination of dry farming (attested mainly in the valleys) and sheep/goat herding (mainly in the highlands). Horticulture can be postulated, but is hardly attested; at least at Dan, large quantities of beef were consumed. Ceramics at all these sites comprise mainly domestic vessels—mostly cooking pots and pithoi. The latter are predominantly different variants of the so-called collared-rim pithoi, some of local Galilean types and others resembling types prevalent in the central hill country. Several sites also produced pithoi of the Cypriot-inspired 'wavy band' variety, of which some were imported from the northern Canaanite coast, but others, especially in Iron Ib, were produced in Galilee. Pithoi were used mainly for storing agricultural commodities, as water containers, and in industrial applications. Beyond agriculture, sites such as Dan and Tel Harashim produced evidence of bronze recycling, conducted in domestic contexts.

An exceptional site is Har Adir (Stratum III), where a large casemate 'fortress' (perhaps a storage or redistribution centre) was constructed apparently in the Ir1/2 transition. Evidence of cultic practices is scant. At Dan (Stratum V), a small oblong structure with a back room (*adyton*) may have been of cultic function and, by its plan and associated metallurgical activities, recalls similar installations in the lowlands and in Cyprus. Stratum V also produced evidence of 'standing stones' (biblical *mazevot)*. No evidence of anthropomorphic cult objects exists in these regions, in contrast to the Late Bronze Age and concurrent practices in the lowlands. Burials sites are unknown, indicating that they were very modest affairs.

Despite the remote locations of some of the sites, there is ample evidence of interregional contacts, especially with the northern Canaanite/Phoenician coast, as evidenced mainly by the import of pithoi and Phoenician commercial containers, and occasionally, especially at Dan, Philistine containers arriving from the south. Some of the collared-rim pithoi originate in the Central Highlands, and exchanges are also attested with the more southerly regions of the Rift Valley—the environs of the Sea of Galilee and the Beth Shean Valley. Some peculiar painted vessels at Dan, resembling contemporary 'Sea People' pottery (mainly open vessels adorned with birds), and ring-kernoi at Dan and Har Adir (the latter in a cultic context), may point to some Cypriot-derived customs.

The mountainous areas of the Galilee are considered in the Bible to be part of Israel's inheritance (the tribes of Dan, Naphtali, Asher, Zevulun, and Issachar). Traditionally, therefore, most Iron I sites were considered Israelite. The destruction of Late Bronze Age Hazor and the humble settlement constructed over it were especially associated with the biblical account of Joshua's conquest. It seems, however, that the overriding factor in understanding these new settlements is the final collapse of the political and economic megacentre at Hazor, its kingdom, other contemporary centres in these regions, and the general collapse of the Levantine economic system. It is probably this Canaanite population, reverting to more basic and fragmented modes of subsistence, which accounts for most of the Iron I population here. Rapidly, however, intensive interregional commercial ties were formed—mostly with the lowlands to the west and south, and also with the central hill country.

Concurrently, however, the presence of other populations may be detected: Cypriot cult and other elements are indicative in this respect, and the infiltration of people from other regions cannot be ruled out. Both these phenomena are perhaps reflected in biblical traditions regarding the tribe of Dan. New group identities must have been forged and eventually, in Iron II, with the rise of territorial kingdoms, settlements like Hazor, Dan, and others were superimposed and apparently developed into the major towns of Israel. Others may have been incorporated into neighbouring polities, notably Tyre.

The central hill country and foothills

A similar process may be traced in the Central Highlands stretching between the Jezreel and Beer-Sheva Valleys—the hills of Samaria and Judea. The fate of the two major Bronze Age centres in these regions (Shechem and Jerusalem) is not entirely clear. At Shechem some continuity into the 12th century is attested (Stratum XI) and the Late Bronze broad house temple was apparently still functioning, but the town was destroyed apparently soon after. In Jerusalem, not a single structure has yet been unequivocally assigned to Iron I. A possible exception is a massive stepped stone revetment abutting the eastern slope of the 'City of David' spur, which probably supported a large structure; its date, however, is contested.

The very few Late Bronze sites in these regions are replaced by hundreds of new small settlements, most of them unfortified and with hardly any evidence of intra- and inter-site hierarchy, though at Khirbet Raddana, for example, some structures were larger and better constructed than others. Mostly these were established at new locations or (such as at et-Tell/'Ai near Bethel) on sites that had been desolate for centuries, and only rarely (e.g. at

Bethel) on the ruins of Late Bronze sites. Some sites, like Giloh south of Jerusalem and sites in the Jordan Valley, are no more than the poor habitations of pastoralists and accompanying animal pens.

At locales like Shiloh, ʿAi, and Khirbet Raddana, villages were established. Architecturally, they are characterized by clusters of pillared buildings, whereby some spaces of the houses are divided by stone or wooden pillars, the former either monolithic or constructed of superimposed stone drums. Most notably and surprisingly, a fairly uniform house plan is in use—the 'three- or (rarely) four-room house' (with two-room house variations: Faust and Bunimovitz 2003). It is usually a long-house building comprising a back broad room, typically fronted by two or three perpendicular long and narrow spaces, one of which served as a courtyard, separated by a row of columns/piers (Fig. 41.10). Though attempts have been made to trace this building type to semi-nomadic tent 'architecture', it is probably rooted in a sedentary Bronze Age Canaanite milieu. In Iron I, its main distribution is in the highland of Cisjordan, but it is also known from Transjordan and is destined to become the typical house plan of Israel and Judah in Iron II. Some of these house clusters are arranged peripherally, and at ʿIzbet Sartah, on the western fringes of the Samaria hills (Stratum III),

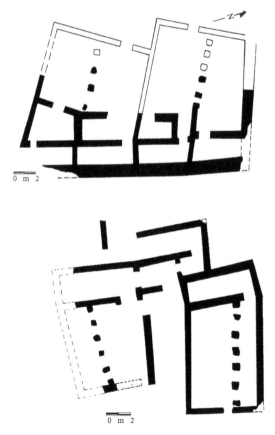

FIG. 41.10 Plan of three-room pillared houses at Khirbet Raddana (courtesy Zvi Lederman)

broad rooms were arranged in a circular belt, enclosing a large open space. This too has been interpreted as an arrangement linking pastoral tent 'settlements' and the town plan typifying Iron II Israelite/Judahite towns. Similarly to Galilee, stone-lined silos abound at these sites, and likewise rock-hewn cisterns. No architecture of an obvious public nature is known, though at Shiloh a large building complex may have served for communal storage and/or redistribution.

Other material media are also very basic, much more so than in the northern highlands. Pottery, rooted in Canaanite tradition, consists mainly of simple household vessels (cooking pots and kraters), and hardly any elaboration (such as painted decoration) is attested (Fig. 41.11). Especially conspicuous are the large 'collared-rim pithoi' (Esse 1991), probably used for storing cereals and water.

Two cultic sites may be associated with this demographic phenomenon. On Mount 'Ebal, above Shechem, a small Iron I cultic enclosure comprising a central edifice was suggested to be the altar erected by Joshua (Josh. 8). On a mountaintop at Daharat et-Tawileh in northern Samaria, a small paved circular enclosure (near which a bronze bull figurine was discovered) was equated with the 'High Places' mentioned in the Bible.

No burials can be associated with these highland settlements, and hardly any of the long-lived Bronze Age burial caves of the region can be demonstrated to have been used in this period.

Due to the shallow stratigraphy and poor material culture of these sites, it is difficult to date them precisely within Iron I and correlate them to the better-known sequences of the lowlands. On the basis of ceramics, it has been suggested that settlements in the east (Judean Desert fringes and the Jordan Valley) are the earliest and thence settlements spread westward. This would also imply a gradual shift from pastoralism to mixed farming, including horticulture. In the arid Judean Hills, pastoralism was always more important.

Traditionally, these new sites have been identified with the Israelite conquest and settlement described in the Bible (mostly in Joshua and Judges: the tribes of Manasseh, Ephraim, Benjamin, and Judah), and thus debates regarding the geographical and socioeconomic origin of their inhabitants and their ethnic affiliation abound. Can this population be traced

FIG. 41.11 Iron I ceramic assemblage from Shiloh (courtesy of Israel Finkelstein)

to a region outside Canaan and to a pastoral background? Can they be defined as Israelites and associated with the 'Israel' mentioned in Merenptah's stele (late 13th century BCE) in a Canaanite context? Can a tribal confederation as portrayed in the Bible be demonstrated, and when (Dever 1995; Finkelstein 1996)?

Alternative hypotheses, which are more rooted in archaeological *realia*, trace at least most of this population to a Canaanite background, though, as in the north, influxes from other regions are likely. Disagreement continues regarding the following points:

1. Specific origin: the urban Canaanite matrix or pastoral semi-nomads and others becoming sedentary; the latter possibly to be compared or even equated with the *Shasu* (possibly worshipping *YHVH*) and/or *'apiru* mentioned in Egyptian and Near Eastern records.
2. The reasons for the highlands settlement phenomenon and its differences versus that of the lowlands. The main possibilities suggested are: just a 'natural' dichotomy between villages and urban modes of life (London 1989); economically 'exploited' elements in the Canaanite cities physically disengaging from their home towns; highlands pastoralists starting to practise variegated agriculture after their economic symbiosis with the urban centres (many of which having been destroyed) has been severed (Whitelam 1994); and a 'realignment' of Canaanite demography following the collapse of the Late Bronze Age commercial networks, establishing settlements destined to exploit the natural resources of the highlands (mainly wood) and practise horticulture (mainly olives and vines) in order to supply Egypt.

Egypt, indeed, may have been a major factor in this process in other respects as well, but her role is impossible to assess due to the difficulty of accurately dating the sites. Dating the beginning of the 'settlement' phenomenon to the last phase of Egyptian control in Canaan (late 13th/early 12th centuries) led to the suggestion that settlement in remote, 'frontier' regions was enabled by the *pax Aegyptiaca*. Alternatively, it may be in fact the elimination of the Egyptian threat around the mid-12th century that helped instigate this process.

Many of these factors were most probably in operation concurrently, and the arrival of some new population from the east is definitely a possibility. As in many other cases, archaeology fails to substantiate or refute the claim that the highland settlers perceived themselves as distinct—religiously or otherwise. Possible indications for this are the apparently deliberate avoidance of using decorated ceramics and abstention from pork consumption, the latter in contrast to the habit found at Philistine sites. Economically, however, the highland settlements were not isolated. Chiefly, some commodities packed in 'collared-rim pithoi' were exchanged with neighbouring regions. But lowland influence on material culture and lowland imports were dramatically less than in Galilee.

In Iron II, these populations formed the backbone of the kingdoms of Israel and Judah. We will probably never be able to tell how many of them, where and when considered themselves 'Israelite'. The Merenptah stele, however, indicates that a significant part of them apparently did. Archaeology's contribution here is thus far limited, other than demonstrating clearly the continuity between the highlands' Iron I material culture and that of Israel and Judah in Iron II.

SUGGESTED READING

Bloch-Smith, E., and B. Alpert Nakai (1999). A landscape comes into life: the Iron I. *Near Eastern Archaeology* 62: 62–92.

Dever, W. G. (2003). *Who Were the Early Israelites, and Where Did They Come From?* Grand Rapids, Mich.: Eerdmans.

Dothan, T. (1982). *The Philistines and Their Material Culture*. Jerusalem: Israel Exploration Society.

Faust, A. (2006). *Israel's Ethnogenesis: Settlement, Interaction, Expansion and Resistance*. London: Equinox.

Finkelstein, I. (1988). *The Archaeology of the Israelite Settlement*. Jerusalem: Israel Exploration Society.

——(2003). City states to states: polity dynamics in the 10th–9th centuries B.C.E. In S. Gitin and G. W. Dever (eds), *Symbiosis, Symbolism, and the Power of the Past: Canaan, Ancient Israel, and Their Neighbors from the Late Bronze Age through Roman Palaestina*. Winona Lake, Ind.: Eisenbrauns, 75–84.

—— and N. Na'aman (eds) (1994). *From Nomadism to Monarchy: Archaeological and Historical Aspects of Early Israel*. Jerusalem: Israel Exploration Society/Washington, DC: Biblical Archaeology Society.

Gitin, S., A. Mazar, and E. Stern (eds) (1998). *Mediterranean Peoples in Transition: Thirteenth to Early Tenth Centuries BCE*. Jerusalem: Israel Exploration Society.

Kempinski, A. (1989). *Megiddo: A City State and Royal Centre in North Israel*. Munich: Beck.

Killebrew, A. E. (2005). *Biblical Peoples and Ethnicity: An Archaeological Study of Egyptians, Canaanites, Philistines, and Early Israel 1300–1100 B.C.E*. Atlanta, Ga.: Society of Biblical Literature.

—— and G. Lehmann (eds) (2013). *The Philistines and Other "Sea Peoples" in Text and Archaeology*. Atlanta, Ga.: Society of Biblical Literature.

Maeir, A. M., L. A. Hitchcock, and L. K. Horwitz (2013). On the constitution and transformation of Philistine identity. *Oxford Journal of Archaeology* 32(1): 1–38.

Mazar, A. (1990). *Archaeology of the Land of the Bible*, vol. 1: *10,000–586 B.C.E*. New York: Doubleday.

McNutt, P. (1990). *The Forging of Israel: Iron Technology, Symbolism and Tradition in Ancient Society*. Sheffield: Almond.

—— (1999). *Reconstructing the Society of Ancient Israel*. Louisville, Ky.: Westminster/John Knox.

Negbi, O. (1998). Were there Sea Peoples in the Central Jordan Valley at the transition from the Bronze Age to the Iron Age? Once again. *Tel Aviv* 25: 184–207.

Raban, A. (1991). The Philistines in the western Jezreel Valley. *Bulletin of the American Schools of Oriental Research* 284: 17–27.

Sherratt, E. S. (1998). 'Sea Peoples' and the economic structure of the late second millennium in the eastern Mediterranean. In Gitin, Mazar, and Stern (1998: 292–313).

Stern, E. (1990). New evidence from Dor for the first appearance of the Phoenicians along the northern coast of Israel. *Bulletin of the American Schools of Oriental Research* 279: 27–33.

—— (2000). The settlement of the Sea Peoples in northern Israel. In E. D. Oren (ed.), *The Sea Peoples and Their World: A Reassessment*. Philadelphia: University Museum, University of Pennsylvania, 197–212.

Thompson, T. (2000). *The Early History of the Israelite People: From the Written and Archaeological Sources*. Leiden: Brill.

Yasur-Landau, A. (2010). *The Philistines and Aegean Migration at the End of the Late Bronze Age.* Cambridge: Cambridge University Press.

REFERENCES

Artzy, M. (2006). *The Jatt Metal Hoard in the Northern Canaanite/Phoenician and Cypriote Context.* Barcelona: Laboratorio de arqueología Universidad Pompeu Fabra.

Barako, T. J. (2000). The Philistine settlement as mercantile phenomenon? *American Journal of Archaeology* 104: 513–30.

Beck, P., M. Kochavi, and E. Yadin (forthcoming). *The Land of Geshur Project I: Tel Hadar Stratum IV—An Early Iron Age Emporium on the Shores of Lake Kinneret.* Tel Aviv: University of Tel Aviv, Emery and Claire Yass Publications in Archaeology.

Ben-Ami, D. (2001). The Iron I at Tel Hazor in light of the renewed excavations. *Israel Exploration Journal* 51: 148–70.

Ben-Shlomo, D., and M. D. Press (2009). A reexamination of Aegean-style figurines in light of new evidence from Ashdod, Ashkelon, and Ekron. *Bulletin of the American Schools of Oriental Research* 353: 39–74.

Biran, A. (1994). *Biblical Dan.* Jerusalem: Israel Exploration Society.

Bunimovitz, S. (1990). Problems in the 'ethnic' identification of the Philistine culture. *Tel Aviv* 17: 210–22.

D'Agata, A.-L., Y. Goren, H. Mommsen, A. Schwadt, and A. Yasur-Landau (2005). Imported pottery of LH IIIC style from Israel: style, provenance and chronology. In R. Laffineur and E. Greco (eds), *Emporia: Aegeans in the Central and Eastern Mediterranean.* Liège: Histoire de l'art et archéologie de la Grèce antique, Université de Liège/Austin: Program in Aegean Scripts and Prehistory, University of Texas at Austin, 371–80.

Dessel, J. P. (1999). Tell 'Ein Zippori and the Lower Galilee in the Late Bronze and Iron Ages: a village perspective. In E. M. Meyers (ed.), *Galilee through the Centuries: Confluence of Cultures.* Winona Lake, Ind.: Eisenbrauns, 1–32.

Dever, W. G. (1995). Ceramics, ethnicity, and the question of Israel's origin. *Biblical Archaeologist* 58.4: 200–213.

Dothan, T. (1998). Initial Philistine settlement: from migration to coexistence. In Gitin, Mazar, and Stern (1998: 148–61).

—— (2003). The Aegean and the Orient: cultic interactions. In W. G. Dever and S. Gitin (eds), *Symbiosis, Symbolism and the Power of the Past: Canaan, Ancient Israel, and Their Neighbors from the Late Bronze Age through Roman Palaestina.* Winona Lake, Ind.: Eisenbrauns, 189–213.

—— and A. Zukerman (2004). A preliminary study of the Myc IIIC:1b pottery assemblages from Tel Miqne-Ekron and Ashdod. *Bulletin of the American Schools of Oriental Research* 333: 1–54.

Esse, D. L. (1991). The collared store jar: scholarly ideology and ceramic typology. *Scandinavian Journal of the Old Testament* 2: 99–116.

Faust, A., and S. Bunimovitz (2003). The four-room house: embodying Iron Age Israelite society. *Near Eastern Archaeology* 66: 22–31.

Finkelstein, I. (1996). Ethnicity and origin of the Iron I settlers in the Highlands of Canaan: can the real Israel stand up? *Biblical Archaeologist* 59.4: 198–212.

—— (2000). The Philistine settlements: when, where and how many? In E. D. Oren (ed.), *The Sea Peoples and Their World: A Reassessment.* Philadelphia: University Museum, University of Pennsylvania, 159–80.

—— (2005). A low chronology update: archaeology, history and the Bible. In T. E. Levy and T. F. G. Higham (eds), *The Bible and Radiocarbon Dating: Archaeology, Text and Science*. London: Equinox, 31–42.

Fritz, V., and S. Münger (2002). Vorbericht über die zweite Phase der Ausgrabungen in Kinneret (*Tell el-x'Orēme*) am See Gennesaret, 1994–1999. *Zeitschrift des Deutchen Palästina-Vereins* 118: 2–32.

Gilboa, A. (1999). The view from the east: Tel Dor and the earliest Cypro-Geometric exports to the Levant. In M. Iacovou and D. Michaelides (eds), *Cyprus: The Historicity of the Geometric Horizon*. Nicosia: Archaeological Research Unit, University of Cyprus, 119–39.

—— (2005). Sea Peoples and Phoenicians along the southern Phoenician coast: a reconciliation— An interpretation of *Šikila* (*SKL*) material culture. *Bulletin of the American Schools of Oriental Research* 337: 47–78.

—— and I. Sharon (2003). An archaeological contribution to the Early Iron Age chronological debate: alternative chronologies for Phoenicia and their effects on the Levant, Cyprus and Greece. *Bulletin of the American Schools of Oriental Research* 332: 7–80.

—— and E. Boaretto (2008). Tel Dor and the chronology of Phoenician 'pre-colonization' stages. In C. Sagona (ed.), *Beyond the Homeland: Markers in Phoenician Chronology*. Louvain: Peeters, 113–204.

Halpern, B. (2000). Centre and sentry: Megiddo's role in transit, administration and trade. In I. Finkelstein, D. Ussishkin, and B. Halpern (eds), *Megiddo III: The 1992–1996 Seasons* II. Tel Aviv: Emery and Claire Yass Publications in Archaeology, Institute of Archaeology, Tel Aviv University, 535–75.

Herzog, Z. (1997). *Archaeology of the City: Urban Planning in Ancient Israel and Its Social Implications*. Tel Aviv: Emery and Claire Yass Archaeology Press.

—— and L. Singer-Avitz (2006). Sub-dividing the Iron Age IIA in northern Israel: a suggested solution to the chronological debate. *Tel Aviv* 33: 163–95.

Higginbotham, C. R. (2000). *Egyptianization and Elite Emulation in Ramesside Palestine: Governance and Accommodation on the Imperial Periphery*. Boston: Brill.

Humbert, J.-B. (1988). Tell Keisan entre mer et montagne: l'archéologie entre texte et contexte. In E.-M. Laperrousaz (ed.), *Archéologie, art et histoire de la Palestine*. Paris: Cerf, 65–83.

Killebrew, A. E. and J. Lev-Tov (2008). Early Iron Age feasting and cuisine: an indicator of Philistine–Aegean connectivity? In L. A. Hitchcock, R. Laffineur and J. L. Crowley (eds), *Dais, The Aegean Feast: Proceedings of the 12th International Aegean Conference, University of Melbourne, Centre for Classics and Archaeology, 25–29 March 2008*. Liège: Histoire de l'art et archéologie de la Grèce antique, Université de Liège/Austin: Program in Aegean Scripts and Prehistory, University of Texas at Austin, 339–46.

London, G. (1989). A comparison of two contemporaneous lifestyles of the late second millennium B.C. *Bulletin of the American Schools of Oriental Research* 273: 37–55.

Martin, M. (2006). The Egyptianized pottery assemblage from Area Q. In A. Mazar (ed.), *Excavations at Tel Beth Shean 1989–1996 I: From the Late Bronze Age IIB to the Medieval Period*. Jerusalem: Israel Exploration Society, 140–57.

Mazar, A. (2000). The temples and cult of the Philistines. In E. D. Oren (ed.), *The Sea Peoples and Their World: A Reassessment*. Philadelphia: University Museum, University of Pennsylvania, 213–32.

—— (2002). Megiddo in the thirteenth–eleventh centuries BCE: a review of some recent studies. In E. D. Oren and S. Ahituv (eds), *Aharon Kempinski Memorial Volume: Studies in Archaeology and Related Disciplines*. Beer Sheva: Ben-Gurion of the Negev University Press, 264–82.

—— (2003). Beth Shean in the second millennium B.C.E.: from Canaanite town to Egyptian stronghold. In M. Bietak and E. Czerny (eds), *The Synchronization of Civilizations in the Eastern Mediterranean in the Second Millennium B.C. II: Proceedings of the SCIEM 2000-Euroconfernece, Haindorff, 2nd of May–7th of May 2001*. Vienna: Österreichische Akademie der Wissenschaften, 323–40.

—— (2005). The debate over the chronology of the Iron Age in the southern Levant: its history, the current situation, and a suggested resolution. In T. E. Levy and T. F. G. Higham (eds), *The Bible and Radiocarbon Dating: Archaeology, Text and Science*. London: Equinox, 13–28.

Oren, E. D. (1984). Governors' residencies in Canaan under the New Kingdom: a case study of Egyptian administration. *Journal of the Society for the Study of Egyptian Antiquities* 14: 37–56.

Panitz-Cohen, N., and A. Mazar (eds) (2009). *Excavations at Tel Beth-Shean (1989–1996)*, vol. 3: *The 13th–11th Century BCE Strata in Areas N and S*. Jerusalem: Israel Exploration Society and Hebrew University of Jerusalem.

Sharon, I., and A. Gilboa (2013). The SKL town: Dor in the Early Iron Age. In A. E. Killebrew and G. Lehmann (eds), *The Philistines and Other "Sea Peoples" in Text and Archaeology*. Atlanta, Ga.: Society of Biblical Literature, 393–467.

—— A. J. T. Jull, and E. Boaretto (2007). Report on the first stage of the Iron Age Dating Project in Israel: supporting a low chronology. *Radiocarbon* 49: 1–46.

Singer, I. (1992). Towards the image of Dagon, the god of the Philistines. *Syria* 69: 431–50.

Stager, L. E. (1995). The impact of the Sea Peoples (1185–1050 BCE). In T. E. Levy (ed.), *The Archaeology of Society in the Holy Land*. London: Leicester University Press, 332–48.

Ussishkin, D. (2004). Area P: the Level VI temple. In *The Renewed Archaeological Excavations at Lachish (1973–1994)*. Tel Aviv: Emery and Claire Yass Publications in Archaeology, 215–81.

Weinstein, J. M. (1992). The collapse of the Egyptian empire in the southern Levant. In W. A. Ward and M. S. Joukowsky (eds), *The Crisis Years: The 12th Century B.C. from Beyond the Danube to the Tigris*. Dubuque, Ia.: Kendall/Hunt, 142–50.

Whitelam, K. W. (1994). The identity of early Israel: the realignment and transformation of Late Bronze Age–Iron Age Palestine. *Journal for the Study of the Old Testament* 63: 57–87.

Yasur-Landau, A. (2001). The mother(s) of all Philistines: Aegean enthroned deities of the 12th–11th century Philistia. In R. Laffineur and R. Hägg (eds), *Potnia: Deities and Religion in the Aegean Bronze Age*. Liège: Histoire de l'art et archéologie de la Grèce antique, Université de Liège/Austin: Program in Aegean Scripts and Prehistory, University of Texas at Austin, 329–43.

CHAPTER 42

THE SOUTHERN LEVANT (TRANSJORDAN) DURING THE IRON AGE I PERIOD

LARRY G. HERR

INTRODUCTION

The Iron I period in Jordan is something of a dark age. Early surveys often assumed that settlement patterns and ceramic development would be like those west of the Jordan River, and misdated some types of pottery in order to match their assumptions. Unfortunately, this happened in some localities even as late as the early 1990s. Thus, Iron I readings in the results of archaeological surveys, such as those of Glueck, should always be treated with the utmost care. There have also been very few excavations at sites that contain Iron I levels. Further, when sites *have* produced Iron I discoveries, they are often exposed in small areas in which coherent archaeological interpretations cannot be supported, such as Sahab. Or, even more problematic, the Iron I levels have been largely destroyed by later constructions, such as Hisban.

We may divide the Iron I sites in Jordan into two principal groups: those in the Jordan Valley and those in the highlands. The sites in the Jordan Valley seem to reflect a more prosperous lifestyle and contain a material culture that is oriented more toward the west than sites on the plateau. However, like the valley sites, prominent Late Bronze sites on the plateau more or less continued to exist into the Iron I period, although with significant changes. Recent research has tended to emphasize the 'tribal' nature of settlement and sedentarization in the highlands, while more established urban connections seem to have existed for the Jordan Valley sites. At the risk of appearing simplistic, it is suggested that clustered settlement patterns may reflect tribal groups or confederacies as they began the settlement process at different paces in different areas, but these groups were never static and interacted with each other in fluid ways (Bienkowski 2009).

Egyptian sources for the Late Bronze and early Iron Ages mention a people group called the Shasu, apparently nomads from a region that included southern Jordan. The only other textual sources relevant to this period are later reports and/or remembrances of the biblical documents. These include stories of the origins of the Arameans, Ammonites, Moabites,

Edomites, and ancient Israelites. Among them are the defeat of Sihon, the king of Heshbon (Num. 21), the victory over King Og in a battle that mentions his astounding iron bed (Deut. 3: 1–11), a series of wars between Israel and the Transjordanian people-groups over who was to control the territories east of the Jordan River (e.g. the Jephthah story in Judg. 11), and even battles that occurred to the west (e.g. the stories of Ehud against the Moabites in Judg. 4 and Gideon against the Midianites in Judg. 6). All these sources certainly reflect interactions among the various groups as they sorted out who they were and how they could best support their clans (Bienkowski 1992).

The settlement process in the highlands was not constant. Regions with high agricultural potential were generally settled first. Thus, northern areas (north of the Zarqa River) continued from Late Bronze settlements; the central areas (from the Zarqa to the Mujib) also continued from Late Bronze settlements or founded new ones near the beginning of the period (Herr and Najjar 2001); the south-central areas (between the Mujib and Hasa) were first settled seriously during the 11th century BCE; and the southern areas (south of the Hasa) do not seem to have been settled clearly until Iron II (Fig. 42.1).

Routledge has produced an important list of features describing the Iron I period as a contrast to the Late Bronze (2004: ch. 5) which I summarize (in part) here:

1. collapse of pan-Mediterranean trade systems;
2. disappearance of palaces and temples with a more egalitarian demography;
3. disappearance of Egyptian hegemony;
4. collapse of the Hittite Empire;
5. the proliferation of pillared houses and the rise of the domestic nature of settlements;
6. increase of sites in the highlands; and
7. episodic occupational patterns (short-term occupation with disruptions).

Much progress has occurred recently in relation to the pottery of Jordan during Iron I, allowing us to re-date older excavated materials. Unfortunately, this has resulted in a net loss of sites rather than gain, because early surveys and small excavations tended to suggest pottery was Iron I when it really was Iron II (see below). No attempt has been made here to isolate all survey sites which have produced Iron I pottery. Indeed, we must significantly reduce the number of Iron I sites many surveys have purported to identify. Even those that I retain in my lists contain probable questionable entries. I have tried to follow the new spelling conventions (but without diacritics) from the Royal Geographic Society for site names which have been adopted by the Department of Antiquities, but in cases where no example occurs, the old spelling is retained; I have also used popular classical site names, such as Pella. Question marks following a site name suggest that I am uncertain about the inclusion of that site.

THE LATE BRONZE AGE/IRON I TRANSITION

This sub-period is necessary in any discussion of the Iron I period in Jordan, because many sites seem to comprise a ceramic horizon which contains forms with strong Late Bronze tendencies, but also forms that reflect the very beginning stages of the Iron I assemblage. Unfortunately, not all the sites discussed below have been extensively excavated or clearly published. Others have finds limited to tombs.

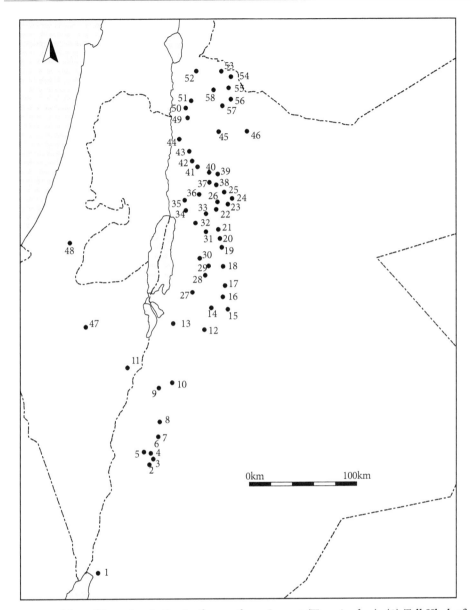

FIG. 42.1 Map of Iron Age I sites in the southern Levant (Transjordan): (1) Tall Khalayfi; (2) Jabal Qsayr; (3) Muallaq; (4) Tawilan; (5) Umm Biyara; (6) Baja III; (7) Ghrareh; (8) Sela; (9) Barqa al-Hatiya/Kh. En-Nabas/Kh. Janyah/Wadi Fidan 40; (10) Busayra; (11) Hatseva; (12) Mudaybi; (13) Numayra; (14) Ader; (15) Arbid and Thamayil; (16) Kh. Mudayna Ulya; (17) Kh. Mudayna Muarraja; (18) Labun; (19) Kh. Mudayna Thamad; (20) Kh. Hari; (21) Tall Jalul; (22) Drayjat; (23) Tall Jawa South; (24) Sahab; (25) Amman; (26) Tall Umayri; (27) Kh. Faris; (28) Balu; (29) Arair; (30) Dhiban; (31) Madaba; (32) Nebo; (33) Tall Hisban; (34) Tall Iktanu; (35) Tall Nimrin; (36) Iraq al-Amir; (37) Tall Safut; (38) Abu Nsayr; (39) Rujm Henu; (40) Umm Dananir; (41) Aijun; (42) Tall Dayr Alla; (43) Tall Mazar; (44) Tall Saidiya; (45) Jarash; (46) Mafraq; (47) Qitmit; (48) Tell Batash; (49) Tall Abu Kharaz; (50) Pella; (51) Jabal Abu Khas; (52) Saham; (53) Abila; (54) Fadayn; (55) Tall Fukhar; (56) Rumayt; (57) Tall Husn; and (58) Tall Irbid

Several sites on the northern and central parts of the plateau seem to have continued from the Late Bronze Age (Abila (?), Amman, the Beqa' Valley, Umm ad-Dananir, Fukhar, Irbid, Jarash, Lahun, Safut (?), Sahab (if the tomb reflects a contemporary settlement), and 'Umayri). At first glimpse, this suggests a peaceful continuity from the Late Bronze into the Iron Age, at least in the north and central plateau, where all of these sites occur. However, at 'Umayri, for instance, there was a complete change in town plan (below). A similar picture appears for the Jordan Valley at Dayr 'Alla, Pella, and Sa'idiya.

Many of the finds on the plateau come from tombs (Amman, Sahab, the Beqa' Valley, Sahem, and Madaba); fragmentary architectural remains are reported for Abila (?), Hisban, Irbid, and Jarash; isolated and/or secondary pottery finds seem to come from 'Ara'ir, Dananir (?), Rujum al-Hinu (?), Safut (?), Jalul, and Jawa South.

The finds at Hisban include a long trench cut into bedrock, possibly a deep, narrow moat at the edge of the hilltop (Ray 2001). Preliminary reports from Irbid indicate a very thick destruction level (up to 4m) which covered the city wall, a tower, and a two-storeyed public building that contained cultic vessels (Herr and Najjar 2001).

The most complete plan of settlement comes from Khirbat al-Lahun (Fig. 42.2), where at least one published pottery vessel, a bi-conical jug, suggests that the site may be dated to this time period (Homès-Fredericq 2009: 173; Homès-Fredericq and Hennessy 1989). The site is very shallow and could be excavated extensively. Scores of houses were enclosed by one of the earliest casemate walls discovered in the southern Levant (Swinnen 2009).

The best-preserved specific remains so far come from 'Umayri (Clark 1997; Herr and Clark 1995; 2009). The defensive system included: a dry moat cut out of the original ridge upon which the site was built; a retaining wall supporting a massive rampart which repaired a crack in bedrock probably caused by an earthquake; and a defensive perimeter wall surrounding the site at the top of the rampart, which has been traced for approximately 70m. The perimeter wall curved into the city.

Inside the perimeter wall were the remains of three houses. Building B, the northernmost house, was preserved over 2m high in places by a massive brick destruction layer which fell from the upper storey of the building. It was a four-room pillared house with post bases separating the long rooms. The broadroom, which used the perimeter wall as its back wall, contained around 70 collared pithoi filling the room and from the collapsed upper storey (Fig. 42.3). Another building to the south (Building A) contained more collared pithoi in the broad room at the back. In a paved area was a standing stone with a votive altar or table in front, but in the nearby courtyard were domestic remains, suggesting a house with a small shrine. Another house is just beginning to appear to the south of Building A within the curve of the perimeter wall.

The best parallels to the objects from these structures are found mostly in the highland regions north of Jerusalem, and range from pottery to potters' marks to seals. The limited variety of the finds in the assemblage suggests a simple economic system brought about by tribal groups beginning a lengthy sedentarization process in the highland areas of Jordan. Although the site was also occupied near the end of the Late Bronze Age, the material culture of this settlement was nothing like that of the LB II level, which included a large public building, either a palace or a temple. A major catalyst of this initial settlement, and perhaps its destruction, may have been frictions arising from the north–south trade routes (Herr 1998).

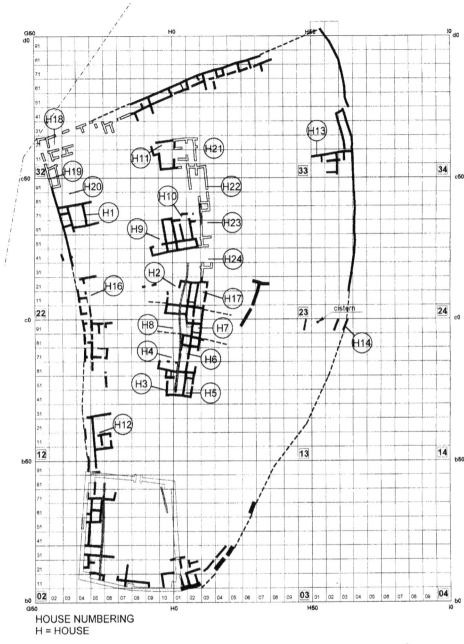

HOUSE NUMBERING
H = HOUSE

FIG. 42.2 Plan of Lehun (courtesy of D. Homès-Fredericq)

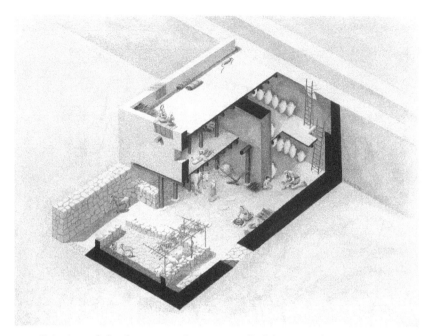

FIG. 42.3 Painting of the four-room house at Tall al-ʿUmayri (courtesy Madaba Plains Project excavations at Tall al-ʿUmayri, Jordan. Artist: Rhonda Root © 2001)

In the Jordan Valley, the most important site is Pella, but the published remains are incomplete. The large and rich cemetery at Saʿidiya, with LB IIB and Iron I pottery, and other objects suggest a significant town or city there. Indeed, recent excavations have uncovered tantalizing hints of its existence, but the exposure is small. The Late Bronze temple at Dayr ʿAlla continued to at least 1180 BCE, as a faience vase with the name of Pharaoh Taousert (Fig. 42.4) has been found inside it (van der Steen 2008a). The Jordan Valley sites generally produced finds of a more varied and luxurious repertoire than the plateau sites, and seem to have continued Late Bronze features more strongly than the plateau sites.

No certain discoveries from this period have been found south of the Wadi Mujib in excavations or surveys. Early published reports may have attributed a few sites to the Transitional period, but almost all the sherds involved can be shown to derive from later periods, such as late Iron I or even Iron II.

Iron I (12th to 11th Centuries)

So far, there are no clear settlements in Jordan that seem to go smoothly from the Transitional period to the main part of Iron I, the late 12th to 11th centuries. Lahun may be an exception. Several sites saw new settlements: Abu al-Kharaz, Dayr ʿAlla, Mazar (?), and Nimrin in the Jordan Valley; and ʿAmman, Baluʿ, Dhiban, Hajjar, ʿIraq al-ʿAmir (?), Mudayna ʿUlya, Mudayna Muʿarraja, Muʿmmariyya, Rujm al-Malfuf South, Sahab, and ʿUmayri on the plateau, and possibly Nahas in the Arabah. This suggests there was dynamic sedentary activity after a disruption. Some sites in both areas were settled only after a destruction level; Dayr ʿAlla A, Pella VII, and ʿUmayri 11 are the clearest examples. But most sites have not produced

FIG. 42.4 Faience vase mentioning Pharaoh Taousert, found at Deir 'Alla (courtesy Gerrit van der Kooij)

clear results or clearly published results for us to be sure if such a relationship extended to other sites. Indeed, many sites have produced only pottery in secondary deposits (and then often not very much): 'Amman, Balu', Dhiban, probably 'Iraq al-'Amir, Jarash, and Rujm al-Malfuf South; others have produced only fragmentary remains: Abila (?), 'Ara'ir, Hajjar, Hisban, Mazar (?), Nimrin, Safut (?), and Nahas (?). Madaba was limited to a tomb; other sites were excavated when Iron I pottery in Jordan was not known very well, and I question their attribution when the pottery is not published: 'Ara'ir, Rujm al-Malfuf South, and Safut.

This period includes several sub-phases of activity which overlap throughout the period. Not all sites were contemporary and some sites probably had more than one phase of occupation, such as 'Umayri. This 'episodic' settlement pattern cannot yet be sorted clearly into a sequential order.

On the northern plateau, Fukhar seems to continue, reusing the Late Bronze palace, while Abila may have extended into this period as well. The Philistine sherd found at Fukhar is still the only one so far discovered on the plateau. Phase 1 at Irbid, which lasted into Iron IIB, included a rebuilt city wall and domestic buildings associated with an industrial installation that the excavators suggest were for wine.

In central areas of the plateau the large amounts of pottery from all sub-periods of Iron I suggest that Hisban continued from the Transitional period into the middle of the Iron I and down into Iron IIA, although the pottery comes only from a secondary fill. A massive destruction at 'Umayri separates the Transitional period (Stratum 12) from this one (Stratum 11). A storeroom was built on top of the brick-filled destruction of Stratum 12. Then at least eighteen collared pithoi were embedded in the fallen bricks. South of the gate area, an open-air sanctuary was constructed and paved with cobbles and plaster, lasting until late Iron II. On one of the lowest floors was a model shrine (Fig. 42.5). In the southern areas of the site in at least three separate fields, several walls were constructed of very large

FIG. 42.5 The reconstructed model shrine found in an open-air sanctuary at Tall al-'Umayri

stones (some are over 2m long). The lowest earth layers sealing against them date to this period.

The Iron I pottery from Sahab was virtually identical to that from 'Umayri at this time. Of special interest are the seal impressions on the rims of many of the Sahab collared pithoi. This is a feature not apparent at other sites in Jordan, except for one example at 'Umayri. None of the house plans at Sahab were complete, but enough was uncovered to characterize the rooms as rectangular and mostly paved with flagstones.

The houses at Lahun may have continued with only minor alterations into this period. They were part of an extensive town of four-room houses which are sometimes pillared; the whole was enclosed by a casemate wall. Possibly over fifty houses existed at the shallow site where the tops of walls are visible on the surface (Fig. 42.2 above) (Swinnen 2009). The excavators date the remains to the Transitional period, but seem to suggest a broader time range as well.

Other central plateau sites were probably new. That is, although they may have had an earlier tomb, the pottery published from the site lacks Transitional forms but matches the later assemblages: Amman (incoherent walls), Madaba (if the late tomb can imply a settlement), and Safut (without published pottery). Certainly, new sites were constructed at Hajjar (a farm or tower, but no published pottery), 'Iraq al-'Amir town (fills and a possible fortification wall), and Rujum al-Malfuf South (the pottery is unpublished). A few potsherds from the period have been published from Dhiban. The unnamed site near Khirbat as-Suq is atop the forested hills on the western fringes of the town almost immediately beneath high-tension wires. It is 1–2km north of Yaduda and was discovered by the Madaba Plains Project survey team (not yet published).

Toward the end of this period, settlements were appearing in the Kerak region at two very similar sites, Mudayna-'Ulya and Mudayna-Mu'arraja. Because the ruins are prominently visible on the surface, it is easy to describe the house plans, city walls, towers, town gates, dry moats severing the sites from neighbouring hills, and the roadways approaching the sites. Four-room pillared houses are visible and are sometimes preserved as high as the lintels above the doors (Routledge 2004). In some cases large slabs of stone are still visible, spanning the rooms of the houses with a corbelling technique. Possibly as many as thirty-five houses existed at Mu'arraja. The pottery from the excavations at both sites seems to date to the late 11th century, perhaps going into the 10th century as well. Similar pottery has been published from Balu' and a nicely preserved citadel has recently been excavated at Mu'mmariyya. Because these excavated sites tend to be limited to the plateau edges overlooking the Wadi Mujib, one should expect a few other sites to turn up in more central areas, probably well hidden beneath later remains.

No Iron I settlements have been excavated south of the Wadi al-Hasa. Various surveys claim to have discovered pottery at several sites. Some of the published 'Iron I' pottery assemblages from surveys prior to the 1990s, however, seem to contain mostly Iron II forms. One suggested Iron I site was actually excavated to test the survey results, but the team discovered only Iron II remains. All this suggests that there was, at best, only an extremely sparse settled population.

The Jordan Valley site of Pella continued from the earlier period, but the wall fragments are not as yet easily interpreted. Remains at Sa'idiya may lead to an entrance to the stepped structure, excavated by Pritchard, which descended to the water source at the foot of the site. A large residency or administrative complex, possibly with Egyptian connections, was also found there. Three major sites began or were resettled at this time: Abu al-Kharaz, Dayr 'Alla, and Mazar. There may have been a citadel at Abu al-Kharaz, but the initial report has not been pursued in later seasons of excavation. At Dayr 'Alla, Iron Age Phases A to G or H all belong to the Iron I period. The first four Iron Age phases (A–D) include a significant bronzesmith's workshop that may have been used to produce large bronze objects. These first four phases probably date to the 12th century. Nearby deposits of clay were probably used for moulds (although none were found) and the metal was fired in a large oven (van der Steen 2008b). Some of the painted pottery has been connected with Philistine wares. The excavators suggest Iron Phase C ended in an earthquake. Phases E–G/H were characterized by a much denser settlement, but with walls often only one brick wide and founded on a layer of reeds. Phase H produced a major building of uncertain use. At Mazar, on the lower mound, toward the end of the period an open court sanctuary was constructed with three rooms at the end of a large courtyard. The pottery, much of which was found together outside the door to one of the rooms, dates to the end of Iron I and the beginning of Iron II. A few wall fragments and potsherds appeared at Nimrin. In the Jordan Valley, the orientation of the material culture still seems to be more toward the west than the sites on the plateau.

At the copper production site of Khirbat an-Nahas in the Wadi Fidan off the Wadi 'Arabah, excavators claim to have found Iron I remains they date from the 12th–11th centuries. But so far, publications have discussed a few architectural remains and ¹⁴C dates, primarily for Iron II. Moreover, the dating for the Iron I phase of activity at the site is ambiguous. The finds from this pre-fortress phase seem to reflect temporary occupation, perhaps during seasonal mining and smelting operations. But without published pottery we cannot relate the ¹⁴C dates to the finds.

THE END OF IRON I

The transition to the Iron II period is very weakly attested on the plateau. Only a few red-slipped, hand-burnished potsherds have been found. The pottery at Hisban includes considerable amounts that can be attributed to Iron IIA, but again it is all from secondary deposits. Most of the sites in the southern plateau in the Karak region were abandoned during this time. Much more work needs to be done on the early Iron II in Jordan.

CONCLUSIONS

We may tentatively suggest the following:

1. The Transitional period seems to be well witnessed in the northern and central plateau. Based on the Late Bronze features in the ceramic assemblages, it would appear to date from the late 13th century to the early 12th century.
2. There are not a significant number of sites from the Transitional period in the Jordan Valley where the orientation of the material culture was toward the valley culture of the west, not toward the eastern highlands.
3. There are no Transitional sites south of the Wadi Mujib.
4. The major part of the Iron I period (from the 12th century to the end of the 11th century and maybe slightly into the 10th century) has no clear subdivisions. Instead, settlements seem to have witnessed individual episodic occupation throughout that time period. Some sites show signs of durative settlement, while others were occupied for only short periods of time.
5. The Iron I sites in the highlands of Jordan do not reflect the small unfortified villages of the western highlands, but were often fortified and many were large enough to be called 'towns'. A possible exception is the area north of the Zarqa River.
6. The Karak region began to be settled only toward the end of Iron I.
7. There are no clear Iron I sites south of the Wadi al-Hasa.
8. The Jordan Valley grew in number of sites during this period, but the orientation of the material culture still seems to be toward the valley culture of the west.

Two things need to happen before our knowledge of the Iron I in Jordan can grow: First, we need more excavations at sites with Iron I levels. One-period sites are fine, but multi-period ones will provide better insights into transitional periods. We especially need excavations at Iron I to early Iron II sites. And second, the Iron I sites that have been excavated need to be fully published.

SUGGESTED READING

Bloch-Smith, E., and B. Alpert Nakhai (1999). A landscape comes to life: the Iron Age I. *Near Eastern Archaeology* 62: 62–92.

Herr, L. G., and D. R. Clark (2001). Excavating the tribe of Reuben. *Biblical Archaeology Review* 27.2: 36–47, 64–6.

—— and M. Najjar (2001). The Iron Age. In B. MacDonald, R. B. Adams, and P. Bienkowski (eds), *The Archaeology of Jordan*. Sheffield: Sheffield Academic, 323–45.

Yassine, K. (1988). *Archaeology of Jordan: Essays and Reports*. Amman: University of Jordan, Department of Archaeology.

Younker, R. W. (1999). The emergence of the Ammonites. In B. MacDonald and R. W. Younker (eds), *Ancient Ammon*. Leiden: Brill, 189–218.

References

Bienkowski, P. (1992). *Early Edom and Moab: The Beginning of the Iron Age in Southern Jordan* Sheffield: National Museums and Galleries on Merseyside.

—— (2009). 'Tribalism' and 'segmentary society' in Iron Age Transjordan. In P. Bienkowski (ed.), *Studies on Iron Age Moab and Neighbouring Areas in Honour of Michèle Daviau*. Leuven: Peeters, 7–26.

Clark, D. R. (1997). Field B: the western defensive system. In L. G. Herr, L. T. Geraty, Ø. S. La Bianca, and R. W. Younker (eds), *Madaba Plains Project: The 1989 Season at Tell el-Umeiri and Vicinity and Subsequent Studies*. Berrien Springs, Mich.: Andrews University, Institute of Archaeology, 53–98.

Herr, L. G. (1998). Tell el-'Umayri and the Madaba Plains region during the Late Bronze–Iron Age I transition. In S. Gitin, A. Mazar, and E. Stern (eds), *Mediterranean Peoples in Transition*. Jerusalem: Israel Exploration Society, 251–64.

—— and D. R. Clark (1995). Madaba Plains Project: excavations at Tall al-'Umayri, 2004. *Annual of the Department of Antiquities of Jordan* 49: 245–60.

—— (2009). From the Stone Age to the Middle Ages in Jordan: digging up Tall al-'Umayri. *Near Eastern Archaeology* 72: 68–97.

—— and M. Najjar. (2001). The Iron Age. In B. MacDonald, R. B. Adams, and P. Bienkowski (eds), *The Archaeology of Jordan*. Sheffield: Sheffield Academic, 323–45.

Homès-Fredericq, D. (2009). The Iron Age II Fortress of al-Lahun (Moab). In P. Bienkowski (ed.), *Studies on Iron Age Moab and Neighbouring Areas in Honour of Michèle Daviau*. Leuven: Peeters, 165–82.

—— and J. B. Hennessy (eds) (1989). *Archaeology of Jordan*. Leuven: Peeters.

Ray, P. J. (2001). *Tell Hesban and Vicinity in the Iron Age*. Berrien Springs, Mich.: Institute of Archaeology, Andrews University.

Routledge, B. E. (2004). *Moab in the Iron Age: Hegemony, Polity, Archaeology*. Philadelphia: University of Pennsylvania Press.

Swinnen, I. M. (2009). The Iron Age I settlement and its residential houses at al-Lahun in Moab, Jordan. *Bulletin of the American Schools of Oriental Research* 354: 29–53.

van der Steen, E. J. (2008a). Introduction: Tell Deir 'Alla in the Late Bronze and Iron Ages. In M. L. Steiner and E. van der Steen (eds), *Sacred and Sweet: Studies on the Material Culture of Tell Deir Alla and Tell Abu Sarbut*. Leuven: Peeters, 17–24.

—— (2008b). Tell Deir 'Alla: the newcomers of the Early Iron Age. In M. L. Steiner and E. van der Steen (eds), *Sacred and Sweet: Studies on the Material Culture of Tell Deir Alla and Tell Abu Sarbut*. Leuven: Peeters, 69–92.

CHAPTER 43

CYPRUS DURING THE IRON AGE I PERIOD (LATE CYPRIOT IIC–IIIA)

Settlement Pattern Crisis (LC IIC–IIIA) to the Restructuring (LC IIIB) of its Settlement Pattern

MARIA IACOVOU

There is a dangerous temptation to link destruction levels together in the interests of tidiness and economy, but history is seldom tidy or notably economical...It is even more hazardous to attempt to bring Cyprus into line with the Egyptian record of events.

(Sandars 1978: 173–4)

INTRODUCTION

Any assessment of Cyprus's 12th-century settlement landscape should not be biased by the preconception that events in Cyprus were the same as events elsewhere in the Mediterranean. The systems failure of the Late Bronze empires triggered different processes in the geopolitical entity of Cyprus from those in the Levant and the Aegean. To comprehend the island's response to the Mediterranean-wide crisis, we have to consider its political status at the time. In the second millennium BC, Cyprus was known to all its commercial partners by the name of only one authority, recorded in their state archives as Alashiya (Knapp 1996a; 2008). Archaeological correlates, however, do not support the view that Alashiya was a unitary state (Peltenburg 1996)—although it was identified by this name almost to the end of the millennium (as we read in the story of the mishaps of the Egyptian emissary Wenamun at Byblos and Alasia of around 1076 BC (Kitchen 1973: 251–2)). It is more likely that it was 'a decentralised polity comprising a patchwork of variably autonomous territories, loosely affiliated to the state' (Peltenburg 2012).

All the same, scholarly consensus supports the view that in the 13th century the island operated on a segmented political model. There is, however, no incontestable evidence (e.g. archives) as to which of the settlements functioned as administrative capitals in Late Cypriot IIC (LC IIC). Furthermore, even though we are justified in thinking that Enkomi or Kalavassos-*Ayios Demetrios* were centres of authority, our understanding of the extent of the territories over which they exercised this authority is based on models of our own making. The fact is that Cyprus's remarkable political geography—its ability to support a multitude of independent polities for as long as a millennium (1300–300 BC) until they were eventually abolished by the Ptolemaic empire system—was shaped by the island's geological and geographical characteristics. Its copper ores are located all around the foothills of the Troodos Massif, which is the heart of the island; beyond this copper-rich zone come the cultivable slopes and plains which produced the foodstuffs that could support a regional system's staple finance; and then, the coastline where harbours could be established. It would appear, therefore, that there was a minimum spatial requirement for the rise of a Cypriot polity: control over a geographically unified economic territory that had access to copper sources, agricultural land, and a port of export (Iacovou 2007).

Scholars have also come to acknowledge that the island enjoyed an equally remarkable immunity from direct military and political interference by land-based empires. Unlike their closest neighbours, the city-states of Syria and Canaan, the Late Cypriot polities suffered neither Egyptian nor direct Hittite control, despite Hittite claims to the contrary (Bunimovitz 1998: 104).

THE LATE 13TH-CENTURY BC CRISIS

No sooner had its first polities been established than Cyprus was stricken by the crisis that swept over the Mediterranean world and caused nearly all of the second-millennium BC states to disintegrate. The blow for Cyprus was serious but not devastating, and there is no unambiguous evidence for large-scale enemy action from across the seas that put urban sites to the torch and left them uninhabited. Its main problem was the 'combination of external disruptions and internal instabilities' (Keswani 1989: 70). In other words, there was reduced demand for Cypriot copper, which caused a production breakdown at home (Knapp 1997: 68). But the *fin de siècle* crisis could not overwhelm an island-wide administrative system, as that did not exist. It affected only the regional systems in different degrees, according to the degree of industrial specialization and administrative complexity the LC IIC polities had developed in the name of running, apparently independently of each other, an overseas exchange system that was based primarily on copper.

THE CULTURAL AND CHRONOLOGICAL CONTEXT OF THE TERM 'LC IIIA'

The 12th century in Cyprus is a series of many different, successful and unsuccessful, settlement histories. By comparing the LC IIC to the LC IIIA settlement pattern, we can assess the cultural losses, the continuities (from LC IIC), and novelties in the material record.

LC IIIA is best regarded as the ultimate phase of the island's Late Bronze Age culture. Its material evidence comes from pre-existing LC IIC sites, not from new ones. LC IIIB, despite the name we give it, is beginning to be recognized as the initial phase of the Early Iron Age (see e.g. Sherratt 2000: 82). Island-wide, its material evidence comes from *new* establishments which, together with a couple of earlier Late Cypriot ones (Paphos and Kition), inaugurated the island's Iron Age settlement pattern as early as the 11th century BC (Iacovou 1994). The absolute age range of LC IIIA covers the better part, if not all, of the 1200s. A start for LC IIIA *c.*1200 is fairly secure (Manning et al. 2001: 328). An end (*c.*1125/1100), however, remains unsubstantiated, as is the start of LC IIIB.

Late Cypriot polities in recession (Fig. 43.1)

Cyprus's own crisis translated into a horizon of settlement abandonments as sites of different types went out of use. Among them were urban centres with ashlar complexes, which contained industrial units and had significant storage capacity: Kalavassos-*Ayios Demetrios*, Maroni-*Vournes*, and Alassa-*Paliotaverna*, where excavation has found no evidence of violent destruction before they were abandoned. At Kalavassos-*Ayios Demetrios* 'most of the town appears to have been peacefully yet thoroughly deserted' (South 1989: 322). The ashlar complex did suffer a fire that may or may not have been contemporary with the settlement's abandonment. Signs of burning are also visible on the monoliths of the central building at Alassa-*Paliotaverna*, but the settlement of Alassa-*Pano Mandilaris* has 'no evidence of violent destruction or fire' (Hadjisavvas 1989: 41).

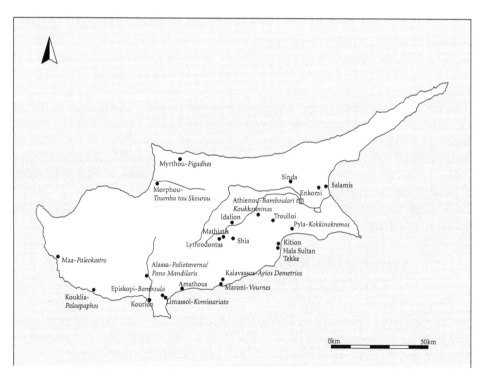

FIG. 43.1 Map of Iron Age I (LC IIC–IIIA) sites in Cyprus

The inhabitants never returned to these settlements, nor did they or any other group revive the monumental central buildings. It was a terminal episode. People were escaping from an irreversible turn of events, which was the failure of their polities to survive the economic crisis. Thus, 12th-century Cyprus was left with a severely shrunk urban pattern.

REGIONAL SYSTEMS IN DISTRESS

The termination of a regional authority entailed the demise of its entire economic region, including its secondary and tertiary dependencies. The abandonment of *Ayios Demetrios* and *Vournes* (Cadogan 1989; 1996) left the valleys of Vasilikos and Maroni without an urban centre from the end of the 13th century to today. In the Iron Age geopolitical pattern, which began to take shape in LC IIIB, much of this region became the eastern border zone of Amathous, a new polity founded down the coast to the west. Likewise, the demise of Alassa affected the whole of the Kouris River Valley. Close to the south coast, Episkopi-*Bamboula*, which, like Alassa, had been inhabited since LC I and may have functioned as its trading port, was also abandoned following a destruction-free transition to LC IIIA (Kling 1989: 17–23). Subsequently, the Kouris region's settlement hierarchy began to be re-established in LC IIIB with the rise of Kourion, which became one of the Iron Age kingdoms of Cyprus.

In the region of Morphou to the west, the mining village of Apliki (Kling and Muhly 2007) and the industrial site at Morphou-*Toumba tou Skourou* went out of use (Vermeule and Wolsky 1990). Myrtou-*Pigadhes*, the most extensive Late Cypriot settlement in the northwest (Taylor 1957), was depopulated at the end of LC IIC (Webb 1999: 53, 287). To the southeast of the Troodos, the mining villages of Mathiatis, Lythrodontas, and Shia went out of use (Hadjicosti 1991). Further to the east, in the heart of the Mesaoria Plain, Athienou-*Bamboulari tis Koukkouninas*, a LC II extramural cult complex with a bronze-working facility, which had served as an intermediary in Enkomi's strategy for the procurement of copper, was given over to the storage of agricultural commodities in LC IIIA but was, nonetheless, abandoned shortly afterwards (Dothan and Ben-Tor 1983: 140; Webb 1999: 21–9, 285).

THE POWER VACUUM

It seems, therefore, that in LC IIIA large settlement hierarchies were eradicated in the Vasilikos and Kouris Valleys and, almost certainly, also in the west of the island. This left a power vacuum, which we can identify as one of the characteristics of the Cypriot 12th century. Industrial and agricultural areas that had an interdependent relation with a primary settlement (Knapp 1997: 69) were laid open for redistribution, once their regional administrative centre had succumbed. At the time, however, the only available claimants were LC IIC polities that survived the crisis and they were not many: Enkomi, Hala Sultan Tekke, Kition, and Paphos (Paphos refers throughout this chapter to Kouklia-*Palaepaphos*). Since no new settlements were founded to fill the gap, the power vacuum persisted to the end of LC IIIA. It began to be remedied in LC IIIB when new sites were founded which, before long, assumed the role of primary centres.

The LC IIIA urban states

The four survivors that continued after the crisis to function as polities form two pairs. Paphos and Kition seem to have profited from everybody else's problems. The LC IIC–IIIA transition began an era of urban nucleation and territorial expansion, which allowed them to remain central places in the Early Iron Age. At Enkomi and Hala Sultan Tekke, however, LC IIIA saw their slow replacement, first as ports and then also as state capitals, followed by complete abandonment during the transition to LC IIIB.

Hala Sultan Tekke

Hala Sultan Tekke (which is also known today as Dromolaxia-*Vyzakia*), the leading Late Cypriot polity of the island's southeast region, had served as a port of entry for elite goods from the beginning of Late Cypriot (Åström 1985: 174; 1996: 10). Apparently, the LC IIIA town had to be abandoned because its port basin silted up. By 1000 BC, it had been transformed into the salt lake of Larnaca (Gifford 1980). Thus Tekke surrendered first its port authority and then its economic zone and much of its population to a successor, Kition, a few kilometres to the east.

Enkomi

Founded as a coastal settlement in MC III/LC IA, Enkomi turned from being a gateway to a capital place after LC IB (Crewe 2004). By LC IIA, when it had consolidated its position, the entire region east of the Troodos was unified under its authority. The closure, therefore, of mining and cult sites east of the Troodos (as noted above) has to be related to Enkomi's crisis and ought to be assessed against the destruction that the urban centre (Level IIB) is believed to have suffered at the end of LC IIC (Dikaios 1969–71: 487). Enkomi, however, was not abandoned. In LC IIIA it was still a polity that traded in copper, but its control over the eastern region had been challenged and almost certainly curtailed. In the first millennium BC, the Cypro-Archaic kingdom of Idalion thrived partly on lands that had once been Enkomi's. It seems possible that the origin of this devolution may date back to the turbulent horizon of LC IIC–IIIA. In fact, *if* the LC IIC–IIIA date for the establishment of a fortified settlement on the summit of the hill of *Ambeleri* can be trusted (Gjerstad et al. 1934: 460; Ålin 1978), it *may* represent an early episode in the establishment of Idalion, whose Iron Age administrative centre was established on the slopes of this hill (Hadjicosti 1997), only 10–15km away from the nearest cupriferous foothills.

Maa-*Palaeokastro* and Pyla-*Kokkinokremos*

These two special-purpose sites (Knapp 1996b: 62), whose topography and lack of water sources emphasize that they were never meant to develop into long-term settlements, are a valuable cultural and chronological indicator of the crisis years and their immediate aftermath. Maa-*Palaeokastro* and Pyla-*Kokkinokremos* were founded at the very end of LC IIC. The former was established on a narrow promontory, 26km west of Paphos. Its landward side is protected by a 50m stretch of defensive wall. In spite of the fact that Maa was planned from scratch as a monumental fortress, it had 'a maximum life of some fifty years' in the first half of the 12th century (Karageorghis and Demas 1988: 260). *Kokkinokremos* was founded on a rocky plateau some 10km east of Kition. The plateau rises steeply from the lowlands and commands a superb view of Larnaca Bay and the fertile plain to the north, which is defined by the hills of the Troulloi mines (Karageorghis and Demas 1984: 3–5). The housing units, estimated as at least 200, were built along the edge of the plateau, forming a continuous outer wall (Karageorghis and Demas 1984: 23). The massiveness of this highly organized operation and the speed with which it was planned and executed on Kition's 'doorstep' are not irrelevant to *Kokkinokremos*'s sudden abandonment only a few decades after its establishment. Pyla means 'gate', and *Kokkinokremos* was meant to guard the Pyla Pass. Whoever had found it necessary to invest in its establishment lost it soon after the end of LC IIC to another claimant who, evidently, established a new frontier.

According to Karageorghis and Demas (1988: 265), Maa was violently destroyed and Pyla-*Kokkinokremos* hurriedly abandoned. What should not be overlooked is how close they were to the two prime urban centres of LC IIIA and how short a time they existed, which makes them like time capsules. Their material record encapsulates region-specific episodes, which open windows onto events that are not irrelevant to the expansion of Paphos and Kition and, particularly, to land claims and the drafting of boundaries between vying polities.

Unlike Enkomi and Hala Sultan Tekke, which were older urban centres, Paphos and Kition turned from being gateways to become true central places in LC IIC/LC IIIA, when other Late Cypriot polities were closing down. During this unsettling period, Paphos and Kition had evidently managed to concentrate so much strength—translated as agricultural and industrial territories as well as manpower—that they could afford to give a monumental expression to their newly acquired political status. For the first time in the island's history, human and material resources were directed towards a hitherto unknown enterprise: the construction of walled *temene* in megalithic ashlar masonry, replacing what had been rather modest sanctuaries (Fig. 43.2). The enhancement plans for Kition Temple 1 and Paphos Sanctuary I followed a common architectural model, using ashlar masonry, horns of consecration, and stepped capitals (Fig. 43.3).

The establishment of Maa and *Kokkinokremos* coincides with the time when Paphos and Kition began monumentalizing their sanctuaries. At this time, Kition acquired a fortification wall constructed in the same 'cyclopean' technique as the wall at Maa (Karageorghis and Demas 1985: 86–7). Its exact circuit is uncertain, but its surviving section to the northeast of the sanctuary was the harbour front of the city (Nicolaou 1976). These large-scale projects at Paphos and Kition were evidently planned and executed by centralized political authorities (Webb 1999: 292). The same, however, could hardly have been the case at Enkomi.

MORE 'CYCLOPEAN' WALLS

Shortly before its destruction at the end of LC IIC, the urban centre of Enkomi was also enclosed in a 'cyclopean' wall (Dikaios 1969–71: 485–6, 512, 909–10). The alignment of its citygates with the town's main north–south and east–west communication arteries suggests that the defensive and the impressive urban grid systems were designed as a whole (Courtois, Lagarce, and Lagarce 1986: 2–7). A 'cyclopean' fort was also erected at Sinda.

FIG. 43.2 *Palaepaphos:* megaliths of the Late Cypriot *temenos* at the sanctuary of the Cypriot Aphrodite (southwest corner) (photograph by author)

FIG. 43.3 Department of Antiquities excavations at Kition Area II (sanctuary area): Temple 1 from the west with workshops and 'cyclopean' wall visible to the north (photo by kind permission of the Director of the Department of Antiquities, Cyprus)

Lying on a rock plateau 15km directly east of Enkomi, Sinda had been established in the Mesaoria Plain to guard the copper route and protect the rich agricultural region that was Enkomi's hinterland. It may have suffered, like Enkomi, a catastrophe at the end of LC IIC but it survived into LC IIIA, to be abandoned before the end of the 12th century (Furumark 1965; Furumark and Adelman 2003).

OLD SALAMIS AND NEW SALAMIS: FROM HETERARCHY TO HIERARCHY

If a *hierarchically* structured administration can be inferred from the concentration of attention in a single sacred quarter at Paphos and Kition, the proliferation of sanctuaries of different types inside the walls of Enkomi in LC IIC points to a *heterarchical* environment, which persisted throughout LC IIIA. Metalworking units and *intra muros* burial chambers also appear in different neighbourhoods (Courtois, Lagarce, and Lagarce 1986) and demonstrate the existence of competing groups within the walled town. No one group managed to become pre-eminent, and thus no one sanctuary was monumentalized on the scale of Paphos and Kition.

Eventually Enkomi or, better, Old Salamis (Yon 1980: 79) was abandoned. The silting of its port basin by alluvial deposits from the Pediaeos River (Lagarce 1993: 91) forced the city to move nearer the coast, to New Salamis. This move, however, encompassed much more than a necessary replacement of harbour facilities: leaving the heterarchical landscape of Old Salamis, it produced the strongly hierarchical Iron Age kingdom of New Salamis under its Greek hegemones. When did Greeks and their language come to Cyprus?

IN SEARCH OF THE GREEK MIGRATION

The sudden proliferation of monumental sacred and defensive structures in the urban centres, as well as in the territories of Paphos, Kition, and Enkomi, was not simply a matter of directing labour to obtain and fetch raw materials. It was a successful application of engineering skills that were up to then unknown. Were the engineers newcomers? The employment of people who had been skilled under a system that specialized in monumental constructions throughout the 14th and 13th centuries BC—as the palace culture of the Greek-speaking Mycenaeans was—must not be excluded. The early Greek dialect (Arcado-Cypriot) that began to be written in the local syllabary by about 1000 BC became in the course of the Iron Age the island's main language and, before the end of the first millennium BC, the island's only language (Iacovou 2006). This phenomenal language change demands that we define the chronology of the new linguistic group's migration into Cyprus and how they established themselves.

FOREIGNERS *INTRA MUROS* AND CULTURAL DIVERSIFICATION

In LC IIIA most of the *intra muros* 'family' chambers, which had been constructed in LC I and LC II, were being abandoned (Keswani 2004). At the same time, there was a noticeable increase in the use of simple shaft graves: they are reported from Enkomi, Kition, Hala Sultan Tekke, and Paphos (Catling 1979; Niklasson 1983: 185; Karageorghis 2000: 257–9). In contrast to the chamber tomb, which was usually constructed by a kin group to receive inhumations over an extended period of time, this type of shallow grave was meant for single use. The proliferation of shaft graves in LC IIIA, side by side with the last of the pre-existing chamber tombs, indicates the presence of people detached from their place of origin (Keswani 1989: 70) who had moved into the 12th-century urban centres. Whether they came from another region of the island or from further afield, they owned no 'family' tombs in these settlements.

Shaft graves were characteristic of the 12th century BC; they disappeared from the mortuary patterns of the Early Iron Age together with the *intra muros* chamber tombs. The most likely reason is that the Early Iron Age settlements were not founded by diverse groups of outsiders but by culturally integrated people. The establishment of extramural, community-organized burial grounds, where the Aegean chamber tomb with the long *dromos* was the preponderant tomb-type, begins from as early as LC IIIB or Cypro-Geometric I. The homogeneity which characterizes the mortuary pattern, and also the material culture, of the Early Iron Age sites could not have been fostered in the course of a migration episode, which would inevitably have left some traces of a cultural diversification in the material record. The horizon which experienced the climax of the migration, therefore, has to predate the 11th–10th centuries BC, by which time Greek, the language of the migrants, began to be recorded in the local syllabary. Cultural diversity can be traced instead in various aspects of the 12th century. Besides shaft graves, bathtubs, Handmade Burnished Ware, and other novel features appeared, but with no homogeneous distribution within or between sites, nor any lasting cultural impact. They created, rather, a short-term lack of balance in the material culture and an inter-site cultural diversity in the 12th century BC (Iacovou 2005).

THE INTRA-URBAN SACRED ENVIRONMENT

The intra-urban sacred environment of LC IIC continued to be prevalent in LC IIIA in Paphos, Kition, and Enkomi. The association of cult and metallurgy, observed in LC IIC, persisted and became marked in LC IIIA, both in functions and iconography: metal workshops were set up inside the sanctuary at Kition, while a male 'smiting' god cast in bronze and standing on an ingot-shaped base was found in a cult site in Enkomi, which is also the likely provenance of his female counterpart, the bronze statuette of the nude 'Ashtarte-on-the-Ingot' that is now in the Ashmolean Museum (Webb 2001).

A new feature, however, was the appearance of anthropomorphic and zoomorphic terracotta votives that do not belong to the traditional Late Cypriot coroplastic types. Prototypes of the bovid terracotta, with a hollow cylindrical body that has been turned on a wheel, can be found in Crete (Karageorghis 1993: 63). The most outstanding examples are the bicephalic centaurs (or sphinxes) from the sanctuary of the Ingot God in Enkomi (Courtois 1971: 300) (Fig. 43.4). As regards the female votive offerings, LC IIIA sees the introduction of the 'goddess' with raised arms, first in its most unassuming representation, like the Psi-type Mycenaean figurine, but by LC IIIB with painted hollow bodies that derive from Cretan prototypes (Karageorghis 1993: 58–60). Three examples associated with the initial use of an extra-urban sanctuary of Limassol-*Komissariato* in LC IIIB/CG I (Karageorghis 1977–8) suggest the establishment of an 11th-century BC cult site by an Aegean group of people (Fig. 43.5).

ENKOMH 1962
Pt. 902A

FIG. 43.4 Proto-White Painted zoomorphic double-headed centaur from the sanctuary of the Ingot God at Enkomi from the Cyprus Museum. (Photo by kind permission of the Director of the Department of Antiquities, Cyprus)

FAST-WHEEL LOCAL PRODUCTION OF AEGEAN-TYPE CERAMICS

The notion that a neat line can be drawn between LC IIC and LC IIIA on ceramic grounds or on a break in cultural continuity belongs to the past (Sherratt 1991: 191). We have come to acknowledge the significance of cultural continua that characterize the transition to LC IIIA without denying that the 12th century also experienced a migration event. Pottery produced on the fast wheel that copied a select few Late Helladic III-painted shapes did not appear suddenly at the end of LC IIC (Kling 1989). Import substitution and the transfer of Aegean-type pottery to local manufacture are attested well before the LC IIC–IIIA site-abandonment horizon (Sherratt 1999: 178). Local imitations of Aegean pottery, now often classified under the umbrella term White Painted Wheelmade III (Kling 1989), were primarily an industrial phenomenon, which gradually led to the eclipse of the traditional slow-wheel ceramic products of Cyprus and their substitution with a wheelmade repertoire.

The 'process of integration into a more or less single spectrum of wheelmade ware' (Sherratt 1991: 193) culminated after LC IIIA in the production of Proto-White Painted

FIG. 43.5 Two female terracotta figurines with raised arms from the Limassol-Komissariato Sanctuary (Limassol Museum; courtesy Vassos Karageorghis)

which represents the primary ceramic definition of LC IIIB. At the time, then, when pottery manufacture in Cyprus arrived at an island-wide, wheelmade, standardized, mass-produced painted product, LC IIIA gave way to LC IIIB.

EPILOGUE

The individual histories of Enkomi, Hala Sultan Tekke, Kition, and Paphos in the course of LC IIIA are different from each other but, together, they tell how urbanism and state functions were kept alive in the 12th century BC. Not surprisingly, cultural continuities seemed to have vied with novelties in LC IIIA polities. Copper was still sourced from their industrial territories and exported from their ports—industrial intensification is evident in three (Tekke excluded) of the coastal survivors (Sherratt 1992: 326)—with the result that these mixed populations would have learned empirically that their livelihood rested on upholding the existing Late Cypriot politico-economic mode; but there was also a novel and much more significant aspect to the metal industries. LC IIIA was the time of early experiments in producing functional iron (Snodgrass 1980: 345; Pickles and Peltenburg 1998). It was a technological breakthrough—certainly the single most impressive achievement of Cyprus in the 12th century—and in time led to a commercial revolution (Sherratt 1994: 85). By LC IIIB, Cyprus was trading its first iron tools and implements (Sherratt 2000: 82), with far-reaching sociopolitical consequences for all Mediterranean cultures.

The successful restructuring of the island's settlement pattern after LC IIIA is therefore partly indebted to a new population that had entered the island not as colonizers—they did not establish separate enclaves—but apparently as skilled economic migrants. It is likely that the execution of monumental urban projects relied on their engineering skills. In the LC IIIA urban environment, which the newcomers shared with the indigenous people, the island's scribal system, having been sheltered from extinction, was adopted by the new linguistic group, who used it to write their own Greek language.

If the Greeks were not a dominant population in the 12th or the 11th centuries, by the 7th century BC individuals who belonged to the Greek linguistic group had become *basileis* (kings) in almost all the Iron Age kingdoms of Cyprus. The process of their ascendancy—the successful claim of royal authority—happened in the Cypriot Early Iron Age horizon (11th–8th centuries BC). To the end of the era of the Cypriot kingdoms, the Cypriot syllabary was the pre-eminent scribal tool of the Greek *basileis*, and to the end of the first millennium BC, a strong identity indicator of Cyprus's Hellenism.

SUGGESTED READING

Georgiou, A. (2011). *Pyla-Kokkinikremos, Maa-Palaeokastro and the Settlement Histories of Cyprus in the Twelfth Century BC.* PhD dissertation, Oxford University.

Iacovou, M. (2013). Aegean-style material culture in Late Cypriot III: minimal evidence, maximal interpretation. In A. E. Killebrew and G. Lehmann (eds), *The Philistines and Other "Sea Peoples" in Text and Archaeology.* Atlanta, Ga.: Society of Biblical Literature, 585–618.

Karageorghis, V. (1990). *The End of the Late Bronze Age in Cyprus.* Nicosia: Pierides Foundation.

—— and J. D. Muhly (1984). *Cyprus at the Close of the Late Bronze Age.* Nicosia: A. G. Leventis Foundation.

Kiely, T. (2005). *From Villages to City-Kingdoms? The Topographic and Political Development of Cypriot Towns during the Later Bronze and Early Iron Ages, ca. 1900–750 BC, with Special Reference to the Spatial and Chronological Relationship of Tombs and Settlement Areas.* PhD dissertation, Oxford University.

Knapp, A. B. (2013). *The Archaeology of Cyprus: From Earliest Prehistory through the Bronze Age.* Cambridge: Cambridge University Press.

Maier, F. G., and M.-L. von Wartburg (1985). Reconstructing history from the Earth, *c.* 2800 B.C.–1600 A.D.: archaeology at Palaepaphos, 1960–1985. In V. Karageorghis (ed.), *Archaeology in Cyprus 1960–1985.* Nicosia: A. G. Leventis Foundation, 142–72.

South, A. K. (2002). Late Bronze Age settlement patterns in southern Cyprus. *Cahier du Centre d'études chypriotes* 32: 59–72.

Steel, L. (2004). *Cyprus before History: From the Earliest Settlers to the End of the Bronze Age.* London: Duckworth.

REFERENCES

Ålin, P. (1978). Idalion pottery from the excavations of the Swedish Cyprus Expedition. *Opuscula Atheniensia* 12: 91–109.

Åström, P. (1985). Hala Sultan Tekke. In V. Karageorghis (ed.), *Archaeology in Cyprus 1960–1985.* Nicosia: A. G. Leventis Foundation, 173–81.

—— (1996). Hala Sultan Tekke: a Late Cypriote harbour town. In P. Åström and E. Herscher (eds), *Late Bronze Age Settlement in Cyprus: Function and Relationship.* Jonsered: Åströms, 9–14.

Bunimovitz, S. (1998). Sea Peoples in Cyprus and Israel: a comparative study of immigration processes. In S. Gitin, A. Mazar, and E. Stern (eds), *Mediterranean Peoples in Transition: Thirteenth to Early Tenth Centuries BCE.* Jerusalem: Israel Exploration Society, 103–13.

Cadogan, G. (1989). Maroni and the monuments. In E. J. Peltenburg (ed.), *Early Society in Cyprus.* Edinburgh: Edinburgh University Press/National Museums of Scotland/A. G. Leventis Foundation, 43–51.

—— (1996). Maroni: change in Late Bronze Age Cyprus. In P. Åström and E. Herscher (eds), *Late Bronze Age Settlement in Cyprus: Function and Relationship.* Jonsered: Åströms, 15–22.

Catling, H. W. (1979). The St Andrews–Liverpool Museums Kouklia Tomb Excavations, 1950–1954. *Report of the Department of Antiquities, Cyprus* 1979: 270–5.

Courtois, J.-C. (1971). Le sanctuaire du dieu au l'ingot d'Enkomi-Alasia. In C. F.-A. Schaeffer (ed.), *Alasia I.* Paris: Mission archéologique d'Alasia, 151–362.

—— J. Lagarce, and E. Lagarce (1986). *Enkomi et le Bronze récent à Chypre.* Nicosia: A. G. Leventis Foundation.

Crewe, L. (2004). *Social complexity and ceramic technology on Late Bronze Age Cyprus: the new evidence from Enkomi.* PhD dissertation, University of Edinburgh.

Dikaios, P. (1969–71). *Enkomi: Excavations 1948–1958* (2 vols). Mainz am Rhein: von Zabern.

Dothan, T., and A. Ben-Tor (1983). *Excavations at Athienou, Cyprus, 1971–1972.* Jerusalem: Institute of Archaeology, Hebrew University of Jerusalem.

Furumark, A. (1965). The excavations at Sinda: some historical results. *Opuscula Atheniensia* 6: 99–116.

—— and C. Adelman (2003). *Swedish Excavations at Sinda, Cyprus: Excavations Conducted by Arne Furumark 1947–1948.* Stockholm: Åströms.

Gifford, J. A. (1980). *Palaeogeography of Archaeological Sites of the Larnaca Lowlands, Southeastern Cyprus.* Ann Arbor, Mich.: University Microfilms International.

Gjerstad, E., J. Lindros, E. Sjöqvist, and A. Westholm (1934). *The Swedish Cyprus Expedition II: Finds and Results of the Excavations in 1927–1931.* Stockholm: Swedish Cyprus Expedition.

Hadjicosti, M. (1991). The Late Bronze Age Tomb 2 from Mathiatis. *Report of the Department of Antiquities, Cyprus* 1991: 75–91.

—— (1997). The kingdom of Idalion in the light of new evidence. *Bulletin of the American Schools of Oriental Research* 308: 49–63.

Hadjisavvas, S. (1989). A Late Cypriot community at Alassa. In E. J. Peltenburg (ed.), *Early Society in Cyprus.* Edinburgh: Edinburgh University Press/National Museums of Scotland/ A. G. Leventis Foundation, 32–42.

Iacovou, M. (1994). The topography of 11th century B.C. Cyprus. In V. Karageorghis (ed.), *Cyprus in the 11th Century B.C.: Proceedings of the International Symposium.* Nicosia: A. G. Leventis Foundation/University of Cyprus, 149–65.

—— (2005). Cyprus at the dawn of the first millennium B.C.E.: cultural homogenization versus the tyranny of ethnic identifications. In J. Clarke (ed.), *Archaeological Perspectives on the Transmission and Transformation of Culture in the Eastern Mediterranean.* Oxford: Oxbow, 125–36.

—— (2006). 'Greeks', 'Phoenicians' and 'Eteocypriots': ethnic identities in the Cypriote kingdoms. In J. Chrysostomides and C. Dendrinos (eds), *Sweet Land: Lectures on the History and Culture of Cyprus.* Camberley: Porphyrogenitus, 24–59.

—— (2007). Site size estimates and the diversity factor in Late Cypriote settlement histories. *Bulletin of the American Schools of Oriental Research* 348: 1–23.

Karageorghis, V. (1977–8). The goddess with the uplifted arms in Cyprus. *Scripta Minora*: 1–45.

—— (1993). *The Coroplastic Art of Ancient Cyprus II: Late Cypriote II–Cypro-Geometric III*. Nicosia: A. G. Leventis Foundation.

—— (2000). Cultural innovations in Cyprus relating to the Sea Peoples. In E. D. Oren (ed.), *The Sea Peoples and Their World: A Reassessment*. Philadelphia: University Museum, University of Pennsylvania, 255–79.

—— and M. Demas (1984). *Pyla-Kokkinokremos: A Late 13th-Century B.C. Fortified Settlement in Cyprus*. Nicosia: Department of Antiquities, Cyprus.

—— (eds) (1985). *Excavations at Kition V: The Pre-Phoenician Levels—Areas I and II*. Nicosia: Department of Antiquities, Cyprus.

—— (eds) (1988). *Excavations at Maa-Palaeokastro, 1979–1986*. Nicosia: Department of Antiquities, Cyprus.

Keswani, P. (1989). Dimensions of social hierarchy in Late Bronze Age Cyprus: an analysis of the mortuary data from Enkomi. *Journal of Mediterranean Archaeology* 2: 49–86.

—— (2004). *Mortuary Ritual and Society in Bronze Age Cyprus*. London: Equinox.

Kitchen, K. A. (1973). *The Third Intermediate Period in Egypt (1100–650 B.C.)*. Warminster: Aris & Phillips.

Kling, B. (1989). *Mycenaean IIIC:1b and Related Pottery in Cyprus*. Gothenburg: Åströms.

—— and J. D. Muhly (2007). *Joan du Plat Taylor's Excavations at the Late Bronze Age Mining Settlement at Apliki Karamallos, Cyprus, part 1*. Sävedalen: Åströms.

Knapp, A. B. (ed.) (1996a). *Near Eastern and Aegean Texts from the Third to the First Millennia BC*, vol. 2: *Sources for the History of Cyprus*. Altamont, NY: Greece and Cyprus Research Center.

—— (1996b). Settlement and society on Late Bronze Age Cyprus: dynamics and development. In P. Åström and E. Herscher (eds), *Late Bronze Age Settlement in Cyprus: Function and Relationship*. Jonsered: Åströms, 54–80.

—— (1997). *The Archaeology of Late Bronze Age Cypriot Society: The Study of Settlement, Survey and Landscape*. Glasgow: University of Glasgow Press.

—— (2008). *Prehistoric and Protohistoric Cyprus: Identity, Insularity, and Connectivity*. Oxford: Oxford University Press.

Lagarce, J. (1993). Enkomi: fouilles françaises. In M. Yon (ed.), *Kinyras: l'archéologie française à Chypre*. Lyon: Maison de l'Orient/Paris: De Boccard.

Manning, S. W., B. Weninger, A. K. South, et al. (2001). Absolute age range of the Late Cypriot IIC period on Cyprus. *Antiquity* 75: 328–40.

Nicolaou, K. (1976). *The Historical Topography of Kition*. Gothenburg: Åströms.

Niklasson, K. (1983). Tomb 23: a shaft-grave of the Late Cypriote III period. In P. Åström, E. Åström, A. Hatziantoniou, K. Niklasson, and U. Öbrink (eds), *Hala Sultan Tekke 8: Excavations 1971–79*. Gothenburg: Åströms, 169–213.

Peltenburg, E. J. (1996). From isolation to state formation in Cyprus, c. 3500–1500 BC. In V. Karageorghis and D. Michaelides (eds), *The Development of the Cypriot Economy from the Prehistoric Period to the Present Day*. Nicosia: Bank of Cyprus/University of Cyprus Archaeological Research Unit and Department of Economics, 17–43.

—— (2012). King Kušmešuša and the decentralised political structure of Late Bronze Age Cyprus. In G. Cadogan, M. Iacovou, K. Kopaka, and J. Whitley (eds), *Parallel Lives: Ancient Island Societies in Crete and Cyprus*. London: British School in Athens, 345–51.

Pickles, S., and E. J. Peltenburg (1998). Metallurgy, society and the Bronze/Iron transition in the east Mediterranean and the Near East. *Report of the Department of Antiquities, Cyprus* 1998: 67–100.

Sandars, N. K. (1978). *The Sea Peoples: Warriors of the Ancient Mediterranean, 1250–1150 B.C.* London: Thames & Hudson.

Sherratt, E. S. (1991). Cypriot pottery of Aegean Type in LCII–III: problems of classification, chronology and interpretation. In J. A. Barlow, D. R. Bolger, and B. Kling (eds), *Cypriot Ceramics: Reading the Prehistoric Record.* Philadelphia: University Museum of Archaeology and Anthropology, University of Pennsylvania, 185–98.

——(1992). Immigration and archaeology: some indirect reflections. In P. Åström (ed.), *Acta Cypria: Acts of an International Congress on Cypriote Archaeology Held in Göteborg on 22–24 August 1991, part 2.* Jonsered: Åströms, 316–47.

——(1994). Commerce, iron and ideology: metallurgical innovation in the 12th–11th century Cyprus. In V. Karageorghis (ed.), *Cyprus in the 11th Century B.C.: Proceedings of the International Symposium Organized by the Archaeological Research Unit of the University of Cyprus and the Anastasios G. Leventis Foundation, Nicosia, 30–31 October 1993.* Nicosia: A. G. Leventis Foundation, 59–107.

——(1999). *E pur si muove*: pots, markets and values in the second millennium Mediterranean. In J. P. Crielaard, V. Stissi, and G. J. van Wijngaarden (eds), *The Complex Past of Pottery: Production, Circulation and Consumption of Mycenaean and Greek Pottery (Sixteenth to Early Fifth Centuries BC).* Amsterdam: Gieben, 163–211.

——(2000). Circulation of metals and the end of the Bronze Age in the eastern Mediterranean. In C. F. E. Pare (ed.), *Metals Make The World Go Round: The Supply and Circulation of Metals in Bronze Age Europe.* Oxford: Oxbow, 82–98.

Snodgrass, A. M. (1980). Iron and early metallurgy in the Mediterranean. In T. A. Wertime and J. D. Muhly (eds), *The Coming of the Age of Iron.* New Haven, Conn.: Yale University Press, 335–74.

South, A. K. (1989). From copper to kingship. In E. J. Peltenburg (ed.), *Early Society in Cyprus.* Edinburgh: Edinburgh University Press/National Museums of Scotland/A. G. Leventis Foundation, 315–24.

Taylor, J. du P. (1957). *Myrtou-Pigadhes: A Late Bronze Age Sanctuary in Cyprus.* Oxford: Department of Antiquities, Ashmolean Museum.

Vermeule, E., and F. Z. Wolsky (1990). *Toumba tou Skourou: A Bronze Age Potters' Quarter on Morphou Bay in Cyprus.* Boston, Mass.: Harvard University, Museum of Fine Arts, Boston Cyprus Expedition.

Webb, J. M. (1999). *Ritual Architecture, Iconography and Practice in the Late Cypriot Bronze Age.* Jonsered: Åströms.

——(2001). The sanctuary of the ingot god at Enkomi: a new reading of its construction, use and abandonment. In P. M. Fischer (ed.), *Contributions to the Archaeology and History of the Bronze and Iron Ages in the Eastern Mediterranean: Studies in Honour of Paul Åström.* Vienna: Österreichische Archäologisches Institut, 69–82.

Yon, M. (1980). La fondation de Salamine. In M. Yon (ed.), *Salamine de Chypre: histoire et archéologie.* Paris: Centre national de la recherche scientifique, 71–80.

THE IRON AGE II PERIOD

CHAPTER 44

INTRODUCTION TO THE LEVANT DURING THE IRON AGE II PERIOD

MARGREET L. STEINER

The Iron II period may easily be the most extensively excavated and intensively researched era of the Levant, especially in the southern part of the region, but it is not the best understood period under investigation. Compared to the Late Bronze Age, we know precious little about the path to statehood that the various regions travelled, or about their economy or history. Both the beginning and the end of the Iron II period are disputed, and there is constant discussion over the dating of the excavated pottery and thus of the strata in which this pottery was found (see also Sharon, Ch. 4 above).[1]

I will not try to discuss or summarize the enormous amount of information provided in the following chapters. What I want to do here is focus on some aspects that have not received much attention in the literature. These concern first the impact of the Assyrians (and later the Babylonians and Persians) on the material culture of the regions they dominated, and secondly the organization of the economy of the various states in the Levant.

THE ASSYRIANS ARE COMING

Starting their expansion at the beginning of the 9th century BC, the Assyrians, and after them the Babylonians and Persians, in the course of several centuries subjected, sometimes destroyed, and in general dominated the peoples and states of the Levant (see for general overviews Schneider and Elayi, Chs 7 and 8 above). I will concentrate on the Assyrians, as they constitute the first Mesopotamian empire that dominated the Levantine scene in the Iron Age.

In general two phases can be distinguished in the contacts that the Assyrians had with the regions surrounding their heartland in the first millennium BC. The first period is the Assyrian expansion in the 9th century under Assurnasirpal II and Shalmaneser III. The

---

[1] The term Iron Age III is sometimes used instead of Iron IIC—see Mazzoni (Ch. 45 below).

latter king regularly crossed the Euphrates to gain access to the Mediterranean Sea, and he subdued the Neo-Hittite states in the north. Most subjected states remained nominally independent, but their rulers became vassals. At the end of the 9th century a period of internal decline set in.

With Tiglath-pileser III (744–727 BC) the second phase started, which is described as the period of 'Assyria's world domination' by van de Mieroop (2004: 232) and 'Assyria's apogee' by Schneider (Ch. 7 above). This is a period of intensive Assyrian control over subjected states, many of which were formally incorporated into Assyria as provinces. This phase ended in 612 BC, when the Babylonians and Medes sacked Assyria's capital, Nineveh.

It is difficult to assess the impact of the Assyrian domination on the daily life of the inhabitants of the region and on the material culture of the Levant. Of course the degree of Assyrianization of the subjugated states varied considerably. Regions on the east bank of the Euphrates were fully incorporated into the empire and 'Assyrianized'. Former capitals such as Dur Katlimmu, Carchemish, and Tell Barsip were rebuilt as Assyrian governor seats, and their architecture and arts display typical Assyrian elements, such as Assyrian-style palaces with mural paintings and sculpture. Imported Assyrian or locally made Assyrian-style pottery can be found in abundance.

The Assyrians considered the Jezireh as part of the Assyrian core, while territories to the west and north were considered more peripheral. This is visible in the archaeological record of the Orontes region and the regions further south in Syria as well as the areas east and west of the River Jordan. Some kingdoms here were eventually incorporated into the empire as provinces (Hamath, Israel, and Damascus), others were reduced to vassal states (Judah and Moab), while the Phoenician and Philistine trading ports continued as more or less independent city-states but had to send tribute to Assyria (see Aubet, Ch. 46 below).[2]

In general scholars are hard-pressed to find traces of Assyrian presence in the middle and southern Levant. Maybe it is not too much to state that without the Assyrian and biblical texts we would not have been able to conclude how, why, and by whom these regions were invaded and subjected. The archaeological records would have shown gradual changes in the material culture, but no major breaks. Over the course of several centuries many cities were destroyed, but it is often hard to find evidence in the ruins to show who the culprits were.

A good example from the Orontes region is Tell Afis. It is identified as ancient Hazrek, capital of the kingdom of Hamath and Lu'ash. The site was conquered by the Assyrians in 738 BC and transformed into a provincial centre, the seat of a governor. But the material culture remained staunchly local (Mazzoni, Ch. 45 below). Several Assyrian seals and a bronze bowl in Assyrian style were excavated, but Assyrian-style pottery (imported or copied) has scarcely been found (Soldi 2009).

Further south, Megiddo presents the same picture. After its destruction at the end of the 8th century BC, the town was completely rebuilt as an Assyrian administrative centre with a pseudo-Hippodamian town plan (see Killebrew, Ch. 48 below). Two Mesopotamian-style open court buildings were excavated just inside the gate. The material culture of this stratum, however, is completely local; hardly any Assyrian-style finds were recorded, as Stern notes with some astonishment (2001: 49).

---

[2] Cyprus was not invaded by the Assyrians but its kingdoms surrendered, apparently of their own free will, and became client states (see Iacovou, Ch. 53 below; she does not mention Assyrian-style finds on Cyprus).

In general, one can say that in the middle and southern parts of the Levant, the Assyrians, and after them the Babylonians and Persians (see Zorn and Lehmann, Chs 54 and 55 below), did not leave many impressive remains of their presence in the area in the form of luxurious palaces and governor residences with orthostats and mural paintings, cuneiform administrative and political inscriptions, majestic temples for the Mesopotamian gods, elite emulations of Assyrian fine wares, or a new kind of pottery.

Of course one can find some traces of Assyrian presence. For the southern Levant (the areas east and west of the River Jordan), Stern has made an inventory of Assyrian finds (2001).[3] But despite his conclusion that the Assyrians 'left rich and important traces in the archaeological record of the country' (2001: 14), the spoils are far from rich. Only four monumental inscriptions in the whole of Palestine are mentioned, as well as some clay cuneiform tablets and Assyrian-style seals. Assyrian-style architecture with walls of *terre pisé*, elevated podiums, the use of burnt bricks, horn-shaped stone thresholds, and vaulted openings and roofs has been identified at only a few sites: Megiddo and Hazor in the north; Tell Jemmeh, Sheikh Zuweid, and Tel Sera', all in Philistia; and Buseirah in Edom.

Three temples built with Assyrian-style elements are mentioned by Stern, at Ekron, Sheik Zuweid, and Buseirah, but the objects found in these temples are not Assyrian but local, and no Assyrian gods were worshipped there (for the Ekron temple, see Ben-Shlomo, Ch. 47 below; for Buseirah, see Bienkowski, Ch. 52). Assyrian-style sculpture is completely absent, while Assyrian-style pottery, mostly locally made, has been found in small quantities only, except at Tell Jemmeh. Assyrian prototypes did influence local pottery styles (which resulted in the production of carinated bowls, handleless bottles, and new types of cooking pots), but this concerns only a small part of the pottery assemblage.

Thus some Assyrian influence on the local traditions, especially in architecture and pottery, can be detected. Were it not for the literary texts, however, these influences could also be explained by other processes such as gift exchange and emulation—and can still be explained that way. In the period before and after the Assyrian conquest, Phoenician architecture and Phoenician or Phoenician-style pottery and arts (ivories, metal, and glass) can be found all over Palestine, probably in greater quantities than the Assyrian material. Nobody would, of course, suggest that the Phoenicians ever conquered the Levant and ruled over it.

This lack of persuasive influence on the material culture of the middle and southern Levant is the more intriguing when compared to the impact of that later empire that subjected the region in a similar way as the Assyrians did—with much sabre-rattling and cruelty: the Roman Empire. The Romans left their lasting mark on almost every aspect of the local culture, from the layout of towns to the building styles of domestic units, from the introduction of new pottery styles to the transformation of the cuisine, from inscriptions in Latin and Greek to new economic and political institutions. Not only was the way of life of the local inhabitants thoroughly transformed, but even their way of thinking. And in every excavation these Roman elements resurface.

Why did the Assyrians, and after them the Babylonians and Persians, not leave such impressive remains? It is not easy to answer this question. The impact of the Assyrians on the material culture in the Levant has not been the subject of many studies, as far as I know. Most research focuses on the historical and political aspects, based mostly on inscriptions. Maybe the Assyrians were not interested in exporting their material culture or their religious

---

[3] No such overview exists for the northern Levant so far.

institutions to the nations they had conquered? On the contrary, they imported many traits from abroad, from building styles to (eventually) the Aramaic language. Or maybe they found the (southern) regions they conquered not interesting enough to which to export their culture?

It's the economy, stupid

There is, however, one aspect of the culture of the local communities that was thoroughly transformed by their inclusion in the Assyrian Empire, and that is the economy. In the 9th and 8th centuries BC the Assyrian onslaught forced the kingdoms that were threatened to unite and work together. They must have geared their economies to a war state of affairs, and were forced to assemble their riches to send as tribute to the Assyrian Empire. In the second phase of Assyrian domination, whenever the (vassal) states rebelled, the Assyrians ruthlessly destroyed their towns and trampled the surrounding countryside, while the policy of forced deportation of large parts of the population must have had a devastating effect on the economy of the regions involved. The number of people 'relocated' by the Assyrians are estimated to be in the millions—van de Mieroop mentions a number of 4.5 million (2004: 219). All this must have had serious social and economic implications.

But there is more. In the 7th and 6th centuries BC, after the campaigns of Tiglath-pileser III and Sargon II, the regions they had conquered became part of what Mazzoni calls 'the Assyrian *koiné*' (Ch. 45 below)—*koiné* not so much in the sense that the peoples shared the same culture or spoke the same language, but in the sense that their economies had been globalized and transformed from the economy of the 'early state' into an open 'world-wide' economy.

In the 9th and first half of the 8th centuries, the kingdoms of the Levant were small, regional states. As I have argued before (Steiner 2001a), in such a state there are usually two economic 'zones of influence'. The first one consists of the royal circle. The king and the small elite live off the returns of their own lands, irregular taxation of the local communities, and taxation of interregional trade. The king lives mostly in his capital, a fortified town, where specialized crafts such as ivory and gold working and the production of luxury pottery are concentrated. Here one can expect to find small palaces and temples, but not large-scale storage facilities, an extensive bureaucratic apparatus creating a lot of economic texts, or a king actively involved in industries and trade. The interest of the ruler in economic matters is small; the state concerns itself foremost with political and ideological matters. Redistribution is an important function of early states, but is ordinarily limited to the distribution of surplus to the (small) administration and the furnishing of sacrifices. The ruler receives food and labour, while his returns are in the ideological sphere: he 'guarantees' fertility, peace, and prosperity. The amounts of goods distributed in these early states are limited.

The local communities (the other 'zone') make a living by agriculture or husbandry combined with the part-time practice of crafts and trade. They are more or less self-sufficient. Land ownership is communal; private landownership is rare. The interaction between the two circuits would have been limited, as taxes were levied on an irregular basis and the local communities had their own industries and markets (see further Steiner 2001a).

This model may apply better to the small kingdoms of the southern Levant than to those of the north. Or maybe one should rather say that we have more archaeological information on the southern than on the northern Levant. Economic information of the Aramean and Neo-Hittite kingdoms is scarce and based on inscriptions rather than on excavated materials. But in the north, as in the south, the kingdoms were small (Mazzoni, Ch. 45, calls them 'petty kingdoms') and the amounts of goods distributed were limited. The Phoenician harbour towns may have been organized in a slightly different way as trade, not agriculture, was the foremost mode of existence.

In the late 8th and 7th centuries, the old economic structure had begun to crumble and the economies changed to a more open, trade-oriented mode. The strategies of deportation or relocation of peoples across the area and the attribution of land to the Assyrians destroyed the old exchange networks and patron relationships. It put an end to the luxury crafts patronized by and meant for the local elite, such as the production of ivory inlays and precious metal vessels (Mazzoni, Ch. 45). And it made way for new forms of interaction and for the production and exchange of goods on a much larger scale.

An impressive example of the expanded scale of production is Ekron in Philistia, which expanded considerably in size (from 4ha to 20ha) after the Assyrian conquest. In and around the tell 115 olive oil presses were excavated, with an estimated annual production capacity of 500–1,000 tonnes of olive oil or 50,000–100,000 filled oil jars (Ben-Shlomo, Ch. 47 below). This enormous amount—about the production of modern-day Lebanon—must have been distributed in a wide market area, possibly all the way to Assyria.

A good example of absorption into the expanded exchange networks can be found in Jerusalem. Because of the wide-scale destruction of Jerusalem by the Babylonians (and the extensive excavations), we can reconstruct the lifestyle and economy in the 7th century BC. The difference between the city in the 10th/9th centuries and the late 7th is enormous (Steiner 2001b). On top of a monumental stepped-stone structure of earlier periods a residential quarter was built, belonging to what may be called the elite of Jerusalem: artisans and traders, and wealthy ones at that. To me this signifies the growing importance of trade and the exchange of luxury goods in this period.

The excavations yielded remains of all kinds of imported luxury goods (see Steiner 2001b): wooden furniture and ivory from north Syria, decorative shells from the Red Sea, wine jars from Greece or Cyprus, and scarabs from Egypt, while bronze must have come from either Cyprus or Transjordan. From Shiloh's excavation 'fine pottery bowls from Assyria' are mentioned. Arab inscriptions on pottery may testify to either trade with Arabia of the presence of Arabian traders in the city.

The small vassal state of Judah may have been insignificant in the eyes of the Assyrians compared to other regions. Nevertheless, in the 7th century BC the city was included in the trade networks of the Assyrian *koiné* and its inhabitants took advantage of the open, 'worldwide' economy of which they were now part.

New studies on the social and economic organization of Iron II societies and the changes brought about by Assyrian domination will lead to new understandings of how the local communities coped with the many changes in this era. A promising project is the new excavations at Zincirli, where one of the main research questions is 'the socioeconomic organization of the Iron Age city' (Schloen and Fink 2009: 218).

REFERENCES

Schloen, J. D., and A. S. Fink (2009). Searching for ancient Sam'al: new excavations at Zincirli in Turkey. *Near Eastern Archaeology* 72: 203–19.

Soldi, S. (2009). Aramaeans and Assyrians in north-western Syria: material evidence from Tell Afis. *Syria* 86: 97–118.

Steiner, M. L. (2001a). Jerusalem in the 10th and 7th centuries BCE: from administrative centre to commercial city. In A. Mazar (ed.), *Studies in the Archaeology of the Iron Age in Israel and Jordan*. Sheffield: Sheffield Academic, 280–88.

—— (2001b). Mesha versus Solomon: two models of economic organization in Iron Age II. *Svensk Exegetisk Årsbok* 67: 37–45.

Stern, E. (2001). *Archaeology in the Land of the Bible*, vol. 2: *The Assyrian, Babylonian, and Persian Periods (732–332 B.C.E.)*. New York: Doubleday.

van de Mieroop, M. (2004). *A History of the Ancient Near East ca. 3000–323 B.C.* Malden, Mass.: Blackwell.

CHAPTER 45

....

THE ARAMEAN STATES DURING THE IRON AGE II–III PERIODS

....

STEFANIA MAZZONI

Syria in the Iron Age presents a multifaceted political, social, and cultural landscape; architecture and sculpture exhibit a strong variety of forms mirroring the articulation in city-states or petty states, each characterized by local traditions and various peoples. Syria is just part of a Near East transformed by the emergence of new components (Arameans and Phoenicians, Philistines, Caldaeans and Hebrews, Ammonites and Moabites, Arabs and Iranians, Urartians, Phrygians, and Ionians) interacting with powerful states (Assyria, the Hittites, and Egypt). This process not only changed the geography of the (already flexible) political borders of the area but also introduced different mechanisms for intercultural interaction; overseas and trans-desertic circulation of goods and tradesmen, military occupation and administrative empire control, and the deportation and forced relocation of populations were new factors that had a tremendous impact, increasing multiculturality and symbiotic processes and prompting manifold national identities and ethnic forces to develop. These trends reached their climax between the 10th and 8th centuries BC, a crucial phase not least because the then emerging societies of the western Mediterranean became familiar with this scenario. Syria, owing to its long-lasting heritage, was a formative component of this landscape.

Different terms are used to label this period and its manifestations: Syro-Hittite, Neo-Hittite, Aramean, and Neo-Syrian, each stressing the significant components involved and the orientation towards continuity or renewal (Bunnens 2000; Mazzoni 2000a; 2000c). It is worth noting, however, that it was precisely the dynamic interlace of these many identities with their individual traits and regional orientations that generated the urban growth and cultural development of the period that archaeology defines as Iron I–III.

Cultural borders were flexible as were the unstable political ones, and the kingdoms of Hittite origin or Aramean new formation were more often allied. Sources document a period of increasing conflict.[1] Damascus to the south with the land of Aram and Karkemish to the

---

[1] For historical sources on the period, see Sader (1987; 2000), Liverani (1992), Klengel (1992: 191–218), and Masetti Rouault (2001: 71–87, 114–27). For the variety of languages, see Lipiński (2000b) and Dalley (2000). The term 'Khatti' was applied to Karkemish, but also to a large geographical area west of the Euphrates (see Hawkins 1975; 1995).

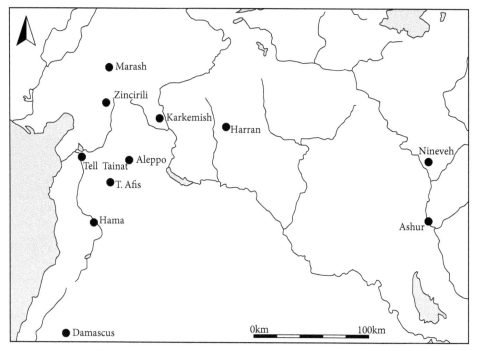

FIG. 45.1 Map of Iron Age II sites in the Aramean states

north with the land of Khatti were the two political poles of the area; the first contended for the fertile land of the Galilean hills with Israel, the second for the Euphrates border with Assyria, who already controlled the northeastern frontier. In northern Syria, dynasties of Hittite origin reigned in Karkemish; in Pattina with its capital in Kunalua (most probably Tell Tainat), exerting control over the renowned Weather God Temple of Aleppo; in Que; and in Gurgum (Marash). Sam'al (Zincirli), on the western bank of the Kara-su, once the land of Usha, was instead controlled by the Aramean Bit Gabbari/Y'dy. Other Aramean kingdoms included Bit Agushi, with a capital first at Arne (Tell Araane?) and then at Arpad (Tell Rifa'at), and Lu'ash, with its capital at Hazrek (Tell Afis?), while Hamath was instead ruled by a dynasty of Hittite tradition. The Bit Adini tribe transformed the Hittite town of Masuwari on the left bank of the Euphrates into the Aramean Til Barsib; the Bit Bakhiani tribe founded Guzana (Tell Halaf) on a branch of the Khabur River, near the old centre of Sikani (probably the old Hurrian capital, Washukanni, but today Tell Fakhariyah). On the Middle Euphrates, the Arameans spread in the country of Laqê (14th–13th-centuries kingdom of Khana) (Fig. 45.1).

THE ARCHAEOLOGICAL FRAMEWORK

Unlike Iron I, which is now well phased on the basis of dense package levels of a few sites,[2] the periodization of Iron II–III is still a work in progress.

---

[2] E.g. Tell Kazel and Tell Afis. On the Iron I and II chronology, see Mazzoni (2000a; 2000b; 2000c; 121–34).

Old excavations in the major capitals of the area provide our main sources of information on architecture, sculpture, and related inscriptions: Karkemish (1878–81, 1911–14), Zincirli (1888–1902), Tell Tainat (1935–8), Tell Halaf (1911–13, 1927–9), and Hama (1934–40). Their ceremonial units experienced a long duration with many rebuildings across the whole of the Iron Age; they consequently yielded many architectural phases (Langenegger, Müller, and Naumann 1950) but only a few assemblages of pottery (Hama: Riis 1948; Fugmann 1958; Riis and Buhl 1990). Tell Abu Danne, near Aleppo (Lebeau 1983) and Ras el-Bassit on the north coast (Braemer 1986) have supplied the first diagnostic well-sequenced materials for building the pottery horizon of the later phase of the period (Lehmann 1996).

Sites currently under excavation offer reliable sequences but mostly for Iron I, the end of Iron II, and Iron III: in coastal Syria, Tell Sianu, Tell Tweini, and Tell Kazel (Simira); along the Afrin River, Tell Jenderes and Tell 'Ain Dara in the 'Amuq Plain, Tell Tainat; along the Orontes, Tell Qarqour (Qarqar) and Tell Atcharneh (Late Bronze Age Tunip); in the trans-Orontic region, Tell Mastuma, Tell Afis, Tell Tuqan, and Tell Mardikh; in central Syria, Tell Mishrifeh and Tell Wardiyat, near Massyaf; on the Euphrates, Karkemish, Tell Ahmar, Tell Shiukh Fawqani (Burmarina), Tell Khamis, Tell Qadahiye, Jurn Kabir II, Tell Sheikh Hassan; and south of the Khabur confluence, Tell Masaikh. On the Khabur, the reappraisal of excavations at Tell Fakhariyah and Tell Halaf will certainly provide reliable data, while excavations in Tell Sheikh Hammad, Tell 'Ajaja, and the survey in the Khabur area have extensively documented the Neo-Assyrian and Neo-Babylonian phases.

It is not easy to organize the data provided by old excavations with their set of monuments occasionally decorated and inscribed, and data offered by new excavations with reliable contexts and pottery sequences (too often only spanning short periods); even less easy to fit them into the scenario documented by the often detailed, but not impartial, historical sources.

THE IRON I/II TRANSITION
(10TH CENTURY BC)

Syria in the 10th century BC was dominated by and divided into three different forces: kingdoms of Hittite origin ('the Great Khatti'), which between the 12th and 10th centuries BC in Iron I had secured political continuity and stability in the area; Assyria, pushing out its western frontier from the Khabur and Balikh Rivers, tributaries of the Euphrates; and the Arameans, who more or less successfully resisted Assyrian expansion, drawing unstable but resistant borders. The Arameans were elements of both trouble and political renewal[3] as is acknowledged in the Old Testament and various Assyrian sources.[4] A 'king of Aram', in the

---

[3] There are different views on this observation: Sader (1987: 81–97), Schwartz (1989), Sader (1992), Dion (1997: 15–21), Lipiński (2000a: 25–76), and Sader (2000: 61–72).

[4] The first reference leaves no doubt as to their nature: Tiglath-pileser I (1114–1076 BC) crossed the Euphrates 28 times, twice a year, to drive the Ahlamu Armayu back to the desert whence, drawn by famine, they arrived in Nineveh in 1082–1081 BC. The broken obelisk of Ashshur-bel-kala (1073–1056 BC) cites many battles with the land of Aram; the inscription of Simbar-Shihu, first king of the 2nd Dynasty of the Land of the Sea (1025–1008 BC), mentions Aramean and Sutean attacks during the reign of King Adad-apla-iddina (1068–1047 BC) (Liverani 1992; Fales 2002).

reign of Ashur-rabi II (1012–972 BC), seized two cities; while Hadad-ezer,[5] son of Rehob, king of Aram-Zobah, unified Beth-Rehob with Zobah, controlled Beqaʾ, formed coalitions with the Arameans of the Euphrates and the Ammonites, and fought against David. Literary sources point to the mid-10th century BC as the period in which the Arameans formed a proper state that eventually turned into a conspicuous focus of political and cultural attraction from the 9th to the mid/end of the 8th centuries BC.

This is the historical scenario in which the Iron I/II transition has to be fixed. Archaeology cannot supply a firm date, as the time and modes of the Iron I/II transition are in fact not well perceived in site sequences. Pottery offers few clues because the period considered is not very extensive and evolutive trends can only be chronologically significant over long periods. However, the decline of the painted wares of the Iron I tradition and the introduction of the burnished Red Slip Ware characterize the change between the two phases.

A few sites present evidence of continuity from the 12th (early Iron I) to the mid-8th centuries BC (mature Iron II), that is to the Assyrian conquest and even after. In Zincirli and Karkemish buildings and sculptures were continuously added, but we still have to rely on old excavations. A different case is offered by sites where the monumental units of Iron II were planned over dense Iron I domestic units, apparently without a destruction level, such as Hama and Tell Afis. Tell Halaf was founded in the 10th century and rebuilt progressively; and Tell ʿAin Dara documents two transitional phases (XIX–XVIII: Stone and Zimansky 1999: 39–74) in the lower town covering Iron I phases without a break, while the decoration of the monumental temple on the acropolis probably fits with not too short a period between the 13th/12th and 11th centuries and was consequently in use during the whole of Iron I (as was the Citadel of Aleppo's Storm God Temple) (Abū ʿAssāf 1990; Gonnella, Khayyata, and Kohlmeyer 2005). In Tell Qarqour a transitional Iron I/II phase in Area E, D in the lower mound is documented (Dornemann 2003: 10–59). In Tell Mishrifeh, a small village from Iron IC of apparently 10th-century date is transformed into a large town with an acropolis and a palace (Area C, Phase IIb) dated to Iron II (Morandi Bonacossi 2006). On the coast, Tell Tweini yields evidence of a limited disruption, which has been linked to the destruction by fire of Temple Area IV of Tell Kazel and a break in Tell Sukas, attributed to the mid-9th-century BC Assyrian attacks (al-Maqdissi et al. 2007). In Tell Kazel, Area I ('the jar building'), Levels 16–14 belong to Iron I and its transition (Badre and Gubel 1999–2000).

Finally, cremation was a distinct cultural trait of the Iron Age, but its precise emergence and origins are not fully understood. Cremation burials were continuously used from LB II (Ugarit and Alalakh) to Iron I (Tell Sukas and Hama), the 10th century (Yunus, Hama, and Tell Sukas), and the 9th–8th centuries (Yunus, Deve Hüyük, Tell Halaf, Hama, and Ras el-Bassit), as in Phoenicia and Palestine, often together with inhumation (Bienkowski 1982; Courbin 1993: 104–9).[6]

To summarize, there is not a single disruption or gap that can account for a regional transition. There are instead many factors showing the emergence of evolutive trends: a general increase in urbanization, new planning of domestic districts, new building of ceremonial

---

[5] Lipiński (2000a: 337–41) raises doubts concerning the historicity of Hadad-ezer and his identification with the 'king of Aram' of the Assyrian sources proposed by Malamat and Hawkins (see Lipiński 2000a: 341).

[6] The pre-crisis emergence of the practice would exclude its association with Sea Peoples in the same way as its later increase and spread on the coast precludes a connection with Late Hittite elements.

and institutional centres, a reappraisal of monumental decoration, and a change in the pottery horizon.

This process was not simultaneous and cannot be precisely dated. I suggest that the end of the 10th century and the start of the 9th century BC fit both the historical and archaeological data. The first date is preferred if we credit the Aramean expansion and the consolidation of the Luwian states with a consistent urban growth and new cultural orientations towards neighbouring partners. The second date is preferred if we credit the Assyrian expansion with a new, not only military, but also cultural impact.

THE IRON II–III ARCHAEOLOGICAL
SEQUENCE

Iron II–III can be phased tentatively by anchoring the site sequences to the historical data. Archaeology provides evidence of different building activities in the main sites of the area.[7] In the Hama citadel two building phases, E2 and E1 (gate and palaces), are documented; E1 was sealed by a fire destruction dated to the 720 BC Assyrian conquest, after which the city was abandoned. In Karkemish, after the building activities of the Katuwas kingdom (end of the 10th century), two architectural phases are documented: in the mid-8th century connected with Yariris, regent for Kamanis, son of Astiruwas, and in the late 8th century linked to a son of Sasturas before the 717 BC Assyrian conquest and destruction of the ceremonial area. Karkemish was then rebuilt and enlarged under the Assyrians in the 7th century. In Sam'al, after an 11th–10th century building phase (city gate and outer citadel gate), we find a building phase in the 9th century, anchored to the dynasty of King Kilamuwa (citadel outer compound with Palaces J and K), a building phase in the 8th century at the time of the dynasty of Barrakib (citadel inner compound with Palaces HII–III), and an Assyrian phase after c.670 BC. In Tell Halaf, the date of the Altbau (1–5) and Kapara architectural phases is debated; the third phase is Assyrian. In Tell Tainat (of the five building periods recognized), Period I was dated to 875–825 BC on the basis of Luwian inscriptions pre-dating later levels; Period II ended in 738 BC with the Assyrian conquest, assuming the identification with Kunalua to be correct; and Periods IV–V were dated to the 7th century. Of the four pottery stages (Oa–Od) that are coherent with but do not perfectly correspond to the building periods, Ob–c are dated from the 9th century until 725 BC and Od to 725–550 BC. At Ras el-Bassit, eight building phases are dated (on the basis of imported Greek pottery) to between the third quarter of the 9th century and the second half of the 6th. Red Slip Assemblages A–H came from Architectural Levels 3–9.

As pointed out above, recent excavations have produced sequences with occupational levels and architecture phases mostly belonging to the periods immediately before or after the Assyrian annexation. The initial part of the period (about the 9th century) is still deceptive, having been obliterated by 8th-century building activities. Also pottery of the later periods is better documented (Tell Mastuma, Tell Afis, and Hama), especially the Neo-Assyrian eastern horizon (Tell Ahmar, Tell Khamis, and Tell Shiukh Fawqani). Moreover, phasing over two centuries is difficult because of the continuity and increasing standardization of pottery.

---

[7] A recent reassessment of the architectural phases and archaeological contexts is presented by Pucci (2008). See for Tell Halaf, Baghdo et al. (2009); for Tainat, Harrison (2012), Harrison and Osborne (2012); and for Karkemish: Marchetti (2012).

A periodization of Iron IIA–B and Iron III has been suggested and is used here, fitting the archaeological sequences, architectural levels, and historical events. Iron IIA was a phase of reurbanization of the main towns which included the rebuilding of monumental quarters as well as new lower towns with residential units. This phase corresponds to the expansion of the kingdoms of Aramean and Hittite origin, and their opposition to Assyria in the 9th century BC. A second phase of reurbanization and rebuilding in the first half of the 8th century defines Iron IIB; its end is linked to the Assyrian conquest and annexation which extends from 738 to 717 BC.[8] The third phase of Iron III is dated to the 7th and 6th centuries BC and is characterized by a new territorial organization, changes in urbanism, and a consistent transformation in arts and crafts (halting of monumental sculpture and a decrease in ivory production), along with the diffusion of Assyrian wares.[9]

Iron IIA: A phase of cultural renewal (9th century bc)

The evidence for Iron IIA is provided by its architecture and monumental buildings with their sculpture and minor arts. Pottery in reliable contexts is not yet well known, although we can assign new diagnostic traits to Iron II (such as the emergence of the Red Slip Ware with hand burnishing). The period attests to a great cultural renewal and consistent reurbanization; new and old towns were planned or rebuilt on a monumental scale, ivory and bronze productions flourished as well as stone sculpture of a variety of genres: funerary statues and stelae, and architectural sculpture.

However, the 9th century also represents the period of Assyrian military expansion: the stele from Terqa by Tukulti-Ninurta II (890–884 BC), with its Assyrian inscription celebrating the conquest of the region and the reliefs in a native style depicting the king, the weather god fighting the serpent, and a fishman *apkallu*, provides a picture of the many components at play (Masetti Rouault 2001: 89–114).[10] There was then the sequence of military campaigns that Ashurnasirpal II (883–859 BC) launched against Kummukh, Bit Halupe, Bit Adini, Karkemish, Bit Agushi, Pattina down to Mount Lebanon and the sea of Amurru, Tyre, Sidon, Byblos, and Arwad. Shalmaneser III (858–824 BC) had to confront many coalitions obtaining rich tributes by Sam'al, Pattina, Karkemish, Bit Agushi, Kummukh, and setting up his victory stelae on Mount Amanus, but also presenting offerings to the weather god Hadad in his celebrated temple in Aleppo. Til Barsib was then conquered in 856 BC and transformed into an Assyrian provincial seat, Kar Shalmaneser. In the battle at Qarqar Shalmaneser III had still to fight against Irhuleni of Hamath, Adad-idri/Hadad-ezer of Aram (the Ben-Hadad of the local sources who succeeded Rezon on the Damascene throne at the time of Asa of Juda and Baasha of Israel), Achab of Israel, the cities of Byblos, Irqata, Arwad, Ushnatu, Siyannu, Gindibu the Arab, Bit-Rehob, and the Ammonites. In 841 BC

---

[8] Cooper and Fortin (2004: 27) isolated the period 720/690 BC as Iron IIC/III on the basis of a thorough analysis of the Atcharneh pottery. Lehmann (1998) also defines the pottery from 720–700 BC as Assemblage 2.

[9] The intensity of the transformations involved precludes terming this phase Iron IIC as elsewhere proposed.

[10] See for comparison the *apkallu* in the west gate of the Aleppo Tempel (Gonnella, Khayyata, and Kohlmeyer 2005: fig. 158).

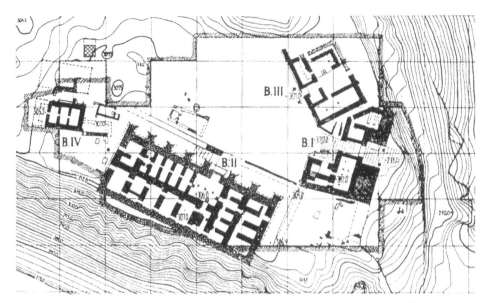

FIG. 45.2 Plan of the citadel of Hama, E2–1 (after Fugmann 1958: fig. 185)

Damascus was conquered; Ben-Hadad was killed by one of his officials, Hazaèl ('the son of nobody' in the Assyrian sources[11]) (2 Kgs. 8:7–15); stelae were then erected on the Amanus and Lebanon Mountains and rich tributes received as the Black Obelisk from Nimrud and the Bronze Gate from Balawat illustrate. Bit Agushi was captured in 834 BC and Lubarna II was killed in 831 BC at Kunalua by the usurper Surri, who was then substituted by Sasi and protected by Assyria.

Many of the cities mentioned in the Assyrian sources furnish archaeological documents that indicate a process of economic and cultural growth, despite the wars. It was in these uneasy times that most of the Luwian and Aramean towns were built *ex novo* or rebuilt on a monumental scale with temples and palaces. A palace with a front porch and columns (*bit hilani*, a name given by Assyrians who later borrowed the conception of the porch) became the most distinct institutional building of the area.[12] The hilanis of Zincirli, Tell Halaf, and Tell Tainat show variations of a similar plan and style of decoration. Portal lions guarding the gates of palaces and citadel entrances were found in many places: Hama, Ahmar, Marash, Zincirli, Harran, Halaf, and Malatya.

The citadel of Hama (Fig. 45.2) was built by King Urhilina and his son Uratami[13] in the 9th century BC (Hawkins 2000: 400, 404, 410–11, 421, pls 219, 220, 232). A monumental

---

[11] It is uncertain if the Ben-Hadad cited in Old Testament was the same as the Hadad-ezer cited in the Assyrian annals; they might have been two kings because in 1 Kgs. 20: 1–34 Ben-Hadad is said to be the enemy of Ahab while Hadad-ezer was his ally against the Assyrians (see Pitard 1987: 114–25; Klengel 1992: 208–9; Lipiński 2000a: 373–5).

[12] On the *bit hilani* after the seminal studies of Frankfort (1952) and Naumann (1955: 411–30), see Hrouda (1975) and the discussions by Fritz (1983), Margueron (1979: 170–75), and Matthiae (2002).

[13] The inscriptions state that fortifications, temples for Pahalatis (Ba'alat) and the storm god, and new towns were built.

gateway (*Bâtiment I*) with a portico and two columns on its external façade and jambs deco-rated with lions[14] (Fugmann 1958: 153–64, figs 186–9, 192, 195, 196, 199, 200; Riis and Buhl 1990: 34, 40–42, nos 11–12 (*Groupe A, porte F*), 13–14 (*Groupe C, porte E*); Mazzoni 2000a: 43) gave access to a central square on the sides of which were residential and official build-ings: *Bâtiments II* and *III*, sharing a plan similar to the hilanis but without a porch, a small shrine and statues of lions, and the tripartite storage house (*Bâtiment IV*).[15] *Bâtiment V* on the western edge of the mound was probably a hilani with a front porch.

Zincirli, whose town and citadel gates had been built and decorated in Iron I (12th–10th centuries BC) (Pucci 2008),[16] experienced a new building phase with an inner citadel com-pound and two palaces of the hilani type (J, K: Stratum IV). Palace J was built by King Kilamuwa (*c.* 830–820 BC), who set his stele at the side of the entrance. As noted elsewhere, this stele, with its Phoenician inscription (*KAI* 24) and relief in Assyrian style representing Kilamuwa,[17] documents the interculturality of the period in a manner similar to the above-mentioned Terqa stele. The same applies to the stele from Brej (north of Aleppo), with its image in Phoenician style and its Aramaic inscription dedicated by Bar-Hadad, son of a king of Aram, to Melkart, god of Tyre (Sader 1987: 255–8; Pitard 1988; Bonnet 1988: 132–6; Puech 1992; Lipiński 1995: 229–39; Dion 1997: 121–2; Lipiński 2000a: 215–16).[18]

The town of Guzana/Tell Halaf was founded at the end of the 10th century BC and then built in the course of the 9th. The citadel was centred on a hilani palace, the 'Tempel-Palast', so named by the German excavators because of its unparalleled grandeur and decoration. Its façade had a porch with three caryatid columns, representing two gods and a goddess on the back of a bull, lion, and lioness, and reliefs inside the porch representing demons, gods, and the hunt. Inscriptions attribute the palace to King Kapara, son of Hadianu; 178 small orthostats of a somewhat rougher carving decorated the rear side of the building. They bear short cuneiform inscriptions citing a 'temple of the Weather-God' and a few citing the reign of Kapara, which in one case was inscribed over an older one, providing evidence of his reuse of the reliefs, probably from an earlier temple. The palace was approached on the side through a gate decorated by scorpion-men, and opened into a place with an altar built of glazed ornamented bricks over a podium and a mausoleum with two vaulted tombs. Two additional tombs with cremation burials topped by the statues of the dead and later obliter-ated by a brick terrace were built near the outer gate of the citadel; a small shrine contained

[14] The proposed dating of these lions to the 10th century on the basis of their schematic style might suggest an initial monumental planning of the citadel in Phases E2–F, in the final phase of Iron I.

[15] Its function is controversial. Busink (1970: 563–5) interpreted it as a temple or treasure house, *Schatzhaus* (*contra* Riis and Buhl 1990: 24–5). On the base of its size and materials, Werner (1994: 81, 141, pl. 60:2) interpreted it as a storage building.

[16] The 10th-century date is provided by the statue of a king on a base flanked by lions grasped by a kneeling hero at the right of Gate Q, similar to the Katuwas bases in Karkemish (see bibliography and discussion in Niehr 2006: 112–16). The statue was not in a primary position and might represent Gabbar, founder of the Bit Gabbar dynasty, as defined by Kilamuwa and dated to the time of Katuwas of Karkemish between the second half of the 10th and early 9th centuries BC.

[17] His name was Luwian and he was the son of Hayanu, an Aramean (Fugmann 1958: 153–64, figs 186–9, 192, 195, 196, 199, 200; Riis and Buhl 1990: 34, 40–42, nos 11–12 (*Groupe A, porte F*), 13–14 (*Groupe C, porte E*); Mazzoni 2000a: 43).

[18] Pitard (1988) identifies the Bar-Hadad of the stele, son of 'Attar-hamek, with a king of a northern Aram, distinct from Aram-Damascus, because his name is not documented in its list. Lipiński (2000a: 215–16) and Dion (1997: 121–2) instead read 'Attar-sumki.

two statues of ancestors and one of a god. The compound was a ceremonial area for the celebration of royal dignity granted by the city gods and dynastic ancestors. The older small orthostats and the later Kapara monuments share a common style and similar figurative conventions and can be dated (on stylistic grounds and historical considerations) to the 9th century (Orthmann 1971: 122–9; 2002).[19] A statue, depicting the traits of the local governor Hadad'isi, son of Shamash-nuri, in a provincial Assyrian style with a bilingual Assyro-Aramean inscription, was found in nearby Tell Fakhariyah (Sikani)[20], indicating that in the 9th century the region was under Assyrian control. The whole Jezirah at that time was in fact Assyrianized and experienced a consistent reurbanization of an Assyrian nature, as evidenced by the residences at Tell Ahmar (Kar Shalmaneser), the 'Ivory Building' at Arslan Tash (Khadatu), and the palace at Tell Masaikh.[21]

In the 9th century BC a consistent ivory production emerged or was reintroduced after the Late Bronze Age on a large scale: a repertory of images was created to decorate furniture, beds, thrones and chairs, luxury objects, handles of fans and mirrors, containers for cult, pyxides, and spoons. Many workshops and regional styles are attributed to northern ('Flame and Frond' group) and southern Syria ('Intermediate' group), and Phoenicia.[22] Most of our documents are provided by the booties documented in the Assyrian capitals, mainly Nimrud.[23] Only sparse remains were found in contexts which escaped in the looted citadels: in a cinerary urn of a tomb of Tell Halaf, in Buildings IV–V at Hama, in the 'ivories palace' at Arslan Tash, in Palaces J, L, and K at Zincirli. The Halaf and Hama ivories and the reliefs of Tell Halaf share all the figurative conventions of the 'Flame and Frond' group and have been attributed to the same source; but they more probably reflect a distinct common style which was adopted in different media and workshops.

Seals reflect the diffusion of common linear styles in a variety of productions: stamp seals prevail with simple figurative motifs (animals and monsters), Syro-Hittite shapes (with hammer-head or human fist handles, studs, stalks, four- or three-lobed), and Levantine and Egyptianizing traditions (conoid, ovoid, tabloid, and scaraboids in frit, glass, and stone).

Bronzes and ivories document the artistic and economic flourishing in the second half of the 9th century BC, when Damascus became the political focus of the area with King Haza'el, a powerful leader known in the Assyrian Annals and in the Old Testament. His name appears in important documents: a stele of Tell al-Qadi (Dan), celebrating his victory over Ahazia of Judah and Jehoram of Israel; a stele from Tell Afis, together with Jehu; a bronze frontlet

---

[19] Pucci (2008: 125–6) dates Kapara to the 8th century on the basis of her analysis of the architectural sequence.

[20] Abū 'Assāf, Bordreuil, and Millard (1982: 98–113) support a 850–825 BC date, identifying Shamash-nuri with the 866 eponym, or a 793–763 BC date when it is known that Assyrian governors had statues sculpted and inscribed. Sader (1987: 23–9) supports an 8th-century date. Lipiński (2000a: 129) identifies Hdys'y ('Haddu is my help') with the Adad-remanni (similarly, 'Hadad show piety on me') eponym of 841 (*contra* Schwemer 2001: 613, n. 4955). Orthmann (2002: 20, 93–4) compares the statue to the Tempel-Palast caryatids.

[21] On the process, see Kühne (1995), Rouault (2001), Fales (2002), and Makinson (1999).

[22] On the ivory production and problem of the identification of workshops and schools in relation to the Halaf reliefs, see Winter (1976a: 15–17; 1976b; 1981: 122–9; 1989: 321–2) and Herrmann (1986: 48–53; 1992: 28–39; 2000: 268–82).

[23] Noteworthy among the mentions of ivory tributes to Assyrians is the one concerning 'a bed and throne in ivory' submitted by King Mari' of Damascus to Adad-Nirari III (810–783 BC) on the occasion of his 805–802 BC campaigns against Syria (Klengel 1992: 210; Lipiński 2000a: 393).

showing nude goddesses under the winged sun from the Heraion of Samos; a bronze cheek-piece at Eretria in Euboeia (*KAI* 311: 'Hadad gave to our lord Haza'el from 'Umqi in the year he crossed the river'); an ivory plaque from Arslan Tash (*KAI* 232: 'to our lord Haza'el in the year of the annexation of...'); and an ivory fragment from Room T10 in Fort Shalmaneser at Nimrud ('our lord Haza'el') (Lipiński 2000a: 388–9, 393 with bibliography).[24] The elegant style of other blinkers and frontlets can be compared with and consequently dated to the same period, notably the 'Lu'ash School', named after the inscription on one of a group of five frontlets from Nimrud (Herrmann 1986: 49).[25]

IRON AGE IIB: THE LAST DEVELOPMENT (8TH CENTURY BC)

The expansion of Aram continued to around 800 BC. The Aramaic stele of King Zakkur (*KAI* 202), probably from Tell Afis, relates a victory against a coalition led by the king of Aram, Bar-Hadad, with the kings of Arpad (Bar-Gushi, 'the son of Gush'), Que, 'Umq, Gurgum, Melid, and Sam'al (Klengel 1992: 212–13; Liverani 1992: 109–10, 115; Dion 1997: 128–9; 139–43; Ikeda 1999: 282–3; Lipiński 2000a: 254–5, 299–312). Zakkur had succeeded in con-trolling Hamath and the adjoining Lu'ash ('Lukhuti' in Assyrian sources) and was possibly supported by Assyrians like the kings of Sam'al. The stele of Antakya relates the arbitration in which the Assyrian governor Shamshi-ilu (for King Adad-Nirari) fixed the Orontes border between Zakkur with Atar-shumki, son of Adramu, king of Arpad (Donbaz 1990; Ponchia 1991: 10–11; Dion 1997: 127–9; Lipiński 2000a: 282–4; Dalley 2000: 85–6). The stele of Pazarcik relates Shamsi-ilu's (Shalmaneser IV) campaign in Kummukh and Gurgum against Hadianu of Damascus and the defeat of Atar-shumki.

These were the political reasons which resulted in the region witnessing further cultural and economic development and new urban and building activities in the 8th century BC. We know that Zakkur rebuilt Hazrek and Panamuwa Sam'al; Yariris rebuilt Karkemish and founded new towns; King Sipi founded a fortress in Tabal (Sader 1987: 207, 209);[26] and Azitawata founded the citadel of Azitawataya (Karatepe) and many fortresses for the protec-tion of the Adanawa (Hawkins and Morpurgo-Davies 1978: 115–16; Hawkins 2000: 45–71), as stated in the bilingual Phoenician and Luwian inscriptions. New reliefs celebrate kings and governors as well as their courts; at Karkemish the outer gate giving access to the hilani was decorated in the mid-8th century with a royal buttress and reliefs representing Kamanis, son of Astiruwas, his regent Yariris, soldiers, courtesans, and the child Tuwarsais with his nurse (Fig. 45.3) (Hawkins 2000: 78; Orthmann 1971: 35, pl. 31).

At the top of the Great Staircase on the upper mound, the upper gate was decorated by a son of King Sasturas, possibly Astirus II, with reliefs representing genii in an Assyrian style, probably shortly before the conquest of the city in 717 BC (Hawkins 2000: 79; Orthmann 1971: 35–6, pls 21d, e, 22). In Sam'al a new compound enclosed the hilanis, whose front

[24] On Haza'el, see Suriano (2007 and bibliography). On the Afis stele, see Amadasi (2005).
[25] For a detailed analysis and attribution of the ivory frontlets, see Wicke (1999) and Gubel (2005).
[26] The statue of Panamuwa II from Gerçin (Orthmann 1971: 75–6, 202, 484; Wartke 2005: 26–8, figs 24–6, 62–4; Sader 1987: 161, 163). The stele of Cekke mentions the foundation of the city of Kamana (Hawkins 2000: 143–54). For Sipi, see the rock inscription of Karaburun (Hawkins 2000: 480–83).

FIG. 45.3 Reliefs at the Royal Buttress, Karkemish (after Hogarth 1914: pl. B8b)

columns stood on bases decorated by sphinxes, and halls were decorated with reliefs showing the court milieu of King Barrakib (*Nordliche Hallenbau* and Hilani III) (Orthmann 1971:
63–4, pls 63–6; 80–82, pls 49–51). In the citadel of Sakçagözü an outer gate decorated by a
relief with a lion hunt opened onto a bit hilani with columns standing on bases adorned with
lions and reliefs depicting a court parade (Orthmann 1971: 63–4, 80–82, pls 49–51, 63–5).
Two gates in the citadel of Karatepe were lavishly decorated by orthostats with reliefs showing images of court celebration, war, navigation, the hunt, and demons, illustrating that local
artists were acquainted with Phoenician, Luwian, and Aramean art (Winter 1979; Çambel
and Özyar 2003). Inside stood the statue of a king, as in the lion gate of Malatya (Melid),
both images representing protective ancestors.

Funerary art had an unprecedented diffusion in this period, with statues of the deceased
or stelae representing the banquet offered by relatives to the deceased. A stele of Sam'al shows
the image of a princess seated at her funerary meal; two statues of the god Hadad celebrated
Panamuwa I (from Gerçin, 7km northeast of Zincirli: *KAI* 214) and Panamuwa II (from
Tahtali Pinar, 2km northeast of Zincirli: *KAI* 215) (Orthmann 1971: 377–80). Marash, capital of Gurgum, has yielded numerous funerary banquet stelae, a few bearing short Luwian
inscriptions, while the Aramaic inscriptions of the stelae from Neirab (near Aleppo) celebrate the priests Sin-zer-ibni and Si'-gabbari, the second shown seated at his funerary
banquet.[27] Numerous stelae representing local weather gods were erected in the many dedicatory shrines in towns, but also in shrines on the mountains and at the springs where these
gods manifested their power.[28]

Ivory production increased and distinct styles emerged in Damascus ('Intermediate' tradition), Zincirli (SW 7 group of Nimrud), and other north Syrian centres ('Roundcheeked
and Ringletted' group) where elabourate masterpieces were created (Winter 1976a; 1976b;
Herrmann 1986: 19, 49; Wicke 2002; 2005 on its association with the Yunus Cemetery

---

[27] For a comprehensive analysis of funerary Syro-Hittite art, see Bonatz (2000a; 2000b).
[28] See Bunnens (2006) for a detailed analysis of the Storm-God stelae and Mazzoni (2000a: 50–51) for
a complete list. For images and cult, see Schwemer (2001).

group of seals). Comparisons are found in other media, such as the seals of the Yunus Cemetery group (near Karkemish) or the Vulture group and a few impressions and seals from Hama bearing Aramean ('I'n, 'Adanlaram) and Luwian scripts (Alani the scribe), all sharing elabourate motifs and the elegant style of the Roundcheeked group. Other distinct figurative stamp seals were diffused especially in funerary contexts ('Lyre Player' and 'Horse' groups). In addition there was a provincial Assyrian and Assyrianized production of cylinder seals in frit and stone with the image of a hero fighting a bull or dragon, or worshippers before various gods, altars, animals, genii, or only their symbols. Moreover, institutional seals were more often provided with short Phoenician, hieroglyphic Luwian, and Aramaic inscriptions. It was a multilingual society that acknowledged literacy: scribes are shown in the Barrakib stele and four funerary stelae from Marash; the Phoenician scribe 'Abd-'ilim signing the inscription on the Hadad statue at Gozana; Ahuzas ('clever scribe') signing the stele of Meharde; and Pedantimuwas signing the stele of Sheizar; while Yariris, prince of Karkemish, declared that he was master of different scripts and twelve languages.[29]

East of the Euphrates, Assyria maintained a firm control through the activity of powerful governors. Nergal-erish, governor of Rasappa and Khindanu between the Khabur and the Euphrates, declared in the Tell Rimah stele that he founded 331 villages, which is confirmed by modern surveys, and documents an unprecedented growth of rural settlements in the area (Morandi Bonacossi 1996; Wilkinson and Barbanes 2000). Similarly, Mannu-ki-Ashur rebuilt Guzana in this phase. Tell Tainat's Gate VII was decorated with orthostats showing soldiers defeating enemies in a provincial Assyrian style; these must have been decorated after 738 BC and were reused in a later Assyrian phase. The outer gate decoration of Arslan Tash can be dated to the same mid-8th century, given the style of the sculptures showing a victory parade of the army (Albenda 1988). This provincial Assyrian art, emerging in the second half of the 8th century, was produced by local artists and shows local traits: in both Arslan Tash and Tell Tainat, in fact, the outer gates of the town were decorated in line with the Syro-Hittite practice.

THE POTTERY HORIZON OF IRON II

Material culture of Iron IIA is not yet well phased,[30] even though we usually assign to it consistent evolutive traits such as Red Slip Ware with vertical burnishing or shapes such as deep bowls with expanded rims, jars with double rims, holemouth cooking pots, and pithoi with thickened rims. Available data increase in Iron IIB, thanks to the abundant materials sealed in the destruction levels left by Assyrian conquest (Lehmann 1998: 9–15, Assemblage 1). Even through regional orientations, the pottery horizon of the period appears to be fairly homogeneous and is characterized by standardization, with prevailing medium-fired simple buff/orange wares for table and storage vessels, and simple burnished and Red Slip burnished wares of fine or common fabrics for table vessels.

[29] See Hawkins (2000: 130–31, 133) for the inscription of Yariris and its mention of the Ashur, Sura (Urartu?), and Taiman (Aramaic?) scripts; and Hawkins (2000: 416–19) for the stelae of Meharde and Sheizar. Lipiński (2000a: 215–16) reads instead Tyrian (Sura) script.

[30] As Dornemann (2003: 41–3) noted for the Qarqour assemblage: 'The Iron Age IIA tradition seems to have a long duration with minimal change, so at this point [it] is difficult to illustrate different chronological phasing in the existing inventory.'

Three main regional assemblages with distinct orientations can be recognized: the coastal, gravitating towards Phoenicia and open to Cypriot and Greek imports; the Jezirah, fully Assyrianized; and a central one, open to both coastal and Assyrian components. The coastal pottery horizon, documented at Ras el-Bassit in Assemblages 3–9 from the tell (Braemer 1986) and the *extra moenia* cremation cemetery, is marked by a lustrous fine Red Slip Ware, commercial jars, Cypro-Geometric, White-Painted, Bichrome, Black-on-Red, and Ionian pottery imports (Courbin 1993: 77–81). Comparisons with materials from the trading port at Al Mina[31] indicate a Phoenician connection probably prompted by direct maritime links. A similar repertory was found in Tell Sianu, Tell Tweini with its Phoenician Sanctuary in Field B and three architectural phases in Area A (al-Maqdissi et al. 2007), and Tell Sukas with its *extra moenia* cemetery (Riis et al. 1996). In Tell Kazel, Levels 13–6 in Area I and Levels 4–3 in Area II date to Iron II (Capet 2003: 115–16). The area of the 'Amuq Plain (Tell Tainat) and the Afrin River (Tell Jenderes and Tell 'Ain Dara: lower Town Square 4, Phase I) is characterized by prevailing Red Slip, Cypro-Geometric pottery, and lingering Iron I-style painted ware.

The assemblage of inland Syria forms a single tradition which includes two subregional variants: the Orontes and the trans-Orontic regions. Hama E1 provides the diagnostic Orontes region assemblage: Red Slip burnished and standard common wares prevail; painted wares are limited to reddish-brownish circles or concentric designs, crosses, and radiating wavy and straight lines inside the open forms or simple lines on the necks of the jars. In this region lay Tell Qarqour (Area A, the Gateway and B, especially B2 with a local sequence of twelve occupation levels and eight architecture phases: Dornemann 2003: 41–7); Tell Atcharneh (Lower Town (CVB): Cooper and Fortin 2004); and Tell Wardiyat, near Massyaf (Level VII: Heitham 2001). Khan Sheikoun (al-Maqdissi 2003) and Tell Mishrifeh (lower town: Areas A–B domestic houses, Maisons 1–2; Area D pottery kiln; Acropolis: Area C Palace, Areas G–H industrial units; and Area J storage and domestic units (al-Maqdissi 2003; Morandi Bonacossi 2006)) gravitate towards the Hama horizon.

The trans-Orontic horizon is defined by Common Orange Ware prevailing over Red Slip; assemblages are furnished by Tell Abu Danne Levels IIc–d (Lebeau 1983); Tell Mastuma Layers I-1-3 (groups of houses and a residence: Wakita et al. 1995; Wakita, Wada, and Nishiyama 2000); Tell Afis (Area D: Levels 1–7; Area B: town wall; Area G: Square Court: levels; and Area A: Temples 1–3: Cecchini 1998); Tell Tuqan; and Tell Mardikh, which give evidence of several phases of occupation (Cecchini and Mazzoni 1998; Fiorentino 2006: 159–61).

In the Jezirah and along the Euphrates, Late Assyrian wares became dominant over the course of the 8th century; glazed wares, distinct standardized fabrics, and individual forms (palace ware, tripod bowls, bowls with inverted and thickened rims, carinated bowls, and pipe lamps) were popular, gradually spreading west of the Euphrates towards the end of the century (Wilkinson and Barbanes 2000; Anastasio 2007).

Standardization was a substantial characteristic of the repertory of forms which show a few regional variants. Table vessels (Fig. 45.4: 1–3, 8–15) consist of plain-rimmed hemispherical or conical bowls; large platters; bowls with deep S-profiles; and bowls with expanded or thickened rims with a low carination and with everted rims, all having ring

---

[31] On the chronology of Al Mina and its pottery documentation, see references in Mazzoni (2001: 299–304) and Luke (2003: 1–3).

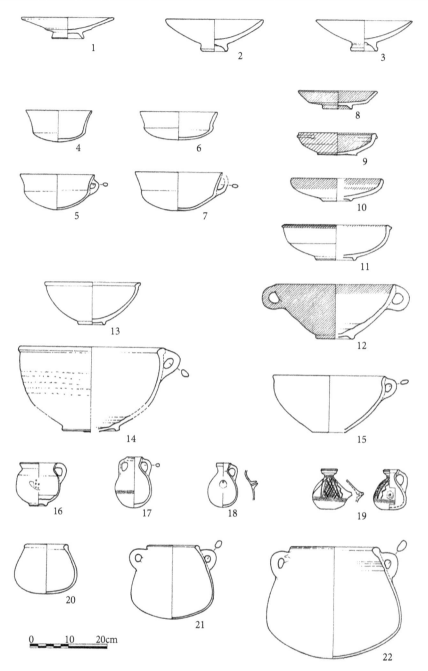

FIG. 45.4 Iron II–III pottery: (1) Tell Afis (TA.89.G.562/1); (2, 3) Hama (after Riis and Buhl 1990: figs 74.531, 76.556); (4, 5) Tell Afis (TA.92.G.342/1, TA.02.B.628/1); (6–8) Tell Mastuma (after Wada 1994: figs 1.5, 7.6; Wakita et al. 1995: fig. 7.4); (9) Tell Abou Danne (after Lebeau 1983: 463, A6–658); (10, 11) Tell Afis (TA.89.G.564/1, TA.89.G.552/1); (12) Tell Mastuma (after Wada 1994: fig. 1.16); (13–18) Tell Afis (TA.86.D.228/1, TA.04.B.432/2, TA.86.D.200/5, TA.86.228/4, TA.04.B.432/1, TA.86.D.244/1); (19) Tell Mastuma (after Wakita et al. 1995: fig. 7.7); and (20–22) Tell Afis (TA.02.B.621/2, TA.86.D.109/1, TA.00.J.213/1) (drawings by Sergio Martelli)

bases and tall or low pedestals (as at Hama, Qatna, and Tell Atcharneh). Kraters, the hall-mark of Iron I, survive but are reduced to a straight profile and expanded or out-turned rims, occasionally with low carination. A distinct type was the carinated bowl of Assyrian imitation (Fig. 45.4: 4–7), appearing in the local assemblages in the late 8th century (Adachi 1997). Jars and juglets show a trend to standardization and regional variations (Fig. 45.4: 16–19): out-turned rims for juglets prevail in the coastal sites; inland the double-rimmed and collared or ridge-necked jars with two handles; and double rims become gradually less sharpened and more rounded, emulating standard Assyrian types.

Storage pithoi (Fig. 45.5) constitute a diagnostic shape. In coastal sites the commercial cigar-shaped or bag jars for maritime transport from the Levantine tradition were wide-spread. Inland, the tall ovoid pithoi show a marked evolution in rims and bases from Iron I to III. At the beginning we find large ovoid pithoi with expanded rims, thickened inside and with small rounded bases and rod-type decoration applied on the shoulder. Then there emerges a cigar-shaped pithos with an outer swollen rim and later flattened outer rim and large solid convex bases, often marked with finger impressions on the rim. Pithoi, used for long periods, were sunk in the soil or set in platforms and lined along the walls of storage rooms as in Qatna or Tell Mastuma; at Building II in Hama, where older and late pithoi were kept together (Riis and Buhl 1990: 137, Figs. 61, 62) (Fig. 45.5: 5, 6); and at Afis, in a house of the lower town (D, Levels 4–2), where they were piled one above the other (Fig. 45.5: 1–4). Cooking ware was represented by the ovoid and globular two-handled holemouth pot with thickened rim (Fig. 45.4: 20–22) definitely replacing the everted-rim Late Bronze type, while the plain rim is a later trait prevailing in Iron III.

IRON III: DECULTURATION IN THE ASSYRIAN *KOINÉ* (7TH AND 6TH CENTURIES BC)

War, annexation, and consequent deportations by Kings Tiglath-pileser III (745–727 BC), Shalmaneser V (726–722 BC), and Sargon II (721–705 BC) resulted in an end to the auton-omy and a halting in the urban and artistic growth of the native kingdoms; only allies and vassals escaped conquest and were assimilated into the Assyrian Empire. The process was not simultaneous, nor everywhere of the same intensity or effect. In 743 BC at Kummukh Tiglath-pileser III defeated the coalition of the Urartian Sarduri II and Mati'ilu of Agushi, whose capital Arpad was besieged for three years, and then the coalition lead by Tutammu of Pattina/Unqi with the nineteen districts of Hamath, Hatarikka (Hazrek), Simira, Usnu, Sianu, and Gubla/Byblos. In 738 BC Kunalua (renamed Kullani), Hatarikka, and Simira were conquered, as was Damascus in 732 BC, answering the call of Ahaz of Judah (attacked in Jerusalem by Resin/Rahianu of Damascus and Pekah of Israel) with their ally, Panamuwa II of Sam'al, dying in the battle. Damascus, Hauran, Qarnim (southwest of Damascus), Masuate, and Zobah became Assyrian provinces. Sargon II defeated the last resistance: Yaubi' of Hamath, allied with Hatarikka, Arpad, Simira, and again Damascus, was defeated at Qarqar in 720 BC; Qarqar and Hamath were conquered and their territory assigned to other peoples, as reported in the victory stelae of Hamath, Sheizar, and Asharne. Karkemish, once the capital of the Great Khatti, was the last to fall in 717 BC, following the alliance between its King Pisiri and Mita, king of Mushku (Phrygian Mida).

These events brought about two processes: a sudden deculturation in arts and decline of genres sponsored by local patrons; and assimilation or emulation of Assyrian culture in the

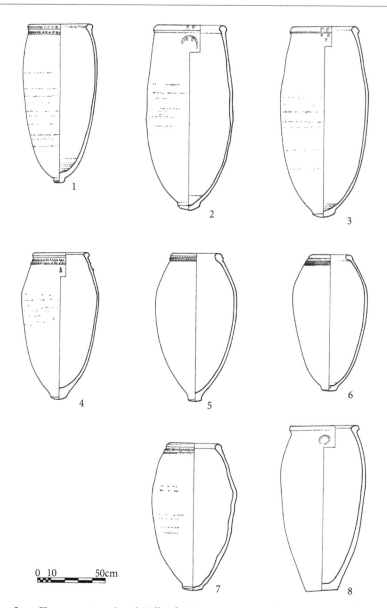

FIG. 45.5 Iron II storage jars: (1–4) Tell Afis (TA.86.D.269/1, TA.86.D.268/1, TA.87.D.285/1, TA.87.D.40/1); (5–6) Hama (after Riis and Buhl 1990: fig. 61.419, 417); and (7, 8) Tell Mastuma (after Egami, Wajita, and Ishida 1988–9: fig. 7.J3, J1) (drawings by Sergio Martelli)

towns under Assyrian administration. The few that were transformed into Assyrian seats were extensively rebuilt, and a new process of urbanization Assyrianized the country over the course of the 7th century BC (Mazzoni 1995). Sam'al was destroyed in 676 BC, a new palace being rebuilt in 671/670 BC, and Esarhaddon had his victory stele set in the outer citadel gate and two others in Til Barsib (Nevling Porter 2000). Karkemish was enlarged with an extensive lower town and also decorated with reliefs in an Assyrian style, probably matching the older regional capitals, such as Dur Katlimmu on the middle Khabur (Tell Sheikh Hammad: Kühne 1995; 2000) with its 120ha occupied by a lower town and a walled upper town with many palaces (F–G, Red House); Shadikanni (today Tell ʿAjaja) and its palace decorated by gate lions; or Tell Barri with its palace and paintings (Pecorella and Pierobon Benoit 2005). On the Euphrates, at Tell Ahmar (Kar Shalmanaser), Assyrian elite houses with cobbled mosaics in Area C of the middle city terrace give evidence of two strata (2A-C–3) (Bunnens 1999; 2002–3; Jamieson 2000). Tell Shiukh Foqani/Burmarina (Areas F–H) (Makinson 1999), Tell Khamis (Matilla Séiquier 1999), Tell Qadahiye, Jurn Kabir II (Buildings I–II) (Eidem and Pütt 1999), and Tell Sheikh Hassan (Gebäude A, Schicht 3) (Boese 1995) document isolated hilanis. Along the coast, local culture survived and gradually developed, as in Phoenicia, opening itself to other Mediterranean components, Cypriots, and Greeks (Lehmann 1998). The settlement of Al Mina, the temples of Tell Sukas and ʿAmrith, and the cemetery of Tartous belong to the Neo-Assyrian and Neo-Babylonian period, extending into the Persian period (Akkermans and Schwartz 2003: 386–94).

The 7th and 6th centuries BC document the final transformation and ultimate decline of native culture. The deportation or relocation of peoples across the area and the attribution of land to the Assyrians were strategies aimed at cultural eradication and colonization; they also favoured new processes of interculturality in an area already receptive to a variety of stimuli and influences which became integrated into a large supraregional *koiné*.

SUGGESTED READING

Akkermans, P. M. M. G., and G. M. Schwartz (2003). *The Archaeology of Syria from Complex Hunter-Gatherers to Early Urban Societies (c. 16,000–300 BC)*. Cambridge: Cambridge University Press.

Aro, S. (2003). Art and architecture. In H. C. Melchert (ed.), *The Luwians*. Leiden: Brill, 281–337.

Bunnens, G. (ed.) (2000). *Essays on Syria in the Iron Age*. Louvain: Peeters.

Dion, P.-E. (1997). *Les Araméens à l'Âge du fer: histoire politique et structures sociales*. Paris: Gabalda.

Hawkins, J. D. (1982). The Neo-Hittite states in Syria and Anatolia. In J. Boardman, I. E. S. Edwards, N. G. L. Hammond, and E. Sollberger (eds), *Cambridge Ancient History*, vol. 3, pt 1, 2nd edn. Cambridge: Cambridge University Press, 372–441.

Klengel, H. (1992). *Syria, 3000 to 300 B.C.: A Handbook of Political History*. Berlin: Akademie.

Lipiński, E. (2000). *The Aramaeans: Their Ancient History, Culture, Religion*. Louvain: Peeters.

Liverani, M. (1992). *Studies on the Annals of Ashurnasirpal*, vol. 2, pt 2: *Topographical Analysis*. Rome: Università di Roma 'La Sapienza', Dipartimento di scienze storiche, archeologiche e antropologiche dell'antichità.

Mazzoni, S. (2000). Syria and the periodization of the Iron Age: a cross-cultural perspective. In Bunnens (2000: 31–59).

Pitard, W. T. (1987). *Ancient Damascus: A Historical Study of the Syrian City-State from Earliest Times until Its Fall to the Assyrians in 732 B.C.E.* Winona Lake, Ind.: Eisenbrauns.

Sader, H. (1987) *Les états araméens de Syrie depuis leur fondation jusqu'à leur transformation en provinces assyriennes*. Beirut: Orient-Institut der Deutschen Morgenländischen Gesellschaft/ Wiesbaden: Steiner.

REFERENCES

Abū Assāf, A. (1990). *Der Tempel von 'Ain Dara*. Mainz am Rhein: von Zabern.

—— P. Bordreuil, and A. R. Millard (1982). *La statue de Tell Fékhérye et son inscription bilingue assyro-araméenne*. Paris: ADPF.

Adachi, T. (1997). The fine carinated bowl in the Iron Age. *Bulletin of the Ancient Orient Museum* 18: 41–55.

Akkermans, P. M. M. G., and G. M. Schwartz (2003). *The Archaeology of Syria from Complex Hunter-Gatherers to Early Urban Societies (c. 16,000–300 BC)*. Cambridge: Cambridge University Press.

Albenda, P. (1988). The gateway and portal stone reliefs from Arslan Tash. *Bulletin of the American Schools of Oriental Research* 271: 5–30.

al-Maqdissi, M. (2003). Recherches archéologiques syriennes à Mishirfeh-Qatna au nord-est de Homs (Émèse). *Comptes-rendus des séances de l'Académie des inscriptions et belles-lettres* 147: 1487–1515.

—— K. Van Lerberghe, J. Bretschneider, and M. Badawi (2007). *Tell Tweini: The Syro-Belgian Excavations*. Damascus: Direction générale des antiquités et des musées.

Amadasi, M. G. (2005). Area A1: il frammento di stele in basalto con iscrizione. *Egitto e Vicino Oriente* 28: 21–3.

Anastasio, S. (2007). *Das obere Habur-Tal in der Jazira zwischen dem 13. und dem 5. Jh. V.Chr. Die Keramik des Projektes Prospection archéologique du Haut-Khabur Occidental (Syrie du N.E.)*. Florence: Centro editoriale toscano.

Badre, L., and É. Gubel (1999–2000). Tell Kazel (Syria): excavations of the AUB Museum, 1993–1998, third preliminary report. *Berytus* 44: 123–203.

Baghdo, A.el-M., L. Martin, M. Novák, and W. Orthmann (2009). *Tell Halaf: Vorberichte über die erste und zweite syrisch-deutsche Grabungskampagne*. Wiesbaden: Harrassowitz.

Bienkowski, P. A. (1982). Some remarks on the practice of cremation in the Levant. *Levant* 14: 80–9.

Boese, J. (ed.) (1995). *Ausgrabungen in Tell Sheikh Hassan*, vol. 1: *Vorläufige Berichte über die Grabungskampagnen 1984–1990 und 1992–1994*. Saarbrücken: Saarbrücker Druckerei.

Bonatz, D. (2000a). *Das syro-hethitische Grabdenkmal: Untersuchungen zur Entstehung einer neuen Bildgattung in der Eisenzeit im nordsyrisch-südostanatolischen Raum*. Mainz am Rhein: von Zabern.

—— (2000b). Syro-Hittite funerary monuments: a phenomenon of tradition or innovation? In Bunnens (2000: 189–210).

Bonnet, C. (1988). *Melqart: cultes et mythes de l'Héraclès tyrien en Méditerranée*. Leuven: Peeters/Namur: Presses universitaires de Namur.

Braemer, F. (1986). La céramique à engobe rouge de l'Âge du fer à Bassit. *Syria* 63: 221–46.

Bunnens, G. (1999). Aramaeans, Hittites and Assyrians in the Upper Euphrates Valley. In G. del Olmo Lete and J. L. Montero Fenollós (eds), *Archaeology of the Upper Syrian Euphrates, the Tishrin Dam Area: Proceedings of the International Symposium Held at Barcelona, January 28th–30th, 1998*. Barcelona: Ausa, 605–24.

—— (2000). Syria in the Iron Age: problems of definition. In Bunnens (2000: 189–210).

—— (2002–3). Til Barsib before the Assyrians. *Les annales archéologiques arabes syriennes* 45–6: 163–72.

—— (2006). *A New Luwian Stele and the Cult of the Storm-God at Til Barsib-Masuwari*. Louvain: Peeters.

Busink, T. A. (1970). *Der Tempel von Jerusalem, von Salomo bis Herodes: Eine archäologisch-historische Studie unter Berücksichtigung des westsemitischen Tempelbaus* (2 vols). Leiden: Brill.

Çambel, H., and A. Özyar (2003). *Karatepe Arslantas, Azitawataya: Die Bildwerke*. Mainz am Rhein: von Zabern.

Capet, E. (2003). Tell Kazel (Syrie): Rapport préliminaire sur les 9e–17e campagnes de fouilles (1993–2001) du Musée de l'Université Américaine de Beyrouth, Chantier II. *Berytus* 47: 63–121.

Cecchini, S. M. (1998). Area G, the Iron I–III levels: architecture, pottery and finds. In Cecchini and Mazzoni (1998: 273–96).

—— and S. Mazzoni (eds) (1998). *Tell Afis (Siria): scavi sullacropoli 1988–1992*. Pisa: ETS.

Cooper, E., and M. Fortin (2004). Tell 'Acharneh in the Middle Orontes Valley and the Assyrian presence in Syria. In G. Frame (ed.), *From the Upper Sea to the Lower Sea: Studies on the History of Assyria and Babylonia in Honour of A. K. Grayson*. Leiden: Nederlands Instituut voor het Nabije Oosten, 17–56.

Courbin, P. (1993). *Fouilles de Bassit: tombes du fer*. Paris: Recherche sur les civilisations.

Dalley, S. (2000). Shamshi-ilu, language and power in the western Assyrian empire. In Bunnens (2000: 79–88).

Dion, P.-E. (1997). *Les Araméens à l'Âge du fer: histoire politique et structures sociales*. Paris: Gabalda.

Donbaz, V. (1990). Two Neo-Assyrian stelae in the Antakya and Kahramanmaras museums. *Annual Review of the Royal Inscriptions of Mesopotamia Project* 8: 5–24.

Dornemann, R. H. (2003). Seven seasons of ASOR excavations at Tell Qarqur, Syria, 1993–1999. In N. L. Lapp (ed.), *Preliminary Excavation Reports and Other Archaeological Investigations: Tell Qarqur, Iron I Sites in the North-Central Highlands of Palestine*. Boston, Mass.: American Schools of Oriental Research, 1–141.

Egami, N., S. Wajita, and K. Ishida (1988-9). Tell Mastuma: a preliminary report of the excavations in Idlib, Syria, 1986–1988. *Bulletin of the Ancient Orient Museum* 10: 47–75.

Eidem, J., and K. Pütt (1999). Tell Jurn Kabir and Tell Qadahiye: Danish excavations in the Tishrin Dam area. In G. del Olmo Lete and J. L. Montero Fenollós (eds), *Archaeology of the Upper Syrian Euphrates, the Tishrin Dam Area: Proceedings of the International Symposium Held at Barcelona, January 28th–30th, 1998*. Barcelona: Ausa, 193–9.

Fales, F. M. (2002). The Djezireh in Neo-Assyrian sources. In M. al-Maqdissi, M. A. Karim, A. Al-Azm, and M. Al-Khoury (eds), *The Syrian Jezira: Cultural Heritage and Interrelations— Proceedings of the International Conference Held in Deir ez-Zor, April 22nd–25th, 1996*. Damascus: République arabe syrienne, Ministère de la culture, Direction générale des antiquités et des musées, 181–99.

Fiorentino, R. (2006). La ceramica. In F. Baffi (ed.), *Tell Tuqan: ricerche archeologiche italiane nella regione del Maath (Siria)*. Lecce: Congedo, 157–61.

Frankfort, H. (1952). The origin of the bît-hilani. *Iraq* 14: 120–31.

Fritz, V. (1983). Die Syrische Bauform des Hilani und die Frage seiner Verbreitung. *Damszener Mitteilungen* 1: 43–58.

Fugmann, E. (1958). *Hama: fouilles et recherches, 1931–1938*, vol. 2, pt 1: *L'architecture des périods pré-hellénistiques*. Copenhagen: Nationalmuseet.

Gonnella, J., W. Khayyata, and K. Kohlmeyer (2005). *Die Zitadelle von Aleppo und der Tempel des Wettergottes: Neue Forschungen und Entdeckungen*. Münster: Rhema.

Gubel, É. (2005). Phoenician and Aramaean bridle-harness decoration: examples of cultural contact and innovation in the eastern Mediterranean. In C. E. Suter and C. Uehlinger (eds),

Crafts and Images in Contact: Studies on Eastern Mediterranean Art of the First Millennium BCE. Fribourg: University Press/Göttingen: Vandenhoeck & Ruprecht, 111–47.

Harrison, T. (2012). West Syrian *megaron* or Neo-Assyrian *Langraum*? The Shifting Form and Function of the *Tell Ta'yīnāt (Kunalua)* Temples. In J. Kamlah (ed.), *Temple Building and Temple Cult. Architecture and Cultic Paraphernalia of Temples in the Levant (2.–1. Mill. B.C.E.)*. Wiesbaden: Harrassowitz: 3–21.

—— and Osborne, J. F. (2012). Building XVI and the Neo-Assyrian Sacred Precinct at Tell Tayinat. *Journal of Cuneiform Studies* 64: 125–43.

Hawkins, J. D. (1975). Ḫatti. *Reallexikon der Assyriologie* 4: 152–9.

—— (1995). Karkamish and Karatepe: Neo-Hittite city-states in north Syria. In J. Sasson (ed.), *Civilizations of the Ancient Near East*, vol. 2. New York: Scribner, 1295–307.

—— (2000). *Corpus of Hieroglyphic Luwian Inscriptions*, vol. 1: *Inscriptions of the Iron Age* (3 vols). Berlin: de Gruyter.

—— and A. Morpurgo-Davies (1978). On the problems of Karatepe: the hieroglyphic text. *Anatolian Studies* 28: 103–19.

Heitham, H. (2001). Tell Wardiyat: récentes recherches archéologiques (1997–1999). *Bulletin of the Canadian Society for Mesopotamian Studies* 36: 107–14.

Herrmann, G. (1986). *Ivories from Nimrud (1949–1963)*, vol. 4: *Ivories from Room 37, Fort Shalmaneser* (2 vols). London: British School of Archaeology in Iraq.

—— (1992). *Ivories from Nimrud (1949–1963)*, vol. 5: *The Small Collections from Fort Shalmaneser*. London: British School of Archaeology in Iraq.

—— (2000). Ivory carving of first millennium workshops: traditions and diffusion. In C. Uehlinger (ed.), *Images as Media: Sources for the Cultural History of the Near East and the Eastern Mediterranean, 1st Millennium BCE*. Fribourg: University Press Fribourg, 267–82.

Hogarth, D. G. (1914). *Carchemish: Report on the Excavations at Djerabis on Behalf of the British Museum*, vol. 1: *Introductory*. London: Trustees of the British Museum.

Hrouda, B. (1975). Ḫilāni, bīt. B. Archäologisch. *Reallexikon der Assyriologie* 4: 406–9.

Ikeda, J. (1999). Looking from Til Barsib on the Euphrates: Assyria and the west in ninth and eighth centuries B.C. In K. Watanabe (ed.), *Priests and Officials in the Ancient Near East: Papers of the Second Colloquium on the Ancient Near East—The City and Its Life, Held at the Middle Eastern Culture Center in Japan (Mitaka, Tokyo), March 22–24, 1996*. Heidelberg: Universitätsverlag Winter, 271–302.

Jamieson, A. S. (2000). Identifying room use and vessel function: a case-study of Iron Age pottery from Building C2 at Tell Ahmar, north Syria. In Bunnens (2000: 259–303).

Klengel, H. (1992). *Syria, 3000 to 300 B.C.: A Handbook of Political History*. Berlin: Akademie.

Kühne, H. (1995). The Assyrians on the Middle Euphrates and the Ḫābūr. In M. Liverani (ed.), *Neo-Assyrian Geography*. Rome: Università degli studi di Roma 'La Sapienza', Dipartimento di scienze storiche, archeologiche e antropologiche dell'antichità, 69–85.

—— (2000). The 'Red House' of the Assyrian Provincial Center of Dur-Katlimmu. In P. Matthiae, A. Enea, L. Peyronel, and F. Pinnock (eds), *Proceedings of the First International Congress on the Archaeology of the Ancient Near East, Rome, May 18th–23rd 1998*. Rome: Università degli studi di Roma 'La Sapienza', Dipartimento di scienze storiche, archeologiche e antropologiche dell'antichità, 761–9.

Langenegger, F., K. Müller, and R. Naumann (1950). *Tell Halaf*, vol. 2: *Die Bauwerke*. Berlin: de Gruyter.

Lebeau, M. (1983). *La céramique de l'Âge du fer II–III à Tell Abou Danné et ses rapports avec la céramique contemporaine en Syrie*. Paris: Recherche sur les civilisations.

Lehmann, G. (1996). *Untersuchungen zur späten Eisenzeit in Syrien und Libanon: Stratigraphie und Keramikformen zwischen ca. 720 bis 300 v. Chr.* Münster: Ugarit-Verlag.

—— (1998). Trends in the local pottery development of the Late Iron Age and Persian period in Syria and Lebanon, ca. 700 to 300 B.C. *Bulletin of the American Schools of Oriental Research* 311: 7–37.

Lipiński, E. (1995). *Dieux et déesses de l'univers phénicien et punique.* Louvain: Peeters.

—— (2000a). *The Aramaeans: Their Ancient History, Culture, Religion.* Louvain: Peeters.

—— (2000b). The linguistic geography of Syria in Iron Age II (c. 1000–600 B.C.). In Bunnens (2000: 125–42).

Liverani, M. (1992). *Studies on the Annals of Ashurnasirpal*, vol. 2, pt 2: *Topographical Analysis.* Rome: Università di Roma 'La Sapienza', Dipartimento di scienze storiche, archeologiche e antropologiche dell'antichità.

Luke, J. (2003). *Ports of Trade, Al Mina and Geometric Greek Pottery in the Levant.* Oxford: Archaeopress.

Makinson, M. (1999). La culture matérielle du Moyen Euphrate au premier millénaire avant J.-C. In G. del Olmo Lete and J. L. Montero Fenollós (eds), *Archaeology of the Upper Syrian Euphrates, the Tishrin Dam Area: Proceedings of the International Symposium Held at Barcelona, January 28th–30th, 1998.* Barcelona: Ausa, 363–91.

Marchetti, N. (2012). Karkemish on the Euphrates: excavating a city's history. *Near Eastern Archaeology* 75: 132–47.

Margueron, J.-C. (1979). Un 'hilani' à Emar. In D. N. Freedman (ed.), *Archaeological Reports from the Tabqa Dam Project, Euphrates Valley, Syria.* Cambridge, Mass.: American Schools of Oriental Research, 153–76.

Masetti Rouault, M. G. (2001). *Cultures locales du Moyen-Euphrate: modèles et événements, IIe–Ier mill. av. J.-C.* Turnhout: Brepols.

Matilla Séiquier, G. (1999). Tell Khamis. In G. del Olmo Lete and J. L. Montero Fenollós (eds), *Archaeology of the Upper Syrian Euphrates, the Tishrin Dam Area: Proceedings of the International Symposium Held at Barcelona, January 28th–30th, 1998.* Barcelona: Ausa, 205–25.

Matthiae, P. (2002). L'origine dell'edificio E di Büyükkale e il problema storico del Hilani. In S. De Martino and F. Pecchioli Daddi (eds), *Anatolia Antica: studi in memoria di Fiorella Imparati.* Florence: LoGisma, 571–92.

Mazzoni, S. (1995). Settlement pattern and new urbanization in Syria at the time of the Assyrian conquest. In M. Liverani (ed.), *Neo-Assyrian Geography.* Rome: Università di Roma, Istituto di studi del Vicino oriente, 181–92.

—— (2000a). Syria and the periodization of the Iron Age: a cross-cultural perspective. In Bunnens (2000: 31–59).

—— (2000b). Crisis and change: the beginning of the Iron Age in Syria. In P. Matthiae, A. Enea, L. Peyronel, and F. Pinnock (eds), *Proceedings of the First International Congress on the Archaeology of the Ancient Near East, Rome, May 18th–23rd 1998.* Rome: Università degli studi di Roma 'La Sapienza', Dipartimento di scienze storiche, archeologiche e antropologiche dell'antichità, 1043–55.

—— (2000c). Syria and the chronology of the Iron Age. *Isimu* 3: 121–38.

—— (2001). La Siria e il mondo greco arcaico. In S. Settis (ed.), *I greci: storia, cultura, arte, società*, vol. 3: *I greci oltre la Grecia.* Turin: Einaudi, 283–328.

Morandi Bonacossi, D. (1996). *Tra il fiume e la steppa: insediamento e uso del territorio nella bassa valle del fiume Habur in epoca neo-assira* (2 vols). Padua: Sargon.

—— (2006). Un centro amministrativo nel regno di Hamath: Tell Mishrifeh e la sua regione nella seconda Età del ferro (IX–VIII secolo a.C.). In D. Morandi Bonacossi, E. Rova, F. Veronese, and P. Zanovello (eds), *Tra Oriente e Occidente: studi in onore di Elena Di Filippo Balestrazzi*. Padua: Sargon, 73–114.

Naumann, R. (1955). *Architektur Kleinasiens von ihren Anfängen bis zum Ende der hethitischen Zeit*. Tübingen: Wasmuth.

Nevling Porter, B. (2000). Assyrian propaganda for the west: Esarhaddon's stelae for Til Barsip and Sam'al. In Bunnens (2000: 143–76).

Niehr, H. (2006). Bestattung und Ahnenkult in der Königshäusern von Sam'al (Zincirli) und Guzana (Tell Ḥalāf) in Nordsyrien. *Zeitschrift der Deutschen Palästina-Vereins* 122: 111–39.

Orthmann, W. (1971). *Untersuchungen zur Späthethitischen Kunst*. Bonn: Rudolf Habelt.

—— (2002). *Die aramäisch-assyrische Stadt Guzana: Ein Rückblick auf die Ausgrabungen Max von Oppenheims in Tell Halaf*. Saarbrücken: Saarbrücker Druckerei.

Pecorella, P., and R. Pierobon Benoit (2005). *Tell Barri/Kahat: la campagna del 2002*. Florence: Florence University Press.

Pitard, W. T. (1987). *Ancient Damascus: A Historical Study of the Syrian City-State from Earliest Times until Its Fall to the Assyrians in 732 B.C.E.* Winona Lake, Ind.: Eisenbrauns.

—— (1988). The identity of the Bar-Hadad of the Melqart stele. *Bulletin of the American Schools of Oriental Research* 272: 3–21

Ponchia, S. (1991). *L'Assiria e gli stati transeufratici nella prima metà dell'VIII sec. a.C.* Padua: Sargon.

Pucci, M. (2008). *Functional Analysis of Space in Syro-Hittite Architecture*. Oxford: Archaeopress.

Puech, É. (1992). La stèle de Bar-Hadad à Melqart et les rois d'Arpad. *Revue biblique* 99: 311–34.

Riis, P. J. (1948). *Hama: fouilles et recherches, 1931–1938*, vol. 2, pt 3: *Les cimetières à crémation*. Copenhagen: Nationalmuseet.

—— and M.-L. Buhl (1990). *Hama: fouilles et recherches, 1931–1938*, vol. 2, pt 2: *Les objets de la période dite syro-hittite (Âge du fer)*. Copenhagen: Fondation Carlsberg.

—— J. Jensen, M.-L. Buhl, and B. Otzen (1996). *Sukas X: The Bronze and Early Iron Age Remains at the Southern Harbour*. Copenhagen: Royal Danish Academy of Sciences and Letters.

Rouault, O. (2001). Terqa et sa région (6e–1er millénaires av. J.-C.). *Akkadica* 122: 1–26.

Sader, H. (1987) *Les états araméens de Syrie depuis leur fondation jusqu'à leur transformation en provinces assyriennes*. Beirut: Orient-Institut der Deutschen Morgenländischen Gesellschaft/ Wiesbaden: Steiner.

—— (1992). The 12th century B.C. in Syria: the problem of the rise of the Aramaeans. In W. A. Ward and M. S. Joukowsky (eds), *The Crisis Years: The 12th Century B.C. from Beyond the Danube to the Tigris*. Dubuque, Ia.: Kendall/Hunt, 157–63.

—— (2000). The Aramaean kingdoms of Syria: origin and formation processes. In Bunnens (2000: 61–76).

Schwartz, G. M. (1989). The origins of the Aramaeans in Syria and northern Mesopotamia: research problems and potential strategies. In O. M. C. Haex, H. H. Curvers, and P. M. M. G. Akkermans (eds), *To the Euphrates and Beyond: Archaeological Studies in Honour of Maurits N. van Loon*. Rotterdam: Balkema, 275–91.

Schwemer, D. (2001). *Die Wettergottgestalten Mesopotamiens und Nordsyriens in Zeitalter der Keilschriftkulturen: Materialien und Studien nach den schriftlichen Quellen*. Wiesbaden: Harrassowitz.

Stone, E. C., and P. E. Zimansky. (1999). *The Iron Age Settlement at 'Ain Dara, Syria: Survey and Soundings*. Oxford: Archaeopress.

Suriano, M. J. (2007). The apology of Hazael: a literary and historical analysis of the Tel Dan inscription. *Journal of Near Eastern Studies* 66: 163–76.

Wada, H. (1994). Pottery vessels in the Iron Age II in the south area of Tell Mastuma. *Bulletin of the Ancient Orient Museum* 15: 51–76.

Wakita, S., I. Asano, H. Wada, et al. (1995). Tell Mastuma: a preliminary report of the excavations at Idlib, Syria, in 1994 and 1995. *Bulletin of the Ancient Orient Museum* 16: 1–73.

——H. Wada, and S. Nishiyama (2000). Tell Mastuma: change in settlement plans and historical context during the first quarter of the first millennium B.C. In Bunnens (2000: 537–57).

Wartke, R.-B. (2005). *Sam'al: Ein aramäischer Stadtstaat des 10. bis 8. Jhs. v. Chr. und die Geschichte seiner Erforschung.* Mainz am Rhein: Staatliche Museen zu Berlin.

Werner, P. (1994). *Die Entwicklung der Sakralarchitektur in Nordsyrien und Südostkleinasien vom Neolithikum bis in das 1. Jt. v. Chr.* Munich: Profil.

Wicke, D. (1999). Altorientalische Pferdescheuklappen. *Ugarit-Forschungen* 31: 803–52.

——(2002). Die elfenbeinerne Kosmetikpalette IM 79501: zwischen Kosmologie und Ornament. *Baghdader Mitteilungen* 33: 229–71.

—— (2005). 'Roundcheeked and ringletted': Gibt es einen nordwestsyrischen Regionalstil in der altorientalischen Elfenbeinschnitzerei? In C. E. Suter and C. Uehlinger (eds), *Crafts and Images in Contact: Studies on Eastern Mediterranean Art of the First Millennium BCE.* Fribourg: University Press Fribourg/Göttingen: Vandenhoeck & Ruprecht, 67–110.

Wilkinson, T. J., and E. Barbanes (2000). Settlement patterns in the Syrian Jazira during the Iron Age. In Bunnens (2000: 397–422).

Winter, I. J. (1976a). Phoenician and north Syrian ivory carving in historical context: questions of style and distribution. *Iraq* 38: 1–22.

—— (1976b). Carved ivory furniture panels from Nimrud: a coherent subgroup of the north Syrian style. *Metropolitan Museum Journal* 11: 25–54.

—— (1979). On the problems of Karatepe: the reliefs and their context. *Anatolian Studies* 29: 115–51.

—— (1981). Is there a south Syrian style of ivory carving in the early first millennium B.C.? *Iraq* 43: 101–30.

—— (1989). North Syrian ivories and Tell Halaf reliefs: the impact of luxury goods upon 'major' arts. In A. Leonard Jr and B. B. Williams (eds), *Essays in Ancient Civilization Presented to Helene J. Kantor.* Chicago: Oriental Institute of the University of Chicago, 321–32.

CHAPTER 46

PHOENICIA DURING THE IRON AGE II PERIOD

MARÍA EUGENIA AUBET

INTRODUCTION

During Iron Age II (900–600 BC) Phoenician history became aligned with the history of Tyre. Archaeological evidence shows that the city of Tyre took the initiative in transforming Phoenicia into a commercial, territorial, and colonial power (Fig. 46.1). The transformation began at the end of Iron I in the middle of the 11th century BC, when the whole region of the Bay of Akko and Mount Carmel became part of a southerly extension of Phoenicia, and Tyre set up its first trading post in Palaepaphos, on southwest Cyprus.

The causes of Tyre's ascendancy during Iron II are the result of a number of factors that came together at the end of Iron I. In the first place, with the destruction of Ugarit at the beginning of the 12th century BC, the chief maritime and commercial power in the region disappeared, shifting the main focus of interregional trade southwards. Secondly, the decline of Egypt left Phoenicia free of administrative interference, conferring a high degree of independence on its cities. Lastly, the absence of competitors in Levantine trade after the 'crisis years' left the Phoenician cities in a position to resume the long-range economic strategy that had caused cities like Byblos and Ugarit to prosper: that of acting as intermediaries between the great empires of the interior and the peripheral regions of Syria, Galilee, and the Mediterranean, and supplying strategic raw materials like copper, silver, and tin. Recent excavations in the region, moreover, demonstrate that the Phoenician cities remained at the margins of the serious destructions that devastated the region at the end of the Bronze Age. They were thus able quickly to regain control of the maritime circuits of exchange and connect them with the principal land networks, thanks to the privileged position of their ports, which afforded them good communication along the roads to the Beqa' Valley, Damascus, Lower Galilee, and Jordan Valley. So it can be said that at the beginning of Iron II the Phoenician cities had become genuine regional markets. Neither Tyre nor Sidon were a great centre of production, and their political institutions and merchant corporations succeeded in monopolizing the distribution of products and raw materials created by others.

It had been thought that the transition from the Late Bronze to the Iron Age in Phoenicia had implied the replacement of a palace-administered exchange by a decentralized and

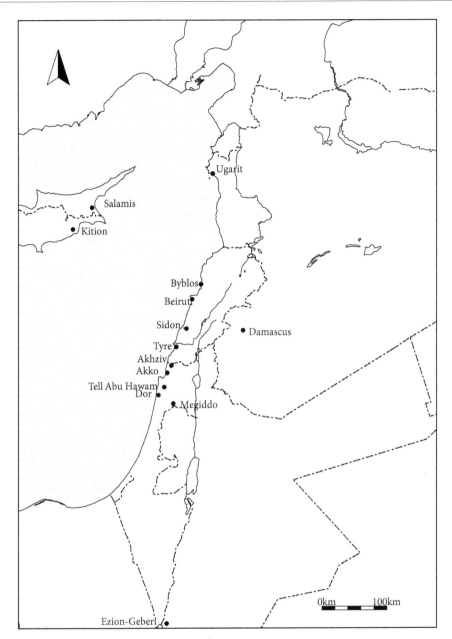

FIG. 46.1 Map of Iron Age II sites in Phoenicia

entrepreneurial trade, and Phoenician trade was described as an activity characteristic of 'merchant capitalism'. This interpretation was undoubtedly strongly influenced by the Homeric texts. The reality is much more complex and, as in so many other cases, archaeology reflects a strong continuity with Late Bronze Age traditions in which private trade and institutional trade were intermixed and coexisted.

We know the archaeological sequence of Iron II thanks to important stratified deposits of ceramics and architecture identified in Tyre, Sarepta, Cyprus, Dor, Tell Abu Hawam, and Tel Keisan. These sequences, together with the Tyre stratigraphy established by Bikai in 1973–4 in the centre of the island (Bikai 1978), show the main features of the evolution of Phoenician pottery, easily recognizable and sober, standardized with conservative shapes and simple decoration. In its general evolutionary tendency we can observe three fundamental changes:

1. The presence of Phoenician pottery, as in Strata XIII–X in Tyre (1050–850 BC) where the types characteristic of Phoenician Iron Age pottery appear for the first time, was strongly imbued with the traditions of the Late Bronze Age, together with Cypriot pottery, and the so-called Philistine pottery. Known as the 'Kouklia horizon' in Cyprus (Bikai 1987: 50–53), its most representative forms are the pilgrim flask, the palm tree jar, the dipper juglet, the strainer-spouted jar, and the round-based juglets with Bichrome decoration of concentric circles. At a later point in this period, during the first half of the 9th century BC (= Tyre X), burials began in the recently excavated zone of the Al-Bass cemetery.
2. The pottery of Tyre IX–IV (850–760 BC), or 'Salamis horizon' in Cyprus, shows transitional forms in which the circle decoration gives way to horizontal bands. Red Slip Ware makes an appearance and gradually increases, the most representative forms being the trefoil juglet with a long neck and the square-rimmed juglet (Fig. 46.2a), a forerunner of the famous mushroom-lipped jug.
3. In Strata III–II at Tyre, or the 'Kition horizon' in Cyprus (760–700 BC), the classic forms of the colonies in the West appear: the square-rim juglet becomes the mushroom-lip jug (Fig. 46.2b), the trefoil globular juglet becomes firmly established,

FIG. 46.2 Juglets from Al-Bass (Tyre)

and oil bottles, plates, the so-called Fine Ware, and the crisp-ware storage jar or 'torpedo' jar proliferate.

This is the time of the pinnacle of Red Slip Ware and of the absolute dominion of Tyre in the Mediterranean. In the time of Stratum I in Tyre, or the 'Amathus' horizon in Cyprus (700–600 BC), all these forms evolve into types further removed from the original models, although the Tyre III–II pottery continues to be predominate. Thus the body of the mushroom-lip jug becomes wider, the trefoil juglet acquires a biconical form, and Red Slip Ware starts to decline.

The presence and distribution of these three groups of pottery in Cyprus and Galilee allow us to reconstruct the main stages of Phoenician external expansion.

THE 10TH–8TH CENTURIES BC AND THE MAKING OF TYRE

From the 10th century BC on, the archaeological record and written sources reveal strong growth in the city of Tyre. We do not know why Tyre imposed her supremacy on other Phoenician city-states. According to the written tradition, both classical and biblical, Iron II Tyre arose from an urban project and large-scale restructuring undertaken by just one person, King Hiram I (969–936 BC), who gave the city its monumental urban appearance that was to last for centuries (Fig. 46.3). The legend, as reported by Flavius Josephus (*Contra Ap.* I, 113), tells us that Hiram joined the two islands or reefs together, forming a single island, on which he erected temples for Melqart, Astarte, and Ba'al Shamem. Centuries later some historians were able to visit the famous temple of Melqart, the patron deity of the city and the monarchy, evoking its two famous columns, one of pure gold and the other of emerald, which shone at night (Herodotus II, 44). As late as the Hellenistic period, the temple still received annual tributes in the name of the king, sent by the colonies. Other important projects of Hiram I were the construction of the walls and of the *Eurychoros* or 'open space', a big marketplace near the north port, the most ancient documented in eastern sources.

We have very little archaeological data from Tyre during Iron II. On the island a large industrial quarter of the 10th–8th centuries BC has been identified, devoted to the production of pottery and precious metals. This sector was discovered by Bikai (1978) very close to the city's acropolis, where the temple of Melqart and the royal palace must have stood. Part of the main necropolis was excavated in 1997–2009 opposite the island, in the Al-Bass district, where in antiquity there had been a beach on the mainland less than 2km from the city. This is the biggest Iron Age necropolis known in Phoenicia (Aubet 2004). It was found at a depth of more than 4m near the Roman necropolis and has a high density of adult burials; so far 225 cremation urns have been located. The majority of the burials date to the 9th–7th centuries BC and reveal homogeneous mortuary practices: each cremation burial is accompanied by standard grave goods consisting of a mushroom-lip jug, a trefoil-rim jug, and a drinking bowl. Once the grave was closed, several fires were lit and vessels and pitchers were thrown onto the tomb. Inside the urn, near the bone remains, objects for personal use, such as rings, scarabs, bracelets, and jewels, were deposited. Some burials were found associated with stone stelae on which inscriptions commemorating the deceased and symbolic motifs had been carved. The Al-Bass necropolis has provided a few novelties concerning the

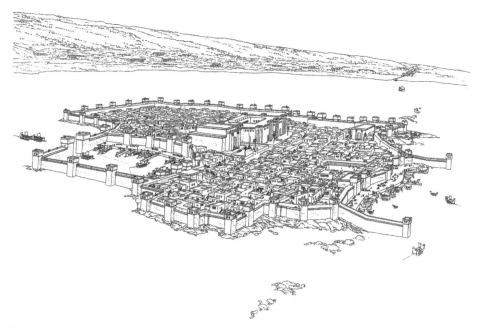

FIG. 46.3 Reconstruction of Tyre in Iron Age II

mortuary practices of Tyre. In many cases the bone remains of the same individual had been distributed between a pair of urns; one of the two contained most of the individual's bone remains, while the contiguous urn preserved some bones and ash. In Al-Bass most of the graves are double-urn.

For the period when Tyre assumed hegemony over the other Phoenician cities, the most relevant information about the Phoenician heartland comes from cemeteries. Only Sarepta, 13km south of Sidon, has yielded stratigraphic sequences as complete (or more so) as Tyre. Two large sondages in the 1970s in the centre of this small coastal city, termed Areas II,Y and II,X, have provided important data about Iron II (Anderson 1988). As in Tyre, the Iron Age displays absolute continuity with the Late Bronze and starts in Strata E–D (1025–850 BC) with the first elements characteristic of Phoenician material culture: Bichrome ceramics and, for the first time, ashlar masonry that uses the header-and-stretcher technique typical of Phoenician architecture. This stratum is defined by a large quantity of Cypriot imports, whose early presence demonstrates that relations with Cyprus continued uninterrupted at the start of the Iron Age. Stratum C, dated to 800–650 BC, coincides with the industrial zone, which centred on the production of pottery and the processing and distribution of olive oil, as evidenced by the large number of kilns, stone olive presses, and storage and commercial amphorae found in its installations. The typical building technique of this period is the header-and-stretcher system alternating with rubble in domestic buildings and industrial installations, a technique only previously known in the colonies of the West.

The excavations in the town centre of Beirut (ancient Biruta) in 1993–6 revealed the importance of a Phoenician city that is barely mentioned in the written sources of the first millennium BC. The most notable find is a huge stone glacis (Fig. 46.4) of which a 160m stretch, 7.5m high, has been preserved (Finkbeiner and Sader 1997; Badre 1997). The glacis

FIG. 46.4 The glacis of Beirut

corresponds to an impressive fortress wall, the upper part of which is not preserved, erected in the Late Bronze Age and reused in the Iron Age after a long period of abandonment. The use of the Iron Age glacis dates to the 10th–7th centuries BC and shows several levels of destruction and abandonment. The archaeological evidence tells us that the Beirut tell was formed by a fortified citadel surrounded by a low-lying city. A few kilometres south of Beirut in Khaldé, near the international airport, an extensive necropolis, made up of 150 burials, was excavated in 1961–4 (Saidah 1966). Scattered at various levels, most of the tombs are inhumations from the 10th–8th centuries BC. Level IV dates to the 10th–9th centuries BC, and contains Tombs 166 and 167 with materials similar to Tyre X and Sarepta D. Particularly interesting is Tomb 121, made up of a stone cyst containing rich inhumations and a crema-tion, all associated with a stone stele.

In north Lebanon, the previous excavations at Byblos failed to identify the Iron II levels, of which a few burials outside the walls are known. Only the excavations of 1978–81 and 1992–8 in the centre of Tell Arqa have provided evidence of a northern city during Iron II (Stratum 10), which arose following a long period of abandonment after the Late Bronze Age (Thalmann 2000). This is an extensive centre showing a violent level of destruction at the beginning of the 7th century BC. A casemate wall delimited the town centre, and the town is characterized by its paucity of foreign relations, judging by the few imports found in the centre.

THE TERRITORIAL EXPANSION

The transformation of Phoenicia into a territorial power is the work of a single city, Tyre, whose control over Lower Galilee gave it direct access to one of the most fertile agricultural territories in the region. This territorial expansion began in the middle of the 11th century and pre-dates the reign of Hiram I.

The biblical tradition tells us that in the middle of the 10th century BC, Hiram I bought from Solomon twenty cities in the 'land of Cabul' in Galilee for 120 talents of gold (I Kgs.

9:10–14), incorporating the whole agricultural hinterland of Akko into his kingdom. But this biblical episode is contradicted by the archaeological evidence, which shows that the southern frontier of the kingdom of Tyre had already reached the Bay of Akko and Mount Carmel by the mid-11th century BC.

In Tel Dor, Strata XI–X and IX in Area B1 (c.1050–1000 BC) reveal that after the destruction of the city of the 'Sea Peoples', a Phoenician population settled there, using Bichrome pottery with affinities to Tyre XIII. Up until the Hellenistic and Roman periods Dor continued to be a Phoenician city (Stern 1995; Gilboa, Sharon, and Zorn 2004). From the outset, Dor presents itself as a well-planned city with streets, monumental walls, port installations, and large public buildings which, from Stratum VIII (10th century BC) onwards used the typically Phoenician technique of ashlar masonry with a fill of stones between the pillars. In Area 2D one of the largest public buildings in Israel was located, perhaps a palace consisting of ashlars and situated close to the entrance to the city from the port.

Another important southern Phoenician centre is Tell Abu Hawam, in modern Haifa, a small fortified city at the mouth of the River Quishon, where Stratum III reflects a predominantly Phoenician character (Balensi and Herrera 1985; Herrera and Gómez 2004). In the Iron II levels the remains of a city wall, bastion, and several buildings have been found, belonging to a period when, as in the Late Bronze Age, Tell Abu Hawam constituted the chief port of entry to the cross-country roads leading to the Jordan Valley through Megiddo and Beth Shean. Stratum III appears to be sealed by a level of fire dated to 750–700 BC, which is followed by a long period of abandonment.

Tyre's political hegemony is particularly visible in the Bay of Akko. This is a rich coastal plain made up of alluvial valleys with fertile soils and a mountainous zone, less rich but suitable for grazing and dry agriculture. A survey carried out in 1993–6 in the hinterland of Akko resulted in the location of numerous Iron II settlements (Lehmann 2001). Their form and distribution show that the definitive incorporation of this region into the kingdom of Tyre coincides with a profound restructuring of the territory, defined by the appearance of prosperous centres, intensification of agriculture centred on the production of wheat, wine, and olive oil, and a considerable increase in population. The settlement pattern entailed the existence of a system revolving around a regional centre (i.e. Akko), surrounded by subcentres and newly founded villages and settlements. The high point of this territory occurred in the 10th–8th centuries BC, when the city of Akko became the administrative capital of Lower Galilee (Dothan 1976). Within its sphere of influence were the cities of Akhziv (Mazar 2001) and Tel Keisan, the latter less than 7km from Akko, in the heart of the alluvial plain of Lower Galilee (Briend and Humbert 1980). Sited on a hill dominating the bay—the 'land of Cabul'—Keisan shows more or less uninterrupted occupation from the Late Bronze Age. Above Strata 9–10 of Iron I, characterized by early Phoenician elements—Bichrome pottery and ashlar masonry—and after a level of destruction dated to around 1000 BC, a modest settlement was established a bit later (Stratum 8), which had known rapid development throughout Stratum 7 (900–850 BC), when the material culture of the site places Tel Keisan within the orbit of Tyre. After Stratum 6 (850–800 BC), which was very poor, it was abandoned for a brief period, and the settlement was reconstructed in Stratum 5 (750–700 BC), providing an abundance of Red Slip and Fine Wares of a Tyrian type, as well as traces of intense local wheat production. Level 4 (700–600 BC) is characterized by a dense population. The large number of amphorae reveals a prosperous oil trade. The violent abandonment of the site shortly before 600 BC is attributed to the Assyrian conquest.

Forming part of the Tyrian organizational system in the hinterland of Akko, small forti-fied structures are known, like Tel Kabri, and make up part of Tyre's administrative system. The best-known structure was excavated in 1982–92 at Horbat Rosh Zayit—possibly bibli-cal Cabul—situated in a zone midway between the Plain of Akko and the mountains, suit-able for grazing and both dry and irrigated agriculture (Gal and Alexandre 2000). It is a big fortified edifice surrounded by a variety of agricultural installations, which were used for a short time from the end of the 10th century to the middle of the 9th century BC. Its architec-ture is characterized by ashlar masonry, the headers-and-stretchers technique, and the use of dressed stone at the corners, i.e. clearly inspired by Phoenician architecture. The edifice consisted of two storeys and separate areas of activity—a granary, storehouse, kitchen, an area for processing oil, a mill for wheat, a space for worship, and in particular a cellar with a huge quantity of Phoenician amphorae. It is estimated that it could store some 14,000 litres of wheat, oil, and wine. The presence of weights, seals, and stamps indicates that this strong-hold was concerned with administrative management, focusing on the processing, produc-tion, packaging, and distribution of agricultural products. Thus, it functioned as a centre for the receipt of taxes, probably managed by officials dependent on Tyre. The whole organiza-tion of the hinterland of Akko reveals an efficient centralized administration.

FOREIGN TRADE AND COLONIALISM

The interregional connections of the Phoenician cities in the Iron Age reflect networks and trade routes very similar to those of the Late Bronze Age. The presence of large quantities of Phoenician pottery in the Cypriot sites of Palaepahos-Skales and Tomb I at Salamis, as well as a high volume of Cypriot imports in Tyre XIII, Sarepta E–D, and Dor X–IX (Bikai 1978: 74; 1987: 50–3), demonstrates that contacts with Cyprus were hardly affected by the events of the 'crisis years'. In Palaepahos, more than half the burials of the 11th–10th centuries BC contain Phoenician ceramics, which suggests a prosperous regional exchange in western Cyprus, probably associated with a Tyrian trading post. The case of Kouklia-Palaepahos reveals that after the fall of Ugarit the Phoenicians shifted the main trade route to the south of the island. So Tyre maintained the Bronze Age commercial circuits, but used differ-ent routes. Kouklia-Palaepahos could be considered the earliest Phoenician commercial enclave overseas. Phoenician commercial activity in Cyprus would have culminated around 850 BC with the founding of the first 'official' Tyrian colony in the Mediterranean, Kition (Karageorghis 1976). The vast majority of the pottery at Kition is Tyrian, which emphasizes the political and economic importance Tyre attached to the southeast of the island and access by colonial means to the metal-bearing resources of the region. Later, the Phoenician pres-ence in Cyprus increased, as is shown by finds from the 7th century BC in Amathus and the Phoenician character of its cremation necropolis (Christou 1998). However, the Phoenician pottery from the second half of the 8th century BC found in Ayia Irini has a strong affinity with that of Sarepta rather than Tyre, denoting the presence of different Phoenician com-mercial spheres in overseas trade.

The existence of a Phoenician trading post at Palaepahos favoured the renewal of con-tacts with the Aegean. From the end of the 10th down to the 8th centuries BC, Tyre offers the greatest concentration of Greek Proto-Geometric ceramics in the whole of the Levant (Coldstream 1998). Most of it consisted of pendent semicircle skyphoi of the Euboean type, the most popular Greek vessel in the East, appreciated for its quality as a drinking cup. This indicates the direct implication of merchants from the Aegean in Phoenicia from a very early time and the development of joint Phoenicio-Euboean activities. The arrival of Greek ceramics in Tyre coincides with the find of oriental jewels and Phoenician ceramics in the elite tombs at Lefkandi in Euboea. So the Tyre–Euboea trade route across the south of Cyprus would have been inaugurated at the end of the 10th century BC, before the founding of Kition—a scene similar to the Late Bronze Age, when the Phoenician coast and not Ugarit had been the main recipient of Aegean pottery. The route must have passed through the south of Crete, since numerous Phoenician amphorae from the end of the 10th century BC have been discovered in the city of Kommos in the so-called Temple A (925–800 BC) (Shaw 1989). Temple B (800–760 BC), a three-pillar shrine of a Phoenician type—the most ancient known in the Greek world—appeared in association with Phoenician amphorae made with clays from the Lebanese coast. The building of a small Phoenician temple in Kommos suggests the existence of Levantine residents in the south of Crete since at least 800 BC, and reveals one of the most common practices of Phoenician colonialism: the building of a temple to guarantee peaceful commercial transactions and the implication of the temple of Melqart in Tyre in the colonial enterprise. Various finds also signal the presence of Phoenician merchants in other places in Crete, like Knossos and Orthi Petra (Eleutherna) (Stampolidis 2003). At the same date, around 800 BC, the Phoenicians had already initiated commercial contacts with the mining region of Huelva in the south of Spain.

THE ASSYRIAN EPILOGUE

The expansion of the Neo-Assyrian Empire and its pressure on the Phoenician cities corresponds to a fairly brief period (733–630 BC) and was less decisive than was originally thought. For a long time the horizon of the 8th–7th centuries BC was considered to be the beginning of the end of Tyre, due to Assyrian military and political pressure. However, this period corresponds to the zenith of the Phoenician colonial enterprise in the West. Many levels of destruction in Phoenicia have been related to the Assyrian conquest, not always very convincingly. The progressive Assyrian dominion over the Phoenician cities began with Tiglath-pileser III in 733/2 BC, stemming from the conquest of Lower Galilee and Dor. In 701 BC Sennacherib conquered Sidon, Sarepta, Akko, and Akhziv, and his annals mention the Plain of Akko as part of the Assyrian Empire. Asurbanipal (668–626 BC) would have destroyed the hinterland of Tyre and the city of Akko, deporting its inhabitants, an event that has been connected with the destruction level of Stratum 7 of Area A (Dothan 1976: 23). But the Assyrians made sure to preserve the city of Tyre and its zones of influence because of their economic and commercial potential. From the second half of the 8th century BC the whole of the kingdom of Tyre was still open to Assyrian trade and, contrary to the traditional view, it seems to coincide with high levels of prosperity and reactivation of the economy. In Tel Keisan, Assyrian pottery was located from Level 5 (Briend and Humbert 1980: 164). The Assyrian period coincides in Keisan with a rebirth of the city, which can be recognized in Level 4 with new town planning under Assyrian administration, as at Dor, where a flourishing local industry arose—smelting and producing iron. The fall of the Assyrian Empire and the subsequent Neo-Babylonian conquest would eventually drag the city-state of Tyre down with it, and see the shifting of the main centre of power again to Sidon.

Suggested reading

Aubet, M. E. (1993). *Phoenicians and the West: Politics, Colonies, and Trade*, trans. M. Turton. Cambridge: Cambridge University Press.

Baurain, C., and C. Bonnet (1992). *Les phéniciens: marins des trois continents*. Paris: Colin.

Gras, M., P. Rouillard, and J. Teixidor (1989). *L'univers phénicien*. Paris: Arthaud.

Katzenstein, H. J. (1973). *The History of Tyre: From the Beginning of the Second Millennium B.C.E. until the Fall of the Neo-Babylonian Empire in 538 B.C.E.* Jerusalem: Schocken Institute for Jewish Research of the Jewish Theological Seminary of America.

Markoe, G. (2000). *Phoenicians*. London: British Museum Press.

Matoian, V. (ed.) (1999). *Liban, l'autre rive: exposition présentée à l'Institut du monde arabe du 27 octobre au 2 mai 1999*. Paris: Flammarion.

Moscati, S. (ed.) (1988). *I fenici*. Exhibition, Palazzo Grassi, Venice. Milan: Bompiani.

Sader, H. (2005). *Iron Age Funerary Stelae from Lebanon*. Barcelona: Bellaterra.

Stern, E. (1994). *Dor, Ruler of the Seas: Twelve Years of Excavations at the Israelite-Phoenician Harbor Town on the Carmel Coast*, trans. J. Shadur. Jerusalem: Israel Exploration Society.

References

Anderson, W. P. (1988). *Sarepta I: The Late Bronze and Iron Age Strata of Area II, Y*. Beirut: Publications de l'Université Libanaise.

Aubet, M. E. (ed.) (2004). *The Phoenician Cemetery of Tyre-Al Bass*. Beirut: Ministère de la culture, Direction générale des antiquités.

Badre, L. (1997). Bey 003 preliminary report: excavations of the American University of Beirut Museum 1993–1996. *Bulletin d'archéologie et d'architecture libanaises* 2: 6–94.

Balensi, J., and M. D. Herrera (1985). Tell Abu Hawam 1983–1984: rapport préliminaire. *Revue biblique* 92: 82–128.

Bikai, P. M. (1978). *The Pottery of Tyre*. Warminster: Aris & Phillips.

—— (1987). *The Phoenician Pottery of Cyprus*. Nicosia: A.G. Leventis Foundation with the assistance of the J. Paul Getty Trust.

Briend, J., and J.-B. Humbert (1980). *Tell Keisan (1971–76): une cité phénicienne en Galilée*. Fribourg: Éditions universitaires/Göttingen: Vandenhoeck & Ruprecht/Paris: Gabalda.

Christou, D. (1998). Cremations in the Western Necropolis of Amathus. In V. Karageorghis and N. Stampolidis (eds), *Eastern Mediterranean: Cyprus–Dodecanese–Crete, 16th–6th Cent. B.C.* Athens: University of Crete/A. G. Leventis Foundation, 207–15.

Coldstream, J. N. (1998). The first exchanges between Euboeans and Phoenicians: who took the initiative? In S. Gitin, A. Mazar, and E. Stern (eds), *Mediterranean Peoples in Transition: Thirteenth to Early Tenth Centuries BCE*. Jerusalem: Israel Exploration Society, 353–60.

Dothan, M. (1976). Akko: interim excavation report, first season 1973/74. *Bulletin of the American Schools of Oriental Research* 224: 1–48.

Finkbeiner, U., and H. Sader (1997). Bey 20: preliminary report of the excavation 1995. *Bulletin d'archéologie et d'architecture libanaises* 2: 114–205.

Gal, Z., and Y. Alexandre (2000). *Horbat Rosh Zayit: An Iron Age Storage Fort and Village*. Jerusalem: Israel Antiquities Authority.

Gilboa, A., I. Sharon, and J. R. Zorn (2004). Dor and Iron Age chronology: scarabs, ceramic sequence and 14C. *Tel Aviv* 31: 32–59.

Herrera, M. D., and F. Gómez (2004). *Tell Abu Hawam (Haifa, Israel): el horizonte fenicio del Stratum III británico*. Salamanca: Universidad Pontificia de Salamanca/Huelva: Universidad de Huelva.

Karageorghis, V. (1976). *Kition: Mycenaean and Phoenician Discoveries in Cyprus*. London: Thames & Hudson.

Lehmann, G. (2001). Phoenicians in western Galilee: first results of an archaeological survey in the hinterland of Akko. In A. Mazar (ed.), *Studies in the Archaeology of the Iron Age in Israel and Jordan*. Sheffield: Sheffield Academic, 65–112.

Mazar, E. (2001). *The Phoenicians in Achziv: The Southern Cemetery—Jerome L. Joss Expedition, Final Report of the Excavations, 1988-1990*. Barcelona: Laboratorio de arqueología, Universidad Pompeu Fabra de Barcelona.

Saidah, R. (1966). Fouilles de Khaldé: rapport préliminaire sur les première et deuxième campagnes (1961-1962). *Bulletin du Musée de Beyrouth* 19: 51–90.

Shaw, J. W. (1989). Phoenicians in southern Crete. *American Journal of Archaeology* 93: 165–83.

Stampolidis, N. (2003). Phoenician presence in the Aegean. In N. Stampolidis and V. Karageorghis (eds), *ΠΛΟΕΣ—Sea Routes: Interconnections in the Mediterranean 16th-6th c. BC*. Athens: University of Crete/A. G. Leventis Foundation, 217–32.

Stern, E. (ed.) (1995). *Excavations at Dor: Final Report*, vol. 1. Jerusalem: Institute of Archaeology, Hebrew University of Jerusalem in cooperation with Israel Exploration Society.

Thalmann, J.-P. (2000). Tell Arqa. *Bulletin d'archéologie et d'architecture libanaises* 4: 5–74.

CHAPTER 47

PHILISTIA DURING THE IRON AGE II PERIOD

DAVID BEN-SHLOMO

Geographical and Chronological Setting

The region of Philistia is defined here as the coastal strip and inner coastal plains lying between Nahal Gerar (or the modern Egyptian border) in the southwest and the Yarkon River in the north (Fig. 47.1). This region is about 70km long and 27km wide in the south, narrowing to 15km in the north; its eastern boundary can be defined topographically as the area west of the foothills of the Judean Shephelah. The chronological transition between the Iron I and Iron II in southern Palestine is not always sharply defined, and it is therefore constructive to add another short horizon, which could be defined as the transitional Iron I–Iron IIA (Table 47.1). The Iron IIA is seen as a relatively long period of 150–200 years; the latter Iron Age (Iron IIB–C) is also about 200 years long, and can be divided into an earlier, Iron IIB and later Iron IIC phase, ending in the Babylonian destructions around 600 BCE.

Historical Sources

Only few external sources refer to Philistia during the Iron IIA, while the historicity of the abundant biblical reports on collisions between Kings Saul and David and the Philistines during this period is debatable. In Adad-Nirari III 'Calah Slab' of the end of the 9th century BCE Philistia is mentioned among several states sending him tribute (Shai 2006: 355), and thus is treated as an integral political entity. Most other external texts dealing directly with the Philistine city-states are dated to the 8th–7th centuries, and relate to the Assyrian rule in Philistia, which started after Tiglath-pileser III's campaign in 734 BCE (Tadmor 1966). The absence of Philistia from Iron II Egyptian sources stands in contrast to the Iron I. It seems that the Philistine cities preserved a degree of independence under Assyrian rule as tribute-bearing states. The trade between the Philistine cities (Gaza, Ashkelon, and Ashdod), the southern Egyptian Delta, and the northern Phoenician ports (Byblos, Arvad, Tyre, and

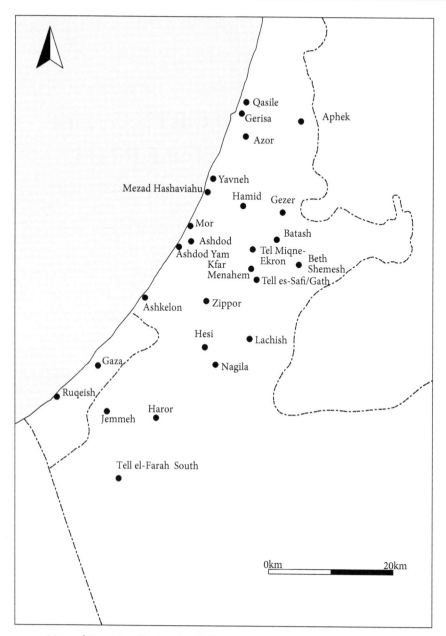

FIG. 47.1 Map of Iron Age II sites in Philistia

Sidon) probably benefited the Assyrian interest (Tadmor 1966: 87–8; Master 2003: 49–51). The participation of the Philistine cities in campaigns, either against Judah or in revolts against Assyria, is minimal during the initial years of Assyrian rule. It is also mentioned that Uzziah, king of Judah (785–733 BCE), made war against the Philistines, destroyed the walls of Gath and Ashdod, and built cities in the territories of Ashdod (2 Chr. 26:6); this passage shows the strength of Ashdod during the 8th century. During the reign of Sargon II there

Table 47.1 Chronological comparison of the main sites in Iron Age I–II Philistia and its vicinity

Site	Iron Age I (c.1175–975 BCE)	Iron Age IIA (c.975–800 BCE)	Iron Age IIB (800–701 BCE)	Iron Age IIC (701–604/586 BCE)
Tell es-Safi/Gath	A7 A6 A5	A4 A3	A2	gap
Tel Miqne-Ekron	VII VI V IVB	IVA III	II	IB IA
Ashdod	XIII XII XI	X (IX)	VIII	VII VI
Ashkelon Grid 38	20 19 18	17 16	15	14
Lachish	VI gap	V IV	III	II
Tell Qasile	XII XI X	IX	VIII	VII
Tel Batash (Timnah)	VI V	IV gap	III	II

were several rebellions against Assyria, probably with some Egyptian support. In 722/721 King *Hanun* of Gaza joined such a rebellion with other cities, and was suppressed by Sargon in 720 BCE. The siege of Ekron by Sargon II is depicted on his palace walls at Dur-Sharukkin. In 712 BCE *Yamani* replaced the king of Ashdod and revolted against the Assyrians. *Yamani* is mentioned as a 'Greek', as his name is reminiscent of the term 'Greek' in Semitic languages. As retaliation Sargon II attacked the city in 712, leaving a basalt victory stele (Dothan 1971: 192–7).

After Sargon II's death in battle, numerous rebellions broke out against the Assyrian administration and Ekron and Ashkelon joined in; these were crushed by Sennacherib's campaign to Philistia and Judah in 701 BCE. In the Sennacherib annals, Ashdod, Gaza, and Ekron are mentioned; in Ekron, the Assyrian king reinstated the original king *Padi* after a local revolt. It seems that the Assyrians preserved the independence of the Philistines to some degree as a buffer zone between Assyria and Egypt and even transferring territory from Judah to them (Tadmor 1966: 97). Historical evidence from the Iron IIC includes texts from the reigns of Sennacherib, Essarhaddon, and Ashurbanipal (Pritchard 1969: 287, 291, 294), mentioning Ashdod and Ekron; various ostraca testify to the flourishing of the wine industry at this city at Ashkelon (Stager 2008: 1584–5). The royal inscription from Ekron is of primary importance (Fig. 47.2) (Gitin 2003: 284–6, fig. 3, see below); it reads: 'The house (which) Akhayush (Ikausu/Achish), son of Padi, son of Ysd, son of Ada, son of Ya'ir, ruler (*sar* ') of Ekron, built for Pythogaia (*Ptgyh*), his lady. May she bless him, and protect him, and prolong his days, and bless his land.'

Herodotus mentions that Ashdod (referred to as Azotus) was besieged by King Psamtich I (663–609 BCE) for no fewer than twenty-nine years (Herodotus, *Histories* II, 157). Ashdod is also mentioned as one of the six coastal sites in the prism of Nebuchadnezzar (Pritchard 1969: 308), while the reference to the 'remnants of Ashdod' together with Ashkelon, Gaza, and Ekron (Jer. 25:20) possibly indicates the relative weakness of Ashdod during this period. Gath is notably absent from the Iron IIC texts. Around the year 600 BCE the Philistines cities of Ashdod, Ekron, Ashkelon, and Gaza were destroyed by Nebuchadnezzar. During the Persian and Hellenistic periods, Philistia was probably still viewed as a geopolitical entity, although the Philistines as a people ceased to exist. Settlements near Nippur were probably

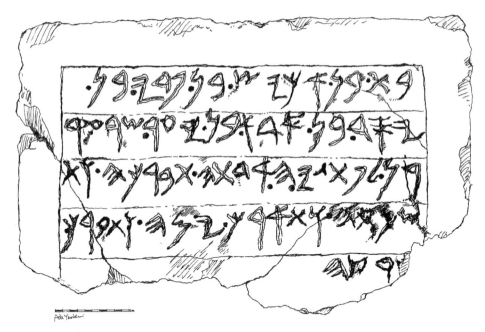

FIG. 47.2 The royal dedicatory inscription from Ekron (Gitin 2003: fig 3; courtesy Seymour Gitin)

named after Gaza (*Hasatu*) and Ashkelon (*Iskalanu*) as they were populated by exiles from Philistia (Zadok 1978: 61).

ARCHAEOLOGICAL RECORD

The main Philistine cities or pentapolis known from the Iron I are still the major sites to be considered during Iron II. Each of the four excavated cities, Tel Miqne-Ekron, Ashdod, Ashkelon, and Tell es-Safi/Gath, displays variable characteristics in the different sub-periods of the Iron II. Surveys also indicate a rise in sites in the Shephelah and Philistia during this period (Shavit 2000: 215–16).

Iron IIA (*c.* 975–800 BCE)

While Tel Miqne-Ekron was a large fortified city at the turn of the Iron I, after the violent destruction of Stratum IVA the site becomes much smaller, as the lower city (Fields IV and III) is not occupied until the Iron IIC (Dothan and Gitin 1993: 1056). Stratum IVA already exhibits Iron IIA pottery forms and probably represents a transitional Iron I–IIA phase dated to the early 10th century BCE. Otherwise, only scanty remains on the acropolis reflect Iron IIA material (Stratum III), and the site shrinks to an area of 4ha. At Ashdod there is no clear violent destruction of the final Iron I stratum, XI, and the city grows during the Iron IIA, with several residential quarters uncovered in Areas G, H, K, and M. A continuation of architecture is evidenced in Stratum X together with a change in material culture represented by the absence of Philistine Bichrome pottery and the introduction of Iron IIA pottery forms. During this period there is clear evidence that the site is fortified, including a city wall and a four-chambered gate in Area M, Strata X–IX (Dothan and Porath 1982: 7–30, plan 5). The lower city largely expands to a size of 22ha. The evidence from Tell es-Safi shows an expansion of the site during the Iron IIA to an area of 50ha, especially during the latter part of this period (Phase A3) (Maeir 2003; Uziel and Maeir 2005). Especially important is Stratum A3 in Area A on the eastern slope of the tell, where an extensive destruction is probably dated to the campaign of Hazaʾel (the end of the 9th century BCE). This stratum included several domestic and industrial units and a rich assemblage of complete pottery vessels, reflecting both the 'Late Philistine Decorated' style and typical late Iron IIA forms (in similarity to the Lachish, Level IV assemblage). During this period a 2km-long trench surrounded the tell, probably related to the Aramean siege of the city. The evidence from Ashkelon is still fragmentary concerning the Iron IIA; building remains and pits in Phase 16 of Grid 38 represent this period (Stager 2008: 1584). The fortifications erected during the Iron I continued to be in use until the end of the Iron II (Stager 2008: 1584). The Iron IIA is also represented in other excavated sites in Philistia and its borders, though in relatively limited remains, as at Tel Batash Stratum IV, Beth Shemesh Stratum IIB, Tell Qasile Stratum IX, and at Gezer Strata VIII–VI, with a six-chamber gate and fortifications, as well as Tel Zippor Stratum I, Tel Zeitah, Tel Nagila Stratum IV, Tel Hamid Stratum VI, the cemetery at Azor, Tell el-Hesi, a small settlement in Tel Gerisa, and Tel Mor Stratum 3. More extensive evidence was reported from Tel Haror (Oren 1993a) and Tel Seraʿ Stratum VII (Oren 1993b), but is not published yet.

Iron IIB (800–701 BCE)

During this period Ekron remains a small site (Stratum IIB–A), while Ashdod expands to an area of 26ha with an industrial zone in Area D including mostly a large potter's workshop (Dothan 1971: 89–92) and possibly a shrine related to it (Dothan and Freedman 1967: 132). The fortification in Area M continues and the gate area is expanded to a six-chambered structure (Stratum VIII, Dothan and Porath 1982: 19–25, plans 9, 12), which probably dates to the late 9th and 8th centuries. The destruction of Stratum VIII at Ashdod, evidenced at Area D by mass burials, is associated with Sargon II's campaign against the revolt of *Yamani* in 712 BCE (Dothan 1971: 92, 101). During this period, to the north of the tell, an impressive fortress or palace of Assyrian style was built (Kogan-Zehavi 2006). Oren reconstructs a large Assyrian complex at Ruqeish (Oren 1993b, Phases III–II). Assyrian influence or control is also evidenced in a well-preserved vaulted building from Tell Jemmeh (van Beek 1993: 672), also including many Assyrian 'palace ware' vessels. A rampart and a glacis from the Iron IIB at Tel Haror Areas D, E, and G (Oren 1993a: 584) were destroyed in the 7th century and could also be related to the Assyrian administration. The Stratum V fortress at Tel Seraʿ Area C is possibly Assyrian in style (Oren 1993b: 1333–4) as well. The Iron IIB at Tell es-Safi/Gath shows a decrease to an area of 25ha; the main area is characterized by domestic buildings and agricultural activities (Stratum A2) and the majority of its pottery assemblage is Judahite (Uziel and Maeir 2005: 62). During this same period excavations at the nearby site of Kfar Menahem indicated a large-scale industrial industrial activity of some sort (Ben-Shlomo, Shai and Maeir 2004: 22). Ashkelon has yielded little information on this period (Phase

15). The Iron IIB is also evidenced at Gezer Stratum VI, Beth Shemesh Stratum IIA, Batash Stratum III, a city wall at Ashdod-Yam, a massive fortification system at Tell el-Hesi Stratum VII, Tel Nagila Stratum II, Tell Qasile Stratum VIII with a large public building, Tel Hamid Stratum V, and Tel Mor Stratum 2.

Iron IIC (701–604/586 BCE)

The final phase of the Iron Age, the Iron IIC, illustrates another change in settlement pattern in Philistia. The site of Ekron largely expands to the areas settled in the Iron I (Strata IC–IB, Fields III and IV in the lower city) to about 20ha, and fortifications are restored, including a three-entryway gate built in Field III; the upper city was also rebuilt. On and around the tell 115 olive oil installations were built (Dothan and Gitin 1993: 1056) with a production capacity of 500–1000 tonnes, making Ekron the largest industrial centre for the production of olive oil in antiquity thus far excavated. An assemblage of four-horned limestone altars was found in relation to these installations.

The hallmark of this period is the temple-palace complex in upper Field IV (Complex 650) (Fig. 47.3), built directly above a series of Iron I public buildings (Gitin 2003: 284–6, fig. 1). In the complex a royal dedicatory inscription of Padi, king of Ekron, was found (Fig. 47.2 above). The main building and additional auxilary structures contained thousands of storage jars and other vessels, caches of silver and iron, a Phoenician figurine, stone altars, silver hoards, and a large number of ivory objects, some of them very large, and probably dated and sourced to Late Kingdom Egypt. This temple-palace complex shows possible Assyrian affinities in its plan, while the sanctuary resembles Kition's Phoenician temple. The complex probably administrated olive oil production at the site, which is estimated to be the largest of its period in the Near East. This industry was conducted under either the auspices or the direct control of the Assyrians in the earlier part of this period (Stratum IC). Yet the latter part of the 7th century (Stratum IB), while the Assyrian Empire falls and the Egyptians return to control parts of Canaan, the structure and the industry continue. The fortified settlement and olive oil industry of nearby Tel Batash (Stratum II) should be understood in relation to the prosperity of Ekron (Mazar and Panitz-Cohen 2001: 281–2).

At Ashkelon there is evidence of a large commercial city, a 'market quarter' in Grid 50 (Stager 2008), and a 'royal' wine press (Stager 2008: 1584) in Grid 38, Phase 14. The market included a row of shops and storerooms and yielded finds such as juglets and ostraca, indicating commerce in wine. A large amount of agricultural products was found *in situ* in the commercial quarter (Stager 2008: 1584) and is dated to 600–604 BCE; it contained cereals imported from the Shephelah and Judah. Evidently, the city was a major port of the region. However, Ashdod during this period is probably reduced in size; the residential areas are less planned and indicate more outdoor agricultural activities. The Iron IIC is not evidenced at Tell es-Safi/Gath and this city was largely deserted after it was captured by Judah earlier in the Iron IIB. Some of the other Iron IIB settlements, such as Tel Sera', Tel Haror, Tell Jemmeh, Ashdod Yam, and Yavneh, continue into the Iron IIC, but otherwise there is a decrease in the remains in most sites. The destruction of Ekron (604 BCE, Stratum IB), Ashdod (c.600 BCE, Stratum VI), and Ashkelon (604 BCE) by Nebuchadnezzar II is well attested by destruction levels at the sites. The early 6th century BCE is represented at Ekron (Stratum IA) by fragmentary architectural remains and pottery.

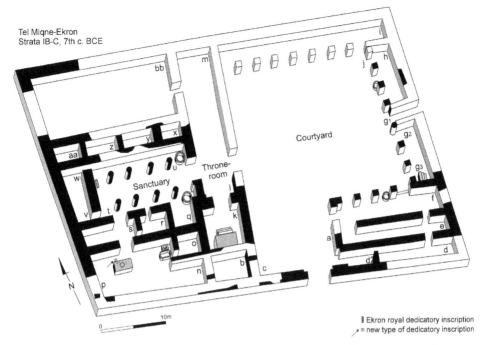

Tel Miqne-Ekron
Strata IB-C, 7th c. BCE

Courtyard

Throne-room

Sanctuary

10m

0

N

▌ Ekron royal dedicatory inscription
⚹ ⊠ new type of dedicatory inscription

FIG. 47.3 Temple-Palace Complex 650, Ekron (Gitin 2003: fig 1; courtesy Seymour Gitin)

MATERIAL CULTURE

Pottery and relative chronology

The end of the Iron II in southern Palestine is well defined by the Babylonian destructions; however, the beginning of this period as well as its sub-phasing are often less distinct and not related to historical events, but rather to the definition of cultural-ceramic horizons. A possible exception could be the late 8th-century Assyrian campaigns.

Therefore, the beginning of the Iron IIA is defined by the appearance of new forms and decoration styles, namely the red slipped and burnished ware (see Fig. 47.4), and the virtual disappearance of Philistine Bichrome style. In several cases, as at Ekron (Stratum IVA) and Tell Qasile (Stratum X–IX), late degenerated Philistine forms appear together with red slipped and burnished ware, and thus this phase could be defined as intermediate or transitional Iron I–IIA. The Iron IIA pottery is characterized by a development of late Iron I forms, as carinated bowls and chalices, and an introduction of new forms, such as open bowls with ridges under the rim and various types of rounded and holemouth kraters, and holemouth and sack-shaped jars. Various globular jugs and dipper juglets become much more popular during this period. Towards the end of the Iron IIA the Iron I forms completely disappear. Many of the undecorated forms appearing in Philistia are typical of this region, and a coastal pottery tradition can be defined (Gitin 1998: 165–7); types popular in Judah and the Shephelah, as well as in northern Israel, are rare in Philistia. Various types of cooking jugs

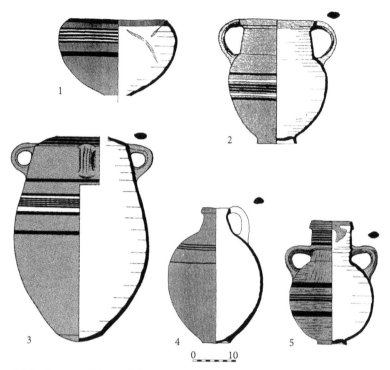

FIG 47.4 Main forms of Late Philistine Decorated Ware ('Ashdod Ware')

appear in Philistia during the Iron II and possibly continue the tradition of the use of jugs for cooking introduced during the Iron I in the Philistine cities.

A distinct group of decorated pottery ware that is also typical for Philistia during the Iron IIA–B is defined as 'Ashdod Ware' or 'Late Philistine Decorated Ware' (Fig. 47.4) (Ben-Shlomo, Shai, and Maeir 2004). This ware is characterized mostly by Iron II 'coastal' forms (as the globular kraters, amphorae, various jugs, and sack-shaped jars), and a distinct decoration technique of thick red slip, meticulous vertical burnish, and black and white linear decoration. Various zoomorphic vessels and terracottas from Ashdod and Ekron also appear with this decoration style (Dothan 1971: figs 68–71; Ben-Shlomo, Shai, and Maeir 2004: 9, 12). The ware appears in various sites of Philistia and its vicinity, such as Ashdod, Ekron, Tell es-Safi/Gath, Ashkelon, Tel Mor, Ruqeish, Tel Batash, Tel Zeitah, Tel Sera', Gezer, Tel Hamid, and Tel Nagila in the respective Iron IIA and occasionally Iron IIB strata. It is most common, so far, at Ashdod and Tell es-Safi/Gath. While the forms and decorative motifs do not show an Aegean connection, this style can be defined as 'Philistine' on account of its well-defined spatial and temporal appearance, and it probably replaced the Philistine Bichrome pottery as fine table ware, although appearing in much smaller relative quantities. This pottery also shows certain 'Phoenician' attributes, but was found to be locally made at Ashdod and Tell es-Safi, according to its find spots in pottery kilns at Ashdod (Areas M and D) and to petrographic and chemical analysis (Ben-Shlomo, Shai, and Maeir 2004). Iron IIA imported 'Red on Black' and White Painted as well as Phoenician pottery are quite rare in Iron IIA Philistia, and only appear commonly in the Yarkon Basin region at Tell Qasile, Azor, Tel Gerishe, and Aphek.

The late Iron IIB ceramic horizon is characterized by appearance of some new forms, including Assyrian-influenced forms such as carinated bowls and bottles, and ridged cooking pots and small jugs; the red slip and burnish treatment is not as commonly used, while the pottery itself seems to be more mass produced and standardized (similar to Lachish, Level III). 'Late Philistine' ('Ashdod Ware') pottery still appears, but generally, the differences between Philistia and the Shephelah gradually diminish. There is a gradual change in the pottery assemblages of the Iron IIB and IIC; the appearance of several imported groups from the west and the cessation of the Late Philistine Ware during the Iron IIC should be noted, yet the separation between these horizons is based usually on the Assyrian destruction levels (as at Lachish, Level III). During this period a rich assemblage of Archaic and 'East Greek' and 'wild-goat' style pottery as well as Egyptian metal cultic items were uncovered in the commercial market quarter of Ashkelon (Master 2003: 59–61) and at Mezad Hashaviahu (Fantalkin 2001), where it was suggested to represent the presence of Greek mercenaries (Niemeier 2001: 23). Some of the forms of the final Iron II continue to appear and develop during the Babylonian and early Persian periods.

Other aspects of material culture

The iconography and religion of Iron IIA–B Philistia is not very well known to us yet, as there is hardly any direct evidence from temples except several cultic rooms in domestic or industrial buildings at Ashdod, Area D (Dothan and Freedman 1967: 132–3, Pl. xix) and Area K (Dothan and Ben-Shlomo 2005: 47). However, a group of terracottas can attest indirectly to both the iconography and cult of Iron II Philistia. This includes the new find of a large favissa near Tel Yavneh (Ziffer 2007), which includes hundreds of house models/stands and other cultic vessels (mostly chalices), probably dated to the late Iron IIA or early Iron IIB. The favissa was probably related to a temple on the tell or its vicinity. The iconography of this assemblage includes depictions of animals (mostly bovines, but also lions) and humans (mostly female) as well as pastoral and architectural depictions. Most compositions are similar to the traditional Canaanite and Syrian cultic representations, but show stylistic Philistine iconographic elements echoing Iron I figurines (Ziffer 2007: 19, 28–9). Somewhat earlier, the musician's stand from Ashdod (Fig. 47.5; Dothan and Ben-Shlomo 2005: 180–84), as well as another house model fragment found with it, resemble the Yavneh assemblage. At Ashdod 'debased' examples of Aegean-style 'Ashdoda' figurines were found in Iron II contexts, showing a certain continuation in Aegean-style cult practices.

During the Iron IIC, Complex 650 at Ekron was probably partly a cultic building. The inscription in the *cella* of the temple (Figs 47.2 and 47.3 above) was dedicated to the goddess *Ptgya* (Gitin 2003: 284), who is possibly connected to the Aegean goddess *Potnia*. Other finds from the temple include ostraca reading to 'Ba'al and to Padi' (Gitin 2003: 288, fig. 5) and other cultic vessels. This assemblage, which is yet to be published, possibly indicates again a mixture of Aegean and Canaanite traditions, or probably a situation in which the Aegean deity is amalgamated into a local religious structure (Gitin 2003: 292).

Burial practices are hardly evidenced in Iron II Philistia, especially in the major cities—a situation similar to that of the Iron I. Late Iron I and Iron IIA tombs at Azor show variable mortuary practices including pit burials, brick-case burials, and multiple burials as well as rarer forms of jar burials and cremation (Dothan 1961). During the Iron IIB, cremation

FIG. 47.5. The musician's stand from Ashdod (courtesy Israel Antiquities Authority)

burials also appear at Ruqeish and Tell el-Farah South. The rising popularity of this practice during the Iron IIB–C could be strongly influenced by the Phoenician culture. It is hoped that new results from Tell es-Safi/Gath and Ashkelon will help to clarify this issue.

DISCUSSION

An evaluation of the Iron Age II in this region must address the issue of the continuation of Philistine material culture, as well as its social and political organization initiated during the Iron Age I, in relation to the immigrant society from the Aegean and/or Cyprus. The 'urban imposition' suggested for Philistia during the Iron I (as at Ekron) may be more evident during the Iron IIA in the sites of Ashdod and Gath. The influence of external powers such as the Arameans during the 9th and the Assyrians during the 8th century BCE on the urbanization of Philistia and the southern Levant is crucial, but its nature is not clear to us yet. It is often postulated that the political structure of the Philistine cities was probably some sort of city-state, as seems to be indicated in the biblical descriptions (Shai 2006: 348–52), although the Philistines are often mentioned as a collective (as in 1 Kgs. 15: 27, 16: 15–17). During the Iron IIA, this situation may have continued (Shai 2006: 358) with shifting dominance of the cities. The possibility of a more centralized monarchy type of organization is also suggested (Machinist 2000: 57–9), with some similarity to the situation in the hill-lands. During the Iron IIB, there is no longer a reference to a unified Philistine entity, but only to the separate cities, which became more independent. The archaeological data suggests that during the Iron II, power shifted between the various Philistine centres. Ashdod and Tell es-Safi/Gath were dominant; in the following Iron IIB Ashdod was the major Philistine site. During the

Iron IIC, Ashkelon and Ekron prospered as trade centres for all the Near East, a development probably initiated by the Assyrians but which continued after the fall of the Assyrians, under Egyptian control, until the Babylonian destructions. Ekron was a centre for production and distribution of olive oil, while Ashkelon was a centre for production and distribution of wine (Stager 2008: 1585) as well as a major port.

Preliminary observations of the very rich assemblage from Yavneh show certain stylistic similarities to Iron I Philistine iconographic traditions as well as to a more 'Canaanite' tradition of iconography and motifs. This cultic mixture probably reflects the situation in the Tell Qasile temples of the final Iron I. It is still difficult to identify direct contacts between Philistia and the Aegean region during the Iron II, although the suggestion of a late wave of immigrants from the Aegean or 'Archaic mercenaries' has occasionally been raised (Niemeier 2001). So far, it seems that certain Aegean-affiliated elements of the material culture are preserved or modified during this period (as terracottas and cooking jugs), but their presence is gradually decreasing. It seems that Philistia during the Iron II, while not necessarily a unified political entity, had its cultural identity still stemming from the immigrant culture of the Iron I. The cities were ruled by local Philistine kings, as attested by the external texts and the Ekron inscription, appearing as late as the early 7th century BCE, in which both the king of Ekron and its main goddess have Aegean names. Nevertheless, many aspects of the Iron II culture in Philistia are not yet sufficiently known.

Suggested reading

Ehrlich, C. S. (1996). *The Philistines in Transition: A History from ca. 1000–730 B.C.E.* Leiden: Brill.

Finkelstein, I . (2002). The Philistines in the Bible: a late monarchic perspective. *Journal for the Study of the Old Testament* 27: 131–67.

Gitin, S . (1995). Tel Miqne-Ekron in the 7th century B.C.E.: the impact of economic innovation and foreign cultural influences on a Neo-Assyrian vassal city state. In S. Gitin (ed.), *Recent Excavations in Israel: A View to the West—Reports on Kabri, Nami, Miqne-Ekron, Dor and Ashkelon*. Dubuque, Ia.: Kendall/Hunt, 61–79.

—— (1997). Late Philistines. In E. M. Meyers (ed.), *The Oxford Encyclopedia of Archaeology in the Near East*, vol. 4. New York: Oxford University Press, 311–13.

—— T. Dothan, and J. Naveh (1997). A royal dedicatory inscription from Ekron. *Israel Exploration Journal* 48: 1–16.

Herzog, Z., and L. Singer-Avitz (2004). Redefining the centre: the emergence of state in Judah. *Tel Aviv* 31: 209–44.

Na'aman, N . (2003). Ekron under the Assyrian and Egyptian Empires. *Bulletin of the American Schools of Oriental Research* 332: 81–91.

Stone, B. J. (1995). The Philistines and acculturation: culture change and ethnic continuity in the Iron Age. *Bulletin of the American Schools of Oriental Research* 298: 7–32.

References

Ben-Shlomo, D., I. Shai, and A. M. Maeir (2004). Late Philistine Decorated Ware (Ashdod Ware): typology, chronology, and production centers. *Bulletin of the American Schools of Oriental Research* 335: 1–35.

Dothan, M. (1961). Excavations at Azor, 1960. *Israel Exploration Journal* 11: 171–5.

—— (1971). *Ashdod II–III: The Second and Third Seasons of Excavations, 1963, 1965—Soundings in 1967* (2 vols). Jerusalem: Department of Antiquities and Museums, Ministry of Education and Culture/Department of Archaeology, Hebrew University of Jerusalem/Israel Exploration Society.

—— and D. Ben-Shlomo (2005). *Ashdod VI: The Excavations of Areas H and K (1968–1969)*. Jerusalem: Israel Antiquities Authority.

—— and D. N. Freedman (1967). *Ashdod I: The First Season of Excavations, 1962*. Jerusalem: Department of Antiquities and Museums, Ministry of Education and Culture/Department of Archaeology, Hebrew University of Jerusalem/Israel Exploration Society.

—— and Y. Porath (1982). *Ashdod IV: Excavation of Area M—The Fortifications of the Lower City*. Jerusalem: Department of Antiquities and Museums, Ministry of Education and Culture/Department of Archaeology, Hebrew University of Jerusalem/Israel Exploration Society.

Dothan, T., and S. Gitin (1993). Miqne, Tel (Ekron). In E. Stern (ed.), *The New Encyclopedia of Archaeological Excavations in the Holy Land*, vol. 3. Jerusalem: Israel Exploration Society/New York: Simon & Schuster, 1051–9.

Fantalkin, A. (2001). Mezad Hashavyahu: its material culture and historical background. *Tel Aviv* 28: 3–165.

Gitin, S. (1998). Philistia in transition: the tenth century B.C.E. and beyond. In S. Gitin, A. Mazar, and E. Stern (eds), *Mediterranean Peoples in Transition: Thirteenth to Early Tenth Centuries BCE*. Jerusalem: Israel Exploration Society, 162–83.

—— (2003). Israelite and Philistine cult and the archaeological record in Iron Age II: the 'smoking gun' phenomenon. In W. G. Dever and S. Gitin (eds), *Symbiosis, Symbolism and the Power of the Past: Canaan, Ancient Israel, and Their Neighbors from the Late Bronze Age through Roman Palaestina*. Winona Lake, Ind.: Eisenbrauns, 279–95.

Kogan-Zehavi, E. (2006). Tel Ashdod. *Hadashot Arkheologiyot* 118. http://www.hadashot-esi.org.il/report_detail_Eng.asp?id=340&mag_id=111 (accessed 26 Aug. 2010).

Machinist, P. (2000). Biblical traditions: the Philistines and Israelite history. In E. D. Oren (ed.), *The Sea Peoples and Their World: A Reassessment*. Philadelphia: University Museum, 53–83.

Maeir, A. M. (2003). Notes and news: Tell es-Safi/Gath. *Israel Exploration Journal* 57: 237–46.

Master, D. M. (2003). Trade and politics: Ashkelon's balancing act in the seventh century B.C.E. *Bulletin of the American Schools of Oriental Research* 330: 47–64.

Mazar, A., and N. Panitz-Cohen (2001). *Timnah (Tel Batash) II*. Jerusalem: Institute of Archaeology, Hebrew University of Jerusalem.

Niemeier, W.-D. (2001). Archaic Greeks in the Orient: textual and archaeological evidence. *Bulletin of the American Schools of Oriental Research* 322: 11–32

Oren, E. D. (1993a). Haror, Tel. In E. Stern (ed.), *The New Encyclopedia of Archaeological Excavations in the Holy Land*, vol. 2. Jerusalem: Israel Exploration Society/New York: Simon & Schuster, 580–84.

—— (1993b). Tel Sera'. In E. Stern (ed.), *The New Encyclopedia of Archaeological Excavations in the Holy Land*, vol. 4. Jerusalem: Israel Exploration Society/New York: Simon & Schuster, 1329–35.

Pritchard, J. B. (ed.) (1969). *Ancient Near Eastern Texts Relating to the Old Testament*, 3rd edn with suppl. Princeton, NJ: Princeton University Press.

Shai, I. (2006). The political organization of the Philistines. In A. M. Maeir and P. de Miroschedji (eds), *'I Will Speak the Riddles of Ancient Times': Archaeological and Historical Studies in*

Honor of Amihai Mazar on the Occasion of His Sixtieth Birthday, vol. 1. Winona Lake, Ind.: Eisenbrauns, 347–59.

Shavit, A. (2000). Settlement patterns in the Ayalon Valley in the Bronze and Iron Ages. *Tel Aviv* 27: 189–230.

Stager, L. E. (2008). Tel Ashkelon. In E. Stern (ed.), *The New Encyclopedia of Archaeological Excavations in the Holy Land*, vol. 5: *Supplementary Volume*. Jerusalem: Israel Exploration Society/Washington, DC: Biblical Archaeology Society, 1578–86.

Tadmor, H. (1966). Philistia under Assyrian rule. *Biblical Archaeologist* 29: 86–102.

Uziel, J., and A. M. Maeir (2005). Scratching the surface at Gath: implications of the Tell es-Safi/Gath surface survey. *Tel Aviv* 32: 50–75.

van Beek, G. (1993). Jemmeh, Tell. In E. Stern (ed.), *The New Encyclopedia of Archaeological Excavations in the Holy Land*, vol. 2. Jerusalem: Israel Exploration Society/New York: Simon & Schuster, 667–74.

Zadok, R. (1978). Phoenicians, Philistines, and Moabites in Mesopotamia. *Bulletin of the American Schools of Oriental Research* 230: 57–65.

Ziffer, I. (2007). *In the Field of the Philistines: Cult Furnishings from the Favissa of a Yavneh Temple*. Tel Aviv: Eretz Israel Museum.

CHAPTER 48

··

ISRAEL DURING THE IRON
AGE II PERIOD

··

ANN E. KILLEBREW

INTRODUCTION

··

Israel, as a person, people, region, and kingdom, plays a prominent role in the biblical narrative. Israel (literally 'struggles with God') is first mentioned in the Bible as an alternative
name given to Jacob after he wrestled with an angel (Gen. 32: 28–9). It also appears as a collective name for the twelve sons of Jacob (the 'Children of Israel'), the eponymous founders
of the twelve tribes who traced their ancestry back to Jacob (Gen. 32: 32; 49: 16, 28; Exod. 1:
9). According to the Bible, following the rebellion of the northern tribes (House of Joseph
(Ephraim and Manasseh) and the tribes of Galilee and Transjordan) against Solomon's
successor, Rehoboam, 'Israel' is used to distinguish them from the southern tribes (Judah,
Simeon, and Benjamin) that remained loyal to the house of David (e.g. 1 Kgs. 12).[1] The
archaeology of Israel as a regional territory, also referred to as the northern kingdom, is the
topic of this chapter.

The earliest appearance of name 'Israel' in the Pharaoh Merenptah's late 13th-century
account of his campaign to the Levant provides tantalizing clues to a pre-Iron Age Israel.
Although there is a consensus that the hieroglyphs in his victory stela do translate as Israel
and refer to a 'people', the particular geographic region inhabited by this group remains
less certain.[2] Approximately 350 years pass until 'Israel', as a political entity and territorial
kingdom, reappears in non-biblical texts and inscriptions (see below), most notably the Tel

---

[1] In post-monarchic biblical texts, Israel refers to the peoples of both kingdoms; however, these
may reflect later idealized notions of a unified 'Israel'. For a detailed analysis and survey of the relevant
literature, see Naʾaman (2009a; 2009b). For an alternative interpretation, see Davies (1992: 11–74), who
argues that 'Israel' was a late invention, referring only to the kingdom of Judah at the end of the Iron Age.
Regarding the appearance of 'Israel' in post-monarchic texts, see also Ben Zvi (1995) for a discussion of
the use of the Books of Kings as a source in reconstructing a history of the northern kingdom of Israel,
see Naʾaman (2007).

[2] See e.g. Killebrew (2005: 154–5) for a review of the literature relevant to the appearance of Israel
in the Merenptah Stele. Liverani (2005: 25) and others suggest the central highlands of Canaan as a
probable area of activity for Merenptah's 'Israel'.

Dan and Mesha Stelai. In addition to the biblical account, especially 1 and 2 Kings, the most important sources for constructing a political, social, economic, and material culture history for Iron Age Israel include Egyptian, Assyrian, Moabite, and Aramaic royal inscriptions, ostraca, and other inscribed objects from the southern Levant, and the archaeological evidence, including surveys and excavations (see Grabbe 2007 for an overview of relevant biblical and extra-biblical texts).

Territorial definition

Attempts to reconstruct the borders of the northern kingdom during the Iron II period (c.1000–600 BCE) rely on biblical descriptions of tribal boundaries in the Book of Joshua, chapters 13–19 (see e.g. Aharoni 1979: 248–67) and the twelve administrative districts of Solomon as outlined in 1 Kgs. 4: 7–19 (see e.g. Aharoni 1979: 309–20). The historicity of these boundaries is debated from viewpoints which range from maximalist to minimalist (e.g. Ash 1995; Hess 1997). Additionally, the territorial and political borders of the kingdom of Israel fluctuated over time, according to historical circumstance.[3] For the purposes of this chapter, 'Israel' is defined geographically as encompassing the northern central hill country (bordered by Bethel in the south), the Galilee (bordered to the north by the Litani River and mountains of Lebanon and to the east by the Golan Heights), the Sharon Plain, and the Jordan, Jezreel, and Huleh Valleys. Phoenicia (Aubet, Ch. 46 above) lies to the north and west, Aram and the Aramean territories (Mazzoni, Ch. 45 above) mark the northern and eastern limits, with Judah (Hardin, Ch. 49 below) and Ammon (Younker, Ch. 50 below) forming the eastern and southern borders, respectively (Fig. 48.1). This geographical designation does not necessarily reflect shifting political, cultural, religious, linguistic, or ethnic boundaries that the region witnessed during the Iron II period.

Historical and chronological cornerstones

The dating of Iron II sites, particularly strata traditionally attributed to the 10th and 9th centuries BCE, remains a topic of spirited debate (see Finkelstein and Mazar 2007; Hardin, Ch. 49 below). At stake is the historical reliability of the biblical account describing a highly developed 10th-century united monarchy during the reigns of David and Solomon; challenges to the reliability of a nearly century-long tradition of ceramic analyses that form the basis for dating Iron II strata; and questions regarding state formation in the southern Levant. Pharaoh Shoshenq's (Shishak's) campaign to the southern Levant in c.926 BCE is the most significant 10th-century chronological linchpin. Although the historicity of this event is not disputed, the nature, extent, and physical evidence at locations mentioned in his itinerary are debated (see e.g. Wilson 2005 for a recent treatment; for the parallel biblical account, see 1 Kgs. 14: 25–8). Neo-Assyrian military incursions into Israel, which culminated in the conquest of the capital city Samaria by Sargon II in 722/721 or 720 BCE, serve as 8th-century chronological pegs for dating northern kingdom Iron II sites (see e.g. Kelle 2002 and Tappy

---

[3]   See Na'aman (2009a; 2009b: esp. 335–8) for a discussion of this territory, and Finkelstein (2011b) for a recent interpretation of the changing boundaries of the northern kingdom.

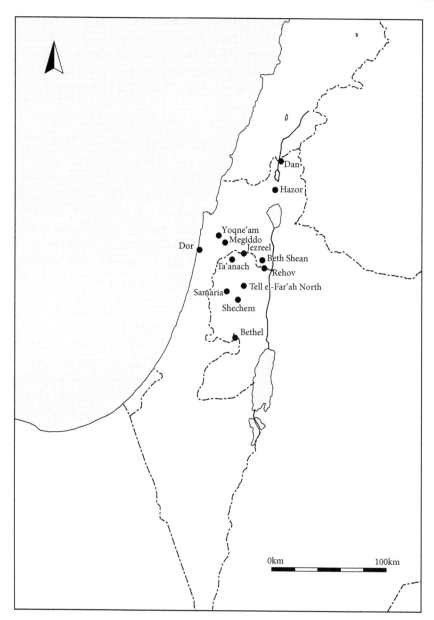

FIG. 48.1 Map of Iron Age II sites in Israel

2007 for an overview of the various views and dates for the fall of Samaria). These events, often also attested in the biblical account, together with Syro-Palestinian inscriptions, are invaluable for our understanding of Iron II Israel. Among the latter group of texts, the most noteworthy include the Tel Dan and Mesha Stelae and the Samaria Ostraca (see below; for a recent analysis of these texts within their larger historical and archaeological context, see Rainey and Notley 2006: chs 12 and 13, esp. 185–9, 203–5, 211–13, 221–2, and bibliography therein).

ARCHAEOLOGICAL EVIDENCE FROM
SURVEYS AND EXCAVATIONS

Settlement patterns during the Iron Age II period

Surveys conducted in the central hill country (Samaria), in the Jezreel Valley, and in Upper and Lower Galilee provide the framework for reconstructing Iron Age settlement patterns. The results present a mixed picture of Iron II settlement in northern Palestine. Surveys in the Upper Galilee indicate a decline in settlements from 71 documented sites during the Iron I, dropping to 36 settlements in the subsequent Iron II period. Part of this perceived decline may be due to the difficulties in precisely dating the Iron Age ceramics collected during the survey (Frankel et al. 2001: esp. 128). In the Lower Galilee, surface survey has revealed a different settlement picture. During the Iron IIA, earlier Iron I settlements were deserted and appear to have been replaced by new large fortified sites. In the southern sector, a number of fortified settlements are documented. Due to the paucity of Late Bronze and Iron I settlements in the northern region of the Lower Galilee, the increase in rural settlement activity during the Iron IIA is particularly noteworthy. By the later 9th century, some of these settlements were abandoned, which Gal attributes to the Aramean threat. The population increased during the 8th century until the Assyrian conquest, which resulted in the devastation of the Lower Galilee. Several centuries passed before the region began to recover from the Assyrian destruction and deportations (Gal 1992: 94–109).

Zertal's landmark survey of northern Samaria (the territory of Manasseh) demonstrates a doubling of the number of sites from the Iron I to II, reaching an apex of over 300 during the 9th and 8th centuries BCE. Most of the Iron II sites are newly founded. Approximately half of these are farmsteads, one third are villages, and the remaining c.20 per cent are towns and cities. On the basis of his survey results, Zertal concludes that the majority of the population lived on farms or in villages. Smaller numbers of enclosures, caves sites, fortresses/tower/ camps, and cultic sites have also been documented. Following the Assyrian destruction of Samaria in 722/721, there was a dramatic decrease in settlements that he attributes to the Assyrian deportation and resettlement policies (for a summary of the survey results, see Zertal 2001 and references therein).

Further to the south, Finkelstein and Lederman's survey of the territory of Ephraim revealed a similar settlement pattern. The Late Bronze Age is represented by only a handful of sites. The Iron I period witnessed a noteworthy increase in settlements, with nearly 100 sites attributed to the Iron I/II transition. Settlement density peaks in the later Iron II period, with over 200 sites identified, representing one of the most densely populated periods in this region (Finkelstein, Lederman, and Bunimovitz 1997: 893–902, 948–51).

Two views have emerged regarding the interpretation of this survey data. Gal (1992: 94–6) and Faust (2003; 2007) propose an abandonment of villages at the end of the 11th century BCE, with the population shifting to fortified settlements. In Faust's opinion, this abandonment of the rural sector represents the emergence of an 'Israelite polity' that coincides with the rise of a 10th-century united monarchy in the southern Levant. Others have challenged this interpretation, on both methodological and archaeological grounds (e.g. Finkelstein 2005; Herzog 2007), disputing the claim of widespread desertion of rural settlements and pointing out that early Iron II centres are largely administrative, not residential. The debate remains unresolved. Survey evidence presents a partial and unstratified record of the past. This, combined with the problematic nature of our understanding of ceramic development during the late 11th–9th centuries, especially in rural areas, limits our ability to interpret the data.

The rise of regional kingdoms: Israel during the 10th and 9th centuries BCE (Iron IIA)

Traditionally dated to the 10th century, the Iron II period has been linked to the united monarchy in the biblical account; more recently, however, this association has undergone intense scrutiny. At stake are the historicity of Kings David and Solomon and the nature of state formation in the region. A re-examination of the ceramic and stratigraphic evidence, combined with the analysis of hundreds of ^{14}C samples, indicates that features associated with the Iron IIA period extend into the 9th century (see e.g. Levy and Higham 2005 for a variety of views). Based on these recent studies, estimates for the beginning of the Iron II period ranges in date between 980 and 920 BCE, continuing through the mid- to late 9th century (see e.g. Finkelstein 2011c and Mazar 2011 for two differing viewpoints and bibliography therein). The latter part of this period coincides with increased Aramean interactions with Israel. Aram's incursions into northern Palestine are best illustrated by the Tel Dan Stele, which contains the victory boasts of an Aramean king, most likely Hazael, who had conquered the city (for a recent discussion of the stela, see e.g. Suriano 2007 and bibliography therein). In my discussion of the Iron IIA, I follow Herzog and Singer-Avitz's (2006) division into two phases: the Early and Late Iron IIA.[4]

The initial stages of the Iron II are identified by a distinctive change in material cultural, most notably red slipped hand-burnished pottery (see Zarzeki-Peleg 1997 and Herzog and Singer-Avitz 2006 for a detailed ceramic discussion). In northern Palestine, many Iron I sites are characterized by the continuation of Late Bronze Age Canaanite material culture, especially at sites located along the coast or in the valleys (see Gilboa, Ch. 41 above). Some of these Iron I settlements met a violent end (e.g. Iron I levels at Megiddo Stratum VIA, Yoqne'am Stratum XVII, and Ta'anach Stratum IB). At other key sites, early Iron II strata rest on scant remains and/or an occupational gap or represent a newly established settlement (e.g. Iron I levels at Hazor XII–XI, Jezreel, and Samaria). The Early Iron IIA is often characterized by modest, unfortified settlements that lack large public structures, especially domestic structures (e.g. Megiddo VB, the modest or pre-settlement remains at preenclosure Jezreel and Samaria Period 0, Yoqne'am Strata XVI–XV, Ta'anach Stratum IIA, and Tell el-Far'ah North Stratum VIIa). At Dor, the transition is more complex. During the Early Iron IIA (which equals Gilboa and Sharon's Transitional Iron I/II), an urban coastal Canaanite/Phoenician culture continues, punctuated by a material cultural break and the appearance of red slipped hand-burnished ware and imported Black-on-Red Ware (Cypro-Geometric III) during the subsequent Late Iron IIA (Gilboa and Sharon 2008; see also Aubet, Ch. 46 above).

---

[4] This has also been termed the transitional Iron I/Iron II (= Early Iron IIA) and Iron IIA (= Late Iron IIA), see e.g. Gilboa and Sharon (2008: 161–3).

The larger settlements of the Late Iron IIA are typified by public architecture marked by the construction of residencies/palaces (e.g. Megiddo VA/IVB), large royal enclosures (e.g. Samaria Periods I–II and Jezreel), and high places (e.g. Dan Strata IVA ('Bamah A')–III (early phases—'Bamah B')); fortifications including walls and gates at a number of sites (e.g. Dan Stratum III (early phases), Jezreel, Yoqne'am Stratum XIV, and Hazor Strata X–VIII); and clear signs of increased prosperity and political consolidation. A remarkable aviary from Rehov Stratum V also dates to this period (Fig. 48.2).

In addition to elite-controlled centralized religious centres, such as the high place at Dan, there is also evidence of popular cultic activities, some clearly in domestic contexts. These include offering stands, model shrines, and incense altars (e.g. Ta'anach, Megiddo, Tell el-Far'ah North, and Rehov (Fig. 48.3); see especially Mazar and Panitz-Cohen 2008 regarding the evidence of popular household religious worship from Rehov). The typical Iron IIA ceramic repertoire includes red slipped hand-burnished bowls (often carinated) and jugs, carinated kraters, holemouth jars, 'Hippo'-type storage jars, amphoriskoi, and imported wares, such as a Cypriot Bichrome jug from Tel Rehov Stratum V (see e.g. Fig. 48.4).

State formation and the rise of regional kingdoms

The appearance of impressive monumental public architecture and clear signs of political and economic consolidation during the Iron IIA period in Israel, considered together with the biblical accounts, have raised questions regarding the process of state formation during the early first millennium in the southern Levant. As N. Yoffee (2005) points out, state formation is context-specific and should be considered within its broader, individual environmental and geopolitical setting (see also Herzog and Singer-Avitz 2006: 188). Proposals range from the rise of ethnicized secondary states beginning in the 9th century, partially in reaction to Assyrian imperialistic expansionist policies in the Levant (e.g. Joffe 2002), to interpretations that reject traditional statehood theoretical models, such as kin-based,

FIG. 48.2 General view of the Iron IIA apiary in Area C, Tel Rehov (Stratum V), looking northeast (courtesy Tel Rehov Expedition, The Hebrew University of Jerusalem)

FIG. 48.3 Iron IIA altar from Area C, southeastern end of the apiary, Tel Rehov (Stratum V) (photograph David Haris; courtesy Tel Rehov Expedition, The Hebrew University of Jerusalem)

FIG. 48.4 Iron IIA ceramic assemblage from Building CH in Area C at Tel Rehov (Stratum V) (photograph Gabi Laron; courtesy Tel Rehov Expedition, The Hebrew University of Jerusalem)

authority patrimonial relationships that served as a substratum throughout the Iron II period (Master 2001 and bibliography therein) or regionally based tribal states or kingdoms (see Steiner, Ch. 44 above, and Bienkowski, Ch. 52 below). These regional kingdoms, which flourished in the southern Levant during the first centuries of the Iron II period, ultimately succumbed to the Neo-Assyrian Empire.

FIG. 48.5 General view of the Iron II high place at Tel Dan (photograph Ann E. Killebrew)

In the shadow of the Assyrian Empire: Israel during the late 9th–mid-/late 8th centuries BCE (Iron IIB)

The decline of Aramean influence in Israel's affairs coincided with an expanding Assyrian empire, as expressed by intensified commercial and trade relations with the West and increased military campaigns to the Levant (see Schneider, Ch. 7 above). The Assyrian imperial relationship with western regional kingdoms, including Israel, is best defined as one between an imperial power and client-states, who acquired wealth via tribute from its vassal kings and war booty. Assyria's primary motivation underlying campaigns to the west seems to be mainly economic, with the goal of controlling trade routes in western Asia, in particular access to the Phoenician ports. Thus the purpose of clientship that character-ized Assyria's relationship with Israel during this period was mainly related to the control of goods and surpluses, rather than territory (see also Bedford 2009: 43–56).

Freed of Aramean interference in the early 8th century following Adad-nirari III's sub-jugation of Damascus, the kingdom of Israel experienced a revitalization that resulted in territorial growth and economic prosperity, particularly during the reign of Jeroboam II. Archaeologically this is expressed at Dan with additional development of the high place (Fig. 48.5)[5] and city fortifications of Stratum II (both attributed by the excavator to Jeroboam II: see e.g. Biran 1994: 203–6, 260–70, figs 167, 168); the construction of extensive 'stables', fortifications, and other impressive structures assigned to Megiddo Stratum IVA; the massive citadel and fortification system of Hazor Stratum Va; the monumental city walls of Yoqne'am Stratum XIIa–b; Samaria Periods IV–VI, or possibly Period II;[6] Beth Shean

---

[5] See Greer (2010) regarding the *marzeah* cultic practices at Dan's high place and its broader implications for the northern kingdom during this period.

[6] Flawed excavation reports and fieldwork limit our understanding of Iron Age Samaria; see e.g. Tappy (2007). For an alternative views, see Franklin (2004; 2005) and most recently Finkelstein (2011a).

Stratum IV; and the multi-towered city wall, three-entryway and lower gate systems, and Palace 8000 of Gezer Stratum VI (see Dever 2007 for an overview). The expansion of Israel's cultural and, most likely, political influence is discerned at Dor sometime during the 9th and 8th centuries. This is best expressed by the 'Israelization' of Dor's pottery repertoire, representing a shift from a northern coastal Iron I 'Canaanite/Phoenician' tradition to one more closely affiliated with inland 'Israelite' assemblages (Gilboa and Sharon 2008: 166).

Cultural and commercial interconnections

Two artefact assemblages—a group of ivories and a collection of ostraca both originating from Samaria, capital of the kingdom of Israel—provide invaluable insights into pre-Assyrian conquest cultural and economic systems. The Samaria ivories, comprising approximately 1000 fragments, embody the prosperity and cosmopolitan character of Israel during this period and are alluded to in the 8th-century oracles of Amos (see e.g. Amos 3:15). These ivory carvings are similar to Phoenician-style ivories discovered elsewhere, most notably from Nimrud, located today in Iraq (see e.g. Winter 2010: 187–334). Although most of the ivories were found in secondary or disturbed deposits, on the basis of typological comparisons they most probably date to the late 9th–mid-8th centuries BCE (see Tappy 2006 and bibliography therein). The presence of Phoenician-style luxury items (e.g. ivories and metal vessels) and ceramic figurines, as well as the widespread appearance of utilitarian pottery vessels, such as 'torpedo' storage jars at both inland and coastal sites, attest to well-developed cultural and commercial ties between Israel and the Phoenician coast, especially with Tyre.

The Samaria Ostraca are a collection of over 100 inscribed sherds, of which 63 are legible. Traditionally dated to the reigns of both Joash and Jeroboam II or only to a period of the latter's rule, these inscriptions preserve administrative notations of wine and oil shipments from agricultural estates in the Manassite tribal region to the capital city. These ostraca provide an unprecedented glimpse into the socioeconomic relationship between Samaria's royal centre and elite members of Manassite clans in its hinterland, and geographical insights that include a corpus of place names within the tribal inheritance of Manasseh (see recent treatments by Rainey and Notley 2006: 221–3 and Niemann 2008 for various interpretations).

Iron IIC: Israel under Assyrian rule (late 8th–7th centuries BCE) and the impact of empire

The relationship between Assyria and Israel deteriorated during the second half of the 8th century, characterized by increasing unrest and even open revolt against Neo-Assyrian policies in the region. Military intervention and campaigns to Israel escalated (see Schneider, Ch. 7 above). The northern kingdom was conquered in two waves: during the reigns of Tiglath-pileser III (733/732 BCE) and later by Shalmaneser V and/or Sargon II (722/721; 720 BCE). Attempts to correlate these documented historical events, and particularly the accounts of conquest and destruction as depicted in the biblical and Assyrian sources, with the stratigraphic sequences at key sites are central in efforts to establish Iron Age II chronological benchmarks and to reconstruct a political history of Israel. Heavy destruction layers from Tiglath-pileser's 732 BCE campaign have been identified at Dan (Stratum II), Hazor (Stratum V), Beth Shean (Strata IV and parts of V), Rehov (Stratum III), Megiddo (Stratum IVA), Ta'anach (City, Stratum IV),

Yoqneʿam (Stratum VIII), and Dor (see e.g. Dever 2007 for an analysis of destruction levels associated with Assyrian military actions at Iron II sites). The Neo-Assyrian response culminated in two waves of destruction at numerous cities in the northern kingdom including its capital, deportation of a significant number of Israel's inhabitants to Mesopotamian towns, and their replacement by foreign populations from elsewhere (see e.g. 2 Kgs. 17: 24). These actions also triggered a massive influx of refugees from the north to Judah (see Hardin, Ch. 49 below), resulting in a massive expansion of Jerusalem at the end of the 8th century BCE. Following the region's conquest, Assyria administratively subdivided the territories previously under Israelite and Aramean control into six Assyrian provinces, including three west of the Jordan River: Megiddo, Samaria, and Dor (see Stern 2001: 3–12 for an overview).

Archaeologically, the impact of Assyrian rule is most apparent in construction projects that heralded the appearance of new architectural traditions at select sites. Excavations at Megiddo (Stratum III) provide our best example of an Assyrian administrative centre. The Stratum III city is constructed on a well-laid-out orthogonal plan that included geometrically shaped insulae, domestic quarters that constitute c.75 per cent of the site, a public granary, and Assyrian-style public buildings consisting of a series of rooms around a central courtyard that closely follow Assyrian design (Fig. 48.6; Reich 1992: 214–22).

Surveys have revealed that the province of Megiddo and the Galilee experienced a dramatic reduction in population. However, Assyrian policy varied from province to province, as is reflected in the archaeological record. In contrast to the Galilee, the region of Samaria underwent a building and population boom, presumably as a result of the arrival of new peoples. Assyria's imprint is evident, but not dominant, in other aspects of Israelite 7th-century material culture. Excavated Assyrian-style objects include clay burial containers, pottery, glyptic art, metal vessels, and other objects, which appear alongside local, Phoenician, and Greek-style material culture (see e.g. Stern 2001: 14–101 for a summary). At Tel Rehov

FIG. 48.6 Assyrian-style administrative building at Megiddo (Stratum III). (Courtesy of the Megiddo Expedition)

(Stratum II) and nearby Beth Shean (local Stratum P6), evidence of squatters, settling on the ruins after the Assyrian destruction, was uncovered. At Rehov, several burials that included Assyrian-shaped vessels suggest to the excavator that Assyria may have established a modest settlement at the site, as yet undiscovered, similar to the Assyrian-period citadel established at Hazor (Mazar and Aḥituv 2011).

Assyrian provincial rule was short-lived. By the final decades of the 7th century, Assyria was in retreat. During the twilight of the Assyrian Empire, biblical tradition portrays an assertive Judah, which briefly extended its influence into the lands of the former northern kingdom (2 Chron. 34: 3–7), only to fall prey to Egyptian and Babylonian imperial ambitions.

SUGGESTED READING

Dever, W. G. (2007). Archaeology and the fall of the northern kingdom: what really happened? In S. W. Crawford, A. Ben-Tor, J. P. Dessel, W. G. Dever, A. Mazar, and J. Aviram (eds), 'Up to the Gates of Ekron': Essays on the Archaeology and History of the Eastern Mediterranean in Honor of Seymour Gitin. Jerusalem: W. F. Albright Institute of Archaeological Research/ Israel Exploration Society, 78–92.

Finkelstein, I., and A. Mazar (2007). The Quest for the Historical Israel: Debating Archaeology and the History of Early Israel. Atlanta, Ga.: Society of Biblical Literature.

Rainey, A. F., and R. S. Notley (2006). The Sacred Bridge: Carta's Atlas of the Biblical World. Jerusalem: Carta, 157–258.

Stern, E. (2001). Archaeology of the Land of the Bible, vol. 2: The Assyrian, Babylonian and Persian Periods (732–332 B.C.E.). New York: Doubleday.

REFERENCES

Aharoni, Y. (1979). The Land of the Bible: A Historical Geography, 2nd edn, trans. and ed. A. F. Rainey. Philadelphia: Westminster Press.

Ash, P. S. (1995). Solomon's? district? list. Journal for the Study of the Old Testament 67.3: 67–86.

Bedford, P. R. (2009). The Neo-Assyrian Empire. In I. Morris and W. Scheidel (eds), The Dynamics of Ancient Empires: State Power from Assyria to Byzantium. Oxford: Oxford University Press, 30–65.

Ben Zvi, E. (1995). Inclusion and exclusion from Israel as conveyed by the use of the term 'Israel' in post-monarchic biblical texts. In S. W. Holloway and L. K. Handy (eds), The Pitcher is Broken: Memorial Essays for Gösta W. Ahlström. Sheffield: Sheffield Academic, 95–149.

Biran, A. (1994). Biblical Dan. Jerusalem: Israel Exploration Society/Hebrew Union College/ Jewish Institute of Religion.

Davies, P. R. (1992). In Search of 'Ancient Israel'. Sheffield: JSOT Press.

Dever, W. G. (2007). Archaeology and the fall of the northern kingdom: what really happened? In S. White Crawford, A. Ben-Tor, J. P. Dessel, W. G. Dever, A. Mazar, and J. Aviram (eds), 'Up to the Gates of Ekron': Essays on the Archaeology and History of the Eastern Mediterranean in Honor of Seymour Gitin. Jerusalem: W. F. Albright Institute of Archaeological Research/ Israel Exploration Society, 78–92.

Faust, A. (2003). Abandonment, urbanization, resettlement and the formation of the Israelite state. Near Eastern Archaeology 66: 147–61.

—— (2007). Rural settlements, state formation, and 'Bible and archaeology'. *Near Eastern Archaeology* 70: 4–9.

Finkelstein, I. (2005). (De)formation of the Israelite state: a rejoinder on methodology. *Near Eastern Archaeology* 68: 202–8.

—— (2011a). Observations on the layout of Iron Age Samaria. *Tel Aviv* 38: 194–207.

—— (2011b). Stages in the territorial expansion of the northern kingdom. *Vetus Testamentum* 61: 227–42.

—— (2011c). The Iron Age chronology debate: is the gap narrowing? *Near Eastern Archaeology* 74: 50–54.

—— Z. Lederman, and S. Bunimovitz (1997). *Highlands of Many Cultures: The Southern Samaria Survey* (2 vols). Tel Aviv: Institute of Archaeology, Tel Aviv University.

—— and A. Mazar (2007). *The Quest for the Historical Israel: Debating Archaeology and the History of Early Israel*. Atlanta, Ga.: Society of Biblical Literature.

Frankel, R., N. Geztov, M. Aviam, and A. Degani (2001). *Settlement Dynamics and Regional Diversity in Ancient Upper Galilee: Archaeological Survey of the Upper Galilee*. Jerusalem: Israel Antiquities Authority.

Franklin, N. (2004). Samaria: from the bedrock to the Omride palace. *Levant* 36: 189–202.

—— (2005). Correlation and chronology: Samaria and Megiddo redux. In Levy and Higham (2005: 310–22).

Gal, Z. (1992). *Lower Galilee during the Iron Age*, trans. M. R. Josephy. Winona Lake, Ind.: Eisenbrauns.

Gilboa, A., and I. Sharon (2008). Between the Carmel and the sea: Tel Dor's Iron Age reconsidered. *Near Eastern Archaeology* 71: 146–70.

Grabbe, L. L. (2007). The kingdom of Israel from Omri to the fall of Samaria: if we only had the Bible.... In L. L. Grabbe (ed.), *Ahab Agonistes: The Rise and Fall of the Omri Dynasty*. London: T & T Clark, 54–99.

Greer, J. S. (2010). An Israelite Mizrāq at Tel Dan? *Bulletin of the American School of Oriental Research* 358: 27–44.

Herzog, Z. (2007). State formation and the Iron Age I–Iron Age IIA transition: remarks on the Faust–Finkelstein debate. *Near Eastern Archaeology* 70: 20–1.

—— and L. Singer-Avitz (2006). Sub-dividing the Iron Age IIA in northern Israel: a suggested solution to the chronological debate. *Tel Aviv* 33: 163–95.

Hess, R. S. (1997). The form and structure of the Solomonic district list in 1 Kings 4: 7–19. In G. D. Young, M. W. Chavalas, and R. E. Averbeck (eds), *Crossing Boundaries and Linking Horizons: Studies in Honor of Michael C. Astour on His 80th Birthday*. Bethesda, Md.: CDL, 279–92.

Joffe, A. H. (2002). The rise of secondary states in the Iron Age Levant. *Journal of the Economic and Social History of the Orient* 45: 425–67.

Kelle, B. E. (2002). What's in a name? Neo-Assyrian designations for the northern kingdom and their implications for Israelite history and biblical interpretation. *Society of Biblical Literature* 121: 639–66.

Killebrew, A. E. (2005). *Biblical Peoples and Ethnicity: An Archaeological Study of Egyptians, Canaanites, Philistines, and Early Israel 1300–1100 B.C.E.* Atlanta, Ga.: Society of Biblical Literature.

Levy, T. E., and T. Higham (eds) (2005). *The Bible and Radiocarbon Dating: Archaeology, Text and Science*. London: Equinox.

Liverani, M. (2005). *Israel's History and the History of Israel*, trans. C. Peri and P. R. Davies. London: Equinox.

Master, D. (2001). State formation theory and the kingdom of Ancient Israel. *Journal of Near Eastern Studies* 60: 117–31.

Mazar, A. (2011). The Iron Age chronology debate: is the gap narrowing? Another viewpoint. *Near Eastern Archaeology* 74: 105–11.

—— and S. Aḥituv (2011). Tel Reḥov in the Assyrian period: squatters, burials and a Hebrew seal. In I. Finkelstein and N. Na'aman (eds), *The Fire Signals of Lachish: Studies in the Archaeology and History of Israel in the Late Bronze Age, Iron Age, and Persian Period in Honor of David Ussishkin*. Winona Lake, Ind.: Eisenbrauns, 265–80.

—— and N. Panitz-Cohen (2008). To what god? Altars and a house shrine from Tel Rehov puzzle archaeologists. *Biblical Archaeology Review* 34.4: 40–7.

Na'aman, N. (2007). The northern kingdom in the late tenth–ninth centuries BCE. In H. G. M. Williamson (ed.), *Understanding the History of Ancient Israel*. Oxford: Oxford University Press, 399–418.

—— (2009a). Saul, Benjamin and the emergence of 'Biblical Israel' (Part 1). *Zeitschrift für die Alttestamentliche Wissenschaft* 121: 211–24.

—— (2009b). Saul, Benjamin and the emergence of 'Biblical Israel' (Part 2). *Zeitschrift für die Alttestamentliche Wissenschaft* 121: 335–49.

Niemann, H. M. (2008). A new look at the Samaria ostraca: the king–clan relationship. *Tel Aviv* 35: 249–66.

Rainey, A. F., and R. S. Notley (2006). *The Sacred Bridge: Carta's Atlas of the Biblical World*. Jerusalem: Carta.

Reich, R. (1992). Palaces and Residencies in the Iron Age. In A. Kempinski and R. Reich (eds), *The Architecture of Ancient Israel from the Prehistoric to the Persian Periods in Memory of Immanuel (Munya) Dunayevsky*. Jerusalem: Israel Exploration Society, 202–22.

Stern, E. (2001). *Archaeology of the Land of the Bible*, vol. 2: *The Assyrian, Babylonian and Persian Periods (732–332 B.C.E.)*. New York: Doubleday.

Suriano, M. J. (2007). The apology of Hazael: a literary and historical analysis of the Tel Dan inscription. *Journal of Near Eastern Studies* 66: 163–76.

Tappy, R. E. (2006). The provenance of the unpublished ivories from Samaria. In A. M. Maeir and P. de Miroschedji (eds), *'I Will Speak the Riddles of Ancient Times': Archaeological and Historical Studies in Honor of Amihai Mazar on the Occasion of His Sixtieth Birthday*. Winona Lake, Ind.: Eisenbrauns, 637–56.

—— (2007). The final years of Israelite Samaria: toward a dialogue between texts and archaeology. In S. W. Crawford, A. Ben-Tor, J. P. Dessel, W. G. Dever, A. Mazar, and J. Aviram (eds), *'Up to the Gates of Ekron': Essays on the Archaeology and History of the Eastern Mediterranean in Honor of Seymour Gitin*. Jerusalem: W. F. Albright Institute of Archaeological Research/Israel Exploration Society, 258–79.

Wilson, K. A. (2005). *The Campaign of Pharaoh Shoshenq I into Palestine*. Tübingen: Mohr Siebeck.

Winter, I. J. (2010). *On Art in the Ancient Near East*, vol. 1: *Of the First Millennium B.C.E.* Leiden: Brill.

Yoffee, N. (2005). *Myths of the Archaic State: Evolution of the Earliest Cities, States and Civilizations*. Cambridge: Cambridge University Press.

Zarzeki-Peleg, A. (1997). Hazor, Jokneam and Megiddo in the tenth century B.C.E. *Tel Aviv* 24: 258–88.

Zertal, A. (2001). The heart of the monarchy: pattern of settlement and historical considerations of the Israelite kingdom of Samaria. In A. Mazar (ed.), *Studies in the Archaeology of the Iron Age in Israel and Jordan*. Sheffield: Sheffield Academic, 38–64.

CHAPTER 49

··

JUDAH DURING THE IRON
AGE II PERIOD

··

JAMES W. HARDIN

Iron II Judah, which lasted some 400 years (*c.*1000–586 BCE), has attracted as much interest from archaeologists as perhaps any place on earth of similar size and duration. What has been revealed through archaeological investigation is a small, territorial- and/or tribal-based kingdom with a settlement pattern that differed markedly from the preceding Iron I and with a recognizable material culture that developed out of local traditions. This chapter provides an overview of what has been revealed archaeologically, while taking into account more theoretical considerations for processing the archaeological data and critically referring to some textual sources. First, Judah's boundaries are identified. Next the archeological remains from the 10th century through the beginning of the 6th century are outlined. Discussed within this outline are Judah's material culture, its suggested social and political organization, its relationships with its neighbors (both near and far), and its religion.

BORDERS

While the borders of Judah shifted, its backbone always was the Hebron Ridge, which runs south from Jerusalem through Hebron before dropping into the Negev Desert (Fig. 49.1). To the west were the forests and maquis of the Judean Hills, which drop gradually to the low, rolling hills of the Shephelah and coastal plain. To the east were more arid environs that drop more precipitously into the Jordan Valley and Arabah. Judah's northern border generally followed an east–west line just north of Jerusalem to the vicinity of Gezer, which straddled the Via Maris. From Gezer, the western border of Judah ran southward where the Shephelah gave way to the coastal plain down to where both meet the Negev Desert, north of Beer Sheva. If the Hebron Ridge was the backbone of Judah, the Shephelah was its heartland and the most densely occupied area for much of its history. During times of prosperity, Judah was able to extend its political sway further south than Beer Sheva, certainly to Kadesh Barnea near the Brook of Egypt, likely to the fortified caravanserai of Kuntillet Ajrud perched atop a hill overlooking the Gaza–Gulf of Eilat/Aqaba trade route, and possibly even to the Gulf of Eilat/Aqaba region. The eastern border of Judah generally followed the Arabah up to the western shore of the Dead Sea before turning west toward Jerusalem near Jericho.

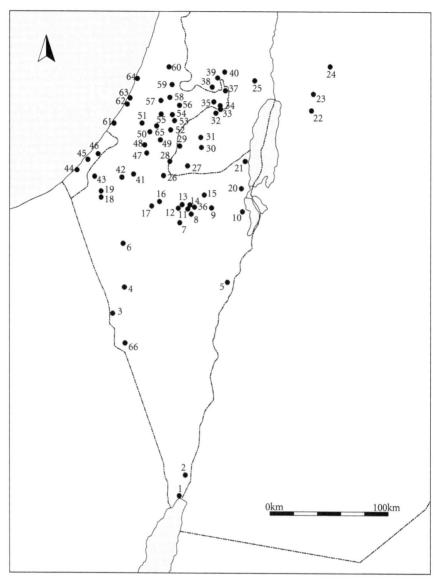

FIG. 49.1 Map of Iron Age II sites in Judah: (1) Tell el-Kheleifeh; (2) Timna'; (3) Kadesh-Barnea; (4) Be'er Resisim; (5) Mezad Hazeva; (6) Rehovot-in-the-Negev; (7) Aroer; (8) Horvat Qitmit; (9) Horvat 'Uza; (10) En Boqeq; (11) Tel Mahata; (12) Tel Masos; (13) Tel 'Ira; (14) Tel Mahata (small); (15) Arad; (16) Tel Beersheba; (17) Beersheba; (18) Tell el-Far'ah (South); (19) 'En Besor; (20) Masada; (21) En-Gedi; (22) Medeba (Medaba); (23) Heshbon; (24) Rabbat-Amman; (25) Jericho; (26) Tel Halif; (27) Kh. Rabut; (28) Tell Beit Mirsim; (29) Kh. El-Qom; (30) Hebron; (31) Beth-Zur; (32) Bethlehem; (33) Giloh; (34) Ramat Rahel; (35) Jerusalem; (36) Tel Malhata; (37) Tell el-Ful; (38) Gibeon; (39) Tell en-Nasbeh; (40) Bethel; (41) Tel Sera'; (42) Tel Haror; (43) Tell Jemmeh; (44) Ruqeish; (45) Tell el-'Ajjul; (46) Gaza; (47) Tel Nagila; (48) Tell el-Hesi; (49) Lachish; (50) Tel 'Erani; (51) Tel Zippor; (52) Tell Judeideh; (53) Kh. Qeiyafah; (54) Azekah; (55) Tell Zafit; (56) Beth Shemesh; (57) Tel Miqne (Ekron); (58) Tel Batash; (59) Gezer; (60) Lod; (61) Ashkelon; (62) Ashdod-Yam; (63) Ashdod; (64) Mezad Hashavyahu; (65) Eitun; and (66) Kuntillet Ajrud

Iron IIA (1000–930 bce)

Exactly when the kingdom of Judah existed within these borders is a topic of heated debate. W. F. Albright was among the first to associate specific archaeological remains with historical events taking place during the 10th century bce (his Iron IIA) and to use them to demonstrate the historicity of the monarchy established by David and Solomon (see Sharon, Ch. 4 above). However, this widely accepted association has been challenged over the last two decades on the basis of two debates. The first is historical and concerns the veracity of the biblical texts, and is beyond the scope of this work. The second is archaeological and attempts to 're-anchor' the well-established relative typological sequence of the Iron II material culture[1] (Finkelstein 1996).

Finkelstein (1996) recently suggested that Iron IIA materials traditionally dated to the 10th century bce should actually be re-dated to the 9th. This removes all remains one might associate with an emergent state as biblically accorded to David (e.g. destructions at Qasile Stratum X and Megiddo Stratum VI) and Solomon (e.g. the gates at Gezer Stratum VIII, Megiddo Strata VA–IVB, and Hazor Stratum X; see 1 Kgs. 9: 15) and associates them with events surrounding the divided monarchy almost a century later. To make this work, a flurry of reshuffling has been undertaken to undo the established relationships between archaeological materials and historically known events—especially military campaigns (e.g. campaigns of Pharaoh Sheshonq I or the Arameans Bir Hadad and Hazael).

Carbon-14 dating has been employed extensively in this debate (Levy and Higham 2005), with both sides demonstrating some support for their temporal conclusions. While the lower dates have gained some support, most archaeologists still lean toward the more traditional chronology. A recent suggestion for moving the archaeological debate forward was made by Mazar (2005). Following Barkay (1992), he suggests a longer duration (c.150 years) than most archaeologists presently accept for the Iron IIA archaeological materials. Mazar's case generally supports the traditional chronology, while allowing for a longer continuation of the assemblages in question. Regardless of its absolute date, the archaeological data suggest a marked change from the preceding Iron I.

Many of the typical Iron I farmsteads and villages are abandoned, destroyed, or morph into the towns and cities of the early Iron II. Faust has noticed that, at least in the highlands, virtually no Iron I settlements continue as rural villages or farmsteads into the early Iron IIA (2006: 114–18). While there are a number of small Iron IIA settlements and farmsteads dotting the Central Negev Highlands, these are accompanied by fifty-some fortified enclosures giving the appearance of a deliberate effort to settle the area and to control trade movement through it (royal efforts? See Cohen 1979). Other Iron II settlements throughout Judah begin modestly—some without fortifications—but they grow into the fortified

---

[1] While there are a number of changes in the material culture that take place between the Iron I and Iron II, there is much continuity. This especially is demonstrated in the ubiquitous three- and four-room houses which dominate Iron Age domestic architecture (discussed below) and in ceramic production. Developments, especially in the surface treatment of various bowls, have been used to differentiate various sub-phases in the Iron Age. Generally, bowls with a red slip were associated with Iron I (c.11th century), bowls with a red slip and an applied irregular or hand burnish were associated with the Iron IIA (c.10th century), and bowls with red slip and wheel burnishing were associated with the Iron IIB–C (9th–7th centuries). The appearance and disappearance of artefact types and imports also was used to further refine subdivisions within Iron II.

towns and cities, regional centres, and fortresses occupied throughout Iron II. Some notable examples that develop into fortified towns and cities include: Tell el-Full/Gibeah Stratum II (maybe a little earlier), Jerusalem Stratum 14, Gibeon, en-Nasbeh Stratum 3, Bethel, Tell Qasile Strata X–IX, Gezer Stratum IX, Beth Shemesh Stratum IIa, Tell Batash Stratum IV, Tell Zayit, Khirbet el-Qom, Tell Beit Mirsim Stratum B3, and Tell Halif Stratum VII (though poorly known). Developing regional centres include Lachish Level V and Beer Sheva Strata VII–VI, and fortresses and caravanserais include Arad Strata XII–XI, Kadesh Barnea Early Fort, Kuntillet Ajrud, Khirbet Qeiyafa, and perhaps Hesi Stratum IX.

Faust suggested a number of possible explanations for this shift to an urban settlement pattern, including: (1) nomadization (see Bienkowski, Ch. 52 below); (2) economic opportunism created by new markets—especially in the lowlands and Shephelah; (3) ecology (e.g. less rain, more silting, salting); (4) present methodological constraints (making identification of early, rural Iron IIA sites difficult); (5) outside threat (e.g. Philistines, Egyptians); or (6) forced settlement by a newly established monarchy (Faust 2006: 120–34).

Given the recent settlement of 'Sea Peoples' to the west, textual assertions of the presence of other outside elements (Egyptians and a little later Arameans), and on the basis of extant archeological data, Faust's Nos 2, 5, and 6 are the most plausible explanations and probably important for political changes accompanying or causing the settlement pattern shift. Late in the Iron IIA, a number of sites were destroyed or abandoned. Destructions are noted at Qasile Stratum VIII, Gezer Stratum VIII, Timnah Stratum IV, several of the central Negev Highland fortresses (which are all abandoned at this time), Kadesh Barnea, probably Gibeon and Bethel, and possibly Arad Stratum XI. Traditionally these were associated with Pharaoh Sheshonq I/Shishak around 925 BCE, whose Levantine campaign is detailed in relief on the Amun temple at Karnak and referred to in biblical texts (1 Kgs. 14: 25–9). Proponents of the lower chronology implicate in these destructions endemic warfare or perhaps campaigning Arameans (see Finkelstein 2002).

Regardless of the causes, the archaeological picture during the Iron IIA is one of increasing urbanization and centralization and perhaps even ethnic consciousness. These changes culminate in the formation of a monarchy, certainly by the mid–late Iron IIB—a period when we have much better synchronisms between the archaeological record and contemporary historical documents (especially those of the Neo-Assyrians). While it is problematic to determine archaeologically when state formation first occurred and how it was done, the Iron IIA archaeological data certainly suggest trends in that direction.

In addition to the increasing urbanism, archaeological data demonstrate a recovery during the late Iron I/early Iron IIA of the long-distance trade typical of earlier periods but recently dormant. Blakely (2002) noticed a striking similarity between a map created by Kochavi (1998), which identifies the location of known Iron I/Iron IIA tripartite pillared buildings (usually associated with stables and/or trade), and a map of the borders of the United Monarchy as described in 1 Kgs. 4: 7–19 and discussed by Halpern (2001). The location of these buildings along the borders of Judah (and Israel) implicates the monarchy's responsibility in their construction and maintenance to make sure the trade items moving from areas south (Arabia and Africa) passed through their (Israel and Judah) territories. This trade would have been administered from the newly forming regional centres, fortresses, and caravanserais. Economically, this trade would have supplemented agriculture, viticulture, horticulture, animal husbandry, textile weaving—all evidenced archaeologically in Judah and Israel—and probably other locally produced goods as well.

Though trade re-emerged during the Iron IIA, the traditional Near Eastern power centres were unable to dominate or directly control the southern Levantine corridor. In the forming power vacuum, spaces opened for local populations to expand their own contacts (Joffe 2002: 431). The local leaders who took advantage of this may have been elites at city-states or perhaps rural headmen or tribal leaders who began coalescing kin-based groups into larger tribal entities of folks who may even have been linked by cosmological and/or theological orientations (LaBianca and Younker's (1994) supra-tribal kingdom). Whatever the case, some polities managed to expand, control, and maintain areas large enough— and eventually reach a level of sociopolitical complexity high enough—to allow for their consideration as small states (Frick 1985; Joffe 2002; Portugali 1994; McNutt 1999; a differing view of sociopolitical complexity and state formation in Master 2001; Schloen 2001; Stager 2003).

For Israel and Judah, the biblical texts tell us that this reorganization began with the rise of David and Solomon, who began to affect changes in all facets of society. Politically, a king involved in problems of state (military campaigns, judicial matters, border control, etc.) was installed, a new elite class was formed, and positions of service and servitude were created. A new capital was established by David at Jerusalem, a site not embedded geographically, politically, economically, and socially in northern and southern territories and groups. The town and crown were legitimized by the state-sanctioned cult of Yahweh (brought to Jerusalem by David and institutionalized by Solomon). On the basis of the archaeological evidence from Jerusalem, however, we cannot say much about these processes, as little Iron IIA material has been recovered from the City of David excavations—mainly due to later removal of earlier materials and limited access to excavation areas caused by modern development and problematic political and socio-religious issues. The absence of Iron IIA evidence from Jerusalem has been cited by some as evidence for the absence of a politically powerful united monarchy in the 10th century BCE (e.g. Steiner 1997).

IRON IIB (930–700 BCE)

In the early Iron IIB there is a continuation of the trends toward increasing urbanism demonstrated by increases in the size, number, and new appearances of fortresses, regional centres, palaces, and fortified cities, towns, and villages (e.g. Ramat Rachel Stratum Vb). These developed along borders, major thoroughfares, crossroads, or the limited number of locations that adequately met certain needs: a constant water supply, arable land, and a defensible position. These needs limited settlement size during the Iron II to 8–10 acres (3–4ha) with populations of perhaps 500–1000 people (Mazar 1990: 435).[2] Most estimates for Judah's population during the 8th century are between 150,000 and 200,000 people (see Broshi and Finkelstein 1992: 56–7).

Already in the 9th century BCE, if not earlier, public works included fortifications (gates, towers, walls—mainly solid but later casemates—and glacis), water retrieval and storage systems demonstrating an understanding of hydrology. Complex water systems have been

---

[2] Exceptions included 8th-century Jerusalem, which dwarfed other settlements in both population and area (approx. 15,000 people on 60–150 acres = 5–60ha) and Lachish, a massive regional capital in the southwestern Shephelah (several thousand people on approximately 20 acres = 8ha).

discovered at Gibeon, Jerusalem, Gezer, Lachish, and Beer Sheva. More typical are the many cisterns hewn out of the bedrock and lined with plaster or drainage systems which include channels and gutters that moved water into cisterns or out of towns. Other examples of public works and planning included administrative buildings; large storage buildings (Beer Sheva, el-Hesi, Lachish, and Gezer); houses forming a perimeter around settlements; and 'blocks' of buildings (Barkay 1992: 329–30; Herzog 1992; 1997; Mazar 1990: 463–5). More recently, other elements have been noted, including cosmological considerations for the orientation of doorways and gates (Bunimovitz and Faust 2003) and the maintenance of free and quick access to city walls via corridors strategically located to link the city wall to an inner-ring road, aiding the defence capabilities of the settlement (Faust 2002: 300–12). Outer-ring roads (outside the walls) have been identified at Jerusalem and Beer Sheva.

During this time, the three- or four-room house becomes the dominant architectural type in Judahite settlements (Fig. 49.2). This house type, probably indigenous to the southern Levant, first proliferated in the small, spatially liberal Iron I settlements and was easily adapted to the more crowded, fortified settlements of the Iron IIB before disappearing completely at the end of the Iron Age. It is an astonishingly uniform house type, generally ranging in size from 35m² to 80m² and in a few examples more than 100m² squared. They frequently existed in Iron II settlements in a peripheral ring backed against or built into the fortification system. In interior spaces, they were clustered into smaller groups, districts, or quarters. It is likely that the clusters were occupied by extended households of probably two to four generations or perhaps larger kinship groups at the 'clan' level. They probably would have been patrilineal, patrilocal, and endogamous and belonging to a larger collective also based on kinship (real or fictive), a pattern typical throughout the eastern littoral of the Mediterranean (see McNutt 1999; Schloen 2001; Stager 1985).

Judahite burial practices closely resemble the architectural features of the four-room house (Bunimovitz and Faust 2003). These tombs, known especially from the 8th century BCE, typically contained individuals of both sexes and all ages, accommodating 15–30 individuals (Bloch-Smith 1992: 217). It seems reasonable to assume that each tomb represented small extended households, serving as a dwelling or house for the deceased.

By the late Iron IIB (8th century BCE), Judahite occupation reached its greatest extent with regard to population and settlement size and number. This increase is especially evident at

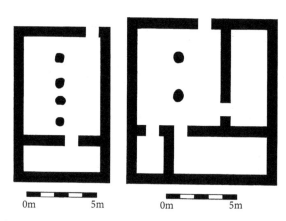

0m   5m   0m   5m

FIG. 49.2 Plan of typical three- and four-room houses (drawn by Dylan P. Karges)

Jerusalem, near the end of the 8th century, when its population exploded and the size of the city increased dramatically. One possible explanation for this population increase is the influx of refugees from the northern kingdom after its fall to the Assyrians in 722/721 BCE.

During the last third of the 8th century, the Neo-Assyrian Empire came to dominate Levantine events by wielding its military might, especially in siegecraft, and reducing smaller states and kingdoms, including Judah, to vassalage or client status. Judah was essentially left unmolested so long as it remained loyal and protected and nurtured Assyria's economic and political interests in the area. This included passing along taxes and duties as annual tribute, serving as a buffer between Assyria and its enemies (especially Egypt), aiding in the consoli-dation of an Assyrian military presence, and keeping open the lucrative trade and commer-cial routes that passed through its territories (see Borowski 1987: 182). Failure to comply could lead to the penal reduction of the kingdom through military occupation—a fate that befell Judah at the end of the century.

Assyrian military activity began to impact Judah directly during the reign of the Assyrian Tiglath-pileser III (*c*.745–727). His successors, Shalmaneser V (*c*.727–722) and Sargon II (*c*.721–705), conquered Israel, destroyed its capital, and deported and/or replaced its population. Perceiving Assyrian weakness after the death of Sargon II, Judah, under King Hezekiah (*c*.727–698 BCE), a king noted by the biblical writers for his piety and early pros-perity (e.g. 2 Kgs. 18: 1–8; Isa. 38: 10–20), revolted against his Assyrian overlords. The events surrounding this episode produced perhaps the most amazing convergence of historical and archaeological sources of data in the entire Iron Age.

IRON IIC (700–586 BCE)

Assyrian texts describe how Sennacherib (*c*.704–681 BCE) was greeted to the throne with open rebellion throughout his empire. Hezekiah, for his part, probably stopped paying trib-ute (perhaps encouraged by Babylon, Tyre, and Egypt) and began taking territories from vassals who remained loyal to Assyria (e.g. Ashkelon and King Padi's Ekron) while strength-ening his own cities and laying stores (including goods distributed in '*lmlk*'-stamped storage jars: Fig. 49.3). Jerusalem's massive solid wall enclosing the Western Hill and its water tunnel connecting the Gihon Spring with the Siloam Pool were probably part of these efforts (2 Kgs. 20:20). Sennacherib responded in 701 BCE, as attested in biblical texts (2 Kgs. 18–20; 2 Chr. 32; Isa. 37), Assyrian records (the Sennacherib Prism), and on the dramatic bas-relief on the walls of his throne room in Nineveh.

Archaeological attestations to Assyrian activity in Judah are prevalent. Nearly every Iron II site investigated in the Shephelah and northern Negev regions yield a destruction level probably associated with Assyrian campaign activities (e.g. Beth Shemesh Stratum IIB, Gezer Stratum VI, Batash/Timnah Stratum III, 'Ira Stratum VII, Malhata Stratum IV, Khirbet Rabud Stratum B-II, Lachish Level III, Tell Judeideh, Tell el-Hesi, Tel Zayit, Tell el-'Erani VI, Arad Stratum VIII, Beer Sheva Stratum II, Tell Eitun, Tell Beit Mirsim A (Fig. 49.4), Tell Halif Stratum VIB, among others—but see Blakely and Hardin 2002).

None of these yields evidence so dramatically as the large regional capital of Lachish (Level III), sitting atop a high mound surrounded by a double wall and gate system. Revealed here are a siege ramp along the southwestern slope, a counter-ramp inside the city, and massive burning throughout the city accompanied by many arrowheads, sling stones,

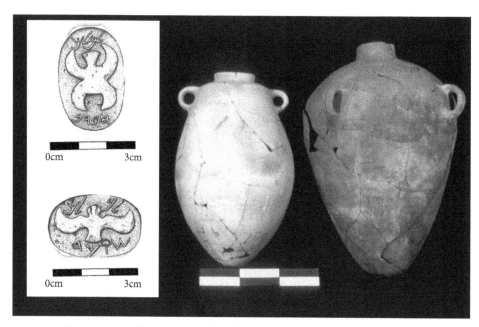

FIG. 49.3 Large storage jars typical of the late 8th century BCE. The example on the far right is typical of the *lmlk* type, sometimes stamped with 'belonging to the king' and mentioning one of four place names (example here drawn by Dylan P. Karges; photograph courtesy Lahav Research Project)

scale armour fragments, and a mass grave (over 1500 individuals) beneath the site. These remains provide one of the most important linchpins for correlating a historically recorded event with a specific material culture of the Iron Age, and this correlation is one of the few almost unanimously agreed upon among scholars studying Judah.

LIFE AFTER SENNACHERIB

The Shephelah and northern Negev never fully recovered from the devastation wrought by Sennacherib, as evidenced by the decreased number of sites there (Blakely and Hardin 2002). It seems likely that the Assyrians forced mass deportations of its inhabitants or, due to Hezekiah's rebellion, removed the Shephelah and northern Negev from Judahite autonomy.

However, not all regions suffered so greatly. From the archaeology, it appears that areas north and east of Jerusalem (ancient Benjamin) experienced continued occupation without interruption (e.g. Gibeon and en-Nasbeh). Also from archaeology, Jerusalem and its environs continued to experience heavier population densities than other areas of Judah. More marginal regions were also settled during the 7th and early 6th centuries BCE more intensely than at any other time during the Iron Age. This especially includes an unparalleled wave of settlement in the region of the Judean Desert between Jerusalem and the Dead Sea, from the Boqe'ah to the vicinities of Jericho and Ein Gedi. Grain from this area has been found in Ashkelon, attesting to the regional trade in which Judah participated (Faust and Weiss

N

0   10
meters

FIG. 49.4 Plan of domestic areas from Tell Beit Mirsim's Stratum A (adapted by Dylan P. Karges from Albright 1943: pls 3 and 4)

2005). The Beer Sheva Basin experienced the same kind of extensive expansion as the eastern deserts (e.g. Ira, Masos, 'Aroer, Malhata, and Uza). Perhaps these expansions originated with émigrés from the Shephelah.

Apparently, a reconfigured Judah continued to prosper as a vassal of Assyria until the campaigns of the Babylonian king Nebuchadnezzar in 597 and 586 BCE. These were as devastating as Sennacherib's (see Hab. 1: 6–10; affected sites include Ein Gedi Stratum V, Arad Strata VII/VI, Horvat Uza Stratum IV, Ira Stratum V, Malhata Stratum III, Lachish Level II, es-Shariah, Timnah, Gezer Stratum V, Jerusalem, Ramat Rachel Stratum VA, and possibly 'Aroer). With these activities, the kingdom of Judah and the Iron Age came to a close.

CULTURAL FINDS

Archaeology demonstrates that the kingdom of Judah carved out a niche for itself among other Levantine entities and the imperial states that constantly threatened its autonomy. Its similarity and full integration with its neighbours is seen in epigraphic finds, its counting systems of weights and measures, and its religion. Writing materials in Judah are known from the very beginning of the Iron II, when the Phoenician alphabet was adopted and developed as a local, Hebrew version. The earliest Iron II alphabet-based texts known from Judah (late Iron I/early Iron IIA), notably include the Gezer Calendar, an abecedary from Tel Zayit, and a large ostracon from Khirbet Qeiyafa. From the 9th century, two very important inscriptions for the history of early Judah but not from within its geographical territories are the 'Bet David' Aramaic inscription from Dan (in Israel) and the Mesha Stele from Dhiban (in ancient Moab). Both mention the 'House/City of David'.

There was an explosion of writing during the 8th century when stamp seals (with Egyptian rather than Mesopotamian iconography—scarabs, winged griffins, etc.), bullae, writing on ceramic vessels, and monumental inscriptions become more common. Important inscriptions and iconography from Kuntillet Ajrud exist mainly as graffiti on walls, jars, and bowls. Notable among these is the mention of 'Yahweh of Samaria and his Asherah' and depictions of individuals/gods/goddesses, which provide a glimpse into religious practices at this site and suggest a possible connection with Israel. Another inscription mentioning 'Yahweh and his Asherah' was discovered in a tomb at Khirbet el-Kom in the Hebron area. Both of these lend evidence to the prominence of Asherah in cultic activity in Judah, possibly as a consort of the male deity (see below).

An invaluable collection of ostraca was excavated from the southern fortress of Arad (fortress Strata VIII–VII), providing a window into the royal presence in the southeastern portions of the kingdom. Commanders of the fortresses are mentioned along with a king of Egypt, Greek mercenaries, Edomite confrontations, royal Judahite policies, and the dispensing of food supplies. In Jerusalem, a dedicatory inscription from Hezekiah's Water Tunnel and an inscription in a Silwan tomb provide examples from the kingdom's capital. Another important collection of eighteen ostraca was found in a room off the piazza at Lachish's gate (Level II). Collections of bullae are well known from the 7th century, including a collection of more than fifty from a burned house in Jerusalem. Also from Jerusalem is the 7th-century silver amulet from a Khetef Hinnom tomb incised with the earliest known fragment of a biblical text (Num. 6:24–5). While this list is not exhaustive, it demonstrates the high level of literacy among royal administrators and those conducting transactions.

With regard to economic transactions, Judah began to pursue its own policies by the 8th century and possibly already in the 9th. A system of measures and weights was distinct to Judah, and some weights were inscribed with paleo-Hebrew or Egyptian hieratic numeric values representing fractions and multiples of four shekels (Kletter 1998). Weight units appear to follow the Egyptian rather than the Mesopotamian system. Goods moving through Judah include gold, silver, copper, bronze, iron, other metals, ivory, precious and semi-precious stones, rare woods, monkeys, horses, textiles, Cypriot and East Greek pottery, and especially perfumes/unguents, oils, wine, fish (Mediterranean and Nile), and other victuals—all attested archaeologically (for trade, see Defonzo 2005; Holladay 2001; 2006).

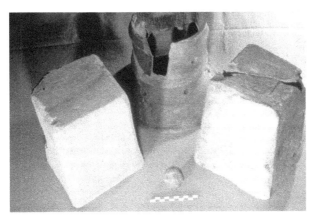

FIG. 49.5 Cultic remains found in the broadroom of a four-room house at Tell Halif include a fenestrated ceramic stand, two bevel-edged stone altar/stands, and the head of a pillar figurine (photograph courtesy Lahav Research Project)

With regard to cultic activity, a picture is developing of religious activities that were much like those of Judah's neighbors; apparently the orthodoxy described in biblical texts was not the norm for most times, as some texts assert (e.g. 2 Kgs. 16: 10–16, 21: 1–17, 23:10; Jer. 7: 18, 44: 17–25; Zeph. 1: 5). From the 10th century, Cult Room 49 is known from Lachish Level V, complete with stands, a horned altar, chalices, and other objects. An 8th-century domestic shrine at Tell Halif contained the head of a pillar figurine, a fenestrated stand, two shaped rectangular stands, and possibly a 'standing stone' (Fig. 49.5). The ubiquitous pillar figurines found throughout Judah (especially in domestic contexts) have been associated with the goddess Asherah by some but understood as votives by others. They were probably used predominantly, if not exclusively, by women, thereby demonstrating women's active roles in ritual activities (Meyers 2005).

Any discussion of religion in this period must include Solomon's Temple. To date there are no known archaeological remains securely associated with this structure. However, its description is rooted in the religious architecture of Iron Age Canaan, including its tripartite plan (known in northern Syria), double columns (Tell Qasile), and use of cedar as a building material (Lachish and Tell Qasile). An 8th-century temple was found deliberately buried at Arad (Strata IX–VIII)—complete with a tripartite division, a sacrificial altar made of field-stones, and a niche or 'holy of holies' with two altars/stands and two standing stones. At Beer Sheva, the stones of a dismantled horned altar were found reused in a storehouse. The burying of the former and dismantling of the latter may have been associated with the bibli-cally described cultic reforms of either Hezekiah or Josiah. Over twenty tumuli were found in the area of Jerusalem with perimeter walls, large platforms, paved areas, and some pits and enclosure walls. Many were filled with burned animal bones. These have been associ-ated with high places (*bamot*) or royal cenotaphs (Barkay 1992). Also near Jerusalem is the enigmatic Cave I, which contained many bowls and other ceramic forms and different types of figurines (a *bamah*? See Steiner 1997).

Based on the discussion above, a setting is revealed where not only religious special-ists but all members of society participated in religious activities. The abundance of cultic materials, the types, and their contexts suggest that Judahite religion was steeped in Levantine traditions where food or liquids were presented, libated and/or consumed; anointing or ritual purifications and cleansings were performed; and sacred and/or communal meals were served and consumed by the Judahites, their guests, and their deity. For some 400 years, all of these acts insured the company of the deity (see Holladay 1997) and secured the participants' relative wellbeing as they experienced life among other groups in the Levant.

This very brief overview of the small territorial kingdom of Judah imparts only a very small portion of what has been revealed through archaeological investigation and the critical analyses of biblical and other textual sources. It also attests to how the state of our understanding of Iron II Judah in the context of its neighbours continues to be refined by the immense and continually growing data available to researchers.

SUGGESTED READING

Dever, W. G. (2001). *What Did the Biblical Writers Know and When Did They Know It? What Archaeology Can Tell Us about the Reality of Ancient Israel*. Grand Rapids, Mich.: Eerdmans.

Herr, L. G. (1997). Iron II Palestine: emerging nations. *Biblical Archaeologist* 60.3: 114–83.

King, P. J., and L. E. Stager (2001). *Life in Biblical Israel*. Louisville, Ky.: Westminster/John Knox.

Master, D. M. (2001). State formation theory and the kingdom of ancient Israel. *Journal of Near Eastern Studies* 60: 117–31.

Mazar, A. (1990). *Archaeology of the Land of the Bible*, vol. 1: *10,000–586 B.C.E.* New York: Doubleday.

REFERENCES

Albright, W. F. (1943). *The Excavations of Tell Beit Mirsim III: The Iron Age*. New Haven, Conn.: American Schools of Oriental Research.

Barkay, G. (1992). The Iron Age II–III. In A. Ben-Tor (ed.), *The Archaeology of Ancient Israel*. New Haven, Conn.: Yale University Press/Tel Aviv: Open University of Israel, 302–73.

Blakely, J. A. (2002). Reconciling two maps: archaeological evidence for the kingdoms of David and Solomon. *Bulletin of the American Schools of Oriental Research* 327: 49–54.

—— and J. W. Hardin (2002). Southwest Judah in the late eighth century B.C.E. *Bulletin of the American Schools of Oriental Research* 326: 11–64.

Bloch-Smith, E. (1992). *Judahite Burial Practices and Beliefs about the Dead*. Sheffield: JSOT Press.

Borowski, O. (1987). *Agriculture in Iron Age Israel*. Winona Lake, Ind.: Eisenbrauns.

Broshi, M., and I. Finkelstein (1992). The population of Palestine in Iron Age II. *Bulletin of the American Schools of Oriental Research* 287: 47–60.

Bunimovitz, S., and A. Faust (2003). Building identity: the four-room house and the Israelite mind. In W. G. Dever and S. Gitin (eds), *Symbiosis, Symbolism, and the Power of the Past: Canaan, Ancient Israel, and Their Neighbors from the Late Bronze Age through Roman Palaestina*. Winona Lake, Ind.: Eisenbrauns, 411–23.

Cohen, R. (1979). The Iron Age fortresses in the central Negev. *Bulletin of the American Schools of Oriental Research* 236: 61–79.

Defonzo, R. J. P. (2005). *Iron II Judah: an intra-regional study of production and distribution.* PhD dissertation, University of Toronto.

Faust, A. (2002). Accessibility, defence, and town planning in Iron Age Israel. *Tel Aviv* 29: 297–317.

—— (2006). *Israel's Ethnogenesis: Settlement, Interaction, Expansion, and Resistance.* London: Equinox.

—— and E. Weiss (2005). Judah, Philistia, and the Mediterranean world: reconstructing the economic system of the seventh century B.C.E. *Bulletin of the American Schools of Oriental Research* 338: 71–92.

Finkelstein, I. (1996). The archaeology of the united monarchy: an alternative view. *Levant* 28: 177–87.

—— (2002). The campaign of Shoshenq I to Palestine: a guide to the 10th century BCE polity. *Zeitschrift des Deutchen Palästina-Vereins* 118: 109–35.

Frick, F. S. (1985). *The Formation of the State in Ancient Israel: A Survey of Models and Theories.* Sheffield: Almond.

Halpern, B. (2001). *David's Secret Demons: Messiah, Murderer, Traitor, King.* Grand Rapids, Mich.: Eerdmans.

Herzog, Z. (1992). Administrative structures in the Iron Age. In A. Kempinski and R. Reich (eds), *The Architecture of Ancient Israel from the Prehistoric to the Persian Periods in Memory of Immanuel (Munya) Dunayevsky.* Jerusalem: Israel Exploration Society, 223–30.

—— (1997). *Archaeology of the City: Urban Planning in Ancient Israel and Its Social Implications.* Tel Aviv: Emery and Claire Yass Archaeology Press.

Holladay, J. S., Jr. (1997). Four-room house. In E. M. Meyers (ed.), *The Oxford Encyclopedia of Archaeology in the Near East*, vol. 2. New York: Oxford University Press, 337–42.

—— (2001). Toward a new paradigmatic understanding of long-distance trade in the ancient Near East: from the Middle Bronze II to the Early Iron II. In P. M. M. Daviau, J. W. Wevers, and M. Weigl (eds), *The World of the Arameans II: Studies in History and Archaeology in Honour of Paul-Eugene Dion.* Sheffield: Sheffield Academic, 136–98.

—— (2006). Hezekiah's tribute, long-distance trade, and the wealth of nations ca. 1000–600 BC: a new perspective. In S. Gitin, J. E. Wright, and J. P. Dessel (eds), *Confronting the Past: Archaeological and Historical Essays on Ancient Israel in Honor of William G. Dever.* Winona Lake, Ind.: Eisenbrauns, 309–32.

Joffe, A. H. (2002). The rise of secondary states in the Iron Age Levant. *Journal of Economic and Social History of the Orient* 45: 425–67.

Kletter, R. (1998). *Economic Keystones: The Weight System of the Kingdom of Judah.* Sheffield: Sheffield Academic.

Kochavi, M. (1998). The eleventh century B.C.E. tripartite pillar building at Tel Hadar. In S. Gitin, A. Mazar, and E. Stern (eds), *Mediterranean Peoples in Transition: Thirteenth to Early Tenth Centuries BCE.* Jerusalem: Israel Exploration Society, 468–78.

LaBianca, Ø. S., and R. W. Younker (1994). The kingdoms of Ammon, Moab and Edom: the archaeology of society in Late Bronze/Iron Age Transjordan (ca. 1400–500 BCE). In T. E. Levy (ed.), *The Archaeology of Society in the Holy Land.* New York: Facts on File, 399–415.

Levy, T. E., and T. Higham (eds) (2005). *The Bible and Radiocarbon Dating: Archaeology, Text and Science.* London: Equinox.

Master, D. M. (2001). State formation theory and the kingdom of Israel. *Journal of Near Eastern Studies* 60: 117–31.

Mazar, A. (1990). *Archaeology of the Land of the Bible*, vol. 1: *10,000–586 B.C.E.* New York: Doubleday.

—— (2005). The debate over the chronology of the Iron Age in the southern Levant: its history, the current situation, and a suggested resolution. In Levy and Higham (2005: 15–30).

McNutt, P. M. (1999). *Reconstructing the Society of Ancient Israel*. Louisville, Ky.: Westminster/ John Knox.

Meyers, C. L. (2005). *Households and Holiness: The Religious Culture of Israelite Women*. Minneapolis: Fortress.

Portugali, J. (1994). Theoretical speculations on the transition from nomadism to monarchy. In I. Finkelstein and N. Na'aman (eds), *From Nomadism to Monarchy: Archaeological and Historical Aspects of Early Israel*. Jerusalem: Ben-Zvi/Israel Exploration Society/Washington, DC: Biblical Archaeological Society, 203–17.

Schloen, J. D. (2001). *The House of the Father as Fact and Symbol: Patrimonialism in Ugarit and the Ancient Near East*. Winona Lake, Ind.: Eisenbrauns.

Stager, L. E. (1985). The archaeology of the family in ancient Israel. *Bulletin of the American Schools of Oriental Research* 260: 1–35.

—— (2003). The patrimonial kingdom of Solomon. In W. G. Dever and S. Gitin (eds), *Symbiosis, Symbolism, and the Power of the Past: Canaan, Ancient Israel, and Their Neighbors from the Late Bronze Age through Roman Palaestina*. Winona Lake, Ind.: Eisenbrauns, 63–74.

Steiner, M. L. (1997). Two popular cult sites of ancient Palestine. *Scandinavian Journal of the Old Testament* 11: 16–28.

CHAPTER 50

....

AMMON DURING THE IRON AGE II PERIOD

....

RANDALL W. YOUNKER

INTRODUCTION

....

The Ammonites were an ancient people who became an important local polity on the central Jordanian plateau from about the middle of the 2nd millennium BCE until the latter part of the first millennium BCE. Their country was known as Ammon, while their capital was called Rabbath-Ammon, or simply, Amman. They are best known for their numerous encounters with the biblical Israelites. However, the Ammonites are also known from extra-biblical literature largely because their territory was astride major caravan routes that connected Arabia with the major cultural centres of the Fertile Crescent. Their control over part of these critical trade routes led to important interactions with the great powers in Mesopotamia (Assyria and Babylon) and Egypt that greatly impacted the history of both western Palestine and Jordan.

Geographic extent of Ammon

According to Deut. 2:26–37, the boundary of Ammon, over which Israel was not to cross, was defined by the course of the Jabbok (modern Zerqa) River—'neither the land along the course of the Jabbok nor that around the towns in the hills' (Deut. 2:37). This would seem, at first glance, to be a rather straightforward delineation. However, unlike other rivers in Jordan, which flow in an fairly true east-to-west direction, the course of the Jabbok forms an almost complete circle from its head at Ras al-Ain near the base of the ancient capital Rabbath-Ammon (modern Amman), from which it sets out in an easterly direction, then makes a broad northward arch until it bends back due west, emptying into the Jordan River. This has led to much consternation and discussion among biblical geographers, who have tended to prefer nice straight borders and have restricted the use of the Jabbok as a boundary to either its east–west stretch in the north or its south–north stretch in the east (Younker 1994: 61). I have suggested that the ancient understanding was more simple and straightforward: the Jabbok was the border and essentially surrounded the territory of ancient Ammon. However, the ancients did not view the Jabbok simply as the main course but would have included all of its tributaries, which extend the land of the Ammonites considerably. The fact that typical Ammonite settlements (see below) are found on hills all along the various tributaries of the Jabbok supports this understanding.

Research

In spite of their importance to biblical and Syro-Palestinian history, there have been only a couple of comprehensive studies of the Ammonites, neither from a purely archaeological perspective. George Landes completed an historical study of the Ammonites in 1956 (which did incorporate the archaeological findings known up to that time) and a literary/ historical study has been undertaken by Ulrich Hübner (1992). Apart from these studies and occasional incidental references, treatments of the Ammonites have generally been limited to either brief surveys or encyclopedia articles (e.g. Glueck 1937; Albright 1953; Landes 1961; Oded 1971; Horn 1976; Thompson 1982a; 1982b; MacDonald 1994). MacDonald and Younker (1999) and Younker (2003) have provided the most comprehensive review of Ammonite archaeology to date. Daviau and Dion (2007: 301–7) have provided a brief overview of Ammon during Iron II with a helpful discussion on ceramics and connections with Assyria.

Ammonite culture is characterized by a number of unique features. These include a unique ceramic corpus (see below), architectural styles (see below), Ammonite inscriptions (found at Amman, Umm Udhayna, Umayri, Siran, Jalul, and elsewhere), and the appearance of stone and ceramic statues and figurines of males wearing various styles of the Egyptian *atef* crown (Daviau and Dion 2007). Sites that have been dated to the Iron Age and identified as Ammonite include a number of tombs found in Amman and the Sahab Tomb excavations, including Sahab, Amman, and Meaqbalein (Fig. 50.1).

A number of rujms and qasrs (towers and fortified structures) were excavated that date to Iron II; these served a number of functions including fortified farmsteads, watchtowers, and caravanserai. Settlement sites that include most or all of these Ammonite material culture features include the Beqaʿ Valley, Safut, Amman, Sahab, Tall al-Umayri, Tall Jawa, Hesban, Madaba, Jalul, and other sites. Important pillared domestic structures have been found at Tell Jawa, Umayri, and Jalul—a tripartite building was also found at the later site. Iron Age casemate walls have been found at Jawa and Umayri, and a solid offset wall at Jalul. Excavations continue at Madaba, Hesban, Umayri, and Jalul.

Periodization

There is a discussion of periodization for Iron II in the general introduction to this volume. The periodization which I have used dates Iron IIA from the early part of the 10th century BCE (*c.*1000) down to Pharaoh's Shishak's invasion of Palestine (*c.* 925 BCE). Iron IIB covers the 9th to the late 8th centuries BCE (900–721 BCE). Iron IIC is dated from the 7th to the 5th centuries BCE (see below).

Regardless of when precisely one begins the Iron II, most scholars agree that from a socio-political viewpoint, the beginning of Iron II in the eastern Levant—especially Cisjordan and Transjordan—witnessed the coalescence of local tribal groups into territorial monarchies (sometimes called 'tribal kingdoms or states') that we know as Israel, Ammon, Moab, and Edom.

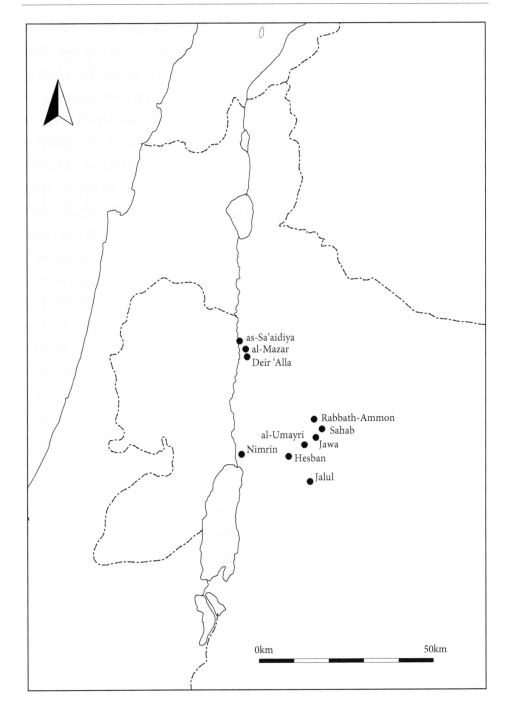

FIG. 50.1 Map of Iron Age II sites in Ammon

AMMON DURING THE IRON IIA–B

History

Historical sources for the beginning of the early Iron II (A–B) in Ammon are, unfortunately, lacking. There are a couple of biblical references to Ammon in 2 Chronicles that seem to apply to this period. While some scholars are uncertain of the historical veracity of some biblical sources, the references to Ammon do not contradict any known historical sources and, indeed, seem in harmony with what is known about the relationships between Ammon and the kingdoms of Israel and Judah. For example, according to 2 Chr. 26: 8; 27: 5, which correspond to the time of the divided monarchy, the Ammonites were forced to pay tribute to the southern kingdom of Judah. The occasional subjugation of Transjordan kingdoms by Cisjordan ones is supported by some extra biblical evidence such as the Mesha Inscription, thus many scholars are inclined to think that Ammon's subjection to Judah is plausible (e.g. Barton 2002: 516).

However, when the rising Assyrian Empire moved into the area, the Ammonites joined other Syro-Palestinian polities in a coalition to resist Assyrian advances (Luckenbill 1926: 223; Younker 2003). The Ammonite army led by King Ba'sa, son of Ruhubi, joined the coalition against Shalmaneser III at Qarqar in 853 BCE. After this battle, however, the western alliance unraveled and the Israelites became entangled in a confrontation with the Arameans.

With Israel thus distracted, the Ammonites, who may have enjoyed a degree of independence after the division of the Israelite monarchy, joined forces with the Moabites and Meunites in an invasion of Judah—possibly at the instigation of the Arameans (2 Chr. 20: 1, 10). Although Judah's king, Jehoshaphat, was able to rally his army to meet this threat, the Transjordan coalition unravelled before the Judahite army arrived (de Tarragon 1992: 195).

Ammon was later forced to pay tribute to Uzziah, king of Judah (767–740 BCE), and his son Jotham (2 Chr. 26: 8; 27: 5). In 734 the Ammonite king, Sanipu, was a vassal of Tiglath-pileser III, and his successor, Pudu-ilu, held the same position under Sennacherib and Esarhaddon (de Tarragon 1992: 195).

Ceramics and ceramic chronology

At present it is difficult to separate Iron IB from Iron IIA in Ammon; the ceramic chronology is not yet well enough developed for a definitive separation of these two periods in the Ammon region. Moreover, as noted above, there has not been a scholarly consensus on when to begin the Iron II, and many early survey and excavation reports fail to provide enough specificity to make a distinction—either in what dates they mean when they say Iron IIA or any description of the appearance of the ceramics. Since some researchers may have assumed that Iron IB included the 10th century BCE, it is likely that some early Iron II readings are skewed to the 9th–8th centuries BCE or what we might call Iron IIB. Thus for the purposes of this chapter I will discuss the periods together as Iron IIA–B, covering the 10th–8th centuries BCE.

As Daviau has noted, two styles of surface treatment distinguish Ammonite pottery from Moabite and Judean: red slipped and painted pottery in Iron IIB, and a black-slipped and burnished ware which appears toward the end of Iron IIB and goes into Iron IIC and the Persian period (see below; Daviau and Dion 2007: 304). For Iron IIB, the dominant forms are red slipped and burnished small hemispherical bowls, large hemispherical bowls with black-painted bands, thin-walled unburnished bent-sided bowls, shallow thick-walled bent-sided burnished bowls, large platters with red slip and black-and-white painted bands, juglets, and jugs with black-and-white painted bands on red slip.

Settlement pattern

Regardless of the difficulties of separating the sub-periods of early Iron II in Ammon, one fact that jumps out when examining the data is the clear and obvious increase in the number of settlements over and against those of the preceding Iron I. Whereas survey and excavations have identified some fifteen sites in Ammon during early Iron I, that number increased dramatically to 97 sites during early Iron II (Younker 2003: 154–8). While most of the principal Iron I sites in Ammon, such as Rabbath-Ammon, Hesban, Tall al-Umayri, Jalul, Safut, Jawa, Umm ad-Dananir, and Safut, continued to be occupied in early Iron II, the majority of Iron II sites were new.

While a couple of these new sites (Khilda and the Sports City Site) were of medium size, ranging between 5ha and 10ha in size, the rest, were 'small sites' of 2.5ha or less. Of the 97 early Iron II sites, 36 appear to be actual settlements—small towns or villages consisting of several houses. The remaining sites—nearly two-thirds—mostly consist of one or two rectangular buildings built of chert or limestone blocks. The structures are variously described as blockhouses, forts, qasrs, tower forts, towers/rujms, farmsteads, or agricultural complexes. The author's own study of these sites has led him to conclude that the principal function of most of these is properly classified as agricultural complexes or fortified farmhouses (Fig. 50.2). This is because most of these sites exhibit a number of distinctive agricultural features such as prime agricultural fields (flat with good soil), field walls, perimeter walls around the compound, terraces, cisterns, bedrock food preparation areas (e.g. cup-holes),

FIG. 50.2 Ammonite fortified tower or farmstead north of Amman (courtesy Horn Archaeology Museum)

bedrock winepresses, mill stones, and storage caves. Excavations of a couple of these sites show remains consistent with an agricultural complex (store-jars, etc.) (Younker 2003: 157).

The presence of a clear three-tiered settlement hierarchy (made up of large sites such as Rabbath-Ammon, medium sites like Khilda, and small agricultural compounds) would support the existence of a more complex, integrated sociopolitical organization in the region during Iron IIA–B. This would be in harmony with textual data (biblical and extra-biblical) that describe the presence of an Ammonite kingdom. However, when compared with the scale of both individual site size and the settlement hierarchy in Mesopotamia, that of Transjordan cannot be understood as equivalent. The smaller scale, combined with the persistence of strong tribal traditions (as indicated in both biblical and extra-biblical literature), suggests that different terminology would be appropriate to describe the Ammonite polity. Some have suggested terms such as a 'tribal state' (Younker 2003: 162, 163).

Fortifications and architecture

A city gate and walls were found at Tall Jawa, south of Amman. The wall was a casemate fortification and dated from Iron IIB—it continued in use during Iron IIC (Daviau and Dion 2007: 302). A small stretch of a possible city wall was found at Jalul in Field A on the north side of the site. It has been dated to the 8th century BCE and was widened during the 7th century BCE (Younker 2007). The presence of a volute of a proto-Ionic capital at Amman suggests the presence of monumental architecture in the Ammonite capital (Fig. 50.3).

At Tall Jawa, Daviau excavated a variety of pillared walls that supported upper-storey rooms in buildings whose overall plans differed from one another. Most notable is the difference between the 'agglutinative plan' of Building 300 of Iron IIB (Stratum VIII) and the more orthogonal plan of Building 7000 of the later Iron IIC (Daviau and Dion 2007: 302). A possible pillared building was also recovered at Jalul from the 8th century BC (Younker 2007: 132).

FIG. 50.3 Proto-Ionic capital found on the Amman Citadel (courtesy Horn Archaeology Museum)

Material culture

One characteristic class of artefacts from this period is the stone statue of a male wearing a variation of the Egyptian *atef* crown (Fig. 50.4). A number of these have been recovered in the immediate vicinity of Amman (Dornemann 1983: 156–7), while several smaller ceramic figurine versions have been recovered at Amman, Tall Jawa, and Jalul (Younker 1994: 308–9). It is thought that these statues depict noble or royal personages. One of the statues has an inscription that Fawzi Zayadine translates as 'of Yarah-'azar, son of Zakir (?), son of Shanib' (Zayadine 1974). He equates Shanib with an Ammonite king known as Shanipu, listed in the second campaign account of Tiglath-pileser III (745–727 BCE). Zayadine also believes that both Yarah-'azar and Zakir were Ammonite kings, thus extending the Ammonite king-list by two. Daviau and Dion believe that the *atef* statues and figurines represent an independent Ammonite artistic tradition (Daviau and Dion 1994). Siegfried Horn suggests that these headdresses represent the crown worn exclusively by Ammonite kings (Horn 1973). Although Horn suggests that this style of crown may date back to the time of David, Daviau and Dion note that it appears to be restricted mostly to Iron IIB (1994).

There are also a small number of female stone sculptures (busts), but they are restricted to double-faced heads that appear to have served an architectural function—perhaps as part of a balustrade (Dornemann 1983: 160–62). The reverential attitude that many of the statues display leads Dornemann to suggest that much of the Ammonite statuary was intended for display within a sacred precinct, perhaps a temple or shrine. Although Egyptian and Syrian influences can be seen in the work, the statues all appear to be the work of indigenous artisans who created a distinctive tradition.

Inscriptions

The 9th-century Amman Citadel Inscription was found in 1961 (Fig. 50.5). The text consists of thirty-three words carved on a limestone block, approximately 10.25×7.5in

FIG. 50.4 *Atef*-crowned figurine found at Jalul (courtesy Horn Archaeology Museum)

FIG. 50.5 Amman Citadel Inscription (courtesy Horn Archaeology Museum)

(Aufrecht 1989). Because the inscription is incomplete it has been subjected to a variety of interpretations. Several scholars understand it as a building inscription, perhaps of a temple or citadel. Others see it as an oracle from the Ammonite god Milcom, ordering the construction of defensive towers around the perimeter of Rabbah-Ammon. In spite of its uncertain meaning, it provides important clues about the linguistic and paleographic characteristics of the Ammonite language.

The Balaam Inscription—found in a shrine at Deir ʿAlla, east of the Jordan River—recounts the vision and prophecies of Balaam, son of Beor, known also from the Bible (Num. 22–4). There is a debate about the language and script—whether it is Aramaic or Ammonite (Hackett 1980; Aufrecht 1989).

AMMON DURING THE IRON IIC (7TH–5TH CENTURIES BCE)

History

During the 2nd half of Iron II (IIC: 7th–5th centuries BCE), Ammon reached its florescence, in terms both of political power and material culture. This would have occurred during the time of Assyrian, Babylonian, and then Persian sovereignty. Ammon's political success and prosperity is reflected in Jer. 49, where the prophet rebukes the Ammonites for taking advantage of Judah's misfortunes by moving into the territory or Gad: 'Why do you boast of your valleys, boast of your valleys so fruitful? O unfaithful daughter, you trust in your riches and say, "Who will attack me?"' (Jer. 49: 4). Surveys conducted throughout Ammon's hinterland by the Madaba Plains Project (Younker 1989) have recorded numerous structures that appear to be part of well-planned agricultural complexes. These complexes included features such as enclosure walls, cisterns, wine presses, cup-holes, terraces, small field towers, and other elements associated with food production. The archaeological evidence supports the biblical suggestion that Ammonite agricultural success had provided a firm economic base that in turn had created the political confidence that led to the prophetic rebuke.

This growth is already suggested during the time of Ashurbanipal (668–627 BCE), whose records indicate that the Ammonites had become the wealthiest of all the Palestinian kingdoms by virtue of the fact that they were required to pay the highest tribute to the Assyrian coffers (assuming that this higher tribute can be taken as a measure of wealth and not disloyalty!).

It was this same economic and political success that probably led to the events described in Jer. 27 and 40, where the prophet accuses an unnamed Ammonite king of leading a rebellion against Babylon. It would appear that Ammon's success gave their king confidence in undertaking such a risky adventure, that included assassinating Babylon's hand-picked governor of Judah, Gedaliah. Jeremiah later implicated the Ammonite king, Baalis, as the one responsible for the assassination of Gedaliah. An Ammonite seal impression with an inscription reading 'Belonging to Milkom-'ur, servant of Ba'al-yahsa' was found at Tall al-Umayri in 1984 (Herr 1985). The iconography includes a four-winged scarab, often used as a royal motif in the region, suggesting that the owner of this seal worked for Baalis, the Ammonite king (Younker 1985).

It would seem unlikely that the Babylonians would ignore the murder of their own appointed leader of Judah (Gedaliah) and, indeed, Josephus claims that Nebuchadnezzar ordered a punitive campaign against the Ammonites during his twenty-third year (582–581 BCE).

In spite of any damage that resulted from this campaign, it appears that the Ammonites continued to thrive within their land well into Hellenistic times and beyond.

Ceramics and ceramic chronology

Herr describes the Ammonite pottery of Iron IIC as achieving its most distinctive and superior level of development (1999: 224). Interesting is the fact that a very local Ammonite tradition emerged with few of the typical pottery forms found outside the region (Lugenbeal and Sauer 1972; Herr 1999: 224). Distinctive fine ware bowls—possibly used by the more wealthy inhabitants—appear including elegant shallow bowls or plates; decorative burnished bowls, some with grey burnish made with a manganese tool; and a distinctive variety of burned black bowls—'black burnished wares'.

Material culture

A large number of male ceramic figurines, including the 'horse and rider figurines', are common to this period. Landes (1961) suggests that the horse and rider figurines represented Ammonite cavalry. Such figurines have been found in Ammonite tombs at al-Muqabelein and Amman, as well as at Tall Jawa, Tall al-Umayri, and Jalul. Female figurines are also common at Ammonite sites during this period. Daviau notes the greater diversity in form and style when compared with the contemporary pillar figurines which are dominant in Judah (Daviau and Dion 2007: 302). The well-known 'woman holding a tambourine' (continued from Iron I) is also found in Ammon, either as a plaque (handmade or moulded) or as a pillar figurine. Other Ammonite figurines of the Iron Age include depictions of horses, camels, fish, and the Egyptian household god Bes.

Settlement pattern

Rabbath-Ammon, of course continued to be the largest and principle Ammonite site during this period. Other key sites that are dated to this period include Safut to the north, Jawa, Sahab, Umayri, and Jalul to the south, and several sites in the Jordan Valley, such as Dayr 'Alla (VI), al-Mazar, Nimrin, and as-Sa'aidiya (IV). These would be smaller cities or large towns. Smaller agricultural settlements include Rujm Salim, and two Khirbat al-Hajjars. Many of the farmsteads that existed in Iron IIB appear to have continued to be occupied in Iron IIC, although surveys of these sites are not usually specific in differentiating between Iron IIB and C. Rather, the reports simply designate them as Iron II (see Herr and Najjar 2001: 334–8).

Also dating to this period are the numerous Ammonite megalithic 'towers' and fortresses that were strategically placed on hilltops around Rabbath-Ammon to provide protection against, or at least an early warning system of the appearance of, invaders (local polities such as the Judahites and Israelites) and raiders (desert Arabs) who might pose a threat to the Ammonites (Younker 1989; Kletter 1991).

As in Iron IIB, a significant number of small well-constructed sites might be best classified as fortified farmsteads—indeed, many of these probably continued to be occupied from the previous period. The precise number is difficult to ascertain because many reports date these sites simply to Iron II without indicating a sub-period. Herr and Najjar (2001: 336) suggest that there may be as many as 150 sites or structures dating to this period. They count 35 circular towers and 122 rectangular fortresses. The fortified agricultural sites are characterized by a number of distinctive features, including perimeter walls, terraces, cisterns, wine presses, and watch towers. These 'fortified' farmsteads would support the increase of the sedentary population of Ammon during this period, and were undoubtedly the foundation for the prosperity indicated in literary sources. Ammon's prosperity and increasing sociopolitical complexity are also reflected in the larger settlement sites such as Amman, Hesban, Umayri, Jalul, and Jawa, which all continue to be occupied during this time. At Jalul there are several large domestic buildings—the site was surrounded by a wall and entered through a chambered gate. The tripartite building continued to be in use. An administrative building with thick walls was found at Tall al-Umaryi (Herr and Najjar 2001: 336). At Amman, the volute of a proto-Ionic capital speaks of monumental architecture at the Ammonite capital city.

PERSIAN PERIOD (5TH–4TH CENTURIES BCE)

History

There are few literary references to shed light on Ammon during the Persian period. The best-known biblical reference is to Tobiah the Ammonite (Neh. 4:3) (who was actually of

Judahite heritage), whose family had long held land in Ammonite territory in the area of the modern Wadi es-Sir (west of Amman). According to the book named after him, Nehemiah, a Jewish cup bearer to Artaxerxes Longimanus (Neh. 2: 1), was commissioned by that Persian king to return to Jerusalem and rebuild the city (Neh. 2: 1–10). Tobiah, who had actually moved into the Temple compound in Jerusalem, was one of the local leaders who tried to oppose Nehemiah's project; Nehemiah ejected him. Some scholars believe that Tobiah may have served as an Ammonite governor. While the later Tobiad castle and family tombs can still be found at Iraq al-Amir in Jordan, there is little actual archaeological material from the Persian period.

Apart from the Tobiah account, there is little written record of Ammon in the Persian period. However, the amount of archaeological material recovered from the Persian period in Ammon has increased in recent years. Dating material remains from the Persian period in Jordan has been greatly facilitated by the refined ceramic chronology of Sauer (1986: 18) and Herr (1997: 244–6). The presence of Attic ware at Umayri and Jalul, typical Persian-period incense altars at Jalul, along with the discovery of two Persian-period 'provincial' seals at Umayri, have helped in securing the dating of Persian material in Amman. Recognizing the Persian ceramic horizon in Ammon has helped in identifying Persian-period occupation at several sites, including Hesban, Tall al-Umayri, Tall Jawa, Jalul, and Dreijat (a fortified site southwest of Umayri).

SUGGESTED READING

Aufrecht, W. E. (1989). *A Corpus of Ammonite Inscriptions.* Lewiston, NY: Mellen.

Dornemann, R. H. (1983). *The Archaeology of Transjordan in the Bronze and Iron Ages.* Milwaukee: Milwaukee Public Museum.

Herr, L. G. (1993). Whatever happened to the Ammonites? *Biblical Archaeology Review* 19.6: 26–35, 68.

Hübner, U. (1992). *Die Ammoniter: Untersuchungen zur Geschichte, Kultur und Religion eines Transjordanischen Volkes im 1. Jahrtausend v. Chr.* Wiesbaden: Harrassowitz.

MacDonald, B., and R. W. Younker (eds) (1999). *Ancient Ammon.* Leiden: Brill.

Younker, R. W. (1994). Ammonites. In A. J. Hoerth, G. L. Mattingly, and E. M. Yamauchi (eds), *Peoples of the Old Testament World.* Grand Rapids, Mich.: Baker, 293–316.

REFERENCES

Albright, W. F. (1953). Notes on Ammonite history. In R. M. Díaz (ed.), *Miscellaneous Biblica B. Ubach.* Montserrat: Spain, 130–35. Reprinted 1986 in L. T. Geraty and L. G. Herr (eds), *The Archaeology of Jordan and Other Studies: Presented to Siegfried H. Horn.* Berrien Springs, Mich.: Andrews University Press, 503–9.

Aufrecht, W. E. (1989). *A Corpus of Ammonite Inscriptions.* Lewiston, NY: Mellen.

Barton, J. (2002). *The Biblical World,* vol. 1. London: Routledge.

Daviau, P. M. M., and P.-E. Dion (1994). El, the god of the Ammonites? The Atef-crowned head from Tell Jawa, Jordan. *Zeitschrift des Deutschen Palästina-Vereins* 110: 158–67.

—— (2007). Independent and well-connected: the Ammonite territorial kingdom in the Iron Age II. In T. E. Levy, P. M. M. Daviau, R. W. Younker, and M. Shaer (eds), *Crossing Jordan: North American Contributions to the Archaeology of Jordan.* London: Equinox, 301–8.

de Tarragon, J.-M. (1992). Ammon. In D. N. Freedman (ed.), *The Anchor Bible Dictionary*, vol. 1. New York: Doubleday, 194–6.

Dornemann, R. H. (1983). *The Archaeology of Transjordan in the Bronze and Iron Ages.* Milwaukee: Milwaukee Public Museum.

Glueck, N. T. (1937). Explorations in the land of Ammon. *Bulletin of the American Schools of Oriental Research* 68: 13–21.

Hackett, J. A. (1980). *The Balaam Text from Deir 'Alla.* Chico, Calif.: Scholars.

Herr, L. G. (1985). The servant of Baalis. *Biblical Archaeologist* 48: 169–72.

—— (1997). The pottery. In L. T. Geraty, L. G. Herr, Ø. S. LaBianca, and R. W. Younker (eds), *Madaba Plains Project 3: The 1989 Season at Tell el-'Umeiri and Vicinity and Subsequent Studies.* Berrien Springs, Mich.: Andrews University Press in cooperation with the Institute of Archaeology, 228–49.

—— (1999). The Ammonites in the Late Iron Age and Persian period. In MacDonald and Younker (1999: 219–38).

—— and M. Najjar (2001). The Iron Age. In B. MacDonald, R. Adams, and P. Bienkowski (eds), *The Archaeology of Jordan.* Sheffield: Sheffield Academic, 323–45.

Horn, S. H. (1973). The crown of the king of the Ammonites. *Andrews University Seminary Studies* 11: 170–80.

—— (1976). Heshbon. In K. R. Crim, V. P. Furnish, and L. R. Bailey (eds), *The Interpreter's Dictionary of the Bible: An Illustrated Encyclopedia Identifying and Explaining All Proper Names and Significant Terms and Subjects in the Holy Scriptures, including the Apocrypha, with Attention to Archaeological Discoveries and Researches into the Life and Faith of Ancient Times—Supplementary Volume.* Nashville, Tenn.: Abingdon, 410–11.

Hübner, U. (1992). *Die Ammoniter: Untersuchungen zur Geschichte, Kultur und Religion eines Transjordanischen Volkes im 1. Jahrtausend v. Ch.* Wiesbaden: Harrassowitz.

Kletter, R. (1991). The Rujm el-Malfuf buildings and the Assyrian vassal state of Ammon. *Bulletin of the American Schools of Oriental Research* 284: 33–50.

Landes, G. M. (1961). The material civilization of the Ammonites. *Biblical Archaeologist* 24: 65–86.

Luckenbill, D. D. (1926). *Ancient Records of Assyria and Babylonia*, vol. 1: *Historical Records of Assyria from the Earliest Times to Sargon.* Chicago: University of Chicago Press.

Lugenbeal, E. N., and J. A. Sauer (1972). *Pottery from Heshbon.* Berrien Springs, Mich.: Andrews University Press.

MacDonald, B. (1994). *Ammon, Moab and Edom: Early States/Nations of Jordan in the Biblical Period (End of the 2nd and During the 1st Millennium B.C.).* Amman: Al Kutba.

—— and R. W. Younker (eds) (1999). *Ancient Ammon.* Leiden: Brill.

Oded, B. (1971). Ammon, Ammonites. In *Encyclopedia Judaica*, vol. 2. Jerusalem: Keter, 854a–860a.

Sauer, J. A. (1986). Transjordan in the Bronze and Iron Ages: a critique of Glueck's synthesis. *Bulletin of the American Schools of Oriental Research* 263: 1–26.

Thompson, H. O. (1982a). The Biblical Ammonites, pt 1. *Bible and Spade* 11.1: 1–14.

—— (1982b). The Biblical Ammonites, pt 2. *Bible and Spade* 11.2–4: 47–61.

Younker, R. W. (1985). Israel, Judah and Ammon and the motifs on the Baalis Seal from Tell el-'Umeiri. *Biblical Archaeologist* 48: 173–80.

—— (1989). Towers in the region surrounding Tell Umeiri. In L. T. Geraty, L. G. Herr, Ø. S. LaBianca, and R. W. Younker (eds), *Madaba Plains Project 1: The 1984 Season at Tell el-Umeiri and Vicinity and Subsequent Studies.* Berrien Springs, Mich.: Andrews University Press in cooperation with the Institute of Archaeology, 195–8.

—— (1994). Ammonites. In A. J. Hoerth, G. L. Mattingly, and E. M. Yamauchi (eds), *Peoples of the Old Testament World*. Grand Rapids, Mich.: Baker, 293–316.

—— (2003). The emergence of Ammon: a view of the rise of Iron Age polities from the other side of the Jordan. In B. A. Nikhai (ed.), *The Near East in the Southwest: Essays in Honor of William G. Dever*. Boston: American Schools of Oriental Research, 153–76.

—— (2007). Highlights from the heights of Jalul. In T. E. Levy, P. M. M. Daviau, R. W. Younker, and M. Shaer (eds), *Crossing Jordan: North American Contributions to the Archaeology of Jordan*. London: Equinox, 129–36.

Zayadine, F. (1974). Note sur l'inscription de la statue d'Amman J.1656. *Syria* 51: 129–36.

CHAPTER 51

....

MOAB DURING THE IRON
AGE II PERIOD

....

MARGREET L. STEINER

In the late summer of 1868, a missionary by the name of F. A. Klein travelled on horseback through Moab, together with his guide Zattam, son of a sheikh of the Bene Sacher tribe. Near ancient Dhiban, north of the Wadi Mujib, they were shown a black basalt stone with an ancient inscription. The story of how the stele was destroyed, reconstructed, and eventually ended up in the Louvre has been told many times before (Horn 1986; Graham 1989). The inscription attracted the attention of biblical scholars, as it mentions both Mesha, king of Moab, and Omri, king of Israel. It is dated to the end of the 9th century BC. The discovery of the Mesha Inscription put Moab on the archaeological map and revealed that King Mesha was more than a 'sheep master', as he is called in biblical texts (2 Kgs. 3: 4). The excavation of Dhiban, home city of King Mesha according to the inscription, was the first large-scale excavation in Moab.

THE REGION

....

Moab is the region both north and south of the Wadi Mujib (Fig. 51.1). The name is mentioned in the Hebrew Bible, the Mesha Inscription, and in Assyrian inscriptions from the Iron Age. Earlier references to Moab in Egyptian texts are still being debated.

The region consists of rolling highlands, fertile and well suited for agriculture. Several deep wadis run from east to west toward the Dead Sea, which constitutes Moab's western border. East of Moab the great desert begins. The area between the Wadi Mujib and the Wadi Hasa has long been defined by scholars as the original heartland of Moab; however, few large settlements have been found on the central plateau and most settlements mentioned in the Mesha Inscription are located north of the Wadi Mujib.

The northern border of Moab was heavily disputed terrain. According to the Mesha Inscription, in the 9th century BC Madaba, Nebo, Jahas, and Atharot were Israelite territory, later captured by King Mesha. But not only the Israelites struggled with the Moabites for control over the northern part of Moab, the Ammonites did too (Dearman 2009). In the biblical prophecies against Moab, Heshbon is attributed alternately to Moab (Isa. 15: 4; 16: 8–9) and Ammon (Jer. 48: 2, 34, 45; 49: 3). At Jalul an engraved seal was found with

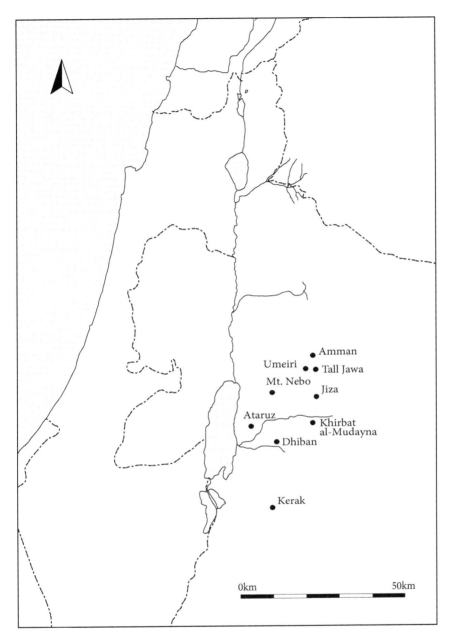

FIG. 51.1 Map of Iron Age II sites in Moab

Ammonite script from the 7th century BC. According to the excavator, the presence of this seal might suggest that Jalul was Ammonite then and that the border of the Ammonite king-dom extended as far south as Madaba during the latter part of the Iron Age (see Younker, Ch. 50 above).

Daviau suggests that during the 8th and 7th centuries BC the Wadi Wala/Wadi ath-Thamad constituted the northern border of Moab, as the pottery found at sites north of that line differs from sites south of it (Daviau 1997: 225–7). However, borders of pottery repertoires and political borders do not necessarily coincide (Steiner 2009).

State formation

It is generally accepted that Mesha's Moab was some form of state, with a formalized leadership, a (small) administration, and a capital. The discussion is rather about what kind of state. Steiner (2001) suggests it conformed to the 'Early State' as described by Claessen and Skalník (1978), with limited control of the king over the local communities and over economical matters (see below). Others (Younker 1997) have suggested that Mesha's Moab was a tribal state (see also Bienkowski, Ch. 52 below and 2009). Routledge (2004) argues for a 'segmentary' state, in which the segments are formed by the population of the towns that are mentioned in the Mesha Inscription, together with their hinterlands. As the archaeological evidence is limited and most excavations have not been fully published, the final word on this matter has not been said.

Archaeological evidence

The problems surrounding the archaeological evidence of southern Jordan are succinctly summarized by Bienkowski in his contribution on Edom (Ch. 52 below). The problems he mentions apply equally well to Moab: most excavations and surveys are ongoing and have not been fully published. The excavation of Dhiban has yielded disappointing results because of later Hellenistic and Roman building activities on the site which have largely destroyed the Iron Age remains. Survey work, from Nelson Glueck's in the 1930s to recent ongoing work, lacks a firm base in the form of an established pottery chronology. This is caused by the dearth of final publications, but also by of the lack of multi-layered sites in Moab. Most sites are one-period, and no site thus far has yielded a good sequence of pottery shapes. Thus the dates attached to pottery and settlements in publications are to be treated with caution. Apart from the Mesha Inscription, very few inscriptions have been found in Moab.

Settlement patterns

In contrast to Ammon and Israel, Moab seems to boast a two-tiered settlement hierarchy, with on the one hand fortified towns and fortresses, and on the other small agricultural settlements. The excavated towns of Khirbat al-Mudayna ath-Thamad and Dhiban are 1ha and 3ha in size respectively. These towns can be interpreted as the seats of the king and his court—in other words, the elite of Moab surrounded themselves with fortification walls, impressive gates, and small-sized 'palaces'. These small but well-defended towns functioned as centres of administration, regional trade, and industry. Most are located in the northern part of Moab, north of the Wadi Mujib. The fortresses, on the other hand, were located mainly on the eastern border of the region, where incursions by Arab tribes were threatening, as attested in Assyrian texts.

The many small villages, farmsteads, and agricultural installations have largely remained unexcavated. Surveys have revealed a dramatic growth of small settlements in the course of the Iron Age, both north of the Wadi Mujib (Ji 2007) and south of it (Miller 1991).

Towns

Tell Dhiban was excavated from 1950 to 1953 (Winnett and Reed 1964; Tushingham 1972) and again in 1955, 1956, and 1965 (Morton 1989). The excavations concentrated on the Iron II period, when Dhiban was supposed to be ancient Dhibon, the capital of King Mesha. Later building activities from the Hellenistic period onwards had, however, severely disturbed the Iron Age layers. What was found are massive earth fills, up to 11m deep. They constitute an extension of the site by some 0.75ha in Iron IIB, enlarging the town to 3ha. Morton excavated part of a large Iron II building, interpreted as a palace (for plan, see Routledge 2004; Morton 1989). The architectural remains and pottery of Dhiban have generally been dated to the 9th–7th centuries BC.

The best example of a fortified town may be Khirbat al-Mudayna on the Wadi ath-Thamad. The settlement is 1.1ha in size and is surrounded by a casemate wall that is visible on the surface above an earth embankment. At the north side a six-chambered gate leads into a plaza, at least 16×7m wide. From there a road runs southwards alongside a complex of tripartite pillared buildings with industrial functions on the east side. At the other side of the road is a large public building adjacent to a domestic complex (Daviau et al. 2006). Between the plaza and the casemate wall a small temple was excavated (Daviau and Steiner 2000), in which an inscribed incense stand was found (Dion and Daviau 2000).

The buildings excavated on the east, west, and south sides of the mound all hug the casemate wall and use the casemate room as storage space (Daviau et al. 2008). The finds in the pillared buildings include large stone basins, giant millstones, cuboid incense altars, and plain and painted pottery. The textile industry may have been an important economic activity, as loomweights and other related finds (low stone tables and dyeing equipment) have been excavated (Daviau and Chadwick 2007). The main strategic function of the town must have been to guard the northern and eastern frontiers of the kingdom.

Carbon-14 samples date the construction of the site in the middle of the 9th century BC. Some centuries later Mudayna was violently destroyed; the gate and pillared buildings were burnt down, although the shrine shows no sign of burning and may have been respected by the attackers. The pottery (see below) dates this destruction to around 600 BC—but note that dating the pottery of Moab is still in its infancy (see above). The attackers may be sought among the Babylonians, who (according to Josephus) campaigned against Moab in 582 BC. Alternatively the town may have been destroyed by nomadic tribes from the east or by the Ammonite kingdom trying to extend its control to the south.

Other Moabite Iron Age towns north of the Wadi Mujib include Tell Madaba (Harrison, Foran, and Graham 2007); Khirbat al-Mukkhayat or ancient Nebo (not excavated); Khirbat al-Ataruz, where a large temple complex has been unearthed (see below); and possibly Hesban (Ray 2001) and Tell Jalul (see Younker, Ch. 50 above, who however assigns Tell Jalul, unequivocally to Ammonite territory).

South of the Wadi Mujib only the Iron Age town of Balu' was identified (Worschech 1995). According to the excavator it may have reached a size of 10ha, but very little of this area has actually been uncovered. Kerak is often equated with Kir Hareseth from the Mesha Inscription, but no Iron Age remains have been identified up to date.

Fortresses

Several forts have been ascribed to this period, but most have not or only very partially been excavated and their pottery has not been published so far, including square enclosures at

Arair, Akuzeh, Iktanu and Lehun, and a round fortification at Rumeyl. Their dating and the interpretation of their function have to await the final publication of the data. The material of Lehun has now been analysed; the Iron II material generally dates to the end of the period, the 7th–6th centuries BC (Steiner forthcoming).

Mudaybi is a large fortress located on the Karak Plateau, south of the Wadi Mujib. The enclosure is 0.75ha in size, surrounded by a casemate wall with large towers at the corners and in the wall. A four-chambered gate at the east side provided an entrance; several proto-aeolic volute capitals have been found nearby. It has been dated by the excavators to the late Iron II/Persian period on the basis of ^{14}C dating (Mattingly and Pace 1989).

Villages and isolated buildings

In a survey of the eastern edge of the Kerak Plateau, 61 sites dating to Iron II were identified in an area of 15×50km, among which were 45 isolated structures including towers and small rectangular enclosures (see Routledge 1996: 94). According to Routledge, the towers did not have a defensive function as they were not located on top of the hills but overlooking arable lands. In Ammon, where several of these towers have been found, they tend to cluster with agricultural installations: wine presses, oil presses, and terraces (Kletter 1991). On the Kerak Plateau no agricultural installations were found near the towers except cisterns. Routledge excavated several of these towers and isolated structures, and found they contained the complete range of grain and food preparation tools. They were probably used for storage and as field shelters. He dated most of these structures to the 7th century BC and later (Routledge 1996: 95). They were abandoned at the end of Iron IIC. Small nucleated villages have been identified during surveys, but so far none have been excavated.

Burial tombs

Several rock-cut tombs from the region of Moab provide insight into the burial practices of the elite of Moab. At Dhiban, several Iron II tombs were found, three of which were full of pottery and other finds (Tushingham 1972). Besides pottery dated to the 9th–6th centuries BC (for a description, see below), these bench tombs contained cylinder seals, pendant beads, and jewellery. In one tomb a (broken) anthropoid pottery coffin was found. In several tombs human remains were found, but as the tombs had been robbed, no intact skeletons could be retrieved.

Two tombs were excavated at Khirbat al-Mukhhayat (Mt Nebo), containing hundreds of complete vessels dated by the excavator to the 10th–7th centuries BC as well as cylinder seals, pendant beads, and fragments of pottery coffins (Saller 1966). A large tomb near Madaba was in use during Iron I and II (Piccirillo 1975; Thompson 1984).

RELIGION

Moab's main god Kemos is mentioned a dozen times in the Mesha Inscription as well as eight times in the Hebrew Bible. His name also appears in theophoric names on seals found in Moab (Van Zyl 1960) and in the name of Kemos-yat, the father of Mesha, in the Mesha Inscription (see further Mattingly 1989).

So far four religious complexes have been identified in Moab. At Khirbat 'Ataruz, a multi-chambered sanctuary was excavated with at least three parallel rooms. They contained a variety of cultic objects including jars decorated with bull heads and a fenestrated architectural model with two male figures. The excavator dates the complex to the late Iron I and early Iron II periods, and presumes it was destroyed by King Mesha (as narrated in the Mesha Inscription). A village was built over the ruins later in Iron II.

A smaller temple was unearthed at Khirbat al-Mudayna ath-Thamad, dating to the 7th–early 6th centuries BC (Daviau and Steiner 2000) (Fig. 51.2). The structure was 5×5m with plastered benches at three sides. One libation altar and two shaft altars were found inside the building, one containing an inscription saying 'the incense altar that Elishama made for YSP, the daughter of "WT"' (Dion and Daviau 2000; but see Rainey 2002 for an alternative translation; Routledge 2003). Other finds in the temple include oil lamps, female figurines, and beads. It seems most material was removed from the temple when the town was attacked. Near the entrance stood a stone mortar surrounded by ashes and iron slag, suggestive of smithing activities (making arrowheads?) in this last stage of the town. To which deity the shrine was dedicated is not clear.

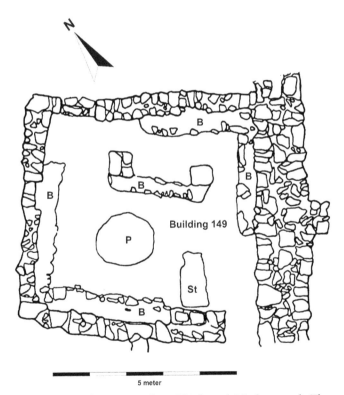

FIG. 51.2 Plan of the temple excavated at Khirbat al-Mudayna ath-Thamad (courtesy Wadi Thamad Project). Several benches (B) lined the walls, while another bench was flanked by two stone pillars. A pit (P) had been cut through the floor and was then resealed. It contained only some pottery and a stone with a rectangular impression. The flat stone (St) may have served as an offering table

Outside the gate of Mudayna several standing stones were found, bordering the pathway to the gate. This was interpreted as a small place of worship by the excavator, although no cultic or special objects were found nearby (Daviau et al. 2006).

Some 2km west of Khirbat al-Mudayna an open-air sanctuary has been excavated (Site WT-13 of the Wadi ath-Thamad survey: Daviau et al. 2006). On a flat hilltop a perimeter wall was built, enclosing an area of c.7×14m. Large stones inside the wall may have served as benches. The finds inside the enclosure wall consisted of a large collection of ceramic statuettes and pillar figurines with a disc in their hands—comparable to the figurines of Horvat Qitmit and 'Ein Hazeva in the Negev. Other special finds include miniature vessels, architectural models, faience amulets, scarabs, and shells (see Daviau 2008 and Dolan 2009 for illustrations of some of the material). The pottery dates this sanctuary firmly in the later Iron II period. An earlier occupation phase consisted of five cooking installations from the Iron I/IIA period, but it is unclear if these finds constitute an earlier phase of the sanctuary or are the remains of household activities.

POTTERY

The Iron II pottery of Moab is well known from tombs, but very little has been published from secure layers at excavated sites. The pottery from the first six seasons of excavations at Khirbat al-Mudayna (1996–2004) is in the process of being published by the author (see also Steiner 2006; 2009) (Fig. 51.3). The pottery comes mainly from the uppermost floors and the destruction debris on top of the floor, and consists of ordinary household vessels: cooking pots, storage jars, kraters, medium and small bowls and jugs, and juglets. In the absence of ^{14}C dates this pottery can only very generally be dated to the end of the Iron II period (c.600 BC).

The repertoire is rather monotonous. Most kraters belong to the same type: a large, deep, four-handled, holemouthed vessel with a folded rim (Fig. 51.3a–b). Almost half of the medium bowls consist of a smaller version of this vessel. In Moab, close parallels have so far only been found (in very small quantities) at Dhiban, some 20km away, and on the Kerak Plateau. In Edom two- and four-handled deep bowls with thickened rims and a ring base seem to be common too.

Half of the cooking pots excavated at Mudayna are of a type that has so far only been reported from the region of Moab and the eastern Jordan Valley. It is a sturdy vessel with a squared rim and two handles. Several of the large storage jugs have three handles (Fig. 51.3c, d), a feature also found at Dhiban. The small cups (Fig. 51.3e, f) are also found at Ammonite sites such as Tell Jawa and Umeiri.

Only a very small number of the sherds are painted with black/dark brown and red stripes or slipped and burnished. White paint was seldom applied. Black-burnished bowls are scarce. This is in stark contrast to the pottery from the same period found in the area of Ammon to the north (where most bowls are red slipped and highly burnished) and Edom to the south (with a large amount of painted pottery). It may be that in Moab these ways of decorating pottery were not *en vogue*, or that Khirbat al-Mudayna was an outpost within the Moabite territory with little demand for fine wares.

The pottery from the tombs of Dhiban and Mukkhayat (Mount Nebo) is more varied, with painted kraters with three-looped bases, carrot bottles, censers, decorated jugs and juglets, and lamps. Slip and polishing are rare. In these tombs, hundreds of small oil or perfume juglets were deposited, commonly called 'Cypro-Phoenician' juglets, although they originate

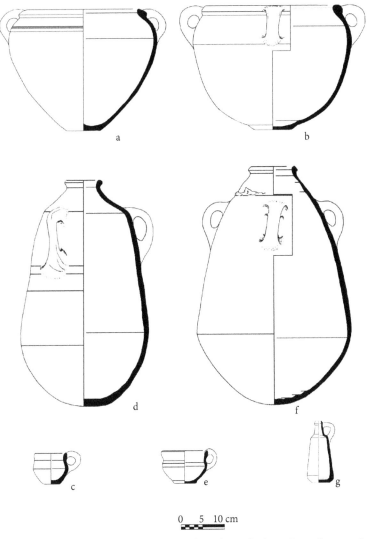

0   5   10 cm

FIG. 51.3 A selection of the complete vessels found at Khirbat al-Mudayna ath-Thamad

neither from Cyprus nor Phoenicia. The painted motifs generally consist of horizontal bands or lines on the neck and the body; a few have concentric circles on two sides of the body. The colour of these lines is mostly black and sometimes black and red (Fig. 51.4). Similar juglets have been found in settlements, but in small quantities only. At Khirbat al-Mudayna some thirty juglets (complete or large fragments) have been counted, which is the largest collection outside of the tombs thus far.

MOAB IN CONTEXT

Evidence from the beginning of the Iron II period (Iron IIA, 10th–first half of 9th centuries BC) is almost completely lacking from Moab. The beginning of state formation and the building of towns and fortresses have generally been attributed to the mid-9th century BC (Iron

FIG. 51.4 'Cypro-Phoenician' juglet (P135) from Khirbat al-Mudayna with dark-brown-painted lines on an unslipped burnished surface (photo Bernard Haberstroh, courtesy Wadi Thamad Project)

IIB). King Mesha's text has influenced this dating to a large extent, but ^{14}C dates at Khirbet al-Mudayna and Madaba are beginning to corroborate it. Moab experienced a short period of independence, in which it fought with the Israelites over the Madaba Plains (according to the Mesha Inscription).

One way to look at Moab is as an 'early state', according to Claessen and Skalník (1978)—that is, a state that experiences state formation for the first time in its history (Steiner 2002). In such a state there are usually two economic 'zones of influence'. The first one consists of the royal circle. The king and the small elite live off the returns of their lands, irregular taxation of the local communities, and taxation of interregional trade. The king lives mostly in his capital, a fortified town, where specialized crafts such as ivory and gold working and the production of luxury pottery are concentrated. Here one can expect to find small palaces and temples, but not large-scale storage facilities, an extensive bureaucratic apparatus creating a lot of economic texts, or a king actively involved in industries and trade. The interest of the ruler in economic matters is small; the state concerns itself foremost with political and ideological matters. Redistribution is an important function of early states, but is ordinarily limited to the distribution of surplus to the (small) administration and the furnishing of sacrifices. The ruler receives food and labour, while his returns are in the ideological sphere: he 'guarantees' fertility, peace, and prosperity. The amounts of goods distributed in these early states are limited.

The local communities (the other 'zone') make a living by agriculture or husbandry combined with the part-time practising of crafts and trade. They are more or less self-sufficient. Land ownership is communal; private land ownership is rare. The interaction between the two circuits will have been limited, as taxes were levied on an irregular basis and the local communities had their own industries and markets (see further Steiner 2001).

In the 9th century BC the small emerging state of Moab displayed the paraphernalia of what Routledge calls 'kingly things': palaces, gate complexes, proto-aeolic capitals, and royal inscriptions. The elite of Moab, who lived in the fortified towns the king had built by his workforce of commoners and prisoners of war (as stated in the Mesha Inscription), were laid to rest in rock-cut tombs near the important towns of Dhiban, Madaba, and Mukhhayat (Mount Nebo). They were buried with nicely decorated pottery, lamps, and jewellery. The decorated bowls and the many 'Cypro-Phoenician' juglets may signify their wish to distinguished themselves from the common people by the conspicuous consumption of wine and scented oil and the ostentatious display of riches. The juglets are clearly inspired by the more expensive but very rare Cypriot Black-on-Red juglets (Schreiber 2003). Such was the demand for these perfume juglets that a local production of this pottery developed in the region.

The Assyrian campaigns, which started in the 8th century BC, did not seriously alter the organization of the state, although Moab became a vassal of the Assyrians and had to pay tribute. Vera Chamaza (2005) has analysed the Assyrian sources concerning Moab. According to one clay tablet, King Salamānu of Moab submitted to the Assyrians and presented gifts (tribute) following the 734–732 BC campaign of Tiglath-pileser III, during which Tiglath-pileser probably did not enter Transjordan. Texts of later Assyrian kings confirm that Moab paid tribute or presented gifts. What exactly Moab paid remains unclear, because it is mentioned together with other vassal states as Judah and Ammon. Moab did not have much to offer to Assyria. Its importance lay in the (trade) routes from Egypt to Syria that Assyria wanted to control. The Assyrians probably left the task of protecting the routes to the Moabites, as no Assyrian stations or fortresses have been found so far. In Iron IIC (7th and 6th centuries BC), when the Neo-Babylonian Empire succeeded the Neo-Assyrian one, the situation changed. It seems that the Transjordanian vassal states rebelled against Babylon. According to Josephus, in the year 582 BC King Nebuchadnezzar II campaigned against Ammon and Moab, defeating them. Archaeological evidence shows that while several Ammonite towns recovered from this blow and flourished during the Neo-Babylonian and Persian periods, the same cannot be said for Moab, as there is no archaeological evidence for these periods. Khirbat al-Mudayna was attacked and destroyed (see above), and Dhiban and the fortresses seem to have been deserted. It would be a long time before the region regained its strength.

SUGGESTED READING

Biblical Archaeologist, The (1997). 60.4 (on the archaeology of Moab).

Bienkowski, P. (ed.) (2009). *Studies on Iron Age Moab and Neighbouring Areas in Honour of Michèle Daviau*. Leuven: Peeters.

Dearman, J. A. (ed.) (1989). *Studies in the Mesha Inscription and Moab*. Atlanta, Ga.: Scholars.

Dion, P.-E., and P. M. M. Daviau (2010). The Moabites. In A. Lemaire and B. Halpern (eds), *The Books of Kings: Sources, Composition, Historiography and Reception*. Leiden: Brill: 205–24.

Routledge, B. E. (2004). *Moab in the Iron Age: Hegemony, Polity, Archaeology*. Philadelphia: University of Pennsylvania Press.

REFERENCES

Bienkowski, P. (2009). 'Tribalism' and 'segmentary society' in Iron Age Transjordan. In P. Bienkowski (ed.), *Studies on Iron Age Moab and Neighbouring Areas in Honour of Michèle Daviau*. Leuven: Peeters: 7–26.

Claessen, H. J. M., and P. Skalník (eds) (1978). *The Early State*. The Hague: Mouton.

Daviau, P. M. M. (1997). Moab's northern border: Khirbat al-Mudayna on the Wadi ath-Thamad. *Biblical Archaeologist* 60: 222–8.

—— (2008). Ceramic architectural models from Transjordan and the Syrian tradition. In H. Kühne, R. M. Czichon, and F. J. Kreppner (eds), *Proceedings of the 4th International Congress of the Archaeology of the Ancient Near East, 29 March–3 April 2004, Freie Universität Berlin*, vol. 1: *The Reconstruction of Environment—Natural Resources and Human Interrelations through Time*. Wiesbaden: Harrassowitz, 293–308.

—— and R. Chadwick (2007). Shepherds and weavers in a 'global economy': Moab in Late Iron Age II—Wadi ath Thamad Project (Khirbat al-Mudayna). In T. E. Levy, P. M. M. Daviau, R. W. Younker, and M. Shaer (eds), *Crossing Jordan: North American Contributions to the Archaeology of Jordan*. Sheffield: Equinox, 309–14.

—— M. L. Steiner, et al. (2006). Excavation and survey at Khirbat al-Mudayna and its surroundings: preliminary report of the 2001, 2004 and 2005 Seasons. *Annual of the Department of Antiquities of Jordan* 50: 249–84.

—— A. Dolan, J. Ferguson, et al. (2008). Preliminary report of excavations and survey at Khirbat al-Mudayna ath-Thamad and in its surroundings (2004, 2006 and 2007). *Annual of the Department of Archaeology of Jordan* 52: 343–74.

—— and M. L. Steiner (2000). A Moabite sanctuary at Khirbat al-Mudayna. *Bulletin of the American Schools of Oriental Research* 320: 1–21.

Dearman, J. A. (2009). Moab and Ammon: some observations on their relationship in light of a new Moabite inscription. In P. Bienkowski (ed.), *Studies on Iron Age Moab and Neighbouring Areas in Honour of Michèle Daviau*. Leuven: Peeters, 97–116.

Dion, P., and P. M. M. Daviau (2000). An inscribed incense altar of Iron Age II at Hirbet el-Mud ēyine (Jordan). *Zeitschrift des Deutschen Palästina-Vereins* 116: 1–13.

Dolan, A. (2009). Defining sacred space in ancient Moab. In P. Bienkowski (ed.), *Studies on Iron Age Moab and Neighbouring Areas in Honour of Michèle Daviau*. Leuven: Peeters, 129–44.

Graham, M. P. (1989). The discovery and reconstruction of the Mesha inscription. In J. A. Dearman (ed.), *Studies in the Mesha Inscription and Moab*. Atlanta, Ga.: Scholars, 41–92.

Harrison, T. J., D. Foran, and A. Graham (2007). Investigating 5,000 years of urban history: the Tall Madaba Archaeological Project. In T. E. Levy, P. M. M. Daviau, R. W. Younker, and M. Shaer (eds), *Crossing Jordan: North American Contributions to the Archaeology of Jordan*. Sheffield: Equinox, 143–52.

Horn, S. H. (1986). Why the Moabite stone was blown to pieces: ninth-century B.C. inscription adds new dimension to biblical account of Mesha's rebellion. *Biblical Archaeology Review* 12.3: 50–61.

Ji, C.-H. (2007). The 'Iraq Al-Amir and Dhiban Plateau regional surveys. In T. E. Levy, P. M. M. Daviau, R. W. Younker, and M. Shaer (eds), *Crossing Jordan: North American Contributions to the Archaeology of Jordan*. Sheffield: Equinox, 137–42.

Kletter, R. (1991). The Rujm El-Malfuf buildings and the Assyrian vassal state of Ammon. *Bulletin of the American Schools of Oriental Research* 284: 33–50.

Mattingly, G. L. (1989). Moabite religion and the Mesha Inscription. In J. A. Dearman (ed.), *Studies in the Mesha Inscription and Moab*. Atlanta, Ga.: Scholars, 211–38.

——and J. H. Pace. (1989). Crossing Jordan: by way of the Karak Plateau. In J. A. Dearman (ed.), *Studies in the Mesha Inscription and Moab*. Atlanta, Ga.: Scholars, 153–60.

Miller, J. M. (ed.) (1991). *Archaeological Survey of the Kerak Plateau: Conducted during 1978–1982 under the Direction of J. Maxwell Miller and Jack M. Pinkerton*. Atlanta, Ga.: Scholars.

Morton, W. H. (1989). A summary of the 1955, 1956, and 1965 excavations at Dibon. In J. A. Dearman (ed.), *Studies in the Mesha Inscription and Moab*. Atlanta, Ga.: Scholars, 237–46.

Piccirillo, M. (1975). Una tomba del Ferro I a Madaba. *Liber annuus* 25: 199–224.

Rainey, A. F. (2002). The new inscription from Khirbet el-Mudeiyineh. *Israel Exploration Journal* 52: 81–6.

Ray, P. J. (2001). *Tell Hesban and Vicinity in the Iron Age*. Berrien Springs, Mich.: Andrews University Press.

Routledge, B. E. (1996). *Intermittent agriculture and the political economy of Iron Age Moab*. PhD dissertation, University of Toronto.

——(2003). A comment on Rainey's 'The new inscription from Khirbet el-Mudeiyineh'. *Israel Exploration Journal* 53: 192–5.

——(2004). *Moab in the Iron Age: Hegemony, Polity, Archaeology*. Philadelphia: University of Pennsylvania Press.

Saller, S. J. (1966). Iron Age tombs at Nebo, Jordan. *Liber annuus* 16: 165–298.

Schreiber, N. (2003). *The Cypro-Phoenician Pottery of the Iron Age*. Leiden: Brill.

Steiner, M. L. (2001). I am Mesha, king of Moab, or: Economic organization in Iron Age II. *Studies in the Archaeology and History of Jordan* 8: 327–30.

——(2002). Mesha versus Solomon: two models of economic organization in Iron Age II. *Svensk Exegetisk Årsbok* 67: 37–45.

——(2006). The pottery of Khirbat al-Mudayna and Site WT-13 in Jordan. *Leiden Journal of Pottery Studies* 22: 101–10.

——(2009). Khirbat al-Mudayna and Moabite pottery production. In P. Bienkowski (ed.). *Studies on Iron Age Moab and Neighbouring Areas in Honour of Michèle Daviau*. Leuven: Peeters, 145–64.

——(forthcoming). The Iron Age Pottery of Khirbat al-Lahun, Area D. *Bulletin of the Amerian Schools of Oriental Research*.

Thompson, H. O. (1984). Madaba: an Iron Age tomb. In H. O. Thompson (ed.), *The Answers Lie Below: Essays in Honor of Lawrence Edmund Toombs*. Lanham, Md.: University Press of America, 147–83.

Tushingham, A. D. (1972). *The Excavations at Dibon (Dhibân) in Moab: The Third Campaign 1952–53*. Cambridge, Mass.: American Schools of Oriental Research.

Van Zyl, A. H. (1960). *The Moabites*. Leiden: Brill.

Vera Chamaza, G. W. (2005). *Die Rolle Moabs in der neuassyrischen Expansionspolitik*. Münster: Ugarit-Verlag.

Winnett, F. V., and W. L. Reed (1964). *The Excavations at Dibon (Dhibân) in Moab*. Cambridge, Mass.: American Schools of Oriental Research.

Worschech, U. (1995). City planning and architecture in the Iron Age city of al-Bālū in central Jordan. *Studies in the History and Archaeology of Jordan* 5: 145–9.

Younker, R. W. (1997). Moabite social structure. *Biblical Archaeologist* 60: 237–48.

....

CHAPTER 52

EDOM DURING THE IRON AGE II PERIOD

....

PIOTR BIENKOWSKI

THE NATURE OF THE EVIDENCE

As with any geographical area or chronological period, what we can say with confidence about Iron II Edom (Fig. 52.1) is constrained by the nature of the evidence and the type of archaeological work carried out and published. The particular constraints for Iron II Edom are that much of the evidence comes from surface surveys; relatively few sites have been excavated and even fewer of those have been published in final form. Indeed, at the time of writing, only three Iron II sites in Edom have been properly published in final form—Tawilan (Bennett and Bienkowski 1995), Busayra (Bienkowski 2002), and Umm al-Biyara (Bienkowski 2011).

This makes it difficult to give an authoritative or comprehensive overview of sites and finds. Other than the three fully published sites, the rest of the evidence available falls into the following categories:

- surface surveys carried out in the 1930s by Nelson Glueck;
- more recent intensive surface surveys, some fully published, others only ever published in preliminary form or still ongoing;
- excavations which were either published only in preliminary form (e.g. Ghrareh: Hart 1988) or technically problematic, thus leaving many problems unresolved (e.g. Glueck's 1938–40 excavations at Tall al-Kheleifeh: Pratico 1993); and
- ongoing excavations which have yielded some preliminary publications, but often without details of finds or contextual data (e.g. recent work in the Faynan region: Levy, Adams, and Shafiq 1999; Levy et al. 2004).

Archaeological coverage of Edom in general—including the Iron II period—is extremely patchy. Large areas have still not been systematically surveyed, and even those that have been surveyed more intensively give us data that is not stratigraphically controlled. This means that questions about precise dating, use of sites and the nature of the material culture cannot be answered effectively. These constraints should be borne in mind when reading this section.

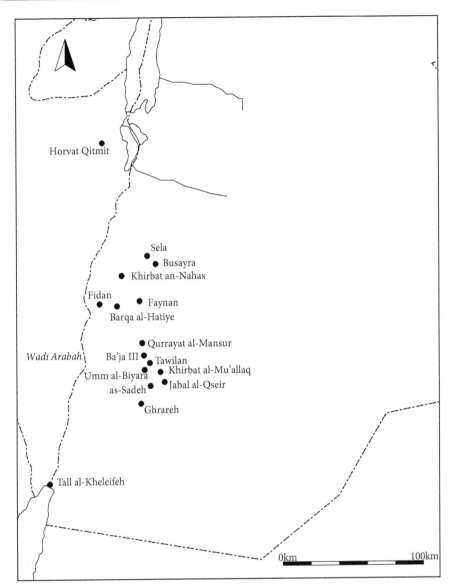

FIG. 52.1 Map showing Iron Age II sites in Edom

The other types of evidence which have a bearing on interpretation of Iron II in Edom are:

- Hebrew Bible: this mentions Edom directly as a neighbour and frequent enemy of Israel and Judah, but the historicity of many of the passages is disputed, so they must be carefully evaluated in order to extract worthwhile historical information (Bartlett 1989).
- Contemporary historical references: Edom appears in Egyptian, Assyrian, and Neo-Babylonian inscriptions and these are useful for evaluating Edom's relationships with imperial powers.

- Epigraphic sources: a few inscriptions on bullae and ostraca have been found from Edom itself. While the information they provide is of limited use, occasionally the royal names can be connected with those in Assyrian inscriptions to provide a useful dating framework.

DATING

Exact dates for Iron II settlement in Edom cannot yet be established with certainty. There are four sources for dating:

- A bulla from a stratified context at Umm al-Biyara inscribed 'belonging to Qos-Gabr, king of Edom' has been dated on paleographic grounds to the first three-quarters of the 7th century BCE (Fig. 52.2). It is possible, though not certain, that the name is the same as the *Qaušgabri*, king of Edom, known from the annals of the Assyrian kings Esarhaddon (dated 673 BCE) and Ashurbanipal (dated 667 BCE), which would provide a more precise date. The identification is plausible, but it cannot be discounted that the bulla refers to another Qos-Gabr, king of Edom, later in the 7th century BCE, since no names of kings of Edom are attested in the Assyrian annals after 667 BCE. Nevertheless, a date within the first three-quarters of the 7th century BCE is certain.
- Inscriptions on ostraca from Busayra, Umm al-Biyara, and Tall al-Kheleifeh, and a Neo-Babylonian bulla from Umm al-Biyara are dated by paleography and parallels to symbolism between the late 8th and 6th centuries BCE.
- Pottery: assigning precise dates to Iron II pottery from Edom is hugely problematic. Until a few years ago it was widely believed that Iron II settlement in Edom and its associated pottery dated between the late 8th and 6th centuries BCE. Recent work in the Faynan area and a re-evaluation of the pottery from Busayra have caused these dates to be stretched both earlier and later. In the Faynan area, pottery from Barqa al-Hatiye and Khirbat an-Nahas has been associated with ^{14}C dates in the 9th century

FIG. 52.2 Bulla inscribed 'belonging to Qos-Gabr, king of Edom' from Umm al-Biyara (courtesy Piotr Bienkowski)

BCE (Bienkowski 2001). The Busayra pottery dates between the late 8th century and
c.300/200 BC, the later date indicated by the presence of Attic and Hellenistic sherds
alongside characteristic 'Iron II' pottery. Late Iron II forms appear to continue virtually
unchanged to the end of the Persian period and perhaps into the early Hellenistic
period, with the probable addition of some new forms but no discernible break
between the periods (Bienkowski 2002: 349–51).

- Radiocarbon dates from the Faynan area have been claimed to show settlement there
between the 12th and 9th centuries BCE (Levy et al. 2004). However, at the time of this
writing, the contexts of those dates have not been published, and only a preliminary
account of some of the pottery (Smith and Levy 2008). Furthermore, the claims for the
early, 12th–9th-century BCE settlement are based on artificially pushing the ¹⁴C dates on
average 100 years earlier than the standard calibrated radiocarbon evidence allows for,
using the 'Bayesian' calibration system (see critique in van der Steen and Bienkowski
2006); furthermore, when a different Bayesian calibration system was used as a test,
the results differed significantly. The Faynan ¹⁴C dates therefore must be used with
caution, depending on whether they have been calibrated by the Bayesian system, and
this has implications for interpretation of early Iron Age settlement, metallurgy, and
statehood in Edom (see below).

Currently the dating evidence indicates some activity in the Faynan region between the
12th and 9th centuries BCE, the vast majority of sites on the Edomite plateau flourishing
between the late 8th and 6th centuries BCE, and continuity of settlement at certain sites
through the Persian period and perhaps into the Early Hellenistic period.

THE 'TRIBAL KINGDOM' MODEL
AND ALTERNATIVES

Until the end of the 20th century, the Iron II in Edom was interpreted almost exclusively
according to an understanding of the archaeology derived from the Hebrew Bible: we can
term this the 'traditional' or 'biblical archaeology paradigm'. Edom and its neighbours were
interpreted as discrete, bounded nation-states with formal political borders, following the
19th-century European model. Within each 'state', the material culture was linked to ethnicity: so, for example, a particular type of pottery was identified as characteristically 'Edomite'
and its presence was seen as denoting the presence of ethnic Edomites who identified with
the nation-state. The state of Edom was constructed as centralized and hierarchical with
a king, a capital, a state religion, and a centralized administrative system. The presence of
'Edomite' pottery, for example, outside the 'borders' of Edom, across the Wadi Arabah in
the Negev within what was regarded as Judah, was interpreted as evidence of invasion, conquest, and settlement by Edomites (Bienkowski 2007).

This 'traditional paradigm' did not account for the complexity of the archaeological record,
and Bienkowski and van der Steen (2001) proposed a new framework, building empirically on
previous theoretical work. This approach is generally termed the 'tribal kingdom' model.

According to the tribal kingdom model, the basic unit of subsistence in Iron II Edom
(indeed, throughout most periods in the southern Levant), historically, is the tribe. A working definition of 'tribe' is:

- a small group defined by traditions of common descent (real or fictive kinship, generative genealogies);
- temporary or permanent political integration above the family level;
- shared language, culture, and ideology;
- inhabits a core geographical area but can move around, contract, and expand depending on circumstances: can be sedentary, nomadic, or both;
- works together in such joint endeavours as trade, agriculture, house construction, conflict (blood feud and warfare), and ceremonial activities;
- usually composed of a number of smaller local communities (e.g., families, bands, villages, or neighbourhoods); and
- may be aggregated into temporary or permanent higher-order clusters—confederations, nations, or kingdoms.

Based on such criteria, in an archaeological model the tribes in Iron II Edom would have been kin-based, partially range-tied and nomadic, and partially land-tied and settled with a mixed economy of pastoralism, agriculture, trade, protection, and copper-mining, the balance changing according to circumstances. They would have had core areas but moved around, and negotiated movement across areas controlled by other tribes. They had relations with towns, nominal 'central' governments, and with imperial powers, but in practice they were independent—although clearly their ability to act 'independently' was constrained—and their affiliation ('identity') was to kin groups within the tribe, not to a 'kingdom'. Within such a model, Edom was not a monolithic nation-state, but a tribal kingdom composed of largely independent groupings held together by bonds of cooperation and allegiance to a supra-tribal monarchy at the so-called capital, Busayra, which was in fact probably more of a supra-tribal centre. Each tribe continued to control its own area and had its own power base, so the relationship between tribes, and between Busayra and the other tribes, was heterarchical, not hierarchical.

These tribal groups did not suddenly stop their pastoral migrations when political 'Edom' was formed—or, more accurately, when a monarchy was generated from the tribal coalitions. They continued to move independently across the Wadi Arabah and interacted with other groups from Arabia and the west. The tribal groups controlled and sometimes raided the incense trade between Arabia and the Mediterranean. The characteristic pottery of these different groups is found mixed together at the sites where they mingled, especially in the Negev, and much of it was probably manufactured at these sites; here, they probably had grazing grounds and engaged in small-scale agriculture. Other archaeological correlates of this model include the decentralization of Edom, with widely varying settlement types and ceramic assemblages between different regions—the Petra area of southern Edom, for example, having quite distinctive mountain-top sites with long-room houses and a paucity of painted pottery (see below).

A critique of the 'tribal kingdom' model by Routledge (2004) substitutes an alternative model of hegemony, focusing on Iron Age Moab as a case study. Routledge's definition of hegemony is force and consent operating together, the cumulative effect of specific projects carried out by particular agents, the bounding of the social space of the state, and the differentiation of rulers from the ruled. Within this framework, he emphasizes the concept of segmentation as a form of identification: essentially, how identity is formed through differentiation and hierarchy, and forms taxonomic categories that can be applied to the archaeological and historical evidence (for a critique of Routledge's model, especially its failure to account for the archaeological evidence, see Bienkowski 2007). Porter (2004) has attempted to apply Routledge's framework, established for Moab, to the evidence from Iron Age Edom in order to develop an alternative to the 'tribal kingdom' model, focusing on ways that segmentary systems constructed and promoted the ability of 'elites' to organize disparate tribal alliances. Nevertheless, his basic premiss is that Edom was a centralized, hierarchical state within set borders, and in many ways, this is no more than an elaboration of the traditional paradigm.

THE NATURE OF IRON II SETTLEMENT IN EDOM

There is no evidence for settlement in Edom during the Middle and Late Bronze Age. Egyptian inscriptions of the late second millennium BCE record that Edom was inhabited by the *Shasu*, nomadic pastoralists who lived in tents and kept flocks of sheep.

Current evidence suggests that, in the early Iron Age, mining recommenced in the Wadi Faynan after a gap of nearly 1,000 years. Ongoing work in the Faynan area has proposed that there is ^{14}C and ceramic evidence for a main phase of copper production in the 12th–11th centuries BCE, with the construction of a fortress at Khirbat an-Nahas in the 10th century (Levy et al. 2004). It has also been claimed that the presence of the copper industry and the fortress indicates state formation in Edom considerably earlier than previously thought. Problems with interpreting the ^{14}C dates have been outlined above. An alternative proposal (van der Steen and Bienkowski 2006: 17–18) is that there is evidence at Faynan of aceramic, non-settled cooking activity and possibly mining by pastoralist groups between the late 12th and 11th centuries, and some definite mining activity at the very end of the 11th century BCE. Burials ^{14}C-dated to the 10th–9th centuries BCE have been found in the nearby Wadi Fidan. They contained beads, textiles, leather, metal jewellery, and wooden bowls, perhaps indicating that these were pastoralist groups known from Egyptian inscriptions to have inhabited this area (Levy, Adams, and Shafiq 1999). The Nahas fortress, belonging to the 10th or 9th century BCE, was an isolated, short-lived phenomenon—indeed, there are indications that its construction was never completed—unconnected to later developments and state formation on the Edomite plateau.

On current evidence, the activity at Faynan between the 12th and 9th centuries BCE is isolated from the rest of Edom: outside the Faynan area, nothing has been found to date to that period, and there is no evidence of archaeological continuity between the Faynan activities and later developments on the Edomite plateau (the little pottery published so far from Khirbat an-Nahas does not have as close parallels to pottery from the Edomite plateau as the excavators claim, see Smith and Levy 2008). It is possible that the activities at Faynan were connected with copper mining and trade to the west, rather than with state formation and settlement on the Edomite plateau.

Iron II settlement on the Edomite plateau dates from the late 8th century BCE. From this date, surface surveys indicate intensive settlement across the whole of Edom, though few sites have been excavated. A characteristic of Iron II settlement in Edom is how very different the sites are: there is no consistency in site type, no hierarchy of settlements, and huge regional variation, which is what one would expect of the pattern of settlement in a heterarchical tribal kingdom with little central control.

Busayra, often called the 'capital' of Edom, and certainly the main city of Edom mentioned in the Hebrew Bible (Bozrah), was clearly some sort of administrative and religious centre, located in the north of Edom (Bienkowski 2002). It is a natural stronghold on a high spur surrounded on three sides by wadis, with a route leading towards the Wadi Arabah and the crossing to the Negev used by Arabian trade. Excavations revealed two large public buildings, probably a temple and a palace, constructed on stone and earth platforms which raised them up above the surrounding houses, the whole area bounded by a perimeter wall (Fig. 52.3). The architecture and town plan are quite unique in Edom: certainly no other structure in Iron Age Edom has yet been identified as a temple or shrine (see below).

Many Iron Age settlements in Edom appear to have been open villages and farms, such as Tawilan (Bennett and Bienkowski 1995) and Khirbat al-Mu'allaq (Lindner, Knauf, and Zeitler 1996). Ghrareh is an exception, since it was on a spur surrounded by an enclosure wall, but it is most likely to be interpreted as a fortified farmstead with perhaps some involvement in trade (Hart 1988). Ongoing excavations at Khirbat ad-Dabba, near Petra, have revealed two large casemate wall systems and two large rectilinear buildings, indicating that this may be more than simply an agricultural settlement (Whiting 2006). Tall al-Kheleifeh on the Red Sea is an enigmatic site, variously described as a border fortress, a grain storage facility, or a fortified caravanserai. It was excavated by Nelson Glueck in 1938–40, who proposed two main phases: a casemate fortress with a six-roomed building in the centre, followed by a fortified settlement with a four-chambered gate (Pratico 1993). However, a season of new excavations in 1999 by the late M.-L. Mussell suggests a drastic revision to Glueck's stratigraphy and plans, and questions his division into strata. Kheleifeh's unique mixture of pottery of different origins and other objects strongly suggests that its role was connected with the Arabian trade as a gateway town on the Red Sea coast trade route.

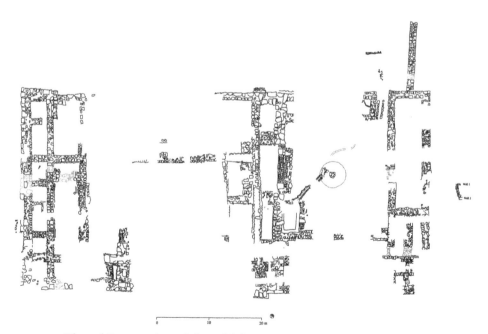

FIG. 52.3 Plan of Busayra Area A 'temple' (courtesy Piotr Bienkowski)

A particular characteristic of Iron II sites in the Petra region are mountain-top sites: Umm al-Biyara, as-Sadeh, Ba'ja III, Jabal al-Qseir, and Qurayyat al-Mansur (see Knauf and Lindner 1997). These are barely accessible with no direct access to spring water—cisterns are either rain-fed, or water has to be carried up to the summit from springs at the mountain base. These mountain sites are nevertheless situated among terraces and small fields that are suitable for small-scale agriculture, grazing, viticulture, and horticulture. The people living on the mountain sites obtained grain and other products of agriculture—presumably by exchange—from sites on the plateau with whom they had a reciprocal but shifting relationship. Some of the characteristic 'longhouse' buildings and installations at the mountain sites might be explained as secure storage areas, protecting food and other goods that were painstakingly acquired and carried up. Many of the mountain sites have a pottery assemblage largely restricted to cooking and storage (of liquid or grain), with little painted pottery. This lack of fine 'table ware' may reflect the function of these sites—some may have been temporary camps, although for most there is little to suggest they were not permanently occupied—but can also be explained in other ways, such as economic status or tribal tradition and culinary habits.

The largest of these mountain-top sites is Qurayyat al-Mansur (Hübner 2004). The summit and terraces have dense concentrations of dry-stone buildings, apparently broadroom houses, divided into discrete areas on the northern, southern, and eastern ends of the plateau. There is evidence of a town wall, with a gateway at the northern point. On the basis of his surface survey, Hübner (2004) concludes that the site was the second largest settlement so far discovered in Edom, after Busayra, and suggests it was a customs post on the Iron II trade route for copper from Faynan and incense from Arabia, situated almost exactly halfway between the Petra area and Busayra.

'EDOMITE' POTTERY

The regional variation in pottery throughout Iron II Edom mirrors the variation in site type. A type of pottery generally known as 'Edomite' pottery is a painted ware particularly characteristic of Busayra (hence it has also been labelled 'Busayra Painted Ware') (Fig. 52.4).

Approximately half of the bowls from Busayra were decorated, mainly with lines and bands of slip, and similar decoration appears also on many jars, jugs, and a few other vessels. The most common type of decoration is an arrangement of concentric horizontal bands and lines, appearing on most vessel types with the exception of cooking pots and lamps. An elaborate type of painted slip decoration consists of horizontal bands and lines supplemented with a variety of motifs, normally geometric (e.g. diagonal strokes, triangles, zigzags, 'tree of life', blobs and spots, saltires, and cross-hatching). Denticulated decoration is found at Busayra, Tall al-Kheleifeh, and Tawilan, but is particularly common in the Negev. Although denticulation is often regarded as diagnostic of 'Edomite' pottery, the fact that it occurs apparently in even greater profusion in the Negev perhaps suggests that this was a form of decoration common over a wide area, including the Negev and southern Jordan, rather than being specific to one group.

The pottery assemblage at Busayra is very rich, and many types are not found elsewhere in Edom: indeed, many of the parallels are from the Negev. This suggests an assemblage characteristic of northern Edom and the Negev, demonstrably different from that in southern

FIG. 52.4 Decorated pottery from Busayra (courtesy Piotr Bienkowski)

Edom. The most noticeable characteristics of the pottery assemblage from Umm al-Biyara inside Petra are how restricted it is compared with Busayra, and the paucity of painted decoration and its relative simplicity. This suggests that there is a complex mix of ceramic assemblages throughout Edom, undermining attempts to define a characteristic 'Edomite' assemblage.

RELIGION

The only 'temple' so far tentatively identified in Edom is the Area A building at Busayra. In its developed phase it consisted of two wings, each with rooms around an inner courtyard. Four symmetrically placed major doorways were found, two central and two off-centre. The courtyard of the northeastern wing contained a stone-lined cistern associated with two drains, one emerging from a small room with plastered floor and walls. At one end of the courtyard, stone paving led to shallow stone steps flanked by two circular stone bases bearing the imprint of columns, statues, or cult objects. A small plastered room, from which one drain exited, might be identified as a 'purification room'. This led to a long, narrow plastered room reached by the steps, described as a *cella* or 'holy of holies', associated with two low stone podia and copper alloy chair fittings, perhaps suggesting that it originally contained an impressive chair or throne. There was no direct access between the two courtyards, and it is possible that these functioned separately.

There is no evidence from epigraphic finds or Hebrew Bible references to indicate the identity of the deity or deities who might have been worshipped in the 'temple'. It has been suggested that the shrine at Horvat Qitmit in the Negev was Edomite and dedicated to Qos, but the architecture and cultic finds there are completely different and it cannot be used as a parallel. Nevertheless, there is some temptation to identify the Busayra 'temple' as dedicated to Qos, since two kings of Edom had names compounded with this theophoric element, but this is speculation (Bartlett 1989: 203). While this argument might allow the identification of Qos as the deity of the royal line at Busayra, there is no clear evidence that Qos was a 'state' god of Edom or the head of a pantheon. Certainly Qos is known to have been worshipped in Edom, the Hijaz, and the Negev (Bartlett 1989: 200–4; Dearman 1995: 123–7), but there is also some evidence that other gods were known, such as Hadad, El, Baal, Astarte, and perhaps Sin, some of them perhaps assimilated within Qos (Bartlett 1989: 194–6; Dearman 1995: 123–31). It is possible that different tribal or kin groups in Edom recognized different deities or aspects of deities (Dearman 1995: 128–31), as may have also been the case in Ammon.

RELATIONS WITH THE IMPERIAL POWERS OF ASSYRIA, BABYLON, AND PERSIA

The Assyrian king Adad-nirari III claimed that Edom submitted and paid tribute after his campaign to Palestine in 796 BC, but no specific king of Edom was named. Qos-malak, Ayarammu, and Qos-gabr are mentioned as tributary kings of Edom in the inscriptions of Tiglath-pileser III and his successors. Edom, along with Moab and Ammon, remained independent states, paying tribute when required and performing some other tasks. They were not annexed as provinces nor considered part of Assyria (Bienkowski 2000). There is no evidence for permanent Assyrian presence in Edom: no officials, garrisons, or an Assyrian road network. Delegations of high officials from Edom brought tribute to the Assyrian capital, as is attested by letters and wine lists from Nimrud which show that they were well looked after. Maybe the king of Edom sometimes led the delegations: one tablet from Nimrud mentions gifts of gold and silver given by the Assyrian king to the king of Ammon and his attendants.

FIG. 52.5 Neo-Babylonian relief at Sela (courtesy Jane Taylor)

The only firm evidence for Mesopotamian presence during the Iron Age in Edom is the relief at Sela near Busayra (Dalley and Goguel 1997) (Fig. 52.5). This shows a standing king, above him a crescent and a star, and an illegible inscription. Analysis of the style of the relief identifies the figure almost certainly as the Neo-Babylonian king, Nabonidus (555–539 BCE). It may have been carved to commemorate Nabonidus' journey through Edom towards Tayma, and may suggest that Edom was under Babylonian administration at that time, although this cannot be proven.

There is evidence that at least certain sites in Edom continued to be occupied beyond the traditional end of the Iron II period and through the Persian period. When exactly Edom ceased to exist as an independent kingdom is not clear. It is possible that the localized destruction of parts of Busayra was the work of Nabonidus during his campaign of 553 BC. Edom may have been annexed at this point and ceased to exist as an independent state. If this was the case, then the 'palace' can be interpreted as the residence of the king of Edom, but, following selective destruction and some alteration, it may later have become the residency of an official appointed by the Babylonians.

It is unlikely that Edom survived as an independent kingdom into the Persian period. In the Persian sources, the area from the Euphrates to southern Palestine (including Transjordan) is known by the term 'Beyond the River'. After 486 BCE, 'Beyond the River' became a satrapy in its own right. Therefore, Edom probably came under the overall rule of the Persian satrap of 'Beyond the River'. At present, there is no evidence that Edom became a separate province within that satrapy, although there is evidence that Ammon was a separate province. Evidence from elsewhere indicates the likelihood that governors were members of indigenous groups rather than external appointees. It is therefore probable that Edom continued to be represented by the supra-tribal authority at Busayra under the Babylonians and Persians, and possibly into the early Hellenistic period under the Ptolemies. Just as the Ptolemies maintained the Tobiads' status under the Persians in Ammon, with their stronghold at 'Iraq al-Amir, so too the tribal family at Busayra may have continued as a leading family, perhaps in the role of 'client-shaykhs' of the Persians and Ptolemies, but how far their authority over the tribes of southern Edom remained at this period is conjectural.

Suggested reading

Bartlett, J. R. (1989). *Edom and the Edomites*. Sheffield: JSOT Press.

Bienkowski, P. (ed.) (1992). *Early Edom and Moab: The Beginning of the Iron Age in Southern Jordan*. Sheffield: Collis/National Museums and Galleries on Merseyside.

——and E. J. van der Steen. (2001). Tribes, trade and towns: a new framework for the Late Iron Age in southern Jordan and the Negev. *Bulletin of the American Schools of Oriental Research* 323: 21–47.

Edelman, D. V. (ed.) (1995). *You Shall Not Abhor an Edomite, For He Is Your Brother: Edom and Seir in History and Tradition*. Atlanta, Ga.: Scholars.

LaBianca, Ø. S., and R. W. Younker (1985). The kingdoms of Ammon, Moab and Edom: the archaeology of society in Late Bronze/Iron Age Transjordan (ca. 1400–500 BCE). In T. E. Levy (ed.), *The Archaeology of Society in the Holy Land*. London: Leicester University Press, 399–415.

MacDonald, B. (1994). *Ammon, Moab and Edom: Early States/Nations of Jordan in the Biblical Period (End of the 2nd and During the 1st Millennium B.C.)*. Amman: Al Kutba.

References

Bartlett, John R. (1989). *Edom and the Edomites*. Sheffield: JSOT Press.

Bennett, C.-M., and P. Bienkowski (1995). *Excavations at Tawilan in Southern Jordan*. Oxford: Oxford University Press.

Bienkowski, P. (2000). Transjordan and Assyria. In L. E. Stager, J. A. Greene, and M. D. Coogan (eds), *The Archaeology of Jordan and Beyond: Essays in Honor of James A. Sauer*. Winona Lake, Ind.: Eisenbrauns, 44–58.

——(2001). Iron Age settlement in Edom: a revised framework. In P. M. M. Daviau, J. W. Wevers, and M. Weigl (eds), *The World of the Aramaeans: Biblical, Historical and Cultural Studies in Honour of Paul-E. Dion*, vol. 2. Sheffield: Sheffield Academic, 257–69.

——(2002). *Busayra: Excavations by Crystal M. Bennett 1971–1980*. Oxford: Oxford University Press.

——(2007). Tribes, borders, landscapes and reciprocal relations: the Wadi Arabah and its meaning. *Journal of Mediterranean Archaeology* 20: 33–60.

——(ed.) (2011). *Umm al-Biyara: Excavations by Crystal M. Bennett in Petra 1960–1965*. Oxford: Oxbow.

——and E. J. van der Steen (2001). Tribes, trade and towns: a new framework for the Late Iron Age in southern Jordan and the Negev. *Bulletin of the American Schools of Oriental Research* 323: 21–47.

Dalley, S., and A. Goguel (1997). The 'Sela' sculpture: a Neo-Babylonian rock relief in southern Jordan. *Annual of the Department of Antiquities of Jordan* 41: 169–76.

Dearman, J. A. (1995). Edomite religion: a survey and an examination of some recent contributions. In D. V. Edelman (ed.), *You Shall Not Abhor an Edomite, For He Is Your Brother: Edom and Seir in History and Tradition*. Atlanta, Ga.: Scholars, 119–36.

Hart, S. (1988). Excavations at Ghrareh, 1986: preliminary report. *Levant* 20: 89–99.

Hübner, U. (2004). Qurayyat el-Mansur und Hirbet el-Faid in Südjordanien. *Zeitschrift des Deutschen Palästina-Vereins* 120: 141–56.

Knauf, E. A., and M. Lindner (1997). Between the plateau and the rocks: Edomite economic and social structure. *Studies in the History and Archaeology of Jordan* 6: 261–4.

Levy, T. E., R. B. Adams, M. Najjar, et al. (2004). Reassessing the chronology of biblical Edom: new excavations and 14C dates from Khirbat en-Nahas (Jordan). *Antiquity* 78: 865–79.

—— and R. Shafiq (1999). The Jebel Hamrat Fidan Project: excavations at the Wadi Fidan 40 Cemetery, Jordan (1997). *Levant* 31: 293–308.

Lindner, M., E. A. Knauf, and J. P. Zeitler (1996). An Edomite fortress and a Late Islamic village near Petra (Jordan): Khirbat al-Muallaq. *Annual of the Department of Antiquities of Jordan* 40: 111–35.

Porter, B. W. (2004). Authority, polity, and tenuous elites in Iron Age Edom (Jordan). *Oxford Journal of Archaeology* 23: 373–95.

Pratico, G. D. (1993). *Nelson Glueck's 1938–1940 Excavations at Tell el-Kheleifeh: A Reappraisal.* Atlanta, Ga.: Scholars.

Routledge, B. E. (2004). *Moab in the Iron Age: Hegemony, Polity, Archaeology.* Philadelphia: University of Pennsylvania Press.

Smith, N.G., and T.E. Levy (2008). The Iron Age pottery from Khirbat en-Nahas, Jordan: a preliminary study. *Bulletin of the American Schools of Oriental Research* 352: 41–91.

van der Steen, E. J., and P. Bienkowski (2006). How old is the kingdom of Edom? A review of new evidence and recent discussion. *Antiguo Oriente* 4: 11–20.

Whiting, C. (2006). The South Jordan Iron Age II Excavation and Survey Project. *Bulletin of the Council for British Research in the Levant* 1: 36–8.

··

CHAPTER 53

CYPRUS DURING THE IRON AGE THROUGH THE PERSIAN PERIOD

From the 11th Century BC to the Abolition of the City-Kingdoms (c.300 BC)

··

MARIA IACOVOU

[I]n order to understand the role of the Greeks in the eastern Mediterranean during the years *ca.* 1100–600 BC, it is necessary to move away from Syria and Palestine and to concentrate upon the island of Cyprus. Cyprus, I argue, provides the best evidence, both archaeological and philological, for the establishment of the Greeks in the far reaches of the eastern Mediterranean world.

James Muhly (2009: 23)

INTRODUCTION

··

From at least as early as the 13th century to the end of the 4th century BC, when Ptolemy I Soter abolished the royal dynasties of Cyprus, the Mediterranean's easternmost island stood staunchly in support of a segmented model of statehood: for as long as a millennium, Late Bronze Age *Alashiya* (*Iadnana* to the Neo-Assyrians and *Kypros* to the Greeks) was divided into a multiple though fluctuating number of variably autonomous politico-economic territories (Fig. 53.1).

Throughout this long era which, ever since the groundbreaking work of the Swedish-Cyprus Expedition in the 1930s, has been divided into the Late Cypriot (LC IIC–IIIB), the Cypro-Geometric (CG I–III), the Cypro-Archaic (CA I–II), and the Cypro-Classical (CC I–II) periods, the island sustained a homogeneous, strongly indigenous and, to the eye of the archaeologist, easily recognizable material culture; a versatile extrovert culture that did not lose its individuality when it adopted or was inspired by foreign prototypes, such as ceramic (e.g. Black-on-Red ware) or sculptural (e.g. Egyptianizing statuary) styles, which were then

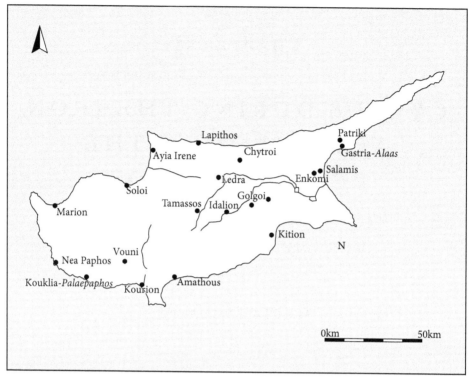

FIG. 53.1 Map of Iron Age II sites in Cyprus

traded far and wide. Moreover, stylistic as well as provenance studies conducted on metal artefacts, pottery, terracotta, and limestone figures that have been found in the Levant, the Aegean, and Italy have increasingly highlighted the fact that, from the 12th century BC to the end of the Cypro-Archaic period (around 475 BC), different aspects of the material culture of the island (e.g. Cypriot-type statues) exercised a strong influence with a purposely maintained Cypriot trademark, on its Mediterranean environment (see below).

RESEARCH PROBLEMS: URBAN LONGEVITY, LIMITED SETTLEMENT VISIBILITY

Sinister though it may sound, archaeologists in Cyprus have come to lament the absence of destruction levels or abandonment episodes that could have preserved the basic internal structure of settlements in the Cypro-Geometric and Cypro-Archaic periods. In fact, with the exception of a few sites where excavators were able to isolate 5th- and/or 4th-century levels—e.g. Kition, Idalion, Amathous, and Paphos (as in Chapter 43, 'Paphos' refers throughout this chapter to Kouklia-*Palaepaphos*)—even the Cypro-Classical strata have an extremely poor archaeological visibility. As a rule, we deal with a scatter of settlement evidence fortuitously discovered during the excavation of monumental structures of late antiquity (gymnasia, theatres, baths, etc.) that have eradicated the secular and sacred environment in many of the once autonomous Iron Age polities of Cyprus (e.g. Salamis and Kourion).

The longevity of the first-millennium BC settlements constitutes a major research problem which, admittedly, renders the study of the socioeconomic structure of the island a daunting task, and the interpretations of its urban and political development a controversial issue. There is, however, a much more positive aspect to this impressive *longue durée*, which calls for a constructive evaluation: granted that for more than a millennium the urban demography of the island did not undergo drastic changes, it becomes evident that from as early as the 11th century BC the island operated on a successful economic system. We do not observe in 11th-century Cyprus human resources wasted in the establishment of short-lived, failing settlements. One need only compare the sheer longevity of the settlements in Cyprus to the contemporary situation in Greece, where after the 12th century, and for as long as three centuries, there was an unnaturally high failure factor in the establishment of new settlements (Iacovou 2005a: 23). In the Aegean there was 'a remarkable discontinuity in occupation between what appear to be some of the most prominent settlement sites of the Early Iron Age and those of the ensuing period' (Snodgrass 1987: 173).

Nevertheless, due to the inherent shortcomings of settlement archaeology in Cyprus, the rich and diverse Iron Age material culture of the island—in many cases the loot of intensive 19th-century treasure hunting that destroyed hundreds of tombs and dozens of sanctuaries (cf. Goring 1988; Marangou 2000)—has until recently been approached from an art-historical point of view. In the absence of secure provenance or substantial contextual information, greater emphasis was placed upon the identification of external artistic influences (e.g. Phoenician, Assyrian, or Egyptian) on Cypriot pottery, metal objects, and sculpture. This was then mistakenly used as evidence for colonization (see below, the Phoenician 'colonization' of Kition) or political subjection (see below, the Egyptian 'domination' of Cyprus). In this chapter, the migration and permanent establishment of Greek and Phoenician people on the island, as well as the often elusive relation of the Cypriot polities to the Near Eastern empires, will be interpreted from an internal, a 'Cyprocentric' point of view (Iacovou 2007a). By contextualizing the material data and the epigraphic evidence, we may begin to reconstruct the separate regional histories of the different polities that participated, for longer or shorter periods of time, in the island's first-millennium political geography.

ONE POLITICAL CULTURE, THREE LANGUAGE GROUPS

Three distinct languages were in use on the island during the better part of the first millennium BC: a Semitic one that was written in the Phoenician alphabet; an Indo-European one (the Arcado-Cypriot Greek dialect) that was written in the Cypriot syllabary and, after the 5th century, also in the Greek alphabet; and an undecipherable language christened 'Eteocypriot' that was also inscribed in the Cypriot syllabary (cf. Collombier 1991a; Panayotou-Triantafyllopoulou 2006). Much ink has been spilled in attempts to associate each linguistic group with a distinct ethnic culture—a fact that altogether distorts the cultural and political configuration of Cyprus in the first millennium BC. A contextual approach to the mortuary pattern, the sacred landscape, and the symbols of statehood employed by the Iron Age city-kingdoms indicate that the material culture in the various polities made no concerted effort to construct a distinctly Phoenician, Greek, or 'Eteocypriot' identity (Iacovou 2006a; 2008a). The 'Cyprus phenomenon' (i.e. a largely unified material culture sustained by three different linguistic groups) has its roots in the island's successful handling of the 'crisis years'. The evidence analysed in the previous chapter on Cyprus, which is primarily devoted to the archaeology of the 12th century BC, rejects the idea that an island-wide sharp break was imposed for any length of time after LC IIIA. The Mediterranean-wide crisis that had put an end to the second-millennium economic system and trade pattern, which centred on the exchange of high-value goods between heads of empires and palace states, did not obliterate all the regional economies of Cyprus. This made the island a desirable migrants' destination. The newcomers were neither invaders nor colonists; they made no attempt to establish separate enclaves. Instead, they infiltrated economically vibrant Cypriot centres, like Enkomi, Paphos, and Kition, that were in the process of revolutionizing the metal industry with the production of 'working iron' (Snodgrass 1980) and where the Late Cypriot economic system—identified in the close association of cult, metallurgy, and trade in metals—had remained prevalent (Sherratt 1998: 300, 304; Webb 1999: 287).

CONTINUITIES AND SETTLEMENT PATTERN RESTRUCTURING

The power vacuum suffered mostly by southern and western settlement hierarchy systems in LC IIIA (Iacovou, Ch. 43 above) did not last long. In the Vasilikos and Kouris River Valleys it healed with the foundation of Amathous and Kourion in LC IIIB (the 11th century BC). These two settlements, which were first and foremost ports of export, became the management centres of the agricultural and industrial hinterland of their respective regions. Alison South provides a magisterial summary of the settlement pattern transformation in the Vasilikos and Maroni Valleys:

> To what extent the Late Bronze Age 'chiefdoms' were the ancestors of the Iron Age kingdoms is a very complicated question [...]; it is well known that while there was continuity at some sites (Enkomi-Salamis, Kition, Kouklia [Paphos]), many others were abandoned, and immense changes took place following the upheavals at the end of the Bronze Age. In the case of Kalavassos and Maroni, these two prosperous Late Bronze Age polities, well endowed with agricultural and mineral resources, were completely abandoned by about 1200 BC, and although there is plentiful evidence for occupation having resumed in the Iron Age, they never regained their previous wealth and importance. Indeed, in this region the political pattern changed out of all recognition, with Amathus taking over as the centre of a kingdom, and the Maroni and Vasilikos valleys found themselves in the borderlands at the outer edge of the hypothesized extent of the kingdom...(South 2002: 68)

The island's Iron Age settlement pattern was, therefore, structured from old as well as new establishments and, as adroitly pointed out by Anthony Snodgrass (1994), survivals played a far more important role than losses in the construction of the Cypriot Iron Age. The long-term continuities, which bridge the divide between the island's Late Bronze and Iron Ages, are evident in the material record. The most important ones are the following:

(a) continuity of the Late Cypriot script, which was adopted and adapted by two different languages (Greek and 'Eteocypriot'), both of which served state functions in the Cypro-Archaic and Cypro-Classical periods (e.g. legends on coins and royal dedicatory inscriptions) (Iacovou 2008a) (Fig. 53.2);

FIG. 53.2 Greek Cypro-Syllabic inscription of the king of Paphos Onasicharis (Kouklia Museum Inv. No. 2141, with the kind permission of the Director of Antiquities, Cyprus)

(b) continuity of an economy based on trading the island's metallic wealth, as copper remained Cyprus's primary export commodity from the Late Bronze Age to the end of antiquity (cf. Kassianidou 2000) and, in addition, trade in metals was optimized with the production and marketing of iron tools and weapons, since Cypriot metalworkers played a 'major role in unlocking the secrets of working with iron' (Muhly 2003); and

(c) continuity of the same open-air cult model not only in the Late Cypriot urban *temene* of Paphos and Kition but also in Late Bronze extra-urban sanctuaries that were refurbished in the Cypro-Geometric and Cypro-Archaic periods (e.g. Ayia Irene: cf. Gjerstad et al. 1935: 820–44) and in new sanctuaries established by Iron Age authorities (e.g. Amathous: cf. Fourrier and Hermary 2006; Fourrier 2007).

The preservation of the old Cypriot cult model that had been developed in the Bronze Age and came to be closely associated with the management of the copper trade in LC IIC–IIIA was more important than the promotion of Greek, Phoenician, or 'Eteocypriot' identities (Iacovou 2006a). Significantly, neither the Greek kings of Paphos nor the Semitic dynasty of Kition felt compelled to replace the indigenous cult practice with one that would have underlined their distinct origins from 'motherlands' that lay on opposite sides of the Mediterranean. They did not operate as colonists, which is why they have little in common with Greeks established in Syracuse or Akragas, or with Phoenicians established on the isle of Motya. Unlike the Archaic and Classical city-states of the other big Mediterranean island of Sicily, the Iron Age polities of Cyprus were not implanted on an island that until the arrival of colonists from east and west had not developed its own urban and literate culture (Iacovou 2008b: 250).

TERRITORIAL FRAGMENTATION, SOCIAL HOMOGENIZATION

The Early Iron Age polities were operating in a transformed economic environment in which institutionalized commercial exchanges between heads of state were a feature of the past (cf. Bell 2006: 105). From the 12th century and until the rise of the Assyrian Empire, Mediterranean trade was largely an entrepreneurial enterprise carried out by merchant groups and petty kingdoms. In the absence of a powerful unifying regulator, the number of regions trying to establish their own autonomous politico-economic territory kept multiplying. In Cyprus, ten is the highest reliable number we have and is based on Neo-Assyrian records of the early 7th century (see below).

Despite the fact that territorial fragmentation is a key feature of the Cypro-Geometric period—it was put into reverse gear once the island joined the Assyrian Empire (in 707 BC)—a common organizational concept is evident behind the selection of exclusively extramural cemeteries in the periphery of the otherwise invisible Cypro-Geometric settlements. All of them were newly designated burial grounds. They had been established in LC IIIB or CG I and most of them remained in use for centuries. The long-term maintenance and gradual expansion of the 'towns of the dead' (*necropoleis*) imply a secure and stabilized demography; and the basic structure of Early Iron settlements may be inferred from the spatial distribution of their extensive cemeteries (cf. Iacovou 2005b: 129, 131).

The Cypriot-type chamber tomb, which had been in use since the Early Cypriot, is not attested after the 12th century—it was not even retained in Amathous, the new Iron Age harbour town whose foundation is traditionally attributed to an autochthonous stock (cf. Iacovou 2002a). The prevalent type of tomb in every Cypro-Geometric cemetery is the chamber tomb with the long *dromos*, which in the Late Helladic period but not after the 12th century had served as the family tomb of the Mycenaean society. In Cyprus, however, where it makes its first appearance in the 11th century in association with Proto-White Painted pottery (e.g. at Gastria-*Alaas*: Karageorghis 1975), it is not reserved for the inhumation of a particular group of migrants. Thus, the evidence provided by Cypro-Geometric burial assemblages from all over the island (e.g. Paphos, Kourion, Amathous, Salamis, and Lapithos) suggests that Cyprus entered the first millennium with a highly homogenized society (Iacovou 2005b: 128). We do not observe in either the burial customs or the ceramic industry (especially the tableware), or in the rest of the Cypro-Geometric material culture, a differential use that could underscore a distinction between indigenous groups and newcomers.

The Cypro-Geometric culture was an island-wide *koiné*. Cremation, the prevailing rite in post-12th-century ('Dark Age') Greece, is rarely observed in Cyprus. It was, however, practised in the case of extraordinary individuals with evident Aegean affiliations, as is the case of the deceased in the LC IIIB *Kaloriziki* T 40 at Kourion (McFadden 1954). The placement of the cremated remains in elaborate bronze kraters and the exceptional burial gifts (a superb gold sceptre, two bronze tripod stands (Fig. 53.3), and arms of bronze, to mention only a few) belong to the milieu of the warrior grave tradition, and link the dead warrior of Kourion-*Kaloriziki* to near-contemporary heroic burials from Knossos (Subminoan), Tiryns (Submycenaean), and Lefkandi (Proto-Geometric) (Catling 1995: 126–7; Coldstream and Catling 1996: 646–8).

Phoenician *tophets* have not been found in Cyprus, not even in Kition, which has been repeatedly described as the Phoenicians' first colony to the west. Only one cemetery with funerary urns of the Cypro-Archaic period—found during rescue operations on the coast of Amathous but still unpublished—bears resemblances to a *tophet* (Karageorghis 1995: 330; 2002a: 151, fig. 319; Christou 1998). It supports the presence of a foreign, most probably Semitic, community that had established its burial ground separately from the extensive

FIG. 53.3 Bronze tripod stand from *Kaloriziki* T.40 (Cyprus Museum, with the kind permission of the Director of Antiquities, Cyprus)

Iron Age cemeteries of the harbour town of Amathous (with hundreds of chamber tombs with a *dromos*), which spread around the citadel hill (cf. Hermary 1999: fig. 3).

NEW COMMERCIAL STRATEGIES: AFTER THE CRISIS AND PRIOR TO EMPIRE RULE

Early Cypro-Geometric tombs contain impressive evidence as to the Mediterranean markets the Cypriots were exploiting and their ability to access rare exotica (e.g. a West Mediterranean *obelos* of Atlantic bronze from Amathous: Karageorghis and Lo Schiavo 1989) and raw materials, including precious metals that were made into jewellery by local craftsmen employing largely simple techniques (e.g. gold rings, gold plaques, and silver fibulae: Goring 1983). Evidently, Cypriot commercial enterprises were not brought to a standstill in the 11th century, but the strategies that began to make up for the losses were new (cf. Bell 2006: 102–3). In fact, the coastal urban centres of Cyprus are thought to have been in the forefront of this alternative trading system since the 12th century (Sherratt 1998: 292) and the same sites provide the earliest evidence for the introduction of the new iron technology (carburization and quenching: cf. Wheeler and Maddin 1980).

The oxhide ingot, the exchange unit *par excellence* of Cypriot copper, was one of the victims of the new trading pattern: it is not recorded after the 12th century. Considering its weight—about 28kg of raw copper—and the fact that it was shipped in considerable numbers to customers who were heads of Late Bronze states (cf. Knapp 2008: 308–12), its abandonment was inevitable. We have no evidence regarding the shape or weight of the units in which Cyprus traded its raw metal after the 'crisis years', but we know instead of Cypriot metal artefacts, which become increasingly visible in the freelance trade of the post-Sea Peoples era. Although they are usually presented as exclusively Late Cypriot products, the rod tripods and four-sided stands were apparently made and exported from Cyprus to the end of the 11th century. Their presence in CG I tombs (together with hemispherical bowls and spearheads) has been increasing (e.g Kourion-*Kaloriziki* T 39; Paphos-*Skales* T 49, 58; and Amathous-*Diplostrati* T 109: cf. Iacovou and Hermary 1999: 154), and it is becoming harder and harder to explain them all as heirlooms or antiques in CG I burial assemblages. In fact, beyond Cyprus, especially in Crete, Italy, and Sardinia, Cypriot stands continued to be imitated throughout the Early Iron Age (Karageorghis 2000: 60; Papasavvas 2001: 206–11; Kourou 2008: 363). Not surprisingly, the clay mould fragments for casting tripod legs found in *Xeropolis* (the settlement site of Lefkandi in Euboea) in a Late Proto-Geometric context (*c*.900 BC), are associated with Cypriot craftsmen (Catling and Catling 1980: 96, pls 12, 13a).

Bronze stands were not the only items with a Cypriot trademark that were reproduced/imitated in different parts of the Mediterranean. Iron knives, at times with an ivory handle and often bimetallic (with bronze rivets), made in Cyprus from as early as the 12th century, were among the first utilitarian iron implements that circulated in the 'post-Ugarit' Mediterranean maritime trade. 'The Cypriot knives were a great success and appear to have been exported to or copied in Palestine and the Levant' (Pickles and Peltenburg 1998: 84). They have been traced in Syria (e.g. Hama), the southern Levant (e.g. Tell Qasile, Tell el-Far'ah, and Megiddo), Anatolia (e.g. Tarsus), and the Aegean (Sherratt 1994), especially Crete.

The Early Iron Age cemeteries of Knossos, in particular, have produced some exceptional metal artefacts from Cyprus: e.g. a Cypriot bronze bowl with a Phoenician inscription from a Middle Proto-Geometric tomb dated *c*.900 BC (Coldstream and Catling 1996: 30, T.Jf1, fig. 157); and iron *oboloi* (roasting spits) from two 10th-century tombs at *Fortetsa* (Brock 1957: 22, 202, no. 203; Coldstream 1977: 164, n. 22). In Cyprus, *oboloi* are an 11th-century novelty; they appear first in LC IIIB/CG I tombs and it is quite likely that they were a Cypriot invention (Coldstream 1977: 146; 1985: 54). The earliest, e.g. a group of three from Kition (Myres 1910: 107, pl. 29) and a second group of three from Paphos-*Skales* T 49, were of bronze (Karageorghis 1983: 60–61, pl. 88), though spits made of iron are reported from CG I–III tombs at Lapithos (Lapithos T 409:7; T 11: 32a–c; T 417:12a; T 422:10: Gjerstad et al. 1934). In CA I–II iron spits were deposited, often together with a pair of fire-dogs, in warrior burials (e.g. Paphos-*Kato Alonia*: Karageorghis 1963). Most of these elite burials come from monumental built tombs (e.g. Salamis T 79: Karageorghis 1973: 118; Patriki T 1: Karageorghis 1972: 169; Tamassos T 12: Buchholz, Matthäus, and Walcher 2002: 228–9). Their original function as spits for roasting meat is not in doubt (Karageorghis 1970). In Cyprus, as well as in Greece, where they were also often deposited with fire-dogs—as in the Argos warrior grave (Courbin 1957) and the North Cemetery of Knossos (Coldstream and Catling 1996: 591)—they were an acknowledged symbol of male status (cf. Coldstream 1977: 146–8). But what is more intriguing is that these thin rods, of which the hand could grasp six at once (hence, the Greek *drachma*) were deposited in numbers that can be divided or multiplied by six, which suggests that 'they had become an index of wealth, a primitive currency' (Coldstream 1977: 148) in the pre-monetary economy.

Standardized products were part of the response to the decentralized long-distance trade that began to flourish after the collapse of the second-millennium BC state economies, and this strategy could not have excluded ceramic containers and tablewares. Beginning in the 11th century, the local ceramic industry of Proto-White Painted (PWP) in LC IIIB and White Painted I (WP)/Bichrome I in CG I, achieved (for the first time) the standard-ization and fast-wheel mass production of an impressive range of high-quality utilitarian vessels (Sherratt 1991). The repertoire of PWP, published by Pieridou in her irreplaceable study of 1973, also includes a fascinating range of specialized vases (e.g. kernoi, zoomorphic and bird-shaped askoi (Pieridou 1970; 1971), pyxides, and horn- and boat-shaped vessels (Pieridou 1973)) that may have been used in cultic as well as funerary practices. The major-ity of PWP shapes are indebted to the repertoire of LH IIIC painted vases (e.g. amphorae, stirrup-jars, kylikes, cups, deep bowls, and kalathoi (Fig. 53.4) or have local antecedents in the slow-wheel shapes of the Cypriot Bronze Age (e.g. the ring kernos).

The impact of contemporary Levantine containers and slow-pouring vessels, on the other hand, becomes more pronounced in the production line of WP I/Bichrome I (cf. globular jugs: Iacovou 1988: 36). The imported originals that had reached Cyprus with their content are not plentiful and the same may be said of WP I/Bichrome I pottery on the Phoenician coast. PWP has not been securely identified outside Cyprus—though a wavy-band bowl from Sarepta is assigned to LC IIIB (Koehl 1985: 118–22). The earliest, most abundant and well-stratified CG I pottery ever found outside Cyprus is contained in assemblages from Tyre (cf. Aubet and Nuñez 2008) and Tel Dor; surprisingly, the shapes are mostly open tableware (Gilboa 1999: 122; 2005: 60). In CG IB/II, when Tel Dor witnessed an influx of Cypriot pottery, some bowl fragments were found to be local imitations (Gilboa 1999: 123, fig. 5: nos 7–8).

Seen in their chronological milieu, the modest ceramic exchanges described above were not insignificant (cf. Karageorghis 2002a: 132, figs 278–81; 2008: 330). They suggest that the traffic between Cyprus and the Phoenician coast never ceased—not even in LC IIIA–IIIB (on the artefactual evidence, see Gilboa 2005: 53), when exchanges may have been largely

Kouklia skales
T. 9/7

FIG. 53.4 Proto-White Painted kalathos with pictorial decoration from Kouklia T.9 No. 7 (Cyprus Museum, with the kind permission of the Director of Antiquities, Cyprus)

limited to Cypriot-type wavy-band pithoi in the Levant cf. (cf. Gilboa 2001; Karageorghis 2008: 328) and Cannanite-type amphorae (cf. Hadjicosti 1988) in Cyprus. This strictly bilateral phenomenon becomes more pronounced when compared with the absence of exchanges between the southern Levantine coast (i.e. Philistia) and Cyprus. Like the coastal polities of southeast Cyprus, the northern Levantine coast (Phoenicia) was 'one of the few areas that were least affected by the dramatic demographic and other terminal Late Bronze Age upheavals' (cf. Gilboa 2005: 49).

In the Aegean region PWP and WP I/Bichrome I have not been identified to this date—not even in Crete, where three WP III/Bichrome III vases from the North Cemetery of Knossos are described as the first of this Cypriot fabric to be recorded on the island (Coldstream and Catling 1996: 406). Even in Rhodes the earliest ceramic evidence for Cypriot imports (two barrel jugs), as well as Cypriot imitations or influences on Rhodian Geometric pottery production, date to the early 9th century BC (Bourogiannis 2009: 114–15), but it is quite likely that future work will push the evidence backwards. Thus, today, Lefkandi in Euboea continues to hold the earliest confirmed arrival of a CG II vase in the Aegean: a Bichrome II jug from a Late Proto-Geometric tomb, dating to 920–900 BC (Desborough 1980: 350, pl. 137: 19; Lemos 2002: 227). At the same time, around the end of the 10th century, the first Euboean pendent semicircle skyphoi appear in Cyprus, at the port site of Amathous (Desborough 1957; Lemos and Hatcher 1991; Lemos 2002: 228). Coldstream, who has published and discussed (practically single-handedly) all Greek Geometric and Archaic imports to Cyprus, underlines that 'of all the city-kingdoms of Cyprus, Eteocypriot Amathus has been the most prolific of Early Greek imported pottery' (1995: 195). More importantly, Greek pottery exports to Amathous 'closely match those reaching Tyre, and therefore place Amathus firmly on the route from the Aegean to the Phoenician metropolis' (Coldstream 1998: 6).

The development of common ceramic styles in the Levant and Cyprus—as in the production of Bichrome Wheelmade and Red Lustrous Wheelmade—is well attested in the Late Cypriot period (cf. Steel 2004: 154), and it should not cause surprise when it reoccurs in the Early Iron Age. In the 1980s, however, following the rescue excavations of the Paphos-*Skales* Iron Age cemetery (Karageorghis 1983) and also of a few hundred Cypro-Geometric chamber tombs from the cemeteries of Amathous (Tytgat 1989), the problem of differentiating between Phoenician imports and local imitations of some closed vessel types (pilgrim flasks and round-based jugs) reached a climax. The solution was given by Patricia Bikai, who after having published the Tyre sounding (Bikai 1978), was able to identify the Phoenician imports in the Cypro-Geometric tombs of Cyprus and also group them into four horizons on the basis of their Cypriot contexts (Bikai 1987).

BLACK-ON-RED WARE

Granted that the most conspicuous shapes that were adopted by the Cypriot ceramic industry, and were incorporated into the local production of Cypro-Geometric, were contemporary Phoenician closed vessels, it is hardly surprising that in the advanced Cypro-Geometric period a type of ware began to be manufactured on the island that was inspired by various traits associated with Phoenician pottery production. According to Bikai, the inspiration for the much-discussed Black-on-Red (BoR) lies in the Phoenician 'Red Ware' imports identified in CG I tombs (Bikai 1983: 405; Schreiber 2003: 231, 275). BoR, however, is not a Phoenician ware. Bikai 'has always been mystified by the suggestion that Black-on-Red is

Phoenician' (Coldstream and Bikai 1988: 37); and it should certainly not be labelled 'Cypro-Phoenician'—a misnomer that has been used in Levantine archaeology. In the Tyre assemblage, for instance, BoR is described as an imported alien element. Schreiber's important work on BoR has shown that the ware was made 'meaningful as a recognizable and marketable commodity' in Cyprus (Schreiber 2003: 1), from where it was widely exported and also imitated in different parts of the Mediterranean. BoR's distribution pattern in Israel/Palestine, Phoenicia, Syria, Asia Minor, and Egypt shows 'a broad but relatively minimal distribution, over a lengthy period of time' (Schreiber 2003: 80). In Cyprus the ware is closely associated with CG III and CA I burial assemblages. It is quite likely that the inception of its production in Cyprus occurred in CG II (conventionally dated to c.950–850), but this does not by any means make it a 'hallmark' of the 10th century (Iacovou 2004 *contra* Schreiber 2003: 84). BoR exports to the Aegean are also of Cypriot manufacture and are largely confined to the 8th century (cf. Bourogiannis 2009: 122). In Rhodes, Kos, and Crete, BoR was 'copiously imitated' from the late 9th to the 7th centuries BC (Stampolides 2009: 95). When pottery from Cyprus 'began to arrive at Knossos in a steady flow from about 800 onwards', the preponderant ware among the imports was BoR, and it inspired the frequently imitated shape of the BoR juglet (Coldstream 1984: 136–7).

Consequently, a survey of Cypro-Geometric and Cypro-Archaic pottery exports and their local imitations would underline that these preponderantly small- and medium-size closed vases (jugs and juglets) were primarily traded as containers for marketing different kinds of liquid, especially perfumed oil (cf. Schreiber 2003: 65). In the first millennium BC, no Cypriot open shape managed to match the popularity of the Late Cypriot White Slip bowls that were exported all over the Mediterranean as vessels on their own right—apparently because of their impermeable surface (cf. Karageorghis 2008: 327–8). The fine ware open shapes (mainly WP I) that dominate the Tel Dor and Tyre assemblages in CG I constitute an unusual phenomenon, which is currently attributed to the presence of Cypriots—established with their tableware—on the Phoenician coast (cf. Gilboa 2005: 337). Later, during the transitional period from CG III to Cypro-Archaic, a large number of Cypriot amphoroid kraters were used as urns for cremation burials in the Iron Age cemetery of Tyre-Al Bass (Aubet 2004).

Cypro-Archaic: Return to empire rule

The rise of Assyria, the first Iron Age empire that reached as far west as the Mediterranean and incorporated the coastal city-states of the Levant into its centrally controlled market economy, worked as a catalyst for the political geography of Cyprus. A primary goal of Neo-Assyrian imperialism was the control of a vast interregional trading network that rendered the redistribution of goods an essential operation. Militarily, however, their westward expansion had stopped short of Cyprus: the island did not suffer a military intervention (cf. Yon and Malbran-Labat 1995). It was the collective decision of Cyprus's regional representatives that apparently led, shortly before the end of the 8th century (c.707 BC), to the negotiation of a profitable liaison with Sargon II of Assyria, which appears to have given the Cypriots a 'favoured nation' status (Muhly 2009: 24). They became client states and operated primarily as the empire's Mediterranean *entrepôts* (Iacovou 2002b). The royal stele, which Sargon II ordered be erected at Kition to mark the western frontier of his dominion, is inscribed with the only Near Eastern decree ever found beyond the continent. The cuneiform text suggests that the Cypriot leaders went of their own accord to offer Sargon II gifts and allegiance; they returned having secured the emperor's recognition as heads of kingdoms (Yon 2004: 345–54).

In an invaluable royal inscription on a prism (dated to 673/2 BC), Esarhaddon (680–669) identifies by name ten Cypriot kings and their capital seats. Although each had his own kingdom, they all belonged geographically to *Iadnana*. The etymological 'history' of the term and its variants (Adnana and Iadanana: cf. Stylianou 1989: 384–6) has recently been thoroughly discussed (with a critical review of all earlier interpretations) by James Muhly, who concludes that this term describes Cyprus 'as the predominant island in the land of the Danunians', or the 'Eastern Ionians' (2009: 28). The transliteration of the kings' names on the list runs as follows: Akestor of Edil (Idalion), Pylagoras (or Phylagoras) of Kitrusi (Chytroi), Kisu of Sillua (Salamis), Eteandros of Pappa (Paphos), Eresu (Aratos?) of Silli (Soloi), Damasos of Kourion (Kuri), Admesu (Admitos?) of Tamesi (Tamassos), Damusi of Qardihadasti, Onasagoras of Lidir (Ledra), and Bususu of Nuria (Lipiński 1991; 2004: 74). Thus, Esarhaddon's prism reveals that in the first quarter of the 7th century more than half the Cypriot polities were ruled by kings who bore Greek proper names.

MANIFESTATIONS OF ROYALTY AND EXPANSION OF CYPRIOT TRADING ACTIVITIES TO EAST AND WEST FROM C.700 BC

Although there are no Assyrian royal records referring to the Cypriot polities after the reign of Asurbanipal (668–663 BC), we are exceptionally well informed by archaeological evidence as to the new wealth that began to pour into the island from the beginning of the Cypro-Archaic period. No sooner had Cyprus become a tributary to Assyria than its material culture acquired architectural monumentality befitting its royal dynasties. With Salamis leading the way—as Enkomi, its predecessor, had done in the Late Cypriot era—the territorial monarchs constructed the first true monuments of Iron Age Cyprus: the built tombs. Salamis possesses the earliest (late 8th century) and the greatest concentration of 'royal tombs', which held ostentatious burial gifts of unsurpassed craftsmanship (cf. Karageorghis 2002a: 157–73) (Fig. 53.5). In fact, the high-quality wood and ivory 'Phoenician' furniture witnessed in the Salamis tombs of the late 8th century are considered among the first examples of the Egyptianizing iconography that was imported to Cyprus on a large scale during the 7th century (Faegersten 2003: 257).

These sepulchral monuments also served for staging extravagant funerary ceremonies, which in Salamis, in particular, are evocative of Homeric burial customs (Karageorghis 1969; 2002b). The display of exotica and status symbols before their deposition was of paramount importance. Burial processions often involved horse-drawn chariots and hearses and the sacrifice of the animals that were then buried with the deceased lord. Built tombs were also constructed in Amathous—where the second highest number has been recorded—Kition, Tamassos, Idalion, Kourion, and elsewhere (Christou 1996).

Besides built tombs, a whole range of new Cypriot phenomena are dated within the fifty years covered by the last quarter of the 8th and the first quarter of the 7th century, alternatively between the dating of Sargon's stele and Esarhaddon's prism; collectively they define the sociopolitical environment of the Cypro-Archaic period. The most important is the

FIG. 53.5 Salamis, 'Royal' Tomb No. 79 (Cyprus Museum photographic archive, with the kind permission of the Director of Antiquities, Cyprus)

earliest recorded use of the Cypriot syllabary by Greek *basileis* (kings), the political leaders of almost all the Cypriot kingdoms in the Cypro-Archaic and Cypro-Classical periods (Iacovou 2006b). Thus, use of the Greek syllabary for state functions in Cyprus pre-dates that of the Phoenician alphabet by two centuries (Iacovou 2013: 141–2).

Two of the earliest known royal syllabic inscriptions—the one reads Akestor *basileus* of Paphos, the other mentions only the title *basileus*—are engraved on silver bowls dated *c*.725–675 (Karageorghis 2000; 2002a: figs 321, 322). Like the bronze stands in earlier days, these so-called Cypro-Phoenician bowls (in bronze or silver), recovered from contexts dating from the 9th to the 7th centuries BC (Markoe 1985; 2000: 148), are associated with Mediterranean elites in Italy, the Aegean, and Cyprus. There are twenty-two examples known from Cyprus and most of them come from sanctuaries and built tombs (Karageorghis 2000: 180, nos 297–307). A group of these vessels has been assigned to a workshop in Cyprus that was active around 700 BC (Markoe 2000: 149–50).

Meanwhile to the east, at the trading port of Al Mina—established at the mouth of the Orontes River that provided access to Syria and to Assyria beyond—the predominantly Euboean pottery of the first generation suddenly gives way around 700 BC to pottery of Cypriot type (Boardman 1999). At the same time, to the west, merchant seals in the Cypriot syllabary occur on two Greek vases dated around 700 BC; one was found in northern Greece and the other in Italy (Vokotopoulou and Christides 1995). And, almost simultaneously, Cypriot terracotta figurines make their debut in the Greek sanctuaries of Ionia, along the coast of Asia Minor and in the adjacent islands of the eastern Aegean (Samos, Rhodes, Cos, and Chios).

Terracotta and limestone sculpture

On the basis of securely dated evidence from the Heraion of Samos, the import of Cypriot terracotta figurines started steadily at the beginning of the 7th century—if not a little earlier, in the late 8th century—and, without delay, they began to be produced with Samian clay. Moulds, a novelty for Samian potters of the 7th century, played a major role in the production of Cypriot-type figurines, which continued down to the 6th century. Recently, it has been confirmed that even large Cypriot-type terracottas were made with local Samian clay (Karageorghis et al. 2009: 20, 204–5).

Technically demanding large and even life-size terracotta sculptures began to be produced on Cyprus in the mid-7th century (cf. Karageorghis 2000: 139). The best examples of this early phase are the sculptures found *in situ* and in the hundreds around the altar of the Iron Age sanctuary of Ayia Irene (Gjerstad 1948: 93) (Fig. 53.6). Impressive examples of 7th-century large-size Cypriot terracotta figures found at Miletus have been classified as fragments of female votive statues, like the life-size figure from Old Smyrna (Henke 2009: 209).

Sculpture in limestone (Cyprus has no marble) also began in the second half of the 7th century (cf. Karageorghis 2000: 106), and the earliest are votives from the sanctuary of Golgoi which, like Idalion, Arsos, and Kition—the main workshops of stone sculpture in Cyprus—is close to the limestone sources situated in the centre and the southeastern parts of the island. Interestingly, the early development of limestone sculpture in Cyprus has been attributed by Antoine Hermary, the leading authority on Cypriot sculpture, to the prestige enjoyed by the Cypriot terracottas (Hermary 1991: 146). Hermary posits that sculptors from Idalion moved with their material first to Samos—where the earliest Cypriot limestone sculpture outside Cyprus is recorded—and not much later to other eastern Aegean sites, as well as to Naukratis and to small kingdoms on the Levantine coast (Hermary 2009: 247). Large numbers of Cypriot-type sculptures in limestone and terracotta were found at the Temple of Eshmun near Sidon (Stucky 1993; Karageorghis 2007). The terracotta fragments, most of them moulded, date primarily to the 6th century BC. Some were imported from Cyprus, others were locally made; and the same seems to be true of the limestone statues

FIG. 53.6 Terracotta statues from the sanctuary of Ayia Irene on display in the Cyprus Museum (Cyprus Museum photographic archive, with the kind permission of the Director of Antiquities, Cyprus)

(cf. Karageorghis 2008: 332). The greatest number of 6th-century Cypriot statues come from the sanctuary of Amrit (Lembke 2004); it belongs to the class known as Cypro-Ionian (Hermary 2008: 172).

Two recent provenance studies on limestone (Kourou et al. 2002) and terracotta (Karageorghis et al. 2009) statuettes of Cypriot type found in the Aegean have shown that the distribution pattern of Cypriot and Cypriot-type terracotta figurines is exactly the same as that of the contemporary class of Cypriot limestone statuettes—despite the fact that the presence of the latter in the Aegean is dated to a shorter period (from the late 7th to the middle of the 6th century) (Kourou et al. 2002: 5). In fact, the trend of dedicating terracotta and stone figurines of Cypriot origin or style in Greek sanctuaries of the eastern Aegean, to the near complete exclusion of the rest of the Greek world, is a phenomenon confined to the Archaic period (Karageorghis et al. 2009: 19).

The impressive visibility of Cypriot and Cypriot-type sculpture abroad throughout the Cypro-Archaic period justifies the term 'Cyprianizing trend', coined to describe the prestige enjoyed by this sculpture in the eastern Aegean and the Levant.

SANCTUARIES AND KINGDOM TERRITORIES

Dedications of sculptures in clay and stone are another means through which royal agendas were manifested (cf. Hermary 1989; Fourrier 2007; Satraki 2008). Numerous dedications by kings or members of their families have been identified in extra-urban sanctuaries, whose proliferation and enhancement during the Cypro-Archaic period is interpreted as a gesture on behalf of the rulers to legitimize state boundaries and to protect routes that facilitated the transfer of copper and raw materials to the ports of export.

As to whether Cyprus was forced to pay tribute to Egypt some time in the 6th century, this is largely a modern academic construct built from Herodotus's unfounded claim that Amasis was the first man to seize the island (*Hist.* 2.182.2) and from a group of Egyptianizing male votive statues (cf. Karageorghis 2002a: 195). As Reyes has stated after a thorough review of the debate, 'it is not possible to associate anything Egyptian in the material record with an "Egyptian domination", if only because, historically, there need not have been any such phenomenon' (Reyes 1994: 78).

The 'Egyptianizing horizon' on Cyprus begins in the late 8th century, but Cypriot Egyptianizing votive objects in the round (e.g. sphinxes, Hathoric stelae and capitals, and the kilt-wearing male figures) are encountered from the early 6th century onwards, executed in the local limestone. They are closely tied to the carved and incised iconography of the ivory plaques and the bronze and silver bowls in Cyprus since the end of the 8th century (Faegersten 2003: 13–14). Karageorghis has justifiably described this tendency as 'Egyptomania' (2002a: 197). In her indispensable study of the Egyptianizing male limestone statuary from Cyprus, Faegersten identifies three distinct craft traditions on these statues: the indigenous Cypriot votive tradition, the East Greek sculptural tradition, and the Phoenician wood and ivory repertoire (2003: 264). The Egyptianizing limestone figure was a characteristic Cypriot votive type, strongly related to the Cypriot clay and limestone votive figures manufactured in the island's workshops, and it was dedicated in the sanctuaries during the entire 6th century. Despite the fact that from the last quarter of the 7th century, Cypriot merchants and craftsmen are established in the Nile Delta *emporion* of

Naukratis—where Cypriot sculptors produced statuary for the local market (Hermary 2001: 27)—the Egyptianizing sculpture was not created under the influence of contemporary Saite-period Egypt (Faegersten 2003: 263–4). Egyptianizing statues have also been found at various sites in Lebanon (e.g. Amrit, Byblos, and Sidon: Faegersten 2003: 178).

In Cyprus itself the most remarkable examples of Egyptianizing sculpture—the portrait of a king-priest from Paphos, who sports a Cypriot version of the Egyptian double crown (cf. Maier 1989: 378, fig. 40; Faegersten 2003: 293, Cat. 58), and a Hathoric capital from the palace of Amathous (Hermary 2000: 146, no. 969)—date from the c.500 BC, by which time Cyprus was under the Persians. On both examples we can see how the Cypriots employed carefully selected imperial insignia in the name of the development of their own royal and religious iconography (Hermary 2001: 29). The Egyptian Hathor was protectress of mining operations, and Edgar Peltenburg has established a link between the goddess and faience and copper production in Late Bronze Age Cyprus (2007). It is no wonder, therefore, that in the Iron Age Hathoric capitals have been found in monumental buildings identified as palaces at Vouni and Amathous (Hermary 2000: 165). In the Iron Age, Hathor may have been an image of the Great Cypriot Goddess (invoked as *wanassa* by the Greeks and as Astarte by the Phoenicians).

In Amathous and Idalion the palace compounds have supplied evidence for record keeping, large-scale storage, and industrial activities—quantities of copper slag and fragments of crucibles in Amathous and olive-oil presses in Idalion (Aupert 1996: 103; Hadjicosti 1997). In addition, the Amathousian palace produced votive offerings associated with a number of palatial sanctuaries (cf. Petit 2002). Religion and state were not two distinct institutions in a Cypriot kingdom, which explains the role of kings as priests in Paphos and, judging from the infrequent use of the term 'priest' or 'priestess' on inscriptions (Masson 1983: 438), why priesthood in Cyprus seems to have been insignificant before the Hellenistic period.

In the case of Paphos in particular, the Greek rulers sought to become identified as legitimate heirs to the legendary figure of Kinyras, the pre-Greek king of the island, who was also the Goddess's beloved high priest. As late as the 4th century, Greek syllabic inscriptions from Paphos show that Timarchos, Nikokles, and others insisted on being identified by their double title as king-priests (cf. Masson 1983: 95, 112–14; Maier 1989). In this manner, they stressed their undivided authority over the sacred and secular environment (Iacovou 2013: 146).

NUMISMATIC ECONOMY

The dynamism with which numismatic economy was introduced in Cyprus in the second half of the 6th century, when first Salamis, Paphos, and Idalion issued silver coins with exclusively syllabic Greek legends (Figs 53.7a, b) is considered a surprisingly early phenomenon (cf. Kraay 1976: 301; Destrooper-Georgiades 1984). Despite the fact that around this time the Cypriot kings had offered their allegiance to the Persian Empire—probably shortly after the subjection of the Levantine city-states (c.525 BC)—the style and weight of the silver sigloi of Cyprus does not imitate that of the Persian coins. It should also be noted that in the Phoenician city-states numismatic economy was introduced almost a century later than in Cyprus (around the middle of the 5th century) (Iacovou 2012). Even the earliest coins of Byblos and Tyre (cf. Elayi 1992: 21–2, 26) are later than the 5th-century issues of Kition and Lapethos, which have Phoenician inscriptions (cf. Markoe 2000: 98).

A.S.69

FIG. 53.7A Idalion silver siglos (obverse); sphinx seated, syllabic signs in the field (Cyprus Museum photographic archive, with the kind permission of the Director of Antiquities, Cyprus)

FIG. 53.7B Paphos silver siglos (reverse) from the Vouni hoard; eagle standing, syllabic signs in the field (Cyprus Museum photographic archive, with the kind permission of the Director of Antiquities, Cyprus)

With the exception of Idalion, the inland kingdoms identified on the prism of Esarhaddon—Chytroi, Ledra, and Tamassos—have failed to provide any kind of inscriptional evidence that could defend their independent status in the period following the inception of numismatic economy. Despite the fact that the oldest coin hoard ever found in Cyprus (dating c.500–498 BC) was recently excavated in Nicosia (thought to be ancient Ledra), numismatists are unable to associate with any degree of certainty the thirty-six silver sigloi to any one of the inland polities (Pilides and Destrooper-Georgiades 2008: 327). The case of Tamassos is particularly intriguing, since it has built tombs and all kinds of elite artefacts and status symbols in the burial assemblages which, according to Matthäus (2007), define a royal ideology of the late Archaic period.

The fact that neither coins nor royal inscriptions have yet been associated with these three inland sites suggests a major reorganization of the political geography of the island. The pact with the Assyrians created a new economic environment that worked in favour of coastal polities but undermined the significance of inland centres. This was paramount for the territorial consolidation of fewer (than ten) autonomous politico-economic regions. Although we do not have a Persian list of the late 6th-century Cypriot kingdoms, the material evidence suggests that before the end of the Cypro-Archaic period (c.475 BC), the history of the Cypriot states becomes a history of port authorities, which reaches its climax with the takeover of the last inland kingdom, Idalion, by the Phoenician dynasty of Kition before the middle of the 5th century (Stylianou 1989: 403–4; Collombier 1991b: 34–5).

PERSIAN RULE AND THE GRAECO-PERSIAN CONFLICT

Achaemenid archives are silent as to the date and the circumstances under which Persian rule began in Cyprus. We are unaware as to how it was enforced or what obligations it entailed. Cyprus was one of the many subdivisions of the district of Syria but its governmental structure is not known (cf. Mehl 2004: 14). Persian domination did not disrupt or interfere with the commercial enterprises of the Cypriots. In fact, the Persians seem to have treated the Cypriot kings like 'sacred cows' despite repeated incidents of disobedience and rebellious behaviour in the course of the Graeco-Persian conflict, which began with the Ionian Revolt in 499/498 BC.

The unsuccessful attempt of Onesilos of Salamis to unite the Cypriot kingdoms under his authority and to join the Ionian uprising (Herodotus, *Hist.* 5.103–16) marked the end of the kingdoms' smooth relations with whichever empire had until then imposed the rules of trade in the Mediterranean. From that day on, caught in the middle of the long-drawn-out clash of the Persians with the Aegean city-states, headed first by Athens and later by Alexander the Great, the Cypriot kings fought a losing battle against the polarization of political and economic interests in the Mediterranean. It was under these new geopolitical circumstances that a powerful Phoenician dynasty made its appearance in Kition at the start of the 5th century.

Although neither Idalion nor Kition are mentioned by Herodotus in the episodes of the Ionian Revolt, it is not coincidental that the attacks against Idalion begin after the failure of the revolt. The Kitian kings' aggressive attitude should be considered in the context of the southeastern geo-economic (catchment) area to which both sites belong. Idalion was nearer, and in control of, the mines but it also had to have a port of export within its geographically consolidated territory. Kition was a port of export but had to have access to mines if it were to claim the status of a Cypriot kingdom (Iacovou 2007b). For Kition to take over as the region's administrative capital and port of trade, it had to undermine the supremacy of the last remaining inland capital that blocked the route to the mining region. And it did just that, in the years after the Ionian Revolt—probably not until the second quarter of the 5th century. This interpretation would also explain why there is minimal overlap between the last coin issues of Idalion and the first of Kition (e.g. a siglos of Idalion is struck over a siglos of Baalmilk I: Destrooper-Georgiades 2002: 353–5, nn. 16, 22). The takeover is now confirmed by the fascinating discovery of an economic archive—the first ever to be found in Cyprus—in a building identified as the administrative centre of Idalion in the 4th century BC. The archive rooms were full of accounts inscribed on ostraca or written on gypsum plaques, almost all in the Phoenician alphabet (Hadjicosti 1997: 58–9, fig. 24).

THE PHOENICIANS AND KITION

'[A] Phoenician *presence* on the Island before *c*.800 still needs to be demonstrated and not invoked uncritically' (Gilboa, Sharon, and Boaretto 2008). Like the establishment of Greek people on Cyprus, the establishment of Phoenicians on the island is not heralded by a distinct cultural package (nor should it be defended on the basis of ceramic imports: Iacovou 2005b: 131–2) but by Phoenician inscriptions (Iacovou 2008a: 643). Despite the fact that the Phoenician alphabetic scribal tool is attested in Cyprus from as early as the late 10th century (Lipiński 2004: 42–6), there is no indication that it was used consistently and continuously by a Semitic royal authority other than that of Kition. The case of Lapethos, where there is no record of a Greek syllabic inscription, remains a puzzle, as Greek (e.g. Dimonikos or Dimonax) and Semitic (e.g. Sidqimilk) names of kings alternate on its 5th-century coins but the inscriptions are all in the Phoenician alphabet (Masson and Sznycer 1972: 98–9; Lipiński 2004: 81). Late in the 4th century, the Greek alphabet replaces the Phoenician one on the coins of its last king, Praxippos (Destrooper-Georgiades 1995: 163). In Marion, where the earliest coins were issued by Sasmas (*c*.480–460 BC), with a syllabic legend on the obverse and a Phoenician on the reverse (Masson and Sznycer 1972: 79; Destrooper-Georgiades 1993), the later 5th-century coins of Stasioikos I and Timocharis are inscribed in the Greek syllabary (Masson 1983: 181). Kition, therefore, is the only Cypriot state where the kings bore purely Semitic names and were addressed with the Semitic term *mlk,* throughout the 5th and 4th centuries, but not before the 5th century. The earliest evidence that supports the presence of a Phoenician royal authority in Kition is provided by the legends on the early 5th-century coinage of Baalmilk I, founder of the Phoenician dynasty.

If we, therefore, contextualize the evidence of script types used around Cyprus in the first millennium, we are bound to realize that Kition is a Cypriot polity from where the syllabary is conspicuously absent: from the 9th to the 4th centuries, Kition produced 150 exclusively Phoenician inscriptions, which cover the secular, funerary, and sacred domain, but hardly any in the syllabary (Yon 2004: 159). This implies that the establishment of a literate Phoenician population in Kition was a particularly early event that should be held responsible for the discontinuity of the Cypriot syllabary into the first millennium.

The opposite phenomenon is observed in Paphos, the only Cypriot polity from where the Phoenician alphabet is almost totally absent and where the adoption of the Cypriot syllabary by Greek speakers is evident from the 10th century. The earliest epigraphically recorded Cypriot statesmen are 7th-century kings of Paphos; they are Akestor and Eteandros and their title is described with the Greek term *basileus* written in syllabic Greek. Although Mycenaean *basileis* were low-ranking regional officers—*quasireu* on the Linear B tablets from the palace archives of Knossos and Pylos—with this Greek term alone, which was evidently upgraded after the establishment of Greeks on Cyprus, the Cypriots defined the office of their supreme rulers not only in Paphos, but also in Salamis, Idalion, Marion, Soloi, and Kourion (Iacovou 2006b). Even in Amathous, where the syllabary expressed the unknown Eteocypriot language, the Amathousian rulers, whose names were mostly Greek, such as Lysandros, Epipalos, and Androkles, used the syllabary to inscribe their coins and royal dedications (cf. Amandry 1984: 60–3; Hermary and Masson 1982: 235–42).

THE CYPRO-CLASSICAL PERIOD

Following the abolition of the Greek dynasty of Idalion, Ozibaal, son of Baalmilk I, began to identify himself as king of Kition and Idalion and, for a period in the 4th century, Pumayaton, the last king of Kition, ruled over Kition, Idalion, and Tamassos. Thus, in the 5th and 4th centuries, when Kition acted as a steadfastly pro-Persian authority whose mission was to keep Cyprus within the Persian sphere, its kingdom reached the apogee of its political and economic supremacy. During this period commercial contacts with the Levant were intensified and the style of the 5th-century votive statuary from the sanctuary of Amrit changed: its closest stylistic and iconographic parallels are now found on the 5th-century limestone sculpture of Kition (Fig. 53.8). Hermary suggests that this 'phenomène unique en son genre' was the result of the establishment of a Kitian community at Amrit (Hermary 2008: 175). Two Phoenician inscriptions from Amrit, which seem to have been dedicated to Eshmoun by Cypriot Phoenicians, render further support to this view. But Cypriot Greeks must also have been present in the small Cypriot communities that sprang up on the Levantine coast: three dedicatory inscriptions (of the 5th and 4th centuries)—one from Tel Dor, one from Sarepta, and the third probably from Sidon—are in the Greek syllabary (Hermary 2008: 176–7).

From the middle of the 5th century and especially from the reign of Evagoras I of Salamis, who was an ardent supporter of the Athenians and is credited with the introduction of the

FIG. 53.8 Limestone statue of Herakles-Milqar (h. 123cm) from Kition-*Bamboula* (Cyprus Museum photographic archive, with the kind permission of the Director of Antiquities, Cyprus)

Greek alphabet in Cyprus (cf. Collombier 1991a), the Greek art of the Classical period became the predominant cultural prototype on the island—not only in kingdoms ruled by Greeks but equally in Kition and Amathous. On the coins, especially those of 4th-century Salamis, busts of Greek gods (Aphrodite, Athena, Artemis, and Apollo) appear for the first time. At Paphos, Zeus enthroned is depicted on the obverse of the 4th-century silver siglos of King Timocharis, which portrays on the reverse a standing Aphrodite (for the first time). In Cyprus, the first time that the goddess is invoked as *Kypria Aphrodite* is on a 4th-century bilingual inscription of the last king of Amathous, Androkes (Fourrier and Hermary 2006: 9, fig. 6).

In the mortuary sample of Kition, Phoenician anthropoid sarcophagi (also known from Amathous: cf. Karageorghis 2000: 226–9), often made of Parian marble, occur—even in the same chamber tomb—with sarcophagi bearing Greek iconography and lids imitating Greek temple pediments (cf. Georgiou 2009). Greek marble stelae with the name of the deceased inscribed in the Phoenician alphabet also abound in Kition (Yon 2006: 124). In the 4th century even the Phoenician language opened up to Greek loans: when the triumphant King Milkiathon (392–362 BC) dedicated a trophy in celebration of his victory against the Salaminians and their allies the Paphians, he used on the inscription the Greek word *tropaion* (Yon 2004: 201).

In spite of the political ascendancy of Kition in the Cypro-Classical period, Phoenician failed to become the predominant language on the island. In fact, even within Kition, the Phoenician alphabet had a precise expiration date. No sooner had Cyprus been made a Ptolemaic colony than the inscriptions from Kition were written in alphabetic Greek (Yon 2004: 154, 160–61; 2006: 125, fig. 80).

A SYMBOLIC DEATH AND THE END OF TRILINGUALISM

A population confined on an island that shared the same environment and a largely identical culture for hundreds of years should have also come to share the same language; but this did not happen. Instead, for as long as Cyprus was divided into autonomous states, Greek, Phoenician, and Eteocypriot were able to survive as three distinct languages. When the kingdoms were abolished by Ptolemy I and the people of Cyprus were forced to accept a unified political environment, Eteocypriot and Phoenician disappeared from the written record in no time. In the 3rd century BC, Greek had become the only language: the *koiné* was written in the Greek alphabet but the Arcado-Cypriot dialect, which had made its first appearance *c.*1000 BC inscribed on the *obelos* of *Opheltas* from Paphos-*Skales* T 49 (Karageorghis 1983: 60, pl. 88), continued to make use of the syllabary to the end of the first millennium BC (Michaelidou-Nicolaou 1993).

The first time the island achieved linguistic coherence was also the first time that territorial boundaries had been lifted. The abolition of the kingdoms at the end of the 4th century BC, aptly defined by Papantoniou (2008) as the transfer of authority from *basileis* to *strategos*, is the first major break in the political and cultural history of ancient Cyprus. It was decided by an external authority and was inflicted with considerable violence against the ruling families. In eliminating the hereditary kings of Cyprus, Ptolemy did not differentiate between the Phoenician Pumayaton of Kition, the 'Eteocypriot' Androkles of Amathous, or the Greek kings of Paphos and Salamis, Nikokles, and Nikokreon (Iacovou 2007a: 464). All of them stood for the same indigenous, millennium-old political culture—a culture so ingrained in the identity of the Cypriots that Ptolemy knew he had to kill and bury it with its last royal representatives if he were to stand a chance of subjugating the Cypriots to the colonial administration of his newly founded empire.

KYPRIOI: ONE CULTURAL IDENTITY

In the literary record of antiquity, the Cypriots, whether kings or commoners, are not identified as Greeks, Phoenicians, or natives but as *Paphioi, Salaminioi, Kourieis, Soleis, Lapitheis,* and *Marieis* from the name of their kingdom. The Greek authors of antiquity, who identify the Giblites, the Tyrians, and the Sidonians collectively as Phoenicians, do not refer to the people or the kings of Kition as Phoenicians but as *Kitiois* (cf. Diodorus 14.98.2; 19.59.1). The Phoenicians of Kition do not seem to have ever been grouped under the umbrella term 'Phoenicians'; they are instead invariably covered by the term *Kyprioi*. In fact, the terms *Phoinikes* and *Kyprioi* occur in apposition in many historiographies in reference to the people or the kings of the Levantine coast and Cyprus respectively (cf. Herodotus, *Hist.* 3.19.3; 6.6.1; Arrian, *Anab.* 2.13.7; 2.20; Diodorus 16.40). Irrespective of their linguistic identity, the different *ethne* of the island identified themselves and were collectively identified as *Kyprioi*.

SUGGESTED READING

Aupert, P., and M.-C. Hellmann (eds) (1984). *Amathonte I: Testimonia, pt 1: Auteurs anciens, monnayage, voyageurs, fouilles, origines, géographie.* Paris: Recherche sur les civilisations/ Athens: École française d'Athènes.

Carbillet, A. (2011). *La figure hathorique à Chypre (IIe-Ier mill. av. J.-C.).* Münster: Ugarit-Verlag.

Chavane, M.-J., and M. Yon (1978). *Salamine de Chypre X: Testimonia Salaminia,* pt 1: *Première, deuxième et troisième parties.* Paris: De Boccard.

Christodoulou, P. (2009). Nicokréon: le dernier roi de Salamine de Chypre—Discours idéologique et pouvoir politique. *Cahiers du Centre d'études chypriotes* 39: 235–58.

Counts, D. (2001). Prolegomena to the study of Cypriot sculpture. *Cahiers du Centre d'études chypriotes* 31: 129–81.

Iacovou, M. (ed.) (2012). *Cyprus and the Aegean in the Early Iron Age: The Legacy of Nicolas Coldstream.* Nicosia: A. G. Leventis Foundation.

——and D. Michaelides (eds) (1999). *Cyprus: The Historicity of the Geometric Horizon.* Nicosia: Archaeological Research Unit, University of Cyprus.

Karageorghis, J. (2005). *Kypris, the Aphrodite of Cyprus: Ancient Sources and Archaeological Evidence.* Nicosia: A. G. Leventis Foundation.

Karageorghis, V. (1993–8). *The Coroplastic Art of Ancient Cyprus: The Cypro-Archaic Period,* vols 3–6. Nicosia: A. G. Leventis Foundation.

Satraki, A. (2012). *Κύπριοι Βασιλείς από τον Κόσμασο μέχρι το Νικοκρέοντα.* Athens: University of Athens.

Walcher, K. (2009). *Die Architektur und Bauornamentik der archaischen Konigsgraber von Tamassos auf Zypern.* Rahden: Leidorf.

References

Amandry, M. (1984). Le monnayage d'Amathonte. In P. Aupert and M.-C. Hellmann (eds), *Amathonte I: Testimonia, pt 1: Auteurs anciens, monnayage, voyageurs, fouilles, origines, géographie.* Paris: Recherche sur les civilisations/Athens: École française d'Athènes, 57–76.

Aubet, M. E. (2004). *The Phoenician Cemetery of Tyre-Al Bass: Excavations 1997–1999.* Beirut: Ministère de la culture, direction générale des antiquités.

—— and F. J. Nuñez (2008). Cypriot imports from the Phoenician cemetery of Tyre Al-Bass. In C. Doumet-Serhal (ed.), *Networking Patterns of the Bronze and Iron Age Levant: The Lebanon and Its Mediterranean Connections.* London: Lebanese British Friends of the National Museum, 71–104.

Aupert, P. (1996). *Guide d'Amathonte.* Athens: École française d'Athènes/Nicosia: A. G. Leventis Foundation/Paris: De Boccard.

Bell, C. (2006). *The Evolution of Long Distance Trading Relationships across the LBA/Iron Age Transition on the Northern Levantine Coast: Crisis, Continuity and Change—A Study Based on Imported Ceramics, Bronze and Its Constituent Metals.* Oxford: Archaeopress.

Bikai, P. M. (1978). *The Pottery of Tyre.* Warminster: Aris & Phillips.

—— (1983). Appendix II: The imports from the East. In Karageorghis (1983: 396–406).

—— (1987). *The Phoenician Pottery of Cyprus.* Nicosia: A. G. Leventis Foundation with the assistance of the J. Paul Getty Trust.

Boardman, J. (1999). The excavated history of Al Mina. In G. R. Tsetskhladze (ed.), *Ancient Greeks, West and East.* Leiden: Brill, 135–61.

Bourogiannis, G. (2009). Eastern influence on Rhodian geometric pottery: foreign elements and local receptiveness. In V. Karageorghis and O. Kouka (eds), *Cyprus and the East Aegean: Intercultural Contacts from 3000 to 500 BC.* Nicosia: A. G. Leventis Foundation, 114–30.

Brock, J. K. (1957). *Fortetsa: Early Greek Tombs Near Knossos.* Cambridge: Cambridge University Press.

Buchholz, H.-G., H. Matthäus, and K. Walcher (2002). The royal tombs of Tamassos. *Cahiers du Centre d'études chypriotes* 32: 219–42.

Catling, H. W. (1995). Heroes returned? Subminoan burials from Crete. In J. B. Carter and S. P. Morris (eds), *The Ages of Homer: A Tribute to Emily Townsend Vermeule.* Austin: University of Texas Press, 123–36.

—— and E. A. Catling (1980). The mould and crucible fragments: the foundry refuse. In M. R. Popham, L. H. Sackett, and P. G. Themelis (eds), *Lefkandi I: The Iron Age. The Settlements, the Cemeteries.* London: Thames & Hudson for the British School of Athens, 93–7.

Christou, D. (1996). *Κυπρο-Αρχαϊκή Μνημειακή Ταφική Αρχιτεκτονική.* Nicosia: Department of Antiquities, Cyprus.

—— (1998). Cremations in the Western Necropolis of Amathous. In V. Karageorghis and N. C. Stampolides (eds), *Eastern Mediterranean: Cyprus, Dodecanese, Crete, 16th–6th Cent. B.C.* Athens: University of Crete/A. G. Leventis Foundation, 207–16.

Coldstream, J. N. (1977). *Geometric Greece.* New York: St. Martins.

—— (1984). Cypriaca and Cretocypriaca from the North Cemetery of Knossos. *Report of the Department of Antiquities, Cyprus* 1984: 122–37.

—— (1985). Archaeology in Cyprus 1960–1985: the Geometric and Archaic periods. In V. Karageorghis (ed.), *Archaeology in Cyprus 1960–1985.* Nicosia: A. G. Leventis Foundation, 47–59.

—— (1995). Amathus Tomb NW 194: the Greek pottery imports. *Report of the Department of Antiquities, Cyprus* 1995: 187–98.

—— (1998). *Light from Cyprus on the Greek 'Dark Age'? A Lecture Delivered at the Ashmolean Museum, Oxford, on 5th May, 1997.* Oxford: Leopards Head Press.

—— and P. M. Bikai (1988). Early Greek pottery in Tyre and Cyprus: some preliminary comparisons. *Report of the Department of Antiquities, Cyprus*: 35–44.

—— and H. W. Catling (1996). *Knossos North Cemetery: Early Greek Tombs* (4 vols). London: British School at Athens.

Collombier, A.-M. (1991a). Écritures et sociétés à Chypre à l'Âge du fer. In C. Baurain, C. Bonnet, and V. Krings (eds), *Phoinikeia Grammata: lire et écrire en Méditerranée*. Namur: Société des études classiques, 425–47.

—— (1991b). Organisation du territoire et pouvoirs locaux dans l'île de Chypre à l'époque perse. *Transeuphratène* 4: 21–43.

Courbin, P. (1957). Une tombe géométrique d'Argos. *Bulletin de correspondance hellénique* 81: 322–86.

Desborough, V. d'A. (1957). A group of vases from Amathus. *Journal of Hellenistic Studies* 77: 212–19.

—— (1980). The Dark Age Pottery (SM–SPG III) from settlement and cemeteries. In M. R. Popham, L. H. Sackett, and P. G. Themelis (ed.), *Lefkandi I: The Iron Age*. London: Thames & Hudson for the British School at Athens, 281–350.

Destrooper-Georgiades, A. (1984). Le trésor de Larnaca (IGCH) 1272 réexaminé. *Report of the Department of Antiquities, Cyprus*: 140–61.

—— (1993). Continuités et ruptures dans le monnayage chypriote à l'époque achéménide. *Transeuphratène* 6: 87–101.

—— (1995). La numismatique *partim* Orient. In V. Krings (ed.), *La civilisation phénicienne et punique: manuel de recherche*. Leiden: Brill, 148–65.

—— (2002). Les royaumes de Kition et Idalion aux Ve et IVe siècles. *Cahiers du Centre d'études chypriotes* 32: 351–68.

Elayi, J. (1992). Le phénomène monétaire dans les cités phéniciennes à l'époque perse. In T. Hackens and G. Moucharte (eds), *Numismatique et histoire économique phéniciennes et puniques: Actes du colloque tenu à Louvain-la-Neuve, 13–16 mai 1987*. Louvain-la-Neuve: Séminaire de numismatique Marcel Hoc, Université Catholique de Louvain, 21–31.

Faegersten, F. (2003). *The Egyptianizing Male Limestone Statuary from Cyprus: A Study of a Cross-Cultural Eastern Mediterranean Votive Type*. Lund: Department of Archaeology and Ancient History, Lund University.

Fourrier, S. (2007). *La coroplastie chypriote archaïque: identités culturelles et politiques à l'époque des royaumes*. Paris: Maison de l'Orient et de la Méditerranée.

—— and A. Hermary (2006). *Amathonte VI: le Sanctuaire d'Aphrodite des origines au début de l'époque impériale*. Paris: École française d'Athènes.

Georgiou, G. (2009). Three stone sarcophagi from a Cypro-Classical tomb at Kition. *Cahiers du Centre d'études chypriotes* 39: 113–39.

Gilboa, A. (1999). The view from the east: Tel Dor and the earliest Cypro-Geometric exports to the Levant. In M. Iacovou and D. Michaelides (eds), *Cyprus: The Historicity of the Geometric Horizon*. Nicosia: Archaeological Research Unit, University of Cyprus, 119–39.

—— (2001). The significance of Iron Age 'Wavy-Band' pithoi along the Syro-Palestinian littoral, with reference to the Tel Dor pithoi. In S. R. Wolff (ed.), *Studies in the Archaeology of Israel and Neighboring Lands in Memory of Douglas L. Esse*. Chicago: Oriental Institute of the University of Chicago/Atlanta, Ga.: American Schools of Oriental Research, 163–74.

—— (2005). Sea Peoples and Phoenicians along the southern Phoenician coast: a reconciliation. An interpretation of Sikila (SKL) material culture. *Bulletin of the American Schools of Oriental Research* 337: 47–78.

—— I. Sharon, and E. Boaretto (2008). Tel Dor and the chronology of Phoenician 'pre-colonisation' stages. In C. Sagona (ed.), *Beyond the Homeland: Markers in Phoenician Chronology*. Leuven: Peeters, 113–204.

Gjerstad, E. (1948). *The Swedish Cyprus Expedition IV, pt 2: The Cypro-Geometric, Cypro-Archaic and Cypro-Classical Periods*. Stockholm: Swedish Cyprus Expedition.

—— J. Lindros, E. Sjöqvist, and A. Westholm (1934). *The Swedish Cyprus Expedition I: Finds and Results of the Excavations in Cyprus 1927–1931*. Stockholm: Swedish Cyprus Expedition.

—— (1935). *The Swedish Cyprus Expedition II: Finds and Results of the Excavations in Cyprus 1927–1931*. Stockholm: Swedish Cyprus Expedition.

Goring, E. (1983). Appendix VI: Techniques of the Palaepaphos-Skales jewellery. In V. Karageorghis (ed.), *Palaepaphos-Skales: An Iron Age Cemetery in Cyprus*. Konstanz: Universitätsverlag, 418–22.

—— (1988). *A Mischievous Pastime: Digging in Cyprus in the Nineteenth Century—With a Catalogue of the Exhibition 'Aphrodite's Island: Art and Archaeology of Ancient Cyprus' Held in the Royal Museum of Scotland, Edinburgh from 14 April to 4 September 1988*. Edinburgh: National Museums of Scotland/Bank of Cyprus Cultural Foundation.

Hadjicosti, M. (1988). Appendix IV, pt 1: 'Canaanite' jars from Maa-Palaeokastro. In V. Karageorghis and M. Demas, *Excavations at Maa-Palaeokastro, 1979–1986*. Nicosia: Department of Antiquities, Cyprus, 340–81.

—— (1997). The kingdom of Idalion in the light of new evidence. *Bulletin of the American Schools of Oriental Research* 308: 49–63.

Henke, J.-M. (2009). Cypriote terracottas from Miletus. In V. Karageorghis and O. Kouka (eds), *Cyprus and the East Aegean: Intercultural Contacts from 3000 to 500 BC*. Nicosia: A. G. Leventis Foundation, 206–17.

Hermary, A. (1989). *Catalogue des antiquités de Chypre: sculptures, Musée du Louvre, Département des antiquités orientales*. Paris: Réunion des Musées Nationaux.

—— (1991). Les débuts de la grande plastique chypriote en terre cuite. In F. Vandenabeele and R. Laffineur (eds), *Cypriote Terracottas: Proceedings of the First International Conference of Cypriote Studies, Brussels–Liège–Amsterdam, 29 May–1 June 1989*. Brussels: A. G. Leventis Foundation/Vrije Universiteit Brussel/Université de Liège, 139–47.

—— (1999). Amathous before the 8th century BC. In M. Iacovou and D. Michaelides (eds), *Cyprus: The Historicity of the Geometric Horizon*. Nicosia: Archaeological Research Unit, University of Cyprus, 55–68.

—— (2000). *Amathonte V: les figurines en terre cuite archaïques et classiques—Les sculptures en pierre*. Paris: Ecole française d'Athènes/Nicosia: A. G. Leventis Foundation.

—— (2001). Naucratis et la sculpture égyptisante à Chypre. In U. Höckmann and D. Kreikenbom (eds), *Naukratis. Die Beziehungen zu Ostgriechenland, Ägypten und Zypern in archaischer Zeit*. Möhnesee: Bibliopolis, 27–38.

—— (2008). Les liens entre Kition et Amrit au Ve siècle avant J.-C. *Cahiers du Centre d'études chypriotes* 37: 167–84.

—— (2009). Ionian styles in Cypriote sculpture of the sixth century BC. In V. Karageorghis and O. Kouka (eds), *Cyprus and the East Aegean: Intercultural Contacts from 3000 to 500 BC*. Nicosia: A. G. Leventis Foundation, 244–51.

—— and O. Masson (1982). Inscriptions d'Amathonte IV. *Bulletin de correspondance hellénique* 106: 235–44.

Iacovou, M. (1988). *The Pictorial Pottery of Eleventh Century B.C. Cyprus*. Göteborg: Åströms.

——(2002a). Amathous: an Early Iron Age polity in Cyprus—The chronology of its foundation. *Report of the Department of Antiquities, Cyprus* 2002: 101–26.

——(2002b). From ten to naught: formation, consolidation and abolition of Cyprus' Iron Age polities. *Cahier du Centre d'études chypriotes* 32: 73–87.

——(2004). Phoenicia and Cyprus in the first millennium BC: two distinct cultures in search of their distinct archaeologies. *Bulletin of the American Schools of Oriental Research* 336: 61–6.

——(2005a). The Early Iron Age urban forms of Cyprus. In R. Osborne and B. W. Cunliffe (eds), *Mediterranean Urbanization 800–600 B.C.* Oxford: Oxford University Press for the British Academy, 17–43.

——(2005b). Cyprus at the dawn of the first millennium BC: cultural homogenization versus the tyranny of ethnic identifications. In J. Clarke (ed.), *Archaeological Perspectives on the Transmission and Transformation of Culture in the Eastern Mediterranean*. Oxford: Oxbow, 125–34.

——(2006a). 'Greeks', 'Phoenicians' and 'Eteocypriots': ethnic identities in the Cypriote kingdoms. In J. Chrysostomides and C.Dendrinos (eds), *'Sweet Land': Lectures on the History and Culture of Cyprus*. Camberley: Porphyrogenitus, 24–59.

——(2006b). From the Mycenaean *qa-si-re-u* to the Cypriote *pa-si-le-wo-se*: the *Basileus* in the kingdoms of Cyprus. In S. Deger-Jalkotzy and I. S. Lemos (eds), *Ancient Greece from the Mycenaean Palaces to the Age of Homer*. Edinburgh: Edinburgh University Press, 315–36.

——(2007a). Advocating Cyprocentricism: an indigenous model for the emergence of state formation on the Mediterranean's easternmost island. In S. W. Crawford, A. Ben-Tor, J. P. Dessel, W. G. Dever, A. Mazar, and J. Aviram (eds), *'Up to the Gates of Ekron': Essays on the Archaeology and History of the Eastern Mediterranean in Honor of Seymour Gitin*. Jerusalem: Israel Exploration Society, 461–75.

——(2007b). Site size estimates and the diversity factor in Late Cypriote settlement histories. *Bulletin of the American Schools of Oriental Research* 348: 1–23.

——(2008a). Cultural and political configurations in Iron Age Cyprus: the sequel to a protohistoric episode. *American Journal of Archaeology* 112: 625–57.

——(2008b). Cyprus from migration to Hellenisation. In G. R. Tsetskhladze (ed.), *Greek Colonisation: An Account of Greek Colonies and Other Settlements Overseas*, vol. 2. Leiden: Brill, 219–88.

——(2012). From regional gateway to Cypriot kingdom: copper deposits and copper routes in the *chora* of Paphos. In V. Kassianidou and G. Papasavvas (eds), *Eastern Mediterranean Metallurgy and Metalwork in the Second Millennium BC: A Conference in Honour of James D. Muhly*. Oxford: Oxbow, 58–69.

——(2013). The Cypriot syllabary as a royal signature: the political context of the syllabic script in the Iron Age. In P. Steele (ed.), *Syllabic Writing on Cyprus and Its Context*. Cambridge: Cambridge University Press, 133–52.

——and A. Hermary (1999). Amathus Diplostrati T.109. *Report of the Department of Antiquities, Cyprus* 1999: 151–62.

Karageorghis, V. (1963). Une tombe de guerrier à Palaepaphos. *Bulletin de correspondance hellénique* 87: 265–300

——(1969). *Salamis: Recent Discoveries in Cyprus*. New York: McGraw-Hill.

——(1970). Note on sigynnae and obeloi. *Bulletin de correspondance hellénique* 94: 35–44.

——(1972). Two built tombs at Patriki, Cyprus. *Report of the Department of Antiquities, Cyprus* 1972: 161–80.

—— (1973). *Excavations in the Necropolis of Salamis*, vol. 3. Nicosia: Department of Antiquities.

——(1975). *Alaas: A Protogeometric Necropolis in Cyprus*. Nicosia: Department of Antiquities.

—— (1983). *Palaepaphos-Skales: An Iron Age Cemetery in Cyprus*. Konstanz: Universitätsverlag.

——(1995). Cyprus and the Phoenicians: achievement and perspectives. In *I fenici—ieri, oggi, domani: ricerche, scoperte, progetti*. Rome: Gruppo editoriale internazionale, 327–34.

—— (2000). *Ancient Art from Cyprus: The Cesnola Collection in the Metropolitan Museum of Art*. New York: Metropolitan Museum of Art.

—— (2002a). *Early Cyprus: Crossroads of the Mediterranean*. Los Angeles: J. Paul Getty Museum.

——(2002b). La nécropole 'royale' de Salamine quarante ans après. *Cahier du Centre d'études chypriotes* 32: 19–29.

—— (2007). Cyprus and Sidon: two thousand years of interconnections. *Cahiers du Centre d'études chypriotes* 37: 41–52.

—— (2008). Interconnections between Cyprus and Lebanon from the Bronze Age to the end of the Archaic period. In C. Doumet-Serhal (ed.), *Networking Patterns of the Bronze and Iron Age Levant: The Lebanon and Its Mediterranean Connections*. London: Lebanese British Friends of the National Museum, 325–37

—— N. Kourou, V. Kilikoglou, and M. D. Glascock. (2009). *Terracotta Statues and Figurines of Cypriote Type Found in the Aegean: Provenance Studies*. Nicosia: A. G. Leventis Foundation.

—— and F. Lo Schiavo (1989). A west Mediterranean obelos from Amathus. *Rivista di studi fenici* 17: 15–29.

Kassianidou, V. (2000). Hellenistic and Roman mining in Cyprus. In G. K. Ioannides and S. A. Hadjistyllis (eds), *Acts of the Third International Congress of Cypriot Studies (Nicosia, April 1996)*, vol. 1. Nicosia: Society of Cypriot Studies, 745–56.

Knapp, A. B. (2008). *Insularity, Connectivity and Identity: Prehistoric and Protohistoric Cyprus*. Oxford: Oxford University Press.

Koehl, R. B. (1985). *Sarepta 3: The Imported Bronze and Iron Age Wares from Area II, X—The University Museum of the University of Pennsylvania Excavations at Sarafand, Lebanon*. Beirut: Librairie Orientale.

Kourou, N. (2008). The Aegean and the Levant in the Early Iron Age: recent developments. In C. Doumet-Serhal (ed.), *Networking Patterns of the Bronze and Iron Age Levant: The Lebanon and Its Mediterranean Connections*. London: Lebanese British Friends of the National Museum, 361–74.

——V. Karageorghis, Y. Maniatis, K. Polikreti, Y. Bassiakos, and C. Xephontos (2002). *Limestone Statuettes of Cypriote Type Found in the Aegean: Provenance Studies*. Nicosia: A. G. Leventis Foundation.

Kraay, C. M. (1976). *Archaic and Classical Greek Coins*. London: Methuen.

Lembke, K. (2004). *Die Skulpturen aus dem Quellheiligtum von Amrit: Studie zur Akkulturation in Phönizien*. Mainz am Rhein: von Zabern.

Lemos, I. S. (2002). *The Protogeometric Aegean: The Archaeology of the Late Eleventh and Tenth Centuries BC*. Oxford: Oxford University Press.

——and H. Hatcher (1991). Early Greek vases in Cyprus: Euboean and Attic. *Oxford Journal of Archaeology* 10: 197–208.

Lipiński, E. (1991). The Cypriot vassals of Esarhaddon. *Scripta Hierosolymitana* 33: 58–64.

——(2004). *Itineraria Phoenicia*. Leuven: Peeters.

Maier, F. G. (1989). Priest kings in Cyprus. In E. J. Peltenburg (ed.), *Early Society in Cyprus*. Edinburgh: Edinburgh University Press/National Museums of Scotland/A. G. Leventis Foundation, 376–91.

Marangou, A. (2000). *The Consul Luigi Palma di Censola, 1832–1904: Life and Deeds*. Nicosia: Cultural Centre of the Popular Bank Group.

Markoe, G. (1985). *Phoenician Bronze and Silver Bowls from Cyprus and the Mediterranean*. Berkeley: University of California Press.

—— (2000). *The Phoenicians*. Berkeley: University of California Press.

Masson, O. (1983). *Les inscriptions chypriotes syllabiques: recueil critique et commenté*. Paris: De Boccard.

—— and M. Sznycer (1972). *Recherches sur les Phéniciens à Chypre*. Paris: Droz.

Matthäus, H. (2007). The royal tombs of Tamassos. *Cahiers du Centre d'études chypriotes* 37: 211–30.

McFadden, G. H. (1954). A Late Cypriote III tomb from Kourion Kaloriziki No. 40. *American Journal of Archaeology* 58: 131–42.

Mehl, A. (2004). Cypriot city kingdoms: no problem in the Neo-Assyrian, Late Egyptian and Persian empires, but why were they abolished under Macedonian rule? *Epetirida Kentrou Epistimonikon Erevnon* 30: 9–21.

Michaelidou-Nicolaou, I. (1993). Nouveaux documents pour le syllabaire chypriote. *Bulletin de correspondance hellénique* 117: 346–7.

Muhly, J. D. (2003). Trade in metals in the Late Bronze Age and the Iron Age. In N. C. Stampolidis and V. Karageorghis (eds), *Sea Routes: Interconnections in the Mediterranean 16th–6th c. BC*. Nicosia: University of Crete/A. G. Leventis Foundation, 141–9.

—— (2009). The origin of the name 'Ionian'. In V. Karageorghis and O. Kouka (eds), *Cyprus and the East Aegean: Intercultural Contacts from 3000 to 500 BC*. Nicosia: A. G. Leventis Foundation, 23–30.

Myres, J. L. (1910). A tomb of the Early Iron Age from Kition. *Liverpool Annals in Archaeology and Anthropology* 3: 107–17.

Panayotou-Triantafyllopoulou, A. (2006). Languages and scripts in ancient Cyprus. In J. Chrysostomides and C. Dendrinos (eds), *'Sweet Land': Lectures on the History and Culture of Cyprus*. Camberley: Porphyrogenitus, 61–75.

Papantoniou, G. (2012). *Religion and Social Transformations in Cyprus: From the Cypriot Basileis to the Hellenistic Strategos*. Leiden: Brill.

Papasavvas, G. (2001). *Chálkinoi ypostátes apó tin Kýpro kai tin Kríti tripodikoí kai tetrápleuroi ypostátes apó tin ýsteri epochi tou chalkoú éos tin proïmi epochi tou sidirou*. Nicosia: A. G. Leventis Foundation.

Peltenburg, E. J. (2007). Hathor, faience and copper on Late Bronze Age Cyprus. *Cahier du Centre d'études chypriotes* 37: 375–94.

Petit, T. (2002). Sanctuaires palatiaux d'Amathonte. *Cahier du Centre d'études chypriotes* 32: 289–326.

Pickles, S., and E. J. Peltenburg (1998). Metallurgy, society and the Bronze/Iron transition in the east Mediterranean and the Near East. *Report of the Department of Antiquities, Cyprus* 1998: 67–100.

Pieridou, A. (1970). Κυπριακά Πλαστικά Αγγεία. *Report of the Department of Antiquities, Cyprus* 1970: 92–102.

—— (1971). Κυπριακά Τελετουργικά Αγγεία. *Report of the Department of Antiquities, Cyprus* 1971: 18–26.

—— (1973). *O protogeometrikos rythmos en Kypro*. Athens: Archaiologike Hetaireia.

Pilides, D., and A. Destrooper-Georgiades (2008). A hoard of silver coins from the plot on the corner of Nikokreontos and Hadjopoullou Streets. *Report of the Department of Antiquities, Cyprus* 2008: 307–35.

Reyes, A. T. (1994). *Archaic Cyprus: A Study of the Textual and Archaeological Evidence*. Oxford: Clarendon Press/New York: Oxford University Press.

Satraki, A. (2008). Manifestations of royalty in Cypriot sculpture. In G. Papantoniou (ed.), *POCA 2005: Postgraduate Cypriot Archaeology*. Oxford: Archaeopress, 27–35.

Schreiber, N. (2003). *The Cypro-Phoenician Pottery of the Iron Age*. Leiden: Brill.

Sherratt, E. S. (1991). Cypriot pottery of Aegean type in LCII–III: problems of classification, chronology and interpretation. In J. A. Barlow, D. R. Bolger, and B. Kling (eds), *Cypriot Ceramics: Reading the Prehistoric Record*. Philadelphia: University Museum of Archaeology and Anthropology, University of Pennsylvania, 185–98.

—— (1994). Commerce, iron and ideology: metallurgical innovation in 12th–11th century Cyprus. In V. Karageorghis (ed.), *Cyprus in the 11th Century B.C.: Proceedings of the International Symposium Organized by the Archaeological Research Unit of the University of Cyprus and the Anastasios G. Leventis Foundation, Nicosia, 30–31 October 1993*. Nicosia: A. G. Leventis Foundation, 59–107.

—— (1998). Sea Peoples and the economic structure of the late second millennium in the eastern Mediterranean. In S. Gitin, A. Mazar, and E. Stern (eds), *Mediterranean Peoples in Transition: Thirteenth to Early Tenth Centuries BCE*. Jerusalem: Israel Exploration Society, 292–313.

Snodgrass, A. M. (1980). Iron and early metallurgy in the Mediterranean. In T. A. Wertime and J. D. Muhly (eds), *The Coming of the Age of Iron*. New Haven, Conn.: Yale University Press, 335–74.

—— (1987). *An Archaeology of Greece: The Present State and Future Scope of a Discipline*. Berkeley: University of California Press.

—— (1994). Gains, losses and survivals: what we infer for the 11th century BC. In V. Karageorghis (ed.), *Cyprus in the 11th Century B.C.: Proceedings of the International Symposium Organized by the Archaeological Research Unit of the University of Cyprus and the Anastasios G. Leventis Foundation, Nicosia, 30–31 October 1993*. Nicosia: A. G. Leventis Foundation, 167–73.

South, A. K. (2002). Late Bronze Age settlement patterns in southern Cyprus: the first kingdoms? *Cahier du Centre d'études chypriotes* 32: 59–72.

Stampolides, N. C. (2009). Can Crete be excluded? Direct or indirect contacts among Cyprus, the east Aegean and Crete during the Geometric–Archaic periods. In V. Karageorghis and O. Kouka (eds), *Cyprus and the East Aegean: Intercultural Contacts from 3000 to 500 BC*. Nicosia: A. G. Leventis Foundation, 94–102.

Steel, L. (2004). *Cyprus before History: From the Earliest Settlers to the End of the Bronze Age*. London: Duckworth.

Stucky, R. A. (1993). *Die Skulpturen aus dem Eschmun-Heiligtum bei Sidon: Griechische, römische, kyprische and phönizische Statuen und Reliefs vom 6. Jahrhundert vor Chr. bis zum 3. Jahrhundert nach Chr*. Basel: Vereinigung der Freunde antiker Kunst.

Stylianou, P. J. (1989). *The Age of the Kingdoms: A Political History of Cyprus in the Archaic and Classical Periods*. Nicosia: Archbishop Makarios III Foundation.

Tytgat, C. (1989). *Les nécropoles sud-ouest et sud-est d'Amathonte I: les tombes 110–385*. Nicosia: École française d'Athènes/A. G. Leventis Foundation.

Vokotopoulou, I., and A.-P. Christides (1995) A Cypriot graffito on an SOS amphora from Mende, Chalcidice. *Kadmos* 34: 5–12.

Webb, J. M. (1999). *Ritual Architecture, Iconography and Practice in the Late Cypriot Bronze Age.* Jonsered: Åströms.

Wheeler, T. S., and R. Maddin (1980). Metallurgy and Ancient Man. In T. A. Wertime and J. D. Muhly (eds), *The Coming of the Age of Iron.* New Haven, Conn.: Yale University Press, 99–126.

Yon, M. (2004). *Kition dans les textes: testimonia et corpus épigraphique.* Paris: Recherche sur les civilisations.

——(2006). *Kition de Chypre.* Paris: Recherche sur les civilisations.

—— and F. Malbran-Labat (1995). La stèle de Sargon II à Chypre. In A. Caubet (ed.), *Khorsabad, le palais de Sargon II, roi d'Assyrie: Actes du colloque organisé au musée du Louvre par le Service culturel les 21 et 22 janvier 1994.* Paris: La Documentation française, 159–79.

CHAPTER 54

THE LEVANT DURING THE BABYLONIAN PERIOD

JEFFREY R. ZORN

INTRODUCTION: DEFINING THE BABYLONIAN PERIOD

In order to define the material culture of the Babylonian period (Fig. 54.1) one would ideally like to be able to identify a site destroyed at the beginning of the period, then immediately rebuilt, then destroyed again at the beginning of the Persian period (all established
unequivocally by textual documentation). Ideally one would like a series of such sites in different parts of the Levant. This would provide clear brackets for discussing the archaeological character of the period. However, these ideals do not (yet) exist. Besides the lack of these
desiderata, defining the material culture of the Babylonian period in the Levant is extremely
problematic for a number of other reasons.

First, the period is defined by political transitions, not substantial material cultural
changes. It begins when the Babylonians under Nebuchadnezzar II cross the Euphrates River
in August 605 BC, defeat the Saitic Egyptian army under Pharaoh Necho II at Carchemish,
and pursue them as far as Hamath. It ends with the defeat of the Babylonian armies, capture
of the last Babylonian king, Nabonidus, and the assimilation of the Babylonian Empire into
the rising Persian Empire by Cyrus II in October 539 BC. This is a period of less than seventy years, a brief time in which to expect significant material cultural changes to manifest.
Because a clear artefactual horizon for the period is lacking, there can be no reliable analysis
of settlement patterns based on survey data.

Also, without such benchmarks it is impossible to say at what point the material culture
of the Iron Age II makes the transition to that of the Persian period. One cannot say how the
material culture of 586 compares to that of 556. Indeed, there is evidence that many aspects
of the Iron Age persisted into the Persian period. This in turn leads to debate over the terminology of the period. Should it even be defined as a 'Babylonian period' or as Iron III, Iron
IIC, Iron IID, or something else?

It is common to find claims that particular sites were destroyed in some Babylonian campaign, but often this is based only on the site's Iron Age material culture coming to an end,
and not on a clear destruction deposit. It may well be that the site persisted much longer, or

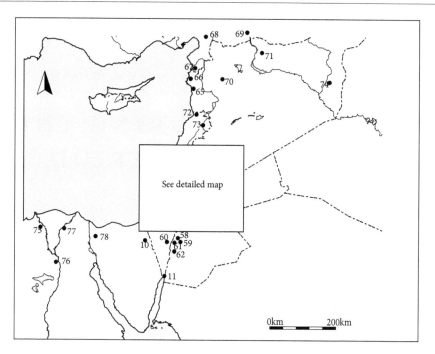

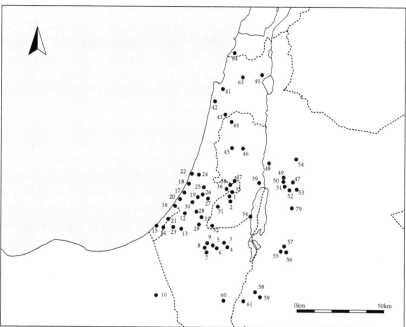

FIG. 54.1 Map of Babylonian-period sites in the Levant: (1) Jerusalem + Ketef Hinnom; (2) Ramat Raḥel; (3) Arad; (4) Ḥorvat 'Uza; (5) Malḥata; (6) Qitmit; (7) 'Aroer; (8) Tel Masos; (9) Tel 'Ira; (10) Kadesh Barnea; (11) Tell el-Kheleifeh; (12) Tell el-Ḥesi; (13) Tel Sera'; (14) Tell Jemmeh; (15) Ruqeish; (16) Ashkelon; (17) Ashdod; (18) Meṣad Ḥashavyahu; (19) Ekron; (20) Ashdod Yam; (21) Gaza; (22) Yavneh-Yam; (23) Tel Haror; (24) Rishon le-Zion; (25) Gezer; (26) Timnah; (27) Beth Shemesh; (28) Lachish; (29) Tell Beit Mirisim;

did come to an end during the Babylonian period, but perhaps because the site was aban-doned due to changing geopolitical conditions, rather than because of violent attack. Similar problems can occur with surveys because they cannot often provide fine chronological dis-tinctions or solid evidence on a site's built-up area. A related issue is the degree of architec-tural continuity that may have existed between the end of the Assyrian Empire in the west and the rise of the Persians, a mere century later. Public buildings which have yielded only Persian-period artefacts were not necessarily constructed then; they may be earlier, perhaps continuing in use from the Assyrians or Babylonians.

Another issue is the destructive impact of Babylonian rule across much of this region. Many sites, especially in the south, were indeed destroyed at this time and witness little, if any, imme-diate resettlement. Even if they were resettled, the remains are often those of flimsy squatter occupations that are difficult to trace and often receive cursory descriptions in reports.

Yet another problem is the meagre nature of textual evidence available for understanding the Babylonian impact on the Levant. Unlike their Assyrian predecessors, the Babylonian kings did not decorate their palaces with reliefs depicting their far-flung campaigns, nor did they have annals compiled to document their military achievements. The fragmentary Babylonian Chronicle preserves only the first eleven years of Nebuchadnezzar's reign, the third year of Neriglissar, and about six years of the reign of Nabonidus, a total of little more than a quarter of this period (Grayson 1975: 99–112). This is only marginally supplemented by the Harran inscriptions of Nabonidus and his mother (Pritchard 1969: 311–12, 560–63), and the so-called Verse Account (Pritchard 1969: 312–15). The Bible is the major source of data for ancient Israel and some of its immediate neighbours, but really only for Judah and then only before 582 BC, when the third Babylonian deportation is carried out. The bibli-cal data is supplemented by epigraphic finds, such as the ostraca from Arad and Lachish, the Ketef Hinnom amulets, and a few other inscriptions. Josephus, though usually depen-dant on the biblical text, preserves a few independent witnesses to the period, as do Greek authors such as Herodotus and others. Few texts covering this period have originated from Philistia, Jordan, Syria, or Lebanon (e.g. Pritchard 1969: 307).

ISRAEL

The territory of ancient Israel, including the modern West Bank, must be treated as two separate entities because of their different political fates going into the Babylonian period: the area of the old northern kingdom of Israel, and that of the southern kingdom of Judah.

FIG. 54.1 (*Continued*) (30) Tel Ḥarasim; (31) Khirbet Abu Tuwein; (32) Tell Rabud; (33) Khirbet Beit Liyeh; (34) En Gedi; (35) Tell el-Ful; (36) Gibeon; (37) Bethel; (38) Tell en-Naṣbeh; (39) Jericho; (40) Hazor; (41) Akko; (42) Shiqmona; (43) Yoqneam; (44) Megiddo; (45) Samaria; (46) Tell el-Far'ah; (47) 'Amman; (48) Tell Mazar; (49) Khilda; (50) Meqabelein; (51) Umm Uthainah; (52) Tell el-'Umeiri; (53) Jawa; (54) Safut; (55) Hisban; (56) Khirbat 'Arbid and Khirbat ath-Thamayil; (57) Qasr al-Dabba; (58) Sela'; (59) Busayra; (60) 'En Ḥaṣeva; (61) Wadi Feinan; (62) Tawilan; (63) Tell Kabri; (64) Tyre; (65) Tell Sukas; (66) Ras al-Bassit; (67) Al Mina; (68) Zinçirli; (69) Carchemish; (70) Mardikh; (71) Til Barsib; (72) Tell 'Arqa; (73) Wadi Brisa; (74) Shaykh Hamad; (75) Naucratis; (76) Memphis; (77) Daphnae; (78) Migdol; and (79) Khirbat al-Mudayna ath-Thamad

The former had been divided into Assyrian provinces for over a century by the time the Babylonian armies arrived, while the latter was a vassal kingdom.

The picture in the north is complicated because a great many sites were either destroyed, abandoned, or rebuilt toward the end of the Iron Age II; there is, however, no clear way to identify either the mechanism(s) for these changes or their timing. That is, it is impossible to say who initiated these changes, under what circumstances, or when. For example, there is no guarantee that all the sites were destroyed as the result of any single king's military campaign. Compounding the problem is a lack of texts which specify other than the most general activity of foreign rulers in the area. There are many possibilities. Settlements could have been destroyed by the military activities of the Egyptians as they took over the former Assyrian provinces, by the Babylonians as they drove the Egyptians out, or even by King Josiah of Judah. An Assyrian governor may have switched sides and joined first the Egyptians, then the Babylonians, then revolted against the latter (much as happened in Judah). Some sites may simply have undergone urban redevelopment for some reason unclear today, or been abandoned as a result of changing economic-political fortunes (the Babylonians seem to have been more interested in looting their provinces for short-term building projects in Mesopotamia, rather than in long-term building of a successful, ongoing provincial system).

At Hazor, Stratum III contains a Mesopotamian-style residence (Stern 2001: 312–13) which could be Assyrian and/or Babylonian in construction that continued in use into the Persian-period Stratum II. At Ayelet Hashahar, beyond the main tell at Hazor, part of a reception hall for a Mesopotamian-style residence was found. The combination of Mesopotamian-style architecture and ceramics from the Persian period may indicate continued use through the Babylonian period (Kletter and Zwickel 2006: 168–9, 174–5, 178–9). At Megiddo the Assyrian Strata III/II suffer some destruction and are followed by Stratum I. A fortress somewhat like that found at Hazor was the major addition to Stratum II and seems to have continued in use into Stratum I (Stern 2001: 313–17). Little can be said about the initial phase of construction of most structures assigned to Stratum I because they are a hodgepodge of different periods, but some were destroyed in the Persian period, indicating that they might be as early as the Babylonian period. The picture at both Hazor and Megiddo is similar: major administrative centres and little else. At Samaria a few walls and objects may be Babylonian. Paltry remains have also been found at Yoqneam XI, Tell el-Far'ah North VIIe1, Akko, and perhaps Shiqmona (Stern 2001: 315–16, 319–20). The Galilee, largely depopulated during the Assyrian invasions of the 8th century BC, seems to remain so under the Babylonians, and there seems to be a decline in settlement in the northern hill country as well (Stern 2001: 312).

Thus, it seems that a decline in settled urban life in northern Israel begun under the Assyrians continued under the Babylonians, with only a few regional centres of note and many sites, if occupied at all, only sparsely settled. Many sites, probably destroyed by Assyrian campaigns of the 8th–7th centuries BC, were not rebuilt, or the evidence is questionable.

Babylonian activity in Judah is easier to trace than to the north. The Babylonian campaign of 587/6 BC resulted in the destruction of many Judean cities and towns: Jerusalem 10, Ramat Raḥel VA, Gezer V, Beth Shemesh IIc, Tell Batash II, Lachish II, Tell Beit Mirisim A1, Arad VI, 'Aroer II, Kadesh Barnea, En Gedi V, Jericho, and others come to a fiery end (Stern 2001: 321–6). Surveys in Judah may supplement the evidence gathered from excavations, suggesting a great decline in the number of settlements during the Babylonian period (Lipschits 2005: 258–71; Faust 2012: 33–72, 119–47).

Even among the sites which were destroyed there is, however, often meagre evidence of survivors, refugees, and squatters. For example, some tombs at Ketef Hinnom in Jerusalem and a few other sites have been suggested to show continuity of burial through the 6th century BC (Stern 2001: 324; Faust 2004: 161–2), indicating that some elite segments of society remained in the land (burials of commoners being rare in the Iron Age). Other sites in Judah that seem to possess evidence of post-destruction occupation include Tel Ḥarasim IIIc, Lachish I, Khirbet Abu Tuwein, and Tell Rabud A-1. Caves in the Judean Hills were also probably used as refuges before and after the Babylonian invasion, such as Khirbet Beit Liyeh (Parker 2003).

Despite this invasion, however, not every site in the kingdom of Judah was destroyed. The area north of Jerusalem seems to have been spared devastation. Tell el-Ful IIIb has some walls and cisterns of this period, and Gibeon has yielded important inscriptions perhaps connected with the post-destruction administration. Bethel may have been occupied (Stern 2001: 321–2). Tell en-Naṣbeh 2 (biblical Mizpah; Fig. 54.2) was the administrative centre for the area providing examples of architecture such as securely dated four-room houses (*contra* Faust 2004: 165), ceramics, stamp impressions, inscriptions, and ceramic coffins that may be connected with the Babylonian administration (Zorn 2003).

Certainly much of Judah, though not all, was devastated by the Babylonian attacks and suffered a steep decline in population. How many people continued to live on among the ruins and in the areas largely spared by the Babylonians is impossible to say.

SINAI AND EGYPT

When Ashurbanipal invaded Egypt in 667 he mustered troops from Syria-Palestine (including Judah) and Cyprus to aid his endeavour (Pritchard 1969: 294); some may have been left behind to help garrison the land. There were also no doubt merchants, military men, and diplomats from the same area who plied their professions in Egypt in the 7th–6th centuries BC. In the wake of punitive actions taken by the Babylonians, especially in the southern Levant, which brought an end to their sponsoring countries, many may have found themselves voluntarily or involuntarily stranded there. Moreover, many Judeans, including military men, fled to Egypt in the wake of the Babylonian conquest (Jer. 42:1–43: 7). The Egyptians even held the deposed Judean king Jehoahaz (and his entourage?) hostage (2 Kgs. 23: 34). It is not surprising then to find a Jewish garrison at the island of Elephantine in the Persian period, but which was of Saitic origins (6th century BC). Archaeological (primarily ceramic) evidence for Levantine and Greek presence in Egypt and the Sinai in the late 7th–6th centuries BC is attested at sites such as Daphnae, Naucratis, Memphis, and Migdol (Weinberg 1971: 92–4; Oren 1984: 24–8; Maeir 2002; Holladay 2004, 407–11; Jer. 44: 1).

PHILISTIA

Textual evidence relating to Philistia at this time is sparse. The prophets Jeremiah (47) and Zephaniah (2:4–7) condemn the Philistine cities and promise various destructive

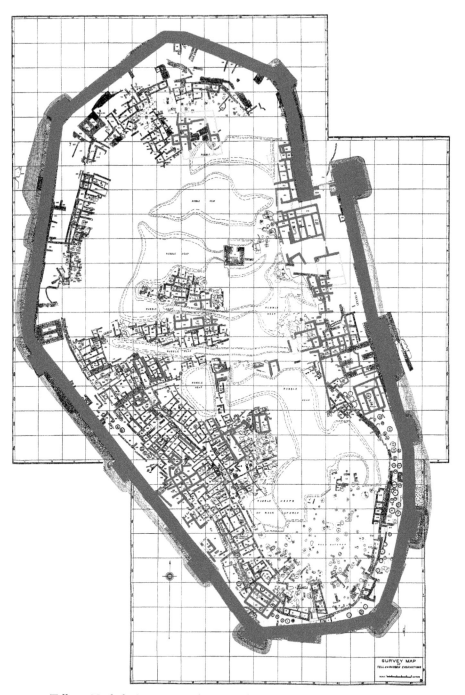

FIG. 54.2 Tell en-Naṣbeh Stratum 2 showing the Babylonian-period structures against other remains (image based on 1:400 site plan; courtesy Badè Institute of Biblical Archaeology)

punishments, which they appear to believe will be brought by the Babylonians, as does Ezekiel briefly (25: 15–17). The Babylonian Chronicle records that in his first regnal year (604 BC; Grayson 1975: 100) Nebuchadnezzar captured and destroyed Ashkelon (Fig. 54.3), though no reason is given, nor is any mention made of the fate of other Philistine cities at that time. This is the only securely dated Babylonian attack in Philistia. Scholars have had a tendency to ascribe the destructions found at other Philistine sites to this single campaign. However, given the incomplete nature of the Babylonian Chronicle this is only an assumption. Indeed, Nebuchadnezzar would have passed through Philistia on his campaigns against Egypt (601, 568 BC) and possibly during his campaigns against Judah (597, 586 BC).

Other pertinent texts for understanding the fate of the Philistines include the following: The letter of Adon, possibly the king of Ekron, found at Saqqara, Egypt, reports the approach of the Babylonian army to Aphek (Porten 1981). Rations lists dated 592 BC and after from Babylon mention the sons of Aga', king of Ashkelon, and other Ashkelonites (Porten 1981: 50). A list of officials and foreign rulers dated c.570 BC mentions kings of Gaza and Ashdod (Pritchard 1969: 307–8).

Whatever their dates, the major Philistine cities of Ashkelon, Ekron Stratum Ib, and perhaps Ashdod Stratum VII were all destroyed by the Babylonians (Stern 2001: 316–18); only Gaza escaped this fate, probably due to its importance as a staging ground for invasions into Egypt (Katzenstein 1994: 42–3). Other sites destroyed toward the end of the 7th century BC, possibly by the Babylonians, include: Tel Batash II (Timnah), Ashdod Yam, Yavneh-Yam IX, Rishon le-Zion, Tel Sera' V, Tel Haror G3, and Tell el-Ḥesi VIIa (Stern 2001: 316–18). The Greek mercenary fortress at Meṣad Hashavyahu was, however, apparently abandoned, not destroyed (Waldbaum and Magness 1997: 38). The former Assyrian centre at Ruqeish II may have continued into the 6th century.

FIG. 54.3 Babylonian-era destruction at Ashkelon (image courtesy Leon Levy Expedition to Ashkelon)

While many sites were destroyed, Babylonian-period attempts at rebuilding by refugees and squatters have been identified at a number of sites, including: Tell Jemmeh, Tel Sera' IV, Tell el-Ḥesi VI, Ekron IA (which also possesses a Mesopotamian-style open court building), Tel Batash IIa (Timnah), and possibly Ashdod VI. Again, it is impossible to estimate the number of survivors following the Babylonian campaigns.

Jordan

As a result of his pioneering surveys in Jordan in the 1930s Nelson Glueck came to the conclusion, based on comparing pottery from Jordan with Israelite forms, that settlement ceased in Ammon, Moab, and Edom from the 6th century BC until the 3rd. His assumption that there would be reasonably broad similarity between the ceramics of the two regions was eventually proved incorrect. While there are some forms in common, there is also strong regionality, especially at the end of the Iron Age. It has become clear that there is great longevity to Iron Age pottery traditions in Jordan, and that these forms continue well after the end of the Iron Age in Israel.

Ammon

There is very little textual data on Ammon during the Babylonian period to assist in the understanding of the archaeological material (for Ammon in general, see Herr 1999; Herr and Najjar 2001: 335–8; Stern 2001: 328–30). Nebuchadnezzar used Ammonites in his 597 BC campaign against Judah (2 Kgs. 24:1–2); they flirted with joining Judah in its final disastrous revolt (Jer. 27: 1–7; Ezek. 21: 18–20); Judeans found refuge there during the 586 campaign (Jer. 40: 11). The Ammonite king, Baalis, is credited with instigating the assassination of Gedaliah, the Babylonian-appointed ruler of Judah after the fall of Jerusalem, and of then giving the assassin refuge in Ammon (Jer. 40: 11, 41: 15). Josephus (*Antiquities* 10.9.7) recounts a campaign by Nebuchadnezzar in his twenty-third year (582 BC) against Ammon and Moab, perhaps in retaliation for this act. In his second and third years (554–553 BC) Nabonidus campaigned in the west, apparently reaching as far as Edom (Grayson 1975: 105, 282). If so, his probable route would have taken him through both Ammon and Moab.

So far nothing clearly of this period has been found at 'Amman itself, but tombs thought to be of the 6th century have been found at Meqabelein, Umm Uthainah, Khilda, just west of 'Amman, and in the cemetery at Tell Mazar in the Jordan Valley. The most important finds from these sites are probably the chalcedony stamp seals in Babylonian style.

Tell el-'Umeiri and its vicinity are especially important. Excavations on the western side of the site have so far revealed three large public buildings and a large domestic complex dated to the 6th century BC by the script found on an ostracon in a pit beneath one of the walls of the domestic unit. This date is strengthened by the recovery of a seal impression of Milkom'ur, servant of Ba'alyasha', found in the debris above one of the public buildings. Ba'alyasha' is almost certainly the Baalis of the biblical text. At or in the vicinity of Tell el--'Umeiri, 75 seal impressions or seals have been found. Dozens of farmsteads, with ceramics similar to Tell el-'Umeiri, and an associated wine press were found in the same region.

Material from the vicinity of 'Amman and south (Safut, Hisban, Jawa, and especially Tell el-'Umeiri) seems to indicate a material cultural high point during the 6th century BC (Lipschits 2004). The texts and material remains may indicate that Ammon continued as a vassal kingdom as late as *c.*580 BC, but its political fate after that date is uncertain, though its reduction to a province is possible since Nehemiah 2:10, 19 refer to Tobiah as an Ammonite official, not a ruler.

Moab

Little is known about Moab in this period owing to the still preliminary state of knowledge of Moabite ceramics. There is the account in Josephus (above) crediting Nebuchadnezzar with a campaign in Moab in his twenty-third year, and the possibility that Nabonidus passed through on his way to Edom. There is at present slender evidence for site abandonment in Moab in the mid-6th century BC at Khirbat 'Arbid, Khirbat ath-Thamayil, and Qasr al-Dabba, perhaps due to either shifting trade routes or a Babylonian attack (Routledge 2004: 210–12). Khirbat al-Mudayna ath-Thamad was destroyed either at the end of the 7th or in the 6th century (Steiner 2009: 148).

Edom

Edom at the end of the Iron II period stretched across both sides of the Arabah (on the history of Edom at this time, see Bartlett 1989: 147–61; Crowell 2008). Biblical texts suggest that save for a brief moment (Jer. 27: 3) Edom was solidly in Nebuchadnezzar's camp in the 597 and 586 BC campaigns against Judah. While Josephus recounts Babylonian campaigns against Ammon and Moab in Nebuchadnezzar's twenty-third year (582 BC), there is no mention of a campaign against Edom. It seems that, save for sheltering some Judean refugees after the 586 BC fall of Jerusalem (Jer. 40: 11), the kings of Edom gave Nebuchadnezzar no cause for war at this time and Edom probably continued as a vassal state. The Harran Inscription of Nabonidus briefly describes his campaigns in Arabia, in which he reached as far as Medina (Pritchard 1969: 562). The Babylonian Chronicle for his third year (553 BC) may record a campaign against Edom, though because of the broken nature of the first sign certainty is impossible (Grayson 1975: 105, 282). The likelihood of a Babylonian campaign in Edom at this time was strengthened by the discovery of a badly worn inscription and relief, probably of Nabonidus, cut into a cliff face at Sela', just northwest of Busayra (Dalley and Goguel 1997).

A lack of a clear terminus for Iron Age II Edomite pottery confounds the understanding of the Babylonian period. Excavations in Area A at the Edomite capital of Busayra (biblical Bozrah) are especially important in this regard (for Edom in general, see Bienkowski 1995: 54–62; 2001; Stern 2001: 273–5, 330–31).

Work at Busayra uncovered remains of an Assyrianizing temple which was constructed in Phase 3, suffered some fire damage, but continued in use with modifications through Phase 4, which was destroyed by fire; Phases 1–4 in Area A correspond with similar phases in Area C, possibly a palace. All four phases contain Iron Age Edomite painted pottery, but Area A, Phase 4 also contained two late 4th-century BC Attic sherds, suggesting continuity of occupation at the site from the late 8th century BC through the Babylonian period, to the end of the Persian period. This may indicate that Iron Age Edomite pottery persisted well beyond the end of the Iron Age. The partial Phase 3 destruction might be attributed to Nabonidus. It is therefore possible that the village of Tawilan and the fortified town of Tell el-Kheleifeh continued through the 6th century; both contain some evidence of occupation in the Persian period and no clear destruction deposits. Indeed, the destruction of many Edomite sites attributed to the 7th–early 6th BC may need to be reconsidered. Presumably the Babylonians would have been interested in exerting some control over the southern branches of the King's Highway, and a devastated Edom might not serve this purpose. Edomite pottery was also found in the vicinity of the Wadi Feinan copper mines. There is no a priori reason to exclude the possibility of the continued exploitation of these mines under the Babylonian regime.

Edomite material is (currently) even more plentiful in the Israelite Negev than in Edom (Stern 2001: 276–94, 325–6). These may be divided between actual Edomite sites and Edomite finds from Judean sites. Among the former are the forts at ʿen Ḥaṣeva, where a small Edomite shrine and an array of cultic figurines and a seal were found, and Ḥorvat ʿUza, which produced an Edomite ostracon. Extensive material, including a seal and an array of cultic figurines, was found at the Edomite shrine at Qitmit.

Judean sites that have produced painted Edomite pottery and other objects are primarily located in the southern Beer Sheba Valley. These include Malḥata (where it constitutes up to 25 per cent of the total), ʿAroer, Tel Masos, and Tel ʿIra. Lesser quantities have been found in the southern and western Negev at sites such as Kadesh Barnea, Tel Haror, Tel Seraʿ, and Tell Jemmeh. Edomite names have been found on ostraca from Malḥata and Arad, and on a seal from ʿAroer. The military threat posed by Edomites is mentioned in ostraca from Arad. Clearly a strong Edomite presence was growing in this region at the expense of the Judeans (military, commercial, or both).

Unfortunately, reports on Qitmit and ʿen Ḥaṣeva only assert that they were destroyed at the end of the Iron Age, but without mentioning if any destruction debris was found, and generally assume that the ends of these sites are connected with Babylonian attacks. Because Edomite pottery is found at sites with parallels to Judean pottery known from sites thought to have been destroyed in one of Nebuchadnezzar's campaigns, it is sometimes assumed that these Edomite sites were destroyed at the same time, even though there is no evidence for Babylonian hostility toward Edom under Nebuchadnezzar or that Nabonidus ever campaigned west of the Arabah. Given the emerging evidence from Busayra and the lack of texts documenting widespread and destructive military campaigns by the Babylonians against Edom (other than threats made by some Judean prophets), these assumptions may need to be revised. The Edomite Negev sites are generally found on trade routes extending from the Red Sea to the Mediterranean. If Nabonidus was interested in dominating the Arabian incense trade, control over the Edomite sites in the Negev, rather than their destruction, may have been to his advantage.

Syria, Lebanon, and Turkey

Even more so than in the southern Levant, clear remains from the Babylonian period in Syria, Lebanon, and Turkey are scant. Nebuchadnezzar besieged Tyre for thirteen years (c.587–574 BC), but so far no evidence of this attack has come to light. Unequivocal evidence for Babylonian activity in the area is provided by remains of five sets of reliefs and inscriptions carved by Nebuchadnezzar along roads, such as Wadi Brisa, in northern Lebanon (Da Riva 2010). Some sites reported to contain material from this period include: Mardikh VC2, Ras al-Bassit F–G and 8, Tell Sukas G3 and G2, Al Mina 5, Tell 'Arqa 9C, Shaykh Hamad F2, and others (Lehmann 1998: 12; Akkermans and Schwartz 2003: 364). Other material may come from sites excavated in the early days of archaeology, such as Zinçirli II (Lehmann 1994: 111), but the reporting of data is often problematic. Cypriot imports diminish in quantity, while imports from the Greek mainland increase; Syria is increasingly part of the Mediterranean economy (Lehman 1998: 19, 21, 32; Weinberg 1971: 90–92). Imports and imitations of Assyrian ceramics die out soon after the end of the empire (Lehman 1998: 21). There is relatively little difference in ceramics between coastal and inland sites, a change from clear regionalism in earlier periods (Lehmann 1998: 29) (Fig. 54.4).

Excavations at Dur-Katlimmu/Shaykh Hamad on the Habur revealed a Mesopotamian-style courtyard 'Red House' built over the burned remains of an Assyrian residence (Akkermans and Schwartz 2003: 389). Four cuneiform tablets were found there written in good Neo-Assyrian form, but date early in the reign of Nebuchadnezzar, indicating that the structure belongs to the Babylonian period. The pottery from the 'Red House' shows continuity with forms known from Assyrian sites from the end of the empire (Kreppner 2006: 127). A similar picture emerges at Til Barsib, where an Assyrian phase in two courtyard buildings seems to be followed by two of the Babylonian period (Bunnens 1997: 21, 25, 28). This suggests that while regime change in the northern Levant, which had been carved up into Assyrian provinces for over a century, may have been accompanied by some violence, there was also continuity in material culture and personnel. In other words the Assyrian governors and other administrative personnel in the north may have seen the collapse of the empire as more of a civil war between Assyria and Babylonia, and simply switched sides as the dust settled (Dalley 2003: 27*–8*).

GREEKS IN THE EAST

One of the hallmarks of the late 7th to early 6th centuries BC in the Levant is the limited but increasing presence of imports from the (mostly east) Greek world at many sites, though usually only a few pieces at each site. Most of these are table wares, perfume containers, or transport amphorae. However, the reason for this increase and its nature is much debated. Are they evidence for the presence of Greek merchants or mercenaries, or are they simply trade items? The limited quantities of Greek pottery at most sites may be best explained as a result of trade, rather than as evidence for merchant colonies or stations at this time. A few other Greek artefacts and inscriptions, dated c.600 BC, are scattered along the Levantine coast (Waldbaum 1997: 8–10). A greater variety of Greek imports seems available in the late 7th century compared to the middle of the 6th, suggesting that the change from Assyrian to Babylonian rule may have had an impact on Greek trade (Weinberg 1971: 78, 90–91; Vanderhooft 1999: 83–4).

Types of Greek pottery known from either side of 600 BC from the southern Levant include various forms of Early–Middle Corinthian Ware and East Greek Ware such as Ionian cups, Middle Wild Goat II (possibly Late Wild Goat; Fig. 54.5), cooking pots, and transport amphorae (Waldbaum 1994: 59–60; Waldbaum and Magness 1997: 27). There seems to be little Greek

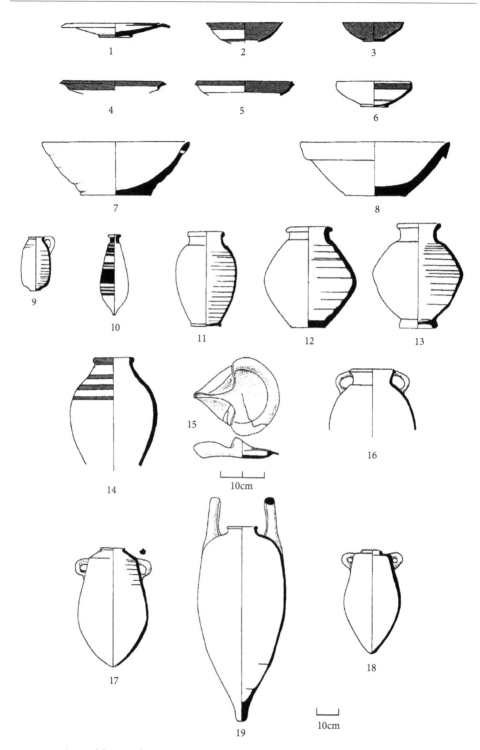

FIG. 54.4 Assemblage 5 from Syria, c.580–540 BC (Lehmann 1998: fig. 8; used with the author's permission)

FIG. 54.5 Wild Goat Ware from the end of the 7th century BC at Ashkelon (image courtesy Leon Levy Expedition to Ashkelon)

pottery from the mid-6th century BC in the south (Faust 2012: 73–92). Attic pottery does not
seem to appear until early in the Persian period. With much of the south in ruins, and many
elites exiled, there may not have been much of a market for imported prestige items.

Tell Kabri, destroyed c.600 BC, and Meşad Hashavyahu, abandoned about the same time,
contained imported Greek cooking pots among other Greek vessels. These have been taken
to indicate the presence of actual Greeks living at these sites, most probably mercenaries.
The Greeks at Kabri may have been in the service of Tyre. Meşad Hashavyahu is more problematic because Hebrew inscriptions have been found there. Some suggest that it was a garrison of Greek mercenaries in the service of Judah, others that it was an Egyptian garrison
site (like Migdol), even though no Egyptian materials were found there (Waldbaum and
Magness 1997: 38–9).

In the north, Wild Goat, Bucchero, Fikellura, Middle and Late Corinthian, Vroulian,
Clazomenian, and Attic Black Figure pottery are represented along with Ionian bowls,
Rosette bowls, Chian chalices, SOS amphorae, and Samian bottles (Lehmann 1998: 19–22;
his Assemblages 4 (c.650–580 BC) and 5 (c.580–540 BC)).

SUMMARY

The Babylonians seem little interested in the Levant other than as a source of natural and
human plunder to be used in the rebuilding of Babylonia. There is debate over whether the
Babylonians took over the earlier Assyrian provincial system, or even whether they had a
clear administrative system at all for the Levant. Much depends on the nature of the approximately quarter-century of Egyptian hegemony in the area and whether it maintained
Assyrian political structures (Vanderhooft 1999: 82–3, 90–110; Lipschits 2005: 3–8, 36–42,
48–9, 66; Stern 2001: 348–50). It may be that old Assyrian provinces and their governors,
city-states, and vassal kingdoms (perhaps some re-emerging after being provinces) that

rendered regular tribute were left alone, but those which rebelled were crushed, leaving only modest, often poor, resettlement afterwards.

N.B. Summaries of many of the sites listed in the above discussion can be found in Stern (1993), Meyers (1997), and Herr and Najjar (2001).

Suggested Reading

Beaulieu, P.-A. (1989). *The Reign of Nabonidus, King of Babylon, 556–539 B.C.* New Haven, Conn.: Yale University Press.

Lipschits, O., and J. Blenkinsopp (eds) (2003). *Judah and the Judeans in the Neo-Babylonian Period.* Winona Lake, Ind.: Eisenbrauns.

Spalinger, A. J. (1977). Egypt and Babylonia: a survey (*c.*620–550 B.C.). *Studien zur altägyptischen Kultur* 5: 221–44.

Stager, L. E. (1996). The fury of Babylon: Ashkelon and the archaeology of destruction. *Biblical Archaeology Review* 22.1: 57–69, 76–7.

Wiseman, D. J. (1991). Babylonia, 605–539 B.C. In J. Boardman, I. E. S. Edwards, N. G. L. Hammond, and E. Sollberger (eds), *Cambridge Ancient History III, pt 2: The Assyrian and Babylonian Empires and Other States of the Near East, from the Eighth to the Sixth Centuries B.C.* Cambridge: Cambridge University Press, 229–51.

References

Akkermans, P. M. M. G., and G. M. Schwartz (2003). *The Archaeology of Syria: From Complex Hunter-Gatherers to Early Urban Societies (c.16,000–300 BC).* Cambridge: Cambridge University Press.

Bartlett, J. R. (1989). *Edom and the Edomites.* Sheffield: JSOT Press.

Bienkowski, P. (1995). The Edomites: the archaeological evidence from Transjordan. In D. V. Edelman (ed.), *You Shall not Abhor an Edomite, For He Is Your Brother: Edom and Seir in History and Tradition.* Atlanta, Ga.: Scholars, 41–92.

—— (2001). New evidence on Edom in the Neo-Babylonian and Persian periods. In J. A. Dearman and M. P. Graham (eds), *The Land That I Will Show You: Essays on the History and Archaeology of the Ancient Near East in Honor of J. Maxwell Miller.* Sheffield: Sheffield Academic, 198–213.

Bunnens, G. (1997). Til Barsib under Assyrian domination: a brief account of the Melbourne University excavations at Tell Ahmar. In S. Parpola and R. M. Whiting (eds), *Assyria 1995: Proceedings of the 10th Anniversary Symposium of the Neo-Assyrian Text Corpus Project, Helsinki, September 7–11, 1995.* Helsinki: Neo-Assyrian Text Corpus Project, 17–28.

Crowell, B. L. (2008). Nabonidus, as Sila, and the beginning of the end of Edom. *Bulletin of the American Schools of Oriental Research* 348: 75–88.

Da Riva, R. (2010). A lion in the cedar forest: international politics and pictorial self-representation of Nebuchadnezzar II (605–562 BC). In J. Vidal (ed). *Studies on War in the Ancient Near East: Collected Essays on Military History.* Münster: Ugarit-Verlag, 165–91.

Dalley, S. (2003). The transition from Neo-Assyrians to Neo-Babylonians: break or continuity? *Eretz-Israel* 27: 25*–8*.

—— and A. Goguel (1997). The Sela' sculpture: a Neo-Babylonian rock relief in southern Jordan. *Annual of the Department of Antiquities of Jordan* 41: 169–76.

Faust, A. (2004). Social and cultural changes in Judah during the 6th century BCE and their implications for our understanding of the nature of the Neo-Babylonian period. *Ugarit-Forschungen* 36: 157–76.

—— (2012). *Judah in the Neo-Babylonian Period: The Archaeology of Desolation*. Atlanta, Ga.: Society of Biblical Literature.

Grayson, A. K. (1975). *Assyrian and Babylonian Chronicles*. Locust Valley, NY: J. J. Augustin.

Herr, L. G. (1999). The Ammonites in the Late Iron Age and Persian period. In B. MacDonald and R. Younker (eds), *Ancient Ammon*. Leiden: Brill, 219–37.

—— and M. Najjar (2001). The Iron Age. In B. MacDonald, R. Adams, and P. Bienkowski (eds), *The Archaeology of Jordan*. Sheffield: Sheffield Academic, 323–45.

Holladay, J. S., Jr (2004). Judaeans (and Phoenicians) in Egypt in the late seventh to sixth centuries B.C. In G. N. Knoppers and A. Hirsch (eds), *Egypt, Israel and the Ancient Mediterranean World: Studies in Honor of Donald B. Redford*. Leiden: Brill, 405–38.

Katzenstein, H. J. (1994). Gaza in the Neo-Babylonian period (626–539 B.C.E.). *Transeuphratène* 7: 35–49.

Kletter, R., and W. Zwickel (2006). The Assyrian building of 'Ayyelet ha-Shahar. *Zeitschrift des Deutschen Palästina-Vereins* 122: 151–86.

Kreppner, F. J. (2006). *Die Keramik des 'Roten Hauses' von Tall Šēḫ Ḥamad/Dūr-Katlimmu: Eine Betrachtung der Keramik Nordmesopotamiens aus der zweiten Hälfte des 7. und aus dem 6. Jahrhundert v. Chr.* Wiesbaden: Harrassowitz.

Lehmann, G. (1994). Zu den Zerstörungen in Zincirli während des frühen 7. Jahrhunderts v. Chr. *Mitteilungen der Deutschen Orient-Gesellschaft zu Berlin* 126: 105–22.

—— (1998). Trends in the local pottery development of the Late Iron Age and Persian period in Syria and Lebanon, ca. 700 to 300 B. C. *Bulletin of the American Schools of Oriental Research* 311: 7–37.

Lipschits, O. (2004). Ammon in transition from vassal kingdom to Babylonian province. *Bulletin of the American Schools of Oriental Research* 335: 37–52.

—— (2005). *The Fall and Rise of Jerusalem: Judah under Babylonian Rule*. Winona Lake, Ind.: Eisenbrauns.

Maeir, A. M. (2002). The relations between Egypt and the southern Levant during the Late Iron Age: the material evidence from Egypt. *Ägypten und Levante* 12: 235–46.

Meyers, E. M. (ed.) (1997). *The Oxford Encyclopedia of Archaeology in the Near East* (5 vols). New York: Oxford University Press.

Oren, E. D. (1984). Migdol: a new fortress on the edge of the eastern Nile Delta. *Bulletin of the American Schools of Oriental Research* 256: 7–44.

Parker, S. B. (2003). Graves, caves and refugees: an essay in microhistory. *Journal for the Study of the Old Testament* 27: 259–88.

Porten, B. (1981). The identity of King Adon. *Biblical Archaeologist* 44: 36–52.

Pritchard, J. B. (ed). (1969). *Ancient Near Eastern Texts Relating to the Old Testament*, 3rd edn with supplement. Princeton, NJ: Princeton University Press.

Routledge, B. E. (2004). *Moab in the Iron Age: Hegemony, Polity, Archaeology*. Philadelphia: University of Pennsylvania Press.

Steiner, M. L. (2009). Khirbet al-Mudayna and Moabite pottery production. In P. Bienkowski (ed.), *Studies on Iron Age Moab and Neighbouring Areas in Honour of Michèle Daviau*. Leuven: Peeters, 145–64.

Stern, E. (ed.) (1993). *The New Encyclopedia of Archaeological Excavations in the Holy Land* (4 vols). Jerusalem: Israel Exploration Society & Carta/New York: Simon & Schuster.

—— (2001). *Archaeology of the Land of the Bible*, vol. 2: *The Assyrian, Babylonian, and Persian Periods (732–332 B.C.E.)*. New York: Doubleday.

Vanderhooft, D. S. (1999). *The Neo-Babylonian Empire and Babylon in the Latter Prophets.* Atlanta, Ga.: Scholars.

Waldbaum, J. C. (1994). Early Greek contacts with the southern Levant, ca. 1000–600 B.C: the eastern perspective. *Bulletin of the American Schools of Oriental Research* 293: 53–66.

——(1997). Greeks *in* the east or Greeks *and* the east? Problems in the definition and recognition of presence. *Bulletin of the American Schools of Oriental Research* 305: 1–17.

——and J. Magness (1997). The chronology of early Greek pottery: new evidence from seventh-century B.C. destruction levels in Israel. *American Journal of Archaeology* 101: 23–40.

Weinberg, S. S. (1971). Post-Exilic Palestine: an archaeological report. *Proceedings of the Israel Academy of Sciences and Humanities* 4: 78–97.

Zorn, J. R. (2003). Tell en-Naṣbeh and the problem of the material culture of the 6th century. In O. Lipschits and J. Blenkinsopp (eds), *Judah and the Judeans in the Neo-Babylonian Period.* Winona Lake, Ind.: Eisenbrauns, 413–47.

CHAPTER 55

THE LEVANT DURING THE PERSIAN PERIOD

GUNNAR LEHMANN

INTRODUCTION

The Persian (or Achaemenid) period is a time of such profound changes that this epoch is also known as the 'Axial Age'. Some of the processes involved began already in the preceding centuries when world powers emerged such as the Assyrian and the Neo-Babylonian Empires. The Achaemenid Empire was the continuation of this, followed by the Hellenistic empires. During the Persian period new political elites emerged as well as new religious and economic ones. The world was growing together; the Mediterranean was increasingly interacting with the Near East. Authoritative religious texts were composed, among them the Bible. The foundations of philosophy and science were laid. A new vision of man and humanity was forged.

The Levant as an interface between East and West was at the heart of many of these processes, and its material culture reflects both the traditions and the innovations of this period. The changes in the material culture do not follow directly political developments. The most significant innovations had already begun during the 6th century BCE, at least one generation before the Achaemenid Empire. The following major changes occurred *during* the Persian period: new artistic styles were adopted from Greece and the Levant increasingly merged with the Mediterranean economy. After Alexander's conquests, many of the markers of the material culture from the Persian period continued into the first two or three generations of the Hellenistic period and were slowly replaced by the innovations of that age.

CHRONOLOGY

In the northern Levant the archaeology of the period between c.538 and 333 BCE is often called the 'Achaemenid period', a notion with strong historical connotations. In the southern Levant archaeologists prefer the label 'Persian period'; this notion, too, reflects the historical changes rather than the development of the material culture. In addition, the notion

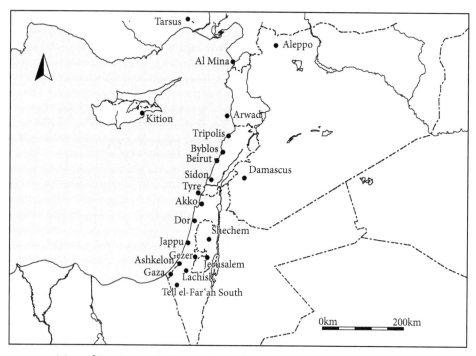

FIG. 55.1 Map of Persian-period sites in the Levant

'Persian period' suggests wrongly that the material culture in the Levant is of 'Persian' character. Indeed, the study of the material culture of this period was long somewhat neglected, with the unsaid implication that everything essential about this time can be found in the historical record. To counter this perception, archaeologists introduced archaeological notions such as 'Iron Age III' for this period to stress the development of the material culture independent of the historical record (Lehmann 1996; Elayi 2000). Unfortunately, the term 'Iron Age III' is already used by other archaeologists working in Syria and Palestine to label the period between the 7th and the early 6th century BCE. Currently, there seems to be no solutionto this dilemma. In this chapter, the period will be labelled 'Iron III/Persian period'.

EXCAVATIONS AND SURVEYS

The excavations and surveys in the Levant with evidence of the Iron III/Persian period are conveniently listed by Stern (1982; 2001), Lehmann (1996; 2002), and Nunn (2000) (Fig. 55.1). Among the most important sites are Deve Höyük, Kinet Höyük (ancient Issos), and Al Mina in Turkey; Tell Mardikh (ancient Ebla), Tell Kazel, and Tell Sukas in Syria; and Tell 'Arqa, Byblos, Beirut, Sidon, and Kamid el-Loz in Lebanon. In Israel one should point out Tel Keisan, Tel Megadim, Tel Michal, and Ashkelon along the coast. Qadum, Shechem, Jerusalem, Lachish, Tell el-Hesi, and Tel Halif have provided important finds in inner Palestine. In Transjordan, Tell es-Sa'idiyeh, Tell el-Mazar, Tell Nimrin, Heshbon, and Tell el-'Umeiri should be mentioned.

SETTLEMENT PATTERN

Only a few urban sites of the Iron III/Persian period have been excavated. Important cities in Syria such as Aleppo, Arwad, and Damascus, mentioned in historical records, remain unexcavated. Likewise, little is known about the urban structure or city planning of most Phoenician cities like Tyre, Sidon, or Byblos. Beirut is the only Phoenician city where urban quarters have been fully studied (Elayi and Sayegh 1998; 2000). In the southern Levant, Akko, Dor, Ashdod, and Ashkelon have been excavated, but large cities like Gaza and Jaffa have only partially been investigated (Stern 2001).

Important urban centres developed in the Levant only along the Mediterranean coast, with the possible exceptions of Aleppo and Damascus. Urbanism is best studied in the southern Levant, where cities seem to appear only after some stagnation during the Babylonian period. Interestingly, there are indications that urbanism only re-emerged around 480 BCE, rather than earlier during the transitional Iron III–early Persian period (Shalev 2008).

Most excavations in the Levant exposed small rural towns or villages. Even historically well-known sites like Jerusalem (Lipschits and Oeming 2006) and Shechem were only small rural towns during the Iron III/Persian period (Campbell 2002). Many tell sites of Iron Age I–II were abandoned before the Iron III/Persian period. When these tells were resettled during the 5th and 4th centuries BCE, the character of the sites changed radically. While most of the tells were towns and villages during Iron I–II, the settlement of the Iron III/Persian period is characterized by estates and small fortified structures. Villages and towns of the Iron III/Persian period are often found on new locations.

At many sites, a regular plan of settlement was noted that was compared with Hippodamic concepts and explained with Greek influence. Recently, scholars have pointed out that regular plans may originate in the Near East, where similar plans appear in the Levant during the Assyrian period (e.g. Megiddo Stratum III).

The settlement density can be reconstructed to some extent with the results of archaeological surveys. Such surveys cover especially Palestine, but there is increasing evidence from Jordan, Lebanon, and Syria. Surveys and excavations provide evidence for a relatively dense pattern of settlements that is similar to the density of the 7th and early 6th centuries BCE. The coastal regions of the Levant were especially densely populated. The settlement included also areas bordering the desert such as Transjordan and central Syria.

Although there were attempts to distinguish between early and later settlements during the Iron III/Persian, it is very difficult to differentiate the pottery of most surveys into early and late assemblages (see below). Any suggestions to distinguish a development of the settlement pattern as by Charles E. Carter (1999) are misleading and based on a wrong understanding of the evidence.

Cautious estimates of the population during the Iron III/Persian period are currently possible only with the data available in Palestine. There, a population around c.200,000 is possible. Such a population size is close to that of the preceding Iron II and underlines the continuity, especially in the rural sector.

ARCHITECTURE

Urban architecture of the Iron III/Persian period is characterized by public structures such as palaces, temples, and fortifications. Although no palace has so far been excavated in the Levant, a few architectural elements found can be interpreted as evidence for palatial buildings, such as Persian-style double-bull column capitals in Sidon and the reliefs from Arwad.

A number of sacral buildings have been investigated, among them the important Eshmun Temple at Bustan ash-Shaykh, near Sidon, and the temple at ʿAmrit, the so-called Maabed (Dunand and Saliby 1985). A large podium building in Byblos with column rows in the inner central hall may either be interpreted as a temple or palace. The character of *Bâtiments* I and II in Byblos remains unclear due to the chaotic excavations at the site and the lack of publication. Another monumental temple complex was excavated at Umm al-ʿAwamid in Lebanon, south of Tyre (Dunand and Duru 1962). Both the Eshmun Temple and the building at Umm al-ʿAwamid display Greek architectural influence. At the Eshmun Temple two building phases are distinguished, an early one dated to the 6th and 5th centuries BCE and a later one with an amphiprostyle plan of the 4th century BCE. At Umm al-ʿAwamid most of the architecture dates to the Hellenistic period, but the *in antis* temple at the site could go back to the 4th century BCE as well.

One of the most famous temples of the Iron III/Persian period, the temple at Jerusalem, remains of course completely unknown and there is currently no evidence for this building. A sacral complex that is probably very similar to the temple at Jerusalem was recently discovered at Mount Gerizim near Shechem. Although the evidence for the oldest Samaritan shrine known today is only scant, the excavator has dated these remains to the 4th century BCE. There is, however, a dispute as to the early date of the building. At Mount Gerizim a courtyard can be reconstructed, but the main temple plan did not survive (Magen, Misgav, and Tsfania 2004; Magen 2008).

The so-called Solar Shrine at Lachish may have been initially constructed during the Iron III/Persian period (Aharoni 1968; 1975). It resembles the administrative open-court buildings (see below) and its interpretation as a shrine is not entirely clear. More small shrines and sanctuaries were discovered; those in Palestine were discussed by Kamlah (1999). To this discussion one has to add the sanctuary at Kharayab in Lebanon (Chéhab 1951–4).

The plans of sanctuaries in the Levant during the Iron III/Persian period develop out of a long-room plan that was already characteristic for the earlier Iron Age. Since the 5th and especially during the 4th centuries there is distinctive Greek influence of the Classical period. Kamlah has emphasized the Phoenician role in the construction of sanctuaries, especially in the prosperous coastal regions. Greek stylistic elements were employed by Phoenicians, who were apparently the agents of Greek cultural influence on the architecture of the Levant during the Iron III/Persian period.

Evidence for urban fortifications is rare, and such remains were excavated only in Byblos and mainly at Dor, where a tower and casemate-like walls were found (Stern 1994: fig. 93). The harbour of Issos, modern Kinet Höyük, in the Bay of Iskenderun was also fortified with a still-unpublished wall that surrounded the town during the Iron III/Persian period.

A relatively large number of fortresses were excavated, especially in the southern Levant. The fortresses are typically constructed with a central courtyard and rooms around it that form a casemate-like fortification wall. Many such buildings were found scattered between villages or fortifying the desert border, including the border to Egypt. A list of buildings in Palestine can be found in Stern (2001: 371–2) and Hoglund (1992). To this list one has to add the Persian-period Buildings I and IV (that form *one* structure) at Ugarit and a recently discovered building at Tell Sianu, erroneously interpreted by Michel al-Maqdissi as a sanctuary (2003: 92–4).

Another type of public structure is administrative, a continuation of the Assyrian open-court building. This type of building was also in use during post-Assyrian times in Tell Shaykh Hamad (northeast Syria) and Zincirli (southeast Turkey). The open-court buildings must have existed throughout the 6th century BCE, because they appear again during the Iron III/Persian period in slightly modified form. One of the best examples in Palestine is the 'residency' building at Lachish (Aharoni 1975).

BURIALS

Burials reflect religious beliefs and group identities, and offer important information about the social, economic, and ethnic differentiation within a society. The coastal regions again display the more developed and elaborate evidence. Here, shaft-tombs and freestanding constructed tombs were noticed. Some of the constructed tombs have monumental appearance like the 'Maghazil' tombs, large rock structures with underground chambers at 'Amrit that were in use during the Persian and Hellenistic periods (Nunn 2000: 204–6).

At Sidon, elaborate burial chambers of the royal family and the city's elites were discovered. Anthropomorphic sarcophagi of various types stood in the chambers. The earliest anthropomorphic sarcophagi were Egyptian imports that were reused for the burial of Sidonian kings, among them Tabnit (*c*.550? BCE) and his son Eshmun'azar II (525? BCE). Later variations of anthropomorphic sarcophagi display increasingly classical Greek stylistic features. Thus, a specific form of Phoenician burial developed out of Egyptian models and later under Greek influence.

The highly decorated architectural sarcophagi found in Sidon from the period between 430 and 300 BCE are an exception (Nunn 2000: 27–9). These sarcophagi, among them the Satrap-Sarcophagus, the Lycian Sarcophagus, the Sarcophagus with Mourning Women, and the Sarcophagus of Abdalonymos ('Alexander Sarcophagus'), display a splendid figurative decoration. While the artwork implies familiarity with Greek art, it is still debated whether these sarcophagi were manufactured by Greek or Phoenician artists.

Another less exceptional form of burial during the Iron III/Persian period was cist tombs. These graves were either built with stones or cut into rock to form rectangular burials for a single person. In the Levant they appear at Khilda (Jordan), Khirbet Ibsan (Lower Galilee), the Beth Shean region, Makhmish, Gezer, Lachish, Tell el-Far'ah South, Kamid el-Loz, Ugarit, Deve Hüyük, and Tall Ahmar, but they were also noticed at Tall Billa, Ur, Susa, and Persepolis in Mesopotamia and Iran. This specific burial practice during the Iron III/Persian period seems to be 'foreign' to the Levant, and may be a custom of mercenaries and official state functionaries.

A local earlier Iron tradition, rock-cut family tombs, seems to have continued in the central hill country of Israel and Judah at least in the beginning of the Iron III/Persian period. Only future research will show whether there is a continuation of such family graves or individual burials replaced them during this period. Tumuli graves in the Jordan Valley were identified with burials of nomadic populations living in the valley and the Judean Desert (Magen 2004).

CERAMICS

Pottery is the most important criterion for dating archaeological contexts during the Iron III/Persian period. A distinctive Babylonian assemblage during the 6th century BCE did not apparently exist, and Iron II ceramic styles are around 550 BCE increasingly replaced by pottery types characteristic of the 'Persian' period. Although a few ceramic types can be dated to either the early or late Iron III/Persian period, it is generally very difficult to distinguish such an early or late phase. In excavations and surveys the relevant types that do allow such a distinction are often missing, or the stratigraphic record is not detailed enough for such a precise dating. The most important types are just continuing from the 6th century BCE into the early Hellenistic period. Even the 'Basket-Handle' amphorae and mortaria with high pedestal ring bases continue well into the early 3rd century BCE (Lehmann 1996; Stern 2001: 514–22; Thalmann 1978: fig. 44:7–9).

Local Iron II ceramics were still characterized by regional productions throughout the Levant. During the 6th and the 5th centuries BCE there is an increasing standardization in the repertoire of the pottery. The same types appear now from northern Syria to southern Palestine. Although there are still regional workshops, the pottery forms are very similar and comparable.

A significant part of the pottery in the Levant was imported and includes Cypriot styles, among them the ubiquitous 'Basket-Handle' amphorae and mortaria with high pedestal ring bases. In the late 6th century Late Corinthian, Clazomenian, and Vroulian vessels appeared in the Levant. But after c.480 BCE, this variety of Greek ceramics is almost exclusively replaced by Attic, Black-Figured, Red-Figured, and Black-Glazed. Among the local decorated pottery there is mainly the so-called Band-Decorated style that reflects eastern Greek influences (Lehmann 2000).

FIGURATIVE ARTS

Most of the figurative arts of the Iron III/Persian period were found in Phoenicia or in Phoenician contexts. With the exception of simple clay figurines, Phoenicia (and to some extent also northern Syria) is richer in sculptures, reliefs, and seals than Palestine or Transjordan. The works of figurative art have been comprehensively analysed and conveniently published by Nunn (2000, with further references). The sculpture of the early Iron III/Persian period is characterized by Late Archaic Cypriot style (550/540–475 BCE) and represents a continuation of Middle Archaic Cypriot sculpture that reached especially Phoenicia during the 6th century BCE. The most important early examples of Phoenician sculpture, such as the torsos from Tyre and Sarepta, were at least inspired by Middle Archaic Cypriot sculpture. The Late Archaic Cypriot style is already dominated by Greek Archaic influence.

The other major influence on figurative arts in the Levant during the Iron III/Persian period came from Egypt. Egyptianizing scarabs as well as Egyptian metal figurines and sarcophagi were found frequently in the early part of the Iron III/Persian period before 480 BCE.

According to Nunn there is a major change around 480 BCE in the artistic production of the Levant. Now Greek Classical influence becomes dominant, almost exclusively replacing the previously dominant Cypriot and Egyptian styles. Greek clay figurines were favoured and common. Sarcophagi clearly displayed Greek classical stylistic influence, although they were produced locally. The so-called Temple Boy sculptures found in the Eshmun Temple near Sidon and elsewhere are another example of a specific Phoenician object with Greek stylistic features. Reliefs on the royal Sidonian sarcophagi and the 'Tribune of Eshmun' are further evidence for this trend. Attic painted pottery (Black-Figured and Red-Figured styles) and Greek glyptics appeared throughout the Levant.

Against these influences, true Achaemenid, Iranian influences remain very rare. Some of the clay figurines such as the Persian Riders or the relief on the Yehawmilk or Byblos Stele show such an influence with the iconographic display of persons in Persian garments.

The development of figurative arts during the Iron III/Persian period demonstrates the Phoenician flexibility in adapting foreign artistic influences without giving up their own traditions. They produced specific Phoenician objects such as the Temple Boy sculptures that were created in Greek style and used in specific Phoenician contexts. It was apparently rather a matter of form than of content. In a similar way, Phoenician artistic production had opened itself to Egyptian influence earlier during the 8th–6th centuries BCE. On the other hand, monumental sculpture in general was rather rare during Iron I–II and becomes more common in the Levant only from the 6th century BCE.

SMALL FINDS

Among the small finds, many metal objects were made of bronze. Iron and precious metals such as gold and silver do occur, however, and the craftspeople mastered the technical aspects of working with all these metals. During the Iron III/Persian period the traditional Iron Age fibula was still in use in the Levant. This kind of decorated safety pin was part of local dress. Until the early 6th century BCE, fibulae were still distributed in the Levant and further east to Mesopotamia and Iran. During the 6th century, fibulae went out of fashion in areas east of the Euphrates. Only in a small pocket in southern Babylonia did they still appear (Pedde 2000: 365–6), where they were most probably worn by deported populations from the Levant. From the 5th century BCE, fibulae appear only in the Levant, and are thus a distinct marker of Levantine material culture during the Iron III/Persian period.

Another typical find of the period is Egyptian metal situlae. A situla is a small ritual metal vessel in the form of a bucket with a loop handle. Originally they are dedications in the Egyptian cult of Isis and designed to carry holy water for rituals. Although they are popular between 1000–700 BCE, most finds in the Levant date between 650–400 BCE; here they were in use as votive offerings in funerals and sanctuaries.

The so-called Irano-Scythian arrowheads have appeared in the Near East since the 7th century BCE. While they are clearly in use during the Iron III/Persian period, it is difficult to assign a more precise chronology. Irano-Scythian arrowheads are usually made of bronze and appear to be introduced to the Levant by foreign soldiers from Iran or Scythia. Greek types of arrowheads are rare in the Levant during the Iron III/Persian period, and more typical of the Hellenistic period.

Decorated metal bowls with carination and flaring rims were part of luxurious drinking sets. While usually in bronze, such bowls were also made in gold and silver. The bowls of the Iron III/Persian period are deeper than earlier flat bowls of the late Iron Age. Sets for wine consumption included decorated metal dippers and jugs, as in the set found in Tomb 650 at Tell el-Far'ah South. Similar metal bowls were also found in other parts of the Achaemenid Empire. Metal fittings for furniture were found in Samaria and Tell el-Far'ah South. Pictures of furniture with similar fittings can be studied in reliefs in Persepolis.

Glass beads with grotesque faces are typical of jewellery manufactured in Phoenicia. Such beads also appear in the Phoenician colonies of the western Mediterranean (Haevernick 1977). A necklace could include faience amulets of Egyptian gods such as Bes. Small miniature vessels were also made of glass. Since these are small, it is likely that they contained a valuable liquid, most probably cosmetics. Although these vessels seem to be a Phoenician product, they often copy Greek pottery shapes such as jugs or amphorae. Metal bracelets with facing animal heads, often rams, are typical for the Iron III/Persian period. Such bracelets appear in bronze, silver, or gold and clearly reflect an Iranian style of jewellery

COINS

After their first appearance around 630 BCE in Lydia, coins were already being minted around c.600 BCE in Athens, and an Attic silver standard called 'tetradrachma' with a unit of 17.5 grams of silver became widely used around c.540 BCE in the Levant. In Levantine cities a multitude of coins were in circulation during the Iron III/Persian period, including Greek, Persian, and local satrap coins from Cilicia, Cyprus, Egypt, and Palestine. While many Thraco-Macedonian coins circulated in the Levant until about 475 BCE, most Greek coins were Attic in origin between 474–400 BCE.

Persian coins were introduced after c.510 BCE by Darius I. They included the gold dareikos, with 8.4gm of gold = 20 silver sigloi (shekels), and silver siglos (shekel), with 5.5gm of silver (after 475 BCE with 5.5–5.6 grams of silver).

Phoenician coins seem to appear only after c.500 BCE at Kition, followed by coins of Byblos (from c.470 BCE), Tyre, Sidon (450 BCE), and later Arwad, Tripolis, and Dor. Syrian cities such as Damascus and Bambyke may have minted coins since the 4th century BCE. There is also a distinct Iron-III/Persian-period coinage in Cilicia with coins from Tarsus.

An important group of Levantine coins are the so-called Philisto-Arabian silver coins (Gitler and Tal 2006). These are also known as Graeco-Phoenician, Graeco-Persian, or Egypto-Arabian coins.

Some of the coins bear the inscription עז that may stand for the city of Gaza (עזה). This was small money, mostly made of silver. Unfortunately, most Philisto-Arabian coins were not found in excavations, but appeared on the antiquities market and in private collections. The date of minting of Philisto-Arabian coins is thus unclear. They may have been manufactured between 450–330 BCE or only after 404 BCE. This group of coins is characterized by a remarkable diversity of types, and it is often difficult to find two coins that are identical. Most Philisto-Arabian coins have no inscription; on some, however, there are inscriptions in Phoenician signs such as עזה– עז – ע – אנ – ב – ד – שׁ . These signs could refer to Gaza, Ashkelon, or Antheodon. The diversity of the coins may be due to a great number of different minting authorities of local Persian officials.

Coins and weights from the region of Yehud have attracted considerable research interest. The so-called Yehud coins are inscribed 'Yehud' in Aramaic, rarely in paleo-Hebrew 'Yehudah'. A Yehud coin was small silver money, minted probably at the very end of the Iron III/Persian period between 360–292/283 BCE (Mildenberg 1988: 727). Coins were also minted by Samaritans, dated between 360–332 BCE with the assumption that they ended with the conquest by Alexander.

SUMMARY

The Iron III/Persian period was a time of intensive cultural, social, and economic exchange between various continental regions of the Near East with Mediterranean societies. In figurative arts, architecture, ceramics, and small finds, a profound process of Hellenization took place, long before the conquest of Alexander and Hellenism. This was not a one-way exchange: the continuous 'orientalization' of Greece was a parallel phenomenon in the Aegean. The material culture of the Levant underlines also the ethnic and social differentiation of the region. The coastal plain and the continental lowlands were much more involved in processes of exchange and cultural syncretism than were the more remote highlands and the arid margins of the Levant. While some areas embraced and developed foreign influences, others rejected them and resisted innovations that were considered foreign and wrong.

SUGGESTED READING

Briant, P. (2002). *From Cyrus to Alexander: A History of the Persian Empire*, trans. P. Daniels. Winona Lake, Ind.: Eisenbrauns.

—— and R. Boucharlat (2006). *L'archéologie de l'empire achéménide: nouvelles recherches*. Paris: De Boccard.

Lehmann, G. (1996). *Untersuchungen zur späten Eisenzeit in Syrien und Libanon: Stratigraphie und Keramikformen zwischen ca. 720 bis 300 v.Chr.* Münster: Ugarit-Verlag.

Nunn, A. (2000). *Der figürliche Motivschatz Phöniziens, Syriens und Transjordaniens vom 6. bis zum 4. Jahrhundert v.Chr.* Freiburg: Freiburg Universitätsverlag/Göttingen: Vandenhoeck & Ruprecht.

Stern, E. (1982). *Material Culture of the Land of the Bible in the Persian Period 538–332 B.C.* Warminster: Aris & Phillips/Jerusalem: Israel Exploration Society.

—— (2001). *Archaeology of the Land of the Bible*, vol. 2: *The Assyrian, Babylonian, and Persian Periods, 732–332 BCE*. New York: Doubleday.

REFERENCES

Aharoni, Y. (1968). Trial excavation in the 'solar shrine' at Lachish: preliminary report. *Israel Exploration Journal* 18: 157–69.

——(1975). *Investigations at Lachish: The Sanctuary and the Residency (Lachish V)*. Tel Aviv: Gateway.

al-Maqdissi, M. (2003). The Syrian coast: one thousand years of archaeology (1600–600 BC). In N. C. Stampolides (ed.), *Sea Routes from Sidon to Huelva: Interconnections in the Mediterranean 16th–6th c. BC*. Athens: Museum of Cycladic Art, 90–4.

Campbell, E. F. (2002). *Shechem III: The Stratigraphy and Architecture of Shechem/Tell Balâtah* (2 vols). Boston, Mass.: American Schools of Oriental Research.

Carter, C. E. (1999). *The Emergence of Yehud in the Persian Period: A Social and Demographic Study*. Sheffield: Sheffield Academic.

Chéhab, M. H. (1951–4). *Les terres cuites de Kharayeb* (2 vols). Paris: Librarie d'Amérique et d'Orient.

Dunand, M., and R. Duru (1962). *Oumm el-'Amed: une ville de l'époque hellénistique aux échelles de Tyr*. Paris: Librairie d'Amérique et d'Orient.

——and N. Saliby (1985). *Le temple d'Amrith dans la Pérée d'Aradus*. Paris: Geuthner.

Elayi, J. (2000). Les sites phéniciens de Syrie au Fer III/Perse: bilan et perspectives de recherche. In G. Bunnens (ed.), *Essays on Syria in the Iron Age*. Louvain: Peeters, 327–48.

——and H. Sayegh (1998). *Un quartier du port phénicien de Beyrouth au Fer III/Perse: les objets*. Paris: Gabalda.

——(2000). *Un quartier du port phénicien de Beyrouth au Fer III/Perse: archéologie et histoire*. Paris: Gabalda.

Gitler, H., and O. Tal (2006). *The Coinage of Philistia of the Fifth and Fourth Centuries BC: A Study of the Earliest Coins of Palestine*. Milan: Ennerre/New York: Amphora/B & H Kreindler.

Haevernick, T. E. (1977). Gesichtsperlen. *Madrider Mitteilungen* 18: 152–231.

Hoglund, K. G. (1992). *Achaemenid Imperial Administration in Syria-Palestine and the Missions of Ezra and Nehemiah*. Atlanta, Ga.: Scholars.

Kamlah, J. (1999). Zwei nordpalästinische 'Heiligtümer' der persischen Zeit und ihre epigraphischen Funde. *Zeitschrift des Deutschen Palästina-Vereins* 115: 163–90.

Lehmann, G. (1996). *Untersuchungen zur späten Eisenzeit in Syrien und Libanon: Stratigraphie und Keramikformen zwischen ca. 720 bis 300 v.Chr*. Münster: Ugarit-Verlag.

——(2000). East Greek or Levantine? Band-decorated pottery in the Levant during the Achaemenid period. *Transeuphratène* 19: 83–113.

——(2002). *Bibliographie der archäologischen Fundstellen und Surveys in Syrien und Libanon*. Rahden: Marie Leidorf.

Lipschits, O., and M. Oeming (eds) (2006). *Judah and the Judeans in the Persian Period*. Winona Lake, Ind.: Eisenbrauns.

Magen, Y. (2004). Two tumuli in the Jordan Valley (Yafit). In H. Hizmi and A. De Groot (eds), *Burial Caves and Sites in Judea and Samaria: From the Bronze and Iron Ages*. Jerusalem: Israel Antiquities Authority, 285–99.

——(2008). *Mount Gerizim Excavations 2: A Temple City*, trans. E. Levin and M. Guggenheimer. Jerusalem: Israel Antiquities Authority.

——H. Misgav, and L. Tsfania (2004). *Mount Gerizim Excavations 1: The Aramaic, Hebrew and Samaritan Inscriptions*, trans. E. Levin and M. Guggenheimer. Jerusalem: Israel Antiquities Authority.

Mildenberg, L. (1988). Yehud-Münzen. In H. Weippert (ed.), *Palästina in vorhellenistischer Zeit*. Munich: Beck, 719–28.

Nunn, A. (2000). *Der figürliche Motivschatz Phöniziens, Syriens und Transjordaniens vom 6. bis zum 4. Jahrhundert v. Chr*. Freiburg: Freiburg Universitätsverlag/Göttingen: Vandenhoeck & Ruprecht.

Pedde, F. (2000). *Vorderasiatische Fibeln: Von der Levante bis Iran*. Saarbrücken: Saarbrücker Druckerei.

Shalev, Y. (2008). *Tel Dor as a test-case for urbanization in the coastal plain during the Persian period*. MA thesis, Hebrew University of Jerusalem.

Stern, E. (1982). *Material Culture of the Land of the Bible in the Persian Period 538–332 B.C.* Warminster: Aris & Phillips/Jerusalem: Israel Exploration Society.

——(1994). *Dor, Ruler of the Seas: Twelve Years of Excavations at the Israelite-Phoenician Harbor Town on the Carmel Coast*, trans. J. Shadur. Jerusalem: Israel Exploration Society.

——(2001). *Archaeology of the Land of the Bible*, vol. 2: *The Assyrian, Babylonian, and Persian Periods, 732–332 BCE*. New York: Doubleday.

Thalmann, J.-P. (1978). Tell 'Arqa (Liban nord): campagnes I–III (1972–1974)—Chantier I: rapport préliminaire. *Syria* 55: 1–151.

INDEX

Note: Page numbers in *italic* refer to figures. Entries and sub-entries are arranged alphabetically, except for archaeological periods, which are arranged chronologically.

CPSIA information can be obtained
at www.ICGtesting.com
Printed in the USA
LVHW110726040322
712617LV00004B/32

9 780198 822561